WEST'S LEGAL FORMS

SECOND EDITION

VOLUME 2

BUSINESS ORGANIZATIONS

With Tax Analysis

JOINT VENTURES

CORPORATIONS

By

PAUL LIEBERMAN
of the Michigan Bar

Sections 26.1 to 49

ST. PAUL, MINN.
WEST PUBLISHING CO.
1981

Library of Congress Catalog Card Number: 81-51744

SUMMARY OF CONTENTS

Volume 1

DIVISION I. CHOICE OF BUSINESS FORM

DIVISION II. TAX LAWS—SOURCES AND ADMINISTRATION

DIVISION III. INDIVIDUALS IN BUSINESS (PROPRIETORSHIPS)

DIVISION IV. PARTNERSHIPS

PART A. FORMATION AND OPERATION OF PARTNERSHIP

SUMMARY OF CONTENTS

PART B. TRANSFERS AND LIQUIDATIONS OF PARTNERSHIP INTERESTS

Volume 2

DIVISION V. JOINT VENTURES

DIVISION VI. CORPORATIONS

PART A. PREINCORPORATION MATTERS

PART B. INCORPORATION PROCEDURES

TABLE OF CONTENTS

DIVISION V. JOINT VENTURES

CHAPTER 26. JOINT VENTURES

DIVISION VI. CORPORATIONS

PART A. PREINCORPORATION MATTERS

CHAPTER 27. PREINCORPORATION CHECKLIST AND WORKSHEET

CHAPTER 28. SELECTING THE INCORPORATION STATE

CHAPTER 29. PREINCORPORATION AGREEMENTS

A. AGREEMENTS—GENERALLY

B. PREINCORPORATION AGREEMENTS

CHAPTER 30. SPECIAL PROBLEMS OF CLOSE CORPORATIONS

CHAPTER 31. ENTITIES TREATED AS CORPORATIONS FOR STATE LAW AND TAX LAW PURPOSES

TABLE OF CONTENTS

PART B. INCORPORATION PROCEDURES

CHAPTER 32. STEPS OF INCORPORATION—GENERALLY

CHAPTER 33. ARTICLES OF INCORPORATION

CHAPTER 34. BY-LAWS

A. INTRODUCTION

B. BY-LAW FORMS

CHAPTER 35. ORGANIZATION MEETING(S)

A. IN GENERAL

B. MEETING OF INCORPORATORS

TABLE OF CONTENTS

PART C. CORPORATE FINANCE—GENERALLY

CHAPTER 38. CORPORATE FINANCE

A. METHODS OF FINANCING—GENERALLY

B. EQUITY (STOCK)

C. DEBT FINANCING

D. TAX IMPLICATIONS OF THE ISSUANCE OF STOCK AND DEBT

CHAPTER 39. SUBSCRIPTIONS AND ISSUANCE OF SHARES

TABLE OF CONTENTS

CHAPTER 40. AUTHORIZED SHARES

TABLE OF CONTENTS

CHAPTER 41. STOCK CERTIFICATES

TABLE OF CONTENTS

CHAPTER 45. STOCKHOLDER MEETINGS AND CONSENTS

A. STOCKHOLDER MEETINGS

1. Introduction

2. Notices and Calls for Meetings

3. Stockholder Meeting—Minute Formats

B. STOCKHOLDER CONSENTS

C. STOCKHOLDER DISSENTS

D. MISCELLANEOUS FORMS

CHAPTER 46. BOARD OF DIRECTORS

A. INTRODUCTION

B. DIRECTORS' MEETINGS

C. DIRECTORS' RESOLUTIONS

TABLE OF CONTENTS

CHAPTER 47. VOTING OF SHARES

A. VOTING RIGHTS GENERALLY

B. PROXIES

C. VOTING TRUSTS

D. STOCKHOLDER VOTING AGREEMENTS

E. POOLING AGREEMENTS

TABLE OF CONTENTS

CHAPTER 48. RESOLUTIONS AND MINUTES (STOCKHOLDERS AND BOARD OF DIRECTORS)

A. IN GENERAL

B. RESOLUTIONS AND MINUTES

TABLE OF CONTENTS

TABLE OF CONTENTS

CHAPTER 49. INSPECTION OF BOOKS AND RECORDS

TABLE OF CONTENTS

*

BUSINESS ORGANIZATIONS

DIVISION V
JOINT VENTURES

CHAPTER 26
JOINT VENTURES

Table of Sections

§ 26.1 Introduction [1]

A Joint Venture (JV) or Joint Adventure is a business association distinguishable from Partnership (if at all) only by narrowness of purpose and scope. A Partnership may be formed for a single undertaking, but is usually intended to encompass an indefinite number of transactions within a relatively broad line of business for an indefinite duration. Typically, some or all of the Partners devote their entire time to the business. A JV is commonly a single undertaking or series of related undertakings, not requiring the entire attention of the participants, and having a fairly short duration. A wide variety of formal and informal financial and business arrangements may be JVs,[2] whether or not the phrase is used by the parties.

1. Adapted from Crane and Bromberg, Law of Partnerships, § 35.

2. Joint Venture examples include:

Real estate speculation, Adams v. Bruce, 265 Mich. 137, 251 N.W. 328 (1934); Saunders v. McDonough, 191 Ala. 119, 67 So. 591 (1914); Fitzhugh v. Thode, 221 Iowa 533, 265 N.W. 893 (1936); Cecil v. Montgomery, 95 Okl. 184, 218 P. 311 (1923).

Subdivision and sale of real estate, Fishback v. U. S., 215 F.Supp 621 (D.C.S.D.1963). By Agreement with

JVs are commonly used to carry out a single transaction (such as constructing a single building) or to develop and lease or sell a particular property. The participants may number in the dozens or hundreds when they are mainly suppliers of capital, or there may be only two. There is no easy dividing line between JV and Partnership, whether the question is to classify the operation or to find the consequences of its classification one way or the other. If anything, a court is more likely to find a JV than a Partnership when a plaintiff tries to enforce vicarious liability on a member of a loose group with which he dealt.

As in Partnership, there is confusion about the essential elements, similarly attributable to the effort to do equity in a variety of situations. Sometimes an outsider is urging the existence of the relation in order to find a solvent defendant he can hold liable. Other times the dispute is among the alleged Venturers themselves, one claiming a right to profits or property in the hands of another, or to contribution for losses incurred by him. Speaking generally, a JV, like a Partnership, requires a business purpose as distinct from a social one,[3] or from an incidental economic benefit. For example, an effort to enforce a zoning law, joined in by several property owners, resulting in a settlement and payment of damages, is not a JV for the purpose of requiring an equal division of the funds received.[4] There must be co-ownership of the enterprise, as distinguished from a principal and agent relation,[5] and probably a degree of common

landowner, real estate agent advanced funds for improvement and subdivision, and sold lots. Proceeds were allocated to pay landowner $400 per lot, to reimburse him for certain earlier improvements, and to reimburse the agent for funds advanced; any surplus was to be divided equally between them. Held: landowner not entitled to capital gain on $400 per lot; land passed to Joint Venture created by them, and was held primarily for sale to customers.

Production of a play, Selwyn & Co. v. Waller, 212 N.Y. 507, 106 N.E. 321, L.R.A.1915B, 160 (1914), motion to amend remittitur denied 213 N.Y. 678, 107 N.E. 1085.

Co-authorship of a play, Losch v. Marcin, 251 N.Y. 402, 167 N.E. 514 (1929).

Building construction, Zech v. Bell, 94 Wash. 344, 162 P. 363 (1917).

Purchase, holding and sale of bank stock, Chisholm v. Gilmer, 81 F.2d 120 (4th Cir. 1936), affirmed 299 U.S. 99, 57 S.Ct. 65, 81 L.Ed. 63, rehearing denied 29 U.S. 623, 57 S.Ct. 229, 81 L.Ed. 458.

Acquiring, financing and operating utility projects by banking firms, Smith, Landeryou & Co. v. Hollingsworth, 218 Iowa 920, 251 N.W. 749 (1934).

Association of fighter and manager, Safro v. Lakofsky, 191 Minn. 532, 255 N.W. 94 (1934).

Jaeger, Joint Ventures: Membership, Types and Termination, 9 Am.U.L. Rev. 111, 117–27 (1960) exhaustively lists the kinds of enterprises which have appeared in JV litigation.

3. Krause v. Hall, 195 Wis. 565, 217 N.W. 290 (1928).

4. Sappenfield v. Mead, 338 Ill.App. 236, 87 N.E.2d 220 (1949).

5. Ross v. Burrage, 233 Mass. 439, 124 N.E. 267 (1919) (employer had no fiduciary duty to disclose as he would in a JV).

control (although this may be unimportant where one person is conducting the entire activity with others as investors). There must be an intention to submit the capital investment (if any) of each associate to the risks of the enterprise, as distinguished from a loan to be returned absolutely.[6] The sharing of profits is presumptive of Joint Venture, but not conclusive, as it is for Partnership.[7] No express Agreement to share losses seems necessary, since this will be a consequence if the JV exists.[8] And no express agreement to form a JV is requisite; the relation may be inferred from conduct.[9] A JV

Chapman v. Dwyer, 40 F.2d 468 (2d Cir. 1930). Arrangement between attorneys for mutual assistance in certain cases held not to show intent to enter a JV so that accounting in equity (as distinct from law action for compensation) would be maintainable.

The essentials of a JV have been said to be at least (a) community of interest in the object of the undertaking, (b) equal right to direct and govern the conduct of each other therein, (c) share in loss, (d) close and even fiduciary relation. Beck v. Cagle, 46 Cal.App.2d 152, 115 P.2d 613 (1941). Some of these elements are consequences rather than prerequisites. Another judicial formulation and extended discussion is Ford v. McCue, 163 Ohio St. 498, 127 N.E.2d 209 (1955) (owner of truck and bakery route not in JV with one who took them over for several weeks during his vacation; no sharing of receipts or expenses, no control). Cf. Zorich v. Petroff, 152 Cal.App.2d 806, 313 P. 2d 118 (1957) (no JV for production of film; plaintiff, by agreement, was to be associate producer and share profits but did not assume financial risks or have right of control, hence he had no property interest in the film).

6. Treat v. Murdock, 55 P.2d 547 (Cal. App.1936); Waldman v. Shoemaker, 367 Pa. 587, 80 A.2d 776 (1951) (P lent $18,000 to operator of turkey raising project and was to receive share of profits; held: P entitled to repayment of loan though project was unsuccessful; Ds retained sole title to turkeys, eggs and proceeds of sale; Ps had no voice in control; no express or implied Agreement to share losses).

7. See Garner v. Maxwell, n. 84 above and, generally, U.P.A. § 7, Secs. 14–20 above. Mere royalty payments or commissions are not enough, Nizuk v. Gorges, 180 Cal.App.2d 699, 4 Cal. Rptr. 565 (1960) (furniture store with franchised thrift plan paid franchiser fixed fee per member and fixed percentage of gross sales to members); Bates v. Simpson, 121 Utah 165, 239 P.2d 749 (1952) (used car dealers operating on same lot and sharing expenses; each received $25 for selling a car belonging to the other, and a commission for arranging any financing).

8. The conflict and confusion on this point are traced in Comment, Joint Adventures—The Sharing of Losses Dilemma, 18 U.Miami L.Rev. 429 (1963).

Of course, within the firm, an Agreement (express or implied) for one member to bear all the losses is binding. Allison v. Dilsaver, 387 S.W.2d 206 (Mo.App.1965).

9. Ditscher v. Booth, 13 N.J.Super. 568, 80 A.2d 648 (1951); Stein v. George B. Spearin, Inc., 120 N.J.Eq. 169, 184 A. 436, 437 (1936); Ditis v. Ahlvin Constr. Co., 408 Ill. 416, 97 N.E.2d 244 (1951).

A husband-wife relationship in operating a household is said to be not the result of contract but of status under which he must provide her with a home. Accordingly, it is not a JV, and he is not responsible for her negligent performance of household chores injuring a third person. State ex rel. McCrory v. Bland, 355 Mo. 706, 197 S.W.2d 669, 168 A.L.R. 929 (1946). Cf. Lemon v. Lonker, 97 Pa. Super. 240 (1929).

may exist by estoppel, when one holds himself out as a Joint Venturer or consents to another's doing so.[10]

Whether a JV is considered a Partnership or merely analogized to one, the Venturers are governed by the rules applicable to Partners.[11] The U.P.A. applies, e. g., to the results of wrongful dissolution.[12] There are the usual fiduciary duties to account for profits and joint property,[13] although the more limited purpose and part-time participation may shrink the area in which non-competition aspects of fiduciary duty are operative.[14] Quite generally, the agreement among Joint Venturers has the same central role as in Partnership.[15] It fully binds the members, though not ignorant outsiders.

JV members are personally liable for debts, like Partners. Each Venturer has authority to act and bind within the scope of the business.[16] Such authority is limited to the actual or apparent scope of

10. John's, Inc. v. Long Island Garden Center of Nassau, Inc., 49 Misc.2d 1086, 269 N.Y.S.2d 231 (Dist.Ct.1966). See Garrison v. Place, 92 Ohio App. 239, 109 N.E.2d 569 (1952).

11. Few v. Few, 239 S.C. 321, 122 S. E.2d 829 (1962). See Homestake Mining Co. v. Mid-Continent Exploration Co., 282 F.2d 787 (10th Cir. 1960) (N.M. law) (this Limited Partnership could be more accurately described as several JVs among subgroups of its members, but same fiduciary duties apply either way).

The assignment of an interest in a JV is similar to that in Partnership. Meinhard v. Salmon, n. 13, infra.

12. Zeibak v. Nasser, 12 Cal.2d 1, 82 P.2d 375 (1938). Although a JV's purpose has not been accomplished, a member has power to dissolve, exposing himself to liability for breach of contract. See Comment, 38 Calif. L.Rev. 860, 868 (1950).

A JV without a fixed term can be ended without liability by any party at any time. Harrington v. Sorelle, 313 F.2d 10 (10th Cir. 1963) (N.M. law).

13. Homestake Mining Co. v. Mid-Continent Exploration Co., n. 93 above; Allen v. Steinberg, 244 Md. 119, 223 A.2d 240 (1966).

Smith, Landeryou & Co. v. Hollingsworth, 218 Iowa 920, 251 N.W. 749 (1934); Mendelsohn v. Leather Mfg. Corp., 326 Mass. 226, 93 N.E.2d 537 (1950) (one Venturer buying out interest of the other); Johnson v. Ironside, 249 Mich. 35, 227 N.W. 732 (1929) (dealings in property within scope of JV).

14. See Homestake Mining Co. v. Mid-Continent Exploration Co., n. 93 above, finding no usurpation of "partnership opportunity" in one Partner's building a uranium mill similar to the firm's. In a General Partnership the result might well have been different. Members entering a JV of narrow scope may impliedly waive some of the non-competitive phases of fiduciary duty, although the court in Homestake did not employ this theory.

15. If the existence of a JV depends entirely on the effect of a written agreement, it must be sufficiently definite and complete in its terms to be a valid contract in general. Mason :. Rose, 176 F.2d 486 (2d Cir. 1949), noted 18 Geo.Wash.L.Rev. 559, 48 Mich.L.Rev. 701 (1950), 1950 U.Ill. L.F. 136 (actor-movie producer contract incomplete). A very sketchy agreement that "any future purchase of stock shall be made on a 50-50 basis" was recognized as valid and enforceable, without calling it a JV, in Butler v. Attwood, 369 F.2d 811 (6th Cir. 1966) (Mich. law).

16. Bushman Constr. Co. v. Air Force Academy Housing, Inc., 327 F.2d 481 (10th Cir. (1964) Colo. law) (payment and lien waiver certificates in conthe Venture. The usual narrow purpose puts constraints on actual authority and, to a lesser extent, on apparent authority. Agreements to limit authority further are effective only among members and against third parties with notice.[17] It is a great mistake to think (as some businessmen do) that a Joint Venture offers significant protection from liability.

A Joint Venturer may have an accounting in equity.[18] This remedy is not always exclusive, and he may be allowed a suit at law for delivery of joint property or contribution to expenses incurred.[19] But, as in Partnership, if there are many transactions and the financial relations are complicated, component claims will not be passed on piecemeal by the courts, and an accounting will be necessary.

If not considered technically a Partnership, a group of Joint Venturers could not be adjudicated bankrupt as a single entity. Rules of creditor priority in joint and separate property would not apply. But, in the many states where JVs are deemed Partnerships, there is no reason why they should not be so treated in bankruptcy.

Where JVs are distinguished from Partnerships, they are likely to be accorded less entity status. Even so, there is recognition of an equivalent of the Partners' equities doctrine at common law.[20]

While the death of a Joint Venturer will normally bring about a technical dissolution, the typical limited objective of the firm makes it easier to find an implied agreement that the objective be carried out, and the firm continued by the survivors. Such a conclusion is strengthened if the survivor was given powers of representation by the original Agreement,[21] or if there are a number of Venturers and

struction subcontracting JV); Foote v. Posey, 164 Cal.App.2d 210, 330 P. 2d 651 (1958) (note and mortgage in real estate JV); Deicher v. Corkery, 205 Cal.App.2d 654, 23 Cal.Rptr. 270 (1962) (agreement with selling agent to reimburse him for crediting part of his commission against sale price in order to avoid revision of escrow documents when acreage discrepancy discovered; real estate JV); Bond v. O'Donnell, 205 Iowa 902, 218 N.W. 898, 63 A.L.R. 901 (1928); Daily v. Scott, 74 S.W.2d 881 (Mo.App.1934) (collection of JV debt).

17. Taylor v. Brindley, 164 F.2d 235 (10th Cir. 1947) (Okl. law; constructive knowledge of limitation from instrument recorded in chain of title).

18. Saunders v. McDonough, 191 Ala. 119, 67 So. 591 (1914); Butler v. Union Trust Co., 178 Cal. 195, 172 P. 601 (1918); Waldo Lumber Co. v. Metcalf, 132 Me. 374, 171 A. 395 (1934); Adams v. Bruce, 265 Mich. 137, 251 N.W. 328 (1934).

19. Clark v. Sidway, 142 U.S. 682, 12 S.Ct. 327, 35 L.Ed. 1157 (1892); Brudvik v. Frosaker Blaisdell Co., 56 N.D. 215, 216 N.W. 891 (1927); Cecil v. Montgomery, 95 Okl. 184, 218 P. 311 (1923); Kingsley Clothing Mfg. Co. v. Jacobs, 344 Pa. 551, 26 A.2d 315 (1942).

20. Twyford v. Sonken-Galamba Corp., 177 Okl. 486, 60 P.2d 1050 (1936) (Venturer's mortgage of his interest held subject to Co-venturer's equities).

21. Pownall v. Cearfoss, 129 W.Va. 487, 40 S.E.2d 886 (1946). If the decedent was to participate personally in the Venture, his death should dissolve. Roberts v. Weiner, 137 Conn. 668, 81 A.2d 115 (1951).

they have agreed that the majority can make decisions [22] and take action. If the firm is to be wound up, the job should, as in Partnership, devolve on the survivors.

A JV is a Partnership for income tax purposes.[23] In particular, profits are taxable to the members as earned, whether or not distributed.[24]

Where Corporations are not permitted to be Partners, the JV takes on added significance since Corporations may nonetheless enter JVs. The distinction is made that a JV involves less delegation of managerial authority of the Board of Directors. Corporate Joint Ventures are now often themselves incorporated, so that the vehicle is technically a commonly-owned subsidiary rather than a JV.

Library References:

C.J.S. Joint Adventures § 1.
West's Key No. Digests, Joint Adventures ⚷1 et seq.

§ 26.2 Basic Joint Venture Agreement

COMMENT

This form only covers certain substantive matters. The practitioner is urged to also consult the sophisticated Joint Venture Agreement at § 26.3, infra.

[*Name*]

JOINT VENTURE AGREEMENT

This Agreement, made and entered into as of the [*Date*], by and among [*Names*] (all of whom together are hereinafter collectively sometimes referred to as "Venturers").

WITNESSETH

Whereas, the Parties hereto desire to form a Joint Venture (hereinafter referred to as the "Venture") for the term and upon the conditions hereinafter set forth;

Now, therefore, in consideration of the mutual covenants hereinafter contained, it is agreed by and among the Parties hereto as follows:

Article I

BASIC STRUCTURE

§ 1.1 Form

The Parties hereby form a Venture pursuant to the Laws of [*Name of State*].

22. Harmon v. Martin, 395 Ill. 595, 71 N.E.2d 74 (1947).

23. IRC § 761(a).

24. For discussion of Partnership taxation, see Chapters 17 and 18, supra.

§ 1.2 Name

The business of the Venture shall be conducted under the name of [*Name*].

§ 1.3 Place of Business

The principal office and place of business of the Venture shall be located at [*Describe*], or such other place as the Venturers may from time to time designate.

§ 1.4 Term

The Venture shall commence on [*Date*], and shall continue for [*Number*] years, unless earlier terminated in the following manner:

(a) By the completion of the purpose intended, or

(b) Pursuant to this Agreement, or

(c) By applicable [*State*] law, or

(d) By death, insanity, bankruptcy, retirement, withdrawal, resignation, expulsion, or disability of all the then Venturers.

Alternative A

§ 1.5 Purpose—Manufacture

The purpose for which the Venture is organized is to manufacture, fabricate and assemble the following products: ______; and to sell, lease and otherwise promote and deal in the same and in related products and services and to manufacture, fabricate and assemble the tools, materials and equipment reasonably necessary for such manufacturing processes.

Alternative B

§ 1.5 Purpose—Publication and Broadcasting

The purpose for which the Venture is organized is to create, prepare, draft, design, print, broadcast and publish material relating to the following subject matters: ______ in and for all forms of broadcasting and publication including radio, television, newspaper, magazines, and all other forms of commercial and noncommercial media.

Alternative C

§ 1.5 Purpose—Real Estate

The purpose for which the Venture is organized is to operate, manage, improve, repair, rent, lease, own, acquire, sell, assign, mortgage, hypothecate, and otherwise deal in the following real property and its appurtenances and fixtures and to deal in direct interests, Partnership interests, Stockholder interests and joint venture interests which represent shares in such property to build or contract for the building or buildings and other structures on such property for such uses: ______.

Alternative D

§ 1.5 Purpose—Research

The purpose for which the Venture is organized is to conduct under its employment (or through independent contracts or Joint Ventures) research, design and development of the following: ______; and to experiment, test and test market the products, services and processes resulting from such research and development and to investigate, consult, report, and render advice as to the development of similar products and the techniques and methods of their manufacture and sale.

Alternative E

§ 1.5 Purpose—Sales

The purpose for which the Venture is organized is to lease, sell, import, export and to finance purchases and sales of the following products and services: ______; and to promote the sale thereof and to install, maintain and improve the products so sold and to maintain an inventory of the products to be sold and their repair parts and to finance such inventory by factoring or other forms of finance or hypothecation.

Alternative F

§ 1.5 Purpose—Services—Business

The purpose for which the Venture is organized is to render the following services: ______; and to own and operate the associated facilities, equipment and real estate to render such services to the public at large.

Alternative G

§ 1.5 Purpose—School

The purpose for which the Venture is organized is to conduct and offer to the public educational training in the following areas: ______.

Alternative H

§ 1.5 Purpose—Wholesale

The purpose for which the Venture is organized is to purchase, sell, warehouse, hold, take on consignment, receive, store, forward, factor, collaterally assign and otherwise borrow against and finance inventory of the following kind and nature: ______.

§ 1.6 Investment Representative of Venturers

Each Venturer represents and warrants that he is acquiring his interest in the Venture for his own account, for investment, and not with a view to the sale or distribution thereof.

Article II

FINANCIAL ARRANGEMENTS

§ 2.1 Initial Contributions of Venturers

Each Venturer has made available to the initial capital of the Venture property in the amount and form indicated on Schedule A attached hereto and made a part hereof.

§ 2.2 Additional Capital Contribution

If at any time during the existence of the Venture it shall become necessary to increase the available capital with which the said Venture is doing business, then (upon the vote of the Managing Venturer(s)):

[*Names*] shall contribute to the capital of this Venture within ______ days notice of such need in an amount (according to their then Percentage Share of Profits) as called for by the Managing Venturer(s).

§ 2.3 Percentage Share of Profits

(a) The Percentage Share of Profits of each Venturer shall be (unless otherwise modified by the terms of this Agreement) as follows:

Names	Initial Percentage Share of Profits

§ 2.4 Return of Capital Contributions

Each Venturer shall have the right to demand the return of the capital made available to the Venturer upon its dissolution, subject to Article IV.

§ 2.5 Rights of Priority

Except as herein provided, the individual Venturers shall have no right to any priority over each other as to the return of capital.

§ 2.6 Distributions

Distributions to the Venturers of net operating profits of the Venture, as hereinafter defined, shall be made [*at least monthly/at such time as the Managing Venturers shall reasonably agree*]. Such distributions shall be made to the Venturers simultaneously.

For the purpose of this Agreement, net operating profit for any accounting period shall mean the gross receipts of the Venture for such period, less the sum of all cash expenses of operation of the Venture, and such sums as may be necessary to establish a reserve for operating expenses.

Option

In determining net operating profit, deductions for depreciation, amortization, or other similar charges not requiring actual current expenditures of cash shall *not* be taken into account.

Option

In any case, [*Number*] percent of Venture income shall be left in the Venture as a further contribution capital by each Venturer.

§ 2.7 Compensation

Alternative A—1

No Venturer shall be entitled to receive any compensation from the Venture, nor shall any Venturer receive any drawing account from the Venture.

Alternative A—2

The Managing Venturers may pay compensation to any Venturer as they deem reasonable.

Article III

MANAGEMENT

§ 3.1 Managing Venturers

The Managing Venturers shall be: [[*Name*]/*all Venturers*].

§ 3.2 Voting

Alternative A

All Managing Venturers shall have the right to vote as to the management and conduct of the business of the Venture according to their then Percentage Share of Income. Except as otherwise herein set forth a majority of such Income shall control.

Alternative B

The Managing Venturers shall have the right to vote as to the management and conduct of the business of the Venture as follows:

Names	**Vote**

Article IV

DISSOLUTION

§ 4.1 Dissolution

In the event that the Venture shall hereafter be dissolved for any reason whatsoever, a full and general account of its assets, liabilities and transactions shall at once be taken. Such assets may be sold and turned into cash as soon as possible and all debts and other amounts due the Venture collected. The proceeds thereof shall thereupon be applied as follows:

(a) To discharge the debts and liabilities of the Venture and the expenses of liquidation.

(b) To pay each Venturer or his legal representative any unpaid salary, drawing account, interest or profits to which he shall then be entitled.

(c) To repay to any Venturer the capital he made available.

(d) To divide the surplus, if any, among the Venturers or their representatives according to each Venturer's then Percentage Share of Profits.

Article V

MISCELLANEOUS

§ 5.1 Accounting Year, Books, Statements

The Venture's fiscal year shall commence on *January 1st* of each year and shall end on *December 31st* of each year. Full and accurate books of account shall be kept at such place as the Managing Venturers may from time to time designate, showing the condition of the business and finances of the Venture; and each Venturer shall have access to such books of account and shall be entitled to examine them at any time during ordinary business hours. At the end of each year, the Managing Venturers shall cause the Venture's accountant to prepare a balance sheet setting forth the financial position of the Venture as of the end of that year and a statement of operations (income and expenses) for that year. A copy of the balance sheet and statement of operations shall be delivered to each Venturer as soon as it is available.

Each Venturer shall be deemed to have waived all objections to any transaction or other facts about the operation of the Venture disclosed in such balance sheet and/or statement of operations unless he shall have notified the Managing Venturers in writing of his objectives within thirty (30) days of the date on which such statement is mailed.

§ 5.2 Banking

The Venture shall maintain a bank account or bank accounts in the Venture's name in a national or state bank in the State of [*Name*]. Checks and drafts shall be drawn on the Venture's bank account for Venture purposes only and shall be signed by the Managing Venturers, or their designated agent.

§ 5.3 Titles and Subtitles

Titles of the paragraphs and subparagraphs are placed herein for convenient reference only and shall not to any extent have the effect of modifying, amending or changing the express terms and provisions of this Venture Agreement.

§ 5.4 Words and Gender or Number

As used herein, unless the context clearly indicates the contrary, the singular number shall include the plural, the plural the singular, and the use of any gender shall be applicable to all genders.

§ 5.5 Execution in Counterpart

This Venture Agreement may be executed in any number of counterparts, each of which shall be taken to be an original.

§ 5.6 Severability

In the event any parts of this Agreement are found to be void, the remaining provisions of this Agreement shall nevertheless be binding with the same effect as though the void parts were deleted.

§ 5.7 Effective Date

This Agreement shall be effective only upon execution by all of the proposed Venturers.

§ 5.8 Waiver

No waiver of any provisions of this Agreement shall be valid unless in writing and signed by the persons or party against whom charged.

§ 5.9 Assignment

This Agreement shall be binding upon and inure to the benefit of the parties hereto and their respective heirs, legal representatives, executors, administrators, successors and assigns.

Preferred as a Matter of Practical Experience

§ 5.10 Arbitration

Any controversy or claim arising out of or relating to this Agreement shall only be settled by arbitration in accordance with the rules of the American Arbitration Association, one Arbitrator, and shall be enforceable in any court having competent jurisdiction.

Witnesses	Venturers
______________________	______________________
______________________	______________________

Dated: ______.

Schedule A

Capital Contributed	Name of Venturer
______________________	______________________
______________________	______________________

Library References:

C.J.S. Joint Adventures § 3.
West's Key No. Digests, Joint Adventures ⚷1.10.

§ 26.3 Comprehensive Joint Venture Agreement

GENERAL COMMENT

The following Joint Venture Agreement is presented as a jumbo set list of possible provisions. It should be noted that many of these are mutually exclusive or serve conflicting goals.

Table of Sections

Article II. Financial Arrangements

Section

2.1 Definitions.
2.2 Initial Contribution of Venturers.
2.3 Additional Capital Contribution.
2.4 Percentage Share of Capital.
2.5 Shift in Venturer's Share of Capital.
2.6 Venturer's Share of the Profits and Losses.
2.7 Allocation of Liquidation Preferences.
2.8 Return of Capital Contributions.
2.9 Rights of Priority.
2.10 Distributions.
2.11 Compensation.

Article III. Management

Section

3.1 Managing Venturers.
3.2 Voting.
3.3 Rights, Powers and Restriction of Payments.
3.4 Powers of (Names).
3.5 Liability.

Article IV. Right to Assign Venture Interest

Section

4.1 Venturer's Right of Assignment of Profits and Losses.

Article V. Dissolution

Section

5.1 Dissolution.

Article VI. Miscellaneous—Substantive Provisions

Section

6.1 Miscellaneous—Substantive Provisions.
6.2 Venture's Agents.
6.3 Transfers to Living Trusts.
6.4 Checks.
6.5 Conflicts of Interest.

Article VII. Miscellaneous

Section

7.1 Execution in Counterpart.
7.2 Indemnification.
7.3 Notice.
7.4 Modifications.
7.5 Agreement Binding.
7.6 Amendments.
7.7 Banking.
7.8 Titles and Subtitles.

[*Name*]

JOINT VENTURE AGREEMENT

This Agreement, made and entered into as of the [*Date*], by and among [*Names*] (all of whom together are hereinafter collectively sometimes referred to as "Venturers").

WITNESSETH

Whereas, the Parties hereto desire to form a Joint Venture (hereinafter referred to as the "Venture") for the term and upon the conditions hereinafter set forth;

Now, therefore, in consideration of the mutual covenants hereinafter contained, it is agreed by and among the Parties hereto as follows:

Article I
BASIC STRUCTURE

§ 1.1 Form

The Parties hereby form a Joint Venture pursuant to the Laws of [*Name of State*].

§ 1.2 Name

The business of the Venture shall be conducted under the name of [*Name*].

§ 1.3 Place of Business

The principal office and place of business of the Venture shall be located at [*Describe*], or such other place as the Venturers may from time to time designate.

§ 1.4 Term

The Venture shall commence on [*Date*], and shall continue for [*Number*] years, unless earlier terminated in the following manner:

(a) By the completion of the purpose intended, or

(b) Pursuant to this Agreement, or

(c) By applicable [*State*] law, or

(d) By death, insanity, bankruptcy, retirement, withdrawal, resignation, expulsion, or disability of all of the then Venturers.

Alternative A

§ 1.5 Purpose—Farming

The purpose for which the Venture is organized is to cultivate, raise, grow, produce and sell the following products: ______.

Alternative B

§ 1.5 Purpose—Finance

The purpose for which the Venture is organized is to subscribe or, acquire, purchase, invest in and deal in, interests in public and private security offerings and to underwrite and participate in security offerings of every type, including stock, securities, warrants, options, bonds, notes, indentures and other secured and unsecured equity and debt instruments.

Alternative C

§ 1.5 Purpose—Manufacture

The purpose for which the Venture is organized is to manufacture, fabricate, and assemble the following products: ______; and to sell, lease and otherwise promote and deal in the same and in related products and services and to manufacture, fabricate and assemble the tools, materials and equipment reasonably necessary for such manufacturing processes.

Alternative D

§ 1.5 Purpose—Publication and Broadcasting

The purpose for which the Venture is organized is to create, prepare, draft, design, print, broadcast and publish material relating to the following subject matters: ______ in and for all forms of broadcasting and publication including radio, television, newspaper, magazines, and all other forms of commercial and noncommercial media.

Alternative E

§ 1.5 Purpose—Wholesale

The purpose for which the Venture is organized is to purchase, sell, warehouse, hold, take on consignment, receive, store, forward, factor, collaterally assign and otherwise borrow against and finance inventory of the following kind and nature: ______.

Alternative F

§ 1.5 Purpose—Real Estate

The purpose for which the Venture is organized is to operate, manage, improve, repair, rent, lease, own, acquire, sell, assign, mortgage, hypothecate, and otherwise deal in the following real property and its appurtenances and fixtures and to deal in direct interests, Partnership interests, Stockholder interests and Joint Venture interests which represent shares in such property to build or contract for the building or buildings and other structures on such property for such use: ______.

Alternative G

§ 1.5 Purpose—Research

The purpose for which the Venture is organized is to conduct under its employment (or through independent contracts or Joint Ventures) research, design and development of the following: ______; and to experiment, test and test market the products, services and processes resulting from such research and development and to investigate, consult report, and render advice as to the development of similar products and the techniques and methods of their manufacture and sale.

Alternative H

§ 1.5 Purpose—Sales

The purpose for which the Venture is organized is to lease, sell, import, export and to finance purchases and sales of the following products and services: ______; and to promote the sale thereof and to install, maintain and improve the products so sold and to maintain an inventory of the products to be sold and their repair parts and to finance such inventory by factoring or other forms of finance or hypothecation.

Alternative I

§ 1.5 Service—Business

The purpose for which the Venture is organized is to render the following services: ______; and to own and operate the associated facilities, equipment and real estate to render such services to the public at large.

Alternative J

§ 1.5 Purpose—School

The purpose for which the Venture is organized is to conduct and offer to the public educational training in the following areas: _______.

§ 1.6 Investment Representative of Venturers

Each Venturer represents and warrants that he is acquiring his interest in the Venture for his own account, for investment, and not with a view to the sale or distribution thereof.

Article II

FINANCIAL ARRANGEMENTS

§ 2.1 Definitions

For purposes of this document "capital" shall be defined as property made available to and owned by the Venture other than property of a kind which would be includable in the inventory of the Venture or which is held for sale to customers of the Venture in its ordinary course of business. The gain on such property and the losses, deductions, amortization and depreciation associated with such property shall be added to or subtracted from the Venturer's capital accounts (using the [*initial/then*] capital accounts as a base) according to their then share of [*capital/income*].

All other ("operating") profits (or losses) of the Venture shall be (if income) deemed to be income of the Venturers according to their share of profits and losses. If losses, these shall be deducted from the Venturer's capital accounts according to their share of profits and losses. Undistributed profits shall be added to the relevant Venturer's capital accounts. Amounts distributed in excess of current profits shall be deducted from the relevant Venturer's capital accounts.

Upon dissolution, any Venturer having a negative capital account balance shall:

Alternative A

be required to make up such a balance.

Alternative B

have no obligation to the Venture.

COMMENT TO § 2.1

By separating the initial capital (which will be repaid to the contributing Venturers as a priority item upon liquidation) from increases (and decreases) in the Venture capital accounts (see § 2.-5, infra), the Venturer may receive a higher or lower share of capital increases than his contribution of property warrants.

COMMENTS TO ALTERNATIVE A

It may be necessary to include this provision in order for the Venture to specially allocate capital gains and *losses* in a system which disregards capital contributions when allocating such gains and losses (except to the extent to which the system is merely allocating potential gains of contributed property (as set forth in Options 1 and 2 of § 2.4, infra.) This is especially true if the Venture can reasonably expect a capital loss on such property.

It may also be necessary to include this provision in order for the Venture to specially allocate *income and operating losses* in a system which disregards capital contributions and services rendered. This is especially true if the Venture can reasonably expect an operating loss to be generated from the ownership of such property.

The reason why this is necessary is that special allocations of tax consequences must relate to the economic impact of the Venturer's rights. If losses are deducted, then those Venturers must either suffer economic losses or (in the case where the tax loss will exceed the Venturer's actual economic loss), make up such losses at some future date.

§ 2.2 Initial Contribution of Venturers

Each Venturer has made available to the initial capital of the Venture property in the amount and form indicated on Schedule A attached hereto and made a part hereof. An individual capital account shall be maintained for each Venturer.

§ 2.3 Additional Capital Contribution

If at any time during the existence of the Venture it shall become necessary to increase the capital with which the said Venture is doing business, then (upon the vote of the Managing Venturers):

[*Names*] shall contribute to the capital of this Venture (within _______ days notice of such *need*) an amount according to his then Percentage Share of Profits as called for by the Managing Venturer(s).

§ 2.4 Percentage Share of Capital

(a) The Percentage Share of Capital of each Venturer shall be (unless otherwise modified by the terms of this Agreement) as follows:

Names	Initial Percentage Share of Capital

(b) The gains, losses, deductions and credits relating to the following capital assets are specially allocated to the following Venturers (and they shall not be taken into account in the general allocation provided for above, which general allocation shall be supplemental to such special allocation):

Option 1

Any investment credit recaptured on the following property shall be allocated to the Venturer(s) as follows:

Property	Venturer(s)

Option 2

Any recapture under Internal Revenue Code §§ 1245, 1250, or 1252 shall be allocated to the following Venturers:

Property Upon Whose Disposition Recapture Is Charged	Venturer(s) Recapture Is Allocated To

Option 3

All Internal Revenue Code § 1251 gain on the following properties shall be allocated to the following Venturers:

Venturers	Percentage § 1251 of Gain So Allocated	Property

Option 4

The following assets had potential investment credit recapture or a fair market value in excess of their basis when contributed to the Venture; it is agreed that the income (and losses and recaptured investment credits) for tax purpose (but not for distribution purposes) shall be allocated to the following Venturer(s) who contributed such property to the extent that income tax gain (and losses and recaptured investment credits) is recognized on the disposition of such property:

Assets	Venturer

Option 5

Item: [*Describe Asset*]

Name	Venturer's Names Who Will Share in the Special Allocation	Percentage of Allocation Among the Venturers Sharing the Special Allocation

Not Preferred as a Matter of Practical Experience

(c) Election under Internal Revenue Code § 754. The Venturer shall make the special election to allocate basis under Internal Revenue Code § 754.

COMMENT TO OPTIONS 1, 2 AND 3

Recapture gains will not be recognized by contributing Venturer, but will have to be recognized to the Venture upon disposition (even though the Venture has not benefited from the tax deduction or credit). Thus, a special allocation of such gain to the contributing Venturer may be in order when the capital contributed has, already, such recapture potential.

COMMENT TO OPTION 3

The purpose of this option is to avoid tax upon the formation of the Venture when Internal Revenue Code § 1251 Farm Recapture Property is being contributed by Venturers in different proportions than their Venture interests will be.

COMMENT TO OPTION 4

The ability to allocate the already existing potential gain to the Venturer contributing such assets is well accepted.

COMMENT TO (c)

The election under Internal Revenue Code § 754 will:

(a) Allow a new Venturer of the existing Venture to get the full tax benefit (or suffer the burden) of the greater (or lesser) basis in his Venturer interest relative to the original Venturers' then basis, and

(b) Allow the existing Venturers to incur the burden of the tax deduction which a Venturer who joined the Venture after its inception and who received a distribution of Venture property would otherwise have taken upon a Venture distribution of property whose basis is lower than the distributee's basis in his Venture interest (see Chapter 8, supra).

The financial advisor should assess the trouble of making the adjustments called for before such election is agreed to.

The election can be made, if all Venturers later agree in any year an adjustment would be made; but, once made, it can not be readily revoked.

§ 2.5 Shift in Venturer's Share of Capital

(a) [*Name*]'s capital interest shall increase by [*Describe Amount of Increase*] and [*Name*]'s capital interest shall decrease by [*Describe Amount of Decrease*] upon the following event: [*Describe*].

COMMENT TO (a)

This clause is used when the Venture (or a Venturer) wants to compensate another Venturer for the Venture reaching certain goals or having existed for a certain amount of time. Generally this type of shift in capital accounts will result in income to the Venturer being compensated and a deduction by the Venture. If it is desired that the Venturer(s) giving up part of their share receive this deduction, the special allocation of (b) below must be made.

(b) Upon the shift of a capital interest as provided in (a) above to [*Name*], the amount includable in such Venturer's income shall be deducted by [*Name*] who shall also bear the burden of any gain on the distribution. It shall be presumed that the amount transferred is:

Alternative A

Its value on the date of Venture formation.

Alternative B

Its value on the date of transfer.

COMMENT TO (b)

If the shift in capital interests is compensation to a Venturer then (in order to have the tax results follow the purpose of the shift) an Internal Revenue Code § 704 allocation should be made of the compensation which will be taxed to the Venture and (since Venturer(s) who suffer a reduction in interest provided the capital from which such capital was transferred) the deduction should be deducted by such other Venturer(s) and not by the Venture as a whole. If the Venture as a whole gets the deduction, then the Venturer receiving the increased benefit would share in this deduction.

§ 2.6 Venturer's Share of the Profits and Losses

(a) *Except as specially allocated,* the individual Venturers shall share in the profits and losses of the Venture according to the following priority:

(a) First Priority Venturers:

Names	Description of Priority

(b) Second Priority Venturers:

Names	Description of Priority

§ 2.7 Allocation of Liquidation Preferences

The following liquidating preferences shall be effective among Venturers:

Preference	Venturer
First $______________	[*Names*]
The rest	According to all Venturers' share of profits and losses

COMMENT TO § 2.7

This Section can provide the special distribution which will hopefully avoid gain on formation of the Venturer when one Venturer is contributing capital and the other services.

§ 2.8 Return of Capital Contributions

No Venturer shall have the right to demand the return of the capital he made available, except as herein provided.

§ 2.9 Rights of Priority

Except as herein provided, the individual Venturers shall have no right to any priority over each other as to the return of capital contributions.

§ 2.10 Distributions

Distributions to the Venturers of net operating profits of the Venture, as hereinafter defined, shall be made [*at least monthly/at such time as the Managing Venturers shall reasonably agree.*] Such distributions shall be made to the Venturers simultaneously.

For the purpose of this Agreement, net operating profit for any accounting period shall mean the gross receipts of the Venture for such period, less the sum of all cash expenses of operation of the Venture, and such sums as may be necessary to establish a reserve for operating expenses.

Option 1

In determining net operating profit, deductions for depreciation, amortization, or other similar charges not requiring actual current expenditures of cash [*shall be taken into account in accordance with generally accepted accounting principles/shall not be taken into account*].

Option 2

In any case, [*Number*] percent of Venture income shall be left in the Venture as a further contribution capital by each Venturer.

§ 2.11 Compensation

Alternative A

No Venturer shall be entitled to receive any compensation from the Venture, nor shall any Venturer receive any drawing account from the Venture.

Alternative B

The Managing Venturers may pay compensation to any Venturer as they deem reasonable.

Alternative C

(a) The Venture shall employ [*Name*] as the [*Describe*] of the Venture for a period of not less than [*Number*] months and shall pay him $[*Dollars*] per year for his services as such; said amount to be paid in [*Period*] installments of $[*Dollars*], the first such payment to be paid on [*Date*].

(b) [*Name*] shall have the authority to:

(1) Acquire and dispose of assets.

(2) Borrow money and give security therefor.

(3) Enter into contracts.

(4) Deposit and withdraw Venture funds.

(5) Employ and dismiss employees and establish their wages and benefits.

(6) Establish Venture procedures.

(7) Determine hours of operation.

(8) Advertise.

(9) [*Purchase/construct/lease*] the following plant and equipment: [*Describe*].

(10) Purchase the following inventory: ______.

(11) Establish the following sales representatives: ______.

(12) Determine the sales price of the Venture inventory.

(13) Do such other things, as he in his sole and reasonably exercised discretion, shall deem necessary to successfully establish, operate and manage the Venture.

(c) [*Name*]'s employment contract shall have the following fringe benefits:

(1) Medical Insurance with the following features:

(A) Hospital:

Room and board: ______.

Maximum no. of days: ______.

Intensive care additional: ______.

Intensive care no. of days: ______.

Maximum extra charges: ______.

Surgical schedule: ______.

Anesthesia: ______.

In-hospital benefit: ______.

Hospital-out-patient: ______.

(Supplemental accident): ______.

Radiation therapy: ______.

Diagnostic x-ray and lab: ______.

Maternity: ______.

(1) Medical Insurance with the following features:—Continued

(B) Major medical:

Maximum: ______.

Deductible: ______.

Co-insurance: ______.

Prescription drugs: ______.

Out-patient: ______.

Convalescent care: ______.

(C) Dental:

Deductible family: ______.

Oral exams, etc.: ______.

X-rays, fillings, etc.: ______.

Bridges, dentures, crowns, etc.: ______.

Maximum benefit: ______.

(D) Carrier: ______.

(2) Disability insurance with the following features:

(A) Carrier: ______.

(B) Wait upon accidental disability: ______.

(C) Wait up sickness: ______.

(D) Benefit per week: $______.

(E) Reduction for partial disability: ______.

(F) Reduction for ability to be employed full time in some other job: ______.

(G) Benefit period upon accident: ______.

(H) Benefit period upon sickness: ______.

(3) Group term life insurance:

(A) Death benefit: $______.

(4) Group whole life insurance:

(A) Death benefit: $______.

(5) Fully paid vacation days per year: ______.

(6) Fully paid sick days per year: ______.

(7) Use of car as follows:

(A) Make and model: ______.

(B) Reimbursement per business mile: ______.

(C) Repair policy: [*Describe*].

(8) Educational benefits—work related:

(A) Days fully paid: ______.

(B) Maximum course charge/day: $______.

(C) Maximum hotel allowance: $______/day.

(D) Maximum meal allowance: $______/day.

(E) Maximum entertainment: $______/day.

(9) Education benefits—non-work related:

(A) Maximum course cost and book costs per Venture fiscal year: $______.

(10) Personal liability insurance coverage: $______.

(11) A *qualified* retirement plan benefit which has the following features:

(A) Name of plan: ______.

(B) Minimum age for participation: ______.

(C) Minimum service for participation: ______.

(D) Employment status (categories): ______.

(E) Vesting: ______.

(F) Venture contribution formula: ______.

(G) Employee contribution formula: ______.

(H) Effective date of plan: ______.

(I) Initial trustees: ______.

(J) Initial contribution: $______.

(12) A deferred compensation plan which has the following features:

(A) Benefit on death: $______.

(B) Benefit on disability: $______.

(C) Benefit on retirement or termination before age 65: $______.

(D) Benefit on retirement or termination after age 65: $______.

(13) Reimbursement for:

(A) Entertainment (not to exceed $______ per ______).

(B) Travel not to exceed $______ per day excluding mileage which shall be at [*Cents*] per mile and

hotel per day: $______.

meals per day: $______.

entertainment per day: $______.

Alternative D

The Managing Venturers shall be compensated as follows: [*Describe*].

Article III

MANAGEMENT

§ 3.1 Managing Venturers

The Managing Venturers shall be: [[*Name*]/*all Venturers*].

§ 3.2 Voting

Alternative A

All Managing Venturers shall have the right to vote as to the management and conduct of the business of the Venture according to their then Percentage Share of Income. Except as otherwise herein set forth a majority of such Income shall control.

Alternative B

The Managing Venturers shall have the right to vote as to the management and conduct of the business of the Venture as follows:

Names	Vote

Option 1

Abstentions and refusals to act upon any measure shall be considered as a vote in favor of the proposed measure. A Venturer shall be deemed to have abstained whenever a response by said Venturer shall not have been received by [*Name*] within the time specified in this Agreement or in the notice for the response, whichever is applicable.

§ 3.3. Rights, Powers and Restriction of Payments

No Venturer without the consent of all the other Venturers shall:

(a) Do any act in contravention of this Agreement.

(b) Do any act which would make it impossible to carry on the ordinary business of the Venture.

(c) Confess judgment against the Venture.

(d) Possess Venture property, or assign his interest or rights in specific Venture property, for other than a Venture purpose.

§ 3.4 Powers of [Names]

(a) The [*Names*] shall have the following authority:

Alternative A

(1) To exercise the powers reasonably necessary in order to pursue the Venture's purposes; provided however, that the consent of all of the Managing Venturers shall be necessary for any decision in contravention of the express desires of any other Venturer or involving One Hundred ($100.00) Dollars or more.

Alternative B

(1) To purchase, invest in, reinvest in, or otherwise acquire, and to retain, whether originally a part thereof or subsequently acquired, any and all stocks, bonds, notes, or other securities, or any variety of real or personal property, including stocks or interests in investment trusts and common trust funds operated and managed by a corporate trustee, as he may deem advisable.

(2) To obtain, sell and convey, mortgage, encumber, lease, exchange, pledge, partition, plat, subdivide, improve, repair, surrender, abandon or otherwise deal with or dispose of any and all property of whatsoever character and wheresoever situated real property forming a part of this Venture, at such time or times and in such manner and upon such terms as, in his absolute and uncontrolled discretion, it may be deemed expedient and proper; to give options therefore; to execute deeds, transfers, leases, pledges, mortgages, and other instruments of any kind. Any leases and contracts may extend beyond the term of the Venture.

(3) To borrow money upon terms acceptable to from any person or Corporation, and to pledge or mortgage any property as security therefor and to renew any indebtedness incurred;

(4) To open and to close checking or savings accounts, in banks or similar financial institutions, [and/or] safety deposit boxes in his name or in the name of a nominee, *with or without indication of any fiduciary capacity;* to deposit cash in and withdraw cash from such accounts [and/or] boxes, *with or without indication of any fiduciary capacity;* to hold such accounts [and/or] securities in bearer form, or in his or in the name of a nominee *with or without indication of any fiduciary capacity;*

(5) To give general or special proxies or powers of attorney for voting or acting in respect of shares or securities, which may be discretionary and with power of substitution; to deposit shares or securities with, or transfer them to, protective commit-

tees or similar bodies; to join in any reorganization and to pay assessments or subscriptions called for in connection with shares or securities held by the Venture.

(6) To adjust, arbitrate, compromise, sue or defend, abandon or otherwise deal with and settle any and all claims in favor of or against the Venture;

(7) To employ investment counsel, brokers, accountants, attorneys, and any other agents to act in his behalf; generally to do any act or thing and execute all instruments necessary, incidental or convenient to the proper administration of the Venture property;

(8) To make payments, division, or distribution of the Venture property wholly or partly in kind;

(9) To make employment contracts and pay pensions and establish pension and other incentive plans for any or all of its employees; provided, that no contract shall be made in favor of such Venturer *without the consent of* [*Number*] *percentage of the Venturers.*

Option 1 *(Not Generally Preferred as a Matter of Practical Experience)*

(10) Provided that approval of ______% of the Venturers shall be required for the approval of the following actions:

(A) To sue and complain, in the Venture's name.

(B) To purchase, take, receive, lease, or otherwise acquire, own, hold, improve, use and otherwise deal in and with, real or personal property, or any interest therein, wherever situated.

(C) To sell, convey, mortgage, pledge, lease, exchange, transfer and otherwise dispose of all or any part of the Venture's property and assets.

(D) To lend money and use its credit to assist its employees.

(E) To purchase, take, receive, subscribe for, or otherwise acquire, own, hold, vote, use, employ, sell, mortgage, lend, pledge, or otherwise dispose of, and otherwise use and deal in and with, shares or other interests in, or obligations of, other domestic or foreign corporations, associations, partnerships or individuals, or direct or indirect obligation of the United States or of any other government, state, territory, governmental district or municipality or of any instrumentality thereof.

(F) To make contracts and guarantees and incur liabilities, borrow money, issue notes, bonds, and other obligations, or secure any of its obligations by mortgages or pledge of all or any of the Venture property, franchises and income.

(G) To lend money.

(H) To make donations for the public welfare or for charitable, scientific or educational purposes.

(I) To pay pensions and establish pension and other incentive plans for any or all of its managers and employees.

(J) To be a promoter, venturer, member, associate, or manager of any venture, joint venture, trust or other enterprise.

Option 2 (Not Generally Preferred as Being too Restrictive)

(11) The Venture and its agents shall not exercise the following powers:

(A) To sue or complain in the Venture name.

(B) To purchase, take, receive, lease, or otherwise acquire, own, hold, improve, use and otherwise deal in and with, real or personal property, or any interest therein, wherever situated.

(C) To sell, convey, mortgage, pledge, lease, exchange, transfer and otherwise dispose of all or a substantial part of the Venture property and assets.

(D) To lend money and use its credit to assist Venture employees.

(E) To purchase, take, receive, subscribe for, or otherwise acquire, own, hold, vote, use, employ, sell, mortgage, lend, pledge, or otherwise dispose of, and otherwise use and deal in and with, shares or other interests in, or obligations of, other domestic or foreign corporations, associations, partnerships or individuals, or direct or indirect obligations of the United States or of any other government, state, territory, governmental district or municipality or of any instrumentality thereof, or direct or indirect obligations of the United States or of any other government, state, territory, governmental district or municipality or of any instrumentality thereof.

(F) To make contracts and guarantees and incur liabilities, borrow money, issue its notes, bonds, or other obligations, or secure any of its obligations by mortgage or pledge of all or any of the Venturer's property and income.

(G) To lend money.

(H) To make donations for the public welfare or for charitable, scientific or educational purposes.

(I) To pay pensions and establish pension plans, pension trusts, profit sharing plans, stock bonus plans, stock option plans and other incentive plans for any or all of its employees.

(J) To be a promoter, partner, member, associate, or manager of any partnership, joint venture, trust or other enterprise.

(K) Assign, transfer, pledge, compromise or release any Venture claim or debt, except upon payment in full.

§ 3.5 Liability

No Venturer shall incur any liability for any mistakes or errors in judgment made in good faith and in the exercise of due care in connection with the Venture business, and no Venturer shall be deemed to have violated any of the provisions of this Venture Agreement for any such mistakes or errors in judgment.

Article IV

RIGHT TO ASSIGN VENTURE INTEREST

§ 4.1 Venturers Right of Assignment of Profits and Losses

An interest in the Venture shall not be assigned without the approval of all Venturers.

Article V

DISSOLUTION

§ 5.1 Dissolution

In the event that the Venture shall hereafter be dissolved for any reason whatsoever, a full and general account of its assets, liabilities and transactions shall at once be taken. Such assets may be sold and turned into cash as soon as possible and all debts and other amounts due the Venture collected. The proceeds thereof shall thereupon be applied as follows:

(a) To discharge the debts and liabilities of the Venture and the expenses of liquidation.

(b) To pay each Venturer or his legal representative any unpaid salary, drawing account, interest or profits to which he shall then be entitled.

(c) To repay to any Venturer the capital he made available.

(d) To divide the surplus, if any, among the Venturers or their representatives according to each Venturer's then Percentage Share of *Income/Capital.*

Article VI

MISCELLANEOUS—SUBSTANTIVE PROVISIONS

§ 6.1 Miscellaneous—Substantive Provisions

The Venture's fiscal year shall commence on *January 1st* of each year and shall end on *December 31st* of each year. Full and accurate books of account shall be kept at such place as the Managing Venturers may from time to time designate, showing the condition of the business and finances of the Venture; and each Venturer shall have access to such books of account and shall be entitled to examine them at any time during ordinary business hours. At the end of each year, the Managing Venturers shall cause the Venture's accountant to prepare a balance sheet setting forth the financial position of the Venture as of the end of that year and a statement of operations (income and expenses) for that year. A copy of the balance sheet and statement of operations shall be delivered to each Venturer as soon as it is available.

Each Venturer shall be deemed to have waived all objections to any transaction or other facts about the operation of the Venture disclosed in such balance sheet and/or statement of operations unless he shall have notified the Managing Venturer in writing of his objectives within thirty (30) days of the date on which such statement is mailed.

The Venture books shall be kept on the [*cash/accrual*] basis and *in accordance with generally accepted accounting principles* consistent with those employed for determining its income for federal income tax purposes.

§ 6.2 Venture's Agents

Pursuant to the Venture's day to day activity the Managing Venturers shall have the power to employ investment counsel, brokers, accountants, attorneys, and any other agents to act in the Venture's behalf, generally to do any act or thing and execute all instruments necessary, incidental or convenient to the proper administration of the Venture property; otherwise said employment shall only be made if agreed to by all the Venturers.

Option 1

§ 6.3 Transfers to Living Trusts

For purpose of this Agreement, any Venturer may transfer his or her interest to said Venturer's Living Trust. Upon such transfer, legal title shall rest in such Living Trust but such interest shall be subject to the same events and circumstances as if the transferring Venturer continued to own such interest. Further, said transferring

Venturer shall continue to exercise all rights and be liable for all duties imposed by this Agreement.

§ 6.4 Checks

All checks or demands for money and notes of the Venture shall be signed by the Managing Venturer(s) or such other person or persons as the Managing Venturers may from time to time designate.

§ 6.5 Conflicts of Interest

Venturers may engage in or possess interest in other business ventures of every kind and description for their own accounts. Neither the Venture nor any of the Venturers shall have any rights by virtue of this Agreement in such independent business Ventures or to the income or profits derived therefrom.

Article VII

MISCELLANEOUS

§ 7.1 Execution in Counterpart

This Agreement may be executed in any number of counterparts, each of which shall be taken on to be an original.

§ 7.2 Indemnification

The Venture shall indemnify any person who is made, or threatened to be made, a party to any action, suit or proceeding (whether civil, criminal, administrative or investigative) by reason of the fact that he, his testator or intestate is or was a manager, employee or agent of the Venture or serves or served any other enterprises at the request of the Venture as follows:

Alternative A

to the full extent permitted by law;

Alternative B

to the extent to which such Venturer was not acting with gross negligence or wilful or wanton disregard of either this Agreement or the criminal statutes.

Provided, however, that any indemnity under this Section shall be provided out of and to the extent of Venture assets only, and no Venturer shall have any personal liability with regard to said indemnity.

§ 7.3 Notice

Any and all notices provided for herein shall be given in writing by registered or certified mail, return receipt requested which shall be addressed to the last address known to the sender or delivered to the recipient in person.

§ 7.4 Liability

The doing of any act or the failure to do any act by any Venturer (the effect of which may cause or result in loss or damage to the Venture) if pursuant to opinion of legal counsel employed by the Managing Venturers on behalf of the Venture, shall not subject such Venturer to any liability.

Further, the Managing Venturers shall not be liable for any error in judgment or any mistake of law or fact or any act done in good faith in the exercise of powers and authority conferred upon *them* but shall be liable only for gross negligence or wilful default.

§ 7.5 Agreement Binding

This Agreement shall be binding upon the parties hereto and upon their heirs, executors, administrators, successors or assigns, and the parties hereto agree for themselves and their heirs, executors, administrators, successor and assigns to execute any and all instruments in writing which are or may become necessary or proper to carry out the purpose and intent of this Agreement.

Option 1

§ 7.6 Amendments

This Agreement may be altered at any time by the decision of the Venturers holding not less than two-thirds (⅔) of the then capital of the Venture confirmed by an instrument in writing, which instrument the Venturers hereby agree to execute. Provided that no authority conferred upon the Managing Venturers shall be reduced or eliminated without *their* consent.

§ 7.7 Banking

The Venture shall maintain a bank account or bank accounts in the Venture's name in a national or state bank in the State of [*Name*]. Checks and drafts shall be drawn on the Venture's bank account for Venture purposes only and shall be signed by the Managing Venturers, or *their* designated agent.

§ 7.8 Titles and Subtitles

Titles of the paragraphs and subparagraphs are placed herein for convenient reference only and shall not to any extent have the effect of modifying, amending or changing the express terms and provisions of this Agreement.

§ 7.9 Words and Gender or Number

As used herein, unless the context clearly indicates the contrary, the singular number shall include the plural, the plural the singular, and the use of any gender shall be applicable to all genders.

§ 7.10 Severability

In the event any parts of this Agreement are found to be void, the remaining provisions of this Agreement shall nevertheless be binding with the same effect as though the void parts were deleted.

§ 7.11 Effective Date

This Agreement shall be effective only upon execution by all of the proposed Venturers.

§ 7.12 Waiver

No waiver of any provisions of this Agreement shall be valid unless in writing and signed by the person or party against whom charged.

Preferred as a Matter of Practical Experience

§ 7.13 Arbitration

No civil action concerning any dispute arising under this Agreement shall be instituted before any court and all such disputes shall be submitted to final and binding arbitration under the auspices of the American Arbitration Association, [*City*], [*State*]. Such arbitration shall be conducted in accordance with the rules of such association before a single arbitrator. The parties agree that the interest of the Joint Venture cannot be readily sold in the open market, and for that reason among others, the parties will be irreparably damaged in the event that this Agreement is not specifically enforced. Therefore, in addition to any award of damages, any such award shall, if the party entitled to the same demands it, grant specific performance of this Agreement. All costs and expenses of the arbitration, including actual attorney's fees, shall be allocated among the parties according to the arbitrator's discretion. The arbitrator's award resulting from such arbitration may be confirmed and entered as a final judgment in any court of competent jurisdiction and enforced accordingly. Further, the parties hereto expressly agree that proceeding to arbitration and obtaining an award thereunder shall be a condition precedent to the bringing or maintaining of any action in any court with respect to any dispute arising under this Agreement, except for the institution of a civil action to maintain the status quo during the pendency of any arbitration proceeding.

SIGNATURE PAGE

In witness whereof, [*Describe*], do hereby, as of the day and year below written, execute this Agreement.

Witnesses	**Venturer**
____________________	____________________
____________________	Date Signed: ____________

STATE OF ____________ }
County of ____________ } ss

On this ______ day of ______, 19__, before me a Notary Public in and for said County, personally appeared ______, known to me to be the persons whose names are subscribed to the foregoing instrument and acknowledged to me that they executed the same as their own free act and deed.

____

Notary Public, ______ County

My Commission Expires: ______.

Schedule "A"

Initial Capital Contributions

Venturer	Property Contributed

§ 26.4 Joint Venture in the Construction and Sale of a Building (One Party Contributes Labor, the Other Cash)

Agreement made this ______ day of ______, 19__, by and between ______ of ______, and ______ of ______.

Whereas, ______ has entered into a contract for the purchase of the following described property in the City of ______, County of ______, State of ______: [*Here Describe*];

Whereas, the parties desire to associate together in constructing on said lot a dwelling house and in selling the same upon completion;

It is agreed as follows:

§ 1. Purchase of Lot. The parties will immediately pay to the owner of the lot herein referred to the sum of $______ in full payment of said lot. Each of the parties will contribute an equal amount to make up this sum and title shall be taken in the names of ______ and ______, husband and wife, and ______ and ______, husband and wife.

§ 2. Labor and Materials Paid for. ______ shall pay to ______ the sum of $______ in cash, being one-half of the labor and materials paid for to the present time by ______ in respect to said property.

§ 3. Labor and Materials to Be Paid for. All unpaid bills for labor and materials heretofore put in said property and not paid for, and all materials and outside labor necessary for the completion of said property, shall be paid for one-half by ______ and one-half by ______.

§ 4. Labor Performed by Parties. For any labor performed by the parties to this Agreement in the completion of the dwelling upon said property, or other building, ______ shall be allowed the sum of $______ per hour and ______ shall be allowed the sum of $______ per hour.

§ 5. Sale of Building. Upon the completion of said building, the property shall be placed on the market for sale at a price and upon terms to be mutually agreed upon between the parties, and after deducting from the sale price, and paying, any unpaid bills for materials or outside labor, any amounts due either party for labor, and the cost of sale, including a broker's commission, if any, escrow fees, title insurance policy, etc., the remainder of the sale price shall be divided equally between the parties.

§ 6. Execution of Documents. Each of the parties, and their respective wives whose consent is hereto attached, shall sign any and all papers necessary to carry out the terms of this Agreement.

Parties

______

______

His Wife

______

______

His Wife

Library References:

C.J.S. Joint Adventures § 3 et seq.
West's Key No. Digests, Joint Adventures 🔑2.

§§ 26.5–27.0 are reserved for supplementary material.

DIVISION VI
CORPORATIONS

PART A
PREINCORPORATION MATTERS

INTRODUCTION

After having determined that the corporate form is the most appropriate organizational form for doing business (see Chapter 1, supra, "Available Forms of Business," and Chapter 2, supra, "Factors in Selecting Business Form"), the next steps are to select a state for incorporation, enter into promotional Agreements (if necessary), and take such other steps as are necessary prior to actual incorporation. The chapters which follow in this subdivision will treat these various preincorporation matters.

In order to appreciate the tax implications of various corporate transactions, the following terms of art must be understood:

Basis; Adjusted Basis; Taxable Income

The concept of "*basis*" is at once one of the most difficult and easiest concepts to understand.[1] The concept of basis attempts to create the foundation for a calculation of a base (thus the term "basis") for present or future exclusion of gain from taxation. In other words, the intent of most of the Internal Revenue Code is to tax a taxpayer once on a particular economic gain but not again (i. e.: the taxpayer may further invest the gain without tax on that gain). The concept of basis is a statutory calculation to arrive at what previously taxed amounts were used to acquire the asset in question.

The concept of "*adjusted basis*" is used to reflect what adjustments to the acquisition basis have been made during the ownership of the asset in question to reflect tax benefits (like depreciation) and expenses (like improvements). Often, the term "basis" is used to mean adjusted basis.

Once we know on what amount the taxpayer has already been taxed and what adjustments to the acquisition basis should have been made, we can subtract this amount from the total amount being received by the taxpayer for the asset and the difference will generally be taxable. This difference is generally called "*taxable income*." Gen-

1. IRC § 1011.

erally, taxable income plus the basis of the assets surrendered will equal what has actually or theoretically been received for the surrender of the asset in question.

Without exception, the basis of an actual dollar of U. S. currency (called "*money*" in the Internal Revenue Code) is always one dollar.

Generally, the basis of property other than money owned by a taxpayer is:

(a) Its cost to him in money, plus

(b) The basis to him of property (other than money) which he gave up in order to acquire the property in question, plus

(c) Any taxable gain which he "recognized" (i. e., paid taxes on) when he received the property in question, plus

(d) A variety of adjustments which the Internal Revenue Code may have required the taxpayer to make during the ownership of the property in question (i. e., to arrive at the adjusted basis).

It can be seen that, in part, the question of basis is quite circular: the basis of the property being given up will often partially determine the basis of the property in question (i. e., the property received). Thus, the basis of the property in question depends on knowing the basis of the property preceding it and so on. However, basis questions are generally not so difficult. This is because they can be categorized into several categories:

> (1) Property received in a transaction that was completely taxable (that is, where the receiving taxpayer pays tax on the difference between the value of what he received in the transaction and the basis of what he gave up) has a basis equal to the value of what he received. This is the result in the normal barter transaction where goods are traded for services, services for services or goods for goods. Note: in the case where a person has received services, these services, if they add value to goods already owned or received at the same time or in the future, will increase the basis of these goods rather than have a basis of their own. In these barter transactions, each person receiving goods for services must pay tax on receipt (which tax will be calculated to reflect the fair market value of what is received less the basis of what is given up) unless a particular exception to the income tax law applies. Since the transaction is fully taxable, the taxpayer starts with a new basis as to the goods (and/or services) received equal to the fair market value of what he received. Although technically his basis is equal to the basis of what he gave up plus the amount of taxable gain he realized, the net result is that his basis is (upon receipt) equal to the fair market value of what he received.
>
> Thus, most basis questions revolving around goods for goods, services for services, or goods for services questions can be re-

solved by stating that the basis upon receipt is equal to the fair market value of what is received. Thereafter, basis adjustments will be made to the property according to the relevant provisions of the Internal Revenue Code which determine the adjusted basis of property being held by a taxpayer. One major exception to this is the concept of part "gift" and part "exchange" (see (4), (5) and (6) below).

(2) The basis of property which is received solely in exchange for money will generally be the value of the money itself. This is because it is presumed in the tax law that the fair market value of property received for money is the money itself (money being our basic medium of exchange). One major exception to this is that a transaction can be labeled as part "gift" and as part "exchange" (see (4), (5) and (6) below).

Thereafter, basis adjustments will be made to the property according to the relevant provision of the Internal Revenue Code which determines the adjusted basis of property being held by a taxpayer.

(3) Thus, *for all completely taxable transactions, the basis of the property received will be either (1) the money paid for it (if only money was paid) or (2) its value when received.* This rule is the key rule to most basis questions.

(4) If a transaction is not fully taxable, then it is either partially (or completely) a gift or it escapes taxation because of one of the numerous (and important) exceptions to the taxation rules. Only in these *nontaxable transactions* do the complete rules of basis have to be applied (and thus understood). Fortunately, these rules always start with the basis of the property being *surrendered* and thus (one can hope and expect) that the property being surrendered or its predecessor property can be traced back to a fully taxable transaction or to money, and thus the basic rule can be applied. The rules relating to the basis of property received in a partial or fully nontaxable transaction are spelled out in the sections relating to such transactions and will be dealt within such sections.

(5) *The basis of property received in a transaction which is fully a gift* (that is: no property or services are surrendered by the recipient) is the basis of the property in the hands of the giver (i. e., the donor) plus any gift taxes paid by him (or the receiver).

(6) The basis of property received in a transaction in which the property given up is given up partially as a gift should be calculated as follows: the fair market value of what is *surrendered* is calculated. The portion of what is *received* for this sur-

rendered property is thought of as a normal business transaction and the basis *of this portion* of what is received is calculated as set forth above for calculating normal transactions (whether or not fully taxable). The rest of the fair market value of what is received is considered a gift. Its basis is the basis *of this portion* in the hands of the donor plus any gift tax paid by him (or the receiver). The new basis is the total of these two basises.

Depreciation, Amortization, and Accelerated Cost Recovery System

Depreciation is the tax law's approach to the loss in value that certain tangible assets (at least theoretically) undergo.

Amortization is the same approach applied to intangible assets whose value is reducing. Often, amortization is referred to as depreciation as it will be in these volumes. The tax law permits the taxpayer to subtract from his income the theoretical loss in value involved. Prior to the Economic Recovery Tax Act of 1981 [2] (summarized below), all depreciation and amortization was based upon the useful life of an asset to the taxpayer and its salvage value at the end of the useful life. The useful life of the asset was generally left up to the reasonable estimate of the taxpayer. However, a set of tables (called ADR or class life asset depreciation range system) allowed taxpayers to depreciate assets according to the useful life associated with their classification by the Internal Revenue Service.

The Economic Recovery Tax Act of 1981 generally replaced the Asset Depreciation Range (ADR) system for depreciating property with the Accelerated Cost Recovery System (ACRS) [3] for property placed in service after December 31, 1980.

The former depreciation system was designed to allocate depreciation deductions over the period the asset was used in business so that deductions for the cost of an asset were matched with the income produced by the asset. Under the new ACRS, the cost of an asset is recovered over a predetermined period shorter than the useful life of the asset or the period the asset is used to produce income.

Summary of Eligible Property Under Accelerated Cost Recovery System

Under old tax law (i. e. for property in service as of December 31, 1980), assets used in a trade or business or for the production of income are depreciable if they are subject to wear and tear, decay or decline from natural causes or obsolescence. Assets that do not decline in value on a predictable basis or that do not have a determinable useful life, such as land, goodwill, and stock, are not depreciable.

Under the new ACRS, most tangible depreciable property (real and personal) placed in service after December 31, 1980, is eligible re-

2. Pub.Law 97–34.

3. ERTA, § 201, adding IRC § 168.

covery property [4] and is covered by the accelerated cost recovery system (ACRS). However, ACRS does not apply to (1) property not depreciated in terms of years (except certain railroad property), and (2) property amortized (e. g., leasehold improvements and low-income rehabilitation expenditures). The cost recovery methods and periods are the same for both new and used property. Salvage value is disregarded in computing ACRS allowances.

The cost of eligible recovery property is recovered over a 3-year, 5-year, 10-year, or 15-year period, depending upon the type of property. In general, eligible personal and real property is broken down into the following four categories: [5]

- Automobiles, light trucks, research-and-development equipment, racehorses older than two years and other horses older than 12 years all will be written off in three years.
- Virtually all other equipment, except some assets of public utilities, will be written off in five years.
- Public-utility property, which previously was written off after it had been in service between 18 and 25 years, will be written off in 10 years.
- Buildings, along with public-utility property, which previously were written off after more than 25 years, will be written off in 15 years. (The bill also provides bigger tax credits for the rehabilitation of old and historic buildings.)

Special Depreciation Deduction for Small Business

Under pre 1981 law, there were no special provisions specifically applicable to the depreciation of assets by a small business. Pre 1981 law, however, does provide a deduction for "bonus" first-year depreciation in an amount not exceeding 20 percent of the cost of eligible property (Internal Revenue Code 179). The cost of the property that may be taken into account may not exceed $10,000 ($20,000 for individuals who file a joint return). Thus, the maximum additional first-year depreciation deduction is limited to $2,000 ($4,000 for individuals filing a joint return).

The Economic Recovery Tax Act of 1981, however, repeals Internal Revenue Code § 179 and replaces it with a new § 179 election to immediately deduct (expense) the cost of new or used personal property up to $5,000 per year in 1982 and 1983, $7,500 in 1984 and 1985 and $10,000 in years after 1985.

4. "Recovery property" is defined in IRC § 168(c).

5. See IRC § 168 for Tables of cost recovery periods for specific types of recovery property.

Optional Recovery Periods and Write-Offs Methods

Under pre 1981 law, taxpayers have several options that permit flexibility in computing depreciation deductions and net operating losses. Taxpayers have an option to use a useful life 20 percent shorter or longer than the ADR midpoint life. There is an option to use straight-line or accelerated methods, where allowed. In determining the date or additions to and retirements from a depreciation account, taxpayers have an option to use an averaging convention for personal property. In general, net operating losses and operating losses of certain insurance companies may be carried back three years and forward seven years.

Under the ERTA taxpayers have an option to use one of two additional recovery periods that are longer than the recovery period prescribed for each class of property or a non-term of years method of depreciation or amortization. In addition, taxpayers have an option to use an accelerated or straight-line method over the regular (ACRS) recovery period.

Earnings and Profits

Distributions by a Corporation to its Stockholders are taxable as dividends only to the extent the distribution is out of current or accumulated earnings and profits. Under present law, earnings and profits for U.S. Corporations are computed using straight-line depreciation over the useful life of property. The 20-percent ADR useful life variance may be used to determine the useful life for this purpose. Under the ERTA [6] earnings and profits for U.S. Corporations are based on straight-line depreciation over extended recovery periods as set forth below:

Extended Recovery Period

Property	**Year**
3-year property	5
5-year property	12
10-year property	25
15-year property	35

Stock, Securities and Short Term Debt

The concept of "*stock or securities*" is a term of tax law "art". It must be distinguished from *short term debt* instruments. Clearly stock and securities includes stock. It may also include a debt instrument if it has, in effect, the characteristics of an equity instrument or of long term debt. Thus, debt may be classified as: (1) debt which is neither a stock nor a security (short term debt), (2) stock or (3)

6. ERTA, Sec. 206, amending IRC § 312(k). Such new rules apply to property placed in service after 1980 in tax years ending after 1980.

securities. Some of the factors considered by the courts [7] in making these distinctions are:

(A) Does this debt instrument have an interest provision? This weighs in favor of it being debt.[8]

(B) Is the debt-equity ratio too high? Over 10:1 may be excessive and thus the debt will probably be held to be "stock" because it represents an equity interest.[9]

(C) Is the debt held proportionate to stockholdings? This weighs in favor of it being stock.[10]

(D) Is the debt subordinate to other debt holders? This weighs in favor of it being stock.[11]

(E) Is the debt secured? This weighs in favor of it being a security or non-security debt.

(F) Is this type of loan realistic? This weighs in favor of it being a security or non-security debt.[12]

(G) Does the business have likely prospects for success? This weighs in favor of it being stock.[13]

(H) Whether the debt was given in exchange for the Corporation's primary asset. This weighs in favor of it being stock.[14]

(I) When is the note due? Generally only debt due in more than 5 years will be considered a security rather than a non-security debt. However, a one year note has been held to be a security.[15]

This latter factor is the most important factor in distinguishing non-security and security debt because the other factors recited above generally arise in the context of whether or not the debt is to be classified as "stock".

The concept of "*preferred stock*" is a term of both practical state law and tax law. In practical terms, preferred stock can be distinguished from bonds, notes and other debt because such stock represents either (1) an obligation owed to a Stockholder which depends upon the profitability of the Corporation (whereas debt generally is not conditional), or (2) no obligation is actually owed to the Stock-

7. IRC § 385 and its Regulations are designed to modify this criterion. As of this date the effect of such modification, if any, is not clear.

8. IRC § 385.

9. Ibid.

10. Ibid.

11. Ibid.

12. Rev.Rul. 68–54, 1968–1 C.B. 69.

13. Ibid.

14. Schnitzer v. Comm'r, 13 T.C. 43 (1949), affirmed per curiam 183 F.2d 70 (9th Cir.), certiorari denied 340 U.S. 911, 71 S.Ct. 291.

15. Campbell v. Carter Foundation Production Co., 322 F.2d 827 (5th Cir. 1963); Camp Wolters Enterprises, Inc. v. Comm'r, 22 T.C. 737, 750–751 (1955), affirmed 230 F.2d 555 (5th Cir.), cert. denied 352 U.S. 826, 77 S.Ct. 39, 1 L.Ed.2d 49.

holder (whereas with debt there is an obligation). Preferred stock can be distinguished from common stock because its holder will receive, under one or more stated conditions, a preference over the rights of the common stock.

For purposes of the tax law, preferred stock "generally refers to stock which, in relation to other classes of stock outstanding enjoys certain limited rights and privileges (generally associated with specified dividend and liquidation priorities) but does not participate in corporate growth to any significant extent."

Tax Rates—Generally

A basic understanding of *corporate* and *individual tax rates* is necessary in order to fully grasp the interrelationship of corporate tax planning.

Generally individuals pay income tax rates and Corporations income tax rates as described below. However, with the exception of certain capital gains taxes, Subchapter S (also known as tax option or Small Business) Corporations will pay no corporate tax (see Chapter 86, infra). Rather their taxable income will be combined in proportion to stock ownership with their Stockholders' taxable income and this combined income will be taxable to their Stockholders at personal income tax rates. Similarly, if the Subchapter S Corporation suffers a loss, to the extent of the basis of the Stockholder in question in his stock and loans he makes to the Corporation, such loss will be netted against his personal taxable income.

Tax Rates—Ordinary Income Tax on Individuals (Generally)

Under pre 1982 law, individual income tax rates started at 14 percent on taxable income above $3,400 on a joint return and $2,400 on a single return. The rates ranged up to 70 percent on taxable incomes, in excess of $215,400 on a joint return, and $108,300 on a single return.

The highest marginal rate was 70 percent on taxable income in excess of $215,400 on a joint return and $108,300 on a single return. However, the top rate on personal service income was limited to 50 percent (the maximum tax). This rate applied above $60,000 on a joint return and $41,500 on a single return.

A deduction from gross income was allowed for 60 percent of any net capital gain for the year. The remaining 40 percent of any net capital gain was taxed at the ordinary rates up to 70 percent. Thus, the top effective tax rate on capital gains was 28 percent (70 percent rate times the 40 percent included in taxable income).

The Economic Recovery Tax Act of 1981 (ERTA) provides for cumulative across-the-board reductions of 23 percent by 1984 on the following schedule:

	Percent
1981	1¼
1982	10
1983	19
1984	23

Withholding changes take place on October 1, 1981, July 1, 1982, and July 1, 1983. The bill makes several other withholding changes to give the Secretary the authority to issue regulations, which would permit workers to adjust their withholding to more closely match their tax liability.

Deduction for Two-Earner Married Couples

Under prior law, married taxpayers generally were treated as a single taxpaying unit. If married taxpayers elected to file separate rather than joint returns, they usually paid a higher tax. The differing rate schedules for single and married taxpayers gave rise to a marriage penalty when two single wage earners of relatively equal income married each other.

The ERTA of 1981 allows couples filing a joint return a deduction in computing adjusted gross income equal to a percentage of the lower earning spouse's qualified earned income (up to $30,000 of income). In 1982, the percentage will be 5 percent (up to a $1,500 maximum deduction) and in 1983 and subsequent years the percentage will be 10 percent (up to a $3,000 maximum deduction).

Indexing

Under present law, the individual income tax is based on various fixed amounts including the amounts that define the tax brackets, the zero bracket amount, and the personal exemption. These amounts are set by statute and are not adjusted for inflation.

Under the Ecoonmic Recovery Tax Act of 1981, the income tax brackets, zero bracket amount, and personal exemption are adjusted for inflation (as measured by the Consumer Price Index), starting in 1985.

Maximum Tax Repealed

Under old tax law (i. e. until January 1, 1982), the maximum tax on personal service income was enacted to limit the tax on wages, salaries, professional fees, compensation for services, pension and annuity income, and deferred compensation to 50 percent. However, because the highest marginal tax rate on all types of income is reduced to 50 percent, effective January 1, 1982, the need for this limitation no longer exists. Accordingly, the ERTA repeals the maximum tax on personal service income with respect to tax years beginning after December 31, 1981.

Alternative Minimum Tax

The ERTA reduces the top alternative minimum tax rate from 25 percent to 20 percent. The rate for amounts between $20,000 and $60,000 is 10 percent, and the 20 percent rate applies to any amount in excess of $60,000. Therefore, the 10 percent alternative minimum tax rate follows that of prior law, which applied the 20 percent rate to the $60,000 to $100,000 range and a rate of 25 percent to income exceeding $100,000.

Tax Rates—Preference Tax on Individuals (Generally)

Individuals may pay a tax in part based upon the *preference ("minimum") tax*[16] of 15%. This is charged on the amount by which the following items of income exceed the higher of $10,000 or 50% of the normal income tax taxpayer would pay in the year in question:

(1) 60% of all capital gains income.

(2) The amount of depreciation taken on real and personal property leased to others over straight line depreciation.[17]

(3) The percentage depletion available less the adjusted basis of the property being depleted.

(4) The amount of the special Internal Revenue Code accelerated amortization of pollution control facilities, railroad rolling stock, on the job training facilities and child care facilities over normal forms of depreciation.

(5) The fair market value of stock received pursuant to the exercise of a stock option over the stock option price.

(6) The excess of itemized deductions (other than medical expenses and casualty losses) over 60% of adjusted gross income.

(7) The amount of intangible drilling costs over certain basic depletion methods.

Tax Rates—Capital Gains on Individuals (Generally)

Under the ERTA of 1981 the maximum capital gains tax rate has been reduced from 28 to 20 percent to conform to the reduction in the maximum marginal tax rate to 50 percent, beginning with the 1982 calendar year, but a special exception from current rates is made for

16. IRC § 56 et seq.

17. As provided by the ERTA of 1981, § 205, the amount of the tax preference item for accelerated depreciation is the excess of the depreciation taken over the amount that would have been allowable using the straight-line method over periods as set forth in IRC § 57(a)(12).

capital gains on sales or exchanges occurring after June 9, 1981. Even though the exclusion from gross income of 60 percent of net capital gains (i. e., the capital gains deduction) remains unchanged, the application of the adjusted highest tax rate results in this difference. Formerly, the maximum 70 percent tax rate on the remaining 40 percent of net capital gains includible in gross income resulted in a tax of 28 percent. Accordingly, the 50 percent maximum tax rate similarly applied to 40 percent of net capital gains results in the tax of 20 percent.

Ordinary Income Tax on Corporations (Generally)

Under pre 1982 law, the corporate (except Subchapter S Corporations, see Chs. 85, 86) income tax is imposed at the following rates [18]:

Taxable income	Rate (Percent)
Less than $25,000	17
25,000–50,000	20
50,000–75,000	30
75,000–100,000	40
Over $100,000	46

The Economic Recovery Tax Act of 1981 reduces the tax rates on the two lowest brackets, *i. e.,* those imposing tax on taxable income below $50,000. The change will go into effect in 1982 and 1983.

The brackets below $50,000 will be adjusted as follows:

Taxable income In 1982	Rate (Percent)
Less than 25,000	16
$25,000–50,000	19
1983 and later years	
Less than $25,000	15
$25,000–$50,000	18

Accumulated Income Tax on Corporations (Generally)

Corporations may pay a tax [19] in part based upon any income which is not distributed but is *"unreasonably accumulated"* (see Chapter 53, infra, for a more complete explanation) equal to an additional 27½% of the first $100,000 of unreasonable accumulation and 38½% of the rest.[20]

18. IRC § 11.

19. IRC § 531 et seq.

20. There is an exception for $150,000 of accumulation for taxable years ending December 31, 1981, which was increased by the ERTA of 1981 to $250,000 for taxable years beginning after December 31, 1981 for non-professional Corporations. See IRC § 535(c)(2).

Personal Holding Company Tax on Corporations (Generally)

During the course of corporate operations, unintentionally or unavoidably, the Corporation may incur a 50% tax on *"personal holding company income."*[21] This tax can be avoided by paying a dividend within 90 days after the deficiency in tax is determined.

The personal holding tax on personal holding company income may be charged if: (1) the Corporation has 5 or fewer Stockholders who directly (or indirectly through a series of constructive receipt rules) own more than 50% of the Corporation and (2) the sum of the following incomes equals or exceeds 60% of the Corporation's adjusted gross income: dividend, interest, royalties, rents, production film rentals, compensation when the contracting party has (or has the right to) designate the person to furnish a particular personal service, compensation received by the Corporation for the use of corporate property which a 25% or more Stockholder has the right to personally use, and amounts received by the Corporation as the grantor or beneficiary of a trust or the beneficiary of an estate. The determination of whether there will be any personal holding company tax, at all, is a Herculean task not suited for those of short attention span, temper or time. See Chapter 53, infra, for a more complete explanation.

Preference Tax on Corporations (Generally)

Corporations may pay a tax in part based upon a *preference ("minimum") tax*[22] equal to 15% of the amount by which the following items exceed the greater of $10,000 or the full amount of the normal income tax which would otherwise be paid in the year in question:

(1) The capital gains "savings" achieved by the Corporation's use, if any, of the alternative capital gains tax.

(2) The amount of depreciation taken on real property over straight line depreciation.

(3) The percentage depletion available less the adjusted basis of the property being depleted.

(4) The amount of the special Internal Revenue Code accelerated amortization of pollution control facilities, railroad rolling stock, on the job training facilities and child care facilities over normal forms of depreciation.

(5) The fair market value of stock received pursuant to the exercise of a stock option over the stock option price.

21. IRC § 541 et seq. This tax was reduced from 70% to 50% for taxable years beginning after December 31, 1981 by the ERTA of 1981.

22. IRC § 56 et seq.

(6) The excess of itemized deductions (other than casualty losses) over 60% of adjusted gross income.

(7) The amount of intangible drilling costs over certain basic depreciation methods.

Capital Gains Tax on Corporations (Generally)

Corporations may pay a *capital gains income* tax [23] in part based upon a tax equal to the lower of the ordinary income rate or 28% on all capital gains income.

Dividend Income (Generally)

The concept of *dividend* [24] income is of great importance in the area of corporate taxation because dividend income is generally the least desirable type of income to pay taxes upon. Simply put, dividend income (with a few statutory exceptions) is any distribution made by a Corporation which is a benefit to stock owners and which is paid as a return on their investment.

Generally we can say the following about dividend income:

(1) The tax impact on the payment of a dividend may be lower to the recipient than the tax on other distributions. However, it is not deductible. Actually, there are three types of taxation of distributions from Corporations as a return on the Stockholder's stock ownership (as distinguished from distributions which are for services or goods or which are in redemption of stock). Technically speaking, although all three types of taxation are generally referred to in the literature as *dividends*, the Internal Revenue Code only refers to one of these types of taxation (the one made out of "Earnings and Profits", as defined below), as being truly a dividend. For purposes of this text, the term "dividend" will be used in its popular sense—to refer to all distributions made as a return on the Stockholders *total stock ownership*—and not to its strict technical meaning. However, it is still of the utmost importance that the three types of dividends (in the practical sense) taxation be fully understood.

The three types of dividends (in the practical sense) taxation are:

(A) A full ordinary income tax will be paid by the taxpayer-Stockholder when property is distributed to him as a return on his investment and, as of the close of the corporate fiscal year, if Earnings and Profits (see below) were earned by the Corporation for that taxable year or when Earnings and Profits (see below) had been accumulated for prior taxable years by the Corporation.

23. IRC § 1201.

24. IRC § 301. See Chapter 57, infra.

(B) Any property distributed when the Corporation has no accumulated Earnings and Profits for prior years and will have none for the current fiscal year will be tax free to the extent of the taxpayer's basis in his stock. These distributions will accordingly reduce his basis in his stock.

(C) Any property distributed in excess of the above two calculations (i. e., in excess of Earnings and Profits and stock basis) are considered capital gain items.

Since the last two tiers of dividends treatment may be only as burdensome or less burdensome as in the case where the distribution is not considered a dividend, it may be (in rare circumstances) that the taxpayer will try to structure a dividend transaction rather than trying to structure a transaction "not essentially equivalent to a dividend". However, in most cases, great effort is made to structure transactions which are not essentially equivalent to a dividend for tax purposes.

In any case—the corporation can not deduct the payment.

(2) Rental payments, interest payments, earned income payments (i. e., salaries and payments to independent contractors, if reasonable) do not receive dividend treatment, but receive more favored tax treatment since these are deductible to the Corporation.

(3) Redemptions of stock (that is, the Corporation is buying back its own stock) will be treated as a dividend unless certain factual situations are present.[25] The factual situations are intended to allow the redeeming Stockholder to receive capital gains treatment for the gain on his stock in those situations where (A) it is thought that the Stockholder has significantly reduced his percentage of economic ownership in the Corporation or (B) special tax treatment was thought to be reasonable because of the circumstances of the redemption. It should be noted that if capital gains treatment is not available, then the complete dividend treatment rules set forth above are applicable. (See Chapter 57, infra, for a more complete description).

Earnings and Profits

(1) The concept of *Earnings and Profits* [26] (commonly referred to as *E & P)* is basically a concept of retained taxable income. That is: it is the historical net effect of taxable and non-taxable income, taxable losses and non-deductible distributions.

Non-taxable income includes life insurance proceeds and tax exempt interest.

25. IRC § 302 and § 303.

26. IRC § 312.

Non-deductible distributions include dividends paid and distributions for capital redemptions of stock and partial liquidations and life insurance premiums paid which do not increase cash values. The amount to be subtracted as a result of such distributions is the basis of the property distributed except for corporate obligations which are valued at their face amount.

Applying Internal Revenue Code § 312 to various transactions results in the following adjustments to E & P:

(1) Salary. Reduce E & P to extent of the deduction.

(2) Rents. Reduce E & P to extent of deduction.

(3) Interest. Reduce E & P to extent of the deduction.

(4) Sales. Gain or loss in E & P is computed by starting with adjusted basis and then increasing or decreasing E & P for the gain or loss recognized.

(5) Dividends. Decrease E & P by the amount of money; the principal (face) amount of the Corporation's notes and other debt and the adjusted basis of other property distributed and *increase* E & P by the amount of gain recognized upon the distribution.

(6) Distribution of Inventory at the Time of a Partial or Complete Liquidation or Redemption of Stock. No increase is made in E & P due to any gain recognized on distribution.

(7) Distribution Property Changeable to the Corporations Capital Account. Don't reduce E & P.

(8) Inventory. E & P will *increase* on the distribution of inventory to the extent its fair market value exceeds its adjusted basis, even though there is no taxable gain (except in the event of a liquidation—see below).

(9) Unrealized Receivables. E & P will increase on the distribution of the unrealized receivables (except in the event of a liquidation—see below).

(10) Other Tax Free Distributions. There will be no reduction of E & P.

(11) Where Corporation Splits. An allocation of E & P between the two Corporations takes place.

(12) Liquidations. No reduction of E & P is made to extent the liquidation is charged to the Corporation's capital account; otherwise it is treated as a distribution in respect to stock (see above).

The calculation of E & P which results from corporate income depends upon the Corporation's accounting methods. However, the calculation of E & P resulting from distributions and increases of capita are independent of the accounting method.

(13) Depreciation. See *Earnings and Profits* under discussion of "Depreciation, Amortization and Accelerated Cost Recovery System" on page 44, supra.

Redemptions (Generally)

A *redemption* will be considered as not essentially equivalent to a dividend if [27] and only if (1) a limited set of circumstances exist concerning the nature of the redemption and (2) the persons or entities whose stock ownership the Internal Revenue Code deems [28] (that is, arbitrarily and artificially implies) as being "*constructively*" owned by the redeeming Stockholder either after the redemption (A) do not in fact own such stock or (B) if they do own such stock, the amount of stock which they own both before and after the redemption is statutorily *deemed* to entitle the Stockholder to claim that he falls within the circumstances which are necessary for him to avoid dividend treatment and (3) the Corporation is not a *"collapsible Corporation."* [29]

Briefly, the circumstances which will avoid dividend treatment (described more extensively at Chapter 63 et seq., infra) are circumstances where Internal Revenue Code provides that the Stockholder's actual (and deemed) ownership percentage was, as a result of the redemption, materially reduced. Briefly, the circumstances where stock will be *deemed* to be owned by the redeeming Stockholder are those where the family or entity who actually own the stock are thought to have such a close economic relationship to the redeeming Stockholder that the redeeming Stockholder and the "constructively redeeming Stockholder(s)" are probably acting in tandem with one another.

Cash and Accrual Basis Taxes

First, it should be noted that the tax term "basis" here is a confusion of technical use. In this context "basis" means *method* and does not mean "basis" as used in definition above.

A *cash basis taxpayer* is a taxpayer who accounts for his income and deductions based on when he actually receives and expends money and distributes other property. This fundamental rule has a growing list of exceptions, however, since the Internal Revenue Service is beginning to clamp down on persons who have used the cash basis

27. IRC § 302.

28. IRC § 318.

29. IRC § 341.

method of accounting to circumvent the taxation rules. Some of these exceptions are:

(1) Pension and profit sharing contributions are deductible by cash basis taxpayers when accrued if they are paid before the taxpayer's tax return (including extensions) is due.[30]

(2) Certain real estate deductions for construction real estate are not deductible until they would otherwise be accrued.[31]

(3) All capital expenses are amortized and depreciated[32] over the life of the asset (unless a special rule applies), or written off under the Accelerated Cost Recovery System (for property placed in service after December 31, 1980), and not deducted when paid for.[33] If the asset has no ascertainable life, then these items are generally not depreciable or amortizable.

An *accrual basis taxpayer* accounts for his income and deductions *in the period to which they properly relate.* For instance, a taxpayer who pays taxes based on a calendar year period and who pays an insurance premium one year in advance or one year late will still deduct the premium in the year he receives the insurance protection.

Taxpayers who own inventory or manufacture goods must be on an accrual system. Taxpayers who have service business (which are traditionally cash basis taxpayers) and who also have a separate business operation which requires accrual accounting can set up one set of accounting methods for each separate business even though only one tax return is to be filed, which will reflect both approaches.[34]

Fiscal Year

The *fiscal year* of a taxpayer is the period for which the taxpayer must account for the tax results of his operations. Generally, the taxpayer will also keep his financial books attuned to such year. Fiscal year ends must end on the last day of a calendar month.

The importance of the choice of a fiscal year is:

(1) It will determine when many accounting functions (such as closing the books and filing tax returns) are required to be done and thus (since the heaviest burden of these falls shortly after the corporate year end) the choice should generally be made when it will be convenient to do such work (trying to stay away from March, April and December year ends when tax advisors are traditionally rushed).

30. IRC § 404(a)(6).

31. IRC § 189.

32. IRC § 167.

33. See however IRC § 179 as revised by the ERTA of 1981 which gives small businesses an election to immediately deduct (expense) the cost of new or used personal property up to $5,000 per year in 1982 and 1983, $7,500 in 1984 and 1985, and $10,000 in years after 1985.

34. IRC § 446(c).

(2) A deferral of income taxes can often be accomplished by the selection of a year end. For example, if the Corporation will traditionally receive a great deal of its income in October, a year end which ends in October, November or December will not postpone taxes for a cash basis Corporation's Stockholders because a cash basis taxpayer must (in order to get a deduction before year end) actually pay its expenses (with the exception of qualified pension and profit sharing) before its year end and thus these amounts will be taxable to the Stockholders (assuming they are on a calendar year) in such calendar year.

If our example is an accrual basis taxpayer, a year end in October may cause problems also. This is because, although an accrual basis taxpayer may deduct costs which relate to the fiscal year in question when it binds itself to pay these (such as employee salary payments and payments to employee benefit plans), such payments will not be deductible in the fiscal year in question if they are owed to a Stockholder or related party who owns directly or indirectly more than 50% of the stock of the Corporation and such payments are not made until more than 2½ months after the corporate year end. In fact, such payments, if not made within the 2½ month period, will never be deductible.[35]

The reason that in the example the October, November and December cash basis corporate taxpayer and the October accrual basis corporate taxpayer did not postpone taxes is because all payments, to be deductible, to the Corporation's individual Stockholders will be made before December 31, and these individual taxpayers will generally have fiscal years which end in December. Therefore all income earned by the Corporation will be earned by the Corporation and taxed to its Stockholders (to the extent distributed) in the same tax period.

On the other hand if the Corporation had a January 31 year end, then all income earned from February 1 to December 31 of one calendar year could be paid (or accrued if the Corporation is an accrual basis taxpayer) to the Stockholders in the next calendar year and they would only pay tax on the receipt of such moneys in the following calendar year. They will have postponed the tax on such income being earned for one year since the Corporation received a deduction in the year it was earned as a result of the fact that it paid the income (or accrued its payment) to the Stockholder in one year but the Stockholder only received the income in the next fiscal year (and thus paid taxes on it in that year).

Library References:

C.J.S. Internal Revenue §§ 93–95.

West's Key No. Digests, Internal Revenue ⚷231 et seq.; 3065 et seq.

35. IRC § 267.

CHAPTER 27

PREINCORPORATION CHECKLIST AND WORKSHEET

Table of Sections

---

§ 27.1 Interview Checklist and Worksheet

INTRODUCTORY COMMENTS

The interview sheet appearing below is designed for the attorney interviewing the client who desires to form a new Corporation.

By filling in the checklist interview sheet the attorney will be assisted in obtaining the information necessary for preparation of the Articles of Incorporation, By-laws, organizational minutes, stock issuance, and supplementary agreements. The checklist also contains a reminder about important federal income tax points to be observed including Internal Revenue Code Subchapter S, §§ 1371–1379 (election of Corporation and Stockholders to have profit and loss of Corporation taxed to the Stockholders and not to the Corporation, with Corporation net operating losses deductible by the Stockholders to the extent of their basis in their stock).

This checklist assumes the decision to incorporate has already been made. Before this decision is made the lawyer should face the problem whether or not to incorporate the client's business. This may be a difficult question for the closely held and relatively small firm. It requires consideration of the long-range tax effect of operating under the corporate tax laws, the personal, family and business relationships of the client, income of the client from sources other than the business and other factors. These questions are considered in detail in Chapters 1 and 2, supra.

CONSIDERATIONS FOR ESTABLISHMENT OF A CORPORATION

CONSIDERATIONS

1. Name of the Corporation: ______________________________
   Phone Number: (__________) ______________
2. Office Address: ______________________________
   ____
3. Corporate Mailing Address: ______________________________
   ____

4. Principal Parties:

List Directors, Officers, and Stockholders.

(a) Name ____________________
Residence Address ____________________
____
Residence Phone (________)____________
Social Security Number ____________________
Birthdate ____________________
Driver's License Number ____________________

(b) Name ____________________
Residence Address ____________________
____
Residence Phone (________)____________
Social Security Number ____________________
Birthdate ____________________
Driver's License Number ____________________

(c) Name ____________________
Residence Address ____________________
____
Residence Phone (________)____________
Social Security Number ____________________
Birthdate ____________________
Driver's License Number ____________________

(d) Name ____________________
Residence Address ____________________
____
Residence Phone (________) ____________
Social Security Number ____________________
Birthdate ____________________
Driver's License Number ____________________

(e) Name ____________________
Residence Address ____________________
____
Residence Phone (________) ____________
Social Security Number ____________________
Birthdate ____________________

5. Name(s) of Incorporators: ____________________
____

6. Number of Directors: ____________________

7. Name(s) of Directors: ____________________
____
____
____

8. Name(s) of Stockholders: ______________________________
____
____
____
____

9. Officers:

Any one person may hold two offices, except the office of President and Secretary.

Alt. A–1. There will be no Chairman of the Board.

Alt. A–2. There will be a Chairman of the Board—he will be the chief operating officer.
Name: ______________________________

Alt. A–3. There will be a Chairman of the Board—he will merely run Board meetings.
Name: ______________________________

10. President: Name ______________________________

11. Vice-President: Name ______________________________

12. Secretary: Name ______________________________

13. Treasurer: Name ______________________________

14. Resident Agent: Name ______________________________

15. Assets Transferred:

Alt. B–1: The assets to be transferred are to be listed.

Q: Will the client supply the list? Yes/No

Q: Should we ask the accountants to prepare a list of the business equipment, business supplies, fixtures, and other operating assets indicating the adjusted tax cost basis and fair market values of such assets and any liabilities to be transferred to the Corporation? Yes/No

Alt. B–2: The assets to be transferred will not be listed—reference will be made to the opening books of the Corporation.

Alt. B–3: $______ of cash will be transferred.

Alt. B–4: ______ (name of business) will be transferred.

Q: Will all liabilities be transferred or will this result in possible tax upon incorporation?

All liabilities/except the liabilities on the attached list.

Q: Will the accounts receivable be transferred. Yes/No

STOCKS AND SECURITIES ISSUED

16. Will securities (long term notes) be issued? Yes/No

17. Shares Authorized:

	Par Value	Number
Voting Common		
Not-voting Common		
Preferred		

(a) Enough stock should be authorized in the Articles, over and above the original issue, to permit additional shares to be sold without amending the Articles of Incorporation.

(b) Cumulative voting: Minority Stockholders will normally want to elect members of the Board of Directors by the existence of cumulative voting rights. Yes/No

(c) Pre-emptive rights: Should existing Stockholders have the first right to buy newly offered shares? Yes/No

18. Preferred rights and preferences:
Dividend of ______% of par
Dividend of $______ per share
Call: Yes/No
Put: Yes/No
Other: ______________________

19. The amount of cash working capital necessary to operate the business must be determined and a decision made regarding whether a part of this working capital will be loaned to the Corporation rather than raised through the issuance of stock.

Should the accountant make the determination of whether there should be a loan? Yes/No

If we know there is to be a loan, describe.

Payee: ______________________________

Interest Length: ______________________________

Face Amount: ______________________________

Payment Period: ______________________________

Including Interest/Plus Interest

Note: notes under 5 years run the risk of being declared stock.

20. List Stock and Securities to be issued and to whom issued:

Name	**Common Stock** Voting	Non Voting	**Preferred Stock**	**Face Amount of Securities (or notes)**

21. Bank Accounts:

Open a new corporate account and maintain the present Proprietorship or Partnership account to phase out the old operation.

(a) Name of bank (corporate account) ____________

____

(b) Authorized signer's office: ____________

____

____

____

____

22. Will the following be adopted?

	Yes	No
(a) Medical Expense Reimbursement Plan (note: discrimination problems)		
(b) Cafeteria Plan		
(c) Welfare Plan		
(d) Profit Sharing Plan		
(e) Pension Plan		
(f) Disability Plan		
(g) Lease		

If so:

Monthly Rent $____________

Address ____________

____

(h) Buy-Sell Agreement

(i) Employment Agreement with: ____________

(j) Seal

23. Compensation:

Salary levels of officer-employees should be determined.

Name	Salary

24. Should a double dip provision be included? Yes/No

25. Status:

    (a) Should the corporation elect Subchapter S?
    This would enable Stockholders to continue being taxed as a Proprietor or Partnership and also participate in corporate fringe benefit programs, subject to certain limitations imposed by the Tax Reform Act of 1969. Yes/No

    (b) Should the Corporation have a special effective date? Yes/No
    If so, what? __________

    (c) Should the Corporation have an assumed name? Yes/No
    If so, what? __________

    (d) Should the Corporation protect its name by the Stockholders filing d/b/a's in certain counties? Yes/No
    Which counties: __________
    ____
    ____

    (e) What is the specific corporate purpose?
    ____
    (This information is reflected on the SS–4 form.)
    Should the Articles use a general purpose clause? Yes/No

26. Should transfer of the assets to be transferred to the Corporation in exchange for stock be documented by a bill of sale from the present owner? Yes/No

27. By-law considerations:
    (a) Fiscal Year End __________
    (b) Indemnification of Directors and Officers. Yes/No

28. Miscellaneous information:

    (a) Is the business location within the city limits? Yes/No

    (b) Number of employees? __________

    (c) Anticipated monthly withholding liability for State taxes?
    $______

    (d) Anticipated annual gross receipts: $______

    (e) Will the Corporation require a sales tax license? Yes/No

    (f) Anticipated monthly sales tax liability will be: $______

    (g) First date you paid or will pay wages? ______. 19__.

29. Accountant:
    Name ______________________________________
    Address ____________________________________
    ____
    Phone (__________) ____________________

30. Transfer of Accounts Receivable:
Should the accountant be asked to prepare a list showing the present total accounts receivable for the Corporation? Yes/No
Will the accounts receivable be transferred to the new Corporation? Yes/No

31. Lease:
   (a) Who owns the present business offices?
   (b) Is there a written lease? Yes/No
   (c) Does the lease permit assignment (with or without consent of the landlord?) Yes/No
   (d) Should we formally assign the present lessee's interest to the new Corporation? Yes/No
   (e) Should we prepare a new lease or rental agreement? Yes/No
   (f) Should lease assignment be prepared for any equipment or fixtures which are leased presently? Yes/No

32. Miscellaneous insurance:
Are there presently any:
   1. Wage continuation and/or disability policies,
   2. Life Insurance policies,
   3. Medical Expense insurance policies, or
   4. Any other insurance.

If not, consideration should be given to the use of the Corporation in the purchasing of such insurance.
   (a) If a disability insurance policy exists or is contemplated, a disability income plan or cafeteria should be prepared to make possible deductibility to the Corporation for the premiums.
   (b) In order for the Corporation to pay for and deduct employees medical expenses, a medical expense reimbursement plan or cafeteria is required. Titles of classifications of covered employees and terms of the plan must be determined.

Library References:

C.J.S. Corporations §§ 36, 47, 48.
West's Key No. Digests, Corporations ⚷14(1) et seq.

§§ 27.2–28.0 are reserved for supplementary material.

CHAPTER 28

SELECTING THE INCORPORATION STATE

Table of Sections

---

§ 28.1 General Considerations

It is generally recommended that a local business incorporate in the state where it is doing business. This is so even though the laws of such state are somewhat burdensome. The reason is that local incorporation avoids (1) the disadvantage of being sued in a distant state, (2) double taxation, and (3) the added organization expenses of foreign incorporation. Such advice is particularly appropriate for the small or medium sized enterprise with a simple capital structure. However, where the Corporation proposes to carry on business in a number of states or where the tax or corporate statutes of the state are unusually oppressive, the possibility of incorporating in a state outside the principal place of business may profitably be considered.

If it is decided to incorporate in a state other than that in which the principal place of business is located, Delaware is favored at the present time although Michigan and New Jersey are also good choices. It is the state of incorporation of many of the major business enterprises in this country. The reason is fairly obvious. The Delaware statutes are traditionally "liberal" granting to management great flexibility in the control and conduct of the affairs of the Corporation. The court decisions interpreting the statutes are numerous, provide a reasonably certain guide, and on the whole are sympathetic to management. Further, the corporate taxes imposed are reasonable, and are likely to continue to be because of the importance to the state of foreign Corporations. All these considerations are looked upon with favor by management and management usually employs the lawyers who decide the state of incorporation.

It should be emphasized that in recent years a number of states have undertaken a revision of their corporate statutes in order to bring them up to date and encourage local businesses to incorporate at home. A very substantial influence in this direction has been the Model Business Corporation Act prepared by the Committee on Corporate Laws (Section of Corporation, Banking and Business Law) of the American Bar Association. It has been used as the pattern for modernizing the Corporation laws in a majority of the states.

Where the business enterprise is doing, or is to do, business in more than one jurisdiction, the initial question also arises as to whether there should be one or more Corporations. Perhaps a separate Corporation in each jurisdiction might offer advantages. When a single Corporation is to be formed to engage in multi-state activities, choice of jurisdiction of incorporation becomes important. Sound selection requires comparison of the features involved not only in incorporating in one jurisdiction or another but also in doing business (and often formally qualifying) in the jurisdiction or jurisdictions other than the jurisdiction of incorporation.

Various factors might be relevant in the selection process.

Corporate statutes which are "enabling", "liberal", "permissive", and flexible, along with legislative, judicial and administrative attitudes sympathetic to business Corporations—so-called "corporate climate", are the prime choice of corporate management and corporate counsel.

Counsel here can be aided substantially by retaining correspondent counsel in the other jurisdictions or requesting the assistance of one of the Corporation service companies.

Relative advantages and disadvantages may change from time to time. One possibility might be to dissolve, liquidate, and reincorporate in another jurisdiction. A preferable alternative might be to form a new Corporation in the other jurisdiction and then merge, tax-free, into it.

Library References:

C.J.S. Corporations § 176 et seq.
West's Key No. Digests, Corporations 🔑52.

§ 28.2 Checklist as to State Selection [1]

Among the more relevant factors in selecting the preferable state for incorporation are the following:

(1) Are there express provisions for preincorporation share subscriptions?

(2) May a Corporation be formed for perpetual or limited duration?

1. The source of the following checklist is Henn, Law of Corporations (2d ed. 1970) § 92. A third edition is being prepared by Professor Henn for 1982 publication.

(3) How restrictive are the provisions concerning corporate names?

(4) Are there express provisions permitting use of a similar corporate name with the consent of the existing Corporation? In the case of affiliated Corporations? Otherwise?

(5) Is reservation of a corporate name possible? By express statutory provisions? By administrative courtesy?

(6) For what period may a corporate name be reserved?

(7) What renewals of reservation of corporate name are possible?

(8) Is a single incorporator permissible?

(9) Are there any requirements that the incorporator or incorporators subscribe for shares? What are the qualifications required of an incorporator or incorporators with respect to: Residence? Citizenship? Age? Otherwise?

(10) May a Corporation serve as an incorporator?

(11) Are there express provisions for informal action by the incorporator(s)?

(12) For what purposes may a Corporation be incorporated?

(13) Are broad purposes permissible?

(14) Must specified purposes be set forth in the Articles of Incorporation?

(15) Are there any constitutional or statutory restrictions on corporate ownership of real property? Agricultural land? Personal property? Shares in other Corporations? Are there any constitutional or statutory debt limitations?

(16) Are there express provisions on the ultra vires doctrine?

(17) How broad are the statutory general corporate powers? Do they include power to make charitable contributions irrespective of corporate benefit? To carry out retirement, incentive and benefit plans for Directors, Officers, and employees? To be a Partner? To adopt emergency By-laws? Must the statutory general corporate powers be set forth in the Articles of Incorporation?

(18) What are the fees for filing or recording the Articles of Incorporation?

(19) What are the organization taxes? Other initial taxes?

(20) Do such taxes discriminate against shares without par value?

(21) Are filings subject to close administrative scrutiny and conservatism, with resulting filing delays?

(22) Is there a state stamp tax on the issuance of securities?

(23) Are "blue sky" law requirements burdensome?

(24) What, if any, is the minimum authorized or paid-in capital requirement? Must evidence of compliance be filed? Who are liable, and to what extent, for noncompliance?

(25) What qualitative and quantitative consideration requirements apply to par value shares? To shares without par value? With respect to the valuation of property or services, does the "true value" or "good faith" rule apply? Do Preincorporation services satisfy such consideration requirements?

(26) To what extent may a portion of the consideration received for shares be allocated to capital surplus? Within what period after the issuance of the shares may this be done?

(27) May partly-paid shares be issued? May certificates for partly-paid shares be issued?

(28) Are there express provisions for fractions of shares? Scrip?

(29) What provisions may be made with respect to: Dividend preferences? Liquidation preferences?

(30) When two or more classes of shares are authorized, must the provisions concerning them be stated or summarized on the share certificates?

(31) Are express provisions made for issuing preferred or other "special" classes of shares in series? What are the limitations on permissible variations between series of the same class?

(32) To what extent may preferred shares be made redeemable? To what extent may common shares be made redeemable?

(33) To what extent may shares be made convertible?

(34) What are the record date provisions? Are bearer shares permissible? What rights attach to them?

(35) What are the express statutory provisions for, and judicial and administrative attitudes toward, close Corporations?

(36) To what extent may voting rights of Stockholders be denied or limited? Absolutely? Contingently? May shares carry multiple votes? Fractional votes?

(37) What are the minimum quorum requirements for Stockholder action?

(38) Are there express provisions permitting greater-than-normal requirements for: Stockholder quorum? Stockholder vote?

(39) Are there express provisions for holding Stockholder meetings outside the state? On dates to be set by Board of Directors? What are the notice requirements?

(40) Are there express provisions for informal action by Stockholders? Unanimously? By required percentages?

(41) Is cumulative voting permissive or mandatory?

(42) What are the provisions for Stockholder class voting for Directors?

(43) Are there express provisions for Stockholder Voting Agreements?

(44) Are there express provisions permitting Stockholder control of Directors?

(45) Are there express provisions for irrevocable proxies?

(46) Are there express provisions for voting trust, permitting closed voting trusts and renewals?

(47) Are there express provisions for purchase and redemption by the Corporation of its own shares, including use of stated capital if the purchase is made for specified purposes?

(48) Are there provisions concerning the validity and enforceability of agreements by the Corporation to purchase its own shares?

(49) Is insolvency, in either the equity or the bankruptcy sense, a limitation on the redemption or purchase by the Corporation of its own shares?

(50) Are there express provisions for rights and options to purchase shares, including the issuance of shares, and the share certificates therefor, even partly-paid, to Directors, Officers and Employees? What are the judicial attitudes with respect thereto?

(51) Is Stockholder approval required for the issuance of share options, either generally or to Directors, Officers and Employees?

(52) Do preemptive rights exist or not exist absent provision in the Articles of Incorporation? Are they adequately defined? May they be denied, limited, amplified, or altered in the Articles of Incorporation?

(53) What is the minimum number of authorized Directors?

(54) What are the qualifications required of Directors with respect to: Residence? Citizenship? Stockholding? Age? Otherwise?

(55) May the Board of Directors be classified? Staggered?

(56) What are the minimum quorum requirements for Board of Directors action?

(57) Are there express provisions permitting greater-than-normal requirements for: Board of Directors quorum? Board of Directors vote?

(58) Are there express provisions for holding Board of Directors meetings outside the state?

(59) Are there express provisions for informal action by the Board of Directors? By means of conference telephone or some comparable communication technique?

(60) What are the provisions for removal of Directors? For cause? Without cause?

(61) Are there express provisions for filling vacancies on the Board of Directors? By Stockholder action? By Board of Directors action?

(62) Are there provisions for increasing the size of the Board of Directors? By Stockholder action? By Board of Directors action?

(63) Are there provisions for filling newly-created Directorships? By Stockholder action? By Board of Directors action?

(64) Are there express provisions for executive Committees of the Board of Directors? Other Committees of the Board of Directors? Informal action by Committees? What powers may be exercised by Committees? What is the minimum number of Committee members?

(65) Are there express interested Directors/Officers provisions?

(66) What corporate Officers are required?

(67) May the same person hold more than one office?

(68) What are the required qualifications of the various officers with respect to: Residence? Citizenship? Stockholding? Being a Director? Age? Otherwise?

(69) Are there provisions for the election of Officers by Stockholders? For the removal of Officers by Stockholders?

(70) To what standards are Directors and Officers held accountable? Standard of care? Fiduciary standards? Statutory duties? What are the possible liabilities of Directors? Officers?

(71) To what extent may Directors immunize themselves from liability by filing their written dissents? By reliance on records?

(72) What are the express provisions for deadlock, arbitration, and dissolution, and the judicial attitudes concerning the same?

(73) Are cash and property dividends payable out of surplus? Capital surplus? Earned surplus? Net profits?

(74) Is insolvency, in either the equity or the bankruptcy sense, a limitation on cash or property dividends?

(75) Are unrealized appreciation and depreciation recognized in computing surplus? Capital surplus? Earned surplus?

(76) Are there express "wasting assets" Corporation dividend provisions?

(77) Are there express provisions for share dividends? Share splits? Other share distributions?

(78) To what extent do statutory requirements of notice or disclosure to Stockholders apply in the event of: Cash or property dividends or other distributions from sources other than earned surplus? Share distributions? Reduction of stated capital by cancellation of reacquired shares? Reduction of stated capital made by Board of Directors? Elimination of deficit in earned surplus account by application of capital surplus ("quasi-reorganization")? Conversion of shares? Who are liable for noncompliance? Corporation? Directors or Officers for subjecting Corporation to liability?

(79) What are the provisions for Stockholder class voting for extraordinary corporate matters? May filings effecting extraordinary corporate matters have delayed effective dates?

(80) What Stockholder approval is required for a sale, lease, exchange, or other disposition of corporate assets?

(81) What Stockholder approval is required for a corporate mortgage or pledge?

(82) What Stockholder approval is required for a corporate guaranty?

(83) Do the statutory provisions provide for expeditious amendment of the Articles of Incorporation? Including elimination of preemptive rights? Elimination of cumulative voting? Elimination of cumulative preferred dividend arrearages? Making nonredeemable shares redeemable? Are there provisions for "restated" Articles of Incorporation?

(84) What are the statutory provisions permitting merger or consolidation?

(85) Are there provisions for short-merger of a Subsidiary into a Parent Corporation? Of a Parent into a Subsidiary Corporation?

(86) What are the statutory provisions concerning nonjudicial dissolution?

(87) What are the statutory provisions concerning judicial dissolution?

(88) How extensive are the appraisal remedies afforded dissenting Stockholders? To what extent are appraisal remedies exclusive?

(89) What are the express provisions relating to Stockholder derivative actions?

(90) Are there express provisions for derivative actions by a Director? By an Officer? By a creditor? By others?

(91) Is there statutory differentiation between Stockholder derivative actions and other actions brought by Stockholders?

(92) What are the provisions for indemnification for litigation expenses of Directors? Of Officers? Of other corporate personnel? Are there provisions for insurance?

(93) Are the statutory indemnification provisions exclusive or not with respect to Directors? Officers? Other corporate personnel?

(94) What books and records must be kept within the state?

(95) What are the requirements with respect to annual and other reports?

(96) What are the annual franchise tax rates?

(97) What are the state share transfer tax rates?

(98) Are nonresident security holders subject to local taxes? Personal property taxes? Inheritance taxes?

(99) Are there express provisions to accommodate small business investment companies?

(100) Are there express provisions to accommodate open-end investment companies ("mutual funds")?

(101) To what extent are foreign Corporations doing business in the state subject to the corporate statute's regulatory provisions? Local "blue sky" laws? Local fees and taxes?

(102) To what extent has the corporate statute been construed by the courts? Are judicial and administrative attitudes sympathetic?

(103) Does the state have a statute or regulations similar to Subchapter S?

ADDITIONAL FACTORS IN THE SELECTION OF THE INCORPORATING STATE

(104) Out-of-state incorporations usually impractical where all business operations to be in a single state—unless there is public-issue of shares contemplated.

(105) There is a greater likelihood of diversity jurisdiction in federal courts.

(106) Disadvantages in out-of-state incorporation:

Danger of attachment of property in local litigation.

Local prejudice against "outsiders."

Reports required in two states (nature of information required to be disclosed).

(107) Does the state allow delegation of Board of Director authority to non-Board members (as Michigan does)?

§ 28.3 Consequences of Doing Business as Foreign Corporation—In General

The consequences of doing business in jurisdictions other than the jurisdiction of incorporation must be considered in selecting the jurisdiction of incorporation. By doing such business, the foreign Corporation becomes subject to local litigation, regulation, and taxation, including requirements of formal admission. Various sanctions are imposed for noncompliance with admission requirements.

The judicial jurisdiction and legislative jurisdiction of the states over Corporations and other forms of business enterprise tend to be governed by the same ultimate constitutional standard: whether the state's contacts with a person, thing, or occurrence are sufficient to make the state's action reasonable. If reasonable there is no denial of due process or undue burden on interstate commerce. Practical considerations determine the extent to which a state will actually exercise the jurisdiction which it constitutionally may.

§ 28.4 Consequences of Doing Business as Foreign Corporation—Taxation

The domestic Corporation is subject to taxation by its state of incorporation.

The foreign Corporation is subject to taxation by states where any of its activities enjoy benefit or protection or involve sufficient minimum contact, even though such activities involve interstate or foreign commerce, so long as the tax is commensurate with the Corporation's activities in such states, subject to the limitations of the Federal Interstate Income Law of 1959.[2]

§ 28.5 State Tax Rates

In that state taxes are commonly one of the primary factors to be considered in selecting the incorporation state, the following listing of taxes in the respective states is set forth. This listing appeared in, and is reprinted with the permission of, Iron Age (issue of November 13, 1978). A check should of course be made to determine any interim changes in tax rates.

2. The Federal Interstate Income Act of 1959, 15 U.S.C.A. §§ 381–384, granted immunity from state income tax to income derived within a state by any person (except a domestic Corporation) from interstate commerce if the only business activities within such state by or in behalf of such person during the taxable year are either or both of the following:

"(1) the solicitation of orders by such person, or his representative, in such State for sales of tangible personal property, which orders are sent outside the State for approval or rejection, and, if approved, are filled by shipment or delivery from a point outside the State; and

"(2) the solicitation of orders by such person, or his representative, in such State in the name of or for the benefit of a prospective customer of such person, if orders by such customer to such person to enable such customer to fill orders resulting from such solicitation are orders described in paragraph (1)."

	Personal Income Tax	Corporate Income Tax	Inventory	Real Property: Plant, Machinery, Land	Corporate Franchise	Sales & Use on Mfg.	Unemployment Ins. Rates
AK	5%°	5.4% of Net, + 4% Surtax on Net	Assess at 100% Rate: $3 per $100	Assess at 100%° Rate: $3 per $100°	0	0	2.6% of $10,000 Range: 5.1%–2.6%
AL	5%	5% of Net Use Use Fed. Deductions	0	Assess at 25% Rate: $3.50 per $100	$3 per $1000 (on Alabama investment)	0	2.7% of $6000 Range: 4.0%–1.0%
AZ	8%	10.5% less Fed. & State	0	Assess at 24% Rate: $1.60 per $100	0	3%°	2.7% of $6000 Range: 4%–15%
AR	6%°	6% of Net°	Assess at 20% Rate: $6.40 per $100	Assess at 20% Rate: $6.40 per $100	$1.10 per $1000 of Capital Stock	0	3.1% of $6000 Range: 4.9%–1.4%
CA	3.1%	9% of Net°	Assess at 100% 62% of Mar. 1 invent.	Assess at 100% Rate: 1.25%	9% of State Net Income	6%°	3.6% of $6000 Range: 4.9%–1.4%
CO	8%	5% of Net	Assess at 5% Rate: $8.20 per $100	Assess at 5% Rate: $8.20 per $100	22¢ per $1000 on sales over $1 million	0	3.6% of $4200 Range: 3.6%–0.3%
CT	0	10% of Net	0	Assess at 70% Rate: $4.98 per $100 (Av.)	0	0	4.5% of $6000 Range: 6.0%–1.5%
DE	$390 + 8.8% of amt. over $8,000	8.7%	0	0	Base + .4% of Gross	0	4.2% of $6000 Range: 4.5%–1.6%
FL	0	5% of Net Fed. Income	Assess at 10% Rate: 10%°	Assess at 10% Rate: $14.96 per $100	$1.50 per $100, Florida Gross	0	2.7% of $6000 Range: 4.2%–1.1%
GA	$340 + 6% of amt. over $10,000	6% of Net	0	Assess at 40% Rate: $4.55 per $100	To $5000, based on Capital Stock	0	2.7% of $6000 Range: 4.2%–1.1%
HI	4.27°	6.43% of Net	0	Assess at 60%° Rate: $2.82 per $100	0.5% of Gross°	3.5%°	3.5% of $9800 Range: 3.5%–3.5%
ID	7.5%	6.5% of Gross	0	Assess at 20% Rate: $7.50 per $100	0	0	3.1% of $6000 Range: 4.2%–1.1%
IL	2.5%	4.0%	0	Assess at 33% Rate: $7.19 per $100	0	0	3% of $6000 Range: 4.3%–2.9%
IN	2%	3% of Gross	0	Assess at 33% Rate: $7.44 per $100	5¢ per $100 Corp. value	0	2.7% of $6000 Range: 3.3%–0.0%
IA	7%	9% less 50% of Fed. Income Tax	0	Assess at 100% Rate: $3 per $100	0	0	2.7% of $6000 Range: 6.0%–0.6%
KS	4.5%	6.75%°	Assess at 30%° Rate: $8.77 per $100	Assess at 30% Rate: $8.77 per $100	0	0	3.6% of $6000 Range: 3.6%–0.0%
KY	$280 + 6% of amt. over $8000	5.8% of Net	Assess at 100% Rate: 15¢ per $100°	Assess at 100% Rate: 70¢ per $100° Machinery: 15¢ per $100	70¢ per $1000 of stock	0	2.7% of $6000 Range: 5.5%–0.5%
LA	2%	4% of Net	Assess at 15% Rate: $5.50 per $100°	Assess at 15% of value Rate: $5.50 per $100°	$1.50 per $1000 stock & cash	3%	2.7% of $6000 Range: 2.7%–0.1%
ME	4%	7% of Net	0	Assess at 75% Rate: $2.45 per $100	0	5%°	5% of $6000 Range: 5.4%–2.4%

All estimates are for manufacturing corporations only.
°Indicates further exemptions not included in estimates used for table

IRON AGE: November 13, 1978

	Personal Income Tax	Corporate Income Tax	Inventory	Real Property: Plant, Machinery, Land	Corporate Franchise	Sales & Use on Mfg.	Unemployment Ins. Rates
MD	5%	7%	0	Assess at 45% Rate: $3 per $100	0	5%*	5% of $6000 Range: 5.4%–2.4%
MA	5%	9.5%	0	0	0	0	3.0% of $6000 Range: 6.4%–2.6%
MI	4.8%	Single Tax (Approx. 13% of taxable income)	0	Assess at $50% Rate: $5.39 per $100	0	0	2.7% of $6000 Range: 7.5%–1.0%
MN	16% of Federal Tax	12% of Net	0	Assess at 43% Rate: $10.50 per $100 on buildings, land. 0% Tax on Machinery	0	0	2.7% of $6000 Range: 7.5%–1.0%
MS	4%	4%	0	Assess at 20% (Av.) Rate: $6.80 per $100 *	$2.50 per $1000 on capital in use	5%*	1.0% of $6000 Range: 2.7%–2.6%
MO	6%	5% less Fed. Income Tax (2.6%)	Assess at 20.45% (Av.)* Rate: $5.46 per $100 (Av.)*	Assess at 20.45% (Av.) Rate: $5.46 per $100 (Av.)*	.5% of stock & surplus	3%	3.2% of $6000 Range: 3.1%–3.1%
MT	12.1%	6.75%	4.2% of whole-sale value *	Assess at 100% Rate: 8.55%	0	0	3.1% of $6000 Range: 3.7%–0%
NE	16% of Federal Tax	4.4%	0	Assess at 35% Rate: $3 per $100	0	3%	2.7% of $6000 Range: 3.7%–0%
NV	0	0	0	Assess at 35% Rate: $6.50 per $100	0	3%	3.5% of $6900 Range: 3.7%–1.1%
NH	0	8% of net	0	Assess at 100 pct. Rate: $2.50 per $100 (Av.) 0% on machinery	0	0	2.7% of $6000
NJ	2%	7.5% of Net	0	Assess at 76.9% (Av.) Rate: $3.30 per $100 (Av.)*	1¢ per $5	0	3.4% of $6200
NM	9%	9% of Net	Assess at 33%* Rate: $2 per $100 0% on finished goods	Assess at 33% Rate: $2 per $100	55¢ per $1000 of capital stock	3.75%	2.7% of $6100 Range: 4.2%–0.6%
NY	11–12%	10%*	0	Assess at 100% Rate: $4.25 per $100 (Av.)	0	0	3.7% of $6000 Range: 5.2%–0.1%
NC	7%	6% of Net	72¢ per $100 * of assessed value	Rate: 72¢ per $100	$1.50 per $1000 of stock, or same rate of 55% of property value	0	2.7% of $6000 Range: 5.7%–0.1%
ND	7.5%	6% of Net Less Fed. Income Tax	0	Assess at 50% Rate: $1.37 per $100 Machinery exempt	1% of net income	0	2.7% of $6000 Range: 4.27%–0.5%
OH	2.1%	1% (local tax)	Assess at 39% Rate: $4.38 per $100 *	Assess at 35% Rate: $4.38 per $100	8% of net income	0	3.0% of $6000 Range: 4.8%–1.1%
OK	3.4%	4%	Assess at 35% Rate: $8.50 per $100	Assess at 35% Rate: $8.50 per $100	$1.25 per $1000 of capital stock; cash	0	3.1% of $6000 Range: 5.2%–0.3%

All estimates are for manufacturing corporations only.
* Indicates further exemptions not included in estimates used for table.

45

	Personal Income Tax	Corporate Income Tax	Inventory	Real Property: Plant, Machinery, Land	Corporate Franchise	Sales & Use on Mfg	Unemployment Ins. Rates
OR	10%	7.5%	0	Assess at 100% Rate: $2.41 per $100 (Av.)	0	0	3.5% of $8000 Range: 4.0%–2.6%
PA	2.2%	10.5% of net income	0	0	1% of corp.* value	0	2.0% of $6000 Range: 4.0%–1.0%
PR	3%*	2.1% of Net (est.)*	0	Assess at 60%* Rate: $4.03 per $100	0	0	3.45% of total Range: 3.45%–3.45%
RI	9%*	6%*	0	Assess at 50% Rate: $5.03 per $100 Machinery exempt	$2.50 per $1000 of capital stock	0	2.7% of $6000 Range: 4.0%–2.2%
SC	7%	6%	0	Assess at 10.5% Rate: $1.67 per $1000	$1 per $1000 or stock, surplus	0	2.7% of $6000 Range: 4.1%–1.3%
SD	0	0	0	Assess at 60% Rate: 43¢ per $100	40¢ per $100 of cash & credit	0	2.7% of $6000 Range: 4.5%–0.0%
TN	0	6% of Net	Assess at 30% Rate: $4 per $100 Raw mat'l only; 0% for fin. goods	Assess at 40%, land Assess at 30%, mach. Rate: $4 per $100	$1.50 per $1000 Capital property	0	2.7% of $6000 Range: 4.0%–4%
TX	0	0	Assess at 10%–100% Rate: (Av. $1.20 per $100*	Assess at 10%–100% Rate: $1.21 per $100	$4.25 per $1000 of stock, surplus *	0	.4% of $6000 Range: 4.0%–0.1%
UT	8%	6% less Fed. Income Tax Eff. rate, 3.12%	0	Assess at 30% Median rate: $2.70 per $100	0	0	2.7% of $9600 Range: 2.8%–1.3%
VT	25% of Fed. Tax payment	7.5% of Net	0	0	0	3%*	3.29% of $6000 Range: 6.2%–1.7%
VA	5.75%	6% of net	0	Assess at 100% Rate: $9.00 per $1000; $8.00 per $1000 on machinery (av.)	30¢ per $100 of capital	0	7% of $6000 Range: 3.2%–0.5%
WA	0	0	0	Assess at 100% Rate: 1%	Business & Occupation Tax 46% of gross taxable in-state income	6%*	3.3% of $6000 Range: 3.3%
WV	3.5%	$8.80 per $1000 of gross income	Assess at 100% Rate: $2.40 per $100	Assess at 100% Rate: $2.40 per $100	$340 plus 15¢ per $1000	0	1.5% of $6000 Range: 3.3%–1.1%
WI	6%	7.9%*	0	Assess at 100% Rate: $2.50 per $100. 0 on machy. & equip.	7.9% of Wisc. net * Double weight state sales	0	3.7% of $6,000 Range: 6.5%–0.5%
WY	0	0	0	Assess at 25% Rate: $7.16 per $100	$50 per $1 million of corp. assets	0	3.77% of $6000 Range: 4.0%–1.5%

All estimates are for manufacturing corporations only.
*Indicates further exemptions not included in estimates used for table

IRON AGE, November 13, 1978

§§ 28.6–29.0 are reserved for supplementary material.

*

CHAPTER 29

PREINCORPORATION AGREEMENTS

Table of Sections

A. AGREEMENTS—GENERALLY

§ 29.1 Types of Preincorporation Agreements

"Preincorporation Agreement" is a broad term which is often used to encompass at least four distinguishable kinds of Agreements:

(a) "Agreements of association" or Preincorporation Agreements or Agreements to Form a Corporation;

(b) Agreements between promoters and non-stockholder third persons;

(d) Promoter's contracts.

"Stockholder Agreements" are executed after Incorporation, and may or may not involve the Corporation as a party.[1]

1. See Chapter 47 infra, with respect to Voting and Pooling Agreements.

"Agreement of association" (or "articles of Agreement") or Preincorporation Agreements or Agreements to Form a Corporation are the terms for a formal preliminary instrument. It is required by statute in a few jurisdictions as part of the incorporation procedure or as a convenience to the Stockholders. Such Preliminary Agreements usually deal with where and how the Corporation is to be formed, the respective contributions of each associate to the initial assets, the source of future funds if needed, the allocation of shares and other securities, and such intracorporate provisions as voting control, the names of the Directors and Officers, and their salaries, the taking over of the property assembled by the promoters for the business and adoption of outstanding Preincorporation Agreements with third persons, employment contracts, share transfer restrictions, etc.

When Preincorporation Agreements between promoters and third parties are made, there is generally no Corporation in existence. Absent statute or provision in the Articles of Incorporation, the Corporation is not automatically bound when it is incorporated. Although the parties have an enforceable Agreement which can be enforced to bind the Corporation.

Subscriptions (see Chapter 39, infra) are Agreements to purchase shares (as compared to an Agreement to form a particularly described Corporation and purchase shares). Subscription agreements may describe a Corporation yet to be formed (although it does not bind anyone to form this Corporation).

Promoter's contracts are agreements between the initial subscribers or the Corporation and a promoter to pay a fee to the promoter to locate additional subscribers.

Library References:

C.J.S. Corporations § 119 et seq.
West's Key No. Digests, Corporations ⚿30.

§ 29.2 Agreements to Form Corporation—Generally

The first step in the process of organizing a Corporation may be the preparation of a Preincorporation Agreement between the organizers. When not a necessary step in the sense of being required by statute it is wise practice for the parties to put in writing their understanding of the terms and conditions that will govern the formation and conduct of the proposed Corporation.[2] The Agreement will cover such matters as: (a) the contents of the Articles of Incorporation; (b) who will occupy the various corporate offices; (c) what

2. C.J.S. Corporations, §§ 134, 135.

salaries will be paid; (d) what each is to contribute in the way of cash and property, and, (e) how many shares each is to receive.

A Preincorporation Agreement may be either a mere memorandum outlining the main points of an oral agreement or a complete written document describing all the details of the understanding. The formal Agreement is the preferred method of establishing a legally binding commitment to invest in a Corporation to be formed.

Normally, a Preincorporation contract will be fully executed by the formation of a Corporation as provided in the Agreement. If it is desired to have certain provisions of the Agreement survive the Incorporation and continue to bind the parties, the Agreement should specifically so state. If the Agreement is to survive it should usually be adopted by the Corporation.

An Agreement to form a Corporation usually places the parties to the Agreement in the relationship of Joint Venturers, with the formation of the Corporation and the establishment of its business as the object of the Venture. There is a conceptual difficulty, after the Corporation is formed, in simultaneously treating the parties as having the rights of Stockholders in the Corporation and as Joint Venturers with a fiduciary relationship to each other. As a result, some courts have taken the view that when the parties adopt the corporate form, with the corporate shield to protect them, they necessarily "cease to be partners and have only the rights, duties and obligations of stockholders".[3] Other courts have taken the position that the Joint Venture may continue after the formation of the Corporation, at least where the parties' intention to this effect is clear.[4]

§ 29.3 Promoters—Generally [5]

A promoter is a person who takes the initiative in developing and organizing a new business Venture. He may act either alone or with co-promoters. The promoter is often an aggressive, imaginative entrepreneur who fulfills the essential economic function of taking an idea and creating a profitable business to capitalize on the idea.

The activities of promoters fall into three principal areas. (1) The promoter must arrange for the necessary capital for the Corpo-

3. The leading case adopting this view is Jackson v. Hooper, 76 N.J.Eq. 592, 75 A. 568 (Ct.Err. & App.1910). See also, Weisman v. Awnair Corp. of America, 3 N.Y.2d 444, 165 N.Y.S.2d 745, 144 N.E.2d 415 (1957).

4. E. g. De Boy v. Harris, 207 Md. 212, 113 A.2d 903 (1955). This view seems to accord better with modern theories of corporate enterprise, particularly close Corporations.

5. This Section, and §§ 29.4–29.7, infra, have their source in Hamilton, Corporations in a Nutshell (1980) Ch. 5.

ration. He may invest only his personal funds, or use his personal funds plus loans from banks to obtain the necessary capital. He may seek outside capital from a small number of investors, who may be friends or neighbors. If so, he must negotiate with the outside investors to determine their share in the forthcoming enterprise, and arrange either by contract or subscription to ensure that the capital will be forthcoming when needed. If a public offering is to be made (which is rare for a newly-commenced business) he must secure compliance with the Federal Securities Laws and state "blue sky" laws as well as arranging for the distribution and sale of the securities, often through an underwriter. (2) The promoter must obtain the necessary assets and personnel so that the Corporation may function. He may obtain a lease or an option to purchase needed land, or may enter into a contract to purchase with a view of assigning the contract to the Corporation. He may negotiate construction contracts to build or remodel the necessary buildings. He must secure the necessary employees which often will include himself. He may secure the necessary machinery, equipment or fixtures. He may contact customers or arrange for advertising. Obviously, in this area, the kinds of activities promoters engage in are numerous and varied, depending on the nature of the business being promoted. (3) The promoter must arrange for the formation of the Corporation itself. He must arrange for the filing of the Articles of Incorporation, the preparation of the necessary papers, the issuance of shares, and the like. If the promoter first forms the Corporation, subsequent contractual problems are usually minimized since he may thereafter conduct all the necessary steps in the name of the Corporation, and there is little chance of confusion between the promoter's individual liability and the corporate liability on the arrangements he negotiates. Thus, actions may be taken in the corporate name, and only if a third person desires the personal liability of the promoter as well as the Corporation, as may be the case with banks, will the promoter execute an obligation individually or separately guaranteeing its performance.

Often, however, the formation of the Corporation turns out to be one of the last steps in the promotional process. The promoter may begin investigation of the profitability of the proposed business, determine that the prospects of success are good, and proceed at once with business negotiations in the areas of capital formation and obtaining business assets and contracts without actually forming the Corporation. In this situation there is great likelihood of confusion and uncertainty, and most of the contractual litigation involving promoters arises in this way.

§ 29.4 Promoter's Contracts with Non-Stockholders

Let us assume that a promoter enters into a contract to purchase machinery for the new business he is promoting, and consider whether the promoter is personally liable on that contract. No single, simple answer is possible. In some circumstances he is, in other circumstances he is not. If the Corporation has been duly formed and the contract is entered into and executed by the promoter in the corporate name, he would normally not be personally liable since he has executed the contract merely as an agent and not as a principal. On the other hand, if the Corporation has not been formed, and the promoter enters into the contract in his own name without referring to the Corporation with the thought of subsequently assigning the contract to the Corporation, he is clearly personally liable. These are the easy cases. The more difficult cases fall into two major categories:

(1) Contracts Entered in the Name of the (Not Yet Formed) Corporation. In this class of case the promoter executes a contract in the corporate name *in a way that makes it appear that the Corporation has been formed when it actually has not been.* Many cases say that such a promoter is personally liable on the theory that a person acting as agent represents that his principal exists, and the promoter is liable because of a misrepresentation. Other cases merely state that a person who purports to act as agent for a nonexistent principal thereby automatically becomes a principal. The latter theory is based on contract and the former on tort, though in most cases they should lead to the same result.

These cases holding the promoter personally liable when the Corporation has not been formed often give the third person a windfall because that person is usually not relying on the promoter's credit when entering into the contract; rather he is relying on the Corporation's credit or, more likely, on the possibility that the Corporation will do well and be able to pay off the obligations. (If he was relying on the promoter's credit he would require the promoter to guarantee the "Corporation's" obligation.) However, virtually all courts in this situation hold the promoter personally liable despite the potential windfall.

If the Corporation is thereafter formed and adopts the contract, the promoter may then seek to avoid liability on the basis of several possible arguments. He may contend that the subsequent formation of the Corporation corrected any misrepresentation or deception that may have occurred. He may also argue that the manner of execution of the Agreement indicates that the third party was content to accept the liability of the Corporation, and that therefore the adoption of the contract should release him—in other words, that the transaction should be construed as a novation. Also, depending to some extent on the wording of the Agreement, the promoter may be able to argue that he should not be held liable on the basis of the parol evidence rule (since only the Corporation was referred to in the contract). Finally, the promoter may also seek to defend on the ground that the Corporation was sufficiently formed so that it was a "Corporation de facto," or a "Corporation by estoppel" and therefore it was "in existence" when the contract was entered into. Even though these arguments are superficially plausible, the chances of success are problematic.

To summarize: if the promoter enters into a contract with a third person in the name of the Corporation without disclosing that it is not in existence, he is personally liable on the contract. If the Corporation is thereafter created and takes over the contract, the promoter has a better chance of being relieved of liability but he still probably will be found liable.

(2) Contracts Referring to the Fact the Corporation Is Not Yet Formed. In this class of case the contract is executed by the promoter and the third party when both are aware that the Corporation has not been formed. The contract itself usually reveals this fact, as for example when it is executed in a name such as "ABC Corporation, a Corporation to be formed." Or the promoter may advise the third person that the Corporation has not yet been formed when he executes the contract in the corporate name. It will be noted that this situation differs from situation (1) in that both parties are aware that the Corporation is not yet in existence and there is no possible misrepresentation as to that fact.

This pattern may be analyzed in several different ways with widely divergent consequences. For example, it may be analyzed as an offer to the Corporation which is revocable by either party and will result in a contract only if the Corporation is thereafter formed and accepts the offer before it is withdrawn. Or it may be analyzed as an irrevocable option running to the Corporation, with the consideration being a promise, express or implied, by the promoter to form the Corporation and use his best efforts to cause the Corporation to adopt the contract. Or, it may be analyzed as a present contract between the third person and the promoter by which the promoter is bound, with the understanding that if the contract is adopted by the Corporation the promoter will nevertheless remain secondarily liable in the contract.

Which of these various alternatives is the proper one in any specific situation depends on the elusive "intention of the parties." If an attorney is called upon to draft a Preincorporation Agreement it is relatively simple for him to ascertain the parties' intention and describe it in a written Agreement in terms so precise that there can be no cause for misunderstanding. If the promoter is to be bound until the Corporation adopts the contract, and then is to be released from liability, the contract that specifically so provides should avoid later disputes.

Litigation in this area generally involves Agreements in which the intention is not clearly spelled out. The contract may have been negotiated by the parties without legal assistance, or the language chosen may not illuminate the specific problem one way or the other. Or the parties may have been unable to agree on their respective rights in the event of some remote contingency. Rather than forego a lucrative transaction, the parties use language such as "ABC Corporation, a Corporation to be formed," hoping that the question of the liability of the promoter will not arise. In such situations, the search for intent is truly hopeless, though the courts must resolve the dispute one way or another.

Generalizations about tests which courts use to find "intention" are hazardous. Probably most courts feel that it is likely that the third person intended for *someone* to be liable. Hence, there is a distinct tendency to hold the promoter at least initially liable, especially where the Corporation is never formed. Indeed, some cases flatly state that the promoter is personally liable in this situation unless there is specific agreement to the contrary. This view is strengthened where the third person is to receive payments or partial performance before the Corporation is formed; presumably the promoter intends to make those payments or render the performance himself until the Corporation is formed.

Professor Williston has suggested that most persons assume that even if the promoter is initially liable, he is nevertheless to be released if the Corporation is later formed and adopts the contract. In other words, there is to be a novation. The testimony of the plaintiff in Bradshaw v. Jones, 152 S.W. 695, 697 (Tex.Civ.App.1912), writ refused, is representative of this understanding: "I understood that I was working for [Mr. Jones] personally until the railroad was organized; and after the railroad was organized, I was working for the railroad, of course,". Not surprisingly, the court concluded that a novation was intended. There are, however, some holdings and a considerable amount of dicta to the contrary. One problem with the Williston approach is that it may encourage promoters to create "straw" Corporations to take over contracts even after it is clear that the Venture should be abandoned.

If the promoters are held liable, they are considered to be Partners, and liable for all promotional contracts on a joint and several basis.

Where both parties are aware that the Corporation has not yet been formed, several recent cases have held the promoter not personally liable on the contract. In Quaker Hill, Inc. v. Parr, 148 Colo. 45, 364 P.2d 1056 (1961), for example, the court concluded that on the facts the third party never intended to rely on the promoters' performance of the contract and therefore should not be able to hold the promoters personally liable. These recent cases may signal the beginning of a more realistic judicial attitude towards ascertaining the "intention of the parties," since it is probable in many cases that the third person intended to look only to the Corporation for performance of the contract.

§ 29.5 Liability of Corporations for Promoter's Contracts

A Corporation, after it is formed, is not automatically liable on obligations incurred by its promoters in its behalf. The reason usually given is that the promoter cannot be the Corporation's agent since the Corporation is not in existence. This conceptualistic argument can be partially justified on the practical ground that the rule permits investors in a Corporation an opportunity to consider and reject undesirable arrangements agreed to by the promoter. Of particular importance, it permits review by subsequent investors of contracts entered into between the promoter himself and the Corporation. This practical justification is not particularly persuasive since it does not provide a systematic review of all promoters' contracts by subsequent investors.

The theory on which Corporations voluntarily become liable on contracts negotiated by their promoters has been the subject of a great deal of confusing discussion. Much depends on how the relationship between the third person and the promoter is originally categorized. If the arrangement constitutes an "offer" by the third person to the Corporation or an "option" running to the Corporation (without personal liability on the promoter) the Corporation becomes liable by "accepting" the offer. If the arrangement constitutes a contract between the promoter and third person where it is understood that a Corporation will be formed, the Corporation "adopts" the contract. Technically, "ratification" is not the proper word to describe this situation because "ratification" assumes that the Corporation was in existence at the time the contract was entered into. Courts nevertheless sometimes use the words "ratification" and "adoption" interchangeably. If the promoter is then relieved from liability, the "adoption" or "ratification" becomes a "novation." If the arrangement between the promoter and third person is contractual and the third person was unaware that formation of the Corporation was contemplated, the Corporation may be an "assignee" of the promoter, and becomes liable by "agreeing to assume" the obligation.

In the last analysis, the legal words used are not particularly important. What is necessary is some form of assent by the Corporation to the contract after it has been formed. If this assent is manifested, it may serve as an "acceptance," an "adoption," or an "assumption," as the case may be.

The necessary assent may be express, or it may be implied from the circumstances. If a Corporation takes the benefits of a contract made by its promoter, it will usually be concluded that it has assented to the burdens of the contract. For example, if a promoter negotiates a contract by which a third person agrees to become an employee of the Corporation for a specified period, the Corporation "accepts" (or "adopts" or "assumes") the contract if it permits the employee to render services for the Corporation, and thereafter cannot fire the employee without cause during the contract period.

Since the Corporation becomes liable on the contract only when it assents, it has been held that the contract term begins when the assent occurs. This may be of importance for purposes of the statute of limitations or the one year statute of frauds provision.

§ 29.6 Promoter's Fiduciary Duties

Co-promoters of a single Venture owe fiduciary duties to each other. In effect they are treated as Partners in a Venture to organize the business.

Much more difficult questions are raised where a promoter enters into transactions with the Corporation before outside creditors, investors, or Stockholders are brought into the Venture. The transaction may involve the receipt of shares of the Corporation by the promoter, or the creation of corporate indebtedness in favor of the promoter for services or property. The transaction may be entered into when the promoter is the sole Stockholder, or with the approval of the then Stockholders. Later or subsequent creditors, investors or Stockholders may object to the transaction on the ground that the services or property were overvalued or the amount awarded to the promoter was excessive. In many cases of this kind the courts have used language of fiduciary duty in reviewing and often setting aside such transactions to the extent they are believed to be unfair. The leading case finding a fiduciary duty is Old Dominion Copper Mining & Smelting Co. v. Bigelow, 203 Mass. 159, 89 N.E. 193 (1909), affirmed 225 U.S. 111, 32 S.Ct. 641, 56 L.Ed. 1009, announcing the so-called "Massachusetts rule." Not all courts have agreed, however; see particularly Old Dominion Copper Mining & Smelting Co. v. Lewisohn, 210 U.S. 206, 28 S.Ct. 634, 52 L.Ed. 1025 (1908), involving the same transaction and announcing the "federal rule" that subsequent Stockholders or investors may not set aside previously approved promoters' transactions.

As a practical matter, the issue in these cases is not so much whether or not a fiduciary duty exists as whether or not there has been full disclosure of the transaction. If there has been full disclosure subsequent creditors, investors, or Stockholders may readily protect themselves by refusing to deal with the Corporation or by reducing the price at which they acquire shares to reflect the reduction in value caused by the promoter's transaction. Indeed, the fiduciary duty described above is basically a duty of full disclosure rather than a duty of fair dealing. Cases continue to arise, however, in which subsequent investors attack promoter's transactions, and some courts have set them aside on the basis of a vague discussion of "fiduciary" duties.

Since failure to disclose may constitute a violation of federal or state securities acts, many cases that fifty years ago would have been analyzed as "promoter's fraud" cases are now analyzed as securities act cases.

§ 29.7 Organizational Expenses Incurred by Promoters

Logically, expenses incurred in connection with the organization of a Corporation should be treated no differently than other contracts entered into by promoters. For example, if an attorney is employed by promoters to draw up the Articles of Incorporation, the promoter should be liable for the attorney's fee unless the attorney agrees to look only to the Corporation. If the Corporation is formed and adopts the contract, it becomes liable for the fee, and whether or not the promoter is released from his obligation depends on whether the transaction is deemed a novation.

There are complications, however. Organizational expenses such as attorneys' fees are peculiar in that the mere corporate existence is in effect a use of the benefits of the contract by the Corporation. Arguably, therefore, by its mere existence the Corporation has agreed to pay whatever fee was negotiated by the promoter. Some courts have so held, but the majority view is that the Corporation is not automatically bound. Rather the Corporation—since it cannot refuse the services—can only be compelled to pay a reasonable fee under the circumstances.

Many states have statutes that permit the payment of reasonable charges and expenses of organization of a Corporation out of the capital received by it in payment for its shares without impairing capital or rendering such shares not fully paid and non-assessable. (See e. g., Model Bus.Corp.Act § 22.)

Often the promoter or the attorney will wish to take shares in the Corporation for organizational expenses and services. There is nothing inherently wrong with this practice; indeed, it somewhat resembles a contingent fee based on the success of the business rather than on litigation. The value of the consideration received by an attorney or promoter for services is, of course, taxable income to them and may be deducted by the Corporation as an expense over a 60 month period.

Promoters naturally expect to be compensated for their efforts, and in view of the nature of their innovative efforts, they often may legitimately expect compensation which would be considered generous by a salaried person. Typically, a promoter will form a Corporation with nominal capital, and then seek outside financial support to make his promotion a success. The subsequent investors will usually purchase shares in the Corporation at a higher price than the shares previously issued to the promoter. The investors' interest is thereby diluted and the promoters' interest increased in value. In a sense this increase in value represents partial compensation to the promoter.

§ 29.8 Preincorporation Services

At the time of any preincorporation services, the Corporation is not in existence, and the only possible present contract is with the promoters. After incorporation, the Corporation can, expressly or sometimes impliedly, assume responsibility for such services. Preincorporation services in most jurisdictions do not qualify as valid consideration for the issue of shares since the services were not rendered to the Corporation as required.

§ 29.9 Agreement to Form Corporation—Drafting Techniques

The Preincorporation Agreement is an Agreement among the promoter and the Stockholders or the Stockholders alone for the formation of the Corporation and is to be distinguished from Agreements between promoters and non-Stockholder third persons, which have been previously discussed.

Sometimes the Preincorporation Agreement includes provisions typically found in Stockholder Agreements.

The Preincorporation Agreement can take the form of a simple memorandum, but the more careful practice is to draft a relatively elaborate and detailed Agreement, in which the persons interested in the enterprise agree (1) on the persons who are to serve as incorporators and as initial Directors; (2) to execute and acknowledge and cause to be filed the Articles of Incorporation; (3) to subscribe to shares and/or debt securities for prescribed consideration; (4) at the organization meetings of the Incorporators and of the Board of Directors (i) to vote to adopt the By-laws in the form attached, (ii) to authorize the acceptance of any subscriptions and the issue of any debt securities and of shares, (iii) to approve the form(s) of the share certificates with legends in the forms attached, (iv) to appoint certain persons to certain offices at certain salaries, (v) to approve the execution by the Corporation of any desired employment contracts with certain persons in the forms attached, and (vi) to authorize the payment by the Corporation of a certain fee to the attorney for his fees and disbursements in connection with the organization of the Corporation. If there are any "accommodation" or dummy subscribers, they can agree to transfer any of their subscriptions as the real parties in interest desire. Those with a continuing interest in the enterprise can also agree to enter into a "Stockholder Agreement" either among themselves or among themselves and the Corporation.

§§ 29.10–29.20 are reserved for supplementary material.

B. PREINCORPORATION AGREEMENTS

§ 29.21 Agreement to Form Corporation

INTRODUCTORY COMMENT

The following is the form for a Preincorporation Agreement. It differs from a Subscription Agreement by being much more detailed in its assumptions (and thus requirements) as to the form of the Corporation and its operational format and in as much as it binds the signators to form the Corporation described. It differs from a promoters contract inasmuch as it assumes that some (if not all) of the future Stockholders are identified already.

AGREEMENT TO FORM A CORPORATION AND OPERATE A BUSINESS

This Agreement made [*Date*], by and among [*Names*] (herein jointly and individually referred to as the "parties");

Whereas, the parties have agreed to organize a profit Corporation under the laws of the State of [*Name*] for the purpose of operating a business.

Whereas, the parties have agreed to subscribe for the [*Describe*] stock and debt of the Corporation (herein referred to as "securities") as hereinafter set forth.

Now, therefore, in consideration of mutual covenants and other valuable consideration exchanged, the Stockholders agree as follows:

§ 1.1 Incorporation

[*Names*] will incorporate a profit Corporation under the laws of the State of [*Name*] known as [*Name of Corporation*], (the "Corporation").

§ 1.2 Corporate Purpose

The Corporation shall have the following purpose:

Alternative A (General)

The purpose for which the Corporation will be organized is to transact all lawful business for which Corporations may be organized under the Business Corporation Act of [*State of Incorporation*].

Alternative B (Agent)

The purpose for which the Corporation will be organized is to represent, consult with, render reports to, and act as agent or independent contractor for the following types of concerns: ______; and to represent their interests and pursue their goals in every manner as if their purposes and goals were the purposes and goals of this Corporation.

Broadcasting. see *Alternative I* below.

Alternative C (Brokerage)

The purpose for which the Corporation will be organized is to arrange for the import, export, trade, purchase, sale, consignment and warehousing of the following: ______; and to act as agent for others who want to accomplish the same.

Alternative D (Farming)

The purpose for which the Corporation will be organized is to cultivate, raise, grow, produce and sell the following products: ______.

Alternative E (Finance)

The purpose for which the Corporation will be organized is to subscribe for, acquire, purchase, invest in and deal in, interests in public and private security offerings and to underwrite and participate in security offerings of every type, including stock, securities, warrants, options, bonds, notes, indentures and other secured and unsecured equity and debt instruments.

Alternative F (Holding Company)

The purpose for which the Corporation will be organized is to acquire, invest in, hold, distribute, hypothecate and sell interests in Partnerships and corporate business enterprises, and to exercise all of the powers of an interest holder under the terms of such entities' charters and By-laws.

Alternative G (Management)

The purpose for which the Corporation will be organized is to render accounts receivable, accounts payable, organizational, sales, inventory, manufacturing, financial advance planning and technical advice to the following types of businesses: ______; and to act to said businesses' general production merchandizing, organization, reorganization and operations and to act as promoter, investigator, systems analyzer, agent, representative and consultant for said business operations.

Alternative H (Manufacture)

The purpose for which the Corporation will be organized is to manufacture, fabricate and assemble the following products: ______; and to sell, lease and otherwise promote and deal in the same and in related products and services and to manufacture, fabricate and assemble the tools, materials and equipment reasonably necessary for such manufacturing processes.

Alternative I (Publication and Broadcasting)

The purpose for which the Corporation will be organized is to create, prepare, draft, design, print, broadcast and publish material relating to the following subject matters: ______ in and for all forms of broadcasting and publication including radio, television, newspapers, magazines, and all other forms of commercial and noncommercial media.

Alternative J (Real Estate)

The purpose for which the Corporation will be organized is to operate, manage, improve, repair, rent, lease, own, acquire, sell, assign, mortgage, hypothecate, and otherwise deal in real property and its appurtenances and fixtures and to deal in direct interests, Partnership interests, Stockholder interests and Joint Venture interests which represent shares in such property and to build or contract for the building of buildings and other structures on such property for such uses.

Alternative K (Research)

The purpose for which the Corporation will be organized is to conduct under its employment (or through independent contracts or Joint Ventures) research, design and development of the following: ______; and to experiment, test and market the products, services and processes resulting from such research and development and to investigate, consult, report, and render advice as to the development of similar products and the techniques and methods of their manufacture and sale.

Alternative L (Sales)

The purpose for which the Corporation will be organized is to lease, sell, import, export and to finance purchases and sales of the following products and services: ______; and to promote the sale thereof and to install, maintain and improve the products so sold and to maintain an inventory of the products to be sold and their repair parts and to finance such inventory by factoring or other forms of finance or hypothecation.

Alternative M (Service Business)

The purpose for which the Corporation will be organized is to render the following services: ______; and to own and operate the associated facilities, equipment and real estate to render such services.

Alternative N (School)

The purpose for which the Corporation will be organized is to conduct educational training in the following areas: ______.

Alternative O (Wholesale)

The purpose for which the Corporation will be organized is to purchase, sell, warehouse, hold, take on consignment, receive, store, forward, factor, collaterally assign and otherwise borrow against and finance inventory of the following kind and nature: ______.

§ 1.3 Initial Stockholders

The initial Stockholders of the Corporation shall be the undersigned, who shall subscribe for and purchase the following securities on or before [*Date*], for the consideration indicated:

Security Description	Stockholder	Number of Securities	Consideration

Option 1

There shall be no other securities outstanding at the time of incorporation.

§ 1.4 Close Corporation Status

The Corporation shall be qualified as a "close Corporation". Accordingly, all things shall be done to insure qualification of the Corporation as a close Corporation. In the event that any thing necessary to qualify as a close Corporation is overlooked during the organization of the Corporation or thereafter, the parties agree that they shall take such steps as are appropriate to qualify the Corporation as a close Corporation.

After organization of the Corporation the associates shall observe all the requirements necessary to continue close Corporation status, until such time as the close Corporation status is terminated as provided herein. Notwithstanding anything to the contrary herein, no actions may be taken by the Corporation, or by any of the Stockholders, including issuance of additional shares, which would have the effect of disqualifying the Corporation as a close Corporation under the General Corporations Law, unless such action is agreed to *by the unanimous vote/by a vote of ——% of the voting power* of all parties to this Agreement and any transferees of shares of the parties to this Agreement.

§ 1.5 Articles of Incorporation

The parties shall cause the execution and filing of Articles of Incorporation in the form set forth as Exhibit A which is attached hereto and incorporated by reference.

§ 1.6 By-laws

Attached hereto as Exhibit B and incorporated by reference are a set of By-laws which shall be the By-laws of this Corporation and which the parties shall cause to be adopted after formation of the Corporation.

§ 1.7 Subchapter S Status

This Corporation shall elect to be a Subchapter S Corporation.

All the parties to this Agreement agree to cause the Corporation to file, and shall execute as Stockholders, any form necessary to be filed with the Internal Revenue Service in order to obtain Subchapter S status. It is understood by all parties hereto that Subchapter S status would be terminated if there is any transfer of shares of this Corporation to a party who elects to terminate the Subchapter S election, or to sufficient parties to increase the number of Stockholders beyond the maximum allowed under the Subchapter S provision of the Internal Revenue Code. Accordingly, all parties hereto agree not to transfer their stock in any way that would cause a termination of the Corporation's Subchapter S election except pursuant to unanimous agreement to the contrary hereafter entered into by written amendment of this Agreement. Therefore, any party hereto who desires to transfer shares of the Corporation to someone who is not a party to this Agreement shall have no right to transfer such shares to any third party who does not agree prior to such transfer, in writing, to join in the election of Subchapter S status. The foregoing restriction upon transfer of shares is in addition to, and not in place of, any other restrictions created by this Agreement and shall appear as a legend on the Corporation's stock certificates.

§ 1.8 Termination

This Corporation shall be terminated, and the parties agree thereupon to wind up the affairs of Corporation and to liquidate and dissolve Corporation upon thirty (30) days written notice in the event of any of the following, in which case the mutual rights and duties of the parties may also be settled in the manner set forth herein.

(1) Claimed breach of this Agreement, coupled with failure of the other Stockholders to negotiate and consummate a purchase of the Corporation's stock from such claimant.

(2) Conduct of a Stockholder detrimental to the Corporation, coupled with failure of the Stockholders to negotiate and consummate a purchase of the Stockholder's stock pursuant to the terms hereof.

(3) Filing of a petition in bankruptcy against a Stockholder, coupled with failure of the Stockholders to negotiate and consummate a purchase of the shares of Stockholder whose assets have become subject to a petition in bankruptcy.

(4) Adjudication of insanity or incompetence of a Stockholder coupled with failure of the Stockholders (including any guardian or conservator of an associate) to negotiate and consummate a purchase of the insane or incompetent Stockholder's stock.

(5) Issuance of a lien or levy of writ of attachment or writ of execution against the shares of any Stockholder herein without immediate removal of such lien or levy, coupled with failure of the Stockholders to negotiate and consummate a purchase of the shares of the Stockholder whose shares have been subject to such attachment or execution. Any transfer of ownership of shares of a Stockholder by operation of law pursuant to a writ of execution or otherwise shall be deemed a breach of the Agreement.

If any Stockholder attempts to transfer his shares in violation of the restrictions on such transfer contained in the Agreement, the remaining parties shall have the option and the right to cause voluntary dissolution of Corporation at once, and shall have an irrevocable proxy to vote the shares in favor of a voluntary dissolution of the Corporation.

§ 1.9 Continuing Obligation

A party's withdrawal shall not release such withdrawing party from any obligation(s) he has to Corporation or to the other parties.

§ 1.10 Cessation of Business

Upon termination and dissolution of the Corporation, no further business will be transacted other than winding up of Corporation affairs, collection of outstanding accounts and payment of outstanding liabilities, and liquidation of the Corporation.

§ 1.11 Division of Corporation Assets Upon Liquidation

Upon liquidation, Corporation assets shall be divided in the following order:

(a) Expenses of liquidation and debts of the Corporation other than debts owing to Stockholders shall be paid first.

(b) Next, there shall be paid debts owing to Stockholders, including business loans and advances by Stockholders to or for the benefit of the Corporation.

(c) The remaining assets shall be distributed to the Stockholders of the Corporation in proportion to their rights thereto under the Articles of Incorporation, or under the terms of this Agreement, whichever is controlling.

§ 1.12 Restrictions on Distributions

No dividends, distributions or payments for or upon shares shall be made by the Corporation if such dividends, distributions or payments for or upon shares would be in violation of any provision of the General Corporation Law. Before any dividends, distributions or payments for or upon shares are made, the Stockholders, Directors and Officers shall consult with the Corporation's legal counsel and accountant to obtain their opinion as to whether such dividends, distributions or payments for or upon shares may be made legally.

§ 1.13 Identification of Source of Distribution Upon Shares

Each distribution to Stockholders other than one chargeable to retained earnings shall be identified in a notice to Stockholders as being made from a source other than retained earnings, stating the accounting treatment thereof. Such notice shall accompany the distribution or shall be given within three months after the end of the fiscal year in which the distribution has been made.

§ 1.14 Irrevocable Proxy

Alternative A

(a) All parties to this Agreement shall vote their own shares. However, all parties hereto agree to vote their shares in favor of all actions required explicitly or implicitly to be taken under this Agreement and against any action explicitly or implicitly contrary to this Agreement.

If any party to this Agreement should attempt to vote his shares contrary to the provisions of this Agreement, such vote shall be disregarded and shall have no force and effect, and immediately and automatically upon the attempt to vote such shares contrary to the terms of this Agreement, the other parties hereto shall have a proxy to vote such shares in the manner required by the terms of this Agreement. Such proxy shall be deemed an irrevocable proxy which continues during the term of this Agreement.

Alternative B

(a) ______ hereby constitute and appoint ______ as their attorney-in-fact and proxy to vote all of the shares of this Corporation standing in the names of ______ upon any and all matters upon which Stockholders are entitled to vote.

(b) Each party hereto agrees that if he is employed by the Corporation, and if such employment is ever terminated by voluntary resignation, permanent physical disability or death, then the shares of Corporation stock owned by such party (referred to as "the terminated Stockholder-employee") may, at the option of all other parties hereto, be voted by such other parties subject to the following proxy provisions. The phrase "permanent disability" shall have the meaning stated elsewhere herein or in any other agreement between the parties defining such term. The terminated Stockholder-employee hereby grants a proxy to all other parties hereto to vote all shares of the Corporation owned by the terminated Stockholder-employee. This proxy is, however, granted to, and only to, those other parties hereto who acquire from the terminated Stockholder-employee a right to purchase all shares of the Corporation owned by the terminated Stockholder-employee, either (1) by acceptance of an offer of the terminated Stockholder-employee or his estate or personal representative to sell all shares owned by the terminated Stockholder-employee or (2) by *the exercise of the option/the fulfillment of the obligation* an option to purchase all shares owned by the terminated Stockholder-employee or his estate or personal representative pursuant to the terms of § 1.19, infra.

The proxy which is granted and arises by reason of satisfaction of the foregoing conditions shall be an irrevocable proxy. The proxy shall remain in effect until the completion of the purchase of the shares owned by the terminated Stockholder-employee or his estate or personal representative or until otherwise terminated as provided below. The irrevocable proxy shall terminate if the holders thereof are ever in default in their agreement to purchase the shares owned by the terminated Stockholder-employee, or his estate or personal representative. If more than one party hereto is purchasing shares from a terminated Stockholder-employee or his estate or personal representative, pursuant hereto, each purchasing Stockholder shall have an irrevocable proxy to vote the number of shares which he is purchasing.

§ 1.15 Additional Stockholders

(a) It is agreed that [*Names*] (hereinafter referred to as the "Promoter"): is authorized to sell for a period ending [*Date*] together up to [*Number and Description of securities*] (but not in blocks of less than [*Number*] per owner or joint owner), all of which securities shall be subject to the Corporation's Buy-Sell Agreement and to a securities legend, to persons who fit the following criterion: [*Describe*] at a price not less than $[*Dollars*] per security.

(b) The promoter agrees that *he/she* shall only represent the Corporation in the following manner:

(1) All solicitations shall be made by [*Personal contact/telephone/mailings*] to persons who fit the following description [*Describe*].

(2) The only advertising materials to be used shall be first approved by ______.

(3) The only description of the Corporation and its prospects to be used shall be the materials attached hereto and made a part hereof; the Promoter agrees that he will not, in any manner whatsoever, suggest, hint or indicate that such materials underestimate the condition or prospects of the Corporation or fail to give a copy of such materials to each and every prospective purchaser as follows: [*Describe When Copy is to be Given*].

The Promoter agrees that if he has failed to comply with this subparagraph for any reason, such failure and its facts shall be immediately disclosed to ______.

COMMENT TO (a) AND (b)

There is no area of the law which is fraught with more danger than state and federal security laws and regulations. A careful review of the applicable law as it relates to the following questions is strongly advised:

(a) Who can sell?

(b) What commissions, if any can be paid?

(c) Who can buy?

(d) How many offerings can be made in a certain period?

(e) What exemptions there are for certain offerings?

(f) What can be said about the Corporation?

(g) What price can be charged for the security?

(h) How offers can be communicated?

(i) What is an offer?

(j) What is a security?

(c) The Promoter shall be remunerated as follows: [*Describe*].

§ 1.16 Initial Directors

The Corporation initially shall have [*Number*] Directors who shall be: [*Names*].

§ 1.17 Initial Officers

The initial Officers of the Corporation shall be:

Chairman: ________________.

President: ________________.

Vice-President: ____________.

Secretary: ________________.

Treasurer: ________________.

§ 1.18 Employment Contract

The Corporation shall employ [*Name*] as the [*Describe Position*] of the Corporation for a period of not less than [*Number*] months and shall pay him $[*Dollars*] per year for his services as such; said amount to be paid in bi-weekly installments of $[*Dollars*], the first such payment to be paid on [*Date*]. [*Name*] shall have the authority to:

(a) Acquire and dispose of assets.

(b) Borrow money and give security therefor.

(c) Enter into contracts.

(d) Deposit and withdraw corporate funds.

(e) Employ and dismiss employees and establish their wages.

(f) Establish corporate procedures.

(g) Determine hours of operation.

(h) Advertise.

(i) [*Purchase/construct/lease*] the following plant and equipment: _______.

(j) Do such other things, as he in his sole and reasonably exercised discretion, shall deem necessary to successfully establish, operate and manage the Corporation.

The Corporation and [*Name*] shall enter into an employment contract with the following fringe benefits:

(a) Medical Insurance with the following features:

(1) Hospital:

Room and Board: $______ day.

Maximum no. of days: _______.

Intensive care additional: $______ day.

(a) Medical Insurance with the following features:—Continued

(1) Hospital:—Continued

Intensive care no. of days: ______.

Maximum extra charges: $______.

Surgical schedule: ______.

Anesthesia: ______.

In-hospital benefit: ______.

Hospital-out-patient: ______.

(Supplemental accident): ______.

Radiation therapy: ______.

Diagnostic x-ray and lab: ______.

Maternity: ______.

(2) Major medical:

Maximum: $______.

Deductible: $______.

Co-insurance: ______ (percent).

Prescription drugs: ______.

Out-patient: ______.

Convalescent care: ______.

(3) Dental:

Deductible/family: ______.

Oral exams, etc.: ______.

X-Rays, fillings, etc.: ______.

Bridges, dentures, crowns, etc.: ______.

Maximum benefit: ______.

(4) Carrier: ______.

(5) Disability insurance with the following features:

(A) Carrier: ______.

(B) Wait upon accidental disability: ______.

(C) Wait up sickness: ______.

(D) Benefit per week: $______.

(E) Reduction for partial disability: ______.

(F) Reduction for ability to be employed: ______.

(G) Benefit period upon accident: ______.

(H) Benefit period upon sickness: ______.

(b) Medical reimbursement:

(1) Maximum benefit per corporate fiscal year: $______.

(c) Group term life insurance:

(1) Death benefit: $______.

(d) Group whole life insurance:

(1) Death benefit: $______.

(e) Fully paid vacation days per year: ______.

(f) Fully paid sick days per year: ______.

(g) Use of car ______.

(1) Make and model: ______.

(2) Reimbursement per business mile: ______.

(3) Repair policy: [*Describe*].

(h) Educational benefits-work related:

(1) Days fully paid: ______.

(2) Maximum course charge/day: $______.

(3) Maximum hotel allowance: $______/day.

(4) Maximum meal allowance: $______/day.

(5) Maximum entertainment: $______/day.

(i) Education benefits—non work related.

(1) Maximum course cost and book costs per corporate fiscal year: $______.

(j) Professional liability insurance coverage: $______ per occurrance and $______ per year.

(k) Personal liability insurance coverage: $______ per person and $______ per occurrance.

(l) A stock warrant which has the following features: [*Describe*].

(m) A stock option which has the following features: [*Describe*].

(n) A qualified retirement plan benefit which has the following features:

(1) Name of plan: ______.

(2) Minimum age for participation: ______.

(3) Minimum service for participation: ______.

(4) Employment status (categories): ______.

(5) Vesting: ______.

(6) Corporation contribution formula: ______.

(7) Employee contribution formula: ______.

(8) Effective date of plan: ______.

(9) Initial committee members: ______.

(10) Initial trustees: ______.

(11) Initial contribution: $______.

(o) A deferred compensation plan which has the following features:

(1) Benefit on death: $______.

(2) Benefit on disability: $______.

(3) Benefit on retirement or termination before age 65: $______.

(4) Benefit on retirement or termination after age 65: $______.

(p) Reimbursement for:

(1) Entertainment (not to exceed $______ per ______).

(2) Travel not to exceed $______ per day (excluding mileage which shall be at [*Cents*] per mile.

(3) Hotel per day: $______.

(4) Meals per day: $______.

(5) Entertainment per day: $______.

(q) A Split Dollar Plan with the following features:

(1) Name of plan: ______.

(2) Type of plan:

Alternative A–1

Collateral assignment.

Alternative A–2

Endorsement method.

Alternative A–3

Fractional assignment method.

Alternative A–4

Reverse split dollar.

(3) Type of policy:

Alternative B–1

Face value of $______.

Alternative B–2

Premium of $______.

(4) Corporation's contribution:

Alternative C–1

the increase, if any, in the tabular cash surrender value of the policy which will result from the premium payment in question and the application of dividends toward the purchase of additional insurance.

Alternative C–2

the difference, if any, in the premium then due and the "PS–58" costs of the policy in question.

Alternative C–3

the total premium, net of dividends and premium waivers.

(5) The insured's obligation will be:

Alternative D–1

the PS–58 cost.

Alternative D–2

none.

Alternative D–3

the difference between the premium due and the Company's obligation set forth above.

(6) The "total loan" shall be defined as:

Alternative E–1

the then cash value.

Alternative E–2

the total amount actually paid by the Corporation.

§ 1.19 Buy-Sell Agreement

The parties *and additional Stockholders (if any)* shall enter into a Buy-Sell Agreement *as attached hereto as Exhibit C/ with the following features:*

Triggering Event	Price	Terms	Do Remaining Stockholders Have Option or Is There a Mandatory Buy Out
(a) Stockholder has offer from third party.			
(b) Disability.			
(c) Death.			
(d) Termination of employment before age 65.			
(e) Retirement after age 65.			
(f) Force out of Stock ownership by remaining Stockholders.			

§ 1.20 Voting Trust

It is agreed that a Voting Trust Agreement shall be entered into by the parties *and additional Stockholders (if any) as attached hereto/with the following features:*

(a) Trustee: ______.

(b) Termination Date: ______.

§ 2.1 Notice

Any and all notices provided for herein shall be given in writing by registered or certified mail, return receipt requested which shall be addressed to the last address known to the sender or delivered to the recipient in person.

§ 2.2 Modifications

No modification of this Agreement shall be valid unless such modification is in writing and signed by the parties hereto.

§ 2.3 Waiver

No waiver of any provision of this Agreement shall be valid unless in writing and signed by the person or party against whom charged.

§ 2.4 Applicable Law

This Agreement shall be subject to and governed by the laws of the State of [*Name*].

§ 2.5 Assignment

This Agreement shall be binding upon and inure to the benefit of the parties hereto and their respective heirs, legal representatives, executors, administrators, successors and assigns.

§ 2.6 Agreement to Be Filed with Corporation Secretary

A copy of this Agreement shall be filed with the Secretary of the Corporation for inspection by any prospective purchaser of shares.

§ 2.7 Legend on Certificates

Each certificate for shares issued by the Corporation shall bear a notation or legend giving notice of all of the following which are applicable: (a) the fact that the shares represented by the certificate are subject to restrictions upon transfer imposed by the Stockholders' Agreement; (b) the fact that the shares represented by the certificate are subject to a Voting Agreement or an irrevocable proxy; (c) the legend prescribed by law; (d) Sub-Chapter S status legend; and Blue Sky legend.

§ 2.8 Arbitration

No civil action concerning any dispute arising under this Agreement shall be instituted before any court and all such disputes shall be submitted to final and binding arbitration under the auspices of the American Arbitration Association, [*City*], [*State*]. Such arbitration shall be conducted in accordance with the rules of such association before a single arbitrator. The parties agree that the stock of the Corporation cannot be readily sold in the open market, and for that reason among others, the parties will be irreparably damaged in the event that this Agreement is not specifically enforced. Therefore, in addition to any award of damages, any such award shall, if the party entitled to the same demands it, grant specific performance of this Agreement. All costs and expenses of the arbitration, including actual attorney's fees, shall be allocated among the parties according to the arbitrator's discretion. The arbitrator's award resulting from such arbitration may be confirmed and entered as a final judgment in any court of competent jurisdiction and enforced accordingly. Further, the parties hereto expressly agree that proceeding to arbitration and obtaining an award thereunder shall be a condition precedent to the bringing or maintaining of any action in any court with respect to any dispute arising under this Agreement, except for the institution of a civil action to maintain the status quo during the pendency of any arbitration proceeding.

In witness whereof, the parties have hereunto set their hands and seals the ______ day of ______, 19__.

Witnesses	**Stockholders**
______________________	______________________
______________________	______________________
	Promoter
	______________________

§ 29.22 Agreement to Incorporate Partnership

This contract, made the ______ day of ______, 19__, between ______ and ______, his wife, hereafter referred to as the party of the first part, ______ and ______, his wife, hereafter referred to as the party of the second part, and ______ and ______, his wife, hereafter referred to as the party of the third part,

Witnesseth, that,

Whereas the parties hereto are Partners in a Partnership known as ______, with offices located at ______, and

Whereas the parties desire to incorporate said business and conduct the said business hereafter as a Corporation under the name ______, at the same location,

Now therefore it is agreed that:

1. The parties agree to form a Corporation under the ______ Business Corporation Act under the name ______. The Articles of Incorporation and By-laws of said Corporation shall be in the forms set forth in Exhibits A and B hereto.

2. The parties hereto agree to transfer their interests in the Partnership to said Corporation in exchange solely for shares of stock in the manner set forth below. The interests in the Partnership transferred hereunder shall include all of the assets and business of said Partnership, including inventory, fixtures, equipment, books and records, bank deposits, goodwill, all other personal property, tangible and intangible, and all real property or interests therein owned by the Partnership. The parties hereto agree to execute such legal instruments as may be appropriate or necessary to accomplish the transfer of such assets and business.

3. Said Corporation shall assume and agree to pay and discharge all liabilities and obligations of the Partnership, and the parties hereto agree to cause the Corporation to execute such legal instruments as may be appropriate or necessary to accomplish the assumption of liabilities. The Corporation shall indemnify against, and hold harmless the parties hereto from, such liabilities and obligations.

4. The parties hereto shall constitute the initial Board of Directors of the Corporation.

5. The number of shares to be issued to each party hereto shall be determined on the basis of the value of the interest of each Partner in the Partnership as reflected by the books of the Partnership as of the close of business on ______, 19__. One share shall be issued for each $100 or fraction thereof of such value.

6. Each party agrees to enter into employment contracts with the Corporation for a period of one year at the following compensation: Party of the First Part ______; Party of the Second Part ______; Party of the Third Part ______. Each of the parties hereto agree to devote their full time and attention to the conduct of business and affairs of the Corporation. Each party further agrees that for a period of ______ years after he ceases to be an employee or director of the Corporation he will not engage in the same or any similar business in ______ County, or within a distance of ______ miles of the boundaries of the City of ______.

7. The parties hereto agree to give such notices of dissolution and of intention to incorporate without change of firm name as may be required to avoid personal liability of the parties hereto with re-

spect to liabilities or obligations of the business conducted by the Corporation.

In witness whereof, the parties have executed this Agreement.

Parties:

____

____

____

____

____

____

COMMENTS

This is a skeletal form which will need elaboration depending on the nature of the business being transferred, the possibility that Partners will also be creditors of the Partnership, the possibility that property was lent by the Partners rather than being contributed, and so forth.

The transfer of a business to a newly formed Corporation is usually tax free under section 351 of the Internal Revenue Code of 1954. There are pitfalls, however, and one should not simply assume without investigation that the transaction is tax free. See Chapter 37, infra, for further discussion.

§ 29.23 Agreement Between Sole Proprietor and Cash Contributor to Form a Corporation

Agreement entered into this ______ day of ______, 19__, between A_____ B______, residing at ______, herein called B______, and C______ D______, residing at ______, herein called D______.

Whereas, B______ now owns and operates a ______ business at ______ under the name ______; and

Whereas, the parties desire to form a Corporation for the purpose of associating together in carrying on such business.

Now, therefore, it is agreed as follows:

1. **Formation.** A Corporation shall be organized forthwith under the laws of the State of ______.

2. **Name.** The name of the Corporation shall be ______.

3. **Duration.** The period of duration of the Corporation shall be perpetual.

4. **Purposes.** The purposes for which the Corporation is to be organized shall be limited as follows: [*Insert Statement of Purposes*].

5. **Capital Stock.** The capital stock of the Corporation shall be $100,000, consisting of 1000 shares of common stock of the par value of $100 per share.

6. **Subscription of B______.** B______ hereby subscribes for and agrees to take 600 shares of the aggregate par value of $60,000 and to pay for the same by transferring to the Corporation, when formed, free and clear of all encumbrances of every kind, the assets and good will of the ______ business now carried on by him under the name of ______, which assets shall include ______.

7. **Subscription of D______.** D______ hereby subscribes for and agrees to take 400 shares of the aggregate par value of $40,000 and to pay for the same $40,000 in cash.

8. **Board of Directors.** The initial Board of Directors shall consist of ______ persons who shall be ______.

9. **Employment and Salaries.** B______ shall be the president of the Corporation at a salary of $______ per annum for the first year as compensation for full time services. D______ shall be the secretary-treasurer of the Corporation at a salary of $______ per annum for the first year as compensation for full time services.

10. **Transfer of Stock.** It is agreed that neither party will sell, pledge or otherwise encumber his shares without first offering the same to the other party at a price to be fixed by mutual agreement and in the absence of agreement by an appraiser appointed by the ______ Trust Company. The offer shall be in writing and shall remain open for ______ days.

11. **Organization Expenses.** The expenses of organization shall be paid by the Corporation.

12. **On Whom Binding.** This Agreement shall be binding upon each of the parties and their respective heirs, representatives and assigns.

In witness whereof, *etc.*

§ 29.24 Promoter's Contract and Preincorporation Agreement

COMMENT

The following form can be used to bind prospective Stockholders, to reserve a certain share of the Corporation to certain Stockholders, and to allow a promoter to sell additional stock to others.

PROMOTER'S CONTRACT AND PREINCORPORATION AGREEMENT

This Agreement by and between [*Name of Promoter*] (herein referred to as "Promoter") and [*Name of Corporation or the Incorporators*] (herein referred to as "Seller"),

Whereas the Seller desires that [*Name of Corporation*] sell [*Number*] shares of [*Describe Stock*] (herein referred to as the "Shares") in addition to existing commitments to sell the same;

Now for mutual covenants exchanged and other valuable consideration, it is agreed:

§ 1.1 Preexisting Commitments

The following shares have been already committed for and the Promoter shall not receive any remuneration for their sale:

Name of Subscriber	Number of Shares

COMMENT TO § 1.1

If stock is received for services, this will be immediately taxable to the person receiving the stock (see Chapter 37, infra). Most incorporations can be made taxfree to the incorporators if certain rules are followed. See Chapter 37, infra, in this regard.

§ 1.2 Promoter's Authority

The Promoter is authorized to sell for a period ending [*Date*] up to [*Number*] shares (but not in blocks of less than [*Number*] shares per owner or joint owner), all of which stock shall be subject to the Corporation's Buy-Sell Agreement and to a Securities legend, to persons who fit the following criterion: [*Describe*] at a price not less than [*Dollars*] per share.

§ 1.3 Promoter's Representations

The Promoter agrees that he shall only represent the Corporation in the following manner:

(a) All solicitations shall be made by [*personal contact/telephone/mailings*] to persons who fit the following description [*describe*].

(b) The only advertising materials to be used shall be first approved by the Sellers.

(c) The only description of the Corporation and its prospects to be used shall be the materials attached hereto and made a part hereof. The Promoter agrees that he will not, in any manner whatsoever, suggest, hint, or indicate that such materials underestimate the condition or prospects of the Corporation or shall such Promoter fail to give a copy of such materials to each and every prospective purchaser as follows: [*Describe When Copy Is to Be Given*].

The Promoter agrees that if he has failed to comply with this subparagraph for any reason, such failure and its facts shall be immediately disclosed to Seller.

COMMENTS TO §§ 1.2 AND 1.3

There is no area of the law which is fraught with more danger than state and federal security laws and regulations. A careful review of the applicable law as it relates to the following questions is strongly advised:

(a) Who can sell?

(b) What commissions, if any can be paid?

(c) Who can buy?

(d) How many offerings can be made in a certain period?

(e) What are the exemptions for certain offerings?

(f) What can be said about the Corporation?

(g) What price can be charged for the stock?

(h) How offers can be communicated?

(i) What is an offer?

(j) What is a security?

§ 1.4 Promoter's Compensation

The promoter shall be remunerated as follows: [*Describe*].

§ 2.1 Incorporation

The Corporation will be a profit Corporation under the laws of the State of [*Name*] known as [*Name of Corporation*], (the "Corporation").

§ 2.2 Corporate Purpose

The Corporation shall have the following purpose: [*See § 1.2 of Agreement at § 29.21, supra.*]

§ 2.3 Initial Directors

The Corporation initially shall have [*Number*] Directors who shall be: [*Names*].

§ 2.4 Initial Officers

The initial Officers of the Corporation shall be:

Chairman: ___________.

President: ___________.

Vice President: ___________.

Secretary: ___________.

Treasurer: ___________.

§ 2.5 Employment Contract

[*See § 1.7 in Agreement of § 29.21, supra, this Chapter.*]

§ 2.6 Buy-Sell Agreement

The Stockholders *and additional Stockholders (if any)* shall enter into a Buy-Sell Agreement *as attached hereto/with the following features*:

Triggering Event	Terms	Price	Do Remaining Stockholders Have Option or Is There a Mandatory Buy Out
(a) Stockholder has offer from third party.			
(b) Disability.			
(c) Death.			
(d) Termination of employment before age 65.			
(e) Retirement after age 65.			
(f) Force out of Stock ownership by remaining Stockholders.			

§ 2.7 Voting Trust

It is agreed that a Voting Trust Agreement shall be entered into by the Stockholders *and additional Stockholders (if any) as attached hereto as Exhibit C/ with the following features:*

(a) Trustee: ___________.

(b) Termination Date: ___________.

§ 2.8 Subchapter S Status

The Stockholders agree that they will cause the Corporation to elect to be taxed under Subchapter S of the Internal Revenue Code and that they will not transfer the stock of the Corporation if such transfer will cause the Corporation to lose its election to be taxed under Subchapter S of the Internal Revenue Code.

§ 3.1 Notice

Any and all notices provided for herein shall be given in writing by registered or certified mail, return receipt requested, which shall be addressed to the last address known to the sender or delivered to the recipient in person.

§ 3.2 Modifications

No modification of this Agreement shall be valid unless such modification is in writing and signed by the parties hereto.

§ 3.3 Waiver

No waiver of any provision of this Agreement shall be valid unless in writing and signed by the person or party against whom charged.

§ 3.4 Applicable Law

This Agreement shall be subject to and governed by the laws of the State of [*Name*].

§ 3.5 Assignment

This Agreement shall be binding upon and inure to the benefit of the parties hereto and their respective heirs, legal representatives, executors, administrators, successors and assigns.

§ 3.6 Arbitration

No civil action concerning any dispute arising under this Agreement shall be instituted before any court and all such disputes shall be submitted to final and binding arbitration under the auspices of the American Arbitration Association, [*City*], [*State*]. Such arbitration shall be conducted in accordance with the rules of such association before a single arbitrator. The parties agree that the stock of the Corporation cannot be readily sold in the open market, and for that reason among others, the parties will be irreparably damaged in the event that this Agreement is not specifically enforced. Therefore, in addition to any award of damages, any such award shall, if the party entitled to the same demands it, grant specific performance of this Agreement. All costs and expenses of the arbitration, including actual attorney's fees, shall be allocated among the parties according to the arbitrator's discretion. The arbitrator's award resulting from such arbitration may be confirmed and entered as a final judgment in any court of competent jurisdiction and enforced accordingly. Further, the parties hereto expressly agree that proceeding to arbitration and obtaining an award thereunder shall be a condition precedent to the bringing or maintaining of any action in any court with respect to any dispute arising under this Agreement, except for the institution of a civil action to maintain the status quo during the pendency of any arbitration proceeding.

In witness whereof, the parties have hereunto set their hands and seals the ______ day of ______, 19__.

Witnesses	Promoter
______________________	______________________
______________________	Seller
	______________________

§§ 29.25–30.0 are reserved for supplementary material.

CHAPTER 30

SPECIAL PROBLEMS OF CLOSE CORPORATIONS

Table of Sections

A. INTRODUCTION

B. FINANCIAL STRUCTURE

C. MANAGEMENT STRUCTURE

D. SHARE TRANSFER RESTRICTIONS

E. DRAFTING CONSIDERATIONS FOR CLOSE CORPORATIONS

A. INTRODUCTION

§ 30.1 In General [1]

The "close corporation", "closed corporation" or "closely-held corporation"—or "one-man corporation", "family corporation", "incorporated partnership", or "chartered partnership", as it is variously called—is, as its name implies, a Corporation whose shares are held by a single Stockholder or by a closely-knit group of Stockholders. It differs from the public-issue Corporation in that there is no public issue or trading of its voting shares.

Although the Corporation is generally thought of as a small business enterprise, no distinction between the close Corporation and the public-issue Corporation along such lines can be drawn in all cases. Not all large business Corporations have publicly-held voting shares outstanding. Most close Corporations, however, are relatively small business enterprises. Numerically, the vast majority of business Corporations are closely-held.

The close Corporation desires to function and does function very differently from the larger Corporations with public Stockholders. In the close Corporation, there are usually no public investors; its Stockholders are active in the conduct and management of the business (with resulting coincidence of control and management); the insiders want to keep out outsiders; and the emphasis is on simplified and informal procedures with all participating, with attendant possible risk of deadlock. In short, its member or members desire to gain certain corporate advantages, such as limited liability and certain corporate tax consequences (with minimization of double taxation),

1. This section and several other parts of this chapter are adapted from Henn, Law of Corporations (2d ed. 1970). A third edition is being prepared by Professor Henn for 1982 publication.

at the same time preserving many of the internal attributes of an individual Proprietorship or Partnership.

In contrast with the close Corporation, Corporations with public Stockholders and other investors necessarily involve substantial separation of ownership and control, have a form of representative government-by-the-majority, with management delegated to a Board of Directors, generally following rather formal procedures, and operate in a relatively institutionalized and depersonalized manner, which is not susceptible to deadlock. The transfer of its shares is often not only free from transfer restrictions but is facilitated by securities exchange listing or an active over-the-counter market.

Despite the basic differences between the close Corporation and the larger Corporation with public Stockholders, most are organized under and governed in the various American jurisdictions by the same Corporation statutes, which only in recent years have shown concern for the basic interests of the close Corporation.[2]

This chapter will concentrate on the peculiar problems of close Corporations, first exploring the practical distinctions between the "one-man corporation" and the "incorporated partnership";[3] then enumerating the growing number of provisions in modern state corporate statutes to accommodate them to the special needs of close Corporations;[4] then highlighting Board of Directors considerations[5] and the typical deviations of close Corporations from the statutory norms with respect to financial structure,[6] management structure,[7] and transferability of shares;[8] and concluding with a summary of the drafting problems involved in obtaining the desired individual Proprietorship or Partnership attributes within the permissible theoretical and practical limitations of the corporate mold.[9] However, it must be emphasized that except in rare instances (1) the legal foundation for close Corporations and other Corporations is identical and (2) the selection of various attributes (whether or not usually associated with close Corporations) depends on practical and tax factors and (3) from the author's view, treating close Corporations separately can be counterproductive. However, certain Corporation concepts should especially be considered in the context of a close Corporation. These are reviewed here.

Library References:

C.J.S. Corporations § 14 et seq.
West's Key No. Digests, Corporations ⚷3.

2. See § 30.4, infra, for discussion of state statutes governing close Corporations.

3. See § 30.2, infra.

4. See §§ 30.3, 30.4, infra.

5. See § 30.5, infra.

6. See §§ 30.21, 30.22, infra.

7. See §§ 30.31–30.45, infra.

8. See § 30.51, infra.

9. See §§ 30.62–30.69, infra.

§ 30.2 One-Man Corporation—Incorporated Partnership

One, two, or more individuals might desire to form a business Corporation.

Where one person is involved, except for possible nominal stockholdings in others when necessary to qualify them to serve as Directors, incorporation results in a "one-man corporation".

Where two or more persons are involved, the resulting close Corporation is sometimes loosely called an "incorporated partnership" or "chartered partnership". The associates might all be members of the same family, giving rise to the term "family corporation" ; or members of two or more families; individuals who are completely unrelated; or even a combination of Corporations or of Corporations and individuals (including so-called "joint venture" corporations).

An entity may be given corporate tax status for state law purposes even though it is not entitled to (and does not want) corporate status. In fact, a Partnership or Business Trust or other entity may be given tax status unwittingly and unwillingly. The foundation for this determination is the Kintner Regulations (see Chapter 31, infra, for a more complete description of the Kintner Regulations).

Basically, these Regulations provide for the following tests:

(a) Does the entity in question have centralized management? If so, this is considered a corporate characteristic.

(b) Do the owners of the entity in question have limited liability? If so, this is considered a corporate characteristic.

(c) Do the owners of the entity in question have free transferability of their ownership interests? If so, this is considered a corporate characteristic.

(d) Does the entity in question continue in its theoretical status as an entity for state law purposes in all cases even if one or more owner dies, is disabled, withdraws or becomes bankrupt? If so, this is considered a corporate characteristic.

(e) Does the entity have associates (i. e., more than one owner)? If so, this is considered a corporate characteristic.

(f) Is the object of the equity's existence to carry on a business for profit? If so, this is considered a corporate characteristic.

The purpose of the Kintner Regulations is to use the above characteristics to classify the entity in question for tax purposes as a Corporation or not.

Generally, the Kintner Regulations are applied as follows:

(a) The characteristics that are shared by both types of entities are ignored. Thus, items (e) and (f) above are ignored if the question is Partnership or Corporation and items (a), (b), (c) and (d) above are ignored if the question is Business Trust or Corporation.

(b) The entity label is presumed to control. Thus, if 50% or more of the relevant characteristics match the entity's format, the entity's format will control the tax results. If less than 50% of the relevant characteristics match the entity's format, the alternative entity's tax rules will be applied.

Even if the Kintner Regulations substantiate the Corporation's claim to corporate tax treatment, this treatment may be denied if the facts of corporate operation (not status) do not have enough "indices" of corporate being.

Thus, indices of corporate being are important for two reasons:

(a) Their lack of existence may be used under state law to pierce the corporate veil and deny corporate benefits to Stockholders, and

(b) Their lack of existence may be used under the tax law to disallow corporate tax status and tax benefits.

What are these corporate indices? Generally, corporate indices will be the same for both tax and state law. As one might expect, they are physical acts which Corporations generally do. Therefore, the indices are many of the incorporation actions and documents described in this text.

Since some of these documents and actions are more important than others, the important ones have been noted below.

These are:

(a) Articles of Incorporation properly filed and accepted by the state of incorporation.

(b) Issuance of stock certificates.

(c) Adoption of By-laws.

(d) Filing corporate tax returns.

(e) Using the corporate name and executing documents by corporate agents in the name of the Corporation.

(f) Use of a corporate bank account and, when other assets are titled, holding them in the corporate name.

(g) The existence of a reasonable ratio of debt to equity (3 to 1 is reasonable; 9 to 1 is often thought to be unreasonable). (See Reg. § 1.385–6 (1981).)

§ 30.3 Statutory Differentiation

In most states, close and other Corporations are organized and operate under the corporate statutes which are equally applicable to all Corporations. The older statutes were not drafted with particular concern for the special problems of close Corporations, though newer state corporate statutes have provisions favorable to the special needs of close Corporations.[10] In addition, several states have

10. The Model Business Corporation Act was drawn to be equally applicable to the needs of both large and small incorporated business enterpris-

separate close Corporation acts or separate statutory provisions for close Corporations as elect to become subject thereto.[11] In any event, reference should be made to respective state corporate statutes for such special acts or provisions.

Several modern statutory provisions, while theoretically available to all Corporations, are as a practical matter invocable only by close Corporations.

Statutory provisions enacted primarily for close Corporations include those permitting the fixing of greater-than-normal quorum and voting requirements for Stockholder action [12] or Board of Directors action,[13] permitting greater informality on the part of Stockholders [14] and Directors,[15] and, in fewer jurisdictions, permitting rather substantial impingement by Stockholders of close Corporations on the management functions traditionally vested in the Board of Directors and permitting provision for Stockholder dissolution at will or upon the occurrence of a specified event.

Most court decisions have required close Corporations to adhere to the statutory norm, but occasionally greater judicial tolerance of the close Corporation has been afforded.

Ingeniousness on the part of counsel in drafting arrangements for the formation and operation of close Corporations has, notwithstanding lack of statutory and judicial differentiation, enabled close Corporations to achieve most of their legitimate objects thereby rendering the present situation tolerable to numerous small business Corporations.

es. Campbell, "The Model Business Corporation Act", 11 Bus.Law. 98, 104–106 (July 1956). The Model Business Corporation Act presently has several provisions helpful to close Corporations: Section 53, permitting one or more incorporators; Section 145 permitting Stockholder action by prior unanimous written consent without a meeting; Section 32, permitting the Articles of Incorporation to require greater-than-normal quorum for Stockholder meetings and permitting the Articles of Incorporation or By-laws to require greater-than-normal vote for Stockholder action; Section 143, recognizing the effectiveness of provisions in the articles of incorporation requiring greater-than-normal vote for Stockholder action; Section 44, permitting Board of Directors action by prior unanimous written consent without a meeting; Section 40, permitting the Articles of Incorporation or bylaws to require greater-than-normal quorum for Board of Directors meetings and greater-than-normal vote for Board of Directors action; and Section 97, authorizing judicial dissolution in event of deadlock. The 1969 Model Act revision expressly recognizes (a) Stockholder voting Agreements, free from voting trust provisions, (b) Articles of Incorporation provisions for management of the business and affairs of Corporations by a person or persons other than the Board of Directors and (c) a Board of Directors of a single director.

See also proposed "Model Statutory Close Corporation Act" at footnote 17, infra.

11. See § 30.4, infra, with respect to special close Corporation statutes.

12. See § 30.34, infra.

13. See § 30.42, infra.

14. See § 30.33, infra.

15. See § 30.41, infra.

At the federal regulatory level, the statutes have been drafted for primary application to larger Corporations issuing their securities to the public or engaging in activities with substantial impact on the economy.

Also at the federal level, tax relief has been provided to certain small business Corporations.[16]

Library References:

C.J.S. Corporations § 41.
West's Key No. Digests, Corporations ⚷12½.

§ 30.4 Special Close Corporation Statutes

State statutes assume that Corporations will be conducted with a degree of formality: Stockholders will meet to elect Directors who will in turn meet to elect or appoint Officers and to direct the affairs of the Corporation. Even a moment's reflection will indicate that these assumptions are unjustified for the small closely held Corporation. With only a few Stockholders, all or most of whom are active in the conduct of the business, corporate matters are likely to be resolved by unanimous consent with a minimum of formality and no regard for the statutory niceties. This entirely understandable practice creates several possible legal issues:

(1) Will the ignoring of corporate formalities give rise to an argument that the corporate veil should be "pierced" and the participants held personally liable on corporate obligations?

(2) Will the participants agree upon a control arrangement that is reasonable under the circumstances but violates the "statutory norms" so that the arrangement is legally unenforceable?

(3) Will decisions made informally and without following the statutory norms be binding on the Corporation and third parties?

Special statutes [17] relating to closely held Corporations have been adopted in California, Delaware, Texas, Florida, Maryland, Minnesota,

16. See Chapter 85, infra, "Subchapter S Corporations."

17. The following is a listing of the respective sections in the proposed "Model Statutory Close Corporations Act":

Sec.
1. [Model] Statutory Close Corporation Act.
2. Application of [general] business corporation act and [ ] professional corporation act.
3. Definition of a statutory close corporation; articles of incorporation.
4. Share restrictions.
5. Notice of statutory close corporation status on issued shares.
6. Transfer of shares in breach of transfer restrictions.
7. Mergers, consolidations, share exchanges, and sale of assets.
8. Termination of statutory close corporation status.

New York and a number of other states. These statutes are designed to permit such Corporations to conduct their affairs with essentially the same formalities as if they were Partnerships. While there is considerable variation in the state statutes relating to close Corporations they generally provide the following—

(1) Agreements that restrict the discretion of Directors (and are therefore probably invalid under conventional principles) are specifically validated.[18]

18. E. g. proposed Model Statutory Close Corporation Act § 11 provides:

§ 11. Agreements Among Shareholders

(a) The shareholders of a statutory close corporation may by unanimous action enter into one or more written agreements to regulate the exercise of the corporate powers and the management of the business and affairs of the corporation or the relations among the shareholders of the corporation.

(b) Any agreement authorized by this section shall be valid and enforceable according to its terms notwithstanding the elimination of a board of directors, any restriction on the discretion or powers of the board of directors, or any proxy or weighted voting rights given to directors and notwithstanding that the effect of the agreement is to treat the corporation as if it were a partnership or that the arrangement of the relations among the shareholders or between the shareholders and the corporation would otherwise be appropriate only among partners.

(c) If the corporation has a board of directors, the effect of an agreement authorized by this section restricting the discretionary powers of the directors shall be to relieve the directors of, and to impose upon the person or persons in whom such discretion or powers are vested, the liability for acts or omissions imposed by law upon directors to the extent that the discretion or powers of the directors are controlled by the agreement.

(d) An election not to have a board of directors in an agreement authorized by this section shall not be valid unless the articles of incorporation contain a statement to that effect in accordance with section 10.

(e) An election granting one or more shareholders the right to have the corporation dissolved at will or upon the occurrence of any specified event or contingency shall not be valid unless a statement of this right is included in the articles of incorporation in accordance with section 15.

(f) A shareholder agreement authorized by this section shall not be amended except by the unanimous written consent of the shareholders unless otherwise provided in the agreement.

(g) Any action permitted by this section to be taken by shareholders may be taken by the subscribers to shares of the corporation if no shares have been issued at the time of the agreement authorized by the section.

(h) This section shall not prohibit any other agreement among two or

(2) The Corporation may elect to dispense with the Board of Directors entirely and have the business and affairs of the Corporation conducted by the Stockholders as though they were Partners.[19] If this option is elected, the liabilities otherwise imposed on Directors are imposed on the Stockholders acting as Directors.

(3) The Corporation may adopt special dissolution provisions that permit a minority Stockholder, in specified circumstances, to compel the dissolution of the Corporation. This provision, designed to eliminate the "locked in" feature of the close Corporation is the principal substantive provision of these statutes that addresses the basic problem of the minority Stockholder in a closely held Corporation. However, it has only limited

more shareholders not otherwise prohibited by law.

See also Md.Corp. and Ass'ns Code Ann. § 4–401, V.A.T.S.Tex.Bus.Corp.Act art. 2.30–2, and Minn.Bus.Corp.Act § 302A.457 for similar provisions.

19. E. g. proposed Model Statutory Close Corporation Act § 10 provides:

§ 10. Election Not to Have a Board of Directors

(a) A statutory close corporation may operate without a board of directors if the articles of incorporation contain a statement to that effect. While this statement is effective:

(1) All corporate powers shall be exercised by or under authority of, and the business and affairs of the corporation shall be managed under the direction of, the shareholders of the corporation, and all powers and duties conferred or imposed upon the board of directors by the [general] business corporation act shall be exercised or performed by the shareholders.

(2) No liability that would otherwise be imposed on the directors shall be imposed on a shareholder by virtue of any act or failure to act unless the shareholder was entitled to vote on the action.

(3) Any requirement that an instrument filed with any governmental agency contain a statement that a specified action has been taken by the board of directors shall be satisfied by a statement that the corporation is a statutory close corporation having no board of directors and that the action was duly approved by the shareholders.

(4) The shareholders by resolution may appoint one or more shareholders to sign any documents as "Designated Directors."

(5) Unless the articles of incorporation otherwise provide, any action requiring director approval or both director and shareholder approval shall be sufficiently authorized by shareholder approval and any action otherwise requiring a vote of a majority or greater percentage of the board of directors shall require the affirmative vote of the holders of a majority, or such greater percentage, of the shares entitled to vote thereon.

(b) An amendment to the articles of incorporation to include the provisions authorized by subsection (a) shall be approved by the holders of all the shares of the corporation whether or not otherwise entitled to vote thereon, or all the subscribers to such shares, or the incorporators, as the case may be. An amendment to the articles of incorporation to delete the election shall be approved by the affirmative vote of the holders of at least two-thirds of each class of the shares of the corporation whether or not otherwise entitled to vote thereon.

See Md.Corp. and Ass'ns Code § 4–302 for similar provision.

usefulness since it is applicable only when specifically agreed to.

(4) In the event of a deadlock at the directoral level, courts are specifically empowered to break the deadlock by the appointment of impartial "provisional Directors." This provision is designed to provide a simpler, more flexible and less drastic solution to deadlocked Corporations than either the appointment of a receiver or dissolution. It is applicable to all close Corporations and not limited to those that elect it; it is likely that the mere threat of the appointment of one or more provisional Directors will be a strong stimulus to quarreling Stockholders to make some kind of a mutual accommodation. [See e. g., Proposed Model Statutory Close Corporation Act § 16, and similar provisions in Calif., Mich., Minn., N. J. and So. Car. statutes.]

Close Corporation statutes tend to be complex; much of the complicated language is addressed to problems such as determining which Corporations are eligible to take advantage of these special provisions and what happens when an electing Corporation loses its eligibility. Since Corporations form a continuum in terms of size and number of Stockholders, lines must to some extent be arbitrary, and the possibility that an electing Corporation might become ineligible because of events over which it has little control has to be faced. A few states originally made the special statutes applicable to all Corporations that fell within a broad statutory definition, but the trend is clearly toward making the special provisions completely elective by including appropriate provisions in the Articles of Incorporation of qualified Corporations.

The definition of an eligible Corporation involves a limitation on the number of Stockholders (ranging from as low as 10 in some states to 35 or more in others [20]), a requirement that there have been no registered public offering of shares, and a requirement that share transfer restrictions be imposed on all outstanding shares limiting their free transferability. Statutes also usually require appropriate notations on all certificates describing which special provisions the Corporation has elected to make applicable.

Even though a number of states have adopted close Corporation statutes, a rather limited sampling of the actual experience in several states indicates that they are not widely used. Florida even repealed its close Corporation statute in 1975, but includes provisions accommodating close corporations in its present corporations statute. While the reasons for the lack of use are speculative, it is probable that most attorneys are able to work out basic control relationships under the general Corporation statutes and therefore do not feel it is necessary

20. Not to exceed *30* in Delaware, Del.Gen.Corp.Law § 342(a)(1); not to exceed 50 in proposed Model Statutory Close Corporation Act § 3.

to use or experiment with these new and largely untried statutes. It is also possible that the sheer complexity of some of these statutes may have discouraged their widespread use.

§ 30.5 Board of Director(s)

A Board of Directors of at least three individual Directors must be authorized under older corporate statutes, relieved by some modern corporate statutes permitting one-Director or two-Director boards, at least in one-Stockholder or two-Stockholder Corporations, or no board of directors.[21]

In a close Corporation composed of two equal interests held by two individuals, families, or groups, an even-numbered Board is often established to reflect the 50–50 share ownership. Where at least a three-man Board of Directors must be authorized, as under older statutes, and Directors are required to be Stockholders (an even less prevelant modern requirement), the qualification of at least three Directors is dependent upon there being no less than three Stockholders, with at least nominal interest. Although the initial Directors named in the Articles of Incorporation who attend to the initial formal arrangements at the outset, can be "accommodation" or "dummy" Directors, the duties imposed on management militate against the use of "accommodation" or "dummy" Directors in a going concern. In the case of two equal Stockholders, one practical solution under older statutes might be to authorize a three-man Board but after the initial formalities are completed have the Board carry on with each of the two Stockholders as a Director and with one vacancy.

Another device, where permissible, would be to have an executive committee composed of the real parties in interest with as much authority delegated to it as applicable law permits.[22]

So far as the Board of Directors is concerned, desired representation on it of the Stockholders (by themselves or their designees) should be assured; its functions and procedures formally circumscribed so far as lawful, and the individual Directors subjected to maximum Stockholder control by, for example, appropriate removal provisions in the Articles of Incorporation or By-laws, and in "shareholder agreement" binding the parties, as Directors, so far as legally possible, to exercise their Director functions (e. g., voting for Officers

21. The 1969 Model Bus.Corp.Act (§ 36) revision and the statutes of a number of states (e. g. Minn.Bus.Corp.Act § 302A.203; West's Ann.Cal.Corp.Code § 301) permit a single director. See note 19, supra, regarding election to not have board. See § 30.4, supra, with respect to special close Corporation statutes in certain states that provide for management by Stockholders rather than by the Board.

22. See Ch. 46 infra.

and other matters) to effectuate the legitimate interests of the parties; and appropriate provision made for deadlock at the Board of Directors level.[23]

§§ 30.6–30.20 are reserved for supplementary material.

B. FINANCIAL STRUCTURE

§ 30.21 Financial Structure—Generally

The structuring of a close Corporation's equity is dealt with in the context of Chapters 38–40, infra, while debt financing is dealt with in the context of Chapters 38 and 43, infra, and methods of the Stockholders withdrawing funds from the close Corporation is covered in the Chapter dealing with transactions with a related party (Chapter 54, infra).

§§ 30.22–30.30 are reserved for supplementary material.

C. MANAGEMENT STRUCTURE

§ 30.31 Management Structure—Generally[1]

The management structure of the close Corporation can follow a variety of patterns, depending on whether the close Corporation is to be a "one-man corporation", subsidiary, affiliated Corporation, "family corporation", etc., and the extent to which those concerned desire to function in ways different from the normal corporate pattern. The considerations especially applicable to the close Corporation will be stressed in this section and succeeding sections, in contrast to the more traditional corporate management structure.

In setting up the management structure, the respective traditional managerial functions of Stockholders, directors, and officers must be considered. Under the "concession theory", Corporations are created by the state and must conform to the "statutory norms", which may or may not have built-in flexible provisions. At the opposite extreme is the idea, often expressed but too infrequently applied, that Stockholders may agree among themselves to do what they want so long as there is no damage to creditors or others.

In many close Corporation situations, centralizing managerial functions as fully as permissible in Stockholders (as such, as Directors, and as Officers) may be desirable, despite the traditional sepa-

23. See § 30.4, supra.

1. This section, and §§ 30.32–30.45, infra, are adapted from Henn, Law of Corporations (2d ed. 1970) §§ 263–280. A third edition is being prepared by Professor Henn for 1982 publication.

ration of ownership (in Stockholders) and management (in Board of Directors and Officers) in the Corporation.[2]

Library References:

C.J.S. Corporations §§ 715–720, 725, 726.
West's Key No. Digests, Corporations ⚷281 et seq.

§ 30.32 Stockholders—Initial and Subsequent

At the time of incorporation, the initial Stockholder group, and their respective share interests, are fixed. Subsequent changes can be controlled by appropriate share transfer restrictions (along with options or buy-sell agreements) relating to issued shares [3] and by appropriate limitations on the authorization and issue of additional shares.

Obviously, to the extent that any close Corporation managerial setup is based on arrangements among Stockholders in one capacity or another, changes in the identity of Stockholders or in their proportionate interests might dislocate such managerial setup.

§ 30.33 Stockholders' Voting Rights

Where shares are to be issued in proportion to consideration received and to the desired respective interests of the Stockholders, a single class of shares would ordinarily be authorized. Such shares would carry one vote per share for each matter, unless cumulative voting were in effect with respect to elections of Directors.

Formalities of Stockholder Action. A growing number of modern statutes permit Stockholder action to be taken by unanimous written consent, or majority consent, in lieu of the otherwise required Stockholder vote at a duly-convened Stockholder meeting.[4]

Cumulative Voting. Cumulative voting is mandatory in some jurisdictions, permissive in others.[5] In the latter jurisdictions, a provision authorizing cumulative voting can be inserted in the Articles of Incorporation.[6] Cumulative voting is a form of proportional representation to assure any desirable minority representation on the Board. In the usual close Corporation situation, where the Board of Directors is of small size, holders of small minority interests may not be assured of any representation on the Board by cumulative voting.

2. See § 30.4, supra, and § 30.35, infra, with respect to special statutory provisions in certain states which provide for Stockholder (rather than director) management.

3. See § 30.51 and Chapters 42, 52 and 68, infra.

4. See Chapter 45, infra.

5. See Chapter 47, infra.

6. E. g., McKinney's N.Y.Bus.Corp. Law, § 618.

More satisfactory methods of assuring representation on the Board by minority Stockholders in close Corporations than cumulative voting are Stockholder Agreements requiring the parties to vote for certain persons as Directors [7] or sufficiently high greater-than-normal quorum/voting requirements for Stockholder election of Directors to render ineffective any such election without the concurrence of minority Stockholders.[8]

Class Voting. Another means of assuring representation on the Board of Directors of different Stockholders is to authorize classes of shares and a classified Board of Directors, so that each class of shares elects its class of Directors.[9] In all other respects, the rights of the holders of the different classes can be identical. Or class voting requirements can in effect give a veto power to a class, which might consist of only a single Stockholder. As indicated in connection with cumulative voting, there are often satisfactory alternative methods of achieving the same results.

Miscellaneous. Where shares are classified because of financial considerations,[10] there is normally no need in the close Corporation for authorizing shares with contingent voting rights, shares with disproportionate voting rights, or non-voting shares.

Library References:

C.J.S. Corporations §§ 548, 550.
West's Key No. Digests, Corporations ⚷197 et seq.

§ 30.34 Stockholder Quorum—Voting Requirements

There are two ways of giving a minority Stockholder protection against his fellow Stockholders' doing something objectionable to such Stockholder: (a) Stockholder veto provisions, and (b) greater-than-normal quorum/voting requirements for Stockholder action. Both devices, unlike "Stockholder Agreements" which are often positive in terms, are negative.

Stockholder veto provisions are inconsistent with the idea of corporate-government-by-majority-or other required vote- and, unless of rather limited scope, run the risk of invalidity.[11]

7. See § 30.35, infra. Even where cumulative voting is in effect, Stockholders can nevertheless agree among themselves to vote in a certain way for Directors. Sensabaugh v. Polson Plywood Co., 135 Mont. 562, 342 P.2d 1064 (1959); E. K. Buck Retail Stores v. Harkert, 157 Neb. 867, 62 N.W.2d 288, 45 A.L.R.2d 774 (1954).

8. See § 30.34, infra.

9. See Chapters 40 and 47, infra.

10. See Chapter 40, infra.

11. See Matter of William Faehndrich, Inc., 2 N.Y.2d 468, 161 N.Y.S.2d 99, 141 N.E.2d 597 (1957); Benintendi v. Kenton Hotel, Inc., 294 N.Y. 112, 60 N.E.2d 829, 159 A.L.R. 280 (1945). Cf. Roland Park Shopping Center, Inc. v. Hendler, 206 Md. 10, 109 A.2d 753 (1954); Katcher v. Ohsman, 26 N.J.Super. 28, 97 A.2d 180 (1953); Ripin v. U. S. Woven Label Co., 205 N. Y. 442, 98 N.E. 855 (1912).

Greater-than-normal quorum/voting requirements for Stockholder action are also inconsistent with majority rule, but are being sanctioned by statutes in a growing number of states.[12]

§ 30.35 Stockholder Agreements

Because of the traditional separation of ownership and control in the Corporation, Stockholders of close Corporations often agree among themselves to vote collectively in certain matters.[13]

An Agreement among Stockholders to combine in the exercise of their Stockholder functions is valid in the majority of jurisdictions, on the ground that Stockholders are generally under no fiduciary duties, and what they may do individually they may do collectively,[14] assuming lack of fraud by controlling Stockholders against minority Stockholders or some other illegal object. By such a Stockholder Agreement, the Stockholders usually agree either to cast their votes in a certain way for various matters or to pool their votes and cast them jointly as they agree or an arbitrator determines.[15]

Such Agreements usually do not run afoul of prohibitions on Stockholders' selling their votes or proxies.

"Stockholder Agreements" often have provisions dealing with matters other than the exercise of Stockholder voting rights, such as matters within the proper purview of the management functions of the Board of Directors or share transfer restrictions, deadlock, and arbitration provisions, etc.

If an Agreement among Stockholders binds them with respect not only to their Stockholder functions but also to any Director functions they might have, the Agreement can be said to be one among Directors as well as among Stockholders. If such a "Stockholder Agreement" (it being to such an extent a "Director Agreement") contains provisions limiting the discretion of the Board of Directors in managing the Corporation in the best interests of the Corporation, such provisions might be invalid unless otherwise authorized by statute.[16]

12. See, e. g., Model Bus.Corp.Act § 32 (per articles of incorporation or bylaws); Del.Gen.Corp.Law, § 216 (1967), Minn.Bus.Corp.Act § 302A.443 (per articles of incorporation or bylaws); McKinney's N.Y.Bus.Corp.Law, § 616 (per certificate of incorporation, though such provision may also be deleted by ⅔ amendment unless greater vote specifically required). See also Chapter 47, infra.

13. See Chapter 47, infra.

14. Ringling Bros.-Barnum & Bailey Combined Shows, Inc. v. Ringling, 29 Del.Ch. 610, 53 A.2d 441 (Sup.Ct. 1947); McQuade v. Stoneham, 263 N. Y. 323, 189 N.E. 234 (1934), reargument denied 264 N.Y. 460, 191 N.E. 514. See also Chapter 47, infra.

15. See Chapter 47, infra.

16. For liberal statutory treatment of such agreements; see McKinney's N. Y.Bus.Corp.Law, § 620 (Stockholder

Several state corporate statutes include a special subchapter or set of sections to which eligible close Corporations may elect to be subject.[17] Such close Corporations remain subject to the other provisions of the corporate statute to the extent that they are not inconsistent with the close Corporation sections. Expressly permitted in close Corporations are written Stockholder Agreements, whether embodied in the Articles of Incorporation, By-laws, or side agreement.[18]

Stockholder Agreements, unlike irrevocable proxies and voting trusts, are not self-executing. For breach of valid provisions, the most adequate remedy is usually specific performance. Damages are usually inadequate. Special statutory proceedings are generally not available to enforce such an Agreement.

If the shares are transferable, as they would be absent a valid share transfer restriction, a transferee without notice would take them free from the obligations of any Stockholder Agreement. Accordingly, sound practice requires that the share certificates involved bear an appropriate legend referring to the Stockholder Agreement.

The Agreement should have an ascertainable duration to avoid its being construed as terminable at will, and should be sufficiently definite to prevent its invalidity for vagueness.

Other aspects of "Stockholder Agreements" in the close Corporation, such as share transfer restrictions, deadlock and arbitration provisions, etc., will be explored more fully later.[19]

Library References:

C.J.S. Corporations § 551.
West's Key No. Digests, Corporations ⚷199.

§ 30.36 Fiduciary Relationship Among Stockholders

In the close Corporation, not only do the normal fiduciary duties of controlling Stockholders apply, but in addition the courts are prone to require a higher standard of fiduciary responsibility.[20]

agreements; provision in articles of incorporation as to control of directors); Model Bus.Corp.Act § 35 (business and affairs of Corporation to be managed by Board of Directors except as may be otherwise provided in articles of incorporation). A number of states have close Corporation statutes permitting sterilization or even abolition of the Board of Directors. See § 30.4, supra.

17. See § 30.4, supra.

18. See e. g. V.A.T.S.Bus.Corp.Act, art. 2.30–2; Maryland Corp.Act § 104; Maine Bus.Corp.Act § 618; West's Ann.Cal.Corp.Code § 204; Minn.Bus.Corp.Act §§ 302A.455, 457. See also Model Bus.Corp.Act § 34 which authorizes shareholder voting Agreements.

19. See §§ 30.37, 30.45, 30.51, infra.

20. Helms v. Duckworth, 101 U.S. App.D.C. 390, 249 F.2d 482 (1957); Manis v. Miller, 19 N.Y.2d 875, 280 N.Y.S.2d 675, 227 N.E.2d 596 (1967); Mendelson v. Blatz Brewing Co., 9 Wis.2d 487, 101 N.W.2d 805 (1960).

§ 30.37 Provisions Against Stockholders Deadlock

Wherever Stockholders are equally divided, enjoy a veto, or are subject to greater-than-normal quorum/voting requirements, the likelihood of deadlock at the Stockholder level is increased.

Generally, there are three alternative methods of dealing with deadlock: (a) Buy-Sell Agreements, (b) arbitration, and (c) dissolution.

Buy-Sell Agreements. Apart from *Buy-Sell Agreements* in connection with share transfer restrictions [21] and in connection with the death, disability or termination of employment of a Stockholder [22] are provisions, usually in Stockholder Agreements, whereby in the case of deadlock (as well as other contingencies), one faction can be bought out, thus preserving the Corporation as a going concern and assuring a fair price to those whose interests are bought out.[22]

Arbitration. Provision for arbitration of future controversies among Stockholders is more or less possible in several jurisdictions. In some states, the enforcement of Agreements to arbitrate future disputes is precluded by common-law rules or by limited statutory arbitration provisions.[23]

Arbitration clauses, when desirable, are probably best inserted in Stockholder and other Agreements.[24] Problems of drafting such clauses can be formidable.

Dissolution. Dissolution in the event of Stockholder deadlock might possibly be effected either with or without judicial proceedings.

Dissolution without judicial proceedings in case of deadlock might be achieved pursuant to an advance Agreement among the necessary Stockholders to vote for or consent to such dissolution.[25]

Dissolution with judicial proceedings is rarely ordered by a court in the absence of enabling legislation. Even where there is such legislation, as under the Model Business Corporation Act,[26] dissolution in the event of deadlock will be ordered only if the court is satisfied "that irreparable injury to the Corporation is being suffered or is threatened by reason" of such deadlock. This subject is explored more fully later.[27]

21. See § 30.51, infra.

22. See Chapter 68, infra.

23. Uniform Arbitration Act, 7 U.L.A. 76; approved in 1955; adopted in nearly one half of the states.

24. See Chapter 29(B), infra.

25. See § 30.35, supra.

26. Model Bus.Corp.Act § 97.

27. See Chapter 78, infra.

§ 30.38 Voting Trust and Irrevocable Proxy

Voting Trusts. The voting trust is a device for concentrating Stockholder voting rights, at least for the permissible duration of voting trusts, in the hands of one or more persons—the voting trustees.[28]

The principal disadvantages of the voting trust are the expenses of setting it up and exchanging the shares for voting trust certificates, the necessity of strict compliance with technical statutory requirements, the problems of selecting the voting trustees, and its limited maximum duration (e. g., 10 or 15 years). Despite the fact that the voting is self-executing, these disadvantages, coupled with the fact that desired control can be achieved in less cumbersome and more effective ways, have relegated the voting trust to a relatively minor role in close Corporations.

Where shares are held in a voting trust, the share certificates should refer to such fact or voting trust certificates should be issued in lieu of such shares.[29]

Irrevocable Proxies. Irrevocable proxies also provide a means, sometimes for a shorter period and sometimes for a longer period than that allowed for a voting trust, of enabling one or more persons —the proxyholders, as agents of the Stockholders giving the proxies— to exercise the voting rights belonging to such Stockholders. To be irrevocable, a provy must either be "coupled with an interest" or "given as security" in jurisdictions which adhere to such concept or comply with statutory requisites in jurisdictions with statutes governing irrevocable proxies.[30]

Available only in limited situations, irrevocable proxies sometimes may be useful in a close Corporation as a means of insuring performance of voting obligations of Stockholders under a Stockholders' Agreement, since irrevocable proxies, unlike Stockholders' Agreements, are self-executing.[31]

28. See Chapter 47, infra, for voting trust and pooling Agreements.

29. E. g., Del.Gen.Corp.Law § 218 (1967); McKinney's N.Y.Bus.Corp. Law § 621.

30. See Chapter 47, infra.

31. E. g., McKinney's N.Y.Bus.Corp. Law § 609(f)(5); West's Ann.Cal.Corp. Code § 705(e). See generally Comment, "Voting Trusts and Irrevocable Proxies", 41 Temp.L.Rev. 480 (1968); Note, "The Irrevocable Proxy and Voting Control of Small Business Corporations", 98 U.Pa.L.Rev. 401 (1950). Compare Ringling Bros.-Barnum & Bailey Combined Shows, Inc. v. Ringling, 29 Del.Ch. 610, 53 A.2d 441 (Sup.Ct.1947), with Smith v. San Francisco & N. P. Ry., 115 Cal. 584, 47 P. 582 (1897).

If the share certificate on its face refers to the proxy and its irrevocability, the irrevocable proxy should be effective against any purchaser of the shares.[32]

Library References:

C.J.S. Corporations §§ 550, 552.
West's Key No. Digests, Corporations ⚷198, 198.1.

§ 30.39 Directors—Generally

Corporate management being vested in the Board of Directors, the Stockholders in a close Corporation in order to exercise the desired control must assure themselves of such control at the Board of Directors level as well as at the Stockholder level. Stockholder control over Board of Directors action can be achieved by (a) giving minority Stockholders a veto over Board of Directors action; (b) giving Directors who represent minority Stockholders a veto over Board of Directors action; and (c) binding Directors in advance to act in prescribed ways; and, where permitted by statute, agreements restricting discretion of Directors or provisions in the Articles providing for management by Stockholders rather than by Directors.[33]

While giving a minority Stockholder a veto over Board of Directors action would appear to be the most simple and direct approach, any such veto provision sufficiently broad in scope to accomplish the purpose might well be held invalid as unduly impinging on the statutory norm vesting management in the Board of Directors, except in those few jurisdictions allowing Stockholder control.

Giving a minority Director a veto over Board of Directors action might run counter to a statutory policy that Board of Directors action should be by a majority of Directors present (assuming a quorum), except in those jurisdictions specifically allowing this.

A possible variation is to have classified Directors, with each class of Directors elected by a different class of shares, and to require approval of each class of Directors for any Board of Directors action. The validity of such provisions, when broad in scope, is questionable in many jurisdictions.

A sounder approach, in jurisdictions which permit, is to impose sufficiently greater-than-normal quorum/voting requirements for Board of Directors action, thereby giving a Director who absents himself from a board meeting, or who does not vote in favor of any Board of Directors action, an effective veto.[34]

Any such Director veto approach, of course, protects a minority Stockholder only if he or his obedient representative is a Director.

32. E. g., McKinney's N.Y.Bus.Corp. Law § 609(h); West's Ann.Cal.Corp. Code § 418.

33. See § 30.4, supra, in this regard.

34. See § 30.34 (n. 12), supra, and § 30.42 infra.

Methods of assuring Stockholder representation on the Board have been previously discussed.[35]

Attempts to bind the Directors to act in advance in prescribed ways encounter two major difficulties. The first is the legal barrier against unduly fettering (or "sterilizing") the Board of Directors; the second difficulty is the practical one of anticipating in advance matters which will require Board of Directors action in the future.[36]

See also § 30.4, supra, for special close Corporation statutory provisions providing for Stockholder management.

Library References:

C.J.S. Corporations §§ 741, 742.
West's Key No. Digests, Corporations ⚷296, 297.

§ 30.40 Directors—Number, Election, and Removal

The number of Directors is usually fixed in the Articles of Incorporation or By-laws. A statutory minimum of three Directors generally once had to be authorized, but modern statutes increasingly permit two Directors in a two-Stockholder Corporation and one Director in a one-Stockholder Corporation, or no board of directors.[37]

Where a managerial setup is predicated upon an assumption of a certain size Board of Directors, safeguards should be imposed to assure against changes in the size of the Board. Provision in Articles of Incorporation requiring unanimous Stockholder consent to any change in the size of the Board of Directors should be upheld.[38]

In assuring Stockholder representation on the Board, the corollary problem of removing any Director who is not carrying out the wishes of the Stockholder or Stockholders who elected him should not be overlooked. Classified Directors, with any class of Stockholders empowered to remove, with or without cause, any Director elected by such class, is one possible solution. Advance power to remove Directors without cause is probably most important where any Director has no financial interest in the Corporation, such as in the case of Directors serving as representatives of a parent Corporation on the Board of its subsidiary, of the required two additional Directors in a "one-man Corporation", or of the required third Director in a two-Stockholder Corporation.

See also Chapter 46, infra, for additional coverage of election and removal of Directors.

Library References:

C.J.S. Corporations §§ 716 et seq., 738.
West's Key No. Digests, Corporations ⚷283, 294.

35. See § 30.35 supra.

36. See § 30.43 infra.

37. See note 21 to 30.5, supra. See also note 19 to § 30.4, regarding election to not have board.

38. See § 30.34, supra.

§ 30.41 Formalities of Director Action

Under a growing number of statutes, unanimous written Director consent without a meeting is effective in lieu of a formal board meeting.[39] In addition, a number of state statutes provide for board meeting by means of electronic communications.

Even in jurisdictions without any statutory exception to the Board meeting requirement,[40] informal action by Directors of close Corporations without a meeting has been upheld by the courts in some cases.

See Chapter 46, infra, for additional coverage.

§ 30.42 Director Quorum—Voting Requirements

Greater-than-normal Board of Directors quorum/voting requirements in effect enable minority Directors to veto action at the Board of Directors level. Such requirements, if broad in application, might be invalid except as sanctioned by statute.[41] Modern statutes tend to permit such requirements when imposed by the Articles of Incorporation or possibly the By-laws. Such requirements often enhance the probability of deadlock at the Board of Directors level.

See Chapter 46, infra, for additional coverage of quorum requirements.

Library References:

C.J.S. Corporations § 749.
West's Key No. Digests, Corporations ⚷297.

§ 30.43 Director Agreements

Any Agreement to bind Directors in advance to vote in a certain way is in effect a "Director Agreement" although the parties might have entered into the Agreement nominally as Stockholders. The validity of such Agreements depends upon applicable statutes and judicial attitudes toward "statutory norms".[42] Such Agreements completely fettering the discretion of the Directors so as to result in a "sterilized" Board ordinarily are found invalid, except in jurisdictions specifically allowing stockholders or others to control the Board.

39. See Chapter 46, infra. Such statutes often provide that the Articles of Incorporation or By-laws can preclude Board of Directors action without a meeting. Such statutes are construable as preempting the field and prohibiting Corporations from acting informally without complying with the statute. Village of Brown Deer v. City of Milwaukee, 16 Wis.2d 206, 114 N.W.2d 493 (1962), certiorari denied 371 U.S. 902, 83 S.Ct. 205, 9 L. Ed.2d 164.

40. E. g., McKinney's N.Y.Bus.Corp. Law § 708 ("at a meeting of the board").

41. Many statutes in general terms expressly authorize such provisions in Articles of Incorporation or By-laws not inconsistent with law. See e. g. Model Bus.Corp.Act §§ 32 and 54. See also § 30.34 (n. 12) supra.

42. The Texas, Maryland, and Delaware close Corporation statutes ex-

Agreements to keep named persons as named officers so long as faithful, efficient, and competent, to pay them reasonable salaries, to pay reasonable dividends, etc., especially when all Stockholders are parties to the Agreement, have been upheld.

Library References:

C.J.S. Corporations § 742.

§ 30.44 Fiduciary Duties of Directors

Directors of a close Corporation are, of course, subject to the usual fiduciary duties, and might even be held to a higher fiduciary standard.[43]

§ 30.45 Provision Against Director Deadlock

Board of Directors deadlock can be dealt with by three alternative methods: (a) arbitration, (b) appointment of provisional Director, and (c) dissolution.

Arbitration. Besides the usual problems of arbitration, previously discussed in connection with the arbitration of Stockholder deadlock,[44] arbitration of deadlock at the Director level presents the additional problem of delegating managerial discretion—a responsibility vested by statute in the Board of Directors—to someone else—the arbitrator. For example, Articles of Incorporation containing a provision that in the event of deadlock among the Directors their differences will be arbitrated might not be accepted for filing by the Secretary of State. The problem is analogous to binding in advance the Directors' discretion.[45]

Appointment of Provisional Director. A few jurisdictions by statute provide for the court appointment, under prescribed circumstanc-

pressly permit "shareholder agreements", whether in the Articles of Incorporation, By-laws, or a side Agreement, restricting the discretion or powers of the Directors of electing close Corporations. See § 30.4, supra, in this regard. See also 1969 Model Act revision ("except as may be otherwise provided in the articles of incorporation"); McKinney's N.Y. Bus.Corp.Law § 701 (subject to any provision in Articles of Incorporation authorized by § 620(b) as to control of Directors or by § 715 for election of officers by Stockholders, business of Corporation shall be managed by its Board of Directors); id. § 620(b) Articles of Incorporation provision as to control of Directors); id. § 715(b) (Articles of Incorporation provision as for Stockholder election of officers); id. § 716 (Stockholder removal of officers elected by Stockholders); West's Ann.Cal.Corp.Code §§ 204, 300(b).

43. E. g., Matter of Gearing v. Kelly, 11 N.Y.2d 201, 227 N.Y.S.2d 897, 182 N.E.2d 391 (1962) (holding that where Director of close Corporation absented herself from Board of Directors meeting to prevent quorum to fill vacancy, neither such Director nor her associate Stockholder could then seek to set aside election of Director on ground quorum was not present).

See e. g. Model Bus.Corp.Act § 41 which governs Director conflicts of interest.

44. See § 30.37, supra.

45. See § 30.42 supra. Statutes increasingly permit broad delegation of the management functions of the Di-

es, of a disinterested "provisional Director" when the Corporation has an even number of Directors who are equally divided and cannot agree as to management of its affairs. Quite apart from some disfavor against a court-appointee's running a business Corporation—with its overtones of political patronage and his expense, even though his decisions require the concurrence of half of the Directors, such statutes suffer from the shortcoming of being limited to Director deadlock situations caused by an equally-divided even-numbered Board.

Dissolution. Where the Board of Directors is deadlocked, courts hesitate to order such a drastic remedy as dissolution absent statutory authorization to do so. Even when there is a statute, the courts might tend to construe it strictly. The Model Business Corporation Act authorizes judicial dissolution in the event of Director deadlock which cannot be resolved by the Stockholders if "irreparable injury to the Corporation is being suffered or is threatened by reason thereof".[46]

Since the same dissolution statutes usually deal with Director and Stockholder deadlock, they will be treated together in a more comprehensive manner in a later section.[47]

§§ 30.46–30.50 are reserved for supplementary material.

D. SHARE TRANSFER RESTRICTIONS

§ 30.51 Rules as to Validity[1]

In General. Shares in a close Corporation, at least shares with voting rights, are by definition closely-held. Mutual Agreement, usually is the means of selecting the original Stockholders and their respective interests.

Since shares in a close Corporation are rarely traded, much less listed on a securities exchange, their value is usually difficult to determine, and there is, as a practical matter, very little market for such shares. Besides the practical difficulties, the shares in most close Corporations under specific Close Corporation Statutes are subjected to the legal limitations of share transfer restrictions.

The prime function of share transfer restrictions, when imposed by statute or agreement is to keep the Corporation close. Apart from such transfer restrictions, corporate shares are usually freely alienable; in fact, ready transferability of interest is one of the traditional

rectors, at least in close Corporations by provisions in the Certificate of Incorporation (New York), or in the Articles of Incorporation, By-laws or a side Agreement. See § 30.4, supra, in this regard.

46. Model Bus.Corp.Act § 97; proposed Model Statutory Close Corporation Act.

47. See Chapter 78, infra.

1. Adapted from Henn, Law of Corporations (2d ed. 1970), § 281. A third edition is being prepared by Professor Henn for 1982 publication.

attributes of a Corporation. Corporate statutes generally provided that shares are transferable in the manner provided by law and in the By-laws or Articles.

Share transfer restrictions also help to preserve the management structure of a close Corporation which is often predicated on the assumption that certain persons will be holders of certain share interests and should control the business as Stockholders, Directors, and Officers. Shifts in Stockholding, by changing the respective proportionate interests or introducing outsiders, can seriously dislocate the initial desires of the Stockholders.

Share transfer restrictions also tend to maintain relative secrecy in corporate affairs, since the requirements of Corporation law do not require substantial public disclosure of information in most close Corporation situations.

Validity of Restrictions. The question of the validity of share transfer restrictions is sometimes confused by the fact that shares have both contractual and property aspects. The freedom to restrain the alienation of shares thus can vary, depending on whether the contract or property rule be applied. However, shares should be regarded as *sui generis* and neither rule should control. Thus, the validity of share transfer restrictions turns upon corporation law rules developed by the courts with or without the aid of a statute.

Generally, restrictions to be valid must be adopted for a lawful purpose.

The purposes of preventing outsiders from obtaining ownership in the Corporation and of maintaining the proportionate interests of Stockholders are ordinarily recognized as proper.

The nature of the business being conducted may have some bearing upon the validity of a restriction. This is particularly true where special statutes control the business being conducted, as in the case of banking Corporations. The special statutory rules are likely to differ from the general principles determining the validity of restrictions.

The type of restraint employed is the most important factor in determining the validity of a transfer restriction. It is now generally accepted that a share transfer restriction will be upheld if it does not constitute an unreasonable restraint on alienation. An absolute restraint on alienation would be unreasonable *per se* and therefore void. On the other hand, absolute restraints have been upheld where they are to last only for a limited period. However, restrictions having a limited duration are not usually desirable and the draftsmen will rarely employ them.

By far the most common restriction is that making use of an *option or first right of refusal* provision. Typically, they provide that a Stockholder must offer his shares to the Corporation and/or proportionately to the other Stockholders before transferring the shares to an outsider. They might also provide for an absolute option in, or a binding Buy-Sell Agreement with, the Corporation and/or other Stockholders exercisable upon a specified event. Such provisions are generally held to be reasonable and therefore valid. See Chapters 41 and 68, infra, for further coverage of this subject.

A less common restraint is the "consent" restriction, which requires the consent of the Board of Directors or of the remaining Stockholders as a prerequisite to the transfer of the shares. While these restrictions are valid in some states,[2] they operate virtually to bar the alienation of the shares and are more likely to be considered unreasonable. Consent restrictions when adopted by Corporations running Cooperative apartment houses have been upheld on the ground that the restriction is similar to a provision in a lease against assignment. However, other uses of consent restrictions will at least invite litigation, with no assurances that the restriction will be upheld.

Despite the hostility of some courts to consent restrictions, other restraints of a more severe type have been upheld.

In the absence of special factors demanding a different type of restriction, the wisest course would seem to be to adopt restrictions of the option type, Buy-Sell type, or of another type whose validity is beyond question in the jurisdiction involved.

Uniform Commercial Code.[3] In addition to the common-law rules affecting the validity—or enforceability—of a restraint, there is also one widely adopted statute—section 8–204 of the Uniform Commercial Code.

Section 8–204 provides that unless noted conspicuously on the security a restriction on transfer imposed by the issuer even though otherwise lawful is ineffective except against a person with actual knowledge of it.

Even under the majority view, however, a restriction may have had some binding effect despite the absence of any reference to it on the share certificate. Thus, it has been held that a restriction by way of an option provision may be considered as a continuing offer to the optionee which may be accepted until its withdrawal by the Stockholder.[4]

Since the Uniform Commercial Code provision is limited to transfer restrictions imposed by the issuer, such as in the Articles of In-

2. See, e. g., Del.Gen.Corp.Law § 202(a)(3) (1967) (permitting restriction which requires Corporation or holders of any class of securities to consent to any proposed transfer); Colbert v. Hennessey, 351 Mass. 131, 217 N.E.2d 914 (1966) (upholding Stockholder Agreement not to transfer shares without consent of other Stockholders); Longyear v. Hardman, 219 Mass. 405, 106 N.E. 1012 (1914).

3. See also Chapter 52, infra, with respect to U.C.C. Article 8 governing transfer of securities.

4. Larson v. Superior Auto Parts, Inc., 207 Wis. 613, 72 N.W.2d 316 (1955). Cf. Costello v. Farrell, 234 Minn. 453,

corporation, the By-laws, or an Agreement to which the Corporation is a party, the lack of reference on the share certificate should affect the enforceability of the transfer restriction only against bona fide purchasers without knowledge or notice.

However, share transfer restrictions imposed prior to the repeal of the Uniform Stock Transfer Act by the Code, and not stated upon the certificate, will be invalid under the majority construction of that Act, even though attempted enforcement of the restriction occurs after such repeal.[5]

Cross Reference

For additional coverage of share transfer restrictions, including drafting considerations and forms, see Chapter 41, infra.

Library References:

C.J.S. Corporations § 391.
West's Key No. Digests, Corporations ⚿113.

§§ 30.52–30.61 are reserved for supplementary material.

E. DRAFTING CONSIDERATIONS FOR CLOSE CORPORATION

§ 30.62 Close Corporations—Articles of Incorporation

The Corporation is a close Corporation; no shares and no securities evidencing the right to acquire shares shall be issued by means of public offering, solicitation or advertisement. All such shares and securities shall be subject to restrictions on transfer as permitted by [*applicable statutory citation*] such Act. All issued shares, excluding treasury shares, and all issued securities evidencing the right to acquire shares of the Corporation shall be held of record by no more than ______ persons in the aggregate.

Library References:

C.J.S. Corporations, § 52 et seq.
West's Key No. Digests, Corporations ⚿18.

§ 30.63 Close Corporations—Separate Stockholders Agreement

This Agreement, made this ______ day of ______, 19__, by and between ______, ______, and ______.

Witnesseth that,

48 N.W.2d 557, 29 A.L.R.2d 890 (1951), in which it was stated in a dictum that the Uniform Stock Transfer Act could not be used by the transferee to avoid a contractual obligation.

5. Goodar Inv. Co. v. Detroit Bank & Trust Co., 4 Mich.App. 218, 144 N.W.2d 649 (1966) (holding invalid share transfer restriction not stated on share certificate under Uniform Stock Transfer Act, since replaced by Uniform Commercial Code).

Whereas, the parties hereto are all the Stockholders and subscribers of the capital stock of ______, a ______ Corporation; and

Whereas, the parties hereto desire to make certain Agreements relating to the manner in which the business and affairs of the Corporation shall be conducted,

Now, therefore, the parties agree as follows:

1. The Corporation shall at all times qualify as a close Corporation under the ______ Business Corporation Act. Each party agrees to take no action that may jeopardize or cause the loss of the status of close Corporation under said Act.

2. The business and affairs of the Corporation shall be conducted pursuant to the following principles: [*Here Insert Desired Provisions Set Forth in the Preincorporation or Voting Trust Forms, Whichever is Applicable Forms*].

3. The foregoing principles shall be set forth in the By-laws of the Corporation, and appropriate notations shall be placed on the certificates representing shares of the Corporation, to the end that such principles shall be binding on the Corporation and the parties hereto.

4. This Agreement shall remain in force so long as any party hereto desires to continue the business of the Corporation. This Agreement shall be binding upon and inure to the benefit of the parties hereto, and to the extent permitted by this Agreement, their respective heirs, successors, legal representatives and assigns.

5. This Agreement shall be governed by the laws of the State of ______.

In witness whereof, the parties have executed this Agreement.

Dated: ______, 19__.

____

____

His Wife

____

____

His Wife

COMMENTS

Since special close Corporation elections, including Agreements as to the conduct of the business of the Corporation, must appear in the Articles of Incorporation or By-laws, a separate Agreement between the Stockholders is not necessary. It may often be convenient, however, to have the basic understandings established prior to the filing of the Articles or the preparation of the By-laws.

Article 2 of this form should in every case contain provisions restricting the transfer of securities, providing some mechanism for terminating the interest of a Stockholder, and providing for the death of a Stockholder. Since shares of stock may be community property, it is desirable for the spouses of the parties to execute the Agreement. It may also be desirable to name the spouses as parties in the heading of the form.

§ 30.64 Close Corporations—Election to Be Managed by Stockholders—Provision for Articles of Incorporation

(a) Articles of Incorporation. This Corporation elects to have its business and affairs managed by the Stockholders rather than by a Board of Directors.

(b) Bylaws. The business and affairs of the Corporation shall be managed by the Stockholders rather than by a Board of Directors. Actions by the Stockholders shall be approved on the basis of the vote, cast in person or by proxy, of the holders of shares having a majority of the total voting power of all outstanding shares entitled to vote with respect to such action. Actions consented to by the Stockholders shall be binding on the Corporation. Actions taken with the full knowledge of all the Stockholders shall be deemed consented to unless a Stockholder objects thereto in a timely manner.

(c) Share Certificate. Article ______ of the Articles of Incorporation reads as follows:

"This Corporation elects to have its business and affairs managed by the Stockholders rather than by a Board of Directors."

COMMENTS

The election to dispense with the Board of Directors and provide for Stockholder management of the business of the Corporation when provided for by statute is peculiarly appropriate for the small Corporation with few Stockholders—perhaps three or less. Even though a close Corporation may consist of as many as 35 persons, direct management by the Stockholders is unlikely to be attractive in the larger Corporations, though many Partnerships with as many as 35 Partners function well.

The rule that voting is on a per share rather than a per capita basis is statutory, though the Articles of Incorporation may provide that a greater percentage of votes, or voting on some other basis, e. g., per capita, is required. The broad consent provision of the statute is included in the By-laws because, as a practical matter, it is likely to reflect the predominant way in which corporate action is actually taken.

The provision with respect to the election to have a Board of Directors is not required since the same clause may appear in the articles of amendment necessary to remove the original election from the Articles of Incorporation. It is included only so that the By-laws will reflect an option that all electing close Corporations have under the statute.

The requirement that a conspicuous notation of this election appear on the share certificate is statutory.

A Corporation that does not elect close Corporation status must have a Board of Directors. The Board, however, may consist of one or more members and may act by unanimous consent; such a Corporation may possess nearly the flexibility and simplicity of a Corporation that has elected to dispense entirely with the Board of Directors.

See also § 30.4, footnotes 18 and 19, supra.

Library References:

C.J.S. Corporations § 495.
West's Key No. Digests, Corporations ⚷180.

§ 30.65 Close Corporations—Stockholder Agreement in By-laws or Articles

(i) The Corporation may not borrow money from any person or institution not a Stockholder in an amount in excess of $______ without the prior written consent of ______, or the person or persons entitled to vote the shares now owned by ______.

(ii) To the extent permitted by law, the Corporation shall pay and declare, each year, a dividend of not less than $______, or, in the event such a dividend cannot be lawfully made, the Corporation shall distribute from capital surplus the amount of $______, or such lesser amount that may be permitted by law.

(iii) No Stockholder may transfer or convey his shares to any other person, except that any Stockholder may at any time terminate his relationship with the Corporation by selling his shares to the Corporation at [*Describe*].

(iv) The Stockholders shall vote per capita on all matters so long as ______, ______, and ______ are Stockholders. No heir, successor, or assign of any Stockholder shall have any right to vote whatsoever; but such heir, successor, or assign shall have the rights set forth in article ______ hereof.

(v) ______ shall be employed as President of the Corporation at a salary of $______ per year (or such other amount as may be agreed to by the Stockholders) for a term of ______ years; thereafter ______ shall be employed as a consultant at a salary of $______ per year for the balance of his lifetime. During his term as President, ______ shall devote at least ______ percent of his time to the business and affairs of the Corporation.

(vi) The Directors and Officers of the Corporation, and their compensation, shall be as follows:

______, Director and President, at a salary of not less than $______ per month;

_______, Director, Vice President, Secretary and Treasurer, at a salary of not less than $_______ per month.

(vii) No civil action concerning any dispute arising under this Agreement shall be instituted before any court and all such disputes shall be submitted to final and binding arbitration under the auspices of the American Arbitration Association, [*City*], [*State*]. Such arbitration shall be conducted in accordance with the rules of such association before a single arbitrator. The parties agree that the stock of the Corporation cannot be readily sold in the open market, and for that reason among others, the parties will be irreparably damaged in the event that this Agreement is not specifically enforced. Therefore, in addition to any award of damages, any such award shall, if the party entitled to the same demands it, grant specific performance of this Agreement. All costs and expenses of the arbitration, including actual attorney's fees, shall be allocated among the parties according to the arbitrator's discretion. The arbitrator's award resulting from such arbitration may be confirmed and entered as a final judgment in any court of competent jurisdiction and enforced accordingly. Further, the parties hereto expressly agree that proceeding to arbitration and obtaining an award thereunder shall be a condition precedent to the bringing or maintaining of any action in any court with respect to any dispute arising under this Agreement, except for the institution of a civil action to maintain the status quo during the pendency of any arbitration proceeding.

(viii) The business and affairs of this Corporation shall be conducted as though the Stockholders were general Partners conducting business under the [*State*] Uniform Partnership Act, subject to the following Agreements: [*Herein State Any Such Agreements*].

(ix) The foregoing provisions of the *By-laws* may be amended only by the unanimous vote of the Stockholders of the Corporation.

(b) Notation on Certificates. These shares are subject to an agreement of Stockholders set forth in the By-laws. The Corporation will furnish to the record holder of the certificate without charge upon written request to the Corporation at its principal place of business or registered office a copy of such By-law provisions.

COMMENTS

Most (or all) of the illustrative provisions in this form would be considered against public policy and unenforceable in most non-electing Corporations. In an electing close Corporation, such provisions are squarely contemplated.

Such provisions may be placed either in the Articles of Incorporation or the By-laws. It is usually preferable to place them in the By-laws for reasons of privacy and ease of amendment, except that this leaves open the possibility of the Stockholder amending these out of the By-laws.

It is important to follow precisely the procedural requirements of the Statute: counterparts of such Agreements must be on file and subject to Stockholder inspection at both the registered office of the Corporation and its principal place of business, and an appropriate notation must be placed conspicuously on each share certificate.

Such provisions build a considerable amount of inflexibility into the Corporation and may lead to undesirable consequences if the Stockholders are unable to agree upon modifications. Hence they should be used cautiously.

Library References:

C.J.S. Corporations § 179 et seq.
West's Key No. Digests, Corporations ⚷54.

§ 30.66 Close Corporations—Stockholder's Option to Dissolve Close Corporation

(a) Articles of Incorporation. Article ______. This Corporation may be dissolved at any time [*upon the affirmative vote of ______ per cent of any class of shares*], [*at the express will of any Stockholder*], [*if any Stockholder desires dissolution upon the occurrence of any of the following events*:].

(b) Bylaws. Section ______. This Corporation may be dissolved at any time [*Here Repeat Provision of the Articles of Incorporation*]. Any Stockholder desiring to dissolve the Corporation shall give 30 days written notice thereof by certified mail to all other Stockholders. Dissolution of the Corporation shall occur upon the expiration of said 30 day period and the filing of Articles of Dissolution executed by the appropriate corporate Officers.

(c) Notation on Certificates. Article ______ of the Articles of Incorporation provides that the Corporation may be dissolved at any time as follows: [*Here Repeat the Provision of the Articles of Incorporation.*]

COMMENTS

Some statutes permit the Articles of Incorporation to grant any Stockholder the right to compel dissolution of the Corporation. The alternatives set forth in this form should cover the principal types of provisions. Events which might trigger dissolution include significant disagreements, the death of a participant, the failure to pay specified salaries and/or dividends, and similar matters.

The power to compel dissolution is a significant revision of the typical rules about corporate dissolution. A nonelecting Corporation may be dissolved only by the vote of at least a majority of the Stockholders, by unanimous consent, or by decree of court after a significant period of deadlock. The power to compel dissolution may avoid deadlocks where voting power is evenly divided; it may give a minority Stockholder, who usually is at the mercy of the majority Stockholder, a significant weapon. In effect it permits a Stockholder to have the same power to terminate a relationship as a Partner possesses.

It is possible to use voting devices, such as a standby voting trust or pooling Agreement, to give a Stockholder the effective power to compel dissolution in a non-electing Corporation. See Form § 30.69, infra.

Library References:

C.J.S. Corporations § 1684 et seq.
West's Key No. Digests, Corporations ⚷610.

§ 30.67 Close Corporations—Notice of Election to Dissolve Corporation

To: ____________

I hereby notify you that I have exercised the option given to me under Article ______ of the Articles of Incorporation of ______ Corporation, a close Corporation incorporated under the ______ Business Corporation Act, to dissolve the Corporation. After 30 days from the date of this notice Articles of Dissolution should be filed with the office of the Secretary of State.

Dated: ______, 19__. ____________________________.

§ 30.68 Close Corporations—Articles of Dissolution

Pursuant to the provisions of of the ______ Business Corporation Act, the undersigned Corporation adopts the following Articles of Dissolution for the purpose of dissolving:

1. The name of the Corporation is ______.
2. The names and respective addresses of its Officers are:

Name	Office	Address
____________	____________	____________
____________	____________	____________
____________	____________	____________

3. The names and respective addresses of the Directors are:

Name	Address
____________	____________
____________	____________
____________	____________

4. A written notice that ______ has exercised the power to dissolve the Corporation given to him by Article ______ of the Articles of Incorporation, a copy of which *is attached*, has been signed by ______ or in his behalf by his duly authorized attorney as contemplated by the ______ Business Corporation Act, and written notice of such dissolution has been given to all other Stockholders.

5. [*Check Either Statement A or Statement B Below.*]

Alternative A

All debts, obligations and liabilities of the Corporation have been paid, discharged, or adequate provision has been made therefor.

Alternative B

The Corporation's property and assets are not sufficient to satisfy and discharge all its liabilities and obligations, and all property and assets have been applied so far as they would go to the payment thereof in a just and equitable manner, and no property or assets remain available for distribution among its Stockholders.

6. [*Check Either Statement A or Statement B Below.*]

Alternative A

All remaining property and assets of the Corporation have been distributed among its Stockholders in accordance with their respective rights and interests.

Alternative B

No property remains for distribution to Stockholders after applying it so far as it would go to the just and equitable payment of the liabilities and obligations of the Corporation.

7. [*Check Either Statement A or Statement B Below.*]

Alternative A

There are no suits pending against the Corporation in any court.

Alternative B

Adequate provision has been made for the satisfaction of any judgment, order, or decree which may be entered against it in any pending suit.

Dated this the ______ day of ______, 19__.

______________________	______________________
By: ______________________	By: ______________________
Its ______ President	Its ______ Secretary

STATE OF __________
County of ______

Sworn to __________.

[*Seal*]

____
Notary Public, ______ County, ______

COMMENTS

The Stockholders exercising the option to dissolve have the responsibility of notifying all other Stockholders in writing of the exercise of the option.

§ 30.69 Close Corporations—Stand-By Trust Operative Only if Deadlock Exists

An Agreement made this ______ day of ______, 19__, between ______ and ______, the sole Stockholders of ______ Corporation, a Corporation organized and existing under the laws of the State of ______ (said Stockholders being hereafter referred to as the beneficiaries) and ______, ______ and ______, or other persons who may be selected as trustees pursuant to the terms hereof (said persons being hereafter referred to as the trustees).

Whereas the beneficiaries each own precisely one half of all the issued and outstanding capital stock of ______ Corporation; and

Whereas in the event of disagreement between the beneficiaries, the affairs of the Corporation may be deadlocked; and

Whereas the beneficiaries desire to create a swift and efficient remedy for a deadlock should one occur;

Now, therefore, it is hereby agreed as follows:

§ 1. The beneficiaries shall indorse in blank and assign and deliver to the trustees the certificates representing the shares of stock owned by them in ______ Corporation, and shall do all things necessary for the transfer of their respective shares to the trustees on the books of said Corporation.

§ 2. The trustees shall hold the shares of stock transferred to them for the benefit of the beneficiaries under the following terms and conditions:

(a) In the event a deadlock (as hereafter defined) does not exist, the trustees shall vote said shares as directed by the beneficiaries representing a majority in interest of the shares held by the trustees hereunder;

(b) In the event a deadlock (as hereafter defined) exists at any meeting of beneficiaries or Directors, and said deadlock is not broken (as hereafter defined) within 30 days after the meeting at which the deadlock exists, the trustees shall—

(i) Call a special meeting of Stockholders, and (1) execute a written consent to dissolve the Corporation pursuant to the ______ Business Corporation Act, as amended, and (2) elect themselves as the sole Directors of the Corporation, removing all prior Directors of the Corporation;

(ii) As Directors and Stockholders, take all steps as may be necessary to cause the Corporation to cease carrying on its business and to wind up its affairs as required by the ______ Business Corporation Act, as amended; and

(iii) File with the Secretary of State Articles of Dissolution of the Corporation pursuant to the ______ Business Corporation Act, as amended.

§ 3. A "deadlock" shall be deemed to exist under this Agreement if either (1) the beneficiaries are unable to agree upon all the persons to be elected by the trustees as Directors, or (2) at a meeting of Directors, the Directors are unable to act because of the absence of a quorum or because they are evenly divided upon an issue, and the beneficiaries are unable, at a meeting called by the trustees for that purpose, to agree upon a Board of Directors which is able to act upon the issue. A deadlock shall be deemed "broken" only if beneficiaries representing a majority in interest of the shares held by the trustees hereunder execute a written instrument containing directions to the trustees which, if followed, will eliminate the deadlock.

§ 4. At any time prior to the issuance of a certificate of dissolution by the Secretary of State, the trustees shall execute a written consent to the revocation of voluntary dissolution proceedings at the request of beneficiaries representing a majority in interest of the shares held by the trustees hereunder.

§ 5. This trust shall continue for 10 years from the date hereof but may be terminated at any time prior thereto by a written instrument executed by beneficiaries representing a majority in interest of the shares held by the trustees hereunder and delivered to the trustees.

§ 6. While this trust is outstanding, no further shares of ______ Corporation shall be issued. The trustees shall not vote to approve any amendment to the Articles of Incorporation or merger or consolidation affecting the Corporation without the consent of all the beneficiaries hereunder. The trustees shall not dispose of any shares deposited hereunder without the consent of all the beneficiaries hereunder.

§ 7. The trustees shall collect all dividends that may accrue upon the shares of stock and pay them over to the beneficiaries in interest of such shares.

§ 8. The trustees shall, upon request, issue trust certificates representing the shares deposited hereunder, and such certificates may be transferred or assigned, subject to any reasonable restrictions on transfer on which the beneficiaries may agree.

§ 9. In the event a trustee fails to qualify or ceases to act hereunder, the surviving or other trustee shall appoint a trustee to fill the vacancy, and the person so appointed shall be vested with all the duties, powers, and authority of a trustee originally named herein.

§ 10. This trust shall become effective when a counterpart of this Agreement is deposited with the Corporation and the shares are transferred hereunder pursuant of the ______ Business Corporation Act, as amended, and this Agreement.

In witness whereof, the parties hereto have executed this Agreement.

Dated: ______, 19__.

______________________	______________________
	Trustee
______________________	______________________
His Wife	Trustee
______________________	______________________
	Trustee
______________________	
His Wife	

Library References:

C.J.S. Corporations § 552.
West's Key No. Digests, Corporations ⚷198.1.

§§ 30.70–31.0 are reserved for supplementary material.

CHAPTER 31

ENTITIES TREATED AS CORPORATIONS FOR STATE LAW AND TAX LAW PURPOSES

Table of Sections

---

§ 31.1 Distinguishing Considerations Between State and Tax Laws

The tax benefits and burdens of incorporation (see Chapter 2, supra), depend upon a particular entity in fact attaining "corporate" status under the applicable state and/or tax laws.

Although the vast majority of tests which determine corporate status under the state and tax laws overlap, at the fringes we can find some significant differences; these are as set forth in the following sections.

Library References:

C.J.S. Taxation § 1093.
West's Key No. Digests, Taxation ⚷1015.

§ 31.2 Articles of Incorporation

An entity will not be entitled to corporate status for state law purposes unless it has at least filed its *Articles of Incorporation* under some state law at some time before the date in question. Unfortunately, no clear state law test can be given as to where or when such filing has to occur. Essentially there are three types of relevant state law situations:

(a) The entity in question claims an incorporation in the state in question. In this situation, all states will only recognize as a Corporation an entity that has filed its Articles of Incorporation and received the appropriate state agency's approval of such filing. Thereafter, states require that Corporations file annual reports with the state and pay a fee. Some states make such annual report filing and fee payment a precondition to continuous status as a Corporation. However, the trend is towards giving the state the right to revoke such status but not making such revocation automatic. In addition, all states have statutes and judicially wrought rules which deny even a properly incorporated Corporation corporate status if the activities of the Stockholders are thought to be against state policy. This denial is called "piercing the corporate veil" and is rarely done except in extreme circumstances. States will generally recognize an incorporation which is merely meant to profunctorily meet state requirements when no one will be harmed (these are called Form Corporations). The largest use of Form Corporations is to allow a lender to avoid the individual usury laws in favor of the corporate usury laws.

(b) The entity in question claims an incorporation in another state and claims that it is *not* doing business in the state in question. As to the claim of incorporation, this will be tested (if at all) by the above rules as interpreted by the state of the claimed incorporation.

The doing business question is quite complex:

> Under general U. S. Consitutional law a state can not tax or burden interstate commerce. Therefore, it is thought that any Corporation that merely engages in interstate commerce across the borders of a state need not ask that state for permission to conduct this business (by registering as a *foreign* Corporation). Any Corporation which is to engage in intrastate commerce will have to register however (see Chapters 28, supra, and 36, infra, for a more complete description). If it is determined that the foreign Corporation should have registered, then (depending on the facts and the state): (1) the entity may not be entitled to claim the benefits of incorporation or (2) the entity may have to register before claiming such benefits.

(c) The entity in question claims an incorporation in another state and agrees that it must register as a foreign Corporation in the state in question (see Chapter 36, infra). In this case, corporate status may or may not be granted to such entity before such registration depending on the state and the circumstances.

§ 31.3 Unintentional Corporate Status for Tax Law Purposes

An entity may be given corporate tax statute for state law purposes even though it is not entitled to (and does not want) corporate status. In fact, a Partnership or Business Trust or other entity may be given corporate tax status unwittingly and unwillingly. The foundation for this determination is the Kintner Regulations (see § 2.32, supra, for a more complete description of Kintner Regulations).

Basically, these regulations provide for the following tests:

(a) Does the entity in question have centralized management? If so, this is considered a corporate characteristic.

(b) Do the owners of the entity in question have limited liability? If so, this is considered a corporate characteristic.

(c) Do the owners of the entity in question have free transferability of their ownership interests? If so, this is considered a corporate characteristic.

(d) Does the entity in question continue in its theoretical status as an entity for State law purposes in all cases even if one or more owner dies, is disabled, withdraws or becomes bankrupt? If so, this is considered a corporate characteristic.

(e) Does the entity have associates (i. e., more than one owner)? If so, this is considered a corporate characteristic.

(f) Is the object of the equity's existence to carry on a business for profit? If so, this is considered a corporate characteristic.

The purpose of the Kintner Regulations is to use the above characteristics to classify the entity in question for tax purposes as a Corporation or not.

Generally, the Kintner Regulations are applied as follows:

(a) The characteristics that are shared by both types of entities are ignored. Thus, items (e) and (f) above are ignored if the question is Partnership or Corporation and items (a), (b), (c) and (d) above are ignored if the question is Business Trust or Corporation.

(b) The entity label is presumed to control. Thus, if 50% or more of the relevant characteristics match the entity's format, the entity's format will control the tax results. If less than 50% of the relevant characteristics match the entity's format, the alternative entity's tax rules will be applied.

§ 31.4 General Indices of Corporate Status

Even if the Kintner Regulations substantiate the Corporation's claim to corporate tax treatment, this treatment may be denied if the facts of corporate operation (not status) do not have enough "indices" of corporate being.

Thus, indices of corporate being are important for two reasons:

(a) Their lack of existence may be used under state law to pierce the corporate veil and deny corporate benefits to Stockholders, and

(b) Their lack of existence may be used under the tax law to disallow corporate tax status and tax benefits.

What are these corporate indices? Generally, corporate indices will be the same for both tax and state law. As one might expect, they are physical acts which Corporations generally do. Therefore, the indices are many of the incorporation actions and documents described in this Text.

Since some of these documents and actions are more important than others, the important ones are:

(a) Articles of Incorporation properly filed and accepted by the state of incorporation.

(b) Issuance of stock certificates.

(c) Adoption of By-laws.

(d) Filing corporate tax returns.

(e) Using the corporate name and executing documents by corporate agents in the name of the Corporation.

(f) Use of a corporate bank account and, when other assets are titled, holding them in the corporate name.

(g) The existence of a reasonable ratio of debt to equity (3 to 1 is reasonable; 9 to 1 is often thought to be unreasonable. (See Reg. 1.385–6 (1981)).

(h) Holding annual meetings and keeping the corporate record book up to date.

§§ 31.5–32.0 are reserved for supplementary material.

PART B

INCORPORATION PROCEDURES

CHAPTER 32

STEPS OF INCORPORATION—GENERALLY

Table of Sections

---

§ 32.1 Introduction

After resolving the inquiry of the most suitable form of business enterprise [1] and, assuming that incorporation is deemed best, and after determining the most advantageous jurisdiction in which to incorporate,[2] the next steps after the promotional stage [3] are to comply with the required incorporation procedures in the selected jurisdiction of incorporation and admission procedures in other jurisdictions where the Corporation is to do business.

Sound incorporation requires a thorough understanding and appreciation of many relevant facts concerning the proposed enterprise. Many of these facts should have already been considered in selecting the form of enterprise and jurisdiction of incorporation, in anticipation of the problems of complying with the incorporation and admission procedures.

In general, counsel must know all the information relevant to drafting the Articles of Incorporation, By-laws, Stockholder Agreements, minutes of organization meetings, form(s) of share certificates, and any other documents relevant to the financing and management of the Corporation. This might require some prodding of the client, who has probably not worked out in his own mind all the legally-significant details. Obviously, counsel should be thoroughly conversant with applicable Corporation and other relevant laws.

1. See Chapters 1 and 2, supra.

2. See Chapter 28, supra.

3. See Chapter 29, supra.

In this chapter, the various steps in the incorporation procedures are first outlined in general terms.[4] Thereafter, the general problems involved in drafting the Articles of Incorporation,[5] and the By-laws [6] are treated. Then, the organization meetings, their agenda and minutes, are discussed.[7] Problems encountered in drafting Preincorporation Agreements between promoters and third persons [8] have already been discussed. Drafting problems unique to the close Corporation, including the drafting of close Corporation provisions for the Articles of Incorporation and By-laws, Stockholder and other Agreements, and share certificate legends, have previously been treated in the context of the discussion of the special problems of close Corporations, although specific/form provisions are found in the related chapter.[9]

Library References:

C.J.S. Corporations §§ 1 et seq., 4, 5, 8, 32.
West's Key No. Digests, Corporations ⚷1 et seq.

§ 32.2 Process of Incorporation—Generally

The process of incorporation involves a number of steps which vary somewhat from state to state. A composite listing of incorporation procedures follows. It should be cautioned that no state prescribes all of these steps, and different states prescribe varying combinations of some of the steps in different chronological order. In addition, business considerations will dictate whether certain nonmandatory steps are taken.

(1) Preparation and execution of Preincorporation Agreements between the organizers of the Corporation and, if required by statute, the publication thereof. (See Chapter 29, supra.)

(2) Preparation and execution of contracts to be entered into by the organizers on behalf of the proposed Corporation. (See Chapter 29, supra.)

(3) Solicitation of Preincorporation subscriptions to shares if desired, subject to the requirements of state blue sky laws and the federal securities laws, if applicable. (See Chapter 39, infra.)

(4) Adoption of appropriate plans for meeting the capital requirements of the proposed Corporation. (See Chapter 38, infra.)

4. See § 32.2, infra.

5. See Chapter 33, infra.

6. See Chapter 34, infra.

7. See Chapter 35, infra.

8. See Chapter 29, supra.

9. See Chapter 30, supra.

(5) Choice,[10] clearance and reservation or registration[11] of the corporate name.

(6) Preparation and execution of the Articles of Incorporation. (See Chapter 33, infra.)

(7) Filing of the Articles of Incorporation with state of incorporation and payment of fees.

(8) Issuance of "Certificate of Incorporation."[12] Publication of incorporation, if required.

(9) Preparation and adoption of By-laws. (See Chapter 33, infra.)

(10) Organization meeting and preparation of minutes. In some states this is a meeting of the Incorporators and subscribers. In other states, especially where the Articles of Incorporation name the initial Directors, this is a meeting of Directors. Still other states require organization meetings of both. (See Chapter 35, infra.)

(11) First meeting of Directors and preparation of minutes. (See Chapter 35, infra.)

(12) Solicitation of post-incorporation subscriptions and issuance of shares, subject to the requirements of state blue sky laws and the federal securities laws, if applicable. (See Chapter 39, infra.)

(13) Securing of a stock (or record) book with stock certificates, stock ledger, minute books, and corporate seal.

(14) Payment of minimum paid-in capital and performance of other conditions precedent to engaging in business operations.

(15) Filing for a Certificate of Authority to Transact Business in States other than the State of Incorporation (see Chapter 36, infra.)

(16) Filing of a Sub-Chapter S election with Internal Revenue Service (see Chapter 85, infra.)

10. Model Bus.Corp.Act § 7 requires the corporate name to contain the word "corporation", "company", "incorporated", or "limited", or an abbreviation thereof; prohibits the use of any word or phrase indicating that the Corporation is organized for any purpose other than its purposes as stated in its articles of incorporation; and provides that the name shall not be the same as, or deceptively similar to, the name of any domestic Corporation or of any qualified foreign Corporation, or to any reserved or registered name. Many jurisdictions do not recognize the word "company" or its abbreviation as a sufficient indication of corporateness. For additional discussion of corporate name, see § 33.3, infra.

11. Model Bus.Corp.Act § 9 (reservation of corporate name for 120 days). The majority of states have such statutory provisions, with time periods ranging from 10 days to 12 months, with possible renewals. In several jurisdictions without such statutes, administrative officials as a matter of courtesy will reserve names under varying terms and conditions. Some jurisdictions by statute authorize "registration" of corporate names, effective until the end of the calendar year, with possible annual renewals. Model Bus.Corp.Act §§ 10 and 11.

12. Model Bus.Corp.Act § 55.

(17) Execution of documents transferring assets to the Corporation.

(18) Execution of qualified retirement program(s) and filing of same with Internal Revenue Service for approval.

(19) Execution of nonqualified employee benefit programs.

(20) Execution of Employment Agreement(s).

(21) Issuance of stock, securities and short term notes to investors (see Chapters 38 et seq., infra.)

(22) Execution of a Stockholders Agreement (see Chapter 29).

(23) Filing of forms necessary to comply with the following tax authorities demands:

(A) Federal ID (identification) number.

(B) State tax number(s) for income, sales, use, cigarette, gasoline, etc. taxes.

(C) State unemployment forms.

(D) Federal unemployment forms.

(24) Preparation of the following documents and doing the following activities ancillary to an incorporation:

(A) Obtaining new letterhead for stationery, statements, etc., reflecting the new business name.

(B) Obtaining business cards to reflect the new name.

(C) Obtaining checks reflecting the new name.

(D) Requesting that the telephone book listing show the new name.

(E) Changing business signs to reflect the new name.

(F) Signing correspondence identifying principals as an Officer or Director of the Corporation.

(G) Notifying suppliers and customers of the name change.

(H) Giving consideration to the freezing of an existing Keogh Plan. A Keogh Plan is a form of non-corporate retirement program which has tax benefits and which can (with difficulty) be incorporated into a Corporation's retirement program. Practical experience has taught the author to freeze the Keogh Plan, rather than incorporate it. As an alternative, a Keogh Plan may be terminated, which involves a small tax penalty. This should be done if it is believed the funds would generate greater results or if the practical problems and costs of freezing the plan exceed the benefit.

(I) Discontinue the old form of organization. If an Assumed Name Certificate was filed, a Certificate of Discontinuance should be prepared and filed. Are there any other matters in connection with the discontinuance of the old Proprietorship or Partnership which are not specifically covered above (e. g., the termination of the Partnership Agreement and distribution of its assets).

SUMMARY

As indicated above, incorporation procedures involve various steps in different states. Some of such steps are regarded as mandatory; others as directory; some as conditions precedent to incorporation or to the doing of business; others as conditions subsequent. Corporate existence begins at different steps of the incorporation procedure in different jurisdictions depending upon applicable statutes and decisional law, most usually upon the filing of the Articles of Incorporation or upon the issue of a formal "certificate of incorporation".

§ 32.3 Incorporators

The person or persons who execute the Articles of Incorporation are called "incorporators." The number required varies from state to state, with three being the traditional number but with a large number of states requiring only a single incorporator. A few states may still have residency or age requirements, or limit incorporators to natural persons, but most states now permit an incorporator to be anyone over the age of 18 without regard to residency and many states also permit artificial entities such as Corporations to serve as incorporators. Some states require that each incorporator subscribe for at least one share of stock, but most states do not have a similar requirement.

The relaxation of the requirements relating to incorporators reflects the minor role they play in the formation of a modern Corporation. Depending on the state, incorporators may serve one or more of the following roles:

(1) They execute and deliver the Articles of Incorporation to the Secretary of State;

(2) They, or their representatives, receive the charter or Certificate of Incorporation back from the Secretary of State;

(3) They meet to complete the organization of the Corporation;

(4) They call the first meeting of the initial Board of Directors (often named in the Articles of Incorporation), at which meeting the organization of the Corporation is completed;

(5) They may voluntarily dissolve the Corporation if the Corporation has not commenced business and has not issued any shares; and

(6) They may amend the Articles of Incorporation by unanimous consent if the Corporation has not commenced business and has not issued any shares.

In most states today the initial Directors named in the Articles complete the organization of the Corporation. In these states, the role of Incorporators is basically limited to the ceremonial function of signing the Articles of Incorporation. As a result, acting as incorporator does not appear to give rise to any risk of liability. Indeed, many attorneys or their secretaries or other law office employees routinely serve as incorporators.

An "incorporator" must be sharply distinguished from a "subscriber." The latter agrees to buy shares in the Corporation; in other words, he is an investor and participant in the venture. An "incorporator" on the other hand serves the largely ceremonial or ministerial functions described in this section.

Library References:

C.J.S. Corporations §§ 36, 48, 119 et seq.
West's Key No. Digests, Corporations ⚷15, 30(1).

§§ 32.4–33.0 are reserved for supplementary material.

CHAPTER 33

ARTICLES OF INCORPORATION

Table of Sections

---

§ 33.1 General Considerations

Every state, by statute, requires the filing of Articles or Certificate of Incorporation as a condition precedent to corporate existence, although some states will allow a functioning corporation to retroactively file for certain purposes. The form and content of these Articles should closely follow the statutory requirements of the state of incorporation.

Most business Corporations (other than Professional Corporations) are organized today under general incorporation statutes. The basic instrument which upon filing usually creates the Corporation is called in most states "Articles of Incorporation" [1] or "Certificate of Incorporation". The contents thereof are prescribed in the general incorporation statutes. In many states, official forms are also pre-

1. See e. g. Model Bus.Corp.Act § 2(c).

scribed [2] and are made available on request. In most states, corporate existence begins with the filing, usually with the Secretary of State, of the Articles or Certificate of Incorporation.[3] In some jurisdictions, duplicate Articles of Incorporation are filed, and corporate existence begins with the issue of a formal certificate appended thereto called a "Certificate of Incorporation". Various conditions precedent to doing business might also be imposed.

While the corporate laws of the fifty states are not uniform, there is, however, considerable similarity in respect to what the Articles shall contain and also as to what they may set forth. While the Articles must stay within these limitations there is a great deal of room to tailor the Articles to fit the business needs of the proposed enterprise. The statutes of a number of states are very liberal in allowing optional provisions to be inserted for regulating the affairs of the Corporation.

Typical requirements for the Articles of Incorporation are found in the Model Business Corporation Act: [4]

(a) The name of the Corporation; [5]

(b) The period of duration, which may be perpetual; [6]

(c) The purpose or purposes for which the Corporation is organized which may be stated to be, or to include, the transaction of any or all lawful business for which Corporations may be incorporated under the Act; [7]

2. See e. g. Model Bus.Corp.Act § 142 (forms to be furnished by Secretary of State upon request, but their use, unless otherwise specifically prescribed in the Act, not to be mandatory).

See Model Bus.Corp.Act Official Forms in §§ 33.12, 33.13, infra.

3. See § 33.2, infra, discussion of filing requirements.

4. Section 48. See Official Model Bus. Corp.Act Forms in §§ 33.12, 33.13, infra.

5. All states require the Articles (or certificate) of Incorporation to set forth the name of the Corporation (See e. g. § 54(a); Del.Gen.Corp.Law, § 102(a)(1); West's Ann.Cal.Corp.Code § 202(a). Requirements applicable to corporate names, and their clearance and possible advance reservation, or registration, are discussed at § 33.3, infra. In setting forth the corporate name, it should be done precisely, with correct spelling, capitalization, punctuation, inclusion of the definite article, "The", if desired, use of abbreviations where desired (e. g., "Corp.", "Co.", "Ltd."), and use of the ampersand, "&", for "and" if desired. Obviously, the name as set forth in the Articles of Incorporation should conform to its use in any required title or endorsement of the Articles. Subsequent display and other use of the name should be consistent with the name set forth in the Articles.

6. Most states require that the Articles of Incorporation set forth the duration of the Corporation (e. g. Model Bus.Corp.Act § 54(b)), at least when it is not to be perpetual (e. g. Del. Gen.Corp.Law § 102(b)(5) (1967); McKinney's N.Y.Bus.Corp.Law § 402(a)(9)). Some states impose constitutional or statutory limitations on corporate duration, which should be observed in setting forth the duration in the Articles of Incorporation.

7. All states require the Articles of Incorporation to set forth the corporate

(d) The aggregate number of shares which the Corporation shall have authority to issue; if such shares are to consist of one class only, the par value of each of such shares, or a statement that all of such shares are without par value; or, if such shares are to be divided into classes, the number of shares of each class, and a statement of the par value of the shares of each such class or that such shares are to be without par value; [8]

purposes or objects, the two terms being synonymous (e. g. Model Bus. Corp.Act § 54(c); see also West's Ann.Cal.Corp.Code § 202; McKinney's N.Y.Bus.Corp.Law § 402(a)(2)).

Most states permit incorporation of business Corporations for "any lawful business" or "any lawful purpose or purposes", subject to various exceptions (e. g. Model Bus.Corp.Act § 3). Some bar Corporations from engaging in certain activities, such as practicing professions, in their Corporation statutes, other statutes, or by case law. Most exceptions are stated in terms of specific classes of Corporations or Corporations formable under other statutes or both, and often refer to banks and trust companies, loan companies, insurance companies, public utilities, and railroads (e. g. Model Bus.Corp.Act § 3).

A growing number of modern statutes allow the Articles of Incorporation to set forth either specific purposes or a general statement that the Corporation may pursue any and all lawful purposes under the statute.

In other states, the statement of purposes must be reasonably clear and definite; a mere paraphrase of the broad statutory language is usually not sufficient, although an omnibus-purpose clause following a more specific statement might be acceptable; however, its future construction would be conjectural. The usual practice is to define the principal business actually contemplated in the main purpose clause, and thereafter enumerate additional activities related and unrelated thereto, often without differentiation between purposes and powers.

The purpose clause or clauses should express the nature and scope of the business and risk as agreed upon among the Stockholders. Therefore, the purpose clause or clauses should be so drafted as to be definite enough to curb excursions into unauthorized ventures and yet sufficiently general to permit reasonable operations and expansion without the necessity of future amendment of the Articles of Incorporation. Careful drafting of the purpose clause or clauses, using available forms and precedents as a checklist, is highly desirable from several points of view. In most situations, a relatively general statement of purposes to the extent permissible is preferable to specific enumeration.

The purpose clause might state that the purposes shall be construed as powers as well as purposes, and the matters expressed in any clause shall in nowise be limited by reference to or inference from the terms of any other, but shall be regarded as independent purposes and powers; and the enumeration of specific purposes and powers shall not be construed to limit or restrict in any manner the meaning of general terms of the general powers; nor shall the expression of one thing be deemed to exclude another not expressed, although it be of like nature.

The extent to which the stated purposes will be carried out is within the discretion of the Board of Directors.

8. Most states *require* that the Articles of Incorporation set forth the number of authorized shares, the number of shares in each class if shares are classified, and the par value of any par value shares, and if there are to be shares without par value a statement to such effect (e. g. Del.Corp. Law § 102(a)(4).) Other statutes provide that the articles *may* contain provisions relating to the par value of any authorized shares (e. g. Model Bus.Corp.Act § 54(3). Still other statutes (e. g. West's Ann.Cal.Corp.Code § 202), make no mention of par value.

(e) If the shares are to be divided into classes, the designation of each class and a statement of the preferences, limitations and relative rights in respect of the shares of each class; [9]

(f) If the Corporation is to issue the shares of any preferred or special class in series, then the designation of each series and a statement of the variations in the relative rights and preferences as between series in so far as the same are to be fixed in the Articles of Incorporation, and a statement of any authority to be vested in the Board of Directors to establish series and fix and determine the variations in the relative rights and preferences as between series; [10]

(g) A statement that the Corporation will not commence business until consideration of the value of at least one thousand dollars has been received for the issuance of shares; [11]

(h) If any preemptive right is to be granted to Stockholders, the provisions therefor; or, alternatively, any provision limiting or denying to Stockholders the preemptive right to acquire additional or treasury shares of the Corporation; [12]

Choice between par value shares and shares without par value is usually based upon applicable requirements of consideration for their issue; rates of organization and capital, issue, and transfer taxes, and the desirability of allocating part of the consideration to capital surplus. Some states require the Articles of Incorporation to include certain prescribed statements concerning stated capital.

9. All states require that the Articles of Incorporation, if the shares are to be divided into classes, set forth the designation of each class and a statement of the preferences, limitations, and relative rights in respect of the shares of each class (e. g. Model Bus.Corp.Act § 54(e); West's Ann.Cal. Corp.Code § 202; McKinney's N.Y. Bus.Corp.Law § 402(a)(5)). Preferences may exist with respect to dividends and/or net assets upon liquidation. Dividend preferences may be cumulative, cumulative-to-the-extent-earned, or noncumulative, and participating or nonparticipating. Liquidating preferences may or may not include any preferred dividend arrearages, and may be participating or nonparticipating. The Articles of Incorporation may usually deny or limit the voting rights, absolutely or conditionally, of some classes (e. g. Model Bus.Corp.Act § 33; McKinney's N.Y. Bus.Corp.Law §§ 501, 612, 613); provide for the redemption by the Corporation of preferred shares; make shares convertible by the holder into other securities; contain protective or other provisions for preferred or other shares; and authorize the issue of share warrants. Apart from shares and other equity securities, debt securities, such as bonds, debentures, and notes, may be issued.

10. Most states permit the Articles of Incorporation to authorize the issue of a class or classes in series, as provided therein or as fixed from time to time by the Board of Directors (e. g. Model Bus.Corp.Act § 54(f) preferred or special class or classes). Various limitations may limit the variations between series of the same class.

11. The Articles of Incorporation in some jurisdictions are required to state that the Corporation will not commence business until consideration of the value of a specified minimum amount has been received for the issuance of shares. Even in states which may not require such statement in the Articles, minimum paid-in capital might be required before commencing business.

12. Most states expressly permit the Articles of Incorporation to deny or

(i) Any provision, not inconsistent with law, which the incorporators elect to set forth in the Articles of Incorporation for the regulation of the internal affairs of the Corporation, including any provision restricting the transfer of shares and any provision which under the Act is required or permitted to be set forth in the By-laws; [13]

(j) The address of its initial registered office, and the name of its initial registered agent at such address; [14]

(k) The number of Directors constituting the initial Board of Directors and the names and addresses of the persons who are to serve as Directors until the first annual meeting of Stockholders or until their successors be elected and qualify; [15]

(*l*) The name and address of each incorporator.[16]

limit preemptive rights. In several other states, preemptive rights exist unless otherwise provided in the Articles of Incorporation (e. g. Model Bus.Corp.Act § 26). In other states, preemptive rights exist only to the extent that provision is made for them in the Articles of Incorporation (e. g. Model Bus.Corp.Act alt. § 26). As a general rule, preemptive rights might be avoided in Corporations whose shares are to be widely held, especially those with complicated share structures, but secured in the case of close Corporations.

13. Most states expressly *permit* (i. e. do not require) the Articles of Incorporation to include provisions, not inconsistent with law, for the regulation of the internal affairs of the Corporation (e. g. Model Bus.Corp.Act § 54). Some states also provide that the Articles of Incorporation may include any provision required or permitted to be set forth in the By-laws (e. g. Model Bus.Corp.Act § 54; West's Ann.Cal.Corp.Code § 204. Many statutory substantive provisions are expressly subject to variation by provisions in the Articles of Incorporation or By-laws.

14. All states require the Articles of Incorporation to set forth the address of the registered office or place of business of the Corporation (e. g. Model Bus.Corp.Act § 54(h)). Several states also require the designation of a registered agent for service of process upon the Corporation, either in the Articles or in a separate instrument (e. g. M.B.C.A. § 54(h); West's Ann.Cal.Corp.Code § 202).

Some states require the Corporation to have and to maintain continuously in the state a registered office, which may but need not be the same as its place of business, and a registered agent whose business office is identical with such registered office (e. g. M.B.C.A. § 12).

Provision is often made for changing the Corporation's registered office or registered agent without the necessity of amending the Articles of Incorporation (e. g. M.B.C.A. § 13).

15. Many states require the Articles of Incorporation to name the initial Director or Directors (e. g. Model Bus.Corp.Act § 54(i)). Some states require the Articles to set forth the number of Directors. In several states, the Articles of Incorporation may prescribe qualifications for Directors, or possibly dispense with certain requirements (e. g. Model Bus.Corp.Act § 35). Most states allow classification of the Directors, subject to some limitations (e. g. Model Bus.Corp.Act § 37).

16. Most states require the Articles of Incorporation to set forth the names and addresses of the Incorporators (e. g. Model Bus.Corp.Act § 54(1); West's Ann.Cal.Corp.Code § 202). Traditionally, at least three adult natural persons are required as incorporators, but a growing number of jurisdictions permit one incorporator, or even a corporate incorporator (e. g. Model Bus. Corp.Act § 53; West's Ann.Cal.Corp. Code § 200). Some states impose citizenship or residence requirements; a few still require that the incorporators

It is not necessary to set forth in the Articles of Incorporation any of the corporate powers enumerated in the Model Act.[17]

Some states require the Articles of Incorporation to be entitled and possibly endorsed or to contain the drafter's name as prescribed by statute.

In addition, state statutes provide that a Corporation may elect to be governed by certain statutory provisions, the election of which must be reflected by an appropriate provision in the Articles of Incorporation. For example, many statutes provide that a majority shall constitute a quorum of Stockholders except that the quorum may be reduced to as low as one-third by specific provision in the Articles of Incorporation (Model Business Corporation Act § 32). Of more practical importance, many statutes provide that the Stockholders shall have a preemptive right to acquire new shares (see § 18.1 of § 33.16, infra) or to vote shares cumulatively (see § 7.10 of § 33.16, infra) unless these rights are specifically negated by appropriate provisions in the Articles of Incorporation. Some states instead provide "opt in" provisions for these rights—e. g., a Corporation's Stockholders will not have preemptive rights unless the Articles of Incorporation specifically provide for them (e. g., Model Business Corporation Act § 26). The statute of each specific state must be consulted to determine the pattern adopted by that state.

Finally, Corporations may elect to place provisions relating to the governing of its internal affairs in the Articles of Incorporation in order to make them more permanent, more difficult to amend, and, hopefully, binding on persons who may not have actual knowledge of them. Such provisions may also be placed in the Corporation's By-laws. However, it is good practice for provisions denying customary rights to Stockholders or others to appear in the Articles of Incorporation rather than the By-laws so that the Directors can't change these provisions.

Library References:

C.J.S. Corporations § 52 et seq.
West's Key No. Digests, Corporations 🔑18.

§ 33.2 Execution and Filing

The Articles of Incorporation in all states must be signed by the Incorporator or Incorporators.[18] Some states require verification; others acknowledgment.[19]

subscribe to shares, sometimes in the Articles of Incorporation.

17. See e. g. Model Bus.Corp.Act § 54.

18. E. g. Model Bus.Corp.Act § 53; Del.Gen.Corp.Law § 103.

19. E. g. McKinney's N.Y.Bus.Corp. Law § 402(a).

In most states only the original Articles must be filed, usually with the Secretary of State.[20] In some states, duplicate originals of the Articles must be delivered to the Secretary of State, who, upon finding that they conform to law and that all fees and taxes have been paid, files one of the duplicate originals and issues a "certificate of incorporation" to which is affixed the other duplicate original.[21]

Some states also require either prior or subsequent recording or filing in some county office or offices. In some states this is the only way of fully protecting the corporate name. In a few states, the state official with whom the Articles are filed is required to attend to the local recording or filing.

Court orders or approval of the state attorney general is sometimes required. Publication is occasionally required.

Upon the filing of the Articles,[22] or possibly upon the issue of a "Certificate of Incorporation",[23] corporate existence usually begins. The "Certificate of Incorporation" or other specified evidence of incorporation might be conclusive[24] or presumptive evidence of compliance with all conditions precedent to incorporation.

20. E. g. Del.Gen.Corp.Law § 101(a), 103(c)(1) (with duplicate copy); McKinney's N.Y.Bus.Corp.Law, § 402(a).

21. E. g. Model Bus.Corp.Act §§ 55, 56, 127, 128.

In most every state, the filing is reviewed by the state officer or his staff. If the document is approved, the corporate existence is usually deemed to begin as of the date and time the document is filed. The filing authority reflects its approval of the document by some step, such as the issuance of a formal "Certificate of Incorporation," attaching it to a duplicate original or copy of the document, or increasingly, by the mere issuance of a receipt for the filing fee. The original document is retained by the Secretary of State in most states, and the same information may also be kept in computer-readable form. Some states have additional filing requirements. Delaware, for example, requires local filing in the county in which the Corporation's registered office is located (as well as filing in a state office) 8 Del.C. § 103(c)(5). Arizona requires that the Articles be published in a newspaper of general circulation in the county in which the Corporation's known place of business is located three consecutive times within 60 days after the articles are filed (A.R.S. § 10–055). A handful of states still require recording in every county in which the Corporation transacts business.

These additional filing requirements may also create legal problems as to when the corporate existence begins if some, but not all of them, are complied with. A few states have statutes that deal with this question. Delaware, for example, provides that corporate existence begins with the acceptance of the filing by the Secretary of State, and the failure to file locally within the specified period increases the filing fee but does not affect the existence of the Corporation [8 Del.C. § 103(d)]. Some states, however, condition the existence of the Corporation on the completion of all filing and advertising requirements.

22. E. g. McKinney's N.Y.Bus.Corp. Law § 403.

23. E. g. Model Bus.Corp.Act § 56.

24. E. g. Id.

Some states impose various conditions precedent to the doing of business.

Where filing of the Articles of Incorporation is refused by the Secretary of State or other official, mandamus or its modern equivalent is the usual remedy to test such refusal in the courts.[25]

There are often statutory provisions for the correction of Articles of Incorporation.[26]

The Articles of Incorporation are subject to amendment (See Chapter 51, infra.) Such amendments require Stockholder consent (with possible appraisal right to dissenting Stockholders), and involve filing fees and other expenses.

Library References:

C.J.S. Corporations §§ 59, 62.
West's Key No. Digests, Corporations ⚿22.

§ 33.3 Corporate Name

Most statutes set up minimum requirements with respect to the corporate name.[27] Typical provisions include:

(1) The name must contain a word indicating corporateness, such as "corporation," "company" or "incorporated," or an abbreviation of one or more such words.

(2) The name may not contain any word or phrase which indicates that it is organized for a purpose that it is not permitted to engage in. As a practical matter, with the development of very general purposes clauses, the principal impact of this restriction is to preclude the use of names which suggest a purpose for which Corporations may not be organized under the state business Corporation act. Thus, in many states, "bank," "bank and trust," "certificate of deposit," "title guaranty," and "cemetery" may not appear in corporate names since there are special regulatory requirements in statutes relating to formation of Corporations for such purposes.

(3) The name may not be the "same or deceptively similar" to any other corporate name. The purposes of this requirement are apparently in part to make sure that each Corporation has a unique name, and in part to prevent unfair competition.

(4) If the name is "similar" (as contrasted with the "same or deceptively similar") to any other corporate name, it may be

25. Some jurisdictions provide for appeal from the Secretary of State. E. g., Model Bus.Corp.Act § 140.

26. E. g. McKinney's N.Y.Bus.Corp. Law § 105.

27. See e. g. Model Bus.Corp.Act § 8.

used only if a "letter of consent" is obtained from the owner of the similar name which expressly permits the name to be used. The purpose of this requirement appears to be solely to prevent unfair competition.

Secretaries of States usually maintain lists of corporate names that are not currently available, and check proposed new names against that list. However, the issue as to whether a name is available or whether it is "deceptively similar" often involves questions of judgment; some Secretaries of State have developed "rules of thumb" or "house rules" to guide their discretion on judgments as to name availability. As a practical matter, the issue whether or not a specific name is available is seldom litigated. Even if an attorney strongly disagrees with the Secretary of State as to the availability of a name, it is much simpler and cheaper to select another name than to litigate over name availability. However, when two Corporations or businesses have used similar names in the past, the right to the continued use of such name may be so valuable as to lead to bitter litigation over whether the use of the name constitutes unfair competition. Secretaries of State are usually directed by statute to accept the results of such litigation in establishing name availability.

Because corporate names are handled on a first-come first-serve basis, many state statutes permit the *reservation* of a proposed corporate name for a limited time for a nominal fee while corporate papers are prepared. This *reservation* of a corporate name should be contrasted with the *registration* of a name by a foreign Corporation permitted in some states. A *registration* of a corporate name allows a foreign Corporation with long-term plans to expand into the state to reserve the exclusive use of its name and prevent a local Corporation from using the same name.[28] A *reservation* of a name is for a brief period, usually three or four [29] months, and is usually not renewable; a *registration* is for a year or more and may be renewed indefinitely.[30]

§ 33.4 Period of Duration

All business Corporation acts now permit a Corporation to have perpetual existence.[31] In the past some statutes limited Corporations to a fifty year or some other specified life span. These provisions are now obsolete though rarely Articles are filed pro-

28. Id. § 10.

29. Id. § 9 (120 days).

30. Id. § 11.

31. Model Bus.Corp.Act § 54(b) requires that the Articles of Incorporation set forth the period of duration, "which may be perpetual."

viding for a term less than perpetual as part of internal corporate planning.

Library References:

C.J.S. Corporations § 78.
West's Key No. Digests, Corporations ⚷36.

§ 33.5 The Purposes Clause

Many state statutes provide that a Corporation may be organized for any lawful purpose or purposes, which purposes shall be "fully stated" in the Articles of Incorporation.[32] This language has often been interpreted to mean that extremely broad phrases such as "for general business purposes" or "to engage in any lawful business" are unacceptable.

The requirement that the purposes of a Corporation be "fully stated," however, has one major drawback. There is no limitation on the number of purposes for which a single Corporation may be formed. It is theoretically possible for a Corporation's purposes clause to list every conceivable business in which a Corporation may engage, including mining diamonds on the moon. Purposes clauses therefore had a tendency to become increasingly prolix, increasingly unreadable, and often completely uninformative as to what business the Corporation planned to engage in. As a result the modern trend is clearly away from the "fully stated" approach of purposes clauses, and toward the direction of requiring either no specific statement of purposes at all or a very general one, e. g., "this corporation may engage in any lawful business." Where a state permits such a clause to be used, the requirement of a purposes clause has been reduced to a formality, and there seems to be little reason to require such a clause. Even in such states, Articles may sometimes be filed with a narrow purposes clause as part of internal corporate planning.

Library References:

C.J.S. Corporations § 47.
West's Key No. Digests, Corporations ⚷14.

§ 33.6 Capitalization

The Articles of Incorporation must include information about the types or kinds of securities the Corporation is authorized to issue.[33] Separate chapters of this work are devoted to corporate securities, and the requirements applicable to Articles of Incorporation are discussed there. (See Chapters 38 and 43, infra.)

32. See e. g. Model Bus.Corp.Act § 54(c); West's Ann.Cal.Corp. Code § 202.

33. Id. § 54.

The number and par value of shares authorized need not be the number of shares actually issued—the Corporation may authorize more or the same number (but not less) shares than it issues. Those shares not issued are called "authorized but unissued" shares. These authorized but unissued shares are not the same as treasury shares. Treasury shares are shares which were once issued and outstanding (in the hands of Stockholders) and were later reacquired by the Corporation but were not retired. The Corporation owns these treasury shares and they are issued and outstanding. The importance of this is that in some states treasury shares are considered to have value and therefore in these states the annual franchise fee (if any) and intangible taxes (if any) on shares owned may be collected upon the Corporation's normal tangible and intangible assets *plus* the treasury shares held by the Corporation. When a Corporation is either incorporated or doing business in such a state, it should consider retiring such treasury stock (see § 38 of Model Bus.Corp.Act).

For additional discussion of authorized shares, see Chapter 40, infra.

The amount of franchise fees, if any, a Corporation will pay upon incorporation usually depends upon the number of shares authorized and/or the amount of par value of each of those shares. If stock has no par value, then it is often deemed to have a value of $1.00 per share for franchise fee purposes.

Often, there is a minimum franchise fee which allows the Corporation to issue a certain amount of total par value. However, any amount (equal to or in excess of par value) may be paid for these shares. It generally makes no sense to authorize a number of shares which (when multiplied by their par value) will be in total par value less than (or greater than) the minimum fee would permit. In some situations unsophisticated Stockholders will want to have the par value of the shares they receive equal their investment, and in these cases it may be necessary to authorize more stock than the minimum fee would allow in order to issue shares with a total par value equal to the Corporation's initial capital. Also, when preferred shares are being issued whose dividend, liquidation or redemption value depends upon par value, the Corporation may have to issue such preferred stock with a par value in excess of the minimum fee schedule.

In any case the value of assets transferred to the Corporation for particular shares should at least equal their par value. If it is not, the Stockholders receiving such stock will be liable for the difference.

In certain limited situations when the franchise fee is based on total par value, it may be beneficial to have the number of shares issued and their par value as low as possible. This will be the case when the book value of the Corporation's net equity is less than what was paid for the stock. This can only happen if the Corporation has been in operation and has lost money. The value of issuing a low total par value is that most annual franchise fees are based on the greater of issued par value or net book equity value. When net book equity value is very low, some franchise fee might be saved by having a low total par value for the then issued stock. However, the Corporation will not be taking advantage of the full franchise fee.

Another value in a low total par is that redemptions and dividends are limited to being paid out of capital surplus (Model Bus.Corp. Act §§ 6 and 45). The lower the par value, the more capital surplus there will be.

The way to plan for this possibility is to originally issue (a) as few shares as reasonably possible and (b) use as low a par value as reasonably possible.

One reason not to follow the above suggestion of issuing a few shares of low par value is that some lenders are of the opinion that a high par value for the Stockholder's equity shows that the Corporation is "substantial". Of course, this is not necessarily true, but their opinions should be considered in making a decision.

Example of balance sheet emphasizing equity section when low par has been used and the issue price exceeds the par value:

Value of assets to be transferred to Corporation:

$10,000 by one Stockholder.

Assume that the States minimum initial franchise fee is based upon a minimum authorized equity of $50,000.

Balance Sheet

Assets	**Net Equity**		**Liabilities**
	1,000 shares $0.01 common		
	Issued ($5,000,000 authorized)	$ 10	$0
	Capital surplus	9,990	
$10,000	Total net equity	$10,000	

The required information about types or kinds of securities in the Articles of Incorporation relates to the securities the Corporation *is authorized to issue.* In addition, the statutes of several states require disclosure of what securities *will actually be issued,* or more commonly, prohibit the Corporation from commencing business before it has received a specified minimum amount of capital. The most popular amount is $1,000, but some statutes require $500 or some other amount, and some require some specified percentage of authorized capital. Minimum capital requirements in state statutes were practically universal twenty years ago, but a large number of states, including all of the important commercial ones, have eliminated such requirements on the theory that any minimum amount of capitalization is arbitrary and does not provide meaningful protection to creditors.

The major problem with minimum capital provisions is that they take no account of the specific capital needs of the particular business. Also, the requirement of $1,000, while perhaps meaningful in the 1950's and 1960's, has become the victim of inflation and is much less significant today. The Model Business Corporation Act eliminated its minimum capitalization requirement in 1969. In states that have eliminated the minimum capitalization requirement it is theoretically possible to form a Corporation with a capitalization of one cent.

In most states with a minimum capital requirement, the principal enforcement mechanism is to make Directors who assent to the Corporation commencing business before it has received the required capital liable jointly and severally for such part of the capital as has not been received. Usually this liability terminates when the required consideration is received. A few states make the Directors personally liable for *all* corporate obligations incurred before the minimum capital was paid in, even if the shortfall of capital was small and the liabilities incurred are large.

Library References:

C.J.S. Corporations § 64 et seq.
West's Key No. Digests, Corporations ⚷16.

§ 33.7 Registered Office and Registered Agent

Every Corporation must maintain a registered office and a registered agent at that office.[34] The registered office may but need not be also the Corporation's business office. The primary purpose of a registered office and registered agent is to provide an agent for service of process. The underlying idea is that it should be possible at all times to find a Corporation and to have a person upon whom, and a place at which, any notice or process required or permitted by law may be served. A second purpose is to have an office to which tax notices and other official communications from the state may be sent. The original registered office and registered agent must usually be specified in the Articles of Incorporation; if either is changed thereafter a statement describing the change must be filed with the Secretary of State.

Often a Corporation designates its principal business office to be its registered office. In such a case, the registered agent usually is a corporate Officer or employee. The principal disadvantage of

34. See e. g., Model Bus.Corp.Act § 12; Minn.Bus.Corp.Act §§ 302A.111, 121.

this is the possibility that summons, legal documents, or other communications may be mixed in with routine business mail and not receive the attention they deserve. For this reason, many attorneys suggest that they be designated as the registered agent and their office be designated as the registered office, although they are therefore creating liability for themselves.

§ 33.8 Initial Board of Directors

In states where the incorporators meet to complete the formation of the Corporation, there is usually no requirement that the initial Board of Directors be named in the Articles of Incorporation since they will be selected by the incorporators at the initial meeting or by the Stockholders at a meeting immediately thereafter. However, in most states the role of incorporators is nominal and the organization of the Corporation is completed by the initial Directors who are named in the Articles.

Where the initial Board of Directors is named in the Articles,[35] it serves as the board until the first annual meeting of Stockholders or until the Directors' successors are elected and qualify. The first annual meeting of Stockholders may be set immediately after the organizational meeting of the initial Board of Directors so that elected Directors take office almost immediately. It is therefore possible to refer to nominal Directors (that is, directors who have no continuing interest in the business and cease to serve as Directors immediately after the organizational meeting) in the Articles. In this way disclosure of the identity of the permanent Board of Directors may be avoided. Whether or not this is desirable depends on the wishes of the clients.

Unlike incorporators or registered agents, Directors may sometimes incur liabilities by virtue of their office. Hence, it may be unwise for an attorney or his employees to serve as Directors, nominal or otherwise, though the risk may be slight as a practical matter if the directorship is for a short period.

Library References:

C.J.S. Corporations §§ 36, 48.
West's Key No. Digests, Corporations ⚷15.

§ 33.9 Corporate Powers

The Articles of Incorporation are usually not required to set forth corporate powers. Some modern statutes expressly provide

35. E. g. Model Bus.Corp.Act § 54(i) requires that the initial board be named in the Articles. See also Del. Gen.Corp.Law § 102(a)(6); Minn.Bus. Corp.Act § 302A.111.

that the Articles need not or should not set forth the powers.[36] However, a frequent practice is to include numerous power clauses, often commingling them with purpose clauses. Powers clauses should contain any desired lawful limitations on powers conferred by statute or implied apart from statute and any lawful provision for desired powers which exist only if provision is made for them in the Articles.

Modern statutes usually enumerate corporate powers, in a reasonably logical arrangement.[37]

Apart from statute, implied power not inconsistent with statute or the "statutory norm" will be recognized to do all things reasonably necessary to enable the Corporation to carry out it purposes and powers. Besides such implied powers, which defy cataloguing, are incidental powers or traditional corporate attributes:

(a) To have existence independent of the death or withdrawal of members;

(b) To sue and be sued in the corporate name;

(c) To acquire, hold, and convey property for corporate purposes in the corporate name;

(d) To have a seal;

(e) To make By-laws.

All of which may be said to inhere in a Corporation as a legal entity or in corporateness as such.

Certain statutory powers are conferred without apparent exception, other statutory powers exist unless otherwise provided in the Articles of Incorporation, and certain implied or incidental powers apart from statute clearly exist in the absence of any contrary provision in the Articles of Incorporation; and other statutory powers exist only if mentioned in the Articles of Incorporation clearly do not exist unless so mentioned. The extent to which any of the several types of powers may be amplified, limited, or denied in the Articles of Incorporation may present unresolved problems of statutory construction. Certainly, they should not be amplified beyond the bounds prescribed by statute such as statutes which prohibit a Corporation from possessing or exercising any powers unless given by law or necessary to the powers so given.

For the Corporation to enjoy powers which exist only if mentioned in the Articles of Incorporation, enumeration would be necessary. Here, too, enumeration should be within the bounds of statute and "statutory norms", and care should be taken that the enumeration is so drafted as not to exclude desired powers which would otherwise exist without mention.

36. See e. g. Model Bus.Corp.Act § 54; McKinney's N.Y.Bus.Corp.Law § 402(b); Del.Gen.Corp.Law § 102(c).

37. See e. g. Model Bus.Corp.Act § 4; Minn.Bus.Corp.Act § 302A.161; West's Ann.Cal.Corp.Code § 207; Del.Gen. Corp.Law § 121 et seq.

In summary, then, the powers clauses in the Articles of Incorporation should, at least contain any desired denials or limitations on the powers conferred by statute or implied apart from statute and any provision for desired powers which exist only if provision is made for them in the Articles, but in all such cases only to the extent lawful.

Library References:

C.J.S. Corporations § 52 et seq.
West's Key No. Digests, Corporations ⚷18.

§ 33.10 Drafting Techniques

The Articles of Incorporation must state the various matters required by statute,[38] and may include other provisions not inconsistent with law.

Such additional provisions may be specifically or generally authorized by statute.[39]

Among the provisions which in some jurisdictions may be specifically authorized by statute are those (a) authorizing cumulative or class voting;[40] (b) providing that Directors need not be Stockholders; (c) requiring that meetings of the Board of Directors be held only within the state; (d) requiring that Stockholder meetings be held only within the state; (e) imposing greater-than-normal quorum/voting requirements for Stockholder and/or Board of Directors action; (f) permitting action by unanimous written consent in lieu of a meeting by Stockholders;[41] (g) permitting action by unanimous written consent in lieu of a meeting by Directors;[42] providing for Stockholder election of Officers; (h) imposing control over Directors; (i) requiring Stockholder approval for corporate mortgages; (j) requiring indemnification of Directors, Officers, and employees by the Corporation for reasonable litigation expenses incurred by them as such in defending litigation;[43] (k) providing for

38. See § 33.1, supra.

39. E. g. Model Bus.Corp.Act §§ 18 (second paragraph), 26 (second paragraph), 27 (second sentence), 32 (second sentence), 33 (first paragraph), 35 (second sentence), 35 (last sentence), 36 (second sentence), 40 (first sentence), 40 (second sentence), 42 (first sentence), 45 (first sentence), 45(b), 45(e), 48(a), 67 (second sentence), 143 (specific references), 54(i) (general provision).

40. See Chapter 47, infra.

41. See Chapter 45, infra.

42. See Chapter 46, infra.

43. As alternatives to insertion in the Articles of Incorporation, such provisions may take the form of a Stockholder By-laws or Stockholder resolution, thereby possibly achieving broader indemnification than is possible under the standards applied by the Secretary of State in accepting for filing Articles of Incorporation containing such provisions. See Model Bus.Corp.Act § 5.

nonjudicial dissolution by a Stockholder or the holders of a specified number of proportion of shares at will or upon the occurrence of a specified event; [44] and (*l*) restricting the power of Stockholders to petition for judicial dissolution in the event of deadlock.[45]

Generally authorized by statute may be provisions regulating the business of the Corporation, the conduct of its affairs, its rights or powers, or the rights or powers of its Stockholders or Directors, not inconsistent with law, including possibly any provision required or permitted to be set forth in the By-laws. The initial language of such authorization is very broad, but the "not inconsistent with law" concluding clause is often construed by the courts as restrictive, permitting no more than possibly slight impingement on the "statutory norms".

Among provisions which may be included in the Articles of Incorporation are: those to the effect that any transaction between the Corporation and another shall not be affected because one or more of its Directors has a personal interest in the transaction or is connected with such other person; [46] provisions authorizing Stockholder removal of Directors without cause; [47] provisions reasonably restricting the transfer of shares; [48] provisions fixing the compensation for Directors or Officers or authorizing the Board of Directors to fix their own compensation.[49]

Examples of special provisions which might not be allowed in Articles of Incrporation by some Secretaries of States are: provisions that the incorporators shall assign their subscriptions immediately after incorporation; provisions delegating management of the busi-

44. See 30.66, infra.

45. See Chapter 68, infra.

46. Everett v. Phillips, 288 N.Y. 227, 43 N.E.2d 18 (1942), reargument denied 289 N.Y. 625, 43 N.E.2d 841, reargument denied 289 N.Y. 675, 45 N.E.2d 176. Such an interested director provision may be important in a close Corporation where a Director's approval might be required for matters personally affecting him, such as appointment to office, salary, loans by him to the Corporation, etc. Quaere, whether such a provision, if inserted only in the By-laws, would be valid. See e. g. Model Bus.Corp.Act § 41.

47. See e. g. Model Bus.Corp.Act § 39. Such a removal provision might validly be included in the By-laws, even without a parallel provision in the Articles of Incorporation.

48. Instead of being inserted in the Articles of Incorporation, or paralleling insertion therein, such restriction might be included in the By-laws and/or Stockholders' Agreement. In the event of multiple insertion, consistency should be maintained. Because the Articles of Incorporation and By-laws are impersonal in nature, any share transfer restriction or options of a more personal type should be effected by a Stockholders' Agreement. See § 30.51, supra and Chapter 68, supra.

49. In lieu of insertion in the Articles of Incorporation, such provisions can be included in the By-laws or a Stockholder resolution or, except for possible self-dealing complications, Board of Directors resolution.

ness to an individual or another Corporation; provisions purporting to authorize the sale of corporate assets or other extraordinary matters beyond the statutes governing such matters; absolute prohibitions on share transfers, or provisions making transfer contingent upon the consent of Directors or Stockholders, or provisions barring employees from transferring their shares and requiring them to sell their shares to the Corporation upon termination of their employment; provisions that preferred shares shall be redeemed out of surplus at a stated time, but if surplus is insufficient, steps shall be taken to reduce stated capital in order to create surplus for such purpose; provisions giving Stockholders an all-inclusive power to veto Board of Directors action;[50] provisions requiring greater-than-normal quorum/vote for Stockholder action in terms of number of shares rather than percentage; provisions authorizing various matters upon less-than-normal vote or consent of Stockholders; provisions authorizing removal of Directors without cause by the Board of Directors; provisions authorizing Directors to act otherwise than collectively as a board or giving certain Directors more than one vote; provisions that if the Directors disagree or are evenly divided, their differences should be arbitrated; provisions for the unqualified delegation of powers of the Board of Directors to an executive committee; provisions that the right of the Directors to manage the business shall be subject to the By-laws, provisions limiting the powers of Directors to appoint or remove Officers and authorizing the Stockholders to fix the compensation of officers; provisions conferring on the Board excessively broad powers to amend the By-laws; provisions for reimbursement of litigation expenses incurred by corporate personnel where the litigation is settled without court approval, or except where such person is adjudged "guilty of wilful malfeasance or misfeasance in the performance of his duties".

Thus, in jurisdictions with less modern statutes or where administrative officials adhere strictly to traditional notions, there are many restrictions on the special close Corporation provisions which may be inserted in the Articles of Incorporation. Some such provisions which may not be inserted in the Articles of Incorporation might validly be included in other documents. Statutes which give greater recognition to the special problems of the close Corporation afford more flexibility.[51]

50. However, a type of veto which empowers Stockholders or a class of Stockholders to overrule board action in *particular* matters may be acceptable.

51. See Chapter 30, supra.

§ 33.11 Check List for Use in Preparing Articles of Incorporation

1. Corporate name.

(a) Clear intended name with Secretary of State of incorporation.

(b) Clear intended name with Secretary of State of other states where Corporation intends to transact business.

(c) Desirability of trade-mark search of intended name.

(d) Desirability of filing name as a trade name.

2. Location of principal office.

(a) County.

(b) City.

(c) Street and number.

3. Resident agent.

(a) Name of individual or Corporation.

(b) Address (including street and number).

4. Purposes.

(a) Nature of business in general.

(b) Scope of activities in detail.

5. Powers.

(a) Is it desired to set out the statutory powers?

(b) Are there to be any limitations of the customary powers, such as the right to deal in real and personal property, to borrow money, to deal in securities, etc.?

6. Capital stock.

(a) Total number of shares of all classes.

(b) Number of shares of each class having a par value:
Common;
Preferred;
Other.

(c) Par value of each class:
Common;
Preferred;
Other.

(d) Number of shares without par value:
Common;
Preferred;
Other.

(e) Price at which par value stock is to be sold:
Common;
Preferred;
Other.

(f) Price at which no par value stock is to be sold:
Common;
Preferred;
Other.

(g) Are incorporators planning to exchange property for stock; if so, description and agreed value of property.

(h) How is the price at which subsequently issued stock shall be sold to be determined?

7. Characteristics of preferred stock.

(a) Dividends:
Source;
Rate;
Dates of payment;
Cumulative or noncumulative.

(b) Redemption:
Price;
Notice;
Manner.

(c) Priority of shares in event of dissolution.

(d) Conversion rights of preferred stock.

(e) Sinking fund for redemption or retirement.

8. Minimum amount of capital with which Corporation will commence business.

9. Incorporators.

(a) Names and addresses of each of the incorporators (dummies or principals).

10. Period of duration.

(a) Is Corporation to have perpetual existence?

(b) If for a fixed term, commencing ______; ceasing ______.

11. Liability of Stockholders.

(a) Is private property of Stockholders to be subject to payment of corporate debts?

12. Is the Certificate to include the provision for compromises and arrangements between the Corporation and its creditors?

13. Is the preemptive right of Stockholders to be denied?

14. Are there special situations, such as a sale of assets, which should require the approval of more than a majority of the outstanding stock?

15. Voting rights.

(a) Any limitations on the right of each Stockholder to one vote for each share of stock.

(b) Is the preferred stock to have full, limited, or no voting power?

16. Is the transfer of stock to be restricted?

17. Is there to be a provision for a stock option plan?

18. Are the Directors to have the power to amend By-laws?

19. Are the Directors to have the power to set apart reserves?

20. Is the requirement that Directors be elected by ballot to be eliminated?

§ 33.12 Skeleton Articles of Incorporation—Model Business Corporation Act

COMMENT

The following Articles of Incorporation cover only certain substantive matters. The practitioner is urged to also consult the Sophisticated Articles of Incorporation at § 33.16, infra, and the Checklist at § 33.11, supra.

ARTICLES OF INCORPORATION OF ______

The undersigned, acting as incorporator(s) of a Corporation under the ______ Business Corporation Act, adopt(s) the following Articles of Incorporation for such Corporation:

(Note 1)

First: The name of the Corporation is ______.

Second: The period of its duration is ______.

Third: The purpose or purposes for which the Corporation is organized are: ______.

Fourth: The aggregate number of shares which the Corporation shall have authority to issue is ______.

(Note 2)

Fifth: Provisions granting preemptive rights are:

(Note 3)

Sixth: Provisions for the regulation of the internal affairs of the Corporation are:

(Note 4)

Seventh: The address of the initial registered office of the Corporation is ______, and the name of its initial registered agent at such address is ______.

Eighth: The number of directors constituting the initial Board of Directors of the Corporation is ______, and the names and addresses of the persons who are to serve as Directors until the first annual meeting of Stockholders or until their successors are elected and shall qualify are:

Name	**Address**
______________________	______________________
______________________	______________________
______________________	______________________

Ninth: The name and address of each incorporator is:

Name	**Address**
______________________	______________________
______________________	______________________
______________________	______________________

Dated ______, 19__.

____

____

____

Incorporator(s) (Note 5)

1. One or more persons or domestic or foreign Corporations may be the incorporator or incorporators.

2. If the authorized shares are to consist of one class only, insert a statement of the par value of such shares or a statement that all of such shares are to be without par value. [Note: The Model Business Corporation Act no longer provides for par value shares.]

If the authorized shares are to be divided into classes, insert a statement of the number of shares of each class, a statement of the par value of the shares of each such class or that such shares are to be without par value, and a statement of the preferences, limitations and relative rights in respect of the shares of each class.

If the authorized shares of any preferred or special class are to be issued in series, insert a statement of the designation of each series, a statement of the variations in the relative rights and preferences as between series insofar as the same are to be fixed in the Articles of Incorporation, and a statement of any authority to be vested in the Board of Directors to establish series and fix and determine the variations in the relative rights and preferences as between series.

3. If preemptive rights are not to be granted, omit this article or insert "None."

4. If no provisions for the regulation of the internal affairs of the Corporation are to be set forth, omit this article or insert "None."

5. Corporate incorporators should sign by a duly authorized officer.

Source of Form

Form No. 11 (Model Bus.Corp.Act § 54), Official Forms for Use Under the 1969 Revision of the Model Business Corporation Act, prepared by the Committee on Corporate Laws of the American Bar Association.

§ 33.13 Skeleton Articles of Incorporation—Model Business Corporation Act (Alternative Short Form)

COMMENT

The following Articles of Incorporation cover only certain substantive matters. The practitioner is urged to also consult the Sophisticated Articles of Incorporation at § 33.16, infra, and the Checklist at § 33.11, supra.

ARTICLES OF INCORPORATION*

1. The name of the Corporation is ______.

2. The period of its duration is perpetual.

3. Its purpose is to transact the business of ______ and all other business not forbidden by law.

4. It shall have authority to issue ______ shares, all of one class, ______ par value.**

5. The address of its initial registered office is ______. The name of its initial registered agent at such address is ______.

6. The number of Directors constituting its initial Board of Directors is ______, whose name(s) and address(es) is (are):

____

____

____

*** ______________________
Signature of Incorporator

Dated ______, 19__.

* This is a shorter alternative to Form No. 11.

** The Model Bus.Corp.Act no longer provides for par value shares.

*** If more than one incorporator, add additional blanks.

Source of Form

Form No. 12 (Model Bus.Corp.Act § 54), Official Forms for Use Under the 1969 Revision of the Model Business Corporation Act, prepared by the Committee on Corporate Laws of the American Bar Association.

§ 33.14 Articles of Incorporation—Delaware (1967 General Corporation Law)

COMMENT

The following Articles of Incorporation cover only certain substantive matters. The practitioner is urged to also consult the Sophisticated Articles of Incorporation at § 33.16, infra, and the Checklist at § 33.11, supra.

CERTIFICATE OF INCORPORATION
OF
______ CORPORATION

§ 1. **Name.** The name of the Corporation is ______ Corporation.

§ 2. **Registered Office and Registered Agent.** The address of the Corporation's registered office in Delaware is ______ Street in the City of ______ and County of ______, and the name of its registered agent at such address is ______.

§ 3. **Purposes.** The purpose of the Corporation is to engage in any lawful act or activity for which Corporations may be now or hereafter organized under the General Corporation Law of Delaware.

Alternative A

§ 4. **Capital Stock (Providing for One Class of Par Value Stock).** The Corporation is authorized to issue only one class of stock. The total number of such shares is ______ and the par value of each of such shares is ______ dollars.

Alternative B

§ 4. **Capital Stock (Providing for Two Classes of Stock, One Voting and One Non-voting).** The total number of shares of all classes of stock which the Corporation shall have authority to issue is ______, all of which are to be without par value. ______ of such shares shall be Class A voting shares and ______ of such shares shall be Class B non-voting shares. The Class A shares and the Class B shares shall have identical rights except that the Class B shares shall not entitle the holder thereof to vote on any matter unless specifically required by law.

Alternative C

§ 4. Capital Stock (providing for two classes of stock, preferred and common). The total number of shares of all classes of capital stock which the Corporation shall have authority to issue is ______ shares, of which ______ shares shall be shares of Preferred Stock without par value (hereinafter called "Preferred Stock"), and ______ shares shall be shares of Common Stock of the par value of $______ per share (hereinafter called "Common Stock").

Any amendment to the Certificate of Incorporation which shall increase or decrease the authorized capital stock of the Corporation may be adopted by the affirmative vote of the holders of a majority of the outstanding shares of stock of the Corporation entitled to vote.

The designations and the powers, preferences and rights, and the qualifications, limitations or restrictions thereof, of the Preferred Stock shall be as follows:

(1) The Board of Directors is expressly authorized at any time, and from time to time, to provide for the issuance of shares of Preferred Stock in one or more series, with such voting powers full or limited but not to exceed one vote per share, or without voting powers and with such designations, preferences and relative, participating, optional or other special rights, and qualifications, limitations or restrictions thereof, as shall be expressed in the resolution or resolutions providing for the issue thereof adopted by the Board of Directors and as are not expressed in this Certificate of Incorporation or any amendment thereto, including (but without limiting the generality of the foregoing) the following:

(a) the designation of such series;

(b) the dividend rate of such series, the conditions and dates upon which such dividends shall be payable, the preference or relation which such dividends shall bear to the dividends payable on any other class or classes or on any other series of any class or classes of capital stock of the Corporation, and whether such dividends shall be cumulative or noncumulative;

(c) whether the shares of such series shall be subject to redemption by the Corporation, and, if made subject to such redemption, the times, prices and other terms and conditions of such redemption;

(d) the terms and amount of any sinking fund provided for the purchase or redemption of the shares of such series;

(e) whether the shares of such series shall be convertible into or exchangeable for shares of any other class or classes or of any other series of any class or classes of capital stock of the Corporation, and, if provision be made for conversion or exchange, the times, prices, rates, adjustments, and other terms and conditions of such conversion or exchange;

(f) the extent, if any, to which the holders of the shares of such series shall be entitled to vote as a class or otherwise with respect to the election of Directors or otherwise; provided, however, that in no event shall any holder of any series of Preferred Stock be entitled to more than one vote for each share of such Preferred Stock held by him;

(g) the restrictions and conditions, if any, upon the issue or reissue of any additional Preferred Stock ranking on a parity with or prior to such shares as to dividends or upon dissolution;

(h) the rights of the holders of the shares of such series upon the dissolution of, or upon the distribution of assets of, the Corporation, which rights may be different in the case of a voluntary dissolution than in the case of an involuntary dissolution.

(2) Except as otherwise required by law and except for such voting powers with respect to the election of Directors or other matters as may be stated in the resolutions of the Board of Directors creating any series of Preferred Stock, the holders of any such series shall have no voting power whatsoever.

5. **Incorporators.** The names and mailing addresses of the incorporators are:

Name	Mailing Address
____________	____________
____________	____________

Option

§ 6. **Initial Directors (if the Powers of the Incorporator or Incorporators Are to Terminate Upon the Filing of the Certificate of Incorporation).** The names and mailing addresses of the persons who are to to serve as Directors until the first annual meeting of Stockholders or until their successors are elected and qualify are:

Name	Mailing Address
____________	____________
____________	____________

Option

§ 7. Regulatory Provisions. The following additional provisions are inserted for the management of the business and for the conduct of the affairs of the Corporation, and creating, defining, limiting, and regulating the powers of the Corporation, the Directors and the Stockholders, or any class of Stockholders.

(a) Power of Directors to Amend Bylaws. The Board of Directors is authorized and empowered from time to time in its discretion to make, alter or repeal the By-laws of the Corporation, except as such power may be limited by any one or more By-laws of the Corporation adopted by the Stockholders.

(b) Books. The books of the Corporation (subject to the provisions of the laws of the State of Delaware) may be kept outside of the State of Delaware at such places as from time to time may be designated by the Board of Directors.

(c) Cumulative Voting. At all elections of Directors of the Corporation, each Stockholder shall be entitled to as many votes as shall equal the number of votes which he would be entitled to cast for the election of Directors with respect to his shares of stock multiplied by the number of Directors to be elected, and that he may cast all of such votes for a single Director or may distribute them among the number to be voted for, or for any two or more of them as he may see fit.

(d) Consent of Stockholders in Lieu of Meeting. Whenever the vote of Stockholders at a meeting thereof is required or permitted to be taken for or in connection with any corporate action by any provision of the General Corporation Law of the State of Delaware the meeting and vote of Stockholders may be dispensed with if such action is taken with the written consent of the holders of not less than a majority of all the stock entitled to be voted upon such action if a meeting were held; provided that in no case shall the written consent be by the holders of stock having less than the minimum percentage of the vote required by statute for such action, and provided that prompt notice is given to all Stockholders of the taking of corporate action without a meeting and by less than unanimous written consent.

(e) Elections of Directors. Elections of Directors need not be by written ballot.

(f) Removal of Directors. The Stockholders may at any time, at a meeting expressly called for that purpose, remove any or all of the Directors, with or without cause, by a vote of the holders of a majority of the shares then entitled to vote at an election of Directors. No Director may be removed when the votes cast against his removal would be sufficient to elect him if voted cumulatively at an election at which

the same total number of votes were cast and the entire Board were then being elected. [*When by the provisions of the Certificate of Incorporation the holders of the shares of any class or series, voting as a class, are entitled to elect one or more Directors, any Director so elected may be removed only by the applicable vote of the holders of the shares of that class or series, voting as a class.*]

Option

§ 8. **Creditor Arrangements.** Whenever a compromise or arrangement is proposed between this Corporation and its creditors or any class of them and/or between this Corporation and its Stockholders or any class of them, any court of equitable jurisdiction within the State of Delaware may, on the application in a summary way of this Corporation or of any creditor or Stockholder thereof or on the application of any receiver or receivers appointed for this Corporation under the provisions of section 291 of Title 8 of the Delaware Code or on the application of trustees in dissolution or of any receiver or receivers appointed for this Corporation under the provisions of section 279 of Title 8 of the Delaware Code order a meeting of the creditors or class of creditors, and/or of the Stockholders or class of Stockholders of this Corporation, as the case may be, to be summoned in such manner as the said court directs. If a majority in number representing three-fourths in value of the creditors or class of creditors, and/or of the Stockholders or class of Stockholders of this Corporation, as the case may be, agree to any compromise or arrangement and to any reorganization of this Corporation as consequence of such compromise or arrangement, the said compromise or arrangement and the said reorganization shall, if sanctioned by the court to which the said application has been made, be binding on all the creditors or class of creditors, and/or on all the Stockholders or class of Stockholders, of this Corporation, as the case may be, and also on this Corporation.

Option

§ 9. **Preemptive Rights.** The holders from time to time of the shares of the Corporation shall have the preemptive right to purchase, at such respective equitable prices, terms, and conditions as shall be fixed by the Board of Directors, such of the shares of the Corporation as may be issued, from time to time, over and above the issue of the first ______ shares of the Corporation which have never previously been sold. Such preemptive right shall apply to all shares issued after such first ______ shares, whether such additional shares constitute a part of the shares presently or subsequently authorized or constitute shares held in the treasury of the Corporation, and shall be exercised in the respective ratio which the number of shares held by each Stockholder at the time of such issue bears to the total number of shares outstanding in the names of all Stockholders at such time.

§ 10. Greater Voting Requirements. The affirmative vote of a majority of the Directors shall be necessary for the transaction of any business at any meeting of Directors, except in the case of a proposal to borrow money on the Corporation's credit, in which case the favorable vote of all of the Directors shall be necessary.

Option

§ 11. Duration. The duration of the Corporation's existence shall extend for the period beginning on the date the Certificate of Incorporation of the Corporation is filed with the Secretary of State of Delaware, and ending December 31, 19__.

Option

§ 12. Personal Liability. The Stockholders shall be liable for the debts of the Corporation in the proportion that their stock bears to the total outstanding stock of the Corporation.

§ 13. Amendment. The Corporation reserves the right to amend, alter, change or repeal any provision contained in the Certificate of Incorporation, in the manner now or hereafter prescribed by statute, and all rights conferred upon Stockholders herein are granted subject to this reservation.

We, the undersigned, being all of the incorporators above named, for the purpose of forming a Corporation pursuant to the General Corporation Law of Delaware, sign and acknowledge this Certificate of Incorporation this 1st day of ______, 19__.

Acknowledgment

STATE OF __________ }
County of __________ } ss.

On this ______ day of ______, 19__, before me personally came ______, one of the persons who signed the foregoing certificate of incorporation, known to me personally to be such, and acknowledged that the said certificate is his act and deed and that the facts stated therein are true.

____
Notary Public

[*Seal*]

§ 33.15 Basic Articles of Incorporation

COMMENT

The following Articles of Incorporation cover only certain substantive matters. The practitioner is urged to also consult the Sophisticated Articles of Incorporation at § 33.16, infra, and the Checklist at § 33.11, supra.

ARTICLES OF INCORPORATION

These Articles of Incorporation are signed by the Incorporator(s) for the purpose of forming a profit Corporation as follows:

Library References:

C.J.S. Corporations, § 52 et seq.
West's Key No. Digests, Corporations ⚷18.

Required by Statute

Article I

NAME

§ 1.1 Name

The name of the Corporation is [*Name*].

COMMENTS TO ARTICLE I

The Articles must set forth the corporate name (Model Bus. Corp.Act § 54).

The corporate name:

(a) Shall contain the word "corporation," "company," "incorporated" or "limited," or shall contain an abbreviation of one of these words.

(b) Shall not contain any word or phrase which indicates or implies that it is organized for any purpose other than one or more of the purposes contained in its Articles of Incorporation.

(c) Shall not be the same as, or deceptively similar to, the name of any domestic Corporation existing or authorized to do business under the laws of the state of incorporation, or a name the exclusive right to which is, at the time, reserved or registered in the relevant state of incorporation, except that this provision shall not apply if the Corporation files the written consent of such other Corporation or holder of a reserved name to use the same or deceptively similar name and one or more words are added to make such name distinguishable from such other name (Model Bus. Corp. Act § 8).

For additional discussion of corporate name, see 33.3, supra.

Required in Some Form by Statute

Article II
PURPOSE

§ 2.1 Purpose

The purpose or purposes for which the Corporation is organized is to transact all lawful business for which Corporations may be organized under the Business Corporation Act of [*State of Incorporation*].

COMMENTS TO ARTICLE II

The Articles must state the purposes for which the Corporation has been organized. They are permitted to state that "the Corporation was organized to transact all lawful business for which Corporations may be organized."

Professional Corporations are generally required to state a specific purpose (see Chapter 85, infra).

In some cases the Stockholders may fear that the Board may engage in business transactions which the Stockholders have not contemplated. In these cases, the Articles should set forth the specific purpose(s) for which the Corporation has been organized so that the Board will be appropriately restricted (see § 33.16, infra, for examples).

The problem with specifying a corporate purpose is that it may be used by the Internal Revenue Service against the Corporation's claim that the sale of a particular piece of corporate property was *not* in the ordinary course of corporate business and therefore is not entitled to capital gain treatment.

For additional discussion pertaining to corporate "purpose", see § 30.5, supra.

Required in Some Form by Statute

Article III
SHARES

§ 3.1 Authorized Stock

The total authorized stock is ______ common shares of ______ par value per share.

COMMENTS TO ARTICLE III

This form is only for a simple incorporation where only one class of common stock is to be issued. If more than one class of common is to be issued or if preferred stock is to be issued see Chapter 40, infra, for the appropriate form.

Article IV

NO NEED FOR ACTUAL STOCKHOLDER MEETING

Alternative A (If Allowed, Preferred as a Matter of Practical Experience)

§ 4.1 Majority Consent Voting

Any action required or permitted by the Business Corporation Act of [*State of Incorporation*] at an annual or special meeting of Stockholders may be taken without a meeting, without prior written notice and without a vote if consented to in writing by the holders of outstanding shares having at least the minimum number of votes necessary to authorize or ratify such action if taken at a meeting at which all shares entitled to vote were present and voted. Prompt written notice of the taking of said action shall be given to the non-consenting Stockholders by (among other methods) mailing said notice to said Stockholders by first class mail, postage prepaid, to their address of record.

Alternative B (Not Generally Preferred as a Matter of Practical Experience)

§ 4.1 Unanimous Consent Voting

Any action of the Stockholders may be taken with the unanimous written consent or a meeting.

COMMENTS TO ARTICLE IV

(a) Many modern corporation statutes (but not the Model Bus.Corp.Act) permit one of the following:

(1) Actions may be taken without a Stockholders meeting and without unanimous consent if the procedure is specifically authorized in the Articles of Incorporation with certain exceptions; or

(2) Actions may be taken without unanimous consent unless specifically prohibited in the Articles of Incorporation.

(b) If the Corporation is closely held, then one of these provisions are highly recommended for the following reasons:

(1) The controlling Stockholders will control the voting at the Stockholder meeting in any case.

(2) Stockholder meetings are often hard to arrange. Consents to the waiver and/or notices of the meeting are often not obtained at the correct time, thus jeopardizing the validity of the meeting.

(3) Often business must be conducted quickly and this procedure will speed the approval process.

The problem with the procedure of Alternative A is it does not give an articulate or well-informed Stockholder the right to pursuade others of his views.

For additional discussion of consent voting, see Chapter 47, infra.

Required by Statute

Article V

DIRECTORS

§ 5.1 Initial Directors

The initial Board shall consist of ______ Directors and the names and addresses of the persons who shall serve as Directors until the first annual meeting of Stockholders or until their successors can be elected and qualified are:

____________________	____________________
Name	Address
____________________	____________________
Name	Address

COMMENTS TO ARTICLE V

This information is required by Model Bus.Corp.Act. § 54.

The number of Directors of a closely held Corporation should generally be a number which just meets minimum statutory requirements (Model Bus.Corp.Act. § 36) and which is convenient to assemble for a meeting.

It is recommended that when the Corporation is closely held that the Board include only persons who are familiar with the day to day operations of the Corporation. The reasons for this are:

(a) Directors face substantial personal liability.

(b) The input of consultants is generally only required on an intermittent basis.

(c) If a consultant is a CPA, he will not be able to certify to the independence of the opinion if he is on the Board.

(d) If the consultant is an attorney, he will not be able to render truly independent advice if he is on the Board.

(e) The Corporation may want to seek outside advice and ignore the advice of normal advisors. This will be more difficult if the advisor being ignored is a Board member.

Board seats are often given to loyal employees, although it should be always remembered that in situations of adversity a majority of the Board can meet and a majority of that majority can act. Thus, one or a few dissidents could control the Board in unusual circumstances.

Only one Director is required under Model Bus.Corp.Act § 36. For additional discussion of Directors, see Chapter 46, infra.

Required by Statute

Article VI

REGISTERED OFFICE

§ 6.1 Registered Office

The address of the initial registered office is:

______________	______________	______________
(No. and Street)	(Town or City)	(State and Zip Code)

The mailing address of the initial registered office is:

______________	______________	______________
(No. and Street)	(Town or City)	(State and Zip Code)

COMMENTS TO ARTICLE VI

The Articles must state the address of the Corporation's initial registered office and the name of its initial registered agent at such address. The registered office need not be the same as the Corporation's place of business (Model Bus.Corp.Act § 12).

The registered agent may either be an individual resident or a Corporation authorized to do business in the State so long as he, she or its business office is identical to the registered office (Model Bus.Corp.Act § 12).

The purpose of the registered office is to designate a place where the service of legal documents can occur. The registered agent should be responsible enough to contact appropriate advisors upon the receipt of any legal documents and tax forms.

Required by Statute

Article VII

INCORPORATORS

§ 7.1 Incorporators

The name(s) and business address(es) of the Incorporator(s) are as follows:

Name	**Address**
______________	______________
______________	______________
______________	______________

COMMENTS TO ARTICLE VII

One or more persons may be the incorporator(s) of the Corporation. There is no need for such person(s) to ultimately become Stockholders (Model Bus.Corp.Act § 53). The name and address of each Incorporator must be stated (Model Bus.Corp.Act § 54).

For additional discussion of incorporators, see Chapter 32, supra.

Required by Statute

Article VIII

TERM

§ 8.1 Term

The term of existence of the Corporation shall be *perpetual.*

COMMENTS TO ARTICLE VIII

The Articles must state the period of corporate duration (Model Bus.Corp.Act § 54). See also § 33.4, supra, this Chapter.

Required in Order to Get Practical Result Sought

Article IX

EFFECTIVE DATE

COMMENT TO ARTICLE IX

When a Corporation wants to limit its authority to do business until a certain date in the future, this provision will be necessary. A Corporation can not be retroactively incorporated.

§ 9.1 Effective Date

The effective date of Incorporation shall be [*fill in date*].

In witness whereof, the undersigned, the incorporator(s) of the above-named Corporation, [*has (have)*] hereunto signed these Articles of Incorporation on this ______ day of ______, 19__.

______________________	______________________
[*Type Name Under Signature*]	Address
______________________	______________________
	Address
______________________	______________________
	Address

GENERAL COMMENT

The following are possible Article of Incorporation clauses not included in the above form:

(1) Cumulative Voting (See § 7.10 of § 33.16, infra).

(2) Preemptive Rights (§ 18.1 of § 33.16, infra).

(3) Indemnification of Board members, Directors and agents (Art. 20 of § 33.16, infra).

(4) Stockholder restrictions on sale of stock (Chapter 52, infra).

(5) More than one class of common stock (Chapter 40, infra).

(6) Preferred stock (Chapter 40, infra).

(7) Specific Purpose Clauses (Art. II of § 33.16, infra).

(8) Specific Power Clauses (Art. III of § 33.16, infra).

(9) Form of Stock Certificate (Chapter 40, infra).

(10) Stockholder meetings (Art. V of § 33.16, infra).

(11) Stockholder voting (Art. VI of § 33.16, infra).

(12) Amendment of Articles (Chapter 51, infra).

(13) Stockholders control number of Directors (§ 9.2 of § 33.16, infra).

(14) Special Percentage for Board voting (§ 10.1 of § 33.16, infra).

(15) Board voting procedures (§ 11.1 of § 33.16, infra).

(16) Board powers (§ 11.6 of § 33.16, infra).

(17) Classes of Directors (§ 11.12 of § 33.16, infra).

(18) By-laws (Art. XII of § 33.16, infra).

(19) Dividends (Art. XIII of § 33.16, infra).

(20) Changes in Balance Sheet (Art. XIV of § 33.16, infra).

(21) Record Book (Art. XV of § 33.16, infra).

(22) Conflicts in interest (Art. XVI of § 33.16, infra).

(23) Committees (Art. XVII of § 33.16, infra).

(24) Corporate Director, Officer and agent liability (Art. XIX of § 33.16, infra).

(25) Close Corporation Election (Art. XXI of § 33.16, infra).

§ 33.16 Sophisticated Articles of Incorporation

The following form is presented as a comprehensive set of possible provisions for Articles of Incorporation. It should be noted that many of these provisions are mutually exclusive or serve conflicting goals. Accordingly, care must be taken in selecting and tailoring such provisions to the particular wishes of the incorporators and to the needs of the type of business contemplated. Also, of course, reference must be made to the requirements of state statutes governing Articles of Incorporation.

Table of Sections

Article XII. By-laws

Section

12.1 Initial By-laws.
12.2 Emergency By-laws.
12.3 Officers.

Article XIII. Dividends

Section

13.1 Dividends in General.
13.2 Dividends to Other Classes.
13.3 Class Split-Ups.

Article XIV. Changes in Balance Sheet

Section

14.1 Reductions in Stated Capital.
14.2 Increase in Stated Capital.
14.3 Elimination of Deficits.
14.4 Creation of Reserves.

Article XV. Record Book and Financial Statements

Section

15.1 Books.
15.2 Inspection of Books.
15.3 Financial Statements.

Article XVI. Conflicts in Interest

Section

16.1 Contracts with Directors and Officers.
16.2 Lending to Directors.

Article XVII. Board Has Power to Appoint a Committee

Section

17.1 Committees.
17.2 Denial of Authority.
17.3 Further Denials of Authority.
17.4 Meetings.

Article XVIII. Preemptive Rights

Section

18.1 Preemptive Rights.

Article XIX. Board of Director, Officer, Employee and Agent Liability

Section

19.1 Stock Transfer Liability.
19.2 General Director Liability.
19.3 Refusal to Allow Inspection of Books.

Article XX. Indemnification of Directors, Officers, Employees and Agents

Section

20.1 Indemnification. (Alternative A)
20.1 Indemnification. (Alternative B)
20.2 Insurance.

Article XXI. Special Provisions for Close Corporations Requiring a Special Statutory Election

Section

21.1 Special Provisions for Close Corporations Requiring a Special Statutory Election.

Article XXII. Redemption of Shares

Section

22.1 Redemption of Shares.

Article XXIII. Dissolution

Section

23.1 Non-Judicial Dissolution.

Article XXIV. Registered Office

Section

24.1 Office.

Article XXV. Incorporators

Section

25.1 Incorporators.

Article XXVI. Term

Section

26.1 Term.

Article XXVII. Effective Date

Section

27.1 Effective Date.

ARTICLES OF INCORPORATION

These Articles of Incorporation are signed by the incorporator(s) for the purpose of forming a profit Corporation as follows:

Required by Statute

Article I

NAME

§ 1.1 Name

The name of the Corporation is ________.

COMMENTS TO ARTICLE I

The Articles must set forth the corporate name (Model Bus. Corp.Act § 54).

The corporate name:

(a) Shall contain the word "corporation," "company," "incorporated" or "limited," or shall contain an abbreviation of one of such words.

(b) Shall not contain any word or phrase which indicates or implies that it is organized for any purpose other than one or more of the purposes contained in its Articles of Incorporation.

(c) Shall not be the same as, or deceptively similar to, the name of any Corporation existing or authorized to do business under the laws of the State of Incorporation, or a name the exclusive right to which is, at the time, reserved or registered (see § 33.3, supra) except that this provision shall not apply if the Corporation files the written consent of such other Corporation or holder of a reserved or registered name to use the same or deceptively similar name and one or more words are added to make such name distinguishable from such other name (Model Bus.Corp.Act § 8).

For additional discussion of corporate name, see § 33.3, supra.

Required by Statute in Some Form

Alternative A

Article II

PURPOSE

§ 2.1 General

The purpose for which the Corporation is organized is to transact all lawful business for which Corporations may be organized under the Business Corporation Act of [*State of Incorporation*].

Alternative B

§ 2.1 Agent

The purpose for which the Corporation is organized is to represent, consult with, render reports to, and act as agent or independent contractor for the following types of concerns: ______; and to represent their interests and pursue their goals in every manner as if their purposes and goals were the purposes and goals of this Corporation.

Alternative C

§ 2.1 Brokerage

The purpose for which the Corporation is organized is to arrange for the import, export, trade, purchase, sale, consignment and warehousing of the following: ______; and to act as agent for others who want to accomplish the same.

Alternative D

§ 2.1 Farming

The purpose for which the Corporation is organized is to cultivate, raise, grow, produce and sell the following products: ______.

Alternative E

§ 2.1 Finance

The purpose for which the Corporation is organized is to subscribe for, acquire, purchase, invest in and deal in, interests in public and private security offerings and to underwrite and participate in security offerings of every type, including stock, securities, warrants, options, bonds, notes, indentures and other secured and unsecured equity and debt instruments.

Alternative F

§ 2.1 Holding Company

The purpose for which the Corporation is organized is to acquire, invest in, hold, distribute, hypothecate and sell interests in other partnerships and corporate business enterprises, and to exercise all of the powers of an interest holder under the terms of such entities' charters and By-laws.

Alternative G

§ 2.1 Management

The purpose for which the Corporation is organized is to render accounts receivable, accounts payable, organizational, sales, inventory, manufacturing, financial advance planning and technical advice to the following types of businesses: ______; and to aid said businesses' general manufacturing, merchandizing, organization, reorganization and operations and to act as promoter, investigator, systems analyzer, agent, representative and consultant for said business operations.

Alternative H

§ 2.1 Manufacture

The purpose for which the Corporation is organized is to manufacture, fabricate and assemble the following products: ______; and to sell, lease and otherwise promote and deal in the same and in related products and services and to manufacture, fabricate and assemble the tools, materials and equipment reasonably necessary for such manufacturing processes.

Alternative I

§ 2.1 Publication and Broadcasting

The purpose for which the Corporation is organized is to create, prepare, draft, design, print, broadcast and publish material relating to the following subject matters: ______ in and for all forms of broadcasting and publication including radio, television, newspapers, magazines, and all other forms of commercial and noncommercial media.

Alternative J

§ 2.1 Real Estate

The purpose for which the Corporation is organized is to operate, manage, improve, repair, rent, lease, own, acquire, sell, assign, mortgage, hypothecate, and otherwise deal in real property and its appurtenances and fixtures and to deal in direct interests, partnership interests, stockholder interests and joint venture interests which represent shares in such property and to build or contract for the building of buildings and other structures on such property.

Alternative K

§ 2.1 Research

The purpose for which the Corporation is organized is to conduct under its employment (through independent contracts or joint ventures) research, design and development of the following: ______; and to experiment, test and test market the products, services and processes resulting from such research and development and to investigate, consult, report, and render advice as to the development of similar products and the techniques and methods of their manufacture and sale.

Alternative L

§ 2.1 Sales

The purpose for which the Corporation is organized is to lease, sell, import, export and to finance purchases and sales of the following products and services: ______; and to promote the sale thereof and to install, maintain and improve the products so sold and to maintain an inventory of the products to be sold and their repair parts and to finance such inventory by factoring or other forms of finance or hypothecation.

Alternative M

§ 2.1 Service Business

The purpose for which the Corporation is organized is to render the following services: ______; and to own and operate the associated facilities, equipment and real estate to render such services.

Alternative N

§ 2.1 School

The purpose for which the Corporation is organized is to conduct educational training in the following areas: ______.

Alternative O

§ 2.1 Wholesale

The purpose for which the Corporation is organized is to purchase, sell, warehouse, hold, take on consignment, receive, store, forward, factor, collaterally assign and otherwise borrow against and finance inventory of the following kind and nature: ______.

COMMENTS TO ALTERNATIVES A–O:

The Articles must state the purposes for which the Corporation has been organized. They are permitted to merely state that the Corporation is organized to transact all lawful business for which Corporations may be organized (Model Bus.Corp.Act § 3).

Professional Corporations are generally required to state a specific purpose (see Div. VII, infra, for examples).

In some jurisdictions, Corporations are required to state a specific purpose.

Stockholders may fear that the Board may engage in business transactions which the Stockholders have not contemplated. In these cases, the Articles should set forth the specific purpose(s) for which the Corporation has been organized so that the Board will be appropriately restricted.

A danger in specifying a corporate purpose is that it may be used by the Internal Revenue Service to claim that the sale of a particular piece of corporate property was in the ordinary course of corporate business and therefore is not entitled to capital gain treatment.

For additional discussion of corporate "purpose", see § 33.5, supra.

Article III

POWERS OF THE CORPORATION

Use if Specific Powers Are to Be Listed (These Are Preferred)

§ 3.1 Powers

As needed to pursue the corporate purposes, the following powers are hereby granted to the Board of Directors:

(a) To sue, complain and defend in the corporate name.

(b) To adopt a corporate seal which may be altered at pleasure, and to use the same by causing it, or a facsimile thereof, to be impressed or affixed or in any other manner reproduced.

(c) To purchase, take, receive, lease, or otherwise acquire, own, hold, improve, use and otherwise deal in and with, real or personal property, or any interest therein, wherever situated.

(d) To sell, convey, mortgage, pledge, lease, exchange, transfer and otherwise dispose of all or any part of the corporate property and assets.

(e) To lend money and use its credit to assist corporate employees.

(f) To purchase, take, receive, subscribe for, or otherwise acquire, own, hold, vote, use, employ, sell, mortgage, lend, pledge, or otherwise dispose of, and otherwise use and deal in and with, shares or other interests in, or obligations of, other domestic or foreign corporations, associations, partnerships or individuals, or direct or indirect obligations of the United States or of any other government, state, territory, governmental district or municipality or of any instrumentality thereof.

(g) To make contracts and guarantees and incur liabilities, borrow money at such rates of interest as it may determine, issue its notes, bonds, and other obligations, and secure any of its obligations by mortgage or pledge of all or any of the Corporation's property and income.

(h) To lend money for any corporate purpose, invest and reinvest its funds, and take and hold their payment of funds so loaned or invested.

(i) To conduct its business, carry on its operations and have offices and exercise the powers granted herein, within or without this state.

(j) To make donations for the public welfare or for charitable, scientific or educational purposes.

(k) To transact any lawful business which the Board of Directors shall find will be an aid of governmental policy.

(*l*) To pay pensions and establish pension plans, pension trusts, profit sharing plans, stock bonus plans, stock option plans and other incentive plans for any or all of its Directors, Officers and employees.

COMMENTS

Corporate powers are, generally, implied and statutorily granted. Therefore none need be specified. However, listing the corporate powers will have the following benefits:

(1) It will satisfy the rule that a document should be reasonably complete.

(2) It will remind the advisers and Directors and Officers what powers are granted.

This list is the list of corporate powers statutorily granted (Model Bus.Corp.Act § 54). It is probably impossible for the Stockholders to deny these powers to themselves. However, they can deny these powers to the Board of Directors (Model Bus.Corp. Act § 35).

For additional discussion of corporate powers, see § 33.9, supra.

Not Generally Preferred as Being too Restrictive

§ 3.2 Limitations

The Corporation's Board of Directors or its agents shall not exercise the following powers:

(a) Sue, complain and defend, in the corporate name.

(b) Purchase, take, receive, lease, or otherwise acquire, own, hold, improve, use and otherwise deal in and with, real or personal property, or any interest therein, wherever situated.

(c) Sell, convey, mortgage, pledge, lease, exchange, transfer and otherwise dispose of all or any part of the corporate property and assets.

(d) Lend money and use its credit to assist corporate employees.

(e) Purchase, take, receive, subscribe for, or otherwise acquire, own, hold, vote, use, employ, sell, mortgage, lend, pledge, or otherwise dispose of, and otherwise use and deal in and with, shares or other interests in, or obligations of, other domestic or foreign corporations, associations, partnerships or individuals, or direct or indirect obligations of the United States or of any other government, state, territory, governmental district or municipality or of any instrumentality thereof.

(f) Make contracts and guarantees and incur liabilities, borrow money, issue its notes, bonds, and other obligations, or secure any obligation by mortgage or pledge of all or any of the Corporation's property and income.

(g) Lend money for any purpose.

(h) Conduct its business, carry on its operations and have offices and exercise the powers granted herein, without this state.

(i) Make donations for the public welfare or for charitable, scientific or educational purposes.

(j) Pay pensions and establish pension plans, pension trusts, profit sharing plans, stock bonus plans, stock option plans and other incentive plans for any or all of its Directors, Officers or employees.

(k) Be a promoter, partner, member, associate, or manager of any partnership, joint venture, trust or other enterprise.

Article IV

SHARES

Required by Statute in Some Form

Alternative A

§ 4.1 Authorized Shares

The total authorized stock is: ______ common shares of par value per share.

COMMENTS TO ALTERNATIVE A

This form is only for an Incorporation where only one class of common stock is to be issued. See Chapter 40, infra, if more than one class of common is to be issued or if preferred stock is to be issued. Call rights are set forth in Article XXII, infra.

Not Preferred Because, as a Matter of Practical Experience, This Provision Is Preferably Included in the By-Laws

§ 4.2 Certificates

The shares of a Corporation shall be represented by certificates signed by the President or a Vice-President and the Secretary or an Assistant Secretary of the Corporation, and may be sealed with the seal of the Corporation or a facsimile thereof. The signatures of the President or Vice-President and the Secretary or Assistant Secretary upon a certificate may be facsimiles if the certificate is manually signed on behalf of a transfer agent or a registrar, other than the Corporation itself or an employee of the Corporation. In case any Officer who has signed or whose facsimile signature has been placed upon such certificate shall have ceased to be such officer before such certificate is issued, it may be issued by the Corporation with the same effect as if he were such Officer at the date of its issue.

COMMENTS TO § 4.2

This section repeats Model Bus.Corp.Act § 23.

For additional discussion of share certificates, see Chapter 40, infra.

Article V
STOCKHOLDER MEETINGS

Not Preferred Because as a Matter of Practical Experience These Provisions Are Preferably Included in the By-laws

§ 5.1 Meetings

Meetings of Stockholders may be held at such place within or without this state as may be stated in or fixed in accordance with the By-laws. If other place is stated or so fixed, meetings shall be held at the registered office of the Corporation.

An annual meeting of the Stockholders shall be held at such time as may be stated in or fixed in accordance with the By-laws.

A special meeting of the Stockholders may be called by the Board of Directors, the holders of not less than one-tenth of all the shares entitled to vote at the meeting, or such other persons as may be authorized in the By-laws.

§ 5.2 Notice

Written notice stating the place, day and hour of the meeting and, in case of a special meeting, the purpose or purposes for which the meeting is called, shall be delivered not less than *ten* nor more than *fifty* days before the date of the meeting, either personally or by mail, by or at the direction of the President, the Secretary, or the Officer or persons calling the meeting, to each Stockholder of record entitled to vote at such meeting. If mailed, such notice shall be deemed to be delivered when deposited in the United States mail addressed to the Stockholder at his address as it appears on the stock transfer books of the Corporation, with postage thereon prepaid.

COMMENTS TO § 5.2

This provision repeats Model Bus.Corp.Act §§ 28 and 29.

For additional discussion of Stockholder meetings, see Chapter 45, infra.

§ 5.3 Calling Special Meetings

A special meeting of the Stockholders may be called by the President or Secretary or any two Board members. The purpose of such meeting must be stated in the notice.

COMMENTS TO § 5.3

Special meetings are permitted by Model Bus.Corp.Act § 28. Use of this language will help the Corporation to function more efficiently. See also § 3.6 of 34.14, infra, for the implementing By-law language. Model Bus.Corp.Act § 29 requires that the purpose of a special meeting be stated.

For additional coverage of special Stockholder meetings, see Chapter 45, infra.

Article VI
CONSENT MEETINGS

Alternative A (Majority Consent)

Preferred, if Allowed, as a Matter of Practical Experience

§ 6.1 Majority Consent Meetings

Any action required or permitted to be taken at an annual or special meeting of Stockholders may be taken without a meeting, without prior written notice and without a vote if consented to in writing by the holders of outstanding shares having at least the minimum number of votes necessary to authorize or ratify such action if taken at a meeting at which all shares entitled to vote were present and voted. Prompt written notice of the taking of said action shall be given to the non-consenting Stockholders by (among other methods) mailing said notice to said Stockholders by first class mail, postage prepaid, to the address of record.

Alternative B (Unanimous Consent)

Preferred if Alternative A Is Not Allowed

§ 6.1 Unanimous Consent Meetings

Any action required or permitted to be taken at a meeting of the Stockholders of the Corporation, or any action which may be taken at a meeting of the Stockholders, may be taken without a meeting if a consent in writing, setting forth the action so taken, shall be signed by all of the Stockholders entitled to vote with respect to the subject matter thereof.

Such consent shall have the same effect as a unanimous vote of the Stockholders.

COMMENTS TO ALTERNATIVE B

This provision allows Stockholder action without the necessity of a meeting only if all Stockholders consent (Model Bus.Corp.Act § 145).

For additional discussion of consent meetings, see Chapter 45, infra.

COMMENTS TO § 6.1

Many modern business law statutes (but not the Model Bus. Corp.Act) permit one of the following:

(a) Action without a meeting without majority consent if the situation is specifically authorized in the Articles of Incorporation (Michigan) with certain exceptions; or

(b) All actions may be taken without majority consent unless specifically prohibited in the Articles of Incorporation (Delaware).

(c) If the Corporation is closely held (see Chapter 30, supra) then one of the above provisions is highly recommended for the following reasons:

(1) The controlling Stockholders will control the vote at the Stockholder meeting in any case.

(2) Stockholder meetings are often hard to arrange. Consents to waiver and/or notices of the meeting are often not obtained at the correct time, thus jeopardizing the validity of the meeting.

(3) Ofter business must be conducted quickly and this procedure will speed the approval process.

The problem with the Alternative A procedure is it does not give an articulate or well informed Stockholder the right to persuade others of his views.

For additional discussion of consent meetings, see Chapter 45, infra.

Article VII

STOCKHOLDER VOTING

Not Preferred Because as a Matter of Practical Experience These Provisions Are Preferably Included in the By-Laws

§ 7.1 Close of Transfer Books

For the purpose of determining the Stockholders entitled to notice of or to vote at any meeting of Stockholders or any adjournment thereof, or entitled to receive payment of any dividend, or in order to make a determination of Stockholders for any other proper purpose, the Board of Directors of a Corporation may provide that the stock transfer books shall be closed for a stated period but not to exceed, in any case, *fifty* days. If the stock transfer books shall be closed for the purpose of determining Stockholders entitled to notice of or to vote at a meeting of Stockholders, such books shall be closed for at least *ten* days immediately preceding such meeting. In lieu of closing the stock transfer books, the By-laws, or in the absence of an applicably By-law the Board of Directors, may fix in advance a date as the record date for any such determination of Stockholders, such date in any case to be not more than *fifty* days and, in case of a meeting of Stockholders, not less than *ten* days prior to the date on which the particular action, requiring such determination of Stockholders, is to be taken. If the stock transfer books are not closed and no record date is fixed for the determination of Stockholders entitled to notice of or to vote at a meeting of Stockholders, or Stockholders entitled to receive payment of a dividend, the date on which notice of the meeting is mailed or the date on which the resolution of the Board of Directors declaring such dividend is adopted, as the case may be, shall be the record date for such determination of Stockholders. When a determination of Stockholders entitled to vote at any meeting of Stockholders has been made as provided in this section, such determination shall apply to any adjournment thereof.

§ 7.2 List of Voting Stockholders

The Officer or agent having charge of the stock transfer books shall make a complete record of the Stockholders entitled to vote at such meeting or any adjournment thereof, arranged in alphabetical order, with the address of and the number of shares held by each. Such record shall be produced and kept open at the time and place of the meeting and shall be subject to the inspection of any Stockholder during the whole time of the meeting for the purposes thereof.

Failure to comply with the requirements of these sections shall not affect the validity of any action taken at such meeting.

§ 7.3 Quorum

(a) A *majority* of the shares entitled to vote, represented in person or by proxy, shall constitute a quorum at a meeting of Stockholders.

(b) If a quorum is present, the affirmative vote of the majority of the shares represented at the meeting and entitled to vote on the subject matter shall be the act of the Stockholders, unless the vote of a greater number or voting by classes is required by the By-laws.

COMMENTS TO §§ 7.1–7.3

This language follows Model Bus.Corp.Act §§ 30, 31, 33, 34 and 144.

The minimum quorum is a third of the shares entitled to vote.

For additional discussion of Stockholder voting, see Chapter 45, infra.

Not Generally Preferred as a Matter of Practical Experience

§ 7.4 Class Voting

All voting shall be by classes. A majority of each class of shares shall approve of any action to be taken by the Stockholders.

COMMENT TO § 7.4

This provision is permitted by Model Bus.Corp.Act § 30.

Not Generally Preferred as a Matter of Practical Experience

§ 7.5 Percentage for Action

As to the following matters, __% of the shares voting shall be required to approve any proposed Stockholder action:

(a) The amendment of this section.

(b) Removal of one or more of the corporate Directors.

(c) To sue, complain and defend, in the corporate name.

(d) To purchase, take, receive, lease, or otherwise acquire, own, hold, improve, use and otherwise deal in and with, real or personal property, or any interest therein, wherever situated.

(e) To sell, convey, mortgage, pledge, lease, exchange, transfer and otherwise dispose of any part of the Corporation's property and assets.

(f) To lend money and use credit to assist its employees.

(g) To purchase, take, receive, subscribe for, or otherwise acquire, own, hold, vote, use, employ, sell, mortgage, lend, pledge, or otherwise dispose of, and otherwise use and deal in and with, shares or other interests in, or obligations of, other domestic or foreign Corporations, Associations, partnerships or individuals, or direct or indirect obligations of the United States or of any other government, state, territory, governmental district or municipality or of any instrumentality thereof.

(h) To make contracts and guarantees and incur liabilities, borrow money, issue the Corporation's notes, bonds, and other obligations, or to secure any of the Corporation's obligations by mortgage or pledge of all or any of its property, franchises and income.

(i) To lend money for the Corporation's purposes.

(j) To conduct corporate business, carry on its operations and have offices and exercise the powers granted herein, outside of this state.

(k) To make and alter By-laws, for the administration and regulation of the affairs of the Corporation.

(*l*) To make donations for the public welfare or for charitable, scientific or educational purposes.

(m) To establish pension plans, pension trusts, profit sharing plans, stock bonus plans, stock option plans and other incentive plans for any or all of its Directors, Officers and employees.

(n) To cause the Corporation to be a promoter, partner, member, associate, or manager of any partnership, joint venture, trust or other enterprise.

COMMENT TO § 7.5

This language (permitted by Model Bus.Corp.Act § 30) will be helpful in protecting minority Stockholders against the oppression of the majority. Although permitted in the By-laws it is recommended that this language be in the Articles so that the Board does not undermine the rights to be protected by changing the By-laws.

Preferred as a Matter of Practical Experience

§ 7.6 Shares Entitled to Vote

(a) Each outstanding share, regardless of class, shall be entitled to one vote on each matter submitted to a vote at a meeting of Stockholders, except as may be otherwise provided herein. If these Articles of Incorporation provide for more or less than one vote for any share, on any matter, every reference in these Articles to a majority or other proportion of shares shall refer to such a majority or other proportion of votes entitled to be cast.

(b) Neither treasury shares, nor shares held by another Corporation if a majority of the shares entitled to vote for the election of Directors of such other Corporation is held by this Corporation, shall be voted at any meeting or counted in determining the total number of outstanding shares at any given time.

COMMENT TO § 7.6

This section must be changed if it is inconsistent with provisions of stock or securities issued or authorized.

§ 7.7 Who Votes

(a) A Stockholder may vote either in person or by proxy executed in writing by the Stockholder or by his duly authorized attorney-in-fact. No proxy shall be valid after eleven months from the date of its execution, unless otherwise provided in the proxy.

(b) Shares standing in the name of another Corporation, domestic or foreign, may be voted by such officer, agent or proxy as the

By-laws of such other Corporation may prescribe, or, in the absence of such provision, as the Board of Directors of such other Corporation may determine.

(c) Shares held by an administrator, executor, guardian or conservator may be voted by him either in person or by proxy, without a transfer of such shares into his name. Shares standing in the name of a trustee may be voted by him, either in person or by proxy, but no trustee shall be entitled to vote shares held by him without a transfer of such shares into his name.

(d) A Stockholder whose shares are pledged shall be entitled to vote such shares until the shares have been transferred into the name of the pledgee, and thereafter the pledgee shall be entitled to vote the shares so transferred.

Option

(e) On and after the date on which written notice of redemption of redeemable shares has been mailed to the holders thereof and a sum sufficient to redeem such shares has been deposited with a bank or trust company with irrevocable instruction and authority to pay the redemption price to the holders thereof upon surrender of certificates therefor, such shares shall not be entitled to vote on any matter and shall not be deemed to be outstanding shares.

(f) Whenever any notice is required to be given to any Stockholder under the provisions of a waiver thereof in writing signed by the person or persons entitled to such notice, whether before or after the time stated therein, such waiver shall be equivalent to the giving of such notice.

§ 7.8 Voting Trusts

Any number of Stockholders of the Corporation may create a voting trust for the purpose of conferring upon a trustee or trustees the right to vote or otherwise represent their shares, for a period of not to exceed ten years, by entering into a written voting trust agreement specifying the terms and conditions of the voting trust, by depositing a counterpart of the agreement with the Corporation at its registered office, and by transferring their shares to such trustee or trustees for the purposes of the agreement. Such trustee or trustees shall keep a record of the holders of voting trust certificates evidencing a beneficial interest in the voting trust, giving the names and addresses of all such holders and the number and class of the shares in respect of which the voting trust certificates held by each are issued, and shall deposit a copy of such record with the Corporation at its registered office. The counterpart of the voting trust agreement and the copy of such record so deposited with the Corporation shall be subject to the same right of examination by a Stockholder of the Corporation, in person or by agent or attorney, as are the books and records of the Corporation, and such counterpart and such copy of such record shall be subject to examination by any holder of record of voting trust certificates, either in person or by agent or attorney, at any reasonable time for any proper purpose.

COMMENT TO § 7.8

See Chapter 47, infra, with respect to voting trusts.

§ 7.9 Stockholder Agreements

Agreements among Stockholders regarding the voting of their shares shall be valid and enforceable in accordance with their terms. Such agreements shall not be subject to the provisions of this Article regarding voting trusts.

COMMENT TO § 7.9

See Chapter 47, infra, for coverage of stockholder voting agreements.

COMMENT TO §§ 7.7, 7.8, AND 7.9

These Sections follow Model Bus.Corp.Act §§ 33 and 34.

§ 7.10 Cumulative Voting

As to the election of a Board of Directors, the Stockholders of the Class ______ common stock shall have the following right: such Stockholders may vote the number of shares owned by him for as many persons as there are Directors to be elected and for whose election he has a right to vote, or to cumulate his votes by giving 1 candidate as many votes as the number of such Directors multiplied by the number of his shares, or by distributing his votes on the same principle among any number of the candidates.

Article VIII

AMENDMENT OF ARTICLES OF INCORPORATION

Alternative A (Generally Preferred as a Matter of Practical Experience)

§ 8.1 Amendments to Articles

The Corporation may amend its Articles of Incorporation, from time to time, so as:

(a) To change its corporate name.

(b) To change its period of duration.

(c) To change, enlarge or diminish its corporate purposes.

(d) To increase or decrease the aggregate number of shares, or shares of any class, which the Corporation has authority to issue.

(e) To limit, deny or grant to Stockholders of any class the preemptive right to acquire additional or treasury shares of the Corporation, whether then or thereafter authorized.

(f) To increase or decrease the par value of the authorized shares of any class having a par value, whether issued or unissued.

(g) To exchange, classify, reclassify or cancel all or any part of its shares, whether issued or unissued.

(h) To change the designation of all or any part of its shares, whether issued or unissued, and to change the preferences, limitations, and the relative rights in respect of all or any part of its shares, whether issued or unissued.

(i) To change shares having par value, whether issued or unissued, into the same or a different number of shares without par value, and to change shares without par value into the same or a different number of shares having a par value.

(j) To change the shares of any class, whether issued or unissued, and whether with or without par value, into a different number of shares of the same class or into the same or a different number of shares, either with or without par value, of other classes.

(k) To create new classes of shares having rights and preferences either prior and superior or subordinate and inferior to the shares of any class then authorized, whether issued or unissued.

(*l*) To cancel or otherwise affect the right of the holders of the shares of any class to receive dividends which have accrued but have not been declared.

(m) To divide any preferred or special class of shares, whether issued or unissued, into series and fix and determine the designations of such series and the variations in the relative rights and preferences as between the shares of such series.

(n) To authorize the Board of Directors to establish, out of authorized but unissued shares, a series of any preferred or special class of shares and fix and determine the relative rights and preferences of the shares of any series so established.

(*o*) To authorize the Board of Directors to fix and determine the relative rights and preferences of the authorized but unissued shares of series theretofore established in respect of which either the relative rights and preferences have not been fixed and determined or the relative rights and preferences theretofore fixed and determined are to be changed.

(p) To revoke, diminish, or enlarge the authority of the Board of Directors to establish a series out of authorized but unissued shares of any preferred or special class and fix and determine the relative rights and preferences of the shares of any series so established.

COMMENTS TO ALTERNATIVE A

Provisions (f)–(p) may undermine the rights which were theoretically given a Stockholder, since these sections make the stock rights subject to the whims of the Stockholders and Board.

See Chapter 51, infra, for coverage of amendments to the Articles of Incorporation.

COMMENT TO § 8.1

These amendment rights are statutorily granted (Model Bus. Corp.Act § 58); but the Stockholders could deny the Board the right to exercise the same.

Alternative B (Not Generally Preferred as a Matter of Practical Experience)

§ 8.2 Amendments to Articles—Change in Certain Stockholder Rights

As to the ______ class of stock, the Corporation may not amend its Articles of Incorporation, without the consent of [*Describe*] so as:

(a) To increase or decrease the par value of the authorized shares of this class.

(b) To exchange, classify, reclassify or cancel all or any part of these shares.

(c) To change the designation of all or any part of these shares or to change the preferences, limitations, and the relative rights in respect of all or any part of these shares.

(d) To change these shares having par value into the same or a different number of shares without par value, or to change these shares without par value into the same or a different number of shares having a par value.

(e) To change these shares into a different number of shares of the same class or into the same or a different number of shares, either with or without par value, of other classes.

(f) To create new classes of shares having rights and preferences either prior and superior or subordinate and inferior to these shares.

(g) To cancel or otherwise affect the right of the holders of these shares to receive dividends which have accrued but have not been declared.

(h) To divide these shares into a series.

COMMENT TO ALTERNATIVE B

The Stockholders may want (or may be obligated) (see (e), infra, of the form at Chapter 40, § 40.6, infra,) to protect certain classes of stock against the arbitrary exercise of power. It is questionable whether the Corporation can absolutely be denied these powers.

Not Generally Preferred Because as a Matter of Practical Experience These Provisions Are Preferably Included in the By-laws

§ 8.3 Manner of Amending Articles

Amendments to the Articles of Incorporation shall be made in the following manner:

(a) The Board of Directors shall adopt a resolution setting forth the proposed amendment and, if shares have been issued, directing that it be submitted to consideration by the Stockholders, which may be either the annual or a special meeting. If no shares have been issued, the amendment shall be adopted by resolution of the Board of Directors and the provisions for adoption by Stockholders shall not apply.

(b) Unless waived, written notice setting forth the proposed amendment or a summary of the changes to be effected thereby shall be given to each Stockholder of record entitled to vote thereon within the time and in the manner provided for the giving of notice of meetings of Stockholders. If the meeting be an annual meeting, the proposed amendment of such summary may be included in the notice of such annual meeting.

(c) By consent or by meeting a vote of the Stockholders entitled to vote thereon shall be taken on the proposed amendment. The proposed amendment shall be adopted upon receiving the affirmative vote of the holders of a majority of the shares entitled to vote thereon, unless a higher percentage is required; or unless any class of shares is entitled to vote thereon as a class, in which event the proposed amendment shall be adopted upon receiving the affirmative vote of the holders of a majority (or higher percentage, if applicable) of the shares of each class of shares entitled to vote thereon as a class and of the total shares entitled to vote thereon.

Any number of amendments may be submitted to the Stockholders, and voted upon by them, at one meeting.

COMMENT TO § 8.3

This language follows Model Bus.Corp.Act §§ 58 and 59 and is statutorily implied to make it clear that consent meetings may also adopt amendment; the Stockholders could deny the Board these powers. See also Chapter 51, infra, "Amendment of Articles of Incorporation."

Article IX

DIRECTORS

Required by Statute

§ 9.1 Directors

The initial Board shall consist of Directors and the names and addresses of the persons who shall serve as Directors until the first annual meeting of Stockholders or until their successors be elected and qualified are:

____________________ ____________________

Address

____________________ ____________________

Address

COMMENTS TO § 9.1

This information is required by Model Bus.Corp.Act § 54.

The number of Directors can be one or more (Model Bus. Corp.Act § 36). The number of Directors (unless actually specified in the Articles) may vary from time to time.

The number of Directors of a closely held Corporation should generally be a number which meets statutory requirements and which is convenient to assemble for a meeting.

It is recommended that when the Corporation is closely held that the Board include only persons who are familiar with the day to day operations of the Corporation. The reasons for this are:

(a) Directors face substantial personal liability.

(b) The input of consultants is generally only required on an intermittent basis.

(c) If the consultant is a CPA, he will not be able to certify to the independence of the opinion if he is on the Board.

(d) If the consultant is an attorney he will not be able to render truly independent advice if he is on the Board.

(e) The Corporation may want to seek outside advice and ignore the advice of normal advisors. This will be more difficult if the advisor being ignored is a Board member.

Often the Board seats are given to loyal employees, although it should be always remembered that in situations of adversity a quorum of the Board can meet and a majority of that majority can act. Thus, one or a few dissidents could control the Board in unusual circumstances.

Alternative A (Generally Preferred as a Matter of Practical Experience; However, This Provision Is Preferably Included in the By-laws)

§ 9.2 Number of Directors

The Board of Directors of the Corporation shall consist of one or more members. The number of Directors shall be fixed by, or in the manner provided in, the By-laws, except as to the number constituting the initial Board of Directors, which number has been fixed by these Articles of Incorporation. The number of Directors may be increased or decreased from time to time by amendment to, or in the manner provided in these Articles of Incorporation or the By-laws, but no decrease shall have the effect of shortening the term of any incumbent Director. In the absence of a By-law providing for the number of Directors, the number shall be the same as that provided for in these Articles of Incorporation.

Alternative B (Not Generally Preferred as a Matter of Practical Experience)

§ 9.2 Number of Directors

The number of Directors shall be ______ and said number may only be increased or decreased upon approval by the holders of ______ (__%) percent of the outstanding shares then entitled to vote.

COMMENTS TO ALTERNATIVE B

This provision is only recommended when the Stockholders fear the independence of the Board of Directors. It is intended to avoid the following scenario: The Board is made up of five members and split 3–2. Two of the three who are part of the majority quit or die and the remaining Board members, rather than replacing the deceased members continue the Board with a reduced number.

If the By-laws (see § 34.13 (§ 4.2), infra) permit the Board of Directors to fill vacancies, the two dissident members could fill the two vacancies with their cohorts.

Of course, the statutory provision allowing the Stockholders to replace the Board (Model Bus.Corp.Act § 39) will tend to eliminate this problem since the Stockholders could, in time, regain control over the Board.

Article X

SPECIAL PERCENTAGE FOR BOARD QUORUM

Not Generally Preferred as a Matter of General Experience

§ 10.1 Board Quorum

A quorum shall consist of ______ (__%) percent of the members of the Board of Directors then in office.

COMMENT TO § 10.1

This provision will prevent a minority of Directors becoming the majority at a particular Director's meeting and thus thwarting the will of a majority of Directors. By statute, a quorum must be at least a majority (Model Bus.Corp.Act § 40).

Article XI

BOARD OF DIRECTOR MEETINGS

Not Preferred Because as a Matter of Practical Experience This Provision Is Preferably Included in the By-laws

§ 11.1 Voting

A majority of the number of Directors fixed by or in the manner provided in these Articles or in the absence of an Article fixing or providing for the number of Directors, then the number stated in the By-laws, shall constitute a quorum for the transaction of business. The act of the majority of the Directors present at a meeting at which a quorum is present shall be the act of the Board of Directors, unless the act of a greater number is required by these Articles in the By-laws.

Option 1

At all meetings of the Board of Directors all questions shall be decided by a majority of votes, but, in case of an equality of votes, the President shall have a second or deciding vote.

§ 11.2 Place

Meetings of the Board of Directors, regular or special, may be held either within or without this state.

COMMENTS TO § 11.2

Omit this provision if the Articles do not allow business to be conducted outside the state of incorporation.

For additional discussion of Directors meetings, see Chapter 46, infra.

§ 11.3 Notice

Regular meetings of the Board of Directors may be held with or without notice as prescribed in the By-laws. Special meetings of the Board of Directors designated thereby shall be held upon such notice as is prescribed in the By-laws. Attendance of a Director at a meeting shall not constitute a waiver of notice of such meeting if such attendance is for the express purpose of objecting to the transaction of any business because the meeting is not lawfully called or convened. Neither the business to be transacted at, nor the purpose of, any regular or special meeting of the Board of Directors need be specified in the notice or waiver of notice of such meeting unless required by the By-laws.

§ 11.4 Conference Telephone Calls

Except as may be otherwise restricted by these Articles of Incorporation or by the By-laws, members of the Board of Directors may participate in a meeting of such Board by means of a conference telephone or similar communications equipment by means of which all persons participating in the meeting can hear each other at the same time and participation by such means shall constitute presence in person at a meeting.

COMMENT

Conference telephone calls are commonly permitted by statute; see e. g. Model Bus.Corp.Act § 44.

§ 11.5 Consent Actions

Unless otherwise provided by the By-laws, any action to be taken at a meeting of the Directors of the Corporation, or any action which may be taken at a meeting of the Directors may be taken without a meeting and if a consent in writing, setting forth the action so taken shall be signed by all of the Directors. Such consent shall have the same effect as a unanimous vote.

COMMENT TO § 11.5

Section 11.5 will promote Director efficiency. However, it may result in a decision which is not fully debated or thought out. See Chapter 46, infra, for additional discussion.

§ 11.6 Powers

All corporate powers shall be exercised by or under authority of, and the business affairs of the Corporation shall be managed under the direction of the Board of Directors. Directors need not be residents of this state or Stockholders of the Corporation unless the By-laws so require. The By-laws may prescribe other qualifications for Directors.

COMMENT TO § 11.6

Section 12.6 should be modified if certain powers are given to others (see Article XII, § 12.13 of this form, infra).

§ 11.7 Term

The members of the first Board of Directors shall hold office until the first annual meeting of Stockholders and until their successors shall have been elected and qualified. At the first annual meeting of Stockholders and at each annual meeting thereafter the

Stockholders shall elect Directors to hold office until the next succeeding annual meeting, except in case of the classification of Directors. Each Director shall hold office for the term for which he is elected until his successor shall have been elected and qualified.

§ 11.8 Vacancy

Any vacancy occurring in the Board of Directors may be filled by the affirmative vote of a majority of the remaining Directors though less than a quorum of the Board of Directors. A Director elected to fill a vacancy shall be elected for the unexpired term of his predecessor in office. Any directorship to be filled by reason of an increase in the number of Directors may be filled by the Board of Directors for a term of office continuing only until the next election of Directors by the Stockholders.

§ 11.9 Removal of Directors

By consent or at a meeting of Stockholders called expressly for that purpose, Directors may be removed by vote of the Stockholders. Any Director or the entire Board of Directors may be removed, with or without cause, by a vote of the holders of a majority of the shares then entitled to vote at an election of Directors.

§ 11.10 Removal of Officers

Any Officer or agent may be removed by the Board of Directors whenever in its judgment the best interests of the Corporation will be served thereby, but such removal shall be without prejudice to the contract rights, if any, of the person so removed. Election or appointment of an Officer or agent shall not of itself create such contractual rights.

COMMENT TO §§ 11.1–11.10

These sections are statutorily implied and follow Model Bus. Corp.Act §§ 35, 36, 38, 39, 40, 43, 44, 51 and 57; except § 12.9, infra has been modified to provide for consent meetings. See Part 46.31 et seq., infra, for appropriate regular and special Board meeting notice provisions. The Stockholders could deny the Board the right to exercise these powers.

Not Generally Preferred as a Matter of Practical Experience

§ 11.11 Delegation of Authority

Provided that [*Fill in Names of Persons or Positions or Leave Choice to Board of Directors*] shall exercise the following powers of the Board of Directors (and the Board shall have no power to exercise the same):

(a) To sue, complain and defend, in the corporate name.

(b) To use the corporate seal by causing it, or a facsimile thereof, to be impressed or affixed or in any other manner reproduced.

(c) To purchase, take, receive, lease, or otherwise acquire, own, hold, improve, use and otherwise deal in and with, real or personal property, or any interest therein, wherever situated.

(d) To sell, convey, mortgage, pledge, lease, exchange, transfer and otherwise dispose of all or any part of the corporate property and assets.

(e) To lend money and use corporate credit to assist employees or Directors.

(f) To purchase, take, receive, subscribe for, or otherwise acquire, own, hold, vote, use, employ, sell, mortgage, lend, pledge, or otherwise dispose of, and otherwise use and deal in and with, shares or other interests in, or obligations of, other domestic or foreign corporations, associations, partnerships or individuals, or direct or indirect obligations of the United States or of any other government, state, territory, governmental district or municipality or of any instrumentality thereof.

(g) To make contracts and guarantees and incur liabilities, borrow money at such rates of interest as they determine, issue corporate notes, bonds, and other obligations, and secure any of the Corporation's obligations by mortgage or pledge of all or any of its property, franchises and income.

(h) To lend money for the Corporation's purposes, invest and reinvest its funds, and take and hold payment of funds so loaned or invested.

(i) To conduct the Corporation's business, carry on corporate operations and have offices and exercise the powers granted herein, within or without this state.

(j) To elect or appoint officers and agents of the Corporation, and define their duties and fix their compensation.

(k) To make and alter By-laws, not inconsistent with these Articles of Incorporation, or the laws of the state of incorporation, for the administration and regulation of the affairs of the Corporation.

(*l*) To make donations for the public welfare or for charitable, scientific or educational purposes.

(m) To pay pensions and establish pension plans, pension trusts, profit sharing plans, stock bonus plans, stock option plans and other incentive plans for any or all of its Directors, Officers and employees.

(n) To have the Corporation act as a promoter, partner, member, associate, or manager of any partnership, joint venture, trust or other enterprise.

COMMENTS TO § 11.11

This can be a very useful provision. It is permitted (but not implied) by Model Bus.Corp.Act § 35. Among its uses are:

(a) To divide the power of the Board among two or more groups, each one of which is knowledgable in its area.

(b) To give to all or certain Stockholders (or others) powers without making them liable for general Board liabilities.

(c) To give a minority Stockholder or a lending source control over certain corporate functions.

This provision should be distinguished from the provision at Article XVII, infra, of this form which is a mere delegation of the Board's authority to a Committee whereby the Board remains liable for its mismanagement of the committee, and can cancel its authority at any time.

Generally Preferred as a Matter of Practical Experience if Permitted by Statute

§ 11.12 Classes of Directors

The Directors shall be divided into three classes, each class to be as nearly equal in number as possible; the term of office of Directors of the first class to expire at the first annual meeting of Stockholders after their election, that of the second class to expire at the second annual meeting after their election, and that of the third class to expire at the third annual meeting after their election. At each annual meeting after such classification the number of Directors equal to the number of the class whose term expires at the time of such meeting shall be elected to hold office until the third succeeding annual meeting. No classification of Directors shall be effective prior to the first annual meeting of Stockholders.

COMMENT TO § 11.12

Permitted (but not implied) only when there are nine or more Directors (Model Bus.Corp.Act § 37).

§ 11.13 General Authorization of Board's Authority to Issue Stocks and Bonds

The following certificates may be issued from time to time by the Board of Directors in one or more series:

Alternative A–1

[*Describe*] class of [*Describe*] stock only.

Alternative A–2

any stock or security except [*Describe*] class of [*Describe*] stock or security.

The Board of Directors is authorized to determine:

Alternative B–1

the dividend rate.

Alternative B–2

the price and term of issuance.

Alternative B–3

liquidation value and terms.

Alternative B–4

redemption value terms and condition.

Alternative B–5

whether there shall be a sinking fund to retire such certificates and, if so, what the terms and conditions of such fund shall be.

Alternative B–5

conversion rights.

Alternative B–6

voting rights.

§ 11.14 Restrictions on the Issuance of Certificates

The following restrictions upon the issuance of stock shall apply:

Option 1

Only stock authorized at this time may be issued.

Option 2

Only stock whose purchase price is at least book value may be issued.

Option 3

Only stock with rights and preference equal to or less than that of ______ class of [*common/preferred*] stock may be issued.

Option 4

Only stock which does not have any of the following rights and preferences may be issued:

Alternative D–1

The right to vote.

Alternative D–2

The right to vote; except upon default in any dividend.

Alternative D–3

Preemptive rights.

Alternative D–4

The right to vote on a cumulative basis.

Alternative D–5

A dividend preference.

Alternative D–6

A redemption preference.

Alternative D–7

A liquidation preference.

Recommended as a Matter of Practical Experience

Article XII

BY-LAWS

§ 12.1 Initial By-laws

The initial By-laws of the Corporation shall be adopted by the Board of Directors. The power to alter, amend or repeal the By-laws or adopt new By-laws, subject to repeal or change by action of the Stockholders, shall be vested in the Board of Directors. The By-laws may contain any provisions for the regulation and management of the affairs of the Corporation not inconsistent with law or the Articles of Incorporation.

COMMENTS TO § 12.1

This provision is statutorily implied and follows Model Bus. Corp.Act § 27. It must be deleted however if Article XII, § 12.11, infra, of this form granted this power to others or if § 11.6, infra, has denied this power to the Board.

For additional coverage of By-laws, see Chapter 34, infra.

Not Generally Recommended as a Matter of Practical Experience; May Not Be Legal In Some States

§ 12.2 Emergency By-laws

The Board of Directors of the Corporation may adopt emergency By-laws, subject to repeal or change by action of the Stockholders, which shall, notwithstanding any different provision elsewhere in the statutes of the State of Incorporation or in the Articles of Incorporation or By-laws, be operative during any emergency in the conduct of the business of the Corporation resulting from an attack on the United States or any nuclear or atomic disaster. The emergency

By-laws may make any provision that may be practical and necessary for the circumstances of the emergency, including provisions that:

(a) A meeting of the Board of Directors may be called by any Officer or Director in such manner and under such conditions as shall be prescribed in the emergency By-laws;

(b) The Director or Directors in attendance at the meeting, or any greater number fixed by the emergency By-laws, shall constitute a quorum; and

(c) The Officers or other persons designated on a list approved by the Board of Directors before the emergency, all in such order of priority and subject to such conditions, and for such period of time (not longer than reasonably necessary after the termination of the emergency) as may be provided in the emergency By-laws or in the resolution approving the list shall, to the extent required to provide a quorum at any meeting of the Board of Directors, be deemed Directors for such meeting.

The Board of Directors, either before or during any such emergency, may, effective in the emergency, change the head office or designate several alternative head offices or regional offices, or authorize the officers so to do.

To the extent not inconsistent with any emergency By-laws so adopted, the By-laws of the Corporation shall remain in effect during any such emergency and upon its termination the emergency By-laws shall cease to be operative.

Unless otherwise provided in emergency By-laws, notice of any meeting of the Board of Directors during any such emergency may be given only to such Directors as it may be feasible to reach at the time and by such means as may be feasible at the time, including by publication or radio.

To the extent required to constitute a quorum at any meeting of the Board of Directors during any such emergency, the Officers of the Corporation who are present shall, unless otherwise provided in emergency By-laws, be deemed, in order of rank and within the same rank in order of seniority, Directors for such meeting.

No Officer, Director or employee acting in accordance with any emergency By-laws shall be liable except for willful misconduct. No Officer, Director or employee shall be liable for any action taken by him in good faith in such an emergency in furtherance of the ordinary business affairs of the Corporation even though not authorized by the By-laws then in effect.

COMMENT TO § 12.2

This provision is not permitted by all states (it is a Model Bus.Corp.Act optional provision—§ 27A). Even if it is permitted, the Stockholders may deny this right to the Board. It may be very helpful to large Corporations or Corporations with two or more locations which are far apart.

Preferred as a Matter of Practical Experience; However, This Provision Is Preferably Included in the By-Laws

§ 12.3 Officers

The Officers of a Corporation shall consist of a *Chairman,* a President, *one or more Vice Presidents as may be prescribed by the By-laws,* a Secretary, and a Treasurer, each of whom shall be elected by the Board of Directors at such time and in such manner as may be prescribed by the By-laws. Such other Officers and assistant officers and agents as may be deemed necessary may be elected or appointed by the Board of Directors or chosen in such other manner as may be prescribed by the By-laws. Any two or more offices may be held by the same person, except the offices of President and Secretary.

All Officers and agents of the Corporation, as between themselves and the Corporation, shall have such authority and perform such duties in the management of the Corporation as may be provided in the By-laws, or as may be determined by resolution of the Board of Directors not inconsistent with the By-laws.

COMMENT TO § 12.3

This provision is statutorily implied and follows Model Bus. Corp.Act § 50. The Stockholders may modify this language; provided that the Corporation must have a President, Secretary and Treasurer.

Article XIII

DIVIDENDS

Preferred as a Matter of Practical Experience

§ 13.1 Dividends in General

The Board of Directors of the Corporation may, from time to time, declare and the Corporation may pay dividends in cash, property, or its own shares, except when the Corporation is insolvent or when the payment thereof would render the Corporation insolvent, subject to the following provisions:

Alternative A

(a) Dividends may be declared and paid in cash or property only out of the unreserved and unrestricted earned surplus of the Corporation, except as otherwise provided in this section.

Alternative B

(a) Dividends may be declared and paid in cash or property only out of the unreserved and unrestricted earned surplus of the

Corporation, or out of the unreserved and unrestricted net earnings of the current fiscal year and the next preceding fiscal year taken as a single period, except as otherwise provided in this section.

(b) Dividends may be declared and paid in cash out of depletion reserves, but each such dividend shall be identified as a distribution of such reserves and the amount per share paid from such reserves shall be disclosed to the Stockholders receiving the same concurrently with the distribution thereof.

(c) Dividends may be declared and paid in treasury shares.

(d) Dividends may be declared and paid in authorized but unissued shares out of any unreserved and unrestricted surplus of the Corporation upon the following conditions:

(1) If a dividend is payable in shares having a par value, such shares shall be issued at not less than the par value thereof and there shall be transferred to stated capital at the time such dividend as a paid in amount of surplus equal to the aggregate par value of the shares to be issued as a dividend.

(2) If a dividend is payable in shares without par value, such shares shall be issued at such stated value as shall be fixed by the Board of Directors by resolution adopted at the time such dividend is declared and there shall be transferred to stated capital at the time such dividend is paid an amount of surplus equal to the aggregate stated value so fixed in respect of such shares; and the amount per share so transferred to stated capital shall be disclosed to the Stockholders receiving such dividend concurrently with the payment thereof.

COMMENT

For additional discussion of dividends, see Chapter 57, infra.

§ 13.2 Dividends to Other Classes

No dividend payable in shares of any class shall be paid to the holders of shares of any other class unless such payment is authorized by the affirmative vote or the written consent of the holders of at least a majority of the outstanding shares of the class in which the payment is to be made.

Option 1

Provided that the following classes may receive shares of another class: _______.

COMMENTS TO OPTION 1

This provision may be helpful in reorganizations and in situations where the authorized shares of a particular class are completely issued.

For additional discussion of dividends, see Chapter 57, infra.

§ 13.3 Class Split-Ups

(a) A split-up or division of the issued shares of any class into a greater number of shares of the same class without increasing the stated capital of the Corporation shall not be construed to be a share dividend within the meaning of this section.

(b) The Board of Directors of the Corporation may, from time to time, distribute to its Stockholders out of capital surplus of the Corporation a portion of its assets, in cash or property, subject to the following provisions:

(1) No such distribution shall be made at a time when the Corporation is insolvent or when such distribution would render the Corporation insolvent.

(2) No such distribution shall be made unless such distribution is authorized by the affirmative vote of the holder of a majority of the outstanding shares of each class whether or not entitled to vote thereon by the provisions of the Articles of Incorporation of the Corporation.

(3) No such distribution shall be made to the holders of any class of shares unless all cumulative dividends accrued on all preferred or special classes of shares entitled to preferential dividends shall have been fully paid.

(4) No such distribution shall be made to the holders of any class of shares which would reduce the remaining net assets of the Corporation below the aggregate preferential amount payable in event of involuntary liquidation to the holders of shares having preferential rights to the assets of the Corporation in the event of liquidation.

(5) Each such distribution, when made, shall be identified as a distribution from capital surplus and the amount per share disclosed to the Stockholders receiving the same concurrently with the distribution thereof.

(6) The Board of Directors of a Corporation may also, from time to time, distribute to the holders of its outstanding shares having a cumulative preferential right to receive dividends, in discharge of their cumulative dividend rights, dividends payable in cash out of the capital surplus of the Corporation, if at the time the Corporation has no earned surplus and is not insolvent and would not thereby be rendered insolvent. Each such distribution when made, shall be identified as a payment of cumulative dividends out of capital surplus.

Article XIV

CHANGES IN BALANCE SHEET

Generally Preferred as a Matter of Practical Experience; However, These Provisions Are Preferably Included in the By-Laws

§ 14.1 Reductions in Stated Capital

A reduction of the stated capital of a Corporation, where such reduction is not accompanied by any action requiring an amendment of the Articles of Incorporation and not accompanied by a cancellation of shares, may be made in the following manner:

(a) The Board of Directors shall adopt a resolution setting forth the amount of the proposed reduction and the manner in which the reduction shall be effected, and directing that the question of such reduction be submitted to a vote at a meeting of Stockholders, which may be either an annual or a special meeting.

(b) Written notice, stating that the purpose or one of the purposes of such meeting is to consider the question of reducing the stated capital of the Corporation in the amount and manner proposed by the Board of Directors, shall be given to each Stockholder of record entitled to vote thereon within the time and in the manner provided for the giving of notice of meetings of Stockholders.

(c) At such meeting a vote of the Stockholders entitled to vote thereon shall be taken on the question of approving the proposed reduction of stated capital, which shall require for its adoption the affirmative vote of the holders of a majority of the shares entitled to vote thereon.

(d) When a reduction of the stated capital of the Corporation has been approved as provided in this section, a statement shall be executed in duplicate by the Corporation by its President or a Vice-President and by its Secretary or an Assistant Secretary, and verified by one of the Officers signing such statement, and shall set forth:

(1) The name of the Corporation.

(2) A copy of the resolution of the Stockholders approving such reduction, and the date of its adoption.

(3) The number of shares outstanding, and the number of shares entitled to vote thereon.

(4) The number of shares voted for and against such reduction, respectively.

(5) A statement of the manner in which such reduction is effected, and a statement, expressed in dollars, of the amount of stated capital of the Corporation after giving effect to such reduction.

(e) No reduction of stated capital shall be made which would reduce the amount of the aggregate stated capital of the Corporation to an amount equal to or less than the aggregate preferential amounts payable upon all issued shares having a preferential right in the assets of the Corporation in the event of involuntary liquidation, plus the aggregate par value of all issued shares having a par value but no preferential right in the assets of the Corporation in the event of involuntary liquidation.

(f) The surplus, if any, created by or arising out of a reduction of the stated capital of the Corporation shall be capital surplus.

§ 14.2 Increase in Stated Capital

The capital surplus of a Corporation may be increased from time to time by resolution of the Board of Directors directing that all or a part of the earned surplus of the Corporation be transferred to capital surplus.

§ 14.3 Elimination of Deficits

A Corporation may, by resolution of its Board of Directors, apply any part or all of its capital surplus to the reduction or elimination of any deficit arising from losses, however incurred, but only after first eliminating the earned surplus, if any, of the Corporation by applying such losses against earned surplus and only to the extent that such losses exceed the earned surplus, if any. Each such application of capital surplus shall, to the extent thereof, effect a reduction of capital surplus.

§ 14.4 Creation of Reserves

A Corporation may, by resolution of its Board of Directors, create a reserve or reserves out of its earned surplus for any proper purpose or purposes, and may abolish any such reserve in the same manner.

COMMENTS TO ARTICLE XIV

These provisions are statutorily implied (Model Bus.Corp.Act §§ 69 and 70); however, the Stockholders can deny the Board of Directors these rights.

Article XV

RECORD BOOK AND FINANCIAL STATEMENTS

These Provisions Are Preferably Included in the By-laws

§ 15.1 Books

The Corporation shall keep correct and complete books and records of account and shall keep minutes of the proceedings of its

Stockholders and Board of Directors and shall keep at its registered office or principal place of business, or at the office of its transfer agent or registrar, a record of its Stockholders, giving the names and addresses of all Stockholders and the number and class of the shares held by each. Any books, records and minutes may be in written form or in any other form capable of being converted into written form within a reasonable time.

§ 15.2 Inspection of Books

Any person who shall have been a holder of record of shares or of voting trust certificates therefor at least six months immediately preceding his demand or shall be the holder of record of, or the holder of record of voting trust certificates for at least six months and who shall own at least five percent of all the outstanding shares of the Corporation, upon written demand stating the purpose thereof, shall have the right to examine, in person, or by agent or attorney, at any reasonable time or times, for any proper purpose the Corporation's relevant books and records of accounts, minutes, and the record of Stockholders and to make extracts therefrom.

COMMENT

See Chapter 49, infra, with respect to inspection of books and records.

§ 15.3 Financial Statements

Upon the written request of any Stockholder or holder of voting trust certificates for shares of the Corporation, the Corporation shall mail to such Stockholder or holder of voting trust certificates its most recent financial statements showing in reasonable detail its assets and liabilities and the results of its operations.

COMMENT TO ARTICLE XV

Follows rights statutorily implied by Model Bus.Corp.Act § 52. It is doubtful whether these rights can be constricted or eliminated by the Stockholders.

Article XVI

CONFLICTS IN INTEREST

Preferred as a Matter of Practical Experience

§ 16.1 Contracts with Directors and Officers

No contract or other transaction between the Corporation and one or more of its Directors or any other corporation, firm, association or entity in which one or more of its Directors are Directors or officers or are financially interested, shall be either void or voidable because of such relationship or interest or because such Director or Directors are present at the meeting of the Board of Directors or a committee thereof which authorizes, approves or ratifies such contract or transaction or because his or their votes are counted for such purpose if:

(a) The fact of such relationship or interest is disclosed or known to the Board of Directors or committee which authorizes, approves or ratifies the contract or transaction by a vote or consent sufficient for the purpose without counting the votes or consents of such interested Directors; or

(b) the fact of such relationship or interest is disclosed or known to the Stockholders entitled to vote and they authorize, approve or ratify such contract or transaction by vote or written consent; or

(c) The contract or transaction is fair and reasonable to the Corporation.

Common or interested Directors may be counted in determining the presence of a quorum at a meeting of the Board of Directors which authorizes, approves or ratifies such contract or transaction.

COMMENT

See Model Bus.Corp.Act § 41 with respect to director conflict of interest.

§ 16.2 Lending to Directors

The Corporation shall not lend money to or use its credit to assist its Directors without authorization in the particular case by its Stockholders, but may lend money to and use its credit to assist any employee of the Corporation or of a subsidiary, including any such employee who is a Director of the Corporation, if the Board of Directors decides that such loan or assistance may benefit the Corporation.

COMMENT TO ARTICLE XVI

The statute grants this protection (Model Bus.Corp.Act § 47) subject to denial by the Articles (see Article III, § 3.2, supra, of this form).

Article XVII

BOARD HAS POWER TO APPOINT A COMMITTEE

§ 17.1 Committees

The Board of Directors shall have the power to designate one or more committees, each committee to consist of one or more of the Directors of the Corporation. The Board may designate one or more Directors as alternate members of a committee, who may replace an absent or disqualified member at a meeting of the committee. The

By-laws may provide that in the absence or disqualification of a member of a committee, the members thereof present at a meeting and not disqualified from voting, whether or not they constitute a quorum, may unanimously appoint another member of the Board to act at the meeting, and each member thereof, shall serve at the pleasure of the Board. A committee designated pursuant to this paragraph, to the extent provided in the resolution of the Board or in the By-laws may exercise all powers and authority of the Board in management of the business and affairs of the Corporation not prohibited by the relevant Business Corporation Act.

COMMENTS TO § 17.1

The related By-law provisions are in §§ 11.2, 11.38 of the By-laws at § 34.14, infra.

For additional coverage of executive and other committees, see Chapter 46(D), infra.

§ 17.2 Denial of Authority

Provided that no such committee shall have authority to (a) declare dividends or distributions, (b) approve or recommend to Stockholders actions or proposals required to be approved by Stockholders, (c) designate candidates for the office of Director, for purposes of proxy solicitation or otherwise, or fill vacancies on the Board of Directors, or any committee thereof, (d) amend the By-laws, (e) approve a plan of merger not requiring Stockholder approval, (f) reduce earned or capital surplus, (g) authorize or approve the reacquisition of stock unless pursuant to a general formula or (h) authorize or approve the issuance or sale of, or any contract to issue or sell, shares or designate the terms of a series of a class of shares; provided that the Board of Directors, having acted regarding general authorization for the issuance or sale of shares, or any contract therefor, and, in the case of a series, the designation thereof, may, pursuant to a general formula or method specified by the Board by resolution or by adoption of a stock option or other plan, authorize a committee to fix the terms of any contract for the sale of the shares and to fix the terms upon which such shares may be issued or sold, including, without limitation, the price, the dividend rate, provisions for redemption, sinking fund, conversion, voting or preferential rights, and provisions for other features of a class of shares, or a series of a class of shares, with full power in such committee to adopt any final resolution setting forth all the terms thereof and to authorize the statement of the terms of a series.

COMMENTS TO §§ 17.1 and 17.2

This provision follows Model Bus.Corp.Act §§ 41 and 42 but other rights may also be denied the committee by the Stockholders.

This provision is different from the provision at § 12.13, supra, of this form. The latter completely separates the Board from certain items of authority and appoints in its stead another person or persons. This provision merely delegates the Board's authority and the Board will remain liable for its own mismanagement.

The committee clause (although permitted in the Articles of Incorporation) is more appropriately found in the By-laws where it can be amended at will. No purpose is served by having it in the Articles since enabling action will be required by the Board in any case, except in that case where the Stockholders want to limit the committee's powers (see infra).

Generally Some of the Following Will Be Preferred as a Matter of Practical Experience

§ 17.3 Further Denials of Authority

Provided further, that no such committee shall have authority to:

(a) Fix the compensation of the Board of Directors.

(b) Increase or decrease their own number or qualifications.

(c) Sue, complain and defend in the corporate name.

(d) Use the corporate seal.

(e) Purchase, take, receive, lease, or otherwise acquire, own, hold, improve, use or otherwise deal in and with, real or personal property, or any interest therein, wherever situated.

(f) Sell, convey, mortgage, pledge, lease, exchange, transfer and otherwise dispose of all or any part of the corporate property and assets.

(g) Lend money and use the Corporation's credit to assist corporate employees or Directors.

(h) Purchase, take, receive, subscribe for, or otherwise acquire, own, hold, vote, use, employ, sell, mortgage, lend, pledge, or otherwise dispose of, and otherwise use and deal in and with, shares or other interests in, or obligations of, other domestic or foreign corporations, associations, partnerships or individuals, or direct or indirect obligations of the United States or of any other government, state, territory, governmental district or municipality or of any instrumentality thereof.

(i) Make contracts and guarantees and incur liabilities, borrow money, issue corporate notes, bonds, and other obligations, or secure any of the Corporation's obligations by mortgage or pledge of all or any of its property, franchises and income.

(j) Lend money, invest and reinvest the Corporation's funds, or take and hold real and personal property as security for the payment of funds so loaned or invested.

(k) Elect or appoint officers and agents of the Corporation, or define their duties and fix their compensation.

(*l*) Make donations for the public welfare or for charitable, scientific or educational purposes.

(m) Pay pensions and establish pension plans, pension trusts, profit sharing plans, stock bonus plans, stock option plans and other incentive plans for any or all of the corporate Directors, Officers and employees.

(n) Have the Corporation act as a promoter, partner, member, associate, or manager of any partnership, joint venture, trust or other enterprise.

COMMENT TO § 17.3

These are examples of powers which the Stockholders may not want to grant to the committee.

§ 17.4 Meetings

Regular or special meetings of the committee may be held either within or without this state.

Regular meetings of the committee thereby may be held with or without notice as prescribed in the By-laws. Special meetings of the committee designated thereby shall be held upon such notice as is prescribed in the By-laws. Neither the business to be transacted at, nor the purpose of, any regular or special meeting of the committee need be specified in the notice or waiver of notice of such meeting unless required by the By-laws.

Except as may be otherwise restricted by the By-laws, members of the Board may participate in a meeting of such committee by means of a conference telephone or similar communication equipment by means of which all persons participating in the meeting can hear each other at the same time and participation by such means shall constitute presence in person at a meeting.

Unless otherwise provided by the By-laws any action to be taken at a meeting of a committee may be taken without a meeting if a consent in writing, setting forth the action so taken, shall be signed by all of the members of the committee. Such consent shall have the same effect as a unanimous vote.

COMMENT TO § 17.4

See §§ 11.4, 11.5 and 11.6, supra, of the form at § 34.14, infra, for implementing By-laws. This language can be eliminated or modified.

Article XVIII

PREEMPTIVE RIGHTS

§ 18.1 Preemptive Rights

Except to the extent limited or denied by this section or by the Articles of Incorporation, Stockholders shall have a preemptive right to acquire unissued or treasury shares or securities convertible into such shares or carrying a right to subscribe to or acquire shares.

Unless otherwise provided in the Articles of Incorporation,

(a) No preemptive right shall exist

(1) to acquire any shares issued to Directors, Officers or employees pursuant to approval by the affirmative vote of the holders of a majority of the shares entitled to vote thereon or when authorized by and consistent with a plan theretofore approved by such a vote of Stockholders; or

(2) to acquire any shares sold otherwise than for cash.

(b) Holders of shares of any class that is preferred or limited as to dividends or assets shall not be entitled to any preemptive right.

(c) Holders of shares of common stock shall not be entitled to any preemptive right to shares of any class that is preferred or limited as to dividends or assets or to any obligations, unless convertible into shares of common stock or carrying a right to subscribe to or acquire shares of common stock.

(d) Holders of common stock without voting power shall have no preemptive right to shares of common stock with voting power.

Article XIX

BOARD OF DIRECTOR, OFFICER, EMPLOYEE AND AGENT LIABILITY

Not Generally Preferred as a Matter of Practical Experience

§ 19.1 Stock Transfer Liability

An Officer or agent having charge of the stock transfer books who shall fail to prepare the record of Stockholders, or produce and keep it open for inspection at the meeting, as provided in this section, shall be liable to any Stockholder suffering damage on account of such failure, to the extent of such damage.

§ 19.2 General Director Liability

A Director shall perform his duties as a Director, including his duties as a member of any committee of the Board upon which he may serve, in good faith, in a manner he reasonably believes to be in the best interests of the Corporation, and with such care as an ordinarily prudent person in a like position would use under similar circumstances. In performing his duties, a Director shall be entitled to rely on information, opinions, reports or statements, including financial statements and other financial data, in each case prepared or presented by:

(a) One or more Officers or employees of the Corporation whom the Director reasonably believes to be reliable and competent in the matters presented.

(b) Counsel, public accountants or other persons as to matters which the Director reasonably believes to be within such person's professional or expert competence, or

(c) A committee of the Board upon which he does not serve, duly designated as to matters within its designated authority which committee the Director reasonably believes to merit confidence.

(d) But he shall not be considered to be acting in good faith if he has knowledge concerning the matter in question that would cause such reliance to be unwarranted.

(e) A person who so performs his duties shall have no liability by reason of being or having been a Director of the Corporation.

(f) A Director of a Corporation who is present at a meeting of its Board of Directors at which action on any corporate matter is taken shall be presumed to have assented to the action taken unless his dissent shall be entered in the minutes of the meeting or unless he shall file his written dissent to such action with the Secretary of the meeting before the adjournment thereof or shall forward such dissent by registered mail to the Secretary of the Corporation immediately after the adjournment of the meeting. Such right to dissent shall not apply to a Director who voted in favor of such action.

(g) Each Officer, Director or member of any committee designated by the Board of Directors in the manner hereinafter provided shall in the performance of his duties be fully protected in relying in good faith upon the books of account or reports made to the Corporation by any of its officials, or by an independent certified public accountant, or by an appraiser selected with reasonable care by the Board of Directors or by any such committee, or in relying in good faith upon other records of the Corporation.

(h) Any transaction questioned in any Stockholders' derivative suit on the ground of lack of authority, defective or irregular execution, adverse interest of Director, Officer or Stockholder, nondisclosure, miscomputation, or the application of improper principles or practices of accounting may be ratified before or after judgment, by the Board of Directors or by the Stockholders in case less than a quorum of Directors are qualified; and, if so ratified, shall have the same force and effect as if the questioned transaction had been originally duly authorized, and said ratification shall be binding upon the Corporation and its Stockholders and shall constitute a bar to any claim or execution of any judgment in respect of such questioned transaction.

§ 19.3 Refusal to Allow Inspection of Books

Any Officer or agent who, or a Corporation which, shall refuse to allow any such Stockholder or holder of voting trust certificates, or his agent or attorney, so to examine and make extracts from its books and records of account, minutes, and record of Stockholders, for any proper purpose, shall be liable to such Stockholder or holder of voting trust certificates in a penalty of ten percent of the value of the shares owned by such Stockholder, or in respect of which such voting trust certificates are issued, in addition to any other damages or remedy afforded him by law. It shall be a defense to any action for penalties under this section that the person suing therefor has within two years sold or offered for sale any list of Stockholders or of holders of voting trust certificates for shares of such Corporation or has aided or abetted any person in procuring any list of Stockholders or of holders of voting trust certificates for any such purpose, or has improperly used any information secured through any prior examination of the books and records of account, or minutes, or record of Stockholders or of holders of voting trust certificates for shares of such Corporation or any other Corporation, or was not acting in good faith or for a proper purpose in making his demand.

COMMENTS TO ARTICLE XIX

The provisions in this Article follow Model Bus.Corp.Act §§ 30, 35, 43 and 52. These provisions cannot be constricted or eliminated.

For additional coverage of inspection rights, see Chapter 49, infra.

Article XX

INDEMNIFICATION OF DIRECTORS, OFFICERS, EMPLOYEES AND AGENTS

Alternative A (Preferred in Some Form as a Matter of Practical Experience)

§ 20.1 Indemnification

The Corporation shall indemnify to the full extent permitted by law any person who is made, or threatened to be made, a party to any action, suit or proceeding (whether civil, criminal, administrative or investigative) by reason of the fact that he, his testator or intestate is or was a Director, Officer, employee or agent of the Corporation or serves or served any other enterprise at the request of the Corporation.

COMMENTS TO ALTERNATIVE A

This provision can be eliminated.

This indemnification clause has the advantage of being all encompassing. Its drawback is that it violates the drafting rule that the document should be as informative as reasonably possible. Sweeping indemnifications may result in the Corporation paying for an abuse which it wouldn't otherwise pay for.

Therefore, a case by case approach to indemnification may be more appropriate.

See Model Bus.Corp.Act § 5 with respect to indemnification of Officers, Directors, employees and agents.

Alternative B (Preferred in Some Form)

§ 20.1 Indemnification

(a) To the extent the law permits: the Corporation shall indemnify any person who was or is a party or is threatened to be made a party to any threatened, pending or completed action, suit or proceeding, whether civil, criminal, administrative or investigative (other than an action by or in the right of the Corporation) by reason of the fact that he is or was a Director, Officer, employee or agent of the Corporation, or is or was serving at the request of the Corporation as a Director, Officer, employee or agent of another corporation, partnership, joint venture, trust or other enterprise, against expenses (including attorneys' fees), judgments, fines and amounts paid in settlement actually and reasonably incurred by him in connection with such action, suit or proceeding if he acted in good faith and in a manner he reasonably believed to be in or not opposed to the best interests of the Corporation, and, with respect to any criminal action or proceeding, had no reasonable cause to believe his conduct was unlawful. The termination of any action, suit or proceeding by judgment, order, settlement, conviction, or upon a plea of nolo contendere or its equivalent, shall not, of itself, create a presumption that the person did not act in good faith and in a manner which he reasonably believed to be in or not opposed to the best interests of the Corporation and, with respect to any criminal action or proceeding, had reasonable cause to believe that his conduct was unlawful.

COMMENT TO (a)

This provision indemnifies the actor's actions in civil, criminal and administrative actions for costs (i. e., court fees and legal fees) and judgments except it does not cover Stockholder ("derivative") suits against the Corporation.

(b) The Corporation shall indemnify any person who was or is a party or is threatened to be made a party to any threatened, pending or completed action or suit by or in the right of the Corporation to procure a judgment in its favor by reason of the fact that he is or was a Director, Officer, employee or agent of the Corporation, or is or was serving at the request of the Corporation as a director, officer, employee or agent of another corporation, partnership, joint venture, trust or other enterprise against expenses (including attorneys' fees) actually and reasonably incurred by him in connection with the defense or settlement of such action or suit if he acted in good faith and in a manner he reasonably believed to be in or not opposed to the best interests of the Corporation and except that no indemnification shall be made in respect of any claim, issue or matter as to which such person shall have been adjudged to be liable for negligence or misconduct in the performance of his duty to the Corporation unless and only to the extent that the court in which such action or suit was brought shall determine upon application that, despite the adjudication of liability but in view of all circumstances of the case, such person is fairly and reasonably entitled to indemnity for such expenses which such court shall deem proper.

COMMENT TO (b)

This provision indemnifies the actor's actions in civil suits by Stockholders for costs (i. e., court fees and legal fees) only.

(c) To the extent that a Director, Officer, employee or agent of a Corporation has been successful on the merits or otherwise in defense of any action, suit or proceeding referred to in paragraphs (a) and (b) of this Article, or in defense of any claim, issue or matter therein, he shall be indemnified against expenses (including attorneys' fees) actually and reasonably incurred by him in connection therewith.

(d) Any indemnification under paragraphs (a) or (b) of this section (unless ordered by a court) shall be made by the Corporation only as authorized in the specific case upon a determination that indemnification of the Director, Officer, employee or agent is proper in the circumstances because he has met the applicable standard of conduct set forth in paragraphs (a) or (b). Such determination shall be made (1) by the Board of Directors by a majority vote of a quorum consisting of Directors who were not parties to such action, suit or proceeding, or (2) if such a quorum is not obtainable, or, even if obtainable a quorum of disinterested Directors so directs, by independent legal counsel in a written opinion, or (3) by the Stockholders.

(e) Expenses (including attorneys' fees) incurred in defending a civil or criminal action, suit or proceeding may be paid by the Corporation in advance of the final disposition of such action, suit or proceeding as authorized in the manner provided in paragraph (d) of this Article upon receipt of an undertaking by or on behalf of the

Director, Officer, employee or agent to repay such amount unless it shall ultimately be determined that he is entitled to be indemnified by the Corporation as authorized in this section.

(f) The indemnification provided by this section shall not be deemed exclusive of any other rights to which those indemnified may be entitled under any By-law, agreement, vote of Stockholders or disinterested Directors or otherwise, both as to action in his official capacity and as to action in another capacity while holding such office, and shall continue as to a person who has ceased to be a Director, Officer, employee or agent and shall inure to the benefit of the heirs, executors and administrators of such a person.

COMMENT TO ALTERNATIVE B

This provision has the problem of possibly indemnifying persons whom the Corporation wouldn't indemnify if the facts were then being reviewed. A complete recitation of the law is a drafting virtue; however, if the law is not exactly as set forth it may be too restrictive. This right may be denied.

§ 20.2 Insurance

The Corporation shall have power to purchase and maintain insurance on behalf of any person who is or was a Director, Officer, employee or agent of the Corporation, or is or was serving at the request of the Corporation as a director, officer, employee or agent of another corporation, partnership, joint venture, trust or other enterprise against any liability asserted against him and incurred by him in any such capacity or arising out of his status as such, whether or not the Corporation would have the power to indemnify him against such liability under the provisions of this section.

Article XXI

SPECIAL PROVISIONS FOR CLOSE CORPORATIONS REQUIRING A SPECIAL STATUTORY ELECTION

§ 21.1 Special Provisions for Close Corporations Requiring a Special Statutory Election

The Corporation is a close Corporation; no shares and no securities evidencing the right to acquire shares shall be issued by means of public offering, solicitation or advertisement. All such shares and securities shall be subject to restrictions on transfer as permitted by [*applicable statutory citation*]. All issued shares, excluding treasury shares, and all issued securities evidencing the right to acquire shares of the Corporation shall be held of record by no more than [*any number not greater than 35*] persons in the aggregate.

Option

This Corporation elects to have its business and affairs managed by the Stockholders rather than by a Board of Directors.

Option

This Corporation may be dissolved at any time [*upon the affirmative vote of ______ per cent of any class of shares*], [*at the express will of any Stockholder*], [*if any Stockholder desires dissolution upon the occurrence of any of the following events:* (*list*)].

COMMENTS

The election to dispense with the Board of Directors and provide for Stockholder management of the business of the Corporation when provided for by statute is peculiarly appropriate for the small Corporation with few Stockholders—perhaps three or less. Even though a close Corporation may consist of as many as 35 persons, direct management by the Stockholders is unlikely to be attractive in the larger Corporations, though many Partnerships with as many as 35 Partners function well.

The rule that voting is on a per share rather than a per capita basis is statutorily presumed, though the Articles of Incorporation may provide that a greater percentage of votes, or voting on some other basis, e. g., per capita, is required. The broad consent provision of the statute is included in the By-laws because, as a practical matter, it is likely to reflect the predominant way in which corporate action is actually taken.

The requirement that a conspicuous notation of this election appear on the share certificate is statutory.

A Corporation that does not elect close Corporation status must have a Board of Directors in most states. The Board, however, may consist of one or more members and may act by unanimous consent; such a Corporation may possess nearly the flexibility and simplicity of a Corporation that has elected to dispense entirely with the Board of Directors.

See also § 30.4, supra.

Article XXII

REDEMPTION OF SHARES

§ 22.1 Redemption of Shares

Alternative A

The Corporation at its option may redeem the whole or any part, pro rata or by lot, of the ______ shares outstanding at any time, by paying therefor in cash [*Number*] [______%] per cent of the par value thereof, together with any accumulated dividends due thereon, by mailing notices of such redemption to the holders of the ______ shares to be redeemed at their respective addresses as the same may appear on the record of Stockholders of the Corporation, specifying the time and place of redemption within the [*Name of City*], such notice to be mailed at least ______ days and not more than ______ days prior to the date specified therein for redemption. From and after the date specified in any such notice as the redemption date, unless the Corporation shall fail to provide moneys at the time and place specified in such notice for the payment of the redemption price, all rights of the holders thereof as Stockholders of the Corporation, except the right to receive the redemption price, shall cease and terminate. Any redemption hereunder shall be had in the manner determined by the Board of Directors and in accordance with all applicable provisions of law.

COMMENT

Open-end investment companies, if the certificate of incorporation so provides, must redeem their shares at the option of the holder. See Investment Company Act of 1940, 15 U.S.C.A. § 80a et seq. Other Corporations are permitted to redeem their redeemable preferred shares as well as their redeemable common shares if nonredeemable common shares are outstanding, but they are not "redeemable" at the option of the holder.

Alternative B

This Corporation shall have the right at any time (or after ______, 19__,) to purchase in the market or at private sale, its ______ redeemable ______ shares, or any number of shares thereof, issued and outstanding, at a cost to it of not exceeding ______ ($______) Dollars per share. Also, this Corporation shall have the option and absolute right at any time (or after ______, 19__) to redeem any part or all of its said ______ redeemable ______ shares issued and outstanding by paying to the respective holders thereof the sum of ______ ($______) Dollars for each share redeemed (together with the amount of such accrued dividends as may have accumulated thereon at time of redemption).

The Corporation may apply toward the purchase or redemption of ______ shares as herein provided an amount out of its surplus which shall not exceed the amount represented by the shares purchased or redeemed. The purchase or redemption of any such share shall not be effected where the effect of any such purchase or redemption and application of surplus thereto shall be to render the Corporation insolvent.

The Board of Directors of this Corporation shall have full power and discretion to determine upon and select from the outstanding ______ redeemable ______ shares of this Corporation particular shares for redemption and its proceedings and action in this connection shall not be subject to attack except for actual and intentional fraud. In all instances, the Board shall have full power and authority to determine upon and take the necessary proceedings to fully effect the redemption and purchase of the shares selected for redemption, and the cancellation of the certificates representing such shares; and upon the completion of such proceedings, the rights of holders of the shares of such ______ shares which have been redeemed and called in shall in all respects cease and determine, except, of course, such holders shall be entitled to receive the redemption price for their respective shares.

Whenever any shares of such redeemable ______ shares of the Corporation shall be purchased or redeemed as herein authorized, the Corporation may, by resolution of its Board of Directors, cancel said shares, and thereupon this Corporation shall, in connection with the cancellation of shares prohibited by this Certificate of Incorporation from being reissued, deliver to the Department of State a Certificate of amendment, pursuant to Business Corporation Law eliminating such shares from the number of authorized shares.

Alternative C

The ______ stock is subject to redemption, out of funds legally available therefor, in whole, or from time to time in part, at the option of the Board of Directors of the Corporation. If only a part of the ______ stock is to be redeemed, the shares to be redeemed shall be selected by lot or the redemption shall be carried out prorata, at the option of the Board of Directors. The redemption price shall be $______ per share [if redeemed on or before ______, $______ per share if redeemed after ______ and on or before ______, and $______ per share if redeemed after ______] plus cumulative dividends as provided in subdivision (b) of this Article accrued and unpaid to the date fixed for redemption (herein called the "redemption price").

(2) The Corporation shall mail a notice of redemption to each holder of record of shares to be redeemed addressed to the holder at the address of such holder appearing on the books of the Corporation or given by the holder to the Corporation for the purpose of notice, or if no such address appears or is given at the place where the principal executive office of the Corporation is located, not earlier than 60 nor later than 20 days before the date fixed for redemption. The notice of redemption shall include (i) the class of shares or the part of a class of shares to be redeemed, (ii) the date fixed for redemption, (iii) the redemption price and (iv) the place at which the Stockholders may obtain payment of the redemption price upon surrender of their share certificates, (v) *the last date prior to the date of redemption that the right of conversion may be exercised.* If funds are available on the date fixed for the redemption, then whether or not the share certificates are surrendered for payment

of the redemption price, the shares shall no longer be outstanding and the holders thereof shall cease to be Stockholders of the Corporation with respect to the shares redeemed on and after the date fixed for redemption and shall be entitled only to receive the redemption price without interest upon surrender of the share certificate. If less than all the shares represented by one share certificate are to be redeemed, the Corporation shall issue a new share certificate for the shares not redeemed.

Option 1

(3) The Corporation shall also cause a copy of the notice of redemption to be published in a newspaper of general circulation in the county in which the principal executive office of the Corporation is located at least once a week for two successive weeks, in each instance on any day of the week, commencing not earlier than 60 nor later than 20 days before the date fixed for redemption. If the Corporation publishes the notice of redemption as provided in this paragraph (3), the failure of the Corporation to comply with the provision for mailing of notice of redemption in paragraph (2) shall not invalidate the redemption of the shares.

Option 2

(4) If, on or prior to any date fixed for redemption, the Corporation deposits with any bank or trust company in this state as a trust fund a sum sufficient to redeem, on the date fixed for redemption thereof, the shares called for redemption, with irrevocable instructions and authority to the bank or trust company to publish the notice of redemption thereof (or to complete such publication if theretofore commenced) and to pay, on and after the date fixed for redemption or prior thereto, the redemption price of the shares to their respective holders upon the surrender of their share certificates, then from and after the date of the deposit (although prior to the date fixed for redemption) the shares so called shall be redeemed and dividends on those shares shall cease to accrue after the date fixed for redemption. The deposit shall constitute full payment of the shares to their holders and from and after the date of the deposit the shares shall no longer be outstanding and the holders thereof shall cease to be Stockholders with respect to such shares and shall have no rights with respect thereto except the right to receive from the bank or trust company payment of the redemption price of the shares without interest, upon surrender of their certificates therefor.

Option 3 In the Event the ______ Stock is convertible, add the following at the end of the preceding sentence

and the right to convert the shares in accordance with subdivision (g) of this Article. The bank or trust company forthwith shall return to the corporation funds deposited for shares converted. After two years, the bank or trust company shall return to the Corporation funds deposited and not claimed and thereafter the holder of a share certificate for shares redeemed shall look to the Corporation for payment.

Alternative D

The Corporation may, at its option expressed by resolution adopted by a majority of the shares of common stock, upon ten (10) days' written notice to the holders of the ______ stock, or without notice if agreed to in writing by all holders thereof, redeem all shares of the ______ stock then outstanding at the following prices:

$______ if redeemed on or before ______, 19__; and

$______ if redeemed after ______, 19__,

together in each case with a sum equal to all dividends accrued or in arrears to the redemption date. The Corporation, however, without obtaining the prior written consent of the holders of all outstanding ______ stock shall not

(1) Redeem less than all outstanding shares of ______ stock; or

(2) Redeem any ______ stock before ______, 19__.

Alternative E

The ______ stock may be redeemed in whole or in part on any quarterly dividend payment date, at the option of the Board of Directors, upon not less than sixty (60) days prior notice to the holders of record of the ______ stock, published, mailed and given in such manner and form and on such other terms and conditions as may be prescribed by the By-laws or by resolution of the Board of Directors by payment in cash for each share of the ______ stock to be redeemed of ______ per cent (______%) of the par amount thereof and in addition thereto all unpaid dividends accrued on such share.

From and after ______, 19__, the Board of Directors shall retire not less than ______ shares of ______ stock per annum; but the Board of Directors shall first set aside a reserve to provide full dividends for the current year on all ______ stock which shall be outstanding after such purchase or retirement, and provided further that no such purchase or retirement shall be made if the capital of the Corporation would thereby be impaired.

If less than all the oustanding shares are to be redeemed, such redemption may be made by lot or pro-rata as may be prescribed by resolution of the Board of Directors; provided, however, that the Board of Directors may alternatively invite from Stockholders offers to the Corporation of ______ stock at less than ______ (______), and when such offers are invited, the Board of Directors shall then be required to buy at the lowest price or prices offered, up to the amount to be purchased.

From and after the date fixed in any such notice as the date of redemption (unless default shall be made by the Corporation in the payment of the redemption price), all dividends on the ______ stock thereby called for redemption shall cease to accrue and all rights of the holders hereof as Stockholders of the Corporation, except the right to receive the redemption price, shall cease and determine.

Any purchase by the Corporation of shares of its ______ stock shall not be made at prices in excess of said redemption price.

Alternative F

So long as any of the ______ shares shall be outstanding, the Corporation shall set aside, from the surplus profits remaining after the aforesaid cumulative dividends on the ______ shares have been paid or set apart for payment, on or before the ______ day of ______, 19__, and on or before the first day of [*Designate Month*] in each succeeding year, a sinking fund for the redemption or purchase of the ______ shares, in the sum of ______ ($______) Dollars plus the amount, if any, by which ______ per cent of the net earnings and income of the Corporation for the preceding twelve months should exceed ______ ($______) Dollars. The obligation to set aside the sinking funds from the surplus profits remaining after the cumulative dividends have been paid or set aside shall be cumulative, so that if in any year the remaining surplus profits shall be insufficient to permit the full amounts required as aforesaid to be set aside, the deficiency shall be made out of the surplus profits thereafter made, before dividends shall be declared or paid upon the common shares. The sinking fund shall be applied to the redemption of the ______ shares, as herein provided, whenever, and to such extent as the members of the Board of Directors of the Corporation in their discretion may determine, except, that in the event of any such share being offered for sale, at less than the redemption price, such share shall be purchased at the lowest price obtainable not exceeding the redemption price herein specified. ______ shares redeemed or purchased as herein provided shall not be reissued and no ______ shares shall issue in lieu thereof or in exchange therefor, and such shares shall be eliminated from time to time in a manner permitted by law. Moneys credited to the sinking fund and not for the time being used for the purpose of the redemption or purchase of ______ shares shall not be required to be withdrawn from the business, provided, however, that the same must be kept available for the purpose of the redemption or purchase of ______ shares. Moneys credited to the sinking fund shall, so long as any of the ______ shares shall be outstanding, be unavailable as a basis for dividends or for other charges against surplus. No dividend shall be declared upon the common shares, unless the sinking fund above provided shall have been credited in the aggregate with at least ______ ($______) Dollars and no dividend in excess of ______ per cent per annum shall be declared upon the ______ shares unless said sinking fund shall have been credited in the aggregate with at least ______ ($______) Dollars.

Library References:

C.J.S. Corporations § 277 et seq.
West's Key No. Digests, Corporations ⚷68.

Article XXIII

DISSOLUTION

§ 23.1 Non-Judicial Dissolution

Option 1

Upon the following event(s), the Corporation shall be dissolved:

Option 1–A

(a) A vote of ______% of the outstanding common shares.

Option 1–B

(b) The Corporation suffering a loss (as accounted for by generally accepted accounting principles) in ______ consecutive fiscal quarters.

Option 1–C

(c) [*list other events*].

Option 2

The Stockholders may not petition for judicial dissolution unless:

Option 2–A

(a) ______% of the outstanding common shares so petition.

Option 2–B

(b) The Corporation has suffered a loss (as accounted for by generally accepted accounting principles) in ______ consecutive fiscal quarters.

Option 2–C

(c) [*list other events*].

Article XXIV
REGISTERED OFFICE

Required by Statute

§ 24.1 Office

The address of the initial registered office is:

____________	____________	____________
(No. and Street)	(Town or City)	(Zip Code)

The mailing address of the initial registered office is:

____________	____________	____________
(No. and Street)	(Town or City)	(Zip Code)

The name of the initial resident agent at the registered office is: ____________

COMMENTS TO ARTICLE XXIV

The Articles must state the address of the Corporation's initial registered office and the name of its initial registered agent at such address. See Model Bus.Corp.Act § 54(g).

The registered office (Model Bus.Corp.Act § 12) need not be the same as the Corporation's place of business.

The registered agent may either be an individual resident or Corporation authorized to do business in the State so long as he, she or its business office is identical to the registered office (Model Bus.Corp.Act § 12).

The purpose of the registered office is to designate a place where the service of legal documents can occur. The registered agent should be responsible enough to contact appropriate advisors upon the receipt of any legal documents and/or tax forms.

Article XXV
INCORPORATORS

Required by Statute

§ 25.1 Incorporators

The name(s) and address(es) of the incorporator(s) are as follows:

Name	Residence or Business Address
____________	____________
____________	____________
____________	____________
____________	____________

COMMENTS TO ARTICLE XXV

One or more persons may be the incorporator of the Corporation. There is no need for such person(s) to ultimately become Stockholders (Model Bus.Corp.Act § 53). The name and address of each incorporator must be stated (Model Bus.Corp.Act § 54).

For additional discussion of incorporators, see Chapter 32, supra.

Article XXVI

TERM

Required by Statute

§ 26.1 Term

The term of existence of the Corporation shall be *perpetual.*

COMMENT TO ARTICLE XXVI

The Articles must state the period of Corporate duration (Model Bus.Corp.Act § 54(b)).

Article XXVII

EFFECTIVE DATE

Not Generally Preferred as a Matter of Practical Experience

§ 27.1 Effective Date

The effective date of Incorporation shall be [*Fill in Date*].

COMMENT TO ARTICLE XXVII

When a Corporation wants to limit its authority to do business until a certain date in the future, this language will be necessary.

In witness whereof, the undersigned, the incorporator(s) of the above named Corporation, has [*have*] hereunto signed these Articles of Incorporation on the ______ day of ______, 19__.

______________________	______________________
[*Type Name Under Signature*]	Address
______________________	______________________
	Address
______________________	______________________
	Address
______________________	______________________

§ 33.17 Certificate of Incorporation Issued by Secretary of State —Model Business Corporation Act

STATE OF ______

OFFICE OF THE SECRETARY OF STATE

CERTIFICATE OF INCORPORATION

OF ______

The undersigned, as Secretary of State of the State of ______, hereby certifies that duplicate originals of Articles of Incorporation for the incorporation of ______, duly signed pursuant to the provisions of the ______ Business Corporation Act, have been received in this office and are found to conform to law.

Accordingly the undersigned, as such Secretary of State, and by virtue of the authority vested in him by law, hereby issues this Certificate of Incorporation of ______ and attaches hereto a duplicate original of the Articles of Incorporation.

Dated ______, 19__.

____

Secretary of State

Source of Form

Form No. 13 (Model Bus.Corp.Act § 55), Official Forms for Use Under the 1969 Revision of the Model Business Corporation Act, prepared by the Committee on Corporate Laws of the American Bar Association.

Library References:

C.J.S. Corporations § 59.
West's Key No. Digests, Corporations ⚷21.

§§ 33.18–34.0 are reserved for supplementary material.

CHAPTER 34

BY-LAWS

Table of Sections

A. INTRODUCTION

§ 34.1 Scope and Purpose of By-laws

By-laws are the rules and regulations or private laws enacted by the Corporation to regulate, govern, and control its own actions, affairs, and concerns, and its Stockholders, Directors, and Officers.

The existence of such By-laws: (a) smooth the functioning of Stockholder meetings, (b) outline the authority and limitations of the Board of Directors and smooth their meetings, and (c) outline the authority and limitations of the Officers. The By-laws are an indication of incorporation (i. e., that the Corporation is a separate entity—see Chapter 31, supra). In addition, the adoption of special By-law clauses may give to the Corporation rights which it otherwise would not have.

The corporate laws of the fifty states do not specify what the By-laws must contain. Their contents are largely determined by the purpose which they serve. That purpose is to guide the Directors, Officers and Stockholders in the exercise of their management powers. This allows considerable discretion to the draftsman. Actually By-laws follow a fairly uniform pattern setting out the rules governing (a) location of corporate offices, (b) Stockholders' meetings, (c) composition of the Board of Directors, (d) Directors' meetings, (e) Officers, (f) certificates of stock and their transfer, (g) execution of instruments, (h) fiscal year, (i) seal, and (j) amendments.

The provisions of the By-laws are derived from both statutory and non-statutory sources. A number of the By-laws repeat the language of the applicable statute. This is done as a convenience to the Directors, Officers and Stockholders to whom the By-laws are more accessible than the statutes. Again, many of the By-laws, while not a restatement of the statute, are responsive to it, as where the statute sets out a rule to govern unless otherwise provided in the By-laws. Again, many of the By-laws are without statutory basis, but adopt customary procedures consistent with statute.

The By-laws of a large Corporation and a closely held Corporation follow similar lines. There may be some clauses providing for committees and election inspectors which are more appropriate for the large Corporation than for the closely held Corporation. Conversely, there may be others granting enlarged management powers to the Stockholders and restricting the transfer and issuance of stock which are more appropriate for a closely held Corporation than for a large Corporation.

Unlike the Articles of Incorporation, By-laws are usually not filed in any public office, and hence avoid any administrative scrutiny. By-laws like the Articles of Incorporation, must be consistent with constitutional and statutory provisions and "statutory norms" and, in addition, with any valid provisions in the Articles of Incorporation.[1]

While it is often said that every Corporation as such has power to make By-laws, this is frequently confirmed by statute.[2]

Many states provide that By-laws may contain any provision for the regulation and management of the affairs of the Corporation not inconsistent with law or the Articles of Incorporation.[3] Some states spell out by statute those matters which must or may be regulated by By-laws.

1. C.J.S. Corporations, § 179 et seq. See Cary, Law of Corporations, § 133.

2. E. g. Model Bus.Corp.Act § 4(*l*); West's Ann.Cal.Corp.Code § 207(b); McKinney's N.Y.Bus.Corp.Law § 202(a)(22); Minn.Bus.Corp.Act § 302A.161(16).

3. E. g. Model Bus.Corp.Act §§ 27, 52 (at organization meeting of Board of Directors).

Formulation of the initial By-laws is a power variously enjoyed in different jurisdictions by the Incorporators, the Stockholders, or the Board of Directors.[4] Power to adopt, amend, and repeal the By-laws is sometimes vested in the Stockholders, or Board of Directors,[5] or left to treatment in the Articles of Incorporation or in the By-laws themselves.

A growing number of states empower the Board of Directors to adopt emergency By-laws, subject to repeal or change by Stockholders, to be operative, notwithstanding contrary provisions elsewhere in the corporate statutes, or in the Articles of Incorporation or By-laws, during any emergency in the conduct of the business of the Corporation resulting from an attack on the United States or any nuclear or atomic disaster.[6]

By-laws range from the briefest statement of rules for the internal management of the Corporation to what almost amounts to a manual of such rules which includes a restatement of the applicable statutes and provisions in the Articles of Incorporation for the guidance of corporate personnel. A compromise approach is to include such statutes and other provisions in a memorandum or addendum to the By-laws proper.

Some states provide that any provision required or permitted to be set forth in the By-laws may instead be set forth in the Articles of Incorporation,[7] but in the absence of such a provision the By-laws should provide for: penalties for failure to pay installments or calls for subscriptions for shares; [8] place of holding meetings of Stockholders and time of holding annual meeting of Stockholders; [9] number of Directors, except as to first Board of Directors; [10] division of Directors into classes having different terms; [11] fixing of quorum of Directors at a number greater than a majority thereof, and requiring action of the Board to be taken by vote of more than a majority of

4. E. g. Model Bus.Corp.Act § 27 provides:

"The initial by-laws of a corporation shall be adopted by its board of directors. The power to alter, amend or repeal the by-laws or adopt new by-laws, subject to repeal or change by action of the shareholders, shall be vested in the board of directors unless reserved to the shareholders by the articles of incorporation. The by-laws may contain any provisions for the regulation and management of the affairs of the corporation not inconsistent with law or the articles of incorporation."

5. E. g. Model Bus.Corp.Act § 27 (unless reserved to the Stockholders by the articles of incorporation).

6. E. g. Model Bus.Corp.Act § 27A.

7. E. g. Model Bus.Corp.Act § 54(4); West's Ann.Cal.Corp.Code § 204; McKinney's N.Y.Bus.Corp.Law § 402(b).

8. E. g. Model Bus.Corp.Act § 19.

9. E. g. Model Bus.Corp.Act § 28.

10. E. g. Model Bus.Corp.Act § 36.

11. E. g. Model Bus.Corp.Act § 37.

a quorum; [12] notice of Directors' meetings; [13] and election or appointment of Officers.[14]

Certain other provisions either may be prescribed in the By-laws or the Articles of Incorporation or may be omitted entirely: calling special meetings of Stockholders in a manner other than as provided for by statute; [15] fixing record dates; [16] qualifications of Directors; [17] and creation of an executive committee.[18]

By-laws can be adopted or amended impliedly as well as expressly, but the burden is on the party asserting such implied adoption or amendment.

Occasionally, upon sufficient proof, a court will order reformation of the By-laws to reflect representations among the Stockholders.

A provision which is invalid as a By-law might be enforced as a contract among the Stockholders who approved it.

Library References:

C.J.S. Corporations § 179 et seq.
West's Key No. Digests, Corporations ⚿54.

§ 34.2 Check List for Use in Preparing By-laws

1. Location of principal office.
2. Meetings of Stockholders.

(a) Annual meetings of Stockholders:

Time (day and hour);

Place;

Notice.

(b) Special meetings of Stockholders:

By whom called;

Place;

Notice.

(c) Quorum:

Any reason for requiring more or less than a majority?

(d) Voting requirements:

Any reason for requiring more than a majority?

(e) Written consent in lieu of meeting.

12. E. g. Model Bus.Corp.Act § 40.

13. E. g. Model Bus.Corp.Act § 43.

14. E. g. Model Bus.Corp.Act § 50.

15. E. g. Model Bus.Corp.Act § 28.

16. E. g. Model Bus.Corp.Act § 30.

17. E. g. Model Bus.Corp.Act § 35.

18. E. g. Model Bus.Corp.Act § 42.

3. Directors.

(a) Number.

(b) Qualifications:

Are Directors required to be Stockholders?

(c) Election:

Is ballot to be required?

Is cumulative voting authorized?

(d) Term:

Are there to be staggered terms?

(e) Vacancies:

How filled?

(f) Compensation.

(g) Removal:

By whom?

For cause only, or with or without cause?

4. Meetings of Directors.

(a) Regular meetings:

Time;

Place;

Notice.

(b) Special meetings:

By whom called?

Place;

Notice.

(c) Written consent in lieu of meeting.

(d) Quorum.

(e) Voting requirements.

5. Committees of Board of Directors.

6. Officers.

(a) What Officers?

Chairman;

President;

Vice-President (one or more);

Secretary;

Treasurer.

(b) Qualifications:

Is any Officer required to be a Director?

(c) Manner of election—by Directors or Stockholders.

(d) Term of office.

(e) Removal.

(f) Duties of each Officer:

Chairman;

President;

Vice-President;

Secretary;

Treasurer.

(g) Salaries:

Are salaries to be fixed by Board of Directors?

(h) Bond to be furnished:

If so, by whom?

7. Capital Stock:

Transfer agent and registrar;

Determining Stockholders entitled to vote, etc. (closing stock transfer book or fixing record date);

Restrictions on transfer.

8. Execution of instruments:

Who has authority to execute.

(a) Contracts.

(b) Checks, drafts, etc.

(c) Proxies.

9. Form of seal.

10. Fiscal year.

11. Amendments to By-laws:

By whom?

§§ 34.3–34.10 are reserved for supplementary material.

B. BY-LAW FORMS

§ 34.11 By-laws—Model Business Corporation Act *

COMMENT

This set of By-laws only covers certain substantive provisions. The practitioner is urged to also consult the Sophisticated By-laws at § 34.14, infra, and the checklist at § 34.2, supra.

BY-LAWS OF ______

* Numbers in [brackets] are references to Sections of the Model Business Corporation Act.

Article I

OFFICES

The principal office of the Corporation in the State of ______ shall be located in the City of ______, County of ______. The Corporation may have such other offices, either within or without the State of ______, as the Board of Directors may designate or as the business of the Corporation may require from time to time.

The registered office of the Corporation, required by the ______ Business Corporation Act to be maintained in the State of ______ may be, but need not be, identical with the principal office in the State of ______, and the address of the registered office may be changed from time to time by the Board of Directors. [§ 12] [§ 13, Clause (g)]

Article II

STOCKHOLDERS

§ 2.1 **Annual Meeting.** The annual meeting of the Stockholders shall be held on the ______ in the month of ______ in each year, beginning with the year 19__, at the hour of ______ o'clock __. M., or such other time on such other day within such month as shall be fixed by the Board of Directors, for the purpose of electing Directors and for the transaction of such other business as may come before the meeting. If the day fixed for the annual meeting shall be a legal holiday in the State of ______, such meeting shall be held on the next succeeding business day. If the election of Directors shall not be held on the day designated herein for any annual meeting of the Stockholders, or at any adjournment thereof, the Board of Directors shall cause the election to be held at a special meeting of the Stockholders as soon thereafter as conveniently may be. [§ 28] [§ 36]

§ 2.2 **Special Meetings.** Special meetings of the Stockholders, for any purpose or purposes, unless otherwise prescribed by statute, may be called by the President or by the Board of Directors, and shall be called by the President at the request of the holders of not less than one-tenth of all outstanding shares of the Corporation entitled to vote at the meeting. [§ 28]

§ 2.3 **Place of Meeting.** The Board of Directors may designate any place, either within or without the State of ______, as the place of meeting for any annual meeting or for any special meeting called by the Board of Directors. A waiver of notice signed by all Stockholders entitled to vote at a meeting may designate any place, either within or without the State of ______, as the place for the holding of such meeting. If no designation is made, or if a special meeting be otherwise called, the place of meeting shall be the principal office of the Corporation in the State of ______. [§ 28]

2.4 Notice of Meeting. Written notice stating the place, day and hour of the meeting and, in case of a special meeting, the purpose or purposes for which the meeting is called, shall, unless otherwise prescribed by statute, be delivered not less than ten nor more than fifty days before the date of the meeting, either personally or by mail, by or at the direction of the President, or the Secretary, or the Officer or other persons calling the meeting, to each Stockholder of record entitled to vote at such meeting. If mailed, such notice shall be deemed to be delivered when deposited in the United States mail, addressed to the Stockholder at his address as it appears on the stock transfer books of the Corporation, with postage thereon prepaid. [§ 29]

§ 2.5 Closing of Transfer Books or Fixing of Record Date. For the purpose of determining Stockholders entitled to notice of or to vote at any meeting of Stockholders or any adjournment thereof, or Stockholders entitled to receive payment of any dividend, or in order to make a determination of Stockholders for any other proper purpose, the Board of Directors of the Corporation may provide that the stock transfer books shall be closed for a stated period but not to exceed, in any case, fifty days. If the stock transfer books shall be closed for the purpose of determining Stockholders entitled to notice of or to vote at a meeting of Stockholders, such books shall be closed for at least ten days immediately preceding such meeting. In lieu of closing the stock transfer books, the Board of Directors may fix in advance a date as the record date for any such determination of Stockholders, such date in any case to be not more than fifty days and, in case of a meeting of Stockholders, not less than ten days prior to the date on which the particular action, requiring such determination of Stockholders, is to be taken. If the stock transfer books are not closed and no record date is fixed for the determination of Stockholders entitled to notice of or to vote at a meeting of Stockholders, or Stockholders entitled to receive payment of a dividend, the date on which notice of the meeting is mailed or the date on which the resolution of the Board of Directors declaring such dividend is adopted, as the case may be, shall be the record date for such determination of Stockholders. When a determination of Stockholders entitled to vote at any meeting of Stockholders has been made as provided in this section, such determination shall apply to any adjournment thereof. [§ 30]

§ 2.6 Voting Record. The Officer or agent having charge of the stock transfer books for shares of the Corporation shall make a complete record of the Stockholders entitled to vote at each meeting of Stockholders or any adjournment thereof, arranged in alphabetical order, with the address of and the number of shares held by each. Such record shall be produced and kept open at the time and place of the meeting and shall be subject to the inspection of any Stockholder during the whole time of the meeting for the purposes thereof. [§ 31]

§ 2.7 Quorum. A majority of the outstanding shares of the Corporation entitled to vote, represented in person or by proxy, shall constitute a quorum at a meeting of Stockholders. If less than a majority of the outstanding shares are represented at a meeting, a majority of the shares so represented may adjourn the meeting from time to time without further notice. At such adjourned meeting at which a quorum shall be present or represented, any business may be transacted which might have been transacted at the meeting as originally noticed. The Stockholders present at a duly organized meeting may continue to transact business until adjournment, notwithstanding the withdrawal of enough Stockholders to leave less than a quorum. [§ 32]

§ 2.8 Proxies. At all meetings of Stockholders, a Stockholder may vote in person or by proxy executed in writing by the Stockholder or by his duly authorized attorney-in-fact. Such proxy shall be filed with the Secretary of the Corporation before or at the time of the meeting. No proxy shall be valid after eleven months from the date of its execution, unless otherwise provided in the proxy. [§ 33]

§ 2.9 Voting of Shares. Subject to the provisions of Section 12 of this Article II, each outstanding share entitled to vote shall be entitled to one vote upon each matter submitted to a vote at a meeting of Stockholders. [§ 33]

§ 2.10 Voting of Shares by Certain Holders. Shares standing in the name of another Corporation may be voted by such officer, agent or proxy as the By-Laws of such Corporation may prescribe, or, in the absence of such provision, as the Board of Directors of such other Corporation may determine. [§ 33]

Shares held by an administrator, executor, guardian or conservator may be voted by him, either in person or by proxy, without a transfer of such shares into his name. Shares standing in the name of a trustee may be voted by him, either in person or by proxy, but no trustee shall be entitled to vote shares held by him without a transfer of such shares into his name. [§ 33]

Shares standing in the name of a receiver may be voted by such receiver, and shares held by or under the control of a receiver may be voted by such receiver without the transfer thereof into his name if authority so to do be contained in an appropriate order of the court by which such receiver was appointed. [§ 33]

A Stockholder whose shares are pledged shall be entitled to vote such shares until the shares have been transferred into the name of the pledgee, and thereafter the pledgee shall be entitled to vote the shares so transferred. [§ 33]

Neither treasury shares of its own stock held by the Corporation, nor shares held by another Corporation if a majority of the shares entitled to vote for the election of Directors of such other Corporation are held by the Corporation, shall be voted at any meeting or counted in determining the total number of outstanding shares at any given time for purposes of any meeting. [§ 33]

§ 2.11 Informal Action by Shareholders. Any action required or permitted to be taken at a meeting of the Stockholders may be taken without a meeting if a consent in writing, setting forth the action so taken, shall be signed by all of the Stockholders entitled to vote with respect to the subject matter thereof. [§ 145]

§ 2.12 Cumulative Voting. (Optional) At each election for Directors every Stockholder entitled to vote at such election shall have the right to vote, in person or by proxy, the number of shares owned by him for as many persons as there are Directors to be elected and for whose election he has a right to vote, or to cumulate his votes by giving one candidate as many votes as the number of such Directors multiplied by the number of his shares shall equal, or by distributing such votes on the same principle among any number of such candidates. [§ 33]

Article III

BOARD OF DIRECTORS

§ 3.1 General Powers. The business and affairs of the Corporation shall be managed by its Board of Directors. [§ 35]

§ 3.2 Number, Tenure and Qualifications. The number of Directors of the Corporation shall be ______. Each Director shall hold office until the next annual meeting of Stockholders and until his successor shall have been elected and qualified. Directors need not be residents of the State of ______ or Stockholders of the Corporation. [§ 35] [§ 36]

§ 3.3 Regular Meetings. A regular meeting of the Board of Directors shall be held without other notice than this By-law immediately after, and at the same place as, the annual meeting of Stockholders. The Board of Directors may provide, by resolution, the time and place, either within or without the State of ______, for the holding of additional regular meetings without other notice than such resolution. [§ 43]

§ 3.4 Special Meetings. Special meetings of the Board of Directors may be called by or at the request of the President or any two Directors. The person or persons authorized to call special meetings of the Board of Directors may fix any place, either within or without the State of ______, as the place for holding any special meeting of the Board of Directors called by them. [§ 43]

§ 3.5 Notice. Notice of any special meeting shall be given at least two days previously thereto by written notice delivered personally or mailed to each Director at his business address, or by telegram. If mailed, such notice shall be deemed to be delivered when deposited in the United States mail, so addressed, with postage thereon prepaid. If notice be given by telegram, such notice shall be deemed to be delivered when the telegram is delivered to the telegraph company. Any Director may waive notice of any meeting. The attendance of a Director at a meeting shall constitute a waiver of notice of such meeting, except where a Director attends a meeting for the express purpose of objecting to the transaction of any business because the meeting is not lawfully called or convened. Neither the business to be transacted at, nor the purpose of, any regular or special meeting of the Board of Directors need be specified in the notice or waiver of notice of such meeting. [§ 43]

§ 3.6 Quorum. A majority of the number of Directors fixed by Section 2 of this Article III shall constitute a quorum for the transaction of business at any meeting of the Board of Directors, but if less than such majority is present at a meeting, a majority of the Directors present may adjourn the meeting from time to time without further notice. [§ 40]

§ 3.7 Manner of Acting. The act of the majority of the Directors present at a meeting at which a quorum is present shall be the act of the Board of Directors. [§ 40]

§ 3.8 Action Without a Meeting. Any action required or permitted to be taken by the Board of Directors at a meeting may be taken without a meeting if a consent in writing, setting forth the action so taken, shall be signed by all of the Directors. [§ 44]

§ 3.9 Vacancies. Any vacancy occurring in the Board of Directors may be filled by the affirmative vote of a majority of the remaining Directors though less than a quorum of the Board of Directors. A Director elected to fill a vacancy shall be elected for the unexpired term of his predecessor in office. Any directorship to be filled by reason of an increase in the number of Directors may be filled by election by the Board of Directors for a term of office continuing only until the next election of Directors by the Stockholders. [§ 38]

§ 3.10 Compensation. By resolution of the Board of Directors, each Director may be paid his expenses, if any, of attendance at each meeting of the Board of Directors, and may be paid a stated salary as director or a fixed sum for attendance at each meeting of the Board of Directors or both. No such payment shall preclude any Director from serving the Corporation in any other capacity and receiving compensation therefor. [§ 35]

§ 3.11 Presumption of Assent. A Director of the Corporation who is present at a meeting of the Board of Directors at which action on any corporate matter is taken shall be presumed to have assented to the action taken unless his dissent shall be entered in the minutes of the meeting or unless he shall file his written dissent to such action with the person acting as the secretary of the meeting before the adjournment thereof or shall forward such dissent by registered mail to the Secretary of the Corporation immediately after the adjournment of the meeting. Such right to dissent shall not apply to a Director who voted in favor of such action. [§ 48]

Article IV

OFFICERS

§ 4.1 Number. The Officers of the Corporation shall be a President, one or more Vice-Presidents (the number thereof to be determined by the Board of Directors), a Secretary, and a Treasurer, each of whom shall be elected by the Board of Directors. Such other Officers and assistant Officers as may be deemed necessary may be elected or appointed by the Board of Directors. Any two or more Offices may be held by the same person, except the Offices of President and Secretary. [§ 50]

§ 4.2 Election and Term of Office. The Officers of the Corporation to be elected by the Board of Directors shall be elected annually by the Board of Directors at the first meeting of the Board of Directors held after each annual meeting of the Stockholders. If the election of Officers shall not be held at such meeting, such election shall be held as soon thereafter as conveniently may be. Each Officer shall hold office until his successor shall have been duly elected and shall have qualified or until his death or until he shall resign or shall have been removed in the manner hereinafter provided. [§ 50]

§ 4.3 Removal. Any Officer or agent may be removed by the Board of Directors whenever in its judgment the best interests of the Corporation will be served thereby, but such removal shall be without prejudice to the contract rights, if any, of the person so removed. Election or appointment of an Officer or agent shall not of itself create contract rights. [§ 51]

§ 4.4 Vacancies. A vacancy in any office because of death, resignation, removal, disqualification or otherwise, may be filled by the Board of Directors for the unexpired portion of the term.

§ 4.5 President. The President shall be the Principal Executive Officer of the Corporation and, subject to the control of the Board of Directors, shall in general supervise and control all of the business and affairs of the Corporation. He shall, when present, preside at all meetings of the Stockholders and of the Board of Directors. He may sign, with the Secretary or any other proper Officer of the Corporation thereunto authorized by the Board of Directors, certificates for shares of the Corporation and deeds, mortgages, bonds, contracts, or other instruments which the Board of Directors has authorized to be executed, except in cases where the signing and execution thereof shall be expressly delegated by the Board of Directors or by these By-laws to some other Officer or agent of the Corporation, or shall be required by law to be otherwise signed or executed; and in general shall perform all duties incident to the office of President and such other duties as may be prescribed by the Board of Directors from time to time. [§ 23]

§ 4.6 The Vice-Presidents. In the absence of the President or in the event of his death, inability or refusal to act, the Vice-President (or in the event there be more than one Vice-President, the Vice-Presidents in the order designated at the time of their election, or in the absence of any designation, then in the order of their election) shall perform the duties of the President, and when so acting, shall have all the powers of and be subject to all the restrictions upon the President. Any Vice-President may sign, with the Secretary or an Assistant Secretary, certificates for shares of the Corporation; and shall perform such other duties as from time to time may be assigned to him by the President or by the Board of Directors. [§ 23]

§ 4.7 The Secretary. The Secretary shall: (a) keep the minutes of the proceedings of the Stockholders and of the Board of Directors in one or more books provided for that purpose; (b) see that all notices are duly given in accordance with the provisions of these By-laws or as required by law; (c) be custodian of the corporate records and of the seal of the Corporation and see that the seal of the Corporation is affixed to all documents the execution of which on behalf of the Corporation under its seal is duly authorized; (d) keep a register of the postoffice address of each Stockholder which shall be furnished to the Secretary by such Stockholder; (e) sign with the President, or a Vice-President, certificates for shares of the Corporation, the issuance of which shall have been authorized by resolution of the Board of Directors; (f) have general charge of the stock transfer books of the Corporation; and (g) in general perform all duties incident to the office of Secretary and such other duties as from time to time may be assigned to him by the President or by the Board of Directors. [§ 23]

§ 4.8 **The Treasurer.** The Treasurer shall: (a) have charge and custody of and be responsible for all funds and securities of the Corporation; (b) receive and give receipts for moneys due and payable to the Corporation from any source whatsoever, and deposit all such moneys in the name of the Corporation in such banks, trust companies or other depositaries as shall be selected in accordance with the provisions of Article V of these By-laws; and (c) in general perform all of the duties incident to the office of Treasurer and such other duties as from time to time may be assigned to him by the President or by the Board of Directors. If required by the Board of Directors, the Treasurer shall give a bond for the faithful discharge of his duties in such sum and with such surety or sureties as the Board of Directors shall determine.

§ 4.9 **Assistant Secretaries and Assistant Treasurers.** The Assistant Secretaries, when authorized by the Board of Directors, may sign with the President or a Vice-President certificates for shares of the Corporation the issuance of which shall have been authorized by a resolution of the Board of Directors. The Assistant Treasurers shall respectively, if required by the Board of Directors, give bonds for the faithful discharge of their duties in such sums and with such sureties as the Board of Directors shall determine. The Assistant Secretaries and Assistant Treasurers, in general, shall perform such duties as shall be assigned to them by the Secretary or the Treasurer, respectively, or by the President or the Board of Directors. [§ 23]

§ 4.10 **Salaries.** The salaries of the Officers shall be fixed from time to time by the Board of Directors and no Officer shall be prevented from receiving such salary by reason of the fact that he is also a Director of the Corporation.

Article V

CONTRACTS, LOANS, CHECKS AND DEPOSITS

§ 5.1 **Contracts.** The Board of Directors may authorize any Officer or Officers, agent or agents, to enter into any contract or execute and deliver any instrument in the name of and on behalf of the Corporation, and such authority may be general or confined to specific instances.

§ 5.2 **Loans.** No loans shall be contracted on behalf of the Corporation and no evidences of indebtedness shall be issued in its name unless authorized by a resolution of the Board of Directors. Such authority may be general or confined to specific instances.

§ 5.3 **Checks, Drafts, etc.** All checks, drafts or other orders for the payment of money, notes or other evidences of indebtedness issued in the name of the Corporation shall be signed by such Officer or Officers, agent or agents of the Corporation and in such manner as shall from time to time be determined by resolution of the Board of Directors.

§ 5.4 Deposits. All funds of the Corporation not otherwise employed shall be deposited from time to time to the credit of the Corporation in such banks, trust companies or other depositaries as the Board of Directors may select.

Article VI

CERTIFICATES FOR SHARES AND THEIR TRANSFER

§ 6.1 Certificates for Shares. Certificates representing shares of the Corporation shall be in such form as shall be determined by the Board of Directors. Such certificates shall be signed by the President or a Vice-President and by the Secretary or an Assistant Secretary and sealed with the corporate seal or a facsimile thereof. The signatures of such Officers upon a certificate may be facsimiles if the certificate is manually signed on behalf of a transfer agent or a registrar, other than the Corporation itself or one of its employees. Each certificate for shares shall be consecutively numbered or otherwise identified. The name and address of the person to whom the shares represented thereby are issued, with the number of shares and date of issue, shall be entered on the stock transfer books of the Corporation. All certificates surrendered to the Corporation for transfer shall be cancelled and no new certificate shall be issued until the former certificate for a like number of shares shall have been surrendered and cancelled, except that in case of a lost, destroyed or mutilated certificate a new one may be issued therefor upon such terms and indemnity to the Corporation as the Board of Directors may prescribe. [§ 23] [§ 52]

§ 6.2 Transfer of Shares. Transfer of shares of the Corporation shall be made only on the stock transfer books of the Corporation by the holder of record thereof or by his legal representative, who shall furnish proper evidence of authority to transfer, or by his attorney thereunto authorized by power of attorney duly executed and filed with the secretary of the Corporation, and on surrender for cancellation of the certificate for such shares. The person in whose name shares stand on the books of the Corporation shall be deemed by the Corporation to be the owner thereof for all purposes.

Article VII

FISCAL YEAR

The fiscal year of the Corporation shall begin on the first day of January and end on the thirty-first day of December in each year.

Article VIII

DIVIDENDS

The Board of Directors may, from time to time, declare and the Corporation may pay dividends on its outstanding shares in the manner and upon the terms and conditions provided by law and its Articles of Incorporation. [§ 45]

Article IX

CORPORATE SEAL

The Board of Directors shall provide a corporate seal which shall be circular in form and shall have inscribed thereon the name of the Corporation and the state of incorporation and the words "Corporate Seal". [§ 4, Clause (c)]

Article X

WAIVER OF NOTICE

Whenever any notice is required to be given to any Stockholder or Director of the Corporation under the provisions of these By-laws or under the provisions of the Articles of Incorporation or under the provisions of the ______ Business Corporation Act, a waiver thereof in writing signed by the person or persons entitled to such notice, whether before or after the time stated therein, shall be deemed equivalent to the giving of such notice. [§ 144]

Article XI

AMENDMENTS

These By-laws may be altered, amended or repealed and new By-laws may be adopted by the Board of Directors or by the Stockholders at any regular or special meeting. [§ 27]

Article XII

EXECUTIVE COMMITTEE (OPTIONAL)

§ 12.1 Appointment. The Board of Directors by resolution adopted by a majority of the full Board, may designate two or more of its members to constitute an executive committee. The designation of such committee and the delegation thereto of authority shall not operate to relieve the Board of Directors, or any member thereof, of any responsibility imposed By-law. [§ 42]

§ 12.2 Authority. The executive committee, when the Board of Directors is not in session shall have and may exercise all of the authority of the Board of Directors except to the extent, if any, that such authority shall be limited by the resolution appointing the executive committee and except also that the executive committee shall not have the authority of the Board of Directors in reference to amending the Articles of Incorporation, adopting a plan of merger or consolidation, recommending to the Stockholders the sale, lease or other disposition of all or substantially all of the property and assets of the Corporation otherwise than in the usual and regular course of its business, recommending to the Stockholders a voluntary dissolution of the Corporation or a revocation thereof, or amending the By-laws of the Corporation. [§ 42]

§ 12.3 Tenure and Qualifications. Each member of the executive committee shall hold office until the next regular annual meeting of the Board of Directors following his designation and until his successor is designated as a member of the executive committee and is elected and qualified.

§ 12.4 Meetings. Regular meetings of the executive committee may be held without notice at such times and places as the executive committee may fix from time to time by resolution. Special meetings of the executive committee may be called by any member thereof upon not less than one day's notice stating the place, date and hour of the meeting, which notice may be written or oral, and if mailed, shall be deemed to be delivered when deposited in the United States mail addressed to the member of the executive committee at his business address. Any member of the executive committee may waive notice of any meeting and no notice of any meeting need be given to any member thereof who attends in person. The notice of a meeting of the executive committee need not state the business proposed to be transacted at the meeting.

§ 12.5 Quorum. A majority of the members of the executive committee shall constitute a quorum for the transaction of business at any meeting thereof, and action of the executive committee must be authorized by the affirmative vote of a majority of the members present at a meeting at which a quorum is present.

§ 12.6 Action Without a Meeting. Any action required or permitted to be taken by the executive committee at a meeting may be taken without a meeting if a consent in writing, setting forth the action so taken, shall be signed by all of the members of the executive committee. [§ 44]

§ 12.7 Vacancies. Any vacancy in the executive committee may be filled by a resolution adopted by a majority of the full Board of Directors.

§ 12.8 Resignations and Removal. Any member of the executive committee may be removed at any time with or without cause by resolution adopted by a majority of the full Board of Directors. Any member of the executive committee may resign from the executive committee at any time by giving written notice to the President or Secretary of the Corporation, and unless otherwise specified therein, the acceptance of such resignation shall not be necessary to make it effective.

§ 12.9 Procedure. The executive committee shall elect a presiding officer from its members and may fix its own rules of procedure which shall not be inconsistent with these By-laws. It shall keep regular minutes of its proceedings and report the same to the Board of Directors for its information at the meeting thereof held next after the proceedings shall have been taken.

Article XIII

EMERGENCY BY-LAWS [§ 27-A]

The Emergency By-laws provided in this Article XIII shall be operative during any emergency in the conduct of the business of the Corporation resulting from an attack on the United States or any nuclear or atomic disaster, notwithstanding any different provision in the preceding Articles of the By-laws or in the Articles of Incorporation of the Corporation or in the ______ Business Corporation Act. To the extent not inconsistent with the provisions of this Article, the By-laws provided in the preceding Articles shall remain in effect during such emergency and upon its termination the Emergency By-laws shall cease to be operative.

During any such emergency:

(a) A meeting of the Board of Directors may be called by any Officer or Director of the Corporation. Notice of the time and place of the meeting shall be given by the person calling the meeting to such of the Directors as it may be feasible to reach by any available means of communication. Such notice shall be given at such time in advance of the meeting as circumstances permit in the judgment of the person calling the meeting.

(b) At any such meeting of the Board of Directors, a quorum shall consist of ______ [*here insert the particular provisions desired.*]

(c) The Board of Directors, either before or during any such emergency, may provide, and from time to time modify, lines of succession in the event that during such an emergency any or all Officers or agents of the Corporation shall for any reason be rendered incapable of discharging their duties.

(d) The Board of Directors, either before or during any such emergency, may, effective in the emergency, change the head office or designate several alternative head offices or regional offices, or authorize the Officers so to do.

No Officer, Director or employee acting in accordance with these Emergency By-laws shall be liable except for willful misconduct.

These Emergency By-laws shall be subject to repeal or change by further action of the Board of Directors or by action of the Stockholders, but no such repeal or change shall modify the provisions of the next preceding paragraph with regard to action taken prior to the time of such repeal or change. Any amendment of these Emergency By-laws may make any further or different provision that may be practical and necessary for the circumstances of the emergency.

Source of Form

Form No. 51, Official Forms for Use Under the 1969 Revision of the Model Business Corporation Act, prepared by the Committee on Corporate Laws of the American Bar Association.

Numbers in [brackets] are references to Sections of the Model Business Corporation Act.

Library References:

C.J.S. Corporations § 187.
West's Key No. Digests, Corporations ⚷56.

§ 34.12 By-laws—Model Business Corporation Act (Alternative Short Form)

COMMENT

This set of By-laws only covers certain substantive provisions. The practitioner is urged to also consult the Sophisticated By-laws at § 34.14, infra, and Checklist at § 34.2, supra.

BY–LAWS OF ______

Article I

STOCKHOLDERS

Meetings of Stockholders shall be held at the registered office of the Corporation unless another place shall have been determined by the Directors and stated in the notice of meeting. Annual meetings shall be held at ______ __M. on the ______ of ______ unless a holiday, and then on the next business day. [§ 28]

Article II

DIRECTORS

§ 2.1 The number of Directors shall be ______. [§ 36]

§ 2.2 A regular meeting of the Board of Directors shall be held without notice immediately following the annual meeting of

Stockholders and at the same place. The Board of Directors may provide for the holding without notice of additional regular meetings. [§ 43]

§ 2.3 Special meetings of the Board of Directors may be called by the President or any two Directors on 24-hour notice given personally or by telephone or telegraph or on four days' notice by mail. Special meetings shall be held at the place fixed by the Board of Directors for the holding of meetings, or if no such place has been fixed, at the principal business office of the Corporation. [§ 43]

Article III

OFFICERS

§ 3.4 The Officers of the Corporation shall be a President, a Vice-President, a Secretary and a Treasurer, who shall be elected annually at the regular meeting of the Board of Directors held after the annual meeting of Stockholders and shall hold office only so long as they are satisfactory to the Board of Directors. [§§ 50, 51]

§ 3.2 The President shall be the principal executive Officer of the Corporation to put into effect the decisions of the Board of Directors. Subject to such decisions, he shall supervise and control the business and affairs of the Corporation. He shall preside at meetings of the Stockholders and Directors. [§§ 35, 50]

§ 3.3 Subject to any specific assignments of duties made by the Board of Directors, the Vice-President, Secretary and Treasurer shall act under the direction of the President. The Vice-President shall perform the duties of the President when the President is absent or unable to act. The Secretary shall prepare and keep minutes of the meetings of the Stockholders and the Directors and shall have general charge of the stock records of the Corporation. [§§ 31, 52] The Treasurer shall have custody of the funds of the Corporation and keep its financial records. [§ 52]

Article IV

MISCELLANEOUS

§ 4.1 The Board of Directors may authorize any Officer or agent to enter into any contract or to execute any instrument for the Corporation. Such authority may be general or be confined to specific instances. [§§ 35, 50]

§ 4.2 Certificates representing shares of the Corporation shall be in such form as the Board of Directors shall determine. [§ 23] Transfers of shares shall be made only on the stock transfer books of the Corporation. [§ 52]

Article V

ACTION WITHOUT MEETING

Any action required or permitted to be taken by the Board of Directors or the Stockholders at a meeting may be taken without a meeting if a consent in writing, setting forth the action so taken, shall be signed by all Directors or Stockholders, as the case may be. [§§ 44, 145]

Article VI

AMENDMENTS

These By-laws may be altered, amended or repealed and new By-laws may be adopted by the Board of Directors or by the Stockholders. [§ 27]

Source of Form

Form No. 52, Official Forms for Use Under the 1969 Revision of the Model Business Corporation Act, prepared by the Committee on Corporate Laws of the American Bar Association.

Numbers in [brackets] are references to Sections of the Model Business Corporation Act.

§ 34.13 Basic By-laws Form

COMMENT

This set of By-laws only covers certain substantive provisions. The practitioner is urged to also consult the Sophisticated By-laws at § 34.14, infra, and Checklist at § 34.2, supra.

BY–LAWS

Article I

REGISTERED OFFICE

§ 1.1 Registered Office

The registered office shall be in the City of [*Name*], County of [*Name*], State of [*State of Incorporation.*]

The Corporation may also have offices at such other places both within or without the State of Incorporation as the Board of Directors may from time to time determine or the business of the Corporation may require.

Article II
FISCAL YEAR

§ 2.1 Fiscal Year

The fiscal year of the Corporation shall end on the last day of [*Month*], of each year unless another date shall be fixed by resolution of the Board of Directors.

After such date is fixed, it may be changed for future fiscal years at any time by further resolution of the Board of Directors.

COMMENTS TO ARTICLE II

The choice of the fiscal year is of the utmost importance. The following considerations apply:

(a) If possible, the fiscal year should end at a time of the year when it is easiest to take an inventory of assets (if this must be done) and assess the Corporation's general economic health.

(b) If possible, the fiscal year should end at a time of the year when financial advisors will be easily accessible. A year end meeting (before actual year end) to make plans for any present year activities which are to occur before year end is very helpful and in most cases must occur in order to insure that the year end planning is effective for the relevant fiscal year. The following plans can be established and made retroactively effective to the beginning of the fiscal year, but they can not predate the year in which this executed:

(1) Health insurance premium payment plans.

(2) Medical expense reimbursement plans.

(3) Legal expense reimbursement plans.

(4) Qualified retirement programs plans.

(5) Cafeteria plans.

Accrual basis taxpayers will want to have certain expenses accrue before year end so that they can be deducted. For such accrual to occur, these expenses must be "committed to" before that date. Among these are payments to majority Stockholders which must not only be accrued before year end, but must also be paid within 75 days after year end.

The Internal Revenue Service must approve any change of fiscal year. The procedure for accomplishing this is provided for in Treas.Reg. § 1.442–1:

REGULATIONS

§ 1.442–1. Change of Annual Accounting Period

(a) Manner of Effecting Such Change. (1) In General. If a taxpayer wishes to change his annual accounting period (as defined in section 441(c)) and adopt a new taxable year (as de-

fined in section 441(b)), he must obtain prior approval from the Commissioner by application, as provided in paragraph (b) of this section, or the change must be authorized under the Income Tax Regulations. A new taxpayer who adopts an annual accounting period as provided in section 441 and §§ 1.441–1 or 1.441–2 need not secure the permission of the Commissioner under section 442 and this section. However, see subparagraph (2) of this paragraph. For adoption of and changes to or from a 52–53-week taxable year, see section 441(f) and § 1.-441–2; for adoption of and changes in the taxable years of Partners and Partnerships, see paragraph (b)(2) of this section, section 706(b), and paragraph (b) of § 1.706–1; for special rules relating to certain Corporations, subsidiary Corporations, and newly married couples, see paragraphs (c), (d), and (e), respectively, of this section.

(2) Taxpayers to Whom Section 441(g) Applies. Section 441(g) provides that if a taxpayer keeps no books, does not have an annual accounting period, or has an accounting period which does not meet the requirements for a fiscal year, his taxable year shall be the calendar year. If section 441(g) applies to a taxpayer, the adoption of a fiscal year will be treated as a change in his annual accounting period under section 442. Therefore, such fiscal year can become the taxpayer's taxable year only with the approval of the Commissioner. Approval of any such change will be denied unless the taxpayer agrees in his application to establish and maintain accurate records of his taxable income for the short period involved in the change and for the fiscal year proposed. The keeping of records which adequately and clearly reflect income for the taxable year constitutes the keeping of books within the meaning of section 441(g) and paragraph (g) of § 1.441–1.

(b) Prior Approval of the Commissioner. (1) In General. In order to secure prior approval of a change of a taxpayer's annual accounting period, the taxpayer must file an application on Form 1128 with the Commissioner of Internal Revenue, Washington, D.C. 20224 to effect the change of accounting period. If the short period involved in the change ends after December 31, 1973, such form shall be filed on or before the 15th day of the second calendar month following the close of such short period; if such short period ends before January 1, 1974, such form shall be filed on or before the last day of the first calendar month following the close of such short period. Approval will not be granted unless the taxpayer and the Commissioner agree to the terms, conditions, and adjustments under which the change will be effected. In general, a change of annual accounting period will be approved where the taxpayer establishes a substantial business purpose for making the change. In determining whether a taxpayer has established a substantial business purpose for making the change, consideration will be given to all the facts and circumstances

relating to the change, including the tax consequences resulting therefrom. Among the nontax factors that will be considered in determining whether a substantial business purpose has been established is the effect of the change on the taxpayer's annual cycle of business activity. The agreement between the taxpayer and the Commissioner under which the change will be effected shall, in appropriate cases, provide terms, conditions, and adjustments necessary to prevent a substantial distortion of income which otherwise would result from the change. The following are examples of effects of the change which would substantially distort income: (i) deferral of a substantial portion of the taxpayer's income, or shifting of a substantial portion of deductions, from one year to another so as to reduce substantially the taxpayer's tax liability; (ii) causing a similar deferral or shifting in the case of any other person, such as a Partner, a beneficiary, or a Stockholder in an electing small business Corporation as defined in section 1371(b); or (iii) creating a short period in which there is either (*a*) a substantial net operating loss, or (*b*) in the case of an electing small business Corporation, a substantial portion of amounts treated as long-term capital gain. Even though a substantial business purpose is not established, the Commissioner in appropriate cases may permit a husband or wife to change his or her taxable year in order to secure the benefits of section 1(a) (relating to tax in the case of a joint return). See paragraph (e) of this section for special rule for newly married couples.

(c) Special rule for certain Corporations. (1) A Corporation may change its annual accounting period without the prior approval of the Commissioner if all the conditions in subparagraph (2) of this paragraph are met, and if the Corporation files a statement with the district director with whom the returns of the Corporation are filed at or before the time (including extension) for filing the return for the short period required by such change. This statement shall indicate that the Corporation is changing its annual accounting period under paragraph (c) of § 1.442–1 and shall contain information indicating that all of the conditions in subparagraph (2) of this paragraph have been met.

(2) The provisions of this paragraph do not apply unless all of the following conditions are met:

(i) The Corporation has not changed its annual accounting period at any time within the ten calendar years ending with the calendar year which includes the beginning of the short period required to effect the change of annual accounting period;

(ii) The short period required to effect the change of annual accounting period is not a taxable year in which the Corporation has a net operating loss as defined in section 172;

(iii) The taxable income of the Corporation for the short period required to effect the change of annual accounting period is, if placed on an annual basis (see paragraph (b)(1)(i) and (ii) of § 1.443–1), 80 percent or more of the taxable income of the Corporation for the taxable year immediately preceding such short period;

(iv) If a corporation had a special status either for the short period or for the taxable year immediately preceding such short period, it must have the special status for the short period or for the taxable year immediately preceding such short period.

Article III

MEETINGS OF STOCKHOLDERS

Preferred as a Matter of Practical Experience

§ 3.1 Meetings

All meetings of the Stockholders for the election of Directors shall either be by waiver of notice and consent or shall be held at such place either within or without the State of Incorporation as shall be designated from time to time by the Board of Directors and stated in the notice of the meeting.

§ 3.2 Annual Meetings

Annual meetings of Stockholders may be held by waiver of notice and consent or shall be held on such date and time as shall be designated from time to time by the Board of Directors and stated in the notice of the meeting; at which meeting the Stockholders shall elect by a plurality vote a Board of Directors and transact such other business as may properly be brought before the meeting.

§ 3.3 Special Meetings

Special meetings of the Stockholders, for any purpose or purposes, unless otherwise prescribed by statute or by the Articles of Incorporation, may be held by waiver of notice and consent or may be called by the President and shall be called by the President or Secretary at the request in writing of any two (2) of the Board of Directors, or at the request in writing of Stockholders owning not less than ten (10%) percent of the entire common stock of the Corporation issued and outstanding and entitled to vote.

COMMENT TO §§ 3.2 and 3.3

This By-law implements an optional provision in the Articles allowing consent meetings (see § —, supra, and is permitted by Model Bus.Corp.Act § 28). For additional discussion of Stockholder meetings, see Chapter 45, infra.

§ 3.4 Notice

When required By-law, written notice of a special meeting stating the place, date and hour of the meeting and the purpose or purposes for which the meeting is called, shall be given not less than ten (10) nor more than fifty (50) days before the date of the meeting, to each Stockholder entitled to vote at such meeting.

COMMENT TO § 3.4

These dates are statutory limits (Model Bus.Corp.Act § 29).

Preferred as a Matter of Practical Experience

Alternative A (Business Not Limited to Specific Purposes)

§ 3.5 Notice of Specific Purposes

Business transacted at a special meeting shall not be limited to the purposes stated in the notice so long as not more than *40%* of the Stockholders present do not object to the consideration of such business.

Not Generally Preferred as a Matter of Practical Experience

Alternative B (Business limited to Specific Purposes)

§ 3.5 Notice of Specific Purposes

Business transacted at a special meeting shall be limited to the purposes stated in the notice.

COMMENTS TO § 3.5

Alternative A will make the Corporation more efficient.

Alternative B avoids the problem of a Stockholder being unprepared or absent for an important vote.

§ 3.6 Quorum

Except as otherwise provided by statute or by the Articles of Incorporation, the holders of *fifty* (*50%*) percent of the stock issued and outstanding and entitled to vote at such meeting, present in person or represented by proxy, shall constitute a quorum at all meetings of the Stockholders for the transaction of business. If, however, such quorum shall not be present or represented at any meeting of the Stockholders, the Stockholders entitled to vote at such meeting, present in person or represented by proxy, shall have power to adjourn the meeting from time to time, without notice other than announcement at the meeting, until a quorum shall be present or represented. Such adjourned meeting at which a quorum shall be present or represented shall constitute the meeting as originally notified. If the adjournment is for more than sixty (60) days, or if after the adjournment a new record date is fixed for the adjourned meeting, a notice of the adjourned meeting shall be given to each Stockholder of record entitled to vote at the meeting.

COMMENT

Model Bus.Corp.Act § 32 provides that "unless otherwise provided in the articles of incorporation, a majority of the shares entitled to vote, represented in person or by proxy, shall constitute a quorum at a meeting of shareholders, but in no event shall a quorum consist of less than one-third of the shares entitled to vote at the meeting."

§ 3.7 Voting Percentage

When a quorum is present at any meeting, the vote of the holders of a majority of the stock having voting power present in person or represented by proxy shall decide any question brought before such meeting, unless the question is one upon which, by express provision of the statutes or of the Articles of Incorporation or of these By-laws, a different vote is required, in which case such express provision shall govern and control the necessary vote for such question.

§ 3.8 Voting list

The Officer who has charge of the stock ledger of the Corporation shall prepare and make, at least ten (10) days before every meeting of Stockholders, a complete list of the Stockholders entitled to vote at the meeting, arranged in alphabetical order, and showing the address of each Stockholder and the number of shares registered in the name of each Stockholder. Such list shall be open to the examination of any Stockholder for any purpose germane to the meeting, during ordinary business hours, for a period of at least ten (10) days prior to the meeting, either at a place within the city where the meeting is to be held, which place shall be specified in the notice of the meeting, or, if not so specified, at the place where the meeting is to be held. The list shall also be produced and kept at the time and place of the meeting during the whole time thereof, and may be inspected by any Stockholder who is present.

§ 3.9 Votes Per Share and Proxies

Each Stockholder shall be entitled to one vote in person or by proxy for each share of capital stock having voting power held by such Stockholder, but no proxy shall be voted on after *three* (*3*) months from its date, unless the proxy provides for a longer period. If the Articles of Incorporation provide for more or less than one vote for any share, on any matter, every reference in this Article to a majority or other proportion of stock shall refer to such majority or other proportion of the total votes of all shares of stock.

Article IV
DIRECTORS

§ 4.1 Number

The number of Directors which shall constitute the whole Board shall consist of [*Number*] Directors. The Directors shall be elected at the annual meeting of the Stockholders, except as provided in § 4.2, infra. Each Director elected shall hold office until his successor is elected and qualified. Directors need not be Stockholders.

COMMENTS TO § 4.1

The number of Directors can be one or more (Model Bus. Corp.Act § 36). The number of Directors (unless actually specified in the Articles) may vary from time to time.

The number of Directors of a closely held Corporation should generally be a number which meets statutory requirements and which is convenient to assemble for a meeting.

It is recommended that when the Corporation is closely held that the Board include only persons who are familiar with the day to day operations of the Corporation. The reasons for this are:

(1) Directors face substantial personal liability.

(2) The input of consultants is generally only required on an intermittent basis.

(3) If the consultant is a CPA, he will not be able to certify to the independence of the opinion if he is on the Board.

(4) If the consultant is an attorney he will not be able to render truly independent advice if he is on the Board.

(5) The Corporation may want to seek outside advice and ignore the advice of normal advisors. This will be more difficult if the advisor being ignored is a Board member.

Often the Board seats are given to loyal employees, although it should be always remembered that in situations of adversity a majority of the Board can meet and a majority of that majority can act. Thus, one or a few dissidents could control the Board in unusual circumstances. However, a later Stockholders meeting could often remedy the situation.

For additional discussion of Directors and Directors meetings, see Chapter 46, infra.

§ 4.2 Vacancies

Vacancies and newly created directorships resulting from any increase in the authorized number of Directors may be filled by a majority of the Directors then in office, though less than a quorum, or by a sole remaining Director. The Director so chosen shall hold office until the next annual election and until their successors are duly elected and shall qualify, unless sooner displaced. If there are no Directors in office, then an election of Directors shall be held in the manner provided by statute.

§ 4.3 Powers

The business of the Corporation shall be managed by its Board of Directors which may exercise all such powers of the Corporation and do all such lawful acts and things as are not by statute or by the Articles of Incorporation directed or required to be exercised or done by the Stockholders.

§ 4.4 Place of Meetings

The Board of Directors of the Corporation may hold meetings, both regular and special, either within or without the State of Incorporation.

§ 4.5 First Meeting

The first meeting of each newly elected Board of Directors shall be held at such time and place as shall be fixed by the vote of the Stockholders at the annual meeting and no notice of such meeting shall be necessary to the newly elected Directors in order legally to constitute the meeting, provided a quorum shall be present. In the event of the failure of the Stockholders to fix the time or place of such first meeting of the newly elected Board of Directors, or in the event such meeting is not held at the time and place so fixed by the Stockholders, the meeting may be held at such time and place as shall be specified in a notice given as hereinafter provided for special meetings of the Board of Directors, or as shall be specified in a written waiver signed by all of the Directors.

§ 4.6 Regular Meetings

Regular meetings of the Board of Directors may be held without notice at such time and at such place as shall from time to time be determined by the Board.

§ 4.7 Special Meetings

Special meetings of the Board may be called by the President on one day's notice to each Director, either personally or by mail or by telegram; special meetings shall be called by the President or Secretary in like manner and on like notice on the written request by two (2) of the Directors.

§ 4.8 Quorum

At all meetings of the Board, a *majority* of the Directors shall constitute a quorum for the transaction of business and the act of a majority of the Directors present at any meeting at which there is a quorum shall be the act of the Board of Directors, except as may be otherwise specifically provided by statute or by the Articles of Incorporation. If a quorum shall not be present at any meeting of the Board of Directors, the Directors present at such meeting may adjourn the meeting from time to time, without notice other than announcement at the meeting, until a quorum shall be present.

§ 4.9 Consent Meetings

Unless otherwise restricted by the Articles of Incorporation or these By-laws, any action required or permitted to be taken at any meeting of the Board of Directors may be taken without a meeting, if all members of the Board or committee consent thereto in writing, and the writing or writings are filed with the minutes of the Board.

COMMENT TO § 4.9

This section follows Model Bus.Corp.Act § 44.

§ 4.11 General Authorization of Boards Authority to Issue Stocks and Bonds

The following certificates may be issued from time to time by the Board of Directors in one or more series:

Option 1

[*Describe*] class of [*Describe*] stock only.

Option 2

any stock or security.

Option 3

any class of stock or security except [*Describe*] class of [*Describe*] stock or security.

As to such certificates, the Board of Directors is authorized to determine:

Option 4

the dividend rate.

Option 5

the price and term of issuance.

Option 6

the liquidation value and terms.

Option 7

the redemption value, terms and conditions.

Option 8

whether there shall be sinking fund to retire such certificates and, if so, what the terms and conditions of such fund shall be.

Option 9

the conversion rights.

Option 10

the voting rights.

§ 4.12 Restrictions on the Issuance of Certificates

The following restrictions upon the issuance of stock shall apply:

Option 1

only stock authorized as of *date* be issued.

Option 2

only stock whose purchase price is at least book value may be issued.

Option 3

only stock with rights and preferences equal to or less than that of class ______ of [*common/preferred*] shares may be issued.

Option 4

only stock which does not have any of the following rights and preferences may be issued:

Option 5

the right to vote.

Option 6

the right to vote; except upon default.

Option 7

in any dividend.

Option 8

preemptive rights.

Option 9

the right to vote on a cumulative basis.

Option 10

a dividend preference.

Option 11

a redemption preference.

Option 12

a liquidation preference.

Article V

NOTICES

§ 5.1 Notices

Whenever, under the provisions of the statutes or of the Articles of Incorporation or of these By-laws, notice is required to be given to any Director or Stockholder, it shall not be construed to require personal notice unless specifically stated. Rather such notice may be given in writing, by mail, addressed to such Director or Stockholder, at his address as it appears on the records of the Corporation, with postage thereon prepaid, and such notice shall be deemed to be given at the time when the same shall be deposited in the United States mail. Notice to Directors may also be given by telegram.

Whenever any notice is required to be given under the provisions of the statutes or of the Articles of Incorporation or of these By-laws, a waiver thereof in writing, signed by the person or persons entitled to said notice, whether before or after the time stated therein, shall be deemed equivalent to such notice.

Article VI

OFFICERS

§ 6.1 Officers

The Board of Directors, within twenty-one (21) days after the annual election of the Directors in each year, shall elect a President, a Vice-President, a Secretary and a Treasurer, who need not be members of the Board. The Board at that time or from time to time may elect more than one Vice-Presidents, Assistant Secretaries and Assistant Treasurers who may or may not be members of the Board. The same person may hold any two or more offices excepting those of President and Vice-President or Secretary, but no Officer shall execute, acknowledge or verify any instrument in more than one capacity. The Board may also appoint such other Officers and agents as it may deem necessary for the transaction of the business of the Corporation.

COMMENT

See Model Bus.Corp.Act § 50.

§ 6.2 Terms

The term of office of all Officers shall be one year or until their respective successors are chosen, but any Officer may be removed from office, with or without cause, at any meeting of the Board of

Directors by the affirmative vote of a majority of the Directors then in office. The Board of Directors shall have power to fill any vacancies in any offices occurring from whatever reason.

§ 6.3 Salaries

The salaries and other compensation of all Officers of the Corporation shall be fixed by the Board of Directors.

§ 6.4 President

The President shall be the chief executive officer of the Corporation and shall have responsibility for the general and active management of the business of the Corporation, and shall see that all orders and resolutions of the Board are carried into effect. He shall execute all authorized conveyances, contracts, or other obligations in the name of the Corporation except where the signing and execution thereof shall be expressly delegated by the Board of Directors to some other officer or agent of the Corporation. He shall preside at all meetings of the Stockholders and Directors and shall be ex-officio a member of all standing committees of the Board.

§ 6.5 Vice-President(s)

The Vice-Presidents in the order designated by the Board of Directors or, lacking such a designation, by the President, shall in the absence or disability of the President perform the duties and exercise the powers of the President and shall perform such other duties as the Board of Directors shall prescribe.

§ 6.6 Secretary

The Secretary shall attend all meetings of the Board and all meetings of the Stockholders and record all votes and the minutes of all proceedings in a book to be kept for that purpose and shall perform like duties for the standing committees when required. He shall give, or cause to be given, notice of all meetings of the Stockholders and of the Board of Directors and shall perform such other duties as may be prescribed by the Board of Directors or by the President, under whose supervision he shall act. He may execute with the President all authorized conveyances, contracts or other obligations in the name of the Corporation except as otherwise directed by the Board of Directors. He shall keep in safe custody the seal of the Corporation and, when authorized by the Board, affix the same to any instrument requiring it and, when so affixed, it shall be attested by his signature or by the signature of the Treasurer or an Assistant Secretary.

The Secretary shall keep a register of the post office address of each Stockholder. Said address shall be furnished to the Secretary by such Stockholder and the responsibility for keeping said address current shall be upon the Stockholder. The Secretary shall have general charge of the stock transfer books of the Corporation.

§ 6.7 Treasurer—Bond

The Treasurer shall have custody of and keep account of all money, funds and property of the Corporation, unless otherwise determined by the Board of Directors, and he shall render such accounts and present such statements to the Directors and President as may be required of him. He shall deposit funds of the Corporation which may come into his hands in such bank or banks as the Board of Directors may designate. He shall keep his bank accounts in the name of the Corporation and shall exhibit his books and accounts at all reasonable times to any Director of the Corporation, upon application, at the office of the Corporation during business hours. If required by the Board of Directors, he shall give the Corporation a bond in such sum and with such surety or sureties as shall be satisfactory to the Board for the faithful performance of the duties of his office and for the restoration to the Corporation in case of his death, resignation or removal from office of all books, papers, vouchers, money and other property of whatever kind in his possession or under his control belonging to the Corporation.

§ 6.8 Assistants

The Assistant Secretaries and the Assistant Treasurers (if any), respectively, (in the order designated by the Board of Directors or, lacking such designation, by the President) in the absence of the Secretary or the Treasurer, as the case may be, shall perform the duties and exercise the powers of such Secretary or Treasurer and shall perform such other duties as the Board of Directors shall prescribe.

Article VII

CERTIFICATES

§ 7.1 Lost Certificates

The Board of Directors may direct a new certificate or certificates to be issued in place of any certificate or certificates theretofore issued by the Corporation alleged to have been lost, stolen or destroyed, upon the making of an affidavit of that fact by the person claiming the certificate or shares to be lost, stolen or destroyed. When authorizing such issue of a new certificate or certificates, the Board of Directors may, in its discretion and as a condition precedent to the issuance thereof, require the owner of such lost, stolen or destroyed certificate or certificates, or his legal representative, to advertise the same in such manner as it shall require and/or to give the Corporation a bond in such sum as it may direct as indemnity against any claim that may be made against the Corporation with respect to the certificate alleged to have been lost, stolen or destroyed.

COMMENT

For additional discussion of lost, destroyed or stolen certificates, see Chapter 41, infra.

§ 7.2 Surrender

Upon surrender to the Corporation of a certificate for shares duly endorsed or accompanied by proper evidence of succession, assignment or authority to transfer, it shall be the duty of the Corporation to issue a new certificate to the person entitled thereto, cancel the old certificate and record the transaction upon its books.

§ 7.3 Record Date

In order that the Corporation may determine the Stockholders entitled to notice of or to vote at any meeting of Stockholders or any adjournment thereof, or to express consent to corporate action in writing without a meeting, or entitled to receive payment of any dividend or other distribution or allotment of any rights, or entitled to exercise any rights in respect of any change, conversion or exchange of stock or for the purpose of any other lawful action, the Board of Directors may fix, in advance, a record date, which shall not be more than sixty (60) days nor less than ten (10) days before the date of such meeting, nor more than sixty (60) days prior to any other action. A determination of Stockholders of record entitled to notice of or to vote at a meeting of Stockholders shall apply to any adjournment of the meeting; provided, however, that the Board of Directors may fix a new record date for the adjourned meeting. Absent Board of Director action, the record date shall be ten (10) days before the date of such meeting.

§ 7.4 Voting

The Corporation shall be entitled to recognize the exclusive right of a person registered on its books as the owner of shares to receive dividends, and to vote as such owner, and to hold liable for calls and assessments a person registered on its books as the owner of shares, and shall not be bound to recognize any equitable or other claim to interest in such share or shares on the part of any other person, whether or not it shall have express or other notice thereof, except as otherwise provided by the laws of the state of incorporation.

COMMENT

For additional discussion, see Chapter 47, infra.

Article VIII

AMENDMENTS

§ 8.1 Amendments

These By-laws may be altered, amended or repealed or new By-laws may be adopted by the Stockholders or by the Board of Directors at any regular meeting of the Stockholders or of the Board of Directors or at any special meeting of the Stockholders or of the Board of Directors if notice of such alteration, amendment, repeal or adoption of new By-laws be contained in the notice of such special meeting.

§ 34.14 Sophisticated By-law Form

INTRODUCTORY COMMENT

The following form is presented as a comprehensive set of possible By-law provisions. It should be noted that many of these provisions are mutually exclusive or, serve conflicting goals, or may be contradictory to certain provisions of the Articles of Incorporation. Accordingly, care must be taken in selecting and tailoring such provisions to the wishes of the incorporators and to the needs of the type of business contemplated. In addition, care must be taken that all such By-laws are not inconsistent (i. e. not contradictory) with the Articles or Certificate of Incorporation or with statutory requirements.

BY-LAWS

Table of Sections

Article IV. Directors

Article V. Notices

Article VI. Officers

Article VII. Certificates of Shares

Article I
OFFICES

Preferred as a Matter of Practical Experience

§ 1.1 Office

The registered office shall be in the City of ______, County of ______, State of [*Incorporation*].

The Corporation may also have offices at such other places both within or without the State of [*Incorporation*] as the Board of Directors may from time to time determine or the business of the Corporation may require.

Article II
FISCAL YEAR

Preferred as a Matter of Practical Experience

§ 2.1 Fiscal Year

The fiscal year of the Corporation shall end on the last day of ______, of each year unless another date shall be fixed by resolution of the Board of Directors.

After such date is fixed, it may be changed for future fiscal years at any time by further resolution of the Board of Directors.

COMMENTS TO ARTICLE II

The choice of the fiscal year is of the utmost importance. The following considerations apply:

(a) If possible, the fiscal year should end at a time of the year when it is most easy to take an inventory of assets (if this must be done) and assess the Corporation's general economic health.

(b) If possible, the fiscal year should end at a time of the year when financial advisors will be easily accessible. A year end meeting (before actual year end) to make plans for any present year activities which are to occur before year end is very helpful and in most cases must occur in order to insure that the year end planning is effective for the relevant fiscal year. Included in this are the establishment of the following plans which can be made retroactive to the beginning of the year, but not pre-date the year executed:

(1) Health insurance premium plans.

(2) Medical expense reimbursement plans.

(3) Legal expense reimbursement plans.

(4) Qualified retirement programs.

(5) Cafeteria plans.

Accrual basis taxpayers will want to have certain expenses accrue before year end so that they can be deducted. For such accrual to occur, these expenses must be "committed to" before that date. Among these are payments to majority Stockholders which must not only be accrued before year end, but must also be paid within 75 days after year end.

Article III

MEETINGS OF STOCKHOLDERS

Preferred as a Matter of Practical Experience

§ 3.1 Meetings

All meetings of the Stockholders for the election of Directors shall be by waiver of notice and consent or shall be held at such place either within or without the State of Incorporation as shall be designated from time to time by the Board of Directors and stated in the notice of the meeting. Meetings of Stockholders for any other purpose may be held at such time and place, within or without the State of Incorporation as shall be stated in the notice of the meeting or in a duly executed Waiver of Notice thereof.

§ 3.2 Annual Meetings

Annual meetings of Stockholders, if actually held shall be held on such date and time as shall be designated from time to time by the Board of Directors and stated in the notice of the meeting, at which they shall elect by a plurality vote a Board of Directors and shall transact such other business as may properly be brought before the meeting.

COMMENTS TO § 3.2

This language may be in conflict with the higher vote requirements set forth in § 3.12, infra, of this form or the Articles of Incorporation (see Chapter 33, § 33.16, § 7.5, supra).

See Chapter 46, infra, for additional discussion of Stockholder meetings.

§ 3.3 Place and Date

When required by law, written notice of the annual meeting stating the place, date and hour of the meeting shall be given to each Stockholder entitled to vote at such meeting not less than ten (10) nor more than fifty (50) days before the date of the meeting.

COMMENT TO § 3.3

These dates are statutory limits (Model Bus.Corp.Act § 29).

Preferred as a Matter of Practical Experience

§ 3.4 Special Meetings

A special meeting of the Stockholders may be called by the President or Secretary or any two Board members.

COMMENT TO § 3.4

This By-law implements an optional provision in the Articles (see Art. V of the form found at Chapter 33, § 33.16, supra) and is permitted by Model Bus.Corp.Act § 28.

§ 3.5 Special Meetings

Special meetings of the Stockholders, for any purpose or purposes, unless otherwise prescribed by statute or by the Articles of Incorporation, may be held by waiver of notice and consent or may be called by the President and shall be called by the President or Secretary at the request in writing of any two (2) of the Board of Directors, or at the request in writing of Stockholders owning not less than ten (10%) percent of the entire common stock of the Corporation issued and outstanding and entitled to vote. Such request shall state the purpose or purposes of the proposed meeting.

§ 3.6 Notice of Special Meetings

When required by law, written notice of a special meeting stating the place, date and hour of the meeting and the purpose or purposes for which the meeting is called, shall be given not less than ten (10) nor more than fifty (50) days before the date of the meeting, to each Stockholder entitled to vote at such meeting.

COMMENT TO § 3.6

These dates are statutory limits (Model Bus.Corp.Act § 29). See Chapter 45, infra, for additional discussion.

Alternative A (Business Not Limited to Stated Purposes) Preferred as a Matter of Practical Experience

§ 3.7 Purposes

Business transacted at a special meeting shall not be limited to the purposes stated in the notice so long as not more than *forty (40%)* percent of the Stockholders present do not object to the consideration of such business.

Alternative B (Business Limited to Stated Purposes) Not Generally Preferred as a Matter of Practical Experience

§ 3.7 Purposes

Business transacted at any special meeting of Stockholders shall be limited to the purposes stated in the notice unless all of said Stockholders agree to do otherwise.

COMMENT TO ALTERNATIVE B

This provision has the benefit of eliminating "surprise" Stockholder votes where the majority gets caught unaware of the proposed action.

§ 3.8 Quorum

Except as otherwise provided by statute or by the Articles of Incorporation, the holders of *fifty* (*50%*) percent of the stock issued and outstanding and entitled to vote at such meeting, present in person or represented by proxy, shall constitute a quorum at all meetings of the Stockholders for the transaction of business. If, however, such quorum shall not be present or represented at any meeting of the Stockholders, the Stockholders entitled to vote at such meeting, present in person or represented by proxy, shall have the power to adjourn the meeting from time to time, without notice other than announcement at the meeting, until a quorum shall be present or represented. At such adjourned meeting at which a quorum shall be present or represented shall constitute the meeting as originally notified. If the adjournment is for more than sixty (60) days, or if after the adjournment a new record date is fixed for the adjourned meeting, a notice of the adjourned meeting shall be given to each Stockholder of record entitled to vote at the meeting.

COMMENT

Model Bus.Corp.Act § 32 provides that "unless otherwise provided in the articles of incorporation, a majority of the shares entitled to vote, represented in person or by proxy, shall constitute a quorum at a meeting of shareholders, but in no event shall a quorum consist of less than one-third of the shares entitled to vote at the meeting."

§ 3.9 Voting Percentage

When a quorum is present at any meeting, the vote of the holders of a majority of the stock having voting power present in person or represented by proxy shall decide any question brought before such meeting, unless the question is one upon which by express provision of the statutes or of the Articles of Incorporation, a different vote is required in which case such express provision shall govern and control the decision of such question.

Not Generally Preferred as a Matter of Practical Experience

§ 3.10 Special Voting Percentage

Provided, that as to the following matters, ______% of the shares voting shall be required to approve any proposed Stockholder action:

(a) To sue, complain and defend, in the Corporation name.

(b) To purchase, take, receive, lease or otherwise acquire, own, hold, improve, use and otherwise deal in and with, real or personal property, or any interest therein, wherever situated.

(c) To sell, convey, mortgage, pledge, lease, exchange, transfer and otherwise dispose of all or any part of the Corporation's property and assets.

(d) To lend money and use its credit to assist its employees or Directors.

(e) To purchase, take, receive, subscribe for, or otherwise acquire, own, hold, vote, use, employ, sell, mortgage, lend, pledge, or otherwise dispose of, and otherwise use and deal in and with, shares or other interests in, or obligations of, other domestic or foreign corporations, associations, partnerships or individuals, or direct or indirect obligations of the United States or of any other government, state, territory, governmental district or municipality or of any instrumentality thereof.

(f) To make contracts and guarantees and incur liabilities, borrow money at such rates of interest as the Corporation may determine, issue its notes, bonds, and other obligations, and secure any of its obligations by mortgage or pledge of all or any of its property, franchises and income.

(g) To lend money for the Corporation's purposes, invest and reinvest its funds, and take and hold payment of funds so loaned or invested.

(h) To conduct its business, carry on its operations and have offices and exercise the powers granted herein, within or without this State.

(i) To elect or appoint Officers and agents of the Corporation, and define their duties and fix their compensation.

(j) To make and alter By-laws, not inconsistent with its Articles of Incorporation, for the administration and regulation of the affairs of the Corporation.

(k) To make donations for the public welfare or for charitable, scientific or educational purposes.

(*l*) To pay pensions and establish pension plans, pension trusts, profit sharing plans, stock bonus plans, stock option plans and other incentive plans for any or all of its Directors, Officers and employees.

(m) To be a promoter, partner, member, associate, or manager of any partnership, joint venture, trust or other enterprise.

COMMENT TO § 3.10

Although permitted in the By-laws (Model Bus.Corp.Act § 30), this language is more appropriate in the Articles where it can better protect minority Stockholders (see Art. III of the form found at Chapter 33, § 33.16, supra).

§ 3.11 Voting List

The officer who has charge of the stock ledger of the Corporation shall prepare and make, at least ten (10) days before every meeting of Stockholders, a complete list of the Stockholders entitled to vote at the meeting, arranged in alphabetical order, and showing the address of each Stockholder and the number of shares registered in the name of each Stockholder. Such list shall be open to the examination of any Stockholder for any purpose germane to the meeting, during ordinary business hours, for a period of at least ten (10) days prior to the meeting, either at a place within the city where the meeting is to be held, which place shall be specified in the notice of the meeting, or, if not so specified, at the place where the meeting is to be held. The list shall also be produced and kept at the time and place of the meeting during the whole time thereof, and may be inspected by any Stockholder who is present.

COMMENT

See Chapter 47, infra, with respect to voting lists.

§ 3.12 Voting

(a) Each Stockholder shall be entitled to one vote in person or by proxy for each share of capital stock having voting power held by such Stockholder, but no proxy shall be voted on after *three* (*3*) months from its date, unless the proxy provides for a longer period.

(b) If the Articles of Incorporation provides for more or less than one vote for any share, on any matter, every reference in this Article to a majority or other proportion of stock shall refer to such majority or other proportion of the votes of such stock.

Alternative A (Unanimous Consent Voting) Preferred Only if Alternative B Is Not Permitted

§ 3.13 Unanimous Consent Voting

Whenever the vote of Stockholders at a meeting thereof is required or permitted to be taken for or in connection with any corporate action, by any provision of the statutes, the meeting and vote of Stockholders may be dispensed with if all of the Stockholders who would have been entitled to vote upon the action if such meeting were held shall consent in writing to such corporate action taken.

Alternative B (Majority Consent Voting) If Available Preferred as a Matter of Practical Experience

§ 3.13 Majority Consent Voting

Whenever the vote of Stockholders at a meeting thereof is required or permitted to be taken for or in connection with any corporate action, by any provision of the statutes, the meeting and vote of Stockholders may be dispensed with if that number of the Stockholders shall consent in writing to such corporate action taken, who have not less than the percentage of the number of votes as may be authorized in the Articles of Incorporation; provided that in no case shall the written consent be by the holders of stock having less than the minimum percentage of the vote required by statute for the proposed corporate action, and provided that prompt notice must be given to all Stockholders of the taking of corporate action without a meeting and by less than unanimous written consent.

COMMENT TO ALTERNATIVES A and B

This section merely repeats language which is either prohibited or permitted to the Corporation by statute and Articles of Incorporation (see § 6.1 of the form found at Chapter 33, § 33.16, supra).

Article IV

DIRECTORS

Alternative A

§ 4.1 Numbers

The number of Directors which shall constitute the whole Board shall consist of ______ *Directors/such number as the Board from time to time shall designate.* The Directors shall be elected at the annual meeting of the Stockholders, except as provided in Section .2 of this Article, and each Director elected shall hold office until his successor is elected and qualified. Directors need not be Stockholders.

Alternative B

§ 4.1 Number and Qualifications of Classified Directors

The Board of Directors shall consist of ______ Directors, none of whom need to be Stockholders or residents of any particular state. The directors shall be classified with respect to the time for which they hold office by dividing them into three classes, each consisting of ______ Directors, and each Director of the Corporation shall hold office until his successor shall be elected and shall qualify. At the first annual meeting of Stockholders, the Directors of the first class shall be elected for a term of one year; the Directors of the second class shall be elected for a term of two years; the Directors of the third class shall be elected for a term of three years; and at each annual election thereafter the successors to the class of Directors whose terms shall expire that year shall be elected to hold office for the term of three years, so that the term of office of one class of Directors shall expire in each year.

COMMENT TO ALTERNATIVE B

The usual justification given for "staggering" the Board is that it provides continuity. It also has the effect of increasing the number of shares needed to elect a director under cumulative voting and makes an unwanted take-over more difficult, since acquisition of a majority of the shares does not permit immediate replacement of the Directors. The latter advantage is lost if a broad Stockholder removal power is included in the By-laws.

COMMENTS TO § 4.1

The number of Directors can be one or more (Model Bus. Corp.Act § 36). The number of Directors (unless actually specified in the Articles) may vary from time to time.

The number of Directors of a closely held Corporation should generally be a number which meets statutory requirements and which is convenient to assemble for a meeting.

It is recommended that when the Corporation is closely held that the Board include only persons who are familiar with the day to day operations of the Corporation. The reasons for this are:

(a) Directors face substantial personal liability (see Chapter —, § —, infra).

(b) The input of consultants is generally only required on an intermittent basis.

(a) Directors face substantial personal liability.

(d) If the consultant is an attorney he will not be able to render truly independent advice if he is on the Board.

(e) The Corporation may want to seek outside advice and ignore the advice of normal advisors. This will be more difficult if the advisor being ignored is a Board member.

Often Board seats are given to loyal employees, although it should be always remembered that in situations of adversity a majority of the Board can meet and a majority of that majority can act. Thus, one or a few dissidents could control the Board in unusual circumstances. However, a later Stockholder meeting could often remedy the situation.

For additional coverage of Directors and Directors' meetings, see Chapter 46, infra.

Alternative A (Usually Preferred as a Matter of Practical Experience)

§ 4.2 Vacancies

Vacancies and newly created directorships resulting from any increase in the authorized number of Directors may be filled by a majority of the Directors then in office, though less than a quorum, or by a sole remaining Director, and the Directors so chosen shall hold office until the next annual election and until their successors are duly elected and shall qualify, unless sooner displaced. If there are no Directors in office, then an election of Directors may be held in the manner provided by statute.

COMMENT TO ALTERNATIVE A

The problem with this provision is that upon the death or resignation of a few Directors, the dissident Directors might control the Corporation. Its benefit is ease of corporate administration. See Model Bus.Corp.Act § 38 and Chapter 46, infra.

Alternative B (Usually Not Preferred as a Matter of Practical Experience)

§ 4.2 Vacancies

Vacancies and newly created directorships shall only be filled by the Stockholders.

COMMENT TO ALTERNATIVE B

This Section may be important. Given the actual and implied powers of the Corporation, and given the fact that the Board may exercise such powers, the Board has great latitude. Thus, the Stockholders may prefer to always control the Board's membership.

§ 4.3 Powers

The business of the Corporation shall be managed by its Board of Directors which may exercise all such powers of the Corporation and do all such lawful acts and things as are not by statute or by the Articles of Incorporation directed or required to be exercised or done by the Stockholders.

Not Generally Preferred as a Matter of Practical Experience

§ 4.4 Power Limitation

Provided, that the Board shall not exercise the following powers (but rather such powers shall be exercised by [*Name or Describe*]):

(a) Sue, complain and defend, in the Corporation's name.

(b) Purchase, take, receive, lease, or otherwise acquire, own, hold, improve, use and otherwise deal in and with, real or personal property, or any interest therein.

(c) Sell, convey, mortgage, pledge, lease, exchange, transfer and otherwise dispose of all or any part of the Corporation's property and assets.

(d) Lend money or use its credit to assist the Corporation's employees and Directors.

(e) Purchase, take, receive, subscribe for, or otherwise acquire, own, hold, vote, use, employ, sell, mortgage, lend, pledge, or otherwise dispose of, and otherwise use and deal in and with, shares or other interests in, or obligations of, other domestic or foreign Corporations, associations, partnerships or individuals, or direct or indirect obligations of the United States or of any other government, state, territory, governmental district or municipality or of any instrumentality thereof.

(f) Make contracts and guarantees and incur liabilities, borrow money at such rates of interest as it may determine, issue its notes, bonds, and other obligations, or secure any of the Corporation's obligations by mortgage or pledge of all or any of its property, franchises and income.

(g) Lend money for any purpose.

(h) Conduct its business, carry on corporate operations and have offices and exercise the powers granted herein, without this State.

(i) Elect or appoint officers and agents of the Corporation, and define their duties and fix their compensation.

(j) Make and alter By-laws, not inconsistent with the Corporation's Articles of Incorporation, for the administration and regulation of the affairs of the Corporation.

(k) To make donations for the public welfare or for charitable, scientific or educational purposes.

(*l*) Pay pensions and establish pension plans, pension trusts, profit sharing plans, stock bonus plans, stock option plans and other incentive plans for any or all of its Directors, Officers and employees.

(m) Be a promoter, partner, member, associate, or manager of any partnership, joint venture, trust or other enterprise.

COMMENTS TO § 4.4

It may be of value to restrict the Board from certain areas of responsibility. However, if this is to be accomplished, such restrictions are best placed in the Articles (see Art. III of the form found at Chapter 33, § 33.16, supra) where they cannot be amended by the Directors themselves. If (i) or (j) is denied to the Board, it should be granted to the Stockholders in the Articles.

Model Bus.Corp.Act § 35 permits a delegation of the Board powers to others. This is very helpful when minority Stockholders (or creditors) want to protect themselves. To do this, provision must be made in the Articles themselves (see § 11.11 of the form at § ——, infra).

Preferred as a Matter of Practical Experience

§ 4.5 Removal of Board Members

The Stockholders may replace all (but not some) of the Board of Directors at any Stockholders meeting and elect in their stead replacement members some or all of whom may have been members of the ousted Board.

COMMENT TO § 4.5

This provision reaffirms the Stockholders' control over the Board of Directors since they can replace an uncooperative Board at any time. See Chapter 47, infra, and Model Bus.Corp.Act § 39.

§ 4.6 Meetings

The Board of Directors of the Corporation may hold meetings, both regular and special, either within or without the State of Incorporation.

COMMENT TO § 4.6

Section 4.6 must be modified if the Articles of Incorporation (see § —— of the form found at Chapter 33, § 11.2, supra) prohibit meetings outside of the State of Incorporation.

§ 4.7 First Meeting

The first meeting of each newly elected Board of Directors shall be held at such time and place as shall be fixed by the vote of the Stockholders at the annual meeting and no notice of such meeting shall be necessary to the newly elected Directors in order legally to constitute the meeting, provided a quorum shall be present. In the event of the failure of the Stockholders to fix the time or place of such first meeting of the newly elected Board of Directors, or in the event such meeting is not held at the time and place so fixed by the Stockholders, or in the case of the initial meeting of the Board of Directors, then the meeting may be held at such time and place as shall be specified in a notice given as hereinafter provided for special meetings of the Board of Directors, or as shall be specified in a written waiver signed by all of the Directors.

§ 4.8 Regular Meetings

Regular meetings of the Board of Directors may be held without special notice at such time and at such place as shall from time to time be determined by the Board.

§ 4.9 Special Meetings

Special meetings of the Board may be called by the President on one day's notice to each Director, either personally or by mail or by telegram; special meetings shall be called by the President or Secretary in like manner and on like notice on the written request by two (2) of the Directors.

§ 4.10 Quorum

At all meetings of the Board, a majority of the Directors shall constitute a quorum for the transaction of business and the act of a majority of the Directors present at any meeting at which there is a quorum shall be the act of the Board of Directors, except as may be otherwise specifically provided by statute or by the Articles of Incorporation. If a quorum shall not be present at any meeting of the Board of Directors the Directors present at such meeting may adjourn the meeting from time to time, without notice other than announcement at the meeting, until a quorum shall be present.

COMMENT

See Chapter 46, infra.

§ 4.11 Voting by Directors

Each Director shall be entitled to one vote on each matter submitted to the Board of Directors.

§ 4.12 Cumulative Voting

At each election for Directors, each Stockholder entitled to vote shall have the right to vote, in person or by proxy, the number of shares owned by him for as many persons as there are directors to be elected and for whose election he has a right to vote, or to cumulate his votes by (i) giving one candidate as many votes as the number of such directors multiplied by the number of his shares shall equal, or (ii) by distributing such votes on the same principle among any number of such candidates. Any Stockholder who intends to cumulate his votes shall give written notice of such intention to the Secretary of the Corporation on or before the day preceding the election at which such Stockholder intends to cumulate his votes.

COMMENT

The effect of cumulative voting is to permit a significant minority of shares to obtain representation on the Board of Directors. Whether or not cumulative voting is desirable depends on one's point of view. In publicly held Corporations, cumulative voting is generally dispensed with on the theory that it is complicated. It also may permit an organized group to obtain representation on the Board over the opposition of management.

In a handful of states, cumulative voting is mandatory while in other states it is permissible. See Chapter 47, infra, for additional discussion.

Not Generally Preferred as a Matter of Practical Experience

§ 4.13 Limitations on Voting

Provided that __% of Board members (whether or not voting) shall be required for the approval of the following actions:

(a) To sue, complain and defend, in the Corporation's name.

(b) To use the corporate seal.

(c) To purchase, take, receive, lease, or otherwise acquire, own, hold, improve, use and otherwise deal in and with, real or personal property, or any interest therein, wherever situated.

(d) To sell, convey, mortgage, pledge, lease, exchange, transfer and otherwise dispose of all or any part of the Corporation's property and assets.

(e) To lend money and use its credit to assist its employees or Directors.

(f) To purchase, take, receive, subscribe for, or otherwise acquire, own, hold, vote, use, employ, sell, mortgage, lend, pledge, or otherwise dispose of, and otherwise use and deal in and with, shares or other interests in, or obligations of, other domestic or foreign corporations, associations, partnerships or individuals, or direct or indirect obligations of the United States or of any other government, state, territory, governmental district or municipality or of any instrumentality thereof.

(g) To make contracts and guarantees and incur liabilities, borrow money at such rates of interest as it may determine, issue the Corporation's notes, bonds, and other obligations, or secure any of its obligations by mortgage or pledge of all or any of the Corporation's property, franchises and income.

(h) To lend money for the Corporation's purposes, invest and reinvest its funds, or take and hold payment of funds so loaned or invested.

(i) To elect or appoint Officers and agents of the Corporation, and define their duties and fix their compensation.

(j) To make and alter By-laws, not inconsistent with its Articles of Incorporation, for the administration and regulation of the affairs of the Corporation.

(k) To make donations for the public welfare or for charitable, scientific or educational purposes.

(*l*) To pay pensions and establish pension plans, pension trusts, profit sharing plans, stock bonus plans, stock option plans and other incentive plans for any or all of its Directors, Officers and employees.

(m) To be a promoter, partner, member, associate, or manager of any partnership, joint venture, trust or other enterprise.

COMMENT TO § 4.3

This provision, if desired, might be made part of the Articles of Incorporation (see § 7.5 of the form found at § 33.16, supra) where it can not be changed by the Board itself. However, if the fear is only that a majority of the Board may change the By-laws, then this provision (especially sub-section (j)) will be sufficient.

§ 4.14 Actions Without Meeting

Unless otherwise restricted by the Articles of Incorporation or these By-laws, any action required or permitted to be taken at any meeting of the Board of Directors may be taken without a meeting, if all members of the Board or committee consent thereto in writing, and the writing or writings are filed with the minutes of proceedings of the Board.

Preferred as a Matter of Practical Experience

§ 4.15 Conference Call Meetings

Members of the Board of Directors may participate in a Board meeting by means of conference telephone or similar communications equipment by means of which all persons participating in the meeting can hear each other, and participation in a meeting pursuant to this section shall constitute presence in person at such meeting.

COMMENT

This section follows and is permitted by Model Bus.Corp.Act § 43.

Preferred as a Matter of Practical Experience

§ 4.16 Fees

The Directors may be paid their expenses, if any, of attendance at each meeting of the Board of Directors and may be paid a fixed sum for attendance at each meeting of the Board of Directors or a stated salary as Director. No such payment shall preclude any Director from serving the Corporation in any other capacity and receiving compensation therefor. Members of special or standing committees may be allowed like compensation for attending committee meetings.

§ 4.17 Removal of Directors

Directors may be removed for cause by the affirmative vote of a majority in number of shares of Stockholders represented in person or by proxy at a special meeting called for that purpose. A Director whose removal is sought shall be entitled to a notice of the charges against him and a reasonable opportunity to respond to such charges.

COMMENT

In the absence of a By-law provision authorizing removal without cause, Directors are entitled to complete their term and may be removed only for cause. Such removal is technically known as "amotion." See Chapter 46, infra, for additional discussion.

A more common provision is to permit removal of Directors without cause upon the affirmative vote of a majority of the shares. For such a form, see Form, § 33.16, § 11.9, supra. Removal without cause ensures fidelity to the views of a majority of the shares, including, in the case of publicly held Corporations, a recent purchaser of a majority of the shares through a public cash tender or exchange offer.

Article V
NOTICES

§ 5.1 How Given

Whenever, under the provisions of the statutes or of the Articles of Incorporation or of these By-laws, notice is required to be given to any Director or Stockholder, it shall not be construed to mean personal notice unless specifically allowed, but such notice may be given in writing, by first class surface mail, addressed to such Director or Stockholder, at his address as it appears on the records of the Corporation, with postage thereon prepaid, and such notice shall be deemed to be given at the time when the same shall be deposited in the United States mail. Notice to Directors may also be given by telegram.

COMMENT TO § 5.1

This provision probably sets forth the minimum legally acceptable method of notice.

§ 5.2 Waiver

Whenever any notice is required to be given under the provisions of the statutes or of the Articles of Incorporation or of these By-laws, a waiver thereof in writing, signed by the person or persons entitled to said notice, whether before or after the time stated therein, shall be deemed equivalent to such notice.

Alternative A (Preferred as a Matter of Practical Experience)

§ 5.3 Purposes Need Not Be Stated in Notice

No notice of a Board of Directors meeting need state the purpose of such meeting.

COMMENT TO ALTERNATIVE A

This section follows Model Bus.Corp.Act § 43. It will help make Board meetings efficient.

Alternative B (Not Generally Preferred as a Matter of Practical Experience)

§ 5.3 Purposes Must Be Stated in the Notice

Any notice of a Board of Directors meeting shall state the purposes for which the meeting is being called and a general description of the matters to be considered. No other matters may come before the Directors.

COMMENT TO ALTERNATIVE B

This section is permitted by Model Bus.Corp.Act § 43. Its value is to avoid surprises and to avoid Directors missing meetings which later turn out to be important and to help Directors come to meetings better informed.

Article VI

OFFICERS

§ 6.1 Officers

The Board of Directors, within twenty-one (21) days after the annual election of the Directors in each year, shall elect from their number a President of the Corporation and shall also elect a *Vice-President*, Secretary and a Treasurer, who need not be members of the Board. *They may/shall also elect a Chairman of the Board.* The Board at that time or from time to time may elect more than one Vice-Presidents, Assistant Secretaries and Assistant Treasurers who may or may not be members of the Board. The same person may hold any two or more offices excepting those of President and Vice-President, but no Officer shall execute, acknowledge or verify an instrument in more than one capacity. The Board may also appoint such other Officers and agents as it may deem necessary for the transaction of the business of the Corporation.

§ 6.2 Term

The term of office of all Officers shall be until their respective successors are chosen, but any Officer may be removed from office, with or without cause, at any meeting of the Board of Directors by the affirmative vote of a majority of Directors then in office. The Board of Directors shall have power to fill any vacancies in any offices occurring from whatever reason.

§ 6.3 Salaries

The salaries and other compensation of all Officers of the Corporation shall be fixed by the Board of Directors.

Alternative A

§ 6.4 Chairman of the Board

The Chairman of the Board, if any, shall preside over all Board meetings. If no Chairman of the Board is present, the President shall exercise this power.

Alternative B

§ 6.4 Chairman of the Board

The Chairman of the Board shall be the chief officer of the Corporation and shall have responsibility for the general and active management of the business of the Corporation, and shall see that all orders and resolutions of the Board are carried into effect. He shall execute all authorized conveyances, contracts, or other obligations in the name of the Corporation except where the signing and execution thereof shall be expressly delegated by the Board of Directors to some other officer or agent of the Corporation. He shall preside at all meetings of the Stockholders and Directors and shall be ex-officio a member of all standing committees of the Board.

Alternative A

§ 6.5 President

The President shall be the chief executive officer of the Corporation and shall have responsibility for the general and active management of the Business of the Corporation, and shall see that all orders and resolutions of the Board are carried into effect. He shall execute all authorized conveyances, contracts, or other obligations in the name of the Corporation except where the signing and execution thereof shall be expressly delegated by the Board of Directors to some other officer or agent of the Corporation. He shall preside at all meetings of the *Stockholders* and (*if there is no Chairman of the Board*) Directors and shall be ex-officio a member of all standing committees of the Board.

Alternative B

§ 6.5 President

The President shall, in the absence or disability of the Chairman of the Board, perform the duties and exercise the powers of the Chairman of the Board. He shall have, as shall the Chairman, power to exercise all conveyances, contracts or other obligations in the name of the Corporation.

§ 6.6 Vice-President

The Vice-Presidents in the order designated by the Board of Directors or, lacking such a designation, by the President, shall in the absence or disability of the President perform the duties and exercise the powers of the President and shall perform such other duties as the Board of Directors shall prescribe.

§ 6.7 Secretary

The Secretary shall attend all meetings of the Board and all meetings of the Stockholders and record all votes and the minutes of all proceedings in a book to be kept for that purpose and shall perform like duties for the standing committees when required. He shall give, or cause to be given, notice of all meetings of the Stockholders and special meetings of the Board of Directors and shall perform such other duties as may be prescribed by the Board of Directors or by the President, under whose supervision he shall act. When required or requested, he shall execute with the President all authorized conveyances, contracts or other obligations in the name of the Corporation except as otherwise directed by the Board of Directors. He shall keep in safe custody the seal of the Corporation and, when authorized by the Board, affix the same to any instrument requiring it and, when so affixed, it shall be attested by his signature or by the signature of the Treasurer or an Assistant Secretary.

The Secretary shall keep a register of the post office address of each Stockholder. Said address shall be furnished to the Secretary by such Stockholder and the responsibility for keeping said address current shall be upon the Stockholder. The Secretary shall have general charge of the stock transfer books of the Corporation.

§ 6.8 Treasurer

The Treasurer shall have custody of and keep account of all money, funds and property of the Corporation, unless otherwise determined by the Board of Directors, and he shall render such accounts and present such statements to the Directors and President as may be required of him. He shall deposit funds of the Corporation which may come into his hands in such bank or banks as the Board of Directors may designate. He shall keep his bank accounts in the name of the Corporation and shall exhibit his books and accounts at all reasonable times to any Director of the Corporation upon application at the office of the Corporation during business hours. If required by the Board of Directors, he shall give the Corporation a bond in such sum and with such surety or sureties as shall be satisfactory to the Board for the faithful performance of the duties of his death, resignation or removal from office of all books, papers, vouchers, money and other property of whatever kind in his possession or under his control belonging to the Corporation.

§ 6.9 Assistants

The Assistant Secretaries and the Assistant Treasurers (if any), respectively, (in the order designated by the Board of Directors or, lacking such designation, by the President) in the absence of the Secretary or the Treasurer, as the case may be, shall perform the duties and exercise the powers of such Secretary or Treasurer and shall perform such other duties as the Board of Directors shall prescribe.

§ 6.10 Suspension of Officers

Any officer of the Corporation may be summarily suspended by the Board of Directors. The Secretary, Treasurer, or any Vice-President may be summarily suspended by the President subject to subsequent action by the Board of Directors. Any such suspension shall be in writing.

§ 6.11 Power to Vote Shares Owned by Corporation

The President of the Corporation, or any Vice-President, is authorized to execute any proxy, consent, or right to vote possessed by the Corporation in shares of stock owned by the Corporation, subject to the direction of the Board of Directors.

COMMENT

The Board of Directors presumably has power to designate proxies to vote shares of stock owned by the Corporation under its general power of management. This clause is in effect a permanent substitute for authorization that otherwise would appear in corporate resolutions. Compare Form, § 34.30, supra.

Article VII

CERTIFICATES OF SHARES

§ 7.1 Stockholders' Certificates

Every holder of shares in the Corporation shall be entitled to have a certificate, signed by, or in the name of the Corporation by the *President/Chairman* or a Vice-President and the Treasurer or an Assistant Treasurer, or the Secretary or an Assistant Secretary of the Corporation, certifying the number of shares owned by him in the Corporation.

Certificates may be issued for partly paid shares and in such case upon the face or back of the certificates issued to represent any such partly paid shares, the total amount paid thereon shall be specified.

If the Corporation shall be authorized to issue more than one class of stock or more than one series of any class, the powers, designations, preferences and relative, participating, optional or other special rights of each class of stock or series thereof and the qualifications, limitations or restrictions of such preferences and/or rights shall be set forth in full or summarized on the face or back of the certificate which the Corporation shall issue to represent such class or series of shares, provided that, except in lieu of the foregoing requirements, there may be set forth on the face or back of the certificate a statement that the Corporation will furnish without charge to each Stockholder who so requests the powers, designations, preferences and relative, participating, optional or other special rights of each class of stock or series thereof and the qualifications, limitations or restrictions of such preferences and/or rights.

COMMENT TO § 7.1

This provision follows Model Bus.Corp.Act § 23. See Chapters 40 and 41, infra.

§ 7.2 Facsimile Signatures

Where a certificate is countersigned (a) by a transfer agent other than the Corporation or its employee, or, (b) by a registrar, other than the Corporation or its employee, any other signature on the certificate may be a facsimile. In case any Officer, transfer agent or registrar who has signed or whose facsimile signature has been placed upon a certificate shall have ceased to be such Officer, transfer agent or registrar before such certificate is issued, it may be issued, by the Corporation with the same effect as if he were such Officer, transfer agent or registrar at the date of issue.

§ 7.3 Lost Certificates

The Board of Directors may direct a new certificate or certificates to be issued in place of any certificate or certificates theretofore issued by the Corporation alleged to have been lost, stolen or destroyed, upon the making of an affidavit of that fact by the owner claiming the certificate or shares to be lost, stolen or destroyed. When authorizing such issue of a new certificate or certificates, the Board of Directors may, in its discretion and as a condition precedent to the issuance thereof, require the owner of such lost, stolen or destroyed certificate or certificates, or his legal representative, to advertise the same in such manner as it shall require and/or to give the Corporation a bond in such sum as it may direct as indemnity against any claim that may be made against the Corporation with respect to the certificate alleged to have been lost, stolen or destroyed.

COMMENTS TO § 7.3

Uniform Commercial Code § 8–404 provides:

(1) Except as otherwise provided in any law relating to the collection of taxes, the issuer is not liable to the owner or

any other person suffering loss as a result of the registration of a transfer of a security if

(a) there were on or with the security the necessary indorsements (section 8–308); and

(b) the issuer had no duty to inquire into adverse claims or has discharged any such duty (section 8–403).

(2) Where an issuer has registered a transfer of a security to a person not entitled to it the issuer on demand must deliver a like security to the true owner unless

(a) the registration was pursuant to subsection (1); or

(b) the owner is precluded from asserting any claim for registering the transfer under subsection (1) of the following section; or

(c) such delivery would result in overissue, in which case the issuer's liability is governed by section 8–104.

Section 8–405: (1) Where a security has been lost, apparently destroyed or wrongfully taken and the owner fails to notify the issuer of that fact within a reasonable time after he has notice of it and the issuer registers a transfer of the security before receiving such a notification, the owner is precluded from asserting against the issuer any claim for registering the transfer under the preceding section or any claim to a new security under this section.

(2) Where the owner of a security claims that the security has been lost, destroyed or wrongfully taken, the issuer must issue a new security in place of the original security if the owner

(a) so requests before the issuer has notice that the security has been acquired by a bona fide purchaser; and

(b) files with the issuer a sufficient indemnity bond; and

(c) satisfies any other reasonable requirements imposed by the issuer.

(3) If, after the issue of the new security, a bona fide purchaser of the origial security presents it for registration of transfer, the issuer must register the transfer unless registration would result in overissue, in which event the issuer's liability is governed by section 8–104. In addition to any rights on the indemnity bond, the issuer may recover the new security from the person to whom it was issued or any person taking under him except a bona fide purchaser.

See Chapter 41, infra, with respect to lost, destroyed or stolen securities.

§ 7.4 Stock Transfers

Upon surrender to the Corporation or the transfer agent of the Corporation of a certificate for shares duly endorsed or accompanied by proper evidence of succession, assignment or authority to transfer, it shall be the duty of the Corporation to issue a new certificate to the person entitled thereto, cancel the old certificate and record the transaction upon its books.

COMMENTS TO § 7.4

Uniform Commercial Code §§ 8–401 to 8–403 provides:

Section 8–401. (1) Where a security in registered form is presented to the issuer with a request to register transfer, the issuer is under a duty to register the transfer as requested if

(a) the security is indorsed by the appropriate person or persons and

(b) reasonable assurance is given that those indorsements are genuine and effective and

(c) the issuer has no duty to inquire into adverse claims or has discharged any such duty and

(d) any applicable law relating to the collection of taxes has been complied with; and

(e) the transfer is in fact rightful or is to a bona fide purchaser.

(2) Where an issuer is under a duty to register a transfer of a security the issuer is also liable to the person presenting it for registration or his principal for loss resulting from any unreasonable delay in registration or from failure or refusal to register the transfer.

Section 8–402. (1) The issuer may require the following assurance that each necessary indorsement is genuine and effective

(a) in all cases, a guarantee of the signature of the person indorsing; and

(b) where the indorsement is by an agent, appropriate assurance of authority to sign;

(c) where the indorsement is by a fiduciary, appropriate evidence of appointment or incumbency;

(d) where there is more than one fiduciary, reasonable assurance that all who are required to sign have done so;

(e) where the indorsement is by a person not covered by any of the foregoing, assurance appropriate to the case corresponding as nearly as may be to the foregoing.

(2) A "guarantee of the signature" in subsection (1) means a guarantee signed by or on behalf of a person reasonably believed by the issuer to be responsible. The issuer may adopt standards with respect to responsibility provided such standards are not manifestly unreasonable.

(3) "Appropriate evidence of appointment or incumbency" in subsection (1) means

(a) in the case of a fiduciary appointed or qualified by a court, a certificate issued by or under the direction or supervision of that court or an officer thereof and dated within 60 days before the date of presentation for transfer; or

(b) in any other case, a copy of a document showing the appointment or a certificate issued by or on behalf of a person reasonably believed by the issuer to be responsible or, in the absence of such a document or certificate, other evidence reasonably deemed by the issuer to be appropriate. The issuer may adopt standards with respect to such evidence provided such standards are not manifestly unreasonable. The issuer is not charged with notice of the contents of any document obtained pursuant to this paragraph (b) except to the extent that the contents relate directly to the appointment or incumbency.

(4) The issuer may elect to require reasonable assurance beyond that specified in this section but if it does so and for a purpose other than that specified in subsection (3)(b) both requires and obtains a copy of a will, trust, indenture, articles of Copartnership, bylaws or other controlling instrument it is charged with notice of all matters contained therein affecting the transfer.

Section 8–403. (1) An issuer to whom a security is presented for registration is under a duty to inquire into adverse claims if

(a) a written notification of an adverse claim is received at a time and in a manner which affords the issuer a reasonable opportunity to act on it prior to the issuance of a new, reissued or re-registered security and the notification identifies the claimant, the registered owner and the issue of which the security is a part and provides an address for communications directed to the claimant; or

(b) the issuer is charged with notice of an adverse claim from a controlling instrument which it has elected to require under subsection (4) of section 8–402.

(2) The issuer may discharge any duty of inquiry by any reasonable means, including notifying an adverse claimant by registered mail, or certified mail, if the receipt of mailing is postmarked, at the address furnished by him or if there be no such address at his residence or regular place of business that the security has been presented for registration of transfer by a named person, and that the transfer will be registered unless within 30 days from the date of mailing the notification, either

(a) an appropriate restraining order, injunction or other process issues from a court of competent jurisdiction; or

(b) an indemnity bond sufficient in the issuer's judgment to protect the issuer and any transfer agent, registrar or other agent of the issuer involved, from any loss which it or they may suffer by complying with the adverse claim is filed with the issuer.

(3) Unless an issuer is charged with notice of an adverse claim from a controlling instrument which it has elected to require under subsection (4) of section 8–402 or receives notification of an adverse claim under subsection (1) of this section, where a security presented for registration is indorsed by the appropriate person or persons the issuer is under no duty to inquiry into adverse claims. In particular

(a) an issuer registering a security in the name of a person who is a fiduciary or who is described as a fiduciary is not bound to inquire into the existence, extent, or correct description of the fiduciary relationship and thereafter the issuer may assume without inquiry that the newly registered owner continues to be the fiduciary until the issuer receives written notice that the fiduciary is no longer acting as such with respect to the particular security;

(b) an issuer registering transfer on an indorsement by a fiduciary is not bound to inquire whether the transfer is made in compliance with a controlling instrument or with the law of the state having jurisdiction of the fiduciary relationship, including any law requiring the fiduciary to obtain court approval of the transfer; and

(c) the issuer is not charged with notice of the contents of any court record or file or other recorded or unrecorded document even though the document is in its possession and even though the transfer is made on the indorsement of a fiduciary to the fiduciary himself or to his nominee.

See Chapter 52, infra, for further coverage of transfer of shares.

§ 7.5 Record Date

In order that the Corporation may determine the Stockholders entitled to notice of or to vote at any meeting of Stockholders or any adjournment thereof, or to express consent to a corporate action in writing without a meeting, or entitled to receive payment of any dividend or other distribution or allotment of any rights, or entitled to exercise any rights in respect of any change, conversion or exchange of stock or for the purpose of any other lawful action, the Board of Directors may fix, in advance, a record date, which shall not be more than fifty (50) days nor less than ten (10) days before the date of such meeting, nor more than fifty (50) days prior to any other action. A determination of Stockholders of record entitled to notice of or to vote at a meeting of Stockholders shall apply to any adjournment of the meeting; provided, however, that the Board of Directors may fix a new record date for the adjourned meeting. Absent Board of Director action, the record date shall be ten (10) days before the date of such meeting.

COMMENT

This section follows Model Bus.Corp.Act § 30. See Chapter 47, infra.

§ 7.6 Registered Stockholders

The Corporation shall be entitled to recognize the exclusive right of a person registered on its books as the owner of shares to receive dividends, and to vote as such owner, and to hold liable for calls and assessments a person registered on its books as the owner of shares, and shall not be bound to recognize any equitable or other claim to interest in such share or shares on the part of any other person, whether or not it shall have express or other notice thereof, except as otherwise provided by the laws of the state of incorporation.

§ 7.7 Shares in Hands of Trustees or Representatives

Shares held by an administrator, executor, guardian, or conservator may be voted by him without a transfer of such shares into his name so long as such shares forming part of an estate are in his possession and form a part of the estate being served by him. Shares standing in the name of a receiver may be voted by him without the transfer thereof into his name if authority so to do is contained in an appropriate order of the court by which such receiver was appointed. Shares standing in the name of a trustee may be voted by him only if such shares have been transferred into his name as trustee. All such shares may be voted in person or by proxy.

§ 7.8 Shares Held by Pledgee

A Stockholder whose shares are pledged shall be entitled to vote such shares until the shares have been transferred into the name of the pledgee. Thereafter the pledgee shall be entitled to vote the shares so transferred.

§ 7.9 Shares Held by Another Corporation

Shares standing in the name of another Corporation, domestic or foreign, may be voted by such officer, agent, or proxy as the By-laws of such Corporation may authorize or, in the absence of such authorization, as the Board of Directors of such Corporation may determine.

§ 7.10 Successive Proxies

Unless a proxy is irrevocable—

(a) The later execution by the Stockholder of a different proxy revokes the earlier one; and

(b) An attempt to vote by the Stockholder who is present at the meeting revokes all other proxies executed by him.

COMMENT

This By-law codifies the common law rule with respect to successive or inconsistent proxies.

Article VIII

INDEMNIFICATION

Alternative A (General Clause)

§ 8.1 Indemnification

The Corporation shall indemnify to the full extent permitted by law any person who is made, or threatened to be made, a party to any action, suit or proceeding (whether civil, criminal, administrative or investigative) by reason of the fact that he, his testator or intestate is or was a Director, Officer, employee or agent of the Corporation or serves or served any other enterprise at the request of the Corporation.

COMMENT ON ALTERNATIVE A

This section fulfills the purpose of protecting the Directors, officers, employees and agents to the extent possible. The section does not recite the applicable rule and therefore violates the rule of drafting that the document should be as complete as possible. See Model Bus.Corp.Act § 5.

Alternative B (Specific Indemnification)

§ 8.1 Indemnification in General

(a) To the extent permitted by the law of the state of incorporation from time to time in effect and subject to the provisions of Section (c) of this Article, the Corporation shall indemnify any person who was or is a party or is threatened to be made a party to any threatened, pending or completed action, suit or proceeding, whether civil, criminal, administrative or investigative (whether or not by or in the right of the Corporation) by reason of the fact that he is or was a Director, Officer, employee or agent of the Corporation, or is or was serving at the request of the Corporation as a director, officer, employee or agent of another corporation, partnership, joint venture, trust or other enterprise, against expenses (including attorneys' fees), judgments, fines and amounts paid in settlement actually and reasonably incurred by him in connection with such action, suit or proceeding if he acted in good faith and in a manner he reasonably believed to be in or not opposed to the best interests of the Corporation, or its Stockholders, and, with respect to any criminal action or proceeding, had no reasonable cause to believe his conduct was unlawful. The termination of any action, suit or proceeding by judgment, order, settlement, conviction, or upon a plea of nolo contendere or its equivalent, shall not, of itself, create a presumption that the person did not act in good faith and in a manner which he reasonably believed to be in or not opposed to the best interests of the Corporation, and, with respect to any criminal action or proceeding, had reasonable cause to believe that his conduct was unlawful.

(b) To the extent permitted by the law of the state of incorporation from time to time in effect and subject to the provisions of Section (c) of this Article, the Corporation shall have power to indemnify any person who was or is a party to or is threatened to be made a party to any threatened, pending or completed action or suit by or in the right of the Corporation to procure a judgment in its favor by reason of the fact that he is or was a Director, Officer, employee or agent of the Corporation, or is or was serving at the request of the Corporation as a director, officer, employee or agent of another corporation, partnership, joint venture, trust or other enterprise against expenses (including attorneys' fees) actually and reasonably incurred by him in connection with the defense or settlement of such action or suit if he acted in good faith and in a manner he reasonably believed to be in or not opposed to the best interests of the Corporation or its Stockholders and except that no indemnification shall be made in respect of any claim, issue or matter as to which such person shall have been adjudged to be liable for negligence or misconduct in the performance of his duty to the Corporation unless and only to the extent that the court in which such action or suit was brought shall determine upon application that, despite the adjudication of liability but in view of all circumstances of the case, such person is fairly and reasonably entitled to indemnity for such expenses which such court shall deem proper.

(c) If a Director, Officer, employee or agent of the Corporation has been successful on the merits or otherwise as a party to any action, suit or proceedings referred to in Sections (a) or (b) of this Article, or with respect to any claim, issue or matter therein (to the extent that a portion of his expenses can be reasonably allocated thereto), he shall be indemnified against expenses (including attorneys' fees) actualiy and reasonably incurred by him in connection therewith.

(d) Expenses incurred in defending a civil, criminal, administrative or investigative action, suit or proceeding, as authorized by the Board of Directors, whether a disinterested quorum exists or not, upon receipt of an undertaking by or on behalf of the Director, Officer, employee or agent to repay such amount unless it shall ultimately be determined that he is entitled to be indemnified by the Corporation as authorized in this Article.

(e) The indemnification provided by this Article shall not be deemed exclusive of any other rights to which those indemnified may be entitled under any Agreement, vote of Stockholders or disinterested Directors, or otherwise, both as to action in his official capacity and as to action in another capacity while holding such office, and shall continue as to a person who has ceased to be a Director, Officer, employee or agent and shall inure to the benefit of the heirs, executors and administrators of such a person.

COMMENT TO ALTERNATIVE B

These provisions satisfy the rule that the document should be as complete as possible, but it may not cover all allowable situations of indemnification.

COMMENT TO (a)

This provision indemnifies the actors in civil, criminal and administrative actions for costs (i. e., court fees and legal fees) and judgments except it does not cover Stockholder ("derivative") suits against the Corporation.

COMMENT TO (b)

This provision indemnifies the actor's actions in civil suits by Stockholders for costs (i. e., court fees and legal fees) only.

§ 8.2 Insurance

The Corporation may purchase and maintain insurance on behalf of any person who is or was a Director, Officer, employee or agent of the Corporation, or is or was serving at the request of the Corporation as a director, officer, employee or agent of another corporation, partnership, joint venture, trust or other enterprise against any liability asserted against him and incurred by him in any such capacity, or arising out of his status as such, whether or not the Corporation would have the power to indemnify him against such liability under the provisions of this Article or of the Business Corporation Law of the state of incorporation.

Article IX

GENERAL PROVISIONS

§ 9.1 Dividends

Dividends upon the capital stock of the Corporation, subject to the provisions of the Articles of Incorporation, if any, may be declared by the Board of Directors at any regular or special meeting, pursuant to law. Dividends may be paid in cash, in property, or in shares of the capital stock.

Before payment of any dividend, there may be set aside out of any funds of the Corporation available for dividends such sum or sums as the Directors from time to time, in their absolute discretion, think proper as a reserve or reserves to meet contingencies, or for equalizing dividends, or for repairing or maintaining any property of the Corporation, or for such other purpose as the Directors shall think conductive to the interest of the Corporation, and the Directors may modify or abolish any such reserve in the manner in which it was created.

COMMENT

See Chapters 56 and 57, infra, with respect to dividends.

§ 9.2 Annual Statement

The Board of Directors shall present at each annual meeting and at any special meeting of the Stockholders a full and clear statement of the business and condition of the Corporation.

§ 9.3 Checks

All checks or demands for money and notes of the Corporation shall be signed by such Officer or Officers or such other person or persons as the Board of Directors may from time to time designate.

§ 9.4 Seal

The corporate seal shall have inscribed thereon the name of the Corporation and the words "Corporate Seal, [*State of Incorporation*]." The seal may be used by causing it or a facsimile thereof to be impressed or affixed or reproduced or otherwise.

§ 9.5 Loans in General

No loans shall be contracted on behalf of the Corporation and no evidence of indebtedness shall be issued in its name unless authorized by a resolution of the Board of Directors. Such authority may be general or confined to specific instances.

§ 9.6 Loans to Persons with a Conflict

The Corporation may lend money to, or guarantee any obligation of, or otherwise assist any Officer or other employee of the Corporation or of its subsidiary, including any Officer or employee who is a Director of the Corporation or its subsidiary, whenever, in the judgment of the Directors, such loans, guaranty or assistance may reasonably be expected to benefit the Corporation. The loan, guaranty or other assistance may be with or without interest, and may be unsecured, or secured in such manner as the Board of Directors shall approve, including, without limitation, a pledge of shares of stock of the Corporation. Nothing in this section contained shall be deemed to deny, limit or restrict the powers of guaranty or warranty of any Corporation at common law.

COMMENTS TO § 9.6

The problem with this provision is that willingness of the Board to make such loan may be influenced by considerations other than strict corporate considerations, such as the friendship of the Board to the borrower. It should be noted that if the Officer or employee is also a major Stockholder, the possibility exists that the Internal Revenue Service will deem such loan to be a non-deductible dividend taxable to the recipient (see Chapter 56, infra). The possibility of this is especially heightened if the borrower(s) borrow in proportion to their stock ownership.

If the recipient is only an employee then the Internal Revenue Service may contend that the loan was the payment of compensation and, although deductible by the Corporation, taxable to the recipient (see Chapter 56, infra).

The Internal Revenue Service's arguments will be bolstered by some or all of the following:

(a) The lack of a note evidencing the loan.

(b) The loan being in proportion to stock ownership or salaries paid.

(c) Lack of a stated interest rate.

(d) Lack of definite repayment terms.

(e) Lack of actual repayment of interest or principal.

As to merely the lack of stated interest, it has been repeatedly held that such loans are permissible and that no interest will be implied if the loan is in the form of a demand note (see § 56.11, infra).

§ 9.7 Contracts in General

The Board of Directors may authorize any Officer or Officers, agent or agents, to enter into any contract or execute and deliver any instrument in the name of and on behalf of the Corporation, and such authority may be general or confined to specific instances.

§ 9.8 Contracts with Persons with a Conflict

No contract or other transaction between a Corporation and one or more of its Directors or any other corporation, firm, association or entity in which one or more of its directors are Directors or Officers or are financially interested, shall be either void or voidable because of such relationship or interest or because such Director or Directors are present at the meeting of the Board of Directors or a committee thereof which authorizes, approves or ratifies such contract or transaction or because his or their votes are counted for such purpose, if:

(a) The fact of such relationship or interest is disclosed or known to the Board of Directors or committee which authorizes, approves or ratifies the contract or transaction by a vote or consent sufficient for the purpose without counting the votes or consents of such interested Directors; or

(b) The fact of such relationship or interest is disclosed or known to the Stockholders entitled to vote and they authorize, approve or ratify such contract or transaction by vote or written consent; or

(c) The contract or transaction is fair and reasonable to the Corporation.

Common or interested Directors may be counted in determining the presence of a quorum at a meeting of the Board of Directors or a committee thereof which authorizes, approves or ratifies such contract or transaction.

COMMENT TO § 9.8

This language follows Model Bus.Corp.Act § 41 which contradicts the common law which permits contracts between the Corporation and interested parties only if (a) all the facts of the conflict in relationship are known and (b) the transaction is fair.

§ 9.9 Stockholders' Inspection Rights

(a) Any person who shall have been a holder of record of shares for at least six months immediately preceding his demand, or shall be the holder of record of at least five per cent of all the outstanding shares of the Corporation, upon written demand stating the purpose thereof, shall have the right to examine, in person or by agent, accountant, or attorney, at any reasonable time or times for any proper purpose, its relevant books and records of account, minutes, By-laws, and record of Stockholders, and to make extracts therefrom. A holder of a beneficial interest in a voting trust complying with the

Business Corporation Act shall be regarded as a holder of record of the shares represented by such beneficial interest.

(b) Any person who has within the previous two years sold or offered for sale any list of Stockholders or of holders of voting trust certificates of any Corporation, or has aided or abetted any person in procuring any list of Stockholders or of holders of voting trust certificates for any such purpose, or has improperly used any information secured through any prior examination of the books or records of the Corporation, or is not acting in good faith or for a proper purpose, shall not be entitled to any right of inspection under subsection (a) hereof.

COMMENT

The provision is often omitted on the theory that any demand for inspection will result in the Corporation's attorney being consulted.

For additional discussion of Stockholders inspection rights, see Chapter 49, supra.

§ 9.10 Reliance on Corporate Records

Any Officer or Director may rely and act upon information contained in the corporate records maintained by the Secretary and Treasurer of the Corporation. Unless he has actual knowledge that such information is incorrect, he shall not be liable to the Corporation or any person for any action based upon such information.

§ 9.11 Unpaid Subscriptions

If at any time any person subscribes to any unissued shares of this Corporation and such subscription is duly accepted by the Corporation and thereafter such subscriber defaults in the payment of any installment of such subscription or, if such subscription does not provide for payment in specified installments, any call for all or part of the then unpaid balance of the principal amount of such subscription, the Board of Directors then may, at its election, resolve upon either of the two following courses of action to be followed by the Corporation:

(1) That the Corporation proceed to collect the amount due in the same manner as any debt due the Corporation; or

(2) That, if the amount due thereon remains unpaid for a period of twenty (20) days after written demand, deposited in the United States mail in a sealed envelope addressed to the subscriber at his last post office address known to the Corporation with postage thereon prepaid, such subscription shall be declared

null and void and of no further force and effect, any and all payments theretofore paid by the subscriber to the Corporation on such subscription shall be considered forfeited to the use and benefit of the Corporation, and the shares subscribed for by such subscriber shall revert from the status of unissued but subscribed for to the status of unissued and unsubscribed for.

Article X

AMENDMENTS

Alternative A (Not Preferred as a Matter of Practical Experience)

§ 10.1 Stockholders Control By-laws

These By-laws may be altered, amended or repealed or new By-laws may be adopted by the Stockholders or by the Board of Directors, when such power is conferred upon the Board of Directors by the Articles of Incorporation or at any regular meeting of the Stockholders or of the Board of Directors or at any special meeting of the Stockholders or of the Board of Directors if proper notice of such proposal has been given in the notice of such special meeting.

COMMENT TO ALTERNATIVE A

The Board's powers are so broad it is often wise for the Stockholders to control the Board through the By-laws. This provision will make it possible.

Alternative B (Preferred as a Matter of Practical Experience)

§ 10.1 Board Controls By-laws

These By-laws may be altered, amended or repealed or new By-laws may be adopted by the Stockholders or by the Board of Directors at any regular meeting of the Stockholders or of the Board of Directors or at any special meeting if notice of such proposed alteration, amendment, repeal or adoption of new By-laws be contained in the notice of such special meeting.

COMMENT TO ALTERNATIVE B

If the Stockholder's trust the Board, allowing the Board to amend the By-laws will make corporate operations more efficient.

Article XI

COMMITTEES OF DIRECTORS

Preferred as a Matter of Practical Experience

§ 11.1 Committees

The Board of Directors may, by resolution passed by a majority of the whole Board, designate one or more committees, to consist of two or more of the Directors of the Corporation. The Board may designate one or more Directors as alternate members of any committee, who may replace any absent or disqualified member at any meeting of the committee. Any such committee, to the extent provided in the resolution, and as otherwise restricted by the Business Corporation Act of the state of incorporation, shall have and may exercise the powers of the Board of Directors in the management of the business and affairs of the Corporation, and may authorize the seal of the Corporation to be affixed to all papers which may require it; provided, however, that in the absence of disqualification of any member of such committee or committees, the member or members thereof present at any meeting and not disqualified from voting, whether or not he or they constitute a quorum, may unanimously appoint another member of the Board of Directors to act at the meeting in the place of any such absent or disqualified member. Such committee or committees shall have such name or names as may be determined from time to time by resolution adopted by the Board of Directors.

COMMENT TO § 11.1

This provision carries out Article XVIII, § 18.1 of the form

This provision carries out Article XVII, § 17.1 of the form found at § 33.16, infra.

§ 11.2 Denial of Authority

Provided that no such committee shall have authority to (a) declare dividends or distributions, (b) approve or recommend to Stockholders actions or proposals required to be approved by Stockholders, (c) designate candidates for the office of Director, for purposes of proxy solicitation or otherwise, or fill vacancies on the Board of Directors, or any committee thereof, (d) amend the By-laws, (e) approve a plan of merger not requiring Stockholder approval, (f) reduce earned or capital surplus, (g) authorize or approve the reacquisition of stock unless pursuant to a general formula or (h) authorize or approve the issuance or sale of, or any contract to issue or sell, shares or designate the terms of a series of a class of shares; provided that the Board of Directors, having acted regarding general authorization for the issuance or sale of shares, or any contract therefor, and, in the case of a series, the designation thereof, may, pursuant to a general formula or method specified by the Board by resolution or by adoption of a stock option or other plan, authorize a committee to fix the terms of any contract for the sale of the shares and to fix the terms upon which such shares may be issued or sold, including, without limitation, the price, the dividend rate, provisions for redemption, sinking fund, conversion, voting or preferential rights, and provisions for other features of a class of shares, or a series of a class of shares, with full power in such committee to adopt any final resolution setting forth all the terms thereof and to authorize the statement of the terms of a series.

COMMENT TO § 11.2

It generally will be preferable to specifically outline the committee's areas of authority. It's important that the committee's authority be at least as restricted as the powers given to the Corporation (see § 17.2 of the form found at § 33.16, supra), and for the powers of the Board (see § 4.3, supra, of this form).

§ 11.3 Authority

A committee may be established to exercise the following powers as agent for the Board of Directors:

(a) To sue, complain and defend.

(b) To use the corporate seal by causing it, or a facsimile thereof, to be impressed or affixed or in any other manner reproduced.

(c) To purchase, take, receive, lease, or otherwise acquire, own, hold, improve, use and otherwise deal in and with, real or personal property, or any interest therein, wherever situated.

(d) To sell, convey, mortgage, pledge, lease, exchange, transfer and otherwise dispose of all or any part of the corporate property and assets.

(e) To lend money and use the Corporation's credit to assist its employees and Directors.

(f) To purchase, take, receive, subscribe for, or otherwise acquire, own, hold, vote, use, employ, sell, mortgage, lend, pledge, or otherwise dispose of, and otherwise use and deal in and with, shares or other interests in, or obligations of, other domestic or foreign corporations, associations, partnerships, or individuals, or direct or indirect obligations of the United States or of any other government, state, territory, governmental district or municipality or of any instrumentality thereof.

(g) To make contracts and guarantees and incur liabilities, borrow money at such rates of interest as the Corporation may determine, issue its notes, bonds, and other obligations, and secure any of its obligations by mortgage or pledge of all or any of its property, franchises and income.

(h) To lend money for the corporate purposes, invest and reinvest its funds, and take and hold payment of funds so loaned or invested.

(i) To conduct corporate business, carry on its operations and have offices and exercise the powers granted herein, within or without this State.

(j) To elect or appoint officers and agents of the Corporation, and define their duties and fix their compensation.

(k) To make donations for the public welfare or for charitable, scientific or educational purposes.

(*l*) To transact any lawful business which it shall find will be an aid of governmental policy.

(m) To pay pensions and establish pension plans, pension trusts, profit sharing plans, stock bonus plans, stock option plans and other incentive plans for any or all of its Directors, Officers and employees.

(n) To be a promoter, partner, member, associate, or manager of any partnership, joint venture, trust or other enterprise.

§ 11.4 Minutes

Each committee shall keep regular minutes of its meetings and report the same to the Board of Directors when required.

§ 11.5 Consent Meeting

Unless otherwise restricted by the Articles of Incorporation any action required or permitted to be taken at any meeting of any committee thereof may be taken without a meeting, if all members of the committee consent thereto in writing, and the writing or writings are filed with the minutes of proceedings of the committee.

COMMENT TO § 11.5

This provision implements the Articles of Incorporation (see § 11.5 of the form found at Chapter 33, § 33.16, supra) and follows Model Bus.Corp.Act § 43.

§ 11.6 Conference Call Meetings

Committee meetings may be held by means of a conference telephone or similar communications equipment by means of which all persons participating in the meeting can hear each other at the same time.

COMMENT TO § 11.6

This provision implements Model Bus.Corp.Act § 43.

§ 11.7 Notice

Whenever, under the provisions of the statutes or of the Articles of Incorporation or of these By-laws, notice is required to be given to any committee member, it shall not be construed to mean personal notice unless specifically allowed, but such notice may be given in writing, by mail, addressed to such member, at his address as it appears on the records of the Corporation, with postage thereon prepaid, and such notice shall be deemed to be given at the time when the same shall be deposited in the United States mail. Notice to members may also be given by telegram.

Whenever any notice is required to be given under the provisions of the statutes or of the Articles of Incorporation or of these By-laws, a waiver thereof in writing, signed by the person or persons entitled to said notice, whether before or after the time stated therein, shall be deemed equivalent to such notice.

COMMENT

See Model Bus.Corp.Act § 144 with respect to waiver of notice.

Alternative A (Preferred as a Matter of Practical Experience)

§ 11.8 Purpose

No notice of a committee meeting need state the purpose of such meeting.

COMMENT TO ALTERNATIVE A

This section follows Model Bus.Corp.Act § 43.

Alternative B

§ 11.8 Purpose

Any notice of a committee meeting shall state the purposes for which the meeting is being called and a general description of the matters to be considered. No other matters may come before the committee.

COMMENT TO ALTERNATIVE B

This section is permitted by Model Bus.Corp.Act § 43. Its value is to avoid surprises and to avoid committee members missing meetings which later turn out to be important and to help members come to meetings better informed.

Article XII

SPECIAL LANGUAGE FOR CLOSE CORPORATIONS REQUIRING A SPECIAL STATUTORY ELECTION

The business and affairs of the Corporation shall be managed by the Stockholders rather than by a Board of Directors. Actions by the Stockholders shall be approved on the basis of the vote, cast in person or by proxy, of the holders of shares having a majority of the total voting power of all outstanding shares entitled to vote with respect to such action. Actions consented to by the Stockholders shall be binding on the Corporation. Actions taken with the full knowledge of all the Stockholders shall be deemed consented to unless a Stockholder objects thereto in a timely manner.

If the Corporation elects to have its business and affairs managed by a Board of Directors, the number of Directors shall be ________.

This Corporation may be dissolved at any time [*Here Repeat Provision of the Articles of Incorporation*]. Any Stockholder desiring to dissolve the Corporation shall give 30 days written notice thereof by certified mail to all other Stockholders. Dissolution of the Corporation shall occur upon the expiration of said 30 day period and the filing of Articles of Dissolution executed by the appropriate corporate Officers.

§§ 34.15–35.0 are reserved for supplementary material.

CHAPTER 35

ORGANIZATION MEETING(S)

Table of Sections

A. IN GENERAL

B. MEETING OF INCORPORATORS

C. MEETING OF DIRECTORS

A. IN GENERAL

§ 35.1 Introduction[1]

Most of the miscellaneous matters relating to the launching of a new Corporation are accomplished at a meeting of the initial Directors, or in some states, the incorporators. Typical actions will include the acceptance of share subscriptions or contracts; the issuance of shares and the establishment of the consideration for them; the selection and election of Officers; the approval of contracts, loans, leases and other business-related matters; the approval of the By-laws and the seal; the approval of the payment of the expenses of incorporation; the adoption of a resolution opening a bank account and the designation of the Officers authorized to sign checks; and numerous other possible business-related matters. As a practical matter, the attorney will normally draft the minutes of this meeting before the meeting takes place. Also, in some circumstances it may be necessary to have a meeting of the Incorporators to elect Directors; the attorney normally also drafts the minutes of this meeting before the meeting takes place. If meetings are held pursuant to waivers of notice, the attorney also prepares the waiver to be executed before or at the meeting.

Of the states with express statutory requirements concerning organization meetings, most require only an organization meeting of the incorporators. Some states require only an organization meeting of the Directors;[2] others impose various requirements for organization meetings of subscribers, incorporators, Stockholders, or Directors.[3]

1. Adapted from Henn, Law of Corporations (2d ed. 1970), § 135. A third edition is being prepared by Professor Henn for 1982 publication.

2. E. g. Model Bus.Corp.Act § 57 provides:

§ 57. Organization Meeting of Directors

After the issuance of the Certificate of Incorporation an organization meeting of the Board of Directors named in the Articles of Incorporation shall be held, either within or without this state, at the call of a majority of the Directors named in the Articles of Incorporation, for the purpose of adopting By-laws, electing Officers and transacting such other business as may come before the meeting. The Directors calling the meeting shall give at least three days' notice thereof by mail to each director so named, stating the time and place of the meeting.

See also e. g. McKinney's N.Y.Bus.Corp. Law § 404; Minn.Bus.Corp.Act § 302A.171.

3. E. g., Del.Gen.Corp.Law § 108 provides:

§ 108. Organization Meeting of Incorporators or Directors Named in Certificate of Incorporation

(a) After the filing of the certificate of incorporation an organization meeting of the incorporator or incorporators, or of the Board of Directors if the initial Directors were named in the Certificate of Incorporation, shall be held, either within or without this state, at the call of a majority of the incorporators or Directors, as the case may

In states without statutes on the subject, a common cautious practice is to hold post-incorporation organization meetings of both the incorporators and the Directors. The practice often resembles a ritual, with "dummies" or "accommodation" personnel, paper meetings, and, when required, token share subscriptions.

Any organization meetings should be held on proper call and with proper notice[4] and with due observance of applicable quorum and other requirements, unless the meeting is held pursuant to waivers or not held at all but is "consented" to.

A meeting held pursuant to waivers is an actual meeting where notices have not been sent out because the participants have waived their right to proper notice.

A meeting held pursuant to consents has the legal effect of a meeting (where this is permitted) but no actual meeting took place; rather the resolutions were consented to by the appropriate participants (generally each incorporator or Director).

The procedures at the organization meetings are rather standardized and follow various patterns, depending on the extent to which "dummy" or "accommodation" incorporator(s) and/or dummy or accommodation Directors are used. As a general rule, dummies should not be expected to assume responsibility for other than formal matters. The turnover by the dummies to the real parties in interest should be timed not only to leave the determination of substantial matters to the real parties in interest but also to comply with applicable quorum and other requirements.

The older practice was to use dummy incorporators and dummy initial Directors followed by a later election of those people who were

be, for the purposes of adopting By-laws, electing Directors (if the meeting is of the incorporators) to serve or hold office until the first annual meeting of Stockholders or until their successors are elected and qualify, electing Officers if the meeting is of the Directors, doing any other or further acts to perfect the organization of the Corporation, and transacting such other business as may come before the meeting.

(b) The persons calling the meeting shall give to each other incorporator or Director, as the case may be, at least 2 days written notice thereof by any usual means of communication, which notice shall state the time, place and purposes of the meeting as fixed by the persons calling it. Notice of the meeting need not be given to anyone who attends the meeting or who signs a waiver of notice either before or after the meeting.

(c) Any action permitted to be taken at the organization meeting of the incorporators or directors, as the case may be, may be taken without a meeting if each incorporator or Director, where there is more than one, or the sole incorporator or Director where there is only one, signs an instrument which states the action so taken.

4. See e. g., McKinney's N.Y.Bus.Corp. Law § 404. Most state statutes, like New York, provide for waiver of notice. With respect to consent meetings, many state statutes have provisions similar to Del.Gen.Corp.Law § 108(c) (see note 3, supra).

to govern the Corporation. The reason for this was to keep secret the actual people behind the Corporation.

§ 35.2 Title Page of Minute Book

MINUTE BOOK

OF

______ CORPORATION

The ______ Corporation was duly organized under the ______ Business Corporation Act on ______, 19__.

This is the Minute Book of ______ Corporation duly approved by the initial Board of Directors on ______, 19__.

Dated: ______, 19__.

____

____

____

COMMENTS

The Minute Book is usually loose leaf. The pages, however, are consecutively numbered in an effort to ensure that a permanent and untampered record is retained.

The first page of the minute book usually identifies the Corporation, the date of incorporation and the date of the organizational meeting of the initial Board of Directors. A statement is sometimes added that the signatures of the Directors have been affixed to the first page "in order to identify and authenticate this Minute Book."

It is customary to place the Certificate of Incorporation and duplicate Articles of Incorporation received from the Secretary of State in the Minute Book immediately following the Title Page.

B. MEETING OF INCORPORATORS

§ 35.3 Formal Agenda

For the first meeting of the incorporators (assuming the presence of a quorum), a very formal, rigid agenda is approximately as follows:

(a) Election of Chairman and Secretary of meeting;

(b) Filing of waiver(s) of notice of meeting;

(c) Presentation and filing in minute book of Certificate of Incorporation or certified copy of Articles of Incorporation and receipt for payment of filing fee and organization tax;

(d) Adoption of By-laws (see Chapter 34, supra);

(e) Election of initial Directors if not named in the Articles of Incorporation; resignation of any accommodation or dummy initial

Directors and replacement, seriatim, where permissible by action of the incorporator(s);

(f) Authorization to Board of Directors to issue shares (see § 35.24, infra);

(g) Presentation and filing of transfers of any subscriptions from accommodations or dummy incorporator(s) (with affixation and cancellation of any required share transfer tax stamps);

(h) Transaction of any other business where permissible by incorporator(s).

At the first meeting of the Board of Directors (assuming the presence of a quorum), a very formal, rigid order of business is approximately the following:

(a) Election of Chairman and Secretary of meeting;

(b) Filing of waivers of notice of meeting;

(c) Resignation of any accommodation or dummy initial Directors and replacement, seriatim, where permissible by action of Board of Directors;

(d) Approval of minutes of first meeting of incorporator(s);

(e) Approval, ratification and confirmation of all action taken at first meeting of incorporator(s);

(f) Approval of By-laws;

(g) Approval of corporate seal [5] (and affixation of seal to margin of minute book page);

(h) Approval of form(s) of share certificate, with appropriate legends (see Chapter 41, infra);

(j) Acceptance of share subscriptions (see Chapter 39, infra); dation or dummy incorporator(s);

(j) Acceptance of share subscriptions (see Chapter 42, infra);

(k) Authorization of issue of shares; fixing of consideration; valuation of any property consideration; allocation, where permissible, of portion of consideration to capital surplus (see Chapter 39, infra);

(*l*) Authorization for payment or reimbursement of incorporation expenses and legal fees;

(m) Adoption of any Preincorporation Agreements (see Chapter 29, supra);

(n) Election of corporate Officers per statute (e. g., the President might have to be a director) and By-laws, bonding of Officers, and fixing of compensation thereof;

5. The power to adopt and use a corporate seal or common seal, is incidental to every Corporation. Leggett v. New Jersey Mfg. & Banking Co., 1 N.J.Eq. 541 (1832). Modern statutes confirm this power. E. g., Model Bus.Corp.Act § 4(c). Such provisions have been construed as permissive rather than mandatory.

(*o*) Adoption of any Employment Agreements (see Employee Benefit Volume 5); acceptance of transfers of property; making of leases;

(p) Adoption of the bank resolution (form supplied by bank and appropriately modified, see § 35.26, infra, for form);

(q) Adoption of resolution under Internal Revenue Code for Subchapter S election (see Part VIII, infra);

(r) Authorization of filing of any required share transfer tax certificate;

(s) Authorization of application for admission or qualification of Corporation as foreign Corporation in any other jurisdiction(s) where Corporation is to do business;

(t) Authorization of appointment of resident agent or agents;

(u) Authorization of designation of Corporation's general counsel and accountant, and setting up of corporate records, including record of Stockholders;

(v) Transaction of any business where permissible by action of Board of Directors.

Where dummy Directors, as well as dummy incorporators, are used, the resignations of the dummy Directors and the election of their successors can take place either near the end of the first meeting of the incorporators or after the disposition of the formal matters at the first meeting of the Board of Directors.

In issuing the shares, applicable requirements of the Federal Securities Act, state "blue sky" laws, and securities exchange listing requirements, should be observed. Any required state share issue stamps should be affixed and cancelled. Obviously, shares should be issued only for proper consideration.

Appropriate action should also be taken to authorize application for admission of the Corporation in other jurisdictions where business is planned, including the appointment of any required resident agents and the designation of any required registered offices. See Chapter 36, infra, for further discussion.

Provision might also be made for the designation of the Corporation's general counsel and accountant, and the setting up of the corporate records, including the share ledger or record of Stockholders.

The minute book should contain, usually in the front thereof, a certified copy of the Articles of Incorporation, or the formal "Certificate of Incorporation" if one has been issued, and a copy of the By-laws certified by the secretary of the organization meeting or other meeting at which the By-laws were adopted.[6]

6. See § 35.14 et seq., infra.

Library References:

C.J.S. Corporations § 545.
West's Key No. Digests, Corporations ⚷196.

COMMENT

See § 35.1, note 3, supra.

§ 35.4 Notice of Organization Meeting of Incorporators

To: The subscribers and incorporators of ______ Company

The first meeting of the subscribers and incorporators of ______ Company, for the purpose of organizing such Corporation, electing Directors, adopting By-laws, and transacting such other business as may come before the meeting, will be held at the office of ______, in ______, on ______, the ______ day of ______, 19__, at ______ o'clock __. m.

[*Signature of Incorporator*]
[*Name of Incorporator*]

Library References:

C.J.S. Corporations §§ 543, 544.
West's Key No. Digests, Corporations ⚷194.

§ 35.5 Affidavit of Mailing or Serving Notice

[*Venue*]

______, being duly sworn, says he is Secretary of ______ Company, a ______ Corporation, and that on ______ day of ______, 19__, he served the notice, a copy of which is hereto annexed, upon the following ______, by leaving with each of them a copy thereof [*or* by mailing to each of them a copy of said notice, inclosed in a sealed envelope, postage prepaid, and addressed to each of said ______ at his last known address appearing on the records of said Corporation].

[*Signature and Jurat*]

§ 35.6 Waiver of Notice of Organization Meeting of Incorporators

We, the undersigned, constituting all of the incorporators of ______, Inc., a Corporation organized and existing under the laws of the State of ______, do hereby severally waive notice of the time, place and purpose of the first meeting of the incorporators of said Corporation, and consent that the same be held at ______, in the City of ______, State of ______, on the ______ of ______, 19__, at ______ o'clock __. m.; and we do further consent to the transaction of any and all business that may come before the meeting, including the adoption of By-laws and election of Directors.

Dated ______, 19__.

____

____

____

COMMENT

See § 35.1, notes 3 and 4, supra.

§ 35.7 Action by Unanimous Consent Without Meeting

We, the undersigned, being all of the Incorporators of ______ Corporation who would be entitled to vote upon the resolutions hereinafter set forth at a formal meeting of the Incorporators of said Corporation held for the purpose of acting upon such resolutions, do hereby consent to the adoption of the following resolutions to the same extent and to have the same force and effect as if adopted at a formal meeting of the Incorporators of said Corporation:

____

____

In testimony whereof witness our respective signatures on the respective dates set opposite thereto.

Signature of Incorporators	Date of Signatures
________________	________________
________________	________________

Library References:

C.J.S. Corporations § 539.
West's Key No. Digests, Corporations ⚷191.

COMMENT

Action by unanimous written consent without a meeting is commonly authorized by statute (e. g. Model Bus.Corp.Act § 145).

§ 35.8 Proxy of Incorporator for Organization Meeting

Know all men by these presents, that I, the undersigned incorporator of ______ Company, do hereby constitute and appoint ______, or any one of them, my true and lawful attorneys or attorney, with power of substitution, to represent me at the first meeting of the incorporators of said company, to be held at ______, on ______, 19__, or at any adjournment thereof, with the right to vote and to exercise all the powers that the undersigned would possess if personally present.

In witness whereof, *etc.*

§ 35.9 Minutes of First Meeting of Incorporators—Actual Meeting

The meeting of incorporators of ______, Inc. was held at ______ o'clock ___.m. on the ______ day of ______, 19___, at ______, in the City of ______, State of ______, pursuant to a written waiver of notice signed by all the incorporators, fixing said time and place.

The following incorporators were present in person: ______, ______, and ______, being all of the incorporators named in the Articles of Incorporation.

Upon motion, ______ was elected Chairman and ______ was elected Secretary of the meeting.

The Secretary presented the waiver of notice of the meeting signed by all the incorporators and it was filed as part of the minutes.

The Chairman reported that the Articles of Incorporation had been filed in the office of the Secretary of State of the State of ______ on the ______ day of ______, 19___, and a certified copy thereof duly recorded in the office of the County Clerk of ______ County, ______ on the ______ day of ______, 19___. A copy of said Articles of Incorporation was ordered inserted in the minute book as a part of the records of the meeting.

The secretary presented a proposed form of By-laws for the regulation of the affairs of the Corporation, which was read, article by article. Upon motion duly made and seconded, the following resolution was unanimously adopted:

Resolved, that the By-laws submitted and read before this meeting be, and the same hereby are, adopted as the By-laws of this Corporation, and the secretary is hereby instructed to cause the same to be inserted in the minute book immediately following the Articles of Incorporation.

The Chairman stated that the next order of business was the election of a Board of Directors to hold office for the ensuing year and until their successors are elected and qualify. The following were nominated: ______, ______, and ______. No further nominations having been made, a ballot was taken and all of the incorporators having voted, and the ballots having been duly canvassed, the Chairman declared that the above named persons were elected Directors of the Corporation by the unanimous vote of all the incorporators.

Upon motion duly made and seconded, the following resolution was unanimously adopted:

Resolved, that the Board of Directors be and it is hereby authorized in its discretion to issue the capital stock of this Corporation to the full amount or number of shares authorized by the Articles of Incorporation in such amounts and for such considerations as from time to time shall be determined by the Board of Directors and as may be permitted by law.

There being no further business, upon motion duly made and seconded, the meeting was adjourned.

Secretary of the Meeting

____

Library References:

C.J.S. Corporations § 545.
West's Key No. Digests, Corporations ⚷196.

§ 35.10 Minutes of Organization Meeting of Incorporators—Actual meeting

The organization meeting of the incorporators of ______, a domestic Corporation, was held at the office of ______, on the ______ day of ______, 19__, at No. ______ ______ Street, City of ______, County of ______, State of ______, pursuant to a written waiver of notice [*or*, waivers of notice] signed by all the incorporators and fixing said time and place [*or*, on notice duly sent by ______, an incorporator, at least *five* (5) *days* prior to the meeting].

The following incorporators were present in person:

____

The following incorporators were represented by proxy:

__________. Name of Proxy __________.

the same being all of the incorporators of ______ [*or* the same being a majority and constituting a quorum].

On motion, made and seconded, ______ was chosen Chairman, and ______ Secretary of the meeting.

[*The Secretary presented and read the waiver of notice of the organization meeting signed by ______, and was instructed to enter said waiver in the minute book.*]

The proxies above mentioned were presented and ordered to be entered in the minute book.

The Chairman reported that the certificate of incorporation of ______ had been filed by the Department of State of the State of ______ on the ______ day of ______, 19__. Thereupon, on motion duly made, seconded, and adopted it was unanimously resolved to accept said certificate, and the secretary was instructed to cause a copy of said certificate of incorporation and the receipt of the Department of State to be entered in the minute book.

The secretary then presented a form of By-laws for the regulation of the affairs of the company, which were read section by section and upon motion duly made, the said by-laws were unanimously adopted, and the secretary was instructed to enter said By-laws in the minute book immediately following the Certificate of Incorporation.

The chairman stated that the next business before the meeting was the election of [*Number*] Directors, being the number fixed in the By-laws, to hold office until the first annual meeting of the Stockholders, Messrs. ______, ______ and ______ were nominated for Directors of the company. No other nominations having been made, nominations were declared closed, the polls were duly opened, and ballot having been duly had, the polls were declared closed, and the chairman announced that the aforesaid gentlemen were duly elected directors of the Corporation to hold office until the first annual meeting of the Stockholders or until their successors are elected and qualified.

[*Recite at this point the fact of any subscription for the purchase of shares, and the acceptance thereof, and any other action taken by motion, duly made, seconded, and carried.*]

There being no further business, on motion duly made, seconded and carried, the meeting thereupon adjourned.

Dated, ______, 19__.

____

Secretary of the Meeting

§ 35.11 Incorporator's Consent Meeting

The Articles of Incorporation of [*Name*] having been filed in the office of the [*State*] Department of Commerce, and,

The undersigned, hereby waive the necessity of notice of the First Meeting of the Incorporators of the Corporation and the necessity of holding a meeting of the Incorporators of the Corporation; and in its stead consent to and adopt as the act and deed of said Corporation the following:

Resolved, that the following shall be elected to the Board of Directors, to serve until the next annual meeting of Shareholders and until the election and qualification of the successor Board of Directors (or until removed, with or without cause, by the Shareholders): [*Name*].

Executed this ______ day of ______, 19__, to be effective the ______ day of ______, 19__.

Incorporators

____

____

____

§ 35.12 Statement of Incorporators in Lieu of Organization Meeting—Another Form

______, incorporator [*or, all the incorporators, or, attorney in fact for the incorporator, or incorporators*] certify that the Certificate of Incorporation of ______, Inc. was duly filed by the Department of State of the State of ______ on ______, 19__. A copy thereof, together with the receipt of the Department of State, are annexed hereto and inserted in the minute book of the Corporation. The annexed By-laws are adopted and inserted in the minute book. The following persons are designated directors to serve until the first meeting of Stockholders. [*Set Forth Any Further Matters.*]

Dated: ______, 19__.

____

Incorporator(s)
[*or Attorney-in-Fact for Incorporator(s)*]

Library References:

C.J.S. Corporations § 539.
West's Key No. Digests, Corporations ⚷191.

§ 35.13 Statement of Sole Incorporator—Actual Meeting

The undersigned, being the sole incorporator [*or attorney-in-fact for the sole incorporator*] of ______, a Corporation organized under the Business Corporation Law of the State of ______, does hereby certify that the following action organizing said Corporation was duly taken:

A copy of the Certificate of Incorporation of [*Name of Corporation*] together with the receipt issued by the Department of State evidencing payment of the statutory organization tax and the date and payment of the fee for filing the original certificate of incorporation was accepted by ______, the sole incorporator, who directed that the copy of the Certificate of Incorporation together with the receipt issued by the Department of State, as hereinabove stated, be appended to these minutes.

By-laws for the regulation of the affairs of [*Name of Corporation*] were adopted by ______, the sole incorporator who directed that a copy of said by-laws be appended to these minutes.

______, the sole incorporator, was nominated as Director to hold office until the first annual meeting of the Stockholder. No other nomination having been made, the polls were duly opened, and ballot having been duly had, the polls were declared closed, and ______, the sole incorporator, was declared the duly elected Director of [*Name of Corporation*], and he, ______, thereupon accepted his nomination and election as Director.

There being no further business, the meeting thereupon adjourned.

Dated, ______, 19__.

____

Sole Incorporator

§§ 35.14–35.20 are reserved for supplementary material.

C. MEETING OF DIRECTORS

§ 35.21 Notice of Organization Meeting by Directors

To: ______, ______ and ______.

We, the undersigned, being at least a majority of the Directors named in the Articles of Incorporation of ______ Corporation, pursuant to [*applicable statutory citation*], do hereby notify you that the organization meeting of the Board of Directors of said Corporation will be held at ______ in the city of ______, State of ______, at ______ o'clock __M on the ______ day of ______, 19__.

This notice is deposited in the United States mail this ______ day of ______, 19__.

____

____

____

Library References:

C.J.S. Corporations § 747.
West's Key No. Digests, Corporations ⚷298(3).

COMMENT

See § 35.1, note 2, supra (Model Bus.Corp.Act § 57).

§ 35.22 Waiver of Notice of Organization Meeting of Directors

We, the undersigned, constituting all of the Directors of ______, a Corporation organized under the laws of the State of ______, do hereby severally waive notice of the time, place and purpose of the first meeting of Directors of said Corporation, and consent that the meeting be held at ______, and on the ______ day of ______, 19__, at ______ o'clock __. m., and we do further consent to the transaction of any and all business that may properly come before the meeting.

Dated ______, 19__.

____

____

____

§ 35.23 Action by Unanimous Consent Without Meeting

We, the undersigned, being all of the Directors of ______ Corporation who would be entitled to vote upon the resolutions hereinafter set forth at a formal meeting of the Directors of said Corporation held for the purpose of acting upon such resolutions, do hereby consent to the adoption of the following resolutions to the same extent and to have the same force and effect as if adopted at a formal meeting of the Directors of said Corporation:

____

____

In testimony whereof witness our respective signatures on the respective dates set opposite thereto.

Signature of Directors	Date of Signatures
______________________	______________________
______________________	______________________

Library References:

C.J.S. Corporations §§ 745, 748.
West's Key No. Digests, Corporations ⚷298(1).

COMMENT

Action by unanimous written consent without a meeting is commonly authorized by statute (e. g. Model Bus.Corp.Act § 144).

§ 35.24 Resolutions of First Meeting of the Board of Directors—Generally

COMMENT

The first meeting of the Board has generally two purposes. One is to adopt certain basic resolutions which are set forth below. The other is to adopt day-to-day operating provisions which are set forth in Chapter 48, supra. The basic resolutions are:

Resolved, that the organization and incorporation activities of the Incorporators are hereby ratified as the act and deed of the Corporation and that all expenses pursuant thereto be an expense of this Corporation.

Option (Not Preferred Unless There is to be a Consent Meeting and All Those Voting Won't Actually Review the Transaction)

The following vote on the above resolution was counted:

(a) yes: ___________

(b) no: ___________

(c) abstain: ___________

(d) persons demanding that their objections be noted and the reasons for their objections: ___________.

COMMENT TO OPTION 1

If a person feels a meeting is improperly called, he must so object and not further participate. If a Director feels an action is illegal, he should state his reason and immediately resign. He may even have to sue the Corporation to stop the contemplated action to fully protect himself from liability.

Resolved, that the following persons shall be Officers of the Corporation to serve until the next annual meeting of the Board of Directors and until the election and qualification of their respective successors (or until removed, with or without cause) by the Board of Directors:

Chairman of the Board: ___________

President: ___________

Vice-President: ___________

Secretary: ___________

Treasurer: ___________

COMMENT

Although permissible, it is not a good idea to have the President and Secretary the same person since most documents call for the Secretary to attest to the President's signature and this is not legal when they are the same person.

Option (Not Preferred Unless There is to be a Consent Meeting and All Those Voting Won't Actually Review the Transaction)

The following vote on the above resolution was counted:

(a) yes: __________

(b) no: __________

(c) abstain: __________

(d) persons demanding that their objections be noted and the reasons for their objections: __________.

COMMENT

If a person feels a meeting is improperly called, he must so object and not further participate. If a Director feels an action is illegal, he should state his reason and immediately resign. He may even have to sue the Corporation to stop the contemplated action to fully protect himself from liability.

Resolved the fiscal year of the Corporation shall end on the last day of [*Month*], of each year.

Option (Not Preferred Unless There is to be a Consent Meeting and All Those Voting Won't Actually Review the Transaction)

The following vote on the above resolution was counted:

(a) yes: __________

(b) no: __________

(c) abstain: __________

(d) persons demanding that their objections be noted and the reasons for their objections: __________.

COMMENT

If a person feels a meeting is improperly called, he must so object and not further participate. If a Director feels an action is illegal, he should state his reason and immediately resign. He may even have to sue the Corporation to stop the contemplated action to fully protect himself from liability.

Resolved, that [*Name*] be and is hereby appointed the agent for this Corporation in charge of the resident office of the Corporation and that the resident office be located at [*Address*].

Option (Not Preferred Unless There is to be a Consent Meeting and All Those Voting Won't Actually Review the Transaction)

The following vote on the above resolution was counted:

(a) yes: __________

(b) no: __________

(c) abstain: __________

(d) persons demanding that their objections be noted and the reasons for their objections: __________.

COMMENT

If a person feels a meeting is improperly called, he must so object and not further participate. If a Director feels an action is illegal, he should state his reason and immediately resign. He may even have to sue the Corporation to stop the contemplated action to fully protect himself from liability.

Resolved, that [*Name(s)*] having offered to transfer to this Corporation all of the net assets described in the offer attached hereto, for issuance to [*it/she/him/them*], fully paid and nonassessable [*Number*] shares (this being all of the issued capital shares) of the Corporation and it being determined that such property is necessary for the use and lawful purposes of this Corporation, this Corporation is hereby authorized to accept the offer of [*Names*], and upon receipt of the necessary documents transferring all the net assets of [*its/her/his/their*] business to this Corporation to issue to [*Name*], fully paid and nonassessable, [*Number*] shares of this Corporation in full payment thereof.

Option (Not Preferred Unless There is to be a Consent Meeting and All Those Voting Won't Actually Review the Transaction)

The following vote on the above resolution was counted:

(a) yes: __________

(b) no: __________

(c) abstain: __________

(d) persons demanding that their objections be noted and the reasons for their objections: __________.

COMMENT

It will be necessary for the proper transfer documents (see § ——, infra) to be drafted and executed in order for the Corporation to obtain the title it is to receive in exchange for its stock (unless, of course, the property is money which merely requires the delivery of a check).

Resolved, that the Board of Directors having reviewed the proposed By-laws, the same are hereby adopted and shall be inserted in the minute book of the Corporation by the Secretary.

Option (Not Preferred Unless There is to be a Consent Meeting and All Those Voting Won't Actually Review the Transaction)

The following vote on the above resolution was counted:

(a) yes: __________

(b) no: __________

(c) abstain: __________

(d) persons demanding that their objections be noted and the reasons for their objections: __________.

COMMENT

If a person feels a meeting is improperly called, he must so object and not further participate. If a Director feels an action is illegal, he should state his reason and immediately resign. He may even have to sue the Corporation to stop the contemplated action to fully protect himself from liability.

Resolved, that the Seal, the impression of which is herewith affixed, be adopted as this Corporation's corporate seal: [*Imprint Seal Here*]

COMMENT

In most states a seal is no longer needed to have a validly executed document.

Resolved, that the Board of Directors having reviewed the proposed [*common/preferred*] stock certificate form, the same is hereby adopted and a copy shall be inserted in the minute book by the Secretary.

COMMENT

Insert Sample Stock Certificate in record book.

Library References:

C.J.S. Corporations § 744 et seq.
West's Key No. Digests, Corporations ⚷298.

§ 35.25 Minutes (Agenda) of Organization Meeting of Directors —Actual Meeting

MINUTES (AGENDA) OF ORGANIZATION MEETING OF DIRECTORS

Time and Place of Meeting. The organization meeting of the Board of Directors of ______ was held at ______, ______, State of ______, on ______, 19__, at ______ p. m. pursuant to waiver of notice signed by all of the Directors.

Initial Directors Present. There were present Messrs. ______, ______, and ______, counsel, constituting all of the Directors.

Selection of Chairman and Secretary of Meeting. Upon motion duly made, seconded, and unanimously adopted, Mr. ______ was chosen Chairman and Mr. ______ was chosen Secretary of the meeting.

Waiver of Notice of Meeting. The Secretary presented the waiver of notice of the meeting signed by all the Directors. The Secretary was instructed to affix such waiver to the minutes.

Filing of Articles of Incorporation and Issuance of Certificate of Incorporation. Mr. ______ reported that Articles of Incorporation of the Corporation had been filed in the office of the Secretary of State of ______ and its Certificate of Incorporation issued on ______, 19__. The Secretary was instructed to insert the Certificate of Incorporation, with a duplicate original of the Articles of Incorporation affixed thereto, in the minute book preceding the minutes.

Adoption of By-laws. Mr. ______ presented proposed By-laws. After discussion and on motion duly made and seconded, the following resolution was unanimously adopted:

Resolved, that the By-laws submitted and read at this meeting be and are adopted as the By-laws of this Corporation, and that the Secretary is instructed to insert a copy of such By-laws certified by him in the minute book immediately following the Certificate of Incorporation with affixed duplicate original of the Articles of Incorporation.

Election of Officers. The meeting then proceeded to the election of officers of the Corporation. Upon motion duly made, seconded, and unanimously adopted, the following were duly elected to the Offices stated beside their respective names to serve during the pleasure of the Board of Directors:

______________	President
______________	Vice-President
______________	Treasurer
______________	Secretary

Salaries of Officer. There was discussion concerning salaries, following which, on motion duly made, seconded, and unanimously adopted, the following salaries were fixed to be paid until further action by the Board of Directors: [*Describe*].

Fees for Legal Services. It was recognized that Mr. ______ would not be expected to devote all of his time to the affairs of the Corporation and that he would be entitled to submit to the Corporation statements for legal services performed by him from time to time for the Corporation.

Fidelity Bonds. After discussion and on motion, duly made, seconded, and unanimously adopted, the Treasurer was instructed to secure in behalf of the Corporation fidelity insurance protecting the Corporation against defalcations by any of its employees up to $______.

Approval of Forms of Share Certificates. The Secretary presented specimen share certificates to represent the 5% Cumulative Preferred Shares and Common Shares of the Corporation. After discussion and on motion duly made and seconded, the following resolution was unanimously adopted:

Resolved, that the forms of certificates to represent the 5% Cumulative Preferred Shares and Common Shares presented at the meeting be and are approved, and that the Secretary is instructed to insert the specimens in the minute book.

Approval of Corporate Seal. The Secretary presented a form of seal for the Corporation. After discussion and on motion duly made and seconded, the following resolution was unanimously adopted:

Resolved, that the seal, an impression of which is hereto affixed, be and is adopted as the corporate seal of the Corporation.

Designation of Depository of Corporate Funds. The President recommended that an account be established at The ______ National Bank. After discussion and on motion duly made and seconded, the following resolution was unanimously adopted:

Resolved, that The ______ National Bank (hereinafter called the "Bank") be and hereby is designated a depository of the funds of the Corporation, and the President and Treasurer of the Corporation, jointly, are hereby authorized to sign, for and on behalf of the Corporation, any and all checks, drafts or other orders with respect to any funds at any time to the credit of the Corporation with the Bank and/or against any account(s) of the Corporation maintained at any time with the Bank, inclusive of any such checks, drafts or other orders in favor of any of the above-designated Officers, and that the Bank be and hereby is authorized (a) to pay the same to the debit of any account of the Corporation then maintained with it; (b) to receive for deposit to the credit of the Corporation, and/or for collection for the account of the Corporation, any and all checks, drafts, notes or other instruments for the payment of money, whether or not endorsed by the Corporation, which may be received by it for such deposit and/or collection, it being understood that each such item shall be deemed to have been unqualifiedly endorsed by the Corporation, and (c) to receive, as the act of the Corporation, reconcilements of accounts when signed by any one or more of the above-designated Officers, or their appointees; and that the Bank may rely upon the authority conferred by this entire resolution until the receipt by the Bank of a certified copy of a resolution of the Board of Directors of the Corporation revoking or modifying the same.

After discussion and on motion duly made and seconded, the following resolutions were unanimously adopted:

Appointment of Resident Agent Within State; Designation of Registered Office Within State. Resolved, the Corporation Service

Company be and is appointed the resident agent of the Corporation in the State of ______ and the office of such agent at ______ Street, ______, ______, State of ______ be and is designated as the registered office of the Corporation in the State of ______.

Office of Corporation; Place of Meetings. Resolved, that an office of the Corporation be established and maintained at ______ Street, ______, ______, State of ______, and that until further action by the Board of Directors, meetings of the Board of Directors and Stockholders shall be held at such office.

Admission as Foreign Corporation in Other Jurisdictions. Resolved, that the Officers of the Corporation be and are authorized and directed to qualify the Corporation as a foreign Corporation authorized to conduct business in the States of ______ and in connection therewith to appoint all necessary agents or attorneys for service of process and to take all other action which any Officer may deem appropriate.

Place and Time of Regular Meetings of Board of Directors. Resolved, that regular meetings of the Board of Directors be held without notice at the Corporation's office at ______, ______, State of ______, at 2:00 p.m., ______ time, on the second Monday in each month except May when the regular meeting shall be held immediately following the annual meeting of Stockholders and at the place thereof.

Fixing of Consideration for Shares Issued for Property. The Treasurer stated that ______ had offered in writing to transfer to the Corporation all his right, title, and interest in and to the "______ tract" for the sum of $______, to be paid for by the issuance to him as fully paid and nonassessable of 5,000 5% Cumulative Preferred Shares of the Corporation. Upon motion duly made and seconded, the following resolution was unanimously adopted:

Resolved, that it is the judgment of the Board of Directors that the value of said property so offered, is the sum of $______, which is the sum stated in said offer, and that the Corporation accept this offer of ______; that the President be and is authorized to accept said offer in writing on behalf of the Corporation; and that the officers of the Corporation be and are authorized and directed to cause to be issued to ______ certificates representing 5,000 5% Cumulative Preferred Shares upon receipt from ______ of all necessary documents transferring said property to the Corporation.

Fixing of Consideration for Shares Issued for Services. The Treasurer stated that ______ had rendered services in the formation of the Corporation and had agreed to accept in payment for such services as fully paid and nonassessable 250 Common Shares of the Corporation. Upon motion duly made and seconded, the following resolution was unanimously adopted:

Resolved, that said compensation is reasonable and that the Officers of the Corporation be and are authorized and directed to cause to be issued to ______ certificates representing 250 Common Shares in full payment for her services.

Acceptance of Share Subscriptions. The Treasurer stated that the Corporation had received the following offers to subscribe to shares of the Corporation:

______: 10,000 Common Shares at $20 per share.

______: 7,500 Common Shares at $20 per share.

Upon motion duly made, seconded, and unanimously adopted, said offers were accepted, and the officers of the Corporation were authorized and directed to cause to be issued to said subscribers certificates representing said shares upon receipt of the agreed subscription price therefor.

Retainer of Accountants; Fiscal Years. The President recommended that ______, certified public accountants, be retained as the Corporation's accountants. Upon motion duly made, seconded, and unanimously adopted, the President was authorized to retain said accounting firm to serve during the pleasure of the Board of Directors. The President further stated that ______ had recommended that the Corporation adopt the calendar year as its fiscal year. Upon motion duly made and seconded, the following resolution was unanimously adopted:

Resolved, that the fiscal year of the Corporation shall be from *January 1* to *December 31* in each year.

Organizational Expenses. The Treasurer reported that the fees and expenses involved in the incorporation and organization of the Corporation other than for the services of ______, amounted to $______. Upon motion duly made and seconded, the following resolution was unanimously adopted:

Resolved, that the Treasurer be and is authorized and directed to pay in cash all fees and expenses incurred in connection with the incorporation and organization of the Corporation, other than for the services of ______, and that such organizational expenditures, amounting to $______, shall be amortized over such period of not less than 60 months as may be selected by the Corporation in accordance with Section 248 of the Internal Revenue Code.

Subchapter S Election. The Treasurer discussed the advantages of Subchapter S election by the Corporation and the requirements and procedures involved. Upon motion duly made and seconded, the following resolution was unanimously adopted:

Resolved, that the Corporation elect under Section 1372(a) of the Internal Revenue Code, with the consent of all the Stockholders, to be treated as a "small business corporation" for income tax purposes, and that the Treasurer be and is authorized to file such election and the Stockholders statement of consent.

Adjournment. There being no further business to come before the meeting, upon motion duly made, seconded, and unanimously adopted, the meeting was adjourned.

[*Signed*] ______

COMMENTS

This form covers the various things that must be done at the initial meeting of Directors and some issues that are likely to arise.

Minutes are legal documents that should be prepared by attorneys. The minutes of the initial meeting should be prepared along with the Articles of Incorporation, By-laws, etc. as part of the formation of a Corporation. In practice, minutes are usually prepared before the meeting in question, and undoubtedly in many situations minutes are prepared and signed even though no meeting is ever held. Where the number of participants is small and there is complete consensus on what should be done, actually holding a meeting is apt to be considered meaningless and time-wasting nonsense. For this reason, it is usually desirable for the minutes to be signed by all participants so that they may act as a consent in the absence of a meeting. (See consent meeting form, § 35.11, supra). Upon the first sign of hesitation to sign, or when the number of participants is larger, it is desirable to hold an actual meeting, however informal. Each item should be explained and approved.

§ 35.26 Resolution Opening a Bank Account

We hereby certify to The ______ Bank that at a meeting of the Board of Directors of ______, a Corporation duly organized and existing under the laws of the State of ______, duly called and held at its Office No. ______, in the City of ______, State of ______, on the ______ day of ______, 19__, the following resolutions were duly adopted, are in conformity with the charter and By-laws of said Corporation, and are in full force and effect;

Resolved that The ______ Bank be and hereby is designated a depository of this Corporation, and that checks, drafts, notes, bills of exchange, acceptances or other orders for the payment of money upon said The ______ Bank, or payable at any of its offices, be signed on behalf of this Corporation by any [*Insert Number*] of its following Officers, to-wit:

Resolved that said The ______ Bank, be and is hereby authorized without limit as to amount and without inquiry as to the circumstances of issue or the disposition of the proceeds even if drawn to any signing or endorsing Officer or other Officer of this Corporation, or tendered in payment of the individual obligation of any such Officer, or for his credit, or for deposit to his personal account:

1. To accept, certify, and/or pay any such instruments or other orders for the payment of money, whether or not negotiable, so signed and to charge the same to the account of this Corporation or to any account containing funds of this Corporation maintained in the name or names of any Officer, or Officers, or agent or agents, of this Corporation.

2. To purchase, give credit for, cash and/or pay any instruments or other orders for the payment of money whether or not negotiable, payable or tendered to this Corporation by such Officer or Officers authorized as aforesaid to sign similar instruments or orders on behalf of this Corporation.

Resolved that any [*Insert Number*] of the following Officers of this Corporation, to-wit: be and hereby are authorized on behalf of this Corporation:

1. To borrow money and obtain credit from said The ______ Bank, on any terms;

2. To discount any bills or notes receivable or other negotiable instruments;

3. As security for any loan, credit or accommodation to pledge, trustee or otherwise create any lien upon any stocks, bonds, accounts, bills or notes receivable, bills of lading, warehouse receipts, delivery orders, commodities, foreign exchange, or any other securities or property whatsoever;

4. To purchase or sell, either through said The ______ Bank, as agent or otherwise and either for immediate or future delivery, and to deliver, receive delivery of, or otherwise dispose of, stocks, bonds, commodities, foreign exchange, or any other securities or property whatsoever;

And, in connection with any of the foregoing to make, execute and deliver in the name of this Corporation and under its corporate seal or otherwise, any and all checks, drafts, notes, bills of exchange, acceptance, assignments, transfers, endorsements, guarantees, agreements, instructions, obligations, or documents whatsoever, in form satisfactory to said The ______ Bank.

Resolved that the Secretary and President of this Corporation be and hereby are authorized to certify to said The ______ Bank, that these resolutions have been duly adopted, that they are in conformity with the charter and By-laws of this Corporation, and that a copy of this resolution certified by the Secretary and President be delivered to said bank with specimens of the signatures of said officers.

Resolved that said The ______ Bank, shall recognize and act upon, in the payment of corporate funds and in the transaction of all corporate business hereinabove referred to and mentioned, the signatures of the hereinafter set forth present Officers of this Corporation, until notified in writing by an instrument of equal dignity of a change in such corporate Officers.

We further agree that present Officers of this Corporation are as follows:

Name	**Title**
______________________	______________________
______________________	______________________
______________________	______________________
______________________	______________________
______________________	______________________

In witness whereof we have hereunto set our hands as Officers of said Corporation, in capacity of Secretary and President respectively, and affix the corporate seal, this the ______ day of ______, 19__.

____
Secretary of the Corporation

____
President of the Corporation

[*Corporate Seal*]

§ 35.27 Resolution of Directors Ratifying Acts of Incorporators Organization Meeting

On motion duly made, seconded, and carried, it was:

Resolved, that the By-laws adopted at the organization meeting of the incorporators and made a part of the minutes of said meeting, be and they hereby are ratified as the By-laws of this Corporation, and it is further

Resolved, that all of the acts taken and decisions made at the organization meeting of Incorporators of this Corporation be and they hereby are ratified and adopted by this Board of Directors.

§§ 35.28–36.0 are reserved for supplementary material.

CHAPTER 36

FOREIGN STATE INCORPORATION—DOING BUSINESS IN MORE THAN ONE STATE

Table of Sections

---

§ 36.1 "Foreign Corporation" Defined

Often a Corporation will be involved in some business relationship in more than one State. When this happens the law of "Foreign Corporations" is relevant. The term "foreign Corporation" actually has two diverse meanings:

(a) It is referred to in the Internal Revenue Code as meaning non United States Corporations. The Internal Revenue Code has special provisions which relate to the taxation of Corporations incorporated in the United States but that are doing business outside the United States. Although these Corporations are *domestic* Corporations, their foreign activities may have special tax treatment (see Chapters 92 et seq., infra). A true Foreign Corporation, for Internal Revenue Code purposes, is a Corporation incorporated outside the United States but with United States source income.

(b) It is referred to by state Corporation laws to mean Corporations which are not incorporated in the state in question but which have some business relationship to the state in question. The term is used in this context in the sections that follow.

Library References:

C.J.S. Corporations § 1783 et seq.
West's Key No. Digests, Corporations ⚷632.

§ 36.2 Doing Business as Foreign Corporation—Generally [1]

A Corporation "doing business" (or "transacting business") in states other than its jurisdiction of incorporation becomes, to a greater or less extent, subject to the laws of such jurisdictions.

Hence, the consequences of doing business in jurisdictions other than the jurisdiction of incorporation are factors relevant in the selection of the jurisdiction of incorporation.

By doing business or even engaging in an isolated transaction in a jurisdiction or having some contact with such jurisdiction, a foreign Corporation theoretically enjoys the benefit and protection of the laws of such jurisdiction, and thereby becomes reasonably subject to such laws. This is the constitutional basis for making such foreign Corporations amenable to process in such jurisdiction at least with respect to a cause of action which arises in such jurisdiction out of such activity and, where there is sufficient local activity, with respect to any cause of action. A similar theory justifies subjecting such foreign Corporation to reasonable taxation and regulation by such jurisdiction.

When a foreign Corporation does business in another jurisdiction, it can be required by the latter, as a condition on its admission, to qualify formally to do such business. This is so even when the business done involves interstate or foreign commerce, so long as there is some element of intrastate commerce.[2] State qualification statutes constitutionally may not require qualification when the business done is exclusively interstate or foreign commerce.[3]

Such qualification requirements have been constitutionally upheld under the privileges-and-immunities-of-citizens clause (because

1. This Section, and Sections 36.3–36.7, are adapted from Henn, Law of Corporations (2d ed. 1970), §§ 96–101. A third edition is being prepared by Professor Henn for 1982 publication.

2. Eli Lilly & Co. v. Sav-On-Drugs, Inc., 366 U.S. 276, 81 S.Ct. 1316, 6 L.Ed.2d 288 (1961), rehearing denied 366 U.S. 978, 81 S.Ct. 1913, 6 L.Ed.2d 1268 (1961); Union Brokerage Co. v. Jensen, 322 U.S. 202, 64 S.Ct. 967, 88 L.Ed. 1227, 152 A.L.R. 1072 (1944). But see International Textbook Co. v. Pigg, 217 U.S. 91, 30 S.Ct. 481, 54 L.Ed. 678 (1910); International Text Book Co. v. Tone, 220 N.Y. 313, 115 N.E. 914 (1917).

3. Allenberg Cotton Co., Inc. v. Pittman, 419 U.S. 20, 95 S.Ct. 260, 42 L.Ed.2d 195 (1974). But see Rehnquist, J., dissenting, 419 at 36, 95 S.Ct. at 269, 42 L.Ed.2d at 208, and Harlan, J., concurring in Eli Lilly & Co. v. Sav-On-Drugs, Inc., 366 U.S. 276, 284 n. 1, 81 S.Ct. 1316, 1321 n. 1, 6 L.Ed.2d 288, 295 n. 1 (1961). The latter views reflect modern developments in related areas.

a Corporation is not a citizen for such purpose),[4] under the interstate commerce clause (where qualification is reasonable and not a discriminatory or undue burden on interstate commerce), and under the due process clause (as a reasonable exercise of state police power).

Modern-day jurisdiction, whether legislative or judicial, is tending to be governed by the same ultimate standard: whether a state's contacts with a person, thing, or occurrence are sufficient to make the state's action reasonable. If reasonable, there is no *un*due process or *un*due burden on interstate commerce.

Of course, what is reasonable for one purpose may not be for another. While degrees of regulation and rates of taxation (with possibilities of apportionment) are infinite, suability can only be denied, limited to causes of action related to the local activity or contact, or not so limited. Furthermore, standards of reasonableness change with the times.

Most significantly of all, the rules governing jurisdiction are tending to be the same for individuals, Partnerships, other unincorporated associations, and Corporations.

The extent to which a state will exercise such jurisdiction, within constitutional limitations, depends on the interplay of a variety of nonlegal considerations. As a result, different states react differently with respect to subjecting the foreign business enterprise to litigation (including method of service of process, venue privilege, and doctrine of forum non conveniens—the tests for which are increasingly resembling the tests of jurisdiction), income tax, privilege or franchise tax, sales and use taxes, gross receipts taxes, personal property (tangible and intangible) taxes, unemployment insurance taxes, occupation taxes, special licenses, annual and other reports, qualification, etc.

Library References:

C.J.S. Corporations § 1828 et seq.
West's Key No. Digests, Corporations ⚿642.
Wright and Miller, Federal Practice & Procedure § 1066 et seq.

§ 36.3 Doing Business as Foreign Corporation—Amenability to Process

The nature of the Corporation has also created theoretical difficulties in litigation involving foreign Corporations.

4. See, e. g., Model Bus.Corp.Act § 148 ("The provisions of this Act shall apply to commerce with foreign nations and among the several states only in so far as the same may be permitted under the provisions of the Constitution of the United States").

A Corporation is entitled to the protection of the due process clauses of the Fifth and Fourteenth Amendments and of the equal-protection-of-the-laws clause of the Fourteenth Amendment of the United States Constitution. A Corporation, unlike an unincorporated Association, is deemed a citizen for purposes of federal diversity-of-citizenship jurisdiction.

One of the most perplexing corporate litigation problems has been the extent of a state's judicial jurisdiction over foreign Corporations.

Judicial jurisdiction grew out of a state's *de facto* power over persons and things within its territory. Hence for natural persons, physical presence—whether permanent or transitory—became the key test of *in personam* jurisdiction; appearance or consent would also suffice.[5]

Domestic corporations are suable regardless of where the cause of action arose or whether the Corporation is transacting any business in the state. Usually as part of the incorporation procedure, the Corporation must designate an agent for the service of process. The principal federal constitutional inhibition is the due process requirement, in the sense of reasonable notice and opportunity to be heard.

In personam jurisdiction over *foreign* Corporations involves far more complications.

Constitutionally there must be not only reasonable notice and opportunity to be heard,[6] but also observance of the additional federal due process requirement that there be sufficient basis for the exercise of judicial jurisdiction by the state. Furthermore, prosecution of an action may not, under the interstate commerce clause of

5. See National Equipment Rental, Ltd. v. Szukhent, 375 U.S. 311, 84 S. Ct. 411, 11 L.Ed.2d 354 (1964). The classic case on *in personam* jurisdiction based upon common-law due process prior to the 14th amendment, was Pennoyer v. Neff, 95 U.S. 714, 735, 24 L.Ed. 565, 573 (1878), (holding that judgment based upon substituted service by publication or otherwise against non-resident was not entitled to full faith and credit) which significantly contained the following dictum: "Neither do we mean to assert that a State may not require a non-resident entering into a partnership or association within its limits, or making contracts enforceable there, to appoint an agent or representative in the State to receive service of process and notice in legal proceedings instituted with respect to such partnership, association, or contracts, or to designate a place where such service may be made and notice given, and provide, upon their failure to make such appointment or to designate such place, that service may be made upon a public officer designated for that purpose, or in some other prescribed way, and that judgments rendered upon such service may not be binding upon the non-residents both within and without the State."

6. Chassis-Trak, Inc. v. Federated Purchaser, Inc., 179 F.Supp. 780 (D.N.J. 1960); Speir v. Robert C. Herd & Co., 189 F.Supp. 432 (D.Md.1960).

the federal constitution, constitute an undue burden on interstate or foreign commerce.[7]

In summary, the Corporation, even though it has not qualified in another state, by engaging in any activity therein which can be imputed to it, becomes subject to that state's in personam jurisdiction over any cause of action arising from such activity. In a foreign state, the Corporation might also have to answer for activity outside that state, provided the contact with that state is sufficiently substantial to make such result reasonable. Reasonableness depends upon such considerations as the nature of the contact with the forum state, convenience of the forum to the parties, and benefit and protection conferred by the law of the forum on such a Corporation. Reasonable notice and opportunity to be heard must be afforded. Under such circumstances, the exercise of judicial jurisdiction is consistent with due process and not an undue burden on interstate or foreign commerce, and therefore constitutional under the federal constitution.[8]

A state need not exercise its judicial jurisdiction to the full extent permitted by the federal constitution. The extent of a state's exercise of judicial jurisdiction is dependent upon the scope thereof as determined by applicable state statutes and court decisions which do not exceed the foregoing constitutional limitations.

Practically all of the states have enacted so-called "long-arm" or "single-act" statutes.[9] The language in which they are couched varies.[10] In each case, of course, the exercise of *in personam* juris-

7. Boyd v. Warren Paint & Color Co., 254 Ala. 687, 49 So.2d 559 (1950) (unlicensed foreign Corporation engaged in interstate commerce in state held amenable to process); Schlesinger v. Italian Line, 303 N.Y. 994, 106 N.E.2d 69 (1952); Banque de France v. Supreme Court, 287 N.Y. 483, 41 N.E.2d 65 (1942), appeal dismissed and certiorari denied 316 U.S. 646, 62 S.Ct. 1279, 86 L.Ed. 1730 (1942); Matter of Baltimore Mail Steamship Co. v. Fawcett, 269 N.Y. 379, 199 N.E. 628, 104 A.L.R. 1068 (1936) (undue burden usually found where foreign cause of action by nonresident original claimant against foreign common carrier corporation); Restatement, Second, Conflict of Laws § 47, Comment h (1971).

8. See International Shoe Co. v. State of Washington, 326 U.S. 310, 66 S.Ct. 154, 90 L.Ed. 95 (1945); McGee v. International Life Ins. Co., 355 U.S. 220, 78 S.Ct. 199, 2 L.Ed.2d 223 (1957); Hanson v. Denckla, 357 U.S. 235, 78 S.Ct. 1228, 2 L.Ed.2d 1283 (1958). World-Wide Volkswagen Corp. v. Woodson, 444 U.S. 286, 100 S.Ct. 559, 567, 62 L.Ed.2d 490, 501 (1980). See also Wright and Miller, Federal Practice & Procedure, § 1066 et seq. for additional discussion.

9. See Wright and Miller, Federal Practice & Procedure § 1068 et seq.

10. Jacobsen, "Enlargement of Jurisdiction Over Unlicensed Foreign Corporations in Missouri—The 'Single-Act Statute'", 31 U.Kan.City L.Rev. 292 (1967); Weissman, "The Georgia Long Arm Statute: A Significant Advance in the Concept of Personal Jur-

diction depends upon the sufficiency of contacts between the defendant and the forum state.[11]

isdiction", 4 Ga.St.B.J. 13 (1967); Comment, "Interpretive Problems of Ohio's Long-Arm Statute", 19 Case W.Res.L.Rev. 347 (1968); Comment, "Personal Jurisdiction over Nonresidents—The Louisiana 'Long-Arm' Statute", 40 Tul.L.Rev. 366 (1966); Comment, "Expanded Basis of Jurisdiction—An Examination of Tennessee's New 'Long-Arm' Statute", 18 Vand.L.Rev. 1484 (1965); Comment, "South Dakota's Single Act Statute: In Personam Jurisdiction Over Foreign Corporations", 9 S.D.L.Rev. 188 (1964); Note, "Jurisdiction under New Ohio 'Long-Arm' Statute—Problems of Interpretation and Application", 35 U.Cin.L.Rev. 157 (1966); Note, "The Virginia 'Long Arm' Statute", 51 Va.L.Rev. 719 (1965).

See e. g. Model Bus.Corp.Act § 14 which provides:

§ 14. Service of Process on Corporation

The registered agent so appointed by a Corporation shall be an agent of such Corporation upon whom any process, notice or demand required or permitted by law to be served upon the Corporation may be served.

Whenever a Corporation shall fail to appoint or maintain a registered agent in this State, or whenever its registered agent cannot with reasonable diligence be found at the registered office, then the Secretary of State shall be an agent of such Corporation upon whom any such process, notice, or demand may be served. Service on the Secretary of State of any such process, notice, or demand shall be made by delivering to and leaving with him, or with any clerk having charge of the Corporation department of his office, duplicate copies of such process, notice or demand. In the event any such process, notice or demand is served on the Secretary of State, he shall immediately cause one of the copies thereof to be forwarded by registered mail, addressed to the Corporation at its registered office. Any service so had on the Secretary of State shall be returnable in not less than thirty days.

The Secretary of State shall keep a record of all processes, notices and demands served upon him under this section, and shall record therein the time of such service and his action with reference thereto.

Nothing herein contained shall limit or affect the right to serve any process, notice or demand required or permitted by law to be served upon a Corporation in any other manner now or hereafter permitted by law.

11. Duple Motor Bodies, Ltd. v. Hollingsworth, 417 F.2d 231 (9th Cir. 1969); Gelfand v. Tanner Motor Tours, Ltd., 385 F.2d 116 (2d Cir. 1967); Curtis Pub. Co. v. Golino, 383 F.2d 586 (5th Cir. 1967); Buckley v. New York Post Corp., 373 F.2d 175 (2d Cir. 1967); New York Times Co. v. Connor, 365 F.2d 567 (5th Cir. 1966); Elliott v. Edwards Engineering Corp., 364 F.2d 991 (10th Cir. 1966); Buckley v. New York Times Co., 338 F.2d 470 (5th Cir. 1964); Insull v. New York World-Telegram Corp., 273 F.2d 166 (7th Cir. 1959), certiorari denied 362 U.S. 942, 80 S.Ct. 807, 4 L.Ed.2d 770 (1960); Marshall Egg Transport v. Bender-Goodman Co., 275 Minn. 534, 148 N.W.2d 161 (1967); O'Brien v. Lanpar Co., 399 S.W.2d 340 (Tex.Sup.Ct.1966); Pavalon v. Fishman, 30 Wis.2d 228, 140 N.W.2d 263 (1966); Golden Gate Hop Ranch v. Velsicol Chem. Corp., 66 Wash.2d 469, 403 P.2d 351 (1965), certiorari denied 382 U.S. 1025, 86 S.Ct. 644, 15 L.Ed.2d 539 (1966); Andersen v. National Presto Indus., Inc., 257 Iowa 911, 135 N.W.2d 639 (1965); Byham v. National Cibo House Corp., 265 N.C. 50, 143 S.E.2d 225 (1965); Abney Mills, Inc. v. Tri-State Motor Co., 265 N.C. 61, 143 S.E.2d 235 (1965).

See Wright and Miller, Federal Practice & Procedure, § 1069 et seq. for additional discussion.

As the result of studies begun in 1958, the Uniform Interstate and International Procedure Act[12] was approved by the National Conference of Commissioners on Uniform State Laws in 1962.

Section 1.03 of the Uniform Act [Personal Jurisdiction Based upon Conduct] reads:

"(a) A court may exercise personal jurisdiction over a person, who acts directly or by an agent, as to a [cause of action] [claim for relief] arising from the person's

"(1) transacting any business in this state;

"(2) contracting to supply services or things in this state;

"(3) causing tortious injury by an act or omission in this state;

"(4) causing tortious injury in this state by an act or omission outside this state if he regularly does or solicits business, or engages in any other persistent course of conduct, or derives substantial revenue from goods used or consumed or services rendered, in this state; [or]

"(5) having an interest in, using, or possessing real property in this state [; or

"(6) contracting to insure any person, property, or risk located within this state at the time of contracting].

"(b) When jurisdiction over a person is based solely upon this Section, only a [cause of action] [claim for relief] arising from acts enumerated in this Section may be asserted against him."

Whether or not a state's "long-arm" or "single-act" statute is substantive and therefore entirely prospective in application only to claims arising after its effective date,[13] or procedural and there-

12. States that have adopted Uniform Act:

Jurisdiction	Laws	Effective Date	Statutory Citation
Arkansas	1963, Act 101	2–28–1963	Ark.Stats. §§ 27–2501 to 27–2507.
Dist. of Columbia	P.L. 91–358	7–29–1970	D.C.C.E. §§ 13–421 to 13–434.
Massachusetts	1968, c. 760	7–25–1968	M.G.L.A. c. 223A §§ 1 to 14.
Michigan	1967, No. 178	11–2–1967	M.C.L.A. §§ 600.1852, 600.2114a, 600.2118a.
Oklahoma	1965, c. 144	10–21–1965	12 Okl.St.Ann. §§ 1701.01 to 1706.04.
Pennsylvania	1976, P.L. 586, No. 142	6–27–1978	42 Pa.C.S.A. §§ 5321 to 5329.
Virgin Islands	1965, Act 1339	7–1–1965	5 V.I.C. §§ 4901 to 4943.

13. State ex rel. Clay Equipment Corp. v. Jensen, 363 S.W.2d 666 (Mo.1963); Krueger v. Rheem Mfg. Co., 260 Iowa 678, 149 N.W.2d 142 (1967).

fore applicable to actions commenced after its effective date on pre-existing claims,[14] is a matter of construction.[15]

In federal diversity cases, the federal courts have tended to apply the rule of the state where they are sitting on the ground that Rule 4 of the Federal Rules of Civil Procedure [16] refers the "manner" of service to state law or that jurisdiction over the person is substantive.[17]

In all cases, process on the corporation, of course, must be served in the manner prescribed by applicable statute or court rule.

Library References:

C.J.S. Corporations §§ 1828 et seq., 1907, 1917 et seq., 1937.
West's Key No. Digests, Corporations ⚷668.
Wright and Miller, Federal Practice & Procedure § 1066 et seq.

§ 36.4 Doing Business as Foreign Corporation—Regulation

The domestic Corporation is subject to the legislative jurisdiction of its state of incorporation, subject to some constitutional limitations.

The foreign Corporation can be excluded by a state from engaging in local intrastate business or admitted subject to constitutional conditions, including requirements of formal qualification. Even foreign corporations and other forms of business enterprise which cannot constitutionally be excluded or required to qualify can be subjected to reasonable regulation under the state police power, without violating due process of law or constituting an undue burden on interstate commerce. Most states have not exercised more than minor aspects of their constitutional power to regulate foreign corporations doing business in the state (see however McKinney's N.Y.Bus.Corp. Law Art. 13; West's Ann.Calif.Corp.Code § 2115).

The United States Constitution prohibits a state from denying to any person (construed to include Corporation) within its jurisdiction the equal protection of the laws.[18] State constitutions [19] and stat-

14. Carvette v. Marion Power Shovel Co., 157 Conn. 92, 249 A.2d 58 (1968); Kilbreath v. Rudy, 16 Ohio St.2d 70, 242 N.E.2d 658 (1968); Simonson v. International Bank, 14 N.Y.2d 281, 251 N.Y.S.2d 433, 200 N.E.2d 427 (1964); Kilian v. Allegheny County Distributors, Inc., 409 Pa. 344, 185 A.2d 517 (1962).

15. Comment, "Retroactive Expansion of State Court Jurisdiction over Persons", 63 Colum.L.Rev. 1105 (1963).

16. Fed.R.Civ.P. 4(d)(3), 4(d)(7). See Wright and Miller, Federal Practice and Procedure, Rule 4.

17. Wilkerson v. Fortuna Corp., 554 F.2d 745 (5th Cir. 1977), certiorari denied 434 U.S. 939, 98 S.Ct. 430, 54 L.Ed.2d 299; Arrowsmith v. United Press International, 320 F.2d 219, 6 A.L.R.3d 1072 (2d Cir. 1963) (en banc), overruling Jaftex Corp. v. Randolph Mills, Inc., 282 F.2d 508 (2d Cir. 1960). See also Wright and Miller, Federal Practice & Procedure, Rule 4.

18. U.S.Const. amend. XIV, § 1. See WHYY, Inc. v. Borough of Glassboro, 393 U.S. 117, 89 S.Ct. 286, 21 L.Ed.2d 242 (1968) (holding New Jersey statute denying tax exemption to foreign nonprofit corporations owning prop-

utes [20] prohibit foreign corporations from transacting business within the state on more favorable conditions than are prescribed by law to similar domestic Corporations. Yet the foreign Corporation traditionally is either not subject to,[21] or is exempted from,[22] most of the regulatory features of the corporate statute applicable to domestic Corporations.[23]

Library References:

C.J.S. Corporations § 1810 et seq.
West's Key No. Digests, Corporations ⚷636.

§ 36.5 Doing Business as Foreign Corporation—Taxation

The domestic Corporation is subject to taxation by its state of incorporation.

The foreign Corporation may be subject to taxation by states where any of its activities enjoy benefit or protection or involve sufficient minimum contact, even though such activities involve interstate or foreign commerce, so long as the tax is commensurate with the corporation's activities in such states, subject to the limitations of the Federal Interstate Income Law of 1959.[24]

erty in state on basis of foreign incorporation unconstitutional denial of equal protection of laws to persons within state).

19. E. g., A.R.S.Const. art. XIV, § 5; West'sAnn.Const. art. XII, § 15; Va. Const., art. XII, § 163; Ariz.Op.Att'y Gen. No. 65–9, May 7, 1965; Mich. Op.Atty.Gen.No. 3652, Oct. 18, 1965.

20. E. g., Model Bus.Corp.Act §§ 107, 148.

21. E. g., Model Bus.Corp.Act § 106.

22. E. g., McKinney's N.Y.Bus.Corp. Law § 1320. See Restatement, Second, Conflict of Laws ch. 12 (Agency and Partnerships), ch. 13 (Business Corporations) (1971).

23. E. g., Model Bus.Corp.Act § 106 (nothing in act to be construed to authorize state "to regulate the organization or the internal affairs" of foreign Corporation).

24. 15 U.S.C.A. §§ 381–384. Required are sufficient contacts with the taxing state ("nexus"), fair relationship of tax to benefits received, nondiscrimination against interstate commerce, and fair apportionment. See, e. g., Mobil Oil Corp. v. Commissioner of Taxes, 445 U.S. 425, 100 S.Ct. 1223, 63 L.Ed.2d 510 (1980); Exxon Corp. v. Wisconsin Dept. of Revenue, 447 U.S. 207, 100 S.Ct. 2109, 65 L.Ed.2d 66 (1980); Japan Line, Ltd. v. County of Los Angeles, 441 U.S. 434, 99 S.Ct. 1813, 60 L.Ed.2d 336 (1979); Moorman Mfg. Co. v. Bair, 437 U.S. 267, 98 S.Ct. 2340, 57 LEd.2d 197 (1978), rehearing denied 439 U.S. 885, 99 S.Ct. 233, 58 L.Ed.2d 201; Department of Revenue v. Association of Washington Stevedoring Companies, 435 U.S. 734, 98 S.Ct. 1388, 55 L.Ed.2d 682 (1978); Complete Auto Transit, Inc. v. Brady, 430 U.S. 274, 97 S.Ct. 1076, 51 L.Ed.2d 326 (1977), rehearing denied, 430 U.S. 976, 97 S.Ct. 1669, 52 L.Ed.2d 371. Besides interstate commerce and due process limitations, there may be other federal constitutional restrictions, e. g. equal protection of the laws.

§ 36.6 Admission as Foreign Corporation

A foreign Corporation is generally required to qualify (or to secure authority or a certificate, permit, or license) to do any intrastate business within a jurisdiction, notwithstanding that it is also there doing interstate business as well.[25] In rare instances the foreign Corporation might be required to reincorporate.[26]

Statutes often specify various activities which do not constitute transacting business for purposes of qualification requirements.[27]

25. Eli Lilly & Co. v. Sav-On-Drugs, Inc., 366 U.S. 276, 81 S.Ct. 1316, 6 L.Ed.2d 288 (1961), rehearing denied 366 U.S. 978, 81 S.Ct. 1913, 6 L.Ed.2d 1268 (1961). A foreign corporation may do exclusively interstate business without qualification. Allenberg Cotton Co., Inc. v. Pittman, 419 U.S. 20, 95 S.Ct. 260, 42 L.Ed.2d 195 (1974). See Walker, "Foreign Corporation Laws: The Loss of Reason", 47 N.C.L.Rev. 1 (1968); Comment, "Corporate Registration: A Functional Analysis of 'Doing Business' ", 71 Yale L.J. 575 (1962); Note, "State Regulation of Foreign Corporations: Qualification: Interstate v. Intrastate Business", 47 Cornell L.Q. 300 (1962).

26. See National Ass'n for Advancement of Colored People v. Alabama, 377 U.S. 288, 84 S.Ct. 1302, 12 L.Ed.2d 325 (1964) (Alabama qualification requirement to do business held inapplicable to foreign membership Corporation formed by individuals exercising freedom to associate for collective advocacy of ideas); Anti-Defamation League of B'Nai B'rith v. American Italian Anti-Defamation League, Inc., 54 Misc.2d 830, 283 N.Y.S.2d 828 (1967) (nonprofit Corporation held not required to qualify under Business Corporation Law); Note, "Qualification of Foreign Partnerships", 52 Cornell L.Q. 157 (1966). Federal Corporations are not required to qualify, although the statutory definitions of "foreign corporation" might not be explicit. ABA–ALI Model Bus.Corp.Act § 2(b). See Home Owners' Loan Corp. v. Gordon, 36 Cal.App.2d 189, 97 P.2d 845 (1939). A few jurisdictions, e. g., Florida, Wisconsin, bar a foreign Corporation from acquiring, holding, or disposing of property in the jurisdiction until it has qualified; Massachusetts requires a foreign Corporation owning real property in the jurisdiction without a usual place of business there to qualify. 21 Corp.J. 183 (1956). Statutes in different jurisdictions variously refer to "admission" as "qualification", "authorization", "registration", "licensing", or "domestication" (Oklahoma, Tennessee), although "domestication" more strictly denotes a foreign Corporation's becoming a domestic Corporation (without surrendering its corporate charter) (Georgia, Mississippi, Nebraska).

27. Model Bus.Corp.Act § 106:

(a) Maintaining or defending any action or suit or any administrative or arbitration proceeding, or effecting the settlement thereof or the settlement of claims or disputes.

(b) Holding meetings of its directors or Stockholders or carrying on other activities concerning its internal affairs.

(c) Maintaining bank accounts.

(d) Maintaining offices or agencies for the transfer, exchange and registration of its securities, or appointing and maintaining trustees or depositaries with relation to its securities.

(e) Effecting sales through independent contractors.

(f) Soliciting or procuring orders, whether by mail or through employees or agents or otherwise, where such orders require acceptance without this State before becoming binding contracts.

The typical corporate statute provides that (a) A foreign Corporation is not entitled to qualify to transact in the state business which a domestic Corporation is not permitted to transact; (b) A foreign Corporation is not to be denied qualification because the laws of its jurisdiction of incorporation governing its organization and internal affairs differ from such statute; and (c) Nothing in such statute should be construed to authorize regulation of the organization or internal affairs of the foreign Corporation.[28]

In doubtful situations, it is probably better to qualify, since the foreign Corporation would in any event be amenable to local process, regulation, and taxation, although qualification prevents the Corporation from taking the position that it is not doing business in the jurisdiction.[29] Failure to qualify when necessary might prevent the Corporation from learning of actions against it and might subject it to various penalties.

Qualification usually involves some filing of applications for certificates setting forth certain appropriate information (often with a copy of the Articles of Incorporation and any amendments thereto appended),[30] the payment of filing fees, and the designation of a resident agent or the Secretary of State, as the foreign Corporation's agent for service of process. Qualification also means that the foreign Corporation is undeniably subject to service of process and the various Corporation law, regulatory, and tax provisions applicable to foreign Corporations. Filings of reports are also required.[31]

(g) Creating evidences of debt, mortgages or liens on real or personal property.

(h) Securing or collecting debts or enforcing any rights in property securing the same.

(i) Transacting any business in interstate commerce.

(j) Conducting an isolated transaction completed within a period of 30 days and not in the course of a number of repeated transactions of like nature. New York lists only the first four. McKinney's N.Y. Bus.Corp.Law § 1301(b). See Ross Construction Co., Inc. v. U. M. & M. Credit Corp., 214 So.2d 822 (Miss.1968); "Qualification and the Sale of Securities", 25 Corp.J. 243 (1968); "Free Port Laws—Effect on Qualification Requirements", 24 Corp.J. 143 (1964); "Isolated Transactions", 23 id. 243 (1962); "Unusual Doing Business Activities", 23 id. 223 (1962); "'Doing Business' Definitions", 23 id. 183 (1962). The California attorney general has ruled that foreign baseball corporations entering California to play professional baseball games are transacting intrastate business and must qualify. Cal.Op.Atty.Gen.No. 64–178 (Jan. 20, 1964).

28. Model Bus.Corp.Act § 106.

29. Farmingdale Steer-Inn, Inc. v. Steer Inn Realty Corp., 51 Misc.2d 986, 274 N.Y.S.2d 379 (1966).

30. The need to file copies of the articles of incorporation has been eliminated in a growing number of jurisdictions, which require instead a certificate from the jurisdiction of incorporation that the Corporation is existing and in good standing. E. g., McKinney's N.Y.Bus.Corp.Law § 1304(b); Pa.Bus.Corp.Law § 1004 (1966).

See § 36.8 et seq. infra for forms.

31. E. g., Model Bus.Corp.Act §§ 106 et seq. The Model Act expressly provides that nothing therein shall be

A number of states require the annual filing of a list of resident Stockholders; a few states also require the inclusion of nonresident as well as resident Stockholders.

Library References:

C.J.S. Corporations §§ 1807, 1813, 1843.
West's Key No. Digests, Corporations ⚿638, 643.

§ 36.7 Sanctions for Noncompliance with Admission Requirements

Various sanctions are imposed for failure to qualify as required: [32]

(a) Fine or penalty on Corporation; [33]

(b) Fine and/or imprisonment of corporate agents;

(c) Fine and/or imprisonment of Directors and/or Officers;

(d) Corporation's contracts made within state "void";

(e) Corporation's contracts made within state "unenforceable";

(f) Corporation's disability to sue or defend;

(g) Corporation's disability to sue; [34]

(h) Denial of benefits to Corporation of statute of limitations;

(i) Directors/Officers/agents personally liable on contracts made within state;

(j) Injunctions against Corporation;

(k) Imposition of specified regulatory features; [35]

(*l*) Reciprocal penalties.

The most prevalent sanction is to bar the maintenance of any action, suit, or proceeding in any court of the state by a foreign Corporation transacting business in the state without a certificate of authority or any successor or assignee.[36] Noncompliance usually does

construed to authorize the state to regulate the organization or the internal affairs of foreign corporations. Id. § 106.

32. For state-by-state tabulation of sanctions, see 1 P–H Corp. Rep.

33. E. g., Model Bus.Corp.Act § 124 (amount equal to all fees and franchise taxes plus penalties); most all states provide for fines or penalties against the Corporation.

34. E. g., Model Bus.Corp.Act § 124.

35. McKinney's N.Y.Bus.Corp.Law §§ 1316(e), 1317(a)(1), 1318, 1319(a)(4), 1320, imposing liabilities on directors of foreign corporations for unlawful dividends and other distributions, corporate purchase of its shares and loans to directors, and liabilities on foreign Corporation for failure to comply with specified notice and disclosure requirements. Only *qualified* foreign corporations are eligible for exemption from such provisions under § 1320.

36. Model Bus.Corp.Act § 124; McKinney's N.Y.Bus.Corp.Law § 1312.

not impair the validity of any contract or act of such Corporation or prevent it from defending litigation.[37]

Statutes which state that a Corporation may not "maintain" an action "until" it shall have qualified are usually construed as permitting an unqualified Corporation to "commence" suit so long as it thereafter qualifies.[38] Where the legislature barred maintenance of the action but deleted from the bill the phrase "until such corporation shall have obtained a certificate of authority", qualification after the claim accrued was held to be too late.[39]

Instead of imposing a general disability to sue—which is applicable to tort as well as contract claims regardless of where the contract was made—some jurisdictions bar actions on contracts made in the jurisdiction prior to qualification.[40]

Of legislation affecting local contracts, most bar maintenance of any action before qualification and are construed to suspend enforcement, permitting enforcement after qualification (with possible penalties for tardy qualification in some cases).[41] A few statutes make the local contract unenforceable in the courts of the state even though the Corporation later qualifies.[42] Statutory provisions often

37. See Model Bus.Corp.Act § 124.

38. Inn Operations, Inc. v. River Hills Motor Inn Co., 261 Iowa 72, 152 N.W.2d 808 (1967); Video Engineering Co. v. Foto-Video Electronics, Inc., 207 Va. 1027, 154 S.E.2d 7 (1967); J. R. Watkins Co. v. Floyd, 119 So.2d 164 (La.App.1960).

39. Parker v. Lin-Co. Producing Co., 197 So.2d 228 (Miss.1967) (where prior law barred subsequent qualification).

40. E. g., New Jersey, Rhode Island, Vermont. "Unlicensed Foreign Corporations Contract Sanctions", 24 Corp.J. 243 (1965); "Statutory Restrictions on Enforcement of Contracts", 23 Corp.J. 323 (1963); "Unlicensed Foreign Corporations: Enforcement of Contracts", 23 Corp.J. 23 (1960). Such a formulation does not bar enforcement of contracts not made in the state. Brown Broadcast, Inc. v. Pepper Sound Studios, Inc., 242 Ark. 701, 416 S.W.2d 284 (1967); Kemp v. Darke County Farm Bureau Co-op Ass'n, 115 Ohio App. 1, 184 N.E.2d 103 (1961). But see Allen Indus., Inc. v. Exquisite Form Brassiere, Inc., 31 Misc.2d 673, 221 N.Y.S.2d 619 (1961) affirmed 15 A.D.2d 760, 224 N.Y.S.2d 579 (contractual provision stating that contract was deemed to have been made in Michigan held not to establish as matter of law that defense of nonqualification had been waived). Where the contract was unenforceable, the enforcement of a mechanic's lien has been held barred. Greene Plumbing & Heating Co. v. Morris, 144 Mont. 234, 395 P.2d 252 (1964); Berkshire Engineering Corp. v. Scott-Paine, 29 Misc.2d 1010, 217 N.Y.S.2d 919 (1961). Foreclosure of mortgage has also been barred. B. & P., Inc. v. Norment, 241 Ark. 1092, 411 S.W.2d 506 (1967).

41. New England Die Co. v. General Products Co., 92 R.I. 292, 168 A.2d 150 (1961); Day v. Stokes, 97 N.J.Eq. 378, 127 A. 331 (1925); Spokane Merchants' Ass'n v. Olmstead, 80 Idaho 166, 327 P.2d 385 (1958).

42. Calvert Iron Works, Inc. v. Algernon Blair, Inc., 284 Ala. 655, 227 So.2d 424 (1969); Wolf Creek v. Haas, 116 F.Supp. 37 (D.Mont.1953); Foreman & Clark Mfg. Co. v. Bartle, 125 Misc. 759, 211 N.Y.S. 602 (1925). Where the statute barred "any action", arbitration *proceedings* on contracts made within the state have been allowed. Tugee Laces, Inc. v. Mary Muffet, Inc., 273 App.Div. 756, 75 N.Y.S.2d 513 (1947), affirmed

prohibit an assignee from enforcing the contract until the assignor Corporation qualifies.[43]

Other problems of statutory construction arise from the particular statutory language employed: the meaning of "void" or "unenforceable"; [44] the effect of the statute when the unqualified foreign Corporation is sued on the contract so far as the plaintiff's enforcement or a counterclaim by the Corporation is concerned; [45] the effect of the statute on contracts made within the state preparatory to doing business.[46]

Since qualification is not required to engage exclusively in interstate commerce or for the enjoyment of federal rights, the sanctions do not apply to actions to enforce interstate contracts [47] or to assert federal rights.[48]

The Corporation's disability to sue must be promptly asserted to avoid waiver of the defense.[49] Dismissal of a corporation's action

memorandum 297 N.Y. 914, 79 N.E.2d 744. Quasi-contractual liability might also be enforced by the Corporation. Thurston v. Cedric Sanders Co., 80 S.D. 426, 125 N.W.2d 496 (1963); American Middle East Corp. v. Barouk, 13 A.D.2d 919, 215 N.Y.S.2d 843 (1961). Evyan Perfumes, Inc. v. Hamilton, 20 Misc.2d 950, 195 N.Y.S.2d 869 (1959). So also might fair trade actions against nonsignatories. Max Factor & Co. v. Janel Sales Corp., 298 F.2d 511 (2d Cir. 1962); Gillette Co. v. Master, 408 Pa. 202, 182 A.2d 734 (1962).

43. E. g., Rhode Island, Vermont. Where the defense goes to enforceability and not validity, a holder in due course may sue on the contract. Allison Hill Trust Co. v. Sarandrea, 134 Misc. 566, 236 N.Y.S. 265 (1929), modified on other grounds 236 App. Div. 189, 258 N.Y.S. 299.

44. Compare Carolin Mfg. Corp. v. George S. May, Inc., 312 Mich. 487, 20 N.W.2d 283 (1945), with Douglass v. Standard Real Estate Loan Co., 189 Ala. 223, 66 So. 614 (1914).

45. Burley Newspapers, Inc. v. Mist Pub. Co., 90 Idaho 515, 414 P.2d 460 (1966); James Howden & Co. v. American Condenser & Engineering Corp., 194 App.Div. 164, 185 N.Y.S. 159 (1920), affirmed memorandum, 231 N.Y. 627, 132 N.E. 915 (counterclaims by corporations allowed).

46. Worcester Felt Pad Corp. v. Tucson Airport Auth., 233 F.2d 44 (9th Cir. 1956) (construing Arizona statute as not voiding such contracts).

47. Allenberg Cotton Co., Inc. v. Pittman, 419 U.S. 20, 95 S.Ct. 260, 42 L.Ed.2d 195 (1974); Cone Mills Corp. v. Hurdle, 369 F.Supp. 426 (N.D.Miss. 1974); R. C. Allen Business Machines, Inc. v. Acres, 111 N.H. 269, 281 A.2d 162 (1971).

48. Grand Bahama Petroleum Co., Ltd. v. Asiatic Petroleum Corp., 550 F.2d 1320 (2d Cir. 1977); Metropolitan Paving Co. v. International Union of Operating Engineers, 439 F.2d 300 (10th Cir. 1971), certiorari denied 404 U.S. 829, 92 S.Ct. 68, 30 L.Ed.2d 58.

49. Elnat of California, Inc. v. Wilkinson Sword, Inc., 44 Cal.Rptr. 256 (Cal.Dist.Ct.App.1965); Outdoor Elec. Advertising Co. v. Saurage, 207 La. 344, 21 So.2d 375 (1945). See Hulburt Oil & Grease Co. v. Hulburt Oil & Grease Co., 371 F.2d 251 (7th Cir. 1966) (allowing action by nonqualified foreign Corporation doing business in jurisdiction against former agent, who, instead of qualifying Corporation, formed competing domestic Corporation with same name, which name barred foreign corporation's qualification), certiorari denied 386 U.S. 1032, 87 S.Ct. 1482, 18 L.Ed.2d 594 (1967); Dari-Delite, Inc. v. Priest & Baker, Inc., 50 Misc.2d 654, 271 N.Y.S.2d 355 (1966) (burden on party challenging corporation's capacity).

for failure to qualify has been held to be not for want of jurisdiction but an adjudication on the merits and hence *res judicata*.[50]

In addition to the disability-to-sue penalties, many states impose other civil and criminal sanctions. These include fines or penalties imposed on the corporation [51] or its directors,[52] officers,[53] and agents [54] conducting business in the state; possible imprisonment of such personnel; [55] imposition of personal liability on corporate personnel for corporate contracts made or even torts committed within the state; [56] injunctions against the corporation; [57] corporation's disability to defend; [58] corporation's disability to plead statute of limitations; [59] or imposition of specified regulatory provisions; [60] or reciprocal penalties.[61]

When a qualified foreign Corporation ceases to do business in the state, or is dissolved in its state of incorporation, it should for-

50. J. R. Watkins Co. v. Kramer, 250 Iowa 947, 97 N.W.2d 303 (1959).

51. E. g., ABA–ALI Model Bus.Corp. Act § 124 (amount equal to all fees and franchise taxes plus penalties). Many jurisdictions provide for fines or penalties against the corporation ranging up to $10,000 in Indiana and Ohio. See "Failure to Qualify: Monetary Penalties," 26 Corp.J. 99 (1970).

52. E. g., Kentucky ($1,000), Oklahoma (any person) ($1,000), Virginia ($1,-000).

53. E. g., Alabama ($1,000), Arkansas ($1,000), Kentucky ($1,000), Maryland ($1,000), Ohio ($1,000).

54. E. g., Alabama ($1,000), Arkansas ($1,000), Kentucky ($1,000), Maryland ($1,000), Nevada ($500), Oklahoma ($1,000).

55. E. g., Louisiana, Ohio, Oklahoma ($1,000 and/or 30 days imprisonment).

56. E. g., Virginia (officers, directors, agents), Idaho (persons assuming to act), Arkansas (officers, agents); Mountain Home Redi-Mix v. Conner Homes, Inc., 91 Idaho 612, 428 P.2d 744 (1967) (limiting liability to participants in negotiations); Texaco, Inc. v. Bosche, 242 Md. 334, 219 A.2d 80 (1966) (indicating Virginia statute, if compensatory to creditors and not penal, might be enforced by Maryland courts); Bachman v. Doerrie, 70 N.M. 277, 372 P.2d 951 (1962) (enforcing then Utah statute imposing personal liability on contract made by agent).

57. E. g., Arizona, Colorado, Delaware, Indiana, Kansas, Maine, New Hampshire, New Jersey, New York.

58. E. g., Nevada.

59. E. g., Maryland, Nevada; Globig v. Greene & Gust Co., 193 F.Supp. 544 (E.D.Wis.1961) (forbidding plea of statute of limitations under disability to defend).

60. McKinney's N.Y.Bus.Corp.Law §§ 1316(e), 1317(a)(1), 1318, 1319(a)(4), 1320, imposing liabilities on directors of foreign corporations for unlawful dividends and other distributions, corporate purchase of its shares and loans to directors, and liabilities on foreign corporation for failure to comply with specified notice and disclosure requirements. Only *qualified* foreign corporations are eligible for exemption from such provisions under section 1320. See § 36.4, supra.

61. E. g., Delaware, New Jersey (prior to 1963); Eli Lilly & Co. v. Sav-On Drugs, Inc., 57 N.J.Super. 291, 154 A.2d 650 (1959) (application of more stringent Indiana rule barring corporation from suing on any claims), aff'd 31 N.J. 591, 158 A.2d 528 (1960), aff'd on other grounds, 366 U.S. 276, 81 S.Ct. 1316, 6 L.Ed.2d 288 (1961), reh. denied, 366 U.S. 978, 81 S.Ct. 1913, 6 L.Ed.2d 1268 (1961). Georgia, prior to 1969 also had a retaliatory provision. See "Enforcement of Contracts: Retaliatory Provisions," 25 Corp.J. 339 (1968–69).

mally withdraw by surrendering its certificate of authority.[62] Such surrender minimizes taxes and other requirements, often reduces its suability, and might restrict its ability to sue.[63]

Library References:

C.J.S. Corporations § 1861.
West's Key No. Digests Corporations ⚷652.

§ 36.8 Forms—Generally

If a Corporation is doing business within a particular state which it is not incorporated in, it must register as a foreign Corporation (and withdraw its registration when it desires to discontinue the right to do business in that State). Simultaneously, it will also have to comply with all local licensing and tax registration and payment laws.

The following forms are the official Model Business Corporation Act forms relating to such registration. It should be noted however that the Secretary of States office (or other office serving a similar function) in many states provides such forms or otherwise specifies the content of such.

§ 36.9 Application for Certificate of Authority to Transact Business in State

Filing fee: $__________

APPLICATION FOR CERTIFICATE
OF AUTHORITY OF ______

To: The Secretary of State of the State of ______

Pursuant to the provisions of Section 110 of the ______ Business Corporation Act, the undersigned Corporation hereby applies for a Certificate of Authority to transact business in your State, and for that purpose submits the following statement:

First. The name of the Corporation is ______.

Second. The name which it elects to use in your State is ______ (Note 1).

Third. It is incorporated under the laws of ______.

62. Some jurisdictions required the certificate of authority to be surrendered physically or accounted for. Georgia, Hawaii, Kansas, Pennsylvania, Utah, and West Virginia require publication of notice of withdrawal.

63. Robinson Brick & Tile Co. v. Copperstate Supply Co., 100 Ariz. 28, 410 P.2d 96 (1966) (holding certificate of authority to remain in full force until certificate of withdrawal issued); Note, 40 Cornell L.Q. 610 (1955); 22 Corp.J. 123 (1958). The Texas attorney general found no constitutional objection to a statute requiring applications for certificates of withdrawal to state that all known creditors or claimants have been provided for and that the applicant "is not involved in or threatened with litigation in any court in this State." Tex.Op.Att'y Gen.No. C–663, Apr. 26, 1966.

Fourth. The date of its incorporation is ______ and the period of its duration is ______.

Fifth. The address of its principal office in the state or country under the laws of which it is incorporated is ______.

Sixth. The address of its proposed registered office in your State is ______, and the name of its proposed registered agent in your State at that address is ______.

Seventh. The purpose or purposes which it proposes to pursue in the transaction of business in your State are ______________

____

____

Eighth. The names and respective addresses of its directors and officers are:

Name	Office	Address
______	______	______
______	______	______
______	______	______
______	______	______

Ninth. The aggregate number of shares which it has authority to issue, itemized by classes, par value of shares, shares without par value, and series, if any, within a class, is:

Number of Shares	Class	Series	Par Value Per Share or Statement That Shares Are Without Par Value

Tenth. The aggregate number of its issued shares, itemized by classes, par value of shares, shares without par value, and series, if any, within a class, is:

Number of Shares	Class	Series	Par Value Per Share or Statement That Shares Are Without Par Value

Eleventh. The amount of its stated capital, as defined in the ______ Business Corporation Act, is $______.

Twelfth. An estimate of the value of all property to be owned by it for the following year, wherever located, is $______.

Thirteenth. An estimate of the value of its property to be located within your State during such year is $______.

Fourteenth. An estimate of the gross amount of business to be transacted by it during such year is $______.

Fifteenth. An estimate of the gross amount of business to be transacted by it at or from places of business in your State during such year is $______.

Sixteenth. This Application is accompanied by a copy of its Articles of Incorporation and all amendments thereto, duly authenticated by the proper officer of the state or country under the laws of which it is incorporated.

Dated ______, 19__.

____________________ (Note 2)

By ____________________
Its ______ President
And ____________________
Its ______ Secretary
(Note 3)

[*Verification*]

STATE OF __________ }
County of __________ } ss

I, ______, a notary public, do hereby certify that on this ______ day of ______, 19__, personally appeared before me ______, who, being by me first duly sworn, declared that he is the ______ of ______, that he signed the foregoing document as ______ of the Corporation, and that the statements therein contained are true.

____

Notary Public

[*Notarial Seal*]

[*Note: Verification in this form may be made by the President or Vice President of the Corporation in the case of Form No. 9; or by the President, Vice President, Secretary or Assistant Secretary of the Corporation.*]

Notes to Form

1. If the name of the Corporation does not contain the word "corporation," "company," "incorporated," or "limited," or an abbreviation of one of such words, insert the name of the Corporation with the word of abbreviation which it elects to add thereto for use in this State.

2. Exact corporate name of Corporation making the application.

3. Signatures and titles of Officers signing for the Corporation.

COMMENT

The above form is Model Business Corporation Act Official Form No. 43 drafted for use under §§ 110 and 111 of the Model Bus.Corp.Act.

Library References:

C.J.S. Corporations § 1814.
West's Key No. Digests, Corporations ⚷644.

§ 36.10 Certificate of Authority to Transact Business in State

STATE OF ______
OFFICE OF THE SECRETARY OF STATE

CERTIFICATE OF AUTHORITY
OF

______

The undersigned, as Secretary of State of the State of ______, hereby certifies that duplicate originals of an Application of ______ for a Certificate of Authority to transact business in this State, duly signed and verified pursuant to the provisions of the ______ Business Corporation Act, have been received in this office and are found to conform to law.

Accordingly the undersigned, as such Secretary of State, and by virtue of the authority vested in him by law, hereby issues this Certificate of Authority to ______ to transact business in this State under the name of ______ and attaches hereto a duplicate original of the Application for such Certificate.

Dated ______, 19__.

____
Secretary of State

§ 36.11 Application for Amended Certificate of Authority to Transact Business in State

Filing fee: $__________

APPLICATION FOR
AMENDED CERTIFICATE OF AUTHORITY
OF

______

To: The Secretary of State of the State of ______

Pursuant to the provisions of Section 118 of the ______ Business Corporation Act, the undersigned Corporation hereby applies for an

Amended Certificate of Authority to transact business in your State, and for that purpose submits the following statement:

FIRST: A Certificate of Authority was issued to the Corporation by your office on ______, 19__, authorizing it to transact business in your State under the name of ______.

SECOND: The corporate name of the Corporation has been changed to ______ (Note 1).

THIRD: The name which it elects to use hereafter in your State is ______.

FOURTH: It desires to pursue in the transaction of business in your State other or additional purposes than those set forth in its prior Application for a Certificate of Authority, as follows:

____

____ (Note 2).

Dated ______, 19__.

______________________ (Note 3)

By ______________________
Its ______ President
And ______________________
Its ______ Secretary
(Note 4)

[*Verification*]

STATE OF ____________
County of ____________ } ss

I, ______, a notary public, do hereby certify that on this ______ day of ______, 19__, personally appeared before me ______, who, being by me first duly sworn, declared that he is the ______ of ______, that he signed the foregoing document as ______ of the Corporation, and that the statements therein contained are true.

____
Notary Public

[*Notarial Seal*]

[*Note: Verification in this form may be made by the President or Vice-President of the Corporation in the case of Form No. 9; or by the President, Vice-President, Secretary or Assistant Secretary of the Corporation.*]

Notes to Form

1. If the corporate name has not been changed, insert "No change."

2. If no other or additional purposes are proposed, insert "No change."

3. Exact corporate name of Corporation making the application.

4. Signatures and titles of officers signing for the Corporation.

COMMENT

This is Model Bus.Corp.Act Official Form No. 42 as drafted for use under § 111 of the Act.

States which require that the original application be accompanied by a copy of Articles of Incorporation and all amendments to date naturally require the filing of amendments thereafter as they become effective. Some states require them to be filed forthwith, others in 30 days, or 60 days or as part of the next annual report to the state. No amendment of the application (or of the certificate of authority) is usually required except when there is a change of name or change in business purposes. The exceptions just noted, moreover, may force such action in case of a merger or consolidation. Failure to file amendments is declared to be ground for revocation of the certificate of authority; change of name to one for which a certificate of authority would not be granted automatically suspends the certificate of authority to do business in the state, and in other states following the Model Act.

§ 36.12 Amended Certificate of Authority to Transact Business in State

STATE OF ______

OFFICE OF THE SECRETARY OF STATE

AMENDED CERTIFICATE OF AUTHORITY

OF

______

The undersigned, as Secretary of State of the State of ______ ______, hereby certifies that duplicate originals of an Application of ______ for an Amended Certificate of Authority to transact business in this State, duly signed and verified pursuant to the provisions of the ______ Business Corporation Act, have been received in this office and are found to conform to law.

Accordingly the undersigned, as such Secretary of State, and by virtue of the authority vested in him by law, hereby issues this Amended Certificate of Authority to ______ to transact business in this State under the name of ______ and attaches hereto a duplicate original of the Application for such Amended Certificate.

Dated ______, 19__.

____

Secretary of State

COMMENT

This is Model Business Corp. Act Official Form No. 43 as drafted for use under § 118 of the Act.

§ 36.13 Application for Certificate of Withdrawal of Authority to Transact Business in State

Filing fee: $__________

APPLICATION FOR CERTIFICATE
OF WITHDRAWAL OF

______

To: The Secretary of State of the State of ______

Pursuant to the provisions of Section 119 of the ______ Business Corporation Act, the undersigned Corporation hereby applies for a Certificate of Withdrawal from your State, and for that purpose submits the following statement:

First. The name of the Corporation is ______.

Second. It is incorporated under the laws of ______.

Third. It is not transacting business in your state.

Fourth. It hereby surrenders its authority to transact business in your state.

Fifth. It revokes the authority of its registered agent in your State to accept service of process, and consents that service of process in any action, suit or proceeding based upon any cause of action arising in your State during the time the Corporation was authorized to transact business in your State may thereafter be made on the Corporation by service thereof on the Secretary of State of your State.

Sixth. The post-office address to which the Secretary of State may mail a copy of any process against the Corporation that may be served on him is ______.

Seventh. The aggregate number of shares which it has authority to issue, itemized by classes, par value of shares, shares without par value, and series, if any, within a class, as of this date is:

Number of Shares	Class	Series	Par Value Per Share or Statement That Shares Are Without Par Value

Eighth. The aggregate number of its issued shares, itemized by classes, par value of shares, shares without par value, and series, if any, within a class, as of this date is:

Number of Shares	Class	Series	Par Value Per Share or Statement That Shares Are Without Par Value

Ninth. The amount of its stated capital as of this date is $______.

Dated ______, 19__.

________________________ (Note 1)

By ________________________
Its ______ President
And ________________________
Its ______ Secretary
(Note 2)

STATE OF __________
County of __________ } ss

I, ______, a notary public, do hereby certify that on this ______ day of ______, 19__, personally appeared before me ______, who, being by me first duly sworn, declared that he is the ______ of ______, that he signed the foregoing document as ______ of the Corporation, and that the statements therein contained are true.

____
Notary Public

[*Notarial Seal*]

[Note: Verification in this form may be made by the President or Vice-President of the Corporation in the case of Form No. 9; or by the President, Vice-President, Secretary or Assistant Secretary of the Corporation. For form of verification, see § 36.13, supra.]

Notes to Form

1. Exact corporate name of Corporation making the statement.

2. Signatures and titles of officers signing for the Corporation.

COMMENT

This is Model Bus.Corp.Act Official Form No. 44 drafted for use under § 119 of the Act.

Library References:

C.J.S. Corporations § 1843.
West's Key No. Digests, Corporations ⚷651.

§ 36.14 Certificate of Withdrawal of Authority to Transact Business in State

STATE OF ______
OFFICE OF THE SECRETARY OF STATE

CERTIFICATE OF WITHDRAWAL
OF

______

The undersigned, as Secretary of State of the State of ______, hereby certifies that duplicate originals of an Application of ______ for a Certificate of Withdrawal from this State, duly signed and verified pursuant to the provisions of the ______ Business Corporation Act, have been received in this office and are found to conform to law.

Accordingly the undersigned, as such Secretary of State, and by virtue of the authority vested in him by law, hereby issues this Certificate of Withdrawal to ______, and attaches hereto a duplicate original of the Application for such Certificate.

Dated ______, 19__.

____
Secretary of State

COMMENT

This is Model Bus.Corp.Act Official Form No. 45 drafted for use under § 119 of the Act.

§§ 36.15–37.0 are reserved for supplementary material.

CHAPTER 37

TAXATION OF INCORPORATION TRANSACTIONS

Table of Sections

Library References:

West's Key No. Digests, Internal Revenue ⚷3640 et seq.
Kahn, Basic Corporate Taxation, 3rd Ed., § 8.1 et seq.

§ 37.1 Introduction

(a) Generally. The incorporation process will generally be structured so as to result in no taxation to any party. It is possible, however, that the incorporation would be only partially tax free or completely taxable. The term "tax free" is a term of tax law art and refers to whether, as a result of the tax laws, part or all of what would normally be gain (that is the value received exceeds the value surrendered) is declared to be not taxable. The Internal Revenue Code sections which deal with tax free and partially tax free incorporations are:

(1) Internal Revenue Code § 351 tax free exchange of property for stock or securities rules.

(2) Internal Revenue Code § 357 rules governing the assumption of liabilities by the Corporation.

(3) Internal Revenue Code § 356 rules governing the receipt by the Stockholders and security holders of assets other than stock or securities.

(b) Utilizing § 351. Effective tax planning with transfers of property to Corporations involves a clear understanding of § 351 and its related Code provisions. The most important question in planning is simply: does compliance (as discussed herein) with the requirements of § 351 yield the desired tax result and, if so, can we comply?

In using § 351(a), one should insure that all parties transferring property (which includes cash) receive 80% control of the Corporation. Although simultaneous transfers are not necessary, a long period of time between transfers could be vulnerable if the transfers are not properly documented as part of a single plan.

> *Example 1.* C, D, and E decide to form the X Corporation with the following investment: cash of $100,000 from C, real estate worth $100,000 (basis of $20,000) from D, and a patent worth $100,000 (basis of zero) from E. In return for this investment, each party is to receive one-third of the Corporation's authorized stock of 300 shares. On June 1, 19X4, after the corporate charter is granted, C transfers cash of $100,000 in return for 100 shares. Two months later, D transfers the real estate for another 100 shares. On December 3, 19X4, E transfers the patent for the remaining 100 shares.

Taken in isolation, the transfers by D and E would result in recognized gain to each. Section 351 would not be applicable because neither D nor E achieves the required 80% control. If, however, the parties are in a position to prove that all transfers were part of the same plan, C's transfer may be counted and the 80% requirement may be satisfied. To do this the parties should document and preserve evidence of their intentions. Also, it would be helpful to have some reasonable explanation for the delay in D's and E's transfer.

To meet the requirements of § 351, mere momentary control on the part of the transferor may not suffice if loss of control is compelled by a prearranged agreement.[1]

> *Example 2.* For many years T operated a business as a sole Proprietor employing R as manager. In order to dissuade R from quitting and going out on her own, T promised her a 30% interest in the business. To fulfill this promise, T transfers the business to newly formed X Corporation in return for all its stock. Immediately thereafter, T transfers 30% of the stock to R. Section 351 probably would not apply to the transfer by T to X Corporation; it appears that T was under an obligation preventing T from retaining 80% control.[2]

(c) Avoiding § 351. Because § 351(a) provides for the nonrecognition of gain on transfers to controlled Corporations it is often

1. Rev.Rul. 54-96, 1954-1 C.B. 111.

2. Compare Fahs v. Florida Machine and Foundry Co., 48-2 USTC ¶ 9329, 36 AFTR 1151, 168 F.2d 957 (5th Cir. 1948) with John C. O'Connor, 16 T.C.M. 213, T.C.Memo. 1957-50, affirmed in 58-2 USTC ¶ 9913, 260 F.2d 358 (6th Cir.).

regarded as a relief provision favoring taxpayers. There could be situations, however, where the avoidance of § 351(a) produces a more advantageous tax result. The transferors might prefer to recognize gain on the transfer of property if they cannot be particularly harmed by the gain, either because they are in low tax brackets or because the gain will receive preferential long-term capital gain treatment. Keep in mind that the basis of the property to the Corporation will be affected by the applicability or inapplicability of § 351(a).

Another reason why a particular transferor may wish to avoid Internal Revenue Code § 351 concerns possible loss recognition. Recall that § 351(a) refers to the nonrecognition of both gains and losses. Internal Revenue Code § 351(b)(2) specifically states: "no loss to such recipient shall be recognized." The course of action for a transferor who desires to recognize loss on the transfer of property with a basis in excess of fair market value could be any of several alternatives.

- Sell the property to the Corporation for its stock. This procedure may be ignored by the IRS. If the sale is disregarded, the transferor ends up under Internal Revenue Code § 351(a) with a realized, but unrecognized, gain or loss.
- Sell the property to the Corporation for "other property" or boot. Because the transferor receives no stock or securities, Internal Revenue Code § 351 is inapplicable unless Internal Revenue Code § 267 prevents loss recognition.

Suppose, however, the loss property is to be transferred to the Corporation and no loss is recognized by the transferor due to § 351(a). This could present an interesting problem in terms of assessing the economic realities involved:

Example 3. E and F form the Corporation with the following investment: property by E (basis of $40,000 and fair market value of $50,000) and property by F (basis of $60,000 and fair market value of $50,000). Each receives 50% of the X Corporation stock. Has F acted wisely in settling for only 50% of the stock? At first blush, it would appear so since E and F each invested property of the same value ($50,000). But what about the tax considerations? Due to the basis carryover of § 362(b), the Corporation now has a basis of $40,000 in E's property and $60,000 in F's property. In essence, then, E has shifted a possible $10,000 gain to the Corporation, while F has transferred a $10,000 potential loss. With this in mind, an equitable allocation of the X Corporation stock might call for F to receive a greater percentage interest than E.

§ 37.2 Tax Free Incorporations

(a) Generally. In order to have the incorporation process not be taxable to the resulting Stockholders, the following general rules must be met:

(1) 80% Rule. The Stock and security holders who are receiving from the Corporation stock or securities must own (among themselves) at the end of the contemplated transaction at least 80% of the stock and securities of the Corporation.[3]

The Definition of Stock or Securities. This includes common and preferred stock and long term debt. It does not include short term debt (see § 38.41, infra, for further discussion). The incorporators may include individuals, trusts, estates, partnerships, associations or corporations.[4] An existing Stockholder's existing holdings may be counted if he receives stock or securities in the exchange. However, if the amount of stock he receives is small in comparison to what he already has, and if the purpose of his exchange was to help qualify the transaction, then his holdings will be ignored.[5]

When previous subscriptions (some of which are paid) are outstanding for stock, then these subscription holders will be counted if the effect is to deny the requisite 80% control.[6]

(2) Significant Ownership Rule. Each stock and security holder who is to be counted in determining whether the transferring stock and security holders own at least 80% of the stock and securities must own a significant amount of stock.[7] If then the 80% test is met, then those who merely exchange property for securities (and own no stock) will also receive tax free treatment.

This means that in order to be included in the control group calculation (to determine if the control group owns at least 80% of the requisite stock) you must receive securities and previously own stock or receive stock in the exchange.[8] The mere previous ownership or present receipt of securities, alone, is not sufficient.

(3) Services Rule. None of the stock or securities issued may be for services.[9]

(4) Liabilities Rule. The liabilities assumed (or which the property was subject to) must not exceed the basis of the prop-

3. IRC § 351(a). For additional discussion of IRC § 351, see § 2.44 in Chapter 2, supra, Vol. 1.

4. Reg. § 1.351(a)(1).

5. Ibid.

6. Charles Hall, 31 BTA 125.

7. Gage Bros. & Co., 13 T.C. 472.

8. Rev.Rul. 73–472, 1973–2 C.B. 114.

9. Reg. 1.351–1(a)(1)(ii).

erty transferred. The rule (which applies only to Internal Revenue Code § 351 transactions) is that the amount of the liabilities of a cash basis Stockholder shall be excluded in calculating the amount of liabilities assumed if the payment of the liabilities assumed would result, when paid, in a deduction (unless when incurred by the taxpayer they increased his basis). In other words, a distinction is made between expense payables and capital payables, the former not being counted and later being counted as liabilities in determining whether liabilities exceed basis, for a cash basis Stockholder.[10]

What appears to be a tax free/partially tax free Internal Revenue Code § 351 issuance of the stock of one Corporation (the subsidiary) for the stock of another (the parent) if it is accompanied with the assumption by the subsidiary of a liability owed by the Stockholder which was connected with his ownership of the stock of the parent will be taxed under Internal Revenue Code § 304 and will probably be taxed as a dividend.

(5) Avoidance of Tax Rule. If the Corporation assumed liabilities of the transferring stockholder(s) or security holder(s) and the property transferred is not subject to such liabilities, then the principal purpose of the Corporation with regard to such assumption must not have been to avoid income tax on the exchange and there must have been a bona fide business purpose to the exchange.[11] For instance: if a Corporation is organized solely to avail itself of the tax free incorporation provisions, this would be a prohibited purpose.[12]

The Regulations attempt to make the taxpayer prove by a clear preponderance of the evidence (rather than by the majority of the evidence) that when liabilities are assumed the tainted motive did not exist.

One excellent use of a § 351 transaction when the Corporation is in a lower bracket than the Stockholder is to have the Corporation assume the liabilities of the Stockholder.

If the liabilities relate to the purchase of a depreciation capital asset which is also transferred, than the taxpayer will gain the "time-use" of the taxes postponed by the transfer. That is, he will lower his taxes now if the principle payments (if not totally off-set by the depreciation deduction) are paid out of dollars taxed at a lower rate; although eventually the total taxes paid will probably be the same (since the depreciation deduction which could

10. IRC § 357(c).

11. Reg. § 1.357–1(c).

12. Rev.Rul. 68–349, 1968–2 C.B. 143.

have been later taken on the Stockholder's return would have, presumably, later offset high bracket income). Taxes will be postponed and this is an economic benefit.

If the liabilities relate to an asset not being transferred or not depreciable, then there will be an actual tax savings by the Corporation's assumption of the liabilities, since the Corporation's (presumably) lower bracket will be used for the non deductible expense.

(6) Nature of Stock Rule. The stock owned by the relevant control group after the transaction must be at least 80% of the combined voting power of all classes of stock entitled to vote and at least 80% of the total number of shares of all other classes of stock.[13]

(b) Tax Results. If the above rules are met, the following will be the result:

(1) The Stockholder will recognize no gain on the transaction (but see exceptions noted below).[14]

(2) The Stockholder's basis in the stock and securities he receives will be equal to the basis of the property he transferred to the Corporation.[15]

Presumably, if he receives more than one form of stock or security, this basis will be divided among them according to their fair market values.

(3) The Corporation will recognize no taxable gain.

(4) The Corporation's basis will be equal to the basis of the property transferred to it.[16]

(5) If the Stockholder's basis in the property given up exceeds the fair market value of the stock and securities received, the Stockholder will not be able to deduct his loss if the transaction meets the requirements for a tax free exchange.[17]

(6) There is some authority for the following proposition: if preincorporation, a person or entity who is a cash basis taxpayer incures debts which are then assumed by an accrual basis Corporation, as part of the incorporation process, the Corporation will not be entitled to deduct these debts. However, if the receivables to which such payables relate are transferred, then the Corporation will be able to deduct the expenses if it also takes into income the receivables.

13. IRC § 368(c).

14. IRC § 351(a).

15. IRC § 358.

16. IRC § 362.

17. IRC § 357(b)(2).

(c) Definitions and Rules of Interpretation. The following definitions and rules of interpretation and operation are applicable to the general rule:

(1) "Persons" includes any entity or individual.[18]

(2) "Stock and securities" does not include warrants or stock rights [19] or short term debt (see § 38.42, infra for definition). It clearly does not include tangible, real or personal property or cash.

(3) The property which can be safely transferred includes all forms of tangible and intangible real and personal property.

Creditor's claims are also property and can be exchanged under the tax free incorporation rules.[20] Money is also property for this purpose [21] (but not generally under the Internal Revenue Code).

Property also includes know how (that is, proprietary ideas which are not patented and trade secrets) even though these are the product of services.[22]

(4) Generally, the stock and security holders must retain ownership of at least 80% of the stock or securities for a substantial period of time (i. e.: an addition transfer or transaction cannot be contemplated).[23] *Except:* a Corporation receiving stock may immediately distribute the stock to its Stockholders without violating this provision that the persons who transferred assets must be in control of the Corporation after the transaction.[24] The immediate distribution of stock received by a Partnership to its Partners will not violate this *continuity of interest* doctrine either. Similarly, the receipt by agents followed by a distribution to their principals [25] is not objectionable.

(5) The Corporation probably cannot be a Corporation incorporated in a foreign country.[26]

(6) These tax free provisions do not always apply when the Corporation is a Regulated Investment Company or Real Estate Investment Trust.[27]

It should be noted that if the Corporation's assets are to primarily consist of readily marketable stocks and if there is

18. Reg. § 1.351–1(a).

19. Ibid.

20. Rockford Brick & Tile Co., 31 BTA 537.

21. George M. Holstein, 23 T.C. 923 (1955).

22. Rev.Rul. 64–56, 1964, (Part 1) C.B. 133.

23. Rev.Rul. 55–36, 1955–1 C.B. 340.

24. Reg. § 1.351–1(a).

25. Dick, 20 BTA 637.

26. IRC § 367(a).

27. Reg. § 1.351–1(c).

more than one Stockholder, the possibility that the Corporation is a Regulated Investment Company [28] exists.

(7) If among the Stockholders there is an uneven distribution of various types of stocks and securities or if the assets transferred were not owned on a prorata basis by the Stockholders, the actual fair market value of the package a Stockholder receives may exceed (or be less than) his share of the fair market value of the total property transferred to the Corporation by all stock and security holders.

If there is such an uneven distribution of stocks and securities, then the Internal Revenue Service may attack the transaction based on any of the following theories explained elsewhere in this section:

(A) The transaction was partially a dividend.

(B) The substance of the transaction was other than what the form appeared to be and therefore the substantive transaction will be taxed (this is called the *"substance over form"* rule—see (h) infra).

(C) The transaction contemplated several steps, of which this was merely one, and the totality of all the steps will be taxed as a unit (this is the *"step transaction"* rule—see (g), infra).

(d) Recapture of Taxes. The Internal Revenue Code provides for the taxation of certain types of income upon a transfer. The effect of Internal Revenue Code § 351 (the general incorporation Code Section) is to generally avoid such taxation. The items of income which are not recognized in a tax free incorporation are:

(1) There will be no recognition of the gain on the transfer of an installment sales obligation.[29]

(2) In general, there will be no investment credit recapture if substantially all of the assets of the business as then run are transferred. Thus when a dental building was found to be an integral part of the dentist's practice, his not contributing the same to the Corporation did not transfer substantially all of its assets and therefore there was investment credit recapture.

(3) There will be no Internal Revenue Code § 1250 recapture of excess real estate depreciation.

(4) There will be no Internal Revenue Code § 1245 recapture of personal property depreciation.

(5) There *may be* no Internal Revenue Code § 1251 farm operating loss recapture.

28. Reg. § 1.351–1(c).

29. IRC § 453(a).

(6) There will be no Internal Revenue Code § 1252 recapture of soil, and water conservation and land clearing expenditures.

(7) There will be no Internal Revenue Code § 1239 ordinary tax on the sale of depreciable assets.

(8) There will be no Internal Revenue Code § 751 recognition of gain on the transfer of Partnership inventory items (uniquely defined) and substantially appreciated property.

(9) The tax on the transfer of collapsible Corporation stock can be postponed.[30]

(10) The tax on the transfer of § 306 stock will not be taxed.[31]

(e) Other Situations Where There Will Be Nonrecognition of Gain. Of course, even if the above rules are not met, the transaction will not result in taxation if the Stockholder's basis in the property transferred to the Corporation equals the fair market value of stock and securities received. Since the fair market value of the stock and securities distributed by the Corporation will (in a new incorporation) equal the value of the property transferred to the Corporation, this rule means that in order to avoid a tax on incorporation (without relying upon the tax free rules described in this section) the property transferred to the Corporation will have to have a basis equal to its fair market value.

(f) Issuance of Debt. It is often recommended that long term debt be distributed to Stockholders along with stock.

(1) The reasons for this recommendation are:

(A) Later, if the original capital contributed is no longer needed by the Corporation, the Stockholders will be able to withdraw tax free that portion of the capital equal to the debt principal.

(B) If the Corporation is successful, the payment of the tax deductible interest upon the debt will reduce the amount of cash which must be withdrawn as a non deductible dividend since it cannot be withdrawn as salaries.

(C) If the Corporation is successful, the payment of interest may be the best way of avoiding restrictions on the amount of compensation considered reasonable (if such compensation is deemed unreasonable it will be treated as dividend, rather than as a earned income). The payment of the tax deductible interest upon the debt will reduce the amount of cash which must be withdrawn as a non-deductible dividend.

30. IRC § 341(f)(3).

31. IRC § 306(b)(3).

(2) The problem with the issuance of debt is that interest will be paid on the debt.

The necessity of paying interest does not arise from Internal Revenue Code § 351 itself since if no interest is paid on the debt (and thus long term debt is held not to be a "security" for tax purposes), then it would be reclassified as "stock." The tax consequences upon incorporation of issuing stock rather than securities is the same or better. Rather, interest should be paid:

(A) In order to establish that the principal repaid is to retire true debt (and is not a dividend distribution with respect to stock). If this is established then the payment will be treated as a return of capital and not as a dividend. In order to establish this fact the debt must carry a reasonable amount of interest.

(B) In order to avoid the application of Internal Revenue Code § 482 which would allow the Internal Revenue Service to determine a reasonable amount of interest based on their rates (see § 54.2, infra), an interest rate of at least 11 percent (if not usurious) should be charged.[32]

(3) Another problem with the issuance of debt is that it will result in a less healthy corporate net worth since the Stockholder's net equity will be reduced to the extent of the debt. If too much debt is issued, the Corporation may be said to have "thin capitalization" and the Corporation might be reclassified as a Partnership for either tax or state law purposes (see Chapter 31, supra).

(4) In the author's view, recent cases allowing interest free loans (see § 56.11, infra) do not avoid the above described problems.

(g) Distribution Of Short Term Notes and Step Transaction Rule. One way to avoid taxation upon the distribution of a short term note (which is not a security—see supra) to a Stockholder is to distribute such note as a dividend to the Stockholder after the smoke has cleared on the initial incorporation. If the Corporation has no Earnings and Profits for the year (by definition, it has no accumulated E & P) this will result in a tax free dividend (see Chapter 57, infra). It may even make sense to have a short year just to avoid taxation in this case. Knowledgeable practitioners would point out that the Internal Revenue Service might try to take the position that the above transaction was part of the initial incorporation (and thus taxable according to the partial tax free incorporation rules) if the debt received is in excess of the basis of the property surrendered to the Corporation. The rule which relates to this type of an argument is commonly referred to as the *step transaction* rule and is often used

32. F. L. Rooney, 305 F.2d 681.

(and ignored) as suits the Internal Revenue Service's purposes. The rule's test for this situation is whether the taxpayers planned the second transaction when the first was transacted.

Even if a transaction is completely tax free in the traditional sense, it may result in taxation to one or more of the Stockholders if the transaction is followed (or preceded) by another transaction and this auxiliary transaction has a separate tax result which would have been recognized if it had not been masked by the incorporation.

As a basic premise, however, a series of steps will be included in the scope of tax free exchange if they were part of the planned transaction and if they are taken expeditiously.[33]

(h) Substance Over Form. If the Internal Revenue Service feels that the facts behind a transaction are not represented by the form of the transaction, it will attempt to tax the transaction by applying a theory called *substance over form.* This theory looks behind the form of the transaction to its various components or hidden purposes.

Internal Revenue Code § 482 (see § 54.2, infra), which is the statutory embodiment of the substance over form rule, was used to reallocate a deduction from a Stockholder to the Corporation when the Corporation was going to be taxable on the income to which the deduction related.

For instance, if the fair market value of the assets that each stock or security holder transfers are not in proportion to the stock or securities received, then even though Internal Revenue Code § 351 will still be applied to make such transaction tax free, it may be implied that an additional transaction (based upon the assumption that the first transaction should have been proportional) will have taken place.[34] An example of what may be implied is:

(1) A gift was made from the person who ended up with less to the person who ended up with more (and thus a gift tax may be due).

(2) The person receiving the disproportionately high amount may be deemed to have received compensation under Internal Revenue Code § 61.

Note: presumably if it was the Corporation itself that owed the compensation, then that portion of the stock would not qualify at all for Internal Revenue Code § 351 since the stock received must be in exchange for property and services is not deemed to be property (see supra).

(i) Installment Sales. The mere transfer of an installment sales receivable will not be taxable[35] (although a later disposition by the

33. Reg. § 1.351(a)(1).

34. Reg. § 1.351-1(b).

35. IRC § 453(a).

Corporation may be if made within 2 years of the creation of the installment obligation or if of marketable securities).[36]

§ 37.3 Partially Tax Free Incorporations

(a) In order to have the incorporation process result in a partially free transaction to the resulting Stockholders the following general rules must be met:

(1) 80% Rule. The Stockholders who are receiving from the Corporation stock or securities must own (among themselves) at the end of the contemplated transaction at least 80% of the stock and securities of the Corporation.[37]

The Definition of Stock or Securities. This includes common and preferred stock and long term debt. It does not include short term debt (see § 38.41, infra, for further discussion).

The incorporators may include individuals, trusts, estates, partnerships, associations or Corporations.[38] An existing Stockholder's existing holdings may be counted if he receives stock or securities in the exchange. However, if the amount he receives is small in comparison to what he already has, and if the purpose of his exchange was to help qualify the transaction, then his holdings will be ignored.[39]

When previous subscriptions (some of which are paid) are outstanding for stock, then these subscription holders will be used to deny the requisite 80% control.[40]

(2) Significant Ownership Rule. Each stock and security holder who is to be counted in determining whether the transferring stock and security holders own at least 80% of the stock and securities must own a significant amount of stock. If this 80% test is met, then those who merely exchange property for securities (and own no stock) will also receive tax free treatment.

This means that in order to be included in the controlled group calculation (to determine if the control group owns at least 80% of the requisite stock) you must either receive securities and previously own stock[41] or receive stock in the exchange.[42] The mere previous ownership or present receipt of

36. IRC § 453(e)(1) and (e)(7).

37. IRC § 351(a).

38. Reg. § 1.351(a)(1).

39. Ibid.

40. Charles Hall, 31 BTA 125.

41. Rev.Rul. 73–473, 1973–2, C.B. 115.

42. Rev.Rul. 73–472, 1973–2, C.B. 114.

securities, alone, is not sufficient. It should be noted that if the above criterion can be met, then the transaction may be completely tax free (see § 37.2, supra).

(3) Services Rule. A Stockholder who solely renders services for stock or securities will not be counted for purposes of the 80% test. If the Stockholder or Security holder transfers any property, in addition to rendering services, then he will be included for purposes of the 80% test (although the part that was received for services will be taxable).[43]

It should be noted that as a matter of practical law, in some states the issuance of stock for future services is prohibited.

(4) Nature of Stock Rule. The stock owned after the transaction must be 80% of the combined voting power of all classes of stock entitled to vote and 80% of the total number of shares of all other classes of stock.[44]

(b) Tax Result. If the above rules are met, the following will be the result:

(1) The Stockholders gain will be limited to the fair market value of the sum of the following amounts if (and to the extent) received by the Stockholder from the Corporation:

(A) (i) The amount of any liabilities assumed and the amount of any liabilities which the property transferred to the Corporation is subject to, to the extent to which such liabilities are in excess of the stock and security holder's basis in all of the property transferred by such stock and security holders.

Note: what appears to be a tax free/partially tax free Internal Revenue Code § 351 issuance of the stock of one Corporation (the subsidiary) for the stock of another (the parent) if it is accompanied with the assumption by the subsidiary of a liability owned by the Stockholder which was connected with his ownership of the stock of the parent will be taxed under Internal Revenue Code § 304 and will probably be taxed as a dividend.

The gain to each transferor is determined separately based upon whether the liabilities assumed are in excess of his basis.[45]

This rule does not apply to some bankruptcy situations.[46]

A problem arises in the situation of a cash basis taxpayer who transfers receivables (which by definition have

43. Reg. § 1.351–1(a)(1)(ii).

44. IRC § 368(c).

45. Rev.Rul. 66–142, 1966–1, C.B. 66.

46. Reg. § 1.357–2(a) and § 368(a)(1)(G).

no basis to a cash basis taxpayer) and the liabilities relating to those receivables to a Corporation in exchange for stock. Before 1979 there was a split of authority as to the tax result. After 1978 the rule (which applies only to Internal Revenue Code § 351 transactions) is that [47] the amount of the liabilities of a cash basis stock or security holder shall be excluded in calculating the amount of liabilities assumed if the liabilities assumed will result when paid in a deduction (unless when incurred by the taxpayer they increased his basis). In other words, a distinction is made between expense payables and capital payables, the former not being counted and later being counted as liabilities in determining whether liabilities exceed basis for a cash basis Stockholder.

(ii) Or, if the principal purpose of the stock or security holder with regard to such assumption was to avoid income tax on the exchange, then the value of all liabilities assumed or which the property was taken subject to will be taxed.[48] The taxpayer has the burden of proving that the tainted purpose did not exist if he is challenged by the Internal Revenue Service. For instance: if a Corporation is organized solely to avail itself of § 351,[49] the tainted purpose will exist.

One excellent use of a § 351 transaction is (when the Corporation is in a lower bracket than the Stockholder) to have the Corporation assume liabilities of the Stockholder. If the liabilities relate to the purchase of a depreciation capital asset which is also transferred, then the taxpayer will gain the time-use of money. That is, he will lower his taxes now by the fact that the principal payments (if not totally offset by the depreciation deduction) are paid out of dollars taxed at a lower rate, although eventually the total cash paid will probably be the same (since the depreciation deduction would have been taken later on the Stockholder's return and would have, presumably, offset higher bracket income). Taxes will be postponed and this is an economic benefit.

If the liabilities relate to an asset not being transferred or not depreciable, then there will be an actual tax savings by the Corporation's assumption of the liabilities since the Corporation's (presumably) lower bracket will be used for a non deductible expense.

47. IRC § 357(c)(3).

48. Reg. § 1.357–1(c).

49. Rev.Rul. 68–349, 1968–2 C.B. 43.

(iii) Or, if the principal purpose of the Stockholder with regard to such assumption was not a bona fide business purpose, then all liabilities assumed will be deemed to be money distributed and thus taxable.[50] The taxpayer has the burden of proving that the tainted purpose did not exist, if he is challenged by the Internal Revenue Service.

The Regulations attempt to make the taxpayer prove by a clear preponderance of the evidence (rather than by the majority of the evidence) that when liabilities are assumed the tainted motive did not exist.[51]

(B) The amount of any money received and the amount of any short term debt (see § 38.42, infra) received [52] will be taxed.

(C) The amount of stock or securities received for services will be taxed.[53]

(D) If the liabilities assumed or which the property is subject to exceed its basis, then an additional ordinary or capital gain (as the case may be) on the difference between the amount of liabilities assumed and the property's basis will be taxed (unless the cash basis taxpayer's exception (explained in ii above) is applicable).[54]

(2) The Stockholder's basis in the stock and securities he receives tax free will be equal to: [55]

(A) The basis of the property he transferred to the Corporation.

(B) Less the value of any money and "other property" distributed to the Stockholder (which includes any property other than stock or securities).

(C) Less the value of any liabilities assumed by the Corporation (except liabilities transferred by a cash basis taxpayer which were taxable as a result of their assumption).[56]

(D) Plus the amount of any asset distributed to the Stockholder and treated as a dividend to him.

(E) Plus the amount of any gain (other than dividends) recognized on the exchange.

(F) Presumably (D) and (E) only apply to the gain on the assumption of a liability, although, by their terms,

50. Reg. § 1.357–1(c).

51. Ibid.

52. IRC § 351(b).

53. Reg. § 1.351–1(a)(1)(ii).

54. Reg. § 1.358–1.

55. IRC § 358.

56. IRC § 358(d)(2).

they also apply to the receipt of other property (where in the Author's view the basis should be allocated to the property and not the stock).

(3) The stock or security holder's basis in any money received will be equal to its value.[57]

(4) The stock or security holder's basis in any "other property" received will be its fair market value.[58]

(5) In determining the amount of gain of each asset transferred by the Stockholder (and presumably the type of gain),[59] the type of gain which will arise is generally a capital gain on the transfer.[60] This rule is fraught with exceptions and additional taxes.

The full gain on each asset (measured by its allocated share of the fair market value of the stock, securities, short term notes and other assets received) is calculated and then (if at all possible) the gains and losses attributable to each asset will be noted on the Stockholder's return.

The following is a list of the ordinary taxes which each Stockholder might be faced with as to each asset transferred to the Corporation (but such tax will not be in excess of the partial recognition of tax rules set forth above; otherwise a capital gain will be taxed):

(A) Internal Revenue Code § 1245 Recapture (but not in excess of the gain) at ordinary tax rates of post 1962:

(i) Depreciation and amortization taken on personal property.

(ii) Depreciation and amortization of tangible property (other than a building or its structural components) used in manufacturing, production or extraction.

(iii) Depreciation and amortization of tangible property (other than a building or its structural components) used to furnish transportation, communications, electrical energy, gas, water or sewage disposal services.

(iv) A research facility used in connection with the activities set forth in (ii) and (iii).

(v) A bulk storage of fungible commodities facility used in connection with the activities set forth in (ii) and (iii).

(vi) An elevator.

57. IRC § 358.

58. Ibid.

59. Rev.Rul. 68–55, 1968–1 C.B. 140.

60. IRC § 1001.

(vii) Real property deducted or amortized as pollution control facilities, child care facilities, railroad grading and bores, removal of architectural and transportation barriers to the handicapped or rehabilitation of historical structures.

(viii) Certain sports player contracts.

(B) Internal Revenue Code § 1250 property recapture at ordinary rates (but not in excess of the gain) of post 1969 and pre 1982 real estate depreciation in excess of straight line depreciation as follows:

(i) Certain government financed apartments—there will be graded recapture if the holding period was at least 100 months.

(ii) Certain low income housing—there will be graded recapture if the holding period was at least 100 months.

(iii) As to the rest, total recapture.

As to post 1981 real property, 100% of all depreciation under the Accelerated Cost Recovery System will be recaptured.

(C) Internal Revenue Code § 1252 recapture of farm soil and water conservation expenditures and land clearing expenses.

(D) Internal Revenue Code § 1251 farm property recapture when operating losses offset non farm income.

(E) Internal Revenue Code § 453(d) accelerated taxation upon the disposition of installment sale obligations.

(F) Internal Revenue Code § 1239 ordinary tax on the taxable transfer of depreciable assets if the Stockholder and Corporation are related.

A transfer (sale) between related persons means:[61]

(i) A sale between an individual and a Corporation which he directly or indirectly owns 80% of. In determining whether he owns indirectly 80% the rule recited in (iii) below applies.

(ii) A sale between two or more Corporations 80% of each of which are owned directly or indirectly by the same individual.

(iii) The following is a recitation of those persons and entities whose stock ownership will be constructive-

61. IRC § 1239(c), modifying IRC § 318.

ly deemed to be owned by the actual selling Stockholder or the Stockholders who own the Corporation; all relationships refer to the Stockholder himself:

* A parent, child, grandchild, and spouse of the Stockholder.

* A Corporation in proportion to the value of the stock of the Stockholder.

* A Partnership in which the Stockholder is a Partner in proportion to his interest in the Partnership.

* A trust of which the Stockholder is either grantor or beneficiary in proportion to his actuarial interest in the trust.

* An estate whose beneficiaries include the Stockholder in proportion to his interest in the estate.

* A Partnership whose Partners include a parent, child, grandchild or spouse of the Stockholder in proportion to their interest in the Partnership.

* A trust whose beneficiaries include a parent, child, grandchild or spouse of the Stockholder in proportion to their actuarial interest in the trust.

* An estate whose beneficiaries include a parent, child, grandchild or spouse of the Stockholder in proportion to their interests in the estate.

* A Corporation whose Stockholders include a parent, child, grandchild or spouse of the Stockholder in proportion to the value of their interest.

(G) Under Internal Revenue Code § 47 a recapture of that portion of the investment credit taken which was based upon a holding period which did not, in fact, materialize.

Substantially all of the assets of the business as then run must be transferred to avoid investment credit recapture. Thus, when a dental building was found to be an integral part of the dentist's practice, his not contributing the same to the Corporation did not transfer substantially all of its assets and therefore there was investment credit recapture.

(H) Under Internal Revenue Code § 751, if a Partnership is transferred in a taxable transaction to a newly formed Corporation, an ordinary tax will be taxed on inventory items of the Partnership which have appreciated substantially and on the unrealized receivables (which has a unique definition).

(I) A transfer of receivables.[62]

(J) If stock of a third Corporation is transferred to the Corporation by the stock or securities holder, then the ordinary taxes may apply if the following types are transferred:

(i) Stock with a Internal Revenue Code § 305 and § 306 preferred stock taint (see Chapter 58, infra, for further description).

(ii) Collapsible Corporation Stock (see ——, infra, (IRC § 341).

(6) The Corporation will recognize no tax.

The Corporation's basis will be equal to the basis of the property transferred to it.

(c) Definitions and Rules of Interpretation. The following definitions and rules of interpretation and operation are applicable to the rules:

(1) "Persons" includes any entity or individual.

(2) "Stock and securities" does not include warrants or stock rights [63] or short term debt (see § 38.42, infra). It clearly would not include tangible real or personal property or cash.

(3) The property which can be transferred tax free includes all forms of tangible and intangible real and personal property but does not include stock or securities issued solely for services.[64]

Creditor's claims are also property and can be exchanged under § 351.

Money is also property for purposes of Internal Revenue Code § 351 [65] (although not generally for purposes of the Internal Revenue Code).

Property also includes know how (that is, proprietary ideas which are not patented and trade secrets) even though these are the product of services.[66]

(4) Generally, to get tax free treatment the stock and security holders must retain ownership of at least 80% of the stock or securities for a substantial period of time (i. e.: an addition transfer or transaction [67] cannot be contemplated) except: a Corporation receiving stock may distribute the stock to its

62. IRC § 61.

63. Reg. § 1.351–1(a).

64. IRC § 351(a).

65. George M. Holstein, 23 T.C. 923 (1955).

66. Rev.Rul. 64–56, 1964 (Part I) C.B. 133.

67. Rev.Rul. 55–36, 1955–1 C.B. 340.

Stockholders without violating this provision that the persons who transferred assets must be in control of the Corporation after the transaction.[68]

The immediate distribution of stock received by a Partnership to its Partners will not violate this *continuity of interest* doctrine.[69] Similarly, the receipt by agents and then distribution to their principals [70] is not objectionable.

(5) Where the transaction contemplates the transfer at a later date of stock, which transfer (if taken into account) would prevent tax free treatment, such tax free treatment will be denied.[71]

(6) The Corporation probably cannot be a Corporation incorporating in a foreign country.[72]

(7) § 351 does not always apply when the Corporation is a Regulated Investment Company or Real Estate Investment Trust.[73] It should be noted that if the Corporation's assets primarily consist of readily marketable stocks and if there is more than one Stockholder, the possibility that the Corporation is a Regulated Investment Company exists.[74]

(8) There is some authority for the following proposition: if preincorporation, a person or entity who is a cash basis taxpayer incurs debts which are then assumed by an accrual basis Corporation as part of the incorporation process, the Corporation will not be entitled to deduct the same. However, if the receivables to which such payables relate are transferred, then the Corporation will be able to deduct the expenses if it also takes into income the receivables.

(d) Stock for Services. A problem with being taxed on stock for services is that the employee-Stockholder has to pay taxes when he has not received the cash to pay the taxes with. One solution to this is to transfer to the employee a stock package whose present value is virtually nothing. Some of the methods of accomplishing this are:

(1) Give the employee stock options which have a present value of almost nothing and have him elect to be taxed upon such present value (see § 56.12, infra). The ability to make this Internal Revenue Code § 83 election is arguable.

68. Reg. § 1.351–1(a).

69. Rev.Rul. 70–239, 1970–1 C.B. 74.

70. Dick, 20 BTA 637.

71. O. J. Sharpe, 15 T.C.Memo 1384, (1956).

72. IRC § 367(a).

73. Reg. § 1.351–1(c).

74. Reg. § 1.351–1(c).

(2) Give preferred stock or debt to the capital contributing Stockholders so that the common stock which the employee thereafter receives is almost worthless.

(3) Create two types of stock, one of which has a liquidation preference equal to the originally capitalization, and give to the employee the other type of stock (whose value would arguably not include the original capitalization value of the Corporation). In reality it is difficult to argue that capital stock which is merely missing liquidation value or represents no present net value is really worthless (or nearly worthless) but this is generally regarded as an acceptable method of solving the problem of avoiding tax upon issuance of stock.

(4) Issue an Incentive Stock Option.

(e) Losses. It should be noted that if the stock or security holder's basis exceeds the fair market value of the stock and securities received, the holder will not be able to deduct his loss if the transaction meets the requirements for a tax free exchange or a partially tax free exchange.[75]

(f) Issuance of Debt. It is often recommended that long term debt be distributed to Stockholders along with stock.

(1) The reasons for this recommendation are:

(A) Later, if the original capital contributed is no longer needed by the Corporation, the Stockholders will be able to withdraw tax free that portion of the capital equal to the debt principal.

(B) If the Corporation is successful, the payment of interest may be the best way of avoiding restrictions on the amount of compensation considered reasonable (if such compensation is deemed unreasonable it will be treated as a dividend, rather than as earned income). The payment of the tax deductible interest upon the debt will reduce the amount of cash which must be withdrawn as a non deductible dividend.

(2) The problem with the issuance of debt is that interest will be paid on the debt.

The necessity of paying interest does not arise from Internal Revenue Code § 351 itself since if no interest is paid and thus the long term debt is not a "security" for tax purposes, then it would be reclassified as "stock", rather than being reclassified as short term debt. (see § 38.41 et seq. infra). The tax consequences upon incorporation of issuing stock and

75. IRC § 351(b)(2).

securities is the same or better. The debt must carry a reasonable amount of interest:

(A) In order to establish that the principal repaid is to retire true debt (and is not a distribution with respect to stock) so that the payment is treated as a return of capital and not as a stock dividend.

(B) In order to avoid the application of Internal Revenue Code § 482 which would allow the Internal Revenue Service to determine a reasonable amount of interest based on their rates (see Chapter 54, infra).

Another problem with the issuance of debt is that it will result in a less healthy corporate net worth since the Stockholder's capital will be reduced to the extent of the debt. If too much debt is issued, the Corporation may be said to have "thin capitalization" and the Corporation may be reclassified as a Partnership for either tax or state law purposes (see § 2.32, supra, Vol. 2).

In the Author's view, recent cases allowing interest free loans (see § 56.11, infra) do not avoid the above described problems.

(g) Distribution of Short Term Notes and Step Transactions. One way to avoid taxation upon the distribution of a short term note to a stock or security holder is to distribute the same as a dividend to him after the smoke has cleared on the initial incorporation. If the Corporation has no Earnings and Profits for the year, this will result in a tax free dividend (see Chapter 57 infra). It may even make sense to have a short year just to avoid taxation in this case. Knowledgeable practitioners would point out that the Internal Revenue Service might try to take the position that the above transaction was part of the initial incorporation (and thus taxable according to the partial tax free incorporation rules) if the debt received is in excess of the basis of the property surrendered to the Corporation. The rule which relates to this type of an argument is commonly referred to as the *step transaction* rule and is often used (and ignored) as suits Internal Revenue Service's purposes. The rule's test in this situation is whether the taxpayers planned the second transaction when the first was transacted.[76]

(h) Substance Over Form. Even if a transaction is partially tax free in the traditional sense, the non taxable portion of the transaction may result in taxation to one or more of the Stockholders if the transaction is followed (or preceded) by another transaction and

76. F. L. Rooney, 305 F.2d 681 (9th Cir. 1962).

part or all of the auxiliary transaction has a separate tax result which would have been recognized if it had not been masked by the incorporation. If it recognizes this fact, the Internal Revenue Service will attempt to tax the auxiliary transaction by applying a theory called *substance over form*. This theory looks behind the form of the transaction to its various components or hidden purposes.

Internal Revenue Code § 482 (see § 54.2, infra), which is the statutory embodiment of the substance over form rule, was used to reallocate a deduction from a Stockholder to the Corporation when the Corporation was going to be taxable on the income to which the deduction related.[77]

For instance if the fair market value of the assets that each stock or security holder transfers is not in proportion to the stock or securities received, then even though Internal Revenue Code § 351 will still be applied to make such transaction tax free, it may be implied that an additional transaction (based upon the assumption that the first transaction should have been proportionate) will have taken place.[78] An example of what may be implied is:

(1) A gift was made from the person who ended up with less to the person who ended up with more (and thus a gift tax may be due).

(2) The person receiving the disproportionately high amount may be deemed to have received compensation under Internal Revenue Code § 61. Note: presumably if it was the Corporation itself that owed the compensation, then that portion of the stock would not qualify at all for Internal Revenue Code § 351 since the stock received must be in exchange for property and services is not deemed to be property (see supra).

§ 37.4 Non Tax Free Incorporations

(a) Generally. If a Corporation is incorporated without meeting either the tax free or partially tax free rules (see §§ 37.2 and 37.3, supra), then the transaction will be treated as a sale or exchange of assets. Although the general rule is that the resulting Stockholders will pay a capital gains (or loss) tax on the transfer,[79] this rule is fraught with exceptions and additional taxes. The full gain and loss on each asset (measured by its allocated share of the fair market value of the stock, securities, short term notes and other assets received) is calculated and then (if at all possible) the gains and losses attributable to each asset will be noted on the Stockholder's return.

77. Ibid.

78. Reg. § 1.351–1(b).

79. IRC § 1001.

(b) Taxes. The following is a list of the non capital gains taxes which each Stockholder might be faced with as to each asset transferred to the Corporation:

(1) Internal Revenue Code § 1245 recapture (but not in excess of the gain) at ordinary tax rates of post 1962:

(A) Depreciation and amortization taken on personal property.

(B) Depreciation and amortization of tangible property (other than a building or its structural components) used in manufacturing, production or extraction.

(C) Depreciation and amortization of tangible property (other than a building or its structural components) used to furnish transportation, communications, electrical energy, gas, water or sewage disposal services.

(D) A research facility used in connection with the activities set forth in (B) and (C).

(E) A bulk storage of fungible commodities facility used in connection with the activities set forth in (B) and (C).

(F) An elevator.

(G) Real property deducted or amortized as:

(i) pollution control.

(ii) child care facilities.

(iii) railroad grading and bores.

(iv) removal of architectural and transportation barriers to the handicapped.

(v) rehabilitation of historical structures.

(H) Certain sports player contracts.

(2) Internal Revenue Code § 1250 property recapture at ordinary rates that portion of post 1969 and pre 1982 of accelerated depreciation which exceeds straight line depreciation (but not in excess of the gain of a certain percentage of real estate depreciation) taxed as follows:

(A) Certain government financed apartments—there will be graded recapture if the holding period was at least 100 months.

(B) Certain other low income housing—there will be a graded recapture if the holding period was at least 100 months.

(C) As to the rest, total recapture.

As to post 1981 real property, 100% of all depreciation under the Accelerated Cost Recovery System will be recaptured.

(3) Internal Revenue Code § 1251 farm property recapture when operating losses offset non farm income.

(4) A § 453(d) accelerated taxation upon the disposition of installment sale obligations.

(5) A § 1239 ordinary tax if the Stockholder and Corporation are related.

A sale between related persons means:

(A) A sale between an individual and a Corporation which he directly or indirectly owns 80% of. In determining whether he owns indirectly 80% the rule recited in (C) below applies.

(B) A sale between two or more Corporations 80% of each of which are owned directly or indirectly by the same individual.

(C) The following is a recitation of those persons and entities whose stock ownership will be constructively deemed to be owned by the actual selling Stockholder or the Stockholders who own the Corporation; all relationships refer to the Stockholder himself:

(i) A parent, child, grandchild, and spouse of the Stockholder.

(ii) A Corporation in proportion to the value of the stock of the Stockholder.

(iii) A Partnership in which the Stockholder is a Partner in proportion to his interest in the Partnership.

(iv) A trust of which the Stockholder is either grantor or beneficiary in proportion to his actuarial interest in the trust.

(v) An estate whose beneficiaries include the Stockholder in proportion to his interest in the estate.

(vi) A Partnership whose Partners include a parent, child, grandchild or spouse of the Stockholder in proportion to their interest in the Partnership.

(vii) A trust whose beneficiaries include a parent, child, grandchild or spouse of the Stockholder in proportion to their actuarial interest in the trust.

(viii) An estate whose beneficiaries include a parent, child, grandchild or spouse of the Stockholder in proportion to their interests in the estate.

(ix) A Corporation whose Stockholders include a parent, child, grandchild or spouse of the Stockholder in proportion to the value of their interest.

(6) Under Internal Revenue Code § 47 a recapture of that portion of the investment credit taken which was based upon a holding period which did not, in fact, materialize.

(7) Under Internal Revenue Code § 751, if a Partnership is transferred to a newly formed Corporation, an ordinary tax will be taxed on inventory items of the Partnership which have appreciated substantially and on the unrealized receivables (which are uniquely defined).

(8) A transfer of receivables.[80]

(9) Internal Revenue Code § 1252 recapture of farm soil and water clearing expenses.

(10) What appears to be a tax free/partially tax free Internal Revenue Code § 351 issuance of the stock of one Corporation (the subsidiary) for the stock of another (the parent) if it is accompanied with the assumption by the subsidiary of a liability owned by the Stockholder which was connected with his ownership of the stock of the parent will be taxed under Internal Revenue Code § 304 and will probably be taxed as a dividend.

(11) Losses from the transfer of § 1231 assets used in the business.

(12) If another Corporation's stock is the asset transferred by the Stockholder, then the ordinary taxes may apply if the following types are transferred:

(i) Stock with a Internal Revenue Code § 305 and § 306 preferred stock taint (see Chapter 58, infra, for further description).

(ii) Collapsible Corporation Stock (IRC § 341).

(c) Basis. The basis of the stock and securities in the hands of the Stockholder after such a taxable incorporation would be equal to the resulting Stockholder's basis in the assets transferred plus the gain they recognize on the transfer (which will total the fair market value of the stock and securities transferred to them).

The Corporation's basis in the property transferred would be equal to its fair market value.

(d) Choice of Tax Results. A taxable transfer to a Corporation in exchange for securities or short term notes but not stock[81] theoretically can be considered a dividend paid to the transferor or an exchange transaction generally resulting in capital gain treatment. Often the tax results are not obvious. Dividend treatment may be assessed when the effect of the transaction is to make a distribu-

80. IRC § 61.

81. IRC § 317(a).

tion of property with respect to the stock ownership, rather than to exchange assets for new stock or securities of equal value.

A dividend will:

(1) have ordinary income treatment only if it is paid out of earnings and profits (see Chapter 57, infra, for definition). tion).

(2) have no gain if it is paid out of the basis of the distributee's stock.

(3) otherwise have capital gain treatment. (see Chapter 57, infra, for a more complete explanation.)

An exchange transaction will generally be capital gains treatment, except for the exceptions listed in (b) above.

§ 37.5 Reports to Be Filed with the Internal Revenue Service

(1) Every person who received the stock or securities of a controlled Corporation, or other property as part of the consideration, in exchange for property under Internal Revenue Code § 351, must [82] return for the taxable year in which the exchange is consummated a complete statement of all facts pertinent to such exchange, including:

(A) A description of the property transferred, or of his interest in such property, together with a statement of the cost or other basis thereof, adjusted to the date of transfer.

(B) With respect to stock of the controlled Corporation received in the exchange, a statement of:

(i) The kind of stock and preferences; if any;

(ii) The number of shares of each class received; and

(iii) The fair market value per share of each class at the date of the exchange.

(C) With respect to securities of the controlled Corporation received in the exchange, a statement of:

(i) The principal amount and terms; and

(ii) The fair market value at the date of exchange.

(D) The amount of money received, if any.

(E) With respect to other property received:

(i) A complete description of each separate item;

(ii) The fair market value of each separate item at the date of exchange; and

(iii) In the case of a corporate holder, the adjusted basis of the other property in the hands of the controlled Corpora-

82. Reg. § 1.357(a).

tion immediately before the distribution of such other property to the corporate Stockholder in connection with the exchange.

(F) With respect to liabilities of the transferors assumed by the controlled Corporation, a statement of:

(i) The nature of the liabilities;

(ii) When and under what circumstances created;

(iii) The corporate business reason for assumption by the controlled Corporation; and

(iv) Whether such assumption eliminates the transferor's primary liability.

(2) Every such controlled Corporation must file with its income tax return for the taxable year in which the exchange is consummated:

(A) A complete description of all the property received from the transferors.

(B) A statement of the cost or other basis thereof in the hands of the transferors.

(C) The following information with respect to the capital stock of the controlled Corporation:

(i) The total issued and outstanding capital stock immediately prior to and immediately after the exchange, with a complete description of each class of stock;

(ii) The classes of stock and number of shares issued to each transferor in the exchange, and the number of shares of each class of stock owned by each transferor immediately prior to and immediately after the exchange; and

(iii) The fair market value of the capital stock as of the date of exchange which was issued to each transferor.

(3) The following information with respect to securities of the controlled Corporation:

(A) The principal amount and terms of all securities outstanding immediately prior to and immediately after the exchange;

(B) The principal amount and terms of securities issued to each transferor in the exchange, with a statement showing each transferor's holdings of securities of the controlled Corporation immediately prior to and immediately after the exchange;

(C) The fair market value of the securities issued to the transferors on the date of the exchange; and

(D) A statement as to whether the securities issued in the exchange are subordinated in any way to other claims against the controlled Corporation;

(E) The amount of money, if any, which passed to each of the transferors in connection with the transaction;

(F) With respect to other property which passed to each transferor:

(i) A complete description of each separate item;

(ii) The fair market value of each separate item at the date of exchange; and

(iii) In the case of a corporate transferor, the adjusted basis of each separate item in the hands of the controlled Corporation immediately before the distribution of such other property to the corporate transferor in connection with the exchange.

(G) The following information as to the transferor's liabilities assumed by the controlled Corporation in the exchange:

(i) The amount and a description thereof;

(ii) When and under what circumstances created; and

(iii) The corporate business reason or reasons for assumption by the controlled Corporation.

(4) Permanent records in substantial form shall be kept by every taxpayer who participates in the type of exchange described in section 351, showing the information listed above, in order to facilitate the determination of gain or loss from a subsequent disposition of stock or securities and other property, if any, received in the exchange.

§ 37.6 Ruling Check List

(a) Purpose. The purpose of this Revenue Procedure [83] is to set forth in a convenient checklist questionnaire the information necessary to be included in a request for a ruling under section 351 of the Internal Revenue Code of 1954, which relates to transfers to a Corporation controlled by the transferor.

(b) Background. The Internal Revenue Service receives many requests for rulings in which the information furnished as to the proposed transaction is not complete enough to permit a determination to be made. In such cases, it is necessary to secure additional facts from the taxpayer before the ruling request can be considered. This procedure is time consuming for both Service personnel and taxpayers and delays issuance of the final ruling letter. This checklist will fa-

83. Rev.Proc. 73–10, 1978–1, C.B. 760.

cilitate the filing of requests for rulings under section 351 of the Code by showing specific information which should be included so that the application will be as complete as possible when originally filed. However, since the information necessary to rule on a particular transaction depends upon all the facts and circumstances of that case, information in addition to that suggested in this Revenue Procedure may be required. Nevertheless, careful use of the checklist should avoid much needless delay and permit the issuance of rulings in the most expeditious fashion possible.

The authority and general procedures of the National Office of the Internal Revenue Service and of the Office of the District Directors of Internal Revenue with respect to the issuance of advance rulings and determination letters are outlined in Revenue Procedure 72–3, C.B. 1972–1, 698. Careful attention to all the requirements of that Revenue Procedure will also serve to minimize needless delays in processing requests for rulings.

§ 37.7 Information to Be Included in Requests for Rulings Under § 351 of the Code

Each of the items included in this Section should be specifically dealt with in the ruling application even though apparent nonapplicability exists. For example, if in subsection 3.01–1 the transferee Corporation has not yet been formed, the application should identify the item and so state. Presentation of the information should follow the format of this Revenue Procedure as closely as possible. If an item is not applicable, the letters "N. A." may be inserted after that section or subsection to so indicate.

.01 Information Regarding Transferee Corporation

1. Name, identification number, and place and date of incorporation of the transferee Corporation.

2. Description of the business of the transferee Corporation.

3. The location of the District Office that will have audit jurisdiction over the return of the transferee Corporation, or other appropriate party to the transaction, and a statement whether, to the best knowledge of the taxpayer or his representative, the identical issue is being considered by any field office of the Service in connection with the active examination or audit of a tax return already filed or is being considered by a branch office of the Appellate Division. See Revenue Procedure 72–3, C. B. 1972–1, 698.

Transfer to Corporation

1. Property. Describe fully all types and categories of property, tangible and intangible, to be transferred to the Corporation by each transferor and identify specifically each transferor.

2. Services. Describe fully all services to be performed by any transferor or other party for or on behalf of the corporate transferee in connection with the transaction and the consideration to be received in exchange therefor.

3. Existing Business. (a) Assets and Liabilities. Identify on a balance sheet of the existing business the assets to be transferred to, and the liabilities to be assumed by, the transferee. Indicate which of these assets, if any, were received by a transferor as part of a plan of liquidation of another Corporation.

(b) Income and Expenses. State the accounting method of the transferors of an existing business:

(1) Unreported Income. Indicate the amount that will be transferred to the Corporation, such as receivables of a proprietorship reporting on the cash receipts and disbursements method of accounting, unfinished construction contracts, commissions due, installment obligations owed by the transferee to the transferor, etc. Identify these amounts on the balance sheet referred to in subsection 3(a) above. Also state the amount of such items of income which will be retained by the transferor. Furnish full information as to the reporting of all unreported income.

(2) Reserve for Bad Debts. State the amount of any reserve for bad debts attributable to accounts or other receivables being transferred.

(3) Liabilities for Expenses. State the amount that will be assumed by the corporate transferee for which a deduction has not been taken for Federal income tax purposes. Identify these amounts on the balance sheet referred to in subsection 3(a) above. Also state the amount of expenses payable of the business which will not be assumed by the transferee. Furnish full information as to the treatment of all these expenses.

(c) Partners and Partnerships. State whether the Partners' interests in the Partnership or the Partnership's assets will be transferred and whether the Partnership will be liquidated.

4. Patents or Patent Applications. Furnish the following information in regard to each:

(a) The country issuing the patent or in which an application has been filed.

(b) The number of each patent or patent application.

(c) Does the patent or patent application cover a product or process? Describe the product or process.

(d) Is the transferee granted the exclusive right to make, use, and sell the product, or the exclusive right to use the process, in the issuing country for the life of the patent?

(e) Are all the rights granted to the transferor by the issuing country being transferred? Describe any limitations on the use of the patent by the transferee, including the right to sublicense or subassign.

(f) Describe the circumstances under which the patent rights granted to the transferee may be revoked or otherwise terminated.

5. Trade-marks or trade names. Furnish the following information or answers requested in regard to each:

(a) The trade name and a description of the trade-mark.

(b) The country or countries in which the transferee will be granted rights to use the trade-mark or trade name.

(c) Is the transferor the registered user of the trade-mark or trade name in those countries referred to in (b) above? Describe the rights granted to the transferor by each country in which it is a registered user. If the transferor is not the registered user in any of the countries, state the rights, if any, which the transferor has with respect to use of the trade-mark or trade name in that country and the laws under which such rights are granted and protected.

(d) Will the transferee have the exclusive right to use in perpetuity the trade-mark or trade name in each case?

(e) Will the transferee be granted all those rights granted to the transferor by each country in which the transferor claims rights exist which are being transferred? Describe any limitations on the use of the trade-mark or trade name, including the right to sublicense or subassign.

(f) Describe the circumstances under which the rights granted to the transferee may be revoked or otherwise terminated.

6. For information and statements required to be included in an application involving an agreement which purports to furnish technical "know-how" in exchange for stock in a transfer within the meaning of section 351 of the Code, see Revenue Procedure 69–19, C.B. 1969–2, 301.

7. Stock of Another Corporation. If stock of another Corporation is part or all of the property transferred, state what percentage of such stock and stock of the corporate transferee is owned actually and constructively by the transferor (see section 304 of the Code).

8. Other Information on Transfer. (a) Retained Rights. State what rights, if any, the transferors will retain in the property transferred.

(b) Licenses, Leases, etc. Describe any licenses, leases, etc., to be granted in exchange for stock or securities.

(c) Leaseback. Describe any property to be transferred to the corporation that will be leased back to a transferor, other Stockholder, or a related party. Furnish the terms of the lease and identify the lessee.

Liabilities

1. Assumption of Liabilities. (a) State the amount and basis of assets:

(1) State the amount of the liabilities that will be assumed by the corporate transferee (including those identified in 3(a) above) or to which the property transferred will be subject with respect to each transferor.

(2) Indicate the tax basis of the property transferred by each transferor.

(b) Nature of Liability and Purpose of Assumption. Describe fully each liability, give the date incurred, and explain the circumstances under which the liabilities that will be assumed by the corporate transferee were created. State the business reason or purpose for the assumption of liabilities.

(c) Liability Owed to Transferee. Identify any of these liabilities to be assumed that are owed to the corporate transferee and explain how they will be discharged.

2. Indicate the amount and types of indebtedness between transferee and transferors, or other Stockholders, other than that created by recurring arm's-length sales, purchases, etc., in the normal course of business. If a Partnership is a transferor, describe any indebtedness between the Partnership and Partners prior to the exchange. Explain when and how any indebtedness included here was created and how it will be discharged in each case. If this indebtedness was acquired at less than face amount, state the original cost and adjusted basis in the hands of the creditor.

Consideration from the Transferee

1. Stock. A description of each class and the number of shares of each class to be issued to each person for:

(a) Property. See .02–2 above and identify the services. Indicate those persons who will also receive stock for property. If the services identified above were not rendered or are not to be rendered for the benefit of the corporate transferee give a full explanation.

2. Indebtedness. State the principal amount of indebtedness and its terms to be created in favor of each person for:

(a) Property. See .02–1 above and identify the property of each transferor.

(b) Services. See .02–2 above and identify the services.

3. Other Property in Addition to Stock and Indebtedness. Indicate the amount and provide a complete description of any other

property that will be issued to each transferor or other person (identify each) including, but not limited to:

(a) Cash.

(b) Stock rights, warrants, or certificates of contingent interest with the terms of each.

4. Consideration Substantially in Proportion to Interest Transferred. Will each person receive stock, securities, or other property substantially in proportion to his interest in the property transferred to the Corporation or services to be rendered for the benefit of the Corporation? If not, give a full explanation.

Control by Transferors

1. Stock Outstanding Immediately Before Transaction. (a) Furnish a description and the total number of shares of each class outstanding.

(b) State the total number of shares of each class held by a Stockholder who will be a transferor in the exchange.

(c) Indicate the total number of shares of each class held by each Stockholder owning five percent or more of a class and the number of Stockholders owning the balance of each class outstanding.

2. Stock Outstanding Immediately after Transaction. (a) Indicate the total number of shares of each class:

(1) Shares outstanding immediately before transaction.

(2) Shares issued for property.

(3) Shares issued for services.

(b) Indicate the total number and percent of shares of each class held by each transferor:

(1) Shares held immediately before transaction.

(2) Shares received for property.

(3) Shares received for services.

3. Plan and Dates of Exchanges. (a) Will the transfers and exchanges occur pursuant to a plan agreed upon prior to the transaction in which the rights of the parties are defined?

(b) Public offering planned:

(1) Indicate the total number of shares of each class involved.

(2) If underwriters are involved, give names and explain whether the underwriter will purchase such shares for their own account or will act as agent for the transferee Corporation.

(c) Stock rights, warrants, or subscriptions:

(1) If any of the rights, warrants, or subscriptions of the corporate transferee are outstanding or will be issued or offered

in the near future give the total number of shares of each class of stock involved.

(2) Explain the circumstances in which they were or will be issued or offered.

4. Disposition of Stock by Transferors. (a) Indicate the number of shares of each class, if any, that each transferor will dispose of after the exchange.

(b) State the consideration to be received.

(c) Provide the names of the acquiring parties and their relationship, if any, to the corporate transferee or Stockholder-transferor.

(d) State the circumstances and reasons for the disposition including any agreements between the parties.

(e) If there are, or will be, any options to purchase stock from any of the transferors, give full particulars.

General

1. Business Reasons or Purpose. Explain the business reasons for the transaction.

2. Activities of Transferee. Will it remain in existence and retain and use the property transferred to it in an active trade or business?

3. Disposition of Property. Identify any of the transferred property that the transferee expects to dispose of other than through normal business operations and give full particulars concerning the proposed disposition.

4. Related, Connected, or Step Transactions. Describe any loans, sales, exchanges, or other transactions, other than recurring arm's-length sales, purchases, etc., in the normal course of business, that will occur or are contemplated whether or not considered as related to or in connection with the exchange.

Special Corporations

1. Investment Company. Furnish any information not otherwise requested necessary to determine that the transfer is not one to any of the investment companies defined in the regulations.

2. Small Business Corporation. Does the Corporation intend to make the election under section 1372(a) of the Code to be taxed as a "small business Corporation" as defined in section 1371 of the Code?

Copies of Documents to Be Submitted with Request

1. Balance Sheets. Latest of transferee Corporation or other business involved.

2. Plan or Agreement of Exchange. If one has been committed to writing.

3. Securities. If it is contended that any part or all of the indebtedness described is "securities" within the meaning of section 351 of the Code submit:

(a) A brief explaining why.

(b) A copy of the note or other evidence of the indebtedness and loan agreement, if any.

Assumptions or Representations if Applicable

1. Foreign Transferee. If the transfer is to a foreign Corporation, see section 367 of the Code and Revenue Procedure 68–23, C.B. 1968–1, 821.

Inquiries

Inquiries in regard to the Revenue Procedure should refer to its number and should be addressed to the Assistant Commissioner (Technical), Attention: T:I:R, Internal Revenue Service, Washington, D. C. 20224.

Library References:

West's Key No. Digests, Internal Revenue ⚷3642.

§ 37.8 Cross References

In addition to the above discussion, the following may be helpful:

(1) Discussion of issuance of stock and securities for Stockholder services (see Chapter 56, infra).

(2) Discussion of the issuance of Corporate liabilities (i. e.: securities and short term debt) at the time of incorporation (see Chapter 38, infra).

§§ 37.9–38.0 are reserved for supplementary material.

PART C

CORPORATE FINANCE—GENERALLY

CHAPTER 38

CORPORATE FINANCE

Table of Sections

A. METHODS OF FINANCING—GENERALLY

B. EQUITY (STOCK)

C. DEBT FINANCING

D. TAX IMPLICATIONS OF THE ISSUANCE OF STOCK AND DEBT

A. METHODS OF FINANCING—GENERALLY

Library References:

C.J.S. Corporations §§ 192 et seq., 197.
West's Key No. Digests, Corporations 🔑60 et seq.

§ 38.1 The Fundamental Difference Between "Equity" and "Debt"

The distinction between "equity" and "debt" underlies much of the modern law and practice relating to Corporation finance. At the simplest level the distinction is easy to grasp. A "debt" is something that must be repaid: it is the result of a "loan", the person making the loan is a "creditor", and if periodic payments are made, they generally include "interest", which is the charge made for the time-use of the money loaned. On the other hand, "equity" represents an ownership interest in the business itself. One thinks in terms of "Stockholders", shares of "capital stock", voting, and "dividends" rather than "interest." This distinction is often expressed in terms of the types of securities involved: typical debt securities are notes, debentures and bonds,[1] while equity securities consist of shares

1. Technically, a debenture is an unsecured corporate obligation while a bond is secured by a lien or mortgage on corporate property. However, the word "bond" is often used indiscriminately to cover both bonds and debentures.

Other characteristics of debt securities are: (1) They are traditionally bearer instruments, negotiable by delivery, with interest payments represented by coupons. However, registered debt securities are well known. Article 8 of the Uniform Commerical Code, gives registered debt securities attributes of negotiability. (2) Interest payments are usually fixed obligations, due in any event, and expressed as a percentage of the face amount of the security. However, so called income bonds, in which the obligation to pay interest is conditioned

of capital stock, common stock, and preferred stock, either participating or non-participating.[2] It is sometimes not realized, however, that as a matter of economics, the distinction between debt and equity may not be at all clear in many situations. For example, how does a subordinated, 100 year income debenture differ from preferred stock? It is also possible to create a mixed or "hybrid" security which has some of the characteristics of debt and some of equity.[3]

Despite the lack of clear distinction between debt and equity in some situations, legal and tax consequences vary substantially depending on how the particular security is classified. Important areas in which this classification is significant are income taxation, rights on bankruptcy or insolvency, and the right to participate in management. The classification of hybrid securities for tax purposes, in particular, has given rise to considerable litigation.[4] In general, a security may be treated as a debt security for some purposes and as an equity security for other purposes.

§ 38.2 General Considerations

The capitalization of a new Corporation involves several decisions on which the advice of an attorney can be most beneficial.

on adequate corporate earnings, are well known. Somewhat rarer are so-called participating bonds, where the interest obligation increases with corporate earnings. (3) Debt securities are usually subject to redemption, which permits the Corporation to pay off the obligation before it is due, often at a premium over the face value. (4) Debt securities may be subordinated to the payment of other obligations of the Corporation. (5) Debt securities may be convertible into other classes of stock, particularly common stock. Convertible debentures are treated as equity securities for many purposes. See, e. g. 15 U.S.C.A. § 78c (a)(11). (6) Some states authorize holders of bonds or debentures to participate in the selection of the board of directors upon specified contingencies.

See §§ 38.31–38.34, infra, for additional discussion of debt securities.

2. See § 38.12, infra, for a discussion of the classes of equity securities.

3. The use of hybrid securities is often questionable as a business matter because of lack of certainty as to how the instruments will be treated for tax purposes. Also, unusual securities may be difficult to market publicly.

4. The leading cases are John Kelley Co. v. Commissioner, Talbot Mills v. Commissioner, 1946, 326 U.S. 521, 698, 66 S.Ct. 299, 90 L.Ed. 278. The Court stated, "The documents under consideration embody elements of obligations and elements of stock. There is no one characteristic, not even exclusion from management, which can be said to be decisive in the determination of whether the obligations are risk investments in the Corporation or debt. So called stock certificates may be authorized by Corporations which are really debt and promises to pay may be executed which have incidents if stock. * * * " Rather unrealistically, the Court added: "These cases now under consideration deal with well understood words as used in the tax statutes—'interest' and 'dividends.' They need no further definition." 326 U.S., at 530, 66 S.Ct., at 304.

For additional discussion see § 38.3 and § 38.43, infra.

How much capital is usually a business decision. Who is to supply it, and in what form, are also basically business decisions, though attorneys should try to make sure that their clients do not inadvertently violate the federal and state securities acts in their attempts to raise capital. However, a combination of corporate law and tax law principles may dictate answers to the following questions:

> First, should the contributions of the Stockholder be in the form of capital contributions or in the form of Stockholder loans to the Corporation? Usually it is desirable for some of the capital to be in the form of Stockholder loans, and in some situations it may be essential, but as is true with most things, it is possible to have too much of a good thing. See chapter 37, supra.
>
> Second, should the Corporation issue more than one class of shares?
>
> Third, should the shares be par value shares or no par value shares; how many should be authorized, how many should be sold, and at what price? Generally, the choice should be between nominal par value or no par value shares. Usually, more shares should be authorized than are planned to be sold.

The organizers of a business must keep in mind the need to furnish the Corporation with sufficient capital, in exchange for shares, to afford a sound financial basis for the business operation. A failure to do this may lead to denial of limited liability; it may also result in denial of claimed "interest" deductions on the corporate income tax return.

Many methods of financing a business, in addition to the sale of shares, are available. Most can be characterized as short-term, long-term, or intermediate, according to the length of time the funds they raise normally can be used by the business. Various governmental aids to business include several types of lending assistance. State municipalities may be willing to provide facilities for industry, under a long-term leasing arrangement or by providing the framework for the issuance by the Corporation of tax free bonds. Leasing of facilities and equipment is inceasing in popularity, and recent years have seen use of the "sale and lease-back".

The lawyer may have to participate actively in the arrangements for some of these types of financing.

§ 38.3 Dividing Investment Between Shares and Debt

The decision whether to treat investment in a Corporation as equity or as debt, or partly as both, is influenced by various factors. These may be characterized as involving tax aspects, other legal aspects, and non-legal aspects.

Provided the investment in "debt" securities will be so treated for tax purposes rather than as a disguised equity investment, there are four reasons why the federal income tax laws [5] favor small equity and large debt. First, interest paid by a Corporation on its outstanding debt is deductible as an expense, for corporate tax purposes; [6] dividends paid to Stockholders are not.[7] Secondly, the "debt" investment may be repaid without tax consequences; a redemption of stock may be treated as the payment of a dividend.[8] Thirdly, accumulation of a large surplus is less likely to be treated as an "improper" or "unreasonable" accumulation, if there is substantial debt to be paid off, than if the Corporation has less debt.[9] Fourth, in the event of loss, the equity investment will be subject to capital loss treatment to the extent Internal Revenue Code § 1244 is not available while the debt may be treated as a fully deductible business bad debt or as a short-term capital loss.[10] If the equity investment is so small that the enterprise obviously is undercapitalized, courts may be inclined to treat the "debt" as actually an equity investment, and to deny the tax advantages just mentioned.

If the Corporation is to elect Subchapter S treatment, under federal tax laws, for part of its life, investment in the Corporation probably should be substantially in equity form. One of the requirements to qualify for the election is that the Corporation have only one class of stock outstanding.[11] Treasury Regulations state that "if an instrument purporting to be a debt obligation is actually stock, it will constitute a second class of stock." [12] If so, the Corporation will be disqualified to elect under Subchapter S. The regulation, if valid, means that "loans from Stockholders will throw a cloud over a small business corporation if their loans are substantially in proportion to their equity holdings. The Tax Court, in a divided opinion, has questioned the validity of the regulation.[13]

If a substantial part of a Corporation's capital is in the form of debt, the legal rights of the creditors may be a threat to successful continuation of the Corporation. In a number of instances, also, the "owners" will be expected to guarantee corporate debts, and their investment is risked as much as if they had taken equity securities. And if too little of their investment is in the form of share capital, a

5. And also state Corporation income tax laws, which follow federal law on the points involved.

6. IRC § 163.

7. IRC § 161.

8. IRC § 302.

9. IRC § 531.

10. IRC §§ 165, 166.

11. IRC § 1371(a)(4). Subchapter S is considered in greater detail in Chapters 85 and 86, infra.

12. Reg. 1.1371–1(g).

13. Gamman, 46 T.C. 1 (1966). See Ury, Subchapter S: A Trap for the Unwary, 44 Taxes 473, 477–480 (1966).

court may be induced either to "pierce the veil" or to require the "owners" to postpone their claims as creditors until the claims of both preferred and general creditors have been satisfied; sometimes even public preferred Stockholders may be entitled to payment of their claims in advance of the "owner-creditor".[14]

A regulatory commission may encourage a Corporation subject to its jurisdiction to use less debt and more equity capital.

Several non-legal factors are influential in determining the choice of securities and the proportion of the various types to be used. The weight given these factors will vary according to whether the debt securities to be used would be taken by the "owners" or by outsiders who have no desire to acquire an equity interest. Funds may be needed later for future expansion. This dictates that initial debt burdens not be so large as to impair the possibility of obtaining credit at a later time in the enterprise's history. Promoters or present management may desire to protect control of the Corporation. This suggests a preference for non-voting shares or debt securities, and tax considerations may influence that choice. When outside investors are sought, their views as to the "optimum capitalization", and the traditions and fashions current in the securities market at the time are of great significance. Ordinarily, bonds should be used only when future earnings are expected to be reasonably stable and sufficient to meet the interest and sinking fund requirements with a large cushion to spare. If outside investors are sought, the cost of obtaining financing is an important consideration, as is the opportunity of the equity investors for leverage, or "trading on the equity".

An investor may not wish to place more than a certain amount of capital at the risk of the business, but he may be willing to advance additional funds as a secured creditor. Debt may be employed to provide the lender with a senior interest—i. e., a preference over Stockholders for the return on his investment and for the return of his investment upon liquidation. Debt instruments can be given by a Stockholder to his family members or to a charitable organization without diluting the transferor's control of the Corporation. Debt can be used as a form of bail-out by selling the same and thus presently realizing the future growth of the Corporation.

If a corporate business fails, a creditor's losses on the Corporation's debt instruments will be treated as ordinary losses. In contrast if the amount loaned had instead been invested in common stock of the Corporation the loss on that stock will only qualify for an ordinary loss deduction if the terms of § 1244 are met. See § 39.4, infra.

14. This is the philosophy of the Deep Rock Doctrine. See Pepper v. Litton, 308 U.S. 295, 60 S.Ct. 238, 84 L.Ed. 281 (1939); Stone v. Eacho, 127 F.2d 284 (4th Cir. 1942), rehearing denied 128 F.2d 16, certiorari denied 317 U. S. 635, 63 S.Ct. 54, 87 L.Ed. 512. Cf. Darling Stores Corp. v. Young Realty Corp., 121 F.2d 112 (8th Cir. 1941), certiorari denied 314 U.S. 658, 62 S. Ct. 111, 86 L.Ed. 527.

If a Subchapter S election were made, the operating losses of the business are deductible by the Stockholder to the extent of his basis in both stock and debt of the Corporation. Thus, debt may be used in conjunction with a Subchapter S election to increase the availability of losses without making an additional capital contribution. See Chapters 85 and 86, infra.

A sharp distinction should be drawn between debts owed to third persons and debts owed to Stockholders. Both may be advantageous to a Corporation, but the reasons are different. Some debt owed to third persons is often desirable because of the factor of *leveraging.* Leveraging arises when the Corporation is able to earn more on the borrowed capital than the cost of the borrowing. The entire excess is allocable to the equity accounts of the Corporation, thereby increasing the rate of return on the equity invested in the Corporation. An example should help to make this clear. Assume that A is a Corporation with a total invested capital of $500,000. Let us consider the earnings per share on two alternative assumptions: (a) all this capital is invested as equity capital, e. g. 50,000 shares sold at $10.00 per share, and (b) half is borrowed on a long term basis, and the other half is contributed capital, e. g. 25,000 shares sold at $10.00 per share.

Alternative A

Assumed net earnings	$25,000	$100,000	$150,000	$200,000
Number of shares	50,000	50,000	50,000	50,000
Earnings per share	$0.50	$2.00	$3.00	$4.00

Alternative B

Assumed net earnings	$25,000	$100,000	$150,000	$200,000
Interest on bonds (8% on $250,000)	$20,000	$20,000	$20,000	$20,000
Earnings allocable to common	$5000	$80,000	$130,000	$180,000
Number of shares	25,000	25,000	25,000	25,000
Earnings per share	$0.05	$3.20	$5.20	$7.20

In alternative B, the interest represents a fixed cost, a charge for obtaining the use of $250,000 of capital. When earnings are low, debt service takes up most of the earnings: in the hypothetical above, if earnings drop below $20,000, alternative B will show losses while alternative A continues to show modest profits until earnings drop to zero. When earnings increase above $20,000, however, the per share earnings under alternative B rises much more rapidly than alternative A even though the shares are otherwise identical. In effect in alternative B the common Stockholders are getting $500,000 to work for them even though they contributed only $250,000 at the cost of the fixed interest charge which they must meet out of their own capital if necessary. Even this fixed charge is partially offset by the tax saving resulting from the deductibility of the interest. This is leveraging, a device well understood by real estate syndicates and promoters who seek to obtain the largest possible mortgage and the smallest possible equity investment of their own. The risk, of course, is that the income from the project may not be sufficient to cover the fixed charges, and the equity investors may quickly be wiped out.

Section 385 authorizes the Secretary to promulgate regulations defining the standards to be employed in determining whether an interest in a Corporation is to be treated as stock or debt. The Secretary is given a free hand to establish guidelines for such a determination, but the statute suggests five factors that the Secretary might wish to include in his list:

- whether there is a written unconditional promise to pay the debt on demand or on a specified date and to pay a fixed rate of interest;
- whether there is a subordination to or preference over a debt of the Corporation;
- whether the debt is convertible into stock;
- the relationship between stock holdings and holdings of the debt;
- the ratio of debt to equity of the Corporation—the "debt-equity ratio."

These standards are set forth in Treas.Regs. § 1.385–1 et seq. (see pages 424–426, infra).

The court decisions on the "hybrid stock" question have relied on a number of different factors which have been accorded varying degrees of significance. In *Fin Hay Realty*,[15] the Third Circuit identified 16 different factors to be weighed in resolving this question. The Third Circuit emphasized in *Fin Hay* that the various factors that have been identified by the courts "are only aids in answering the ultimate question whether the investment, analyzed in terms of its economic reality, constitutes risk capital entirely subject to the fortunes of the corporate-venture or represents a strict debtor-creditor

15. Fin Hay Realty Co. v. U. S., 398 F. 2d 694, 697 (3d Cir. 1968). See also Slappey Drive Indus. Park v. U. S., 561 F.2d 572 (5th Cir. 1977); Scriptomatic, Inc. v. U. S., 555 F.2d 364 (3d Cir. 1977). See Plumb, The Federal Income Tax Significance of Corporate Debt: A Critical Analysis and a Proposal, 26 Tax L.Rev. 369 (1971). See also Kahn, Basic Corporate Taxation (3d Ed.) § 8.33.

relationship."[16] Some of the most important factors that have been examined by the various courts in determining whether a debt instrument constitutes hybrid stock are:

(1) Does this debt instrument have an interest provision? This weighs in favor of it being a security debt.[17]

(2) Is the debt-equity ratio too high? Over 10:1 may be excessive and thus the debt will probably be held to be "stock" because it represents an equity interest.[18]

(3) Is the debt held proportionate to stockholdings? This weighs in favor of it being stock.[19]

(4) Is the debt subordinate to other debt holders? This weighs in favor of it being stock.[20]

(5) Is the debt secured? This weighs in favor of it being a security or nonsecurity debt.

(6) Is this type of loan realistic? This weighs in favor of it being a security or nonsecurity debt.[21]

(7) Does the business have likely prospects for success? This weighs in favor of it being stock.[22]

(8) Whether the debt was given in exchange for the Corporation's primary asset. This weighs in favor of it being stock.[23]

(9) When is the note due? Generally only due in more than 5 years will be considered a security rather than a non-security. However, a one year note has been held to be a security.[24]

This latter factor is the most important factor in distinguishing non-security and security debt because the other factors recited above generally arise in the context of whether or not the debt is to be classified as "stock".

The debt-equity ratio is one of the more important factors to be considered in determining whether debt is hybrid stock. Where the amount of a Corporation's outstanding debt is disproportionately high with respect to the amount of capital invested in the Corporation, the situation is described as a "thin incorporation." The thin incorporation concept is rarely applicable if the debt-equity ratio is less than 3:1, but that ratio should not be regarded as a bench mark.

16. See also Joseph Lupowitz Sons, Inc. v. Commissioner, 497 F.2d 862, 865–66, n. 8 (3d Cir. 1974); Trans-Atlantic Co. v. Commissioner, 469 F.2d 1189, 1193 (3d Cir. 1972).

17. IRC § 385.

18. Ibid.

19. Ibid.

20. Ibid.

21. Rev.Rul. 68–54, 1968–1 C.B. 69.

22. Ibid.

23. Schnitzer v. Comm'r, 13 T.C. 43 (1949), affirmed per curiam 183 F.2d 70 (9th Cir.), certiorari denied 340 U.S. 911, 71 S.Ct. 291.

24. Campbell v. Carter Foundation Production Co., 322 F.2d 827 (5th Cir. 1963); Camp Wolters Enterprises, Inc. v. Comm'r, 22 T.C. 737, 750–751 (1955), affirmed 230 F.2d 555 (5th Cir.), cert. denied 352 U.S. 826, 77 S.Ct. 39, 1 L.Ed.2d 49.

In appropriate circumstances, a very high debt-equity ratio has been sustained.[25] A thin capitalization does not require that the debt be characterized as stock; it is merely one factor, albeit a highly significant factor, in determining whether the debt is hybrid stock.[26] Most commentators feel that a debt-equity ratio of greater than 10:1 virtually conclusive of equity (i. e. stock) characterization in most circumstances.

Where an ongoing business is contributed to a Corporation, goodwill of that business may be added to the Corporation's assets in mitigation of an imbalance in favor of debt.[27] However, the Fifth Circuit has held that the value of many intangible assets should not be taken into account, and that courts should consider such assets only where there is convincing evidence that they have a direct and primary relationship to the well being of the Corporation.[28]

As the foregoing suggests, the question of whether a purported debt instrument constitutes an equity investment has been unsettled and the numerous decisions in this area often contradictory. Recent regulations [29] however have greatly clarified this debt-equity issue by adopting specific criteria and standards for determining when certain interests in a corporation are treated as stock of indebtedness under IRC § 385. While reference should be made to these Regulations in their entirety, Reg. § 1.385–6(g) relating to debt-to-equity ratios provides as follows:

25. E. g., Baker Commodities, Inc., 48 T.C. 374 (1967), sustaining a debt-equity ratio of almost 700:1 where cash flow and earning power of the Corporation were sufficient to pay debts. See also Gloucester Ice & Cold Storage Co. v. Commissioner, 298 F.2d 183 (1st Cir. 1962).

26. Baker Commodities, Inc., 48 T.C. 374 (1967); Gooding Amusement Co., 23 T.C. 408 (1954), affirmed 236 F.2d 159 (6th Cir.), certiorari denied 352 U.S. 1031, 77 S.Ct. 595, 1 L.Ed.2d 599; Lots, Inc., 49 T.C. 541 (1968), acq. 1968–2 Cum.Bull. 2. In *Lots*, the Tax Court held that loans from a principal Stockholder of the Corporation constituted debt even though the Corporation was thinly capitalized. See Berkowitz v. U. S., 411 F.2d 818 (5th Cir. 1969), affirming a judgment n. o. v. which had overturned a jury verdict granting interest deductions on loans made to a Corporation by its Stockholders when the debt-equity ratio exceeded 21:1. In *Berkowitz*, the Fifth Circuit emphasized, however, that no single test was conclusive in determining this issue, and the court listed 11 factors to be considered. In Scriptomatic, Inc. v. U. S., 555 F.2d 364 (3d Cir. 1977), aff'g 397 F.Supp. 753 (E.D.Pa.1975), a jury verdict for the government that a purported debt instrument was actually an equity investment was overturned by the district court who granted a judgment n. o. v. for the taxpayer and held that the purported "debt" instrument was in fact a debt even though the debt-capital ratio was 16:1. The Third Circuit affirmed.

27. E. g. Estate of Miller v. Commissioner, 239 F.2d 729 (9th Cir. 1956); Murphy Logging Co. v. U. S., 378 F. 2d 222 (9th Cir. 1967).

28. Plantation Patterns, Inc. v. Commissioner, 462 F.2d 712 (5th Cir. 1972), certiorari denied, 409 U.S. 1076, 93 S.Ct. 683, 34 L.Ed.2d 664. In *Plantation Patterns*, the court refused to include a value for the business acumen and financial skill of the principal officer and owner of the business. However, the court did state that in appropriate cases the value of intangible assets should be included in determining the debt-equity ratio.

29. Regs. § 1.385–1 to 1.385–10. Adopted T.D. 7747, Dec. 31, 1980; amended

(g) Debt-to-Equity Ratio. The following rules apply for purposes of the regulations under section 385:

(1) In General. The debt-to-equity ratio of a corporation is the ratio that—

(i) The corporation's liabilities (excluding trade accounts payable, accrued operating expenses and taxes, and other similar items) bears to

(ii) The stockholders' equity.

(2) Stockholders' Equity. The stockholders' equity in a corporation is the excess of—

(i) The adjusted basis of its assets (less reserves for bad debts, if applicable, and other similar asset offsets) over

(ii) Its liabilities (including liabilities excluded under paragraph (g) (1) (i) of this section).

(3) Operating Rules. Except as provided in paragraph (g) (5) of this section, the adjusted basis of a corporation's assets and the amount of its liabilities are determined—

(i) In accordance with the tax accounting principles properly used by the corporation in determining taxable income; and

(ii) Without regard to the treatment of any interest as stock or indebtedness by reason of section 385, except that preferred stock is considered a liability if it is treated as indebtedness under the regulations under section 385.

(4) Illustrations. The following examples illustrate the application of this paragraph (g):

Example A. On December 31, 1990, corporation M has assets with an adjusted basis of $150,000 and liabilities of $100,000. The stockholders' equity in M is $50,000 (i. e., $150,000 – $100,000). Assume that M has no trade accounts payable, accrued taxes and operating expenses, etc., and that the special rules in paragraph (g) (5) of this section do not apply. Based on these facts, the debt-to-equity ratio of corporation M on December 31, 1990 is 2:1 (i. e., $100,000:$50,000).

Example B. On December 31, 1990, corporation N has assets with an adjusted basis of $150,000. In addition, N has liabilities of $100,000, including $30,000 of trade accounts payable, accrued taxes and operating expenses, etc. The stockholders' equity in N is $50,000 (i. e., $150,000 – $100,000). Assume that the special rules in paragraph (g) (5) of this section do not apply. Based on these facts, N has a debt-to-equity ratio on December 31, 1990 of 7:5 (i. e., $70,000:$50,000).

T.D. 7744, May 4, 1981. Applicable to instruments (as defined in Reg. § 1.385–3(c)) and preferred stock issued after December 31, 1981, and to loans described in § 1.385–7 and guaranteed loans made after December 31, 1981.

Example C. On December 31, 1982, foreign corporation F organizes domestic corporation D to acquire and operate a coal mine. D uses the calendar year as the taxable year. Assume that F transfers $10 million to D on December 31, 1982, in exchange for $5 million of 28-percent, 25-year debentures and 100 shares of common stock. Also assume that the interest rate generally paid on similar debentures issued to independent creditors by corporations of the same general size and in the same general industry, geographical location, and financial condition is approximately 14 percent and that 28 percent is higher than the 3 rates described in paragraph (e)(2)(i) of this section (relating to the reasonable rate of interest rule of convenience). Based on these facts, the fair market value of the debentures is approximately $9.8 million. Therefore, the balance sheet of D on December 31, 1982 is approximately as follows:

Assets—$10 million cash. Liabilities and stockholders' equity—$5.0 million debentures; $4.8 million bond premium: $9.8 million total liabilities; $0.2 million stockholders' equity = $10.0 million.

Accordingly, D has a debt-to-equity ratio of approximately 49:1 (i. e., $9.8 million:$0.2 million).

An excessive amount of debt may constitute an intolerable burden for a burgeoning Corporation. The Corporation's interest payments on the debt may inhibit its growth and possibly endanger its existence. If the lenders refrain from collecting the interest in order to permit the Corporation to use the funds, and if they do not collect the principal on maturity, the risk of the debt's being characterized as hybrid stock is increased.

Leveraging can be obtained only by the use of other people's money. Nevertheless it is often advantageous for business reasons for Stockholders to advance a portion of their investment in the business in the form of loans rather than capital contributions.[30] (The tax advantages of doing this have previously been discussed.) As a creditor, a Stockholder may have greater rights upon bankruptcy or insolvency than he would as a mere Stockholder. However, if the loans are advanced as part of the original capitalization of the company, there is a substantial risk that Stockholders' claims as a creditor will be subordinated to the claims of general creditors under the so-called "Deep Rock" doctrine. Loans for subsequent business needs may fare better.[31] It is also possible that a creditor Stockholder may become a secured creditor ahead of general trade creditors, though the court may be tempted to set aside the preferred position under the Deep Rock doctrine, or on the general theory that the lien constitutes a fraud on creditors.

30. Some leverage is obtained if the loans by Stockholders are made on a basis other than in proportion to their stockholdings.

31. See Arnold v. Phillips, 117 F.2d 497 (5th Cir. 1941), certiorari denied Phillips v. Arnold, 313 U.S. 583, 61 S.Ct. 1102, 85 L.Ed. 1539.

A common use of Stockholder debt is to equalize the position of the various Stockholders who are investing in a new Corporation. Assume that A and B have agreed to go into a business with A providing the necessary capital of $50,000 and B providing services in the future. A and B have also agreed that A is to have a 60 per cent interest and B a 40 per cent interest in the business.

Since shares cannot normally be issued for promises for future services,[32] the Corporation cannot simply be capitalized by A paying $50,000 for 60 shares and B receiving 40 shares upon entering into a long term employment contract with the new Corporation. While several different solutions may be suggested,[33] the simplest is to establish the capital of the Corporation at the statutory minimum of $1,000; issue A 60 shares for $600, issue B 40 shares for $400, and have A lend $49,000 to the Corporation. In a sense the shares represent nothing but the future potential profitability of the Corporation, while A receives compensation for the use of his capital in the form of interest, the amount and terms of which must be negotiated by A and B. Perhaps one further variation should be added. The suggested Corporation has $49,000 of debt and only $1,000 of equity. As discussed in the following sections, there is a substantial risk that the 49–1 ratio would cause the court to treat the $49,000 as equity for tax and insolvency purposes, or possibly pierce the corporate veil (even though recognizing it as debt for purposes of determining the rights of A and B). These desirable advantages of debt might be preserved if preferred shares rather than debt is issued for perhaps $25,000 of the debt, and debt for the balance.[34]

The pattern of using senior securities to equalize interests where one "investor" is to perform services for his equity interest is equally

32. See e. g. Texas V.A.T.S. Bus.Corp. Act, art. 2.16B.

33. Another solution is to use $1.00 par value shares and issue A 60 shares for $50,000 and B 40 shares for $40.00. There appears to be no requirement in the Texas Business Corporation Act that all shares of the same class be issued for the same consideration. However, this suggestion is manifestly unfair to A if the business does not do well and the parties desire to liquidate since B in effect would have a 40 per cent interest in the remainder of A's capital. Also it may result in the Internal Revenue Service taking the position that the bargain sale to B constituted compensation for services and was taxable income to B to the extent of 40 per cent of $50,000. The use of different classes of common stock might take care of the liquidation rights but probably would not solve the underlying tax problem.

34. In Obre v. Alban Tractor Co. (1962) 228 Md. 291, 179 A.2d 861, one Stockholder contributed equipment appraised at $63,864.86, plus $1,673.24 in cash; the other Stockholder contributed $8,495.00 worth of equipment and $1,505.00 in cash. In order to equalize the relative investments so as to have a 50–50 division of the capital stock, the first Stockholder received $10,000 par value common stock, $20,000 par value non-voting preferred stock, and an unsecured five year note for $35,548.10, with interest at 5%. The second Stockholder received $10,000 par value capital stock. In a state insolvency proceeding, the court considered the $40,000 of capital to be adequate and refused to subordinate the note to claims of general creditors.

applicable where a going Partnership or Proprietorship is to be incorporated with the infusion of new capital or new employees who are to receive an equity interest. In these situations a person may contribute appreciated property to the new Corporation in exchange for debt and/or shares of common stock, and the question may arise whether gain on the exchange will be recognized for Federal income tax purposes. An exchange of equity or debt securities for property is a taxable event unless the gain is not recognized under section 351 of the Internal Revenue Code of 1954. See Chapter 37, supra. Under this section, non-recognition of gain occurs only if the transferor or transferors of "property" receive only "stock or securities" in such Corporation and immediately after the exchange, the transferor or transferors own stock possessing at least 80 per cent of the combined voting power of all classes of stock and 80 per cent of the total number of the nonvoting shares. "Property" includes cash, personal property, real property, and intangible property, but not services. Persons contributing only services are not considered transferors in meeting the 80 per cent requirements. The phrase "stock or securities" covers equity securities and debt instruments if they fall within the concept of "security." Short term, open account indebtedness would not fall within that concept, whereas formal written instruments of fairly long duration probably would fall within that concept.[35] The difficulty of definition of this critical term is heightened because the Internal Revenue Service will ordinarily not issue rulings as to the applicability of section 351 where evidences of indebtedness are received.[36]

Library References:

West's Key No. Digests, Internal Revenue ⚷3785 et seq., 3885 et seq.
Kahn, Basic Corporate Taxation (3d Ed.) § 8.33.

§ 38.4 Allocation of Stock Between Capital and Services

The type of arrangement described above is useful when the primary contribution of one group of Stockholders is capital and the contribution of the second group of Stockholders is entrepreneurial talent, i. e., the latter group will operate the business and provide the management and expertise. The definitive treatment of this subject was written by Professor Herwitz in his excellent article in the Harvard Law Review, Allocation of Stock Between Services and Capital in

35. See generally Comment, Section 351 Transfers to Controlled Corporations: The Forgotten Term—"Securities", 114 U.Pa.L.Rev. 314 (1965). Five years is often suggested as the minimum period for an evidence of indebtedness to be considered a "security." Considerable uncertainty also exists as to whether § 351 covers transactions which take the form of a "sale" of property to a Corporation with the purchase price payable in installments over a long period of time. See Chapter 37, supra, in this regard.

36. Rev.Proc. 64–31, 1964–2 Cum.Bull. 947, § 4.01.4.

the Organization of a Close Corporation, 75 Harv.L.Rev. 1098 (1962). The following discussion summarizes some of the considerations in using preferred stock or debt for this purpose.

S and C desire to form a Corporation for the production and marketing of widgets. C will contribute $40,000 cash plus liquid assets having a fair market value of $20,000 and a tax basis of $5,000 to the enterprise. S will contribute services, including his expertise in the widgets business. S and C decide to form a Corporation to conduct the business. S is not willing to join the enterprise solely for a salary; he demands a proprietary interest in the business so that he can share in its anticipated growth which will be due in large part to his efforts and expertise. C is willing to accept S as a co-venturer, and since he values S's services as approximately equal to his capital contribution, he agrees to an equal split of the profits.

Since S will need some of the profits of the business to meet his living expenses, S will want a salary from the Corporation. Instead, the Corporation could distribute dividends to S, but that would be an extravagant waste of tax deductions, since reasonable salaries for employees are deductible and dividends are not. However, S may not wish all of his compensation in salary, since, if the business is successful, his income tax burden would soon become excessive; consequently, S will wish part of his interest in the Corporation to be reflected in growth common stocks. However, if S is to realize this gain, a market will have to be found for his stock—a prospect which can rarely be counted upon.

On the other hand, while S is receiving a salary which constitutes a senior return on his investment of services, C has no comparable senior return on his capital investment. If S is paid a salary and the net profits after payment of S's salary were then divided equally between S and C, the latter would be seriously disadvantaged. S and C might agree on an unequal distribution of common stock—i. e., 75% to C and 25% to S—to compensate for S's senior return via a salary; but the proper division depends upon the size of S's salary and the profits remaining after payment, and those figures are likely to change each year. It is difficult to estimate those figures with sufficient accuracy to arrive at an appropriate division of the stock. Moreover, an unequal division could provide C with voting control; but that can be resolved by creating two classes of common, each of which elects two directors, and issuing one class to C and one class to S.

The tax consequences present a more serious obstacle to using only common stock. For example, using the 75–25% ratio noted above, C will contribute property valued at $60,000 for his 75 shares of stock, and S will contribute a nominal amount of cash [37]—e. g.,

37. A nominal contribution may be required of S to comply with local corporate law prohibitions against issuing stock for services.

$500—for his 25 shares. But S's 25 shares are worth at least 25% of the value of the assets of the Corporation ($60,500) or $15,125. Since S paid $500 for shares worth $15,125, the difference of $14,625 will constitute ordinary income to S as stock distributed in payment for services rendered or to be rendered. Reg. § 1.351–1(a)(1), (2), Ex. (3). Since S's cash contribution is relatively small in comparison with the stock received for his services, S may not qualify as a transferor under § 351; and since S possesses over 20% of the Corporation's stock, this disqualification would also disqualify C from the protection of § 351, and thus C would then recognize the $15,000 gain realized by him on the exchange of his appreciated liquid assets for stock. Reg. § 1.351–1(a)(1)(ii). Sections 351(a), 368(c).

An additional problem created by using only common stock is that if the business is liquidated, S will receive 25% of the Corporation's assets. C has invested $60,000 in the business, and he should be entitled to a return of his capital before any additional corporate assets are divided.

These problems can be resolved by using preferred stock or debt to represent most of C's capital contribution and by dividing the common stock equally between them. Then C will receive a senior return on his capital investment in a similar manner to the senior return that S receives on his services via a salary, although these may not be equal; and C will have a preference over S upon liquidation of the business so that C can recapture his investment before any assets are divided. Yet, the voting control of the Corporation and the profits in excess of the senior interests of C and S will be equally divided.

The use of preferred stock or debt may also eliminate or mitigate S's recognition of income and may preserve the protection of § 351 for C's contributions. For example, if C contributed $59,500 for preferred stock and securities, and if C and S each contributed $500 for an equal number of shares of common stock, S's shares will not reflect the value of assets contributed by C; and S will likely be deemed to have paid fair value for his shares. Thus, S will not recognize income on the exchange. Even if S's common shares are deemed to be worth more than $500 because of potential future growth of the business (an unlikely event since C paid a like amount for each share of his common stock), the difference should be relatively small and should not cause serious consequences to S or endanger the qualification of C's exchange for nonrecognition under § 351.

The question then remains whether C's senior interest should be represented by preferred stock or by securities, either of which could be issued tax-free under § 351 in exchange for C's assets. Debt (securities) possesses the tax advantages that interest payments are deductible and that the debt can usually be retired without risking dividend treatment. However, debt possesses a number of disadvantages that must be weighed. In order to avoid hybrid stock treatment, the debt will need a fixed maturity date and probably should not be subordinated to the claims of creditors. If it is not subordinated, the Corporation may find it difficult to obtain outside loans for additional capital. The Corporation may not be able to afford the repayment of the debt at the maturity date, and S may not be willing to permit C to withdraw all of his capital from the enterprise while retaining a 50% interest in its profits; although interest payments could be made conditional upon profitability. The required payment of interest may be harmful to the Corporation, especially during the first few years of its operation. If all of C's $59,500 contribution were represented by debt, the Corporation would be thinly capitalized, and the debt would likely be classified as hybrid stock.

Thus, a sizable percentage of C's contribution might be exchanged for preferred stock. The problem with this is that stock dividends are not deductible and interest payments are deductible. In any case, it is likely that a portion of C's contribution (e. g., $20,000) could be exchanged for debt without causing significant difficulties.

§ 38.5 Division Between Junior Executives and Retiring Management

When aging management commences to turn over the control of a corporate business to younger executives, preferred stock can be a useful device. The younger executives represent the future of the business, and any subsequent growth in the Corporation's value will be due to their efforts. The retiring management will want a fixed secure return on the value of the business established by them during their tenure. The younger executives will desire voting control of the business as well as participation in its growth, but they may not have sufficient funds available to purchase the shares owned by the retiring management. One solution would be to have the Corporation recapitalized into common stock and preferred so that the preferred shares represent the major part of the present value of the Corporation. Thus, the common stock will have a relatively low value, but any future growth in the Corporation will be reflected in the common stock and not in the preferred. The older management can then sell common shares to the younger executives at a price they can afford, the older members will retain a fixed return on their interests and will retain an interest in the Corporation equal to its present value; and the future growth of the business will be enjoyed by the younger, active executives.

It is noteworthy that preferred stock could be issued in a tax-free exchange pursuant to a recapitalization or could be issued as a tax-free stock dividend; but if securities were issued in exchange for stock pursuant to a recapitalization or were issued as a dividend, the Stockholders may recognize income. See Chapters 57 and 59, infra.

§§ 38.6–38.10 are reserved for supplementary material.

B. EQUITY (STOCK)

§ 38.11 Equity Securities—Generally [1]

A Stockholder owns shares [2] of stock in a Corporation. Only in a loose sense does he own the Corporation. Instead he has a threefold proportionate interest in the Corporation with respect to: (a) earnings, (b) net assets, and (c) control. His interest, assuming no complications from more than one class of issued shares, is in proportion to the number of shares he owns out of the total number of shares.

His share certificate evidences his share interest, although for most purposes, the Corporation may rely on the record ownership disclosed by the record of Stockholders which it maintains.

To some extent, the Stockholder's proportionate interest is protected by the fiduciary duties of corporate management, which apply to the issue of shares as well as to other corporate matters, and the doctrine of preemptive rights, which, when applicable, requires a pro rata offering of new shares to existing Stockholders.

§ 38.12 Classes of Equity Securities

(a) Common Shares. Common shares are, of course, the basic equity security reflecting the underlying ownership of the Corporation. Another well-known class of equity security are preferred shares, described below. State Corporation statutes give Corporations broad power to create novel types of securities or specially tailored classes of common or preferred securities; this flexibility is often utilized to effectuate intracorporate Agreements in closely held Corporations.[3]

1. See Henn, Law of Corporations (2d ed. 1970) § 157. A third edition is being prepared by Professor Henn for 1982 publication.

2. The term "Shares" has been defined to mean the units into which the proprietary interests in a Corporation are divided. Model Bus. Corp.Act § 2(d).

3. See Chapter 29, supra, with respect to Stockholder Agreements.

The emphasis in this section, like the preceding one, is essentially descriptive, concentrating on broad classes of equity securities.

(b) Classes of Common Stock. State statutes give Corporations broad power to create classes of common stock with different rights or privileges. Such classes are usually designated by alphabetical notations: "Class A common," "Class B common" and so forth. In closely held Corporations, classes of common stock are primarily used to effectuate control, voting, or financial arrangements. The following examples illustrate the variety and flexibility that classes of common stock may provide:

(1) A Class A common may be created that is entitled to twice the dividend per share of Class B common, but in all other respects the two classes are identical.

(2) A Class A common may be created that has two votes per share while Class B common has one vote per share (this is permitted in some but not all states; some state statutes still have a "one vote per share" principle).

(3) A Class A common may be created that has the power to elect two directors; the holders of Class B common may have the power to elect one, two, or more directors, irrespective of the number of shares of each class outstanding.

(4) It may be required that the President of the Corporation be a holder of Class A shares and the Vice-President and Treasurer be holders of Class B shares.

(c) Preferred Shares. Preferred shares differ from common shares in that they have preference over common shares in the payment of dividends and/or preference in the assets of the Corporation upon the voluntary or involuntary liquidation of the Corporation. "Preference" simply means that the preferred shares are entitled to receive some specified payment (either a dividend or a liquidating distribution, or both) before the common shares are entitled to anything. Most preferred shares contain preferences both as to dividends and liquidation.

The dividend preference may be described either in terms of dollars per share (the "$3.20 preferred") or as a percentage of par or stated value (the "five per cent preferred"). A dividend preference does not mean that the preferred is entitled to the payment in the same way that a creditor is entitled to payment from his debtor. A preferred dividend is still a dividend, and the Directors may decide to omit all dividends, common or preferred, and this decision is generally in no way dependent on whether or not there is current income. Shares preferred as to dividends may be *cumulative, noncumulative,* or *partially cumulative.* If cumulative dividends are not paid in some years, they are carried forward and both they and the current year's preferred dividends must be paid in full before any common dividends may be declared. Noncumulative dividends disappear each year if they are not paid. Partially cumulative dividends are usually of the "cumulative to the extent of earnings" type so that such preferred shares continue to have first claim to actual earnings if not paid out as dividends. Unpaid cumulative dividends are not debts of the Corporation, but have continued right to priority in future distributions. Since Directors (who are elected by the common Stockholders) may defer preferred dividends indefinitely if the Directors are willing to forego dividends on the common shares as well, it is customary to provide that preferred shares may elect a specified number of Directors if preferred dividends have been omitted for a specified period.

Preferred shares may also be *participating*, though typically they are not. Nonparticipating shares are entitled to a specified dividend before anything is paid on the common but no more, irrespective of the earnings of the Corporation. Participating preferred shares are entitled to the original dividend, and after the common receives a specified amount, they may share with the common in any additional distributions. Such shares are sometimes referred to as "Class A preferred" or a similar designation reflecting that their right to participate is open-ended.

Like debt securities, preferred shares are often made *convertible* into common shares at a specified price or specified ratio and redeemable by the Corporation at a fixed price. Typically, the original conversion ratio is established so that the common must appreciate substantially before it is profitable to convert the preferred. When the price of the common rises above this level, the preferred shares will fluctuate in price as the price of the common fluctuates. The redemption privilege usually does not limit the price of the convertible preferred since the privilege to convert customarily continues for a limited period of time after a call for redemption. A conversion is described as *forced* when shares are called for redemption at a time when the value of the shares obtainable on conversion exceeds the redemption price. Also like convertible debt securities, convertible preferred usually contain elaborate provisions protecting the conversion privilege from *dilution* in case of stock dividends, stock splits or the issuance of additional common shares. The statutes of some states prohibit the creation of a security which is convertible into shares having superior rights and preferences as to dividends or upon liquidation—in other words, a common may not be made convertible into preferred. State statutes also may limit the redemption privilege to securities that have a liquidation preference. These limitations are virtually the only substantive statutory restrictions on the issuance of classes of shares in most states.

Articles of Incorporation may also authorize preferred shares to be issued in *series*.[4] Such Articles in effect authorize the Board

4. E. g. Model Bus.Corp.Act § 16 provides:

§ 16. Issuance of Shares of Preferred or Special Classes in Series

If the Articles of Incorporation so provide, the shares of any preferred or special class may be divided into and issued in series. If the shares of any such class are to be issued in series, then each series shall be so designated as to distinguish the shares thereof from the shares of all other series and classes. Any or all of the series of any such class and the variations in the relative rights and preferences as between different series may be fixed and determined by the Articles of Incorporation, but all shares of the same class shall be identical except as to the following relative rights and preferences, as to which there may be variations between different series:

(A) The rate of dividend.

(B) Whether shares may be redeemed and, if so, the redemption price and the terms and conditions of redemption.

(C) The amount payable upon shares in event of voluntary and involuntary liquidation.

(D) Sinking fund provisions, if any, for the redemption or purchase of shares.

(E) The terms and conditions, if any, on which shares may be converted.

(F) Voting rights, if any.

If the Articles of Incorporation shall expressly vest authority in the Board of Directors, then, to the extent that the Articles of Incorporation shall not have established series and fixed and determined the variations in the relative rights and preferences as between series, the Board of Directors shall have authority to divide any or all of such classes into series and, within the limitations set forth in this section and in the Articles of Incorporation, fix and determine the relative rights and preferences of the shares of any series so established.

In order for the Board of Directors to establish a series, where authority so to do is contained in the Articles of Incorporation, the Board of Directors shall adopt a resolution setting forth the designation of the series and fixing and determining the relative rights and preferences thereof, or so much thereof as shall not be fixed and determined by the Articles of Incorporation.

Prior to the issue of any shares of a series established by resolution adopted by the Board of Directors, the Corporation shall file in the office of the Secretary of State a statement setting forth:

(a) The name of the Corporation.

(b) A copy of the resolution establishing and designating the series, and fixing and determining the relative rights and preferences thereof.

(c) The date of adoption of such resolution.

(d) That such resolution was duly adopted by the Board of Directors.

Such statement shall be executed in duplicate by the Corporation by its President or a Vice-President and by its secretary or an assistant secretary, and verified by one of the officers signing such statement, and shall be delivered to the Secretary of State. If the Secretary of State finds that such statement conforms to law, he shall, when all franchise taxes and fees have been paid as in this Act prescribed:

(1) Endorse on each of such duplicate originals the word "Filed," and the month, day, and year of the filing thereof.

(2) File one of such duplicate originals in his office.

(3) Return the other duplicate original to the Corporation or its representative.

of Directors to vary any of the substantive terms of the preferred from time to time. Where preferred shares in substantial amounts are to be sold by a Corporation from time to time to raise capital, the privilege of issuing preferred in series simplifies financing since the price, dividend, liquidation preference, sinking fund provision, voting rights, and other terms of each series may be tailored to then-current market conditions. Shares of different series have identical rights except for the specified business terms which may be varied. Before preferred shares are created, a filing with the Secretary of State describing the terms of the new series may be required if not already authorized. As a practical matter, these provisions are of considerably less importance today than they once were because of the decline in preferred share financing.

The various provisions defining the rights of preferred Stockholders appear in the Corporation's Articles of Incorporation, By-laws, or Director's resolutions. Collectively they are often referred to as the preferred Stockholders' "contract" with the Corporation and with other classes of Stockholders.

See Chapter 40, infra, for a more complete description.

(d) Non-voting Shares. In most states, the Articles of Incorporation may limit or deny the right to vote to classes of shares. Preferred shares are usually non-voting shares, but the privilege to vote may be extended to such shares, either with the common shares or as a separate class. In the closely held Corporation, non-voting shares may serve a planning role similar to classes of common shares. For example, the right to vote may be limited or denied to classes of common shares in the election of Directors, on other subjects normally submitted to Stockholders, or both. In such Corporations there seems to be little objection to the theory that a specific limitation on voting is part of the Stockholder's overall "contract" with the Corporation.

In publicly held Corporations, non-voting shares have been treated with greater suspicion. Such shares are somewhat analogous to perpetual voting trusts, and have been criticized on policy grounds for this reason. Corporations with non-voting shares which are held by the public are ineligible for listing on the New York Stock Exchange, and may suffer market and other disadvantages as well.

In the early years of this century, many Corporations were capitalized by the issuance of non-voting shares to the public while the voting shares were held by the members of the family which

Upon the filing of such statement by the Secretary of State, the resolution establishing and designating the series and fixing and determining the relative rights and preferences thereof shall become effective and shall constitute an amendment of the articles of incorporation.

Forms. For provisions in Articles of Incorporation authorizing issuance of preferred shares in series, see Chapter 40, infra.

founded or controlled the Corporation. This practice has declined in importance in recent years. Further, several Corporations that had issued non-voting shares for this reason have later converted the shares into voting shares. This decision creates subtle issues as to the relative value of the right to vote and the fairness of the terms on which the privilege to vote is granted.

Under most state statutes, even non-voting shares are entitled to vote in connection wtih certain mergers, consolidations, and other extraordinary events that may affect the class of non-voting shares as a class.

(e) Options. Options to purchase shares may be used as a capital raising device, to provide employee incentives, and to a lesser extent as part of control devices. Of course, shares under option are not deemed issued and may not be voted until the options are exercised and the purchase price paid, or in some states, a firm commitment to pay the purchase price in the form of a promissory note has been delivered to the Corporation.

Employee stock purchase or stock option plans are largely governed by the Internal Revenue Code, since favorable tax treatment is usually an essential part of the success of such plans. Many state Corporation statutes contain provisions that authorize the issuance of shares in connection with such plans by the Board of Directors and provide that in the absence of fraud the determination by the Board of the consideration for such shares shall be conclusive.[5]

Warrants are transferable options to acquire shares from the Corporation at a specified price. Warrants have many of the qualities of an equity security since their price is a function of the market price of the underlying shares and the specified issuance price. Warrants frequently are issued as a "sweetener" in connection with the distribution of a debt or preferred stock issue; they may be issued in connection with a public exchange offer, or as compensation for handling the public distribution of other shares. Sometimes they are issued in a reorganization to holders of a class of security not otherwise recognized in the reorganization. Warrants are often publicly traded; warrants issued by a number of Corporations are listed from time to time on the New York Stock Exchange or other exchanges. *Rights* are in effect short term warrants. They may also be publicly traded and listed on securities exchanges. Rights are often issued in lieu of a dividend, or in an effort to raise capital from existing Stockholders.

For further discussion of stock options, rights, and warrants, see Chapter 42, infra.

Library References:

C.J.S. Corporations § 194 et seq.
West's Key No. Digests, Corporations ⚷62.

5. See Model Bus.Corp.Act § 20.

§ 38.13 Preferred Stock

(a) Introduction. Preferred stock has many uses for both business planning and estate planning purposes. In some circumstances, however, nonvoting common stock or debt may serve a purpose equally as well as preferred stock. One advantage of preferred stock over debt is that the former can be acquired in a recapitalization or stock dividend without incurring tax liabilities; that generally cannot be done with debt instruments. However, its dividends are not deductible, whereas debt's interest is deductible. Another consideration is that the Corporation's burden of meeting interest obligations may become oppressive and stifle the company's growth, and a mandatory maturity for repayment of the debt may be burdensome to the Corporation. An advantage of preferred stock over nonvoting common stock is that preferrred provides more security to the holder and accordingly may be more marketable.

One of the useful attributes of preferred stock is that because of its preferential rights and because it does not usually participate in the growth of the business, but instead provides a fixed rate of return and a fixed amount on liquidation, it can be valued more readily than common. Another purpose for issuing preferred stock is to reduce the value of the outstanding common stock.

Caveat: The issuance of preferred stock after incorporation is fraught with danger. See Chapter 58, infra.

(b) Estate Planning.

(1) Gifts to the Donor's Family. The controlling Stockholder of a closely held Corporation may wish to divide corporate stock among members of his family, but he may also wish to retain control of the Corporation during his life. One of the advantages of giving away nonvoting corporate stock is that it will reduce the donor's estate tax liability at the cost of a possible gift tax; and if dividends are paid, it is a means of splitting the income among several members of the family. The Stockholder could donate preferred stock[6] for this purpose, or he could give non-voting common stock.

When contemplating making gifts of corporate stock for purposes of reducing the donor's estate, the provisions of § 303, which provide for distributions from the Corporation free of dividend treatment to nonterminating decedents (see Chapter 65, infra), should be considered. When applicable, § 303 provides a valuable device for withdrawing funds from the Corporation after the Stockholder's demise. If the Stockholder's stock in the Corporation will likely

6. The gift of the preferred stock will not cause adverse tax consequences to the donor even where it is section 306 stock (IRC § 306(b)(3)); but if it is section 306 stock, it will maintain that taint in the donee's hands. IRC § 306(c)(1)(C).

qualify for § 303 treatment on the Stockholder's death, the gift of shares of such stock can endanger the availability of § 303 by reducing the percentage of the decedent's estate that is attributable to his stock. Conversely, if it is a close question whether the stock will qualify under § 303, gifts of other assets of the Stockholder (i. e., assets other than such stock) may reduce the size of his gross estate and thereby increase the percentage of his estate represented by the corporate stock.

A Stockholder may wish to retain a fixed income from the corporate business and to divorce himself (and his gross estate on death) from the future growth of the business. One possibility is to recapitalize the Corporation so that the Stockholder acquires preferred stock having a value equal to a large percentage of the net worth of the Corporation. See Chapter 59, infra. The Stockholder can then give his relatives most of his common stock and retain the preferred. Thus, he will stabilize his interest in the business, since a subsequent rise in the value of the Corporation will inure only to the benefit of the owners of the common stock. An added advantage to this arrangement is that the value of the gifts to the Stockholder's family will be depressed, since most of that value will represent the company's potential for future growth rather than its present equity; consequently, the gift tax cost of the arrangement may not prove too burdensome. A major obstacle to this arrangement is that the Corporation may suffer from distributing large amounts as nondeductible dividends on the preferred stock. While preferred stock can be used for this purpose, moderation should be employed. On the Stockholder's death the preferred stock probably can be redeemed pursuant to a complete termination of the estate's (or legatee's) interest in the Corporation (§ 302(b)(3)), unless there are attribution problems that cannot be resolved.[7] If § 303 is applicable, the stock protected by § 303 can be redeemed without adverse tax consequences, irrespective of attribution rules. See Chapter 65, infra.

(2) Protection of Surviving Beneficiaries. It may not be feasible to have the Stockholder's stock redeemed at his death, or he may prefer that it not be redeemed because of his faith in the business. In such event, he may wish to provide his beneficiaries with some security that they will receive income from the business and will not be "squeezed out" of their investment. Preferred stock may be employed as one step toward insuring that the beneficiaries will receive a minimum income from the business, but additional protections against squeeze-outs should be adopted. Moreover, care should be taken to "insure that contemplated dividends are in fact paid."

7. As a consequence of the repeal of carryover basis by the Crude Oil Windfall Profit Tax Act of 1980, section 306 stock will lose its taint on the Stockholder's death and will be subject to the normal redemption rules of IRC §§ 302 and 303.

(c) Business Planning Considerations. Where there are several investors in a business, they may have entirely different wishes as to the nature and productivity of their investment, and different classes of stock can be useful in complying with their disparate goals. For example, one group of investors may desire substantial security for their capital investment and some assurance of a minimum return on their investment. Preferred stock and debt are means of accomplishing that. The other investors, who receive common stock, accept a greater risk; but if the business is successful, they are the principal beneficiaries of its growth.

§ 38.14 Equity Securities—Authorized; Issued; Outstanding Shares [8]

By definition a stock Corporation is a Corporation having shares of stock.[9]

Corporation statutes recognize the power of the stock Corporation to issue shares, but usually require that the exercise of such power be pursuant to proper authorization in the Articles of Incorporation of the Corporation involved.[10] The organization tax imposed by the jurisdiction of incorporation is usually based on the authorized shares; so also may be a capital tax, license fee on foreign Corporations doing business in the jurisdiction, [11] or franchise tax. Unless the shares purported to be issued are duly authorized, they are void.[12]

A few states impose a tax on the issuance of shares.

The capital of a Corporation is generally computed on the basis of the shares issued.[13]

Not all of the authorized shares, of course, need be issued. Unissued shares might be reserved for future sale, to be available for share dividends, exercise of share options, or exercise of conversion privilege in securities convertible into shares.

Shares which have been issued to the holders thereof are said to be outstanding. When such shares are reacquired by the Corpo-

8. See Henn, Law of Corporations (2d ed. 1970) § 158. A third edition is being prepared by professor Henn for 1982 publication.

9. See, e. g., Model Bus.Corp.Act §§ 2(d), 15. A business Corporation is usually regarded as a type of stock Corporation.

10. See, e. g., Model Bus.Corp.Act §§ 2(g), 15. See also Chapter 35, infra.

11. See, e. g., Model Bus.Corp.Act § 130; McKinney's N.Y. Tax Law § 180 (organization tax); Model Bus.Corp. Act § 131; McKinney's N.Y. Tax Law § 181 (license fee on foreign corporations).

12. See U.C.C. § 8–104 (effect of overissue).

13. See, e. g., Model Bus.Corp.Act 18; McKinney's N.Y.Bus.Corp.Law § 102(a)(12).

ration, by donation, forfeiture,[14] purchase,[15] redemption,[16] conversion,[17] or otherwise, they are frequently called "treasury stock" or "treasury shares". The accounting treatment should be descriptively accurate from the point of view of the applicable Corporation law.

Legally, "treasury shares" are authorized and issued but not outstanding. However, the Corporation may and, under certain circumstances, must restore the shares to unissued status or eliminate the shares from authorized shares by reducing the authorized capital.[18]

Treasury shares being somewhat in a state of limbo, have some unusual characteristics.[19] Even if otherwise voting, treasury shares may usually not be voted, since otherwise corporate management would be voting for themselves, or counted for purposes of determining a quorum or sufficient vote or consent of the Stockholders.[20] Nor do treasury shares participate in dividends or distributions of net assets upon dissolution, since such participation would be circuitous. Nor is its reallotment usually subject to preemptive rights or to consideration-for-shares requirements, at least where their original issue complied with such requirements.

§ 38.15 Par Value, Stated Capital and Related Concepts [21]

Par value of a share of common stock is simply the dollar amount designated as par value by the draftsman of the Articles of Incorporation. It may be one mill, one cent, one dollar, ten dollars, whatever the draftsman designates. At one time par value had considerable importance because it was widely viewed as the amount for which the shares would be issued: shares with a par value of one hundred dollars could be subscribed for at one hundred dollars per share with confidence that all other identical shares would also be

14. See, e. g., Model Bus.Corp.Act § 17. The Model Business Corporation Act does not permit the issue of partly-paid shares, but does expressly provide for fractions of shares (§ 24).

15. A Corporation may usually purchase its own shares out of surplus, and under certain circumstances and to a limited extent as allowed by statute out of capital.

16. If shares are redeemable, a Corporation may redeem them out of surplus or, to the extent permitted by statute, out of capital. See Chapter 61 et seq., infra, with respect to redemptions.

17. See, e. g., Model Bus.Corp.Act § 15 (conversion of preferred shares).

18. See e. g. McKinney's N.Y.Bus.Corp. Law § 515.

19. See, e. g., Model Bus.Corp.Act § 18.

20. See, e. g., Model Bus.Corp.Act § 33.

21. This Section, and §§ 38.16–38.18, infra, are adapted from Hamilton, Corporations in a Nutshell (1980), § 7.4 et seq.

issued for $100. This practice, however, long ago fell into disuse. Today, par value serves only a minor function and is in no way an indication of the price at which the shares are issued, with this one exception: *The one basic rule about setting the price for shares of common stock with a par value is that the price must be equal to or greater than par value.* If this rule is violated and shares are issued for less than par value, the recipient Stockholder in most states is automatically liable to the Corporation for the difference.

In order to understand "stated capital" and "capital surplus" and the issues that evolve from them, a brief excursion into fundamental accounting concepts is useful. The basic truism on which financial statements are based is that *net worth* equals *assets* minus *liabilities. Assets* also equal *liabilities* plus *net worth.* This is the formula used in a "balance sheet" where one side of the equation is placed on the left side and the balance on the right side.

Assets	Liabilities + Net Worth

[C3029]

A balance sheet balances because it is simply a restatement of the basic equation.

Let us examine a balance sheet for a new Corporation immediately after it has sold 100 shares of stock for 1,000 dollars in cash. The balance sheet shows:

Assets		Liabilities		-0-
Cash	$1,000	Net Worth		
	$1,000		Common Stock	$1,000
				$1,000

[C3030]

The concepts of stated capital and capital surplus relate to how the common stock item is shown on the right hand side of the balance sheet. Stated capital is defined to be the aggregate par value of all issued shares (plus or minus certain adjustments not relevant for present purposes). Any excess of capital contributed over the par value is allocated to capital surplus. Thus, if in our hypothetical the 100 shares of common stock had a par value of $1 per share and were sold at $10.00 per share the balance sheet would be as follows:

Assets		Liabilities	–0–
Cash	$1,000	Capital Accounts	
		Stated Capital	$100
		Capital Surplus	900
	$1,000		$1,000

In this balance sheet, the phrase "capital accounts" has been substituted for "net worth" to somewhat more closely reflect modern accounting terminology, but its meaning is the same. Under modern statutes, there is no requirement that any specific amount be put in in the form of stated capital (par value) as long as it equals or exceeds par value; even states that establish a minimum capitalization of $1,000 (or some other amount) require only an aggregate capital of the specified amount without differentiating between how much is stated capital and how much is capital surplus.

Now, a logical question that may be asked is what difference does it make if the capital contribution is recorded as stated capital or capital surplus. Rather surprisingly it does make a difference, which can best be appreciated if we first draw up a balance sheet after the Corporation (1) has borrowed $1,000 from a bank and (2) has had two years of operations during which it has earned and accumulated an aggregate of $2,000 over-and-above all costs, taxes, etc. Further, for simplicity we will continue to assume that all of the assets are held by the Corporation in the form of cash. The balance sheet looks like this:

Assets		Liabilities	$1,000
Cash	$4,000	Capital Accounts	
		Earned Surplus (or Retained Earnings)	2,000
		Stated Capital	100
		Capital Surplus	900
	$4,000		$4,000

At this point the Stockholders decide they want to distribute to themselves some or all of the $4,000. If the balance sheet is to continue to balance, every dollar taken from the left-hand column must obviously be reflected by the reduction of a right-hand column entry. The right-hand entries thus in effect limit or monitor the distribution of assets from the left-hand column. For example dividends may be lawfully paid "out of" earned surplus. This means that amounts may be paid from the cash of the Corporation as dividends up to the maximum amount shown in the right-hand column under "earned surplus," or $2,000 in the above example. Of course, a dividend of, say, $500 paid out of earned surplus would in the above example result in the reduction of cash by $500 to $3500, offset by a reduction of earned surplus to $1,500, and the balance sheet will still balance.

Under most state statutes, Corporations have greater freedom to make distributions from capital surplus than from stated capital. In most states stated capital is "locked in" the Corporation and cannot be distributed except upon the liquidation of the Corporation or if transferred to surplus by reducing par value; however, assets may be distributed to the extent of capital surplus simply with the approval of the holders of a specified fraction of the common shares or the Board. Such a distribution is not a dividend in the normal sense of the word but is called by various names, e. g., "liquidating dividend," "distribution in partial liquidation," or the like. Also capital surplus, but not stated capital, may be used to repurchase or redeem outstanding shares previously issued by the Corporation.

If all the capital is put in the form of stated capital (i. e., the par value of the issued shares equals the consideration received) all the capital is "locked in;" if the bulk of the capital contributed is recorded as capital surplus rather than stated capital there is greater flexibility to distribute unneeded capital to Stockholders or reacquire outstanding shares at a later date. In other words, there is greater flexibility in a Corporation with this balance sheet:

Cash	$1,000	Liabilities	
		Capital Accounts	
		Stated Capital	$100
		Capital Surplus	900
	$1,000		$1,000

than there is in a Corporation with this balance sheet:

Cash	$1,000	Liabilities	-0-
		Capital Accounts	
		Stated Capital	$1,000
		Capital Surplus	-0-
	$1,000		$1,000

Such flexibility is viewed by corporate organizers as a mildly positive feature and is an additional reason for the wide-spread use of nominal par value which leads to low stated capital and high capital surplus. Of course, a bank that lends money to a Corporation might be unhappy if large amounts of capital surplus are available for distribution to Stockholders since the capital of the Corporation forms a "cushion" for the creditor and increases the possibility that the Corporation will have the liquid assets to repay the loan when it comes due. As a result, lenders very commonly insist on contractual restrictions on the freedom of Corporations to distribute their contributed capital that modern Corporation statutes provide. Such restrictions are required so routinely by most lenders that they have almost totally replaced the Corporation statutes as the operative restriction on the freedom of Corporations to distribute their capital to their Stockholders.

Library References:

C.J.S. Corporations § 197.
West's Key No. Digests, Corporations ⚷61.

§ 38.16 No Par Shares

In the early period of corporate history, Corporations only issued shares with par value. No par shares are a relatively recent wrinkle, and the rules relating to such shares were developed in the context of the established rules for accounting for par value shares. When no par shares are issued under most state statutes the entire consideration fixed by the Corporation for the shares constitutes stated capital. However, statutes generally permit the directors to allocate some portion or all of the consideration to capital surplus. Some states limit this power to 25 per cent or some other fraction of the consideration received (as did the Model Act before 1969). Such a restriction on creating capital surplus obviously reduces the attractiveness of no par shares to some extent. However, most states today permit allocation of consideration from no par shares to either stated capital or capital surplus without limitation. Apparently under such a provision it is possible to create a Corporation with as little stated capital using no par shares as with nominal par value shares.

Some state statutes provide that the Board of Directors has the power to fix the consideration for which no par shares are issued but the Articles of Incorporation may expressly reserve this power to the Stockholders. It is always simpler and more convenient for the Board of Directors to exercise this power than the Stockholders. This option is apparently a lingering vestige of the long since discredited idea that par value ensures equality of Stockholders while no par shares do not. In the modern context, it is unlikely that the option for Stockholders to set the issuance price is ever elected.

§ 38.17 Current Trends Regarding Par Value

In 1979 the committee that is charged with reviewing and updating the Model Business Corporation Act approved a proposal to amend that Act by deleting all references to par value and all consequences that flow from a distinction between stated capital and capital surplus. Under this amendment, the validity of corporate distributions to Stockholders is measured by the test whether the Corporation is insolvent in either the bankruptcy or the equity sense immediately after the distribution. While the adequacy of the protection to creditors thus provided is still under consideration, the elegance and simplicity thereby created has much to commend it. At least one major state has adopted this approach and many more will probably follow it in the future.

§ 38.18 Fractions of Shares; Scrip [22]

A growing number of jurisdictions have statutory provisions expressly authorizing the issuance of fractions of shares.[23] These statutes, while sanctioning fractions of shares, do not make their issuance mandatory. The issuance of fractions of shares may create administrative and bookkeeping problems for the issuing Corporation. In connection with share dividends, odd share splits, reverse share splits, conversion, merger, consolidation, or corporate reorganizations, the issuance of fractions of shares might be desirable. Where fractions of shares are issued, the rights of their holders with respect to dividends, net assets on liquidation, voting, preemptive rights, etc., having not always been adequately defined, although modern statutes tend to clarify such rights.

Where statutes are silent with respect to the issuance of fractions of shares, Articles of Incorporation, or amendment thereof, purporting to authorize the issuance of fractions of shares might not be accepted for filing by the Secretary of State.

Many statutes also authorize the issuance of scrip.[24]

Scrip is a certificate exchangeable for shares or cash, usually before a specified date. Issued for fractions of shares, sufficient scrip to represent a whole share may be combined and turned over to the Corporation for a share. Scrip is usually transferable. A holder of scrip generally possesses none of the rights of the Stockholders.

22. See Henn, Law of Corporations (2d ed. 1970) § 161.

23. See, e. g., Model Bus.Corp.Act § 24 (issuance of fractional shares or scrip); McKinney's N.Y.Bus.Corp.Law § 509; West's Ann.Calif.Corp.Code § 407.

24. See e. g. Model Bus.Corp.Act § 24; McKinney's N.Y.Bus.Corp.Law § 509.

§ 38.19 Issuance of Shares by a Going Concern—Preemptive Rights

The issuance of shares by a going concern must meet the same requirements as to kind and amount of consideration as on the original formation and capitalization of the Corporation. The number of shares to be sold and the consideration therefor is set by the Board of Directors. In addition, however, the issuance of new shares may affect the financial and voting rights of existing Stockholders, and as a result additional legal requirements may be applicable. If shares are issued to the current Stockholders in strict proportion to their stockholdings, the relative position of each Stockholder is obviously unaffected though the aggregate capital invested in the Corporation has increased. However, if shares are issued to third persons or to existing Stockholders not in strictly proportional amounts, the voting power of some Stockholders will necessarily be reduced. Further, if the shares are issued disproportionately and for less than current value (a term that need not here be precisely defined), the financial interest of some Stockholders in the Corporation will necessarily be diluted.

A "preemptive right" is a common law concept that permits an existing Stockholder, subject to several important exceptions, to subscribe—in preference to strangers and pro rata with other existing Stockholders—for his relative share of new shares to be issued by the Corporation. Ideally, the preemptive right of each existing Stockholder protects him from injury resulting from the issue of shares. However, in practice it often does not work out that way. For one thing, preemptive rights under modern statutes are permissive rather than mandatory and Corporations may limit or deny such rights by provisions in the Articles of Incorporation. However, even if preemptive rights are excluded, equitable principles may limit the power of Corporations to dispose of new shares on an unfair basis and the statutory exceptions tend to be rather broad.

Shares sold by a going Corporation may come from three sources. They may be shares which are newly authorized by the Corporation by an amendment to the Articles of Incorporation. Or, they may be shares which were previously authorized in the Articles but never previously issued. Or they may be "treasury shares," that is, shares that have been issued and subsequently reacquired by the Corporation. Even though the issuance of any additional shares, no matter what the source, has the same dilutive effect, different legal principles may be applicable depending on the source of the shares.

At common law, it was generally held that a Stockholder's preemptive right was an integral part of the ownership of shares. However, the common law preemptive right did not extend to the following types of transactions:

(1) Shares which were originally authorized but unissued. The rationale for this exception was that an implied understanding existed between the original subscribers that sale of the remaining authorized shares to obtain necessary capital may be completed. However, this rationale is not persuasive in light of the modern practice of authorizing additional shares which are not planned to be sold as part of the original capitalization. As a result some modern courts have refused to recognize this exception.

(2) **Treasury Shares.** The rationale for this exception is that Stockholders are not injured since the shares had previously been issued and their reissuance simply restores a dilution that had existed previously.

(3) Shares issued for property or services rather than cash or shares issued in connection with a merger. The theory underlying these exceptions is that preemptive rights in such situations would frustrate or render impractical desirable transactions, or are impossible to work out since existing Stockholders may not own, and therefore cannot contribute, property on a proportional basis.

(4) Shares issued to satisfy conversion or option rights.

(5) Shares issued pursuant to a plan of reorganization or recapitalization under court supervision.

Some recent decisions have refused to apply these exceptions mechanically and have looked to the realities of the particular situation. One court, for example, held that preemptive rights should not be denied when property is the consideration for shares except where because of peculiar circumstances the Corporation has great need for the particular property, and issuance of shares therefor is the only practical and feasible method by which the Corporation can acquire it. In many situations, the Corporation may pay cash to acquire the needed property; to allow the Corporation to acquire it with shares defeats the preemptive right that would exist if shares were issued for cash and the cash used to acquire the property.

Modern state statutes change the common law preemptive right in several respects:

(1) They give Corporations the privilege of dispensing entirely with preemptive rights if they so choose. The choice must be made by a specific provision in the Corporation's Articles of Incorporation. Statutes may grant preemptive rights unless they

are specifically negated in the Articles, or preclude preemptive rights except to the extent specifically granted in the Articles.

(2) They sometimes give preemptive rights more broadly than the common law, e. g., they may extend the right to "authorized but unissued shares," "treasury shares," and securities convertible into common shares, all types of shares to which the common law preemptive right did not extend.

(3) They provide specifically that preemptive rights do not exist between different classes of shares, e. g., holders of preferred do not have a preemptive right to acquire common.

(4) They provide that shares issued pursuant to employee incentive or compensation plans are not subject to preemptive rights if the plan was originally approved by the Stockholders.

What considerations enter into the decision to limit or deny preemptive rights? The argument in favor of preserving preemptive rights is that the Stockholder who subscribes for a given percentage of the original issue of the shares of a Corporation should be entitled to maintain his percentage interest provided he is willing to subscribe for his proportion of additional issues of shares. This sounds like a democratic principle and undoubtedly it is in many cases. There are situations, however, in which preemptive rights are more a nuisance than anything else. Suppose for example that a Corporation with a fairly large number of Stockholders is in need of immediate funds and can obtain them only by a prompt sale of additional shares to bankers or underwriters. It may well find that compliance with and satisfaction of the preemptive rights of its existing Stockholders will be expensive, time-consuming and only partially successful. The result may be that the Corporation will lose its financing.

If it is anticipated that the Corporation will for some time remain a close Corporation preemptive rights are often retained so as to give each Stockholder the maximum protection against dilution. But, if it is anticipated that the Corporation will in the near future engage in public financing or will seek to acquire other companies or properties by the issuance of its shares, preemptive rights are often eliminated to avoid legal complications when the time arrives for the sale of additional shares or the acquisition of other companies or properties. Where preemptive rights have been excluded, the Directors may always later decide to offer additional shares pro rata to existing Stockholders. In fact, existing Stockholders are often the most logical market, and one likely to be pursued.

Preemptive rights give Stockholders considerably less protection against such tactics than is often thought. Indeed, as a practical matter, the protection provided by preemptive rights is often illusory. A minority Stockholder may be frozen out if he lacks the financial ability to exercise his preemptive right and purchase the additional shares in order to protect his proportionate interest. Often, the majority or dominant Stockholders may purchase their allotment by offsetting indebtedness owed to them by the Corporation (thereby exercising their preemptive rights without further financial investment) while other Stockholders have to invest substantial amounts of cash just to stay even. In one case, for example, the court refused to intervene when a Stockholder was given the choice of investing an additional $136,000 to preserve his twenty per cent interest or permitting his interest in the Corporation to be diluted to less than one per cent.[25] In another case, where the reduction was from about 32 per cent to less than one per cent, the court applied the test whether the issuance of shares seemed to serve a substantial corporate purpose or whether it was designed simply to benefit management, and over one dissent, concluded that the issuance of shares should be set aside.[26] The issue in these cases usually comes down to an evaluation of the need of the Corporation for the additional capital, or where indebtedness is cancelled and the Corporation receives no additional cash, whether the improvement in the balance sheet caused by the cancellation of indebtedness is a bona fide purpose.

Library References:

C.J.S. Corporations, §§ 239 et seq., 258–260, 262, 289.
West's Key No. Digests, Corporations ⚷94 et seq.

§ 38.20 Shares Issued for Property or Services

If shares are issued for cash, the cash price of each share is readily established, subject only to the limitation that the price must equal or exceed the share's par value, if any. If the Stockholder-to-be is contributing property or services, however, the situation is more complicated.

In the first place, under state statutes not all types of property or services may serve as acceptable consideration for the issuance of shares. Some state constitutions and many state statutes provide that shares may be issued only "in whole or in part, in cash, in other property, tangible or intangible, or in labor or services actually performed for the Corporation." [27] In addition, many state statutes specifically provide that promissory notes or the promise of future services do not constitute permissible consideration. Shares issued for ineligible consideration under these statutes are not validly issued and may be cancelled or suit brought by other Stockholders; or al-

25. Hyman v. Velsicol Corp., 342 Ill. App. 489, 97 N.E.2d 122 (1951).

26. Browning v. C. & C. Plywood Corp., 248 Or. 574, 434 P.2d 339 (1967).

27. See e. g., Model Bus.Corp.Act § 19; West's Ann.Calif.Corp.Code § 409; McKinney's N.Y.Bus.Corp.Law § 504.

ternatively, persons receiving such shares may be compelled in a suit by creditors to pay in additional consideration on the theory the shares are "watered."

The case law provides additional gloss on what is eligible consideration: preincorporation services are "services actually performed;" patents for inventions, "good will" of a going and profitable business, contract rights, or computer "software" constitute "intangible property" if they appear to have real value. On the other hand, a lease or contract right that is subject to a substantial condition may not constitute "property," at least if it is likely that the condition will not be fulfilled. Secret formulae, processes or plans that lack novelty or substantial value have also been held not to constitute "property." A note secured by a mortgage on real estate is usually considered to be eligible "property" rather than an ineligible "promissory note" in states that prohibit shares to be issued in exchange for promissory notes. Further, if shares are issued partially for services previously rendered and partially for services to be rendered in the future, the entire issue of shares is invalid since the court will not apportion it if the Directors do not. Thus, shares to be issued to employees for services may be validly issued only at the end of the employment period.

Secondly, the value of the property or services must be determined. Many statutes are based on the Model Act provisions that require the Board of Directors to "fix" the "consideration, expressed in dollars" that the Corporation is to receive,[28] and that "in the absence of fraud in the transaction," the judgment of the Board of Directors as to the value of the consideration "shall be conclusive." [29] These provisions are equally applicable to par and no par value shares. Under these provisions, the resolution of the Board of Directors accepting property for shares must do two things: it must specify the specific property involved, and it must express or fix the value of the property in dollars. Of course, the value so expressed must exceed the par value of any shares being issued. Presumably, something close to actual fraudulent intent must be shown before the decision of a Board of Directors as to the value of property received can be overturned.

§ 38.21 Oppressive Issuance of Shares

Additional shares of stock may often be issued oppressively to dilute the interests of other Stockholders in the Corporation. Misuse of this power is often referred to as a *squeeze out* or *freeze out.*

28. Model Bus.Corp.Act § 18.

29. Id. § 20.

A number of cases attest that corporate management has a fiduciary duty of taking corporate action according to the best interests of the Corporation rather than for personal advantage. This principle amply covers situations where, in the absence of preemptive rights, management dilutes the interests of Stockholders simply by issuing additional shares to itself at a bargain price. This principle may also cover situations where management issues shares to itself at a fair price to ensure retention of control without offering the shares more broadly. In the first situation there is dilution of both financial and voting interests; in the second there is only dilution of the voting power.

Much more difficult are cases involving a combination of legitimate and self-serving purposes. Shares may be issued to friendly persons for apparently worthwhile purposes and entirely in accordance with statutory requirements, but the minority Stockholders complain that the real purpose and principal effect of the transaction is to freeze them out or dilute their interest. Most cases have permitted such transactions to stand, at least where the ostensible purpose does seem to have substance. Courts are naturally reluctant to second guess decisions by Directors and interfere in intracorporate disputes, but will do so if they feel that the ostensible purpose is a sham, and the real purpose of the transaction is simply to benefit management.

§§ 38.22–38.30 are reserved for supplementary material.

C. DEBT FINANCING

§ 38.31 Types of Debt Securities—Generally [1]

Corporations usually enjoy implied, if not express, powers to borrow funds for corporate purposes.[2] The Articles of Incorporation rarely expressly authorize issues of debt securities except in the most general terms.

Debt security holders, as creditors, obviously have a claim on corporate assets prior to Stockholders. Debt securities are frequently called "bonds",[3] whether the obligation is secured or not, although

1. See Henn, Law of Corporations, § 155; Hamilton, Corporations in a Nutshell (1980), Ch. 16. See also §§ 38.1–38.3, supra.

2. E. g. Model Bus.Corp.Act § 4(h); West's Ann.Calif.Corp.Code § 207. The New York Business Corporation Law is more comprehensive than most statutes in having a full section devoted to corporate bonds, debentures, and long-term notes. McKinney's N.Y.Bus.Corp.Law § 518.

3. McKinney's N.Y.Bus.Corp.Law § 102(a)(1) (defining "bonds" as including "secured and unsecured bonds, debentures and notes"). The term "bond" is sometimes defined as a formal promise (engraved or printed, signed, sealed) to pay a specific sum ("principal") at a fixed future time

the term "bond" is also used to denote that the obligation is secured by a mortgage or lien (security interest) on real or personal property or both.

The principal amount owed is the "principal"; the date when repayment of the principal is due is termed the "maturity date"; the portion of the periodic payments made in exchange for the time—use of money constitute "interest" (the rate of interest being often called the "coupon rate").

Debt securities may be issued for consideration equivalent to their principal amount, or for a greater consideration ("premium"), or for a lesser consideration ("discount").

In several jurisdictions, limitations may exist with respect to the consideration received by the Corporation for debt securities.

Some states expressly authorize the Articles of Incorporation to confer voting rights on debt security holders. A few jurisdictions permit other rights of Stockholders to be conferred on debt security holders.

Some debt securities are listed on one or more national securities exchanges, although such exchanges are frequently called "stock exchanges", but most are traded over-the-counter. Usually issued in denominations of $1,000 or multiples thereof, debt securities are quoted in terms of the interest paid on the principal amount.

A few states impose issue taxes on the issuance of certain debt securities.

The transfer of debt securities is governed by the Uniform Commercial Code.[4]

For additional discussion of debt financing, see Chapter 43, infra.

Bonds are long term obligations secured by a pledge of corporate property. Debentures are also long term debts but are unsecured promises to pay though usually accompanied by various restrictive covenants. Notes may be short term or long term and may be secured or unsecured. They differ from bonds and debentures in that the rights of bondholders and debenture holders are often expressed in a tripartite Agreement called the "Trust Indenture" or "Deed of Trust." It is entered into between the company, the bondholders or debenture holders, and the trustee who is their representative. There are of course many variations from the conventional.

("maturity date") and fixed interest ("coupon rate") periodically. Bonds are not always so formal; their maturities can be foreshortened by acceleration-in-event-of-default, redemption, or conversion features; the interest payments are not always fixed but may be dependent upon income. Some statutes expressly authorize facsimile signatures of corporate officers.

4. U.C.C. Article 8. See note 2, supra, and see also chapter 52, infra with respect to transfer of securities.

(a) Short-Term Financing. Short term financing is used commonly to raise working capital or funds needed only on a seasonal basis. It is much less desirable for business expansion purposes, as there is no assurance of renewals, and the changes in the money market may cause creditors to press for immediate payment, to demand high interest rates, or to renew only for very short periods.

Suppliers to a business may extend credit to it in various ways. These are called "trade credits". A purchaser may be able to take a discount from invoice price on goods paid for within a certain number of days after invoice date or middle or end of month; he may be expected to pay the full invoice price within 30 days but can take the discount if he pays within the discount period. Waiting to the end of the discount period to pay enables the purchaser to have the use of the goods for a few days interest free. Waiting to the end of the 30 day period in effect enables the purchaser to borrow the price, under terms commonly used, for about 20 days at 2% interest (or 36% per annum).[5] The sale may also be an open account, in which case there may be an understanding that the seller may charge interest if payment is not made within a certain period after sale; or the buyer may give an unsecured promissory note. Use of such notes is considered poor practice by many credit analysts, however.[6] Suppliers may also use trade acceptances, which are time drafts drawn by the supplier on the buyer for the price of goods shipped, accepted by the buyer, and returned to the seller. The acceptance either is held by the seller until maturity and collected through bank channels, or is discounted before maturity. Although the use of trade acceptances has had vigorous advocates, it has not become popular.

Commercial banks are a major source of short term loans, for many businesses. Often a "line of credit" is arranged, which is the maximum amount the bank will permit the business to borrow; the business can borrow against this amount and repay its loans from time to time as long as the line is open. Usually the bank expects the customer to maintain a deposit, called the compensating balance, equal to a specified percentage of the line of credit, and it often expects that all loans outstanding against the line will be paid off periodically (such as once a year). When a business borrows against the line of credit, normally it will give the bank an unsecured promissory note. Where there has been no arrangement for line of credit,

5. In many businesses where profit margins are low and competition great, failure to take advantage of each discount may mean the difference between profit or loss. But trade credit may be easier to get than bank loans, and may permit a greater volume operation on less investment by the entrepreneur.

6. Notes may be taken from delinquent debtors. A business which has unsecured notes payable may find it difficult to obtain other types of credit; a vendor which has notes receivable (unsecured) may be suspected of unwise credit policies or poor collection practices.

a bank may be willing to loan on unsecured notes, but again may expect a "compensating balance" in the borrower's checking account. The effect of this "balance" requirement is to increase the cost of the loan to the buyer, above the stated interest rate. In addition to the expense, a risk of this type of financing is that when money is tight it may be difficult to renew loans. Banks also make secured loans, which may be secured by various types of collateral, such as readily marketable stocks or bonds which the borrower owns, warehouse receipts, bills of lading or trust receipts, real estate, equipment and other chattels, and even savings account pass books. Banks also discount commercial paper, including installment obligations, and engage in accounts receivable financing.

Commercial finance companies and factoring organizations may also make equipment or inventory loans, discount commercial paper, and engage in accounts receivable financing. Life insurance companies, and other institutional investors, may make loans against or secured by insurance on the life of an owner or major officer of the business.

Bankers' acceptances, under letters of credit, are a short-term financing method for acquiring inventories, which are used more commonly by exporters and importers than by those engaged in domestic trade. The drafts drawn by the vendor are accepted by the bank; the bank makes a charge (or commission) for its acceptance. Although the charges are low, the buyer may have to agree to store goods in a public warehouse until they are sold, and the storage fees and handling charges can add considerable expense.

Short-term loans are generally an expensive method of financing acquisition of fixed assets, or for inventory speculation; the funds obtained by these loans should be so invested so that the assets acquired can be converted into cash in time to pay the loan when due.

(b) Intermediate Term Financing. Short-term loans mature in a year or less. Long-term loans mature ten years or more after they are made. Intermediate-term loans fill the gap between; three to five years is most common. Many term loans of this type require repayment in periodic installments over the life of the loan; the loan may be either secured or unsecured. The contract for the loan may contain substantial restrictions on certain acts of the borrower, including limitations on dividend and salary payments. If the loan is for more than five years, a lending bank may share the loan with an insurance company.

Many loans for an intermediate term have been made by or supported by agencies of the federal government.

(c) Long-Term Financing. Long-term financing is obtained primarily by issuing bonds or debentures that are repayable ten years or more in the future. They usually bear interest at a fixed rate, but can be retired through use of sinking funds, or may contain provisions permitting early redemption. Many are issued pursuant to a trust indenture that defines the rights, privileges and obligations of the parties, and provides a trustee to act in the event the debtor fails to perform as required thereunder. See Chapter 43, infra. Long-term financing may be used to raise funds for initial establishment of a business, normal growth, modernization, and expansion into other fields or an enlarged position in the original field.

In recent years "subordinated debt" issues of promissory notes and debentures have been used increasingly to meet long-term capital needs. These have been placed, for the most part, with insurance companies and other institutional investors. The obligations, in the event of insolvency, liquidation or reorganization of the borrower, are made subordinate and junior in right of payment to specified other indebtedness of the borrower (which may include accounts payable and loans from banks).

Library References:

C.J.S. Corporations §§ 1146–1148, 1150, 1158, 1160, 1161, 1192.
West's Key No. Digests, Corporations ⚷469 et seq.

§ 38.32 Leasing—Lease-Purchase—Sale and Lease-Back

Leasing, leasing with option to purchase, and sale with lease-back arrangements in connection with facilities, equipment and rolling stock enable a business to conserve its capital or to make more economic use of capital. Railroad leasing of lines and cars has been a practice of long standing; leasing of industrial equipment, machinery, and motor vehicles is a relatively new practice, though it will be increasingly attractive as a result of favorable tax advantages resulting from the Economic Recovery Tax Act of 1981.

Leasing is a convenient method to acquire the use of an asset without committing substantial capital and without the costs that would be involved in raising the capital. Many leases include provisions under which rental charges can be adjusted for various reasons, and thus continuing costs are less rigidly fixed than for security issues used to finance purchases. The rental costs are deductible for tax purposes, when paid or accrued; interest costs necessitated by financing are deductible in most circumstances,[7] and the cost of purchasing the asset is recoverable for tax purposes through investment credits and cost recovery allowances to the nominal lessor (see IRC § 168 as added by the ERTA of 1981).

7. IRC § 465.

For tax purposes some leases, whether with option to purchase or not, have been treated as if they were sales; as a result, only deductions for depreciation and for "interest" or similar charges may be allowed.[8] This result may occur where a large rental amount, payable over a relatively short period, approximates the purchase price of the asset and the lessee can continue to use the asset after that period by making relatively nominal payments. Internal Revenue Code § 168(f)(8) provides a safe harbor in this regard.

The Economic Recovery Tax Act [9] (in new IRC § 168(f)(8)) creates a safe harbor that guarantees that a transaction will be characterized as a lease for purposes of allowing investment credits and cost recovery allowances to the nominal lessor. To come within the safe harbor, both the lessor and the lessee must affirmatively elect to treat the lessor as the owner of the property. The lessor must be a corporation, a partnership of corporations, or a grantor trust, the grantor and beneficiaries of which are all corporations. At all times during the term of the lease and at the time that the property is placed in service, the lessor must have a minimum "at-risk" investment of not less than 10 percent of the adjusted basis of the property. In addition, the term of the lease (including all extensions) cannot exceed the greater of (1) 90 percent of the useful life of the property under section 167 or (2) 150 percent of the present class life (ADR midpoint as of January 1, 1981). Only property that is new IRC section 38 property [10] (or certain qualified mass commuting vehicles) may come within the safe harbor rules. The leased property must be leased within 3 months after its acquisition or, in the case of a sale-leaseback transaction, it must be purchased by the lessor within 3 months of the lessee's acquisition for a purchase price that does not exceed the adjusted basis of the property in the hands of the lessee at the time of the lessor's purchase. It is anticipated that the Secretary of the Treasury may prescribe regulations under which property which is part of a facility may not be deemed placed in service until the entire facility is placed in service in order to make the leasing rules available with respect to the entire facility.

If a transaction meets the above requirements, the transaction will be treated as a lease and the parties of the transaction will be treated as lessor and lessee as stipulated in their agreement.

§ 38.33 The Trust Indenture

Debt securities are often issued under an indenture or agreement, to which the issuer and a trustee (usually a financial institution) are parties. The issuer of bonds and a "trustee" [11] are the parties who en-

8. Starr's Estate v. C. I. R., 274 F.2d 294 (9th Cir. 1959).

9. ERTA Sec. 201.

10. As defined in IRC § 48(b).

11. The term "Trustee" probably is inaccurate, as he does not have the same fiduciary responsibilities as trustees under deeds of trust.

ter into the supplementary contract known as the "trust indenture"; individual bondholders are beneficiaries thereunder. Under the Trust Indenture Act of 1939, if the bond issue is intended for public distribution, the "trustee" must be a financially responsible bank with capital and surplus of at least $150,000 which has no affiliation with the issuer.[12]

Some of the provisions of the indenture restate or elaborate on statements in the bond. These include the amounts due on each bond, maturity date, interest rate and interest payment date, and any provisions for anticipatory payment (or redemption) of the debt; [13] also the security for the obligation will be described, in character and extent, or the indenture will state that the obligation is unsecured.

Other provisions may be referred to in the bond, indirectly or with little detail. These may include covenants of the debtor to protect and preserve the security (paying taxes; repairing; replacing worn-out equipment; covenants against permitting waste or destruction), provisions as to the remedies available to individual bondholders or the trustee in the event of default, provisions defining the powers and duties of the trustee, and covenants regarding discharge of liens upon full payment by the debtor. Many indentures provide that any of the terms can be modified or altered, if consent thereto is obtained from a substantial proportion (often 80% or more) of the bondholders. The issuer may also covenant to maintain a specific working capital, to limit salaries, to limit dividends, to establish a sinking fund for redemption and pay into that fund periodically, and to keep properties insured. The indenture will also provide to what extent the "trustee" is liable to the individual bondholders if the debtor fails to perform any of his obligations or covenants or is negligent in his performance. Many provide that the individual bondholder cannot bring action against the debtor for defaults; sometimes this is true until he has asked the trustee to act and the trustee has refused to act.[14] There is no indenture form in general use.

12. 15 U.S.C.A. §§ 77aaa–77bbbb. See also Rabinowitz v. Kaiser-Fraser Corp., 111 N.Y.S.2d 539 (1953), involving allegations that the trustee had conflicting interests because it was creditor of a company which acquired the issuer's assets but did not undertake to assume the issuer's obligations under the indenture.

13. Where redemption is permitted, the issuer usually pays a premium above face value to do so. It may be advantageous to pay the premium, if interest rates are down, if the property securing the debt is to be sold free from liens, or if it is expedient to create a larger bond issue. Sinking funds frequently are set up to enable redemption to occur. Some bond issues have serial maturities, so that portions become due periodically; no premium payment is required to redeem that portion of the issue which has become due.

14. See Aladdin Hotel Co. v. Bloom, 200 F.2d 627 (8th Cir. 1953).

§ 38.34 Classification of Debt Securities [15]

Debt securities, as mentioned, usually involve the Corporation's obligation to pay principal when due (the maturity can be from 30 days or less to 100 years or more), and interest (usually at a fixed rate) while the obligation is outstanding.

Debt securities can be classified in various ways, depending upon the feature or features being emphasized. Often the designation or title of the security will reflect one or more such features.

One generally-accepted classification system for corporate debt securities is as to (a) maturity, (b) purpose, (c) security of principal, (d) income, (e) payees of principal and interest, (f) manner of payment of principal, and (g) conversion.

(a) Maturity. While debt securities, in a broad sense, can, from the point of view of maturity, be "short-time" (say, one year or less), "short-term" (say, five or 10 years or less), or "long-term" (say, more than five or 10 years)—there is little general agreement as to the precise lines of demarcation—the term debt securities is often reserved for obligations of more than "short-time" duration, i. e., for "short-term" or "long-term" obligations. Short-term obligations are sometimes referred to as "unfunded debt"; long-term obligations are often called "funded debt".

(b) Purpose. The purpose of the issue, while usually not a very significant feature, provides a classification basis.

Purchase-money securities are those issued in direct payment for property acquired by the Corporation. Such securities are often secured by a lien on such property.

Construction securities are those issued to finance construction of the Corporation's physical property in the sense that the proceeds realized from their issue are intended to be applied to pay for construction. *Extension* securities involve the application of their proceeds to pay for extensions to physical property. *Improvement* securities are issued to raise funds for the improvement of existing physical property. Obviously, these terms have overlapping meanings.

Funding securities involve the creation of a long-term obligation where none existed before. The proceeds are often used to retire short-term obligations. *Refunding* securities involve the issue of long-term obligations to provide funds to retire other long-term obligations. Neither term has any reference to sinking fund or other reserves.

15. See Henn, Law of Corporations (2d ed. 1970) § 156; Hamilton, Corporations in a Nutshell (1980).

Consolidated securities constitute an issue sufficiently large to provide the funds to retire two or more outstanding issues of debt securities.

Adjustment securities are those issued, usually in reorganization, in substitution for outstanding securities. The "adjustments" might involve lower interest charges, extended maturity, [*and/or*] decreased principal.

(c) Security of Principal. Debt securities are also classifiable according to the mortgage, pledge, or other security, if any, enjoyed by the holder in addition to the personal obligation of the issuer or principal obligor. The holder of an unsecured debt security ranks equally with other general creditors. Even the holder of a secured debt security is, after exhaustion of the security, a general creditor with respect to any unsatisfied balance.

Mortgage securities are secured by a mortgage or lien on the property of the issuer. First mortgage bonds are generally the senior issue, although not necessarily a first lien on all the property. There might, for example, be prior tax liens, purchase-money obligations, or prior liens on small segments of the property. Junior mortgage bonds are secured by a second or subsequent lien on the property. While the designations for such a junior issue vary, "General Mortgage Bonds" is frequently used.

Mortgage bonds are usually issued under a several-hundred page mortgage trust indenture (sometimes called a deed of trust or trust agreement) between the corporate issuer (mortgagor) and a trustee or trustees (mortgagee(s)). The trustee, usually a financial institution, represents the frequently numerous, scattered, and sometimes unknown mortgage bondholders. The indenture may be "closed-end" (limited as to amount of bonds to be issued thereunder) or "open-end" (without such limit). In the latter case, the indenture will usually provide for the authentication by the trustee of the initial issue or issues merely upon the request of the issuer and for the authentication of additional bonds of later series (e. g., "Series B", etc., usually under supplemental indentures) on the basis of property additions, retirement of prior liens, refunding of bonds outstanding under the indenture, or the deposit of cash equal to the principal amount of the bonds authenticated. Bonds of the various series are all equally and ratably secured (except as to any sinking fund established for any particular series) by the indenture.

Bridge, Dock, Divisional, or *Terminal* securities are issued to finance such special purpose properties, and are usually secured by a lien thereon.

Collateral trust securities involve a pledge of personal property, usually securities of other issuers, especially subsidiaries, owned by the obligor. Such financing has the possible advantages of being on the credit of the holding company, which might be better known than the subsidiary, of avoiding after-acquired property clauses, and of permitting the holding company to retain any control, at least prior to default, over the subsidiary.

Equipment obligations involve the issue of various types of securities (mortgage bonds, collateral trust bonds, preferred shares, certificates of beneficial interest), secured by equipment. Such financing has been most used with respect to railroad rolling stock, although it has been tried in other situations, including recently with respect to the aircraft of airlines.[16]

Debentures are generally unsecured obligations, involving only the personal obligation of the obligor, in the United States. Debentures are often issued under an indenture (sometimes called a trust agreement or deed of trust) between the issuer and a trustee. Debenture indentures, of course, have no granting clauses, since they do not involve any lien or mortgage. For the same reason, since there is no problem of equal and ratable security for a series of issues usually the indenture is "closed-end" and there is a separate indenture for each issue of debentures.

To protect debenture holders who rank as general creditors, the debentures and/or indenture might limit borrowing, impose a current liabilities-assets margin requirement, restrict dividend payments, limit share redemption or purchase, require the maintenance of certain reserves, or restrict additional issues of securities. Common protective provisions are so-called "negative pledges" and similar covenants.

Long-term loans from commercial banks and insurance companies have become frequent in recent years, a departure from the long-standing tradition in favor of short-term commercial bank loans. Since the issue involves no public offering, Securities and Exchange Commission requirements, with attendant complexities and expense, can be avoided. The loan agreement, compared to an indenture, is a relatively short (say 30 or so pages) and simple instrument. Several commercial banks might form a group to make the loan.

Subordinated debentures and notes are obligations (sometimes called "subordinated debt", "junior debt" or "inferior debt") upon which the right to receive payment is subordinated by a "subordination agreement" or "subordination clause" in the indenture which provides for the prior payment of certain other indebtedness (sometimes called "senior debt", "superior debt", "prior debt", or "bank debt") of the same debtor. The subordination might be "*inchoate*" (not operative until a voluntary or involuntary distribution of as-

16. 15 U.S.C.A. §§ 79–79z–6.

sets by the debtor to its creditors) or "complete" (payment of principal and interest on the "subordinated debt" is deferred until the obligations on the "senior debt" are satisfied). Such arrangements developed in the late 1930's, with issues by sales finance and small loan companies, spreading to the oil and chemical industries and other industrial concerns, most recently to public utilities.

Assumed obligations are obligations originally issued by Corporations involved in corporate mergers or consolidations. In such situations, the Corporation emerging from the amalgamation assumes the obligations of the constituent Corporations whose corporate existences end.

Guaranteed obligations are those issued by one Corporation (primary obligor) and guaranteed as to payment of principal and/or interest by another Corporation the (guarantor—secondary obligor). Technically, there are two securities, the underlying one issued by the principal obligor and the guaranty issued by the guarantor. The common example are securities issued by a subsidiary and guaranteed by its parent.[17]

Receiver's certificates are generally issued by a Corporation in financial difficulties to raise necessary working capital, pursuant to an order of the court having jurisdiction over insolvency, receivership, bankruptcy arrangement, or reorganization proceedings involving the Corporation. Such certificates are usually given a sufficiently high claim priority to assure their repayment out of the assets of the Corporation.

(d) Income. According to their provisions for income ("interest"), debt securities may be classified. Taxwise, interest on debt securities, unlike dividends on shares, has the advantage of being deductible for federal and state income tax purposes. In unusual situations, debt securities might be made noninterest-bearing (although, if related parties are involved, this may create problems. See § 56.11, infra.

Traditionally, debt securities have involved a *fixed* interest charge. The interest rate is usually fixed in one-eighth units of a percent with resulting adjustment in the price of the security, either at a discount or at a premium. The obligation to pay definite interest continues regardless of the financial status of the Corporation, with the result that such a fixed charge can be embarrassing in hard times. In the latter event, "trading on equity" or "leverage" has the effect of magnifying losses.

17. Both securities, therefore, must be issued, and any indentures relating thereto must be qualified, under applicable requirements of state "blue sky" statutes, the Federal Securities Act of 1933, and the Federal Trust Indenture Act of 1939.

Income obligations condition the obligation to pay interest, in whole or part, on corporate earnings. Sometimes the obligation is entirely dependent upon earnings. On the other hand, there might be a fixed obligation to pay a stated percentage of interest regardless of earnings, with the rest of the interest dependent upon earnings. The interest provision, to the extent of its income-dependent feature, might be cumulative or noncumulative.

To the extent that interest is dependent upon earnings, such feature somewhat resembles the dividend feature of shares. However, to the extent of earnings, there is a definite obligation to pay, in contrast to the usual discretionary power of the Corporation to declare dividends even when legally available funds are available.

Income obligations are usually issued to minimize the Corporation's fixed charges in bad times. Such interest provisions are a common feature of adjustment obligations or obligations, usually junior in nature, issued under corporate reorganization plans.

Obligations which call for interest payments in addition to the interest rate are known as "*participating*" obligations. Such a profit-sharing feature is rare but may be used to sweeten securities with otherwise low interest rates or interest-dependent-upon-income features.

(e) Payees of Principal and Interest. Debt securities are classifiable as to the payees of principal and interest into two types: (a) registered, and (b) coupon.[18] Traditionally, the same issue has been available, at the choice of any holder, in either form, and either form has been exchangeable for the other at the request of the holder. When such exchange privilege exists, the security is sometimes called "interchangeable" or "exchangeable".

A *registered* security bears the name of the owner, who is also registered as the owner with his address on the registry books maintained by the registrar for the issue. The principal, upon maturity, and interest, on the interest dates, are paid to such registered owner. Such securities are usually in denominations

18. Similar classifications sometimes list three categories: (a) "registered", (b) "coupon", (c) "registered coupon". The twofold categorization combines the last two. There is growing investor acceptance of registered bonds. More than half of the new bond issues are appearing only in registered form. Listed among the advantages of registered bonds are convenience, safety, better notice procedures, savings in manpower costs, storage costs and human effort, compared to the antiquated wasteful procedures involved in coupon bonds. Sebring, "Registered Bonds—A Brief Progress Report", 20 Bus.Law. 238 (1964); Waldbillig, "Coupon Bonds Have Advantages", 19 Bus.Law. 999 (1964); Sebring, " 'The Coupon Bond: A Costly Paradox'—A postscript", 18 Bus.Law. 429 (1963); Sebring, "The Coupon Bond: A Costly Paradox", 17 Bus.Law. 844 (1962).

of $1,000 or any multiple thereof. Ownership is transferred by a duly-executed assignment either on the security itself or by separate instrument.[19] Registered securities are "negotiable instruments" under the Uniform Commercial Code, which defines a "bona fide purchaser" as a purchaser for value in good faith and without notice of any adverse claim who takes delivery of a security in bearer form or of one in registered form issued to him or indorsed to him or in blank.[20]

A *coupon* security usually provides for the payment of principal to the bearer thereof, and for payment of an installment of interest to the bearer of the respective interest coupons upon presentation thereof upon their respective due dates. Coupon securities are usually in the denomination of $1,000. Ownership of the security and/or coupons is transferred by delivery thereof. Such a security is negotiable under the Uniform Commercial Code.[21]

Coupon securities often may be registered as to principal (sometimes called "*registered coupon*" form), in which case the principal is payable to the registered owner but the interest remains payable to the bearers of the respective interest coupons. When a coupon security so registered is assigned in blank, it, of course, might be negotiable. If a coupon security so registered is made payable to bearer, principal would again become payable to the bearer of the security.

Obviously, the owners of bearer securities are often unknown to the issuer, the trustee, and the other security holders. This accounts for various provisions for publication of notices (e. g., redemption notice) and the difficulty of rounding up sufficient security holders to take effective action or to compel the trustee to act under certain circumstances.

19. See Uniform Commercial Code § 8–102(1)(c), providing: "A security is in 'registered form' when it specifies a person entitled to the security or to the rights it evidences and when its transfer may be registered upon books maintained for that purpose by or on behalf of an issuer or the security so states." This is comparable to the record ownership and transfer of shares.

20. Uniform Commercial Code §§ 8–105, 8–302. Under the former Uniform Negotiable Instruments Act, registered securities were not negotiable instruments because they were not negotiable in form. Landau v. Best, 41 Del.Ch. 1, 187 A.2d 75 (1962), appeal dismissed 375 U.S. 801, 84 S.Ct. 25, 11 L.Ed.2d 37 (1963). Compare Harr v. Market St. Title & Trust Co., 326 Pa. 410, 190 A. 903 (1957), with Reynolds v. Title Guar. & Trust Co., 240 N.Y. 257, 148 N.E. 514 (1925).

21. Uniform Commercial Code §§ 8–105, 8–302. See id. § 8–102(1) (d), providing: "A security is in 'bearer form' when it runs to bearer according to its terms and not by reason of any indorsement." See also Chapter 52, infra, for discussion of applicability of U.C.C. Article 8 to transfer of securities.

(f) Manner of Payment of Principal. Another way of classifying debt securities is by manner of payment of principal.

All debt securities are legal tender obligations.

One of the traditional features of debt securities is fixed maturity. The corporate issuer, like any other debtor, has no implied right of prepayment.[22]

A frequent provision, however, is a *redemption* provision permitting[23] the Corporation to redeem (call) the issue in whole or part prior to maturity at the redemption price. The redemption price is often set forth as the face amount plus a redemption premium which is usually scaled from, say, five or so percentage points above the face amount or public offering price on the first possible redemption date (often the first anniversary of the issue), down to zero on the maturity date, plus any accrued interest. The redemption procedure is prescribed and usually involves the giving of redemption notice by mail and/or publication, and the deposit of the funds necessary for redemption no later than the redemption date. If there has been compliance with such procedure, the security holders on or after the redemption date lose all their rights except to receive the redemption price upon surrender of their securities. Sometimes the redemption feature is tied in with the operation of a sinking fund provision,[24] or a conversion feature.

Redemption before maturity might be desirable to the Corporation to reduce fixed charges, improve credit standing, avoid high interest rates, free property from any mortgage or pledge, invest any sinking fund, refund or refinance at a lower interest rate, or forestall or promote exercise of any conversion privilege. The redemption premium is supposed to compensate the holder for delay in reinvesting his funds returned to him upon redemption and for any less advantageous market at such time.

22. The Corporation might, of course, purchase its securities by negotiating with holders thereof. Acceleration-in-event-of-default provisions can operate to advance the maturity.

23. Redemption provisions are usually discretionary but can be mandatory. The option is usually in the issuer, but can be in the holder. See Chapters 61 et seq., infra, for additional discussion of stock redemptions.

24. Sinking funds are established to provide funds for the payment of principal not only by periodic partial redemption but also for the periodic retirement of serial bonds or for the payment of securities at maturity. Sinking funds are generally created by contract which usually provide for the administration of the fund by a trustee, but in some instances, the Corporation itself may retain control of the fund. The use of a sinking fund will increase the safety of an issue by reducing the amount of the bonds outstanding and by providing funds for their repayment. The amount of the periodic contribution to the fund will vary with the type of security and will usually be stipulated in the bond or trust indenture. The periodic contributions may be based on a percentage of annual earnings, the face value of the bonds divided by the duration of the bonds, or on an actuarial basis. Such amounts

(g) Conversion. A *convertible* debt security involves the privilege, usually at the option of the holder, of converting it into some other debt or equity. If the latter is a more senior debt security, the conversion is said to be "upstream"; if a junior debt security or shares, "downstream".

Debt securities convertible into shares have been frequently issued, because they combined safety (creditor status) with opportunity for possible speculative gain (increase in price of shares beyond conversion price), and result in retirement of debt, reduction of fixed charges, and substitution of equity interests.[25] Obviously, the Corporation should have enough shares of authorized and unissued shares to take care of the exercise of any subsisting conversion privileges.

To prevent dilution of the conversion privilege during the conversion period, which may run from issue to maturity (subject to any prior redemption) or for a shorter period, so-called "anti-dilution" provisions are included to make adjustments of the number of shares issuable upon exercise of the conversion privilege in certain instances, the most common being (a) issuance of shares for less than the conversion price, (b) issuance of rights to subscribe to or purchase shares or securities convertible into shares, (c) issuance of securities convertible into or exchangeable for shares, at a price less than the conversion price, (d) issuance of dividend of shares or securities convertible into shares, (e) share splits, (f) abnormally large cash dividends, (g) distributions of assets, (h) subdivision or combination of shares or securities convertible into shares; and (i) reorganizations, reclassifications, mergers, or consolidations.

might be reduced by the earnings of the sinking funds.

Failure to meet the sinking fund requirements might constitute an event of default which would permit the trustee to accelerate the maturity of the principal.

For additional coverage of redemptions, see Chapters 62 et seq., infra.

25. The New York Business Corporation Law devotes a section to convertible securities. McKinney's N.Y. Bus.Corp.Law § 519 (expressly authorizing bonds convertible into other bonds or shares of Corporation, requiring that sufficient number of authorized but unissued shares be issued to satisfy any conversion privilege and that minimum consideration requirements applicable to shares be met). See generally C. Pilcher, Raising Capital with Convertible Securities (1955); Katzin, "Financial and Legal Problems in the Use of Convertible Securities", 24 Bus.Law. 359 (1969); Note, "Convertible Securities: Holder Who Fails to Convert Before Expiration of the Conversion Period", 54 Cornell L.Rev. 271 (1969). See also West's Ann.Calif.Corp.Code § 403.

§§ 38.35–38.40 are reserved for supplementary material.

D. TAX IMPLICATIONS OF THE ISSUANCE OF STOCK AND DEBT

Library References:

West's Key No. Digests, Internal Revenue ⚷3640 et seq.
Kahn, Basic Corporate Taxation, 3rd Ed., § 8.31 et seq.

§ 38.41 Introduction

When parties form a Corporation, they must determine whether their contributions to the Corporation should be made in the form of an equity investment or whether funds or property should be "loaned" to the Corporation. A loan to the Corporation may be represented by a security or by short-term notes,[1] both of which are debt instruments.

The question whether property contributed to a Corporation should be an investment or a loan does not arise exclusively on formation of the Corporation. Property is frequently contributed to a controlled Corporation that has been in existence for some years, and the issue is also present there. It is possible for the question to arise in a reorganization setting, but the fact that the distribution of securities may be treated as a taxable distribution and that corporate notes will certainly be treated as a taxable distribution will often discourage the shifting of equity interests into debt.

If the parties have decided to use debt instruments, they must give due account to the fact that while (long term) securities do not constitute as a taxable distribution in a § 351 exchange, corporate notes do not enjoy that exclusion. In a few circumstances the transferor may wish to recognize gain on the contribution of his property to the Corporation, so that the Corporation will enjoy a higher basis in the property received by it. The distribution of short-term notes is one means of accomplishing that. In most circumstances the transferor will not wish to recognize gain at the time that the transfer is made. However, when the transferred asset is sold by the Corporation some years later, the Corporation may contend that the transferor received as a taxable distribution in order to increase its basis. The Corporation is particularly likely to make that contention if the statutory period for assessing a deficiency against the transferor has expired.

One of the more significant tax advantages in using debt instruments is that the Corporation's payment of interest on a debt is a deductible expense under § 163. In contrast, the Corporation's pay-

1. Other forms also are possible, but if long-term notes are used, the possibility exists that they will be treated as securities.

ment of dividends on an equity investment is not deductible. The Corporation's repayment of the principal of the debt instrument is a return of the capital of the bondholder or lender and usually will not cause him any tax consequences.[2] Again, in contrast, the Corporation's redemption of its stock from a Stockholder may be treated as a dividend to the Stockholder. See Chapters 61 et seq., infra.

§ 38.42 Securities and Short Term Debt

As pointed out above, whether or not a transaction is taxable may depend on whether or not the instrument distributed is a security (which by definition is long term debt or equity) or short term debt (generally a note). The following seems relevant:

(1) Debt which matures in 10 years or more will generally be considered a security.[3]

(2) Debt which matures in less than 10 years will be a security if an overall evaluation of the nature of the debt, degree of participation and continuing interest in the business of the debt holder indicates that the debt holder has an investment which will fluctuate with the fortunes of the Corporation rather than a highly liquid, similar to cash position.[4] Most commentators feel that a debt of less than 5 years will probably be considered a short term note.

§ 38.43 Hybrid Stock and "Thin Incorporation"

A debt instrument will be treated as corporate stock where the attributes of the instrument more nearly resemble those of an equity investment than those of a debt, i. e., so-called "hybrid stock." In general, the difference between a Stockholder and a creditor is that the Stockholder's intention is to embark on the corporate adventure, accepting the risks of loss so that he may participate in profits; on the other hand, a creditor does not intend to undertake such risks but to loan capital to others who do intend to take such risks.[5] In practice, this generalization is of limited assistance in distinguishing debts from equity investments.

When a debt is treated as stock, it may create unpleasant consequences. Interest paid on the debt is not deductible, and payments made in retirement of the debt may constitute dividends. If the par-

2. If the Corporation had previously made an election under Subchapter S, the lender's basis in his debt instrument may have been reduced because of a pass-through of the Corporation's net operating losses. See Chapter 86, infra. In such event, the lender will recognize income on the repayment of the debt.

3. Rev.Proc. 80–37.

4. Camp Wollers Enterprises, Inc. v. Comm'r., 22 T.C. 737 (1954) and U. S. v. Mills, 399 F.2d 944 (5th Cir. 1964).

5. Motel Corp., 54 T.C. 1433, 1436 (1970).

ties have relied on a different treatment and acted accordingly, this change could prove to be financially embarrassing.

In some circumstances, the taxpayer may wish to have a nominal "debt" instrument treated as an equity investment. It is possible for the taxpayer to invoke the hybrid stock doctrine against the Internal Revenue Service, but the taxpayer will be allowed to do so only in extraordinary circumstances.[6]

It is difficult to ascertain the standards which will be employed by the Service or by the courts in determining whether a purported debt instrument constitutes hybrid stock. The ambiguities and uncertainty engendered by the many court decisions on this issue induced Congress, in the Tax Reform Act of 1969, to add § 385 to the Code for the purpose of providing greater certainty and predictability to this area.[7]

§ 38.44 Loans Guaranteed by Stockholders

As an alternative to making direct loans to a Corporation, the Stockholders might cause the Corporation to borrow the needed funds from a lending institution, and the Stockholders could personally guarantee the repayment of the loan. Since such loans are usually made on reliance of the credit of the Stockholders rather than on the credit of the Corporation, it is arguable that the substance of the transaction is a loan from the bank to the Stockholders and an equity investment of the borrowed funds by the Stockholders. See Rev.Rul. 79–4, 1979–1 Cum.Bull. 150. If the transaction were so characterized, the Corporation would not be allowed an income tax deduction for interest payments made on account of the loan, and all payments made by the Corporation on account of the loan would constitute constructive dividends to the Stockholders who guaranteed it.

The Service has raised this issue in several cases with mixed results.[8] The Service's prospects for so characterizing a corporate

6. Cornelius v. Commissioner, 494 F.2d 465, 471 (5th Cir. 1974).

7. S.Rept.No.91–552, 91st Cong., 2d Sess. 137–38 (1969). In the 1969 Act, Congress also imposed strict conditions on the deduction of interest on a debt incurred by a Corporation to acquire the assets or stock of another Corporation. § 279.

See also Treas.Regs. § 1.385–1 et seq. as discussed on pgs. 424–426, supra.

8. The Service advanced this contention unsuccessfully in Murphy Logging Co. v. U. S., 378 F.2d 222 (9th Cir. 1967), reversing 239 F.Supp. 794 (D.Or.); and again in a different context in Santa Anita Consolidated, Inc., 50 T.C. 536 (1968), acq. 1969–2 Cum.Bull. xxv. Cf. Wheat v. U. S., 353 F.Supp. 720 (S.D.Tex.1973). The Service prevailed on this contention in Plantation Patterns, Inc. v. Commissioner, 462 F.2d 712 (5th Cir. 1972), certiorari denied, 409 U.S. 1076, 93 S.Ct. 683, 34 L.Ed.2d 664. See also Herbert Enoch, 57 T.C. 781 (1972), acq. on this issue, 1974–1 Cum.Bull. 1, where a Corporation's redemption of its stock with borrowed funds pursuant to a bootstrap acquisition of the Corporation by another Stockholder did not cause income to

loan are strongest when the Corporation has a high debt-equity ratio.[9]

In any event, even if the loan is not deemed to have been made by the Stockholder, any loss suffered by the Stockholder for repayment of the debt under his guaranty will usually be treated as a nonbusiness bad debt which is only deductible as a capital loss under § 166(d).[10] The better solution is to have the Stockholder borrow from the bank and reloan the funds to the Corporation. Thus, if the Corporation does not repay (unless the loan to the Corporation is deemed to be hybrid stock), the loss will be deductible against ordinary income.[11]

§ 38.45 Stock Treated as Debt

The typical setting for a dispute over whether a corporate interest should be treated as a debt or as an equity investment is one in which the instrument involved purports to represent a debt. However, the same question can arise where the corporate interest is represented by what purports to be stock. In Joseph Miele, 56 T.C. 556 (1971), affirmed, the taxpayer unsuccessfully contended that a corporate interest owned by him in the nominal form of preferred stock actually represented a debt. While expressly refraining from passing on the issue, the Third Circuit noted in Scriptomatic, Inc. v. U. S., 555 F.2d 364, 368, n. 4 (3d Cir. 1977), that in an appropriate case, a corporate interest "not debt in form might be found to be debt in economic reality."

In Zilkha & Sons, Inc., 52 T.C. 607 (1969), the Commissioner unsuccessfully sought to have a corporate interest in the nominal form of preferred stock characterized as a debt instrument. The Corporation had no earnings and profits, and so the distributions made on its stock did not constitute ordinary income dividends. The Commissioner unsuccessfully sought to have the distributions characterized as interest which would constitute ordinary income to the distributees.

the other Stockholder. See Jassy, The Tax Treatment of Bootstrap Stock Acquisitions: The Redemption Route vs. The Dividend Route, 87 Harv.L.Rev. 1459, 1466–1467 (1974); Rev.Rul. 79–4, 1979–1 Cum.Bull. 150.

9. See Comment, Guaranteed Loans and Direct Loans: Equal Treatment Under the Tax Law, 16 U.C.L.A.L. Rev. 421 (1969). See, e. g., Plantation Patterns, Inc. v. Commissioner, 462 F.2d 712 (5th Cir.), certiorari denied 409 U.S. 1076, 93 S.Ct. 683, 34 L.Ed.2d 664 (1972); and Rev.Rul. 79–4, supra.

10. See Putnam v. Commissioner, 352 U.S. 82, 77 S.Ct. 175, 1 L.Ed.2d 144 (1956); U. S. v. Generes, 405 U.S. 93, 92 S.Ct. 827, 31 L.Ed.2d 62 (1972), rehearing denied 405 U.S. 1033, 92 S.Ct. 1274, 31 L.Ed.2d 491. But see Santa Anita Consolidated, Inc., 50 T.C. 536 (1968), acq. 1969–2 Cum.Bull. xxv, where a Stockholder's payment for release of its guaranty of a corporate debt was treated as an ordinary loss deduction under § 165.

11. IRC 165.

§ 38.46 Tax Considerations in Issuing Preferred Stock—Unfavorable Considerations

The issuance of preferred stock precludes an election under Subchapter S and will terminate an election that was previously made. §§ 1371(a)(4), 1372(e)(3). See Chapters 85 and 86, infra.

Dividends paid on preferred stock are not deductible expenses of the Corporation.

Nonvoting stock[12] will not qualify for redemption under the substantially disproportionate test (§ 302(b)(2)) unless the redemption of the nonvoting stock is made in conjunction with the redemption of voting stock; and even then, if the nonvoting stock is section 306 stock, the substantially disproportionate test will be of no use. Reg. § 1.302–3(a)(3).

Under § 1244(c)(1), preferred stock cannot qualify for ordinary loss treatment under § 1244.

The sale or redemption of preferred stock may cause adverse tax consequences under § 306. See Chapter 58, infra.

§ 38.47 Tax Considerations in Issuing Preferred Stock—Favorable Considerations

In most cases, preferred stock can be exchanged by a Corporation for its stock or securities pursuant to a recapitalization without causing the Stockholder to recognize gain on the transfer,[13] however the stock or securities then issued to the taxpayer will be tainted if they were originally § 306 stock.[14] See Chapter 58, infra.

Under § 305, preferred stock can often be distributed by a Corporation as a stock dividend without causing recognition of income to the Stockholder.

Preferred stock can qualify for the relief from dividend treatment when stock of a decedent is being redeemed afforded by § 303 where the provisions of that section are applicable. (See Chapter 65, infra).

The redemption of preferred stock, whether voting or nonvoting, in complete termination of a Stockholder's interest in a Corporation will qualify for redemption treatment under § 302(b)(3) even where the preferred is section 306 stock. §§ 302(b)(3), 306(b)(1). For purposes of determining whether the Stockholder's interest was terminated, the attribution rules provided by § 318 are applicable, but

12. Preferred stock is usually nonvoting, but it need not be.

13. IRC § 306(b)(3).

14. IRC § 306(c)(1)(B)(i) and § 306(c)(1)(C).

the relief from those attribution rules accorded by § 302(c) is available. Reg. § 1.306–2(a). See Chapters 61 et seq., infra.

§ 38.48 Tax Considerations in Issuing Preferred Stock—Issuing Preferred Stock When the Corporation Is Formed

There can be advantages to issuing preferred stock when the Corporation is first formed, since this preferred stock will not constitute section 306 stock.[15] However, if the preferred stock is subsequently redeemed by the Corporation (when it has substantial earnings), the redemption must meet the not essentially equivalent to a dividend test of § 302(b)(1), or it will be treated as a dividend notwithstanding the inapplicability of § 306. This untainted preferred stock could there be sold by the Stockholder to a third party without adverse tax consequences, but it may be difficult to locate a purchaser unless the stock is invested with sufficient security that dividends will be paid thereon. It will often place too great a burden on the Corporation to require that substantial sums be paid as dividends during the formative years of the business; therefore, preferred stock issued at that time may not contain sufficient security to make it a desirable purchase. If preferred stock does not meet the demand of a prospective purchaser, and if the stock is modified to meet the purchaser's demands, then the advantage of having issued the stock in exchange for property transferred to a controlled Corporation may be lost in that § 306 may then become applicable or the change in rights may result in taxation pursuant to Reg. § 1.305–7 (see Chapter 58, infra).

15. The definition of section 306 stock refers to stock distributed as a stock dividend and preferred stock issued in a reorganization or corporate division. § 306(c). But, note IRC § 306(c)(1)(C).

§§ 38.49–39.0 are reserved for supplementary material.

CHAPTER 39

SUBSCRIPTIONS AND ISSUANCE OF SHARES

Table of Sections

Library References:

C.J.S. Corporations, §§ 196, 199, 210, 212, 222, 283–288.
West's Key No. Digests, Corporations ⚷70 et seq.

§ 39.1 Introductory Comment

This Chapter contains forms relating to the issuance of shares by a Corporation, both to raise the initial capital and to increase the financing of an on-going business.

Whenever the issuance of shares is contemplated, consideration must be given to the possible applicability of the federal securities laws and the state securities laws.

§ 39.2 Issuance of Shares and the Function of the Attorney

The shares to be initially issued by a new Corporation are usually approved at the organizational meeting of the Directors. The corporate attorney has three functions in this regard:

First, he should prepare the form of share certificate itself for approval by the Board, and he should have available at the meeting a supply of certificates suitable for issuance. Blank share certificates may be purchased at legal stationers. Many small Corporations have printed or engraved certificates, which, of course, must be ordered in advance. In order to save future printing expense, perhaps, fifteen or twenty certificates may be printed even though it is planned initially to issue only one or two. However, a printed certificate is not essential; a typed or even a handwritten certificate is entirely proper. Language for a suitable form of certificate is set forth in § 41.3 et seq., supra.

Second, he should make sure that the certificates to be issued are properly filled out by the appropriate corporate Officers.

Third, he should satisfy himself that the consideration for the shares is of the proper type, in the proper amount, and is actually received by the Corporation. These matters are important because there may be personal liability imposed on Directors or Stockholders if improper or insufficient consideration is received for shares.

§ 39.3 Subscriptions for Shares—Generally

A "subscription" or preincorporation subscription agreement or post incorporation subscription agreement is simply an offer to purchase and pay for a specified number of theretofore unissued shares of a Corporation. This should be contrasted with preincorporation agreements which, in addition to including an offer to purchase and pay, also include various agreements as to the structure of the Corporation and (often) the raising of capital. Such Agreements have largely supplanted the common law subscription, though the wording in such Agreements is usually that each investor "agrees to purchase *and subscribe* for * * *" the securities he agreed to purchase. Such Agreements, of course, are enforceable as simple bilateral contracts without reference to the special statutory provision relating to preincorporation subscriptions described above. See Chapter 29, supra. Subscriptions may be divided into "preincorporation subscriptions," that is, subscriptions for shares of a Corporation that has not yet been formed, and "postincorporation subscriptions," that is, subscriptions for unissued shares of an already existing Corporation. Older texts devote a great deal of attention to preincorporation subscriptions as a device by which a new venture may be assured of adequate capitalization before it is launched. At common law, uncertainty existed whether a subscriber might withdraw from such subscriptions before the Corporation came into existence and accepted them. The reason for this uncertainty was that subscriptions which were obtained individually were usually viewed as individual offers running from each subscriber to the Corporation rather than as a contract among subscribers with the promise of each subscriber supporting the promises of other subscribers.

This problem has largely faded away. Corporation statutes make preincorporation subscriptions enforceable by the Corporation for a limited period (six months in the Model Act[1]) after the formation

1. Model Bus.Corp.Act § 17 provides:

§ 17. Subscriptions for Shares

A subscription for shares of a Corporation to be organized shall be irrevocable for a period of six months, unless otherwise provided by the terms of the subscription agreement or unless all of the subscribers consent to the revocation of such subscription.

Unless otherwise provided in the subscription agreement, subscriptions for shares, whether made before or after the organization of a Corporation, shall be paid in full at such time, or in such installments

of the Corporation is completed without regard to technical questions of consideration; until that period has expired, the statute makes the preincorporation subscription irrevocable by the subscriber.

A subscription may be conditioned on the occurrence of certain events, such as obtaining a specified amount of capital, or a specified loan, or a specified lease. The fulfillment of such conditions is a condition precedent to the obligation of the subscribers. The common law developed a rather confusing distinction between such conditions and "subscriptions on special terms" which constituted a type of condition subsequent. There was little practical difference, however, because failure of the Corporation to comply with a "special term" also permitted the subscriber to rescind his subscription. A subscription induced by fraud may be rescinded as any other contract. The fraud may be committed by an agent of the Corporation or a promoter of the Corporation.

Modern distribution techniques for securities permit the meeting of all capital needs of publicly held Corporations without resort to subscriptions. Indeed, the use of subscriptions by such a Corporation is precluded as a practical matter by the federal securities laws and state "blue sky laws," because the subscriptions themselves constitute securities and may have to be registered as provided by those acts. Since the underlying securities themselves also may have to be registered, the use of subscriptions may result in two expensive registrations.

A person who subscribes or agrees to purchase shares does not become a Stockholder until the subscription price has been fully paid, though some states permit shares to be issued for promissory notes for the unpaid portion of the purchase price.

Subscriptions may be assigned or transferred. An assignee or transferee in good faith and without knowledge or notice that the full

and at such times, as shall be determined by the Board of Directors. Any call made by the Board of Directors for payment on subscriptions shall be uniform as to all shares of the same class or as to all shares of the same series, as the case may be. In case of default in the payment of any installment or call when such payment is due, the Corporation may proceed to collect the amount due in the same manner as any debt due the Corporation. The by-laws may prescribe other penalties for failure to pay installments or calls that may become due, but no penalty working a forfeiture of a subscription, or of the amounts paid thereon, shall be declared as against any subscriber unless the amount due thereon shall remain unpaid for a period of twenty days after written demand has been made therefor. If mailed, such written demand shall be deemed to be made when deposited in the United States mail in a sealed envelope addressed to the subscriber at his last post-office address known to the Corporation, with postage thereon prepaid. In the event of the sale of any shares by reason of any forfeiture, the excess of proceeds realized over the amount due and unpaid on such shares shall be paid to the delinquent subscriber or to his legal representative.

See also e. g. McKinney's N.Y.Bus.Corp. Law § 503.

consideration has not been paid, is not personally liable to the Corporation or its creditors. A personal representative or trustee binds the estate he represents by the execution or receipt of a subscription agreement, not himself personally.

§ 39.4 Internal Revenue Code § 1244

Internal Revenue Code § 1244 allows an ordinary deduction for any loss suffered on common stock received by an individual or Partnership to the extent of $50,000 ($100,000 in the case of a husband and wife filing a joint return) if:

(1) The aggregate amount of money and other property received by the Corporation for stock, as a contribution to capital and as paid-in surplus does not exceed $1,000,000. The determination shall be made as of the time of the issuance of the stock in question and will include amounts received for such stock and for all stock theretofore issued.

The amount taken into account with respect to any property other than money shall be the amount equal to the adjusted basis to the Corporation of such property for determining gain, reduced by any liability to which the property was subject or which was assumed by the Corporation as of the time the property was received by the Corporation.

(2) Such stock was issued by such Corporation for money or other property (other than stock and securities).

(3) Such Corporation, during the period of its 5 most recent taxable years ending before the date the loss on such stock was sustained, either (A) derived more than 50 percent of its aggregate gross receipts from sources other than royalties, rents, dividends, interests, annuities, and sales or exchanges of stocks or securities which result in gain or (B) the amount of deductions allowed (other than deductions for net operating losses, dividends received by the Corporation, dividends received on certain preferred stock, and dividends received from certain foreign corporations) exceeded the amount of gross income.

If the Corporation has not been in existence for 5 taxable years ending before the date the loss on the stock was sustained, gross receipts will be measured by the period of the Corporation's taxable years ending before such date, or if the Corporation has not been in existence for 1 taxable year ending before such date, the period such Corporation has been in existence before such date.

§ 39.5 Preincorporation Subscription Agreement—Short Form

[*Short Form*]

I hereby subscribe for and offer to purchase ______ shares of the common stock of ______ Corporation, par value $______ per share, a Corporation to be formed under the laws of the State of ______ for the total sum of $______, payable in cash upon call by the Board of Directors of ______ Corporation.[2]

My obligation hereunder is expressly conditioned on ______ Corporation obtaining enforceable subscriptions for its common stock which, upon acceptance thereof, will produce an aggregate equity capitalization of ______ Corporation of $______, or more.

I understand that this subscription may not be revoked by me within six months from the date hereof except with the consent of all other subscribers. This subscription shall expire six months from the date hereof if not theretofore accepted by ______ Corporation.

Dated: ______, 19__. /s/ ______________

COMMENTS

The classic preincorporation subscription agreement is not widely used today. In the closely held Corporation, agreements to invest usually take the form of a contract to purchase securities or a simple gentlemen's understanding, which is, of course, revocable. Where a public offering is involved, the federal securities laws and state securities acts, render the use of subscriptions impractical because a double registration may be required; both the subscription and the subsequent issue of shares are deemed securities. Under modern underwriting practices, potential investors may withdraw at any time prior to the receipt of a formal prospectus. However, many state close Corporation statutes, refer to "the initial subscribers to shares" at several points, and an attorney forming a close Corporation may wish to utilize subscription forms rather than a formal agreement.

State Corporation statutes commonly regulate preincorporation subscriptions. For a general discussion, see Chapter 29, supra. fra.

2. If subscription is to be paid in labor and/or property, a description of the labor to be performed and/or property to be conveyed to the Corporation and of its value "expressed in dollars" should be spelled out.

§ 39.6 Preincorporation Subscription Agreement—Another Form

SUBSCRIPTION AGREEMENT TO PURCHASE STOCK OF [NAME OF CORPORATION]

The undersigned hereby agree(s) to subscribe for shares of [*Name of Corporation*] upon the following terms and conditions:

Option 1 (Use if Corporation Has Not Yet Been Incorporated)

§ 1.1 Formation

The Features of Corporation to Incorporated are:

(1) Name: ______.

(2) Stock to be issued: [*Describe Stock and Number of Shares*].

(3) Stock to be authorized: [*Number*].

(4) Special Rights of Stockholders:

(A) Preemptive Rights.

(B) Cumulative Voting.

(C) Special Articles of Incorporation: [*Describe*].

(D) Special By-laws: [*Describe*].

§ 1.2 Consideration

The consideration to be paid by the Undersigned is: [*Describe*].

§ 1.3 Terms

The consideration will be paid: [*Describe Terms*].

Option 2

§ 1.4 Subchapter S Status

The Subscribers agree that they will cause the Corporation to elect to be taxed under Subchapter S of the Internal Revenue Code and that they will not transfer the stock of the Corporation if such transfer will cause the Corporation to lose its election to be taxed under Subchapter S of the Internal Revenue Code. It is agreed that a notation of this transfer restriction will appear on all share certificates issued by the Corporation.

§ 1.5 Stock

Upon full performance of (b) and (c) above, the undersigned shall receive: [*Describe Stock and Number*].

§ 1.6 Termination

This Agreement shall only be terminable if:

(a) The terms hereof are not met.

(b) The said stock is not tendered on or before 6 months after the execution of this agreement.

Option 3

(c) $[*Dollars*] is not raised among all [*initial subscribers/all subscribers who subscribe pursuant to this agreement*].

Option 4

(d) [*Describe Other Conditions*].

Subscribers:

____

Date: ______

____

Date: ______

____

Date: ______

____

Date: ______

§ 39.7 Preincorporation Subscription Agreement—Another Form

I do hereby subscribe to and agree to pay $______ in cash, which sum is hereinafter referred to as the principal sum of this subscription, for ______ shares of the common stock of a proposed Corporation, subject to the following terms and conditions:

(a) Such Corporation shall be duly incorporated under the laws of the State of ______ on or before ______. This subscription shall expire without further action by me on said date unless I am advised on or before said date of the creation of a Corporation to exercise this subscription.

(b) This subscription may be accepted by a Corporation only if each of the following conditions exist at the time of the acceptance of this subscription by such Corporation:

(1) At the time of the incorporation of such Corporation one or more of the incorporators thereof have then procured and then hold for the benefit of such Corporation subscriptions, executed in the same form as this by financially responsible persons, to a total of at least ______ shares of its common stock and having principal amounts to be paid therefor in the aggregate of at least $______ at the rate of $______ per share and all of which subscriptions shall be accepted by said Corporation in the manner provided for in the ______ Business Corporation Act.

(2) The incorporators of such Corporation are at the time of formation of such Corporation in possession of a written opinion from an attorney in good standing to the effect that all of such subscriptions have been obtained in compliance with the provisions of the ______ Securities Act and the Federal Securities Act of 1933 or, if applicable, exemptions therefrom.

(c) The principal amount of this subscription shall be paid to the Corporation at its principal office in ______, ______, in full at such time or in such installments and at such time as shall be determined by and called for by the Board of Directors of the aforesaid Corporation.

Alternative 1

(d) At any time before acceptance hereof this subscription may be revoked by me at my will in the manner hereinafter set forth.

Alternative 2

(d) At any time before acceptance hereof this subscription may be revoked by me in the manner hereinafter set forth if any one or more of the following conditions occur: [*Here State Any Desired Conditions Precedent to Exercise of Right of Revocation*].

(e) In order for this subscription to be revoked as above provided, notice of such revocation shall be given in writing to the Corporation at its registered office. If mailed, such written notice shall be deemed to have been given twenty-four hours after the deposit in the United States mails in a certified sealed envelope with postage thereon prepaid addressed to the Corporation at its registered office.

Dated: ______.

/s/ ____________

§ 39.8 Preincorporation Mutual Subscriptions

We, the undersigned, for and in consideration of the mutual promises of each to the other signers hereof, do each hereby agree with all of the other signers hereof that each does hereby subscribe to the number of shares of the common stock of ______ Corporation, a proposed Corporation to be formed under the laws of the State of ______, set opposite our respective signatures and to pay therefor the amounts set opposite our respective signatures in cash in full or in such installments and at such times as call therefor may be made by the Board of Directors of such Corporation, subject to the following terms and conditions: [*Here State Any Desired Conditions Precedent to Exercise of Right of Revocation*].

Name	Address	No. of Shares	Amount of Dollars
____________	____________	____________	____________
____________	____________	____________	____________

§ 39.9 Preincorporation Subscription Agreement—Several Subscribers Contracting with Each Other

Whereas, it is proposed to organize under the laws of the State of ______ a Corporation to be known as ______, or by such other name as the incorporators may select, for the purpose of engaging in the business of ______;

Whereas, it is proposed that said Corporation shall be authorized to issue ______ shares, of which ______ shares shall be ______ shares of a par value of $___ each, and ______ shares shall be ______ shares without par value; and

Whereas, each of the undersigned desires to subscribe for a designated number of the shares of said proposed Corporation.

Now, therefore, we, the undersigned, in consideration of the promises of each other, severally subscribe for the number of shares of said Corporation set opposite our respective signatures below at the price indicated below and, hereby waiving all notice of assessment, we severally agree with each other and with said proposed Corporation to accept and pay the purchase price for such shares in cash at such times and in such amounts as the Board of Directors may direct.

This Agreement is made upon the condition that said proposed Corporation shall be incorporated within the ______ days from the earliest date on which any one of the undersigned first executed this Agreement.

This Agreement may be executed in any number of counterparts which, taken together, shall constitute the same Agreement.

Name and Signature	Address	Date of Signing	Number of Shares Subscribed for	Total Purchase Price
____________	____________	____________	____________	____________
____________	____________	____________	____________	____________

§ 39.10 Preincorporation Subscription Agreement—First Payment to Trustee

We, the undersigned, hereby severally subscribe for and agree to take at $______ per share the number of shares of the ______ Corporation set opposite our respective names, and promise and agree to pay therefor as follows: __ per cent of subscription to and on demand of ______, as trustee for the said Corporation, such payment, or so much thereof as may be necessary, to be used for the preliminary and incorporating expenses of the said Corporation; __ per cent of subscription to the Treasurer of the said Corporation ______ days after its incorporation; and the balance of subscription at such times and in such installments as may be prescribed by the Board of Directors of said Corporation.

Dated ______, 19__.

Names	Addresses	Shares	Amount
______	______	______	______
______	______	______	______

§ 39.11 Individual Preincorporation Subscription Agreement

The ______ Corporation to be incorporated under the laws of the State of ______.

Capital Stock $______ Shares $______ par value

I, the undersigned, hereby subscribe for ______ shares of the capital stock of the ______ Corporation to be incorporated and agreed to pay in cash for said stock the sum of $______ on demand of the Board of Directors of the Corporation.

This Agreement is made upon the condition that ______ per cent of the capital stock of the Corporation is subscribed in good faith by solvent persons on or before the ______ day of ______, 19__, and the Corporation is incorporated within ______ days thereafter.

Dated ______, 19__.

____

§ 39.12 Contract for Security if Issued

CONTRACT FOR SECURITY

(a) This contract is made on [*Date*], between [*Name of Corporation*], of [*Address*], herein called "Corporation," and [*Name of Purchaser*], of [*Address*], herein called "purchaser."

(b) In consideration of the promise of purchaser to pay [*Amount*] therefor, the Corporation promises to distribute to the purchaser [*Number*] shares of [*Specify Kind of Stock*] when, as and if issued by the Corporation.

____________________ ____________________

[*Signature of Purchaser*] [*Signature of Issuer*]

COMMENT

It is fairly common practice for Corporations proposing to issue securities to employ the device of the "when, as, and if issued agreement" under which a purchaser agrees to purchase one or more securities when, as and if they are issued. The Corporation is thus not obligated to issue the securities and may wait until it determines, from a number of when, as and if, contracts which have been obtained, whether it will issue the securities. U.C.C. § 8–202(5) recognizes the right of a purchaser under such a contract to cancel the contract if there should be a material change in the character of the security covered by the contract.

§ 39.13 Preincorporation Subscription Agreement—Securities Law Clause

PREINCORPORATION SUBSCRIPTION AGREEMENT

1. **Sale Contingent Upon Qualification.** The sale of the securities which are the subject of this Agreement has not been qualified with the Commissioner of Corporations of the State of ______, and the issuance of such securities are the payment or receipt of any part of the consideration therefor prior to such qualification is unlawful. The rights of all parties to this Agreement are expressly conditioned upon such qualification being obtained.

2. **Issuance and Payment for Securities.** No part of the purchase price of the securities which are the subject of this Agreement shall be paid or received, and none of the securities shall be issued until the sale of such securities is qualified with the Commissioner of Corporations of the State of ______.

§ 39.14 Acceptance of Preincorporation Subscription—Short Form

Pursuant to the provisions of ______, the Corporation accepts the following subscriptions:

Name of Subscriber	Address of Subscriber	No. of Shares	Amount Paid
__________	__________	__________	__________
__________	__________	__________	__________

Dated: ______.

§ 39.15 Acceptance of Preincorporation Subscription—Another Form

Whereas, the persons whose names and post office addresses are hereinafter listed have heretofore severally subscribed to the number of common shares of ______ Corporation set opposite their respective names and have by such subscriptions severally offered to pay for such number of shares the amount set opposite their respective names, and have actually paid on such subscriptions the amount set opposite their respective names under the column headed "Amount Paid", the total of which latter amount we, jointly and severally, acknowledge we now hold in trust for such Corporation; and

Whereas, it is deemed for the best interests of such Corporation that such subscriptions be accepted by said Corporation;

Now, therefore, in accordance with and pursuant to the provisions of ______ of the ______ Business Corporation Act, we, the undersigned directors of said Corporation, do thereby attach to the original Articles of Incorporation of such Corporation the following list setting forth the names of such subscribers, their respective post office addresses, the respective number of common shares of such Corporation's authorized shares that have been subscribed by each of such persons, the respective amounts subscribed by each of such persons, and the respective amounts paid by each of such persons:

Name and Address of Subscriber	No. of Shares	Amount Subscribed	Amount Paid
______________	______________	$______	$______
______________ Street			
______________, [*State*]			
______________	______________	$______	$______
______________ Street			
______________, [*State*]			
TOTALS	______________	$______	$______

In Testimony whereof, witness our signatures this ______ day of ______, 19__.

Directors of ______ Corporation

____

____

____

§ 39.16 Cancellation of Subscription Agreement Before Incorporation

To: ____

On the ____ day of ____, 19__, I subscribed for ____ shares of the capital stock of ____, a Corporation to be incorporated under the laws of the State of ____ for the purpose of ____. This is to notify you that I hereby withdraw my said subscription and cancel the same.

Dated ____, 19__. ____________

§ 39.17 Treasurer's Certificate for Subscription

THE ____ COMPANY

This is to certify that ____, a subscriber for ____ shares of the capital stock of the ____ Company, has paid into the treasury of the company the sum of $____, in full payment therefor [*or has paid into the treasury of the company on account of his said subscription* $____ *per share in cash, and* $____ *per share by trustee's receipt*]. Upon surrender hereof [*or upon payment of the remaining installments of said subscription, and surrender hereof, with proper vouchers showings such payments*] certificates for said ____ shares of stock will be issued to the order of the said ____ (as soon as the same are ready for delivery).

Dated ____, 19__. ____________

Treasurer

§ 39.18 Assignment of Subscription to Corporate Stock

For value received, I hereby sell, assign, and transfer to ____ my subscription to ____ shares of the capital stock of the ____, Inc., together with the payments made thereon, as evidenced by the within installment certificate, and I hereby authorize and instruct the proper officers of ____, Inc., upon fulfillment of the conditions of my said subscription, to issue said stock to the order of the said ____.

Dated ____, 19__. [*Signature*]

§ 39.19 Resolution Authorizing Postincorporation Subscriptions

Resolved, that the Officers of the Corporation be and they are hereby empowered to accept subscriptions, in cash and for no less than $____ per share, for the balance of the authorized common shares of the Corporation, par value $____ per share, subject to such additional conditions and terms as may to the President appear reasonable.

§ 39.20 Postincorporation Subscription

I, ______, hereby subscribe for ______ shares of the authorized but unissued common stock of ______ Corporation, of the par value of $______ per share, and agree to pay therefor ______ in the following manner: __ per cent of such amount on the execution of this subscription agreement, and __ per cent on the first day of each month thereafter until such amount shall have been paid in full, at which time a certificate or certificates shall be issued to me for said shares.

Dated: ______, 19__. ____________________

The ______ Corporation accepts the foregoing subscription.

Dated: ______, 19__.

__________ Corporation

By ________________

§ 39.21 Postincorporation Subscription—Installment Payments

We, the undersigned do hereby subscribe for ______ (______) shares of the common shares of [*Name of Corporation*], to be issued as fully paid and nonassessable, and agree to purchase and pay for said shares at the price of ______ ($______) Dollars per share upon the following terms and conditions:

The purchase price of ______ ($______) Dollars per share shall be payable in installments as follows, namely: first installment of ______ ($______) Dollars per share due and payable with subscription; second installment of ______ ($______) Dollars per share on the first day of the second calendar month after subscription is taken; and subsequent monthly installments of ______ ($______) Dollars per share each, payable on the first day of each calendar month thereafter. One or more of the unmatured installments may be paid at any time.

Interest at the rate of ______ per cent. per annum will be paid by the Corporation upon each of the installments duly paid on account of such subscriptions from the time of the receipt thereof by the Corporation until the entire subscription price shall have been paid, but the nonpayment of any of such installments when due shall terminate the subscriber's right to interest on all installments theretofore paid by such subscriber.

After full payment of all installments for such shares, there will be issued full-paid and nonassessable share certificates, dated on the day such full payment is made, and the holder of such shares shall be entitled to receive as a dividend thereon, for the quarterly common shares dividend period in which full payment therefor shall be made hereunder, only such proportion of the dividend which shall be declared by the Corporation's Board of Directors on its common shares for such period as the portion of such period succeeding the date of such full payment shall bear to the entire period aforesaid. Subscribers for such shares shall not have or exercise any of the rights of Stockholders until the issuance to them of such full-paid and nonassessable share certificates.

Upon default on the part of any subscriber in the payment of any installment of the subscription price for more than 30 days after written demand therefor after the due date, this Corporation, upon publication for ten days in any newspaper of general circulation in ______, of a notice specifying the time and place of sale, shall have the right, without previous demand or personal notice, to sell at public sale, to the highest bidder for cash, all of the rights of such subscriber under his contract of subscription (upon condition that such purchaser shall assume and agree to pay all unmatured installments to become due under such contract plus the expenses incidental to such sale), and the balance, if any, of the proceeds of such sale shall be paid by the Corporation to the original subscriber, or his assigns, on demand, at the office of the Corporation in ______, and this Corporation shall reject any or all bids for less than the amount of all matured and unpaid installments, plus the expenses incidental to the sale.

No subscriptions will be received for a fractional part of a share.

Subscriptions will not be valid until accepted by [*Specify Officers*] of the Corporation and subscription receipts or full paid and nonassessable certificates of shares have been issued therefor.

Name	Address	Number of Shares	Class of Shares	Amount of Subscription	Date

Dated, ______, 19__. ____________________

____

§ 39.22 Contract for Security if Issued

COMMENT

See Form at 39.12, supra.

§ 39.23 Assignment of Postincorporation Subscription

For value received, I hereby sell, assign, and transfer to ______ my subscription for ______ (______) shares of the ______ Corporation, together with the payments made thereon, as evidenced by the within installment certificate, and I hereby authorize and instruct the proper officers of said Corporation, upon fulfillment of the conditions of my said subscription, to issue said shares to the order of the said ______.

Dated ______, 19__. ______________________

[*Signature*]

COMMENT

There appears to be no reason why a share subscription agreement should not be transferable as are most contract rights and duties. Recognition of transferability, however, may require registration under the federal and/or state securities law.

§ 39.24 Resolution Accepting Postincorporation Subscription

Whereas, ______ of ______ has subscribed to ______ shares of the heretofore authorized but as yet unissued shares of common stock of this Corporation, such subscription being evidenced by a memorandum in writing signed by ______, dated ______, 19__, exhibited to this meeting of the Board of Directors, under the terms of which subscription ______ offers to pay for said number of shares of stock by delivering to the Corporation the sum of $______, and

Whereas, it is deemed to the best interests of the Corporation to accept such subscription; now, therefore,

Resolved, that the aforesaid subscription be and is hereby accepted, and the Secretary of the Corporation shall promptly notify ______ of the acceptance of such subscription.

§ 39.25 Resolution Accepting Multiple Postincorporation Subscription

Whereas, this Corporation is authorized by its Articles of Incorporation to issue a total of ______ common shares, and

Whereas, ______ of such authorized shares have not previously been issued, and

Whereas, the persons whose names and post office addresses hereinafter listed have heretofore severally subscribed to the number of common shares of this Corporation set opposite their respective names and have by such subscriptions severally offered to pay in cash therefor the amount set opposite their respective names, and none of such subscriptions have heretofore been revoked, and

Whereas, the terms of all of such subscriptions are such that the Corporation can now accept all of such subscriptions, and

Whereas, it is deemed for the best interests of the Corporation that all of such subscriptions now be accepted by the Corporation; now, therefore,

Resolved, that each of the subscriptions of each of the following persons for the respective number of shares set opposite their respective names be and the same are hereby accepted by this Corporation:

Name and Post Office Address of Subscriber	**Number of Shares Subscribed**	**Amount Subscribed**
______________		
______________ Street	______________	$__________
______________, [*State*]		
TOTALS	______________	$__________

And Further Resolved, that the Secretary of the Corporation is ordered promptly to notify each of such subscribers that his or her subscription has this day been accepted by the Board of Directors; and the Treasurer of the Corporation is instructed to debit the total of the amount of such subscriptions to the subscriptions receivable account and to credit such amount to the capital stock subscribed but unissued account on the financial records of the Corporation.

COMMENT

When all the subscriptions have been paid and certificates issued, the two accounts referred to in the last paragraph of the form will be closed out.

§ 39.26 Resolution of Directors Fixing Installments and Times of Payments of Subscriptions to Partly Paid Shares

RESOLUTION OF DIRECTORS FIXING INSTALLMENTS AND TIMES OF PAYMENTS OF SUBSCRIPTIONS TO PARTLY PAID SHARES

Resolved:

(a) That this Corporation shall issue ______ [*Number*] of its common shares as partly paid on the terms stated;

(b) That on all shares to be issued as partly paid, there shall be paid by each subscriber __% of the amount of his subscription on the ______ day of ______, 19__ and on the ______ day of each and every month thereafter until the whole amount remaining due shall be paid; and

(c) That the Secretary be and he hereby is directed to send a copy of this resolution by mail to each and every subscriber of partly paid shares, directed to him at his address as shown on the records of the Corporation with a notice of the amount and date of the first call for payment; and

(d) That the Secretary shall notify each subscriber as to the amount and date of all subsequent calls at least ten days before such calls are due, in the manner and form set forth above; and

(e) That on the certificate issued to represent such shares, the total amount of the consideration to be paid therefor and the amount paid thereon shall be stated; and

(f) That upon the declaration of any dividend on fully paid shares, the Corporation shall declare a dividend upon partly paid shares of the same class, but only upon the basis of the percentage of the consideration actually paid thereon; and

(g) That such shares shall be issued only to such subscribers who agree in writing that they are liable to this Corporation for the full consideration agreed to be paid for the shares.

§ 39.27 Resolution Establishing Times and Amounts of Calls

Whereas, the Board of Directors has decided and resolved to make an offering of ______ of its heretofore authorized but as yet unissued and unsubscribed for common shares and has heretofore (*or:* contemporaneously herewith) appointed agents to solicit and accept subscriptions to such shares and has duly and effectively authorized all other matters necessary to be authorized in connection with such offering, and

Whereas, it is the judgment of the Board that the success of such offering will be best assured if the potential subscribers thereto are granted an opportunity to pay the respective principal amounts of their subscriptions over a period of time and in installments as hereinafter resolved and are assured that they will not sooner be called upon to do so; now, therefore,

Resolved, that all subscriptions to common shares of this Corporation hereafter received and accepted by the Corporation during the continuance of the above referred to offering shall be payable in money as follows:

______% of the principal amount of the subscription at time of execution of each respective subscription.

______% thereof on or before one month [*or* two, three, four, etc. months] after date of such subscription.

§ 39.28 Call for Payment of Subscriptions—Resolution

Whereas, the Corporation has heretofore received and accepted subscriptions to ______ shares of its common shares at the rate of $______ per share for a total of $______, and

Whereas, it is deemed for the best interests of the Corporation that all of such subscriptions should presently be called for payment of their full principal amounts on or before the ______ day of ______, 19__; now, therefore,

Resolved, that the full principal amounts of all subscriptions to the common shares of this Corporation which have heretofore been received and accepted shall be paid on or before the ______ day of ______, 19__; and the Secretary is hereby instructed to notify each of the subscribers of this call.

COMMENT

See Model Bus. Corp.Act § 17 as set out in § 39.3, footnote 1, supra, with respect to calls for payment of subscriptions.

§ 39.29 Call for Unpaid Subscription Price

CALL FOR UNPAID SUBSCRIPTION PRICE

______ 19__.

Mr. ______

Dear Sir:

Enclosed is a copy of a resolution of the Board of Directors of ______ Corporation, duly adopted at a regular meeting of the Board on the ______ day of ______, 19__ fixing the amount of calls on shares issued as partly paid and the date of payment of each call.

I hereby notify you that the first call on your subscription for partly paid shares amounts to $______ and will be due and payable at the office of the Corporation on the ______ day of ______, 19__.

Dated ______, 19__.

____

Secretary

§ 39.30 Call to Make Uniform Payments of Subscriptions—Resolution

Whereas, some of the subscribers to common shares of this Corporation have heretofore paid as much as ______% of the principal amount of their respective subscriptions while others have not yet done so, and

Whereas, it is deemed for the best interest of the Corporation that those subscribers who have not yet paid at least ______% of the principal amounts of their respective subscriptions should now be called upon to do so; now, therefore

Resolved, that each subscriber who has not yet paid at least ______% of the principal amount of his subscription shall pay such amount as shall, when added to such amount as he has previously paid, then equal ______% of the principal amount of his subscription; and the Secretary is hereby instructed to notify each of the subscribers of this call.

§ 39.31 Notices of Call for Payment of Subscriptions

______, 19__

To: __________

By order of the Board of Directors of The ______ Corporation, you are hereby notified that on the ______ day of ______, 19__, the Board of Directors determined that all as yet unpaid subscriptions to the common shares of the said Corporation shall be paid to the Corporation at is principal office on or before ______, 19__.

The records of the Corporation show that the amount due on your subscription dated ______, 19__, in the principal sum of $______ for ______ shares is now $______ which you are hereby respectfully called upon to pay.

Share certificates will be issued upon receipt of the above called for payment.

Very sincerely,

____

Secretary of the Corporation

[*Alternative Form*]

_______, 19__

To: ____________

[*Address*]

Dear Sir:

At a regular meeting of the Board of Directors of _______, Inc., held on _______, 19__, a resolution was duly adopted fixing the amount of calls on stock issued as partly paid and the date of payment of each call.

You are hereby notified that the first call on your subscription for partly paid stock amounts to $_______, which sum is due and payable at the office of the Corporation on _______, 19__.

_______________, Inc.

By ___________ Secretary

[*Alternative Form*]

_______, 19__

To: ____________ [*address*] ____________.

You are hereby notified that on _______, 19__, the Board of Directors of the ______ Corporation adopted a resolution to the effect that each subscriber to the common shares of the Corporation who has not yet paid at least _______% of the principal amount of his subscription shall, on or before _______, 19__, pay such amount as shall, when added to whatever amount he has previously paid on such subscription, then equal _______% of the principal amount of the subscription.

According to the Corporation's records, you have heretofore paid $_______ on your subscription dated _______, 19__ for _______ shares in the original principal amount of $_______. In order, therefore, for you to comply with the aforementioned call of the Board of Directors, you should now pay the sum of $_______ to the Corporation on or before _______, 19__.

By order of the Board of Directors.

____

Secretary of the Corporation

§ 39.32 Waiver of Notice of Call

We, the undersigned, being all of the subscribers to the capital stock of _______, do hereby waive notice, statutory or otherwise, of the time, manner, and place of payment of our respective subscriptions to the capital stock of said Corporation, and we severally agree to pay our respective subscriptions as called for and directed by resolution of its Board of Directors, without any further notice.

Dated ______, 19__. [*Signatures*]

§ 39.33 Transferable Receipt for Payment on Share Subscription

No. ___________ Shares: ___________

RECEIPT

Received, of ______, the sum of $______ in payment of first installment for the purchase of ______ shares of common stock of ______ Corporation, pursuant to a subscription agreement dated ______, 19__.

Under ______ law, the holder of this receipt may receive certificates of ______ Corporation for such shares only upon payment of the remaining sum of $______ according to the terms of said subscription agreement.

This receipt is assignable; transfer may be registered by the surrender of this certificate, properly endorsed, at the office of the undersigned.

Dated: ______.

___________ Corporation

By ________________

Payment Dates:	**Payment Received:**
______________	______________
______________	______________

ASSIGNMENT

For value received, I hereby assign to ______ my subscription to ______ shares of common stock of ______ Corporation represented by the foregoing receipt together with all payments thereon.

Dated: ______. ________________________

COMMENT

There appears to be no reason why a share subscription agreement should not be transferable as are most contract rights and duties. Recognition of transferability, however, may require registration under the federal and/or state securities law.

§ 39.34 Installment Receipt for Subscriptions

No. ________ Shares ________

[*Name of Corporation*]

Installment Receipt in Accordance with the Terms of Subscription Agreement, dated ______, 19__.

Received of ______, for account of ______, the sum of ______ ($______) Dollars, in payment of first installment of ______ per share upon a subscription for ______ shares of the share of ______, in accordance with the terms of the subscription agreement.

The holder hereof will be entitled to a certificate for said share of ______ upon payment of the remainder of said subscription according to the terms of said Agreement and upon surrender of this receipt.

This receipt is transferable only at the office of the undersigned upon surrender hereof, properly endorsed.

Dated, ______, 19__.

[*Name of Corporation*]

By ________________

[*Capacity*]

FURTHER PAYMENTS UPON SUBSCRIPTION

Installment due:	Dollars:	Paid:	Received by
2nd installment, ______, 19__	$______,	______, 19__	______ Vice-Pres.
3rd installment, ______, 19__	$______,	______, 19__	______ Vice-Pres.
4th installment, ______, 19__	$______,	______, 19__	______ Vice-Pres.

This receipt may be exchanged for a permanent share certificate on or after the ______ day of ______, 19__, at the office of the [*Name of Corporation*] at No. ______ ______ Street, City of ______, County of ______, State of ______.

§ 39.35 Notice of Potential Forfeiture

To: ________

Demand is hereby made for payment in full of the balance of the subscription price of ______ called by the Board of Directors for payment on ______, 19__. Please be advised that the Corporation's *By-laws/resolutions* provides that if payment is not received within twenty days of the date of this demand, the Corporation may declare the subscription to be forfeited, and in such event, all your rights and obligations with respect to your subscription will be terminated.

__________ Corporation
By ________________

§ 39.36 Notice to Stockholder of Liability to Forfeiture of Shares

______, 19__

To: __________

[*Address*]

You are hereby notified that at a regular meeting of the Board of Directors of ______, the following resolution was duly adopted:

"Resolved, that the entire [*or* ______ *per cent of the*] unpaid balance on all subscriptions to the ______ stock of this Corporation is hereby called for payment forthwith, and the Secretary is hereby directed to demand payment from each subscriber having an unpaid balance, by mailing to him, at his last known address, a written demand requiring payment within 30 days from receipt of such notice, in default of which his shares and all previous payments thereon will be forfeited."

Demand is hereby made upon you for payment in accordance with the provisions of the above resolution, and you are hereby notified that, in default of payment within 30 days from receipt of this notice and demand, your shares and previous payments thereon will be forfeited.

§ 39.37 Resolution Forfeiting Subscriptions

Whereas, the Corporation has previously called all unpaid subscriptions for payment on ______, 19__, and

Whereas, the persons named below have not paid the agreed amounts despite a demand therefor made on ______, 19__, which demand refers to the possibility that nonpayment may result in forfeiture of subscription rights; now, therefore

Alternative A

Resolved that the subscriptions of the following persons: [*Herein List the Names of Persons and the Number of Shares Subscribed*] are hereby declared to be forfeited, and all rights and obligations of the foregoing persons to subscribe to shares of the Corporation are terminated.

Alternative B

Resolved, that the Secretary be directed to send a notice to ______, in accordance with Article ______ of the Articles of Incorporation, requiring him to pay the call due on his shares, with interest, and stating that, unless such call and interest are paid on or before the ______ day of ______, 19__, his shares and all previous payments will be forfeited without further notice.

Alternative C

Resolved, that the shares of $______, each numbered ______ to ______, of which ______, of ______, is the registered holder, be hereby forfeited in consequence of the nonpayment by the said ______ of calls due thereon, and that the Secretary be directed forthwith to give notice to the said ______ of such forfeiture.

__________, Inc.

By __________ Secretary

§ 39.38 Forms Relating to Receipt of Property as Consideration for Shares

(a) Subscription. * * * and by conveying to the Corporation the following described property which has the value of ______ Dollars:

(b) Acceptance of Subscription. Whereas it is the judgment of the Board of Directors that the property offered by ______ to be conveyed to the Corporation in part consideration for such number of shares is reasonably worth the sum of $______.

COMMENT

Unlike the purchase of shares for cash, the purchase of shares with property usually is a taxable transaction for federal income tax purposes. It is possible, however, that the transaction may be exempt under Internal Revenue Code of 1954, § 351.

§ 39.39 Resolution Establishing Consideration for Shares

Resolved that the consideration to be received by this Corporation for its Class ______ common shares shall be cash in the amount of ______ Dollars per share.

COMMENT

Certain state statutes contemplate that shares without par value should be issued for a consideration fixed by the Board of Directors, or (in some states) by the Stockholders if an appropriate provision is included in the Articles of Incorporation. Shares with par value (other than treasury shares) should not be issued for less than par. It is accepted practice to issue par value shares for more than par, with the excess credited to capital surplus rather than stated capital.

§ 39.40 Allocation of Consideration Received for No Par Shares

Whereas, within the past sixty days this Corporation has received $______ in money, and properties whose value in the judgment of the Board of Directors is $______, for the issuance of ______ of its common shares without par value, and

Whereas, in the judgment of the Board of Directors it is expedient and to the best interests of the Corporation that $______ of such consideration, thereof, should be allocated to capital surplus; now, therefore,

Resolved, that $______ of such consideration shall be allocated to stated capital of the Corporation and $______ thereof allocated to capital surplus of the Corporation.

COMMENT

The allocation of part of the consideration received for no par shares to capital surplus by the directors is contemplated by the Model Business Corporation Act. It is usually desirable to make this allocation since Corporations have greater freedom and flexibility with capital surplus than with stated capital. In some states, there is a limit as to how much can be so allocated.

§ 39.41 Resolution Accepting Property and Fixing Values

Whereas, ______ has offered to convey to this Corporation the hereinafter listed items of personal property and the hereinafter described real property in consideration of this Corporation issuing to him ______ of its common shares with a par value of $______ per share, and

Whereas, it is the judgment of the Board of Directors that the dollar value of such properties are as hereinafter set opposite the listing of same; now, therefore,

Resolved, that such offer be accepted and that the Board of Directors, pursuant to the provisions of the ______ Business Corporation Act, hereby fixes said properties as the consideration to be received by it for the issuance by it to ______ of ______ of the Corporation's authorized but unissued common shares, and fixes the value of said consideration as follows: [*Here List the Properties and Their Values*].

§ 39.42 Resolution of Directors Stating Determination of the Value of Property Received by a Corporation for Its Shares

RESOLUTION OF DIRECTORS STATING DETERMINATION OF THE VALUE OF PROPERTY RECEIVED BY A CORPORATION FOR ITS SHARES

Whereas, ______ has offered in writing to sell to this Corporation all of his right, title and interest in and to ______ [*Describe Property Offered in Consideration for Shares*] for the sum of $______ to be paid for by the issuance to him as fully paid and non-assessable, ______ shares of the ______ stock of this Corporation,

Now, therefore, be it resolved, that it is the determination of the Board of Directors that the above-described ______ [*Refer to Property Mentioned in Preceding Paragraph*] has a fair value to the Corporation of $______, which is the sum stated in said offer, and that this Corporation accept the offer of ______; and

Further resolved that the President be and he hereby is authorized and directed to accept said offer in writing on behalf of this Corporation; and

Further resolved that the President or a Vice-President and the secretary or an Assistant Secretary of this Corporation execute and deliver to ______ a certificate or certificates evidencing ______ [*Number*] shares of this Corporation upon receipt from ______ of all documents necessary to transfer the above-described property to this Corporation.

COMMENT

Corporate statutes authorize the Board of Directors to determine the value of consideration received by the corporation in exchange for the issuance of shares. This becomes important where the Corporation issues shares for noncash consideration. The Directors should adopt a formal resolution placing a value on the property received. It is recommended that the Board of Directors be conservative and prudent in making a valuation of the property received, because the Directors could incur liability to creditors of the Corporation for a gross over-valuation of the property received for shares.

§ 39.43 Shares Issued for Property—Resolution of Directors

Upon motion duly made, seconded, and carried, the following resolution was unanimously adopted:

Whereas, ______ has offered in writing to sell to this Corporation all his right, title and interest in and to [*Description of Prop-*

erty] for the sum of ______ ($______) Dollars, to be paid for by the issuance to him as fully paid and nonassessable of [*Number*] shares of the [*Class*] shares of this Corporation, now, therefore, be it

Resolved, that after due deliberation, it is the judgment of the Board of Directors of this Corporation that the value of said property so offered, is the sum of ______ ($______) Dollars, which is the sum stated in said offer, and that this Corporation accept this offer of ______, and, be it further

Resolved, that the President be and hereby is authorized to accept said offer in writing on behalf of this Corporation; and, be it further

Resolved, that the President [*or Vice-President*] and the Secretary [*or Treasurer*] of this Corporation execute and deliver to ______ said certificates representing shares for [*Number*] shares of [*Class*] shares, upon receipt from said ______ of all necessary documents transferring said property to this Corporation.

§ 39.44 Resolution Authorizing Shares for Services Previously Rendered

Whereas ______ has performed services on behalf of the Corporation during the preceding ______ months;

Whereas, the value of said services to the Corporation is fixed at ______ Dollars; and

Whereas ______ has not been compensated for said services, and is willing to accept ______ of the Corporation's common shares with a par value of $______ per share in full compensation for said services; now therefore,

Resolved, that the Board of Directors, pursuant to the provisions of the ______ Business Corporation Act, hereby fixes the value of the services rendered by ______ at ______ and fixes said services as the consideration to be received by it for the issuance by it to ______ of ______ of the Corporation's authorized but unissued common shares with the par value of $______ per share.

COMMENTS

In most states shares may not be issued for promissory notes or the promise of future services. The practical consequence of this rule is that shares to be issued for services must be issued at the end of the rendition of services rather than at the outset.

Shares issued in exchange for services constitute taxable income to the recipient to the extent of their value.

§ 39.45 Resolution Authorizing Shares for Services Previously Rendered—Another Form

RESOLUTION OF DIRECTORS:
ISSUANCE OF SHARES FOR SERVICES

(a) ______ [*Name*] has rendered promotional services for this Corporation in connection with the organization of this Corporation.

(b) ______ [*Name*] has submitted to the Board of Directors of this Corporation a description of such services and a statement of the value he places thereon, and has further expressed his willingness to accept ______ [*Number*] shares of the common stock of this Corporation in payment therefor.

(c) Therefore, it is hereby resolved that the Board of Directors determines that the fair value of the promotional services rendered to the Corporation by ______ [*Name*] is in the sum of $______.

(d) Therefore, it is further resolved, that the Corporation shall issue ______ [*Number*] shares of its common stock to ______ [*Name*] in consideration of such promotional services subject to the following.

(e) It is also further resolved that the sale and issuance of the securities which are the subject of this resolution has not been qualified with the Commissioner of Corporations of the State of ______ and the issuance of such securities prior to such qualification is unlawful. The rights of the Corporation and of ______ [*Name*] who has rendered such promotional services are expressly conditioned upon such qualification being obtained. None of the shares which are to be issued to ______ [*Name*] pursuant to the foregoing resolution shall be issued until the sale of such shares is qualified under the ______ Corporate Securities laws.

§ 39.46 Issuance of Shares to Nominee

Dated: ______, 19__.

To: The President and Treasurer of __________

Referring to the Agreement made on the ______ day of ______, 19__, between the undersigned and said ______, under the terms of which Agreement there are to be issued to me or to such nominees as I may in writing direct ______ shares of the common shares of said Corporation. Accordingly, I hereby direct you to issue share certificates of said Corporation to the following named persons in the amounts set opposite their respective names:

Name	No. of Shares
______________________	______________________
______________________	______________________
______________________	______________________

The respective receipts of the above named persons for such certificates will be a sufficient discharge to your Corporation under said Agreement to the extent of the shares evidenced by such respective certificates.

____

Witnessed by:

____

COMMENT

This form is a simple direction to a Corporation by a Stockholder entitled to receive certificates to issue them in the name of nominees.

§ 39.47 Demand for Purchase of Similar Securities or Payment of Purchase Price

[*Date*]

To: [*Name of Issuer*]

On [*Date*] your authorized agent [*or Officer*] at [*Address*] issued to the undersigned the following security(ies): [*Describe in Detail*] which are invalid as part of an overissue of such securities.

The undersigned hereby demands that by the ______ day of ______, 19__, you purchase identical valid securities in the open market and deliver the same to the undersigned against surrender of those hereinabove described or pay to the undersigned the purchase price(s) thereof as follows:

Security(ies)	Date Purchased	Purchase Price
__________	__________	__________
__________	__________	__________

together with interest at the rate of ______ per cent per annum from the date of your receipt of this demand.

____

[*Signature of Purchaser*]

COMMENTS

This Form is drafted for use under U.C.C. § 8–104.

Where securities have been "overissued" (i. e., issued in excess of the amount the issuer has the corporate power to issue), the holder of a security which is void for that reason may compel the issuer to purchase and deliver to him an identical valid security against surrender of the invalid security which he holds. U.C.C. § 8–104(1)(a). However, if an identical valid security is not "reasonably" available for purchase, the holder of the overissued security may recover from the issuer only the price that he or the last purchaser for value paid for it, with interest from the date of his demand. § 8–104(1)(b). The issuer can, of course, voluntarily amend its certificate of incorporation or take any other action to validate the void security, but the holder cannot compel such action.

§ 39.48 Cancellation of Contract for Security if and When Issued

[*Date*]

To: [*Name of Prospective Issuer*]
[*Address*]

By contract of [*Date*], the undersigned agreed to purchase for the consideration stated [*Number of*] shares of [*Specify Kind of Stock*] when, as and if issued by you.

Because of the following facts, we deem there has been a material change in the character of the security which is the subject of the contract [*or in the plan or arrangement pursuant to which such security is to be issued or distributed*] and we do hereby exercise our right to cancel such contract.

[*Specify Facts Relied Upon*].

____
[*Signature of Prospective Purchaser*]

COMMENTS

U.C.C. § 8–202(5) states that nothing in § 8–202 shall be deemed to affect the right of a party to a "when, as and if issued" or "when distributed" contract to cancel the contract in the event of a material change in the character of the security which is the subject matter of the contract or the plan or arrangement pursuant to which such security is to be issued or distributed.

Apparently the word "cancel" is not used with the same meaning as it is defined in Article 2. U.C.C. § 2–106(4). Rather its Article 8 meaning seems to more nearly approximate the Article 2 term of "termination." U.C.C. § 2–106(3).

No guide is given as to what constitutes a "material change" entitling the party to cancel.

§ 39.49 Notice to Issuer of Adverse Claims

To: [*Name and Address of Issuer*]

and

[*Name and Address of Transfer Agent, if Any*]

Re: [*Issue of Which Security Is a Part*]

Please take notice that the undersigned claims an interest in a certain [*Share, Certificate, Bond, etc.*] previously issued by [*Name of Issuer*] in the name of [*Full Name of Present Registered Security-holder*]. According to my best information, the [*Share, Certificate, Bond, etc.*] was issued by you on or about [*Date of Certificate, etc., if Any and Known*], and is one of a class of such [*Type of Security*] first issued on [*Date*].

My claim arises by virtue of [*State Nature of Adverse Claims, i. e., Purchase, or Contract to Purchase with Registered Owner, Legatee or Distributee of Registered Owner*].

I am enclosing herewith [*Enclose Documents Such as Will, Contract to Purchase, etc., Corroborating Claim*].

You may correspond with me at the following address: [*Name and Address*].

Please acknowledge receipt on the copy at the place indicated below.

____

[*Name of Adverse Claimant*]

Received: ______, 19__

[*Name of Issuer*]

By __________

[*Title*]

COMMENT

An adverse claimant should give prompt specific notice to the issuer or the transfer agent of the nature of his claim.

§§ 39.50–40.0 are reserved for supplementary material.

CHAPTER 40

AUTHORIZED SHARES

Table of Sections

Library References:

C.J.S. Corporations § 52 et seq.
West's Key No. Digests, Corporations 🔑18.

§ 40.1 Authorized Shares—Generally

The Articles of Incorporation in all jurisdictions are required to set forth the number of authorized shares, the number of shares in each class if shares are classified, and the par value of any par value shares, and if there are to be shares without par value a statement to such effect.[1]

Where there is only one class of shares, such shares, regardless of designation, are in effect "common shares". Such shares hold the voting rights, are entitled to such dividends as are distributed, and receive in the event of liquidation the net assets remaining after the payment of all creditor claims.

§ 40.2 Provision in Articles of Incorporation Authorizing Common Shares

The aggregate number of shares which this Corporation shall have authority to issue is ______ common shares which shares are to be *without par value/have a par value of* [*Number*].

COMMENTS

Every Corporation has power to create and issue the number of shares stated in its Articles of Incorporation. Such shares may be all of one class or divided into two or more classes consisting of either shares with or without par value, and having such designation and such relative voting, dividend, liquidation and other

1. E. g. Model Bus.Corp.Act § 15 provides:

> **§ 15. Authorized Shares**
>
> Each Corporation shall have power to create and issue the number of shares stated in its articles of incorporation. Such shares may be divided into one or more classes with such designations, preferences, limitations, and relative rights as shall be stated in the articles of incorporation. The articles of incorporation may limit or deny the voting rights of or provide special voting rights for the shares of any class to the extent not inconsistent with the provisions of this Act.
>
> Without limiting the authority herein contained, a Corporation, when so provided in its articles of incorporation, may issue shares of preferred or special classes:
>
> (a) Subject to the right of the Corporation to redeem any of such shares at the price fixed by the articles of incorporation for the redemption thereof.
>
> (b) Entitling the holders thereof to cumulative, noncumulative or partially cumulative dividends.
>
> (c) Having preference over any other class or classes of shares as to the payment of dividends.
>
> (d) Having preference in the assets of the Corporation over any other class or classes of shares upon the voluntary or involuntary liquidation of the Corporation.
>
> (e) Convertible into shares of any other class or into shares of any series of the same or any other class, except a class having prior or superior rights and preferences as to dividends or distribution of assets upon liquidation.

See also e. g. West's Ann.Calif.Corp. Code § 400; McKinney's N.Y.Bus. Corp.Law § 500.

rights, preferences, and limitations, consistent with the state Corporation statutes. See e. g. Model Bus.Corp.Act § 15 as set out in footnote 1, supra, § 40.1.

See § 38.12, supra, with respect to classes of common stock.

§ 40.3 Provision in Articles of Incorporation Providing for Common Stock Rights

Common Stock. Subject to the preferential rights above provided in this Article with respect to the Original Preferred Stock, the Cumulative Preferred Stock, the $100 Cumulative Preferred Stock, the Preference Stock and the $100 Preference Stock, the Common Stock and/or the holders thereof shall have the following dividend rights, liquidation rights, and voting rights:

(a) Dividend Rights. The holders of the Common Stock shall be entitled, consistent with the participating rights of the Original Preferred Stock, to dividends when and as declared by the Board of Directors out of any funds legally available therefor, in such amounts and at such times as the Board of Directors may from time to time determine.

(b) Liquidation Rights. In the event of any liquidation, dissolution or winding-up, whether voluntary or involuntary, of the Corporation, the holders of the Common Stock shall share equally and be entitled to be paid in full the par value of their shares, and thereafter the remaining assets and funds of the Corporation shall be distributed ratably to the holders of the Original Preferred Stock and the Common Stock.

(c) Voting Rights. The Common Stock shall be entitled to voting rights on the basis of one vote per share.

COMMENT

This form states the basic rights, preferences, privileges, and restrictions of the common stock, the most junior stock in the stock structure of a Corporation. The common stock has the following rights, privileges and restrictions: dividends declared only at the discretion of the Board of Directors; full voting rights, which are cumulative; no distributions in liquidation until all claims of the Preferred shares and of creditors have been met.

§ 40.4 Clause in Articles of Incorporation—Shares of Two or More Classes With and Without Par Value

The aggregate number of shares which this Corporation shall have authority to issue is _______ (_______) shares which are to be divided into classes as follows:

[*Number*] shares of [*Class*] shares, having a par value of _______ ($_______) Dollars per share.

[*Number*] shares of [*Class*] shares, which shares are to be without par value.

The [*Class*] and [*Class*] shares are to have the following relative rights, preferences and limitations: [*List*].

§ 40.5 Clause in Articles of Incorporation—Shares of Two or More Classes with Par Value

The aggregate number of shares which this Corporation shall have authority to issue is ______ (______) shares, divided into ______ (______) shares of common shares of the par value of ______ ($______) Dollars per share and ______ (______) shares of preferred shares of the par value of ______ ($______) Dollars per share.

The preferred shares may be issued as and when the Board of Directors shall determine and shall entitle the holders thereof to receive out of the surplus, and the Corporation shall be bound to pay, a [*Quarterly*] dividend at the rate of ______ (__%) per centum per annum, payable before any dividend shall be set apart or paid on the common shares; Provided, however, that whenever a dividend is paid on the preferred shares the Directors shall have power in their discretion to declare and pay a dividend out of surplus for a like period on the common shares, pursuant to the provisions of law.

The holders of preferred shares, in case of dissolution of the Corporation, before any amount shall be paid to the holders of the common shares, shall be entitled to be paid the par value of their shares and dividends accumulated and unpaid thereon, but shall not participate in any further distribution of the surplus assets of the company.

Such preferred shares, at the discretion of the Corporation, shall be subject to redemption at par on ______, 19__, or any dividend day thereafter.

§ 40.6 Articles of Incorporation Authorizing Issuance of Common Stock (with Alternative Provisions)

Table of Contents

Article ______

COMMON STOCK

Alternative A

The total authorized common capital stock is: ______ shares of Class ______ common stock of $______ par value per share.

Alternative B

The total authorized common capital stock is: ______ shares of Class ______ common stock with no par value.

Option 1

(a) Cumulative Voting. As to the election of a Board of Directors, the Stockholders of the Class ______ common stock shall have the following rights: each Stockholder may vote the number of shares owned by him for as many persons as there are Directors to be elected and for whose election he has a right to vote, or to cumulate his votes by giving one candidate as many votes as the number of such Directors multipled by the number of his shares, or by distributing his votes on the same principle among any number of the candidates.

Option 2

(b) Pre-emptive rights. Class ______ common Stockholders shall have the right to buy upon the price and terms most favorably offered by the Corporation (as he alone shall determine) any stock or security of the Corporation offered for sale of a Class with the same or a higher priority in regards to:

Option 2–A

(1) Voting.

Option 2–B

(2) Dividends.

Option 2–C

(3) Security.

Option 2–D

(4) Redemption rights.

Option 2–E

(5) Conversion rights.

Option 2–F

(6) Liquidation rights.

Such pre-emptive right to buy such shares of stock shall be exercised in proportion to the number of Class ______ common stock shares and [*Describe the Other Stock and Its Class, Series or Preferences, if Any, to Be Taken Into Account*], said Stockholders own at the time such pre-emptive right arises. Any Stockholder entitled to such pre-emptive rights shall also have the right to buy with all other Stockholders who are so entitled, any shares offered to other Stockholders pursuant to their pre-emptive rights when such other Stockholders have not exercised said pre-emptive rights. Unless such Stockholders shall otherwise agree, they shall purchase such excessive shares in proportion to their stockholdings.

Option 3

Provided, however, that the Stockholders of the Corporation shall have no pre-emptive rights prescribed for any shares of stock in the following cases:

Alternative A–1

(1) When the shares of stock are being issued in consideration of services performed or to be performed.

Alternative A–2

(2) When the shares of stock are being issued in consideration of the transfer of tangible personal property to the Corporation.

Alternative A–3

(3) When the shares of stock are being issued in consideration of the transfer of intangible personal property to the Corporation.

Alternative A–4

(4) When the shares of stock are being issued in consideration of the transfer of real property to the Corporation.

Alternative A–5

(5) When the shares of stock are being issued in consideration of the transfer of any property to the Corporation other than cash.

Alternative A–6

(6) When the shares of stock are being issued as dividends of the Corporation.

Alternative A–7

(7) When the shares of stock are being issued in exchange for other stock or securities of the Corporation then outstanding.

Alternative A–8

(8) When the shares of stock are being issued to fulfill any right or option created by the Corporation previous to the granting of this restriction.

Alternative A–9

(9) When the shares of stock are being issued pursuant to the granting of any right or option created by the Corporation after granting of this restriction.

Alternative A–10

(10) When the shares of stock are being issued pursuant to an amendment to the Articles of Incorporation expanding the number of authorized shares.

Alternative A–11

(11) When the offering for sale is for the issuance of or granting of options to purchase up to [*Number*] of shares of [*Describe*] stock to any Director, Officer or employee of the Corporation, which stock may be offered or sold in such amounts and upon such terms and conditions as the Board of Directors from time to time may determine.

Option 4

(c) Voting. The holders of each share of Class ______ common stock shall be entitled to [*Number*] votes; provided that such voting shall be exercised *only* in the following instances:

Alternative B–1

(1) Whenever a matter is put to all of the Stockholders for their consideration.

Alternative B–2

(2) Whenever a matter is put to any group of Stockholders for their consideration.

Alternative B–3

(3) In those specific instances when the Corporation is deciding whether or not it should act regarding any one or more of the following events:

Option 5–A

(A) To sue, complain, and defend.

Option 5–B

(B) To purchase, take, receive, lease, or otherwise acquire, own, hold, improve, use and otherwise deal in and with, real or personal property, or any interest therein, wherever situated.

Option 5–C

(C) To sell, convey, mortgage, pledge, lease, exchange, transfer and otherwise dispose of all or any part of its property and assets.

Option 5–D

(D) To lend money and use its credit to assist its employees.

Option 5–E

(E) To purchase, take, receive, subscribe for, or otherwise acquire, own, hold, vote, use, employ, sell, mortgage, lend, pledge, or otherwise dispose of, and otherwise use and deal in and with, shares or other interests in, or obligations of, other domestic or foreign corporations, associations, partnerships, or individuals, or direct or indirect obligations of the United States or of any other government, State, territory, governmental district or municipality or of any instrumentality thereof.

Option 5–F

(F) To make contracts and guarantees and incur liabilities, borrow money, issue its notes, bonds, and other obligations, and secure any of its obligations by mortgage or pledge of all or any of its property, franchises and income.

Option 5–G

(G) To lend money, invest and re-invest its funds.

Option 5–H

(H) To elect or appoint Officers and agents of the Corporation and define their duties and fix their compensation.

Option 5–I

(I) To make donations for the public welfare or for charitable, scientific, or educational purposes.

Option 5–J

(J) To pay pensions and establish pension plans, pension trusts, profit sharing plans, stock bonus plans, stock option plans and other incentive plans for any or all of its Directors, Officers and employees.

Option 5–K

(K) To be a promoter, partner, member, associate, or manager of any partnership, joint venture, trust or other enterprise.

End of B–3

Alternative B–4

(4) Except such voting rights shall not be exercised in those specific instances when the Stockholders are to vote whether or not the Corporation should act regarding any one or more of the following events:

Option 6–A

(A) To sue, complain, and defend.

Option 6–B

(B) To purchase, take, receive, lease, or otherwise acquire, own, hold, improve, use and otherwise deal in and with, real or personal property, or any interest therein, wherever situated.

Option 6–C

(C) To merge, consolidate, sell, convey, mortgage, pledge, lease, exchange, transfer, and otherwise dispose of all or any part of its property and assets.

Option 6–D

(D) To lend money and use its credit to assist its employees.

Option 6–E

(E) To purchase, take, receive, subscribe for, or otherwise acquire, own, hold, vote, use, employ, sell, mortgage, lend, pledge or otherwise dispose of, and otherwise use and deal in and with, shares or other interests in, or obligations of, other domestic, or foreign corporations, associations, partnerships or individuals, or direct or indirect obligations of the United States or of any other government, State, territory, governmental district or municipality or of any instrumentality thereof.

Option 6–F

(F) To make contracts and guarantees and incur liabilities, borrow money, issue its notes, bonds, and other obligations, and secure any of its obligations by mortgage or pledge of all or any of its property, franchises and income.

Option 6–G

(G) To lend money, invest and re-invest its funds.

Option 6–H

(H) To elect or appoint Officers and agents of the Corporation and define their duties and fix their compensation.

Option 6–I

(I) To make donations for the public welfare or for charitable, scientific or educational purposes.

Option 6–J

(J) To pay pensions and establish pension plans, pension trusts, profit sharing plans, stock bonus plans, stock option plans and other incentive plans for any or all of its Directors, Officers and employees.

Option 6–K

(K) To be a promoter, partner, member, associate, or manager of any partnership, joint venture, trust or other enterprise.

End of B–4

Alternative B–5

(5) Such vote shall be entitled along with the holders of any other voting certificate to vote in any annual or special meeting

called for the purpose of determining a question which it is entitled to vote upon; and such vote shall be included in determining both the quorum present and in determining the number of votes necessary in order to determine any particular matter.

Option 7

(d) First Right of Refusal. Upon a Class ______ common Stockholder desiring to sell or otherwise transfer such stock to any person or entity, such Stockholder may only do so upon the following terms and conditions (which restriction(s) shall be noted on the share certificate):

Option 7–A

(1) If the transferee is a present Stockholder of the Corporation.

Option 7–B

(1) If the transferee is a present Class ______ common Stockholder of the Corporation.

Option 7–C

(1) If the transferring Stockholder has first offered to transfer such stock upon the following terms and conditions:

Alternative A–1

(A) The offer shall be made to all present Stockholders.

Alternative A–2

(A) The offer shall be made to all present Stockholders who are Class ______ Common Stockholders.

Alternative A–3

(A) The offer shall be made to the Corporation.

Alternative B–1

(B) The offer shall be to sell for cash.

Alternative B–2

(B) The offer shall be to sell over time with __% down and __% per month, including interest at __% per annum.

Alternative C–1

(C) The offered price shall be the price of the proposed transfer; except in the case of a proposed gift, in which case it shall be book value.

Alternative C–2

(C) The offered price shall be the price of the proposed transfer; except in the case of a gift, in which case it shall be the average of its high and low traded value on the date [*Number*] days preceding the date of the offer; except, if such stock has not been then traded, on the next preceding trading date on which trading took place.

Alternative C–3

(C) The offered price shall be the price of the proposed transfer; except in the case of a gift, in which case it shall be an appraised value as determined by such reasonable appraisal methods as the Corporation shall from time to time determine. Any one of the following appraisal methods shall be deemed reasonable:

Alternative D–1

(i) An appraisal by a Certified Public Accountant who is not then engaged by the Corporation.

Alternative D–2

(i) An appraisal by one or more persons chosen by the rules of the American Arbitration Association.

Alternative D–3

(i) An appraisal by two persons, each chosen by the two sides to the question. If the higher value is within 10% of the lower value then the average of the two values shall be used; if they are not so close, then the two appraisers shall agree on a third appraiser who shall:

Alternative D–3A

* Choose among the two amounts only.

Alternative D–3B

* Choose any value between the two amounts.

Alternative D–4

(i) The Corporation's appraisal, which shall be deemed final.

C–3 Continued

When a group of two or more Stockholders is involved in the appraisal process, then the chief financial officer of a National Banking Company or his delegate which does no business with the Corporation shall represent such Stockholders' rights.

Option 7–D

Provided that, in any case, the offeree shall also be offered (and shall have the option of accepting) the same terms as the proposed transfer.

Option 8

(e) **Restrictions on the Corporation's Right to Issue Future Certificates.** The following restrictions upon the Corporation's right to issue stock shall apply:

Alternative A

(1) Only stock authorized at this time may be issued.

Alternative B

(2) Only stock whose purchase price is at least book value may be issued.

Alternative C

(3) Stock shall only be issued with rights and preferences equal to or less than those of this Class ______ common.

Alternative D

(4) Stock shall not be issued so that this Class ______ common stock represents less than __% of the Corporation's voting power or __% of the then capital of the Corporation.

(5) Only stock which does not have any of the following rights and preferences may be issued:

Option 8–A

(A) The right to vote.

Option 8–B

(B) The right to vote; except upon default in any dividend.

Option 8–C

(C) Pre-emptive rights.

Option 8–D

(D) The right to vote on a cumulative basis.

Option 8–E

(E) A dividend preference.

Option 8–F

(F) A redemption preference.

Option 8–G

(G) A liquidation preference.

Option 9

(f) Redemption (Call) by the Corporation. The Corporation shall have the following absolute right to redeem a Class ______ common upon the following conditions:

(1) Price. The price for each share Class ______ common stock shall be:

Alternative A–1

(A) Equal to such stocks proportionate share of the Corporation's then net book value exclusive of the par value of all preferred stock.

Alternative A–2

(A) An amount equal to __% of such stocks proportionate share of the Corporation's then net fair market value, as determined by appraisal less the par value of all preferred stock. Any one of the following appraisal methods shall be deemed reasonable:

Alternative A–1

(i) An appraisal by Certified Public Account who is not then engaged by the Corporation.

Alternative A–2

(i) An appraisal by one or more persons chosen by the rules of the American Arbitration Association.

Alternative A–3

(i) An appraisal by two persons, each chosen by the two sides to the question. If this higher value is within 10% of the lower value then the average of the two values shall be used; if they are not so close, then the two appraisers shall agree on a third appraiser who shall:

Alternative A–3(A)

* Choose among the two amounts only.

Alternative A–3(B)

* Choose any value between the two amounts.

Alternative A–4

(i) The Corporation's appraisal, which shall be final. When a group of two or more Stockholders is involved in the appraisal process, then the chief financial officer of a National Banking Company or his delegate which does no business with the Corporation shall represent such Stockholders' rights at the Corporation's expense.

(B) In addition to the redemption price, the Corporation shall be required to pay to any redeemed Stockholder:

Option 10

(i) An amount equal to any then declared current dividend.

Option 11

(ii) An amount equal to any unpaid accrued dividend.

(2) Terms. The terms of such redemption shall be:

Alternative B–1

(A) Cash.

Alternative B–2

(A) __% down and even monthly payments [*including/plus*] __% interest per annum over ______ months.

(3) Conditions. Such redemption shall only be demanded upon the happening of one or more of the following events:

Alternative C–1

(A) The Corporation's right shall be absolute and without restriction.

Alternative C–2

(A) The Corporation shall only do so if the Stockholder being redeemed is terminated as an employee.

COMMENT TO ALTERNATIVES C–1 AND 2

This is one of the most powerful provisions which the Corporation can be granted. Its purpose is to eliminate dissident Stockholders or Stockholders who are no longer employees. Its effect is much swifter and more powerful that a Buy-Sell agreement (see Chapter 68, infra) because the latter is not automatic and self-executing (since a Buy-Sell agreement generally requires the tender of the stock and the execution of the escrow agreement).

Provided, however, that:

Alternative D–1

(A) All certificates of the same Class which a particular certificate holder holds shall be fully redeemed.

Alternative D–2

(A) Any portion of the same Class which a particular certificate holder holds may be fully redeemed.

Alternative E–1

(B) Redemption of any such stock shall not be made when the effect of such redemption shall be to reduce the net book assets of the Corporation below the stated capital which will be outstanding after the cancellation of such stock.

Alternative E–2

(B) The redemption of any such stock shall not be made where the effect of any such redemption shall be to make the Corporation insolvent upon such redemption.

(C) Any stock redeemed shall be cancelled upon the books of the Corporation.

(4) Effective Date. Upon a notice being sent to the certificate holder at his last known address, the Corporation shall redeem such stock upon the terms and conditions herein set forth, such certificate holder shall no longer have any rights in the Corporation except as set forth in (5) below.

(5) Rights Upon Corporate Redemption. Upon a notice of redemption and until such time as the certificate holder shall be completely paid off, the certificate holder's security rights in the Corporation's assets shall be:

Alternative F–1

(A) As a general creditor.

Alternative F–2

(A) With the same security and priority that such holder had before such notice.

(6) Procedures. The Board of Directors of the Corporation, or a committee established by it, shall have the right from time to time to adopt specific rules of procedure to carry out the full intent of this redemption provision and to do all reasonable acts necessary therefore; provided that such rules and acts shall not violate the specific terms of said common stock.

(g) Subchapter S Status. The owner of Class ______ common stock shall not transfer the same if such transfer will void the election of the Corporation to be taxed under Subchapter S of the Internal Revenue Code.

Option 12

(h) Security Laws. The Common Stockholders may be deemed to be "underwriters" under the Securities Act of 1933 (the "Securities Act"), and thus they are required to comply with the requirements of the Securities Act, the Securities Exchange Act of 1934 (the "Exchange Act"), various rules and regulations of the Securities and Exchange Commission (the "Commission") and state securities laws in connection with any offer or transfer of this certificate.

Alternative A–1

The holders acknowledge the Corporation has no obligation under these securities laws to register this instrument or to provide a prospectus for any offer or transfer thereof by the holders.

Alternative A–2

The Corporation hereby agrees and covenants that it will register the stock certificate and provide a prospectus for offers and transfers of the certificate as follows.

Each stock certificate shall be imprinted with a legend in substantially the following form:

"The offer and transfer of the stock represented by this certificate are subject to compliance with the Securities Act of 1933, the Securities Exchange Act of 1934, rules and regulations of the Securities and Exchange Commission, state securities laws and no transfer of the shares represented by this certificate shall be valid or effective unless made in accordance therewith. To the extent provided therein, all transferees of shares represented by this certificate shall be bound by such agreement."

The holders agree, prior to any transfer or attempted transfer of the certificate to give written notice to the Corporation of the intention to make such transfer. Such notice shall describe the manner and circumstances of the proposed transfer in detail, shall contain an undertaking by the holder giving such notice to furnish such further information as may be reasonably required of the Corporation by law to the applicable state securities commissioner and Securities and Exchange Commission and shall be accompanied by an agreement in the form prescribed by the Corporation (said form to be made available at the Corporation's expense within twenty (20) days of notice to the Corporation of a proposed transaction) by each pro-proposed transferee of the shares to be bound by the provisions of this Section with respect to the offer or transfer by such transferee of any certificate. Each certificate issued upon the transfer of any of the Corporation stock shall have the restrictive legend contained herein conspicuously imprinted on it.

The Corporation will authorize the issuance to the holder upon his written request and authorization instrument certificates representing the appropriate amount of stock not bearing the above legend at such time as the registration and delivery requirements of the applicable state securities commissioner and the Securities and Exchange Act no longer require that offers and transfers of the stock be accompanied by a prospectus.

Option 13

The holders shall indemnify and hold harmless the Corporation, each of its Officers who signs any Registration Statement, each person who may be liable as a Director of the Corporation or as a person who controls or shall have controlled Corporation within the meaning of the Securities Act, from and against any such expenses, losses, claims, damages, liabilities or actions arise out of or are based upon any untrue statement or alleged untrue statement or omission or alleged omission based upon information furnished to the Corporation by or on behalf of the holders for use in any Registration Statement or upon the failure of the holders to provide such information after having received a request for such information, and also in respect of any expenses, losses, claims, damages, liabilities or actions, joint or several, to which any such person may become subject under the Securities Act, the Exchange Act, state securities laws, the common law or otherwise with respect to an offer or transfer of the stock or the case of any claim or the commencement of any action in respect of which indemnity may be sought from the then holders on account of the indemnity agreement contained in this subsection.

§ 40.7 Articles of Incorporation Authorizing Issuance of Preferred Stock (Basic Form)

Table of Contents

Article ______

PREFERRED STOCK

The total authorized preferred capital stock is: ______ shares of Class ______ Preferred stock of $______ par value per share.

Option 1

(a) Dividends. The Corporation shall pay a dividend upon such Class__ preferred stock as follows:

Alternative A–1

(1) Such dividend shall be equal to $______ share.

Alternative A–2

(1) Such dividend shall be equal to __% of the par value of each share.

(2) The Corporation shall be obligated to declare such dividend:

Alternative B–1

(A) Each and every *quarter* if it shall then be legally entitled to do so.

Alternative B–2

(A) Each and every *quarter* if it shall then be legally entitled to do so; and if it shall not be legally entitled to do so, it shall take every step possible to rearrange its capital structure and accounting methods to legally allow for the payment of such dividend.

Alternative B–3

(A) Only as the Board of Directors shall from time to time declare; or if they shall delegate such authority to a committee, only as the committee shall from time to time declare.

Alternative B–4

(A) Only as the Stockholders shall from time to time declare.

Alternative B–5

(A) Only as the persons then holding shares of this Class __ preferred or of the [*Describe the Stock and Its Class, Series and Preference*] stock (and who are entitled by the terms of their certificate to vote) shall from time to time vote to declare such dividend.

(3) If the dividend set forth herein is not paid and if such dividend did not under the circumstances have to be paid, then such dividend:

Alternative C–1

(A) Shall be payable in the next period when such payment legally can be made.

Alternative C–2

(A) Shall be payable in the next period when such payment legally can be made, but only if the facts and circumstances then in existence would require such payment.

Alternative D–1

(B) Shall be paid before any future year's current dividend is paid.

Alternative D–2

(B) Shall be paid in the following priority: the dividend owing from the oldest period shall be paid first and among such oldest dividends the amounts available for distribution shall be allocated according to their respective priorities on the date owed.

Alternative D–3

(B) Shall be paid with all accrued and current dividends in the same priority as if such dividend was then owing.

Alternative D–4

(C) Shall no longer be payable.

Option 2

(b) Liquidation. If the Corporation is liquidated, the following terms shall apply:

(1) Liquidation Value. The certificate holder of each share of Class ______ preferred stock shall have the right to a sum equal to the:

Alternative A–1

(A) The par value of each share.

Alternative A–2

(A) The consideration paid to the Corporation for each share.

(2) Rights of Priority Upon Liquidation. Upon liquidation, the certificate holder shall have right of priority over all common shares and Class ______ preferred shares.

(3) Procedures. The Board of Directors of the Corporation, or a committee established by it, shall have the right from time to time to adopt specific rules of procedure to carry out the full intent of this liquidation provision and to do all reasonable acts necessary therefore; provided that such rules and acts shall not violate the specific terms of this preferred stock.

Option 3

(c) Voting. The holders of each share of Class ______ preferred stock shall be entitled to [*Number*] votes; provided that such voting shall be exercised only in the following instances:

Alternative A–1

(1) Whenever a matter is put to the Stockholders in general for their consideration.

Alternative A–2

(1) Whenever a matter is put to any group of Stockholders for their consideration.

Alternative A–3

(1) Whenever a dividend to the preferred Stockholders is in arrearage.

Option 4

(d) Cumulative Voting. As to the election of a Board of Directors, the Stockholders of the Class ______ preferred stock shall have the following right: they may vote the number of shares owned by them for as many persons as there are Directors to be elected and for whose election he has a right to vote, or to cumulate their votes by giving one candidate as many votes as the number of such Directors multiplied by the number of his shares, or by distributing his votes on the same principle among any number of the candidates.

Option 5

(e) Preemptive Rights.

(1) Class ______ common Stockholders shall have the right to buy upon the price and terms most favorably offered (as such holder alone shall determine) any stock of the Corporation of a Class with the same or a higher priority in regards to:

Option 5–A

(A) Voting.

Option 5–B

(B) Dividends.

Option 5–C

(C) Security.

Option 5–D

(D) Redemption rights.

Option 5–E

(E) Conversion rights.

Option 5–F

(F) Liquidation rights.

(2) Such preemptive right to buy such shares of stock shall be exercised in proportion to the number of Class ______ preferred stock shares and [*Describe the Stock and Its Class, Series or Preferences, if any*] said Stockholders own at the time such pre-emptive rights arise.

Option 5–G

(3) In addition to the preemptive right to buy such shares of stock as in proportion to the number of shares said Stockholders own at the time such pre-emptive right arises, any Stockholder entitled to such preemptive rights shall also have the right to buy with all other Stockholders who are so interested any shares offered to Stockholders pursuant to their preemptive rights which Stockholders have not exercised said preemptive rights. Unless such Stockholders shall otherwise agree, they shall purchase such excessive shares in proportion to their Stockholdings.

Option 5–H

(4) Provided, however, that the Stockholders of the Corporation shall have *no* preemptive rights prescribed for any shares of stock in the following cases:

Alternative A–1

(A) When the shares of stock are being issued in consideration of services performed or to be performed.

Alternative A–2

(B) When the shares of stock are being issued in consideration of the transfer of tangible personal property to the Corporation.

Alternative A–3

(C) When the shares of stock are being issued in consideration of the transfer of intangible personal property to the Corporation.

Alternative A–4

(D) When the shares of stock are being issued in consideration of the transfer of real property to the Corporation.

Alternative A–5

(E) When the shares of stock are being issued in consideration of the transfer of any property to the Corporation other than cash.

Alternative A–6

(F) When the shares of stock are being issued as dividends of the Corporation.

Alternative A–7

(G) When the shares of stock are being issued in exchange for other stock or securities of the Corporation then outstanding.

Alternative A–8

(H) When the shares of stock are being issued to fill any right or option created by the Corporation previous to the granting of this restriction.

Alternative A–9

(I) When the shares of stock are being issued pursuant to the granting of any right or option created by the Corporation issued after the adoption of this restriction.

Alternative A–10

(J) When the shares of stock are being issued pursuant to an amendment of the Articles of Incorporation expanding the number of authorized shares.

Alternative A–11

(K) When the offering for sale is for the issuance of or granting of options to purchase up to [*Number*] of shares of Class ______ preferred stock to any Director, Officer or employee of the Corporation which stock may be offered or sold in such amounts and upon such terms and conditions as the Board of Directors from time to time may determine.

Option 6

(f) Security Laws. The Stockholders may be deemed to be "underwriters" under the Securities Act of 1933 (the "Securities Act"), and thus they are required to comply with the requirements of the Securities Act, the Securities Exchange Act of 1934 (the "Exchange Act"), various rules and regulations of the Securities and Exchange Commission (the "Commission") and state securities laws in connection with any offer or transfer of this certificate.

Alternative A–1

The holders acknowledge the Corporation has no obligation under these securities laws to register this instrument or to provide a prospectus for any offer or transfer thereof by the holders.

Alternative A–2

The Corporation hereby agrees and covenants that it will register the stock certificate and provide a prospectus for offers and transfers of the certificate as follows.

Each stock certificate shall be imprinted with a legend in substantially the following form:

"The offer and transfer of the stock represented by this certificate are subject to compliance with the Securities Act of 1933, the Securities Exchange Act of 1934, rules and regulations of the Securities and Exchange Commission, state securities laws and no transfer of the shares represented by this certificate shall be valid or effective unless made in accordance therewith. To the extent provided therein, all transferees of shares represented by this certificate shall be bound by such agreement."

The holders agree, prior to any transfer or attempted transfer of the certificate to give written notice to the Corporation of the intention to make such transfer. Such notice shall describe the manner and circumstances of the proposed transfer in detail, shall contain an undertaking by the holder giving such notice to furnish such further information as may be reasonably required of the Corporation by law in furnishing information to the applicable state securities commissioner and the Securities and Exchange Commission and shall be accompanied by an agreement in the form prescribed by the Corporation (said form to be made available at the Corporation expense within twenty (20) days of notice to the Corporation of a proposed transaction) by each proposed transferee of the shares to be bound by the provisions of this Section with respect to the offer or transfer by such transferee of any certificate. Each certificate issued upon the transfer of any of the Corporation stock shall have the restrictive legend contained herein conspicuously imprinted on it.

The Corporation will authorize the issuance to the holder upon his written request and authorization instrument certificates representing the appropriate amount of stock not bearing the above legend at such time as the registration and delivery requirements of the applicable state securities commissioner and the Securities and Exchange Act no longer require that offers and transfers of the stock be accompanied by a prospectus.

Option 7

The holders shall indemnify and hold harmless the Corporation, each of its officers who signs any Registration Statement, each person who may be liable as a Director of the Corporation or as a person who controls or shall have controlled Corporation within the meaning of the Securities Act, from and against any such expenses, losses, claims, damages, liabilities or actions arise out of or are based upon any untrue statement or alleged untrue statement or omission or alleged omission based upon information furnished to the Corporation by or on behalf of the holders for use in any Registration Statement or upon the failure of the holders to provide such information after having received a request for such information, and also in respect of any expenses, losses, claims, damages, liabilities or actions, joint or several, to which any such person may become subject under the Securities Act, the Exchange Act, state securities laws, the common law or otherwise with respect to an offer or transfer of the stock or the case of any claim or the commencement of any action in respect of which indemnity may be sought from the then holders on account of the indemnity agreement contained in this subsection.

§ 40.8 Articles of Incorporation Authorizing Issuance of Preferred Shares—Another Form

PREFERRED STOCK CLAUSE

The total number of shares of all classes of stock which the Corporation shall have authority to issue is ______ shares, of which ______ shares, $______ par value, shall be a class designated "preferred stock" and ______ shares, $______ par value, shall be a class designated "common stock".

(1) Shares of preferred stock may be issued from time to time in one or more series, each such series to have distinctive serial designations, as shall hereafter be determined in the resolution or resolutions providing for the issue of such preferred stock from time to time adopted by the Board of Directors pursuant to authority so to do which is hereby vested in the Board of Directors.

(2) Each series of Preferred Stock:

(A) may have such number of shares;

(B) may have such voting powers, full or limited, or may be without voting powers;

(C) may be subject to redemption at such time or times and at such prices;

(D) may be entitled to receive dividends (which may be cumulative or noncumulative) at such rate or rates, on such conditions, from such date or dates, and at such times, and payable in preference to, or in such relation to, the dividends payable on any other class or classes or series of stock;

(E) may have such rights upon the dissolution of, or upon any distribution of the assets of, the Corporation;

(F) may be made convertible into, or exchangeable for, shares of any other class or classes (except a class having prior or superior rights and preferences as to dividends or distribution of assets upon liquidation) or of any other series of the same or any other class or classes of stock of the Corporation at such price or prices or at such rates of exchange, and with such adjustments;

(G) may be entitled to the benefit of a sinking fund or purchase fund to be applied to the purchase or redemption of shares of such series in such amount or amounts;

(H) may be entitled to the benefit of conditions and restrictions upon the creation of indebtedness of the Corporation or any subsidiary, upon the issue of any additional stock (including additional shares of such series or of any other series) and upon the payment of dividends or the making of other distributions on, and the purchase, redemption or other acquisition by the Corporation or any subsidiary of any outstanding stock of the Corporation; and

(I) may have such other relative, participating, optional or other special rights, and qualifications, limitations or restrictions thereof;

all as shall be stated in said resolution or resolutions providing for the issue of such preferred stock. Except where otherwise set forth in the resolution or resolutions adopted by the Board of Directors providing for the issue of any series of preferred stock, the number of shares comprising such series may be increased or decreased (but not below the number of shares then outstanding) from time to time by like action of the Board of Directors.

(3) Shares of any series of preferred stock which have been redeemed (whether through the operation of a sinking fund or otherwise) or purchased by the Corporation, or which, if convertible or exchangeable, have been converted into or exchanged for shares of stock of any other class or classes shall have

the status of authorized and unissued shares of preferred stock and may be reissued as a part of the series of which they were originally a part or may be reclassified and reissued as part of a new series of preferred stock to be created by resolution or resolutions of the Board of Directors or as part of any other series of preferred stock, all subject to the conditions or restrictions on issuance set forth in the resolution or resolutions adopted by the Board of Directors providing for the issue of any series of preferred stock and to any filing required by law.

(4) Except as otherwise provided by law or by the resolution or resolutions of the Board of Directors providing for the issue of any series of the preferred stock, the common stock shall have the exclusive right to vote for the election of Directors and for all other purposes, each holder of the common stock being entitled to one vote for each share held.

Subject to all of the rights of the preferred stock or any series thereof, the holders of the common stock shall be entitled to receive, when, as and if declared by the Board of Directors, out of funds legally available therefor, dividends payable in cash, stock or otherwise.

Upon any liquidation, dissolution or winding-up of the Corporation, whether voluntary or involuntary, and after the holders of the preferred stock of each series shall have been paid in full the amounts to which they respectively shall be entitled or a sum sufficient for such payment in full shall have been set aside, the remaining net assets of the Corporation shall be distributed pro rata to the holders of the common stock in accordance with their respective rights and interests, to the exclusion of the holders of the preferred stock.

§ 40.9 Articles of Incorporation Authorizing Issuance of Preferred Shares—Another Form

(a) Authority. The aggregate number of shares which the Corporation shall have authority to issue is ______, of which ______ shall be common shares of the par value of *each* and ______ shall be preferred shares without par value.

(b) Division. The Board of Directors is hereby authorized, at its option, from time to time, to divide all or any part of the preferred shares into series thereof and to fix and determine variations, if any, between any series so established as to any one or more of the following matters:

(1) The rate of dividend,

(2) The price at and the terms and conditions on which shares may be redeemed,

(3) The amount payable upon shares in event of involuntary liquidation,

(4) The amount payable upon shares in event of voluntary liquidation,

(5) Sinking fund provisions for the redemption or purchase of shares, and

(6) The terms and conditions on which shares may be converted, if the shares of any series are issued with the privilege of conversion.

(c) Preferences, Limitations and Relative Rights of the Classes of Shares.

(1) Preferred Dividends. The holders of all preferred shares, regardless of series, at the time outstanding shall be entitled to receive, when and as declared to be payable by the Board of Directors, out of any funds legally available for the payment thereof, dividends at the rate theretofore fixed by the Board of Directors for each series of such preferred shares that have theretofore been established, and no more, payable quarterly on the last days of January, April, July and October in each year.

(2) Cumulativeness of Preferred Dividends. Dividends on all preferred shares, regardless of series, shall be cumulative. No dividends shall be declared on any shares of any series of preferred shares for any dividend period unless all dividends accumulated for all prior dividend periods shall have been declared or shall then be declared at the same time upon all preferred shares then outstanding. No dividends shall be declared on the shares of any series of preferred shares unless a dividend for the same period shall be declared at the same time upon all preferred shares outstanding at the time of such declaration in like proportion to the dividend rate then declared. No dividends shall be declared or paid on the common shares unless full dividends on all the preferred shares then outstanding for all past dividend periods and for the current dividend period shall have been declared and the Corporation shall have paid such dividends or shall have set apart a sum sufficient for the payment thereof.

(3) Preferences on Liquidation. In the event of any dissolution, liquidation or winding up of the Corporation, whether voluntary or involuntary, the holders of each series of the then outstanding preferred shares shall be entitled to receive the amount fixed for such purpose in the resolution or resolutions of the Board of Directors establishing the respective series of preferred shares that might then be outstanding together with

a sum equal to the amount of all accumulated and unpaid dividends thereon at the dividend rate fixed therefor in the aforesaid resolution or resolutions. After such payment to such holders of preferred shares, the remaining assets and funds of the Corporation shall be distributed pro rata among the holders of the common shares. A consolidation, merger or reorganization of the Corporation with any other corporation or corporations or a sale of all or substantially all of the assets of the Corporation shall not be considered a dissolution, liquidation or winding up of the Corporation within the meaning of these provisions.

(4) Redemption Privileges of the Corporation. The whole or any part of the outstanding preferred shares or the whole or any part of any series thereof may be called for redemption and redeemed at any time at the option of the Corporation, exercisable by the Board of Directors upon thirty (30) days' notice by mail to the holders of such shares as are to be redeemed, by paying therefor in cash the redemption price fixed for such shares in the resolution or resolutions of the Board of Directors establishing the respective series of which the shares to be redeemed are a part together with a sum equal to the amount of all accumulated and unpaid dividends thereon at the dividend rate fixed therefor in the aforesaid resolution or resolutions to the date fixed for such redemption. The Corporation may redeem the whole or any part of the shares of any series, or of several series, without redeeming the whole or any part of the shares of any other series; provided, however, that if at any time less than the whole of the preferred shares of any particular series then outstanding shall be called for redemption, the particular shares called for redemption shall be determined by lot or by such other equitable method as may be determined by the Board of Directors. If, on the redemption date specified in any such notice, funds necessary for such redemption shall have been set aside by the Corporation, separate and apart from its other funds, in trust for the pro rata benefit of the holders of the preferred shares so called for redemption, then, notwithstanding that any certificate for shares so called for redemption shall not have been surrendered for cancellation, the shares so called for redemption shall no longer be deemed to be outstanding, the right to receive dividends thereon shall cease to accrue from and after the date so fixed, and all rights of holders of preferred shares so called for redemption shall forthwith after such redemption date cease and terminate, excepting only the right of the holders thereof to receive the redemption price thereof, but without interest. Any interest accrued on funds so deposited shall be paid to the Cor-

poration from time to time. In case the holder of shares which shall have been called for redemption shall not, within five years after the making of such deposit, claim the amount deposited with respect to the redemption of such shares, the bank or trust company in which such deposit was made shall upon demand pay over to the Corporation such unclaimed amounts and thereupon such bank or trust company shall be relieved of all responsibility in respect thereof to such holder. Preferred shares which are redeemed shall be cancelled and shall not be reissued.

§ 40.10 Articles of Incorporation Authorizing Issuance of Preferred Stock (Sophisticated Form)

Table of Contents

(f) Liquidation.
  (1) Liquidation Value.
  (2) Rights of Priority Upon Liquidation.
  (3) Procedures.
(g) Security Interest.
  (1) Property in Which Security Is Held.
  (2) Interest Perfection.
  (3) Priority.
  (4) Restrictions Upon Future Issues.
  (5) Procedures.
(h) Voting.
(i) Cumulative Voting.
(j) Preemptive Rights.
(k) First Right of Refusal.
(*l*) Security Laws.

Article ______

PREFERRED STOCK

The total authorized preferred capital stock is: ______ shares of Class ______ preferred stock of $______ par value per share.

Option 1

(a) Dividends. The Corporation shall pay a dividend upon such Class ______ preferred stock as follows:

Alternative A–1

(1) Such dividend shall be equal to $______ share.

Alternative A–2

(1) Such dividend shall be equal to __% of the par value of each share.

Alternative A–3

(1) Such dividend shall be equal to __% of the consideration originally paid to the Corporation for each share.

Alternative A–4

(1) Such dividend shall be equal to the greater of __% of the par value of each of such shares or __% of the total dividend distributed by the Corporation for the period in question.

Alternative A–5

(1) Such dividend shall be equal to the greater of __% of the par value of each of such shares or __% of the total dividend

distributed by the Corporation for the period in question; provided that upon each of such Class ______ preferred stock having received a total dividend distribution equal to __% of said Class ______ preferred stock's par value, each share of this Class ______ preferred stock shall thereafter receive the greater of __% of the par value of each of such shares or __% of the total dividend distributed by the Corporation for the period in question.

Alternative A–6

(1) Such dividend shall equal __% of the current net profits of the Corporation as calculated according to the procedures generally used by the Corporation's accountants' generally accepted accounting practices.

Option 1–A

(2) Provided, that such dividend shall not exceed $______ per share.

Option 1–B

(2) Provided that such dividends shall be paid prior to any accumulated and current dividends being paid to the following classes of stock and security holders: [*Describe*]; but after the following classes of stock and security holders: [*Describe*].

(3) The Corporation shall be obligated to declare such dividend:

Alternative B–1

(A) Each and every *quarter* if it shall then be legally entitled to do so.

Alternative B–2

(A) Each and every *quarter* if it shall then be legally entitled to do so; and if it shall not be legally entitled to do so, it shall take every step possible to rearrange its capital structure and accounting methods to legally allow for the payment of such dividend.

Alternative B–3

(A) Only as the Board of Directors shall from time to time declare; or if they shall delegate such authority to a committee, only as the committee shall from time to time declare.

Alternative B–4

(A) Only as the Stockholders shall from time to time declare.

Alternative B–5

(A) Only as the persons then holding shares of this Class—preferred or of the [*Describe the Stock and Its Class, Series, and Preference*] stock (and who are entitled by the terms of their certificate to vote) shall from time to time vote to declare such dividend.

COMMENT TO ALTERNATIVE B–5

If other Stockholders have specifically been given the right to vote on all matters (or on this matter), this clause can't be used to exclude them from voting.

Alternative B–6

(A) Only in a manner which would prohibit any other class of stock of the Corporation to be paid a dividend without first paying the current *and accumulated* (if any) dividend set forth above.

Alternative B–7

(A) Only in a manner which would prohibit any other class of stock of the Corporation which has a fixed dividend to be paid a dividend which is disproportionate (based upon the total fixed dividend payable) if this and every other fixed dividend certificate was fully paid.

Alternative B–8

(A) Only in a manner which would prohibit any other class of stock which has no dividend priority over any other stock or security from being paid a dividend which is disproportionate (based upon the priorities of corporate dividend distribution) to the rights of this certificate.

(4) If the dividend set forth herein is not paid and if such dividend did not under the circumstances have to be paid, then such dividend:

Alternative C–1

(A) Shall be payable in the next period when such payment legally can be made.

Alternative C–2

(A) Shall be payable in the next period when such payment legally can be made, but only if the facts and circumstances then in existence would require such payment.

Alternative D–1

(B) Shall be paid before any current period's dividend is paid.

Alternative D–2

(B) Shall be paid in the following priority: the dividend owing from the oldest period shall be paid first and the amounts available for distribution shall be allocated according to their respective priorities on the date owed.

Alternative D–3

(B) Shall be paid with all current dividends in the same priority as if such dividend was then owing.

Alternative D–4

(B) Shall no longer be payable.

Option 2

(b) Redemption (Put) by the Stockholder. Any Class ______ preferred Stockholder shall have the following absolute right to force the Corporation to redeem such shares as follows:

(1) Price. The price for each share of Class ______ preferred stock shall be:

Alternative A–1

(A) Equal to $______

Alternative A–2

(A) Equal to such stock's par value.

Alternative A–3

(A) Equal to __% of the Corporation then book value.

Alternative A–4

(A) Equal to __% of the Corporation's then fair market value as determined by appraisal. Any one of the following appraisal methods shall be deemed reasonable:

Alternative A–4(A)

(i) An appraisal by Certified Public Accountants who are not then engaged by the Corporation.

Alternative A–4(B)

(i) An appraisal by one or more persons chosen by the rules of the American Arbitration Association.

Alternative A–4(C)

(i) An appraisal by two persons, one of whom shall be chosen by the Corporation and one by the holders. If the higher value is within 10% of the lower value then the average of the two values shall be used; if they are not within 10% of each other, then the two appraisers shall agree on a third appraiser who shall:

Alternative A–5(A)

* Choose among the two amounts only.

Alternative A–5(B)

* Choose any value between the two amounts.

When a group of two or more Stockholders is involved in the appraisal process then the chief financial officer of a National Banking Company or his delegate which does no business with the Corporation or any of its officers or directors shall represent such Stockholders rights at the Corporation's expense.

Alternative A–6

(A) A price based upon the date of redemption as follows:

Date		Price
Before ______		$______ per share
After ______	but before ______	$______ per share
After ______	but before ______	$______ per share
After ______	but before ______	$______ per share
After ______		$______ per share

(B) In addition to the redemption price, the Corporation shall be required to pay to any redeeming Stockholder:

Alternative B–1

(i) An amount equal to any declared but unpaid accrued or current dividend.

Alternative B–2

(i) An amount equal to any dividend which was not paid whether or not payment was excused by the fact of its non-cumulation.

(2) Terms. The terms of such redemption shall be:

Alternative C–1

(A) Cash.

Alternative C–2

(A) __% down and even monthly payments [*including/plus*] __% interest per annum over ______ months.

(3) Conditions. The right to demand redemption shall be exercisable:

Alternative D–1

(A) In all events.

Alternative D–2

(A) Upon the Corporation's bankruptcy or assignment of some or all of its assets for the benefit of its creditors.

Alternative D–3

(A) A receiver being appointed to manage any of the Corporation's assets.

Alternative D–4

(A) A levy being issued or other action being taken which results in another claiming a priority interest (whether such claim is of an interest equal to, lesser or greater than the certificate holders).

Alternative D–5

(A) The Corporation selling, exchanging, surrendering a security interest in or liquidating substantially all of its net assets.

Alternative D–6

(A) The Corporation selling, exchanging, surrendering a security interest in or liquidating any of its assets in a manner not consistent with the ordinary course of its business.

Alternative D–7

(A) The Corporation taking any action which reduces the net book value of the assets subject to the security interest set forth herein to an amount equal to less than __% of the then principal and accumulated interest amount being secured and of any interest of equal or greater redemption priority.

Alternative D–8

(A) The Corporation taking any action which reduces the net fair market value of the assets subject to the security interest set forth herein to an amount equal to less than __%

of the then principal and accumulated interest amount being secured.

Provided that:

Alternative F–1

(A) All certificates of the same Class which a particular certificate holder holds shall be fully redeemed.

Alternative G–1

(B) Redemption of any such stock shall not be made when the effect of such redemption shall be to reduce the net book assets of the Corporation below the stated capital which will be outstanding after the cancellation of such stock.

Option 3

(C) The redemption of any such stock shall not be made where the effect of any such redemption shall be to make the Corporation insolvent upon such redemption.

(D) Any stock redeemed shall be cancelled upon the books of the Corporation.

(4) Effective Date. Upon a notice being sent to the Corporation, the redemption shall be deemed to have occurred and the certificate holder shall no longer have any rights in the Corporation except as set forth in (5) below.

(5) Rights Before the Corporate Redemption. Upon notice of a redemption set forth above and until such time as the certificate holder shall be completely paid off, *or the redemption price shall have been escrowed with* ______, the certificate holder's security rights in the Corporation's assets shall only be:

Alternative H–1

(A) as a general creditor.

Alternative H–2

(A) with the same security and priority that such holder before notice.

(6) Series Call:

(A) The following redemption priority is established:

Redemption Priority (From Highest to Lowest)	Class	Series	Earliest Date of Redemption	Price Per Share
1	A	1	______	$______
2	A	2	______	$______
3	A	3	______	$______
4	A	4	______	$______
5	A	5	______	$______

(B) The Corporation shall redeem only those certificates set forth in the above schedule and only at the price relative to the year in which such redemption is to occur (as set forth in said schedule.)

(C) Before any certificate of a lower priority is redeemed, all holders of a higher priority shall be notified that their option to take priority over such lower priorities will expire within sixty (60) days of the notice date if such certificate is not tendered within such period. Upon the expiration of such date:

Alternative A–1

(i) Such certificate shall lose its right to be redeemed.

Alternative A–2

(ii) Such certificate shall have the highest priority of any certificate for which no such notice has been given.

(7) Notice. The holders demanding redemption shall send notice of their demand for such redemption and the certificate to be redeemed duly endorsed to [*Name or Office Title*]. Upon such notice and tender, redemption shall take place within ten (10) days.

(8) Procedures. The Board of Directors of the Corporation, or a committee established by it, shall have the right from time to time to adopt specific rules of procedure to carry out the full intent of this redemption provision and to do all reasonable acts necessary therefore; provided that such rules and acts shall not violate the specific terms of this preferred stock.

Option 4

(c) Redemption (Call) by the Corporation. The Corporation shall have the following absolute right to redeem a Class __ preferred upon the following conditions:

(1) Price. The price for each share of Class ______ preferred stock shall be:

Alternative A–1

(A) Equal to such stock's proportionate share of the Corporation's then book value exclusive of the par value of all common stock.

Alternative A–2

(A) Equal to __% of such stock's proportional share of the Corporation's then fair market value as determined by appraisal less the par value of all common stock.

Any one of the following appraisal methods shall be deemed reasonable:

Alternative B–1

(i) An appraisal by a Certified Public Accountant who is not then engaged by the Corporation.

Alternative B–2

(i) An appraisal by one or more persons chosen by the rules of the American Arbitration Association.

Alternative B–3

(i) An appraisal by two persons, each chosen by the two sides to the question. If this higher value is within 10% of the lower value then the average of the two values shall be used; if they are not so close, then the two appraisers shall agree on a third appraiser who shall:

Alternative B–3(A)

* Choose among the two amounts only.

Alternative B–3(B)

* Choose any value between the two amounts.

Alternative B–4

(i) The Corporation's appraisal, which shall be final. The chief financial officer of a National Banking Company or his delegate which does no business with the Corporation shall represent such Stockholders rights at the Corporation's expense.

(B) In addition to the redemption price, the Corporation shall be required to pay to any redeemed Stockholder:

Option 5

(i) An amount equal to a declared unpaid accrued or current dividend.

Option 6

(ii) An amount equal to any dividend, which was not paid whether or not such payment was excused by the fact of its noncumulation.

(2) Terms. The terms of such redemption shall be:

Alternative C–1

(A) Cash.

Alternative C–2

(B) __% down and even monthly payments [*including/plus*] __% interest per annum over __ months.

(3) Conditions. Such redemption shall only be demanded upon the happening of one or more of the following events:

Alternative D–1

(A) The Corporation's right shall be absolute and without restriction.

Alternative D–2

(A) The Corporation shall only do so if the Stockholder being redeemed is terminated as an employee.

COMMENT TO ALTERNATIVES C–1 AND 2

This is one of the most powerful provisions which the Corporation can be granted. Its purpose is to eliminate dissident Stockholders or Stockholders who are no longer employees. Its effect is much swifter and more powerful than a Buy-Sell Agreement (See Chapter 68, infra) because the latter is not automatic and self-executing (since a Buy-Sell Agreement generally requires the tender of the stock and execution of the escrow agreement).

Provided however, that:

Alternative E–1

(A) All certificates of the same Class which a particular certificate holder holds shall be fully redeemed.

Alternative E–2

(A) Any portion of the same Class which a particular certificate holder holds may be fully redeemed.

Alternative F–1

(B) Redemption of any such stock shall not be made when the effect of such redemption and the application of the stated capital relating thereto shall be to reduce the net book assets of the Corporation below the stated capital which will be outstanding after the cancellation of such stock.

Alternative F–2

(B) Redemption of any such stock shall not be made when the effect of such redemption and the application of the stated capital relating thereto shall be to make the Corporation insolvent upon such redemption.

(C) Any stock redeemed shall be cancelled upon the books of the Corporation.

(4) *Effective Date.* Upon a notice being sent to the certificate holder at his last known address that the Corporation will redeem such stock upon the terms and conditions herein set forth; and he shall no longer have any rights in the Corporation except as set forth in (5) below.

(5) *Rights Upon Corporate Redemption.* Upon a redemption notice set forth above and until such time as the certificate holder shall be completely paid off, *or the redemption price shall have been escrowed with* ______, the certificate holder's security rights in the Corporation's assets shall be:

Alternative G–1

(A) as a general creditor.

Alternative G–2

(A) with the same security and priority that such holder had before such notice.

(6) *Redemption Timing.* The Corporation shall redeem:

Alternative H–1

(A) only those shares set forth in the following schedule and only at the price relative to the year in which such redemption is to occur (as set forth in said schedule):

Redemption Priority	Class	Series	Earliest Date of Redemption	Last Date of Redemption Price
1	A	1	______	$______
2	A	2	______	$______
3	A	3	______	$______
4	A	4	______	$______
5	A	5	______	$______

Alternative H–2

(A) On or before the following respective dates, that number of shares, or more, as set forth in the following schedule:

Redemption Priority	Class	Series	Earliest Date of Redemption	Last Date of Redemption
1	A	1	______	$______
2	A	2	______	$______
3	A	3	______	$______
4	A	4	______	$______
5	A	5	______	$______

(7) Procedures. The Board of Directors of the Corporation, or a committee established by it, shall have the right from time to time to adopt specific rules of procedure to carry out the full intent of this redemption provision and to do all reasonable acts necessary therefore; provided that such rules and acts shall not violate the specific terms of this preferred stock.

Option 7

(d) Sinking Fund. The following sinking fund shall be established for the retirement of certificates:

(1) Use. The sinking fund may only be used to redeem:

Alternative A–1

(A) certificates from holders of Class ______ preferred stock.

Alternative A–2

(A) certificates from holders of Class ______ preferred stock and from holders of certificates with a higher redemption priority.

Alternative A–3

(A) certificates from holders of Class ______ preferred stock and from holders of certificates with an equal or higher redemption priority.

Alternative A–4

(A) certificates from stock or security holders who are exercising their right to demand that the Corporation redeem them.

Alternative A–5

(A) certificates from stock or security holders against whom the Corporation is exercising its right to demand redemption.

(2) Funding. Said sinking fund shall be funded by a contribution of:

Alternative B–1

(A) __% of the net after tax profits of the Corporation in each fiscal year in question.

Alternative B–2

(A) $______ per *quarter.*

Alternative B–3

(A) $______ per quarter for every share of Class ______ preferred stock which may be redeemed out of such fund.

(3) Procedures. The sinking fund shall be operated under the following additional procedures:

Option 7–A

(A) The Trustee of the fund shall be ______.

Option 7–B

(B) The fund shall be continued until all stock *and securities* has been redeemed or the redemption period has expired, whichever is earlier (at which time any of such funds not expended shall be returned to the Corporation's general assets).

Option 7–C

(C) The Trustee shall determine the amount of money held by such fund on the last day of the month of each [*Fiscal quarter/fiscal year*].

Option 7–D

(D) The Trustee shall redeem as many of the certificates as possible out of said fund.

(E) The Board of Directors of the Corporation, or a committee established by it, shall have the right from time to time to adopt other specific rules of procedure to carry out the full intent of this sinking fund provision and to do all reasonable acts necessary therefore; provided that such rules and acts shall not violate the specific terms of this preferred stock.

Option 8

(e) Conversion Rights:

(1) Right. The certificate holders of the Class ______ preferred stock shall have the following conversion rights upon the following events:

Alternative A–1

(A) To convert each share of Class __ preferred stock into ______ shares of [*Describe the Stock and Its Class, Series or Preference, if Any*].

Alternative A–2

(A) To convert ______ shares of Class ______ preferred stock into $______ of principal debt in the form attached as Exhibit B hereto and made a part hereof.

Option 8–A

(2) Consideration. As a condition for such conversion, the certificate holder shall tender to [*Name or position*] at [*Address*] this certificate together with $______ for each share of Class ______ preferred being converted.

Option 8–B

(3) Time Period. The conversion shall only be exercised within the following time period:

Alternative B–1

(A) At any time.

Alternative B–2

(A) Before the ______ day of ______, 19__.

Alternative B–3

(A) After the ______ day of ______, 19__.

Alternative B–4

(A) Upon the Corporation's bankruptcy or assignment of some or all of its assets for the benefit of its creditors.

Alternative B–5

(A) Upon a receiver being appointed to manage any of the Corporation's assets.

Alternative B–6

(A) Upon a receiver being appointed to manage those assets of the Corporation which the holder of this certificate has a direct or indirect security interest, other than as a general creditor.

Alternative B–7

(A) Upon a levy being issued or other action being taken which results in another claiming a priority interest (whether such claim is of an interest equal to, lesser or greater than the certificate holders') in some or all of the assets of the Corporation.

Alternative B–8

(A) Upon the Corporation selling, exchanging, or surrendering a security interest or liquidating substantially all of its net assets.

Alternative B–9

(A) Upon the Corporation selling, exchanging, or surrendering a security interest in or liquidating a substantial portion of its net assets.

Alternative B–10

(A) Upon the Corporation selling, exchanging, or surrendering a security interest in or liquidating any of its assets in a manner not consistent with the ordinary course of its business.

Alternative B–11

(A) Upon the Corporation taking any action which reduces the net book value of the assets subject to the security interest set forth herein to an amount equal to less than __% of the then principal and accumulated interest amount being secured by this certificate and any other certificate with an equal or higher priority.

Alternative B–12

(A) Upon the Corporation taking any action which reduces the net fair market value of the assets subject to the security interest set forth herein to an amount equal to less than __% of the then principal and accumulated interest amount being secured by this certificate.

COMMENT TO ALTERNATIVE B–11 AND B–12

Use only if the preferred stock in question is secured.

(4) General Provisions. Stock which has been converted under this provision shall be retired and shall not be held as an asset of the Corporation.

These provisions for conversion shall be subject to all applicable statutory limits and restrictions; provided however, that the Corporation shall do all things legally possible to arrange for such conversions if the right herein granted is exercised.

Upon such conversion the Corporation shall forthwith issue to the holder of such rights the stock or certificate which he is entitled to and shall deliver to such converting certificate holder the same in due form. Such new certificate shall have the following restrictions:

Alternative C–1

(A) None.

Alternative C–2

(B) The Buy-Sell restrictions, if any, noted on the surrendered certificate.

Alternative C–3

(C) Restrictions if any, relating to security law violations, as may be required by Corporation's counsel from time to time.

(5) Authorization. The number of shares of stock necessary to fully effectuate the conversion privileges set forth herein shall be authorized as of this date and shall be set aside by the Corporation and only issued pursuant to conversion privileges set forth herein. Such shares shall not be cancelled at any time that the conversion privileges set forth herein are outstanding.

(6) Alteration of Conversion Privileges. The conversion privileges set forth herein may be altered at any time by the vote of a majority of the Directors of the Corporation together with a vote of:

Alternative D–1

(A) If the conversion is to be more favorable in every aspect to the certificate holders in question, then by a vote of the majority of corporate shares entitled to vote.

Alternative D–2

(A) If the conversion terms are in any aspect less favorable to the certificate holders, then by vote of __% of all corporate shares entitled to vote.

Alternative D–3

(A) If the terms are in any aspect less favorable to the certificate holder, then the vote of a majority of all stock entitled to vote and by the majority of the shares held by the certificate holders whose rights will be impaired by such change.

(7) Dividends. Upon conversion, the Corporation shall make no payment or adjustment on account of dividends accrued or in arrears; provided that the holders shall be entitled to such dividend, notwithstanding the fact that his conversion took place before such dividend was paid.

(8) Stock Transfer Books. Nothing herein to the contrary withstanding, no conversion shall be made by the Corporation while the stock transfer books are closed.

(9) Fractional Shares. No fractional shares of stock shall be issued upon conversion of preferred shares. Instead of any

fractional share which would otherwise be issued upon conversion, the Corporation will pay a cash adjustment in respect of such fractional interest in an amount equal to the same fraction of the current value per share of stock to have been issued (determined as provided herein) on the day of conversion.

The value of each share of ______ stock shall be:

(A) Equal to $______.

Alternative E–1

(A) Equal to such stock's proportionate share of the Corporation's then book value exclusive of the par value of all common stock.

Alternative E–2

(A) Equal to __% of such stock's proportionate share of the Corporation's then fair market value as determined by appraisal less the par value of all common stock.

Any one of the following appraisal methods shall be deemed reasonable:

Alternative F–1

(i) An appraisal by a Certified Public Accountant who is not then engaged by the Corporation.

Alternative F–2

(i) An appraisal by one or more persons chosen by the rules of the American Arbitration Association.

Alternative F–3

(i) An appraisal by two persons, each chosen by the two sides to the question. If this higher value is within 10% of the lower value then the average of the two values shall be used; if they are not so close, then the two appraisers shall agree on a third appraiser who shall:

Alternative F–3(A)

* Choose among the two amounts only.

Alternative F–3(B)

* Choose any value between the two amounts.

Alternative F–4

(i) The Corporation's appraisal, which shall be final. The chief financial officer of a National Banking Company or his delegate which does no business with the Corporation shall represent such Stockholders rights at the Corporation's expense.

(10) Adjustment of Conversion Price. The conversion price referred to herein shall be subject to adjustment from time to time as follows:

(A) In case the Corporation shall at any time subdivide the outstanding shares of [*Describe Stock to Be Received*] the conversion price in effect immediately prior to such subdivision shall be proportionately decreased, and in case the Corporation shall at any time combine the outstanding shares of [*Describe Stock to Be Received*], the conversion price in effect immediately prior to such combination shall be proportionately increased, effective at the close of business on the date of such subdivision or combination as the case may be. For the purposes of this subparagraph, any distribution of shares of [*Describe Stock to Be Received*] to holders of such shares shall be deemed to be a subdivision, irrespective of the accounting treatment thereof.

(B) In case [*Describe Stock to Be Received*] of the Corporation issuable upon conversion of these shares shall be changed into another kind of capital stock or debt (otherwise than through a subdivision or combination or combination of shares) or shall represent the right to receive some other security or property, as a result of any capital reorganization, reclassification or any merger or consolidation with another Corporation in which the Corporation is not the surviving Corporation, or any sale of all or substantially all of the assets of the Corporation to another Corporation, each share of these shares shall (subject to further adjustment in conversion price as herein provided) thereafter entitle the record holder to acquire upon conversion thereof the kind and number of shares of stock or other securities or property to which such holder would have been entitled if he had held the [*Describe Stock to Be Received*] issuable upon the conversion of his stock immediately prior to such capital reorganization, reclassification, merger, consolidation or sale of assets.

(C) Whenever the conversion price shall be adjusted as provided in this subparagraph, the Corporation shall forthwith file at each office designated for the conversion of shares of this instrument, a statement, signed by the Chairman of the Board, the President, any Vice-President or the Treasurer of the Corporation, showing in reasonable detail the facts requiring such adjustment and the conversion price that will be effective after such adjustment. The Corporation shall forthwith also cause a notice setting forth any such adjustments to be sent by first class mail, postage prepaid, to each registered holder of these shares at his address then appearing on the stock register.

(11) Notice of Change of Rights. In case:

(A) The Corporation shall declare a dividend (or make any other distribution) on its [*Describe Stock to Be Received*] payable otherwise than in cash out of the consolidated earnings surplus of the Corporation *and its subsidiaries*; or

(B) The Corporation shall authorize the granting to the holders of its [*Describe Stock to Be Received*] of rights to subscribe for or purchase any shares of capital stock of any class or any other rights; or

(C) Of any reclassification of the [*Describe Stock to Be Received*] of the Corporation (other than a subdivision or a combination of its outstanding shares of such stock, of any consolidation or merger to which the Corporation is a party and for which approval of any Stockholders of the Corporation is required) or of the sale or transfer of all or substantially all the assets of the Corporation; or

(D) Of the voluntary or involuntary dissolution, liquidation or winding up of the Corporation;

then the Corporation shall cause to be filed at the office of the Corporation and shall cause to be mailed to the holders of this certificate at their addresses as they shall then appear on the records of the Corporation at least ten days prior to the record date specified in (ii) below, a notice stating:

(i) the record date for such dividend, distribution or rights or, if a record is not to be taken, the date as of which the holders of [*Describe Stock to Be Received*] of record to be entitled to such dividend, distribution or rights are to be determined; or

(ii) the date on which such reclassification, consolidation, merger, sale, transfer, dissolution, liquidation or winding up is expected to become effective, and the date as of which it is expected that holders of [*Describe Stock to Be Received*] of record shall be entitled to exchange their shares of [*Describe Stock to Be Received*] for securities or other property deliverable upon such reclassification, consolidation, merger, sale, transfer, dissolution, liquidation or winding up.

(12) The Corporation will pay any documentary stamp taxes attributable to the initial issuance of shares of [*Describe Stock*

to Be Received] upon conversion of any shares of Class ______ preferred pursuant hereto; provided, however, that the Corporation shall not be required to pay any tax or taxes which may be payable in respect of any transfer involved in the issuance or delivery of any certificates of shares or of such debt other than those issued pursuant to the conversion rights herein set forth.

(13) Procedures. The Board of Directors of the Corporation, or a committee established by it, shall have the right from time to time to adopt other specific rules of procedure to carry out the full intent of this conversion provision and to do all reasonable acts necessary therefore; provided that such rules and acts shall not violate the specific terms of this preferred stock.

End of Option 8

Option 9

(f) Liquidation. If the Corporation is liquidated the following terms shall apply:

Option 9–A

(1) Liquidation Value. The certificate holder of each share of Class ______ preferred stock shall have the right to a sum equal to the:

Alternative A–1

(A) The par value of each share.

Alternative A–2

(A) The consideration paid to the Corporation for each share.

Alternative A–3

(A) Any current and accumulated dividend owing.

Alternative A–4

(A) A portion of the then fair market value of the Corporation equal to each share's relative portion of the par value of all shares then outstanding.

Alternative A–5

(A) A portion of the then fair market value of the Corporation equal to the relative consideration paid to the Corporation for the then outstanding certificates.

(2) Rights of Priority Upon Liquidation. Upon liquidation, the certificate holder shall have the following rights of priority:

Alternative B–1

(A) To be paid only as an unsecured general creditor.

Alternative B–2

(A) To be paid out of, and only from, the value of the secured assets in which this certificate had a security priority.

Alternative B–3

(A) To be paid out of the value of the secured assets in which this certificate had a security priority and thereafter as a general creditor in proportion to the amount of unrealized debt as it relates to the claims of all unsecured creditors of the Corporation.

Alternative B–4

(A) To be paid prior to the following Classes of stock and security holders: [*Describe Stock and Its Class, Series or Preferences, if Any*]; but after the following Classes of stock and security holders: [*Describe the Stock and Its Class, Series or Preferences, if Any*].

(3) Procedures. The Board of Directors of the Corporation, or a committee established by it, shall have the right from time to time to adopt specific rules of procedure to carry out the full intent of this liquidation provision and to do all reasonable acts necessary therefore; provided that such rules and acts shall not violate the specific terms of this preferred ______ stock.

End of Option 9

Option 10

(g) Security Interest:

Option 10–A

(1) Property in Which Security Is Held. The holders of Class ______ preferred stock shall have a security interest in the following assets of the Corporation:

Alternative A–1

(A) All assets.

Alternative A–2

(A) All real property.

Alternative A–3

(A) All personal property.

Alternative A-4

(A) All property in excess of $______ value.

Alternative A-5

(A) All non-tangible assets.

Alternative A-6

(A) [List Specific Property].

(2) Interest Perfection. Such security interest shall be secured by the following:

Alternative B-1

(A) A first priority real estate mortgage which shall be properly executed and recorded in the form attached hereto and made a part hereof as *Exhibit A.*

Alternative B-2

(A) A first priority chattel security interest which shall be properly executed and in the form attached hereto and made a part hereof as *Exhibit A* and shall be noticed by the proper UCC-1 statement filed in all locations which the law requires in order to perfect such lien against the claims of others who by statute are not required to have a higher priority.

Alternative B-3

(A) A sinking fund in the form described herein.

(3) Priority. The security interest held by the Class ______ preferred Stockholders shall have a priority over Stockholders of the following types of stock: [*Describe the Stock and Its Class, Series, or Preference, if any*].

Alternative C

(4) Restrictions Upon Future Issues. In no event shall the Corporation issue any stock or other security which shall have a higher or equal security priority than this issue.

(5) Procedures. The Board of Directors of the Corporation, or a committee established by it, shall have the right from time to time to adopt specific rules of procedure to carry out the full intent of this security interest provision and to do all reasonable acts necessary therefore; provided that such rules and acts shall not violate the specific terms of this preferred ______ stock.

End of Option 10

Option 11

(h) Voting. The holders of each share of Class ______ preferred stock shall be entitled to [*Number*] votes; provided that such voting shall be exercised only in the following instances:

Option 11–1

(1) Whenever a matter is put to the Stockholders in general for their consideration.

Option 11–2

(2) Whenever a matter is put to any group of Stockholders for their consideration.

Option 11–3

(3) In those specific instances when the Corporation is deciding whether or not it should act regarding any one or more of the following events:

Option 11–3(A)

(A) To sue, complain and defend.

Option 11–3(B)

(B) To purchase, take, receive, lease, or otherwise acquire, own, hold, improve, use and otherwise deal in and with, real or personal property, or any interest therein, wherever situated.

Option 11–3(C)

(C) To sell, convey, mortgage, pledge, lease, exchange, transfer and otherwise dispose of all or any part of its property and assets.

Option 11–3(D)

(D) To lend money and use its credit to assist its employees.

Option 11–3(E)

(E) To purchase, take, receive, subscribe for, or otherwise acquire, own, hold, vote, use, employ, sell, mortgage, lend, pledge, or otherwise dispose of, and otherwise use and deal in and with, shares or other interests in, or obligations of, other domestic or foreign corporations, associations, partnerships or individuals, or direct or indirect obligations of the United States or of any other government, State, territory, governmental district or municipality or of any instrumentality thereof.

Option 11–3(F)

(F) To make contracts and guarantees and incur liabilities, borrow money, issue its notes, bonds, and other obligations, and secure any of its obligations, and secure any of its obligations by mortgage or pledge of all or any of its property franchises and income.

Option 11–3(G)

(G) To lend money.

Option 11–3(H)

(H) To elect or appoint Officers and agents of the Corporation, and define their duties and fix their compensation.

Option 11–3(I)

(I) To make donations for the public welfare or for charitable, scientific or educational purposes.

Option 11–3(J)

(J) To pay pensions and establish pension plans, pension trusts, profit sharing plans, stock bonus plans, stock option plans and other incentive plans for any or all of its Directors, Officers and employees.

Option 11–3(K)

(K) To be a promoter, partner, member, associate, or manager of any partnership, joint venture, trust or other enterprise.

Option 11–4

(4) Upon the Corporation's bankruptcy or assignment of some or all of its assets for the benefit of its creditors.

Option 11–5

(5) Upon receiver being appointed to manage any of the Corporation's assets.

Option 11–6

(6) Upon a levy of attachment being issued or other action being taken which results in another claiming a priority interest (whether such claim is of an interest equal to, lesser or greater than the certificate holders).

Option 11–7

(7) Upon the Corporation merging, consolidate, selling, exchanging or surrendering a security interest or liquidating substantially all its net assets.

Option 11–8

(8) Upon the Corporation selling, exchanging or surrendering a security interest in or liquidating any of its assets in a manner not consistent with the ordinary course of its business.

Option 11–9

(9) Upon the Corporation taking any action which reduces the net book value of the assets subject to the first security interest set forth herein to an amount equal to less than __% of the then principal and accumulated dividend amount being secured and of any interest of equal or greater redemption priority.

Option 11–10

(10) Upon the Corporation taking any action which reduces the net fair market value of the assets subject to the security interest set forth herein to an amount equal to less than __% of the then principal and accumulated dividend amount being secured.

Alternative B–1

Immediately upon the happening of such event and until such defaults have been cured, all other shares other than the certificates held pursuant to this classification of certificates and [*Describe the Other Stock and Its Class, Series or Preferences, if Any, to Vote*] shall have no voting power whatsoever in the election of the Directors or in any other question (other than the change in the number of shares outstanding, the rights and preferences of any share outstanding, or the relative rights and preferences of any share outstanding) and the entire voting power of the Corporation shall be invested exclusively in the holders of the Class ______ preferred stock.

Alternative B–2

(11) Immediately upon the happening of such event and until such default has been cured no other Stockholder shall have any voting power as to the election of the Board of Directors and the entire voting power as to such elections shall be vested exclusively in the Class ______ preferred certificate is described herein and [*Describe the Other Stock and Its Class, Series or Preferences, if Any, to Vote*].

Option 11–11

(12) Provided, however, that such Class ______ preferred stock shall not be entitled to vote as to the following: [*Describe*].

(13) Such vote shall be entitled along with the holders of any other voting certificate to vote in any annual or special meeting called for the purpose of determining a question which it is entitled to vote.

Option 12

(i) Cumulative Voting. As to the election of a Board of Directors, the Stockholders of the Class ______ preferred stock shall have the following right: they may vote the number of shares owned by them for as many persons as there are Directors to be elected and for whose election he has a right to vote, or to cumulate their votes by giving one candidate as many votes as the number of such Directors multiplied by the number of his shares, or by distributing his votes on the same principle among any number of the candidates.

Option 13

(j) Preemptive Rights:

(1) Class ______ preferred Stockholders shall have the right to buy upon the price and terms most favorably offered (as he alone shall determine) any stock of the Corporation of a Class with the same or a higher priority in regards to:

Option 13–A

(A) Voting.

Option 13–B

(B) Dividends.

Option 13–C

(C) Security.

Option 13–D

(D) Redemption rights.

Option 13–E

(E) Conversion rights.

Option 13–F

(F) Liquidation rights.

(2) Such preemptive right to buy such shares of stock shall be exercised in proportion to the number of Class ______ preferred stock shares and [*Describe the Stock and Its Class, Series or Preferences, if Any*] said Stockholders own at the time such preemptive rights arise.

Option 13–G

(3) In addition to the preemptive right to buy such shares of stock as in proportion to the number of shares said Stockhold-

ers own at the time such preemptive right arises, any Stockholder entitled to such preemptive rights shall also have the right to buy with all other Stockholders who are so interested any shares offered to Stockholders pursuant to their preemptive rights which Stockholders have not exercised. Unless such Stockholders shall otherwise agree, they shall purchase such excessive shares in proportion to their stockholdings.

Option 13–H

(4) Provided, however, that the Stockholders of the Corporation shall have no preemptive rights prescribed for any shares of stock in the following cases:

Alternative A–1

(A) When the shares of stock are being issued in consideration of services performed or to be performed.

Alternative A–2

(A) When the shares of stock are being issued in consideration of the transfer of tangible personal property to the Corporation.

Alternative A–3

(A) When the shares of stock are being issued in consideration of the transfer of intangible personal property of the Corporation.

Alternative A–4

(A) When the shares of stock are being issued in consideration of the transfer of real property to the Corporation.

Alternative A–5

(A) When the shares of stock are being issued in consideration of the transfer of any property to the Corporation other than cash.

Alternative A–6

(A) When the shares of stock are being issued as dividends of the Corporation.

Alternative A–7

(A) When the shares of stock are being issued in exchange for other stock or securities of the Corporation then outstanding.

Alternative A–8

(A) When the shares of stock are being issued to fill any right or option created by the Corporation previous to the granting of this restriction.

Alternative A–9

(A) When the shares of stock are being issued pursuant to the granting of any right or option created by the Corporation issued after the application of this restriction.

Alternative A–10

(A) When the shares of stock are being issued pursuant to an amendment of the Articles of Incorporation expanding the number of authorized shares.

Alternative A–11

(A) When the offering for sale is for the issuance of or granting of options to purchase up to [*Number*] of shares of Class ______ preferred stock to any Director, Officer or employee of the Corporation which stock may be offered or sold in such amounts and upon such terms and conditions as the Board of Directors from time to time may determine.

Alternative A–12

(A) When the Corporation is merging or consolidating.

Option 14

(k) First Right of Refusal. Upon a Class ______ preferred Stockholder desiring to sell or otherwise transfer such stock to any person or entity, such Stockholder may only do so upon the following terms and conditions:

Option 14–A

(1) If the transferee is a present Stockholder of the Corporation.

Option 14–B

(2) If the transferee is a present Class ______ preferred or Class ______ common Stockholder of the Corporation.

Option 14–C

(3) After the transferring Stockholder has first offered to transfer such stock upon the following terms and conditions:

Alternative A–1

(A) The offer shall be made to all present Stockholders.

Alternative A–2

(A) The offer shall be made to all present Stockholders who are Class ______ preferred Stockholders.

Alternative A–3

(A) The offer shall be made to the Corporation.

Alternative B–1

(B) The offer shall be to sell for cash.

Alternative B–2

(B) The offer shall be to sell over time with __% down and __% per month [*including/plus*] interest at __% per annum.

Option 14–D

(4) Provided that, in any case, the offeree shall also be offered (and shall have the option of accepting) the same terms as the proposed transfer.

Alternative C–1

(5) The offered price shall be the price of the proposed transfer.

Alternative C–2

(5) The offered price shall be the price of the proposed transfer; except in the case of a gift, in which case it shall be book value.

Alternative C–3

(5) The offered price shall be the price of the proposed transfer; except in the case of a gift, in which case it shall be the average of its high and low traded value on the date [*Number*] days preceding the date of the offer; except, if such stock has not been then traded, on the next preceding trading date on which trading took place.

Alternative C–4

(5) The offered price shall be the price of the proposed transfer; except in the case of a gift, in which case it shall be an appraised value as determined by such reasonable appraisal methods as the Corporation shall from time to time determine. Any one of the following appraisal methods shall be deemed reasonable:

Alternative D–1

(A) An appraisal by Certified Public Accountants who are not then engaged by the Corporation.

Alternative D–2

(A) An appraisal by one or more persons chosen by the rules of the American Arbitration Association.

Alternative D–3

(A) An appraisal by two persons, each chosen by the two sides to the question. If this higher value is within 10% of the lower value than the average of the two values shall be used; if they are not so close, then the two appraisers shall agree on a third appraiser who shall:

Alternative D–3(A)

(i) Choose among the two amounts only.

Alternative D–3(B)

(i) Choose any value between the two amounts.

Alternative D–4

(A) The Corporation's appraisal, which shall be deemed final.

(B) The chief financial officer of a National Banking Company or his delegate which does no business with the Corporation shall represent such Stockholders' rights at the Corporation's expense.

Option 15

(*1*) **Security Laws.** The preferred Stockholders may be deemed to be "underwriters" under the Securities Act of 1933 (the "Securities Act"), and thus they are required to comply with the requirements of the Securities Act, the Securities Exchange Act of 1934 (the "Exchange Act"), various rules and regulations of the Securities and Exchange Commission (the "Commission") and state securities laws in connection with any offer or transfer of this certificate.

Alternative A–1

The holders acknowledge the Corporation has no obligation under these securities laws to register this instrument or to provide a prospectus for any offer or transfer thereof by the holders.

Alternative A–2

The Corporation hereby agrees and covenants that it will register the stock certificate and provide a prospectus for offers and transfers of the certificate as follows.

Each stock certificate shall be imprinted with a legend in substantially the following form:

"The offer and transfer of the stock represented by this certificate are subject to compliance with the Securities Act of 1933, the

Securities Exchange Act of 1934, rules and regulations of the Securities and Exchange Commission, state securities laws and no transfer of the shares represented by this certificate shall be valid or effective unless made in accordance therewith. To the extent provided therein, all transferees of shares represented by this certificate shall be bound by such agreement."

The holders agree, prior to any transfer or attempted transfer of the certificate to give written notice to the Corporation of the intention to make such transfer. Such notice shall describe the manner and circumstances of the proposed transfer in detail shall contain an undertaking by the holder giving such notice to furnish such further information as may be reasonably required of the Corporation by law in furnishing information to the Securities and Exchange Commission to the relevant state securities commissioner, and shall be accompanied by an agreement in the form prescribed by the Corporation (said form to be made available at the Corporation expense within twenty (20) days of notice to the Corporation of a proposed transaction) by each proposed transferee of the shares to be bound by the provisions of this Section with respect to the offer or transfer by such transferee of any certificate. Each certificate issued upon the transfer of any of the Corporation stock shall have the restrictive legend contained herein conspicuously imprinted on it.

The Corporation will authorize the issuance to the holder upon his written request and authorization instrument certificates representing the appropriate amount of stock not bearing the above legend at such time as the registration and delivery requirements of the Securities and Exchange Act no longer require that offers and transfers of the stock be accompanied by a prospectus

Option 16

The holders shall indemnify and hold harmless the Corporation, each of its officers who signs any Registration Statement, each person who may be liable as a Director of the Corporation or as a person who controls or shall have controlled Corporation within the meaning of the Securities Act, from and against any such expenses, losses, claims, damages, liabilities or actions arise out of or are based upon any untrue statement or alleged untrue statement or omission or alleged omission based upon information furnished to the Corporation by or on behalf of the holders for use in any Registration Statement or upon the failure of the holders to provide such information after having received a request for such information, and also in respect of any expenses, losses, claims, damages, liabilities or actions, joint or several, to which any such person may become subject under the Securities Act, the Exchange Act, State securities laws, the common law or otherwise with respect to an offer or transfer of the stock or the case of any claim or the commencement of any action in respect of which indemnity may be sought from the then holders on account of the indemnity agreement contained in this subsection.

COMMENT

See § 38.13, supra, with respect to characteristics and authorization for issuance of preferred shares.

§ 40.11 Clause in Articles of Incorporation—Preferred Shares Issued in Series

This Corporation shall have authority to issue its preferred shares in series. The designation of each series, the number of shares therein, and variations in the relative rights, preferences, and limitations as between series are as follows: ________________

____

subject to the limitation that, if the stated dividends and amounts payable on liquidation are not paid in full, the shares of all series of the same class shall share ratably in the payment of dividends including accumulations, if any, in accordance with the sums which would be payable on such shares if all dividends were declared and paid in full, and in any distribution of assets other than by way of dividends in accordance with the sums which would be payable on such distribution if all sums payable were discharged in full.

§ 40.12 Clause in Articles of Incorporation—Directors Authorized to Issue Preferred Shares in Series

This Corporation shall have authority to issue its preferred shares in series. The Board of Directors is vested with authority to establish and designate series, to fix the number of shares therein, and the variations in the relative rights, preferences, and limitations as between series, subject to the limitation that, if the stated dividends and amounts payable on liquidation are not paid in full, the shares of all series of the same class shall share ratably in the payment of dividends including accumulations, if any, in accordance with the sums which would be payable on such shares if all dividends were declared and paid in full, and in any distribution of assets other than by way of dividends in accordance with the sums which would be payable on such distribution if all sums payable were discharged in full.

§ 40.13 Clause in Articles of Incorporation—Reservation of the Right to Fix Consideration for No Par Shares to Stockholders

(a) The right to fix the consideration for which shares without par value are to be issued is reserved to the Stockholders.

(b) The right to fix the consideration to be received by the Corporation for the issuance of any of its Class B common shares without par value is reserved to the holders of its Class A common shares.

COMMENTS

In most States the power to fix consideration for shares is vested in the Board of Directors unless specific provision is made in the articles of incorporation reserving such power to the Stockholders; such reservation is only applicable to shares without par value.

It is believed that little purpose is served by reserving this power to the Stockholders.

§ 40.14 Clause in Articles of Incorporation—Convertible Shares

The [*Class*] shares of this Corporation, herein described as convertible shares may, at the option of the holder thereof, at any time on or before [*or, after*] the ______ day of ______, 19__, be converted into [*Class*] shares of the Corporation upon the following terms and conditions, to wit:

(a) The holder of any of said shares of such convertible shares desiring to avail himself of the option for conversion of his shares as herein provided, shall, on or before [*or, at Any Time after*] the ______ day of ______, 19__, surrender up and deliver, duly endorsed in blank, the certificate or certificates representing the shares to be converted to the Secretary of the Corporation at its office, and at the same time notify the said Secretary in writing over his signature that he desires to convert his shares into [*Class*] shares pursuant to these provisions.

(b) At the time of surrendering his shares for conversion as aforesaid, the said holder desiring to avail himself of the option for conversion of his shares as herein provided shall pay to the Corporation the sum of ______ ($______) Dollars for each share of [*Class*] shares to which the holder is entitled upon such conversion under the terms hereof, such payment to be made to said Secretary for the Corporation. The right of conversion of such convertible shares shall exist only upon the payment of such additional value as herein provided for.

(c) Upon receipt by the Secretary of a certificate or certificates representing shares of convertible shares with the notice that the holder thereof desires to convert the same, all as aforesaid, together with the receipt by him of the sum of ______ ($______) Dollars for each share to be received pursuant to the terms of the conversion, the Corporation shall forthwith cause to be issued to the holder of the convertible shares surrendering the same [*Number*] shares of

[*Class*] shares for each share of convertible shares surrendered for conversion, issuing and delivering to such holder a certificate in due form for such [*Class*] shares.

(d) [*Number*] shares of the [*Class*] shares of this Corporation shall be set aside and reserved, and the said shares shall be issued only in conversion for [*Class*] shares as herein provided for.

(e) Shares which have been converted hereunder shall forthwith be cancelled.

(f) It is expressly provided that these provisions for conversion of the [*Class*] shares of this Corporation shall be subject to all the limitations and restrictions contained in [*State*] Business Corporation Law.

(g) It is further provided that the basis of the conversion of the convertible shares herein authorized into the [*Class*] shares of the Corporation, including the terms and conditions upon which such conversion may be made, may be changed by the Corporation by majority vote of the Directors thereof at any meeting lawfully held, provided approval to such change is also given by a majority of the Stockholders of the Corporation either in writing or at a meeting called for the purpose of considering the matter. But the time within which the conversion may be made shall not be altered. Also, it is expressly provided that the basis of conversion shall not be changed by action of the Corporation as herein provided nor shall such action, if taken be effective unless at the time of such action, and thereafter during the entire period in which the conversion is authorized the stated capital represented by the convertible shares plus the additional value, if any, provided to be paid upon the conversion for the shares to be issued, is at least equal to the contribution to stated capital required by law for the shares to be issued pursuant to the conversion.

§ 40.15 Clause in Articles of Incorporation—Cumulative Dividends

The holders of preferred shares shall be entitled to receive thereon from the surplus only a fixed cumulative dividend of ______ (______%) per cent. per annum and no more, payable in cash on the ______ days of ______ and ______ of each year. Should the surplus of said Corporation prior to any dividend day be insufficient to pay the dividend in the preferred shares, such dividend shall be payable from future surplus, but without interest, and no dividend shall at any time be paid on the common shares until the full amount of ______ (______%) per cent. per annum up to such time and for the then current calendar year upon all of the preferred shares issued shall have been paid or set apart.

In the event of dissolution of the Corporation, the holders of preferred shares shall be entitled to receive the par value of their shares, together with accumulated dividends thereon to the date of payment, before holders of the common shares shall be entitled to receive anything thereon. Thereafter, the preferred shares shall not be entitled to share in the assets of the Corporation.

§ 40.16 Clause in Articles of Incorporation—Cumulative Dividends—Another Form

The holders of record of [*Class*] shares shall be entitled to receive, when and as declared from the surplus only by the Board of Directors, cash dividends of ______ per cent per annum per share, payable [*Annually*] on the ______ day of ______ of each year. The cash dividends on the [*Class*] shares shall be cumulative and shall be payable before any dividends or distributions on the [*Other Classes*] shares shall be paid or set apart, so that if in any dividend period, dividends amounting to ______ per cent (______%) shall not have been paid thereon or set apart therefor, the deficiency shall be payable before any dividends or distributions shall be paid upon or set apart for the [*Other Classes*] shares. Cash dividends on the [*Class*] shares shall accrue from their date of issue. Whenever all cumulative dividends on the [*Class*] shares for all previous years shall have been declared, and shall have become payable, and the accrued dividend for the current year, shall have been declared, and the Corporation shall have paid such declared cumulative dividends for previous years, and such accrued dividend for the current year upon said [*Class*] shares, or shall have set aside from its surplus a sum sufficient for the payment thereof, the holders of [*Other Classes*] shares shall be entitled to receive, when and as declared from the remaining surplus of the Corporation after the payment of the cumulative dividends and accrued dividend for the current year upon the [*Class*] shares as aforesaid, yearly dividends at the rate of ______ per cent (______%) per annum, payable [*Annually*] on the ______ day of ______ of each year.

§ 40.17 Clause in Articles of Incorporation—Non-cumulative Dividends

The holders of record of [*Class*] shares shall be entitled to receive, when and as declared from the surplus only by the Board of Directors, non-cumulative cash dividends at the rate of, but never exceeding, ______ per cent per annum per share for the fiscal year ending with the ______ day of ______, 19__, and for each and every fiscal year thereafter, payable on the ______ day of ______ of each year in preference and priority to any payment for and any dividends upon the

[*Other Classes*] shares for such fiscal year; and, if such surplus of any fiscal year is not sufficient to pay a dividend of ______ per cent. per annum per share on said [*Class*] shares, then such dividend declared by the Board of Directors may be paid thereon as such surplus of such fiscal year will suffice to pay.

After the full ______ per cent dividend on the ______ shares for such fiscal year has been paid or declared and a sum sufficient for the payment thereof set apart, dividends on the ______ shares may be paid out of the remainder of the surplus available therefor.

§ 40.18 Clause in Articles of Incorporation—Participating Shares

The holders of record of the [*Class*] shares shall be entitled, out of the surplus, to receive cumulative dividends at the rate of ______ per cent. per annum in each and every year, in preference and priority to any payment of any dividends upon the [*Other Classes*] shares for such year. If after providing for the payment of full dividends for any year on the [*Class*] shares, and for any balance that may remain due on the cumulative dividends on such [*Class*] shares for preceding years, there shall remain any surplus, any and all such surplus not in the opinion of the Board of Directors required to provide for the maintenance, improvement, enlargement, and operation of the property and business of the Corporation, or for the payment of its liabilities, shall be applicable to dividends upon the [*Other Classes*] shares for such year, to the extent of, but not exceeding, ______ per cent. upon the said [*Other Classes*] shares, when and as from the time the same shall be declared by the board of directors; which dividends upon the [*Other Classes*] shares shall not be cumulative, but shall only be paid if earned. The remainder of any such surplus shall then be applicable to the payment of further dividends to be equally participated in by each share of the [*Class*] and [*Other Classes*] shares.

§ 40.19 Resolution Establishing Series of Preferred Shares

Pursuant to the authority vested in the Board of Directors by the provisions of *Section* ______ *of Article* ______ of the Articles of Incorporation, it is hereby Resolved That:

(a) ______ of the preferred shares authorized to be issued by this Corporation are hereby established and designated *Series A Preferred Shares.* Each share in such series shall, in addition to those otherwise provided by law and the Articles of Incorporation, have the rights and preferences and be subject to the limitations hereinafter set forth.

(b) The rate of dividend payable upon *Series A Preferred Shares* shall be ______ Dollars ($__) per annum.

(c) *Series A Preferred Shares* may be redeemed by the Corporation at the redemption price of $__ per share.

(d) The amount payable upon each *Series A Preferred Share* in the event of involuntary liquidation shall be $__.

(e) The amount payable upon each *Series A Preferred Share* in the event of voluntary liquidation shall be $__.

(f) Each *Series A Preferred Share* may be converted into ______ common shares subject to the following conditions: [*Here State Desired Conditions*].

COMMENT

The Board of Directors of a Corporation may be authorized to establish the business terms of series of preferred shares. See e. g. Model Bus.Corp.Act § 16. It is usually desirable to invest the directors with such authority to improve flexibility in establishing such terms of the series in light of current market conditions. Such authorization may be exercised by a simple resolution; in addition, a statement must be filed with the Secretary of State.

§ 40.20 Resolution Increasing (Decreasing) Number of Shares in Previously Authorized Series

RESOLUTION: INCREASE [*DECREASE*] IN NUMBER OF SHARES OF ______ CORPORATION

(a) ______ Corporation has authorized ______ [*List Type, e. g., "Common", "Preferred"*] *shares in series, as follows:* ______ [*Enumerate Details of Stock Structure to Be Affected by Resolution*].

(b) The number of shares in these series has previously been set by the Corporation as follows: ______ [*List Number of Shares in Each Affected Series*].

(c) The Corporation has issued ______ [*Number*] shares of Series ______ [and ______ [*Number*] *shares of Series* ______] [*Specify Details Regarding Issuance of Shares of Any Affected Series*].

(d) Pursuant to the provisions of the [*State*] Corporations Code and Article ______ of the Articles of Incorporation, the Directors have resolved to, and do hereby [*Increase*] [*Decrease*] the number of shares of these series as follows: ______ [*Enumerating Details of Increase or Decrease in Affected Series*].

(e) The Board of Directors has resolved to, and does hereby, authorize and direct the officers of the Corporation to file with the

[*State*] Secretary of State a Certificate specifying the change in number of shares accomplished by this Resolution.

Dated: ______, 19__.

Library References:

C.J.S. Corporations § 268 et seq.
West's Key No. Digests, Corporations ⚷66, 67.

§ 40.21 Directors' Resolution Determining Number and Rights, Restrictions, Preferences or Privileges of Unissued Shares of Stock

RESOLUTION: RIGHTS OF UNISSUED SHARES

(a) ______Corporation has [*Number*] shares previously authorized to be issued and yet unissued by the Corporation.

(b) Article ______ of the Articles of Incorporation empowers the Board of Directors to determine the rights, restrictions, preferences and privileges of any number of shares previously authorized to be issued but yet unissued by the Corporation.

(c) At a meeting held on ______, 19__, at ______, the Board of Directors resolved to, and does hereby, declare that [*Number*] of the authorized but unissued shares shall have rights, restrictions, preferences, and privileges as follows:

(1) The ______ [*Common*] [*Preferred*] shares shall be divided into ______ [*Number*] series, identified as Series ______ ["A"] and Series ______ ["B"].

[*Alternate Sub-paragraph (1).* The first series of ______ [*Common*] [*Preferred*] shares shall be identified as Series "A".]

(2) The number of shares in Series ______ ["A"] [and ______ "B"] shall be [*Number*] [and [*Number*] respectively];

(3) The preferred shares shall have the following dividend rights: ______ [*State Rate, Date Payable, Whether Cumulative or Non-cumulative, Whether Participating or Non-participating*];

(4) The liquidation preference of the preferred shares is as follows: ______ [*State Right of Preferred and Common Shares Respectively to Assets Upon Termination of Corporate Existence*];

(5) The shares of Series ______ of the preferred [*Common*] shares shall be subject to redemption as follows: ______ [*State Any Facts Giving Rise to Right of Redemption, Redemption Price or Formula for Fixing Redemption Price, Manner*

of Payment of Redemption Price, Source of Funds for Redemption Price];

(6) The shares of Series ______ of the preferred [*Common*] shares shall have the following rights to notice of, and to vote at, meetings of Stockholders: ______ [*State Conditions Upon Which These Shares May Have Notice of, Right to Vote at, or Right to Call Meetings of, Stockholders, e. g., Upon Omission of Payment of Dividends for a Given Time*];

(7) For purchase or redemption of Series ______ of the preferred [*Common*] shares, the Corporation shall set aside certain funds from net earnings as follows: ______ [*State Provisions for Sinking Fund*];

(8) Holders of shares of Series ______ of the preferred [*Common*] shares shall have the right to convert such shares to common [*Series* ______ *of Common*] shares, as follows: ______ [*State Facts Giving Rise to Conversion Rights, Exchange Rate Upon Conversion (Conversion Price)*].

(d) The Board of Directors has resolved to, and does hereby, authorize and direct the officers of the Corporation to file with the [*State*] Secretary of State a Certificate of Determination.

COMMENT

This Form was drafted for use under the California Corporations Code.

§ 40.22 Statement of Resolution Establishing Series of Shares to Secretary of State

To: The Secretary of State of the State of __________.

Pursuant to the provisions of Section ______ of the ______ Business Corporation Act, the undersigned Corporation submits the following statement for the purpose of establishing and designating a series of shares and fixing and determining the relative rights and preferences thereof:

First. The name of the Corporation is ____________________

____

Second. The following resolution, establishing and designating a series of shares and fixing and determining the relative rights and preferences thereof, was duly adopted by the Board of Directors of the Corporation on ______, 19__:

(*Insert copy of resolution*)

Dated ______, 19__.

____________________ (Note 1)

By ________________
Its ______ President
And ________________
Its ______ Secretary
(Note 2)

§ 40.23 Directors' Resolution Determining Number and Rights, Restrictions, Preferences or Privileges of Unissued Shares of Stock

RESOLUTION: RIGHTS OF UNISSUED SHARES

(a) ______ Corporation has [*Number*] shares previously authorized to be issued and yet unissued by the Corporation.

(b) Article ______ of the Articles of Incorporation empowers the Board of Directors to determine the rights, restrictions, preferences and privileges of any number of shares previously authorized to be issued but yet unissued by the Corporation.

(c) At a meeting held on ______, 19__, at ______ the Board of Directors resolved to, and does hereby, declare that [*Number*] of the authorized but unissued shares shall have rights, restrictions, preferences, and privileges as follows:

(1) The ______ [*Common*] [*Preferred*] shares shall be divided into ______ [*Number*] series, identified as Series ______ ["A"] and Series ______ ["B"].

[*Alternate Sub-paragraph (a).* The first series of ______ [*Common*] [*Preferred*] shares shall be identified as Series "A".]

(2) The number of shares in Series ______ ["A"] [and ______ "B"] shall be [*Number*] and [*Number*] respectively];

(3) The preferred shares shall have the following dividend rights: ______ [*State Rate, Date Payable, Whether Cumulative or Noncumulative, Whether Participating or Non-participating*];

(4) The liquidation preference of the preferred shares is as follows: ______ [*State Right of Preferred and Common Shares Respectively to Assets Upon Termination of Corporate Existence*];

(5) The shares of Series ______ of the preferred [*Common*] shares shall be subject to redemption as follows: ______ [*State any Facts Giving Rise to Right of Redemption, Redemption Price or Formula for Fixing Redemption Price, Manner of Payment of Redemption Price, Source of Funds for Redemption Price*];

(6) The shares of Series ______ of the preferred [*Common*] shares shall have the following rights to notice of, and to vote at, meetings of Stockholders: ______ [*State Conditions Upon Which These Shares May Have Notice of, Right to Vote at, or Right to Call Meetings of, Stockholders, e. g., Upon Omission of Payment of Dividends for a Given Time*];

(7) For purchase or redemption of Series ______ of the preferred [*Common*] shares, the Corporation shall set aside certain funds from net earnings as follows: ______ [*State Provisions for Sinking Fund*];

(8) Holders of shares of Series ______ of the preferred [*Common*] shares shall have the right to convert such shares to common [*Series ______ of Common*] shares, as follows: ______ [*State Facts Giving Rise to Conversion Rights, Exchange Rate Upon Conversion (Conversion price)*].

(d) The Board of Directors has resolved to, and does hereby, authorize and direct the officers of the Corporation to file with the California Secretary of State a Certificate of Determination.

COMMENT

This form was drafted for use under the California Corporations Code.

§§ 40.24–41.0 are reserved for supplementary material.

CHAPTER 41

STOCK CERTIFICATES

Table of Sections

Library References:

C.J.S. Corporations § 262.
West's Key No. Digests, Corporations ⚷95.

§ 41.1 Share Certificates—Generally

The share certificate, or stock certificate, is the instrument which evidences the Stockholder's interest (or share or stock) in the

Corporation. Such interest, of course, may exist even though no share certificate is issued. The share certificate serves to identify the Stockholder and to facilitate the transfer of his interest.

Statutes usually require the issue of share certificates, and regulate their form and content.[1]

Regulations of the securities exchanges prescribe standards for certificates for securities listed thereon. Share certificates range

1. E. g. Model Bus.Corp.Act § 23 provides as follows:

§ 23. Shares Represented by Certificates and Uncertificated Shares

The shares of a Corporation shall be represented by certificates or shall be uncertificated shares. Certificates shall be signed by the chairman or vice-chairman of the Board of Directors or the president or a vice president and by the treasurer or an assistant treasurer or the secretary or an assistant secretary of the Corporation, and may be sealed with the seal of the Corporation or a facsimile thereof. Any of or all the signatures upon a certificate may be a facsimile. In case any officer, transfer agent or registrar who has signed or whose facsimile signature has been placed upon such certificate shall have ceased to be such officer, transfer agent or registrar before such certificate is issued, it may be issued by the Corporation with the same effect as if he were such officer, transfer agent or registrar at the date of its issue.

Every certificate representing shares issued by a Corporation which is authorized to issue shares of more than one class shall set forth upon the face or back of the certificate, or shall state that the Corporation will furnish to any Stockholder upon request and without charge, a full statement of the designations, preferences, limitations, and relative rights of the shares of each class authorized to be issued, and if the Corporation is authorized to issue any preferred or special class in series, the variations in the relative rights and preferences between the shares of each such series so far as the same have been fixed and determined and the authority of the Board of Directors to fix and determine the relative rights and preferences of subsequent series.

Each certificate representing shares shall state upon the face thereof:

(a) That the Corporation is organized under the laws of this State.

(b) The name of the person to whom issued.

(c) The number and class of shares, and the designation of the series, if any, which such certificate represents.

(d) The par value of each share represented by such certificate, or a statement that the shares are without par value.

No certificate shall be issued for any share until such share is fully paid.

Unless otherwise provided by the articles of incorporation or by-laws, the Board of Directors of a Corporation may provide by resolution that some or all of any or all classes and series of its shares shall be uncertificated shares, provided that such resolution shall not apply to shares represented by a certificate until such certificate is surrendered to the Corporation. Within a reasonable time after the issuance or transfer of uncertificated shares, the Corporation shall send to the registered owner thereof a written notice containing the information required to be set forth or stated on certificates pursuant to the second and third paragraphs of this section. Except as otherwise expressly provided by law, the rights and obligations of the holders of uncertificated shares and the rights and obligations of the holders of certificates representing shares of the same class and series shall be identical.

from simple typewritten ones to engraved certificates, as required by the New York Stock Exchange to minimize the risk of counterfeiting and to facilitate clearance.

Since the usual share certificate is only approximately 8 by 12 inches in size, it can hardly state more than minimal matters without resorting to microscopic type. The importance of requiring comprehensive statements on the share certificate is counterbalanced by the fact that amendments to the Articles of Incorporation might render obsolete such statements on the share certificate.

Printed or engraved forms of share certificates may be obtained from or through legal stationers, Corporation service companies, or banknote companies. Such certificates can be obtained in a bound book, containing numbered certificates and stubs, which for the small Corporation can serve as the share ledger or record of Stockholders. The stubs can state all relevant data and have affixed thereto any required original issue tax stamps.

Only the form and content of share certificates will be discussed in this section. Share transfer problems will be discussed later.

STATUTORY REQUIREMENTS

Most jurisdictions provide that shares of a Corporation shall be represented by certificates signed [2] by two of several designated officers of the Corporation, usually the President or a Vice-President and the Secretary or an assistant Secretary of the Corporation, and *may* be sealed with the seal of the Corporation or a facsimile thereof.

Certificates representing shares issued by a Corporation which is authorized to issue shares of more than one class are often required to set forth upon the face or back of the certificate, or to state that the Corporation will furnish to any Stockholder upon request and without charge, a full (or summary) statement of the designations, preferences, limitations, and relative rights of the shares of each class authorized to be issued and, if the Corporation is authorized to issue any preferred or special class in series, the variations in the relative rights and preferences between the shares of each such series so far as the same have been fixed and determined and the authority of the Board of Directors to fix and determine the relative rights and preferences of subsequent series.

Furthermore, each share certificate usually is required to state upon its face: [3]

(1) That the Corporation is organized under the laws of the state;

2. See e. g. Model Bus.Corp.Act § 23 at fn. 1, supra; West's Ann.Calif. Corp.Code § 416; McKinney's N.Y. Bus.Corp.Law § 508.

3. Id.

(2) The name of the person to whom issued;

(3) The number and class of shares, and the designation of the series, if any, which such certificate represents;

(4) The par value of each share represented by such certificate, or a statement that the shares are without par value.

Some jurisdictions prohibit the *issue* of any share certificate for any share until such share is fully paid.[4]

Furthermore a share certificate should contain appropriate legends where greater-than-normal quorum and/or voting requirements for Stockholder and/or Director action apply,[5] or where the shares it represents are subject to transfer restrictions,[6] Stockholder voting agreement,[7] voting trust,[8] or irrevocable proxy,[9] are not fully paid,[10] or are subject to Articles of Incorporation provisions for non-judicial dissolution [11] or as to control of directors,[12] etc.

Modern share certificates often contain explanatory legends of abbreviations used to describe limitations on ownership or special types of ownership.

§ 41.2 Drafting Suggestions for Close Corporations

See also Chapter 30, supra.

In the close Corporation, where the shares are subject to various provisions, the share certificates representing such shares should contain appropriate legends referring to such provisions, to avoid the risk of such provisions being held void or unenforceable against transferees of the share certificates.

The share certificate, for example, should contain appropriate legends where greater-than-normal quorum/voting requirements for

4. See e. g. Model Bus.Corp.Act, § 23 at fn. 1, supra.

5. E. g., McKinney's N.Y.Bus.Corp. Law §§ 616(c), 709(c); West's Ann. Calif.Corp.Code §§ 417, 418.

6. E. g., Uniform Commercial Code § 8–204. An issuer's lien upon a security is valid against a purchaser only if the right of the issuer to such lien is noted conspicuously on the security. Id. § 8–103. See West's Ann.Calif. Corp.Code § 418.

7. E. g., McKinney's N.Y.Bus.Corp.Law § 620(a); West's Ann.Calif.Corp.Code § 418.

8. E. g., McKinney's N.Y.Bus.Corp.Law § 621(a).

9. E. g., McKinney's N.Y.Bus.Corp.Law § 609(h); West's Ann.Calif.Corp.Code § 418.

10. McKinney's N.Y.Bus.Corp.Law § 505(e); West's Ann.Calif.Corp.Code § 418.

11. E. g., McKinney's N.Y.Bus.Corp. Law § 1002(c).

12. E. g., McKinney's N.Y.Bus.Corp. Law § 620(g); Minn.Bus.Corp.Act § 302A.449.

Board of Directors or Stockholder action apply,[13] or the shares it represents are subject to transfer restrictions [14] or a lien of the Corporation, "Stockholder agreements",[15] voting trusts,[16] or irrevocable proxies,[17] or are not fully paid,[18] or where the Articles of Incorporation contain a provision as to control of Directors,[19] or for dissolution at will or upon the occurrence of any specified event,[20] etc.

Such legends should at least indicate that there are such provisions and specify where their full text may be found. When such legends are printed on the back of the certificate, the front should state "Restrictions Printed on Back."

"Close Corporations", designated as such in their Articles of Incorporation and otherwise subject to recent close Corporation statutes must state such fact on their share certificates.[21]

13. E. g., McKinney's N.Y.Bus.Corp. Law §§ 616(c), 709(c) (to be noted conspicuously on face or back of every share certificate issued by Corporation); West's Ann.Calif.Corp.Code §§ 417, 418.

14. Uniform Commercial Code § 8–204 (to be noted conspicuously on security). Certificates representing shares subject to any agreement for their repurchase by the Corporation ought to refer to such agreement. See McKinney's N.Y.Bus.Corp.Law § 514; West's Ann.Calif.Corp.Code § 418.

15. See Chapter 68, infra. See McKinney's N.Y.Bus.Corp.Law § 620(a) (Stockholder Voting Agreement); West's Ann.Calif.Corp.Code §§ 418, 706.

16. See Chapter 47. E. g., McKinney's N.Y.Bus.Corp.Law § 621(a) (share certificates issued to voting trustee(s) to state that they are issued under voting trust agreement); West's Ann. Calif.Corp.Code §§ 418, 706.

17. See Chapter 47, infra. E. g., McKinney's N.Y.Bus.Corp.Law § 609(h) (to be noted conspicuously on face or back of certificate representing shares subject to irrevocable proxy); West's Ann.Calif.Corp.Code § 418.

18. E. g., McKinney's N.Y.Bus.Corp. Law § 505(e) (to be noted conspicuously on face or back of certificate representing partly-paid shares); Wests' Ann.Calif.Corp.Code § 418.

19. See § 30.64, supra. E. g., McKinney's N.Y.Bus.Corp.Law § 620(g) (to be noted conspicuously on face or back of every share certificate issued by Corporation).

20. See § 30.66, supra. E. g., McKinney's N.Y.Bus.Corp.Law § 1002(c) (to be noted conspicuously on face or back of every share certificate issued by Corporation).

21. See e. g., West's Ann.Calif.Corp. Code § 418.

§ 41.3 Common Stock Certificate

[FACE]

CERTIFICATE

No.

For Shares

Issued to

Dated 19

FROM WHOM TRANSFERRED

Dated 19

No. ORIGINAL CERTIFICATE	No. ORIGINAL SHARES	No. OF SHARES TRANSFERRED

Received CERTIFICATE No.

For Shares

this day of 19

NUMBER

SHARES

INCORPORATED UNDER THE LAWS OF THE STATE OF . . . .

BUSINESS ENTERPRISES, INC.

COMMON SHARES

THIS CERTIFIES THAT ______________________

is the owner of ______________________ COMMON SHARES ($10 PAR VALUE) of **BUSINESS ENTERPRISES, INC.** fully paid and nonassessable, transferable only on the books of the Corporation by the holder hereof in person or by duly authorized Attorney upon surrender of this Certificate properly endorsed.

[Here, in the case of a corporation authorized to issue shares of more than one class, may be set forth that the corporation will furnish to any shareholder upon request and without charge a full statement of the designation, preferences, limitations, and relative rights of the shares of each class authorized to be issued by the corporation; in the case of a corporation authorized to issue any preferred or special class in series, the variations in the relative rights and preferences between the shares of each such series so far as the same have been fixed and determined and the authority of the board of directors to fix and determine the relative rights and preferences of subsequent series; and in the case of a close corporation, may be printed appropriate legends—although these are often set forth on the reverse of the share certificate.]

WITNESS the seal of the Corporation and the signatures of its duly authorized officers.

Dated ______________

Gilbert C. Dee
President

BUSINESS ENTERPRISES, INC. CORPORATE SEAL 19— STATE OF

Robert P. Lawyer
Secretary

[A7958]

[REVERSE]

[Here may be printed appropriate legends, although these are sometimes printed on the face to make them more conspicuous.]

Abbreviations, when used in the inscription on the face of this certificate, shall be construed as though they were written out in full and when so construed shall be given the meaning ascribed by applicable laws or regulations.

FOR VALUE RECEIVED, ______ hereby sell, assign and transfer unto

____

Please print or typewrite name and address of assignee

____

______________ shares of the Common Shares represented by the within certificate, and do hereby irrevocably constitute and appoint ______________ attorney, to transfer the said Common Shares on the books of the within-named corporation, with full power of substitution in the premises.

Dated ______________

In presence of:

______________ ______________

NOTICE: The signature to this assignment must correspond with the name as written upon the face of the Certificate, in every particular, without alteration or enlargement, or any change whatever.

[A7963]

§ 41.4 Common Stock Certificate (With Restrictions)

INCORPORATED UNDER THE LAWS OF THE STATE OF [*STATE*]

No. __________ __________ Shares

[*Name of Corporation*]

AUTHORIZED CAPITAL ______ SHARES
______ PAR VALUE

This certifies that ______ is the owner of ______ fully paid and non-assessable shares of the common capital stock of [*Name of Corporation*] transferable only on the books of this Corporation upon surrender of this Certificate properly endorsed.

In witness whereof, the said Corporation has caused this Certificate to be signed by its duly authorized officers and sealed with the Seal of the Corporation, this ______ day of ______ A.D. 19__.

(SEAL)

______________ ______________

President Secretary

[*Transfer Restrictions Noted on Back*]

[*BACK OF CERTIFICATE*]

For value received, ______ hereby sell(s), assign(s) and transfer(s) unto ____ ____ Shares represented by the within Certificate, and do hereby irrevocably constitute and appoint ______ Attorney to transfer the said Shares on the books of the within named Corporation with full power of substitution in the premises.

Dated ______, 19__.

In presence of

______________________ ______________________

Witness Certificate Owner

NOTICE: The signature of this assignment must correspond with the name as written upon the face of the certificate in every particular, without alteration or enlargement or any change whatever.

This security is subject to the following restrictions:

Option 1

The restrictions contained in a certain Buy-Sell Agreement dated ______, a copy of which is on file at the corporate offices.

Option 2

The owner is restricted from making a transfer of such security if such transfer would void the election of the Corporation to be taxed under Subchapter S of the Internal Revenue Code.

Option 3

The shares represented by this certificate were acquired in a transaction intended to be exempt from registration under the Federal and State Securities Laws under an investment representation made by the purchaser to the issuer. Such shares may not be sold, transferred, pledged or hypothecated except pursuant to an effective registration statement under the Federal and State Securities Laws, or except in a transaction which, in the opinion of counsel for the issuer, is exempt from registration.

THIS SPACE MUST NOT BE COVERED IN ANY WAY

[C3019]

COMMENT

For discussion of transfer restrictions, including additional forms, see Chapter 52(D), infra.

§ 41.5 Common Stock Certificate (With Restrictions)—Another Form

INCORPORATED UNDER THE LAWS OF THE STATE OF [*STATE*]

No. __________ __________ Shares

[*Name of Corporation*]

AUTHORIZED CAPITAL ______ SHARES

______ PAR VALUE

This certifies that ______ is the owner of ______ fully paid and non-assessable Shares of the Common Capital Stock of [*Name of Corporation*] transferable only on the books of this Corporation upon surrender of this Certificate properly endorsed.

In witness whereof, the said Corporation has caused this Certificate to be signed by its duly authorized officers and sealed with the Seal of the Corporation, this ______ day of ______ A.D. 19__.

[*Seal*]

________________________ ________________________

President Secretary

This security is subject to restrictions and preferences.

The Corporation will furnish without charge to each Stockholder who so requests, the powers, designations, preferences and relative participating, optional or other special rights of each class of stock or series and the qualifications, limitations or restrictions of such preferences and/or rights.

[*Transfer Restrictions Noted on Back*]

[*Back of Certificate*]

For value received ______ hereby sell, assign and transfer unto ____
____ Shares
represented by the within Certificate and do hereby irrevocably constitute and appoint ______ Attorney to transfer the said Shares on the books of the within named Corporation with full power of substitution in the premises.

Dated ______, 19__.

In presence of

______________________ ______________________

Witness Certificate Holder

NOTICE: The signature of this assignment must correspond with the name as written upon the face of the certificate in every particular, without alteration or enlargement, or any change whatever.

Option 1

"The sale, assignment, transfer, pledge or other disposition of the shares of capital stock represented by this certificate are subject to a certain restrictive Agreement dated ______. A copy of which Agreement is on file in the office of the Corporation."

Option 2

The shares represented by this certificate were acquired in a transaction intended to be exempt from registration under the Federal and State Securities Laws under an investment representation made by the purchaser to the issuer. Such shares may not be sold, transferred, pledged or hypothecated except pursuant to an effective registration statement under the federal and state securities laws, or except in a transaction which, in the opinion of counsel for the issuer, is exempt from registration.

THIS SPACE MUST NOT BE COVERED IN ANY WAY

[C3019]

COMMENTS

State Corporation acts have materially simplified the problem of including additional material on certificates. Rights of classes of securities, limitations on preemptive rights and restrictions on transfer may be omitted if the certificates conspicuously contain one of the following statements: the Corporation will furnish a full statement to any Stockholder without charge upon written request to the Corporation at its principal place of business or registered office, or there is on file in the Office of the Secretary of State a full statement of the limitation, restriction, etc.

For additional discussion of transfer restrictions, including additional forms, see Chapter 52(B), infra.

§ 41.6 Common Stock Certificate—Another Form

No. __________ __________ Shares

INCORPORATED UNDER THE LAWS OF THE STATE OF ______,
______ MANUFACTURING COMPANY

This certifies that ______ is the owner of ______ fully paid and nonassessable shares of the par value of $______ each of the common stock of the ______ Manufacturing Company, transferable on the books of the Company by the holder in person or by duly authorized attorney, upon surrender of this certificate properly endorsed.

This certificate is not valid until countersigned by the Transfer Agent and registered by the Registrar.

Witness the seal of the Company and the signatures of its duly authorized officers.

Dated ______, 19__.

______________________ ______________________
Treasurer President

[*Corporate Seal*]

§ 41.7 Common Stock Certificate (With Restrictions)—Another Form

No. __________ __________ Shares

INCORPORATED UNDER THE LAWS OF THE STATE OF ______,
______ MANUFACTURING COMPANY

This certifies that ______ is the owner of ______ shares of the capital stock of ______ Manufacturing Company, transferable only on the books of the Company in person or by attorney, upon surrender of this certificate properly indorsed, and upon full compliance with the terms and conditions of the Stockholders' Option Agreement on file with the secretary of the Company.

In witness whereof, the duly authorized officers of this Company have hereunto subscribed their names and caused the corporate seal to be hereto affixed at ______, this ______ day of ______, 19__.

[*Corporate Seal*] ____________________

President

____

Secretary

§ 41.8 Common Stock Certificate (With Restrictions)—Another Form

No. ________ ________ Shares

INCORPORATED UNDER THE LAWS OF THE STATE OF ______, ______, INCORPORATED

This certifies that ______ is the owner of ______ shares of the capital stock of ______, Incorporated, transferable on the books of the Corporation in person or by attorney, upon surrender of this certificate. The holder hereof accepts said shares of capital stock with notice of, and subject to, the provisions of the By-laws printed on the back hereof.

Witness the seal of the Corporation and the signatures of its duly authorized officers this ______ day of ______, 19__.

[*Corporate Seal*]

____

President

____

Secretary

[*On the back should be printed the provisions it is desired that the Stockholder should have notice of.*]

COMMENT

U.C.C. § 8–204, provides: "Unless noted conspicuously on the security a restriction on transfer imposed by the issuer even though otherwise lawful is ineffective except against a person with actual knowledge of it." The Comment to this section (1962 Official Text) states that "noted" makes clear that the restriction need not be set forth in full text, citing Allen v. Biltmore Tissue Corp., 2 N.Y.2d 534, 161 N.Y.S.2d 418, 141 N.E.2d 812 (1957). For additional discussion and forms, see Chapter 52, infra.

§ 41.9 Share Certificate—One Class of Shares

[*Face of Certificate*]

Number ________ ________ Shares

INCORPORATED UNDER THE LAWS OF THE
STATE OF CALIFORNIA

[*Name of Corporation*]

This certifies that ______ is the record holder of ______ shares of the Capital [*Common*] Stock of [*Name of Corporation*] transferable on the records of the Corporation upon surrender of this certificate properly indorsed.

Witness the signatures of the duly authorized officers of the Corporation.

Dated: ______.

____________________ ____________________

President Secretary

§ 41.10 Share Certificate—Form of Endorsement

[*Reverse of Certificate*]

For value received, the undersigned hereby sell, assign and transfer ______ shares represented by the within certificate to ______ and do hereby irrevocably constitute and appoint ______ Attorney to transfer the said shares on the books of the within named Corporation with full power of substitution in the premises.

Dated ______. ____________________.

NOTICE: The signature to this assignment must correspond with the name or names as written upon the face of the certificate in every particular without alteration or enlargement or any change whatever.

COMMENT

As to indorsements, see Uniform Commercial Code, § 8–308. For additional discussion and forms, see Chapter 52, infra.

§ 41.11 Share Certificate—Form of Endorsement—Another Form

ASSIGNMENT
OF

_____ SHARES OF [*NAME OF CORPORATION*]

CERTIFICATE FOR _____ SHARES

Dated _____ Issued to _______

For value received, _____ does hereby sell, assign, and transfer unto _____, [*Number*] shares of the [*Class*] shares of [*Name of Corporation*] represented by the within certificate numbered _____, and standing in the name of _____ on the books of said Corporation, and does hereby irrevocably constitute and appoint _____ attorney to transfer the said shares on the books of the within named Corporation, with full power of substitution.

Dated _____, 19__. [*Signature*]

In presence of ________. ____________________

Stockholder

NOTICE: The signature to this assignment must correspond with the name as written upon the face of the certificate in every particular.

§ 41.12 Share Certificate—Statement re Partly Paid Shares

The shares represented by this certificate are partly paid and subject to call for the remainder of the consideration to be paid therefor. The total amount of the consideration to be paid for the shares represented by this certificate is $_____, and the amount paid thereon is $_____.

COMMENTS

This Form was drafted for use under the California Corporations Code.

When subdivision (a) of § 418 of the West's Ann.Corp.Code requires the share certificate to state the fact that the shares are not fully paid in the case of shares issued as partly paid pursuant to § 409, or under an employee stock purchase plan or agreement or employee stock option plan or agreement pursuant to § 408, the statement on the share certificate is as above and the statement or reference on the face of the certificate must be conspicuous, that is in larger type or in a contrasting type face or in a different color.

§ 41.13 Share Certificate—Statement re Redeemable Shares

(a) The shares represented by this certificate are redeemable at the option of the Corporation.

(b) The shares represented by this certificate are redeemable at the option of the Stockholder.

§ 41.14 Share Certificate—Statement re Convertible Shares

The shares represented by this certificate are convertible and there is no time limit for conversion.

[*or*]

The shares represented by this certificate are convertible and the period for conversion ends [*Date*].

[*or*]

The shares represented by this certificate are convertible and the period for conversion ends [*Statement of Provision*, e. g., "on the close of business on the fifth day prior to the date fixed for redemption in any notice of redemption"].

§ 41.15 Share Certificate—Legend re Restriction on Transfer

The shares represented by this certificate are subject to restrictions upon transfer contained in [*the Articles of Incorporation; the By-laws of the Corporation; an Agreement among the Stockholders dated* ______.]

§ 41.16 Share Certificate—Legend re Assessability

The shares represented by this certificate are assessable.

COMMENT

When the statute requires the share certificate to include a statement that the shares are assessable, the statement is as above and the statement or reference on the face of the certificate must be conspicuous, that is in larger type or in a contrasting type face or in a different color.

§ 41.17 Share Certificate—Legend re Irrevocable Proxy

The shares represented by this certificate are subject to an irrevocable proxy dated ______.

§ 41.18 Share Certificate—Legend re Voting Agreement

The shares represented by this certificate are subject to a voting agreement dated ______.

§ 41.19 Share Certificate—Legend re Contractually Imposed Restrictions Upon Voting Rights

The shares represented by this certificate are subject to restrictions upon voting rights contractually imposed by the Corporation pursuant to an agreement dated ______.

§ 41.20 Share Certificate—Legend re Close Corporation

This Corporation is a close Corporation. The number of holders of record of all classes cannot exceed ______ [*Number Copied from the Statement in the Articles of Incorporation*]. Any attempted voluntary inter vivos transfer which would violate this requirement is void. Refer to the Articles, By-laws and any Agreements on file with the Secretary of the Corporation for further restrictions.

§ 41.21 Share Certificate—One Class of Shares

Notice is hereby given that the Board of Directors on [*Date*] has levied an assessment of [*Amount*] per share upon the [*Name or Designation of Class or Series of Shares*] of the Corporation payable [*To Whom and Where*]. Any shares upon which this assessment remains unpaid on [*Date Fixed*] will be delinquent. Unless payment is made prior to delinquency, the said shares, or as many of them as may be necessary, will be sold at [*Particular Place*] on [*Date*] at [*Hour*] of such day, to pay the delinquent assessment, together with a penalty of ______ percent of the amount of the assessment on such shares, or be forfeited to the Corporation. [*Name of Secretary with Location of Principal Executive Office of the Corporation.*]

§ 41.22 Share Certificate—Legend re Recognition of Preemptive Rights for Holders of Preferred Stock

The holders of the preferred stock of the Corporation shall be entitled to a preemptive right to subscribe for or purchase, in the proportions which their holdings of preferred stock bear to the outstanding preferred stock, any shares of preferred stock issued after [*Date*] but the holders of preferred stock shall have no preemptive right to subscribe for or purchase any new or additional shares of common stock of the Corporation.

§ 41.23 Preferred Stock Certificate

ORGANIZED UNDER THE LAWS OF THE STATE OF ______

Number __________ __________ Shares

[*Name of Corporation*]

This certifies that ______ is the owner of ______ fully paid and non-assessable preferred shares ______ par value of [*Name of Corporation*] transferable on the books of the Corporation upon surrender of this Certificate properly endorsed.

The designations, preferences, qualifications, limitations, restrictions, and special or relative rights of these preferred shares are set forth on the back of this certificate, and the holder hereof, by accepting this certificate, expressly assents to and is bound by all of said provisions.

In witness whereof, the said Corporation has caused this Certificate to be signed by its duly authorized Officers, and its Corporate Seal to be hereunto affixed, this ______ day of ______ A.D. 19__.
[*Seal*]

______________________ ______________________

President Secretary

[*Transfer Restrictions Noted on Back*]

[*Back of Certificate*]

For value received, ______ hereby sell, assign and transfer unto ____
____ Shares
represented by the within Certificate, and do hereby irrevocably constitute and appoint ______ Attorney to transfer the said Shares on the books of the within named Corporation with full power of substitution in the premises.

Dated ______ 19__.

In presence of

______________________ ______________________

Witness Certificate Holder

COMMENT

The rights and preferences set forth in the Articles of Incorporation should be duplicated on the back of the certificate.

Option 1

"The sale, assignment, transfer, pledge or other disposition of the shares of capital stock represented by this certificate are subject to a certain restrictive agreement dated ______. A copy of which agreement is on file in the office of the Corporation."

Option 2

The shares represented by this certificate were acquired in a transaction intended to be exempt from registration under the Federal and State Securities Laws under an investment representation made by the purchaser to the issuer. Such shares may not be sold, transferred, pledged or hypothecated except pursuant to an effective registration statement under the Federal and State Securities Laws, or except in a transaction which, in the opinion of counsel for the issuer, is exempt from registration.

THIS SPACE MUST NOT BE COVERED IN ANY WAY

[C3019]

COMMENT

For discussion of transfer restrictions, including additional forms, see Chapter 52, infra.

§ 41.24 Preferred Stock Certificate—Another Form

[*Front*]

Certificate No. __________ __________ Shares

THE ______ CORPORATION

This Is To Certify That ______ is the owner of ______ (______) fully paid and non-assessable shares, without nominal or par value, of the $______ preferred stock of ______ Corporation, a Corporation duly incorporated under the laws of the State of ______. For a complete description of the classes of shares of stock which the said Corporation is authorized to issue and the characteristics, preferences, rights, privileges and limitations of each class, reference is here made to the provisions of the Articles of Incorporation, as amended, of said Corporation on file in the office of the Secretary of State of ______, a copy of which is on file with the Transfer Agent. A summary statement of the designations, preferences, limitations, and relative rights of the shares of each class authorized to be issued by said Corporation is set forth on the back of this certificate.

Witness the seal of said Corporation and the signatures of its President or a Vice-President and its Secretary or an Assistant Secretary this ______ day of ______, 19__.

[*Corporate Seal*]

____
President [*or a* Vice President]

____
Secretary [*or an* Assistant Secretary]

[*Back*]

The following is a summary statement of all of the designations, preferences, limitations, and relative rights of the shares of each class authorized to be issued by the Corporation. A complete statement of such designations, preferences, limitations and relative rights is contained in the Articles of Incorporation of the Corporation on file with the Secretary of State of ______, the Transfer Agent, and the Secretary of the Corporation.

Classes of Shares. The Corporation is authorized to issue ______ shares. ______ of such shares are designated as shares of common stock and are of the par value of $______ each. The other ______ of such shares are designated as shares of $______ preferred stock and are without par value.

Dividends and Distribution of Assets. The $______ preferred stock in preference to the common stock is entitled and is limited to dividends at the annual rate of $______ per share cumulative from ______, 19__, and to $______ per share plus any unpaid dividends in any distribution of assets.

Redemption Provisions. All or any part of the $______ preferred stock may be redeemed by the Corporation, by affirmative vote of a majority in number of the shares of the outstanding common stock, at any time by payment of a redemption price of $______ per share if redeemed on or prior to ______, 19__.

Voting Rights. Except as may otherwise be required by the provisions of the ______ Business Corporation Act, no holder of any shares of the $______ preferred stock shall, as such, be entitled to notice of or to vote at any meeting of Stockholders of the Corporation; provided, however, that if and when dividends payable on any of the $______ preferred stock shall be in default in an amount equal to four quarterly payments or more per share, and thereafter until all dividends on any of the said preferred stock in default shall have been paid, the holders of the then outstanding shares of $______ preferred stock, voting as a class, shall be entitled to elect the smallest number of Directors necessary to constitute a majority of the Board of Directors at the next annual meeting of the Stockholders after such default and until all default in the payment of such dividends shall have been completely cured.

Pre-emptive Rights. No holders of any class of shares authorized to be issued by this Corporation have any pre-emptive rights to subscribe to any class of shares issued or which may be issued.

Cumulative Voting for Directors. Cumulative voting for Directors is expressly prohibited by the Articles of Incorporation.

§ 41.25 Preferred Stock Certificate—Noncumulative

No. __________ __________ Shares

INCORPORATED UNDER THE LAWS OF THE STATE OF ______, ______ MANUFACTURING COMPANY

Capital Stock $______ Par Value $______
Common Stock $______ Preferred Stock $______

This is to certify that ______ is the owner of ______ fully paid and nonassessable shares of the preferred stock of the ______ Manufacturing company, transferable only in person or by duly authorized attorney on the books of the company upon surrender of this certificate properly endorsed.

The preferred stock is entitled to a preference of ______ per cent noncumulative, in dividends declared in any fiscal year before any dividends are paid upon the common stock of this company.

The preferred stock is subject to redemption at the option of the Company at any time after ______ years from the ______ day of ______, 19__, upon payment of ______ per share and accumulated dividends.

The preferred stock is not entitled to vote at Stockholders' meetings of the company, nor to participate in profits beyond its fixed, preferential annual dividend of ______ per cent.

In witness whereof, the company has caused this certificate to be signed by its President and Secretary and countersigned by its Treasurer, and sealed with its corporate seal of the ______ day of ______, 19__.

[*Corporate Seal*]

____
President

________________ ____________________
Treasurer Secretary

§ 41.26 Preferred Stock Certificate—Cumulative

[*Following preceding form, substituting for the second paragraph the following, and inserting in the last paragraph* "cumulative" *after* "preferential":]

The preferred stock is entitled to an annual dividend of ______ per cent, payable out of the net profits before any dividend is declared upon the common stock of this company. Should the net profits in any year be insufficient to pay such preferred dividend, either in whole or in part, any unpaid portion thereof shall become a charge against the net profits of the company, and shall be paid in full out of such net profits before any dividends are paid upon the common stock.

§ 41.27 Preferred Stock Certificate—Provisions for Redemption and Restriction Against Incumbrance

INCORPORATED UNDER THE LAWS OF THE STATE OF
______, ______ REALTY COMPANY, ______

Shares $______ each
Common Stock $______ Preferred Stock $______

This certifies that ______ is the holder of ______ fully paid and non-assessable shares of the par value of ______ each of the preferred stock of ______ company, transferable only on the books of the company by the holder hereof or his duly authorized attorney, on the surrender and cancellation of this certificate.

The holder hereof shall be entitled to receive cumulative dividends at the rate of ______ per annum from ______, 19__, on the shares of stock presented hereby, payable in equal quarterly installments of ______ on the first day of January, April, July and October of each year before any sum whatever is paid to or set aside for the benefit of the common Stockholders. In event of the liquidation of the company, the preferred Stockholders shall be entitled to receive the par value of their shares, plus all accrued dividends, and no more, before anything shall be paid to the holders of the common stock.

The company agrees to redeem the shares of stock represented hereby at their par value, plus accrued dividends, on the first day of January, 19__, and it reserves the right to redeem any of its shares of preferred stock before the date fixed therefor, at any dividend paying date, at ______% of par, plus accrued dividends, on giving thirty (30) days prior written notice to the holders of the shares selected for redemption.

The company agrees that it will not convey or encumber its property at ______, without the consent of all its preferred Stockholders, that it will maintain insurance against loss by fire on the improvements on such property to the amount of the preferred stock outstanding, and will not permit its taxes to become delinquent.

Upon failure of the company to comply with all the obligations and if the company shall fail on demand to redeem the same, then hereby shall, at the option of the holder, be immediately redeemable, and if the company shall fail on demand to redeem the same, then the holder hereof shall be entitled to require the liquidation of the company and Stockholders in the order provided by law.

This certificate shall not be valid unless registered by ______, as Registrar.

In witness whereof, the said ______ company has caused this certificate to be executed by its duly authorized Officers and its corporate seal to be hereunto affixed this ______ day of ______, 19__.

§ 41.28 Fractional Scrip Certificate

[*Registered Form*]

This certifies that ______ is the owner of a ______ interest in one share of the common stock of ______ Corporation. The holder hereof shall be entitled to receive, upon surrender of this scrip certificate together with one or more similar certificates equal in the aggregate to one or more full shares, a certificate for the full share or shares represented by such surrendered scrip certificates and a scrip certificate for any fraction in excess of such full share or shares. No dividends shall be paid or shall accrue with respect to this certificate, nor shall it entitle the holder to vote or to exercise any other rights of a Stockholder or to participate in any of the assets of the Corporation in the event of liquidation.

[*Bearer Form*]

This certificates that The Bearer, upon surrender on or before the close of business on ______, 19__, of this Scrip Certificate representing a ______ interest in one share of common stock of ______ Corporation, together with other Scrip Certificates of like tenor, aggregating with the interest represented hereby one or more whole shares of the common stock, shall be entitled to receive in exchange therefor a certificate or certificates for the number of fully paid and nonassessable shares of common stock of ______ Corporation equal to the aggregate number of full shares called for by the Scrip Certificates so surrendered, together with a Scrip Certificate (not exchangeable for common stock after ______, 19__) for any fraction of a share of such common stock in excess of the aggregate number of full shares called for by the Scrip Certificates so surrendered.

The right to exchange this Scrip Certificate for shares of common stock shall expire and become void upon the close of business on ______, 19__. After ______, 19__, the certificates of common stock reserved for the conversion of Scrip Certificates shall be sold at public or private sale, and the proceeds thereof shall be distributed among the holders of Scrip Certificates still outstanding, ratably according to the amount thereof held by such owners, upon surrender of such Scrip Certificates to ______ before ______, 19__. The right to obtain a ratable share of the proceeds of such sale shall expire on ______, 19__, and thereafter this Scrip Certificate shall be of no effect whatsoever, and any undistributed proceeds shall revert to ______ Corporation.

§ 41.29 Certificate of Partly Paid Stock

Number __________ __________ Shares

______ CORPORATION

INCORPORATED UNDER THE LAWS OF THE STATE OF ______

This certifies that ______ is the owner of ______ shares of the partly paid capital stock of ______ Company, transferable only on the books of the Company in person or by duly authorized attorney on surrender of this certificate. ______ per cent of the par value has been paid in cash on the shares of stock named in this certificate. The above-named holder of this certificate accepts the same subject to liability for the payment upon said shares of all installments, not noted as paid upon the face or back of this certificate, which shall be called by the Board of Directors, prior to the transfer of this certificate upon the books of the Company.

In witness whereof, *etc.*

[*On the back:*]

2d installment, __%, paid __________

3d installment, __% paid __________, *etc.*

§ 41.30 Stub of Share Certificate for Stock Book

No. ______

Certificate
for
[*Specify Kind*] Shares
Issued to

____

Residence ______________________________

Dated

__________ ______, 19__.

Transferred from

____

Dated

__________ ______, 19__.

No. Original Certificate __________

No. Original Shares __________

No. of Certificate Transferring Shares	No. Shares Transferred
__________	__________

____

Received
Certificate No. ______
for
______ Shares
__________ ______, 19__.

Amount received ________________

Subscription received by ________________

§ 41.31 Temporary Share Receipt

Capital __________

Number __________
Shares __________

TEMPORARY RECEIPT

[*NAME OF CORPORATION*]

No. __________

This certifies that ______ is entitled to [*Number*] shares of the [*Class*] shares of [*Name of Corporation*], of the par value of ______ ($______) Dollars per share, for which full payment has been made at the rate of ______ ($______) Dollars per share, the receipt of which is hereby acknowledged.

This temporary receipt, properly indorsed, may be exchanged for engraved share certificates on or after the ______ day of ______, 19__.

Dated, ______, 19__.

[*Name of Corporation*]

By ________________

[*Capacity*]

Countersigned:

____

[*Capacity*]

[*Form of Indorsement*]

For value received, ______ has bargained, sold, assigned, and transferred, and by these presents does bargain, sell, assign, and transfer unto ______ the shares named in the within certificate, and ______ does hereby constitute and appoint ______ true and lawful attorney, irrevocably, for ______ and in ______'s name and stead, to use, sell, assign, transfer, and set over, all or any part of the said shares, and for that purpose to make and execute all necessary acts of assignment and transfer, and one or more persons to substitute with like full power.

Dated, ______, 19__. ____________________

Signed in the presence of

____

§§ 41.32–42.0 are reserved for supplementary material.

CHAPTER 42

STOCK OPTIONS, RIGHTS, AND WARRANTS

Table of Sections

Library References:

C.J.S. Corporations §§ 388–392, 400 et seq.
West's Key No. Digests, Corporations 🔑111 et seq.

§ 42.1 Stock Options, Rights and Warrants

Options to purchase shares may be used as a capital raising device, to provide employee incentives, and to a lesser extent as part of control devices. Of course, shares under option are not deemed issued and may not be voted until the options are exercised and the purchase price paid, or in some states, a firm commitment to pay the purchase price in the form of a promissory note has been delivered to the Corporation.

Employee stock purchase or stock option plans are largely governed by the Internal Revenue Code, since favorable tax treatment is often an essential part of the success of such plans. Many state Corporation statutes contain provisions that authorize the issuance of shares in connection with such plans by the Board of Directors and provide that in the absence of fraud the determination by the Board of the consideration for such shares shall be conclusive.[1]

1. E. g. Model Bus.Corp.Act § 20 provides:

§ 20. Stock Rights and Options

Subject to any provisions in respect thereof set forth in its articles of incorporation, a Corporation may create and issue, whether or not in connection with the issuance and sale of any of its shares or other securities, rights or options entitling the holders thereof to purchase from the Corporation shares of any class or classes. Such rights or options shall be evidenced in such manner as the Board of Directors shall approve and, subject to the provisions of the articles of incorporation, shall set forth the terms upon which, the time or times within which and the price or prices at which such shares may be purchased from the Corporation upon the exercise of any such right or

Warrants are transferable options to acquire shares from the Corporation at a specified price. Warrants have many of the qualities of an equity security since their value is a function of the market price of the underlying shares and the specified issuance price. Warrants frequently are issued as a "sweetener" in connection with the distribution of a debt or preferred stock issue; they may be issued in connection with a public exchange offer, or as compensation for handling the public distribution of other shares. Sometimes they are issued in a reorganization to holders of a class of security not otherwise recognized in the reorganization. Warrants are often publicly traded; warrants issued by a number of Corporations are listed from time to time on the New York Stock Exchange or other exchanges. *Rights* are in effect short term warrants. They may also be publicly traded and listed on securities exchanges. Rights are often issued in lieu of a dividend, or in an effort to raise capital from existing Stockholders.

The distinction between stock *options* and stock *warrants* is no longer important in practice. Both allow the holder to buy corporate stock or securities or short term debt at a specific price (or formula) on demand or during a specified period. There are however four wholly distinct purposes for which options and warrants are used by Corporations:

(1) Options are frequenty issued to executives and other employees as a means of giving the holder of the option an opportunity to participate in the appreciation of the equity of the Corporation at no initial investment, except a possible tax.

(2) Warrants are frequently issued by a Corporation in connection with the issuance and sale of debt securities, as an alternative to making the debt securities convertible and with the same purpose of giving the holder of the debt security a right, in addition to his priority and fixed rate of return, to participate in the growth of the equity of the Corporation. [See §§ 42.4 and 42.3, infra.]

(3) Warrants have also been used in recent years in takeover bids by conglomerates, where a 'package' of securities of the offeror is offered to the Stockholders of the target company in exchange for their stock in that Corporation. Such a 'package'

option. If such rights or options are to be issued to directors, officers or employees as such of the Corporation or of any subsidiary thereof, and not to the Stockholders generally, their issuance shall be approved by the affirmative vote of the holders of a majority of the shares entitled to vote thereon or shall be authorized by and consistent with a plan approved or ratified by such a vote of Stockholders. In the absence of fraud in the transaction, the judgment of the Board of Directors as to the adequacy of the consideration received for such rights or options shall be conclusive.

See also e. g. West's Ann.Corp.Code §§ 404–406, 408; McKinney's N.Y.Bus. Corp.Law § 505.

might consist of common shares, or preferred shares, or subordinated convertible debt, or all three, with some warrants thrown in. Since most of those issued in such transactions have since become worthless, they have tended to lose their appeal.

(4) A stock purchase warrant or "right" may be issued to the Stockholders of the Corporation in connection with a so-called "rights offering". This is an offering of stock by the Corporation to its existing Stockholders, either to satisfy preemptive rights or simply because the Corporation desires to give its Stockholders the first right to purchase the new issue. Such warrants are typically of very short duration, for example, ten to fourteen days, and are used merely to handle the mechanics of making such a "rights offering".

§ 42.2 Stock Option/Warrant

[*Name*]
CORPORATION
OF
[*State of Incorporation*]
STOCK [*Option/Warrant*]
TO PURCHASE
[*Describe*]

For value received [*Name*] Corporation, a [*State*] Corporation, grants the following stock right to the

Alternative A–1

Bearer.

Alternative A–2

Registered owner.

(a) Issue. Upon tender of the requisite sum the Corporation agrees to issue up to [*Number*] nonassessable and fully [*paid shares of stock/debt*] described as follows: [*Describe*].

(b) Limitations. Provided, that in no case shall:

Option 1

(1) This right be exercised before [*Date*].

Option 2

(2) This right be exercised after [*Date*].

(c) Tender. Tender shall be accomplished by actual delivery of the sum due in lawful money of the United States of America together with this certificate at the office of the Treasurer of the Corporation.

Option 3

(d) Restrictions On Sales. This [*Option/Warrant*] may not be sold or assigned without first offering the same to the Corporation (for a period of 30 days) for a cash price equal to the lower of $______ or (if any) the proposed purchase price.

(e) Time. Such [*shares/debt*] shall be issued for the following consideration:

Alternative A–1

$______ per $______ of face value of said debt.

Alternative A–2

$______ per share.

Alternative A–3

For their then book value.

Alternative A–4

For its traded value as of the date [*Number*] days before the rights under this [*warrant/option*] are exercised.

Alternative A–5

For their then appraised value.

Any one of the following appraisal methods shall be used:

Alternative A–5(A)

An appraisal by Certified Public Accountants who are not then engaged by the Corporation.

Alternative A–5(B)

An appraisal by one person chosen by the rules of the American Arbitration Association.

Alternative A–5(C)

An appraisal by one or more persons, one of whom shall be chosen by the Corporation and one by the [*option/warrant*] holder. If the higher appraised value is within 10% of the lower value then the average of the two values shall be used; if they are not within 10% of each other, then the two appraisers shall agree on a third appraiser who shall:

Alternative A–6(A)

Choose among the two amounts only.

Alternative A–6(B)

Choose any value between the two amounts.

(f) Fractional Shares. Whenever the Corporation shall be obligated to issue a fractional share to any Stockholder or potential Stockholder, it shall have the following options:

(1) Issue the fractional share; or

(2) Issue scrip; such scrip having no rights whatsoever other than the fact that the same represents a fractional [*share/debt instrument*] and sufficient scrip aggregating one whole [*share/debt instrument*] may be from time to time surrendered in exchange for one whole [*share/debt instrument*] of the [*stock/debt instrument*] to which it relates; or

(3) Deliver cash of an equivalent value to the value of such fractional share; or

(4) Give such holder the choice of either receiving cash of an equivalent value or buying one whole [*share/debt* instrument] (by paying the difference between the fractional [*share/debt*] in question and the cash equivalent of one [*share/debt instrument*].

The cash equivalent of one [*share/debt instrument*] shall be:

Alternative B–1

Its book value.

Alternative B–2

The average of its high and low traded value on the date [*number*] days preceding the date of the transaction.

Alternative B–3

Its appraised value determined by such reasonable appraisal methods as the Corporation shall from time to time employ.

Any one of the following appraisal methods shall be used.

Alternative B–4(A)

An appraisal by Certified Public Accountants who are not then engaged by the Corporation.

Alternative B–4(B)

An appraisal by one person chosen by the rules of the American Arbitration Association.

Alternative B–4(C)

An appraisal by one or more persons, one of whom shall be chosen by the Corporation and one by the holders. If the higher appraised value is within 10% of the lower value then the average of the two values shall be used; if they are not within 10% of each other, then the two appraisers shall agree on a third appraiser who shall:

Alternative B–5(A)

Choose among the two amounts only.

Alternative B–5(B)

Choose any amount between such amounts.

(g) Alteration of Conversion Privileges. The conversion privileges set forth herein may be altered at any time by the vote of a majority of the Directors of the Corporation together with a vote of:

Alternative C–1

(1) If the conversion is to be more favorable in every aspect to the *warrant/option* holders in question, then by a vote of the majority of corporate shares entitled to vote.

Alternative C–2

(1) If the conversion terms are in any aspect less favorable to the *warrant/option* holders, then by vote of ______% of all *warrant/option* holders.

Alternative C–3

(1) If the terms are in any aspect less favorable to the *warrant/option* holder, then the vote of a majority of all stock entitled to vote and by the majority of the *warrant/option* holders whose rights will be impaired by such change measured by the voting power of the stock into which said *warrants/options* can be converted.

(h) Adjustment of Conversion Price. The conversion price referred to herein shall be subject to adjustment from time to time as follows:

(1) In case the Corporation shall at any time subdivide the outstanding shares of [*Describe Stock or Debt to Be Received*] the conversion price in effect immediately prior to such subdivision shall be proportionately decreased, and in case the Corporation shall at any time combine the outstanding shares of [*Describe Stock or Debt to Be Received*], the conversion price in effect immediately prior to such combination shall be proportionately increased, effective at the close of business on the date of such subdivision or combination as the case may be. For the purposes of this subparagraph, any distribution of shares of [*Describe Stock or Debt to Be Received*] to holders of such shares shall be deemed

to be a subdivision, irrespective of the accounting treatment thereof.

(2) In case [*Describe Stock or Debt to Be Received*] of the Corporation issuable upon conversion of these *warrants/options* shall be changed into another kind of capital stock or debt (otherwise than through a subdivision or combination or combination of shares) or shall represent the right to receive some other security or property, as a result of any capital reorganization, reclassification or any merger or consolidation with another Corporation in which the Corporation is not the surviving Corporation, or any sale of all or substantially all of the assets of the Corporation to another Corporation, each share of these *warrants/options* shall (subject to further adjustment in conversion price as herein provided) thereafter entitle the record holder to acquire upon conversion thereof the kind and number of shares of stock or other securities or property to which such holder would have been entitled if he had held the [*Describe Stock or Debt to Be Received*] issuable upon the conversion of his stock immediately prior to such capital reorganization, reclassification, merger, consolidation or sale of assets.

(3) Whenever the conversion price shall be adjusted as provided in this subparagraph, the Corporation shall forthwith file at each office designated for the conversion of shares of this instrument, a statement, signed by the Chairman of the Board, the President, any Vice-President or the Treasurer of the Corporation, showing in reasonable detail the facts requiring such adjustment and the conversion price that will be effective after such adjustment. The Corporation shall forthwith also cause a notice setting forth any such adjustments to be sent by first class mail, postage prepaid, to each registered holder of these *warrants/options* at his address then appearing on the stock register.

(i) Notice of Change of Rights. In case:

(1) The Corporation shall declare a dividend (or make any other distribution) on its [*Describe Stock to Be Received*] payable otherwise than in cash out of the consolidated earnings surplus of the Corporation *and its subsidiaries*; or

(2) The Corporation shall authorize the granting to the holders of its [*Describe Stock to Be Received*] of rights to subscribe for or purchase any shares of capital stock of any class or any other rights; or

(3) Of any reclassification of the [*Describe Stock to Be Received*] of the Corporation (other than a subdivision or a combination of its outstanding shares of such stock, of any consolidation or merger to which the Corporation is a party and for which ap-

proval of any Stockholders of the Corporation is required or of the sale or transfer of all or substantially all the assets of the Corporation; or

(4) Of the voluntary or involuntary dissolution, liquidation or winding up of the Corporation;

then the Corporation shall cause to be filed at the office of the Corporation and shall cause to be mailed to the holders of this certificate at their addresses as they shall then appear on the records of the Corporation at least ten days prior to the record date specified in (ii) below, a notice stating:

(A) the record date for such dividend, distribution or rights or, if a record is not to be taken, the date as of which the holders of [*Describe Stock to Be Received*] of record to be entitled to such dividend, distribution or rights are to be determined; or

(B) the date on which such reclassification, consolidation, merger, sale, transfer, dissolution, liquidation or winding up is expected to become effective, and the date as of which it is expected that holders of [*Describe Stock to Be Received*] of record shall be entitled to exchange their shares of [*Describe Stock to Be Received*] for securities or other property deliverable upon such reclassification, consolidation, merger, sale, transfer, dissolution, liquidation or winding up.

(j) Procedures. The Board of Directors of the Corporation, or a committee established by it, shall have the right from time to time to adopt other specific rules of procedure to carry out the full intent of this conversion provision and to do all reasonable acts necessary therefore; provided that such rules and acts shall not violate the specific terms of this *warrant/option*.

§ 42.3 Stock Purchase Warrant—Detachable

——— CORPORATION CAPITAL STOCK PURCHASE WARRANT (DETACHABLE)

This certifies that, for value received, ______, a ______ Corporation, is entitled to purchase and receive from ______ Corporation (hereinafter sometimes called the "Company"), during the period hereinafter provided, ______ [*number*] fully paid and nonassessable shares of the no par common voting stock of the Company (hereinafter called the "Capital Stock" upon surrender hereof, at the principal office of the Company in ______, ______, and simultaneous payment of the purchase price of $______ [*price*] for each share of the Capital Stock so to be purchased; such number of shares and such purchase price per share being subject, however, to adjustment as hereinafter provided. The purchase price per share, as adjusted from time to time, is hereinafter referred to as the "Purchase Price."

This Warrant shall be exercisable commencing ______, 19__, that being the Closing Date of that certain loan agreement between the Company and ______ Corporation, dated ______, 19__ (hereinafter called the "Agreement"), and shall expire at the close of business on ______, 19__; provided, however, that should the Company be in default on ______, 19__ of the Agreement and/or the debentures issued pursuant thereto, this Warrant shall be exercisable until the close of business on ______, 19__, or until such default is cured, whichever is earlier.

(a) If the Company shall at any time or from time to time hereafter:

(1) Sell or issue any additional shares of its Capital Stock (other than upon exercise of this Warrant and any other Warrants issued upon exchange of this Warrant, and other than upon conversion of the Company's __% ______ [*year*] subordinated convertible debentures issued to ______ Corporation on ______, 19__), for a consideration per share less than the Purchase Price in effect immediately prior to such sale or issuance, or without consideration; or

(2) Sell or issue any rights or options to purchase Capital Stock of the Company, or sell or issue any securities of any kind convertible into shares of Capital Stock of the Company, in which the option, purchase, exercise or conversion price (or consideration) per share, as the case may be, is less than the Purchase Price in effect immediately prior to such sale or issuance; then and in each such case the Purchase Price in effect immediately prior to such sale or issuance shall immediately and automatically be reduced to the consideration per share received by the Company upon such sale or issuance as specified in subparagraph (a), above, or to the option, purchase, exercise or conversion price (or consideration) per share upon such sale or issuance as specified in subparagraph (b), above, as the case may be.

Upon each such adjustment of the Purchase Price, the holder hereof shall thereafter (until a subsequent adjustment of the Purchase Price) be entitled to purchase at the adjusted Purchase Price the number of shares of Capital Stock of the Company obtained by multiplying the number of shares specified in this Warrant by the initial Purchase Price (i. e., $______) and dividing the product so obtained by the adjusted Purchase Price.

(b) For purposes of the aforegoing adjustments, the following provisions shall also apply:

(1) In case the consideration for such issuance or sale of additional shares of Capital Stock, or the option, purchase, exercise or conversion price (or consideration) per share provided for in any such right, option or convertible security, shall be cash, in whole or in part, the amount of consideration received shall be deemed to be the amount of cash received by the Company after deducting therefrom any compensation or discount allowed or paid for the selling, underwriting or purchase thereof to underwriters, dealers or others performing similar services, but without deducting therefrom any other expenses incurred in connection therewith.

(2) In case the consideration for such issuance or sale of additional shares of Capital Stock, or the option, purchase, exercise or conversion price (or consideration) per share provided for in any such right, option or convertible security, shall be wholly or partially other than cash, such other consideration shall be deemed to be the value, expressed in monetary terms, of such consideration as fairly determined by the Board of Directors of the Company.

(3) In case the Company shall sell or issue any rights or options to purchase Capital Stock of the Company, or any securities of any kind convertible into shares of Capital Stock of the Company, such sale or issue shall be deemed to be issue or sale (as of the date of the issue or sale of such rights, options or convertible securities) of the maximum number of shares of Capital Stock necessary to effect the exercise, conversion or exchange of all such rights, options or convertible securities, and the amount received by the Company for the issue or sale of such rights, options or convertible securities plus the total amount of additional consideration, if any, payable to the Company on such exercise, conversion or exchange shall be deemed to be consideration actually received for the issue or sale of such shares of Capital Stock, and such shares of Capital Stock shall be deemed to constitute issued shares of Capital Stock as of said date; provided, however, that no further adjustment of the purchase price shall be made upon the actual issuance of any shares of Capital Stock to effect such exercise, conversion or exchange.

(4) No adjustment in the Purchase Price or in the number of shares purchasable upon exercise of this Warrant shall be made as a result of the issuance by the Company of employee stock options covering an aggregate of such number of shares of Capital Stock which, when added to the number of shares of

Capital Stock covered by presently outstanding employee stock options, does not exceed ______ [*number*] shares.

(5) No adjustment in the Purchase Price or in the number of shares purchasable upon exercise of this Warrant shall be made as a result of the sale or issuance by the Company of an aggregate of not to exceed ______ [*number*] shares of Capital Stock upon exercise of employee stock options theretofore validly issued by the Company.

(6) No adjustment in the Purchase Price shall be made as a result of the sale or issuance by the Company of any additional shares of Capital Stock issued as a stock dividend upon outstanding Capital Stock, and no further adjustment in the number of shares of Capital Stock issuable upon exercise of this Warrant shall be made except to the extent:

(A) In case the Company shall declare any dividend upon outstanding Capital Stock payable in cash or in shares of Capital Stock (or fractions thereof), or in case the Company shall make any other distribution upon outstanding Capital Stock, then and in each such case the holder of this Warrant, upon any exercise of all or any part hereof thereafter, will be entitled to receive the number of shares of Capital Stock as to which the right of purchase is being exercised and, in addition but without any further payment, the securities, cash or other property which the holder of this Warrant would have received by way of such dividends or distributions if such holder (i) had continuously since the date hereof been the record holder of the Capital Stock as to which the right of purchase is then being exercised, and (ii) had retained all securities which he would have received as dividends and/or other distributions upon such Capital Stock.

(B) If the Company shall, by subdivision, combination or reclassification of shares or otherwise, change the outstanding shares of its Capital Stock into a different number or class of shares, the number and class of shares issuable upon exercise of this Warrant and the Purchase Price payable upon such exercise shall be adjusted as provided in the immediately preceding paragraph.

In case of any reorganization or merger of the Company into any other Corporation, then each share of stock issuable upon exercise of this Warrant shall be replaced for the purposes hereof by the stock or other securities or property issuable in respect of each share of Capital Stock of the Company upon such reorganization or merger.

(c) In case at any time:

(1) the Company shall declare or pay any dividend, payable in stock or otherwise, upon the Capital Stock or declare or make any other distribution to the holders of its Capital Stock;

(2) the Company shall offer for subscription pro rata or otherwise to the holders of the Capital Stock any additional shares of stock of any class or other rights;

(3) there shall be any capital reorganization or reclassification of the Capital Stock of the Company, or reorganization or merger of the Company with, or transfer of all or substantially all of its assets to, another corporation; or

(4) there shall be a voluntary or involuntary dissolution, liquidation or winding up of the Company;

then, in any one or more of said cases, the Company shall give written notice to the holder of this Warrant of the date (i) on which the books of the Company shall close, or of record fixed, for determining the Stockholders entitled to such dividend, distribution or subscription rights, or (ii) on which such reorganization, reclassification, consolidation, merger, transfer, dissolution, liquidation or winding up shall take place, as the case may be. Such notice shall also specify the date as of which the holders of Capital Stock of record shall participate in such dividend, distribution or subscription rights, or shall be entitled to exchange their Capital Stock for securities or other property deliverable upon such reorganization, reclassification, merger, transfer, dissolution, liquidation or winding up, as the case may be. Such written notice shall be given at least twenty (20) days prior to the action in question and not less than twenty (20) days prior to the record date or the date on which the Company's transfer books are closed in respect thereto.

Upon any adjustment or other change relating to the Purchase Price of the securities issuable upon exercise of this Warrant, then and in such case the Company shall give written notice thereof to the holder hereof, which notice shall state the Purchase Price resulting from such adjustment and the number of securities receivable at such price upon the exercise of the Warrant, and set forth in reasonable detail the method of calculation and the facts upon which such calculation is based.

No fractional shares of Capital Stock will be issued in connection with any purchase hereunder, but the Company shall, in lieu of such fractional shares, make a cash payment therefor on the basis of the Purchase Price then in effect.

(d) The Company covenants that it will at all times maintain an available and adequate reserve of duly authorized but unissued shares of its Capital Stock, free from preemptive rights, sufficient to effect the full exercise of this Warrant as herein provided, and that it will at all times maintain in full force and effect an appropriate permit of the ______ Commissioner of Corporations authorizing the issuance and sale by the Company of all shares of Capital Stock issuable upon exercise of this Warrant by the holder.

The Company covenants that all shares of Capital Stock issuable upon the exercise of this Warrant will, upon issuance, be validly issued, fully paid and nonassessable, and free from all taxes, liens and charges with respect to the issue thereof.

The holder hereof may surrender this Warrant for exchange at the principal office of the Company. Within a reasonable time thereafter and without expense (other than transfer taxes, if any) to each holder, the Company shall issue in exchange therefor, in such denominations (of not less than ______ [*number*] shares) and issued in such name or names as the holder shall designate (if permitted by the Federal Securities laws and the relevant Blue Sky law(s), as amended from time to time), a new certificate or certificates dated the date hereof evidencing the right to purchase the same aggregate number of shares of Capital Stock as are evidenced hereby, and otherwise containing the same provisions and subject to the same terms and conditions as this certificate.

Upon surrender of this Warrant at the office of the Company accompanied by payment of the appropriate Purchase Price of the Capital Stock in cash, the Company shall forthwith cause to be executed, issued and delivered to the holder of the Warrant a certificate or certificates for the proper number of shares of capital stock or other securities of the Company; and the Company covenants that the issuance of this Warrant shall constitute full authority to those of its officers who are charged with the duty of issuing stock certificates to promptly execute, issue and deliver to the holder of the Warrant the necessary certificate for shares of Capital Stock or other securities of the Company required by such exercise.

This Warrant may be exercised in accordance with its terms prior to expiration as a whole, or from time to time in part. In the event of partial exercise of the Warrant, the Company shall, in addition to delivery of the securities thereby purchased, deliver to the holder of the Warrant, a new Warrant for the remaining shares then subject to the unexercised portion of the Warrant; such new Warrant being dated the date hereof and otherwise containing the same provisions and subject to the same terms and conditions as this Warrant. Certificates for shares of Capital Stock or other securities of the Company issuable by reason of the exercise of Warrants shall be dated and shall be effective as of the date of the surrender of the Warrants for exercise or acceptance of the offering of shares or other securities, as the case may be, and the payment of the appropriate Purchase

Price, notwithstanding any delay in the actual execution, issuance or delivery of the certificates or securities so purchased.

This Warrant shall be registered on the books of the Company, which shall be kept by it at its principal office for that purpose, and shall be transferable only on said books by the holder hereof in person or by duly authorized attorney upon surrender of this Warrant properly endorsed.

______, [*State*] ______, 19__.

__________ Corporation

By ________________

President

[*Seal*]

Attest: __________

Secretary

§ 42.4 Stock Purchase Warrant—Non-detachable

STOCK PURCHASE WARRANT (NON–DETACHABLE)

No. ______ 50 Shares

[*Do Not Detach Without Consulting Trustee*]

______ CORPORATION

INCORPORATED UNDER THE LAWS OF THE STATE OF ______

COMMON STOCK PURCHASE WARRANT EXERCISABLE THROUGH ______, 19__

This is to certify that, subject to the conditions herein set forth, the registered owner of the attached Debenture, bearing the same number as this Warrant, is entitled to purchase until the close of business on ______, 19__, ______ shares of fully paid and nonassessable common stock of the par value of $______ per share "Common Stock" of ______ Corporation, hereinafter called the "Company," for each $______ principal amount of the Debenture to which this Warrant is attached upon surrender hereof at the principal office of ______ Bank, ______, ______, or successor agency appointed by the Company for the purpose, and upon the payment of the purchase price at the principal office of the Bank. Subject to adjustment as hereinafter provided for, the purchase price payable upon exercise of this Stock Purchase Warrant shall be [*e. g., $11 per share prior to December 31, 1973; $12 per share from January 1, 1974, to and including December 31, 1976; $13 per share from January 1, 1977, to and including December 31, 1979; $14 per share from January 1, 1980, to and including December 31, 1982; and $15 per share from Janu-*

ary 1, 1983, to and including December 31, 1985, when this Warrant expires.] These amounts, as adjusted from time to time, are hereinafter called the "Purchase Price."

The Purchase Price payable upon exercise of this Stock Purchase Warrant shall be payable in such coin or currency of the United States of America as at the time of such exercise shall be legal tender for the payment of public and private debts.

(a) If the Company shall at any time after the delivery of the Debentures issue any additional shares, then and in each such case the Purchase Price in effect immediately prior to the issuance of such additional shares shall forthwith be reduced to a price determined by dividing

(1) an amount equal to (A) the total number of shares of common stock outstanding immediately prior to the issue of such additional shares multiplied by the Purchase Price in effect immediately prior to such issue, plus (B) the consideration, if any, received by the Company for such additional shares, by

(2) the total number of shares of Common Stock outstanding immediately after the issue of such additional shares;

provided that no such adjustment of the Purchase Price shall be required if the amount of such adjustment shall be less than 25 cents, but any adjustment not so made shall be carried forward and shall be made at the time and together with the next subsequent adjustment which, together with any adjustment or adjustments so carried forward, shall require adjustment of the Purchase Price by an amount not less than 25 cents.

Upon each such adjustment of the Purchase Price the holder of this Stock Purchase Warrant shall thereafter (until a subsequent adjustment of the Purchase Price) be entitled to purchase at the adjusted Purchased Price the number of shares of Common Stock obtained by multiplying the number of shares of Common Stock specified in this Stock Purchase Warrant by the initial Purchase Price hereinabove specified and dividing the product so obtained by the adjusted Purchase Price.

For the purposes of the foregoing the following provisions shall also be applicable:

(1) In case of the issuance of additional shares of Common Stock for a consideration part or all of which shall be cash, the amount of the cash consideration therefor shall be deemed to be the amount of cash received by the Company for such shares (or, if such shares are offered by the Company for subscription, the subscription price, or if such shares are sold to underwriters or dealers for public offering without a subscription offer, the initial public offering price), without deducting therefrom any compensation

or discount allowed or paid for the selling, underwriting or purchase thereof by underwriters or dealers or others performing similar services, and without deduction for any expenses incurred in connection therewith.

(2) In case of the issuance (otherwise than upon conversion or exchange of other securities of the Company) of additional shares of Common Stock for a consideration part or all of which shall be other than cash, the amount of the consideration other than cash received by the Company for such shares shall be deemed to be the value of such consideration as determined by the Board of Directors of the Company.

(3) In case of the issuance by the Company after the original issue date hereof in ______, 19__, of (A) any security that is convertible into shares of Common Stock of the Company, or (B) any rights or options to purchase Common Stock of the Company, the Company shall be deemed to have issued the maximum number of shares of Common Stock into which such convertible security may be converted, and the maximum number of shares of Common Stock deliverable upon the exercise of such rights or options, for the consideration received by the Company for such convertible security or for such rights or options (plus the amount of any underwriting discount), as the case may be, before deducting therefrom any expenses or commissions incurred or paid by the Company for any underwriting of, or otherwise in connection with, the issuance of such convertible security or rights or options, plus (i) any consideration or adjustment payment to be received by the Company in connection with such conversion and (ii) the minimum considerations to be received by the Company for the Common Stock issuable upon the exercise of such rights or options. No further adjustment of the Purchase Price shall be made as a result of the actual issuance of the shares of Common Stock of the Company upon conversion of any convertible security or exercise of any rights or options referred to in this clause (3). On the termination of the right to convert such convertible security, or on expiration of such rights or options, the Purchase Price hereunder shall be readjusted to such Purchase Price as would have obtained had the adjustment made upon the issuance of such convertible security or upon the issuance of such rights or options been made upon the basis of the number of shares of Common Stock actually issued upon the conversion of such convertible security or the exercise of such rights or options, and of the consideration actually received by the Company upon such conversion or exercise.

(4) Any additional shares of Common Stock issued as a stock dividend shall be deemed to have been issued without consideration.

If the Company shall, by subdivision, combination or reclassification of shares or otherwise, change the outstanding shares of its Common Stock into a different number or class of shares, the number and class of shares issuable upon exercise of this Stock Purchase Warrant and the Purchase Price payable upon such exercise shall be correspondingly adjusted.

Whenever the Purchase Price is adjusted, as herein provided, an Officers' Certificate as defined in the Indenture shall be furnished by the Company to the Trustee and Warrant Agent stating the adjusted Purchase Price and reciting in detail the facts upon which such adjustment was based. Such Officers' Certificate shall be conclusive evidence of the correctness of such adjustment insofar as the Trustee and Warrant Agent are concerned.

No fractional shares of common stock will be issued in connection with any purchase hereunder but the Company shall, in lieu of such fractional shares, make a cash payment therefor on the basis of the Purchase Price then in effect.

In case of any reorganization or merger of the Company into any other Corporation, then each share of stock purchasable under this Stock Purchase Warrant shall be replaced for the purposes hereof by the stock or other securities or property issuable in respect of each share of common stock of the Company upon such reorganization or merger.

This Stock Purchase Warrant is issued subject, also, to the following terms and conditions, to all of which, including all the foregoing provisions, each and every holder assents by accepting this Stock Purchase Warrant:

The holder of this Stock Purchase Warrant shall not have any of the rights of a Stockholder of the Company nor be entitled to any notice of any meetings of Stockholders or of any other proceedings of the Company.

All rights under and by virtue of this Stock Purchase Warrant shall pass and be transferred, and title hereto shall be transferable, only in connection with the transfer of the Debenture to which this Warrant is attached, and then only upon the books of the Company by the registered holder hereof in person or by his duly authorized attorney. This Stock Purchase Warrant is not detachable from such Debenture, except for the purpose of exercise and then only by the Trustee, and is void unless accompanied by such Debenture. If any ______ share Warrant (or ______ share portion of any Warrant originally issued for a multiple of ______ shares) is only partially exercised, then the remaining unexercised purchase rights attributable to such Warrant (or portion) shall thereupon expire and become void.

This Stock Purchase Warrant shall become void and all rights hereunder shall expire unless prior to the close of business on December 31, 1985, it shall be surrendered and the rights thereunder exercised. This Stock Purchase Warrant shall also become void and all rights hereunder shall expire on the date of redemption of the Debenture to which it is attached.

This Stock Purchase Warrant shall not be valid for any purpose unless signed by an authorized officer of ______ Bank, as Agent for the Company.

__________ Corporation

By ____________ Bank
Agent

By ________________
Authorized Officer

Dated as of ______, 19__.

COMMENT

This is the type of warrant to be used with a debenture such as is shown in Chapter 43D, infra.

§ 42.5 Warrant to Purchase Shares

Warrant #W ______

To Purchase ______
Shares of Common Stock
($______ par value)

WARRANT OF
______ CORP.

INCORPORATED UNDER THE LAWS OF
THE STATE OF ______

Exercise Form.

§ 1.1 Basic Terms. This certifies that, for value received, the registered owner is entitled, subject to the terms and conditions of this Warrant, until the expiration date, to purchase the number of shares of the Common Stock, par value $______ ("the Common Stock"), of ______ Corp. (the "Corporation") from the Corporation at the purchase price shown below, on delivery of this Warrant to the Corporation with the exercise form duly executed and payment of the purchase price (in cash or by certified or bank cashier's check payable to the order of the Corporation) for each share purchased.

Registered Owner ______________________________

Purchase Price (until 3 p. m. Central Standard Time,

Dec. 31, 1985): Twenty Dollars ($20) a share

Purchase Price (thereafter until 3 p. m., Central Standard Time, Dec. 31, 1995): Twenty Five Dollars ($25) a share.

Expiration date: 3 p. m., Dec. 31, 1995, unless terminated sooner under this Warrant.

§ 1.2 Corporation's Covenants as to Common Stock. Shares deliverable on the exercise of this Warrant shall, at delivery, be fully paid and non-assessable, free from taxes, liens, and charges with respect to their purchase. The Corporation shall take any necessary steps to assure that the par value per share of the Common Stock is at all times equal to or less than the then current Warrant purchase price per share of the Common Stock issuable pursuant to this Warrant. The Corporation shall at all times reserve and hold available sufficient shares of Common Stock to satisfy all conversion and purchase rights of outstanding convertible securities, options and warrants.

§ 1.3 Method of Exercise; Fractional Shares. The purchase rights represented by this Warrant are exercisable at the option of the registered owner in whole at any time, or in part, from time to time, within the period above specified, provided, however, that purchase rights are not exercisable with respect to a fraction of a share of Common Stock. In lieu of issuing a fraction of a share remaining after exercise of this Warrant as to all full shares covered hereby, the Corporation shall either (a) pay therefor cash equal to the same fraction of the then current Warrant purchase price per share or, at its option, (b) issue scrip for the fraction, in registered or bearer form approved by the Board of Directors of the Corporation, which shall entitle the holder to receive a certificate for a full share of Common Stock on surrender of scrip aggregating a full share. Scrip may become void after a reasonable period (but not less than six months after the expiration date of this Warrant) determined by the Board of Directors and specified in the scrip. In case of the exercise of this Warrant for less than all the shares purchasable, the Corporation shall cancel the Warrant and execute and deliver a new Warrant of like tenor and date for the balance of the shares purchasable.

§ 1.4 Adjustment of Shares Purchasable. The number of shares purchasable hereunder and the purchase price per share are subject to adjustment from time to time as specified in this Warrant.

§ 1.5 Limited Rights of Owner. This Warrant does not entitle the owner to any voting rights or other rights as a Stockholder of the Corporation, or to any other rights whatsoever except the rights herein expressed. No dividends are payable or will accrue on this Warrant or the shares purchasable hereunder until, and except to the extent that, this Warrant is exercised.

§ 1.6 Exchange for Other Denominations. This Warrant is exchangeable, on its surrender by the registered owner to the Corporation, for new Warrants of like tenor and date representing in the aggregate the right to purchase the number of shares purchasable hereunder in denominations designated by the registered owner at the time of surrender.

§ 1.7 Transfer. Except as otherwise above provided, this Warrant is transferable only on the books of the Corporation by the registered owner in person or by attorney, on surrender of this Warrant, properly indorsed.

§ 1.8 Recognition of Registered Owner. Prior to due presentment for registration of transfer of this Warrant, the Corporation may treat the registered owner as the person exclusively entitled to receive notices and otherwise to exercise rights hereunder.

§ 1.9 Effect of Stock Split, Etc. If the Corporation, by stock dividend, split, reverse split, reclassification of shares, or otherwise, changes as a whole the outstanding Common Stock into a different number or class of shares, then:

(a) the number and class of shares so changed shall, for the purposes of this Warrant, replace the shares outstanding immediately prior to the change; and

(b) the Warrant purchase price in effect, and the number of shares purchasable under this Warrant, immediately prior to the date upon which the change becomes effective, shall be preportionately adjusted (the price to the nearest cent). Irrespective of any adjustment or change in the Warrant purchase price or the number of shares purchasable under this or any other Warrant of like tenor, the Warrants theretofore and thereafter issued may continue to express the Warrant purchase price per share and the number of shares purchasable as the Warrant purchase price per share and the number of shares purchasable were expressed in the Warrants when initially issued.

§ 1.10 Effect of Merger, Etc. If the Corporation consolidates with or merges into another corporation, the registered owner shall thereafter be entitled on exercise to purchase, with respect to each share of Common Stock purchasable hereunder immediately before the consolidation or merger becomes effective, the securities or other consideration to which a holder of one share of Common Stock is entitled in the consolidation or merger without any change in or payment in addition to the Warrant purchase price in effect immediately prior to the merger or consolidation. The Corporation shall take any necessary steps in connection with a consolidation or merger to assure that all the provisions of this Warrant shall thereafter be applicable, as nearly as reasonably may be, to any securities or other consideration so deliverable on exercise of this Warrant. The Corporation shall not consolidate or merge unless, prior to consummation, the successor Corporation (if other than the Corporation) assumes the obligations of this paragraph by written instrument executed and mailed to the registered owner at the address of the owner on the books of the Corporation. A sale or lease of all or substantially all the assets of the Corporation for a consideration (apart from the assumption of obligations) consisting primarily of securities is a consolidation or merger for the foregoing purposes.

§ 1.11 Notice of Adjustment. On the happening of an event requiring an adjustment of the Warrant purchase price or the shares purchasable hereunder, the Corporation shall forthwith give written notice to the registered owner stating the adjusted Warrant purchase price and the adjusted number and kind of securities or other property purchasable hereunder resulting from the event and setting forth in reasonable detail the method of calculation and the facts upon which the calculation is based. The Board of Directors of the Corporation, acting in good faith, shall determine the calculation.

§ 1.12 Notice and Effect of Dissolution, Etc. In case a voluntary or involuntary dissolution, liquidation, or winding up of the Corporation (other than in connection with a consolidation or merger covered by paragraph (§ 1.10) above) is at any time proposed, the Corporation shall give at least 30 days' prior written notice to the registered owner. Such notice shall contain: (a) the date on which the transaction is to take place; (b) the record date (which shall be at least 30 days after the giving of the notice) as of which holders of Common Shares will be entitled to receive distributions as a result of the transaction; (c) a brief description of the transaction; (d) a brief description of the distributions to be made to holders of Common Shares as a result of the transaction; and (e) an estimate of the fair value of the distributions. On the date of the transaction, if it actually occurs, this Warrant and all rights hereunder shall terminate.

§ 1.13 Method of Giving Notice; Extent Required. Notices shall be given by first class mail, postage prepaid, addressed to the registered owner at the address of the owner appearing in the records of the Corporation. No notice to warrant holders is required except as specified herein.

Witness the seal of the Corporation and the signatures of its authorized Officers.

Dated ______ [*Seal*] ______ Corp.

By

[*Signature*] [*Signature*]

______________________ ______________________

[*Title*] [*Title*]

ASSIGNMENT FORM

[*To be executed by the registered owner to transfer the Warrant*]

For value received the undersigned hereby sells, assigns, and transfers to

Name ____________________

Address ____________________

this Warrant and irrevocably appoints ____________________ attorney (with full power of substitution) to transfer this Warrant on the books of the Corporation.

Date: ______ ____________________

(Please sign exactly as name appears on Warrant)

Taxpayer ID No. ______

In the presence of: Signature guaranteed by

____________________ ____________________

COMMENT

This form appears in A. Bromberg, Corporate Organizational Documents and Securities—Forms and Comments, 28 Sw.L.J. 874, 954 (1974). Copyright © 1974 by Alan R. Bromberg.

§ 42.6 Exercise Form

EXERCISE FORM

[*To be executed by the registered owner to purchase Common Stock pursuant to the Warrant*]

______ Corp.
[*Address*]

The undersigned hereby: (1) irrevocably subscribes for ______ shares of your Common Stock pursuant to this Warrant, and encloses payment of $______ therefor; (2) requests that a certificate for the shares be issued in the name of the undersigned and delivered to the undersigned at the address below; and (3) if such number of shares is not all of the shares purchasable hereunder, that a new Warrant of like tenor for the balance of the remaining shares purchasable hereunder be issued in the name of the undersigned and delivered to the undersigned at the address below.

Date: ______ ____________________

(Please sign exactly as name appears on Warrant)

Address: ____________________

Taxpayer ID No. ______

COMMENT

This form appears in A. Bromberg, Corporate Organizational Documents and Securities—Forms and Comments, 28 Sw.L.J. 874, 954 (1974). Copyright © 1974 by Alan R. Bromberg.

§ 42.7 Employee Stock Options

Coverage of employee stock option, stock purchase, and related plans is covered in a later volume.

§§ 42.8–43.0 are reserved for supplementary material.

CHAPTER 43

DEBT FINANCING

Table of Sections

A. IN GENERAL

B. NOTES

C. BONDS

D. DEBENTURES

E. GENERAL CLAUSES AND PROVISIONS

A. IN GENERAL

§ 43.1 Introduction

For a general discussion of debt financing and of the various types of debt securities, see Chapter 38, supra.

In the absence of charter or statutory restrictions, a Corporation has the power to issue securities for money borrowed or debts contracted, always observing the formalities prescribed by statute or its Articles.[1] These securities may be bonds, debentures or notes.

1. E. g. Model Bus.Corp.Act § 4(h) provides:

> Each Corporation shall have power:
>
> * * *
>
> (h) To make contracts and guarantees and incur liabilities, borrow money at such rates of interest as the Corporation may determine, issue its notes, bonds, and other obligations, and secure any of its obligations by mortgage or pledge of all or any of its property, franchises and income.
>
> * * *

See also e. g. West's Ann.Calif.Corp. Code § 207; McKinney's N.Y.Bus. Corp.Law § 202 for similar powers.

When any of the bonds and debentures issued are to be sold in interstate transactions, the provisions of the federal securities laws and the relevant state blue sky laws should be complied with. In the event such Act applies and the securities covered by the trust indenture exceeds $1,000,000, the requirements of the Trust Indenture Act of 1939 must be satisfied. The tendency to extend protection to investors by the relevant bodies has caused frequent suggestions of particular provisions to be inserted in bonds, debentures and trust deeds as prerequisites to registration. The latest departmental regulations should, therefore, be consulted before any final draft of the securities to be issued is made.

B. NOTES

§ 43.2 General Note Form

PROMISSORY NOTE

For value received, the undersigned does hereby promise to pay to the order of [*Name*], of [*Address*], the sum of $[*Dollars*] plus interest at the rate of [*rate*] percent per annum on the unpaid principal until fully paid. Said principal and accrued interest shall be paid by the undersigned in lawful money of the United States of America, at [*Address of Lender*], as follows:

> The principal and accrued interest shall be payable in equal installments of principal of $[*Dollars*] [*plus/including*] interest due on the ______ day of each [*month/quarter/year*] beginning on the ______ day of ______, 19__; but in any case, all principal and interest shall be due and payable on or before [*Date or Demand*]. This Note may be prepaid in part or in full with accrued interest without penalty at any time.

Should default be made in the payment of interest and/or principal due hereunder, then such default shall mature the entire indebtedness evidenced hereby, without notice, at the option of the holder hereof. Every person at any time liable for the payment of the debt evidenced hereby, waives presentment for payment, demand and notice of non-payment of this Note, and consents that the holder may extend the time of payment of any part of the whole of the debt at any time at the request of any other person liable hereunder.

Any delay on the part of the Payee in exercising any rights hereunder shall not operate as a waiver of said rights; acceptance of any payment after its due date shall not be deemed a waiver of the right to require prompt payment when due of all other sums, acceptance of any payment after the Payee has declared the entire indebtedness due and payable shall not cure any default of the maker or operate as a waiver of any rights of the Payee hereunder.

This Note shall be paid without claim of set-off or deduction of any nature or for any cause whatsoever.

At the option of the Payee, this Note shall become immediately due and payable without notice or demand on the happening of any one of the following events: the filing of a petition by or against the maker (or any guarantor of the maker) under the provisions of any state insolvency law or under the provisions of the Federal Bankruptcy Act (for bankruptcy or reorganization or other relief), or any assignment by the maker (or any guarantor of the maker) for the benefit of his creditors.

Upon default, the maker agrees to pay all costs and actual attorney fees of collection.

Witnesses: Debtor:

____________________ ____________________

____________________ Dated as of the ______ day of ______, 19__.

Library References:

C.J.S. Corporations § 1226.
West's Key No. Digests, Corporations ⚿465.

§ 43.3 Variable Note

The following is the form for a note which has a varying [unstated] principal amount. This form is an attempt to match corporate practice in many small Corporations where the amount loaned varies during the corporate year and depends upon corporate need.

PROMISSORY NOTE

WITH VARIABLE AMOUNTS DUE

For value received, the undersigned does hereby promise to pay to the order of [*Name*] of [*Address*] an amount of up to $[*Dollars*] as such amounts shall be, from time to time advanced, plus interest at the rate of [*Rate*] per annum on the unpaid principal until fully paid. Said principal and accrued interest shall be paid by the undersigned in lawful money of the United States of America, at the main office of the obligee, as follows:

> Accrued interest shall be payable at least quarter-annually starting on the [*Date*]. Principal shall be on demand, but in any case on or before ______. In any case, a partial payment of no less than [*Rate*] of the then principal shall be paid on or before the last day of [*month/quarter/year*] of each year while this Note remains unpaid beginning on the ______ day of ______, 19__.

Should default be made in the payment of interest and/or principal due hereunder, then such default shall mature the entire indebtedness evidenced hereby, without notice, at the option of the holder hereof. Every person at any time liable for the payment of the debt evidenced hereby, waives presentment for payment, demand and notice of non-payment of this Note, and consents that the holder may extend the time of payment of any part of the whole of the debt at any time at the request of any other person liable hereunder.

Any delay on the part of the Payee in exercising any rights hereunder shall not operate as a waiver of said rights; acceptance of any payment after its due date shall not be deemed a waiver of the right to require prompt payment when due of all other sums, and acceptance of any payment after the Payee has declared the entire indebtedness due and payable shall not cure any default of the maker or operate as a waiver of any rights of the Payee hereunder.

This Note shall be paid without claim of set-off or deduction of any nature or for any cause whatsoever.

At the option of the Payee, this Note shall become immediately due and payable without notice or demand on the happening of any one of the following events: the filing of a petition by or against the maker (or any guarantor of the maker) under the provisions of any state insolvency law or under the provisions of the Federal Bankruptcy Act (for bankruptcy or reorganization or other relief), or any assignment by the maker (or any guarantor of the maker) for the benefit of his creditors.

Upon default, the maker agrees to pay all costs and actual attorney fees of collection.

Witnesses:	Debtor:
______________________	______________________
______________________	Dated as of the ______ day of ______, 19__.

COMMENT

If the Payee (lender) is a Stockholder of the Corporation, it is important to make regular payments of principal to avoid the claim that this note is merely a form of stock and the interest is a dividend (see Chapter 56, supra for further discussion).

§§ 43.4–43.10 are reserved for supplementary material.

C. BONDS

Library References:

C.J.S. Corporations, §§ 1146–1148, 1150, 1158, 1160, 1161, 1192.
West's Key No. Digests, Corporations ⚷469 et seq.

§ 43.11 Corporate Bond—Registered Form

No. ______ $______

THE ______ CORPORATION ______% BOND

Due ______, 19__ ______, 19__

For value received, The ______ Corporation, a Corporation organized and existing under the laws of the State of ______ (hereinafter called the "Company") hereby promises to pay to ______ or registered assigns on the ______ day of ______, 19__, the sum of ______ ($______) Dollars, (unless before that date this bond shall have been redeemed [*or converted*]) with interest thereon at the rate of ______ Per Cent (______%) per annum, payable semi-annually on the first day of *February* and *August* in each year. The principal sum of this bond will be payable at the registered office of the Company (or at such other place as may be designated in writing by the Company). Semi-annual interest payments will be mailed to the registered holder of this bond at his address as last furnished the Company in writing.

These bonds are registered both as to principal and interest and are transferable only on the books of the company by presentation of the bond with an instrument of transfer duly executed by the holder or his duly authorized agent.

In witness whereof, The ______ Manufacturing Corporation has caused its corporate name and seal to be signed and affixed as of the ______ day of ______, 19__.

The ______ Manufacturing Corporation

By: ______________________

President

____

Treasurer

Attest: ______________

Secretary

COMMENT

Uniform Commercial Code § 8–102 defines a security as in "registered form" when it specifies a person entitled to the security or to the rights it evidences and when its transfer may be registered upon books maintained for that purpose by or on behalf of an issuer or the security so states. To be negotiable it need not contain the phrase "to the order of."

§ 43.12 Corporate Bond—Registered Form—Secured by Deed of Trust or Mortgage

[*Name of Corporation*]

FIRST MORTGAGE REGISTERED BOND

No. ______ $[*Amount*]

Know all men by these presents, that [*Name of Corporation*] is indebted, and for value received promises to pay to [*Name of Obligee*] or assigns the sum of ______ ($______) Dollars in lawful money of the United States of America on the ______ day of ______, 19__, at the office of the company in the City of ______ with interest at the rate of ______ per cent per annum, payable semi-annually, at said office, in like money, on the first days of [*Month*] and [*Month*] in each year.

This bond is one of a series of *coupon and* registered bonds of the [*Name of Corporation*], bearing interest at the rate of ______ per cent per annum, issued or to be issued in pursuance of and subject to the terms of the mortgage or deed of trust hereinafter referred to, but so that the aggregate amount of said bonds shall not exceed the total sum of ______ ($______) Dollars. All of said bonds are equally secured by a [*mortgage or deed*] of trust, dated ______, 19__, executed by [*Name of Corporation*] to [*Name of Trustee*] of the City of ______, as trustee, conveying the property and franchises of the [*Name of Corporation*] mentioned in said mortgage or deed of trust, to which reference is hereby made for a description of the property and franchises mortgaged, and the nature and extent of the security, and the rights of the holders of said bonds under the same and the terms and conditions upon which said bonds are issued and secured. This bond is transferable by the holder hereof only in person or by attorney, duly authorized, upon the books of the company, at its office in the City of ______.

This bond shall not become obligatory for any purpose until it shall have been authenticated by the certificate thereon indorsed by the trustee under said mortgage or deed of trust.

In witness whereof, the [*Name of Corporation*] has caused these presents to be signed by its President or Vice-President, and its corporate seal to be hereunto affixed, and to be attested by its Secretary, this ______ day of ______, 19__.

[*Name of Corporation*]

By ________________

President

[*Seal*]

Attest: ____________

Secretary

§ 43.13 Corporate Bond Issued Pursuant to Trust Indenture—Bearer Form

______ CORPORATION

Due ______, 19__

$______ [*City and State*] ______, 19__

No. ______

For Value Received, The ______ Corporation, a ______ Corporation, promises to pay to the order of the bearer of this bond the sum of ______ Dollars ($______) on the ______ day of ______, 19__. In addition the undersigned agrees to pay on the 1st day of ______ and ______ in each year interest thereon at the rate of ______ per cent, upon presentation and delivery of the appropriate interest coupon attached hereto at the ______ Bank, ______, ______.

The undersigned may treat any person in possession of this bond as owner for all purposes, including payment of principal or transfer.

This Bond is issued pursuant to a Trust Indenture dated ______, 19__, between the ______ Corporation and the ______ Bank, ______, ______, and is subject to all the provisions thereof and entitled to all the benefits thereunder. Such Trust Indenture contains provisions specifying upon what events the indebtedness evidenced by this and similar bonds may be prepaid by the undersigned and upon what events the indebtedness evidenced hereunder and by similar bonds may be accelerated at the option of the holders of the bonds or otherwise enforced.

In witness whereof by its duly authorized officers, the ______ Corporation has caused this bond to be executed and its seal thereto affixed by its duly authorized officers as of the day, month and year aforesaid.

____
President

Attest: ______________
Secretary

§ 43.14 Coupon Collateral Trust Bond—Coupon Is Not Registered

______ CORPORATION

COLLATERAL TRUST ______ PER CENT BOND

TOTAL AUTHORIZED ISSUE $______

No. ______ $______

______ Corporation, a Corporation organized and existing under the laws of the State of ______, for value received, promises to pay to the bearer, or, in case of registration, to the registered holder hereof, ______ Dollars, on ______ (or earlier), with interest on said sum from the date hereof at the rate of ______ per cent per annum, payable semiannually on the first days of ______ and ______ of each year, at the office of ______ Trust Company, upon surrender of the respective coupons attached hereto as they severally become due.

This bond is one of a series of bonds aggregating $[*Dollars*] in amount, dated ______, maturing [*Date*], issued and to be issued by the Corporation and being as far as may be of like tenor and effect. Bonds of said series may be in the form of bonds of the denomination of $[*Dollars*] each, numbered consecutively from one (1) to [*Number*] inclusive.

All bonds of said series are, as to both principal and interest, issued under and equally secured by a mortgage dated ______, 19__, whereby ______ Corporation has mortgaged and pledged all its property now owned and hereafter acquired to ______ Trust Company and ______, as Trustees, as provided in said mortgage as security for said bonds; and reference is hereby made to said mortgage for a description of the properties mortgaged and pledged to ______ Trust Company and ______ as such Trustees and the rights of the holders of said bonds under the same and the terms and conditions upon which said bonds are issued and secured. Said mortgage provides for the creation of a sinking fund in the hands of ______ Trust Company.

This bond may be called and redeemed from the holder on any interest day in the manner provided in said mortgage on payment of the principal sum hereof with a premium of ______ per cent thereon, and accrued interest. Interest shall cease to be payable to the holder of this bond if it is thus called, and payment is duly provided, from and after the date fixed in the call for payment.

This bond, but not its coupons, is subject to registration from time to time in accordance with the registration privileges endorsed hereon. Registration shall not affect the negotiability of the coupons, which shall continue to be transferable by delivery, and the payment of any coupon to the bearer thereof shall be a discharge of the obligor in respect to the interest therein mentioned. This coupon bond, with all coupons for future interest hereon, is, either singly or together with other bonds of said series, exchangeable for a registered bond without coupons of said series of a denomination equivalent to the sum total of the principal obligations represented by the bond or bonds for which it is exchanged.

In the event of default the principal of this bond may become or be declared due and payable before maturity, as provided in said deed of trust.

This bond shall not become obligatory for any purpose until the certificate hereon shall have been signed by said ______ Trust Company.

In witness whereof, ______ Corporation has caused these presents to be executed in its name and behalf and its corporate seal to be hereto affixed by its President or a Vice-President and its Secretary or an Assistant Secretary, thereunto duly authorized, and has likewise caused the annexed coupons to be authenticated by a facsimile of the signature of its Treasurer as of the first day of ______, 19__.

______ Corporation

Attest: __________ By __________

Secretary President

[*Form of Coupon*]

No. ______ ______

On the first day of ______, 19__, upon surrender hereof, ______ Company will pay to the bearer at the office of ______ Trust Company in ______, or its successor, ______ Dollars in legal tender of the United States of America, being six (6) months' interest then due on its ______ Per Cent Serial Bond No. ______ unless said bond shall have been previously called and payment duly provided therefor.

____

Treasurer

Trustee's Certificate

______ Trust Company, Trustee, hereby certifies that this bond is one of the series referred to in the within-mentioned deed of trust.

______ Trust Company, Trustee

By __________

Secretary

§ 43.15 Sophisticated Debt Instrument

Generally, the Articles of Incorporation will not authorize the issuance of debt since by statute e. g. Model Bus.Corp.Act § 4(h) the Board is already granted the implied power to issue all forms of debt (unless the Articles deny this right to the Board).

However, the nature of the debt instrument set forth below may be so similar to stock in its rights and preferences or it may supercede Stockholders' rights that prudence may require Stockholder approval and authorization by the Articles of Incorporation.

The following is the form for a sophisticated debt instrument.

Table of Contents

$[*Dollars*] [*Name of Corporation*]

of

[*State of Incorporation*]

Alternative A–1

Unsecured Bond

Alternative A–2

Secured Bond

Alternative A–3

Mortgage Bond

No. ______

Class ______

Series ______

COMMENT

The class of a debt instrument should be used to denote different rights and preferences among different debt instruments of the same title. The series should denote a different redemption date or sinking fund (if any) priority among the same class.

For value received [*Name of Corporation*], of [*State of Incorporation*] promises to pay

Alternative B–1

to the bearer

Alternative B–2

to the registered owner

the sum of $[*Dollars*] plus interest at the rate of [*Rate*] percent per annum on the unpaid principal until fully paid. Said principal and accrued interest shall be paid by the undersigned in lawful money of the United States of America, at [*Address of Lender*], as follows.

(a) **Terms.** The principal and accrued interest shall be payable in *equal* installments of principal of $[*Dollars*] [*plus/including*] interest due on the ______ day of each [*month/quarter/year*] beginning on the ______ day of ______, 19__ to holders of record as of ______ days before such date; but in any case, all principal and interest shall be due and payable on or before [*Date or Demand*]. This debt instrument may be prepaid in part or in full with accrued interest without penalty at any time.

(b) **Default.** Should default be made in the payment of interest and/or principal due hereunder, then such default shall mature the entire indebtedness evidenced hereby, without notice, at the option of the holder hereof. Every person at any time liable for the payment of the debt evidenced hereby, waives presentment for payment, demand and notice of non-payment of this debt instrument and consents that the holder may extend the time of payment of any part of the whole of the debt at any time at the request of any other person liable hereunder.

Any delay on the part of the Payee in exercising any rights hereunder shall not operate as a waiver of said rights; acceptance of any payment after its due date shall not be deemed a waiver of the right to require prompt payment when due of all other sums, acceptance of any payment after the Payee has declared the entire indebtedness due and payable shall not cure any default of the maker or operate as a waiver of any rights of the Payee hereunder.

This debt instrument shall be paid without claim of set-off or deduction of any nature or for any cause whatsoever.

At the option of the Payee, this debt instrument shall become immediately due and payable without notice or demand on the happening of any one of the following events: the filing of a petition by or against the maker or any guarantor of the maker) under the provisions of any state insolvency law or under the provisions of the Federal Bankruptcy Act (for bankruptcy or reorganization or other relief), or any assignment by the maker (or any guarantor of the maker) for the benefit of his creditors.

Upon default, the maker agrees to pay all costs and actual attorney fees of collection.

Option 1

(c) Security Interest. The preferences, limitations and conditions which pertain to this debt instrument are as follows:

Alternative B–1

The holder of this debt instrument shall be secured as a general creditor of the Corporation.

Alternative B–2

The holder of this debt instrument shall have a security interest in the following assets of the Corporation:

Alternative B–2(A)

real property described in the mortgage recorded in Liber —— Page —— of the [*Name*] County Records of the State of [*Name*].

Alternative B–2(B)

Personal property described as follows, which security interest is secured by a UCC–1 statement recorded in the records of [*Name*] County of the State of [*Name*] and the office of the Secretary of State, State of [*Name*]: [*Describe Property*].

COMMENT

See UCC–1 financing statement at § 43.22, infra and the Agreement between the Corporation and trustees as to interest and dividends pledged to secure collateral trust bonds.

Alternative B–2(C)

A sinking fund as provided below.

Option 2

(d) Prohibition Against Stock or Security Priorities. In no event shall the Corporation issue any debt, stock or other security:

Alternative C–1

which shall have a higher security priority than this debt instrument.

Alternative C–2

which shall have an equal or higher priority than this debt instrument other than debt instruments totaling $______ of principal value with the same terms as this debt instrument.

Provided that such restrictions shall not apply to security interests which arise by the operation of law.

COMMENT

The Uniform Commercial Code (*or* other commercial code) will determine what security interest arises automatically upon the rendering of services or supplying of goods. The purpose of this provision is to leave open the possibility that the holder of the debt instrument's rights may be subordinate to those rights which arise by operation of law.

Alternative B–3

The holder of this debt instrument shall have a priority, although unsecured against fully secured creditors, against general creditors in the following assets:

Alternative B–3(A)

all assets.

Alternative B–3(B)

all real property.

Alternative B–3(C)

all personal property.

Alternative B–3(D)

all property in excess of $______ value.

Alternative B–3(E)

all non-tangible assets.

Alternative B–3(F)

[*List Specific Property*].

In the instance of one or more of the following events the holders of this debt instrument shall have a priority security interest and

[*Name*], acting as Trustee, shall perfect such priority to the extent possible by filing the [*UCC–1 Statement/mortgage*] already delivered to him. In such case said priority shall be greater than any Stockholder or general creditor. The events upon which such filing shall take place are:

Alternative C–1

All events.

Alternative C–2

The Corporation's bankruptcy or assignment of some or all of its assets for the benefit of its creditors.

Alternative C–3

A receiver being appointed to manage any of the Corporation's assets.

Alternative C–4

A receiver being appointed to manage those assets of the Corporation which the holder of this debt instrument has a direct or indirect security interest, other than as a general creditor.

Alternative C–5

A levy of attachment being issued or other action being issued or other action being taken which results in another claiming a priority interest (whether such claim is of an interest equal to, lesser or greater than the debt instrument holders).

Alternative C–6

The Corporation selling, exchanging or surrendering a security interest in or liquidating substantially all of its net assets.

Alternative C–7

The Corporation selling, exchanging, surrendering a security interest in or liquidating a substantial portion of its net assets.

Alternative C–8

The Corporation selling, exchanging, surrendering a security interest in or liquidating any of its assets in a manner not consistent with the ordinary course of its business.

Alternative C–9

The Corporation taking any action which reduces the net book value of the assets subject to the security interest set forth herein to an amount equal to less than ______% of the principal and accumulated interest amount being secured.

Alternative C–10

The Corporation taking any action which reduces the net fair market value of the assets subject to the security interest set forth herein to an amount equal to less than ______% of the then principal and accumulated interest amount being secured.

Alternative C–11

The Corporation merging or consolidating.

COMMENTS TO ALTERNATIVES B–3 AND C

This language will create a contingent perfected interest which, upon the happening of the recited event(s) will be perfected (and will be subordinate to all then perfected interests). Before such time, the interest will be unperfected and will allow other creditors (such as banks) to fully secure their loans. Upon a named event, the holders will have a priority over all general creditors, unsecured debt holders and Stockholders (subject to the bankruptcy court voiding the same as a fraud against creditors).

The Uniform Commercial Code provides:

Security interest is enforceable against the debtor or third parties if the debtor has signed a security agreement which contains a description of the collateral and in addition, when the security interest covers crops or oil, gas or minerals to be extracted or timber to be cut, a description of the land concerned. In describing collateral, the word "proceeds" is sufficient without further description to cover proceeds of any character.

Any description of personal property or real estate is sufficient whether or not it is specific if it reasonably identifies what is described.

An unperfected security interest is subordinate to the rights of

(a) a person who becomes a lien creditor without knowledge of the security interest and before it is perfected;

(b) in the case of goods, instruments, documents, and chattel paper, a person who is not a secured party and who is a transferee in bulk or other buyer not in ordinary course of business to the extent that he gives value and receives delivery of the collateral without knowledge of the security interest and before it is perfected;

(c) in the case of accounts, contract rights, and general intangibles, a person who is not a secured party and who is a transferee to the extent that he gives value without knowledge of the security interest and before it is perfected.

(d) a security interest perfected by a filing or by operation of law. See Uniform Commercial Code § 9.312.

(e) Procedures. The Board of Directors of the Corporation, or a committee established by it, shall have the right from time to time to adopt specific rules of procedure to carry out the full intent of this security interest provision and to do all reasonable acts necessary therefore; provided that such rules and acts shall not violate the specific terms of this debt instrument.

Option 3

(f) Liquidation. If the Corporation is liquidated, the holder of this debt instrument shall have the right to a sum equal to the then principal and current and accumulated interest (if any) owing.

Option 4

(g) Redemption Demanded by Debt Holder. The debt holder, at his option, may demand that the Corporation redeem this debt instrument upon the following terms and conditions:

(1) Notice. The debt holder shall tender by telegram or personal delivery or registered or certified mail, postage prepaid, this instrument by the following notice directed to the corporate treasurer:

> "take notice that on this date the undersigned hereby demands redemption of a certain debt instrument No. ______ according to the terms and conditions of such debt instrument."

(2) Payment. Upon receipt of this debt instrument properly endorsed and a proper notice, the corporate Treasurer shall, within *ten (10)* working days, forward to the debt holder the full amount herein set forth.

(3) Price. The price for each $100 of face value of such instrument shall be all accrued interest plus the *greater of/lesser of*:

(A) $______ or

Alternative D–1

(B) An amount equal to ______% of the Corporation's then book value plus accrued interest.

Alternative D–2

(B) An amount equal to the Corporation's then book value times a percentage equal to the share of the net value of the Corporation represented by the face value of this certificate as it relates to the par value of all outstanding stock and the face value of all outstanding debt,

Alternative D–3

(B) An amount equal to ______% of the Corporation's then fair market value as determined by appraisal plus accrued interest.

Any one of the following appraisal methods shall be used:

Alternative D–3(A)

(i) An appraisal by Certified Public Accountants who are not then engaged by the Corporation.

Alternative D–3(B)

(i) An appraisal by one person chosen by the rules of the American Arbitration Association.

Alternative D–3(C)

(i) An appraisal by two or more persons, one of whom shall be chosen by the Corporation and one by the bondholders. If the higher appraised value is within 10% of the lower value then the average of the two values shall be used; if they are not within 10% of each other, then the two appraisers shall agree on a third appraiser who shall:

Alternative D–4(A)

* choose among the two amounts only.

Alternative D–4(B)

* choose any value between the two amounts.

The chief financial officer of a National Banking Company or his delegate which does no business with the Corporation or any of its officers or Directors shall represent such debt holder's rights at the Corporation's expense.

(4) Priority. If a demand for redemption is made by more than one debt holder, and the Corporation cannot then honor all such demands then made:

Alternative E–1

such debt instruments shall be redeemed in proportion to the redemption value of all of the debt instruments of similar priority so tendered by the tendering debt holders.

Alternative E–2

the demands shall be honored according to their day of written receipt by the Corporation (with demands received during the same period when the Corporation is not normally open for business being considered to have been received on what would be the next normal business day).

Demands received (*or* deemed to be received) on the same day shall be deemed to be received at the same time and shall be redeemed in proportion to the redemption value of all of the debt instruments of similar priority so tendered by the tendering debt holders.

Option 5

Provided that no redemption shall be made which cannot be effectuated in compliance with the terms and conditions set forth as part of the sinking fund section of this debt instrument.

COMMENT TO OPTION 4

This provision should not be used unless a sinking fund is to be established (see Option below).

(5) Conditions. The right to demand redemption shall only be exercisable:

Alternative F–1

in all events.

Alternative F–2

before the ______ day of ______, 19__.

Alternative F–3

after the ______ day of ______, 19__.

Alternative F–4

upon the Corporation's bankruptcy or assignment of some or all of its assets for the benefit of its creditors.

Alternative F–5

upon a receiver being appointed to manage any of the Corporation's assets.

Alternative F–6

upon a receiver being appointed to manage those assets of the Corporation which the holder of this debt instrument has a direct or indirect security interest, other than as a general creditor.

Alternative F–7

upon a levy of attachment being issued or other action being taken which results in another claiming a priority interest (whether such claim is of an interest equal to, lesser or greater than the debt holders).

Alternative F–8

upon the Corporation selling, exchanging, surrendering a security interest in or liquidating substantially all of its net assets.

Alternative F–9

upon the Corporation selling, exchanging, surrendering a security interest in or liquidating a substantial portion of its net assets.

Alternative F–10

upon the Corporation selling, exchanging, surrendering a security interest in or liquidating any of its assets in a manner not consistent with the ordinary course of its business.

Alternative F–11

upon the Corporation taking any action which reduces the net book value of the assets subject to the security interest set forth herein to an amount equal to less than ______% of the then principal and accumulated interest amount being secured and any other interest with equal or higher priority.

Alternative F–12

the Corporation taking any action which reduces the net fair market value of the assets subject to the security interest set forth herein to an amount equal to less than ______% of the then principal and accumulated interest amount being secured.

COMMENT TO F–12

Use only if debt is secured.

Alternative F–14

as follows:

Redemption Priority (from highest to lowest)	Class	Series	Earliest Date of Redemption	Last Date of Redemption	Price
1	A	1			
2	A	2			
3	A	3			
4	A	4			
5	A	5			

The Corporation shall redeem only those debt instruments set forth in the above schedule and only at the price relative to the year in which such redemption is to occur (as set forth in said schedule).

(6) Procedures. The Board of Directors of the Corporation, or a committee established by it, shall have the right from time to time to adopt specific rules of procedure to carry out the full intent of this security interest provision and to do all reasonable acts necessary therefore; provided that such rules and acts shall not violate the specific terms of this debt instrument.

Option 6

(h) Redemption (Call) by the Corporation. The Corporation shall have the absolute right to redeem this debt instrument upon the following terms and conditions:

(1) Notice. The Corporation shall send by registered or certified mail, postage prepaid, a notice stating that it will deliver the full redemption price to the debt holder upon surrender of the debt instrument.

(2) Interest Accrual. Interest shall:

Alternative G–1

continue to accrue until surrender of the debt instrument.

Alternative G–2

terminate *ten* (*10*) days after such notice.

(3) Full Redemption Price. The price for each $*100* of principal shall be all accrued interest plus the *greater of* $[*Dollars*] or

Alternative H–1

an amount equal to ______% of the Corporation's then book value plus accrued interest.

Alternative H–2

an amount equal to ______% of the Corporation's then fair market value as determined by appraisal plus accrued interest.

Any one of the following appraisal methods shall be deemed reasonable:

Alternative H–2(A)

an appraisal by Certified Public Accountants who are not then engaged by the Corporation.

Alternative H–2(B)

an appraisal by one person chosen by the rules of the American Arbitration Association.

Alternative H–2(C)

an appraisal by two persons, one of whom shall be chosen by the Corporation and one by the holders. If the higher value is within 10% of the lower value then the average of the two values shall be used; if they are not within 10% of each other, then the two appraisers shall agree on a third appraiser who shall:

Alternative H–3(A)

* choose among the two amounts only.

Alternative H–3(B)

* choose any value between the two amounts.

The chief financial officer of a National Banking Company or his delegate which does no business with the Corporation or any of its officers or directors shall represent such holders rights at the Corporation's expense.

(4) Terms. The terms of such redemption shall be

Alternative I–1

cash

Alternative I–2

______% down and even monthly payments [*including/plus*] ______% interest over ______ months.

(5) Conditions. The right to demand redemption shall only be exercisable:

Alternative J–1

in all events

Alternative J–2

before the ______ day of ______, 19__.

Alternative J–3

after the ______ day of ______, 19__.

Alternative J–4

upon the Corporation's bankruptcy or assignment of some or all of its assets for the benefit of its creditors.

Alternative J–5

upon a receiver being appointed to manage any of the Corporation's assets.

Alternative J–6

upon a receiver being appointed to manage those assets of the Corporation which the holder of this debt instrument has a direct or indirect security interest, other than as a general creditor.

Alternative J–7

upon a levy of attachment being issued or other action being taken which results in another claiming a priority interest (whether such claim is of an interest equal to, lesser or greater than the debt holders).

Alternative J–8

upon the Corporation selling, exchanging, surrendering a security interest or liquidating substantially all of its net assets.

Alternative J–9

upon the Corporation selling, exchanging, surrendering a security interest in or liquidating a substantial portion of its net assets.

Alternative J–10

upon the Corporation selling, exchanging, surrendering a security interest in or liquidating any of its assets in a manner not consistent with the ordinary course of its business.

Alternative J–11

upon the Corporation taking any action which reduces the net book value of the assets subject to the first security interest set forth herein to an amount equal to less than ______% of the then principal and accumulated interest amount being secured and any other debt with equal or higher priority.

Alternative J–12

the Corporation taking any action which reduces the net fair market value of the assets subject to the security interest set forth herein to an amount equal to less than ______% of the then principal and accumulated interest amount being secured.

COMMENT TO J–12

Use only if debt is secured.

Alternative J–13

as follows:

Redemption Priority (from highest to lowest)	Class	Series	Earliest Date of Redemption	Last Date of Redemption	Price
1	A	1			
2	A	2			
3	A	3			
4	A	4			
5	A	5			

The Corporation shall redeem only those debt instruments set forth in the above schedule and only at the price relative to the year in which such redemption is to occur (as set forth in said schedule).

Alternative J–14

if the then prime rate of ______ Bank is at least [*Number*] Points less than the interest rate to be paid on this debt instrument.

Alternative J–15

the Corporation merging or consolidating.

(6) Effective Date. Upon a notice being sent to the holder and after the expiration of a *ten* (*10*) day notice period, the redemption shall be deemed to have occurred and he shall no longer have any rights in the Corporation, except as follows below:

Option 6–A

(A) Upon a redemption being noticed and until such time as the debt holder shall be completely redeemed, then the debt holder's security rights in the Corporation's assets shall be:

Alternative M–1

as a general creditor.

Alternative M–2

with the same security and priority that such holder had when he was entitled to this debt instrument.

Option 6–B

(B) Upon a redemption being noticed, the debt holder shall lose any right he may have to convert or demand redemption of this debt instrument.

(7) Procedures. The Board of Directors of the Corporation, or a committee established by it, shall have the right from time to time to adopt specific rules of procedure to carry out the full intent of this redemption provision and to do all reasonable acts necessary therefore; provided that such rules and acts shall not violate the specific terms of this debt instrument.

Option 7

(i) Conversion Rights. The holders of this debt instrument shall have the following conversion rights upon the following events:

To convert each $______ of face value into shares of [*Describe the Stock and Its Class, Series or Preference, if Any*].

Option 7–A

(1) Consideration. To effectuate such conversion, the certificate holder shall tender to [*Name or Position*] at [*Address*] this certificate together with the following consideration: $______ per $______ of face value being converted.

Option 7–B

(2) Terms. The conversion shall only be exercised within the following time period:

Alternative K–1

At any time

Alternative K–2

Before the ______ day of ______, 19__.

Alternative K–3

After the ______ day of ______, 19__.

Alternative K–4

Upon the Corporation's bankruptcy or assignment of some or all of its assets for the benefit of its creditors.

Alternative K–5

Upon a receiver being appointed to manage any of the Corporation's assets.

Alternative K–6

Upon a receiver being appointed to manage those assets of the Corporation which the holder of this debt instrument has a direct or indirect security interest in, other than as a general creditor.

Alternative K–7

Upon a levy of attachment being issued or other action being taken which results in another claiming a priority interest (whether such claim is of an interest equal to, lesser or greater than the debt holders).

Alternative K–8

Upon the Corporation selling, exchanging, surrendering a security interest or liquidating substantially all of its net assets.

Alternative K–9

Upon the Corporation selling, exchanging, surrendering a security interest in or liquidating a substantial portion of its net assets.

Alternative K–10

Upon the Corporation selling, exchanging, surrendering a security interest in or liquidating any of its assets in a manner not consistent with the ordinary course of its business.

Alternative K–11

Upon the Corporation taking any action which reduces the net book value of the assets subject to the first security interest set forth herein to an amount equal to less than _______% of the then principal and accumulated interest amount being secured and any other debt with equal or higher priority.

Alternative K–12

The Corporation taking any action which reduces the net fair market value of the assets subject to the security interest set forth herein to an amount equal to less than _______% of the then principal and accumulated interest amount being secured.

COMMENT TO ALTERNATIVE K–12

Use only if the debt in question is secured.

Alternative K–13

The Corporation merging or consolidating.

These provisions for conversion shall be subject to all applicable statutory limits and restrictions; provided however, that the Corporation shall do all things legally possible to arrange for such conversion if such conversion rights are exercised.

Upon such conversion the Corporation shall forthwith issue to the holder of such convertible debt instrument the stock or instrument which he is entitled to and shall deliver to such converting debt instrument holder the same in due form. Such new certificate or instrument shall have the following restrictions:

Alternative L–1

none

Alternative L–2

restrictions, if any, intended to prevent securities law violations, as may be required by the Corporation's counsel from time to time.

Alternative L–3

the Buy-Sell restrictions, if any, of any Buy-Sell Agreement then of general effect which binds at least *80%* of all issued stock, by value.

The number of shares of stock necessary to fully effectuate the conversion privileges set forth herein shall be authorized as of this date and shall be set aside by the Corporation and only issued pursuant to conversion privileges set forth herein. Such shares shall not be cancelled at any time that the conversion privileges set forth herein are outstanding.

Option 8

The conversion privileges set forth herein may be altered at any time by the vote of a majority of the Directors of the Corporation and by a vote of:

Alternative M–1(A)

if the conversion is to be more favorable in every aspect to the debt instrument holder in question, then by a vote of the majority of the stock of the Corporation then outstanding.

Alternative M–1(B)

if the conversion terms are in any aspect less favorable to the debt instrument holder then by a vote of ______% of all stock entitled to vote.

Alternative M–1(C)

if the terms are in any aspect less favorable to the debt instrument holder, then the vote of a majority of all stock entitled to vote and by the majority (measured by face value) of the debt holders whose rights will be impaired by such change.

(3) Stock Transfer Books. Nothing herein to the contrary notwistanding, no conversion shall be made by the Corporation while the stock transfer books are closed.

(4) Fractional Shares. No fractional shares of common stock shall be issued upon conversion of such debt. Instead of any fractional share which would otherwise be issued upon conversion, the Corporation will pay a cash adjustment in respect of such fractional interest in an amount equal to the same fraction of the current market price per share of common stock (determined as provided herein) on the day of conversion.

The value of each share of stock shall be:

(A) Equal to $______.

Alternative A–2

(A) Equal to such stock's proportionate share of the Corporation's then book value exclusive of the par value of all common stock.

Alternative A–3

(A) Equal to ______% of such stock's proportional share of the Corporation's then fair market value as determined by an appraisal less the par value of all common stock.

Any one of the following appraisal methods shall be deemed reasonable:

Alternative A–1

(i) An appraisal by a Certified Public Accountant who is not then engaged by the Corporation.

Alternative A–2

(i) An appraisal by one or more persons chosen by the rules of the American Arbitration Association.

Alternative A–3

(i) An appraisal by two persons, each chosen by the two sides to the question. If this higher value is within 10% of the lower value then the average of the two values shall be used; if they are not so close, then the two appraisers shall agree on a third appraiser who shall:

Alternative A–3(A)

* Choose among the two amounts only.

Alternative A–3(B)

* Choose any value between the two amounts.

Alternative A–4

(i) The Corporation's appraisal, which shall be final.

The chief financial officer of a National Banking Company or his delegate which does no business with the Corporation shall represent such Stockholders rights at the Corporation's expense.

(5) Adjustment of Conversion Price. The conversion price referred to herein shall be subject to adjustment from time to time as follows:

(A) In case the Corporation shall at any time subdivide the outstanding shares of [*Describe Stock to Be Received*] the conversion price in effect immediately prior to such subdivision shall be proportionately decreased; and in case the Corporation shall at any time combine the outstanding shares of [*Describe Stock to Be Received*], the conversion price in effect immediately prior to such combination shall be proportionately increased, effective at the close of business on the date of such subdivision or combination as the case may be. For the purposes of this subparagraph, any distribution of shares of [*Describe Stock to Be Received*] shall be deemed to be a subdivision, irrespective of the accounting treatment thereof.

(B) In case [*Describe Stock to Be Received*] of the Corporation issuable upon conversion of such debt shall be changed into another kind of capital stock or debt (otherwise than through a subdivision or combination of shares) or shall represent the right to receive some other security or property, as a result of any capital reorganization, reclassification or any merger or consolidation with another Corporation in which the Corporation is not the surviving Corporation, or any sale of all or substantially all of the assets of the Corporation to another Corporation, each $*100* of such debt shall (subject to further adjustment in conversion price as herein provided) thereafter entitle the debt holder to acquire upon conversion thereof the kind and number of shares of stock or other securities or property to which such holder would have been entitled if he had held the [*Describe Stock to Be Received*] issuable upon the conversion of his debt immediately prior to such capital reorganization, reclassification, merger, consolidation or sale of assets.

Whenever the conversion price shall be adjusted as provided in this subparagraph, the Corporation shall forthwith file at each office designated for the conversion of shares of this instrument a statement, signed by the Chairman of the Board, the President, any Vice President or the Treasurer of the Corporation, showing in reasonable detail the facts requiring such adjustment and the conversion price that will be effective after such adjustment. The Corporation shall forthwith also cause a notice setting forth any such adjustments to be sent by first class mail, postage prepaid, to each registered holder of such debt at his address appearing on the stock register.

(6) Notice of Change of Rights. In case:

(A) The Corporation shall declare a dividend (or make any other distribution) on its [*Describe Stock to Be Received*] payable otherwise than in cash out of the consolidated earnings surplus of the Corporation and its subsidiaries; or

(B) The Corporation shall authorize the granting to the holders of its [*Describe Stock to Be Received*] of rights to subscribe for or purchase any shares of capital stock of any class or any other rights; or

(C) Of any reclassification of the [*Describe Stock to Be Received*] of the Corporation (other than a subdivision or a combination of its outstanding shares of such stock), of any consolidation or merger to which the Corporation is a party and for which approval of any Stockholders of the Corporation is required or of the sale or transfer of all or substantially all the assets of the Corporation; or

(D) Of the voluntary or involuntary dissolution, liquidation or winding up of the Corporation;

then the Corporation shall cause to be filed at the office of the Corporation and shall cause to be mailed to the holders of this debt instrument at their addresses as they shall appear on the records of the Corporation at least *ten (10)* days prior to the record date specified in (i) below or *twenty (20)* days before the date specified in (ii) below, a notice stating:

(i) the record date for such dividend, distribution or rights or, if a record is not to be taken, the date as of which the holders of [*Describe Stock to Be Received*] of record to be entitled to such dividend, distribution or rights are to be determined; or

(ii) the date on which such reclassification, consolidation, merger, sale, transfer, dissolution, liquidation or winding up is expected to become effective, and the date as of which it is expected that holders of [*Describe Stock to Be Received*] of record shall be entitled to exchange their shares of such stock for securities or other property deliverable upon such reclassification, consolidation, merger, sale, transfer, dissolution, liquidation or winding up.

The Corporation will pay any documentary stamp taxes attributable to the initial issuance of shares of [*Describe Stock to Be Received*] upon conversion of any shares of such debt pursuant hereto.

(7) Procedures. The Board of Directors of the Corporation, or a committee established by it, shall have the right from time to time to adopt specific rules of procedure to carry out the full intent of this conversion provision and to do all reasonable acts necessary therefore; provided that such rules and acts shall not violate the specific terms of this debt instrument.

Option 9

(j) Sinking Fund. (1) The following sinking fund shall be established to provide the funds necessary for part or all of the retirement of this debt instrument and other debt instruments.

Redemption Priority (from highest to lowest)	Class	Series	Price	Earliest Date of Redemption	Last Date of Redemption
1	A	1	$______		
2	A	2	$______		
3	A	3	$______		
4	A	4	$______		
5	A	5	$______		

(2) The Corporation shall redeem out of the sinking fund only those debt instruments set forth in the above schedule and only at the price relative to the year in which such redemption is to occur (as set forth in said schedule).

(3) The certificates which may be redeemed out of such sinking fund shall only be:

Option 9–A

(A) holders of this debt instrument and those instruments of the same class as this one.

Option 9–B

(B) holders exercising their right to demand redemption.

Option 9–C

(C) holders against whom the Corporation has a right to demand redemption.

Alternative P–1

Provided, that before any certificate of a lower priority is redeemed, all holders of a higher priority shall be notified that their option to take priority over such lower priorities will expire within 60 days of the notice date if such debt instrument is not tendered within such period. Upon the expiration of such date:

Alternative P–1(A)

such debt instrument shall lose its right to be redeemed.

Alternative P–1(B)

such debt instrument shall have highest priority of any debt instrument for which no such notice has been given.

Alternative P–2

Provided, that no redemption of lower priority shall take place without full redemption of all debt instruments of all higher priorities tendered for redemption first being redeemed.

(4) Said sinking fund shall be funded by a contribution of:

Alternative Q–1

______% of the net after tax profits of the Corporation of the fiscal year in question.

Alternative Q–2

$______ per fiscal year.

Alternative Q–3

$______ per fiscal year for every $100 of face value which may be redeemed out of such fund.

(5) The sinking fund shall be operated under the following additional procedures:

Option 10–A

(A) The Trustee of the fund shall be [*Name*].

Option 10–B

(B) The sinking fund shall be continued until all debt instruments have been redeemed or the redemption period has expired, whichever is earlier (at which time any of such funds not expended shall be returned to the Corporation's general assets).

Option 10–C

(C) The Trustee shall determine the amount of money held by such fund on the last day of the ______ month of each [*fiscal quarter/fiscal year*].

Alternative N–1

(D) The Trustee shall redeem as many of the debt instruments as possible out of said fund.

COMMENT TO ALTERNATIVE N–1

Use only if the Corporation has the right to demand redemption.

Alternative N–2

(D) The Trustee shall redeem as many of the certificates as are tendered out of such fund.

COMMENT TO ALTERNATIVE N–2

Use only if the Stockholder has the right to demand redemption.

(E) The Board of Directors of the Corporation, or a committee established by it, shall have the right from time to time to adopt specific rules of procedure to carry out the full intent of this sinking fund provision and to do all reasonable acts necessary therefore; provided that such rules and acts shall not violate the specific terms of this debt instrument.

Option 11

(k) Voting. The holders of each $*100* of face value of debt shall be entitled to ______ votes; provided that such voting shall be exercised only in the following instances:

Alternative R–1

whenever a matter is put to the Stockholders in general for their consideration.

Alternative R–2

whenever a matter is put to any group of Stockholders for their consideration.

Alternative R–3

upon the Corporation's bankruptcy or assignment of some or all of its assets for the benefit of its creditors.

Alternative R–4

upon a receiver being appointed to manage any of the Corporation's assets.

Alternative R–5

upon a receiver being appointed to manage those assets of the Corporation which the holder of this debt instrument has a direct or indirect security interest, other than as a general creditor.

Alternative R–6

upon a levy of attachment being issued or other action being taken which results in another claiming a priority interest (whether such claim is of an interest equal to, lesser or greater than the holders).

Alternative R–7

upon the Corporation selling, exchanging, surrendering a security interest or liquidating substantially all of its net assets.

Alternative R–8

upon the Corporation selling, exchanging, surrendering a security interest in or liquidating a substantial portion of its net assets.

Alternative R–9

upon the Corporation selling, exchanging, surrendering a security interest in or liquidating any of its assets in a manner not consistent with the ordinary course of its business.

Alternative R–10

upon the Corporation taking any action which reduces the new book value of the assets subject to the first security interest set forth herein to an amount equal to less than ______% of the then principal and accumulated interest amount being secured and any other certificate with equal or higher priority.

Alternative R–11

the Corporation taking any action which reduces the net fair market value of the assets subject to the security interest set forth herein to an amount equal to less than ______% of the then principal and accumulated interest amount being secured.

COMMENT TO ALTERNATIVE R–11

This clause should not be used if other Stockholders have been given the right to exclusively vote on a particular matter and if secured interest has been granted.

Alternative R–12

in those specific instances when the Stockholders are to vote whether or not the Corporation should act regarding any one or more of the following events:

Option 12(A)

(1) To sue, complain and defend, in its corporate name.

Option 12(B)

(2) To purchase, take, receive, lease or otherwise acquire, own, hold, improve, use and otherwise deal in and with, real or personal property, or any interest therein, wherever situated.

Option 12(C)

(3) To merge, sell, convey, mortgage, pledge, lease, exchange, transfer and otherwise dispose of all or any part of its property and assets.

Option 12(D)

(4) To lend money and use its credit to assist its employees.

Option 12(E)

(5) To purchase, take, receive, subscribe for, or otherwise acquire, own, hold, vote, use, employ, sell, mortgage, lend, pledge, or otherwise dispose of, and otherwise use and deal in and with, shares or other interests in, or obligations of, other domestic or foreign corporations, associations, partnerships or individuals, or direct or indirect obligations of the United States or of any other government, state, territory, governmental district or municipality or of any instrumentality thereof.

Option 12(F)

(6) To make contracts and guarantees and incur liabilities, borrow money, issue its bonds, and other obligations, or secure any of its obligations by mortgage or pledge of all or any of its property, franchises and income.

Option 12(G)

(7) To lend money.

Option 12(H)

(8) To elect or appoint officers and agents of the Corporation, and define their duties and fix their compensation.

Option 12(I)

(9) To make and alter By-laws, not inconsistent with its Articles of Incorporation, for the administration and regulation of the affairs of the Corporation.

Option 12(J)

(10) To make donations for the public welfare or for charitable, scientific or educational purposes.

Option 12(K)

(11) To pay pensions and establish pension plans, pension trusts, profit sharing plans, stock bonus plans, stock option plans and other incentive plans for any or all of its Directors, Officers and employees.

Option 12(L)

(12) To be a promoter, partner, member, associate, or manager of any partnership, joint venture, trust or other enterprise.

Alternative S–1

Such vote shall be entitled along with the holders of any other voting certificate to vote in any annual or special meeting called for the purpose of determining a question properly put to the Stockholders of this Corporation; and such share shall be included in determining both the quorum present and in determining the number of votes necessary in order to determine any particular matter.

Alternative S–2

Upon such event the holders of this debt instrument shall be divided into a single class and the holders of all other stock and securities issued by the Corporation shall be divided into a second class and each class shall vote separately and shall be entitled to elect ______ Directors. Further the voting power of each class shall be redetermined so that the total number of votes of each class shall be equal between them and the proportionate shares of stock or debt outstanding in each class shall represent that proportion of each classes individual voting strength; with the result that the particular voting shares or instruments of each particular class shall determine (on a cumulative basis) the various positions which each particular class shall take on any particular issue. For instance, the common Stockholders might agree that ⅔ of them desire to vote for position A and ⅓ desire to vote for position B and the debt holders may vote that

¾ of them desire to vote for position B and ¼ desire to vote for position A. In this case the total votes for position A would be ¼ plus ⅔ divided by 2 (or 45%) and the votes for position B would be the remaining number of votes.

Alternative S–3

Immediately upon the happening of such event and until such defaults have been cured, all common and preferred Stockholders shall have no voting power whatsoever in the election of the Directors or in any other question (other than as to any proposed change in the number of shares outstanding, the rights and preferences of any shares outstanding, or the relative rights and preferences of any shares outstanding) and the entire voting power of the Corporation shall be invested exclusively in these [*Describe This Instrument and Class*].

Alternative S–4

Immediately upon the happening of such event and until such default has been cured no common or preferred stock shall have any voting power as to the election of the Board of Directors and the entire voting power as to such elections shall be vested exclusively in these [*Describe This Instrument and Class*].

Option 13

(*l*) **Security Laws.** The debt holders may be deemed to be "underwriters" under the Securities Act of 1933 (the "Securities Act"), and thus they are required to comply with the requirements of the Securities Act, the Securities Exchange Act of 1934 (the "Exchange Act"), various rules and regulations of the Securities and Exchange Commission (the "Commission") and state securities laws in connection with any offer or transfer of this debt instrument.

Alternative A–1

The debt holders acknowledge that the Corporation has no obligation under these securities laws to register this instrument or to provide a prospectus for any offer or transfer thereof by the debt holders.

Alternative A–2

The Corporation hereby agrees and covenants that it will register the debt instrument and provide a prospectus for offers and transfers of the debt instrument as follows.

Each debt instrument shall be imprinted with a legend in substantially the following form:

"The offer and transfer of the debt represented by this instrument are subject to compliance with the Securities Act of 1933, the Securities Exchange Act of 1934, rules and regulations of the Securities and Exchange Commission, State securities laws and no transfer of the debt represented by this instrument shall be valid or effective unless made in accordance therewith. To the extent provided therein, all transferees of shares represented by this instrument shall be bound by such agreement."

The debt holders agree, prior to any transfer or attempted transfer of the debt instrument to give written notice to the Corporation of the intention to make such transfer. Such notice shall describe the manner and circumstances of the proposed transfer in detail shall contain an undertaking by the debt holder giving such notice to furnish such further information as may be reasonably required of the Corporation by law in furnishing information to the Securities and Exchange Commission and the relevant state securities commissioner and shall be accompanied by an agreement in the form prescribed by the Corporation (said form to be made available at the Corporation expense within *twenty (20)* days of notice to the Corporation of a proposed transaction) by each proposed transferee of the debt instrument to be bound by the provisions of this Section with respect to the offer or transfer by such transferee of this debt instrument. Each instrument issued upon the transfer of any of the debt instruments shall have the restrictive legend contained herein conspicuously imprinted on it.

The Corporation will authorize the issuance to the debt holder upon his written request and authorization instruments representing the appropriate amount of debt not bearing the above legend at such time as the registration and delivery requirements of the Security and Exchange Act no longer require that offers and transfers of the debt be accompanied by a prospectus.

Option 14

The debt holders shall indemnify and hold harmless the Corporation, each of its officers who signs any Registration Statement, each person who may be liable as a director of the Corporation or as a person who controls or shall have controlled the Corporation within the meaning of the Securities Act, from and against any such expenses, losses, claims, damages, liabilities or actions arising out of or based upon any untrue statement or alleged untrue statement or omission or alleged omission based upon information furnished to the Corporation by or on behalf of the holders for use in any Registration Statement or upon the failure of the holders to provide such information after having received a request for such information, and also in respect of any expenses, losses, claims, damages, liabilities or actions, joint or several, to which any such person may become subject under the Securities Act, the Exchange Act, state securities laws, the common law or otherwise with respect to an offer or transfer of the debt instrument or the case of any claim or the commencement of any action in respect of which indemnity may be sought from the then debt holders on account of the indemnity agreement contained in this subsection.

(m) Endorsement as to Exchangeability for Other Denominations. As provided in the face of the bond, coupon bonds of this issue are exchangeable for an equal principal amount of coupon bonds of other denominations or of registered bonds, which registered bonds are in turn exchangeable for coupon bonds.

(n) Negative Pledge Clause in Debenture. The Corporation hereby covenants and agrees with the holder hereof that so long as this debenture shall be outstanding and provision for the payment thereof shall not have been made it will not mortgage nor pledge any of its property unless the instrument creating such mortgage or pledge shall provide that this debenture shall be secured thereby equally and ratably with all other obligations issued or to be issued thereunder, except that the Corporation without so securing this debenture (1) may at any time mortgage or pledge any of its property for the purpose of securing loans to the Corporation contracted in the usual course of business for periods not exceeding one year, and (2) may, in order to secure the purchase price or part thereof of any property which it may hereafter acquire, mortgage or pledge any or all of such acquired property.

Dated: ______ [*Name of Corporation*]

Attest: __________, By _______________,

Its ______ Its ______

(*o*) Guaranty Endorsed on Bond—By Another Corporation. For value received, the undersigned, ______ Corporation, a [*State*] Corporation, has guaranteed and does hereby unconditionally guarantee to the bearer of the within bond, or, if registered, to the registered owner hereof, prompt payment by ______ Corporation of ______ of the principal of the within bond, either at the maturity thereof or at such earlier date as the said bond may become due and payable pursuant to the provisions of the indenture referred to therein, and of all interest due or to become due upon the said bond, hereby expressly waiving all demands and notices and the performance of each and every condition precedent to which the undersigned might otherwise be entitled by law.

Dated ______, 19__ [*Name of Corporation*]

Attest: __________ By _______________,

Its ______ President

§ 43.16 Interest Coupon

On the first day of ______, 19__, [*Name of Corporation*] will pay to the bearer at [*Address*] $[*Dollars*], being six months, interest due on its [*Describe*] bond, due ______, 19__.

No. ______ [*Name of Corporation*]

By __________, Treasurer

§ 43.17 Interest Coupon—Another Form

On the first day of ______, 19__, the ______ Corporation will pay to bearer, at its office at ______, ______, ______ Dollars ($______) in lawful money of the United States of America, being six (6) months interest then due on its First Mortgage Bond, No. ______.

____

Treasurer

COMMENT

Bearer bonds and debentures have attached coupons representing each interest payment for the life of the instrument. Coupons are detached as they mature in order to obtain the periodic payment of interest. Coupons are in effect promissory notes and are sometimes phrased in terms of "______ Corporation promises to pay * * *."

§ 43.18 Interest Coupon—Another Form

On the first day of [*Month*], 19__, the [*Name of Corporation*] Company will pay to bearer, at its office at No. ______ ______ Street, City of ______, County of ______, State of ______, ______ ($______) Dollars, in lawful money of the United States of America, being ______ (______) months interest then due on its First Mortgage Coupon Bond, No. ______.

____

Treasurer

§ 43.19 Trust Mortgage as Security for Indebtedness

The following is the mortgage form to be used with an instrument secured by land.

MORTGAGE

This mortgage, made [*Date*] ______ between [*Name of Corporation*] ______ hereinafter referred to as "The Mortgagor", of [*Ad-*

dress] ______ and [*Name of Trustee*] for the benefit of holders of [*Describe Underlying Security*] hereinafter referred to as "The Mortgagee,"

Witnesseth, that the mortgagor mortgages and warrants to the mortgagee, their heirs, successors and assigns, lands described as:

[*Describe*]

Including any part of any street or alley adjacent to said premises, vacated or to be vacated, together with all and singular the buildings, hereditaments, appurtenances, privileges, rights and water rights, including (but not excluding any other fixtures which would ordinarily be construed as part of the realty), any and all storm sash, storm doors, wire screens, wire doors, window shades, awnings, mantels and connecting iron or woodwork, grates, gas and electric fixtures, bathtubs, laundry and bathroom fixtures, oil burner and equipment, plumbing equipment, linoleum, furnaces, hot water heaters, incinerators, ventilators and all steam or hot water radiators and registers and the piping connected therewith, belonging to or used as a part of the building or buildings upon said premises at the time of the execution of this mortgage, or hereafter erected thereon, or which may be attached to said building or buildings or used as a part thereof at any time during the term of this mortgage, all of which are hereby deemed to be a part of this realty and secured by this mortgage, including as well all apparatus and fixtures of every description for watering, heating, ventilating and screening said premises and the rents, income and profits thereof thereunto belonging or in any wise appertaining

to secure the performance of the covenants hereinafter contained and the payment of the principal sum of [*Set Forth Maximum Amount of Principal Indebtedness*] together with interest at the rate of [*Per Cent*] per annum from the date hereof upon the unpaid principal until fully paid, payable according to the terms of said [*Describe Underlying Security*].

And the mortgagor covenants with the mortgagee, while this mortgage remains in force, as follows:

§ 1.1 Indebtedness

To pay said indebtedness and the interest thereon in the manner provided in the *Note/Bond* for which this mortgage is security.

§ 1.2 Taxes

To pay all taxes, assessments, water rates and other charges that may be levied or assessed upon or against said premises, within 30 days after the same shall become due and payable, and also to pay when due and payable any taxes upon the interest or estate in said lands created or represented by this mortgage, or by said indebtedness, whether levied against said mortgagor or otherwise; and to immediately pay off any lien having or which may have precedence over this mortgage, except as herein stated, and to keep all the improvements erected and to be erected on said premises continually intact and in good order and repair, and to promptly pay for all repairs and improvements, and to commit or suffer no waste of said premises, and to permit or suffer no unlawful use thereof.

§ 1.3 Insurance

To keep the buildings and equipment on the premises insured against loss or damage by fire for the benefit of, with loss payable to, and in manner and amount approved by, and deliver the policies as issued, to the mortgagee with the premiums therefor paid in full.

§ 1.4 Default

It is hereby stipulated and agreed by and between the parties hereto, that if default shall be made in the payment of taxes, assessments, water rates, liens, insurance or other charges upon said premises, or any part thereof, the mortgagee, may, at its option, make payment thereof, and the amounts so paid, with interest thereon at the same rate as provided for the principal indebtedness from the date of such payment, shall be impressed as an additional lien on said premises, and shall be added to and become part of the indebtedness secured hereby, and shall become immediately due and payable; and that in case of the payment of taxes, assessments, water rates, liens, insurance or other charges upon said premises by the mortgagee, as hereinbefore provided, the receipt or receipts of the proper officer or person for such payment in the hands of the mortgagee shall be conclusive evidence of the validity and amount of items so paid by the mortgagee.

And it is hereby stipulated and agreed by and between the parties hereto that if default shall be made in the payment of said principal sum or interest or any other sum secured hereby, or any part thereof, or in the payment of taxes, assessments, water rates, liens, insurance or other charges upon said premises, or any part thereof, at the time and in the manner herein specified for the payment thereof, or in the performance of any of the covenants and agreements herein contained, the entire indebtedness secured hereby remaining unpaid shall at once become due and collectible, if the mortgagee so elects, and without notice of such election and the mortgagee may prosecute a suit at law or equity as if all money secured hereby had matured prior to such date. In addition, the mortgagee may apply for a receiver of such property who shall have full rights over the rents, income and profits of the property described herein.

§ 1.5 Change in Laws

That, in the event of the passage of any law or regulation, state, federal or municipal, subsequent to the date hereof in any manner changing or modifying the laws now in force governing the taxation of mortgages or debts secured by mortgages, or the manner of collecting such taxes, the entire principal secured by this mortgage and all interest accrued thereon shall become due and payable forthwith, at the option of the mortgagee.

§ 1.6 Assignment

That, in the event the ownership of the mortgaged premises, or any part thereof, becomes vested in a person other than the mortgagor, the mortgagee may deal with such successor or successors in interest with reference to this mortgage, and the debt hereby secured in the same manner as with the mortgagor, without in any manner vitiating or discharging the mortgagor's liability hereunder, or upon the debt hereby secured.

§ 1.7 Default Remedy

That power is hereby granted by the mortgagor to the mortgagee, if default is made in the payment of said indebtedness, interest, taxes, assessments, water rates, liens or insurance premiums, or any part thereof at the time and in the manner herein agreed, to grant, bargain, sell, release, and convey the premises, with the appurtenances at public auction and to execute and deliver to the purchaser or purchasers, at such sale, deeds of conveyance, good and sufficient at law, pursuant to the statute in such case made and provided, and out of the proceeds to retain all sums due hereon, and the mortgagee may prosecute on action at law or equity as if all money secured hereby had matured prior to such date. In addition, the mortgagee may apply for a receiver of such property who shall have full rights over the rents, income and profits of the property described herein.

The covenants herein shall bind and the benefits and advantages inure to the respective heirs, assigns and successors of the parties. SIGNED by the mortgagor the day and year first above written.

[*Name of Corporation*]

Signed in the Presence of: By ____________________

____________________ and ____________________

____

STATE OF __________ }
County of __________ } SS

On this [*Date*], before me, the subscriber, a Notary Public in and for said county, personally appeared [*Name*] and [*Name*] to me personally known, who being by me duly sworn, did say that they are the [*Office*] and [*Office*] of the [*Name of Corporation*], and that the seal affixed to said instrument is the corporate seal of said Corporation, and that said instrument was signed and sealed in behalf of said Corporation, by authority of its Board of Directors, and [*Name*] and [*Name*] acknowledged said instrument to be the free act and deed of said Corporation.

My Commission Expires: ______ ____________________

Notary Public, ______
County, [*State*]

COMMENT

Use with § 43.20, infra.

Library References:

C.J.S. Corporations §§ 1177, 1214.
West's Key No. Digests, Corporations 🔑477.

§ 43.20 Agreement of Corporation and Trustee as to Assets Mortgaged

This Agreement made this ______ day of ______, 19__ by and between [*Name*] ("The Corporation") and [*Name*] ("The Trustee");

Whereas the Corporation is obligated to mortgage to a Trustee certain collateral described in Exhibit A pursuant to certain bonds to be issued by the Corporation described as [*Describe*];

And whereas the Trustee has agreed to perform the duties of Trustee as herein defined.

Now, it is agreed that:

§ 1.1 Collateral Mortgage

The Corporation has mortgaged as collateral for [*Describe*] bonds the said collateral as described in Exhibit A.

§ 1.2 Default

Upon default of the underlying bonds, the Trustee shall exercise its mortgagee rights under the said mortgage for the benefit of the bondholders.

§ 1.3 Termination

This Trust shall terminate upon the full payment of all of the obligations secured by herein described assignment of collateral.

§ 1.4 Accounting

The Trustee shall not be required to render any accountings to any court or the bondholders except it shall render an account at least annually to each bondholder upon the Corporation's default. The written approval of such account by such person or his or her guardian or legal representative shall, as to all matters and transactions stated therein, be final and binding upon all persons (whether in being or not) who are then or may thereafter become interested in, or entitled to share in, either the income or principal of such trust; provided always, however, that nothing contained in this section shall be deemed to give such person acting in conjunction with the trustee the power to alter, amend, revoke, or terminate such trust.

The trustee shall have the entire care and custody of all of the assets comprising the Trust Estate and shall maintain full and accurate books of account and records of receipts and disbursements and other financial transactions relative to the Trust Estate, all of which shall be available for inspection at any reasonable time by any bondholder, or his or her legal representative.

§ 2.1 Powers

The Trustee of each trust established hereunder shall have the following power and duties:

(a) Upon default of the bonds secured by this Trust, to take possession of the mortgaged property. To receive and to collect the income and profits from such property except as otherwise provided herein.

(b) Upon a default of ______ days upon the bonds secured by this Trust to option, sell and convey, mortgage, encumber, lease, exchange, pledge, partition, plat, subdivide, improve, repair, surrender, abandon or otherwise deal with or dispose of any and all property of whatsoever character and wheresoever situated forming a part of the Trust Estate, at such time or times and in such manner and upon such terms as, in the absolute and uncontrolled discretion of the Trustee may be deemed expedient and proper; to give options therefore; to execute deeds, transfers, leases, pledges, mortgages, and other instruments of any kind. Any leases and contracts may extend beyond the term of the Trust;

(c) To open and to close checking or savings accounts, in banks or similar financial institutions, and/or safety deposit boxes in the name of a Trustee or in the name of a nominee, with or without indication of any fiduciary capacity; to deposit cash in and withdraw cash from such accounts and/or boxes, with or without indication of any fiduciary capacity; to hold such accounts and/or securities in bearer form, or in the name of a Trustee or in the name of a nominee with or without indication of any fiduciary capacity;

(d) To administer any sinking fund securing the said bonds according to the terms of said fund.

§ 2.2 Resignation of Trustee—Successor

The Trustee may resign at any time by delivering thirty (30) days written notice to that effect to the Corporation. The resigning Trustee shall have the right to select and appoint his successor; or if he fails to do so, a successor shall be appointed by a court of competent jurisdiction.

References to the Trustee or Trustees include successor Trustees. A successor trustee shall succeed to all of the title, powers, rights, discretion, obligations and immunities of the original Trustee. Provided, the successor Trustee shall not be obligated to accept, ratify or approve of any of the acts, omissions, or defaults of the Trustee, nor shall he be required to audit or verify the records of the Trustee. Nor shall the fact that the successor Trustee has assumed and carried out his duties without protest or exception be deemed such an acceptance, ratification or approval. The successor Trustee shall be entitled to rely upon any statements and records (which may come into the successor Trustee's possession after a reasonable search) of the Trustee as to the assets of this Trust and, shall have no responsibility or liability hereunder to any person for the assets of this Trust until reduced to the possession of the successor Trustee.

§ 2.3 Validity of Acts

No one dealing with the Trustee need inquire concerning the validity of anything he purports to do, or need see to the application of any money paid or any property transferred to or upon the order of the Trustee.

§ 2.4 Fees

The Trust Estate and the income therefrom shall be chargeable with the reasonable expense of the Trustee in the administration of the trust and with reasonable compensation for the services of the Trustee.

§ 3.1 Miscellaneous

(a) This Agreement of Trust shall always be interpreted under the laws of the State of [*Name*].

(b) To the same effect as if it were the original, anyone may rely upon a copy certified by a notary public to be a true copy of this instrument (and of the writings, if any, endorsed thereon or attached thereto). Anyone may rely upon any statement of fact certified by anyone who appears from the original document or a certified copy thereof to be a Trustee hereunder.

(c) The Trustee shall have the right from time to time to adopt specific rules of procedure to carry out the full intent of this Trust and to do all reasonable acts necessary therefore; provided that such rules and acts shall not violate the specific terms of this Trust or the underlying bonds.

In witness whereof, the Settlor and the Trustee have executed this Agreement this ______ day of ______, 19__.

In the presence of:	Corporation:
______________________	______________________
______________________	______________________
	Trustee:
______________________	______________________
______________________	______________________

STATE OF ____________ }
County of ____________ } SS

On this ______ day of ______, 19__, before me personally appeared ______ ______, who being duly sworn did say that he is ______ of ______, and that he executed the within instrument and acknowledged the same to be the free act and deed of ______

____

Notary Public, ______ County [*State*]

My Commission Expires: ______

STATE OF ____________ }
County of ____________ } SS

On this ______ day of ______, 19__, before me personally appeared ______, to me known to be an officer of Trust Company and who executed the within instrument and who acknowledged the same to be the said Trust Company's free act and deed.

____

Notary Public, ______ County [*State*]

My Commission Expires: ______

Library References:

C.J.S. Corporations §§ 1191, 1222.

West's Key No. Digests, Corporations ⚿479.

§ 43.21 Bonds Issued to Trustee—Agreement of Corporation and Trustee as to Assets Assigned

COMMENT

One method is for the issuer to take a mortgage securing a single note or bond and issue participation shares therein. Another method is for the issuer to accept a number of mortgages in pledge to secure a single note or bond and then issue participation shares in the note or bond secured by such pledge. Still another method is by receiving various stocks or bonds under a depositary agreement and then issuing participation certificates, which are governed by the deposit agreement and the terms of the certificates.

This Agreement made this ______ day of ______, 19__ by and between [*Name*] ("The Corporation") and [*Name*] ("The Trustee");

Whereas the Corporation is obligated to place into Trust certain collateral described in Exhibit A pursuant to certain bonds to be issued by the Corporation described as [*Describe*];

And whereas the Trustee has agreed to perform the duties of Trustee as herein defined.

Now, it is agreed that:

§ 1.1 Collateral Assignment

The Corporation has assigned as collateral for [*Describe*] bonds the said collateral as described in Exhibit *A* and the proper UCC–1 filings have been made.

§ 1.2 Interest and Dividends

The Corporation from time to time shall be entitled to receive and collect any and all interest, dividends and other income from the pledged assets, and the Trustee on demand of the Corporation shall from time to time deliver to it suitable assignments and standing orders for the payment to it of such interest, rents, dividends and other income, and shall pay over to it, upon the receipt of its President, or Treasurer, any and all sums which may be received or held by the Trustee in respect of such interest, rents, dividends and other income. In case default shall have been declared against the Corporation as herein provided, then during the continuance of such default, in addition to the other remedies hereinafter provided, the Trustee may revoke any such assignments and standing orders, and may collect and receive the interest, rents, dividends and other income on the pledged securities, and all such sums so collected or received shall be applicable to the payment of interest then or thereafter to become due on the bonds hereby secured, and until so applied shall be held by the Trustee as a part of the trust property, but after any such default shall have been made good or shall have been waived, the right of the Corporation to receive and collect such interest, rents, dividends and other income, and the duty of the Trustee to execute such assignments and standing orders, shall revive and continue as though such default had not taken place.

§ 1.3 Voting

Unless there shall be some such continuing default, the Corporation shall have the right to vote any shares of any corporation, association, joint stock company or trust constituting a part of the pledged securities with the same force and effect as though such shares were not subject to this assignment, and the Trustee, upon the written request of the President, Vice-President or Treasurer of the Corporation, accompanied by the written consent of the committee from time to time shall execute and deliver to the Corporation or to such person or persons as may be designated by its President, Vice-President, Secretary or Treasurer such proxies and powers of attorney as may be necessary to enable the Corporation or the person or persons so designated by a vote said shares to the same extent and with the same effect as though such shares were absolutely owned by the Corporation and were not subject to this assignment, provided, however, that such proxies and powers of attorney shall specify that none of such shares shall be voted to authorize, and the Corporation covenants that it will not permit any of such shares to be voted to perform, any act contrary to the provisions of this assignment; and provided, further, that the Trustee may, in its discretion, impose any limitations upon such voting power which it may deem necessary to insure the performance of any covenants in this assignment or in the underlying [*Describe*] bonds contained or to be in the best interests of the bondholders.

§ 1.4 Default

In case default shall have been declared against the Corporation as hereinafter provided, then during the continuance of such default, in addition to the other remedies herein provided, the Trustee may revoke any such proxies or powers of attorney and in its discretion may vote upon any such shares of stock in its discretion.

§ 1.5 Other Property Received

All moneys and property at any time received by the Corporation or the Trustee in respect of any of the assigned property, whether by voluntary payment or out of the proceeds of the sale of any property or otherwise, except payments on account of interest, rents, dividends and other income shall be deposited with and held by the Trustee as a part of the trust property (or in the case of property not capable of being deposited otherwise subjected to the lien hereof) until paid over or applied as hereinafter provided.

§ 1.6 Dividends Defined

The term "dividends" as used in this Article shall *not* be deemed to include stock dividends, distributions of capital or distributions made out of the proceeds or as a result of the consolidation or reorganization, or the sale as an entirety or substantially as an entirety of the properties, of any corporation, association, joint stock company or trust, any of whose bonds, shares or other securities shall constitute a part of the assigned property, *but/and* shall only be deemed to include cash dividends paid from current earnings applicable thereto. In case any question shall arise as to whether any particular moneys constitute interest, dividends or other income, the Trustee shall decide such question and its decision in the premises shall be binding and conclusive upon the Corporation and the bondholders.

§ 1.7 Registration and Preservation

The Trustee shall have the right, in its discretion, to cause any of the bonds or other obligations constituting a part of the pledged securities to stand registered in its name or in the name of its nominee or to bearer, and to cause the certificates for any shares constituting a part of the assigned property to stand in its name or in the name of its nominee or in the name of the Corporation, making such arrangements in each case with any such nominee or with the Corporation as it shall deem suitable for the protection of the Trust. The Trustee may, in its discretion, also stamp any of the assigned property with an appropriate notation to the effect that they are held by it under and subject to the provisions of this Indenture.

The Trustee may do whatever in the opinion of counsel selected or approved by it may be necessary for the purpose of maintaining, preserving, renewing or extending the existence of any corporation, association, joint stock company or trust, any of the shares whereof shall constitute a part of the assigned property, and for such purpose from time to time may sell, assign, transfer and deliver the minimum number of shares which may be necessary to qualify persons to act as directors of or in any other official relation to any such corporation, association, joint stock company or trust.

In so far as all persons and corporations, except [*Name of Corporation Issuing These Bonds*] are concerned, the Trustee shall, except as herein otherwise provided, be deemed to be the absolute owner of all of the assigned property for all purposes whatsoever, but the Trustee shall not be required to take any action looking toward the enforcement or protection of its rights in respect of any of the assigned property unless requested to do so by the Corporation and indemnified to its satisfaction, but it may in its discretion at any time take any such action which it shall deem necessary or convenient for the protection and enforcement of any of its rights and interests as such owner.

COMMENT TO § 1.7

Use if bonds are to be held by Trustee; if so, form §§ 43.24, 43.25 or 43.26, infra, should also be used.

§ 1.8 Termination

This Trust shall terminate upon the full payment of all of the obligations secured by hereindescribed assignment of collateral.

§ 1.9 Accounts

The Trustee shall not be required to render any accountings to any court or the bondholders except it shall render an account at least annually to each bondholder upon the Corporation's default. The written approval of such account by such person or his or her guardian or legal representative shall, as to all matters and transactions stated therein, be final and binding upon all persons (whether in being or not) who are then or may thereafter become interested in, or entitled to share in, either the income or principal of such Trust; provided always, however, that nothing contained in this article shall be deemed to give such person acting in conjunction with the Trustee the power to alter, amend, revoke, or terminate such trust.

The Trustee shall have the entire care and custody of all of the assets comprising the Trust Estate and shall maintain full and accurate books of account and records of receipts and disbursements and other financial transactions relative to the Trust Estate, all of which shall be available for inspection at any reasonable time by any bondholder, or his or her legal representative.

§ 2.1 Powers and Duties

The Trustee of each trust established hereunder shall have the following powers:

(a) To take possession of any property forming a part of the Trust Estate. To receive additions to the trust under this instrument otherwise and to hold and administer the same under the provisions hereof; and to collect the income and profits from such property except as otherwise provided herein.

(b) To retain indefinitely all property in the form in which the same shall be received.

(c) To administer any sinking fund securing the said bonds according to the terms of such fund.

(d) Upon a default of ______ days upon the bonds secured by this Trust, to option, sell and convey, mortgage, encumber, lease, exchange, pledge, partition, plat, subdivide, improve, repair, surrender, abandon or otherwise deal with or dispose of any and all property of whatsoever character and wheresoever situated forming a part of the Trust Estate, at such time or times and in such manner and upon such terms as, in the absolute and uncontrolled discretion of the Trustee may be deemed expedient and proper; to give options therefore; to execute deeds, transfers, leases, pledges, mortgages, and other instruments of any kind. Any leases and contracts may extend beyond the term of the trust;

(e) To open and to close checking or savings accounts, in banks or similar financial institutions, and/or safety deposit boxes in the name of a Trustee or in the name of a nominee, with or without indication of any fiduciary capacity; to deposit cash in and withdraw cash from such accounts and/or boxes, with or without indication of any fiduciary capacity; to hold such accounts and/or securities in bearer form, or in the name of a Trustee or in the name of a nominee with or without indication of any fiduciary capacity;

(f) Upon a default of ______ days upon the bonds secured by this Trust to give general or special proxies or powers of attorney for voting or acting in respect of shares or securities, which may be discretionary and with power of substitution; to deposit shares or securities with, or transfer them to, protective committees or similar bodies; to join in any reorganization and to pay assessments or subscriptions called for in connection with shares or securities held by the Trustee;

(g) The Corporation covenants to pay and discharge, as the same shall become due and payable, all taxes, assessments and governmental and other charges lawfully levied and imposed upon the Trust Estate hereby pledged or conveyed, and upon the franchises, earnings and business of the Corporation, or of any Corporation stock or obligations of which are included in the trust estate and/or of any subsidiary Corporation, and also all taxes, assessments and governmental charges lawfully imposed upon the lien or interest of the Trustee in respect of the Trust Estate and the income and profits thereof; provided, however, that nothing contained in this section shall require the Corporation to pay any such tax, assessment, lien or charge so long as the Corporation in good faith shall contest the validity thereof, unless thereby in the opinion of the Trustee or of counsel selected or approved by the Trustee the rights and security of the holders of bonds secured hereby shall be materially endangered.

(h) The Trustee shall have the right from time to time to adopt specific rules of procedure to carry out the full intent of this Trust and to do all reasonable acts necessary therefore; provided that such rules and acts shall not violate the specific terms of this Trust and the underlying Bonds.

§ 2.2 Resignation of Trustee—Successor

The Trustee may resign at any time by delivering thirty (30) days written notice to that effect to the Corporation. The resigning Trustee shall have the right to select and appoint his successor; or if he fails to do so, a successor shall be appointed by a court of competent jurisdiction.

References to the Trustee or Trustees include successor Trustees. A successor Trustee shall succeed to all of the title, powers, rights, discretion, obligations and immunities of the original Trustee. Provided, the successor Trustee shall not be obligated to accept, ratify or approve of any of the acts, omissions, or defaults of the Trustee, nor shall he be required to audit or verify the records of the Trustee. Nor shall the fact that the successor Trustee has assumed and carried out his duties without protest or exception be deemed such an acceptance, ratification or approval. The successor Trustee shall be entitled to rely upon any statements and records (which may come into the successor Trustee's possession after a reasonable search) of the Trustee as to the assets of this Trust and, shall have no responsibility or liability hereunder to any person for the assets of this Trust until reduced to the possession of the successor Trustee.

§ 2.3 Validity of Acts

No one dealing with the Trustee need inquire concerning the validity of anything he purports to do, or need see to the application of any money paid or any property transferred to or upon the order of the Trustee.

§ 2.4 Fees

The Trust Estate and the income therefrom shall be chargeable with the reasonable expense of the Trustee in the administration of the trust and with reasonable compensation for the services of the Trustee.

§ 3.1 Miscellaneous

(a) This Agreement of Trust shall always be interpreted under the laws of the State of [*Name*].

(b) To the same effect as if it were the original, anyone may rely upon a copy certified by a notary public to be a true copy of this instrument (and of the writings, if any, endorsed thereon or attached thereto). Anyone may rely upon any statement of fact certified by anyone who appears from the original document or a certified copy thereof to be a Trustee hereunder.

In witness whereof, the Corporation and the Trustee have executed this Agreement this ______ day of ______, 19__.

In the presence of:	Corporation:
______________________	______________________
	__________ (1) __________
______________________	
	Trustee:
______________________	______________________
	__________ (4) __________
______________________	

STATE OF ____________ }
County of ____________ } SS

On this ______ day of ______, 19__, before me personally appeared ______ ______, to me known to be an officer of ______ Trust company and who executed the within instrument and who acknowledged the same to be the said Trust Company's free act and deed.

____

Notary Public, ______ County [*State*]

My Commission Expires: ______

STATE OF ____________ }
County of ____________ } SS

On this ______ day of ______, 19__, before me personally appeared ______ ______, who being duly sworn did say that he is ______ of ______, and that he executed the within instrument and acknowledged the same to be the free act and deed of ______

____

Notary Public, ______ County [*State*]

My Commission Expires: ______

§ 43.22 UCC–1 Financing Statement

The following financing statement is the form to be filed with an instrument secured by personal property and fixtures.

This **FINANCING STATEMENT** is presented to a Filing Officer for filing pursuant to the Uniform Commercial Code.	1. Maturity date (if any).	2. No. of additional sheets presented (if any). (See Instruction 5). X
3. Debtor(s) (Last Name First) and address(es) Name and Address of Corporation	4. Secured Party(ies) and address(es) (Name) as Trustee Under (Describe Security)	For Filing Officer (Date, Time, Number, and Filing Office)
5. Name and address(es) of assignee(s) (if any)	Check ☒ if applicable 6. ☒ Proceeds of collateral are also covered. 7. ☒ Products of collateral are also covered. 8. ☐ Collateral was brought into this state subject to a security interest in another jurisdiction.	

9. This financing statement covers the following types (or items) of property:

(Describe)

by: ______________________________
Signature(s) of Debtor(s) (not necessary if Item 8 is applicable)

by: ______________________________
(Signature of Secured Party or Assignee of Record. Not Valid until Signed)

[C3006]

§ 43.23 Debt Security Trust

This Trust entered into by and between [*Name*], a [*State*] Corporation (the "Corporation") and [*Name*] ("Trustee"),

Whereas, the Corporation proposes to issue instruments as described in Exhibit A (the "Instrument") secured by property to be held by the Trustee pursuant to this Trust;

And Whereas, the Trustee agrees to hold and dispose of such property as security for the beneficial owners of such instruments (the "Holders");

Now Therefore, for mutual covenants exchanged it is agreed:

§ 1.1 Property

(a) The property described in Exhibit B (the "Property") shall be held by the Trustee until the Corporation's obligations to the Holders secured by this Trust are terminated.

Option 1

(b) Further to the Trustee shall be issued all of the Instruments described herein. The same shall be registered in the Trustee name and the Trustee shall enforce the terms of such instruments for the Holders. As evidence of their beneficial interest, the Trustee shall issue to such Holder a Certificate of Deposit.

Comment

See § 43.24, infra.

§ 1.2 Default

(a) Upon a default in any term of the Instrument for a period of ______ days the Trustee shall take whatever action is appropriate and legal to accelerate the Holder's debt and to liquidate the Property for the benefit of the Holders and to distribute to them (after the payment of all expenses of collection and Trustee's fees) prorata according to the then principal and interest owed to them, such sums as are then owed to them (including the accelerated portions of the debt principal). The Trustee may waive or postpone its actions only upon the following events: [*Describe*].

The remainder shall be held to pay any sums (not then due) at such time as they become due.

When all of the debt secured by the Instruments has been retired (or when the Corporation has made provision with the Trustee for the payment of the same), the Trustee shall pay the remainder of property held by this Trust (after paying the expenses of this Trust) to the Corporation.

Language to Use with Option 1

(b) Further upon default for such ______ day period, the Trustee shall take whatever action is appropriate and legal to enforce the terms of said Instrument and to collect the same in behalf of the Holders.

§ 1.3 Trustee Liability

(a) The Trustee shall not be liable for any error of judgment made in good faith, unless it shall be proven that the Trustee was negligent in ascertaining the pertinent facts.

(b) The Trustee shall not be liable with respect to any action taken or omitted to be taken by it in good faith in accordance with the direction of a majority of the Holders voting on such issue.

(c) The Trustee may rely and shall be protected in acting upon any resolution, certificate, statement, instrument, opinion, report, notice, request, consent, order, approval, appraisal, bond, debenture or other paper, or document believed by it to be genuine and to have been signed or presented by the proper party or parties.

(d) Any request, direction, order, or demand of the corporation mentioned herein shall be sufficiently evidenced by an instrument signed in the name of the Corporation by the President or any Vice-

President and the Secretary or an Assistant Secretary or the Treasurer or an Assistant Treasurer (unless other evidence in respect thereof be herein specifically prescribed); and any resolution of the Board of Directors of the Corporation may be evidenced to the Trustee by a copy thereof certified by the Secretary or an Assistant Secretary of the Corporation.

(e) The Trustee may consult with counsel and any opinion of counsel shall be full and complete authorization and protection in respect of any action taken, suffered, or omitted by it hereunder in good faith and in accordance with such opinion of counsel.

(f) The Trustee shall be under no obligation to exercise any of the rights or powers vested in it by this Indenture at the request, order, or direction of any of the Holders pursuant to the provisions of this Trust, unless such Holders shall have offered to the Trustee reasonable security or indemnity against the costs, expenses, and liabilities which may be incurred therein or thereby; nothing herein contained shall, however, relieve the Trustee of the obligation, upon the occurrence of an event of default (which has not been cured or waived) to exercise such of the rights and powers vested in it by this Trust, and to use the same degree of care and skill in their exercise as a prudent man would exercise or use under the circumstances in the conduct of his own affairs.

(g) The Trustee shall not be liable for any action taken, suffered, or omitted by it in good faith and believed by it to be authorized or within the discretion or rights or powers conferred upon it by this Trust.

(h) Prior to the occurrence of an event of default hereunder and after the curing or waiving of all events of default, the Trustee shall not be bound to make any investigation into the facts or matters stated in any resolution, certificate, statement, instrument, opinion, report, notice, request, consent, order, approval, appraisal, bond, debenture or other paper or document, unless requested in writing so to do by the holders of not less than a majority in aggregate principal amount of the holders then outstanding; provided, that if the payment within a reasonable time to the Trustee of the costs, expenses, or liabilities likely to be incurred by it in the making of such investigation is, in the opinion of the Trustee, not reasonably assured to the Trustee by the security afforded to it by the terms of this Trust, the Trustee may require reasonable indemnity against such expenses or liabilities as a condition to so proceeding.

(i) The Trustee may execute any of the trusts or powers hereunder or perform any duties hereunder either directly or by or through agents or attorneys, and the Trustee shall not be responsible for any misconduct or negligence on the part of any agent or attorney appointed with due care by it hereunder.

§ 1.4 Holder Meetings

The Trustee at its own initiative (or at the request of ______% of the Holders) shall call a meeting of all Holders which shall take place not earlier than 20 nor later than 30 days after said notice. Each Holder shall be entitled to 1 vote for each $1,000 of principal and accrued interest due him. Votes may be cast in person or proxy. Any Holder not present or represented shall be deemed to have assented to any action or waiver or consent approved by a majority of Holders' votes represented and voting.

§ 2.1 Titles and Subtitles

Titles of the paragraphs and subparagraphs are placed herein for convenient reference only and shall not to any extent have the effect of modifying, amending or changing the express terms and provisions of this Trust.

§ 2.2 Words and Gender or Number

As used herein, unless the context clearly indicates the contrary, the singular number shall include the plural, the plural the singular, and the use of any gender shall be applicable to all genders.

§ 2.3 Execution in Counterpart

This Trust may be executed in any number of counterparts, each of which shall be taken to be an original.

§ 2.4 Waiver

No waiver of any provisions of this Trust shall be valid unless in writing and signed by the person or party against whom charged.

§ 2.5 Applicable Law

This Trust shall be subject to and governed by the laws of the State of [*Name*].

In witness whereof, we have executed this Trust this ______ day of ______, 19__.

Witnesses: Corporation:

______________________ BY: ______________

______________________ Trustee:

______________________ ______________

____

STATE OF __________ }
County of __________ } SS

On this ______ day of ______, 19__, before me personally appeared [*Name*] acting on behalf of [*Name of Corporation*], to me known to be the same person described in and who executed the within instrument as the free act and deed of said Corporation.

____
Notary Public, ______ County, ______
My Commission Expires: ______

STATE OF __________ }
County of __________ } SS

On this ______ day of ______, 19__, before me personally appeared [*Name*] to me known to be the same person described in and who executed the within instrument as ______, and who acknowledged the same to be the free act and deed of [*Name*] Trustee.

____
Notary Public, ______ County, ______
My Commission Expires: ______

§ 43.24 Bonds Issued to Trustee—Certificate of Deposit

No. ______ $______

Certificate of Deposit of ______ Corporation ______ Year Sinking Fund Bonds Deposited under Agreement Dated ______, 19__.

This is to certify that ______ is the registered holder of this certificate, representing ______ Dollars principal amount of the above-mentioned bonds, with coupons, due ______, 19__, and all subsequent coupons attached, deposited with ______ Trust Company, depositary under the above-mentioned Agreement. Every Holder hereof by accepting this certificate accepts and becomes bound by all of the provisions of said Agreement, with the same force and effect as if he had signed the same.

This certificate is transferable only on the books of the Trustee, to be kept for that purpose by the depositary or its agent, and until such transfer the registered holder shall be treated as the owner hereof for all purposes.

No. of bond ______, Property ______, Coupons for years ______, ______, ______.

This certificate shall not be valid unless duly signed by the said ______ Trust Company, depositary, or its authorized agent.

Witness the signature of ______ Trust Company, depositary therein, ______, 19__.

______________ Trust Company
By __________, Vice President

COMMENT

Use this form if the bond holders are to get a certificate as to their security interest in the assigned assets.

§ 43.25 Bonds Issued to Trustee—Certificate of Participation in First Mortgage Real Estate Loans

No. ______ $______

The ______ Trust Company, of ______, hereinafter called Trustee, certifies that the holder of this certificate is entitled under the conditions and upon the terms hereinafter named to a participation to the extent of $______, or the pro rata share thereof from the money collected on account of the principal of certain first mortgage loans on real estate in ______ County, ______, and first mortgage real estate bonds held in trust by the Trustee for the equal pro rata benefit of the holders of Certificates of Participation in Trust No. ______.

(1) The undersigned shall at all times have and retain title to and possession, management, and control of said moneys, notes and bonds, and the investment and reinvestment thereof and the arrangement of all details in connection therewith as in its discretion seems best.

(2) As and when the undersigned receives payment of interest upon said securities, and not otherwise, it will pay to the record holder hereof such proportion of said interest so received accruing on said securities from and after the date hereof as the amount of this certificate bears to the entire amount of said securities, but in no event shall the interest so paid be more than ______% per annum on the face value of this certificate, payable semiannually.

(3) The term of this certificate shall expire on the ______ day of ______, 19__, at which time, or as soon thereafter as sufficient funds have been collected in due course of business on account of the notes and bonds held hereunder, the undersigned will pay to the registered holder hereof his pro rata share of the funds so collected, but in no event more than the face value of this certificate.

(4) The undersigned may deduct from the participation represented hereby, and any interest accruing hereon, the holder's proper proportion of any loss, costs, damages, expenses, and charges of every kind and description which may be incurred or sustained by the undersigned or by or incident to said fund or any part thereof.

(5) This certificate is assignable only upon the books of the undersigned upon proper endorsement and surrender hereof to the undersigned for cancellation and is subject to redemption by the undersigned at any time upon mailing a written notice of such redemption directed to the record holder hereof at his address last appearing upon

the books of the undersigned, after which this certificate shall cease to participate in the interest accruing upon said fund.

_______ Trust Company

Date of Issue _______ By _______________

Maturity Date _______ _______ Trust Company

Countersigned:

____

Ass'n Secretary

Assignment

For value received, subject to the terms of the within Certificate, the undersigned hereby sells, assigns and transfers to _______ all his interest represented by the within certificate and does hereby authorize and appoint _______ Attorney to make the necessary transfer on the books of the Company, with full power of substitution in the premises.

Dated _______, 19__.

____

____

In presence of:

____

____

§ 43.26 Bonds Issued to Trustee—Certificate of Participation in First Mortgage Real Estate Loans—Another Form

_______ Company, hereinafter called the Company, has received from _______ the sum of $_______ for the purchase of and hereby assigns to the purchaser an undivided share equal to that amount, with interest thereon at the rate of _______% per annum, in the bond of _______ for $_______ due _______, 19__ and in the first mortgage securing the same, covering _______________

Interest days _______ 1st and _______ 1st.

This bond and mortgage, together with the policy of the _______ Company, guaranteeing to holders of this and similar certificates payment of principal and interest, are held by the Company as depositary and agent for the holders of such certificates which shall never aggregate more than the amount of principal remaining unpaid on said bond and mortgage, upon the following terms and conditions which are agreed to by the holder of this certificate:

(1) The Company holds and shall continue to hold said bond and mortgage, said policy of _______ Company and the other instruments

and evidences of title relating thereto for the equal and pro rata benefit of the purchaser and any other persons interested therein, as holders of like certificates.

(2) The Company, on receipt of the interest and principal of said bond and mortgage, as required therein, shall distribute the same among the persons entitled thereto. If payments not so required are made, certificates for the same amount will be called in and paid off.

(3) The Company shall have full power to take any action it may deem necessary or desirable in order to enforce any of the provisions of said bond and mortgage and to protect the mortgage security.

(4) The Company may for its own corporate account be the holder or pledgee of similar shares in said bond and mortgage.

(5) The Company may cancel this certificate at any time on thirty days' notice in writing to the purchaser and payment at its office, ______, of the amount then owing to the purchaser for principal and interest.

(6) This certificate is not negotiable. The only way that the interest of the purchaser can be transferred is by the surrender of this certificate to the Company duly assigned and the issuing of another certificate to the transferee.

§ 43.27 Pro Rata Provision in Participation Mortgage

Each note of the series hereby secured shall share pro rata in the security irrespective of maturity, priority of assignment, retention or repurchase by the Trustee, and in the event of bankruptcy or insolvency of the mortgagor or by reason of the insufficiency of the security to satisfy all outstanding notes hereby secured, however caused, and irrespective of any guaranty of payment of any or all of said notes.

COMMENT

The above provision makes clear the intent to have all the notes secured by a split mortgage share pro rata in the security, and is of importance on the question of whether each note is secured by first mortgage lien under statutes authorizing investments by fiduciaries.

§ 43.28 Trustee's Certificate

This is one of the bonds described in the within-mentioned mortgage.

______________, Trustee

By ___________, Asst. Secy.

§ 43.29 Serial Bond With Coupons

$______. No. ______

______ COMPANY OF ______

FIRST MORTGAGE ______ PER CENT SERIAL BOND

For value received, ______ Company, a Corporation organized under the laws of the State of ______, promises to pay to the bearer, or, in case of registration, to the registered owner hereof, the sum of ______ Dollars at the office of ______, in the City of ______, State of ______, in such coin or currency of the United States of America as at the time of payment shall be legal tender for the payment of debts, on the first day of ______, 19__, with interest thereon in the meantime at the rate of ______ per cent per annum, payable semiannually, on the first days of ______ and ______ in each year, in like coin or currency, at the same place; said interest to be payable either to the bearers of the annexed coupons upon their surrender as they severally become due, or to the registered owner of the bond, in case of the surrender of all unpaid coupons for cancellation as hereinafter provided.

This bond is one of a series aggregating ______ Dollars in amount, issued and to be issued by ______ Company, ______ bonds of said series being for the sum of ______ Dollars each, and numbered consecutively from ______ upwards, and ______ bonds of said series being for the sum of ______ Dollars each, and numbered consecutively from ______ upwards.

This bond, as well as all others of said series, is secured by a certain first mortgage or deed of trust, dated ______, 19__, conveying to ______ Trust Company, as trustee the lands and buildings of ______ Company therein described, and will be valid only when authenticated by the certificate hereon of said trustee, or its successor in said trust, that it is one of the series referred to in said mortgage.

The principal of this bond may be declared by said trustee due and payable before maturity, in the event of default as provided in said mortgage or deed of trust. This bond shall pass by delivery, or, if registered, by transfer upon the books of the ______ Trust Company, transfer agents, and, after registration of ownership certified hereon by said ______ Trust Company, no transfer of this bond, except on the books of said ______ Trust Company, shall be valid, unless the last transfer is to bearer, which shall restore transferability by delivery, and this bond shall continue subject to successive registrations and transfers to bearer as aforesaid at the option of each holder. In case of registrations as aforesaid, the coupons annexed hereto shall remain negotiable and transferable by delivery, unless the holder shall surrender the unpaid coupons for cancellation, in which case, the interest as well as principal shall be payable only to the registered owner hereof.

In witness whereof, the said ______ Company of ______ has caused these presents to be executed in its name and behalf, and its corporate seal to be hereto affixed, and the annexed coupons to be authenticated by a facsimile of the signature of its treasurer, this first day of ______, 19__, by its president and by its treasurer thereunto duly authorized.

______ Company

By ______ President

__________, Treasurer.

[*Corporate Seal*]

[*On back*]

Notice.—No writing on this bond except by an officer of the Company.

Date of Registry	In Whose Name Registered	Transfer Agent

§ 43.30 Bond Power

Assignment of Bond—Separate from Bond

For Value Received, ____________________

hereby sell, assign and transfer unto ____________________

one bond of the ____________________ for ____________

($______).

No. ______ herewith standing in ______ name on the books of said ______ and hereby irrevocably constitute and appoint ______ attorney to transfer the said bond on the books of the within named company, with full power of substitution in the premises.

Dated ______

____

____

In presence of:

Signature Guaranteed:

[*Name of Guarantor*]

____

By ____________________

__________ [*Title*]

§§ 43.31–43.40 are reserved for supplementary material.

D. DEBENTURES

Library References:

C.J.S. Corporations §§ 1146–1148, 1150, 1158, 1160, 1161, 1192.
West's Key No. Digests, Corporations ⚿469 et seq.

§ 43.41 Coupon Debenture

THE ______ CORPORATION

Issue of ______ debentures, of $______ each, numbered ______ to ______, bearing interest at ______ per cent per annum, payable on the ______ day of ______ and the ______ day of ______ in each year.

Debenture No. ______ $______

§ 1.1 The ______ Corporation (herein called the "Corporation"), in consideration of the sum of $______ paid to the Corporation, hereby binds itself to pay to the bearer of this debenture on the ______ day of ______, 19__, or on such earlier day as the principal moneys hereby secured may become payable by the conditions of this debenture, the sum of $______, and until payment of the said sum of $______ to pay interest thereon at the rate of ______ per cent per annum by equal half-yearly payments on the ______ day of ______ and the ______ day of ______ in each year in accordance with the coupons annexed hereto.

§ 1.2 The Corporation as beneficial owner hereby charges with such payments its undertaking and all its property and assets whatsoever and wheresoever, both present and future, including therein the uncalled capital of the Corporation for the time being.

§ 2.1 This debenture is one of a series of like debentures, numbered ______ to ______, issued or about to be issued by the Corporation. All the debentures of this series are payable pari passu, and will rank equally as a first charge upon the property and assets of the Corporation comprised therein, without any preference or priority one over another.

§ 2.2 The said charge shall constitute a floating security only, not hindering any sale or other dealings in the ordinary course of business by the Corporation with the property or assets comprised in the charge, but the Corporation shall not be at liberty to create any mortgage or charge upon the property or assets comprised in the security, either in priority to or to rank equally with the charge hereby created, without the consent of holders of [*two thirds*] in value of the outstanding debentures of this issue.

§ 2.3 The principal moneys hereby secured shall become immediately payable in any of the following events:

(a) If the Corporation defaults for [*two months*] in the payment of any interest hereby secured, and the holder before such interest is paid by notice in writing to the Corporation calls the said principal.

(b) If a distress or execution, either by writ or appointment of a receiver, is levied on any part of the property or assets charged, and the debt for which such levy is made or receiver appointed is not paid off within seven days.

(c) If an order is made or a special resolution passed for the dissolution and winding up the Corporation.

§ 2.4 This debenture is a negotiable instrument, with all the incidents of negotiability.

§ 2.5 The Corporation is entitled at any time after the ______ day of ______, 19__, to redeem this debenture [*at a premium of ______ per cent*] on giving [*six*] months' notice by advertisement of its intention so to do.

§ 2.6 The principal moneys secured by this debenture will be paid at the ______ Bank, or at other of the Corporation's bankers for the time being. On application for payment this debenture must be produced and surrendered, together with any coupons for future interest.

Given under the seal of the ______ Corporation this ______ day of ______, 19__.

[*Corporate Seal*]

[*Name of Corporation*]
By ______________

§ 43.42 Interest Coupon

THE ______ COMPANY

$______ DEBENTURE TO BEARER No. ______

Interest coupon for $______, being one-half year's interest due the ______ day of ______, 19__.

__________, Secretary

This coupon will be paid on presentation at the ______ bank.

§ 43.43 Debenture—Payable Out of Corporate Income Only

______ Corporation promises to pay to the registered holder hereof on ______, 19__, the sum of $1,000 with interest on such amount from date issued, until paid, at the rate of ______ per cent per annum, payable semiannually on January 1 and July 1 of each year out of the income of the Corporation (computed after deducting taxes, expenses, bond interest, bond sinking fund deposits, and other proper charges). Interest hereon shall be cumulative.

COMMENTS

Interest is payable on this obligation only if the Corporation earns it. Provisions of other forms that are appropriate for all types of debt interests are not repeated.

Such interests are usually subordinated to other bonds and debentures. They are, however, superior to all equity interests, and some restriction on dividends may be appropriate to protect this intermediate interest.

§ 43.44 Receiver's Certificate of Indebtedness

The undersigned ______, duly appointed Receiver (*or* Trustee) for ______ Corporation, defendant (*or* debtor) in cause No. ______ entitled ______ v. ______, in ______ Court, ______ County, by decree entered therein on the ______ day of ______, 19__, hereby certifies that he was, on the ______ day of ______, 19__, by order of said court duly entered, authorized to incur an indebtedness, as such Receiver (*or* Trustee), in the sum of $______, for the purpose of ______ [*Set Forth the Lawful Purpose*] and to issue Receiver's (*or* Trustee's) certificates as evidence of said indebtedness, in denominations of $______, without interest, payable in due course of administration as ordered by the court, out of the income and proceeds of the receivership estate, which certificates are to be given in payment of said indebtedness.

That by virtue of said authorizing decree, the undersigned Receiver (*or* Trustee) did on the ______ day of ______, 19__, incur indebtedness for borrowed money used for said purpose, in the sum of $______, payable to ______.

Therefore, the undersigned, by these presents, certifies and acknowledges himself, as Receiver (*or* Trustee), to be indebted to ______ in the sum of $______, payable in due course of administration, and as ordered by the court, solely out of the income and proceeds of the receivership estate, the undersigned hereby assuming no personal liability by these presents.

The indebtedness evidenced by the certificates numbered from ______ to ______, inclusive, shall be paid as an administrative expense and shall have priority and preference in payment, as such, only out of the income and proceeds of the receivership estate, each certificate being on a parity with every other certificate of this issue, no preference or priority being accorded to any or either of them over another.

This certificate may be transferred by assignment in writing on the back hereof, signed by the payee, and the transferee shall be entitled to all the rights of the payee, both as to the payment of said certificate and its priority and preference rights.

Dated ______, 19__.

____
Receiver (*or* Trustee)
for __________

[*Reverse Side*]

Assignment of Certificate

For value received, the undersigned hereby sells, assigns and transfers the claim represented by the within certificate, to ______, subject to the terms and conditions of the decree entered ______, 19__, and to all the rules and regulations concerning such transfer from time to time established by the receiver (*or* Trustee), and does hereby appoint ______ attorney, to transfer said certificate on the books of the receiver (*or* Trustee), with full power of substitution in the premises.

Dated ______, 19__. __________ [*Seal*]

Witness: __________ [*Seal*]

____

§ 43.45 Notice of Redemption of Debenture

Notice is hereby given that the Five Year Convertible Income Debentures due ______, 19__, of ______ Corporation have been called for redemption at 110% of the principal amount thereof and will be redeemed at the office of the ______ Trust Company, ______, on ______, 19__. From and after ______, 19__, the holders of said Debentures will have no conversion rights or any other rights, except to receive redemption price.

§§ 43.46–43.50 are reserved for supplementary material.

E. GENERAL CLAUSES AND PROVISIONS

Library References:

C.J.S. Corporations § 1150.
West's Key No. Digests, Corporations ⚷471.

§ 43.51 Redemption Clause

The Company may at its option redeem this debenture at any time hereafter upon payment of the principal amount hereof, plus a premium of ______% of such principal amount, plus any unpaid interest payable for any fiscal year ended prior to the date of redemption, plus interest at the rate of ______% per annum upon such principal amount for the period from the first day of the fiscal year in which redemption is so made to the date of redemption, provided that notice of such redemption, stating the time and place of redemption, shall be published at least once each week for four (4) successive weeks prior to the redemption date in a daily newspaper of general circulation published in ______. Thereupon this debenture shall become due and payable at the time and place designated for redemption in such notice, and payment of the redemption price shall be paid to the bearer of this debenture upon presentation and surrender thereof and of all unpaid interest coupons annexed hereto. Unless default shall be made in the redemption of this debenture upon such presentation, interest on this debenture shall cease from and after the date of redemption so designated. If the amount necessary to redeem this debenture shall have been deposited with the ______ Trust Company and if the notice of redemption shall have been duly published as aforesaid, this debenture shall be conclusively deemed to have been redeemed on the date specified for redemption, and all liability of the Company hereon shall cease on such date and all rights of the holder of this debenture, except the right to receive the redemption price out of the moneys so deposited, shall cease and terminate on such date.

§ 43.52 Negative Pledge Clause

That the Company is lawfully possessed of all the pledged securities, that it has good right and lawful authority to pledge the same as provided in and by this Indenture, and that this Indenture is and always will be kept a first lien upon all the property hereby pledged, or agreed or intended to be pledged, and that the Company will not voluntarily create, or suffer to be created, any debt, lien or charge prior to the lien of this Indenture upon the property pledged hereunder, or any part thereof, or upon the income thereof, and will promptly pay and discharge every obligation for which any lien upon the trust estate prior to the lien of this Indenture may exist or could be created; provided that nothing in this Section ______ contained shall require the Company to pay any alleged debt, lien or charge so long as it shall in good faith and by appropriate legal proceedings contest the validity thereof, unless thereby the rights and security of the holders of bonds secured hereby shall be materially endangered.

The Company covenants and agrees that it will not declare or pay at any time any cash dividend or make any other distribution on, or purchase or retire or otherwise acquire for a consideration any shares of its capital stock unless interest on all of the bonds then outstanding under this Indenture shall have been paid at the rate of ______ per cent (______%) per annum from the date of issue thereof to the interest payment date next preceding said proposed payment of dividends, or unless provision for the payment thereof shall have been made prior to the declaration of any such dividend or the making of any such distribution or any such purchase, retirement or acquisition of stock, provided, however, no such cash dividend shall be paid or distribution made unless prior to or concurrently with the payment thereof the Company shall have set aside for the payment of interest on the bonds outstanding hereunder on the interest payment dates provided hereunder a sum equal to all interest accumulated at the rate of ______ per cent (______%) per annum on the bonds then outstanding hereunder from the last preceding interest date to the date of payment of such cash dividend or the making of such distribution, plus a sum equal to the interest at the rate of ______ per cent (______%) per annum to accrue upon the bonds then outstanding during the six months' period next succeeding the payment of such cash dividend or the making of such distribution.

COMMENT

Negative pledge clauses may be used in any form of bond or debenture and serve to protect the holders against corporate action, the effect of which is to impair the security. Such clauses are more generally included in debentures, which create only an equitable charge upon all the assets of the issuer, which can be protected and enforced only in equity. By restricting the issuer, from giving priority to any other charge, the marketability of such securities is enhanced.

§ 43.53 Call Provision

This bond, as a whole or in part, at the election of the Company, is subject to redemption on any interest payment date at the principal amount thereof and the accumulated and unpaid interest thereon as provided in said Indenture, upon thirty days' prior written notice mailed by the Company to the registered holder hereof addressed to him at the address of such holder as shown by the books of the Company for the registration and transfer of bonds, and upon the conditions and in the manner provided in said Indenture. If this bond or any part hereof is called for redemption and payment therefor is duly provided, as specified in the Indenture, interest shall cease to accrue hereon, or on such part hereof, from and after the date fixed for redemption.

§ 43.54 Sinking Fund and Callable Provisions

All bonds of said series are, as to both principal and interest, issued under and equally secured by a *mortgage* dated ______, 19__, whereby ______ Company has mortgaged and pledged all its property now owned and hereafter acquired to ______ Trust Company and ______, as Trustees, as provided in said *mortgage*, as security for said bonds; and reference is hereby made to said *mortgage* for a description of the properties mortgaged and pledged to ______ Trust Company and ______ as such Trustees, and the rights of the holders of said bonds under the same and the terms and conditions upon which said bonds are issued and secured. Said *mortgage* provides for the creation of a sinking fund in the hands of ______ Trust Company.

This bond or any coupon bond in lieu of or in exchange for which this bond is issued may be called and redeemed from the holder on any interest day in the manner provided in said *mortgage* on payment of the principal sum so called, with a premium of ______ per cent thereon, and accrued interest. In the event of such call of one or more coupon bonds in lieu of or in exchange for which this bond is issued, this bond shall be surrendered to ______ Trust Company and thereupon the holder hereof shall be paid the sums payable upon said coupon bond or coupon bonds thus called, and shall in addition thereto receive bonds of said series either coupon or registered without coupons, or both at his option, of a face value equal in the aggregate to the excess of the face value, if any, of this bond over such coupon bond or bonds thus called. If this bond or any such coupon bond is thus called and payment is duly provided, interest shall cease to be payable to the holder hereof on this bond or on that part of the face value of this bond representing a coupon bond which is called or coupon bonds which are called from and after the date fixed in the call for payment.

Library References:

C.J.S. Corporations § 1169.
West's Key No. Digests, Corporations ⚷486.

§ 43.55 Cumulative Interest Provision

Interest at a rate of not exceeding ______ per cent (______%) per annum shall become due and be payable on all bonds outstanding hereunder as hereinafter provided on ______ and ______ of each year to the registered holders thereof on such dates, for the period from the date of issue thereof to ______, 19__, and thereafter for the six months' period ending on the ______ or ______, as the case may be, next preceding such interest date, provided that upon the issuance of any bonds between ______ and ______, both inclusive, or between ______ and ______, both inclusive, of any year, the registered holders thereof shall be entitled to such interest as may become due and payable thereon for the period beginning, but not for the period terminating, on ______ or ______, as the case may be, on or next preceding the date of issuance of said bonds.

Such interest shall be cumulative from and after the date of issue of said bonds respectively, and all accumulated and unpaid interest which shall not theretofore have been paid shall be paid whenever the principal of the bonds shall become due, whether by declaration, call for redemption or at maturity or otherwise. The term "accumulated and unpaid interest" as used in this Indenture and in said bonds shall mean interest on said bonds at the rate of ______ per cent (______%) per annum from the date of issue of said bonds respectively, whether earned or not, to the extent that such interest shall not have been paid as provided in this Article. Such accumulated and unpaid interest shall not bear interest, unless and until the Company shall have made default in paying the same on any date on which the same shall have become due and payable as herein provided, and in that event interest on the amount so in default shall be paid from the date of such default at the rate of ______ per cent (______%) per annum.

COMMENT

The benefit of a provision for cumulative interest in income bonds is to prevent the bondholders from losing their right to interest if not paid from the income of the year in which it accrues because of a diversion to betterments, which in the long run may benefit both Stockholders and holders of income bonds. Central of Georgia Ry. Co. v. Central Trust Co., 135 Ga. 472, 69 S.E. 708 (1911).

§ 43.56 Redemption Provisions

The debentures of this issue are redeemable at the option of the Company, as a whole or in part, on ______ and ______ of any year prior to maturity, in cash and/or refunding debentures and/or bonds of the Company issued as provided herein and in the mortgage, upon notice published at least once in each or not less than three consecutive calendar weeks preceding the date fixed for redemption (the first publication to be at the redemption date) in one daily newspaper of general circulation published in the Cities of ______, ______, and ______, ______, at the principal amounts thereof and accrued interest thereon to the date of redemption.

The Company may hereafter issue, as in the mortgage provided, and the trustee may certify and deliver, on the order of the Company, additional or new debentures and/or bonds which will be ratably and equally secured by the lien of the mortgage, and any indentures supplemental thereto, with such of the aforesaid debentures as may not have been theretofore paid, or may not thereby be refunded, in such form and of such maturities, and with such provisions as the Company may determine, for all or any of the following purposes:

(a) The acquisition, at a fair and reasonable price as fixed by the Board of Directors of the Company, of new properties and/or additions and betterments to existing properties.

(b) The redemption and/or refunding of the debentures and/or bonds issued hereunder.

§ 43.57 Participation Interest Created by Assignment

______ Company hereby assigns to ______, the holder hereof, an undivided share of ______ Dollars ($______) and interest thereon at the rate of ______ per cent per annum from the date hereof, in the bond and mortgage hereinafter specified, equal and coordinate with all other shares assigned or retained by the company, the aggregate amount of all such shares, issued and retained, at no time to exceed the amount then owing on said bond and mortgage.

§ 43.58 Interim Certificate—Negotiable

ISSUED BY ______ TRUST COMPANY

No. ______ $______

Upon the surrender of this certificate properly indorsed, this Company will deliver to ______, or order, ______ Dollars, par value, of ______ per cent ______ bonds, due ______, with coupons attached representing interest accruing thereon from ______, 19__, until maturity, when, if, and as said bonds are issued and delivered to this Company. When said bonds have been received by the undersigned and are ready for delivery, notice to that effect will be transmitted to the above-named holder hereof at registered address.

______ Trust Company

By ____________________

Dated ______, 19__.

§ 43.59 Interim Certificate—Nonnegotiable

ISSUED BY ______ TRUST COMPANY

______, of ______, has made payment for and is entitled to receive the following securities, when, as, and if issued and received by us. Should these securities not be issued and received, the undersigned reserves the right to refund the amount paid and cancel the transaction: ______. With interest accrued thereon from ______, 19__. When these securities are ready, notice to that effect will be mailed to the above address. No person or persons other than the above-named shall acquire or make any claim hereunder.

Return this certificate when calling for above-described securities.

_____ Trust Company

By ________________

Dated ______, 19__.

§ 43.60 Alternative Provisions to Incorporate in a Debenture or Bond—Reference to Agreement Pursuant to Which It Is Issued

This bond is one of the bonds described in and issued pursuant to a Deed of Trust dated ______, 19__, from [*Name of Issuer*] to [*Name of Trustee*] and [*Other Detail Such as:* which deed of trust is to be duly recorded in the Clerk's Office of the ______ Court of the City of ______].

[*or*]

This bond is one of a series of bonds in the aggregate amount of $500,000.00 which are or may be issued pursuant to and secured by a certain Indenture and Deed of Trust dated [*Specify*] from the issuer to [*Name of Trustee*] and is entitled to all of the security and benefits therein provided.

[*or*]

This debenture is one of an issue of debentures of the Company, not limited in principal amount except as in the Indenture hereinafter mentioned provided [*or* limited to the principal amount of $______] all issued and to be issued under and in accordance with the provisions of the Indenture, dated as of ______, 19__, executed by the Company and ______ Trust Company, Trustee (herein, together with any indenture supplemental thereto, called the "Indenture") to which Indenture reference is made for a description of the rights of the holders of the Debenture and of the Company in respect thereof, the rights, duties and immunities of the Trustee, and the terms and conditions upon which the debentures and coupons are and are to be issued.

[*or*]

This bond is one of an issue of bonds by the Company (herein referred to as the bonds) not limited in principal amount except as in the Mortgage hereinafter mentioned provided, all issued and to be issued and equally and ratably secured by an Indenture (herein, together with any indentures supplemental thereto, called the Mortgage) dated as of ______, 19__, executed by the Company to ______ Bank, Trustee, to which Mortgage reference is made for a description of the property mortgaged, the nature and extent of the security, the rights of the holders of the bonds and of the Company in respect thereof, the rights, duties and immunities of the Trustee, and the terms and conditions upon which the bonds are, and are to be, issued and secured.

[*or*]

This security [bond, debenture, note, *etc.*] is one of the securities described in and issued pursuant to a Deed of Trust dated [*Specify*] from [*Name of Issuer*] to [*Specify, Such as Trustee, Etc.*] and [*Other Details May Be Specified Such as Recording Data for Deeds of Trust, Etc.*]. The provisions of that Deed of Trust are incorporated in this security and made a part of it by this reference.

[*or*]

This bond is one of a series of bonds in the aggregate amount of [*Specify*] which are or may be issued pursuant to and secured by a certain Indenture and Deed of Trust dated [*Specify*] from the issuer to [*Specify*] and is entitled to all of the security and benefits therein provided. The provisions of that Deed of Trust are incorporated in this security and made a part of it by this reference.

COMMENT

The terms of a security include those stated on the security and those made a part of the security by reference to other instruments, indentures or documents or to constitutions, statutes, ordinances, rules, regulations, orders and the like, to the extent that the terms so referred to do not conflict with the terms stated on the security. The terms are binding upon all persons, including purchasers for value, but they do not charge a purchaser for value with notice of a defect which goes to the validity of the security, even though the security states that the person accepting it admits such notice.

§ 43.61 Conversion Provision for Trading Securities

§ —.1(a) The holder of any Debenture or Debentures shall have the right at any time prior to maturity, at his option, to convert, subject to the terms and provisions of this Section, the principal amount of any such Debenture or Debentures (or any portion of the principal amount thereof which is an integral multiple of $1000) into fully paid and non-assessable shares of Common Stock at the conversion rate of _______ shares of Common Stock for each $1,000 principal amount of Debentures, subject in each case to any adjustments in such conversion rate pursuant to the provisions of (d) (except that with respect to any Debenture or Debentures which shall be called for redemption such right shall terminate at the close of business on the second business day next preceding the date fixed for redemption of such Debenture or Debentures, unless the Company shall default in payment due upon redemption thereof), upon surrender of the Debenture or Debentures, the principal of which is so to be converted, to the Company at any time during usual business hours at ______, and, if so required by the Company, accompanied by a written instrument or instruments of transfer in form satisfactory to the Company and the Trustee duly executed by the holder or his duly authorized agent or legal representative. Prior to delivery of any certificate or certificates representing shares of Common Stock into which the principal of such Debenture or Debentures is so to be converted, the Company shall have received a written notice at its said office from the holder of the Debenture or Debentures so surrendered specifying the name or names (with address) in which said certificate or certificates are to be issued. For convenience, the conversion of all or a portion, as the case may be, of the principal of any Debenture into Common Stock is hereinafter sometimes referred to as the conversion of such Debenture. All Debentures surrendered for conversion shall if surrendered to the Company or any conversion agent, be delivered to the Trustee for cancelation and cancelled by it or, if surrendered to the Trustee, shall be cancelled by it, and no Debentures shall be issued in lieu thereof. The Trustee within a reasonable time shall upon request return cancelled Debentures to the Company.

In case any Debenture shall be surrendered for conversion of only a portion of the principal amount thereof, the Company shall execute and the Trustee shall authenticate and deliver to the holder of such Debenture, at the expense of the Company, a new Debenture or Debentures in principal amount equal to the unconverted portion of the Debenture so surrendered.

In case of the surrender of any Debenture for conversion (in whole or in part) on a date after the record date (as defined in ______) for the payment of any interest on Debentures and before the date for payment of such interest, such Debenture shall be accompanied by funds in an amount equal to the amount of interest which would have been payable on such interest payment date in respect of the principal represented by the Debenture (or portion thereof) so surrendered for conversion had the same not been so surrendered for conversion; provided, however, that no such funds need be deposited in the case of any Debenture (or portion thereof) which has been duly called for redemption prior to such interest payment date. The funds so deposited shall be paid on the interest payment date to the person in whose name such Debenture (or the Debenture or Debentures in exchange or substitution for which such Debenture shall have been issued) was registered on such record date; provided, however, that if the Company shall default in the payment of interest due on the Debentures on such interest payment date, such funds shall be repaid to the person who deposited the same.

(b) As promptly as practicable after the surrender, as herein provided, of any Debenture or Debentures for conversion, the Company shall deliver or cause to be delivered at the office or agency to be maintained by it in accordance with the provisions of Section ______ to or upon the written order of the holder of the Debenture or Debentures so surrendered a certificate or certificates representing the number of fully paid and non-assessable shares of Common Stock into which such Debenture or Debentures (or portion thereof) shall have been converted. Prior to delivery of such certificate or certificates, the Company shall have received at its said office or agency from the holder of the Debenture or Debentures so surrendered the written notice referred to in (a) with respect to the name or names (with address) in which said certificate or certificates are to be issued. Subject to the following provisions of this Section and of Section (d), such conversion shall be deemed to have been made immediately prior to the close of business on the date that such Debenture or Debentures shall have been surrendered for conversion, so that the rights of the holder of such Debenture or Debentures (or the portion thereof being converted) as a Debentureholder shall cease at such time, and the person or persons entitled to receive the shares of Common Stock upon conversion of such Debenture or Debentures shall be treated for all purposes as having become the record holder or holders of such shares of Common Stock at such time, and such conversion shall be at the conversion rate in effect at such time; provided, however, that no such surrender on any date when the stock transfer books of the Company shall be closed shall be effective to constitute the person or persons entitled to receive the shares of Common Stock upon such conversion as the record holder or holders of such shares of Common Stock on such date, but such surrender shall be effective to constitute the person or persons entitled to receive such shares of Common Stock as the record holder or holders thereof for all purposes at the time immediately prior to the close of business on the next succeeding day on which such stock transfer books are open, and such conversion shall be at the conversion rate in effect at such time on such next succeeding day.

(c) No adjustments in respect of accrued interest or dividends shall be made upon the conversion of any Debenture or Debentures.

(d) The conversion rate from time to time in effect shall be subject to adjustment as follows:

(1) In case the Company shall (A) pay a dividend in shares of its capital stock, (B) subdivide its outstanding shares of Common Stock, (C) combine its outstanding shares of Common Stock

into a smaller number of shares, or (D) issue by reclassification of its shares of Common Stock any shares of the Company, the conversion rate in effect immediately prior thereto shall be adjusted retroactively as provided below so that the holder of any Debenture thereafter surrendered for conversion shall be entitled to receive the number of shares of the Company which he would have owned or have been entitled to receive after the happening of any of the events described above had such Debenture been converted immediately prior to the happening of such event. An adjustment made pursuant to this subsection (1) shall become effective retroactively immediately after the record date in the case of a dividend and shall become effective immediately after the effective date in the case of a subdivision, combination or reclassification.

(2) In case the Company shall issue rights or warrants to all holders of its Common Stock entitling them (for a period expiring within 45 days after the record date mentioned below) to subscribe for or purchase shares of Common Stock at a price per share less than the current market price per share of Common Stock (as defined in subsection (4) below) at the record date mentioned below, the number of shares of Common Stock into which each $1,000 principal amount of Debentures shall thereafter be convertible shall be determined by multiplying the number of shares of Common Stock into which such principal amount of Debentures was theretofore convertible by a fraction, the numerator of which shall be the number of shares of Common Stock outstanding on the date of issuance of such rights or warrants plus the number of additional shares of Common Stock offered for subscription or purchase, and the denominator of which shall be the number of shares of Common Stock outstanding on the date of issuance of such rights or warrants plus the number of shares which the aggregate offering price of the total number of shares so offered would purchase at such current market price. Subject to subsection (5), such adjustment shall be made whenever such rights or warrants are issued and shall become effective retroactively immediately after the record date for the determination of Stockholders entitled to receive such rights or warrants.

(3) In case the Company shall distribute to all holders of its Common Stock evidences of its indebtedness or assets (excluding cash dividends or distributions) or rights to subscribe or warrants to purchase (excluding those referred to in subsection (2) above), then in each such case the number of shares of Common Stock into which each $1,000 principal amount of Debentures shall thereafter be convertible shall be determined by multiply-

ing the number of shares of Common Stock into which such principal amount of Debentures was theretofore convertible by a fraction, the numerator of which shall be the current market price (as defined in subsection (4) below) per share of Common Stock on the date of such distribution, and the denominator of which shall be such current market price per share of the Common Stock, less the then fair market value (as determined by the Board of Directors, whose determination shall be conclusive, and described in a statement filed with the Trustee) of the portion of the assets or evidences of indebtedness so distributed or of such subscription rights or warrants applicable to one share of the Common Stock. Subject to subsection (5), such adjustment shall be made whenever any such distribution is made and shall become effective retroactively immediately after the record date for the determination of Stockholders entitled to receive such distribution.

(4) For the purpose of any computation under subsections (2) and (3) above, the current market price per share of Common Stock at any date shall be deemed to be the average of the daily closing prices for the 30 consecutive business days commencing 45 business days before the day in question. The closing price for each day shall be the last reported sales price regular way or, in case no such reported sale takes place on such day, the average of the reported closing bid and asked prices regular way, in either case on the New York Stock Exchange, or, if the Common Stock is not listed or admitted to trading on such Exchange, on the principal national securities exchange on which the Common Stock is listed or admitted to trading, or if not listed or admitted to trading on any national securities exchange, the average of the closing bid and asked prices as furnished by any New York Stock Exchange firm selected from time to time by the Company for the purpose.

(5) No adjustment in the conversion rate shall be required unless such adjustment would require an increase or decrease of at least 1% in such rate; provided, however, that any adjustments which by reason of this subsection (5) are not required to be made shall be carried forward cumulatively and taken into account in any subsequent adjustment which (including such carry-forward) requires an increase or decrease of at least 1%. All calculations shall be made to the nearest cent or to the nearest one-thousandth of a share, as the case may be.

(6) Whenever the conversion rate is adjusted, as herein provided, the Company shall promptly file with the Trustee a certificate of a firm of independent public accountants selected by the Board of Directors (who may be the regular accountants

employed by the Company) setting forth the conversion rate applicable after such adjustment and setting forth a brief statement of the facts requiring such adjustment. Such certificate shall be conclusive evidence of the correctness of such adjustment. Promptly after receipt of such certificate, the Trustee, in the name of the Company and as its agent, shall mail a notice specifying such adjustment to each Debentureholder at his last address appearing on the registration books of the Company. The Trustee shall not at any time be under any duty or responsibility to any Debentureholder to determine whether any facts exist which may require any adjustment of the conversion rate.

(7) In the event that at any time, as a result of an adjustment made pursuant to subsection (1) of this Section, the holder of any Debenture thereafter surrendered for conversion shall become entitled to receive any shares of the Company other than shares of its Common Stock, thereafter the number of such other shares so receivable upon conversion of any Debenture shall be subject to adjustment from time to time in a manner and on terms as nearly equivalent as practicable to the provisions with respect to the Common Stock contained in subsections (1) to (6), inclusive, of this Section, and the provisions of Sections (b) and (e) to (i), inclusive, with respect to the Common Stock shall apply on like terms to any such other shares.

(e) No fractional shares or scrip representing fractional shares shall be issued upon the conversion of any Debenture or Debentures. If more than one Debenture shall be surrendered for conversion at one time by the same holder, the number of full shares issuable upon conversion thereof shall be computed on the basis of the aggregate principal amount of the Debentures so surrendered. If the conversion of any Debenture or Debentures results in a fraction, an amount equal to such fraction multiplied by the closing price (determined as provided by Section (d)(4)) of the Common Stock on the day of conversion shall be paid to such holder in cash by the Company.

(f) In case of any consolidation of the Company with or merger of the Company into another Corporation, or in case of any sale or other disposition of all or substantially all the property of the Company as an entirety to any person, the Corporation resulting from such consolidation or such successor or acquiring person, as the case may be, shall execute and deliver to the Trustee a supplemental indenture, in form satisfactory to the Trustee, providing that the holder of each Debenture then outstanding shall have the right thereafter to convert such Debenture into the kind and amount of shares of stock and other securities and property receivable upon such consolidation, merger, sale, lease or other disposition by a holder of the number of shares of Common Stock of the Company into which such Debenture might have been converted immediately prior to such consolidation, merger, sale or other disposition. Such supplemental indenture shall provide for adjustments which shall be as nearly equivalent as may be practicable to the adjustments provided for herein. The provisions of this Section shall similarly apply to successive consolidations, mergers, sales or other dispositions. Notice of the execution of such a supplemental indenture shall be given.

The Trustee shall not be under any responsibility to determine the correctness of any provisions contained in any such supplemental indenture relating either to the kind or amount of shares of stock or securities or property receivable by Debentureholders upon the conversion of their Debentures after any such consolidation, merger, sale, lease or other disposition or to any such adjustment, but, may accept as conclusive evidence of the correctness of any such provisions, and shall be protected in relying upon, an Opinion of Counsel with respect thereto.

(g) The Company covenants that it will at all times reserve and keep available out of its authorized Common Stock, solely for the purpose of issuance upon conversion of Debentures as herein provided, such number of shares of Common Stock as shall then be issuable upon the conversion of all outstanding Debentures. The Company covenants that all shares of Common Stock which shall be so issuable shall, when issued, be duly and validly issued and fully paid and non-assessable.

The Company covenants that, upon conversion of Debentures as herein provided, there will be credited to Common Stock capital account, from the consideration for which the shares of Common Stock issuable upon such conversion are issued, an amount per share of Common Stock so issued as determined by the Board of Directors, which amount shall not be less than the amount required by law and by the Certificate of Incorporation of the Company, as amended, as in effect on the date of such conversion. For the purposes of this covenant the principal amount of the Debentures converted, less the amount of cash paid in lieu of the issuance of fractional shares on such conversion, shall be deemed to be the amount of consideration for which the shares of Common Stock issuable upon such conversion are issued.

(h) The Company covenants that if any shares of Common Stock required to be reserved for purposes of conversion of Debentures hereunder require registration with or approval of any governmental authority under any federal or state law before such shares may be issued upon conversion, the Company will in good faith and as expeditiously as possible endeavor to cause such shares to be duly registered or approved, as the case may be. The Company further covenants that, at any time when the Common Stock of the Company is listed on the New York Stock Exchange or any other national securities exchange, the Company will, if permitted by the rules of such exchange, list and keep listed on such exchange, upon official notice of issuance, all shares of Common Stock issuable upon conversion of Debentures.

(i) The issuance of certificates for shares of Common Stock upon the conversion of Debentures shall be made without charge to the converting Debentureholders for any tax in respect of the issuance of such certificates, and such certificates shall be issued in the respective names of, or in such names as may be directed by, the holders of the Debentures converted; provided, however, that the Company shall not be required to pay any tax which may be payable in respect of any transfer involved in the issuance and delivery of any such certificate in a name other than that of the holder of the Debenture converted, and the Company shall not be required to issue or deliver such certificates unless or until the person or persons requesting the issuance thereof shall have paid to the Company the amount of such tax or shall have established to the satisfaction of the Company that such tax has been paid.

(j) In case the Company proposes to take any action (other than actions of the character described in clauses (A), (B) or (C) of subsection (1) of Section (d)) which would require an adjustment of the conversion rate pursuant to Section (d) or proposes to take any action of the type specified in Section (f), the Company shall give notice to the holders of Debentures at their last addresses as they shall appear upon the register or registers at least ten days prior to the applicable record date in the case of action which would require an adjustment of the conversion rate pursuant to Section (d) and at least ten days prior to the taking of any action described in Section (e), which notice shall state (1) in the case of action requiring an adjustment of the conversion rate pursuant to Section (d), the record date as of which such action is to be taken and (2) in the case of action specified in Section (e), the date on which such action is to become effective, and in each case such notice shall describe the action to be taken and, to the extent such effect may be known at the date of such notice, the effect of such action on the conversion ratio and the number, or kind, or class of shares or other securities or property obtainable upon conversion of the Debentures. Failure to give such notice or any defect therein shall not affect the legality or validity of any such action.

(k) The Trustee shall not be accountable with respect to the validity or value (or the kind or amount) of any shares of Common Stock or of any securities or property which may at any time be issued or delivered upon the conversion of any Debentures;

and it makes no representation with respect thereto. The Trustee shall not be responsible for any failure of the Company to make any cash payment or to issue, transfer or deliver any shares of Common Stock or stock certificates or other securities or property upon the surrender of any Debenture for the purpose of conversion, or to comply with any of the covenants of the Company contained herein.

§ 43.62 Convertible Bonds—Resolution of Directors

Upon motion duly made, seconded, and carried, the following resolution was duly adopted:

Resolved, That the holders of any or all of the bonds of the [*Name of Corporation*] Corporation may and shall have the right to convert the principal of the debt evidenced by such bonds into shares of the Corporation, all of which are [*Class*] shares without par value, on the ______ day of ______, 19__, the exchange and conversion to be made on the basis of ______ shares without par value for each ______ ($______) Dollars face value, of the bonds converted. Provided, however, that the right to convert is conferred subject to the condition that holders of such bonds to be converted shall serve upon the Corporation at its office, on or before the ______ day of ______, 19__, a written notice stating the amount of the par value of the bonds which they will present for conversion.

§ 43.63 Simple Redemption Provision in Articles of Incorporation

The whole or any part of the ______ stock of the Corporation, at the option of the Board of Directors, may be redeemed on any quarterly dividend payment date by paying therefor in cash ______ per share and all unpaid and accrued dividends thereon at the date fixed for such redemption, upon sending by mail to the registered holders of the ______ stock at least sixty (60) days' notice of the exercise of such option. If at any time the Board of Directors shall determine to redeem less than the whole amount of ______ stock then outstanding, the particular stock to be so redeemed shall be determined in such manner as the Board of Directors shall prescribe; provided, however, that no holder of ______ stock shall be preferred over any other holder of such stock.

§ 43.64 Complex Redemption Provision in Articles of Incorporation

(a) The Corporation may at any time, at the option of the Board of Directors expressed by resolution, redeem the whole or any part of the ______ stock at the time outstanding, or the whole or any part of any series thereof, upon notice duly given as hereinafter provided by paying or providing for the payment in cash of the redemption price or the respective redemption prices theretofore fixed by the Board of Directors as hereinabove provided, plus dividends accrued thereon to the date fixed for redemption. Not less than thirty (30) days previous notice of every such redemption of preferred stock shall be mailed to holders of record of the preferred stock to be redeemed, at their last known post office addresses as shown by the Corporation's records. In case of the redemption of a part only of any series of the preferred stock at the time outstanding, the shares of the preferred stock of such series to be redeemed shall be selected pro rata or by lot or in such other manner as the Board of Directors may determine. The Board of Directors shall have full power and authority to prescribe the manner in which and, subject to the provisions and limitations herein contained, the terms and conditions upon which such stock shall be redeemed from time to time.

If the aforesaid notice of redemption shall have been duly given, and if on or before the redemption date designated in such notice, the funds necessary for such redemption shall have been set aside, so as to be and continue to be available therefor, then, notwithstanding that any certificate of such ______ stock so called for redemption shall not have been surrendered for cancellation, the dividends thereon shall cease to accrue from and after the date of redemption so designated, and all rights with respect to such ______ stock so called for redemption shall forthwith after such redemption date cease and determine except only the right of the holder to receive the redemption price therefor, but without interest; or if after notice of redemption of any such ______ stock shall have been duly given as hereinabove provided, and if on or before the redemption date designated in such notice, the Corporation shall deposit in trust with any bank or trust company in the continental United States having a capital and undivided surplus aggregating at least five million dollars ($5,000,000), named in such notice, to be applied to the redemption of the ______ stock so called for redemption, funds sufficient to redeem such ______ stock upon the date specified in the notice of redemption, then from and after the time of such deposit all rights of holders of the ______ stock so called for redemption, as Stockholders of the Corporation, shall cease and determine, except the right to receive the moneys so deposited, but without interest, and the right, if any, to convert such shares into other classes of stock of the Corporation within the period theretofore fixed by the Board of Directors, as hereinbefore provided, for the exercise of such right of conversion. Any funds so deposited which shall not be required for such redemption because of the exercise of any such right of conversion subsequent to the date of such deposit shall be returned to the Corporation forthwith. Any interest accrued on such funds shall be paid to the Corporation from time to time. Any funds so set aside or deposited, as the case may be, and unclaimed at the end of six (6) years from such redemption date shall be released and/or repaid to the Corporation, and such holders of such ______ stock so called for redemption as shall not have received the redemption price prior to such release and/or repayment to the Corporation shall be deemed to be unsecured creditors of the Corporation for the redemption price and shall look only to the Corporation for payment thereof.

(b) (1) Shares of ______ stock redeemed pursuant to the provisions hereof or purchased or redeemed pursuant to any obligation of the Corporation to purchase or redeem shares for a sinking fund or for which credit shall have been taken against any sinking fund obligation, or converted into other classes of stock of the Corporation, if convertible, shall not be reissued or otherwise disposed of, and appropriate proceedings by the Corporation to retire such shares and to effect a corresponding reduction of the stated capital of the Corporation shall be taken at least once annually, provided that the Corporation shall not be required to take any such proceedings at any time when the number of shares previously so redeemed or purchased, with respect to which no proceedings shall have theretofore been taken, shall be less than 500.

(2) Subject to applicable restrictions herein contained, the Corporation shall have the right to purchase shares of its stock, of any class, in the open market and, as to all or any part of the stock from time to time purchased, hold same as treasury stock or resell or reissue or cancel said stock, upon such terms as the Board of Directors shall determine.

§ 43.65 Article Provisions Relating to Restrictions on Dividends and a Sinking Fund

(a) (1) In no event, so long as any of the preferred stock shall be outstanding, shall any dividend whatsoever, whether in cash, stock or otherwise, be paid or declared nor any distribution made, on any stock of the Corporation not ranking prior to or on a parity with the preferred stock nor shall any shares of such subordinate stock be purchased, redeemed or otherwise acquired by the Corporation, nor shall any moneys be paid to or set aside or made available for a sinking fund for the purchase or redemption of any such subordinate stock, unless

(A) All dividends on the preferred stock of all series for all past quarterly dividend periods shall have been paid and the full dividends for the then current quarterly dividend period shall have been paid or declared and a sum sufficient for the payment thereof set apart; and

(B) The Corporation shall have set aside all amounts, if any, theretofore required to be set aside as and for all sinking funds, if any, for the preferred stock of all series for the then current year, and all defaults, if any, in complying with any such sinking fund requirements in respect of previous years shall have been made good.

(2) In no event so long as any of the preferred stock shall be outstanding shall any dividend be paid on any stock of the Corporation subordinate to the preferred stock, nor any distribution made on such subordinate stock, nor shall any shares of such subordinate stock be purchased or redeemed by the Corporation, nor shall any moneys be paid to or made available for a sinking fund for the purchase or redemption of any such subordinate stock.

(b) Any sinking fund provided for the purchase or redemption of preferred stock of any series may provide for the purchase or redemption of stock of such series and of any other series of preferred stock created thereafter.

Unless the Corporation shall have set aside all amounts, if any theretofore required to be set aside as and for all sinking funds, if any, for the preferred stock of all series for the then current year and all defaults, if any, in complying with any such sinking fund requirements in respect of previous years shall have been made good, in no event, so long as any of the preferred stock shall be outstanding, shall any dividend whatsoever, whether in cash, stock or otherwise, be paid or declared, nor any distribution made, on any stock of the Corporation, not ranking prior to or on a parity with the preferred stock, nor shall any shares of such subordinate stock be purchased, redeemed or otherwise acquired by the Corporation nor shall any moneys be paid or set aside or made available for a sinking fund for the purchase or redemption of any such subordinate stock. But default by the Corporation in complying with the sinking fund requirements for the preferred stock for any series shall have no other consequence.

Moneys in any such sinking fund not at the time required for the redemption of shares of stock may be applied by the Corporation to the purchase, at public or private sale, as the Board of Directors of the Corporation may determine, of shares of stock of the one or more series for which such sinking fund shall have been provided, if obtainable at not exceeding the redemption price or prices thereof for sinking fund purposes at the respective dates of purchase. Any money remaining in any sinking fund on the fortieth day preceding any dividend payment date shall, if sufficient to redeem at least one hundred (100) shares, be applied (together with an amount equal to the dividends on the shares called for redemption accrued to the date fixed for redemption, which amount the Corporation shall provide out of its general funds) to the redemption of shares of such one or more series on such dividend payment date, provided, however, that with respect to any shares so called for redemption which shall be converted on or prior to such dividend payment date, such moneys shall be returned to the Corporation forthwith.

When no shares of the one or more series for which any such sinking fund shall have been provided shall remain outstanding, any balance remaining in any such sinking fund shall be repaid to and/or become a part of the general funds of the Corporation.

§ 43.66 Protective Provisions for Senior Securities in Articles

(a) The consent of the holders of two-thirds (⅔) of the preferred stock at the time outstanding shall be necessary for effecting or validating any amendment, alteration or repeal of any of the provisions of the Articles of Incorporation, as amended, which would adversely affect the rights or preferences of the preferred stock or the holders thereof. If any such amendment, repeal or alteration would adversely affect the rights or preferences of any particular series of the preferred stock without correspondingly affecting the remaining outstanding preferred stock, then the like consent of the holders of four-fifths (⅘) of the preferred stock of that particular series shall be necessary for such amendment, repeal or alteration. Notwithstanding the foregoing: (1) no transaction of the type referred to in paragraphs (b) and (c) below, and (2) no transaction relating to an increase in the authorized amount of preferred stock, or the authorization or creation of any additional class of stock ranking prior to or on a parity with the preferred stock, or any increase in the authorized amount of any class of stock ranking prior to or on a parity with the preferred stock, or the authorization or creation of any class of stock or obligation convertible into or evidencing the right to purchase any stock of any class ranking on a parity with the preferred stock, shall be deemed to be such an amendment, alteration or repeal.

(b) So long as any shares of preferred stock are outstanding, the consent of the holders of at least a majority of the preferred stock at the time outstanding shall be necessary for effecting or validating any one or more of the following transactions:

(1) The sale, lease or conveyance by the Corporation of all or substantially all of its property or business or the parting with control thereof;

(2) The merger or consolidation of the Corporation with or into any other Corporation, unless the Corporation resulting

from such merger or consolidation will have after such merger or consolidation no class of stock and no other securities either authorized or outstanding ranking prior to or on a parity with the preferred stock except the same number of shares of stock and the same amount of other securities with the same rights and preferences as the stock and securities of the Corporation respectively authorized and outstanding immediately preceding such merger or consolidation, and unless each holder of preferred stock immediately preceding such merger or consolidation shall receive the same number of shares, with the same rights and preferences, of the resulting Corporation;

(3) The authorization or creation of any additional class of stock ranking prior to or on a parity with the preferred stock or the increase in the authorized amount of any class of stock ranking prior to or on a parity with the preferred stock;

(4) The giving by the Corporation or any subsidiary of any guarantee of any stock of any Corporation.

(c) So long as any shares of preferred stock are outstanding, the consent of the holders of at least a majority of the preferred stock at the time outstanding, shall be necessary for effecting or validating any one or more of the following transactions, unless, after giving effect to such transaction or transactions consolidated net tangible assets will be at least two times the sum of (1) all funded debt of the Corporation and its subsidiaries to be outstanding after giving effect to such transaction or transactions and (2) the total amount which would be payable on involuntary liquidation on all shares of prior stock to be outstanding after giving effect to such transaction or transactions, in which event any of the following transactions may be effected, without the consent of the preferred stock and the holders of such stock shall have no right at a meeting or otherwise to consider or pass upon the same;

(1) The creation, authorization or issue (other than to the Corporation and/or one or more wholly owned subsidiaries) by any subsidiary of any stock ranking prior to the common stock of such subsidiary, or of any stock or other securities convertible into or exchangeable for such prior stock, or the sale or other disposition by the Corporation or any wholly owned subsidiary of any such prior stock or convertible stock or convertible security of a subsidiary unless, prior thereto or at the same time, all other stock of such subsidiary owned directly or indirectly by the Corporation and/or its wholly owned subsidiaries is sold or disposed of;

(2) The issue by the Corporation (other than to one or more wholly owned subsidiaries) of (A) shares of any class of stock ranking prior to the preferred stock or (B) shares of preferred

stock or of any other class of stock ranking on a parity with the preferred stock, or the sale or other disposition by any such wholly owned subsidiary of any such stock of the Corporation;

(3) The creation, issue and sale or assumption by the Corporation or any subsidiary (other than to the Corporation and/or one or more wholly owned subsidiaries) of any indebtedness or the giving by the Corporation or any subsidiary of any guarantee or similar obligation for the payment of any debt or other obligation.

Wherever under any of the provisions of section (2) hereof the consent or vote of a proportion of the holders of the preferred stock shall be a prerequisite or shall be otherwise specified such consent or vote shall be given in person or by proxy, either in writing or at a special meeting called for that purpose at which the holders of the preferred stock shall vote as a class.

(d) Except when otherwise herein or by statute specifically provided, the preferred stock shall have no voting power, provided that if and whenever six (6) quarterly dividends thereon whether or not consecutive shall be unpaid, in whole or in part, then the number of directors of the Corporation shall be increased by two and the preferred stock, voting separately as a class, shall be entitled to elect two members of the Board of Directors at any annual meeting of Stockholders or at any special meeting of Stockholders called as herein provided, and such voting power shall so continue to vest in the preferred stock until all arrears in payment of quarterly dividends thereon shall have been paid and the dividends thereon for the current quarter shall have been declared and funds for the payment thereof set aside, and upon the happening of such event the preferred stock shall be divested of such voting power, but subject always to the same provisions for the vesting of such voting power in the preferred stock in the case of any similar future default or defaults.

At any time when such voting power shall be so vested in the preferred stock, the proper officers of the Corporation shall, upon the written request of the holders of record of at least fifteen per cent (15%) in amount of the preferred stock then outstanding, addressed to the secretary of the Corporation, call a special meeting of the holders of the preferred stock for the purpose of electing such additional Directors. Such meeting shall be held at the earliest practicable date thereafter, if such meeting shall not be called by the proper officers of the Corporation within twenty (20) days after personal service of the above request upon the secretary of the Corporation, or within thirty (30) days after mailing of the same within the United States of America by registered mail addressed to the Secretary of the Corporation at its principal office (such mailing to be evidenced by the registry receipt issued by the postal authorities), then the holders of record of at least fifteen per cent (15%) in amount of the preferred stock then outstanding may designate in writing one of their number to call such meeting, and such meeting may be called by such person so designated upon the notice above provided and shall be held at the place for the holding of annual meetings of the Stockholders of the Corporation. Any holder of preferred stock so designated shall have access to the stock books of the Corporation for the purposes of causing such meeting to be called pursuant to these provisions.

At any annual meeting at which the preferred stock shall be entitled to elect Directors or at any special meeting called as above provided, the holders of a majority in interest of the then outstanding preferred stock shall be sufficient to constitute a quorum, whether present in person or by proxy, and the vote of the holders of a majority of the preferred stock so present at any such meeting at which there shall be such quorum shall be sufficient to elect such additional members of the Board of Directors. The persons so elected as Directors, together with the Directors elected by the common stock or other class or classes of stock having voting rights for the election of Directors, shall constitute the Board of Directors of the Corporation. Whenever the preferred stock shall be divested of such voting power as hereinabove provided, the additional Directors so elected by the preferred stock shall thereupon cease to be Directors of the Corporation, either de facto or de jure.

§ 43.67 Subordination Clause

SUBORDINATION

In the event of any insolvency, bankruptcy or reorganization proceedings or other proceedings for the rearrangement or adjustment of debts, relative to the Corporation or its creditors or property, or in the event of any receivership or liquidation of the Corporation or assignment for the benefit of its creditors, or any dissolution or winding up of the Corporation, then all principal and interest on all indebtedness of the Corporation to ______ Bank [*Name of Corporation's Commercial Bank*] (but not in excess of $______ shall first be paid in full before any payment of principal or interest is made hereon, and in any such proceedings any payment or distribution of any kind or character, whether in cash, property or securities, which may be payable or deliverable in respect hereof shall be paid or delivered directly to ______ Bank for application in payment thereof unless and until all indebtedness to ______ Bank has been paid in full. If any event of default specified in this *Debenture/Bond* occurs, no principal hereof or interest hereon shall, except as provided in the foregoing sentence, be paid unless and until all indebtedness of the Corporation to ______

Bank shall have been paid in full together with all interest thereon and all other amounts payable with respect thereto.

COMMENT

One of the principal areas of negotiation in connection with the issuance of a debt, whether public or private, is the degree of subordination of the debt issue to any subsequent indebtedness which may be incurred by the Corporation. Where the issuing Corporation has good financial stability, and is willing to pay a higher rate of interest, it may be able to sell debt with maximum subordination to other debts to be incurred after issuance of the debenture.

§§ 43.68–44.0 are reserved for supplementary material.

PART D

STOCKHOLDERS AND DIRECTORS

CHAPTER 44

STOCKHOLDERS—GENERALLY

Table of Sections

Library References:

C.J.S. Corporations §§ 219, 475–477, 480, 481, 486.
West's Key No. Digests, Corporations ⚿170 et seq.

§ 44.1 Stockholders' Management Functions—Generally

Stockholder management functions *usually* take the form of voting at Stockholder meetings or giving of written consents with respect to (a) election and removal of Directors;[1] (b) adoption, amendment, and repeal of By-laws;[2] (c) Stockholders resolutions, including ratification of Board of Directors action;[3] and (d) extraordinary corporate matters. Traditionally, Stockholders elect the Board of Directors, who manage the Corporation by determining corporate policy and appointing officers to execute such policy. Separation of ownership (in the Stockholders) and management (in the Board of Directors) is inherent in such approach, presenting different problems in the larger Corporations, with occasional lip service to "Stockholder democracy", and in the close Corporation where identity of ownership and management is often desired as in the case of the individual Proprietorship or Partnership.[4]

1. See Chapter 46, infra.
2. See Chapter 34, "By-laws"; supra.
3. See Chapter 48, infra.
4. See Chapter 30, supra.

While the above describes the *usual* role of Stockholders in the management of the Corporation, certain state statutes have special close corporation provisions wherein the Stockholders by agreement can restrict the discretion of the Directors or can even provide in the articles that the Corporation will be managed by the Stockholders rather than the Directors. See Chapter 30, § 30.4, supra, in this regard.

§ 44.2 Stockholder Election and Removal of Directors

See Chapter 48, infra.

§ 44.3 Stockholder Adoption, Amendment and Repeal of By-laws

Initial By-laws are adopted in different jurisdictions by the incorporators, Stockholders, or Board of Directors. Notwithstanding any power in the Board of Directors to amend or repeal the By-laws, Stockholders usually retain inherent power to do so. Statutes sometimes require Stockholder approval for certain By-laws.

For coverage of "By-laws", see Chapter 34, supra.

§ 44.4 Stockholder Meetings and Consents

See Chapter 45, infra.

§ 44.5 Stockholder Voting Agreements

For text and forms relating to voting rights of Stockholders generally, proxies, voting trusts, Stockholder Agreements, Stockholder dissents, and other miscellaneous forms relating to voting, see Chapter 30, supra and Chapter 47, infra.

§ 44.6 Stockholder Stock Purchase Agreements

See Chapter 68, infra.

§ 44.7 Stockholder Resolutions

See Chapter 48, infra.

§ 44.8 Stockholder Inspection Rights

See Chapter 49, infra.

§ 44.9 Transfer of Shares

See Chapter 52, infra.

§ 44.10 Amendment of Articles

See Chapter 51, infra.

§ 44.11 Dividends

See Chapter 57, infra.

§§ 44.12–45.0 are reserved for supplementary material.

CHAPTER 45

STOCKHOLDER MEETINGS AND CONSENTS

Table of Sections

A. STOCKHOLDERS MEETINGS

1. Introduction

2. Notices and Calls for Meetings

3. Stockholder Meeting—Minute Formats

B. STOCKHOLDER CONSENTS

C. STOCKHOLDER DISSENTS

D. MISCELLANEOUS FORMS

A. STOCKHOLDERS MEETINGS

1. INTRODUCTION

Library References:

C.J.S. Corporations §§ 539–548, 553.
West's Key No. Digests, Corporations ⚷191 et seq.

§ 45.1 Types of Stockholder Meetings—Generally [1]

Stockholder meetings are of two principal types: (a) annual and (b) special. Where the incorporators-subscribers are Stockholders, the organization meetings of incorporators can be considered as an additional type. Stockholders of record are entitled to receive notice of, and to be represented in person or by proxy at, such meetings. The Corporation, usually through its Secretary, should keep minutes of all meetings.[2] Such minutes are among the corporate records open to reasonable Stockholder inspection.

1. Adapted from Henn, Law of Corporations (2d ed. 1970) § 191, and Hamilton, Corporations in a Nutshell (1980).

2. Statutes sometimes expressly require the keeping of corporate minutes. E. g., Model Bus.Corp.Act § 52. See also e. g. McKinney's N.Y.

Stockholder meetings, like other meetings, should be conducted with due regard for parliamentary rules.

ANNUAL MEETINGS

Every state statute contains more or less routine provisions about meetings of Stockholders. The Model Business Corporation Act, for example, provides that an annual meeting shall be held "at such time as may be stated in or fixed in accordance with the By-laws," [3], that notice of an annual or special meeting shall be given not less than ten nor more than fifty days before the meeting,[4] and so forth. The failure to hold an annual meeting does not work a dissolution of the Corporation, though any Stockholder may obtain a summary court order to hold an annual meeting if one is not held within any thirteen-month period. So far as notice is concerned, statutes permit written waivers that may be executed before, at, or after the meeting in question.[5] Moreover, the actual meeting may not be held, but the Stockholders may agree to merely consent to certain actions (see § 45.5, infra).

The principal purpose of an annual meeting is the annual election of Directors, but the annual meeting may act on any relevant matter

Bus.Corp.Law § 624; West's Ann. Calif.Corp.Code § 1500. See also Chapter 48, infra.

3. Model Bus.Corp.Act § 28 provides:

§ 28. Meetings of Stockholders

Meetings of Stockholders may be held at such place within or without this State as may be stated in or fixed in accordance with the bylaws. If no other place is stated or so fixed, meetings shall be held at the registered office of the Corporation.

An annual meeting of the Stockholder shall be held at such time as may be stated in or fixed in accordance with the bylaws. If the annual meeting is not held within any thirteen-month period the Court of ——— may, on the application of any Stockholder, summarily order a meeting to be held.

Special meetings of the Stockholders may be called by the Board of Directors, the holders of not less than one-tenth of all the shares entitled to vote at the meeting, or such other persons as may be authorized in the articles of incorporation or the bylaws.

See also e. g. McKinney's N.Y.Bus.Corp. Law § 602; West's Ann.Calif.Corp. Code § 600.

4. Model Bus.Corp.Act § 29 provides:

§ 29. Notice of Stockholders' Meetings

Written notice stating the place, day and hour of the meeting and, in case of a special meeting, the purpose or purposes for which the meeting is called, shall be delivered not less than ten nor more than fifty days before the date of the meeting, either personally or by mail, by or at the direction of the president, the secretary, or the officer or persons calling the meeting, to each Stockholder of record entitled to vote at such meeting. If mailed, such notice shall be deemed to be delivered when deposited in the United States mail addressed to the Stockholder at his address as it appears on the stock transfer books of the Corporation, with postage thereon prepaid.

See also e. g. McKinney's N.Y.Bus.Corp. Law § 605; West's Ann.Calif.Corp. Code § 601.

5. Model Bus.Corp.Act § 144. See also e. g. McKinney's N.Y.Bus.Corp.Law § 606; West's Ann.Calif.Corp.Code § 601.

and is not limited to the purposes set forth in the notice. Indeed, under the Model Act [6] no statement of purposes at all need appear in the notice of annual meeting.

The agenda may include reports of management, the amendment or repeal of By-laws, resolutions introduced in behalf of management or Stockholders, extraordinary corporate matters, or other matters which may properly come before such meetings. The notice of the meeting will usually set forth the purposes thereof.[7] Statutes sometimes provide procedures for special meetings to elect Directors when the required election has not been held.[8]

SPECIAL MEETINGS

Special Stockholder meetings, between the annual meetings, may usually be called pursuant to applicable statutes,[9] the Articles of Incorporation, or more likely the By-laws, for appropriate purposes. Typically, such a meeting may be called by the Directors, the holders of some specified percentage of the outstanding shares of the Corporation, or by certain Officers. Unlike the annual meeting, the only subjects that generally may be considered at a special meeting are matters described in the notice of meeting. There might even be special meetings of particular classes of shares if duly authorized and called for appropriate purposes.

§ 45.2 Place of Stockholder Meetings

Some statutes still require that Stockholder meetings be held in the state of incorporation, but modern statutes expressly permit such meetings to be held within or without the state.[10]

The Articles of Incorporation, or more likely the By-laws, might designate the place of meeting.[11]

§ 45.3 Notice of Stockholder Meetings

Written notice of a Stockholder meeting is usually required to be sent to Stockholders sufficiently in advance of the meeting. There

6. Id. § 29; § 605 of N.Y.Law.

7. See note 4, supra.

8. E. g., McKinney's N.Y.Bus.Corp. Law, § 603.

9. E. g., Model Bus.Corp.Act § 28 (see note 3, supra); McKinney's N.Y.Bus. Corp.Law, § 602(c) (callable by Board of Directors and by such person or persons as may be so authorized by articles of incorporation or bylaws); West's Ann.Calif.Corp.Code § 601.

10. E. g., Model Bus.Corp.Act § 28 (see note 3, supra); Del.Gen.Corp. Law, § 211 (1967) (as bylaws provide). See also McKinney's N.Y.Bus. Corp.Law § 602; West's Ann.Calif. Corp.Code § 600.

11. The 1969 Model Act revision permits the By-laws to prescribe the manner of determining the time and place of meetings and the persons who may call them.

are usually statutory requirements, often implemented by By-law provisions.[12]

Such notice, under the Model Business Corporation Act, for example, must state the place, day, and hour of the meeting and, in case of a special meeting, the purpose or purposes for which the meeting is called, and must be served on or mailed to each Stockholder of record [13] entitled to vote at such meeting not less than 10 nor more than 50 days before the date of meeting.[14]

Notice may be waived in writing before or after a meeting.[15]

If due notice is not given, the meeting, absent waiver or estoppel, is a nullity.[16]

§ 45.4 Quorum at Meetings

A quorum at any annual or special meeting consists of a majority of the outstanding shares, except that the quorum requirement may be increased or decreased by provisions in the Articles or By-laws. Statutes often prescribe a minimum (one-third in the Model Act and in many other statutes) below which the quorum may not be reduced.[17] Statutes, however, do not prescribe a maximum, and it is therefore possible to require the presence of all outstanding shares to constitute a quorum. Such a provision may be adopted in close Corporations as a planning device, even though it increases the risk of a deadlock since a single Stockholder, no matter how small his holding, may prevent the existence of a quorum.

Where a quorum is present, a majority may usually act to bind the Corporation unless a greater vote is required by statute [18] or a

12. See, e. g., Model Bus.Corp.Act § 29 (see note 4, supra).

13. Model Bus.Corp.Act § 29 (see note 4, supra).

14. Model Bus.Corp.Act § 29 (see note 4, supra); cf. Model Bus.Corp.Act § 73 (at least 20 days' notice for Stockholder meeting called to act upon plan of merger or consolidation); McKinney's N.Y.Bus.Corp.Law, § 605 (requiring notice, when proposed action would afford appraisal remedy, to contain statement of purpose of meeting and to effect that proposed action, if taken, would entitle Stockholders fulfilling statutory requirements to appraisal remedy).

15. Model Bus.Corp.Act § 144; West's Ann.Calif.Corp.Code § 601; McKinney's N.Y.Bus.Corp.Law, § 606 (by waiver of notice, signed by any Stockholder in person or by proxy, whether before or after meeting; attendance of any Stockholder at meeting, in person or by proxy, without protesting prior to conclusion of meeting lack of notice of such meeting, to constitute waiver of notice by him).

16. Statutes may excuse lack of notice where delivery of the notice would be impossible. Del.Gen.Corp.Law, § 230 (1967); McKinney's N.Y.Bus. Corp.Law, § 108 (when notice or lapse of time unnecessary; notices dispensed with when delivery prohibited). See also e. g. West's Ann.Calif. Corp.Code § 601.

17. Model Bus.Corp.Act § 32. See also McKinney's N.Y.Bus.Corp.Law § 608; West's Ann.Calif.Corp.Code § 601.

18. Id.

valid provision in the Articles of Incorporation.[19] Where a quorum is present a disgruntled faction may sometimes lose a vote, and leave the meeting seeking to "break" the quorum and prevent the victorious faction from conducting further business. The general rule is that a quorum, once present, continues, and the withdrawal of a faction does not disable the remaining Stockholders from continuing. For this reason, a minority faction usually stays away to prevent a quorum from ever being present rather than appearing and later withdrawing in an attempt to break the quorum.

§ 45.5 Consent Meetings

A number of states authorize Stockholders to conduct business by unanimous written consent without a meeting.[20] Such a provision is particularly helpful in closely held Corporations, where most Stockholders' decisions are unanimous, and the formality of a meeting may be dispensed with. A few states, including Delaware, have gone a step further and authorized holders of the number of shares needed to act on a matter to act by written consent without a meeting.[21]

For additional coverage of consent meetings, see § 45.71 et seq., infra, this Chapter.

§ 45.6 Record of Stockholders—Voting Lists

Statutes frequently require a Corporation to keep at its principal office,[22] or at the office of its transfer agent or registrar, a record of its Stockholders, giving the names and addresses of all Stockholders and the number and class (or series) of the shares held by each. In addition, statutes sometimes require the preparation of a voting list before each Stockholder meeting.

Such record of Stockholders and voting list are among the corporate records open to reasonable Stockholder inspection.[23] Such record ownership is usually conclusively binding on the inspectors of election, and on the courts in certain kinds of court proceedings.

§ 45.7 Inspectors (or Judges or Tellers) of Election

Inspectors (or judges or tellers) of election are, ideally, impartial supervisors of a corporate election when strife is possible. Usually the number is either one or three. When the Corporation is not fraught with strife, inspectors are usually dispensed with.

19. Model Bus.Corp.Act § 143.

20. Model Bus.Corp.Act § 145; West's Ann.Calif.Corp.Code § 601; McKinney's N.Y.Bus.Corp.Law § 615.

21. E. g. Del.Gen.Corp.Law § 228; McKinney's N.Y.Bus.Corp.Law § 615; Minn.Bus.Corp.Act § 302A.441.

22. E. g. Model Bus.Corp.Act § 52. See also Chapter 47, infra.

23. See Chapters 47 and 49, infra.

Obviously, a small number facilitates decision; an odd number avoids a stalemate. In close Corporations, especially, use of inspectors is a burdensome formality frequently disregarded in practice. Statutes do not make their use mandatory but require them pursuant to Stockholder request or By-law requirement.

Stockholders traditionally have the right to appoint the inspectors, but statutes or By-laws might provide for appointment by Directors or the presiding Officer of the meeting. An inspector need not be a Stockholder.[24] Some statutes forbid the appointment of candidates by Director or Officers. Despite lack of express statutory prohibition, an impartial inspector may avoid future lawsuits. A few statutes require the inspectors to be sworn; [25] even when not required, oaths are frequently used in practice.

Inspectors determine the number of shares outstanding and the voting power of each, the shares represented at the meeting, the existence of a quorum, the validity and effect of proxies, receive votes, ballots or consents, hear and determine all challenges and questions arising in connection with the right to vote, count and tabulate all votes, ballots or consents, determine the result, and do such acts as are proper to conduct the election or vote with fairness to all Stockholders. They become important functionaries in cases of contests.[26] The presiding Officer of the meeting must accept the inspectors' certification.[27]

Inspectors' duties are mainly ministerial, but in practice they make quasi-judicial decisions. Their rulings are subject to court review.

§ 45.8 Court Proceedings

To compel or enjoin the holding of a Stockholder meeting, various judicial remedies are available. Mandamus (*or* its statutory counterpart) or injunction are the traditional remedies. In several jurisdictions, special court proceedings are authorized.[28] Exhaustion of remedies within the Corporation, such as demand and refusal, has sometimes been required as a prerequisite to judicial relief.

24. N.J.Bus.Corp.Law, § 14A:5–25 (1969); Pa.Bus.Corp.Law, § 1512 (1966); McKinney's N.Y.Bus.Corp. Law § 610.

25. McKinney's N.Y.Bus.Corp.Law, § 610.

26. E. g., McKinney's N.Y.Bus.Corp. Law, § 610; West's Ann.Calif.Corp. Code § 707.

27. McKinney's N.Y.Bus.Corp.Law, § 611 (any report or certificate of inspectors to be prima facie evidence of facts stated and of vote as certified by them).

28. E. g., McKinney's N.Y.Bus.Corp. Law, § 619; West's Ann.Calif.Corp. Code § 600.

Statutes also authorize summary judicial proceedings to review corporate elections upon the petition of any aggrieved Stockholder.[29] Depending upon the statutory language, the court's power in such proceedings might be limited to confirming the election, ordering a new election, or granting a temporary stay, and might not extend to the determination of various issues or permit the court to go beyond the record ownership.

§ 45.9 Post-Meeting Reports

In recent years, some of the larger Corporations have prepared and mailed to their Stockholders post-meeting reports to promote better Stockholder relations. Prepared shortly after the annual Stockholder meeting, such a report gives an account thereof.

§§ 45.10–45.20 are reserved for supplementary material.

2. NOTICES AND CALLS FOR MEETINGS

Library References:

C.J.S. Corporations §§ 543, 544.
West's Key No. Digests, Corporations ⚷194.

§ 45.21 Notice of Annual Meeting of Stockholders

To: The Stockholders of ______ Corporation.

Notice is hereby given that the annual meeting of the Stockholders of ______ Corporation will be held at the Corporation's registered office, at ______, in the City of ______, State of ______, on the ______ day of ______ at ______ o'clock.

At such meeting only the holders of the common stock of this Corporation of record at the close of business on ______, 19__, will be entitled to vote.

Dated: ______, 19__.

At: ______

____
President

COMMENTS

The notice of an annual meeting generally does not need to specify the purposes of the meeting. See e. g. Model Bus.Corp.Act § 29 and §§ 45.1 and 45.3, supra. Many notices, however, do de-

29. E. g., Del.Gen.Corp.Law, § 225 (1967); McKinney's N.Y.Bus.Corp. Law, § 619.

scribe the purposes of the meeting: e. g., "The purposes of the meeting are to elect directors, to ratify the selection of ______ as auditor for the corporation, and to consider such other matters as may come before the meeting." There also may be included a statement describing enclosed financial or other information, and a request that if the Stockholder cannot attend in person, he should execute a proxy enclosed with the notice.

Some types of actions that may be approved at an annual meeting must commonly be specifically referred to in the notice: e. g., amendment of Articles of Incorporation, or the reduction of stated capital of the Corporation represented by shares without par value.

§ 45.22 Notice of Annual Meeting of Stockholders—Specifying Objects of Meeting

To: The Stockholders of ______ Company.

You are hereby notified that the Annual Meeting of the Stockholders of the ______ Company will be held at the Company's office in ______, on ______, ______, 19__, at 12 o'clock noon, for the following purposes:

1. To elect ______ directors for the ensuing year.

2. To vote upon the question of amending the Charter and Bylaws of the Company to increase the number of directors from ______ to ______.

3. To vote upon the question of amending the Bylaws of the Company to provide that ______ directors shall constitute a quorum of the Board.

4. To transact such other business as may properly come before the meeting.

Stockholders of record at the close of business on ______, 19__ are the only Stockholders entitled to vote at the meeting. The stock transfer books of the Company will remain open.

By order of the Board of Directors.

Dated: ______, 19__. ______________________

Secretary

§ 45.23 Notice of Annual Meeting of Stockholders with Request for Proxy

NOTICE OF ANNUAL MEETING OF STOCKHOLDERS
OF ______, ______, 19__

The Board of Directors of ______ ("the Corporation") requests that the Stockholders of the Corporation take notice that the annual meeting of Stockholders will be held at ______ a. m. on ______, 19__, at [*Street Address*], ______. The following business will be transacted at the meeting: [*Describe*]

2. Transaction of such other business as may properly come before the meeting or any adjournments thereof.

The close of business on ______, 19__, has been fixed as the record date for the determination of Stockholders entitled to notice of and to vote at this meeting.

ALL STOCKHOLDERS ARE INVITED TO ATTEND THE MEETING IN PERSON OR BY PROXY. STOCKHOLDERS WHO DO NOT EXPECT TO BE PRESENT PERSONALLY AT THE MEETING ARE REQUESTED TO SIGN AND RETURN THE ACCOMPANYING PROXY IN THE ENCLOSED SELF-ADDRESSED ENVELOPE WHICH BEARS RETURN POSTAGE.

____
[*Name*], Secretary

§ 45.24 Notice of Special Meeting of Stockholders—General Form

[*Name of Corporation*]

NOTICE OF SPECIAL MEETING OF STOCKHOLDERS

To: The Stockholders of [*Name of Corporation*].

Please take notice, that a special meeting of the Stockholders of [*Name of Corporation*] will be held at No. ______ ______ Street, City of ______, County of ______, State of ______, on the ______ day of ______, 19__, at ______ o'clock __.M., [*Eastern Daylight Saving Time,*] for the purpose of [*Specify Purpose*].

By order of [*Specify Person(s) by or at Whose Direction Meeting Is Called*], the person(s) calling the meeting, this notice is hereby issued.

Dated: ______, 19__. ____________________

Secretary

COMMENTS

This notice may be issued at the direction of the Board of Directors or such person or persons as may be authorized by the Articles of Incorporation or the By-laws.

Statutes commonly require that notices of special meetings specify the purpose or purposes for which the meeting is being called e. g. Model Bus.Corp.Act § 29. See §§ 45.1 and 45.3, supra.

§ 45.25 Notice of Stockholders Meeting—With Waiver and Consent Provisions

NOTICE OF STOCKHOLDERS MEETING
(INCLUDING WAIVER, IF ANY)

To: The Stockholders of [*Corporation*].

Please take notice that on the ______ day of ______, 19__, at ______ o'clock in the ______ noon, a meeting will take place to discuss and vote upon the attached resolution; unless the need for such meeting is waived prior to such meeting by 100% of the Stockholders and the Resolution adopted by 100% of the Stockholders by their execution of a copy of the attached Resolution.

If you wish to waive the proper number of days notice, please sign here:

____

____

____

If you wish to waive the holding of the meeting *and* if you wish to adopt the resolution, please sign here:

____

____

____

§ 45.26 Call of Special Meeting of Stockholders by President

______, 19__

Mr. ______

Secretary, ______ Company

______, [*State*]

Dear Mr. ______:

You are hereby authorized and instructed to give written notice to the Stockholders that a special meeting of the Stockholders of ______ Company is called for ______ a. m. [*p. m.*] ______, 19__ at ______ Street, ______, to consider and vote upon the following proposals:

(1) ______;

(2) ______;

(3) ______.

____

President, ______ Company

§ 45.27 Call of Special Meeting by Stockholders

To: ______, Secretary.

We, the undersigned, Stockholders of the ______ Company, owning the number of shares of stock set opposite our names, pursuant to provisions of the By-laws, do hereby call a special meeting of the Stockholders of said Company to be held at ______, on the ______ day of ______, 19__, at ______ o'clock __. m. for the purpose of ______ and for the transaction of any or all business that may be brought before the meeting and we hereby authorize and direct that you notify the Stockholders of such meeting in accordance with the provisions of the By-laws.

Dated ______, 19__.

Signature of Stockholders	Number of Shares
____________________	____________________
____________________	____________________

____

Secretary, ______ Company

§ 45.28 Resolution of Directors for Special Meeting

Upon motion duly made, seconded, and carried, the following resolution was duly adopted:

Resolved, that a special meeting of the Stockholders shall be held at the office of this Corporation at No. ______ ______ Street, City of ______, County of ______, State of ______, on the ______ day of ______, 19__, at ______ o'clock __.M. for [*Describe*]; and that notice thereof shall be given by the Secretary within five days hereafter in the manner provided in the By-laws in respect to special meetings.

§ 45.29 Stockholder Demand for Special Meeting to Elect Directors

To: ______, Secretary of [*Name of Corporation*].

The undersigned, representing the holders of at least [*Ten*] percent of the shares entitled to vote in an election of Directors of this Corporation, hereby demand, pursuant to the Business Corporation Law of the State of ______, the call of a special meeting for the election of Directors for [*Name of Corporation*] on the ______ day of

______, 19__ at ______ o'clock __.M. [*Eastern Daylight Savings Time*].

Dated: ______, 19__.

[*Signature*]

____
Stockholder

[*Signature*]

____
Stockholder

§ 45.30 Affidavit of Mailing of Notice of Stockholders' Meeting

STATE OF __________

County of ______

______, being first duly sworn, states:

He is Secretary of ______ Company, a ______ Corporation. On ______, 19__ he caused to be placed in the mail notices of the meeting of Stockholders to be held at __ a. m. [*p. m.*] on ______, 19__, at ______ Street, ______, ______. To each Stockholder of record on ______, 19__, and then entitled to vote, there was addressed, at his last known address appearing on the books of the Corporation, one true copy of the notice, enclosed in a sealed envelope with postage thereon fully prepaid.

____
[*Name of Secretary*]

Subscribed and sworn to before me this ______ day of ______, 19__.

____
Notary Public, State of ______

My Commission Expires ______, 19__

§ 45.31 Waiver of Notice of Stockholders' Meeting

We, the undersigned, being all of the Stockholders of ______, do hereby severally waive notice of the time, place, and purposes of the special meeting of the Stockholders of the said Corporation, and do hereby consent that the ______ day of ______, 19__, at ______ o'clock A.M., be and the same hereby is fixed as the time, and the registered office of the Corporation at No. ______ ______ Street, in the City of ______, State of ______, as the place for holding the same; and do further consent to the transaction of the following business: [*Describe*]

[*City and State Where Signed.*]

Dated: ______, 19__.

____

____

____

COMMENTS

Where the various Stockholders are in agreement as to what business should be conducted at a meeting or that a meeting should take place, it is customary to forgo formal notice and have the Stockholders execute a waiver of notice. Such a waiver is commonly expressly permitted by statute. See e. g., Model Bus.Corp.Act § 144. See also § 45.3, supra.

Alternatively, the Stockholders may dispense with the meeting and act pursuant to a signed consent. See § 45.71 et seq., infra, and § 45.5, supra. In the view of the author, where a meeting is not going to actually take place, it is preferable to have the Stockholders execute a consent rather than a waiver of notice.

§ 45.32 Notice of Adjourned Annual Meeting of Stockholders

______ CORPORATION

IMPORTANT NOTICE

FURTHER ADJOURNMENT OF ANNUAL MEETING

To: The Stockholders.

The annual meeting of Stockholders of ______ Corporation will be held on ______, ______, 19__, at ______ P.M. [*as Further Adjourned from ______, 19__*], at its offices, ______ Street, ______ City, for the purpose of acting upon those matters set forth in the Notice of Meeting of Stockholders heretofore mailed under date of ______, 19__. Two of the matters to be acted upon, namely, ______ and ______, each require the affirmative votes of ______ of the outstanding shares—or approximately ______ votes, whereas proxies have been received as of this date to vote only approximately ______ shares. See Proxy Statement heretofore mailed.

To avoid the expense of additional proxy solicitation you are urged, if you have not heretofore done so, to sign, date and return your proxy promptly so that your shares may be voted.

____

President

______ City: ______, 19__.

§§ 45.33–45.60 are reserved for supplementary material.

STOCKHOLDER MEETING—MINUTE FORMATS

§ 45.61 Minutes of Actual Regular Annual Meeting of Stockholders

Minutes of the regular annual meeting of the Stockholders of ______ held on ______ day, ______, 19__, at ______ a. m., at the office of the Company, ______ Avenue and ______ Street, ______, pursuant to due notice to the Stockholders.

The meeting was called to order by ______, the President. ______, Secretary of the Corporation, acted as Secretary of the meeting.

The Chairman announced that the annual meeting of Stockholders was convened pursuant to due notice, and that pursuant to a resolution adopted by the Board of Directors, ______, 19__, had been fixed as a record date for the determination of Stockholders entitled to vote at the meeting.

The Secretary presented the formal notice of the meeting and the affidavit of ______ of the Corporation as to its being mailed to each Stockholder, and upon motion duly seconded and carried, these documents were approved and ordered on file. A copy of the notice of the meeting is annexed hereto as Exhibit *A*, a copy of the proxy as Exhibit *B*, and a copy of the annual report for the year ended ______, 19__, as Exhibit *C*.

The Chairman declared that a quorum was present and that the meeting was competent to transact the business for which it was convened.

The Chairman announced that ______ and ______ had been appointed as Inspectors for the ensuing election of Directors, and had subscribed the oath prescribed by law faithfully to execute the duties of Inspector at such meeting with strict impartiality and according to the best of their abilities. A copy of said oath is annexed hereto as Exhibit *D*.

The Chairman stated that the following Directors were designated by the management for re-election, and upon motion duly made and seconded, they were nominated to serve as Directors for the ensuing year or until their successors should be elected and qualify in their stead:

______________	______________
______________	______________
______________	______________

The Chairman stated that the following Directors were nominated under an agreement made by certain Stockholders dated ______, 19__, and on motion duly made and seconded, they were nominated to serve as directors for the ensuing year or until their successors should be elected and qualify in their stead:

____

____

Following collection and tabulation of the ballots, the Chairman announced that ______ shares had been voted in favor of each of the nominees for Director. He stated that this constituted a plurality and that they had therefore been duly elected Directors of the Company. The Certificate of the Inspectors of Election is hereto annexed as Exhibit *E*.

The next business before the meeting was [*Describe*].

[*Name*] made the following motion which was seconded by [*Name*]: [*Describe*].

After [*Full Discussion/No Discussion*], a ballot was taken and [*Name*] announced the result of the ballot as follows:

for __________

against __________

absentions __________

Therefore, the motion [*Passed/Failed*].

There being no further business to come before the meeting, upon motion duly seconded and carried, the meeting was declared adjourned.

____

Secretary

Dated, ______: ______, 19__.

COMMENT

Minutes of Stockholder meetings are usually required by statute; see e. g. Model Bus.Corp.Act § 52. See also Chapter 48, infra.

§ 45.62 Minutes of Actual Regular Annual Meeting of Stockholders—Another Form

Minutes of the regular annual meeting of the Stockholders of ______, held on ______, 19__, at ______ a. m., at the office of the Corporation located at ______.

The meeting was called to order by the President, ______, who acted as chairman of the meeting pursuant to the By-laws, and ______, Secretary of the Corporation, acted as secretary of the meeting.

The secretary presented the formal notice of the meeting and the affidavit of ______ as to its being mailed to each Stockholder. Upon motion made, seconded, and carried, these documents were ordered on file. A copy of the notice of meeting is appended to these minutes.

The secretary then presented a certified list of Stockholders and reported the presence of a quorum and of all of the Stockholders.

The following Stockholders were present in person:

________________ ________________

________________ ________________

The following Stockholders were present by proxy:

________________ ________________

________________ ________________

All the above listed proxies were then ordered on file with the secretary.

The chairman then declared that a quorum was present and that the meeting was competent to transact the business for which it was convened.

The secretary then read the minutes of the last meeting of the Stockholders which on motion were duly approved.

The Chairman then stated that the Treasurer would present his report.

The Treasurer then reported ________________________.

On motion duly made, seconded, and carried, the report of the Treasurer was ordered on file.

[*Continue as Above for Other Reports*]

The chairman then stated that the election of Directors was in order and that ______ and ______ had been appointed inspectors of election and had taken and signed an oath faithfully to execute the duties of inspector at the meeting with strict impartiality and according to the best of their ability. A copy of said oath is appended to these minutes.

The chairman stated that the following persons were nominated for election as Directors.

________________ ________________

________________ ________________

The polls were duly opened, and ballot having been duly had, the polls were declared closed, and the inspectors of election proceeded to tabulate the ballots. Following the tabulation of the ballots, the chairman announced that ______, ______, ______, and ______ shares had been voted in favor of ______, ______, ______, and ______, respectively. The chairman stated that the following persons were duly elected Directors of the Corporation to serve for the ensuing year or until their successors should be elected and qualify in their stead:

____________________ ____________________

On motion duly made, seconded, and carried, the inspectors of election were directed to file their report with the Secretary of the Corporation.

There being no further business, the meeting was adjourned.

Dated: ______, 19__.

____

Secretary

§ 45.63 Minutes of Annual or Special Meeting of Stockholders

The ______ annual [*or* special] meeting of the Stockholders of the ______ Company was held at the general offices of the Company at ______, on the ______ day of ______, 19__, pursuant to the provisions of the Bylaws [*or* the Articles of Incorporation] and due notice given by the Secretary. [*In Case of Special Meeting It Is a Good Idea to Set Out Here the Notice and Affidavit of Service.*]

______ presided over the meeting and ______ acted as secretary.

The following Stockholders were present in person or by proxy and represented the number of shares of stock set opposite their names:

Name	Proxy	Number of Shares
________________	________________	________________
________________	________________	________________

A majority of the stock being represented, a quorum was declared present.

The minutes of the last meeting of the Stockholders, held on ______, 19__, were read and approved.

The Secretary presented his annual report, and, after answering some questions, it was accepted and filed.

The Treasurer than presented his annual report, showing the result of the audit of the company's books.

The next business before the meeting being the election of a Board of Directors, the members of the present Board were renominated. No other nominations being made, a ballot was taken, and the President [*or* Chairman] announced the result of the ballot, to wit: That ______ and ______ were unanimously elected Directors of the

Company for the ensuing year and until their successors are elected and qualified.

On motion the meeting was adjourned.

____

Secretary

§ 45.64 Approval of Minutes of Stockholders' Meeting

I understand that a [*Special*] [*Regular*] meeting of Stockholders of ______ Company was held on ______, 19__, at ______ Street, ______, ______. I hereby waive notice of that meeting, ratify the actions taken at the meeting as shown by the minutes of the meeting which I also hereby approve, and agree that this Approval shall be made a part of the minutes of that meeting.

Dated: ______, 19__.

____

Stockholder (__ shares)
______ Company

§§ 45.65–45.70 are reserved for supplementary material.

B. STOCKHOLDER CONSENTS

Library References:

C.J.S. Corporations § 545.
West's Key No. Digests, Corporations ⚷196.

§ 45.71 Stockholder Consents—Generally

As previously indicated,[1] Stockholder rights with respect to control are traditionally asserted by voting at Stockholder meetings.

Modern statutes now provide that written Stockholder consent without a meeting, where unanimous or as otherwise prescribed, constitutes Stockholder action in lieu of the required vote at a Stockholder meeting.[2]

Sometimes, even in the absence of statute, Stockholder informal action has been upheld by the courts where the rights of minority Stockholders were not prejudiced.

1. See 45.1 et seq., supra, this chapter.

2. E. g., Model Bus.Corp.Act § 145 (any action required to be or which may be taken at a Stockholder meeting may be taken without such meeting by unanimous written consent of all Stockholders entitled to vote with respect to such matter). See also § 45.5, supra.

§ 45.72 Action by Unanimous Consent Without Meeting

We, the undersigned, being all of the Stockholders of ______ Corporation who would be entitled to vote upon the resolutions hereinafter set forth at a formal meeting of the Stockholders of said Corporation held for the purpose of acting upon such resolutions, do hereby consent to the adoption of the following resolutions to the same extent and to have the same force and effect as if adopted at a formal meeting of the Stockholders of said Corporation:

____

____

In testimony whereof witness our respective signatures on the respective dates set opposite thereto.

Signature of Stockholders	**Date of Signatures**
______________________	______________________
______________________	______________________

COMMENT

Action by unanimous written consent without a meeting is commonly authorized by statute (e. g. Model Bus.Corp.Act § 145).

§ 45.73 Notice of Authorization of Disputed Corporate Action

NOTICE OF AUTHORIZATION

To: [*Name of Stockholder*]

Notice is hereby given, pursuant to the Business Corporation Law, that authorization for the following corporate action was obtained from the requisite Stockholders of [*Name of Corporation*] by a [*Number*] vote of the Stockholders of said Corporation at a meeting held at the office of the Corporation at No. ______ ______ Street, City of ______, County of ______, State of ______, on the ______ day of ______, 19__:

[*Specify Corporate Action Authorized.*]

Dated: ______, 19__.

____

COMMENT

This notice is to be given all Stockholders except those who voted for or consented in writing to the disputed action by registered mail within ten days after the Stockholders' authorization is obtained.

§§ 45.74–45.80 are reserved for supplementary material.

C. STOCKHOLDER DISSENTS

§ 45.81 Notice of Objection by Stockholder

NOTICE OF OBJECTION

To: [*Name of Corporation*]

The undersigned, ______, residing at No. ______ ______ Street, City of ______, County of ______, State of ______, the Stockholder of record of [*Number*] shares of [*Class*] shares of [*Name of Corporation*], which shares are represented by Certificate No. ______, does hereby object, pursuant to the Business Corporation Law, to [*Specify Corporate Action Objected to*] to be taken at a meeting, called pursuant to a notice of meeting dated the ______ day of ______, 19__, and to be held at the office of the Corporation at No. ______ ______ Street, City of ______, County of ______, State of ______, on the ______ day of ______, 19__.

The undersigned intends to demand payment for his shares, as hereinabove set forth, if said corporate action is taken.

Dated: ______, 19__.

____

§ 45.82 Notice of Election to Dissent

NOTICE OF ELECTION TO DISSENT

To: [*Name of Corporation*]

The undersigned, ______, residing at No. ______ ______ Street, City of ______, County of ______, State of ______, the Shareholder of record of [*Number*] shares of the [*Class*] shares of the said [*Name of Corporation*] represented by Certificate No. ______, having filed a notice of objection with said Corporation on the ______ day of ______, 19__, and having received a notice of authorization from said Corporation on the ______ day of ______, 19__, does hereby elect to dissent pursuant to the Business Corporation Law, to [*Specify Corporate Action Objected to*] taken at a meeting held at the office of said Corporation at No. ______ ______ Street, City of ______, County of ______, State of ______, on the ______ day of ______, 19__.

The undersigned hereby demands payment of the fair value of his shares as hereinabove set forth pursuant to the statute and laws in such cases made and provided.

Dated: ______, 19__.

____

COMMENT

This notice is to be filed with the Corporation within twenty days after the giving of notice to the Stockholder by the Corporation as to the authorization of the action objected to by the Stockholders.

§ 45.83 Consent to Withdrawal of Notice of Election to Dissent

To: [*Name of Stockholder*]

[*Name of Corporation*] does hereby consent, pursuant to the Business Corporation Law, to the withdrawal of the notice of election to dissent filed by you with said Corporation on the ______ day of ______, 19__, and does hereby revoke the offer by said Corporation to pay for the shares as to which the aforesaid dissent was presented, subject to the following terms and conditions:

(1) You shall not have the right to receive payment for the shares as to which the aforesaid dissent was made.

(2) You shall be reinstated to all the rights of a Stockholder as of the filing of said notice of election, including any intervening preemptive rights and the right to payment of any intervening dividend or other distribution or, if any such rights have expired or any such dividend or distribution other than in cash has been completed, in lieu thereof, at the election of the Corporation, the fair value in cash as determined by the board of directors as of the time of such expiration or completion, but without prejudice otherwise to any corporate proceedings that may have been taken in the interim.

Dated: ______, 19__.

____

§ 45.84 Notice of Loss of Dissenter's Rights

NOTICE OF LOSS OF RIGHTS

To: [*Name of Stockholder*]

Notice is hereby given, pursuant to the Business Corporation Law, that your rights arising by virtue of the notice of election to dissent filed by you with [*Name of Corporation*], on the ______ day of ______, 19__, have been lost by reason of your failure to submit the certificates representing all the shares standing in your name on the corporate records to said Corporation [*or to the Transfer Agent of Said Corporation*] within one month from the date of filing of said notice of election to have noted thereon that a notice of election has been filed.

Dated: ______, 19__.

____

COMMENT

This notice is to be given within forty-five days from the date of filing of the notice of election to dissent.

§ 45.85 Offer to Pay for Shares of Dissenting Stockholder

OFFER

BY

[*Name of Corporation*]

To: [*Name of Stockholder*]

Whereas, you, as a Stockholder of record of [*Name of Corporation*], have objected to the action of the Corporation in [*Specify Action*], and have demanded payment of your [*Number*] shares of [*Class*] shares in the Corporation.

Now, pursuant to the provisions of the Business Corporation Law of the State of ______ [*Name of Corporation*] hereby offers to pay for such shares the sum of ______ ($______) Dollars in cash for each and every share thereof, which sum is considered by the Corporation to be the fair value thereof.

Enclosed herein is a balance sheet of the Corporation of [*Name of Corporation*] as of a date not earlier than twelve months before the date of this offer, to wit: the ______ day of ______, 19__, and a profit and loss statement for the twelve months' period ended as of such date.

Acceptance of the same must be made within ______ days after the mailing [*or Delivery*] thereof to you by written offer of acceptance duly signed by you and delivered to the Corporation at its office at No. ______ ______ Street, City of ______, County of ______, State of ______, within such period. Upon acceptance of the offer, you may surrender your certificate representing shares to the Corporation at such office. The assignment on the back thereof must be duly signed, and ______ ($______) Dollars per share for tax transfer stamps must be enclosed.

Upon receipt of your certificate representing shares, duly endorsed for transfer, a check will be sent to you for the same in accordance with the terms of this offer; or, if you personally bring the same into the office of the Corporation and require the cash, the amount of the offer will be paid to you in cash.

Dated: ______, 19__.

[*Name of Corporation*]

____

By ______________________
President

§§ 45.86–45.90 are reserved for supplementary material.

D. MISCELLANEOUS FORMS

§ 45.91 Voting List

I, ______, the Secretary of ______ Corporation, having charge of the stock transfer books for shares of the said Corporation, do hereby certify that the following is a complete list of the Stockholders entitled to vote at the annual meeting of the Corporation to be held on ______, 19__:

Name of Stockholder	Address	Number of Shares Held

[*The list must be arranged in alphabetical order*]

Dated: ______, 19__.

____
Secretary

COMMENT

The voting list must be compiled by the officer or agent having charge of the stock transfer books. It must be kept at the registered office of the Corporation and be available for inspection by any Stockholder during regular business hours. (See e. g. Model Business Corporation Act, § 52, and § 48.2, infra.) A failure to comply with this statutory requirement does not affect the validity of the meeting, but may subject the person having the responsibility of creating the voting list to claims for damages for such failure.

§ 45.92 Report of Inspectors of Election

The undersigned inspectors of election for the annual meeting of ______ Corporation held on the ______ day of ______, 19__, hereby report as follows:

(1) We examined the certified list of Stockholders prepared by the Secretary of the Corporation, and we report that the total number of outstanding shares entitled to vote at such meeting was ______;

(2) We tallied the number of Stockholders present in person or by proxy at such meeting, and report that the number present was ______;

(3) We received and tallied the votes cast for directors of the Corporation at such meeting, and we report and certify that the following persons received the number of votes set forth next to their names:

Name	Number of votes cast
______________	______________
______________	______________
______________	______________

(d) We received and tallied the votes cast for and against the proposition to amend Article Four of the Articles of Incorporation, and report and certify that the number of votes cast for and against such proposition was as follows:

For: __________

Against: __________

Respectfully submitted,

____

Dated: ______.

____

Inspectors of Election

§ 45.93 Inspectors of Election—Oath

OATH OF INSPECTORS OF ELECTION

OF

[*Name of Corporation*]

STATE OF ________ }
County of ________ } ss

The undersigned, ______, ______ and ______, being duly sworn, each for himself deposes and says that he will faithfully execute the duties of Inspector of Election at the annual [*or Special*] meeting of the Stockholders of [*Name of Corporation*] to be held at No. ______ ______ Street, City of ______, County of ______, State of ______, on the ______ day of ______, 19__, at ______ o'clock __.M., [*Eastern Daylight Saving Time,*] with strict impartiality and according to the best of his ability.

____

[*Signature*]

____

[*Signature*]

____

[*Signature*]

____

Inspectors

[*Jurat*]

§ 45.94 Inspectors of Election—Certificate

The undersigned, ______ and ______, do hereby certify:

(1) That the annual meeting of the Stockholders of [*Name of Corporation*] was held on the ______ day of ______, 19__, at ______ o'clock in the ______noon of that day, at the office of said Corporation located at ______, for the purpose of electing [*Specify Purpose*].

(2) That, pursuant to the By-laws of said [*Name of Corporation*], the undersigned, ______ and ______, were duly appointed as Inspectors of Election.

(3) That before entering upon the discharge of our duties, we each took and signed an oath, a copy of which is annexed hereto, faithfully to execute the duties of Inspector of Election at the aforesaid meeting with strict impartiality and according to the best of our ability.

(4) That upon our canvass of the votes at said meeting, we determined that the following number of votes had been cast for the following candidates for Directors:

Name of Candidate	Number of Votes Received
____________________	____________________
____________________	____________________
____________________	____________________

(5) That as a result of such canvass, we determined that [*Name of Candidate(s)*] had received a plurality of the votes cast, which were entitled to vote therein, as required by the By-laws of [*Name of Corporation*].

(6) That we declared [*Name of Candidate(s)*] to be elected [*Specify Office*] of [*Name of Corporation*] for the term of office as specified in the By-laws of said [*Name of Corporation*].

(7) That upon our canvass of the votes at said meeting for the election of Inspectors of Election for [*Name of Corporation*] for the ensuing year, we determined that the following number of votes had been cast for the following candidates:

Name of Candidate	Number of Votes Received
____________________	____________________
____________________	____________________
____________________	____________________

(8) That as a result of such canvass, we determined that ______ and ______, having received a plurality of the votes cast, were elected to the office of Inspectors of Election of [*Name of Corporation*] for the ensuing year and were by us duly declared the elected Inspectors of Election of [*Name of Corporation*] for the ensuing year.

In witness whereof, the undersigned have executed and signed this certificate this ______ day of ______, 19__.

____
Inspector of Election

____
Inspector of Election

[*Acknowledgment*]

§ 45.95 Notice of Intention to Vote Cumulatively

To: Secretary of ______ Corporation

Please be advised that I intend to cumulate my votes for the election of Directors at the annual meeting of Stockholders of ______ to be held on the ______ day of ______, 19__.

____
Stockholder

COMMENT

Some statutes provide that if a Stockholder intends to vote cumulatively for Directors, he must give the Secretary of the Corporation notice preceding the election (e. g. Texas Bus.Corp.Act, Art. 2.29D). The purpose is to assure that all Stockholders understand that shares are being voted cumulatively, thereby warning them that "straight" voting may result in a significant diminution of voting power.

§ 45.96 Ballot for Election of Directors

BALLOT FOR ELECTION OF DIRECTORS OF

[*Name of Corporation*]

Name of Stockholder ______________

Number and Class of Shares Entitled to be Voted ______

Number of Directors to be Elected by that Class of Shares ______

Total Number of Votes Entitled to be Cast in Election of Directors (Multiply the First Two Numbers)

Names of Candidates Nominated for Director	**Votes Cast for Each Candidate**
______________________	______________________
______________________	______________________
______________________	______________________

/s/ ______________________
[*Signature of Stockholder*]

§ 45.97 Ballot—Straight Voting

ANNUAL STOCKHOLDERS MEETING

______ CORPORATION

______, 19__

Ballot

For Directors:

____

____

____

Vote for three persons only.

I, the owner of record of ______ shares of common stock, hereby vote such shares for the above named persons as Directors of the Corporation.

Number of Shares: ______ ___________________________

Stockholder

§ 45.98 Ballot—Cumulative Voting

ANNUAL STOCKHOLDERS MEETING

______ CORPORATION

______, 19__

Ballot

I, the owner of record of ______ shares of common stock hereby vote such shares for the following persons as Directors of the Corporation:

Number of shares ______

Directors to be elected ______

Total number of votes (multiply) ______

Names of Directors	**Number of Votes**
___________________________	___________________________
___________________________	___________________________
___________________________	___________________________

Stockholder

COMMENT

These forms of ballot are structured to emphasize the difference between straight and cumulative voting. For a description of these differences see Chapter 47, infra.

Library References:

C.J.S. Corporations § 549.
West's Key No. Digests, Corporations ⚷200.

§ 45.99 Ballot for Voting on Resolution

ANNUAL STOCKHOLDERS MEETING

______ CORPORATION

______, 19__

Resolved, that article four of the Articles of Incorporation be amended to read as follows:

"FOUR. Cumulative voting shall not be permitted."

I, the owner of record of ______ shares of common stock vote such shares as follows:

______ In favor

______ Opposed

Number of shares ______ ____________________
Name of Stockholder

§§ 45.100–46.0 are reserved for supplementary material.

CHAPTER 46

BOARD OF DIRECTORS

Table of Sections

A. INTRODUCTION

B. DIRECTORS' MEETINGS

C. DIRECTORS' RESOLUTIONS

A. INTRODUCTION

§ 46.1 Number and Qualifications of Directors [1]

NUMBER

Formerly, nearly all statutes required that there be at least three Directors, but many of such statutes now permit "one or more" [2] directors or even no board of directors.[2.5] The number is usually stated in the Articles of Incorporation [3] or By-laws,[4] either at a fixed number or at not less than a certain minimum (within statutory limitation) and not more than a certain maximum. Where an indefinite number or no number is stated in the Articles of Incorporation, the number is fixed in the By-laws.[5]

The number can be changed, within any controlling limitations, by amendment of the Articles of Incorporation or By-laws.[6]

To lessen the chance of deadlock, authorization of an odd number of Directors is the more common practice except where an even split is desired.

QUALIFICATIONS

Some statutes expressly require that Directors be at least 18 years of age or of "full age". Statutes do not prescribe a maximum age.

Statutory residence or citizenship requirements, once common, are becoming rarer.[7]

Similarly, statutory requirements that Directors be Stockholders, prevalent in the past, are tending to disappear.[8]

1. This Section, and Sections 46.2–46.16, are adapted from Henn, Law of Corporations (2d ed. 1970) §§ 204–216, and Hamilton, Corporations in a Nutshell (1980). Professor Henn is preparing a third edition for 1982 publication.

2. See, e. g., Model Bus.Corp.Act § 36; West's Ann.Calif.Corp.Code § 301; Minn.Bus.Corp.Act § 302A.203.

2.5 See, e. g., West's Ann.Corp.Calif. Code § 300; Minn.Bus.Corp.Act § 302A.201.

3. E. g., Model Bus.Corp.Act §§ 36, 54(i) (number of initial board of directors; "or in the manner" provided in the Articles of Incorporation or By-laws—1969 Model Act revision). See note 5 infra.

4. E. g., Model Bus.Corp.Act § 36 (except that number of initial Board of Directors shall be fixed in Articles of Incorporation); Del.Gen.Corp.Law, § 141(b) (1967); McKinney's N.Y.Bus. Corp.Law, § 702(a).

5. E. g., McKinney's N.Y.Bus.Corp. Law, § 702(a) (fixed by By-laws, or by action of Board of Directors or Stockholders under specific provisions of By-law adopted by Stockholders; if not so fixed, number to be three).

6. E. g., Model Bus.Corp.Act § 36; Del.Gen.Corp.Law, § 141(b) (1967); McKinney's N.Y.Bus.Corp.Law, § 702(b); Minn.Bus.Corp.Act § 302A.203.

7. E. g., Model Bus.Corp.Act § 35 (Directors need not be residents of jurisdiction unless so required by Articles of Incorporation or By-laws).

8. E. g., Model Bus.Corp.Act § 35 (directors need not be Stockholders un-

Other qualifications for Directors may be prescribed in the Articles of Incorporation or By-laws.[9]

Some Boards of Directors are composed entirely or largely of "insiders", i. e., Directors who are also Officers of the Corporation or of other Corporations affiliated with it; some other Boards consist mainly of "outsiders", i. e., non-Officers; however, most Boards are mixed. Periodically, the advantages and disadvantages of "insider" or "full-time" Directors, and "outsider" or "part-time" Directors, are reviewed.

In any event, the Chairman of the Board, who might be an important executive Officer, obviously must be a Director, and in many jurisdictions so must the President.

Interlocking directorships on the Boards of Directors of competing Corporations is prohibited by the Federal Clayton Act.[10]

Library References:

C.J.S. Corporations §§ 715, 726.
West's Key No. Digests, Corporations ⚷281, 282.

§ 46.2 Election, Tenure and Removal of Directors

ELECTION

The initial Directors are usually named in the Articles of Incorporation or elected at the organization meeting of incorporators.[11] Directors named in the Articles of Incorporation sometimes are accommodation or Dummy Directors (so that the ultimate Directors are not public record) and are replaced by the real initial Directors at one of the organization meetings. The initial Directors serve until the first annual meeting of Stockholders, or until their successors are elected and qualified.

At the first annual meeting of Stockholders, and at each annual meeting thereafter, the Stockholders elect Directors to serve until the next succeeding annual meeting, except where Directors are divided into classes with one class elected each year as permitted by law.

less so required by Articles of Incorporation or By-laws).

9. Model Bus.Corp.Act § 35; McKinney's N.Y.Bus.Corp.Law, § 701. Typical are requirements that a prescribed number of majority of Directors be residents of the jurisdiction of incorporation. Rubin v. Chicago South Shore & South Bend R. R., 217 F.2d 177 (7th Cir. 1954), certiorari denied 348 U.S. 972, 75 S.Ct. 534, 99 L. Ed. 757; McKee & Co. v. First Nat'l Bank, 265 F.Supp. 1 (S.D.Cal.1967) (upholding By-laws requiring that Directors be residents of county for at least one year prior to election, that no Director be attorney for or connected with any other banking institution, and that certain information concerning nominees be furnished). See also McKinney's N.Y.Ins.Law, § 48(8)(c); 15 U.S.C.A. § 80a–9.

10. Clayton Act § 8, 15 U.S.C.A. § 19.

11. See Chapters 33 and 35, supra.

Most statutes expressly permit such classification,[12] often imposing conditions that there be at least a certain number of Directors on the Board [13] or a certain minimum number elected annually, or fixing maximum number of classes or maximum terms. Most prevalent in Corporations where the stagger system is in effect are three classes, which means that one-third are elected annually to serve three-year terms (except at the start when the three classes are elected to serve one-year, two-year, and three-year terms, respectively).[14] Annual election of less than one-fifth of the Board is rare.

VACANCIES

Any vacancy occurring in the Board of Directors, is filled by the Stockholders or remaining Directors, depending on the jurisdiction.[15]

Where the number of Directors is increased by appropriate amendment of the Articles of Incorporation or By-laws, any newly-created directorship, absent provision to the contrary, is filled by the Stockholders. Statutes sometimes codify this rule with or without variations. A growing number of statutes authorize the Board of Directors to fill newly-created directorships.[16]

TENURE

Directors hold office for the terms for which they were elected or until successors are elected and have qualified.[17] Directors elected to fill vacancies serve for the unexpired terms.[18]

12. E. g. Model Bus.Corp.Act § 36; McKinney's N.Y.Bus.Corp.Law § 704.

13. E. g., Model Bus.Corp.Act § 37 (two or three classes, each class to be as nearly equal in number as possible).

14. E. g., Model Bus.Corp.Act § 37 (permitting two or three classes where Board consists of nine or more members).

15. E. g., Model Bus.Corp.Act § 38 (by remaining Directors through less than a quorum); West's Ann.Calif.Corp. Code § 305 (by majority of directors then in office, or by a sole remaining director).

16. See e. g. Model Bus.Corp.Act § 38; West's Ann.Calif.Corp.Code § 305; McKinney's N.Y.Bus.Corp.Law § 705.

Many older statutes distinguish between an "old" and a "new" vacancy. An "old" vacancy is created by the death or resignation of a Director and may be filled by remaining Directors, "though less than a quorum." A successor Director in an "old" vacancy serves only for the unexpired term of his predecessor. A "new" vacancy, on the other hand, is created by an increase in the number of Directors by amendment of the By-laws or Articles. A "new" vacancy may be filled only by the Stockholders not the Directors. The distinction between "old" and "new" vacancies arose in decisions from the State of Delaware, and was reflected in the 1950 version of the Model Act. The Model Act was revised in 1962 to permit "new" vacancies to be filled by the Directors in the same way as "old" vacancies. (§ 38) Many, but not all, statutes reflect this simpler and more sensible provision.

17. E. g. Model Bus.Corp.Act § 36; West's Ann.Calif.Corp.Code § 301.

18. E. g. Model Bus.Corp.Law § 38

Statutes provide that despite the expiration of a Director's term, he continues to hold office until his successor has been "elected and qualified" (Model Bus.Corp.Act § 36). As a result, the failure to hold an annual meeting does not affect the power of a Corporation to continue to transact its business since the Directors presently in office continue in office with power to act.

The hold-over Director provision is particularly important in situations where the Stockholders are deadlocked in voting power and unable to elect successors to Directors whose terms have expired. In this situation, those who are "in" remain as Directors apparently forever; however, the ultimate solution is the involuntary dissolution of the Corporation if the deadlock cannot be broken.

REMOVAL

Directors are removable, with or (in the appropriate circumstances) without [19] cause, by Stockholders even if such power is also validly conferred on the Board of Directors. Before being removed for cause, the Director is entitled to notice of the charges against him and reasonable opportunity to be heard. Stockholder Agreements to keep named persons as Directors do not preclude removal for cause by the required Stockholder vote, although the removing Stockholders may be liable for damages. Directors usually may not be removed without cause, unless advance power to do so was reserved at the time the Director commenced his term. Statutes, the Articles of Incorporation, or By-laws may confer such power on Stockholders. Modern statutes often deal with removal of Directors for cause or without cause, frequently with provisions to protect any applicable cumulative voting rights or class voting rights.[20]

Library References:

C.J.S. Corporations §§ 716 et seq., 732 et seq., 738.
West's Key No. Digests, Corporations ⚷283, 291, 294.

§ 46.3 Directors' Management Functions—Generally

Directors are not agents of the Stockholders who elect them, but are sui generis. As persons in control of the property of others, Directors are fiduciaries, with their duties running primarily to the Corporation. Under the concession theory, Directors' powers are derived from the state, not delegated by the Stockholders. Most statutes vest in the Board of Directors the management of the Corporation.[21]

19. Model Bus.Corp.Act § 39 provides that Directors may be removed, with or "without" cause, by a vote of the holders of a majority of the shares then entitled to vote at an election of Directors.

20. See e. g. Model Bus.Corp.Act § 39; West's Ann.Calif.Corp.Code §§ 303, 304.

21. E. g., Model Bus.Corp.Act § 35 (except as may be otherwise provided

While statutes often expressly permit the Articles of Incorporation or By-laws to contain provisions limiting the powers of the Directors, or otherwise for the regulation and management of the Corporation, such permission is usually qualified by the limitation that such provisions be not inconsistent with law.[22]

In the exercise of their management functions, the Directors, usually as a Board, are required to use their best judgment and independent discretion, and are responsible for the determination and execution of corporate policy, usually including (a) policy decisions with respect to products, services, prices, wages, labor relations; (b) selection, supervision, and removal of officers and possibly other executive personnel; (c) fixing of executive compensation, pension, retirement, etc. plans; (d) determination of dividends, financing, and capital changes; (e) delegation of authority for administrative and possibly other action; (f) possible adoption, amendment, and repeal of By-laws; (g) possible participation, along with Stockholders in approving various extraordinary corporate matters; and (h) supervision and vigilance for the welfare of the whole enterprise.

SPECIAL CLOSE CORPORATION STATUTORY PROVISIONS

See Ch. 30, § 30.4, supra, for special statutory provisions in certain states which permit the Stockholders of close Corporations to restrict by Agreement the discretion of the Board or even provide in the Articles that the management will be in the hands of the Stockholders, or others, rather than the Board or even eliminate the Board

Library References:

C.J.S. Corporations §§ 764 et seq., 779, 780.
West's Key No. Digests, Corporations ⚿310 et seq.

§ 46.4 Formalities of Board of Directors Action—Generally

Traditionally, the Directors could exercise their management functions only when duly convened as a Board, and several statutes still so provide.[23]

Unlike Stockholders, Directors always vote *per capita*, and except for a rare statute to the contrary, may not vote by proxy.

in Articles of Incorporation); West's Ann.Calif.Corp.Code § 303 (except as in statute or Articles of Incorporation otherwise provided).

22. E. g., Model Bus.Corp.Act § 54. West's Ann.Calif.Corp.Code § 300; McKinney's N.Y.Bus.Corp.Law, § 402(b). See also § 30.4, supra.

23. See e. g. Model Bus.Corp.Act, §§ 35, 40, 43.

§ 46.5 Meetings of Board of Directors

Detailed provisions relating to Directors meetings appear in corporate By-laws and only skeletal provisions are set forth in business Corporation statutes.[24] Regular meetings of the Board of Directors may be held weekly, monthly, quarterly or at any regular interval. The By-laws usually specify when such meetings are to be held, or may authorize the Directors themselves to specify, by resolution, when regular meetings are to be held. It is customary to hold a regular meeting of Directors either immediately before or immediately after the annual meeting of Stockholders. Special meetings are meetings other than regular meetings. The principal difference between regular and special meetings is that a regular meeting may be held without notice, while a special meeting may be held "upon such notice as is prescribed in the By-laws." [25] However, unlike a Stockholders meeting, any relevant business may be transacted at a special meeting of Directors even though not referred to in the notice. As a result there is little practical difference between regular and special meetings of Directors. Directors may waive notice in writing before, at, or after the meeting.

PLACE OF BOARD MEETINGS

Statutes generally do not require that meetings of the Board of Directors be held within the state, unless the Articles of Incorporation or By-laws provide otherwise.[26]

NOTICE OF BOARD MEETINGS

For *regular* meetings of the Board of Directors, the time is often fixed in the By-laws, or a standing resolution, or by usage. Accordingly, absent provision to the contrary, no notice of such meetings usually need be given to Directors.[27] For special meetings, absent provision to the contrary, reasonable advance notice is usually required. For ordinary business matters, any required notice may be general, but any extraordinary matters should be enumerated in the notice.

Any required notice is probably waived where all of the Directors are present and participate. Statutes often so provide [28] or provide that the attendance of any Director waives his lack of notice except where he attends for the express purpose of objecting to the

24. E. g. Model Bus.Corp.Act § 43. Minutes are sometimes required by statute. E. g., Model Bus.Corp.Act § 52. Sanctions for noncompliance are not prescribed.

25. Model Bus.Corp.Act § 43. See also McKinney's N.Y.Bus.Corp.Law § 711; West's Ann.Calif.Corp.Code § 307.

26. E. g., Model Bus.Corp.Act § 43; West's Ann.Calif.Corp.Code § 307; McKinney's N.Y.Bus.Corp.Law, § 710.

27. See note 25, supra.

28. E. g., McKinney's N.Y.Bus.Corp. Law, § 711(c).

lack of notice.[29] Some statutes also generally provide that written waiver of notice by any Director entitled to notice, whether before or after the event, is equivalent to the giving of notice.[30]

QUORUM AND ACTION AT BOARD MEETINGS

A quorum of Directors consists of a majority of the number of Directors fixed in the By-laws, or if the number is not fixed in the By-laws, a majority of the number stated in the Articles of Incorporation.[31] The Articles of Incorporation or By-laws may specify that a greater number than a majority constitute a quorum; some states permit a quorum to be reduced to less than a majority [32], but in most states, by negative inference, a quorum may not be set at less than a majority. Provisions increasing a quorum to all the Directors are permitted and sometimes appear as control provisions in closely held Corporations. Where a quorum is present, the act of the majority of the Directors present at the meeting is the act of the Board, unless the Articles of Incorporation or By-laws require a greater number. Again, unanimity requirements sometimes appear as control provisions in closely held Corporations.

With a single exception, if a quorum is not present the Board of Directors may not act. The only exception is where the Directors are filling a vacancy; the Model Business Corporation Act provides that a vacancy "may be filled by the affirmative vote of a majority of the remaining directors though less than a quorum." [33] An ambiguity hides in this language. Even though there are vacancies, the number of Directors *in office* may still be greater than a quorum. However, if two factions are vying for control, the smaller faction may stay away from a meeting called by the larger faction to prevent a quorum from being present. At such a meeting the Directors *present* are less than a quorum even though the Directors are greater than a quorum. The cases are split as to whether the faction present at such a meeting, "though less than a quorum," may fill the vacancies. In Tomlinson v. Loew's, Inc., 135 A.2d 136 (Del.Ch.1957) By-law language similar to the phrase "though less than a quorum" was held to refer to the Directors in office rather than to the Directors present at the meeting. Several other cases, however, adopt the opposite construction.

29. E. g., Model Bus.Corp.Act § 43; McKinney's N.Y.Bus.Corp.Law, § 711(c) (by attendance of any Director at meeting without protesting, prior thereto or at its commencement, lack of notice to him).

30. E. g., Model Bus.Corp.Act § 144; West's Ann.Calif.Corp.Code § 307; McKinney's N.Y.Bus.Corp.Law, § 711(b), (c); as for adjournments see id. § 711(d).

31. Model Bus.Corp.Act § 40. See also West's Ann.Calif.Corp.Code § 307; McKinney's N.Y.Bus.Corp.Law § 707.

32. E. g. N.Y.Bus.Corp.Law § 707—one third.

33. Model Bus.Corp.Act § 38.

Many jurisdictions permit Directors to participate in meetings by means of conference telephone or some comparable communication technique.[34]

The act of the majority of the Directors present at a meeting at which a quorum is present usually constitutes the act of the Board. Statutes might permit the Articles of Incorporation or By-laws to require more than a majority vote.[35]

Whether or not Directors who are personally interested in a transaction with their Corporation may count for quorum or voting purposes, in the absence of a statute permitting such practice, presents questions not yet fully resolved. Modern statutes permit such practice but provide safeguards to try to assure that the transaction is "fair" to the Corporation.[36] In the absence of such statutes, interested Directors may be counted in some jurisdictions but not in others. Even in the latter jurisdictions, they usually may be counted if there are valid provisions to such effect in the Articles of Incorporation or possibly in the By-laws.

Stockholder ratification has different effects in different jurisdictions depending upon the presence of the previously mentioned factors and the differing judicial attitudes toward the same. Thus, Stockholder ratification can replace action by a Board of Directors which cannot muster a disinterested quorum. It might at least estop any Stockholders who voted for such ratification from complaining, or shift the burden of proof or the burden of going forward with the evidence, or even validate an otherwise voidable transaction.

Library References:

C.J.S. Corporations § 744 et seq.
West's Key No. Digests, Corporations ⚷298.

§ 46.6 Action Without a Meeting

Most states now permit Directors to act without a formal meeting "unless otherwise restricted by the Articles of Incorporation or By-laws." The Model Business Corporation Act provision, widely copied in state statutes, provides that "any action which may be taken at a meeting of Directors or of a committee, may be taken without a meeting if a consent in writing, setting forth the action so taken, shall be signed by all of the directors or all of the members of the com-

34. E. g., California, Delaware, Minnesota, New Jersey, New York. See Model Bus.Corp.Act § 43.

35. E. g., Model Bus.Corp.Act § 40 (Articles of Incorporation or By-laws). See Article XI of § 33.16, supra.

36. E. g., Model Bus.Corp.Act § 41; Del.Gen.Corp.Law, § 144 (1967); McKinney's N.Y.Bus.Corp.Law, § 713; West's Ann.Calif.Corp.Code § 310. The Model Business Corporation Act contained no such provision prior to the 1969 revision (§ 41).

mittee * * *." [37] Some statutes allow for action by a consenting majority. Further, such a consent has "the same effect as a unanimous vote." [38] This modest and sensible provision solves most problems created by the rule requiring Directors meetings. Problems still may arise, however. For one thing, obtaining a written consent signed by all the Directors is itself a formality which may be overlooked by a careless attorney; while a consent signed after the transaction has been entered into is effective, it is always possible that by that time one or more Directors may have changed their minds. And, of course, the procedure is inapplicable if one of the Directors objects to the transaction in question and refuses to execute the consent; a formal meeting is then apparently necessary.

The vesting of management in the Board, rather than in the Directors individually, is usually justified on the grounds of the value of consultation, deliberation, and collective judgment. Even in jurisdictions where the statutes make no apparent exceptions to the meeting requirement, some exceptions have been recognized by the courts, especially in close Corporations.[39]

A number of states (e. g. Calif., Del., Minn., New Jersey, New York) permit Directors to participate in meetings by means of telephone conferences or other comparable communication techniques.

§ 46.7 Directors' Objections to Actions

Directors are sometimes faced with the difficult problem of what to do when a majority insists on authorizing the Corporation to enter into transactions which the Director feels to be risky or outright illegal. The concern of such a Director is not entirely theoretical, since in some circumstances he may be held personally liable even though he objected to the transaction and voted against it. To avoid this result a Director must make sure that his dissent appears in writing since otherwise he is presumed to have assented to the action. If his dissent is not recorded in the minutes he must, in the words of the Model Act, "file his written dissent to such action with the secretary of the meeting before the adjournment thereof or * * * forward such dissent by registered mail to the secretary of the cor-

37. Model Bus.Corp.Act § 44.

38. Del.Gen.Corp.Law, § 141(F).

39. Philadelphia Life Ins. Co. v. Crosland-Cullen Co., 234 F.2d 780 (4th Cir. 1956); Linwood State Bank v. Lientz, 413 S.W.2d 248 (Mo.1967); Columbia Stamping & Mfg. Co. v. Reich, 28 Wis.2d 297, 137 N.W.2d 45 (1965) (Upholding Agreement, not formally approved at Board of Directors meeting, when made at meeting at which all Directors and Stockholders were present and none objected to informality); Matter of Stylemaster Dept. Store, Inc., 7 Misc.2d 207, 154 N.Y.S.2d 58 (Sup.Ct.1956); Matter of Kartub, 7 Misc.2d 72, 152 N.Y.S.2d 34 (Sup.Ct.1956), affirmed mem. 3 A.D. 2d 896, 163 N.Y.S.2d 938 (1st Dep't 1957); Simonson v. Helburn, 198 Misc. 430, 97 N.Y.S.2d 406 (Sup.Ct. 1950). But cf. Brent v. Advance Scale Mfg. Co., 66 Ohio L.Abs. 259, 116 N.E.2d 761 (Ct.App.1952); Hurley v. Ornsteen, 311 Mass. 477, 42 N.E.2d 273 (1942) (no acquiescence by third Director).

poration immediately after the adjournment of the meeting." [40] Filing of a dissent not only eliminates liability, but also obviates later questions of proof and may have a psychological effect upon the other Directors who realize that at least one Director considers the conduct sufficiently questionable as to seek legal protection. Also, it affords notice to Stockholders or others examining the records that at least one Director questioned the propriety of a specific transaction. Other steps a Director might take includes requesting the Corporation to obtain an opinion of counsel as to the propriety of the proposed transaction. While Directors may rely in good faith on the opinion of counsel [41], as a practical matter, an unqualified, reliable opinion may be difficult to obtain if the transaction is questionable. Finally, the Director may resign, though if the resignation occurs after the transaction is approved, liability may be avoided only if the Director files the appropriate dissent.

Similarly, even though a meeting is called without proper notice, a Director waives his objection if he attends the meeting, except where he attends for the sole purpose of objecting to the transaction of any business. Any participation by him in the business undertaken at the meeting is likely to be considered a waiver even if he prefaces his participation by objecting to the lack of notice.[42]

§ 46.8 Executive and Other Committees

Where a Board of Directors is large, it may be convenient to appoint a smaller executive committee to perform the functions of the Board of Directors between meetings of the full board. Corporation acts usually specifically authorize an executive committee, and define the area in which it may or may not function with more or less specificity.[43]

Under the Model Business Corporation Act, an executive committee may be created only if specific provision therefor appears in the Articles of Incorporation or By-laws.[44] Many statutes provide that an executive committee must consist of at least two members; in some states the creation of such a committee also requires approval by more votes than is necessary for the adoption of resolution.

The power of an executive committee extends generally to all matters relating to the business and affairs of the Corporation over which the Board of Directors has authority with specified exceptions:

(1) Exceptions set forth in the resolution creating the executive committee, the By-laws, or the Articles of Incorporation; and

40. Model Bus.Corp.Act § 35.

41. Model Bus.Corp.Act § 35, 2d ¶.

42. Id. at 43. See e. g. Minn.Bus.Corp. Act § 302A.251.

43. See e. g. Model Bus.Corp.Act § 38; West's Ann.Calif.Corp.Code § 311; McKinney's New York Bus.Corp.Law § 712.

44. Model Bus.Corp.Act § 42. See also e. g. McKinney's N.Y.Bus.Corp.Law § 712.

(2) Important matters which the applicable business Corporation act specifically vests in the Board of Directors. The Model Act lists eight such actions, including declaring a dividend, approving a merger, authorizing the sale of shares, and so forth. The basic distinction is between routine matters relating to the business of the Corporation and decisions referred to in the business Corporation act which affect the governance of the Corporation or its basic structure. In this way, the possibility of a "run away" executive committee is largely obviated. Delegation of authority to an executive committee generally does not relieve the Board of Directors, or any member thereof, of any responsibility imposed upon it or them.

In addition to committees of Directors, many Corporations create committees of management personnel to consider business-related problems. These committees form part of executive management rather than part of the management structure of the Board of Directors.

Library References:

C.J.S. Corporations § 760.
West's Key No. Digests, Corporations ⚷299.

§ 46.9 Compensation of Directors

The traditional view is that a Director is not entitled to compensation for his ordinary services as Director unless specific provision is made by the Board. The theory is that either Directors are acting as trustees or that they are motivated by the prospect of increasing the return on their shares. However, a Director may be entitled to compensation pursuant to contract entered into in advance or for extraordinary services beyond normal directoral functions, or for service as a corporate Officer or agent. These principles are based on tradition not legal power. A number of state statutes, following the Model Business Corporation Act, provide that the "Board of directors shall have authority to fix the compensation of directors unless otherwise provided in the articles of incorporation." [45]

The traditional view is gradually changing particularly among large public Corporations. Rather than paying their Directors nothing or a small honoraria for attending meetings, an increasing number now pay substantial sums to outside persons to serve as Directors. Many Corporations believe such payments improve the quality and interest of Directors.

Library References:

C.J.S. Corporations § 803 et seq.
West's Key No. Digests, Corporations ⚷308.

45. Model Bus.Corp.Act § 35. See also e. g. Minn.Bus.Corp.Act § 302A.211.

§ 46.10 Selection, Supervision, and Removal of Officers by Board

SELECTION OF OFFICERS

Most statutes provide for election of the corporate Officers—at least the President, Vice-Presidents, Secretary, and Treasurer—by the Board of Directors, sometimes providing that other Officers and assistant Officers, agents, and employees may be elected or appointed by the Board or chosen as prescribed in the By-laws.[46]

Some statutes require that the President be elected from among the Directors. Some statutes provide that any two offices may be held by the same person with stated exceptions.

It is important for a Corporation to have two different people as officers so that one can attest to the other's signature.

A growing number of statutes permit the Officers to be elected by Stockholders.

SUPERVISION OF OFFICERS

Corporate officers have such authority and duties in the management of the Corporation as inhere in their offices and as may be provided in the By-laws or as determined by resolution of the Board of Directors not inconsistent with the By-laws.[47]

REMOVAL OF OFFICERS

Removal of Officers is usually at the pleasure of the Board of Directors.[48]

Even when an officer has a valid employment contract with the Corporation, he may usually be removed with or without cause. Any such removal is without prejudice, however, to his right to recover damages for any wrongful removal in breach of such contract.

§ 46.11 Management Compensation

Executive compensation, absent provision to the contrary, is usually fixed by the Board of Directors.[49]

46. E. g., Model Bus.Corp.Act § 50; West's Ann.Calif.Corp.Code § 312; McKinney's N.Y.Bus.Corp.Law § 715 (a).

47. E. g., Model Bus.Corp.Act § 50; McKinney's N.Y.Bus.Corp.Law, § 715(g).

48. E. g., Model Bus.Corp.Act § 51; McKinney's N.Y.Bus.Corp.Law, § 716(a). Such power is sometimes expressly restricted with respect to Officers elected by Stockholders. McKinney's N.Y.Bus.Corp.Law, § 716(a) (removable, with or without cause, only by vote of Stockholders (but his authority to act as Officer may be suspended by Board of Directors for cause)). See also West's Ann.Calif. Corp.Code § 312 (subject to the rights, if any, of an officer under any contract of employment).

49. E. g., Model Bus.Corp.Act § 4(k).

Some statutes expressly empower the Board also to fix the compensation of Directors unless otherwise provided in the Articles of Incorporation.[50]

§ 46.12 Declaration of Dividends

Absent relatively rare mandatory provisions, and subject to any preferences and other restrictions, the declaration of dividends (limited, of course, to funds legally available for dividends) is within the discretion of the Board of Directors.

§ 46.13 Delegation of Authority by Board

To some extent, at least, the Board of Directors may delegate management authority. Delegation of authority to officers and other agents and employees is common.[51] The exercise by the Officers, etc., of the authority delegated to them is subject to the supervision of the Board of Directors.

Modern statutes also expressly permit delegation by the Board of Directors of at least some of its more discretionary authority to committees composed of Directors with power to act at least during the intervals between meetings of the whole Board of Directors.

The Model Business Corporation Act, for example, authorizes an executive committee and one or more other committees composed of two or more Directors to exercise all of the authority of the Board of Directors in the management of the Corporation, subject to stated limitations.[52] For further discussion, see § 46.8, supra.

Older corporate statutes made no or only oblique references to committees of the Board.

Absent statutory authorization, delegation of authority to committees is usually strictly construed, and any broad delegation runs the risk of being treated as an unlawful abdication by the Board of its management functions.

50. E. g., Model Bus.Corp.Act § 35; Minn.Bus.Corp.Act § 302A.211.

51. E. g., Model Bus.Corp.Act § 50.

52. Model Bus.Corp.Act § 42. The executive or other committees must be authorized in the Articles of Incorporation or By-laws and by a resolution of a majority of the full Board of Directors, which must define the authority delegated. No committee may exercise the authority of the Board with respect to amendments of the Articles of Incorporation, mergers, consolidations, sales, etc., of all or substantially all corporate assets other than in the regular course of business, voluntary dissolutions or revocation thereof, and By-law amendments. The Model Act does not expressly require the keeping of minutes by such committees, and permits a committee as well as the Board of Directors to act by prior written consent without a meeting. Model Bus. Corp.Act § 44.

Delegation of authority to outsiders, such as management companies or even arbitrators in the event of deadlock of the Board, unless minor in scope, is even more difficult to sustain except in a few jurisdictions were specifically permitted.

Delegation of authority to committees or others does not relieve the Directors of their responsibilities imposed by law,[53] unless otherwise provided by statute.[54]

Library References:

C.J.S. Corporations § 758 et seq.
West's Key No. Digests, Corporations ⚷305.

§ 46.14 Adoption, Amendment, and Repeal of By-laws by Board

In some jurisdictions, the Board of Directors adopts the initial By-laws.[55]

In such cases, or even when the initial By-laws are adopted by incorporators or Stockholders and a statute, the Articles of Incorporation, or By-laws so provide, the Board may amend or repeal the By-laws.[56] Notwithstanding any such power in the Board, the Stockholders retain inherent power to amend or repeal the By-laws.

Furthermore, By-laws limiting the power of the Board of Directors, or By-laws specifically requiring Stockholder approval might be capable of adoption, amendment, or repeal only by Stockholders. By-laws limiting the power of Directors or otherwise affecting corporate management in a manner inconsistent with law, even when unanimously adopted by Stockholders, are void.

Library References:

C.J.S. Corporations §§ 186, 187.
West's Key No. Digests, Corporations ⚷55, 56.

53. E. g., Model Bus.Corp.Act § 42; McKinney's N.Y.Bus.Corp.Law, § 712(c) (designation of any executive or other committee and delegation thereto of authority not alone to relieve any director of his duty to Corporation).

54. E. g., McKinney's N.Y.Bus.Corp. Law, § 620(f) (relieving Directors and imposing on Stockholders liability for managerial acts and omissions under Articles of Incorporation provision as to control of Directors).

55. E. g., Model Bus.Corp.Act § 57. In some jurisdictions, the practice (sometimes not formalized by statute) is shortly after incorporation to have the incorporators at their organization meeting adopt the initial By-laws, and the Board of Directors at its organization meeting also approve and adopt such By-laws.

56. E. g., Model Bus.Corp.Act § 27 (unless such power is reserved to Stockholders by Articles of Incorporation); Del.Gen.Corp.Law, § 109 (1967) (if power conferred on Board of Directors in Articles of Incorporation); McKinney's N.Y.Bus.Corp.Law, § 601 (when so provided in articles of incorporation or By-law adopted by Stockholders). See also West's Ann. Calif.Corp.Code § 211.

§ 46.15 Initiation of Extraordinary Corporate Matters by Board

Extraordinary corporate matters, such as amendments of the Articles of Incorporation or transactions beyond the ordinary business, such as sale or lease of all or substantially all corporate assets not in the regular course of business, merger, consolidation, dissolution, are generally beyond the scope of management delegated to the Board of Directors.

Stockholder approval is generally required for such extraordinary matters. Some statutes expressly require Board of Directors approval as well.[57] Even in the jurisdictions which do not require Board of Directors action, the Board of Directors as a practical matter usually initiates such extraordinary matters.

§ 46.16 Director's Inspection Rights

Directors as individuals enjoy, on common-law principles, a right, termed "absolute" in some and "qualified" in other jurisdictions, to inspect the corporate books and records, as corollary to their duties to keep informed on corporate matters. Such rights are rarely affected by statutes.[58]

Removal of the Director ends his Director status, and with it any unqualified inspection rights. After removal, the Director has been held to enjoy a qualified right to inspect records covering the period of his incumbency to protect his "personal responsibility interest".

Library References:

C.J.S. Corporations §§ 779, 780.
West's Key No. Digests, Corporations ⚿311.

57. E. g., Model Bus.Corp.Act §§ 59, 71, 72, 79, 84; Del.Gen.Corp.Law, §§ 242, 251, 271, 275 (1967); McKinney's N.Y.Bus.Corp.Law, § 902 (adoption of plan of merger or consolidation by Board of Directors); id. § 909 (authorization of proposed sale, lease, exchange, or other disposition of assets, requiring Stockholder approval, by Board of Directors). See also e. g. West's Ann.Calif.Corp.Code § 1101 (merger), § 1200 (reorganization).

58. See e. g. West's Ann.Calif.Corp. Code § 1602.

§§ 46.17–46.30 are reserved for supplementary material.

B. DIRECTORS' MEETINGS

§ 46.31 Introductory Comment

See § 46.5, supra, for text discussion.

§ 46.32 Notice of Regular Meeting of Directors—Another Form

To: [*Name and Address of Director*].

You are hereby notified that the regular quarterly meeting of the Board of Directors of ______ Company will be held at the principal office of said Company at ______, on the ______ day of ______, 19__, at ______ o'clock __. m.

[*Date*]

____
Secretary

COMMENT

Under most corporate statutes (e. g. Model Bus.Corp.Act § 43), notice of regular meetings of the Board of Directors may be dispensed with if the time and place of such meetings are fixed by the By-laws or the Board of Directors. Nevertheless, a notice may be useful in such cases to inform the Directors of the agenda proposed for such meeting. See § 46.5, supra.

Library References:

C.J.S. Corporations § 747.
West's Key No. Digests, Corporations ⚷298(3).

§ 46.33 Notice of Regular or Special Meeting of Directors

To: [*Board of Directors*] of [*Name of Corporation*].

From: [*Name of the Corporate Secretary*].

Please take Notice that on [*Date*] at [*Place*] at [*Time*] a special [*Regular*] meeting of the Directors of said Corporation shall be called to consider:

[*Describe*]

And all other business which may properly come before it.

§ 46.34 Call of a Special Meeting of the Board of Directors by the President—Instruction to Secretary to Give Notice

To: ______

Secretary of ______ Co.

I hereby call a special meeting of the Board of Directors of the company to be held on the ______ day of ______, 19__ at the hour of ______ o'clock __M at the principal offices of the company at ______ Street, ______, ______, for the purpose of: [*Describe*].

You are hereby directed to give notice of said special meeting to each director in accordance with the By-laws of the company.

Dated at ______, ______, this ______ day of ______, 19__.

§ 46.35 Call of Special Meeting of Directors by Two or More Directors

To: ______

Secretary of ______,

______ and ______, [*Names*] Directors of said Corporation do hereby call a special meeting of the Board of Directors of the Corporation to be held at ______ o'clock, __M on the ______ day of ______, 19__ at the office of the Corporation at ______, ______ ______, ______ for the purpose of: [*Describe*].

2. Transacting such other and further business as may properly come before the said meeting.

We hereby authorize and instruct you, as Secretary of the Corporation, to give notice of said special meeting to each Director in accordance with the By-laws of the Corporation.

Dated at ______, ______, this ______ day of ______, 19__.

____

____

Directors of:

____

§ 46.36 Waiver of Notice of Special Meeting

The undersigned Directors waive notice of the special meeting of Board of Directors held [*or to be held*] on the ______ day of ______, 19__ at the office of the Corporation, ______, ______, ______, and consent to the holding of that meeting.

Dated: ______, 19__.

____

____

COMMENT

It is the view of the author that a "waiver of notice" is appropriate only if the meeting is actually to be held; if the Directors plan to proceed by unanimous consent without actually holding a meeting, the appropriate form is a "consent" rather than a waiver of notice.

§ 46.37 Notice of Board of Directors' Meeting—With Waiver and Consent Provisions

NOTICE OF BOARD OF DIRECTORS MEETING
(INCLUDING WAIVER, IF ANY)

To: The Directors of [*Corporation*].

Please take notice that on the ______ day of ______, 19__, at ______ o'clock in the ______noon, a meeting will take place to discuss and vote upon the attached resolution; unless the need for such meeting is waived prior to such meeting by 100% of the Directors and the Resolution adopted by 100% of the Directors by their execution of a copy of the attached Resolution.

If you wish to waive the proper number of days notice, please sign here:

____

____

____

If you wish to waive the holding of the meeting *and* if you wish to adopt the resolution, please sign here:

____

____

____

§ 46.38 Board of Directors' Consent Meeting

CONSENT TO THE WAIVER OF NOTICE, THE NECESSITY OF HOLDING A MEETING, AND THE MINUTES OF A MEETING OF BOARD OF DIRECTORS OF [*Name*]

[*We/I*], the undersigned being [*the only Director/all of the Directors*] of [*Name of Corporation*],

Now, [*we/I*] hereby waive the necessity of notice of the annual meeting of the Board of Directors of the Corporation and the necessity of holding a meeting of the Board of Directors of the Corporation; and in its stead [*we/I*] consent to adopt (and do hereby adopt) as [*our/my*] act and deed as of [*Date*] [*Fiscal Year*], the following:

[*Describe*]

Resolved, that the Secretary of the Corporation shall make the original of this consent part of the official minutes of the Corporation.

Directors:

____

____

Dated as of: ______. ____________________

§ 46.39 Dissent by Director

To: The Secretary of the Corporation.

I hereby dissent from the decision by a majority of the Directors to [*Describe*] made at the meeting of the Board of Directors earlier today. You will recall that I strongly opposed such action at the meeting, believing the Corporation could not legally pay a dividend on common shares at this time and that I voted against that proposal.

Dated: ______, 19__.

____

Director

§ 46.40 Notice to Absent Director of Adjournment of Meeting

To: Directors.

Please be advised that the special meeting of directors held on ______, 19__ was adjourned to ______, 19__, at the offices of the Corporation, ______, ______, ______. The meeting will resume at ______ __. m. on that date to consider the following remaining matters:

Dated: ______, 19__.

____

President

§ 46.41 Minutes of Board of Directors' Meeting

MINUTES OF BOARD OF DIRECTORS' MEETING

The meeting of the Directors of [*Name of Corporation*] was held at [*Time*] on [*Date*] at [*Place*] pursuant to

Alternative A–1

Written waiver of notice signed by ___% of the Directors; said waiver is to be filed as part of the minutes by the Secretary of the Corporation.

Alternative A–2

Actual notice given to each Director, ______ having sworn to the giving of such notice in an affidavit, the Secretary of the Corporation is to file such affidavit as part of the minutes.

Alternative A–3

A written waiver of notice signed by some of the Directors and actual notice given to each other Director, ______ having sworn to the giving of such notice in an affidavit the Secretary of the Corporation is to file such affidavit and the waivers as part of the minutes.

Option 1 (Use When There Is No Elected Officers (or Correct Officer Is Absent))

Upon motion duly made and seconded, [*Name*] was elected chairman and ______ was elected secretary of the meeting.

It was reported by the President:

[*Describe*]

It was reported by the Treasurer:

[*Describe*]

It was reported by [*Name*]:

[*Describe*]

After a resolution duly made and seconded, and a full discussion of the motion in question, the following motions were adopted:

[Describe—See Chapter 48, infra for Sample Resolutions]

There being no further business, upon motion duly made and seconded, the meeting was adjourned.

____

Secretary of Meeting

COMMENT

Model Bus.Corp.Act § 52 requires that the Corporation keep minutes of Board of Directors meetings.

§ 46.42 Minutes of Special Meeting

Minutes of a meeting of the Board of Directors of ______, held at ______, at ______ a. m., ______, 19___, in accordance with due notice.

The Chairman of the Board of Directors called the meeting to order. The Secretary of the meeting called the roll and the following Directors were present:

____

____

____

The Secretary stated that notice of the meeting was given to all of the Directors and he then presented the formal notice of the meeting. Upon motion duly made, seconded, and carried, the notice was ordered on file. A copy of the notice is appended to these minutes.

The Chairman then stated that a quorum was present and that the meeting was competent to transact business.

The Chairman then stated that the meeting was called at the request of ______ to consider the following business:

[*Specify Business Considered*]

____

____

[*State Results of Consideration of Such Business*]

____

____

There being no further business, the meeting was adjourned.

Dated: _______, 19__.

____

Secretary

COMMENT

An affidavit of mailing will obviate future claims that notice was not given.

§§ 46.43–46.50 are reserved for supplementary material.

C. DIRECTORS' RESOLUTIONS

§ 46.51 Comment

See Chapter 48, infra, for resolutions of Board of Directors relating to many matters.

§§ 46.52–47.0 are reserved for supplementary material.

CHAPTER 47

VOTING OF SHARES

Table of Sections

A. VOTING RIGHTS GENERALLY

B. PROXIES

C. VOTING TRUSTS

A. VOTING RIGHTS GENERALLY

§ 47.1 Election of Directors: Straight or Cumulative Voting

Directors are elected each year at the annual meeting of Stockholders by a vote of a majority of the shares (1) present at the meeting and (2) entitled to vote, assuming that a quorum is present. In many states the Articles of Incorporation or By-laws may increase, but may not decrease, the percentage of the shares required for election. In close Corporations it is not uncommon to exercise this privilege and require unanimity as a planning device, even though the possibility of a deadlock is thereby increased.

The most important question relating to the election of Directors is whether shares may be voted "cumulatively" or must be voted "straight." In several states cumulative voting is mandatory by state constitution or provisions in the state Corporation statute. Most states, however, give a Corporation an option to exclude cumulative voting; usually this option requires a specific exclusion in the Articles of Incorporation though in some states, cumulative voting is permitted only if specific provision for it is made in the Articles.

STRAIGHT VOTING

In straight voting, each share carries one vote for each matter, including one vote for each Director to be elected.

Thus in a Corporation with a single class of shares, a plurality of the shares generally would elect all of the Directors and the other shares would elect no Director. If there are two or more classes of outstanding voting shares, each vote usually counts the same regardless of class. If the common shares are numerically greater than the preferred shares, the combined votes of the common Stockholders will outvote the preferred Stockholders. Straight voting is the normal method of Stockholder voting for all corporate matters, except where cumulative voting is in effect with respect to the election of Directors; in the latter case, straight voting would be the normal method except in the election of Directors.

CUMULATIVE VOTING

In cumulative voting, which applies only to the election of Directors, each share carries as many votes as there are vacancies to be filled, the Stockholder being permitted to distribute the votes for all his shares among the candidates in any way he desires.

Cumulative voting is a form of proportional representation to assure any desirable minority representation on the Board.

Cumulative voting is required by state constitutions in some jurisdictions [1] and by statutes in some others,[2] and by federal statute for national banking Corporations [3] (known as "mandatory cumulative voting"). Elsewhere, cumulative voting exists, in some jurisdictions, absent a provision to the contrary in the Articles of incorporation or By-laws,[4] or does not exist, in other jurisdictions, unless there is a provision in the Articles of Incorporation or By-laws providing for cumulative voting (known as "permissive cumulative voting").[5]

Some statutes require that where cumulative voting is authorized, any Stockholder intending to vote cumulatively must first announce such intention before doing so. Until the results have been announced by the Chairman, a Stockholder may change his vote.

1. Ariz.Const. art. XIV, § 10; Idaho Const. art. XI, § 4; Ill.Const. art. XI, § 3; Ky.Const. art. 207; Miss.Const. art. 7, § 194; Mo.Const. art. XI, § 6; Mont.Const. art. XV, § 4; Neb.Const. art. XII, § 5; N.D.Const. art. VII, § 135; Pa.Const. art. XVI, § 4; S.C. Const. art. IX, § 11; S.D.Const. art. XVII, § 5; W.Va.Const. art. XI, § 4.

2. E. g., Model Bus.Corp.Act § 33; West's Ann.Calif.Corp.Code § 708.

3. 12 U.S.C.A. § 61.

4. E. g., Model Bus.Corp.Act § 33; Minn.Bus.Corp.Act § 302A.215.

5. E. g., Model Bus.Corp.Act § 33; Del.Gen.Corp.Law, § 214 (1967); McKinney's N.Y.Bus.Corp.Law, § 618 (provision in articles of incorporation).

The right to vote cumulatively can often be diluted by decreasing the number of vacancies to be filled, by reducing the size of the Board of Directors, or classifying the Board and having a stagger system of election.

If Directors are removable without cause by a simple majority vote of Stockholders, a Director elected by a minority of Stockholders could be removd by the majority of Stockholders.[6]

Where the right of cumulative voting exists pursuant to a provision in the Articles of Incorporation or Bylaws, the right might be eliminated by proper amendment thereof, which might require no more than majority vote or a vote which the minority could not muster sufficient opposing votes to block.

Arguments in favor of and against cumulative voting are raised periodically.

The workings of cumulative voting can be most simply described by an illustration. Let us assume a Corporation with two Stockholders, A with 26 shares, and B with 74 shares. Further, let us assume that there are three Directors and each Stockholder nominates three candidates.

A critical point is that candidates do not run for specific places. The three candidates with the most votes in this election are the winners. If only straight voting is permitted, A may cast 26 votes for each of any three candidates, and B may cast 74 votes for each of any three candidates. The result, of course, is that if they do not agree on any candidates, all three of B's candidates are elected. If cumulative voting is permitted, the total number of votes that each Stockholder may cast is first computed and each Stockholder is permitted to distribute these votes as he sees fit over one or more candidates. In the example above, A is entitled to cast a total of 78 votes (26 $\times$ 3) and B is entitled to cast 222 votes (74 $\times$ 3). If A casts all 78 votes for himself, he is assured of election because B cannot divide 222 votes among three candidates in such a way as to give each candidate 79 or more votes and preclude A's election. (If B gives 79 votes to himself and 79 votes to B_1, he will only have 64 votes left for B_2.) Obviously, the effect of cumulative voting is that it increases minority participation on the Board of Directors. In straight voting, the Stockholder with 51 per cent of the vote elects the entire Board; in cumulative voting, a relatively small faction (26 per cent in the above example) obtains representation on the Board.

The difference between cumulative and straight voting may be vividly illustrated by the deadlock situation where all shares are owned

6. A few jurisdictions by statute have attempted to remedy this loophole by providing that removal of a Director, absent removal of the entire Board, can be blocked by vote of the number of shares sufficient to elect such a Director cumulatively. E. g., Model Bus.Corp.Act § 39. See e. g. West's Ann.Calif.Corp.Code § 303.

equally by two Stockholders—say fifty shares each. If only straight voting is permitted and each Stockholder votes only for his own candidates a deadlocked election is inevitable. If there are two places to be filled A will vote 50 shares for himself, and 50 shares for A_2; B will vote 50 shares for himself, and 50 shares for B_2. Thus, four candidates will each have 50 votes for two positions, and the result is that no one is elected. If cumulative voting is permitted on the other hand, A may cast 100 votes for himself and he will be guaranteed election (since B obviously cannot give two candidates more than 100 votes each.) If there are an odd number of Directors to be elected (say 3) straight voting still leads to deadlock: A_1–50, A_2–50, A_3–50, B_1–50, B_2–50, B_3–50. If cumulative voting is permitted, A and B may each elect one Director but the situation is unstable: a deadlock will be created if each tries to elect the tie-breaking Director and the other votes rationally. However, the strategy and counterstrategy can become complex. If A gives A_1 76 votes, A_1 will be guaranteed of election since B has only 150 votes and obviously cannot prevent A_1's election; similarly, if B gives B_1 76 votes, A cannot prevent B_1's election. If both Stockholders follow this conservative strategy, the result will be A_1–76, A_2–74, B_1–76, B_2–74, with A_1 and B_1 each being elected and a tie existing between A_2 and B_2. However, if B knows that A will follow this strategy in voting, B might be tempted to divide his vote equally between two candidates in order to elect two of the three Directors: A_1–76, A_2–74, B_1–75, B_2–75, with A_1, B_1, and B_2 all being elected. A may counter this strategy by also giving his two candidates 75 votes each, thereby creating a four way tie and electing no one. Indeed, it is disastrous if either Stockholder deviates from these very precise voting patterns. If B decides to vote only slightly illogically, for example, B_1–77, B_2–73, he delivers control of the Corporation over to A even if A follows the conservative strategy of guaranteeing the election of one Director: B_1–77, A_1–76, A_2–74, B_2–73, with B_1, A_1 and A_2 elected. In these and the following illustrations it is assumed that A or B, once they have adopted a strategy and cast their votes, cannot thereafter change them. This is true only to a limited extent in the real world. Balloting for Directors is by written ballot rather than voice vote so that each Stockholder must establish his voting strategy without being sure of his opponent's strategy; however, until the vote is announced, a Stockholder may recast his votes and thereby correct mistakes in his voting pattern.

As the preceding discussion illustrates, one undesirable aspect of cumulative voting is that it tends to be a little tricky. If a Stockholder casts votes in an irrational or inefficient way, he may not get the directorships his position entitles him to; when voting cumulatively it is relatively easy to make a mistake in spreading votes around. Another graphic illustration of this are the cases where a majority Stockholder votes in such a way that he elects only a minority of the Directors. This is most likely to occur when one Stockholder votes "straight" and another cumulates. For example, if A has 60 shares and B only 40, with 5 Directors to be elected, B may nevertheless elect a majority of the board if A votes "straight," and B knows that A is doing so. The result might look like this:

A_1–60, A_2–60, A_3–60, A_4–60, A_5–60, B_1–67, B_2–66, B_3–65, B_4–1, B_5–1.

B should not create tie votes among his own candidates. If he does so, and the tie candidates come in fifth and sixth in an election for five Directorships, the tie may be broken by a new election for only the fifth seat; A may be able to vote his shares in the new election for his own candidate, thereby causing B to lose a seat. This strategy is daring of B because he is spreading his vote over three persons when he can be sure only of electing two. If A knows that B will try to elect three persons, A, by properly cumulating his votes, can elect four directors, in effect "stealing" one of B's. The results of such an election might be as follows:

A_1–73, A_2–74, A_3–75, A_4–76, A_5–2, B_1–67, B_2–66, B_3–65, B_4–1, B_5–1.

In states where cumulative voting is mandatory, and sometimes in Corporations formed in other states as well, it is not uncommon to employ devices that minimize the effects of cumulative voting. One device that reduces the impact of cumulative voting is the "classification" (or "staggering") of the Board of Directors if the Board consists of nine or more members. Under most statutes, the Directors of a large board may be divided into two or three classes of as nearly equal numbers as possible, and one class may be elected each year. In a classified Board, each Director serves for two years (if there are two classes) or three years (if there are three classes). The theoretical justification for classification is that it ensures "experience of service" on the board, since only one-half or one-third of the Board may be replaced each year. However, experience of service is usually not a major motivating factor for classifying a Board, since as a practical matter, experience of service is usually provided by the simple process of reelecting the same persons as Directors year after year. Even where a take-over attempt has been successful, or where a controlling interest in a Corporation has been sold to outsiders, there is often a period during which some Directors are continued in office to provide the necessary continuity and experience. Staggering has two basic effects:

(1) It makes it more difficult for a minority faction to elect a Director when there is cumulative voting. For example, if there are nine Directors elected each year, ten per cent of the stock can elect a Director; if the nine Directors are classified and three are elected each year, it takes twenty-five per cent of the stock to elect a Director.

(2) It makes take-over attempts more difficult. Where the Board consists of three classes, a person becoming a majority Stockholder cannot be ensured of electing a majority on the Board for more than two full years. In some instances classification has been proposed in publicly held Corporations primarily for this reason even though the Corporation does not have cumulative voting.

Other devices also limit the impact of cumulative voting. Reduction of the size of the Board of Directors has much the same effect as staggering the election of Directors. Shares may sometimes be tied up in voting trusts or voting agreements; in many states nonvoting shares also may be used consistently with a cumulative voting requirement. The influence of minority Directors may be minimized by having informal Director discussion in advance of meetings, scheduling Board meetings at inconvenient times or places, and delegating functions to committee composed entirely of management Directors. Also, it may be possible to remove the minority Director without cause and replace him with a more congenial person, at least until the next election. The Model Act, however, and the statutes of many states, prohibit the removal of a minority Director elected by cumulative voting unless the votes to remove him would have been enough to prevent his original election in an election for Directors.[7]

Of course, in states where cumulative voting is permissive it may be eliminated by an amendment to the Articles of Incorporation in the same way as any other attribute of shares.

Library References:

C.J.S. Corporations § 720.
West's Key No. Digests, Corporations ⚿283(2).

§ 47.2 Class (Series) Voting

In class (*or* series) voting, which obviously is possible only where two or more classes (series) of shares outstanding, each class (series) of shares votes as a separate unit for one or more purposes. The Board of Directors might be classified, with one class (series) of shares voting for its class of Directors and another class (series) of shares separately voting for its class of Directors.[8]

Either along with or apart from class (series) voting for Directors, class voting for other matters might exist under statute or the Articles of Incorporation. Where such class voting exists, a sufficient vote of each class might be required,[9] or a sufficient vote gen-

7. Model Bus.Corp.Act § 39. See e. g. West's Ann.Calif.Corp.Code § 303; Minn.Bus.Corp.Act § 302A.223.

8. Model Bus.Corp.Act § 143; e. g., McKinney's N.Y.Bus.Corp.Law, § 703(a).

9. See, e. g., Model Bus.Corp.Act § 60; Del.Gen.Corp.Law, § 242 (1967); McKinney's N.Y.Bus.Corp.Law, § 617.

erally plus a sufficient class vote of any class adversely affected by the matter being voted on.[10] Sometimes such a sufficient class vote might be required even though the shares are otherwise nonvoting.[11]

§ 47.3 Contingent Voting

Contingent voting rights, which obviously exist only where two or more classes (*or* series) of shares are outstanding, are those which arise upon the happening of a stated contingency, such as the default of specified dividends. Once the contingency is over, such as the payment of dividend arrearages, a class (series) of shares with contingent voting rights usually reverts to its former voting status. The requirement is occasionally found that preferred shares have at least minimum contingent or class voting rights.[12]

§ 47.4 Disproportionate Voting

Disproportionate voting, which is possible only where two or more classes (*or* series) are outstanding, exists when one class (series) of shares is validly given greater or less votes per share than another class (series). An example would be where one class (series) has normal voting rights and the shares of another class (series) carry multiple or fractional votes.

§ 47.5 Nonvoting Shares

Except for a few jurisdictions which require that all shares have voting rights, nonvoting shares may usually be authorized and issued, so long as voting rights reside in one or more classes (*or* series) of outstanding shares or possibly debt securities.[13]

Statutes sometimes impose limitations on the issue of nonvoting shares.[14]

10. See, e. g., McKinney's N.Y.Bus. Corp.Law, § 804(a) (overall majority and majority of class (or series) for certain amendments of Articles of Incorporation adversely affecting class); id. § 903(a)(2) (overall two-thirds vote and majority of class (or series) for certain mergers or consolidations).

11. Model Bus.Corp.Act § 60.

12. Federal Public Utility Holding Company Act of 1935, § 7(c), 15 U.S.C.A. § 79g(c); Public Utility Holding Company Act Release No. 13,106 (Feb. 16, 1956); Federal National Housing Act § 608, 12 U.S.C.A. § 1743; Sarner v. Mason, 130 F.Supp. 829 (D.N.J.1955), affirmed 228 F.2d 176 (3d Cir.), certiorari denied 351 U.S. 924, 76 S.Ct. 781, 100 L.Ed. 1454. Securities exchange listing requirements sometimes prescribe minimal contingent and class voting rights for otherwise nonvoting preferred shares.

13. See, e. g., Model Bus.Corp.Act § 33; Del.Gen.Corp.Law, § 151 (1967); West's Ann.Calif.Corp.Code § 400.

14. Federal Public Utility Holding Company Act of 1935, § 7(c), 15 U.S.C.A. § 79g(c); Investment Company Act of 1940, § 18, 15 U.S.C.A. § 80a–18.

Even shares which are nominally nonvoting might have mandatory voting rights with respect to certain matters adversely affecting such shares or otherwise.[15]

Shares of a class otherwise entitled to voting rights, under certain circumstances, might not be voted or counted in determining the total number of outstanding shares.[16]

§ 47.6 Voting Debt Securities

Some statutes, as previously mentioned, expressly permit voting rights to be conferred on holders of bonds, debentures, and other debt securities. To the extent such voting rights are conferred, Stockholder control is, of course, diluted.

§§ 47.7–47.20 are reserved for supplementary material.

B. PROXIES

§ 47.21 Proxies—Generally [1]

The term "proxy" sometimes causes initial confusion because of its various meanings: (1) the *authority* given by the Stockholder to his agent; (2) the *instrument* evidencing such authority; (3) the *agent* (called the proxy holder); and (4) the *exercise* of authority by the agent ("voting, etc., by proxy"). In the following discussion, the meaning of the term will vary in different contexts.

Many statutes provide that Stockholders entitled to vote at a Stockholders meeting have the right to be present and to vote at such meeting in person or by proxy.[2] The proxy holder usually need not be a Stockholder, but must have the legal capacity to be an agent.

15. See, e. g., pre-1966 Model Bus. Corp.Act § 60 (certain amendments of Articles of Incorporation), § 73 (certain mergers or consolidations); Del.Gen.Corp.Law, § 242 (1967); McKinney's N.Y.Bus.Corp.Law, § 804(a) (certain amendments of Articles of Incorporation adversely affecting class (or series)); id. § 903(a)(2) (certain mergers or consolidation adversely affecting class (or series)).

16. See, e. g., McKinney's N.Y.Bus. Corp.Law, § 612(b) (treasury shares; its shares held by any other corporation if majority of shares entitled to vote in election of Directors of such other Corporation is held by it); id. § 612(f) (shares called for redemption if redemption proceeds have been irrevocably deposited); Model Bus.Corp. Act § 33.

1. Adapted from Henn, Law of Corporations (2d ed. 1970) and Hamilton, Corporations in a Nutshell (1980). A third edition is presently being prepared by Professor Henn for 1982 publication.

2. E. g., Model Bus.Corp.Act § 33; West's Ann.Calif.Corp.Code § 705; McKinney's N.Y.Bus.Corp.Law, § 609; 12 U.S.C.A. § 61 (national banks).

The standard state statutory provision relating to proxies merely states that a Stockholder may vote "either in person or by proxy executed in writing by the Stockholder or by his duly authorized attorney-in-fact." (Model

Under certain circumstances, courts might compel a Stockholder of record to deliver a proxy to the real or beneficial owner.

Securities exchanges may have rules regulating the giving of proxies by their members who hold shares in the "street name".

Of course, when shares are sold "ex-voting rights" the seller retains the voting rights for the forthcoming election.

Statutes also provide that every proxy must be in writing and signed by the Stockholder or his duly authorized attorney-in-fact.[3]

Library References:

C.J.S. Corporations § 550.
West's Key No. Digests, Corporations ⚷198(1).

§ 47.22 Duration

In larger Corporations, management by its control of the proxy machinery is able to keep itself in power and gain Stockholder ratification of its actions. Any fraud or illegality in procuring proxies, of course, is subject to appropriate relief.

Statutes in different jurisdictions fix different periods of duration for proxies.[4] In most jurisdictions, such period is applicable only where no time is fixed in the proxy; [5] in some jurisdictions, a maximum allowable period is fixed by statute.

Typical of the former would be a statutory provision that no proxy shall be valid after 11 months from the date of its execution unless its duration is specified in the proxy.[6]

Bus.Corp.Act § 33, 3d ¶.) No particular form of proxy is required under this section. Proxies have been ruled valid despite omission of the name of the proxyholder, the date of the meeting, or the date of the proxy. However, the proxy must be in writing, a provision of obvious benefit to the inspector of elections and the Corporation. A proxyholder need not be a Stockholder.

3. Model Bus.Corp.Act § 33.

4. Usually 11 months. See e. g., Model Bus.Corp.Act § 33; McKinney's N.Y.Bus.Corp.Law, § 609(b); West's Ann.Calif.Corp.Code § 705. Delaware fixes three years. Del.Gen.Corp.Law, § 212 (1967).

The usual state statutory provision relating to duration of a proxy provides that "no proxy shall be valid after eleven (11) months from the date of its execution, unless otherwise provided in the proxy." (Model Bus. Corp.Act § 33, 3d ¶.) The theory of the eleven-month provision is that a new proxy would be executed before each annual meeting. However, there is nothing to prevent the parties from agreeing that a much longer period shall be applicable to a specific proxy.

5. E. g., Model Bus.Corp.Act § 33; West's Ann.Calif.Corp.Code § 705; McKinney's N.Y.Bus.Corp.Law § 609(b).

6. E. g., Model Bus.Corp.Act § 33; McKinney's N.Y.Bus.Corp.Law, § 609(b). See note 4 above.

§ 47.23 Revocation

A proxy, being the appointment of an agent, is normally revocable at the pleasure of the person executing it. Thus, even if a long period is designated as the duration of the proxy, it still may be revoked. A proxy may also be revoked by implication. For example, the execution of a later proxy constitutes a revocation of an earlier, inconsistent proxy. Personal attendance at a meeting may also constitute revocation of an earlier proxy, though this depends on the intention of the Stockholder. Since later proxies revoke earlier ones, it is important that proxies be dated as of the time of execution. Inspectors of election, where there is a contest, must determine which is the latest proxy executed by a specific Stockholder in order to determine how the shares are to be voted.

Certain proxies may be irrevocable. Generally a mere recitation that a proxy is irrevocable does not make it so; such a proxy is usually as revocable as any other proxy. The general rule for determining whether a proxy is truly irrevocable is whether it is "coupled with an interest." This phrase, which has its origin in the agency case of Hunt v. Rousmanier's Adm'rs, 8 Wheat. (21 U.S.) 174, 5 L.Ed. 589 (1823), of course, has no inherent meaning of itself and must be fleshed out with examples and further analysis. It is not enough that the proxy merely be supported by consideration. The clearest example of this is a purchase of a proxy for cash. Such a purchased vote almost certainly would be held to be against public policy and unenforceable; rather than being irrevocable, such a proxy might not be enforceable at all. On the other hand, if a person lends a Stockholder money and takes a lien on the shares as security, an irrevocable proxy granted to the creditor almost certainly would be enforced against the Stockholder. What is the difference between these two situations? A person who purchases a vote presumably intends to recoup his investment in the vote by exercising the power to vote in some way. This power may very well be exercised in a manner adverse to the Corporation: the proxyholder's interest is in recouping a personal payment, and in a sense he is antagonistic to the Corporation. The creditor's interest, on the other hand, is to preserve or increase the value of the shares which constitute his security. Thus he has a financial interest consistent with that of the Corporation which the vote purchaser does not.

An irrevocable proxy separates the ownership from the voting power. Because of the possibility of injury to the owners by the abuse of a naked voting power unconnected with a financial interest in the Corporation, the courts have generally refused to recognize the irrevocability of a proxy except where there appears to be little likelihood that the power to vote will be abused. This is the nub of the notion of "coupled with an interest." The following types of proxies have been held to be proxies "coupled with an interest:"

(1) A proxy given to a pledgee under a valid pledge of the shares;

(2) A proxy given to a person who has agreed to purchase the shares under an executory contract of sale;

(3) A proxy given to a person who has lent money or contributed valuable property to the corporation;

(4) A proxy given to a person who has contracted to perform services for the Corporation as an officer; and

(5) A proxy given in order to effectuate the provisions of a valid pooling agreement (described at § 47.71).

Some courts have upheld irrevocable proxies which do not squarely fall within any of the above categories. On the other hand, New York and California have statutes which define the five situations described above as those in which an irrevocable proxy should be recognized (N.Y.Bus.Corp.Law, § 609(F); Cal.Corp.Code, § 705). Such a statute resolves possible future disputes very simply, but there may be a slight danger that a reasonable proxy might be invalidated because it does not fit squarely into any of the above categories.

Library References:

C.J.S. Corporations § 550.
West's Key No. Digests, Corporations ⚷198(6).

§ 47.24 Scope of Proxy

A general proxy authorizes the proxy holder to vote on all matters properly coming before the meeting, even though the matter is not enumerated in the notice of the meeting. While such a vote may be counted (at least on a matter not introduced by management), a Delaware court has held that such vote does not estop the Stockholder giving the proxy from later bringing a derivative action to challenge the action of the Directors which the vote was cast to ratify.[7] The case involved management's mailing to Stockholders before the meeting of a proxy statement which, in accord with the Securities and Exchange Commission Proxy Rules, stated that management knew of no matters which would come before the meeting other than those stated in the notice of the meeting, but that if any other matter

7. Gottlieb v. McKee, 34 Del.Ch. 537, 107 A.2d 240 (Ch.1954). See also State ex rel. Pertuit v. Pioneer Petroleum Corp., 193 So.2d 286 (La.Ct. App.1967), writ refused 250 La. 271, 195 So.2d 148 (holding proxy holder's authority limited to voting shares and not to extend to defending action involving ownership of shares); Jaquith & Co. v. Island Creek Coal Co., 47 N.J. 111, 219 A.2d 514 (1966) (proxy vote against merger held sufficient written notice of dissent for purposes of appraisal remedy).

properly came before the meeting, the proxy would be exercised in accordance with the best judgment of the proxyholder.

An earlier Delaware case had permitted management to whom a general proxy had been given to make a substitution in the slate of Directors in the absence of fraud or misrepresentation in solicitation.[8]

§ 47.25 Exercise of Proxy

Where the proxy is held by two or more persons, they function by majority vote.[9] They are usually given express power of substitution.

While it has been said that a proxy holder, like any other agent, can always abandon his agency at the risk of incurring whatever liability might ensue,[10] the better view would seem to be that the proxyholder is under a duty to exercise the proxy.[11] Otherwise, the Stockholder giving the proxy is disenfranchised. In any event, the presence at the meeting of the proxyholder as such constitutes the presence of the shares represented by the proxy for purposes of quorum.[12]

Where management solicits proxies in its favor and receives an adverse proxy, it should return the proxy promptly to the Stockholder to avoid any duty of exercising it.

§ 47.26 General Proxy

I, the undersigned, being the holder of ______ shares of common stock of ______, do hereby appoint ______, of ______, ______, as my proxy to attend all meetings of the Stockholders of said Corporation, with full power to vote and act for me in the same manner and extent that I might were I personally present at said meetings.

8. Hauth v. Giant Portland Cement Co., 33 Del.Ch. 496, 96 A.2d 233 (Ch. 1953). See also McKee v. Home Sav. & Trust Co., 122 Iowa 731, 98 N.W. 609 (1904) (general proxy held not to extend to extraordinary corporate matters).

9. Callister v. Graham-Paige Corp., 146 F.Supp. 399 (D.Del.1956).

10. Duffy v. Loft, Inc., 17 Del.Ch. 140, 147, 151 A. 223, 227 (Ch.1930), affirmed 17 Del.Ch. 376, 152 A. 849 (Sup.Ct.).

11. Second Consol. Trust, Ltd. v. Ceylon Amalgamated Tea and Rubber Estates, Ltd., [1943] 2 All (letters) E.R. 567 (Ch). Cf. In re Giant Portland Cement Co., 26 Del.Ch. 32, 21 A.2d 697 (Ch.1941). The proxyholder, as an agent, has been held subject to fiduciary duties. Blair v. F. H. Smith Co., 18 Del.Ch. 150, 156 A. 207 (Ch. 1931); see also Matter of Ideal Mut. Ins. Co., 18 Misc.2d 127, 190 N.Y.S.2d 887 (Sup.Ct.1959), affirmed 9 A.D.2d 60, 190 N.Y.S.2d 895 (1st Dept's).

12. Duffy v. Loft, Inc., 17 Del.Ch. 140, 151 A. 223 (Ch.1930), affirmed 17 Del.Ch. 376, 152 A. 849 (Sup.Ct.); Textron, Inc. v. American Woolen Co., 122 F.Supp. 305 (D.Mass.1954).

My proxy shall have full power to substitute another person as my proxy, and to revoke the appointment of any such substitute proxy.

Dated: ______, 19__.

____

COMMENT

This broad and general proxy is not limited to a specific meeting.

Library References:

C.J.S. Corporations § 550.
West's Key No. Digests, Corporations 🔑198(4).

§ 47.27 Proxy for Stockholders' Meeting

PROXY

Know all men by these presents, that I, [*Name of Stockholder*], residing at No. ______ ______ Street, City of ______, County of ______, State of New York, being the holder of [*Number*] shares of [*Class*] shares of the [*Name of Corporation*], do hereby constitute and appoint [*Name of Proxy Holder*], of No. ______ ______ Street, City of ______, County of ______, State of ______, as my proxy to attend all the meetings of the Stockholders of said company to be held between the date hereof and the ______ day of ______, 19__, [*or the Annual (or Special) Meeting of the Stockholders of this Corporation to Be Held on ______, 19__,*] or any continuation or adjournment thereof, with full power to vote and act for me and in my name, place and stead, in the same manner, to the same extent and with the same effect that I might were I personally present thereat, giving to said [*Name of Proxy Holder*] full power of substitution and revocatoin, and I hereby revoke any other proxy heretofore given by me.

Dated at: ______, N.Y., ______, 19__.

[*Signature*]

____
Stockholder

§ 47.28 Proxy Directing a Specific Vote

The undersigned Stockholder hereby appoints ______, ______ and ______, or any of them, with full power of substitution, to act as proxy for and to vote the stock of the undersigned at a special meeting of Stockholders of ______, to be held at its Registered Office, ______, ______, on ______ at ______ o'clock A.M., ______ standard time, or any adjournment thereof, for the purposes stated in the Notice of Special Meeting.

The undersigned hereby directs this proxy to be voted

For ______ Against ______ proposition 1 [*Describe*], and

For ______ Against ______ proposition 2 [*Describe*],

both of which propositions are described in the Notice of Special Meeting and Proxy Statement. THIS PROXY WILL BE VOTED AS DIRECTED. IF NO CONTRARY DIRECTION IS INDICATED, THIS PROXY WILL BE VOTED FOR THE ABOVE PROPOSITIONS.

Dated: ______, 19__.

[*Signed*] ______

§ 47.29 Proxy for Specified Period

The undersigned hereby constitutes and appoints ______, ______, and ______, or any two of them acting jointly, as his, her, or their proxy to cast the votes of the undersigned at all general, special, and adjourned meetings of the Stockholders of ______ Corporation from time to time and from year to year, when the undersigned is not present at any such meeting and if present does not elect to vote in person. This proxy shall be effective for ______ years from the date hereof unless sooner revoked by written notice to the Secretary of the Corporation.

Dated: ______, 19__. ______________

COMMENT

Under section 33 of the Model Business Corporation Act no proxy is valid after eleven months from the date of execution unless otherwise provided in the proxy.

§ 47.30 Revocation of Proxy

Know all men by these presents, that I, ______, do hereby revoke and annul a certain proxy given by me to ______ authorizing him to represent me or to vote or act for me at any meeting or meetings of the Stockholders of the ______ Corporation.

In witness whereof, I have signed this revocation in duplicate intending to file one with the Secretary of said Corporation and to serve the other on ______.

Dated: ______, 19__. ______________

§ 47.31 Irrevocable Proxy

I, the undersigned, being the record owner of ______ shares of common stock, do hereby appoint ______, of ______, ______ as my proxy to attend all meetings of the Stockholders of the Corporation with full power to vote and act for me in the same manner and extent that I might were I personally present at said meetings.

My proxy shall have full power to substitute another person as my proxy and to revoke the appointment of any such substitute proxy.

This proxy is given in connection with [*Describe*] and is irrevocable until [*Describe*].

Dated: ______, 19__.

____

Stockholder

COMMENT

Unless a proxy is "coupled with an interest," it is revocable even though a statement appears in the proxy itself that it is irrevocable. See generally, § 47.23, supra.

§ 47.32 Irrevocable Proxy for (Number) of Years

I hereby constitute and appoint ______ or ______, or either one of them, and in place of either, in case of substitution, his substitute, attorneys and agents for me and in my name, place and stead, to vote as my proxy at the meetings of the Stockholders of the [*Name of Corporation*] upon any question which may be brought before such meetings, including the election of Directors, according to the number of votes I should be entitled to vote if then personally present, with full power to each of my said attorneys to appoint a substitute in his place.

Alternative A

This proxy shall be effective for [*Number*] years from the date hereof unless sooner revoked by written notice to the Secretary of the Corporation.

Alternative B

This proxy shall be effective for [*Number*] years from the date hereof and it shall not be earlier revoked, said proxy holder having the following interest in the Corporation: [*Describe*].

Dated: ______, 19__.

____

[*Name*]

§§ 47.33–47.40 are reserved for supplementary material.

C. VOTING TRUSTS

§ 47.41 In General

The voting trust is a trust created by the transfer of voting shares by Stockholders to a voting trustee or voting trustees, to hold and vote them, until the purpose is fulfilled or for a specified period, usually pursuant to a voting trust agreement. It is a device to concentrate Stockholder control in one or a few persons who, primarily through the election of Directors, can control corporate affairs.

A Voting Trust is to be distinguished from a Stockholders' Agreement in which the Stockholders agree to cause certain actions to occur as follows:

(1) Arguably the Stockholders' Agreement is not constrained by the duration limitations imposed on voting trusts (see § 47.45, infra).

(2) Voting Trusts leave decision making to the Trustees, where Stockholder Agreements spell out the specific action to be taken (and do not effect other actions which the Stockholders may take).

(3) Voting Trusts are self executing whereas Stockholder Agreements may have to be enforced through Court action (which may not be granted).

Library References:

C.J.S. Corporations § 552.
West's Key No. Digests, Corporations ⚷198.1(1).

§ 47.42 Validity

The older cases found voting trusts to be illegal irrespective of purpose on the ground that the separation of voting power from beneficial interest was repugnant to the concept of Corporation law. Absent an illegal object, such as monopoly, many modern courts would probably uphold a voting trust even in the absence of statute.

Many jurisdictions authorize voting trusts by statutes.[1] The Model Business Corporation Act states that a voting trust may be created subject to the following requirements:

(1) The agreement may not extend beyond ten years;

(2) The agreement must be in writing;

1. See, e. g., Model Bus.Corp.Act § 34; West's Ann.Calif.Corp.Code § 706; McKinney's N.Y.Bus.Corp.Law § 621.

(3) A counterpart of the agreement must be deposited with the Corporation at its registered office, to be subject to the same right of inspection by (A) Stockholders or (B) holders of a beneficial interest in the trust that is provided a Stockholder to inspect books and records of the Corporation; and

(4) The shares subject to the trust must be transferred to the trustee or trustees (Model Bus.Corp.Act § 34).

A statement of the formal requisites of a voting trust may be misleading, however, since some states have imposed the further substantial requirement that the essential purpose of the trust must be a proper one. For example, a trust created solely for the purpose of securing control of or lucrative employment with the Corporation would be invalidated in some states. Obviously, proof of such motives depends on subjective testimony; the cautious, close-mouthed creator of a voting trust in such states may create an enforceable voting trust despite wrongful motives, while a talkative person with basically good motives may inadvertently make damaging statements about the underlying purpose of the trust. In a majority of the states, the purpose of a voting trust is not inquired into; a voting trust is valid if it complies with all statutory requirements.

A voting trust agreement that fails to comply with all statutory requirements is considered invalid in its entirety in most states. Even though these requirements are basically simple ones that may be easily complied with, a number of cases have arisen in which these requirements have been ignored.

Library References:

C.J.S. Corporations § 552.
West's Key No. Digests, Corporations ⚷198.1(2).

§ 47.43 Procedure for Setting Up Voting Trusts

To set up a voting trust, a voting trust agreement is usually executed among the voting trustees, such Stockholders as desire to become parties, and possibly the Corporation whose shares are involved. The Stockholders then transfer their shares to the voting trustees; the transfers are recorded, with notation of the voting trust, on the Corporation's record of Stockholders, making the voting trustees the record holders; new share certificates usually bearing an appropriate legend (to preclude the shares being acquired by *bona fide* purchasers free of the voting trust) are issued by the Corporation to the voting trustees; and voting trust certificates are issued by the voting trustees to the Stockholders in exchange for their shares.

§ 47.44 Voting Trust Certificates

The voting trust certificates represent equitable interests in the shares transferred and any shares subsequently allotted as share dividends, and entitle the certificate holders to a ratable distribution of any cash or property dividends paid by the Corporation to the voting trustees, and to receive share certificates evidencing the shares, plus any share distribution thereon, in exchange for the voting trust certificates upon the termination of the voting trust.

Voting trust certificates, like share certificates, are usually registered in the names of the holders thereof. Such certificates, absent a valid transfer restriction, are transferable.

The voting trustees usually maintain voting trust certificate books, which are generally open to inspection by voting trust certificate holders and possibly other Stockholders.[2]

§ 47.45 Duration

Statutes frequently specify the maximum duration of voting trusts, usually to 10 years. Depending on the statutory language, an attempt to set up a voting trust for an excessive period might be completely void or only invalid as to the excess. Statutes sometimes also provide for permissible extensions.[3]

Until its purposes have been achieved or achievement becomes impossible, the voting trust is usually irrevocable except by the mutual consent of all parties.

Library References:

C.J.S. Corporations § 552.
West's Key No. Digests, Corporations ⚿198.1(4).

§ 47.46 Powers and Duties of Voting Trustees

As in the case of more conventional trusts, the voting trustees, absent a provision to the contrary, usually act by majority vote. In

2. See, e. g., Model Bus.Corp.Act § 34; West's Ann.Calif.Corp.Code § 706; McKinney's N.Y.Bus.Corp.Law, §§ 621, 1316.

3. See, e. g., Del.Gen.Corp.Law, § 218 (1967). New York provides that at any time within six months before the expiration of such voting trust agreement as originally fixed or as extended, one or more holders of voting trust certificates may, by agreement in writing, extend the duration of such voting trust agreement, nominating the same or substitute trustee or trustees, for an additional period not exceeding 10 years, but that such extension agreement shall not affect the rights or obligations of persons not parties thereto and shall in every respect comply with and be subject to all the statutory provisions applicable to the original voting trust agreement. McKinney's N.Y.Bus. Corp.Law, § 621. See also West's Ann.Calif.Corp.Code § 706.

the event of deadlock, resort to the courts for appropriate relief is possible.[4] Voting trustees may be removed for cause by appropriate court proceedings. In functioning as voting trustees, they are subject to the usual fiduciary duties of trustees. For breach of trust, any aggrieved voting trust certificate holder may sue directly since the duty breached was to him and not to the Corporation.

Voting trustees may usually vote in the election of Directors and otherwise exercise the ordinary voting rights enjoyed by the entrusted shares. Whether they may vote the shares for extraordinary matters depends upon any applicable statutes and the construction of the voting trust agreement. Voting trustees cannot vote in derogation of the trust.

Even when the voting trustees have the power to vote for some matter, it is questionable whether they can delegate their discretion by giving proxies to others, at least where any statute or the voting trust agreement does not expressly provide for proxy voting by them.[5] Even where a statute or voting trust agreement permits voting trustees to vote by proxy, an irrevocable proxy, absent a provision authorizing such a proxy in the statute or the voting trust agreement, would probably not be recognized as irrevocable.

Voting trusts may contain precise provisions defining the powers and duties of the trustees. Voting trustees often have working control of the Corporation for extended periods of time, but may have little or no financial interest in the Corporation. Problem areas that have arisen include:

(1) May the trustees elect themselves as Directors and/or Officers? The wisdom of permitting dual offices is debatable since it is unlikely that a voting trustee would vote to remove himself as a Director.

(2) May the trustees remaining in office fill a vacancy in the trustees? Trustees are often given this power, though it may also be vested in the holders of voting trust certificates.

(3) May the trustees vote on major corporate changes, such as mergers, dissolution, or the sale of substantially all of its assets? Arguably, consent of the holders of voting trust certificates should be obtained on such major matters, but voting trust agreements often provide that the trustees may vote on such matters as they see fit.

(4) May the trustees dispose of the shares subject to the voting trust? Voting trust agreements often provide that no sale of under-

4. See e. g. McKinney's N.Y.Bus.Corp. Law, § 612(h).

5. Chandler v. Bellanca Aircraft Corp., 19 Del.Ch. 57, 162 A. 63 (Ch.1932) (where voting trust agreement expressly permitted voting trustees to vote by proxy at Stockholder meetings). See also Del.Gen.Corp.Law, § 218 (1967) (expressly permitting voting trustees to vote shares by proxy).

lying shares may be effected without the prior consent of all, or a designated percentage, of the holders of voting trust certificates.

(5) Should the trustees be relieved of liability for errors in business judgment or nonfeasance? Trustees typically desire broad exculpatory clauses, but such clauses may be inconsistent with the legitimate interest of depositing Stockholders. Also, courts may decline to enforce broad exculpatory clauses applicable to fiduciaries or read such clauses very narrowly.

(6) What deductions, if any, may the trustees make from dividends received by them before paying them over to the equitable owners?

(7) What compensation are the trustees entitled to?

Generally, courts tend to construe voting trust agreements narrowly or to imply a broad fiduciary duty by which trustees' actions may be tested.

Library References:

C.J.S. Corporations § 552.
West's Key No. Digests, Corporations ⚷ 198.1(5).

§ 47.47 Other Statutory Requirements

Older statutes sometimes required that every voting trust be open to accession by all Stockholders. Modern statutes permit a closed voting trust.[6] Statutes often require that copies of any voting trust agreement be on file at the principal office of the Corporation or with the voting trustees, and be open to reasonable inspection by voting trust certificate holders and other Stockholders.[7]

§ 47.48 Status of Voting Trust Certificate Holders as Stockholders

Voting trust certificate holders are the beneficial owners, but not the record owners, of the shares. The Corporation may usually rely on the record ownership, and treat the voting trustees as Stockholders for most purposes. Whether the voting trust certificate holders are Stockholders for the purpose of appraisal rights, Stockholder inspection rights, and other Stockholder rights, depends upon applicable statutory language and judicial holdings.

6. See, e. g., Model Bus.Corp.Act § 34; Del.Gen.Corp.Law, § 218 (1967); McKinney's N.Y.Bus.Corp.Law, § 621.

7. Model Bus.Corp.Act § 34. Noncompliance with such filing requirement might invalidate the voting trust. Abercrombie v. Davies, 36 Del. 371, 130 A.2d 338 (Sup.Ct.1957), 36 Del. Ch. 445, 131 A.2d 822 (Ch.1957) (on remand). See also McKinney's N.Y. Bus.Corp.Law, § 621; West's Ann. Calif.Corp.Code § 706.

§ 47.49 Drafting a Voting Trust Agreement

In drafting a voting trust agreement consideration should be given to the following suggestions:

(a) Purpose. The agreement should state a proper purpose, one that is beneficial to the Corporation and to the Stockholders.

(b) Duration. The agreement should be created for a fixed period not to exceed ten years unless a longer period is permitted by statute. Also, unless permitted by statute, it is safer to leave out a renewal provision, but if one is inserted it should provide for withdrawal of dissenters at the end of the original period.

(c) Open-end. Every other Stockholder of the same class or classes should be permitted to transfer his shares to the voting trustees upon the terms and conditions of the agreement if the statute requires this.

(d) Termination. The agreement should state who should have the right to terminate the agreement and upon what terms; for example, is the agreement to be subject to termination by the holders of a majority in interest.

(e) Qualifications of Trustees. Where possible the trustees should be selected from among the Stockholders. Provision should be made as to whether the trustees may become Directors of the Corporation.

(f) Removals and Vacancies. Provision should be made for the removal of trustees and for the filling of vacancies among the trustees.

(g) Powers of Trustees. The trustees should have all voting rights of the stock except that such stock should not be voted by the trustees in favor of the sale, mortgage or pledge of all or substantially all of the assets of the Corporation or for any change in the capital structure or the powers of the Corporation or in connection with a merger, consolidation, reorganization, or dissolution, except with the consent of the holders of voting trust certificates representing at least a majority of the stock subject at the time to the voting trust agreement.

(h) Standard of Care. Careful attention should be given to the matter of excusing the trustees from liability for their actions.

(i) Meetings of Stockholders. Provision should be made for meetings of the Stockholders to vote upon matters that may have been reserved to them under the terms of the agreement.

(j) Voting Trust Certificates. Provision should be made for turning in the share certificates and the issuance of voting trust certificates to evidence the beneficial interest in the shares made subject to the trust.

(k) Filing. A duplicate copy of the agreement, together with a list of the parties thereto, should be filed in the registered office of the Corporation, and it should be open to inspection by both Stockholders and depositors or their attorneys.

(*l*) Amendments. The agreement should state what amendments shall be permissible and who shall have the power to make them. It has been suggested that no power should be given to the trustees to make any modifications in the agreement or even to construe it.

§ 47.50 Voting Trust Agreement

VOTING TRUST AGREEMENT

This agreement is made this ______ day of ______, 19__, among ______ and ______ as Beneficiaries and ______ and ______ as Trustees.

Whereas, ______, ______, and ______, are owners respectively of ______, ______, and ______ shares [*or,* ______, ______, *and* ______ *the Trustees of this Trust Own No Shares*] of the ______ Company, a ______ Corporation, and the persons who sign this agreement as Beneficiaries own shares of the stock of ______ Company in the number set forth opposite their signatures to this agreement.

Now, therefore, the Trustees and Beneficiaries hereby enter into this Agreement and Declaration of Trust for the purpose of insuring stability and continuity in the management and control of the affairs of ______ Company (hereinafter referred to as "the Corporation") as follows:

§ 1.1 Definitions. Unless otherwise stated in the agreement:

"Stock" or "Shares" refers to all voting stock of the ______ Corporation, and includes all shares or other securities that may at any time be exchanged for shares of the common stock of the Corporation pursuant to a merger, consolidation or other reorganization.

"Corporation" refers to ______ Company, and shall include any and all successors to all or substantially all of the assets and business of ______ Company.

"Beneficiaries" means those persons with the rights and duties of Beneficiaries described herein.

"Trustees" means the persons with the rights and duties of the "Trustees" described herein.

"Voting Trust Certificate" means the document given by the Trustees to the Beneficiaries to evidence deposit of stock with the Trustees by the Beneficiaries.

"Majority of Beneficiaries" means Beneficiaries holding Voting Trust Certificates representing a majority of the voting power of the stock deposited with the Trustees pursuant to this agreement.

"Parties to this agreement" means any party hereto or his successor in interest.

§ 1.2 Creation and Termination of the Trust. The effective date of this Agreement is ______, 19__ and the agreement shall be irrevocable until ______, 19__, [*Duration Not to Exceed Ten (10) Years*].

At any time within two (2) years prior to the time of expiration of the agreement as originally fixed or last extended, one or more beneficiaries under the voting trust agreement may, by written agreement and with the written consent of the voting trustee or trustees, extend the duration of the voting trust agreement with respect to their shares for an additional period not exceeding ten (10) years from the expiration date of the trust as originally fixed or last extended.

Provided, that the shares deposited in Trust by any Beneficiary may be required by such Beneficiary to be sold free of this trust pursuant to the terms of § 1.5 of this agreement.

§ 1.3 Delivery of Shares into Trust, Issuance and Delivery of Voting Trust Certificates; Redelivery of Stock Upon Termination of Trust. Each of the Beneficiaries agrees to deliver to the Trustees the certificates of all stock of the Corporation owned by such Beneficiary, and all stock of the Corporation acquired after the effective date of this agreement and before the termination of this agreement, duly endorsed for transfer, together with such sums as are necessary to pay any taxes imposed on the transfer of such shares. The Trustees agree that they will cause the shares of stock to be transferred on the books of the Corporation to the Trustees in their capacity as Trustees. The Trustees agree to issue and deliver to each of the Beneficiaries a Voting Trust Certificate evidencing receipt by the Trustees of Stock subject to the terms of this agreement. The Voting Trust Certificate shall be in the form of Exhibit "A" attached hereto. Within ten (10) days after the termination of this agreement, the Trustees shall redeliver to the holders of record of Voting Trust Certificates, the stock certificates representing the number of shares of stock or the net proceeds thereof for which the Voting Trust Certificates were issued, provided the holder of record of the Voting Trust Certificate surrenders the Voting Trust Certificate properly endorsed and accompanied by payment of sums sufficient to cover any stamp tax or governmental charge attributable to the transfer of or redelivery of the stock certificates.

§ 1.4 Powers and Rights Granted the Trustees. The Beneficiaries in conveying legal title to their stock to the Trustees agree that by virtue of their control of the stock during the term of and pursuant to this agreement the Trustees shall be the sole possessor of the following Stockholders' rights in that stock:

(a) the right to vote the stock in person or by nominee, agent, attorney-in-fact or proxy at all meetings of Stockholders;

(b) the right to participate in, consent to, or ratify any corporate or Stockholders' action;

(c) the right to receive all dividends and distributions in cash, kind, or in any other property;

(d) the right to become financially interested in any matter or transaction to which the Corporation or any company subsidiary to, controlled by, or affiliated with the Corporation may be a party, and the right to contract with or become financially interested in any company subsidiary to, controlled by or affiliated with the Corporation as fully and freely as though the Trustees were not the Trustees hereunder.

It shall be the duty of the Trustees, and they, or a majority of them, shall have full power and authority, and they are hereby fully empowered and authorized, to represent the holders of such trust certificates and the stock transferred to the Trustees as aforesaid, and to vote upon the said stock, as in the judgment of the trustees or of a majority of them may be for the best interest of the said company, at all meetings of the Stockholders of the said Corporation, in the election of Directors and upon any and all matters and questions which may be brought before such meetings, as fully as any Stockholder might do if personally present, provided, however, that the Trustees shall vote on the following matters only as directed by the beneficial owners of two-thirds in amount of the shares of stock subject of this trust:

(1) Proposals to dissolve the Corporation, or to merge or consolidate it with another Corporation or Corporations;

(2) Proposals to amend the Articles of Incorporation of the Corporation;

(3) Proposals to sell substantially all the assets of the Corporation not in the ordinary course of business; and

(4) Proposals which will have the effect, directly or indirectly, of reducing substantially the voting power, right to dividends, or rights to the assets of the Corporation upon liquidation, of the shares of stock subject of the trust.

The Trustees in accepting legal title to the stock deposited pursuant to this Agreement agree to exercise their best judgment in the interest of the Corporation to assure proper, stable, and continuous management of the affairs of the Corporation, but the Trustees are not responsible for the acts of the Directors and Officers of the Corporation whether or not taken pursuant to the vote or consent of the Trustees as Stockholders, or whether ratified afterwards by the Trustees as Stockholders. (The Trustees may, in their discretion, notice and call a meeting of all Beneficiaries to obtain instructions from the Beneficiaries with respect to the voting of the stock on any particular question due to be considered at a Stockholders' meeting. If the Trustees call such a meeting of Beneficiaries the Trustee [*Shall Be/ Shall Not Be*] bound to vote the stock in accordance with the vote of the Beneficiaries holding Voting Trust Certificates representing a majority of the voting power of stock deposited with the Trustees pursuant to this agreement.

The Trustees do not have the right or authority to sell or otherwise dispose of any of the stock deposited in Trust except as provided by this agreement.

Each Trustee hereunder shall, at all times during the term of this Agreement, be elected, by vote of the Trustees, a Director of the [*Name of Corporation*] unless he or she declines, in writing, to act as such.

§ 1.5 Dividends and Other Distributions; Sale of Shares Free of Trust. The Trustees shall distribute to each registered holder of a Voting Trust Certificate or Certificates cash payments equal to the amount of cash dividends received by the Trustee on account of the stock for which such Voting Trust Certificates were issued.

The Trustees may fix a date not exceeding twenty (20) days preceding any date for the payment or distribution of dividends or for the distribution of assets or rights as a record date for the determination of the Voting Trust Certificate holders entitled to receive such payment or distribution, and the holders of Voting Trust Certificates of record on such date shall be exclusively entitled to participate in such payments or distributions. In any case in which the Trustees shall fail to fix such a record date, the date three (3) days prior to the date of payment or distribution of dividends or the distribution of assets or rights, shall constitute the record date for the determination of the holders of Voting Trust Certificates entitled to receive such payment or distribution.

If the Trustees receive, as a dividend or distribution on account of stock held in this Trust, any additional shares of the stock of the Corporation, the Trustees shall hold such additional shares in trust subject to all the terms and conditions of this agreement. Any such dividend or distribution of stock shall be held for the benefit of those Beneficiaries who are the beneficial owners of the stock on account of which the particular stock dividend or distribution was issued and the Trustees shall issue to those Beneficiaries additional Voting Trust

Certificates (in the form of Exhibit "A"), evidencing retention by the Trustees of such stock dividends or distributions subject to this Trust.

If the Trustees receive any moneys (other than cash dividends), or any property (other than shares of stock of the Corporation) through a distribution by the Corporation to its Stockholders, the Trustees shall distribute such money or property to the holders of Voting Trust Certificates to stock on account of which such money or property was distributed.

If any securities of the Corporation shall be offered for subscription to the holders of stock held by the Trustees subject to this agreement the Trustees shall mail to each Voting Trust Certificate holder a copy of the notice of such offer promptly upon the receipt of such notice by the Trustees. Upon receipt of a request from a registered Voting Trust Certificate holder to subscribe to the issuance of securities, the Trustees shall make such subscription and payment on behalf of such Voting Trust Certificate holders; provided that such request is received by the Trustees at least five (5) days prior to the last date fixed by the Corporation for subscription and payment, and provided further that such request is accompanied by the sum of money required to be paid for such securities. Upon receiving from the Corporation the certificates for voting securities so subscribed for the Trustees shall retain such voting securities and issue to the Voting Trust Certificate holder subscribing to such voting securities a Voting Trust Certificate evidencing retention by the Trustee of such voting securities subject to this Trust. Upon receiving from the Corporation the certificates for non-voting securities so subscribed for the Trustees shall deliver such non-voting securities to the Voting Trust Certificate holder subscribing to such non-voting securities.

If any subscription rights are not exercised by any of the Voting Trust Certificate holders entitled to subscribe, the Trustees may subscribe and pay for the new securities on behalf of any other Voting Trust Certificate holder or holders who requests such subscription by sending notice of such request and payment for the securities in the manner described above. Upon receipt of securities so subscribed for the Trustees shall distribute non-voting securities or Voting Trust Certificates for voting securities, as provided above.

Upon the request of any Beneficiary, the Trustees shall sell free of this agreement any or all shares, the beneficial ownership of which is evidenced by a Voting Trust Certificate registered in the name of such Beneficiary on the records of the Trustee. All transfer taxes or other expenses incident to any such sale shall be paid by the Beneficiary requesting such sale. Such sale free of trust shall be on such terms as are approved by the Beneficiary requesting the sale. However, any Beneficiary requesting a sale of shares free of this trust shall redeposit in trust any shares of the Corporation thereafter acquired by such Beneficiary by inter vivos gift or by purchase, but need not deposit shares thereafter received by any bequest or inheritance.

§ 1.6 Administration of Trust Agreement. The Trustee shall maintain a Register of the holders of all outstanding Voting Trust Certificates and the Trustees may treat the duly registered holder of each Voting Trust Certificate as the absolute owner of such Voting Trust Certificate. Upon presentation to the Trustees of a Voting Trust Certificate duly endorsed in blank for Transfer as provided on the Voting Trust Certificate the Trustees shall enter in the register the name of the Transferee as the absolute owner of such Voting Trust Certificate. The Trustees are not bound or affected by any other notification of a change in ownership of a Voting Trust Certificate although the Trustee may, in his discretion, accept other evidence of such a change in ownership of a Voting Trust Certificate and enter such change upon the register.

The Trustees may give any required notice to the registered holders of Voting Trust Certificates by mailing such notice, postage prepaid, to the address appearing on the register for such Voting Trust Certificate holders. Any notice required to be given the Trustees shall be mailed, postage prepaid, to the Trustees at ______ Street, ______, ______, or to such other address hereafter fixed by the Trustees as the place where they are to receive notices. The Trustees shall give to registered holders of Voting Trust Certificates notice of any change of their address. Any notice to the Corporation by any party hereto must be mailed, postage prepaid, to the Officers of the Corporation at its principal place of business, ______ Street, ______, ______, or such other location to which the principal place of business of the Corporation is hereafter removed.

If there are vacancies among the Trustees for any reason, a successor trustee or trustees shall be designated by the Beneficiaries. In the event of failure of the Beneficiaries to agree upon mutually acceptable successor trustees, any party to this agreement may apply to an appropriate court for the appointment of successor Trustees. Successor Trustees shall enjoy all the rights, powers, interests and immunities of the Trustees originally acting hereunder and shall succeed to the title to the shares of the corporation held in this trust.

This Trust agreement is to be governed by the laws of the State of ______. The Trustees are authorized to construe this agreement and their reasonable construction made in good faith shall be conclusive and binding upon holders of Voting Trust Certificates or any party claiming any right under this trust. The Trustees may seek the advice of legal counsel, which counsel may also be counsel for the Corporation, and any action taken in good faith in accordance with the opinion of such counsel shall be conclusive upon the parties to this agreement and the Trustees shall not be liable to the parties to this agreement on account of such action.

The Trustees are authorized to incur and pay those reasonable expenses and charges which they deem necessary to the administration of this agreement, including, but not limited to, necessary fees and charges for the services of legal counsel. The Trustees shall not be required to give any bond or other security for the discharge of their duties under this trust. The Trustees shall be entitled to reasonable compensation for their services as Trustees, and to reimbursement for reasonable expenses and charges incurred in the administration of the agreement, which compensation and reimbursement shall be paid by the Beneficiaries in proportion to their beneficial interests.

§ 1.7 Inspection of Voting Trust Agreement. A duplicate of the voting trust agreement and any extension thereof shall be filed with the Secretary of the Corporation and shall be open to inspection by a Stockholder, a holder of a voting trust certificate or the agent of either upon the same terms as the record of Stockholders of the Corporation is open to inspection.

§ 1.8 Trustees' Indemnity. The trustees shall be entitled to be fully indemnified out of the dividends coming to their hands against all costs, charges, expenses, and other liabilities properly incurred by them in the exercise of any power conferred upon them by these presents; and the subscribers, and each of them, hereby covenant with the Trustees that in the event of the moneys and securities in their hands being insufficient for that purpose the subscribers and each of them will in proportion to the amounts of their respective shares and interests save harmless and keep indemnified the trustees of and from all loss or damage which they may sustain or be put to by reason of anything they may lawfully do in the execution of this trust.

§ 1.9 Additional Trustees. The voting Trustees for the time being shall have the power and authority by [*Number*] consent in writing filed with the [*Name of Corporation*] and a copy of which shall be mailed to each Beneficiary at his address as the same shall appear upon the books of the Trustees, to add from time to time one or more Trustees to the number of Trustees under this Agreement, provided, however, that no person shall be so added as a Trustee unless he shall at the time of his designation as a Trustee be the holder of not less than ______ (______) shares of the [*Class*] shares of the [*Name of Corporation*] of which not less than ______ (______) shares thereof at the time of his acceptance of the designation as a Trustee and as a condition to his becoming such a Trustee, shall be transferred by him to the Trustees under the terms and provisions of this Agreement, and provided further that such person so designated shall continue to be a Stockholder of record with respect to at least ______ (______) shares of the [*Class*] shares of [*Name of Corporation*]. Any Trustee so appointed and added shall immediately become vested with all the rights, property, powers and authority vested in Trustees pursuant to this agreement.

§ 2.1 **Titles and Subtitles.** Titles of the paragraphs and subparagraphs are placed herein for convenient reference only and shall not to any extent have the effect of modifying, amending or changing the express terms and provisions of this Agreement.

§ 2.2 **Words and Gender or Number.** As used herein, unless the context clearly indicates the contrary, the singular number shall include the plural, the plural the singular, and the use of any gender shall be applicable to all genders.

§ 2.3 **Execution in Counterpart.** This Agreement may be executed in any number of counterparts, each of which shall be taken to be an original.

§ 2.4 **Severability.** In the event any parts of this Agreement are found to be void, the remaining provisions of this Agreement shall nevertheless be binding with the same effect as though the void parts were deleted.

§ 2.5 **Effective Date.** This Agreement shall be effective only upon execution by all of the proposed parties.

§ 2.6 **Waiver.** No waiver of any provisions of this Agreement shall be valid unless in writing and signed by the person or party against whom charged.

§ 2.7 **Applicable Law.** This Agreement shall be subject to and governed by the laws of the State of [*Name*].

§ 2.8 **Assignment.** This Agreement shall be binding upon and inure to the benefit of the parties hereto and their respective heirs, legal representatives, executors, administrators, successors and assigns.

Entered into this ______ day of ______ 19__.

[*Signatures*]

____
Trustee

____
Trustee

____
Trustee

Beneficiaries	Number of Shares
________________	________________
________________	________________
________________	________________
________________	________________
________________	________________
________________	________________
________________	________________
________________	________________

EXHIBIT "A"

VOTING TRUST CERTIFICATE FOR SHARES OF COMMON STOCK OF ______ CORPORATION

This document certifies that ______ is the registered beneficial owner of ______ shares of the common stock of ______ Corporation, a ______ Corporation, and that those shares have been transferred to, and are held by, ______, ______, and ______ as Trustees pursuant to the Voting Trust Agreement of ______, 19__, between the Trustees and certain Stockholders of ______ Corporation as Beneficiaries.

Under the terms of the agreement: (1) the Voting Trust will expire on ______, 19__ unless the term thereof is altered pursuant to the Agreement; (2) the Trustees possess the right to vote the above-mentioned shares as the absolute legal owner thereof and the holder of this Voting Trust Agreement possesses no voting rights in such shares.

This Voting Trust Certificate may be transferred. The transferee will be entitled to the rights enjoyed by the above-named registered beneficial owner of the shares only upon surrender of this Voting Trust Certificate properly endorsed. Upon such surrender the Trustees shall issue to the transferee hereof a new Voting Trust Certificate in the name of such transferee and will treat such party as the beneficial owner of the shares represented by this certificate. The transferee agrees to be bound by the terms of the Voting Trust Agreement, a copy of which will be furnished by the Trustees to the holder or transferee of this certificate upon request.

Dated: ______, 19__.

____

____

____

As Trustees under the Voting Trust Agreement

REVERSE OF VOTING TRUST CERTIFICATE:

For value received, ______ hereby transfers to ______ the beneficial ownership of ______ shares of Common Stock of ______ Corporation represented by this Voting Trust Certificate and does hereby irrevocably authorize the transferee to procure the transfer to the transferee or his nominee of beneficial ownership of those shares on the records of the Trustees holding legal title to those shares.

Dated: ______, 19__.

____

Signature *

In the presence of:

____

§ 47.51 Voting Trust Agreement—Clause Enumerating Voting Trustees' Powers

The Trustees may act hereunder either with respect to voting the shares held by them or otherwise, either in person or by proxy. Except as hereinafter otherwise specifically provided, all questions arising among the Trustees from time to time, with respect to voting, with respect to giving Stockholders' consent to any corporate action or change or otherwise, or with respect to any other matter or thing, shall be determined by the decision, vote or consent of not less than ______ (______) of the number of those then acting as Trustees, either at a meeting, or by writing, with or without meeting, and in like manner they may establish their rules of action. In respect of the matters hereinafter enumerated, the decision, vote or act of not less than the following respective numbers of the Trustees shall for and in the exercise of the voting power or in respect of Stockholders' consents and for all purposes of this Agreement, be deemed the decision or act of all the Trustees:

(a) In voting for members of the Board of Directors of [*Name of Corporation*], other than the Trustees, ______ (______) of the number of the then Trustees.

(b) For increasing the amount of the preferred shares of [*Name of Corporation*], the entire number of the then Trustees.

(c) For increasing the amount of the common shares of [*Name of Corporation*], the entire number of the then Trustees.

* *Notice*: The signature of the Transferor must correspond in every particular with the name of the Beneficial owner as it appears upon the face of this certificate.

(d) For the classification or re-classification of shares, preferred or common, of [*Name of Corporation*], the entire number of the then Trustees.

(e) For change of name of [*Name of Corporation*], ______ (______) of the number of the then Trustees.

(f) Giving consent, where required, to mortgage property or franchises of [*Name of Corporation*], the entire number of the then Trustees.

(g) For consolidation of [*Name of Corporation*] with any other Corporation or Corporations, the entire number of the then Trustees.

(h) For the sale of all or substantially all of the property, assets and franchises of [*Name of Corporation*], the entire number of the then Trustees.

(i) For guaranteeing the bonds of another Corporation or Corporations, the entire number of the then Trustees.

(j) For non-judicial dissolution of [*Name of Corporation*], the entire number of the then Trustees.

(k) With respect to all other votes or consents of Stockholders, ______ (______) of the number of the then Trustees.

Provided, however, that the [*Class*] shares of [*Name of Corporation*], in the name of the Trustees, may in any instance be voted by ______ (______) of the number of the then Trustees for the time being for any purpose, and the consent of the Trustees in respect of the [*Class*] shares of [*Name of Corporation*] in the name of the Trustees may be given in the name of or on behalf of all the then Trustees by ______ (______) of the number of the then Trustees if such ______ (______) so voting or consenting shall have received the written consent of such additional number of Trustees as shall, with the ______ (______) actually voting or consenting, make up the required number of Trustees in respect of the vote or consent in question in accordance with the requirements above set forth.

§ 47.52 Voting Trust Agreement—Clause for Construction of Agreement by Trustees

The trustees are hereby empowered to construe this agreement, and their construction of the same shall be final, conclusive and binding upon all holders of Voting Trust Certificates and all other parties interested.

§ 47.53 Contract for Sale of Stock Held in Trust

It is agreed by and between ______, trustees of "Stock Trust No. ______", herein called "trustees," and ______, of ______, ______, herein called "buyer."

The trustees as trustees of "Stock Trust No. ______" and not individually, agree to transfer and assign to the buyer, on or before ______, 19__, all of the shares of the capital stock of ______ Corporation, held in trust by the trustees, for the sum of $______ Dollars per share, and the buyer agrees to pay for the shares the sum of $______ per share of capital stock, subject, however, to the following conditions:

If within a period expiring at the end of 20 days following the submission of the terms of the agreement by the trustees to their beneficiaries, any higher offer or offers are submitted to the trustees, they shall immediately notify the buyer and he shall have until 5 o'clock P.M. of the day following the expiration of the 20 day period to agree in writing to meet any such higher offer or offers. In the event that the buyer fails to meet any such higher offer or offers, the trustees shall have the right to enter into a contract to sell to the party or parties making such higher offer or offers, and upon the execution of any such new sales agreement this contract shall become null and void.

It is further stipulated and agreed that if, on submission of the terms and consideration of this agreement to the beneficiaries of the trust, by the trustees, the holders of participation certificates, representing one-third or more of the shares of ______ Corporation, so held in trust, dissent from the proposed sale, then this contract shall be null and void.

In the event that holders of participation certificates representing over two-thirds of the shares of ______ Corporation do not dissent and if the buyer agrees in writing to meet any higher offer or offers within the time provided herein, the trustees shall then consummate this agreement by the sale, assignment and transfer of ______ shares of stock to the buyer upon payment by him of the purchase price thereof.

§§ 47.54–47.60 are reserved for supplementary material.

D. STOCKHOLDER VOTING AGREEMENTS

§ 47.61 In General

In most jurisdictions,[1] Stockholders may agree in advance to exercise their voting rights in certain ways. The basis for such holdings

1. Ringling Bros.-Barnum & Bailey Combined Shows, Inc. v. Ringling, 29 Del.Ch. 610, 53 A.2d 441 (Sup.Ct. 1947); McQuade v. Stoneham, 263 N.Y. 323, 189 N.E. 234 (1934), reargument denied 264 N.Y. 460, 191 N.E. 514. See e. g. West's Ann.Calif.Corp.Code § 706; McKinney's N.Y.Bus.Corp.Law § 620; Minn.Bus.Corp.Act § 302A.457; Model Bus.Corp.Act § 34.

is that Stockholders are generally under no fiduciary duties, and may do collectively what they may do individually, assuming lack of fraud by controlling Stockholders against minority Stockholders or some other illegal object. By such a Stockholder agreement, the Stockholders usually agree either to cast their votes in a certain way for various matters or to pool their votes and cast them jointly as they agree or as an arbitrator determines.

The most important traditional function of Stockholders is to elect the Directors. Stockholders also have inherent power to remove Directors for cause, and, when such power is conferred upon them, have power to remove, even without cause, Directors thereafter taking office.

Since management of a Corporation is vested in its Board of Directors, any Stockholder who wishes to exercise influence at the Board of Directors level must either have sufficient representation on the Board or have sufficient control over the Directors. The former can be accomplished by "Stockholder agreements" predetermining the personnel of the Board and other matters. Broad Stockholder removal-without-cause power is often desirable as an adjunct to such agreements with respect to any non-Stockholder Directors.

A Stockholder agreement is a contract among the Stockholders, or some of them, to vote their shares in a specified manner on certain matters. Such an agreement is sometimes called a "pooling agreement." Pooling Agreements result in the shares of the participants being voted as a block. Stockholder Agreements result in certain shares being voted a certain way. The purpose may be to maintain control, or to maximize the voting power of the shares where cumulative voting is permitted, or to ensure that some specific object is obtained. The Stockholders pooling agreement extends only to voting on matters that are within the province of Stockholders, such as the election of Directors, and should be sharply distinguished from Stockholder Agreements that may attempt to resolve matters that are vested in the discretion of Directors. The latter type of agreement raises serious questions of validity in some jurisdictions. The pooling agreement does not.

In a pooling agreement, the Stockholders retain all the indicia of ownership of shares except the power to vote. Further, there is generally no planned voting direction expressed in a pooling agreement. In this respect, a pooling agreement differs from a voting trust (discussed in § 47.41 et. seq.) which contemplates that legal title to the shares be transferred to the trustees. Generally, the advantages of a pooling agreement over a voting trust are that it is less formal, easier to establish, and there is no disruption of other ownership attributes. However, it is more difficult to enforce.

The pooling agreement is generally recognized as a valid contract, subject only to the rules applicable to the validity of contracts in general. A few states have adopted statutes regulating pooling agreements, often limiting the period during which a pooling agreement may continue (e. g., to ten years), requiring that copies of the pooling be deposited at the principal office of the Corporation, and so forth. However, in most states, the pooling agreement is essentially an unregulated contractual voting device that may continue for long periods of time.

Where a *bona fide* purchaser takes shares subject to a Stockholder agreement without notice thereof, he usually would not be bound by such agreement. Accordingly sound practice requires that the share certificates involved bear an appropriate legend referring to the Stockholder agreement.

Such agreements usually do not run afoul of prohibitions on Stockholders' selling their votes or proxies.[2]

Stockholder agreements often have provisions dealing with matters other than the exercise of Stockholder voting rights, such as matters within the proper purview of the management functions of the Board of Directors or share transfer restrictions (see Chapter 52, infra), deadlock, and arbitration provisions, etc.

If an agreement among Stockholders binds them with respect not only to their Stockholder functions but also to any Director functions they might have, the agreement can be said to be one among Directors as well as among Stockholders. If such a "Stockholder agreement" (it being to such an extent a "Director agreement") contains provisions limiting the discretion of the Board of Directors in managing the Corporation in the best interests of the Corporation, such provisions might be invalid.[3]

2. But cf. Morgenstern v. Cohon, 2 N.Y.2d 302, 160 N.Y.S.2d 633, 141 N.E.2d 314 (1957) (sustaining defense of illegality under former McKinney's N.Y.Stock Corp.Law § 47 of agreement to indemnify person for loss on resale of shares purchased by person to vote for reelection of directors); Reilly v. Korholz, 137 Colo. 20, 320 P.2d 756 (1958) (New York law). But see McKinney's N.Y.Bus.Corp.Law § 609(e) (prohibiting Stockholder from selling his vote or issuing proxy to vote to any person for any sum of money or anything of value, except as authorized in § 609 (proxies) and § 620 (Stockholder voting agreements; articles of incorporation provisions as to control of directors)).

3. For liberal statutory treatment of such agreements, see N.C.Bus.Corp. Act § 55–73 (1957); McKinney's N.Y. Bus.Corp.Law § 620 (Stockholder agreements; provision in Articles of Incorporation as to control of Directors); 1969 Model Bus.Corp.Act revision (business and affairs of Corporation to be managed by Board of Directors except as may be otherwise provided in Articles of Incorporation). Maryland and Delaware have close Corporation statutes permitting sterilization or even abolition of the Board of Directors. See § 30.4, supra, with respect to Stockholder management powers as provided by certain close Corporation statutes. Compare Manson v. Curtis, 223 N.Y. 313, 323, 119

A few corporate statutes include a special subchapter or set of sections to which eligible close Corporations may elect to be subject. Such close Corporations remain subject to the other provisions of the corporate statute to the extent that they are not inconsistent with the close Corporation sections.[4]

Stockholder agreements, unlike irrevocable proxies and voting trusts, are not self-executing. For breach of valid provisions, the most adequate remedy is usually specific performance.[5] Damages are usually inadequate. Special statutory proceedings are generally not available to enforce such an agreement.[6]

If the shares are transferable, as they would be absent a valid share transfer restriction, a transferee without notice would take them free from the obligations of any Stockholder agreement.[7] Accordingly, sound practice requires that the share certificates involved bear an appropriate legend referring to the Stockholder agreement (see chapter 41, infra).

N.E. 559, 562 (1918) ("Clearly the law does not permit the stockholders to create a sterilized board of directors"). Analogous are situations where the Directors transfer their Corporation's shares in a subsidiary to themselves (and others) as voting trustees. Adams v. Clearance Corp., 35 Del.Ch. 459, 121 A.2d 302 (1956) (voting trust upheld).

4. Pa.Bus.Corp.Law §§ 371–386 (1968); Del.Gen.Corp.Law §§ 341–355 (1967); Vernon's Ann.Tex.Bus.Corp. Act, art. 2.30–1 et seq.; Md.Corp. and Assoc. Code § 4–101 et seq. See § 30.4, supra, for further discussion.

5. Chayes, "Madame Wagner and the Close Corporation", 73 Harv.L.Rev. 1532 (1960); Note, "Corporations—Specific Enforcement of Shareholder Agreements", 45 N.C.L.Rev. 228 (1966); Note, "Specific Enforcement of Shareholder Voting Agreements", 15 U.Chi.L.Rev. 738 (1948). Such a relief was granted in Galler v. Galler, 32 Ill.2d 16, 203 N.E.2d 577 (1964); Lockley v. Robie, 301 N.Y. 371, 93 N.E.2d 895 (1950), reargument denied 301 N.Y. 731, 95 N.E.2d 409 (4–3); Clark v. Dodge, 269 N.Y. 410, 199 N.E. 641 (1936); Clark v. Dodge, 28 N.Y.S.2d 442 (Sup.Ct.1939), affirmed mem. 261 App.Div. 1086, 28 N.Y.S. 2d 464 affirmed mem. 287 N.Y. 833, 41 N.E.2d 102 (except decree for reinstatement as director and officer). In Ringling Bros.-Barnum & Bailey Combined Shows, Inc. v. Ringling, 29 Del. Ch. 610, 53 A.2d 441 (1947), specific performance was not sought.

6. Lockley v. Robie, 301 N.Y. 371, 93 N.E.2d 895 (1950), reargument denied 301 N.Y. 731, 95 N.E.2d 409 (holding that derivative claim to surcharge officer could not be asserted in individual action for specific performance of Stockholder agreement). Matter of Heller v. Clark Merchandisers, Inc., 9 Misc.2d 106, 154 N.Y.S.2d 150 (Sup. Ct.1955).

7. Wohl v. Miller, 145 N.Y.S.2d 84 (1955) (construing former McKinney's N.Y.Pers.Prop.Law § 176), modified on other grounds 5 A.D.2d 126, 169 N.Y.S.2d 233, reargument denied 5 A. D.2d 823, 170 N.Y.S.2d 991. See also Trefethen v. Amazeen, 93 N.H. 110, 36 A.2d 266 (1944) (transferee of shares with notice of agreement held bound thereby). Cf. Nickolopoulos v. Sarantis, 102 N.J.Eq. 585, 141 A. 792 (1928) (Stockholder agreement for voting contrary to articles of incorporation and By-laws held unlawful as secret agreement). The New York statute does not expressly require notice of a Stockholder voting agreement to be on the certificates reporting shares subject to such agreement.

The agreement should have an ascertainable duration to avoid its being construed as terminable at will,[8] and should be sufficiently definite to prevent its invalidity for vagueness.[9]

Library References:

C.J.S. Corporations § 551.
West's Key No. Digests, Corporations ⚷199.

§ 47.62 Drafting Techniques [10]

"Stockholder agreements" are executed by those interested in close Corporations, may be made before [11] (when the term "Stockholder" would be technically a misnomer) or after incorporation, and may or may not, but usually should, involve the Corporation as a party.[12]

In "Stockholder agreements", the parties can, in most jurisdictions, subject to some limitations, bind themselves as Stockholders or as Directors or as both to do or to refrain from doing certain things.[13]

8. See Weil v. Beresth, 154 Conn. 12, 220 A.2d 456 (1966) (upholding voting agreement under which each four Stockholders agreed to vote his shares to elect themselves as Directors, etc., for so-long-as-he-is-Stockholder); Galler v. Galler, 32 Ill.2d 16, 203 N.E.2d 577 (1964), 95 Ill.App.2d 340, 238 N.E. 2d 274 (1968); Tschirgi v. Merchants Nat'l Bank, 253 Iowa 682, 113 N.W.2d 226 (1962) (enforcing Stockholder agreement to elect Directors against representative of one of Stockholders); Roberts v. Whitson, 188 S.W.2d 875 (Tex.Civ.App.1945), error refused; 721 Corp. v. Morgan Guar. Trust Co., 40 Misc.2d 395, 243 N.Y.S.2d 198 (Sup. Ct.1963).

9. Glazer v. Glazer, 374 F.2d 390 (5th Cir. 1967), certiorari denied 389 U.S. 831, 88 S.Ct. 100, 19 L.Ed.2d 90, on remand 278 F.Supp. 476 (E.D.La.) (upholding jury finding in favor of plaintiff's rights to continued compensation as Directors and Officers of Corporation under agreement that they would continue their present relationship, to carry on their various business enterprises successfully, and that they would refrain from unnecessarily interfering with welfare or duties of each other, and that they would make every effort to create good, healthy, and harmonious relationship); Most Worshipful Prince Hall Grand Lodge of Free and Accepted Masons v. Hiram Grand Lodge Masonic Temple, Inc., 32 Del.Ch. 85, 80 A.2d 294 (1951).

10. Adapted from Henn, Law of Corporations (2d ed. 1970). A third edition will be published in 1982.

11. See Chapter 29, supra.

12. The Corporation would not be bound by the agreement unless a party. Matter of Argus Co., 138 N.Y. 557, 34 N.E. 388 (1893). Even if the Corporation is not a party, it might be able to enforce the agreement on third-party beneficiary principles, or it might be bound on the basis of adoption. Weber v. Sidney, 19 A.D. 2d 494, 244 N.Y.S.2d 228 (1963), affirmed mem. 14 N.Y.2d 929, 252 N. Y.S.2d 327, 200 N.E.2d 867; Moss v. Waytz, 4 Ill.App.2d 296, 124 N.E.2d 91 (1955). The agreement should be in writing, not only for purposes of any applicable statute of frauds requirements, but also for evidentiary purposes, certainty, and psychological effect. See Weber v. Sidney, supra; Williams v. Fitting, 157 N.Y.L.J. No. 12, 18 (Sup.Ct.1967). Specific performance of a written agreement might be granted more readily than of an oral agreement; Aldridge v. Franco Wyoming Oil Co., 24 Del.Ch. 126, 141, 7 A.2d 753, 761 (1939), affirmed 24 Del.Ch. 349, 14 A.2d 380.

13. See §§ 30.35 and 30.43, supra.

Stockholders can by agreement reasonably restrict the transfer of their shares. The most common methods are to give the Corporation or the other Stockholders or both an option to buy such shares, or to make such purchase mandatory by "buy-sell agreements".[14]

Stockholders, in voting for Directors, are usually subject to no fiduciary duties, and hence some or all may agree in advance to vote for certain persons as Directors or to pool their votes for Directors and cast them jointly as they agree or an arbitrator determines. Such agreements ordinarily do not run afoul of prohibitions on Stockholders' selling their votes or proxies, but might if consideration other than mutual promises, such as payment of money, is involved.[15]

Stockholders, in voting for extraordinary corporate matters, are subject to fiduciary duties. While less than all might validly agree in advance to vote in certain ways with respect to such matters, the more cautious practice is to have all Stockholders as parties to such agreements.

Provisions binding Stockholders to vote for dissolution in the event of deadlock, if carried out by the parties or enforced by the courts, are a practical means of achieving dissolution of a deadlocked Corporation without encountering the difficulties of judicial dissolution of solvent Corporations.[16]

Provisions binding the parties to arbitrate their future differences as Stockholders might also be included, making sure, of course, to avoid any inconsistency between arbitration and dissolution provisions, and to comply with applicable local restrictions on arbitration.[17]

To the extent that extraordinary matters in some jurisdictions require concurrent Board of Directors action, the rules applicable to "Director agreements" also apply.

Provisions binding Directors with respect to their management functions can also be included where they do not unduly infringe on the discretion of Directors, especially where all Stockholders are parties to such "Director agreements".[18] Such provisions might bind Directors to appoint and keep in office certain persons so long as they are faithful, efficient, and competent, to pay certain salaries to officers, to declare certain dividends, and to follow other cor-

14. See § 52.61 et seq., infra. See also Chapter 68, infra, with respect to Stockholder buy-sell agreements.

15. See § 30.35, supra.

16. See §§ 30.37, 30.45, supra.

17. Matter of Herrman, 155 N.Y.L.J. No. 10, 14 (Sup.Ct.1966) (agreement providing for arbitration of all controversies "arising out of agreement" held not to cover controversies arising out of violation of articles of incorporation). See § 30.37, supra.

18. See §§ 30.35 and 30.43, supra.

porate policies, but such commitments should be properly qualified to allow some continued exercise of Director discretion with respect to such policies, thus avoiding a "sterilized" Board of Directors [19] except in states which clearly recognize such a delegation of authority.

The drafting of provisions for arbitration of Director deadlocks finds fewer guideposts in the decided cases.[20]

Since the "Stockholder agreement", when properly drafted, can effectuate the intentions of the associates in a close Corporation, its preparation should be carefully considered in the light of current developments, including any applicable statutes.[21]

Although it can be argued that an invalid provision in the Articles of Incorporation or By-laws should be construed as an agreement among the Stockholders who approved the same, drafting such provisions in the form of a "Stockholder agreement" is much more likely to assure court enforcement.[22]

The sounder practice is to have all of the Stockholders, even preferred Stockholders, as parties to the "Stockholder agreement" and often also the Corporation itself. The agreement should be made expressly binding on the parties' heirs, executors, administrators, representatives, successors, and assigns.[23]

The provisions of agreement should be sufficiently definite for purposes not only of validity but also of specific performance by a court of equity.[24]

Sometimes a partial self-executing feature can be built into a Stockholder agreement by appropriate provisions for irrevocable proxies.[25]

19. Id.

20. See § 30.45, supra.

21. R. Kessler, New York Close Corporations ch. 8 (1968); Kessler, "Drafting a Shareholder's Agreement for a New York Close Corporation", 35 Fordham L.Rev. 625 (1967); O'Neal, "Protecting Shareholders' Control Agreements against Attack", 14 Bus. Law. 184 (1958); Hornstein, "Stockholders' Agreements in the Closely Held Corporation", 59 Yale L.J. 1040 (1950); Redfern, "Shareholders' Voting Agreements—Drafting Precautions", 46 Mich.L.Rev. 70 (1947); Strecher, "Corporate Buy-Sell Agreements: Tax Problems in Drafting", 15 Wash. & Lee L.Rev. 18 (1958); Winton, "Tax Traps in Stockholders' Agreements," 2 Prac.Law. 78 (Mar. 1956); Comment, " 'Shareholder Agreements' and the Statutory Norm", 43 Cornell L.Q. 68 (1957).

22. See § 30.35, supra.

23. Storer v. Ripley, 12 Misc.2d 662, 178 N.Y.S.2d 7 (1958). Also, in community property states the Stockholders' spouses should be parties.

24. Most Worshipful Prince Hall Grand Lodge of Free & Accepted Masons v. Hiram Grand Lodge Masonic Temple, Inc., 32 Del.Ch. 85, 80 A.2d 294 (1951).

25. McKinney's N.Y.Bus.Corp.Law § 609(f)(5). Compare Ringling Bros.-Barnum & Bailey Combined Shows, Inc. v. Ringling, 29 Del.Ch. 610, 53 A. 2d 441 (1947), with Smith v. San Francisco & N. P. Ry., 115 Cal. 584, 47 P. 582 (1897).

The duration of the agreement should also be specified, such as so long as any of the individual parties are Stockholders of the Corporation or are alive.[26]

Because of judicial attitudes toward such agreements and the risk that the invalidation of part of the agreement will void the rest,[27] there might well be an express provision that in the event any part of the agreement is held invalid, such invalid part shall be deemed severable from the balance of the agreement, and such balance shall be deemed to constitute the agreement of the parties.

Appropriate reference to any Stockholder agreement should be made on all certificates representing shares covered thereby.[28]

§ 47.63 Stockholders' Agreement

AGREEMENT TO OPERATE A BUSINESS

This agreement made [*Date*], by and among [*Names*] (herein jointly and individually referred to as the "Stockholders");

Whereas, the Stockholders have agreed to operate [*Name*] Corporation (the "Corporation") under the laws of the State of [*Name*];

Whereas, the Stockholders own the [*Describe*] stock and debt of the Corporation (herein referred to as "securities", as hereinafter set forth;

Now, therefore, in consideration of mutual covenants and other valuable consideration exchanged, the Stockholders agree to cause the Corporation to be operated as follows:

§ 1.1 Present Stockholders

The present Stockholders of the Corporation are the following, who have subscribed and purchased the following securities:

Security Description	Stockholder	Number of Securities

Option 1

There shall be no other securities issued without the agreement of the Stockholders.

§ 1.2 Directors

The Corporation shall have [*Number*] Directors who shall be: [*Names*].

26. Weil v. Beresth, 154 Conn. 12, 220 A.2d 456 (1966); Galler v. Galler, 32 Ill.2d 16, 203 N.E.2d 577 (1964), 95 Ill.App.2d 340, 238 N.E.2d 274 (1968); Boatright v. Steinite Radio Corp., 46 F.2d 385 (10th Cir. 1931); Ohlstein v. Hillcrest Paper Co., 22 Misc.2d 405, 199 N.Y.S.2d 88 (1960).

27. See §§ 30.35 and 30.43, supra.

28. See Chapter 41, supra.

§ 1.3 Officers

The Officers of the Corporation shall be:

Chairman: ______________.
President: ______________.
Vice-President: ______________.
Secretary: ______________.
Treasurer: ______________.

§ 1.4 Employment Contract

The Corporation shall employ [*Name*] as the [*Describe Position*] of the Corporation for a period of not less than [*Number*] months and shall pay him $[*Dollars*] per year for his services as such; said amount to be paid in bi-weekly installments of $[*Dollars*], the first such payment to be paid on [*Date*]. [*Name*] shall have the authority to:

(a) Acquire and dispose of assets.

(b) Borrow money and give security therefor.

(c) Enter into contracts.

(d) Deposit and withdraw corporate funds.

(e) Employ and dismiss employees and establish their wages.

(f) Establish corporate procedures.

(g) Determine hours of operation.

(h) Advertise.

(i) [*Purchase/construct/lease*] the following plant and equipment: ______

(j) Do such other things, as he in his sole and reasonably exercised discretion, shall deem necessary to successfully establish, operate and manage the Corporation.

The Corporation and [*Name*] shall enter into an employment contract with the following fringe benefits:

(a) Medical Insurance with the following features:

(1) Hospital:
Room and Board: $______ day.
Maximum no. of days: ______.
Intensive care additional: $______ day.
Intensive care no. of days: ______.
Maximum extra charges: $______.
Surgical schedule: ______.
Anesthesia: ______.
In-hospital benefit: ______.
Hospital-out-patient: ______.
(Supplemental accident): ______.

Radiation therapy: ______.
Diagnostic x-ray and lab: ______.
Maternity: ______.

(2) Major medical:
Maximum: $______.
Deductible: $______.
Co-insurance: ______ (percent).
Prescription drugs: ______.
Out-patient: ______.
Convalescent care: ______.

(b) Dental Insurance:

(3) Dental:
Deductible/family: ______.
Oral exams, etc.: ______.
X-Rays, fillings, etc.: ______.
Bridges, dentures, crowns, etc.: ______.
Maximum benefit: ______.

(4) Carrier: ______.

(5) Disability insurance with the following features:
(A) Carrier: ______.
(B) Wait upon accidental disability: ______.
(C) Wait up sickness: ______.
(D) Benefit per week: $______.
(E) Reduction for partial disability: ______.
(F) Reduction for ability to be employed: ______.
(G) Benefit period upon accident: ______.
(H) Benefit period upon sickness: ______.

(c) Medical reimbursement:
(1) Maximum benefit per corporate fiscal year: $______.

(d) Group term life insurance:
(1) Death benefit: $______.

(e) Group whole life insurance:
(1) Death benefit: $______.

(f) Fully paid vacation days per year: ______.

(g) Fully paid sick days per year: ______.

(h) Use of car:
(1) Make and model: ______.
(2) Reimbursement per business mile: ______.
(3) Repair policy: [*Describe*].

(i) Educational benefits-work related:
(1) Days fully paid: ______.
(2) Maximum course charge/day: $______.
(3) Maximum hotel allowance: $______/day.

(4) Maximum meal allowance: $______/day.
(5) Maximum entertainment: $______/day.

(j) Education benefits—non work related.

(1) Maximum course cost and book costs per corporate fiscal year: $______.

(k) Professional liability insurance coverage: $______ per occurrence and $______ per year.

(*l*) Personal liability insurance coverage: $______ per person and $______ per occurrence.

(m) A stock warrant which has the following features: [*Describe*].

(n) A stock option which has the following features: [*Describe*].

(*o*) A qualified retirement plan benefit which has the following features:

(1) Name of plan: ______.
(2) Minimum age for participation: ______.
(3) Minimum service for participation: ______.
(4) Employment status (categories): ______.
(5) Vesting: ______.
(6) Corporation contribution formula: ______.
(7) Employee contribution formula: ______.
(8) Effective date of plan: ______.
(9) Initial committee members: ______.
(10) Initial trustees: ______.
(11) Initial contribution: $______.

(p) A deferred compensation plan which has the following features:

(1) Benefit on death: $______.
(2) Benefit on disability: $______.
(3) Benefit on retirement or termination before age 65: $______.
(4) Benefit on retirement or termination after age 65: $______.

(q) Reimbursement for:

(1) Entertainment (not to exceed $______ per ______).
(2) Travel not to exceed $______ per day (excluding mileage which shall be at [*Cents*] per mile.
(3) Hotel per day: $______.
(4) Meals per day: $______.
(5) Entertainment per day: $______.

(r) A Split Dollar Plan with the following features:

(1) Name of plan: ______.
(2) Type of plan:

Alternative A–1

collateral assignment.

Alternative A–2

endorsement method.

Alternative A–3

fractional assignment method.

Alternative A–4

reverse split dollar.

(3) Type of policy:

Alternative B–1

face value of $______.

Alternative B–2

premium of $______.

(4) Corporation's contribution:

Alternative C–1

the increase, if any, in the tabular cash surrender value of the policy which will result from the premium payment in question and the application of dividends toward the purchase of additional insurance.

Alternative C–2

the difference, if any, in the premium then due and the "PS–58" costs of the policy in question.

Alternative C–3

the total premium, net of dividends and premium waivers.

(5) The insured's obligation will be:

Alternative D–1

the PS–58 cost.

Alternative D–2

none.

Alternative D–3

the difference between the premium due and the Company's.

Alternative E–1

the total amount actually paid by the Corporation.

Alternative E–2

the total amount actually paid by the Corporation.

§ 1.5 Buy-Sell Agreement

The Stockholders shall enter into a Buy-Sell Agreement with the following features:

Triggering Event	Price	Terms	Do Remaining Stockholders Have Option or Is There a Mandatory Buy Out
(a) Stockholder has offer from third party.			
(b) Disability.			
(c) Death.			
(d) Termination of employment before age 65.			
(e) Retirement after age 65.			
(f) Force out of Stock ownership by remaining Stockholders.			

§ 1.6 Cafeteria Plan

The Corporation shall adopt a Cafeteria Plan which has the following features:

(1) Medical Insurance with the following features:

(A) Hospital:

Room and board ______.
Maximum no. of days ______.
Intensive care additional ______.
Intensive care no. of days ______.
Maximum extra charges ______.
Surgical schedule ______.
Anesthesia ______.
In-hospital benefit ______.
Hospital-out-patient ______.
(Supplemental accident) ______.
Radiation therapy ______.
Diagnostic X-ray and lab ______.
Maternity ______.

(B) Major medical: ______.

Maximum ______.
Deductible ______.
Co-insurance ______.

Prescription drugs ______.
Out-patient ______.
Convalescent care ______.

(C) Dental:
Deductible/family ______.
Oral exams, etc. ______.
X-rays, fillings, etc. ______.
Bridges, dentures, crowns, etc. ______.
Maximum benefit ______.

(D) Carrier: ______.

(2) Disability Insurance with the following features:

(A) Carrier: ______.

(B) Wait upon accidental disability: ______.

(C) Wait upon sickness: ______.

(D) Benefit per week: $______.

(E) Reduction for partial disability: ______.

(F) Reduction for ability to be employed full time in some other job: ______.

(G) Benefit period upon accident: ______.

(H) Benefit period upon sickness: ______.

(3) Medical Reimbursement:

(A) Maximum benefit per corporate fiscal year: $______.

(4) Group Term Life Insurance:

(A) Death benefit: $______.

(5) Group Whole Life Insurance:

(A) Death benefit: $______.

(6) A Group Legal Service Plan which has the following features:

(A) Trustees: ______.

(B) Bank: ______.

(7) Participant description: ______.

(8) Contribution per participant per year: $______.

(9) This plan [*will/will not*] reduce existing salaries by $______ per year.

§ 1.7 Day Care Plan

The Corporation shall adopt a Day Care Plan which has the following features:

(a) Care provided: [*Described*].

(b) Participant's: ______.

§ 1.8 Death Benefit Only Plan

The Corporation shall adopt a Death Benefit Only Plan which has the following features:

(a) Name of Plan: ______.

(b) Participant's employment status or name: ______.

(c) Benefit description: ______.

§ 1.9 Deferred Compensation Plan

The Corporation shall adopt a Deferred Compensation Plan which has the following features:

(a) Name of Plan: ______.

(b) Participant's employment status or name: ______.

(c) Benefit Description:

(1) Benefit on Death: ______.

(2) Benefit on Disability: ______.

(3) Benefit on Retirement or Termination before age 65: ______.

(4) Benefit on Retirement or Termination after age 65: ______.

§ 1.10 Disability Income Plan

The Corporation shall adopt a Disability Income Plan which has the following features:

(1) Carrier: ______.

(2) Wait upon accidental disability: ______.

(3) Wait upon sickness: ______.

(4) Benefit per week: $______.

(5) Participant description: ______.

§ 1.11 Group Life Insurance Plan

The Corporation shall adopt a Group Life Insurance Plan which has the following features:

Employees Covered	Amount and Type of Benefit

§ 1.12 Health Insurance Plan

The Corporation shall adopt a Health Insurance Plan which has the following features:

(1) Hospital:
Room & Board ______.
Maximum no. of days ______.

Intensive care additional ______.
Intensive care no. of days ______.
Maximum extra charges ______.
Surgical schedule ______.
Anesthesia ______.
In-hospital benefit ______.
Hospital-out-patient ______.
(Supplemental accident) ______.
Radiation therapy ______.
Diagnostic X-ray and lab ______.
Maternity ______.

(2) Major medical:
Maximum ______.
Deductible ______.
Co-insurance ______.
Prescription drugs ______.
Out-patient ______.
Convalescent care ______.

(3) Dental: ______.
Deductible/family ______.
Oral exams, etc. ______.
X-rays, fillings, etc. ______.
Bridges, dentures, crowns, etc. ______.
Maximum benefit ______.

(4) Carrier: ______.

(5) Participant description: ______.

§ 1.13 Medical Reimbursement Plan

The Corporation shall adopt a Medical Reimbursement Plan which has the following features: maximum reimbursement per corporate fiscal year $______ per Participant.

(a) Participant Description: ______.

Alternative A–1

(A) as determined by the Treasurer.

Alternative A–2

(A) not in excess of $______ per [*Time Period*] for business entertainment.

(B) not in excess of $______ per day for travel, including meals (excluding mileage which shall be paid at $[*Cents*] per mile.

Comments

Salaries paid to a Stockholder who directly or indirectly owns more than 50% of the Corporate stock by a Corporation on the accrued method must be paid within 75 days of the corporate year end to be deductible.

§ 1.14 Officers' Salaries

Beginning on ______, 19__, and until changed by the Board of Directors, the salary of the President shall be ______ Dollars per year, the salary of the Vice-President shall be ______ Dollars per year, the salary of the Secretary shall be ______ Dollars per year, and the salary of the Treasurer shall be ______ Dollars per year; these salaries shall be payable in monthly installments on the last day of each month.

§ 1.15 Qualified Retirement Plan

The Corporation shall adopt a Qualified Retirement Plan which has the following features:

(a) Name of plan: ______.

(b) Minimum age for participation: ______.

(c) Minimum service for participation: ______.

(d) Employment status (categories): ______.

(e) Vesting: ______.

(f) Corporation contribution formula: ______.

(g) Employee contribution formula: ______.

(h) Effective date of plan: ______.

(i) Initial committee members: ______.

(j) Initial trustees: ______.

(k) Initial contribution: ______.

§ 1.16 Stock Option

The Corporation shall issue a Stock Option which has the following features:

(a) Person issued to: ______.

(b) Consideration: ______.

(c) Stock which can be bought: ______.

(d) Option price: ______.

(e) Expiration date: ______.

(f) Transfer restrictions: ______.

(g) Earliest date of option exercise: ______.

§ 1.17 Vacation and Sick Day Plan

The Corporation shall adopt a Vacation and Sick Day Plan which has the following features:

Employee Categories	Vacation Days During Employer Year	Sick Days During Employee Year

(b) Vacation days must be taken before [*Describe*] of the following Employee Year. If not taken, they are:

Alternative A–1

lost

Alternative A–2

to be paid for at [*Percent*] % of base pay:

Alternative A–3

[*percent*] % cumulated.

(c) Pay for each vacation day taken is to be paid for at [*percent*] % of base pay.

(d) Sick days must be taken before [*Describe*] of the following Employee Year. If not taken, they are:

Alternative B–1

lost.

Alternative B–2

to be paid for at [*Percent*] % of base pay.

Alternative B–3

[*percent*] % cumulated.

(e) Pay for each sick day taken is to be paid for at [*percent*] % of base pay.

§ 1.18 By-laws and Articles

The Corporation shall not amend its By-laws or Articles without the consent of ______% of the Stockholders.

§ 1.19 Additional Stock

The Corporation shall not issue additional shares of stock or borrow from any of its Stockholders without the consent of ______% of the Stockholders.

§ 1.20 Compensation

The Corporation shall not pay wages or bonus in excess of the following:

Position	Compensation

without the consent of ______% of the Stockholders.

§ 1.21 Policies and Agreements

The Corporation shall not modify any of the following policies or documents: [*Describe*] without the consent of ______% of the Stockholders.

§ 1.22 Subchapter S Status

The Stockholders agree that they will cause the Corporation to elect to be taxed under Subchapter S of the Internal Revenue Code and that they will not transfer the stock of the Corporation if such transfer will cause the Corporation to lose its election to be taxed under Subchapter S of the Internal Revenue Code.

§ 2.1 Notice

Any and all notices provided for herein shall be given in writing by registered or certified mail, return receipt requested which shall be addressed to the last address known to the sender or delivered to the recipient in person.

§ 2.2 Modifications

No modification of this Agreement shall be valid unless such modification is in writing and signed by the parties hereto.

§ 2.3 Waiver

No waiver of any provision of this Agreement shall be valid unless in writing and signed by the person or party against whom charged.

§ 2.4 Applicable Law

This Agreement shall be subject to and governed by the laws of the State of [*Name*].

§ 2.5 Assignment

This Agreement shall be binding upon and inure to the benefit of the parties hereto and their respective heirs, legal representatives, executors, administrators, successors and assigns.

§ 2.6 Arbitration

Any controversy or claim arising out of or relating to this Agreement shall be settled by arbitration in accordance with the rules of the American Arbitration Association, one Arbitrator, and shall be enforceable in any court having competent jurisdiction.

In witness whereof, the parties have hereunto set their hands and seals the ______ day of ______, 19__.

Witnesses	**Stockholders**
______________________	______________________
______________________	______________________

§§ 47.64–47.70 are reserved for supplementary material.

E. POOLING AGREEMENTS

§ 47.71 In General

A Stockholder agreement is a contract among the Stockholders, or some of them, to vote their shares in a specified manner on certain matters. Such an agreement is sometimes called a "pooling agreement." Pooling Agreements result in the shares of the participants being voted as a block without, generally, being committed to a particular pattern. Stockholder agreements result in certain shares being voted a certain way. The purpose may be to maintain control, or to maximize the voting power of the shares where cumulative voting is permitted, or to ensure that some specific object is obtained. The Stockholders pooling agreement extends only to voting on matters that are within the province of Stockholders, such as the election of Directors, and should be sharply distinguished from Stockholder agreements that may attempt to resolve matters that are vested in the discretion of Directors. The latter type of agreement raises serious questions of validity in some jurisdictions. The pooling agreement does not.

In a pooling agreement, the Stockholders retain all the indicia of ownership of shares except the power to vote. In this respect, a pooling agreement differs from a voting trust (discussed in § 47.41, above) which contemplates that legal title to the shares be transferred to the trustees. Generally, the advantages of a pooling agreement over a voting trust are that it is less formal, easier to establish, and there is no disruption of other ownership attributes. However, it is more difficult to enforce.

The pooling agreement is generally recognized as a valid contract,[1] subject only to the rules applicable to the validity of contracts in general. A few states have adopted statutes regulating pooling agreements, often limiting the period during which a pooling agreement may continue (e. g., to ten years), requiring that copies of the pooling be deposited at the principal office of the Corporation, and so forth. However, in most states, the pooling agreement is essentially an unregulated contractual voting device that may continue for long periods of time.

Pooling agreements, unlike irrevocable proxies and voting trusts, are not self-executing. Absent required arbitration, a declaratory judgment might lie; for breach of a Stockholder agreement, the other party or parties to the agreement could seek damages, injunction, or specific performance.

Where a *bona fide* purchaser takes shares subject to a pooling agreement without notice thereof, he usually would not be bound by such agreement. Accordingly sound practice requires that the share certificates involved bear an appropriate legend referring to the pooling agreement.

Library References:

C.J.S. Corporations § 551.
West's Key No. Digests, Corporations ⚷199.

§ 47.72 Resolution of Disagreements [2]

A basic part of a pooling agreement is the manner of resolution of possible disagreements in the future. While the parties to the agreement are presumably in complete accord as to how their shares should be voted today, there is no assurance that there will be such accord tomorrow. Pooling agreements often specify that participants will consult in advance of the meeting as to how the pooled shares should be voted, and that the shares will be voted as a majority or some other percentage specify. For example, in an important Delaware case, the agreement provided that the six participants in the pool could select eight agents (most selecting one; some two) and the

1. Ringling Bros.-Barnum & Bailey Combined Shows, Inc. v. Ringling, 29 Del.Ch. 610, 53 A.2d 441 (Sup.Ct. 1947); McQuade v. Stoneham, 263 N.Y. 323, 189 N.E. 234 (1934), reargument denied 264 N.Y. 460, 191 N.E. 514.

Model Bus.Corp.Act § 34 provides:

"Agreements among shareholders regarding the voting of their shares shall be valid and enforceable in accordance with their terms. Such agreements shall not be subject to the provisions of this section regarding voting trusts."

See also § 47.61, supra.

2. Sections 47.72 and 47.73, infra, are adopted from Henn, Law of Corporations (2d ed. 1970) §§ 198, 267; and Hamilton, Corporations in a Nutshell § 9.6. A third edition is presently being prepared by Professor Henn for 1982 publication.

shares would be voted as any seven agents specified.[3] Arbitration was provided for in the event seven agents were unable to agree. While this agreement ultimately was held to constitute an invalid voting trust rather than a pooling agreement, the method of dispute resolution is interesting in that it required a high degree of consensus by the participants. Resolution of disagreements is usually by arbitration, an arbiter, or by a decision of some person mutually trusted by all the participants. However, if the pooling agreement covers enough shares to constitute working control of the corporation, arbitration may in fact vest control of the Corporation in the hands of the arbiter, a person with no financial interest in the enterprise. A "runaway" arbiter is unlikely because the Stockholders may, by agreeing between themselves, retake control over the voting of the pooled shares. Pooling agreements also often provide that the participants in the pool may substitute arbiters by mutual agreement. Instead of arbitration, a pooling agreement may give a participant the option of withdrawing his shares if disagreement continues over a period of time. Such a provision, of course, in a sense defeats the original purpose of a pooling agreement.

§ 47.73 Enforcement of Agreements

Enforcement of a pooling agreement creates special problems since the shares are registered in the names of the individual Stockholders. Many courts will enforce a pooling agreement by decreeing specific performance. It is not always certain, however, that specific performance will be available.[4] The leading Delaware case involving pooling agreements, the agreement itself did not specifically grant a proxy to anyone to vote the shares of an objecting Stockholder who refused to follow the arbiter's instructions. Nevertheless, the Chancellor, 49 A.2d 603 (Del.Ch.1946), found by a process of implication that such a proxy existed. On appeal, the Supreme Court held that the proper remedy was simply not to count votes cast in contravention of the instructions of the arbiter. Under the circumstances, the result was to defeat utterly the purpose of the pooling agreement, since the minority Stockholder who was not a party to the pooling agreement had a majority of the remaining shares after giving effect to the disqualification.

Some state statutes specifically address the enforcement issue by authorizing specific performance of pooling agreements. New York, for example, validates and makes irrevocable a proxy granted in connection with a pooling agreement.[5] To take advantage of such a statute, the agreement probably must contain specific reference to the irrevocable proxy. Enforcement of pooling agreements creates

3. Abercrombie v. Davies, 36 Del.Ch. 371, 130 A.2d 338 (1957).

4. Ringling Bros.-Barnum & Bailey Combined Shows v. Ringling, 29 Del. Ch. 610, 53 A.2d 441 (1947).

5. N.Y.Bus.Corp.Law §§ 609(e), 620.

practical problems for inspectors of corporate elections who must decide who is entitled to vote disputed shares. In such circumstances, an inspector may insist that a court decree be first obtained determining how the shares should be voted.

§ 47.74 Drafting a Stockholders' Pooling Agreement

In drafting a Stockholders' pooling agreement consideration should be given to the following suggestions:

1. **Purpose.** The agreement should state fully the legal purpose or purposes for which it is made.

2. **Duration.** The agreement should be created for a reasonable time, but in no case should the period exceed the statutory time limit for proxies.

3. **Irrevocable Proxy.** Each party should be empowered to vote the entire block of stock for the directors selected under the agreement with a stipulation that such power is irrevocable.

4. **Consideration.** The agreement should spell out a valuable consideration.

5. **Coupled with an Interest.** When practicable, the parties to the agreement should be given a property or security interest in the shares of the other parties, such as a provision for a right of first refusal in case of a sale of shares by a party to the agreement, thereby creating a sufficient interest to satisfy the requirement of a "power coupled with an interest," and adequate consideration. However, in the desire to create an "interest" care should be taken not to establish the substantial equivalent of a voting trust which would require compliance with the statutory provisions relating thereto.

§ 47.75 Pooling Agreement

This voting agreement, executed this ______ day of ______, 19__, witnesseth:

Whereas, ______, ______, and ______ presently own, respectively ______, ______, and ______, of the outstanding common shares of ______ Corporation and are desirous of effectively insuring that, so long as this agreement is in effect, all shares owned by the parties hereto will be voted as a unit upon all matters upon which such shares shall be entitled to vote; now, therefore, for and in consideration of the mutual agreements of the parties hereto, we do hereby agree as follows:

§ 1.1 In exercising any voting rights to which any party hereto may be entitled by virtue of ownership of shares of stock in said Corporation, each party will consult and confer with the others and endeavor to agree as to how all of their votes shall be cast upon each specific proposition upon which they are entitled to vote; and, if they do so agree, they will then so cast their votes in person or by duly executed and effective proxy.

§ 1.2 If, for any reason, the parties fail unanimously to so agree, they shall, nevertheless, cast all of their votes in such manner as may be agreed upon by the party or parties hereto then owning a majority of the total common shares of said Corporation then owned by the parties hereto.

§ 1.3 A counterpart of this agreement shall forthwith be deposited with said Corporation at its principal office.

§ 1.4 Each certificate representing shares of the outstanding stock of said Corporation and presently owned by the parties hereto shall, by the owner thereof, promptly after execution of this agreement, have legibly written upon the margin of the face thereof the following statement: "The shares represented by this certificate are subject to the provisions of a voting agreement, dated ______, 19__, a counterpart of which has been deposited with the Corporation at its principal office." And each of the parties hereto further agrees and promises that a similar statement will be written on the margin of the face of each certificate representing any shares of said Corporation which may hereafter be acquired by any party hereto.

§ 1.5 This agreement shall terminate upon the happening of any one of the following events: ______.

§ 1.6 If not sooner terminated as provided in the immediately foregoing paragraph, this agreement shall terminate at the expiration of ten years from the date of its execution.

§ 1.7 Until terminated as above provided, this agreement shall be binding upon each of the parties hereto, their heirs and assigns, and upon all subsequent owners of any of the shares of stock subject hereto.

In testimony whereof, witness our signatures hereto on the date above stated.

____

____

____

COMMENT

A pooling agreement is an agreement by Stockholders (sometimes all, sometimes less than all) to vote as determined by a method specified in the agreement. Frequently it is limited to voting for Directors. In most jurisdictions such an agreement is valid, absent either fraud on non-participating Stockholders or an illegal objective. Some courts may be less willing to enforce an agreement where not all Stockholders are party to it. See § 47.71, supra.

§ 47.76 Pooling Agreement—Another Form—Irrevocable Proxy

We, the undersigned, Stockholders of ______ Incorporated, believing it to be in our interest as such Stockholders to pool the votes to which our shares are so entitled for the time and on the terms hereinafter mentioned, do hereby respectively agree the one with the other and others, as follows:

1. We will respectively execute irrevocable proxies as to all our respective shares in the said ______ Corporation, to be held by the ______ until the ______ day of ______, 19__, subject to the provisions and terms below mentioned.

2. At all meetings of the Stockholders of the ______ Corporation, the said ______ shall vote all the proxies for all the shares held by ______ in accordance with the instructions of a majority of the undersigned [*or, of a Majority in Interest of the Shares Owned by the Undersigned*].

3. Upon the expiration of the period mentioned in paragraph number one hereof the said proxies shall be revoked.

Dated: ______, 19__.

Witness	**Stockholders:**
______________________	______________________
______________________	______________________
______________________	______________________

§ 47.77 Pooling Agreement—Another Form—Arbitration

STOCK POOLING AGREEMENT

This agreement, made this ______ day of ______, 19__, by and between [*Names*] (The "parties").

Now, therefore, in consideration of mutual covenants other valuable consideration parties agree:

§ 1.1 Restriction of Transfer of Stock

Neither party will sell any shares of stock or any voting trust certificates in [*Name of Corporation*] to any other person whomsoever, without first making a written offer to the other party hereto of all of the shares proposed to be sold, for the same price and upon the same terms and conditions as in such proposed sale, and allowing such other party a time of not less than 30 days from the date of such written offer within which to accept same.

§ 2.1 Joint Action

In exercising any voting rights to which either party may be entitled by virtue of ownership of stock or voting trust certificates held by them in said Corporation, each party will consult and confer with the other and the parties will act jointly in exercising such voting rights in accordance with such agreement as they may reach with respect to any matter calling for the exercise of such voting rights.

§ 2.2 Arbitration

In the event the parties fail to agree with respect to any matter covered by paragraph 2.1 above, the question in disagreement shall be submitted for arbitration to [*Name*] as arbitrator and his decision thereon shall be binding upon the parties hereto. Such arbitration shall be exercised to the end of assuring for the Corporation good management.

§ 3.1 Execution of Other Instruments

Each of the parties hereto will enter into and execute such proxies and such other instruments as, from time to time, may be appropriate to effectuate the purposes and objects of this agreement.

§ 3.2 Duration

This agreement shall be in effect from the date hereof and shall continue in effect for a period of ten years unless sooner terminated by mutual agreement in writing by the parties hereto.

§ 3.3 Successors

This agreement shall be binding upon and inure to the benefit of the heirs, executors, administrators and assigns of the parties hereto respectively.

§ 4.1 Notice

Any and all notices provided for herein shall be given in writing by registered or certified mail, return receipt requested which shall be addressed to the last address known to the sender or delivered to the recipient in person.

§ 4.2 Modifications

No modification of this Agreement shall be valid unless such modification is in writing and signed by the parties hereto.

§ 4.3 Waiver

No waiver of any provision of this Agreement shall be valid unless in writing and signed by the person or party against whom charged.

§ 4.4 Applicable Law

This Agreement shall be subject to and governed by the laws of the State of [*Name*].

§ 4.5 Assignment

This Agreement shall be binding upon and inure to the benefit of the parties hereto and their respective heirs, legal representatives, executors, administrators, successors and assigns.

§ 4.6 Arbitration

Any controversy or claim arising out of or relating to this Agreement shall be settled by arbitration in accordance with the rules of the American Arbitration Association, one Arbitrator, and shall be enforceable in any court having competent jurisdiction.

In witness whereof, the parties have hereunto set their hands and seals the ______ day of ______, 19__.

Witnesses	Stockholders
______________________	______________________
______________________	______________________
	______________________

§ 47.78 Agreement with Purchaser of Shares to Vote for Seller as Officer

This agreement, made this ______ day of ______, 19__, between ______, residing at ______, party of the first part, and ______, residing at ______, party of the second part,

WITNESSETH

Whereas, simultaneously with the execution of this agreement, the party of the first part did acquire from the party of the second part and from other parties, certain shares of a Corporation organized under the laws of the State of ______ (hereinafter called the Corporation),

Now, therefore, in consideration of the premises and other good and valuable consideration, it is agreed by and between the parties hereto as follows:

§ 1.1 The party of the first part agrees to and with the party of the second part that the party of the second part shall continue to occupy his official position, relationship, and employment as Treasurer and general business manager of the Corporation for a period of ______ (______) years from the date hereof, at the same salary as at present being drawn and received by the party of the second part from the Corporation, and the party of the first part shall act in the exercise of its share rights so as to enable the party of the second part to perform all the proper functions and duties as such Treasurer and general manager.

§ 1.2 The party of the second part hereby agrees that by virtue and consideration of his continued employment as hereinabove provided, he will consult with the designated representatives of the party of the first part in all matters pertaining to the policy of the Corporation, the fixing of salaries of Officers of the Corporation, and the employment of executives of the Corporation, and any and all kindred matters.

§ 1.3 This agreement shall be binding upon and shall enure to the benefit of the parties hereto and their heirs, legal representatives, and assigns.

In witness whereof, the parties hereto have set their hands the day and year first above written.

____

____

§§ 47.79–48.0 are reserved for supplementary material.

CHAPTER 48

RESOLUTIONS AND MINUTES (STOCKHOLDERS AND BOARD OF DIRECTORS)

Table of Sections

A. IN GENERAL

B. RESOLUTIONS AND MINUTES

A. IN GENERAL

§ 48.1 Stockholder Resolutions [1]

Stockholder resolutions can relate to a wide variety of matters, so long as they are proper subjects for action at Stockholder meetings. For various extraordinary matters, Stockholder approval is often required. Stockholders occasionally act as a substitute corporate organization for the Board of Directors.

Where Stockholders purport to ratify some matter, various questions arise, such as fullness of disclosure, ratifiability of matter, effect of ratification, burden of proof, counting of interested Stockholders, etc.

Stockholder ratification may estop ratifying Stockholders from thereafter complaining, assuming full disclosure.

Library References:

C.J.S. Corporations § 545.
West's Key No. Digests, Corporations ⚷196.

1. See Henn, Law of Corporations (2d ed. 1970), § 194. A third edition is presently being prepared by Professor Henn for 1982 publication.

§ 48.2 Stockholder Approval of Extraordinary Matters

Stockholders invest in the corporate enterprise as defined in the Articles of Incorporation with the expectation that the Board of Directors will manage the enterprise so far as its ordinary business is concerned.

Amendments of the Articles of Incorporation involve, to a greater or less extent, organic changes in the Corporation; extraordinary transactions are beyond the ordinary business whose management is delegated to the Board of Directors.

At common law, such extraordinary matters required unanimous Stockholder approval. Statutes today permit such matters when approved by a prescribed vote or consent of Stockholders (such vote or consent requirements possibly varying for different matters), with or without concurrent Board of Directors action; dissenting Stockholders under such circumstances often enjoy the right to have their shares appraised and purchased by the Corporation. See Chapter 50, infra.

Typically, such extraordinary matters include amendments of the Articles of Incorporation (including reclassification), sale or lease of assets outside of the Corporation's regular course of business, merger, consolidation, and dissolution, etc.

§ 48.3 Directors' Resolutions

Directors' resolutions may cover every aspect of the Corporation's operations, and it is manifestly not possible to prepare forms for every contingency. The forms that follow are believed to be reasonably representative.

When drafting resolutions, it is customary to use the introductory clause "Resolved, that * * *." It is also customary not to have complete sentences within each resolution; where the construction becomes complex, the resolutions should be broken down into separate subresolutions, each beginning "Resolved, that * * *" Where appropriate, the subresolutions may each be numbered to make it clear that they all deal with the same subject. Some attorneys use the phrase "Resolved further, that * * *" to indicate the relationship between the resolutions.

Library References:

C.J.S. Corporations § 744 et seq.
West's Key No. Digests, Corporations ⚷298.

§ 48.4 Secretary's Certification of Resolution

CERTIFICATE

I have compared the foregoing with a resolution adopted by the Board of Directors of [*Name of Corporation*] at a meeting held at the office of said Corporation, a quorum being present, on the ______ day of ______, 19__, as recorded in the minute book of said Corporation, on page ______ thereof, and I hereby certify that the same is a true, correct, and complete copy thereof, and that the same has not been rescinded.

[*Name of Corporation*],
[*Secretary*]

§ 48.5 Secretary's Certification of Resolution—Another Form

I, ______, certify that I am the Secretary of ______ Corporation, and that I have compared the foregoing with a resolution adopted by the Board of Directors of ______ Corporation at a regular meeting held at the office of the Corporation, a quorum being present, on ______, 19__, as recorded in the minute book of the Corporation, on page ______ thereof, and I hereby certify that the same is a true, correct, and complete copy thereof, and that the same has not been rescinded.

____
Secretary

[*or*]

I, ______, do hereby certify that I am the Secretary of ______ Corporation, a ______ Corporation, and as such secretary I have access to all original records of the Corporation. I do further certify that at a meeting of the Directors of the Corporation, duly called, held, and convened, according to law and the bylaws of the Corporation on ______, 19__, a quorum being present and voting thereon, the following resolutions were unanimously adopted; that the following is a full, true, and correct copy of the resolutions as they appear on the records of the Corporation; and that I am one of the duly authorized and proper Officers of the Corporation to make certified copies of its records in its behalf:

[*Resolution*]

I do further certify that the above resolution has not been in anywise altered, amended, or repealed and is now in full force and effect.

In witness whereof, I have hereunto set my hand and attach the seal of the Corporation this ______ day of ______, 19__.

[*Seal*] [*Signature of Secretary*]

COMMENT

The Secretary's certificate that a resolution was duly adopted and remains in force binds the Corporation to third persons who may rely on the certificate and need not inquire into the question whether all corporate formalities were followed. This conclusion is usually placed on the ground of estoppel or actual authority.

§ 48.6 Certificate of Secretary as to Action Taken by Directors Without a Meeting

CERTIFICATE OF SECRETARY

I, ______, Secretary of ______, a ______ Corporation, do hereby certify that the following resolutions were duly adopted by the unanimous written consent of the Board of Directors without a meeting, and that such resolutions have not been rescinded, amended or modified and are in full force and effect as of the date hereof:

[*Resolutions.*]

In witness whereof I have hereunto set my hand this ______ day of ______, 19__.

____

______, Secretary

COMMENT

The Secretary's certificate may be required by third parties to confirm Directors' resolutions made at a meeting or by written consent.

§§ 48.7–48.10 are reserved for supplementary material.

B. RESOLUTIONS AND MINUTES

Library References:

C.J.S. Corporations § 742.
West's Key No. Digests, Corporations ⚿297.

GENERAL COMMENTS

The following resolutions can be adopted by either the Stockholders or the Board of Directors. Generally the Board will adopt these resolutions (except the election of the Board and the amendment of the Articles) except in the following instances:

(a) The Board has no authority to act.

(b) The Stockholders are adopting in order to bar them from a later legal action against the Board.

(c) The Board's right to act is being superceded; for instance, when the Board is to be replaced, but there will not be time for the new Board to act (given statutory or Bylaw notice requirements).

It should be remembered that if a person feels a meeting is improperly called, he must so object and not further participate. If a Director feels an action is illegal, he should state his reason and possibly resign.

§ 48.11 Accountants—Appointment

Resolved, that [*Name*] be hereby appointed Accountants of the Company for the ensuing year, and that the remuneration for their services as such Accountants be the sum of $______.

Option 1 (Not Preferred for Smoothly Running Closely Held Corporations)

The following vote on the above resolution was counted:

(a) yes: [*Number*];

(b) no: [*Number*];

(c) abstentions: [*Number*];

(d) persons demanding that their objections be noted and the reasons for their objections: __________.

§ 48.12 Agent—Appointment

Be it resolved, that ______ be, and he hereby is, appointed agent for this Corporation with full authority covering the following matters: [*Describe*]

§ 48.13 Amendment to Articles

Resolved that the Articles of Incorporation be amended as follows:

(1) Article ______ shall be deleted in its entirety.

(2) Article ______ shall be added as follows: [*Describe*].

(3) Article ______ shall be amended to read: [*Describe*].

Option 1 (Not Preferred for Smoothly Running Closely Held Corporations)

The following vote on the above resolution was counted:

(a) Yes: [*Number*];

(b) No: [*Number*];

(c) Abstentions: [*Number*];

(d) Persons demanding that their objections be noted and the reasons for their objections: ______________.

§ 48.14 Annual Meeting of Stockholders

Resolved that the annual meeting of the Stockholders shall be held at the office of this Corporation, ______, ______, ______ on the ______ day of ______, 19__, at ______ o'clock __.M., for the election of Directors and such other matters as may come before the meeting;

Resolved, further, that the record date for determining the Stockholders entitled to vote is hereby set as the close of business on ______, 19__; and

Resolved further, that the Secretary shall give notice of the annual meeting to all Stockholders entitled to vote within five days hereafter.

Option 1 (Not Preferred for Smoothly Running Closely Held Corporations)

The following vote on the above resolution was counted:

(a) Yes: [*Number*];

(b) No: [*Number*];

(c) Abstentions: [*Number*];

(d) Persons demanding that their objections be noted and the reasons for their objections: ______________.

§ 48.15 Assessment on Call

Resolved, that a call of ______ per cent is hereby made upon each and every share of the capital stock of the Corporation subscribed for, and same is to be paid by each subscriber to the Treasurer of the Corporation, on or before the ______ day of ______, 19__, (and that the President and Secretary issue certificates of full-paid stock therefor).

Option 1 (Not Preferred for Smoothly Running Closely Held Corporations)

The following Officers are authorized to execute the same: President

Option 2 (Not Preferred for Smoothly Running Closely Held Corporations)

The following vote on the above resolution was counted:

(a) Yes: [*Number*];

(b) No: [*Number*];

(c) Abstentions: [*Number*];

(d) Persons demanding that their objections be noted and the reasons for their objections: __________.

§ 48.16 Assessment on Call—In Installments

Resolved, that a call for the balance due from the subscribers to the capital stock of this Company is hereby made, the same being payable in installments as follows:

$_____ per share on or before the _____ day of _____, 19__;
$_____ per share on or before the _____ day of _____, 19__; *etc.*

Further resolved, that the Secretary notify all subscribers of the time, place of payment, and amount to be paid.

Option 1 (Not Preferred for Smoothly Running Closely Held Corporations)

The following vote on the above resolution was counted:

(a) Yes: [*Number*];

(b) No: [*Number*];

(c) Abstentions: [*Number*];

(d) Persons demanding that their objections be noted and the reasons for their objections: ______________.

§ 48.17 Assumed Name

Resolved, that the [*Board of Directors/Stockholders ratify as executed/adopt as proposed*] a Certificate of Assumed Name which has the following features:

(a) Effective date: __________.

(b) Name to be used: __________.

Option 1 (Preferred as a Matter of Practical Experience)

The Secretary shall make part of the minute book a copy of the same.

§ 48.18 Attorney—Appointment

Resolved, that [*Name*] be hereby appointed to act as attorney for the Corporation and that he be paid the ordinary professional charges for his services as attorney.

Option 1 (Not Preferred for Smoothly Running Closely Held Corporations)

The following vote on the above resolution was counted:

(a) Yes: [*Number*];

(b) No: [*Number*];

(c) Abstentions: [*Number*];

(d) Persons demanding that their objections be noted and the reasons for their objections: ________.

§ 48.19 Auditors—Appointment

Resolved, that ______ be hereby appointed auditors of the Company for the ensuing year, and that the remuneration for their services as such auditors be the sum of $______.

Option 1 (Not Preferred for Smoothly Running Closely Held Corporations)

The following vote on the above resolution was counted:

(a) Yes: [*Number*];

(b) No: [*Number*];

(c) Abstentions: [*Number*];

(d) Persons demanding that their objections be noted and the reasons for their objections: ____________.

§ 48.20 Authorization of Transaction in Which a Director Has a Personal Interest

RESOLUTION AUTHORIZING [*Here Insert Appropriate Title*]

1. ______ [*Name of Director(s) Financially Interested in Transaction*] is now a Director of ______ Corporation.

2. The Board of Directors of ______ Corporation has considered the following transaction. [*Here state facts of the proposed transaction*].

3. ______ [*Name of Director(s) Financially Interested in Transaction*] is interested in the transaction in that ______ [*Here state facts showing interest of Director*].

4. ______ [*Name of Financially Interested Director*] has disclosed his interest to the Board of Directors.

or

[4. The interest of ______ [*Name of Director*] in this transaction is known to the Board of Directors.]

5. The Board of Directors finds that the transaction is just and reasonable and for the best interests of the Corporation. ______ [*Name of Financially Interested Director*] has abstained from the vote of the Board of Directors approving this transaction.

6. Therefore, the Directors of this Corporation have resolved to, and do hereby, authorize the Officers of the Corporation to enter into the transaction described herein.

Option 1 (Not Preferred for Smoothly Running Closely Held Corporations)

The following vote on the above resolution was counted:

(a) Yes: [*Number*];

(b) No: [*Number*];

(c) Abstentions: [*Number*];

(d) Persons demanding that their objections be noted and the reasons for their objections: ______________.

§ 48.21 Authorization of Indemnity for Litigation

DIRECTORS' RESOLUTION AUTHORIZING INDEMNITY FOR LITIGATION

Resolution: Payment of Indemnity to ______

1. ______ [*Insert Name of Person to Be Indemnified*] has incurred the following expenses: [*Insert description of appropriate expenses which may be reimbursed*].

2. These expenses were incurred during [*Here state nature of "proceeding"*]. The claims against ______ [*Name of Person to Be Indemnified*] arose out of actions of ______ [*Name of Person to Be Indemnified*] during the employment of ______ [*Name*] by ______ Corporation. ______ [*Name*] was acting in good faith and in a manner which he reasonably believed to be in the best interests of the Corporation.

3. Therefore, the Directors of ______ Corporation have resolved to, and do hereby, authorize the President and Secretary-Treasurer of the Corporation to cause payment of the sum of $______ to be made to ______ [*Name*] as indemnity for the above-mentioned expenses.

Option 1 (Not Preferred for Smoothly Running Closely Held Corporations)

The following vote on the above resolution was counted:

(a) Yes: [*Number*];

(b) No: [*Number*];

(c) Abstentions: [*Number*];

(d) Persons demanding that their objections be noted and the reasons for their objections: ______________.

§ 48.22 Bank Signature Authorization Form

Resolved that the [*Board of Directors/Stockholders ratify as executed/adopt as proposed*] a bank signature authorization form which has the following features:

(a) Bank: __________.

(b) Type of account(s): __________.

(c) Authorized signatures: __________.

(d) Number of signatures required: __________.

Option 1 (Preferred as a Matter of Practical Experience)

The Secretary shall make part of the minute book a copy of the same.

Option 2 (Not Preferred for Smoothly Running Closely Held Corporations)

The following Officers are authorized to execute the same: President and Secretary.

Option 3 (Not Preferred for Smoothly Running Closely Held Corporations)

The following vote on the above resolution was counted:

(a) Yes: [*Number*];

(b) No: [*Number*];

(c) Abstentions: [*Number*];

(d) Persons demanding that their objections be noted and the reasons for their objections: __________.

§ 48.23 Board of Directors Meetings

Resolved, that the regular meetings of the Board of Directors be held on the ______ of every month at the Corporations' office in ______ at ______ o'clock __.M. and that no notice of such meetings need be given.

§ 48.24 Board of Directors Meetings—Another Form

Resolved, that the Stockholders of ______ Corporation deem it advisable, and in the best interests of this Corporation, that the By-laws of this Corporation, as amended, be further amended in the following respects:

1. Delete all of Article ___, Section ___, in lieu thereof insert the following:

"Section ____. *Regular Meetings.* Regular meetings of the Board of Directors shall be held monthly on such dates as the Board may designate. In each calendar quarter at least one regular meeting of the Board of Directors shall be held in open session with employees of the Corporation at various plant locations."

§ 48.25 Board of Directors—Election by Stockholders

Resolved, that the following person(s) shall be elected to the Board of Directors, to serve until the next annual meeting of Stockholders and until the election and qualification of respective successor(s) (or until removed, with or without cause, by the Stockholders): [*Name(s)*].

§ 48.26 Board of Director Fees and Expenses

Resolved that the [*Board of Directors/Stockholders ratify/authorize*] that (but only to the extent to which set forth below), the fee paid to and expenses reimbursed to each member of the Board shall be:

(a) Fee per meeting: $____________.

(b) Maximum Expense reimbursement per meeting: ____________.

(c) Expense reimbursement for:

(1) Travel: $________ per mile.

(2) Hotel: $________ per day.

(3) Meals: $________ per day.

(4) Entertainment: $________ per day.

COMMENT

Fees paid to a controlling Stockholder by a Corporation on the accrued method must be paid within 75 days of the corporate year end to be deductible (see Introduction to Part A of Division VI (preceding Chapter 27, supra).

The following Officer(s) is authorized to carry out the above resolution: The Treasurer.

§ 48.27 Bonuses to Employees

Resolved, that the following bonus(es) be paid for the current fiscal year:

Employee	Bonus

Option 1 (Not Preferred Unless There Is to Be a Consent Meeting and All Those Voting Won't Actually Review the Transaction)

The following vote on the above resolution ______ was counted:

(a) Yes: __________.

(b) No: __________.

(c) Abstentions: __________.

(d) Persons demanding that their objection be noted and the reasons for their objections: __________.

§ 48.28 Borrowing Money

Resolved, that the Officers of the Corporation signing in the following manner: ______________________________
are authorized to borrow money, discount bills receivable or negotiable paper, and to obtain credit for the Corporation from ______ Bank under such terms as they in their discretion may deem advisable, and in connection therewith to make, execute, endorse and deliver any notes, drafts, acceptances, agreements or any other obligations of the Corporation, and as security therefor, to pledge or hypothecate any stocks, bonds, bills receivable, bills of lading, warehouse receipts or other instruments or property of the Corporation, and to execute and deliver any and all endorsements, instruments of assignment, or powers of attorney, as may be necessary or required in connection therewith.

Resolved, that all notes or other obligations of the Corporation heretofore delivered to said ______ Bank evidencing advances, credits or loans to the Corporation, be and the same are hereby in all respects ratified, approved and confirmed.

Resolved, that the foregoing resolutions shall remain in full force and effect until written notice of their revocation or amendment is duly received by said ______ Bank.

§ 48.29 Borrowing Money—Another Form

Resolved, that the Treasurer, with the concurrence of the President, or one of the Vice-Presidents, may from time to time borrow money for the Corporation, and for this purpose may sell the Corporation's promissory notes, running for not more than six months, at a discount of not more than ______ per cent per annum, the notes to be signed in behalf of the Corporation by at least two of its Officers.

§ 48.30 Borrowing Money—Another Form

Resolved by the Board of Directors of ______ Corporation:

1. That the ______ Bank, herein called "Bank," be, and it is hereby, designated as one of the Depositaries of the funds of this Corporation, and that the President or Treasurer of this Corporation be, and each of them hereby, is, authorized to deposit in the Depositary funds of this company and to endorse in the name of this Corporation for that purpose checks, drafts, notes and other like obligations;

2. That the Bank be, and it hereby is, authorized to pay out funds on deposit with it from time to time to the credit of this Corporation upon checks drawn upon the Depositary and signed in the name of this Corporation by its President or Vice-President and countersigned by its Treasurer or Assistant Treasurer;

3. That the President and Treasurer of this Corporation be, and they are hereby, authorized from time to time to borrow money from Bank in such amounts, for such length of time and at such rates of interest and upon such other terms and conditions as the officers may deem expedient, and to secure the payment of money so borrowed, and to evidence the indebtedness thereby created to execute and deliver in the name and behalf of this Corporation promissory notes, judgment promissory notes and other like obligations of this Corporation, signed in the name of this Corporation by the President and Treasurer and to pledge as security for the payment of the notes and other obligations any property or securities now or hereafter belonging to this Corporation, which notes or other obligations shall be in such form and shall contain such terms, provisions and conditions as may be deemed proper by such Officers;

4. That Bank shall not be in any manner responsible for or required to see to the application of any of the funds deposited with it or borrowed from it as hereinabove provided;

5. That the Secretary of this Corporation, shall file with the Bank, a certified copy of this resolution, under the seal of the Corporation, and shall also file with the Bank a list of the persons at the present time holding offices of President, Vice-President, Treasurer and Assistant Treasurer, in this Corporation, and the Bank shall be entitled

as against this Corporation to conclusively presume that the persons so certified as holding such offices continue to respectively hold the same until otherwise notified in writing by the Secretary of this Corporation;

6. That this resolution shall be in full force and effect and binding upon this Corporation until it shall have been repealed and until written notice of such repeal shall have been delivered to the Bank at its office at ______.

§ 48.31 Buy-Sell Agreement

Resolved that the [*Board of Directors/Stockholders ratify as executed/adopt as proposed*] a Buy-Sell Agreement which has the following features:

Triggering Event	Price	Terms	Option or Mandatory Buy Out
(a) Stockholder has offer from third party.			
(b) Disability.			
(c) Death.			
(d) Termination of employment before age 65.			
(e) Retirement after age 65.			
(f) Force out of Stock ownership.			

COMMENT

See Chapter 68, infra, for forms of buy-sell agreements.

Option 1 (Preferred as a Matter of Practical Experience)

The Secretary shall make part of the minute book a copy of the same.

Option 2 (Not Preferred for Smoothly Running Closely Held Corporations)

The following Officers are authorized to execute the same: President & Secretary

Option 3 (Not Preferred Unless There Is to Be a Consent Meeting and All Those Voting Won't Actually Review the Transaction)

The President shall do all things reasonable and necessary to carry out the purposes of the Buy-Sell Agreement and to that end he shall:

(a) Purchase the required insurance

Option 4 (Not Preferred for Smoothly Running Closely Held Corporations)

The following vote on the above resolution was counted:

(a) Yes: [*Number*];

(b) No: [*Number*];

(c) Abstentions: [*Number*];

(d) Persons demanding that their objections be noted and the reasons for their objections: ____________.

§ 48.32 By-laws—Adoption

Resolved, that the Board of Directors having reviewed the proposed By-laws, the same are hereby adopted and shall be inserted in the minute book of the Corporation by the Secretary.

Option 1 (Not Preferred Unless There Is to Be a Consent Meeting and All Those Voting Won't Actually Review the Transaction)

The Secretary shall make part of the minute book a copy of the same.

Option 2 (Not Preferred for Smoothly Running Closely Held Corporations)

The following vote on the above resolution was counted:

(a) Yes: ____________

(b) No: ____________

(c) Abstentions: ____________

(d) Persons demanding that their objections be noted and the reasons for their objections: ____________.

§ 48.33 By-laws—Changes

Resolved, that the Board of Directors, having reviewed the proposed amendment(s) to the By-laws, the following [*are/is*] hereby adopted:

[*Describe*]

Option 1 (Preferred as a Matter of Practical Experience)

The Secretary shall make part of the minute book a copy of the same.

Option 2 (Not Preferred for Smoothly Running Closely Held Corporations)

The following vote on the above resolution was counted:

(a) Yes: [*Number*];

(b) No: [*Number*];

(c) Abstentions: [*Number*];

(d) Persons demanding that their objections be noted and the reasons for their objections: __________.

§ 48.34 Cafeteria Plan—Adoption

Resolved that the [*Board of Directors/Stockholders ratify as executed/adopt as proposed*] a Cafeteria Plan which has the following features:

(1) Medical Insurance with the following features:

(A) Hospital:

Room & board __________.

Maximum # of days __________.

Intensive care additional __________.

Intensive care # of days __________.

Maximum extra charges __________.

Surgical schedule __________.

Anesthesia __________.

In-hospital benefit __________.

Hospital-out-patient __________.

(Supplemental accident) __________.

Radiation therapy __________.

Diagnostic X-ray and lab __________.

Maternity __________.

(B) Major medical: __________.

Maximum __________.

Deductible __________.

Co-insurance __________.

Prescription drugs __________.

Out-patient __________.

Convalescent care __________.

(C) Dental:

Deductible/family __________.

Oral exams, etc. ______.

X-rays, fillings, etc. ______.

Bridges, dentures, crowns, etc. ______.

Maximum benefit ______.

(D) Carrier: ______.

(2) Disability Insurance with the following features:

(A) Carrier: ______.

(B) Wait upon accidental disability: ______.

(C) Wait upon sickness: ______.

(D) Benefit per week: $______.

(E) Reduction for partial disability: ______

(F) Reduction for ability to be employed full time in some other job: ______.

(G) Benefit period upon accident: ______.

(H) Benefit period upon sickness: ______.

(3) Medical Reimbursement:

(A) Maximum benefit per corporate fiscal year: $______.

(4) Group Term Life Insurance:

(A) Death benefit: $______.

(5) Group Whole Life Insurance:

(A) Death benefit: $______.

(6) A Group Legal Service Plan which has the following features:

(A) Trustees: ______.

(B) Bank: ______.

(7) Participant description: ______.

(8) Contribution per participant per year: $______.

(9) This plan [*will/will not*] reduce existing salaries by $______ per year.

(10) This plan is in lieu of the following benefits now being provided: [*Describe*].

(11) Provided that any salary payment or other payment made to or on behalf of an Officer of the Corporation which shall be disallowed in whole or in part as a deductible expense for Federal income tax purposes, shall be reimbursed by such Officer to the Corporation to the full extent of the disallowance. It shall be the duty of the Board of Directors to enforce payment of each such amount disallowed.

COMMENTS

One question that arises in the case of an employee benefit is the reasonableness of the benefit in light of the total compensation paid. If it is reasonable, the deduction will be available; if the total compensation is not reasonable, the deduction will not be available. The Internal Revenue Service will attempt to claim, in the case of a Corporation, that an unreasonably high payment was in the nature of a dividend to a Stockholder-employee, which was not deductible to the Corporation. The popular solution to this problem is a "double dip" provision (the government is dipping twice into the transaction) in the corporate minutes which requires repayment of the disallowed benefit to the Corporation leaving the Corporation and the employee in the same position they would have been in if the payment had not been made. The government is presently trying to thwart the use of such a provision by asserting that its existence is prima facie evidence of the unreasonableness of the payment. Given the pervasive use of this provision, this "damned if you do or don't" assertion is absurd and, if carried to its logical extension, would negate all tax planning which was based upon a written assertion of the tax results being sought.

See Employee Benefit Plans Volume, with respect to cafeteria plans.

Option 1 (Preferred as a Matter of Practical Experience)

The Secretary shall make part of the minute book a copy of the same.

Option 2 (Not Preferred for Smoothly Running Closely Held Corporations)

The following Officers are authorized to execute the same: President and Secretary.

Option 3 (Not Preferred Unless There Is to Be a Consent Meeting and All Those Voting Won't Actually Review the Transaction)

The President shall do all things reasonable and necessary to carry out the purpose of the Cafeteria Plan and to that end he shall:

(a) Distribute the necessary disclosure summary to participants.

(b) Execute and File the necessary EBS–1 form with the Department of Labor.

(c) Pay plan expenses as required or reasonably necessary.

(d) Deliver Internal Revenue Service Form 1099 to all participants to reflect any economic benefit which is not included in income.

Option 4 (Not Preferred For Smoothly Running Closely Held Corporations)

The following vote on the above resolution was counted:

(a) Yes: [*Number*];

(b) No: [*Number*];

(c) Abstentions: [*Number*];

(d) Persons demanding that their objections be noted and the reasons for their objections: __________.

§ 48.35 Cancellation of Debt

Whereas, [*Name*] was on ______, 19__, indebted to this Corporation in the sum of ______ Dollars ($______), as shown by the books of this Corporation;

Now, therefore, be it resolved, that the indebtedness of [*Name*], amounting to the sum of ______ Dollars ($______) as of ______, 19__, be and the same is hereby forgiven and canceled.

Further Resolved, that the President or a Vice-President and the Secretary of this Corporation be and they are hereby authorized and directed to execute and deliver to said [*Name*] such instrument or instruments and to perform such other act or acts as may be necessary or desirable to evidence and render fully effective this resolution.

Option 1 (Not Preferred for Smoothly Running Closely Held Corporations)

The following vote on the above resolution was counted:

(a) Yes: [*Number*];

(b) No: [*Number*];

(c) Abstentions: [*Number*];

(d) Persons demanding that their objections be noted and the reasons for their objections: __________.

§ 48.36 Cancellation of Debt of Affiliate

Whereas, this Corporation is the owner and holder of all the subscribed and issued capital stock of ______ Company, Inc. a corporation organized and existing under and by virtue of the laws of the State of ______; and

Whereas, ______ Company, Inc. is indebted to this Corporation in the sum of ______ Dollars, as shown by the books of this Corporation; and

Whereas, the conduct of the business of ______ Company, Inc. will be facilitated by the cancellation of the indebtedness and the consequent increase of the net worth of the Corporation, and it is therefore for the best interests of this Corporation that action to that end be taken;

Now, therefore, be it resolved; that the indebtedness of ______ Company, Inc. to this Corporation amounting to the sum of ______ Dollars, be and the same is hereby forgiven, remitted and canceled.

Resolved, further, that the President or a Vice-President and the Secretary of this Corporation be and they are hereby authorized and directed, in the name and under the seal of this Corporation to execute and deliver to ______ Company, Inc. such instrument or instruments and to perform such other act or acts as may be necessary or desirable to evidence and render fully effective this resolution.

Option 1 (Not Preferred for Smoothly Running Closely Held Corporations)

The following vote on the above resolution was counted:

(a) Yes: [*Number*];

(b) No: [*Number*];

(c) Abstentions: [*Number*];

(d) Persons demanding that their objections be noted and the reasons for their objections: __________.

§ 48.37 Charitable Subscription

Resolved, that a donation of $______ be given to the ______ Society, and that the Treasurer is hereby authorized to pay the same.

Option 1 (Not Preferred for Smoothly Running Closely Held Corporations)

The following vote on the above resolution was counted:

(a) Yes: [*Number*];

(b) No: [*Number*];

(c) Abstentions: [*Number*];

(d) Persons demanding that their objections be noted and the reasons for their objections: __________.

§ 48.38 Christmas Bonuses

Whereas, this Corporation has made exceptional profits this year and wishes to observe the holiday season: Resolved, that on December 24th next, the Treasurer is directed to pay to each Officer and employé of this Corporation who has been with the Corporation more than *six* months a sum equal to *five* per cent of his annual salary or wages as additional compensation and a sharing of the Corporation's good fortune, and that the Treasurer charge the same to expense account.

Option 1 (Not Preferred for Smoothly Running Closely Held Corporations)

The following vote on the above resolution was counted:

(a) Yes: [*Number*];

(b) No: [*Number*];

(c) Abstentions: [*Number*];

(d) Persons demanding that their objections be noted and the reasons for their objections: ____________.

§ 48.39 Committee Appointment

Resolved that the [*Board of Directors/Stockholders ratify/authorize*] the establishment of the following committee to perform the following acts:

(a) Committee name: ____________.

(b) Members: ____________.

(c) Authority:

(1) To sue, complain and defend.

(2) To use the corporate seal by causing it, or a facsimile thereof, to be impressed or affixed or in any other manner reproduced.

(3) To purchase, take, receive, lease, or otherwise acquire, own, hold, improve, use and otherwise deal in and with, real or personal property, or any interest therein, wherever situated.

(4) To sell, convey, mortgage, pledge, lease, exchange, transfer and otherwise dispose of all or any part of the corporate property and assets.

(5) To lend money and use the Corporation's credit to assist its employees and Directors.

(6) To purchase, take, receive, subscribe for, or otherwise acquire, own, hold, vote, use, employ, sell, mortgage, lend, pledge, or otherwise dispose of, and otherwise use and deal in and with, shares or other interests in, or obligations of, other domestic or foreign corporations, associations, partnerships or individuals, or direct or indirect obligations of the United States or of any other government, state, territory, governmental district or municipality or of any instrumentality thereof.

(7) To make contracts and guarantees and incur liabilities, borrow money at such rates of interest as the Corporation may determine, issue its notes, bonds, and other obligations, and secure any of its obligations by mortgage or pledge of all or any of its property, franchises and income.

(8) To lend money for the corporate purposes, invest and reinvest its funds, and take and hold payment of funds so loaned or invested.

(9) To conduct corporate business, carry on its operations and have offices and exercise the powers granted herein, within or without this State.

(10) To elect or appoint Officers and agents of the Corporation, and define their duties and fix their compensation.

(11) To make donations for the public welfare or for charitable, scientific or educational purposes.

(12) To transact any lawful business which the Board of Directors shall find will be an aid of governmental policy.

(13) To pay pensions and establish pension plans, pension trusts, profit sharing plans, stock bonus plans, stock option plans and other incentive plans for any or all of its Directors, Officers and employees.

(14) To be a promoter, partner, member, associate, or manager of any Partnership, joint venture, trust or other enterprise.

Option 1 (Not Preferred for Smoothly Running Closely Held Corporations)

The following vote on the above resolution was counted:

(a) Yes: __________.

(b) No: __________.

(c) Abstentions: __________.

(d) Persons demanding that their objections be noted and the reasons for their objections: __________.

Library References:

C.J.S. Corporations § 760.
West's Key No. Digests, Corporations ⚷299.

§ 48.40 Committee Appointment—Another Form

Resolved, that ______, ______ and ______ are hereby appointed, a committee to consider ______, and that the quorum for any meeting shall be ______ members, and that such committee shall have all the powers of the Board necessary or convenient for the purpose of carrying out their inquiry, subject to any restrictions that may be imposed upon them by the Board from time to time.

Option 1 (Not Preferred for Smoothly Running Closely Held Corporations)

The following vote on the above resolution was counted:

(a) Yes: [*Number*];

(b) No: [*Number*];

(c) Abstentions: [*Number*];

(d) Persons demanding that their objections be noted and the reasons for their objections: ________________.

§ 48.41 Committee for Corporate Responsibility

Whereas, the Stockholders of ______ are concerned that the present policies and priorities pursued by the management have failed to take into account the possible adverse social impact of the Corporation's activities, it is

Resolved, that:

1. There be established the ______ Stockholders Committee for Corporate Responsibility.

2. The Committee for Corporate Responsibility shall consist of ten persons to be appointed by the Board of Directors. The members of the Committee for Corporate Responsibility shall be chosen to represent the following: ______ management, environmental and conservation groups, consumers, the academic community, civil rights organizations, labor, the scientific community, social service organizations, and small Stockholders.

3. The Committee for Corporate Responsibility shall prepare a report and make recommendations to the Stockholders with respect to the role of the Corporation in modern society and how to achieve a proper balance between the rights and interest of Stockholders, employees, consumers, and the general public. The Committee shall specifically examine, among other things:

(A) The extent to which the Corporation's policies towards suppliers, employees, consumers, and dealers are contributing to the goals of providing products not injurious to health.

(B) The manner in which the Corporation has used its economic power to contribute to the social welfare of the nation.

(C) The manner by which the participation of diverse sectors of society in corporate decision-making can be increased including nomination and election of Directors and selection of members of the committees of the Board of Directors.

4. The Committee's report shall be distributed to the Stockholders and to the public no later than ______, 19__. The Committee shall be authorized to employ staff members in the performance of its duties. The Board of Directors shall allocate to the Committee those funds the Board of Directors determines reasonably necessary for the Committee to accomplish its tasks. The Committee may obtain any information from the Corporation and its employees reasonably deemed relevant by the Committee, provided, however, that

the Board of Directors may restrict the information to be made available to the Committee to information which the Board of Directors reasonably determines to be not privileged for business or competitive reasons.

Option 1 (Not Preferred for Smoothly Running Closely Held Corporations)

The following vote on the above resolution was counted:

(a) Yes: [*Number*];

(b) No: [*Number*];

(c) Abstentions: [*Number*];

(d) Persons demanding that their objections be noted and the reasons for their objections: __________.

COMMENTS

Argument for: The purpose of this resolution is to enable Stockholders to assess the public impact of the Corporation's decisions and to determine the proper role of the Corporation in society. Only a committee representing a broad segment of the public with adequate resources and access to information can prepare a report which will accomplish these objectives.

Argument against: The proposed committee would be inadvisable for two reasons. First, the extremely broad scope of duties of this committee range on the one hand from the day-to-day functioning of the Corporation's business—a full-time task of management which would be disrupted rather than assisted by the committee's work—to broad policy matters which are the sole responsibility of the Board of Directors of the Corporation.

Second, outsiders who have no accountability to the Corporation's Stockholders should not, in our opinion, be permitted to inject themselves into the corporate decision-making process. Directors are *elected* representatives whose responsibility is to the Stockholders, and to the employees, customers and the public. This responsibility should not be shifted to a committee having among its members persons with no accountability to the owners of the Corporation.

§ 48.42 Commuter Van Plan

Resolved that the [*Board of Directors/Stockholders ratify as executed/adopt as proposed*] a Commuter Van Plan which has the following features:

(a) Participants: [*Describe*]

(b) Van routes and time: [*Describe*]

COMMENT

See Employee Benefit Plans Volume, with respect to commuter van plans.

Option 1 (Preferred as a Matter of Practical Experience)

The Secretary shall make part of the minute book a copy of the same.

Option 2 (Not Preferred for Smoothly Running Closely Held Corporations)

The following Officers are authorized to execute the same: President and Secretary.

Option 3 (Not Preferred Unless There Is to Be a Consent Meeting and All Those Voting Won't Actually Review the Transaction)

The President shall do all things reasonable and necessary to carry out the purposes of the Deferred Compensation Plan and to that end he shall:

(a) Distribute the necessary Notice to participants.

Option 4 (Not Preferred for Smoothly Running Closely Held Corporations)

The following vote on the above resolution was counted:

(a) Yes: [*Number*];

(b) No: [*Number*];

(c) Abstentions: [*Number*];

(d) Persons demanding that their objections be noted and the reasons for their objections: ___________.

§ 48.43 Consent to Use of a Name Similar to the Corporate Name

Resolved that the [*Board of Directors/Stockholders ratify as executed/adopt as proposed*] a Written Consent for another Corporation to use a Name similar to the corporate Name which has the following features:

(a) Name to be used: ___________.

(b) Consideration being paid: ___________.

(c) Name of Corporation which will use the name: ___________.

Option 1 (Preferred as a Matter of Practical Experience)

The Secretary shall make part of the minute book a copy of the same.

Option 2 (Not Preferred for Smoothly Running Closely Held Corporations)

The following Officers are authorized to execute the same: President

Option 3 (Not Preferred Unless There Is to Be a Consent Meeting and All Those Voting Won't Actually Review the Transaction)

The President shall do all things reasonable and necessary to carry out the purposes of the Written Consent to Use of a Name Similar to the Corporate Name and to that end he shall:

(a) File the same with the relevant State.

(b) Execute the compensation agreement.

Option 4 (Not Preferred for Smoothly Running Closely Held Corporations or Consent Meetings)

The following vote on the above resolution was counted:

(a) Yes: [*Number*];

(b) No: [*Number*];

(c) Abstentions: [*Number*];

(d) Persons demanding that their objections be noted and the reasons for their objections: ___________.

§ 48.44 Contribution to Privately Endowed University

Whereas, it appears that there is a growing recognition that Corporations which in their own capacities enjoy many of the benefits of citizenship are under an obligation, greater in times of prosperity, to assume their part of the burdens of citizenship, one such burden being the support of voluntary charity, including the privately supported universities and colleges;

Whereas, it appears that in order to maintain, over a period of time, the conditions under which corporations in general and this Corporation in particular can exist and do business for profit, it is necessary that understanding of the benefits to the nation flowing from private enterprise and corporate organization be continued and if possible broadened and strengthened;

Whereas, it appears that fundamental to such understanding is a knowledge of history, government, economics and kindred subjects;

Whereas, it appears that ______ University is one of the most important centers of such teaching in the State of ______;

Whereas, it appears that ______ University is facing a progressively widening gap between the income from its endowment and the budgetary needs of its present program, before taking into consideration needs for expansion and development; and

Whereas, it appears that through a moderate gift to ______ University this Corporation may assume its share of the aforementioned burdens of citizenship and thus gain the present benefit of public recognition of its existence within the civic and social as well as within the legal and economic structure of society.

Now, therefore, it is resolved:

(1) that it is in the best interests of this Corporation that it join with others in the 19__ Annual Giving to ______ University, to the extent of a contribution of $______ toward the maintenance of the University;

(2) that the sum of $______ is hereby appropriated for that purpose, to be transmitted by the treasurer of this Corporation to ______ University.

Option 1 (Not Preferred for Smoothly Running Closely Held Corporations)

The following vote on the above resolution was counted:

(a) Yes: [*Number*];

(b) No: [*Number*];

(c) Abstentions: [*Number*];

(d) Persons demanding that their objections be noted and the reasons for their objections: ______________.

§ 48.45 Contributions to Qualified Retirement Plans

Resolved, that the Treasurer having reported that the following qualifying compensation(s) were paid during the past fiscal year to the Corporation's employees, the following total contributions shall be made to the Corporation's Qualified Retirement plans for the fiscal year:

Participants' Names	Qualifying Compensation	Profit Sharing Plan	Pension Plan	ESOT

Provided, however, that said contribution(s) shall be conditioned on qualification of said plan(s) under Sections 401, 403(a), and 405

(a) of the Internal Revenue Code and if such plan(s) do not so qualify then they shall be returned to this Corporation within one (1) year of the date of denial of qualification of the plan.

Provided further, that any contribution made which was made as a result of a mistake of fact shall be returned to this Corporation within one (1) year of such contribution if the Board of Directors so demands it.

COMMENT

This language is necessary in order to allow the Corporation to take back such contribution if there is a mistake of fact.

Option 1 (Not Preferred for Smoothly Running Closely Held Corporations)

The following vote on the above resolution was counted:

(a) Yes: __________.

(b) No: __________.

(c) Abstentions: __________.

(d) Persons demanding that their objection be noted and the reasons for their objections: __________.

§ 48.46 Day Care Plan

Resolved that the [*Board of Directors/Stockholders ratify as executed/adopt as proposed*] a Day Care Plan which has the following features:

(a) Care provided: [*Describe*].

(b) Participant's: __________.

COMMENT

See Employee Benefit Plans Volume, for such plans.

Option 1 (Preferred as a Matter of Practical Experience)

The Secretary shall make part of the minute book a copy of the same.

Option 2 (Not Preferred for Smoothly Running Closely Held Corporations)

The following Officers are authorized to execute the same: President.

Option 3 (Not Preferred Unless There Is to Be a Consent Meeting and All Those Voting Won't Actually Review the Transaction)

The President shall do all things reasonable and necessary to carry out the purposes of the Deferred Compensation Plan and to that end he shall:

(a) Distribution of the necessary Notice and summary to participants.

(b) Execute and filing of the necessary form with the Department of Labor.

Options 4 (Not Preferred for Smoothly Running Closely Held Corporations)

The following vote on the above resolution was counted:

(a) Yes: [*Number*];

(b) No: [*Number*];

(c) Abstentions: [*Number*];

(d) Persons demanding that their objections be noted and the reasons for their objections: __________.

§ 48.47 Death Benefit Only Plan

Resolved that the [*Board of Directors/Stockholders ratify as executed/adopt as proposed*] a Death Benefit Only Plan which has the following features:

(a) Name of Plan: __________.

(b) Participant's employment status or name: __________.

(c) Benefit description: __________.

COMMENT

See Employee Benefit Plans Volume, for such plans.

Option 1 (Preferred as a Matter of Practical Experience)

The Secretary shall make part of the minute book a copy of the same.

Option 2 (Not Preferred for Smoothly Running Closely Held Corporations)

The following Officers are authorized to execute the same: President and Secretary.

Option 3 (Not Preferred Unless There Is to Be a Consent Meeting and All Those Voting Won't Actually Review the Transaction)

The President shall do all things reasonable and necessary to carry out the purposes of the Death Benefit Only Plan and to that end he shall:

(a) Distribution of the necessary Notice and summary to participants.

(b) Execute and filing of the necessary EBS–1 form with the Department of Labor.

(c) Establish procedures for (and carrying out such procedures) the execution by all participants of beneficiary designations.

Option 4 (Not Preferred for Smoothly Running Closely Held Corporations)

The following vote on the above resolution was counted:

(a) Yes: [*Number*];

(b) No: [*Number*];

(c) Abstentions: [*Number*];

(d) Persons demanding that their objections be noted and the reasons for their objections: ______.

§ 48.48 Deed to Real Property

Resolved, that this Corporation sell and convey to ______, of ______, that certain parcel of land hereinafter described and that the President and Secretary of this Corporation be and they are hereby authorized and directed to execute and deliver to said ______ a deed covering property owned by this Corporation, lying and being in the City of ______, County of ______ and State of ______, known and described as follows: [*Here Describe*].

Option 1 (Not Preferred for Smoothly Running Closely Held Corporations)

The following vote on the above resolution was counted:

(a) Yes: [*Number*];

(b) No: [*Number*];

(c) Abstentions: [*Number*];

(d) Persons demanding that their objections be noted and the reasons for their objections: ______.

Library References:

C.J.S. Corporations § 1098.
West's Key No. Digests, Corporations ⚷442.

§ 48.49 Deferred Compensation Plan

Resolved that the [*Board of Directors/Stockholders ratify as executed/adopt as proposed*] a Deferred Compensation Plan which has the following features:

(a) Name of Plan: ________.

(b) Participant's employment status or name: ________.

(c) Benefit Description:

(1) Benefit on Death: ________.

(2) Benefit on Disability: ________.

(3) Benefit on Retirement or Termination before age 65: ________.

(4) Benefit on Retirement or Termination after age 65: ________.

(d) Any salary payment or other payment made to or on behalf of an Officer of the Corporation which shall be disallowed in whole or in part as a deductible expense for Federal income tax purposes, shall be reimbursed by such Officer to the Corporation to the full extent of the disallowance. It shall be the duty of the Board of Directors to enforce payment of each such amount disallowed.

COMMENT TO (d)

One question that arises in the case of an employee benefit is the reasonableness of the benefit in light of the total compensation paid. If it is reasonable, the deduction will be available; if the total compensation is not reasonable, the deduction will not be available. The Internal Revenue Service will attempt to claim, in the case of a Corporation, that an unreasonably high payment was in the nature of a dividend to a Stockholder-employee, which was both not deductible to the Corporation and not subject to the maximum tax limitations on earned income. The popular solution to this problem is a "double dip" provision (the government is dipping twice into the transaction) in the corporate minutes which requires repayment of the disallowed benefit to the Corporation leaving the Corporation and the employee in the same position they would have been in if the payment had not been made. The government is presently trying to thwart the use of such a provision by asserting that its existence is prima facie evidence of the unreasonableness of the payment. Given the pervasive use of this provision, this "damned if you do or don't" assertion is absurd and, if carried to its logical extension, would negate all tax planning which was based upon a written assertion of the tax results being sought.

GENERAL COMMENT

See Employee Benefit Plans Volume, for deferred compensation plans.

Option 1 (Preferred as a Matter of Practical Experience)

The Secretary shall make part of the minute book a copy of the same.

Option 2 (Not Preferred for Smoothly Running Closely Held Corporations)

The following Officers are authorized to execute the same: President and Secretary.

Option 3 (Not Preferred Unless There Is to Be a Consent Meeting and All Those Voting Won't Actually Review the Transaction)

The President shall do all things reasonable and necessary to carry out the purposes of the Deferred Compensation Plan and to that end he shall:

(a) Distribute the necessary Notice and summary to participants.

(b) Execute and File the necessary EBS–1 form with the Department of Labor.

(c) Establish procedures for (and carrying out such procedures) the execution by all participants of beneficiary designations and the election or refusal of a joint and survivor benefit.

Option 4 (Not Preferred for Smoothly Running Closely Held Corporations)

The following vote on the above resolution was counted:

(a) Yes: [*Number*];

(b) No: [*Number*];

(c) Abstentions: [*Number*];

(d) Persons demanding that their objections be noted and the reasons for their objections: ____________.

§ 48.50 Depositary Bank

Resolved, by the Board of Directors of _______,

1. That the _______ Bank, be, and it is hereby, designated as one of the Depositaries of the funds of this Corporation, and that the _______ or the _______ or the _______ of this Corporation be, and each of them hereby is, authorized to deposit in said Depositary funds of this Corporation and to endorse in the name of this Corporation for that purpose checks, drafts, notes and other like obligations.

2. That said _______ Bank be, and it is hereby, authorized to pay out funds on deposit with it from time to time to the credit of this Corporation upon checks drawn upon said Depositary and signed in the name of this Corporation by its _______ or _______ and countersigned by its _______ or _______.

3. That the ______ or ______ and ______ or ______ of this Corporation be, and they are hereby, authorized from time to time to borrow money from said ______ Bank in such amounts, for such length of time and at such rates of interest and upon such other terms and conditions as said officers may deem expedient, and to secure the payment of money so borrowed, and to evidence the indebtedness thereby created to execute and deliver in the name and behalf of this Corporation promissory notes, judgment promissory notes and other like obligations of this Corporation, signed in the name of this Corporation by said ______ or ______ and ______ or ______ and to pledge as security for the payment of said notes and other obligations any property or securities now or hereafter belonging to this Corporation, which notes or other obligations shall be in such form and shall contain such terms, provisions and conditions as may be deemed proper by such officers.

4. That said ______ Bank shall not be in any manner responsible for or required to see to the application of any of the funds deposited with it or borrowed from it as hereinabove provided.

5. That ______, the Secretary of this Corporation, shall file with the ______, a certified copy of this resolution, under the seal of the Corporation, and shall also file with said ______ Bank a list of the persons at the present time holding offices of ______ and ______, in this Corporation, and said ______ Bank shall be entitled as against this Corporation to conclusively presume that the persons so certified as holding such offices continue to respectively hold the same until otherwise notified in writing by the Secretary of this Corporation.

6. That this resolution shall be in full force and effect and binding upon this Corporation until it shall have been repealed and until written notice of such repeal shall have been delivered to said ______ Bank at its office in the City of ______.

Library References:

C.J.S. Corporations § 768 et seq.
West's Key No. Digests, Corporations ⚿312(1).

§ 48.51 Directors—Qualifications

Resolved that any candidate nominated by management for election to the Board of Directors shall be so nominated without regard to his or her sex. No attorney associated with the Corporation's outside legal counsel shall be eligible for election to the Board of Directors. This resolution shall take effect on ______, 19__.

Option 1 (Not Preferred for Smoothly Running Closely Held Corporations)

The following vote on the above resolution was counted:

(a) Yes: [*Number*];

(b) No: [*Number*];

(c) Abstentions: [*Number*];

(d) Persons demanding that their objections be noted and the reasons for their objections: ______________.

§ 48.52 Disability Income Plan

Resolved that the [*Board of Directors/Stockholders ratify as executed/adopt as proposed*] a Disability Income Plan which has the following features:

(1) Carrier: __________.

(2) Wait upon accidental disability: __________.

(3) Wait up sickness: __________.

(4) Benefit per week: $__________.

(5) Participant description: __________.

(6) Any salary payment or other payment made to or on behalf of an Officer of the Corporation which shall be disallowed in whole or in part as a deductible expense for Federal income tax purposes, shall be reimbursed by such Officer to the Corporation to the full extent of the disallowance. It shall be the duty of the Board of Directors to enforce payment of each such amount disallowed.

COMMENT TO (6)

One question that arises in the case of an employee benefit is the reasonableness of the benefit in light of the total compensation paid. If it is reasonable, the deduction will be available; if the total compensation is not reasonable, the deduction will not be available. The Internal Revenue Service will attempt to claim, in the case of a Corporation, that an unreasonably high payment was in the nature of a dividend to a Stockholder-employee, which was both not deductible to the Corporation and not subject to the maximum tax limitations on earned income. The popular solution to this problem is a "double dip" provision (the government is dipping twice into the transaction) in the corporate minutes which requires repayment of the disallowed benefit to the Corporation leaving the Corporation and the employee in the same position they would have been in if the payment had not been made. The government is presently trying to thwart the use of such a provision by asserting that its existence is prima facie evidence of the unreasonableness of the payment. Given the pervasive use of this provision, this "damned if you do or don't" assertion is absurd and, if carried to its logical extension, would negate all tax planning which was based upon a written assertion of the tax results being sought.

GENERAL COMMENT

See Employee Benefit Plans Volume, for such disability income plans.

Option 1 (Preferred as a Matter of Practical Experience)

The Secretary shall make part of the minute book a copy of the same.

Option 2 (Not Preferred for Smoothly Running Closely Held Corporations)

The following Officers are authorized to execute the same: President.

Option 3 (Preferred as a Matter of Practical Experience)

The President shall do all things reasonable and necessary to carry out the purposes of the Disability Plan and to that end he shall be responsible for the:

(a) Distribution of the necessary disclosure summary to participants.

(b) Execute and File the necessary EBS–1 form with the Department of Labor.

(c) Pay plan expenses as required or reasonably necessary.

Option 4 (Not Preferred for Smoothly Running Closely Held Corporations)

The following vote on the above resolution was counted:

(a) Yes: [*Number*];

(b) No: [*Number*];

(c) Abstentions: [*Number*];

(d) Persons demanding that their objections be noted and the reasons for their objections: ____________.

§ 48.53 Director's Fees

Resolved that the following Director's fees be paid: [*Describe*].

Option 1 (Not Preferred for Smoothly Running Closely Held Corporations)

The following vote on the above resolution was counted:

(a) Yes: [*Number*];

(b) No: [*Number*];

(c) Abstentions: [*Number*];

(d) Persons demanding that their objections be noted and the reasons for their objections: ________________.

§ 48.54 Distribution-in-Kind in Partial Liquidation

Whereas, this Corporation presently is the owner of miscellaneous properties;

Whereas, the Board of Directors deem it good business and advisable to make a partial liquidation of the Corporation and to pay out certain properties of the Corporation valued at $______ as a distribution in kind ratably to the Stockholders of record on the ______ day of ______, 19__; and

Whereas, the payment of a partial liquidating distribution may be changed to the capital surplus of the Corporation,

Now, therefore, be it resolved, that a partial liquidating distribution should be declared and paid as of ______, 19__, said dividend to be paid in properties in kind valued at $______ and consisting of the following described properties: [*Here Describe.*]

Resolved, further, that a special meeting of Stockholders be called on ______, 19__, at ______ __m., to consider approval of the foregoing resolution.

Option 1 (Not Preferred for Smoothly Running Closely Held Corporations)

The following vote on the above resolution was counted:

(a) Yes: [*Number*];

(b) No: [*Number*];

(c) Abstentions: [*Number*];

(d) Persons demanding that their objections be noted and the reasons for their objections: ________________.

COMMENT

Where a partial liquidation in kind is contemplated, the value of the property to be distributed should be expressed in dollars to ensure that the distribution is properly recorded and that the applicable statutory provisions are complied with. Presumably a valuation expressed in good faith will be accepted by a state Court, but not necessarily by the Internal Revenue Service, though there is no provision making the decision of the Directors in this regard final in the absence of fraud.

§ 48.55 Distribution in Partial Liquidation

Resolved, that the Corporation pay each Stockholder of record of the Corporation on ______, 19__, the sum of $______ per share out of the capital surplus of the Corporation in partial liquidation; and

Resolved further, that the foregoing resolution be submitted to a meeting of the Stockholders called for that purpose to consider the advisability of making such a distribution in partial liquidation; and

Resolved further, that if at least two-thirds of the outstanding shares of each class, including nonvoting shares, approve said resolution, then such payment shall be made on ______, 19__;

Resolved, further, that the Corporation advise each Stockholder upon the distribution of such sum that the payment is in partial liquidation of the Corporation and made out of capital surplus.

Option 1 *(Not Preferred for Smoothly Running Closely Held Corporations)*

The following vote on the above resolution was counted:

(a) Yes: [*Number*];

(b) No: [*Number*];

(c) Abstentions: [*Number*];

(d) Persons demanding that their objections be noted and the reasons for their objections: ______________.

COMMENTS

A distribution in partial liquidation out of capital surplus or reduction surplus is commonly authorized by the Model Bus. Corp. Act, 46. Such a payment, which appears to be indistinguishable from a dividend out of capital, is hedged by significant limitations relating not only to the impact of the distribution on the Corporation's financial affairs, but also to its effect on senior securities holders.

The tax treatment of a distribution which is in "partial liquidation" under such Corporation acts is determined by independent considerations. It may constitute a tax-free return of capital that reduces the basis of the stock. Or, it may constitute a taxable dividend if, for example, the Corporation has earnings in the current year even though it has a net deficit overall. See the discussion of the federal income taxation of dividends and distributions in Chapter 57, infra.

"Reduction surplus" is the surplus created by a reduction in the stated capital of the Corporation in any of several ways. Reduction surplus may also be distributed to Stockholders in partial liquidation in the same manner as capital surplus.

§ 48.56 Distribution in Partial Liquidation—Another Form

Resolved, that the Corporation distribute to its Stockholders in partial liquidation, out of capital surplus [*Reduction Surplus*] the sum of $______;

Resolved further, that the Corporation advise each Stockholder upon the distribution of such sum that the payment is in partial liquidation of the Corporation and made out of capital surplus [*Reduction Surplus*].

Option 1 (Not Preferred for Smoothly Running Closely Held Corporations)

The following vote on the above resolution was counted:

(a) Yes: [*Number*];

(b) No: [*Number*];

(c) Abstentions: [*Number*];

(d) Persons demanding that their objections be noted and the reasons for their objections: ________________.

Library References:

C.J.S. Corporations § 462 et seq.
West's Key No. Digests, Corporations ⚷152.

§ 48.57 Dividend

Resolved that the [*Board of Directors/Stockholders ratify as executed/adopt as proposed*] a dividend which has the following features:

(a) Shares on which dividend is being paid: [*Describe*].

(b) Amount per share: $____________.

(c) Record Date of Stockholders who will receive dividends: ____________.

(d) Date of Payment: ____________.

Option 1 (Not Preferred Unless There Is to Be a Consent Meeting and All Those Voting Won't Actually Review the Transaction)

The Treasurer shall do all things reasonable and necessary to carry out the purposes of the dividend and to that end he shall:

(a) Cause the necessary checks to be issued and distributed.

(b) Distribute Internal Revenue Service form 1099 to all Stockholders receiving a dividend and filing the same with the Internal Revenue Service.

Option 2 (Not Preferred for Smoothly Running Closely Held Corporations)

The following vote on the above resolution was counted:

(a) Yes: [*Number*];

(b) No: [*Number*];

(c) Abstentions: [*Number*];

(d) Persons demanding that their objections be noted and the reasons for their objections: ______.

§ 48.58 Dividend-in-Kind

Resolved, that a dividend consisting of three shares of the common stock of the ______ Corporation, par value of $1.00 per share, received in part consideration for the disposition of certain property of this Corporation, on each share of the capital stock of this Corporation be and the same is hereby declared, payable to the holders of record of shares of this Corporation as of the ______ day of ______, payable on the ______ day of ______.

Option 1 (Not Preferred for Smoothly Running Closely Held Corporations)

The following vote on the above resolution was counted:

(a) Yes: [*Number*];

(b) No: [*Number*];

(c) Abstentions: [*Number*];

(d) Persons demanding that their objections be noted and the reasons for their objections: ______.

§ 48.59 Dividend-in-Kind—Another Form

Whereas, the financial statements furnished by the Treasurer of this Corporation to the Board of Directors are believed by the directors to be an accurate statement of the financial condition of the company on the last day of the fiscal year ending the ______ day of ______, 19__, and

Whereas, the balance sheet shows that this Corporation has unreserved surplus, other than surplus arising from unrealized appreciation in value or revaluation of its assets, of $______.

Therefore, be it resolved, that the ______ shares of the common stock of the ______ Corporation, par value ______ dollars each, received in part consideration of the sale of this Corporation's plant at ______, be divided among the Stockholders of this Corporation, and that a dividend of ______ shares of the ______ Corporation, to and for each share of stock of this Corporation, be and the same is hereby declared and made to the Stockholders of this Corporation, which said dividend of stock shall be transferred, delivered, and paid when and as soon as all of the Stockholders of this Corporation shall assent to and ratify the said dividend.

Option 1 *(Not Preferred for Smoothly Running Closely Held Corporations)*

The following vote on the above resolution was counted:

(a) Yes: [*Number*];

(b) No: [*Number*];

(c) Abstentions: [*Number*];

(d) Persons demanding that their objections be noted and the reasons for their objections: ________________.

§ 48.60 Dividend—One Class of Stock

Whereas, the Board of Directors has considered the financial statements of the Corporation for the period ending ______, 19__, represented to be correct by ______, President of the Corporation, and has concluded on the basis of such statements that the Corporation may pay the dividend set forth below.

Resolved, that a dividend of ______ Dollars per share on the issued and outstanding capital stock of this Corporation is hereby declared, payable to the holders of record of shares as of the ______ day of ______, payable on the ______ day of ______.

Option 1 *(Not Preferred for Smoothly Running Closely Held Corporations)*

The following vote on the above resolution was counted:

(a) Yes: [*Number*];

(b) No: [*Number*];

(c) Abstentions: [*Number*];

(d) Persons demanding that their objections be noted and the reasons for their objections: ________________.

COMMENTS

It is belived desirable to make specific reference to the basis on which the decision to declare a dividend is made. If the Corporation employs a certified or independent public accountant, the phrase "certified by ______ fairly to reflect the financial condition of the corporation" should be substituted. A Director is also excused from liability if "in the exercise of ordinary care and in good faith, in determining the amount available for any such dividend or distribution, he considered the assets to be of their book value."

As indicated in other forms, dividend declarations are sometimes phrased as a percentage of the par value of the shares. This is more commonly done with preferred rather than common shares, and probably should be avoided where nominal par value shares are involved.

§ 48.61 Dividend—One Class of Stock—Another Form

Resolved, that a dividend of ______ Dollars a share of the capital stock of this Corporation be declared out of the unreserved and unrestricted earned surplus, and that the Treasurer is directed forthwith to mail checks for the same to the Stockholders of record on the ______ day of ______, 19__.

Option 1 (Not Preferred for Smoothly Running Closely Held Corporations)

The following vote on the above resolution was counted:

(a) Yes: [*Number*];

(b) No: [*Number*];

(c) Absentions: [*Number*];

(d) Persons demanding that their objections be noted and the reasons for their objections: ______________.

§ 48.62 Dividend—One Class of Stock—Another Form

Resolved, that a dividend of ______ dollars per share on the issued and outstanding capital stock of this Corporation is hereby declared, payable to the holders of record of shares as of the ______ day of ______, payable on the ______ day of ______.

Option 1 (Not Preferred for Smoothly Running Closely Held Corporations)

The following vote on the above resolution was counted:

(a) Yes: [*Number*];

(b) No: [*Number*];

(c) Absentions: [*Number*];

(d) Persons demanding that their objections be noted and the reasons for their objections: ______________.

§ 48.63 Dividend—Payable in Stock of Another Corporation

Resolved, that the ______ shares of the common stock of the ______ Corporation, par value ______ Dollars each, received in part consideration of the sale of the Corporation's plant at ______, be divided among the Stockholders of this Corporation, and that a dividend of ______ shares of said common stock of the ______ Corporation, to and for each share of stock of this Corporation, be and the same is hereby declared and made to the Stockholders of this Corporation, which said dividend of stock shall be transferred, delivered, and paid when and as soon as all of the Stockholders of this Corporation shall assent to and ratify the said dividend.

Option 1 (Not Preferred for Smoothly Running Closely Held Corporations)

The following vote on the above resolution was counted:

(a) Yes: [*Number*];

(b) No: [*Number*];

(c) Absentions: [*Number*];

(d) Persons demanding that their objections be noted and the reasons for their objections: ________________.

§ 48.64 Dividend—Payable in Stock of Another Corporation—Another Form

From the report furnished the meeting on the financial condition of the Corporation for the fiscal year ended ______, 19__ and for each of the subsequent months, it appeared that the Corporation was in a position to declare and pay a dividend in property upon its outstanding shares of common stock.

Thereupon, after discussion it was on motion duly made, seconded and unanimously adopted by the affirmative vote of the Directors present:

Resolved, that a dividend on the outstanding shares of common stock of this Corporation be and it hereby is declared and ordered to be paid in property of this Corporation, to-wit, shares of common stock of ______ Company owned by this Corporation at the rate of ______ shares of common stock of said ______ Corporation for each share of common stock of this Corporation issued and outstanding. Said dividend to be payable on ______, 19__ to the holders of record of said common stock of this Corporation at the close of business on ______, 19__ from the net surplus of this Corporation as at the close of business on ______, 19__, or from the net profits of this Corporation for its current fiscal year; and

Further Resolved, that the proper officers of the Corporation be and they hereby are authorized and directed in the name and on behalf of the Corporation to do or cause to be done all acts or things necessary or proper to carry out the foregoing resolution.

Option 1 (Not Preferred for Smoothly Running Closely Held Corporations)

The following vote on the above resolution was counted:

(a) Yes: [*Number*];

(b) No: [*Number*];

(c) Absentions: [*Number*];

(d) Persons demanding that their objections be noted and the reasons for their objections: ________________.

§ 48.65 Dividend—Payable in Stock of Another Corporation—Another Form

Resolved, that the ______ shares of the common shares of the ______ Corporation, of the par value of ______ ($______) Dollars each, representing surplus of this Corporation, (received in part consideration of the sale of the Corporation's plant at No. ______ ______ Street, City of ______, County of ______, State of ______,) be divided among the Stockholders of this Corporation, and that a dividend of ______ shares of said common shares of the ______ Corporation, to and for each share of this Corporation, be and the same is hereby declared and made to the Stockholders of this Corporation, which said dividend of shares shall be transferred, delivered, and paid to Stockholders of record as shown by the records of this Corporation as of the ______ day of ______, 19__.

Option 1 (Not Preferred for Smoothly Running Closely Held Corporations)

The following vote on the above resolution was counted:

(a) Yes: [*Number*];

(b) No: [*Number*];

(c) Absentions: [*Number*];

(d) Persons demanding that their objections be noted and the reasons for their objections: ______________.

§ 48.66 Dividend—Payable in Stock of Another Corporation—Another Form

From the report furnished this meeting on the financial condition of the Corporation for the fiscal year ended ______, 19__ and for each of the subsequent months, it appears that the Corporation is in a position to declare and pay a dividend in property upon its outstanding common shares,

Resolved, that a dividend on the outstanding common shares of this Corporation be declared and is hereby ordered to be paid in property of this Corporation, to-wit: shares of common shares of ______ Company, Inc., owned by this Corporation, at the rate of ______ shares of common shares of said ______ Company, Inc., for each common share of this Corporation issued and outstanding. Said dividend is to be payable on ______, 19__ to the holders of record of said common shares of this Corporation at the close of business on ______, 19__ from the surplus of this Corporation as at the close of business on ______, 19__, and it is further

Resolved, that the proper Officers of the Corporation be and they hereby are authorized and directed in the name and on behalf of the

Corporation to do or cause to be done all acts or things necessary or proper to carry out the foregoing resolution.

Option 1 (Not Preferred for Smoothly Running Closely Held Corporations)

The following vote on the above resolution was counted:

(a) Yes: [*Number*];

(b) No: [*Number*];

(c) Abstentions: [*Number*];

(d) Persons demanding that their objections be noted and the reasons for their objections: ________________.

§ 48.67 Dividend—Preferred and Common Stock

Whereas, the annual inventory has been taken, the accounts closed and it appears from the financial records prepared by ______, a certified public accountant and represented by him fairly to reflect the financial condition of the Corporation that the Corporation has had a net profit of ______ Dollars; and whereas, over ______ Dollars of the profits are deposited in the Corporation's bank account and are not now required in the operation of the business:

Now, therefore, resolved, that a semiannual dividend of ______ per cent be declared on the outstanding preferred stock of this Corporation, and that an extra dividend of ______ per cent be declared on the outstanding common stock of this Corporation, the dividends to be payable to the Stockholders of record of ______, 19__; and it is further resolved, that the Treasurer forthwith notify the Stockholders of the declaration of the dividends, and he is further authorized and directed to pay the dividends on ______, 19__, and to do anything necessary or incidental thereto.

Option 1 (Not Preferred for Smoothly Running Closely Held Corporations)

The following vote on the above resolution was counted:

(a) Yes: [*Number*];

(b) No: [*Number*];

(c) Absentions: [*Number*];

(d) Persons demanding that their objections be noted and the reasons for their objections: ________________.

§ 48.68 Dividend—Preferred and Common Stock—Another Form

Whereas, the financial statements furnished by the Treasurer of this Corporation to the Board of Directors are believed by the

Directors to be an accurate statement of the financial condition of the Corporation on the last day of the fiscal year ending the ______ day of ______, 19__, and

Whereas, the balance sheet shows that this Corporation has unreserved surplus, other than surplus arising from unrealized appreciation in value or revaluation of its assets, of $______.

Therefore, be it resolved, that a dividend of ______ per cent be paid on the preferred stock issued and outstanding, and a dividend of $______ per share on the common stock issued and outstanding, payable to the holders of stock as shown by the records of the Corporation as of the ______ day of ______, 19__, distributable on the ______ day of ______, 19__.

Option 1 (Not Preferred for Smoothly Running Closely Held Corporations)

The following vote on the above resolution was counted:

(a) Yes: [*Number*];

(b) No: [*Number*];

(c) Absentions: [*Number*];

(d) Persons demanding that their objections be noted and the reasons for their objections: ______________.

§ 48.69 Dividend—Preferred and Common Stock—Another Form

Resolved, that a dividend of ______ per cent be paid on the preferred stock, and a dividend of ______ per cent on the common stock, payable to holders of stock as shown by the records of the Corporation as of the ______ day of ______, 19__, distributable on the ______ day of ______, 19__.

Option 1 (Not Preferred for Smoothly Running Closely Held Corporations)

The following vote on the above resolution was counted:

(a) Yes: [*Number*];

(b) No: [*Number*];

(c) Absentions: [*Number*];

(d) Persons demanding that their objections be noted and the reasons for their objections: ______________.

§ 48.70 Dividend—Preferred and Common Stock—Another Form

Whereas, the financial statement of the Treasurer shows surplus net profits arising from the business of this Corporation of $______ for the calendar year just ended; and

Whereas, over $______ of said profits are deposited in the Corporation's bank account and are not now required in the operation of the business:

Resolved, that a semiannual dividend of ______ per cent be declared on the outstanding preferred stock of this Corporation, and that an extra dividend of ______ per cent be declared on the outstanding common stock of this Corporation, the said dividends to be payable to the Stockholders of record on ______, 19__; and

Further resolved, that the Treasurer is authorized and directed to pay said dividends on ______, 19__, and to do anything necessary or incidental thereto.

Option 1 (Not Preferred for Smoothly Running Closely Held Corporations)

The following vote on the above resolution was counted:

(a) Yes: [*Number*];

(b) No: [*Number*];

(c) Absentions: [*Number*];

(d) Persons demanding that their objections be noted and the reasons for their objections: ______________.

§ 48.71 Dividend—Preferred—Payable Out of Capital Surplus

Resolved that a distribution be made from unrestricted capital surplus to the holders of the outstanding preferred shares of the Corporation which have cumulative preferential right to receive dividends in such amount as shall discharge said cumulative dividend rights.

Option 1 (Not Preferred for Smoothly Running Closely Held Corporations)

The following vote on the above resolution was counted:

(a) Yes: [*Number*];

(b) No: [*Number*];

(c) Absentions: [*Number*];

(d) Persons demanding that their objections be noted and the reasons for their objections: ______________.

COMMENTS

Use of capital surplus to discharge cumulative preferential dividend rights is commonly authorized by the Model Bus.Corp. Act, § 46. The theory is that this enables a Corporation to avoid building up a heavy burden of unpaid cumulative dividend obligations in the early years of its operations.

The preferred Stockholders must be advised of the source of the distribution. See Form § 55.36, infra.

§ 48.72 Dividend—Record Date

Resolved, that ______ o'clock ___M., [*Eastern Daylight Saving Time,*] on the ______ day prior to the date fixed for the payment of any dividend on the shares of the Corporation is hereby fixed as the record date for the determination of Stockholders entitled to receive payment of any such dividend, and only Stockholders of record at such time shall be entitled to receive such payment of dividends.

§ 48.73 Dividend—Several Classes of Stock

Whereas, the financial statement of the Treasurer of this Corporation shows earned surplus of the Corporation of ______ ($______) Dollars for the fiscal year beginning on the ______ day of ______, 19___, and ending on the ______ day of ______, 19___.

Therefore, be it:

Resolved, that ______ ($______) Dollars of said surplus be and the same hereby is set aside for the payment of dividends on the shares of this Corporation, and the Treasurer is hereby directed to pay to holders of shares as shown by the records of this Corporation as of the ______ day of ______, 19___, a dividend of ______ ($______) Dollars per share on the [*Class*] shares without par value issued and outstanding, and a dividend of ______ per cent on the par value of the [*Class*] shares issued and outstanding and a dividend of ______ per cent on the amount actually paid upon shares issued and outstanding as partly paid shares.

Option 1 (Not Preferred for Smoothly Running Closely Held Corporations)

The following vote on the above resolution was counted:

(a) Yes: [*Number*];

(b) No: [*Number*];

(c) Absentions: [*Number*];

(d) Persons demanding that their objections be noted and the reasons for their objections: ______________.

§ 48.74 Double Dip

Resolved, that any salary payment or other payment made to or on behalf of an officer of the Corporation which shall be disallowed in whole or in part as a deductible expense for Federal income tax purposes, shall be reimbursed by such officer to the Corporation to the full extent of the disallowance. It shall be the duty of the Board of Directors to enforce payment of each such amount disallowed.

COMMENT

One question that arises in the case of an employee benefit is the reasonableness of the benefit in light of the total compensation paid. If it is reasonable, the deduction will be available; if the total compensation is not reasonable, the deduction will not be available. The Internal Revenue Service will attempt to claim, in the case of a Corporation, that an unreasonably high payment was in the nature of a dividend to a Stockholder-employee, which was both not deductible to the Corporation and not subject to the maximum tax limitations on earned income. The popular solution to this problem is a "double dip" provision (the government is dipping twice into the transaction) in the corporate minutes which requires repayment of the disallowed benefit to the Corporation leaving the Corporation and the employee in the same position they would have been in if the payment had not been made. The government is presently trying to thwart the use of such a provision by asserting that its existence is prima facie evidence of the unreasonableness of the payment. Given the pervasive use of this provision, this "damned if you do or don't" assertion is absurd and, if carried to its logical extension, would negate all tax planning which includes in its documentation assertion of the tax results being sought.

Option 1 (Not Preferred for Smoothly Running Closely Held Corporations)

The following vote on the above resolution was counted:

(a) Yes: [*Number*];

(b) No: [*Number*];

(c) Abstentions: [*Number*];

(d) Persons demanding that their objections be noted and the reasons for their objections: __________.

§ 48.75 Educational Benefit Plan (Work Related)

Resolved that the [*Board of Directors/Stockholder ratify as executed/adopt as proposed*].

(a) A Work Related Educational Benefit Plan which has the following features per Participant:

(1) Days fully paid: __________.

(2) Maximum course charge/day: $__________.

(3) Maximum hotel allowance: $__________/day.

(4) Maximum meal allowance: $__________/day.

(5) Maximum entertainment: $__________/day.

(6) Participant Description: __________.

COMMENT

See Employee Benefit Plans Volume for form.

(b) Any salary payment or other payment made to or on behalf of an Officer of the Corporation which shall be disallowed in whole or in part as a deductible expense for Federal income tax purposes, shall be reimbursed by such Officer to the Corporation to the full extent of the disallowance. It shall be the duty of the Board of Directors to enforce payment of each such amount disallowed.

COMMENT TO (b)

One question that arises in the case of an employee benefit is the reasonableness of the benefit in light of the total compensation paid. If it is reasonable, the deduction will be available; if the total compensation is not reasonable, the deduction will not be available. The Internal Revenue Service will attempt to claim, in the case of a Corporation, that an unreasonably high payment was in the nature of a dividend to a Stockholder-employee, which was both not deductible to the Corporation and not subject to the maximum tax limitations on earned income. The popular solution to this problem is a "double dip" provision (the government is dipping twice into the transaction) in the corporate minutes which requires repayment of the disallowed benefit to the Corporation leaving the Corporation and the employee in the same position they would have been in if the payment had not been made. The government is presently trying to thwart the use of such a provision by asserting that its existence is prima facie evidence of the unreasonableness of the payment. Given the pervasive use of this provision, this "damned if you do or don't" assertion is absurd and, if carried to its logical extension, would negate all tax planning which was based upon a written assertion of the tax results being sought.

Option 1 (Preferred as a Matter of Practical Experience)

(c) The Secretary shall make part of the minute book a copy of the same.

Option 2 (Not Preferred for Smoothly Running Closely Held Corporations)

(d) The following Officers are authorized to execute the same: President and Secretary.

Option 3 (Not Preferred Unless There Is to Be a Consent Meeting and All Those Voting Won't Actually Review the Transaction)

(e) The President shall do all things reasonable and necessary to carry out the purposes of the Work Related Educational Benefit Plan and to that end he shall:

(1) Distribute the necessary disclosure summary to participants.

(2) Execute and File the necessary EBS–1 form with the Department of Labor.

(3) Pay plan expenses as required or reasonably necessary.

Option 4 (Not Preferred for Smoothly Running Closely Held Corporations)

(f) The following vote on the above resolution was counted:

(1) Yes: [*Number*];

(2) No: [*Number*];

(3) Abstentions: [*Number*];

(4) Persons demanding that their objections be noted and the reasons for their objections: __________.

§ 48.76 Educational Benefit Plans Non-Work Related

Resolved that the [*Board of Directors/Stockholders ratify as executed/adopt as proposed*]:

(a) A Non-Work Related Educational Benefit Plan which has the following features:

(1) Maximum Course cost and book costs per corporate fiscal year: $__________ per Participant.

(2) Participant Description: __________.

COMMENT

See Employee Benefit Plans Volume for form.

(b) Any salary payment or other payment made to or on behalf of an Officer of the Corporation which shall be disallowed in whole or in part as a deductible expense for Federal income tax purposes, shall be reimbursed by such Officer to the Corporation to the full extent of the disallowance. It shall be the duty of the Board of Directors to enforce payment of each such amount disallowed.

COMMENT TO (b)

One question that arises in the case of an employee benefit is the reasonableness of the benefit in light of the total compensation paid. If it is reasonable, the deduction will be available; if the total compensation is not reasonable, the deduction will not be available. The Internal Revenue Service will attempt to claim, in the case of a Corporation, that an unreasonably high payment was in the nature of a dividend to a Stockholder-employee, which was both not deductible to the Corporation and not subject to the maximum tax limitations on earned income. The popular solution to this problem is a "double dip" provision (the government is dipping twice into the transaction) in the corporate minutes which requires repayment of the disallowed benefit to the Corporation leaving the Corporation and the employee in the same position they would have been in if the payment had not been made. The government is presently trying to thwart the use of such a provision by asserting that its existence is prima facie evidence of the unreasonableness of the payment. Given the pervasive use of this provision, this "damned if you do or don't" assertion is absurd and, if carried to its logical extension, would negate all tax planning which was based upon a written assertion of the tax results being sought.

Option 1 (Preferred as a Matter of Practical Experience)

(c) The Secretary shall make part of the minute book a copy of the same.

Option 2 (Not Preferred for Smoothly Running Closely Held Corporations)

(d) The following Officers are authorized to execute the same: President and Secretary.

Option 3 (Not Preferred Unless There Is to Be a Consent Meeting and All Those Voting Won't Actually Review the Transaction)

(e) The President shall do all things reasonable and necessary to carry out the purposes of the Non-Work Related Educational Benefit Plan and to that end he shall:

(1) Distribute the necessary disclosure summary to participants.

(2) Execute and File the necessary EBS–1 form with the Department of Labor.

(3) Pay plan expenses as required or reasonably necessary.

Option 4 (Not Preferred for Smoothly Running Closely Held Corporations)

(f) The following vote on the above resolution was counted:

(1) Yes: [*Number*];

(2) No: [*Number*];

(3) Abstentions: [*Number*];

(4) Persons demanding that their objections be noted and the reasons for their objections: ____________.

§ 48.77 Election Inspectors

Resolved that [*Name*] and [*Name*] be and they are hereby appointed inspectors of election, to serve at the next annual meeting of the Corporation, and at any meeting of the Stockholders that may be held prior thereto.

Option 1 (Not Preferred for Smoothly Running Closely Held Corporations)

The following vote on the above resolution was counted:

(a) Yes: [*Number*];

(b) No: [*Number*];

(c) Abstentions: [*Number*];

(d) Persons demanding that their objections be noted and the reasons for their objections: ___________.

§ 48.78 Election of Directors—Staggered

Resolved, that Article ______, Section ______ of the By-laws be amended so as to provide that the Directors of the Company shall be three in number; that each director after those elected at this meeting shall hold office for a period of three years; that said three directorships respectively be designated by classes, "Class A," "Class B," and "Class C;" that in order to implement said continuity the first Class A Director shall hold office for a term of one year from ______, 19__, and thereafter, the Class A Director shall hold office for the customary three year term above established; that the first Class B Director shall hold office for a term of two years from ______, 19__, and thereafter the Class B Director shall hold office for the customary three year term above established, and that the first Class C Director shall hold office for three years from ______, 19__ and thereafter the Class C Director shall hold office for the customary three year term above established; provided that anything above stated to the contrary notwithstanding, each person who is or shall hereafter become a Director of ______ Company shall hold office until his successor to such class of directorship shall have been duly elected and qualified.

Option 1 (Not Preferred for Smoothly Running Closely Held Corporations)

The following vote on the above resolution was counted:

(a) Yes: [*Number*];

(b) No: [*Number*];

(c) Abstentions: [*Number*];

(d) Persons demanding that their objections be noted and the reasons for their objections: ___________.

§ 48.79 Election of Officers

Resolved, that the following persons be, and they hereby are, elected to the following positions:

President	________________
Vice-President	________________
Secretary	________________
Assistant Secretary	________________
Treasurer	________________
Assistant Treasurer	________________,

for the year ending ________, 19___.

Option 1 (Not Preferred for Smoothly Running Closely Held Corporations)

The following vote on the above resolution was counted:

(a) Yes: [*Number*];

(b) No: [*Number*];

(c) Abstentions: [*Number*];

(d) Persons demanding that their objections be noted and the reasons for their objections: ____________.

§ 48.80 Elimination of Deficit in Earned Surplus

Resolved that the capital surplus of the Corporation be, and the same hereby is, applied to eliminate the deficit of earned surplus arising from losses incurred by the Corporation in the amount of $______.

Option 1 (Not Preferred for Smoothly Running Closely Held Corporations)

The following vote on the above resolution was counted:

(a) Yes: [*Number*];

(b) No: [*Number*];

(c) Abstentions: [*Number*];

(d) Persons demanding that their objections be noted and the reasons for their objections: ________________.

COMMENT

Elimination of deficits in earned surplus by directoral action is commonly authorized by Model Business Corporation Act (69).

The effect of this action is to permit dividends to be paid from current or future earnings without first eliminating the deficit in earned surplus. So called "nimble dividends", that is, dividends paid out of current earnings without eliminating an accumulated deficit are not permitted, as such, under most state Corporation statutes.

§ 48.81 Employee Termination

Resolved, that the termination of the employment of the following person(s) be noted:

[*Names*]

Option 1 (Not Preferred for Smoothly Running Closely Held Corporations)

The following vote on the above resolution was counted:

(a) Yes: [*Number*];

(b) No: [*Number*];

(c) Abstentions: [*Number*];

(d) Persons demanding that their objections be noted and the reasons for their objections: __________.

§ 48.82 Employment Ratification

Resolved, that the employment of the following persons hired during the past fiscal year and the [*salary/salaries*] paid to such person(s) [*is/are*] hereby [*ratified/agreed*] to:

Employee	Starting Date	Salary Paid During Fiscal Year

Option 1 (Not Preferred for Smoothly Running Closely Held Corporations)

The following vote on the above resolution was counted:

(a) Yes: [*Number*];

(b) No: [*Number*];

(c) Abstentions: [*Number*];

(d) Persons demanding that their objections be noted and the reasons for their objections: __________.

Option 1 *(Not Preferred Unless There Is to Be a Consent Meeting and All Those Voting Won't Actually Review the Transaction)*

The Secretary shall make part of the minute book a copy of the same.

§ 48.83 Exchange of Corporate Stock for Assets/Stock

Resolved that the [*Board of Directors/Stockholders ratify as executed/adopt as proposed*] an Agreement to Exchange corporate stock for [*assets/stock*] which has the following features:

(a) Effective Date: __________.

(b) Amount and description of corporate stock to be distributed: __________ for [*Describe Assets or Stock to Be Received*].

(c) Closing Date: __________.

(d) Special Features: __________.

Option 1 *(Preferred as a Matter of Practical Experience)*

The Secretary shall make part of the minute book a copy of the same.

Option 2 *(Not Preferred for Smoothly Running Closely Held Corporations)*

The following Officers are authorized to execute the same: President and Secretary.

Option 3 *(Not Preferred Unless There Is to Be a Consent Meeting and All Those Voting Won't Actually Review the Transaction)*

The Secretary shall make part of the minute book a copy of the same.

Option 4 *(Not Preferred for Smoothly Running Closely Held Corporations)*

The following vote on the above resolution was counted:

(a) Yes: [*Number*];

(b) No: [*Number*];

(c) Abstentions: [*Number*];

(d) Persons demanding that their objections be noted and the reasons for their objections: __________.

Library References:

C.J.S. Corporations § 1052.
West's Key No. Digests, Corporations ⚷408.

§ 48.84 Executive Committee (Short Form)

Resolved, that there is hereby created a committee of the Board of Directors designated the "executive committee" to be composed of [*Number*] Directors. [Optional. There also shall be appointed [*Number*] Directors to serve as alternate members of the executive committee.] The executive committee shall report to the Board of Directors the actions which the executive committee has taken since the previous meeting of the Board of Directors. The executive committee shall have all the authority of the Board of Directors except with respect to:

(1) The approval of any action which also requires Stockholder approval.

(2) The filling of vacancies on the Board or in any committee.

(3) The fixing of compensation of the Directors for serving on the Board or on any committee.

(4) The amendment or repeal of By-laws or the adoption of new By-laws.

(5) The amendment or repeal of any resolution of the Board which by its express terms is not so amendable or repealable.

(6) The declaration of a dividend or other distribution to Stockholders, except at a rate or in a periodic amount or within a price range determined by the Board.

(7) The appointment of other committees of the Board or the members thereof.

Option 1 (Not Preferred for Smoothly Running Closely Held Corporations)

The following vote on the above resolution was counted:

(a) Yes: [*Number*];

(b) No: [*Number*];

(c) Abstentions: [*Number*];

(d) Persons demanding that their objections be noted and the reasons for their objections: ________________.

§ 48.85 Forfeiture of Shares—Final Notice

Resolved, that the Secretary send notice to ______, pursuant to section ______ of the By-laws, requiring him to pay the call due on his shares, with interest, within ______ days of such notification; otherwise, his stock will be forfeited without further notice.

Option 1 (Not Preferred for Smoothly Running Closely Held Corporations)

The following vote on the above resolution was counted:

(a) Yes: [*Number*];

(b) No: [*Number*];

(c) Abstentions: [*Number*];

(d) Persons demanding that their objections be noted and the reasons for their objections: __________.

Library References:

C.J.S. Corporations § 366 et seq.
West's Key No. Digests, Corporations ⚷93.

§ 48.86 Forfeiture of Shares—Declaration of Forfeiture

Resolved, that ______ shares of stock, represented by certificate number ______, of which ______ is the record owner, are hereby declared forfeited for the nonpayment of calls due thereon.

Option 1 (Not Preferred for Smoothly Running Closely Held Corporations)

The following vote on the above resolution was counted:

(a) Yes: [*Number*];

(b) No: [*Number*];

(c) Abstentions: [*Number*];

(d) Persons demanding that their objections be noted and the reasons for their objections: __________.

§ 48.87 Future Salary Adjustments

Resolved, that the following person(s) employed by the Corporation shall be paid the following [*salary/salaries*] during the coming fiscal year:

Employee	Salary

Resolved, that any salary payment or other payment made to or on behalf of an Officer of the Corporation which shall be disallowed in whole or in part as a deductible expense for Federal Income Tax purposes, shall be reimbursed by such Officer to the Corporation to the full extent of the disallowance. It shall be the duty of the Board of Directors to enforce payment of each such amount disallowed.

Option 1 (Not Preferred for Smoothly Running Closely Held Corporations)

The following vote on the above resolution was counted:

(a) Yes: [*Number*];

(b) No: [*Number*];

(c) Abstentions: [*Number*];

(d) Persons demanding that their objections be noted and the reasons for their objections: ________________.

§ 48.88 General Contracts

Resolved that the [*Board of Directors/Stockholders ratify/authorize*] (but only to the extent to which set forth below) a contract with the following provisions:

(a) Purpose: [*Describe*].

(b) Terms: [*Describe*].

(c) Effective date: ____________.

COMMENTS

The following is the general rule regarding contracts when there is a conflict of interest (Model Business Corporation Act § 41):

> No contract shall be either void or voidable because of a conflict if:
>
> (A) The fact of such relationship or interest is disclosed or known to the Board of Directors or committee which authorizes, approves or ratifies the contract or transaction by a vote or consent sufficient for the purpose without counting the votes or consents of such interested Directors; or
>
> (B) The fact of such relationship or interest is disclosed or known to the Stockholders entitled to vote and they authorize, approve or ratify such contract or transaction by vote or written consent; or
>
> (C) The contract or transaction is fair and reasonable to the Corporation.
>
> Common or interested Directors may be counted in determining the presence of a quorum at a meeting of the Board of Directors or a committee thereof which authorizes, approves or ratifies such contract or transaction.

Option 1 (Preferred as a Matter of Practical Experience)

The following officer(s) is authorized to carry out the above resolution: President and Secretary.

Option 2 (Not Preferred for Smoothly Running Closely Held Corporations)

The following vote on the above resolution was counted:

(a) Yes: __________.

(b) No: __________.

(c) Abstentions: __________.

(d) Persons demanding that their objections be noted and the reasons for their objections: __________.

§ 48.89 General Manager—Appointment

Resolved, that ______ be hereby appointed general manager of the Corporation, in accordance with the terms contained in a proposed agreement, exhibited at this meeting, to be made between the Corporation and ______, and that the Corporation execute such agreement accordingly.

Option 1 (Not Preferred for Smoothly Running Closely Held Corporations)

The following vote on the above resolution was counted:

(a) Yes: [*Number*];

(b) No: [*Number*];

(c) Abstentions: [*Number*];

(d) Persons demanding that their objections be noted and the reasons for their objections: __________.

Library References:

C.J.S. Corporations § 722.
West's Key No. Digests, Corporations ⚿285.

§ 48.90 General Manager—Specification of Terms of Employment

Resolved that ______ is hereby appointed general manager on the following terms:

1. **Employment.** The Corporation will employ the manager, and the manager will act as the manager of the Corporation, for the term of ______ years from the ______ day of ______ next, and thereafter until his employment shall be terminated.

2. **Duties of Manager.** During the continuance of employment the manager shall devote the whole of his time during the business hours of the Corporation, and shall use his best endeavors to promote the interests and welfare of the Corporation.

3. Manager Not to Deal in Shares. The manager shall not, without the permission of the Directors, directly or indirectly hold or deal in any shares of the Corporation, or of any other company carrying on a similar business;

4. Manager under Control of Directors. The manager shall exercise and carry out all such powers and duties, and shall observe all such directions and restrictions, as the Board of Directors may from time to time confer or impose upon him, but in default thereof the manager shall control the general management of the business of the Corporation, and shall have power to appoint and dismiss all the employees of the Corporation, and to enter into any trade contracts on behalf of the Corporation in the ordinary way of business, and to do all other acts and things which he may consider necessary or conducive to the interests of the Corporation;

5. Remuneration. The manager shall be entitled by way of remuneration for his services to an annual salary of $______, to be paid monthly, and also to a commission of ______ per cent on the "net profits" of the Corporation in each year; as computed and certified by the Treasurer of the Corporation, whose certificate shall be conclusive;

6. Vacations. The manager shall be entitled to take ______ days' vacation in each year, at a period to be approved of by the Board, and such other holidays, not exceeding a total of ______ days in any one year, as the board may from time to time approve;

Option 1 (Not Preferred for Smoothly Running Closely Held Corporations)

The following vote on the above resolution was counted:

(a) Yes: [*Number*];

(b) No: [*Number*];

(c) Abstentions: [*Number*];

(d) Persons demanding that their objections be noted and the reasons for their objections: ________________.

§ 48.91 Gift

Resolved that, the Corporation being of the opinion that the following gift will improve and enhance the Corporations' image in the community and among its employees, the [*Board of Directors/Stockholders ratify as executed/adopt as proposed*] the following gift:

(a) Donee: ____________.

(b) Property to be given: ____________.

(c) Corporate officers to carry out transfer: ____________.

COMMENT

It should be noted that gifts (except charitable gifts) are not deductible to the Corporation.

Option 1 (Preferred as a Matter of Practical Experience)

The Secretary shall make part of the minute book a copy of the same.

Option 2 (Not Preferred for Smoothly Running Closely Held Corporations)

The following Officers are authorized to execute the same: President.

Option 3 (Not Preferred for Smoothly Running Closely Held Corporations)

The following vote on the above resolution was counted:

(a) Yes: [*Number*];

(b) No: [*Number*];

(c) Abstentions: [*Number*];

(d) Persons demanding that their objections be noted and the reasons for their objections: ______.

§ 48.92 Gift to Widow of Employee

Resolved, that as a material expression of sympathy and of kindness to [*Name*], widow of [*Name*], former [*Describe*] of the Board of this Corporation at his death, and, motivated by a deep sense of appreciation and recognition of the past services of [*Name*], as [*Describe*], there shall be paid to said [*Name*] as a gift [*Number*] equal monthly payments of $[*Dollars*]; payable between ______, 19__ and ______, 19__.

Option 1 (Not Preferred for Smoothly Running Closely Held Corporations)

The following vote on the above resolution was counted:

(a) Yes: [*Number*];

(b) No: [*Number*];

(c) Abstentions: [*Number*];

(d) Persons demanding that their objections be noted and the reasons for their objections: __________.

COMMENT

The first $5000 of this gift is income tax free (Internal Revenue Code § 101(b)).

§ 48.93 Group Life Insurance Plan

Resolved that the [*Board of Directors/Stockholders ratify as executed/adopt as proposed*] a Group Life Insurance Plan which has the following features:

Employees Covered	Benefit

Any salary payment or other payment made to or on behalf of an Officer of the Corporation which shall be disallowed in whole or in part as a deductible expense for Federal income tax purposes, shall be reimbursed by such Officer to the Corporation to the full extent of the disallowance. It shall be the duty of the Board of Directors to enforce payment of each such amount disallowed.

COMMENTS

One question that arises in the case of an employee benefit is the reasonableness of the benefit in light of the total compensation paid. If it is reasonable, the deduction will be available; if the total compensation is not reasonable, the deduction will not be available. The Internal Revenue Service will attempt to claim, in the case of a Corporation, that an unreasonably high payment was in the nature of a dividend to a Stockholder-employee, which was both not deductible to the Corporation and not subject to the maximum tax limitations on earned income. The popular solution to this problem is a "double dip" provision (the government is dipping twice into the transaction) in the corporate minutes which requires repayment of the disallowed benefit to the Corporation leaving the Corporation and the employee in the same position they would have been in if the payment had not been made. The government is presently trying to thwart the use of such a provision by asserting that its existence is prima facie evidence of the unreasonableness of the payment. Given the pervasive use of this provision, this "damned if you do or don't" assertion is absurd and, if carried to its logical extension, would negate all tax planning which was based upon a written assertion of the tax results being sought.

See Employee Benefit Plans Volume for form.

Option 1 (Preferred as a Matter of Practical Experience)

The Secretary shall make part of the minute book a copy of the same.

Option 2 (Not Preferred for Smoothly Running Closely Held Corporations)

The following Officers are authorized to execute the same: President

Option 3 (Not Preferred Unless There Is to Be a Consent Meeting and All Those Voting Won't Actually Review the Transaction)

The President shall do all things reasonable and necessary to carry out the purposes of the Group Term Life Insurance Plan and to that end he shall:

(a) Distribute the necessary disclosure summary to participants.

(b) Execute and file the necessary form with the Department of Labor.

(c) Pay plan expenses as required or reasonably necessary.

(d) Deliver Internal Revenue Service Form 1099 to all participants to reflect insurance economic benefit.

Option 4 (Not Preferred for Smoothly Running Closely Held Corporations)

The following vote on the above resolution was counted:

(a) Yes: [*Number*];

(b) No: [*Number*];

(c) Abstentions: [*Number*];

(d) Persons demanding that their objections be noted and the reasons for their objections: __________.

§ 48.94 Health Insurance Plan

Resolved that the [*Board of Directors/Stockholders ratify as executed/adopt as proposed*]:

(a) A Health Insurance Plan which has the following features:

(1) Hospital:

Room & Board __________.

Maximum # of days __________.

Intensive care additional __________.

Intensive care # of days __________.

Maximum extra charges __________.

Surgical schedule __________.

Anesthesia __________.

In-hospital benefit __________.

Hospital-out-patient __________.

(Supplemental accident) __________.

Radiation therapy __________.

Diagnostic X-ray and lab __________.

Maternity __________.

(2) Major medical:

Maximum __________.

Deductible __________.

Co-insurance __________.

Prescription drugs __________.

Out-patient __________.

Convalescent care __________.

(3) Dental: __________.

Deductible/family __________.

Oral exams, etc. __________.

X-rays, fillings, etc. __________.

Bridges, dentures, crowns, etc. __________.

Maximum benefit __________.

(4) Carrier: __________.

(5) Participant description: __________.

COMMENT

See Employee Benefit Plans Volume with respect to health inance plans.

(b) Any salary payment or other payment made to or on behalf of an Officer of the Corporation which shall be disallowed in whole or in part as a deductible expense for Federal income tax purposes, shall be reimbursed by such Officer to the Corporation to the full extent of the disallowance. It shall be the duty of the Board of Directors to enforce payment of each such amount disallowed.

COMMENT

One question that arises in the case of an employee benefit is the reasonableness of the benefit in light of the total compensation paid. If it is reasonable, the deduction will be available; if the total compensation is not reasonable, the deduction will not be available. The Internal Revenue Service will attempt to claim, in the case of a Corporation, that an unreasonably high payment was in the nature of a dividend to a Stockholder-employee, which was both not deductible to the Corporation and not subject to the maximum tax limitations on earned income. The popular solution to this problem is a "double dip" provision (the government is dipping twice into the transaction) in the corporate minutes which requires repayment of the disallowed benefit to the Corporation leaving the Corporation and the employee in the same position they would have been in if the payment had not been made. The government is presently trying to thwart the use of such a provision by asserting that its existence is prima facie evidence of the unreasonableness of the payment. Given the pervasive use of this provision, this "damned if you do or don't" assertion is absurd and, if carried to its logical extension, would negate all tax planning which was based upon a written assertion of the tax results being sought.

Option 1 (Preferred as a Matter of Practical Experience)

(c) The Secretary shall make part of the minute book a copy of the same.

Option 2 (Not Preferred for Smoothly Running Closely Held Corporations)

(d) The following Officers are authorized to execute the same: President and Secretary.

Option 3 (Not Preferred Unless There Is to Be a Consent Meeting and All Those Voting Won't Actually Review the Transaction)

(e) The President shall do all things reasonable and necessary to carry out the purpose of the Health Insurance Plan and to that end he shall:

(1) Distribute the necessary disclosure summary to participants.

(2) Execute and File the necessary form with the Department of Labor.

(c) Pay plan expenses as required or reasonably necessary.

Option 4 (Not Preferred for Smoothly Running Closely Held Corporations)

(f) The following vote on the above resolution was counted:

(1) Yes: [*Number*];

(2) No: [*Number*];

(3) Abstentions: [*Number*];

(4) Persons demanding that their objections be noted and the reasons for their objections: ___________.

§ 48.95 Implementing Resolution—General

Resolved that * * *.

Further resolved that the Officers of the Corporation are directed to take the necessary steps, to execute and file appropriate documents, and to make appropriate entries in the books and records of the Corporation to implement the foregoing resolution.

§ 48.96 Implementing Resolution Authorizing Filing with Secretary of State

Resolved that * * *

Further resolved that the President and Secretary of the Corporation are hereby authorized and directed to execute and file a certificate with the Secretary of State of ______ and to do such other things as may be necessary to implement the foregoing resolution.

COMMENT

Stockholders may be called upon to consider a wide variety of proposed corporate actions. Usually such actions will have first been considered by the Board of Directors, and the form of resolution will have been crystalized at that stage. This form of resolution is intended to be added to a substantive resolution to authorize the appropriate officers to file the appropriate certificate with the Secretary of State, where that step is necessary to complete the contemplated transaction.

§ 48.97 Incorporation Expenses and Acts

Resolved, that the organization and incorporation activities of the Incorporators are hereby ratified as the act and deed of the Corporation and that [*all the following*] expenses be reimbursed to the payor as an expense of this Corporation.

Option 1 (Not Preferred for Smoothly Running Closely Held Corporations)

The following vote on the above resolution was counted:

(a) Yes: [*Number*];

(b) No: [*Number*];

(c) Abstentions: [*Number*];

(d) Persons demanding that their objections be noted and the reasons for their objections: __________.

§ 48.98 Increasing Stated Capital

Resolved, that the stated capital of this Corporation be increased in the sum of $______, by transferring from paid in surplus to stated capital the said sum of $______, and that ______ shares of stock of no par value be issued and held as treasury stock until otherwise disposed of.

Option 1 (Not Preferred for Smoothly Running Closely Held Corporations)

The following vote on the above resolution was counted:

(a) Yes: [*Number*];

(b) No: [*Number*];

(c) Abstentions: [*Number*];

(d) Persons demanding that their objections be noted and the reasons for their objections: __________.

Library References:

C.J.S. Corporations § 268 et seq.
West's Key No. Digests, Corporations ⚷67.

§ 48.99 Indemnification of Officer, Directors, Agents, and Employers

Resolved that the [*Board of Directors/Stockholders*] have authorized President (and the President shall) indemnify Officers, Directors, agents and employees as follows:

Alternative A–1

The Corporation shall indemnify to the full extent permitted by law any person who is made, or threatened to be made, a party to any action, suit or proceeding (whether civil, criminal, administrative or investigative) by reason of the fact that he, his testator, or intestate is or was a Director, officer, employee or agent of the Corporation or serves or served any other enterprise at the request of the Corporation.

Alternative A–2

(a) The Corporation shall indemnify any person who was or is a party or is threatened to be made a party to any threatened, pending or completed action, suit or proceeding, whether civil, criminal, administrative or investigative (other than an action by or in the right of the Corporation) by reason of the fact that he is or was a Director, officer, employee or agent of the Corporation, or is or was serving at the request of the Corporation as a director, officer, employee or agent of another corporation, partnership, joint venture, trust or other enterprise, against expenses (including attorneys' fees), judgments, fines and amounts paid in settlement actually and reasonably incurred by him in connection with such action, suit or proceeding if he acted in good faith and in a manner he reasonably believed to be in or not opposed to the best interests of the Corporation, and, with respect to any criminal action or proceeding, had no reasonable cause to believe his conduct was unlawful. The termination of any action, suit or proceeding by judgment, order, settlement, conviction, or upon a plea of nolo contendere or its equivalent, shall not, of itself, create a presumption that the person did not act in good faith and in a manner which he reasonably believed to be in or not opposed to the best interests of the Corporation, and, with respect to any criminal action or proceeding, had reasonable cause to believe that his conduct was unlawful.

(b) The Corporation shall indemnify any person who was or is a party or is threatened to be made a party to any threatened, pending or completed action or suit by or in the right of the Corporation to procure a judgment in its favor by reason of the fact that he is or was a Director, officer, employee or agent of the Corporation, or is or was serving at the request of the Corporation as a director, officer, employee or agent of another corporation, partnership, joint venture, trust or other enterprise against expenses (including attorneys' fees) actually and reasonably incurred by him in connection with the defense or settlement of such action or suit if he acted in good faith and in a manner he reasonably believed to be in or not opposed to the best interests of the Corporation and except that no indemnification shall be made in respect of any claim, issue or matter as to which such person shall have been adjudged to be liable for negligence or misconduct in the performance of his duty to the Corporation unless and only to the extent that the court in which such action or suit was brought shall determine upon application that, despite the adjudication of liability but in view of all circumstances of the case, such person is fairly and reasonably entitled to indemnity for such expenses which such court shall deem proper.

(c) To the extent that a Director, officer, employee or agent of a Corporation has been successful on the merits or otherwise in defense of any action, suit or proceeding referred to in subsections (a) or (b), or in defense of any claim, issue or matter therein, he shall be indemnified against expenses (including attorneys' fees) actually and reasonably incurred by him in connection therewith.

(d) Any indemnification under subsections (a) or (b) (unless ordered by a court) shall be made by the Corporation only as authorized in the specific case upon a determination that indemnification of the Director, officer, employee or agent is proper in the circumstances because he has met the applicable standard of conduct set forth in subsections (a) or (b). Such determination shall be made:

(1) By the Board of Directors by a majority vote of a quorum consisting of Directors who were not parties to such action, suit or proceeding, or

(2) If such a quorum is not obtainable, or, even if obtainable a quorum of disinterested directors so directs, by independent, legal counsel in a written opinion, or

(3) By the Stockholders.

(e) Expenses (including attorneys' fees) incurred in defending a civil or criminal action, suit or proceeding may be paid by the Corporation in advance of the final disposition of such action, suit or proceeding as authorized in the manner provided in subsection (d) upon receipt of an undertaking by or on behalf of the Director, officer, employee or agent to repay such amount unless it shall ultimately be determined that he is entitled to be indemnified by the Corporation as authorized in this section.

(f) The indemnification provided by this section shall not be deemed exclusive of any other rights to which those indemnified may be entitled under any By-law, agreement, vote of Stockholders or disinterested Directors or otherwise, both as to action in his official capacity and as to action in another capacity while holding such office, and shall continue as to a person who has ceased to be a Director, Officer, employee or agent and shall inure to the benefit of the heirs, executors and administrators of such a person.

Option 1 (Preferred as a Matter of Practical Experience)

The Corporation shall have power to purchase and maintain insurance on behalf of any person who is or was a Director, Officer, employee or agent of the Corporation, or is or was serving at the request of the Corporation as a Director, Officer, employee or agent of another corporation, partnership, joint venture, trust or other enterprise against any liability asserted against him and incurred by him in any such capacity or arising out of his status as such, whether or not the Corporation would have the power to indemnify him against such liability under the provisions of this section.

Option 2 (Not Preferred for Smoothly Running Closely Held Corporations)

The following vote on the above resolution was counted:

(a) Yes: [*Number*];

(b) No: [*Number*];

(c) Abstentions: [*Number*];

(d) Persons demanding that their objections be noted and the reasons for their objections: ____________.

§ 48.100 Inspectors of Election

Resolved, that ______ and ______ be and they are hereby appointed inspectors of election, to serve at the next annual meeting of the Company, and at any meeting of the Stockholders that may be held prior thereto.

§ 48.101 Issuance of Stocks and Bonds

Resolved that the Board of Directors is hereby authorized to issue the following certificates from time to time in one or more series:

Alternative A–1

[*Describe*] class of [*Describe*] stock only.

Alternative A–2

Any stock or security.

Alternative A–3

Any class of stock or security except [*Describe*] class of [*Decribe*] stock or security.

The Board of Directors is authorized to determine:

Option 1

The dividend rate.

Option 2

The price and terms of issuance.

Option 3

Liquidation value and terms.

Option 4

Redemption value terms and conditions.

Option 5

Whether there shall be a sinking fund to retire such certificates and, if so, what the terms and conditions of such fund shall be.

Option 6

Conversion rights.

Option 7

Voting rights.

Option 8 (Preferred as a Matter of Practical Experience)

The Secretary shall make part of the minute book a copy of the same.

Option 9 (Not Preferred for Smoothly Running Closely Held Corporations)

The following Officers are authorized to execute the same: President and Secretary.

Option 10 (Not Preferred for Smoothly Running Closely Held Corporations)

The following vote on the above resolution was counted:

(a) Yes: [*Number*];

(b) No: [*Number*];

(c) Abstentions: [*Number*];

(d) Persons demanding that their objections be noted and the reasons for their objections: __________.

Library References:

C.J.S. Corporations §§ 262, 289.
West's Key No. Digests, Corporations ⚷98.

§ 48.102 Lease

Resolved that the [*Board of Directors/Stockholders ratify as executed/adopt as proposed*] a lease which has the following features:

(a) Lessor: __________.

(b) Lessee: __________.

(c) Description of Property: __________.

(d) Term: __________.

(e) Rent: __________.

(f) Burdens Corporation is assuming: [*Describe*].

Option 1 (Preferred as a Matter of Practical Experience)

The Secretary shall make part of the minute book a copy of the same.

Option 2 (Not Preferred for Smoothly Running Closely Held Corporations)

The following Officers are authorized to execute the same: President and Secretary.

Option 3 (Not Preferred for Smoothly Running Closely Held Corporations)

The following vote on the above resolution was counted:

(a) Yes: [*Number*];

(b) No: [*Number*];

(c) Abstentions: [*Number*];

(d) Persons demanding that their objections be noted and the reasons for their objections: ______.

§ 48.103 Lease of Safe Deposit Box

Resolved, that the leasing of a safe deposit box or boxes now or hereafter in the safe deposit vaults of the ______ Bank, of ______, in the name of this Corporation, by the President, Vice-President, Treasurer, or Secretary of this Corporation, or any one of them, be and hereby is authorized and confirmed.

Further resolved, that authority to have access to and full control of the contents of the safe or safes, to remove any part or all of the contents, to exchange or surrender such safes, to have the same rights and full control of the contents of safe or safes held in such exchange, be and it is hereby given to the following:

[*Here Provide the Titles of the Officers.*]

Option 1 (Not Preferred for Smoothly Running Closely Held Corporations)

The following vote on the above resolution was counted:

(a) Yes: [*Number*];

(b) No: [*Number*];

(c) Abstentions: [*Number*];

(d) Persons demanding that their objections be noted and the reasons for their objections: ______.

§ 48.104 Lease Termination

Resolved, that [*Name*], Secretary of the Corporation, be and he is hereby authorized and directed to serve a notice to quit upon [*Name*], for the reason that he has defaulted in the terms of the lease dated the ______ day of ______, 19__, and that said Secretary is further authorized to enter suit or take such proceedings as they may deem necessary to again obtain possession of the property covered by said lease.

Option 1 (Not Preferred for Smoothly Running Closely Held Corporations)

The following vote on the above resolution was counted:

(a) Yes: [*Number*];

(b) No: [*Number*];

(c) Abstentions: [*Number*];

(d) Persons demanding that their objections be noted and the reasons for their objections: ________.

§ 48.105 Legal Service Plan

Resolved that the [*Board of Directors/Stockholders ratify as executed/adopt as proposed*] a Group Legal Service Plan which has the following features:

(1) Trustees: ________.

(2) Bank: ________.

(3) Initial contribution: $________.

(4) Participant description: ________.

(5) Benefit provided: [*Describe*].

COMMENT

See Employee Benefit Plans Volume for form.

Option 1 (Preferred as a Matter of Practical Experience)

The Secretary shall make part of the minute book a copy of the same.

Option 2 (Not Preferred Unless There Is to Be a Consent Meeting and All Those Voting Won't Actually Review the Transaction)

The President shall do all things reasonable and necessary to carry out the purposes of the Legal Services Plan and to that end he shall be responsible for the:

(a) Distribution of the necessary disclosure summary to participants.

(b) Execution and filing of the necessary form with the Department of Labor.

(c) Pay plan expenses as required or reasonably necessary.

Option 3 (Not Preferred for Smoothly Running Closely Held Corporations)

The following vote on the above resolution was counted:

(a) Yes: [*Number*];

(b) No: [*Number*];

(c) Abstentions: [*Number*];

(d) Persons demanding that their objections be noted and the reasons for their objections: ___________.

§ 48.106 Liability Insurance

Resolved that the [*Board of Directors/Stockholders ratify/authorize*] (but only to the extent to which set forth below) the purchase of liability insurance as follows:

(a) Persons covered: ___________.

(b) Dollar limits of coverage: $___________.

(c) Events covered:

(1) Errors and omissions only.

(2) All acts, including violations of criminal statements.

The following Officer is authorized to carry out the above resolution: Treasurer.

Option 1 (Not Preferred for Smoothly Running Closely Held Corporations)

The following vote on the above resolution was counted:

(a) Yes: ___________.

(b) No: ___________.

(c) Abstentions: ___________.

(d) Persons demanding that their objections be noted and the reasons for their objections: ___________.

§ 48.107 License in Another State

Resolved, that the President and Secretary be and are hereby authorized and directed to execute, in the name and on behalf of this company, the statement required to be filed by foreign Corporations under the laws of the State of _______, to attach the seal of the Corporation thereto, and in the statement to designate _______ as the person upon whom process against the company may be served within the State of _______, and further to do all things necessary to comply with the law of that state so that the Corporation is authorized to transact business in the state of _______.

Option 1 (Not Preferred for Smoothly Running Closely Held Corporations)

The following vote on the above resolution was counted:

(a) Yes: [*Number*];

(b) No: [*Number*];

(c) Abstentions: [*Number*];

(d) Persons demanding that their objections be noted and the reasons for their objections: ____________.

§ 48.108 Liquidation

Resolved that the [*Board of Directors/Stockholders ratify as executed/adopt as proposed*] a Plan of Liquidation which has the following features:

(a) Date of Distribution: ____________.

(b) Trustee after Liquidation: ____________.

(c) Special Features: ____________.

Option 1

(d) Such liquidation shall be carried out under the procedures of Section 333 of the Internal Revenue Code (one calendar month liquidations).

COMMENT

See Chapter 61 et seq., infra.

Option 2 (Preferred as a Matter of Practical Experience)

The Secretary shall make part of the minute book a copy of the same.

Option 3 (Not Preferred for Smoothly Running Closely Held Corporations)

The following Officers are authorized to execute the same: President and Secretary.

Option 4 (Not Preferred Unless There Is to Be a Consent Meeting and All Those Voting Won't Actually Review the Transaction)

The President shall do all things reasonable and necessary to carry out the purposes of the Plan of Liquidation and to that end he shall:

(a) Execute all necessary transfer documents.

(b) Execute and file of Form 966 with the Internal Revenue Service within 30 days of this resolution.

(c) Distribute Form 1099 to all Stockholders and filing the same with the Internal Revenue Service.

(d) Execute and filing of final tax returns.

(e) Execute Resolution of Dissolution and filing of the same with all States the Corporation is registered to do business in.

Option 5 (Not Preferred for Smoothly Running Closely Held Corporations)

The following vote on the above resolution was counted:

(a) Yes: [*Number*];

(b) No: [*Number*];

(c) Abstentions: [*Number*];

(d) Persons demanding that their objections be noted and the reasons for their objections: ____________.

§ 48.109 Loan to the Corporation

Resolved that the [*Board of Directors/Stockholders ratify as executed/adopt as proposed*] a Loan to the Corporation which has the following features:

(a) Lender: ____________.

(b) Principal: ____________.

(c) Interest: ____________.

(d) Term: ____________.

(e) Special features: ____________.

(f) Collateral: [*Describe*].

Option 1 (Preferred as a Matter of Practical Experience)

The Secretary shall make part of the minute book a copy of the same.

Option 2 (Not Preferred for Smoothly Running Closely Held Corporations)

The following Officers authorized to execute the same: President and Secretary.

Option 3 (Not Preferred for Smoothly Running Closely Held Corporations)

The following vote on the above resolution was counted:

(a) Yes: [*Number*];

(b) No: [*Number*];

(c) Abstentions: [*Number*];

(d) Persons demanding that their objections be noted and the reasons for their objections: ____________.

Library References:

C.J.S. Corporations §§ 1144, 1145.
West's Key No. Digests, Corporations ⚷460, 461.

§ 48.110 Loans to Others

Resolved that the [*Board of Directors/Stockholders ratify/authorize*] (but only to the extent to which set forth below) the following loan to the following [*person/entity*]:

(a) Borrower: ____________.

(b) Amount: $____________.

(c) Interest: ____________% per annum.

(d) Term: ____________.

(e) Special features: ____________.

(f) Collateral: [*Describe*].

COMMENTS

Under Internal Revenue Code § 482 the interest rate charged to a related party must be reasonable or the Internal Revenue Service will readjust it (see § 54.2, infra, for further explanation). However, no interest need be charged a related party if the note is a demand note (see § 56.11, infra for further discussion).

Note: If the loan is to a Director, Stockholder approval is necessary (Model Business Corporation Act § 47).

See § 9.5 and § 9.6 of the form at § 34.14, supra, for relevant By-law.

The following Officer(s) is authorized to carry out the above resolution: Treasurer.

Option 1 (Not Preferred for Smoothly Running Closely Held Corporations)

The following vote on the above resolution was counted:

(a) Yes: ____________.

(b) No: ____________.

(c) Abstentions: ____________.

(d) Persons demanding that their objections be noted and the reasons for their objections: ____________.

§ 48.111 Loans, Credits and Security

Resolved, that the President and Treasurer are hereby authorized on behalf of this Corporation:

(a) To borrow money and to obtain credit for this Corporation from ______ Bank on any terms and to make and deliver notes, drafts, acceptances, instruments of guaranty, agreements and any other obligations of this Corporation therefor in form satisfactory to the Bank;

(b) To pledge or assign and deliver, as security for money borrowed or credit obtained, stocks, bonds, bills receivable, accounts, mortgages, merchandise, bills of lading, warehouse receipts, insurance policies, certificates, and any other property held by or belonging to this Corporation with full authority to endorse, assign or guarantee the same in the name of this Corporation;

(c) To discount any bills receivable or any paper held by this Corporation with full authority to endorse the same in the name of this Corporation;

(d) To withdraw from the Bank and give receipt for, or to authorize the Bank to deliver to bearer or to one or more designated persons, all or any documents and securities or other property held by it, whether held as collateral security or for safekeeping or for any other purpose;

(e) To authorize and request the Bank to purchase or sell for account of the Corporation stocks, bonds and other securities; and

(f) To execute and deliver all instruments required by the Bank in connection with any of the foregoing matters and affix thereto the seal of this Corporation.

Resolved, that the Secretary or any other officer of this Corporation be, and hereby is, authorized to certify to the Bank the names of the present Officers of this Corporation and other persons authorized to sign for it and the offices respectively held by them, together with specimens of their signatures, and in case of any change of any holder of any such office or holders of any such offices, the fact of such change and the names of any new Officers and the offices respectively held by them, together with specimens of their signatures; and the Bank be, and hereby is, authorized to honor any instrument signed by any new Officer or officers in respect of whom it has received any such certificate or certificates with the same force and effect as if the officer or the officers were named in the foregoing resolutions in the place of any person or persons with the same title or titles.

Resolved, that the Bank be promptly notified in writing by the Secretary or any officer of this Corporation of any change in these resolutions, such notice to be given to each Office of the Bank in which any account of this Corporation may be maintained, and that until it has actually received such notice in writing it is authorized to act in pursuance of these resolutions, and that until it has actually so received such notice it shall be indemnified and saved harmless from any loss suffered or liability incurred by it in continuing to act in pursuance of these resolutions, even though these resolutions may have been changed.

Option 1 (Not Preferred for Smoothly Running Closely Held Corporations)

The following vote on the above resolution was counted:

(a) Yes: [*Number*];

(b) No: [*Number*];

(c) Abstentions: [*Number*];

(d) Persons demanding that their objections be noted and the reasons for their objections: ________.

§ 48.112 Lost Certificates

Resolved that the [*Board of Directors/Stockholders ratify/authorize*] that (but only to the extent to which set forth below) the following certificates shall be replaced upon the following circumstances:

(a) Certificate number(s): ________.

(b) Registered owner: ________.

(c) Bond to be furnished to the Corporation: $[*Dollars*]; with [*Name*] as Surety.

(d) Advertisement to be done before certificate is replaced: [*Describe*].

COMMENT

See § 7.3 of the By-laws at § 34.14, supra.

The following Officers are authorized to carry out the above resolution: The President and Secretary.

Option 1 (Not Preferred for Smoothly Running Closely Held Corporations)

The following vote on the above resolution was counted:

(a) Yes: ________.

(b) No: ________.

(c) Abstentions: ________.

(d) Persons demanding that their objections be noted and the reasons for their objections: __________.

§ 48.113 Medical Reimbursement Plan

Resolved that the [*Board of Directors/Stockholders ratify as executed/adopt as proposed*] a Medical Reimbursement Plan which has the following features: maximum reimbursement per corporate fiscal year $______ per Participant.

(a) Participant Description: __________.

COMMENT

See Employee Benefit Plans Volume for form.

(b) Any salary payment or other payment made to or on behalf of an Officer of the Corporation which shall be disallowed in whole or in part as a deductible expense for Federal income tax purposes, shall be reimbursed by such Officer to the Corporation to the full extent of the disallowance. It shall be the duty of the Board of Directors to enforce payment of each such amount disallowed.

COMMENT TO (b)

One question that arises in the case of an employee benefit is the reasonableness of the benefit in light of the total compensation paid. If it is reasonable, the deduction will be available; if the total compensation is not reasonable, the deduction will not be available. The Internal Revenue Service will attempt to claim, in the case of a Corporation, that an unreasonably high payment was in the nature of a dividend to a Stockholder-employee, which was both not deductible to the Corporation and not subject to the maximum tax limitations on earned income. The popular solution to this problem is a "double dip" provision (the government is dipping twice into the transaction) in the corporate minutes which requires repayment of the disallowed benefit to the Corporation leaving the Corporation and the employee in the same position they would have been in if the payment had not been made. The government is presently trying to thwart the use of such a provision by asserting that its existence is prima facie evidence of the unreasonableness of the payment. Given the pervasive use of this provision, this "damned if you do or don't" assertion is absurd and, if carried to its logical extension, would negate all tax planning which was based upon a written assertion of the tax results being sought.

Option 1 (Preferred as a Matter of Practical Experience)

(c) The Secretary shall make part of the minute book a copy of the same.

Option 2 (Not Preferred for Smoothly Running Closely Held Corporations)

(d) The following Officers are authorized to execute the same: President and Secretary.

Option 3 (Not Preferred Unless There Is to Be a Consent Meeting and All Those Voting Won't Actually Review the Transaction)

(e) The President shall do all things reasonable and necessary to carry out the purpose of the Medical Reimbursement Plan and to that end he shall:

(1) Distribute the necessary disclosure summary to participants.

(2) Execute and File the necessary form with the Department of Labor.

(3) Payment of plan expenses as required or reasonably necessary.

Option 4 (Not Preferred for Smoothly Running Closely Held Corporations)

The following vote on the above resolution was counted:

(a) Yes: [*Number*];

(b) No: [*Number*];

(c) Abstentions: [*Number*];

(d) Persons demanding that their objections be noted and the reasons for their objections: __________.

§ 48.114 Merger

Resolved that the [*Board of Directors/Stockholders ratify as executed/adopt as proposed*] an Agreement and Plan of Merger which has the following features:

(a) Effective date: __________.

(b) Other Corporations who will be a party to the merger: __________.

(c) Terms: [*Describe*].

(d) Special features: __________.

(e) Closing date: __________.

COMMENT

See Chapter 72, infra, for form.

Option 1 (Preferred as a Matter of Practical Experience)

The Secretary shall make part of the minute book a copy of the same.

Option 2 (Not Preferred for Smoothly Running Closely Held Corporations)

The following Officers are authorized to execute the same: President and Secretary.

Option 3 (Not Preferred Unless There Is to Be a Consent Meeting and All Those Voting Won't Actually Review the Transaction)

The President shall do all things reasonable and necessary to carry out the purposes of the Agreement and Plan of Merger and to that end he shall:

(a) Execute all name changes and documents to consolidate assets.

(b) Execute and file the certificate of merger with the relevant State(s).

(c) Execute new stock certificates to replace those being replaced.

(d) Cause the Corporation to apply for an Internal Revenue Service ruling as to the tax effect of the same.

Option 4 (Not Preferred for Smoothly Running Closely Held Corporations)

The following vote on the above resolution was counted:

(a) Yes: [*Number*];

(b) No: [*Number*];

(c) Abstentions: [*Number*];

(d) Persons demanding that their objections be noted and the reasons for their objections: __________.

Library References:

C.J.S. Corporations § 1621.
West's Key No. Digests, Corporations ⚷582.

§ 48.115 Miscellaneous

Resolved, that the following miscellaneous acts of the Corporation be [*ratified/approved*]:

[*Describe*]

Option 1 *(Not Preferred Unless There Is to Be a Consent Meeting and All Those Voting Won't Actually Review the Transaction)*

The Secretary shall make part of the minute book a copy of the same.

Option 2 *(Not Preferred for Smoothly Running Closely Held Corporations)*

The following vote on the above resolution was counted:

(a) Yes: ___________.

(b) No: ___________.

(c) Abstentions: ___________.

(d) Persons demanding that their objections be noted and the reasons for their objections: ___________.

§ 48.116 Mortgaging Property

Resolved that the following indebtedness be secured by a mortgage on the following property:

(a) Amount of indebtedness: ___________

(b) Term: ___________

(c) Interest Rate: ___________

(d) Property to be mortgaged: [*Describe*]

Option 1 *(Preferred as a Matter of Practical Experience)*

The Secretary shall make part of the minute book a copy of the same.

Option 2 *(Not Preferred for Smoothly Running Closely Held Corporations)*

The following Officers are authorized to execute the same: President

Option 3 *(Not Preferred for Smoothly Running Closely Held Corporations)*

The following vote on the above resolution was counted:

(a) Yes: [*Number*];

(b) No: [*Number*];

(c) Abstentions: [*Number*];

(d) Persons demanding that their objections be noted and the reasons for their objections: ___________.

Library References:

C.J.S. Corporations §§ 1177, 1214.
West's Key No. Digests, Corporations ⚷477.

§ 48.117 Officers (Board of Directors Minutes)

Resolved, that the following persons shall be Officers of the Corporation to serve until the next annual meeting of the Board of Directors and until the election and qualification of their respective successors (or until removed, with or without cause) by the Stockholders:

Chairman of the Board: ________________

President: ________________

Vice-President: ________________

Secretary: ________________

Treasurer: ________________

COMMENTS

Although generally permissible, it is not a good idea to have the President and Secretary the same person since most documents call for the Secretary to attest to the Presidents' signature and this isn't possible when they are the same person.

The By-laws should provide for the same Officers as are being elected (see Art. VI, of the form at § 34.14, supra).

Option 1 (Not Preferred for Smoothly Running Closely Held Corporations)

The following vote on the above resolution was counted:

(a) Yes: ____________

(b) No: ____________

(c) Abstentions: ____________

(d) Persons demanding that their objections be noted and the reasons for their objections: ____________.

§ 48.118 Officers' Salaries

Resolved that the [*Board of Directors/Stockholders ratify/authorize*] that (but only to the extent to which set forth below) the salary of the Officers shall be:

(a) Position: [*Describe*].

(1) Compensation: $____________.

(2) Guaranteed period of employment: ____________.

(3) Expenses reimbursement:

Alternative A–1

(A) as determined by the Treasurer.

Alternative A–2

(A) not in excess of $______ per [*Time Period*] for business entertainment.

(B) not in excess of $______ per day for travel, including meals (excluding mileage which shall be paid at $[*Cents*] per mile.

COMMENT

Salaries paid to a Stockholder who directly or indirectly owns more than 50% of the corporate stock by a Corporation on the accrued method must be paid within 75 days of the corporate year end to be deductible (see Part A Introduction to Division VI (preceding Chapter 27, supra).

The following Officer(s) is authorized to carry out the above resolution: Treasurer

Option 1 (Not Preferred for Smoothly Running Closely Held Corporations)

The following vote on the above resolution was counted:

(a) Yes: __________.

(b) No: __________.

(c) Abstentions: __________.

(d) Persons demanding that their objections be noted and the reasons for their objections: __________.

§ 48.119 Officers' Salaries—Another Form

Resolved that, beginning on ______, 19__, and until changed by this board, the salary of the President shall be ______ Dollars per year, the salary of the Vice-President shall be ______ Dollars per year, the salary of the Secretary shall be ______ Dollars per year, and the salary of the Treasurer shall be ______ Dollars per year, and that these salaries shall be payable in monthly installments on the last day of each month.

Option 1 (Not Preferred for Smoothly Running Closely Held Corporations)

The following vote on the above resolution was counted:

(a) Yes: [*Number*];

(b) No: [*Number*];

(c) Absentions: [*Number*];

(d) Persons demanding that their objections be noted and the reasons for their objections: __________.

§ 48.120 Officers' Salaries—Increase of

Resolved, that the salary of the Vice-President be increased from the sum of $______ per year to the sum of $______ per year, and that the salary of the Treasurer be increased from the sum of $______ per year to the sum of $______ per year.

Option 1 (Not Preferred for Smoothly Running Closely Held Corporations)

The following vote on the above resolution was counted:

(a) Yes: [*Number*];

(b) No: [*Number*];

(c) Abstentions: [*Number*];

(d) Persons demanding that their objections be noted and the reasons for their objections: __________.

§ 48.121 Partial Liquidation

Resolved, that a partial liquidating dividend be declared and paid as of ______, 19__, said dividend to consist of the following described properties: [*Describe Property*]

Be it Further Resolved, that the Certificate of Incorporation of this Corporation be amended, reducing the Class [*Number*] [*common/preferred*] capital stock of the Corporation from ______ shares of Class [*Number*] [*preferred/common*] stock to ______ shares; and that of the net book value of the assets paid out as a liquidating dividend $[*Dollars*] of such amount be charged against the [*common/preferred*] capital stock account and the remainder be charged against the paid-in surplus account.

Option 1 (Not Preferred for Smoothly Running Closely Held Corporations)

The following vote on the above resolution was counted:

(a) Yes: [*Number*];

(b) No: [*Number*];

(c) Abstentions: [*Number*];

(d) Persons demanding that their objections be noted and the reasons for their objections: __________.

§ 48.122 Pension Trust

COMMENT

See § 48.125, infra.

§ 48.123 Purchase of Business

Resolved, that the offer made by ______ to sell and have conveyed to this Corporation the property of ______, Incorporated, as specified in their offer, for the number of shares of common stock and preferred stock and the amount of cash named in the offer, be accepted, and upon the delivery to this Corporation of satisfactory conveyances of the business and property specified in the offer, the proper Officers of this Corporation be and they are hereby authorized to issue and deliver to ______, or their assigns or nominees, in payment therefor, certificates for the number of shares of the common and preferred stock of this Corporation, and to pay to ______ the amount of cash specified to be paid in the offer; to assume in the name of this Corporation the liabilities referred to in the offer and the completion of the unperformed part of contracts referred to in the offer, and to do all things necessary to carry this resolution into effect.

Option 1 (Not Preferred for Smoothly Running Closely Held Corporations)

The following Officers are authorized to execute the same: President

Option 2 (Not Preferred for Smoothly Running Closely Held Corporations)

The following vote on the above resolution was counted:

(a) Yes: [*Number*];
(b) No: [*Number*];
(c) Abstentions: [*Number*];
(d) Persons demanding that their objections be noted and the reasons for their objections: __________.

Option 3 (Preferred as a Matter of Practical Experience)

The Secretary shall make part of the minute book a copy of the same.

§ 48.124 Purchase of Entire Property of Another Corporation by Issue of Shares

Resolved, that this Corporation purchase of the ______ Company all its rights, assets, plant, material, supplies, patents, and property of every kind and description, including good will, and that it pay in consideration thereof ______ shares of the capital shares of this Corporation, the shares to be taken in part payment of the purchase price, and to be issued as full-paid nonassessable shares, for the purchase of the property aforesaid, and to be designated as shares issued for property purchased.

Further resolved, that this Corporation assume the outstanding liabilities of ______ Company, which amount, according to the certificate of the treasurer thereof, to ______ dollars, and that it pay to the several creditors of the ______ Company the sums of money due to the creditors by its own checks and take due receipts therefor.

Further resolved, that this company also assumes the lease of ______ Company on the property at ______, ______, which lease is to run to ______, 19__, and the rent to be at the rate of ______ Dollars per month.

Option 1 (Not Preferred for Smoothly Running Closely Held Corporations)

The following Officers are authorized to execute the same: President

Option 2 (Not Preferred for Smoothly Running Closely Held Corporations)

The following vote on the above resolution was counted:

(a) Yes: [*Number*];
(b) No: [*Number*];
(c) Abstentions: [*Number*];
(d) Persons demanding that their objections be noted and the reasons for their objections: __________.

Option 3 (Preferred as a Matter of Practical Experience)

The Secretary shall make part of the minute book a copy of the same.

§ 48.125 Qualified Retirement Plan

Resolved that the [*Board of Directors/Stockholders ratify as executed/adopt as proposed*] a Qualified Retirement Plan which has the following features:

(a) Name of plan: __________.

(b) Minimum age for participation; __________.

(c) Minimum service for participation: __________.

(d) Employment status (categories): __________.

(e) Vesting: __________.

(f) Corporation contribution formula: __________.

(g) Employee contribution formula: __________.

(h) Effective date of plan: __________.

(i) Initial committee members: __________.

(j) Initial trustees: ____________.

(k) Initial contribution: ____________.

Any salary payment or other payment made to or on behalf of an Officer of the Corporation which shall be disallowed in whole or in part as a deductible expense for Federal income tax purposes, shall be reimbursed by such Officer to the Corporation to the full extent of the disallowance. It shall be the duty of the Board of Directors to enforce payment of each such amount disallowed.

COMMENT

One question that arises in the case of an employee benefit is the reasonableness of the benefit in light of the total compensation paid. If it is reasonable, the deduction will be available; if the total compensation is not reasonable, the deduction will not be available. The Internal Revenue Service will attempt to claim, in the case of a Corporation, that an unreasonably high payment was in the nature of a dividend to a Stockholder-employee, which was both not deductible to the Corporation and not subject to the maximum tax limitations on earned income. The popular solution to this problem is a "double dip" provision (the government is dipping twice into the transaction) in the corporate minutes which requires repayment of the disallowed benefit to the Corporation leaving the Corporation and the employee in the same position they would have been in if the payment had not been made. The government is presently trying to thwart the use of such a provision by asserting that its existence is prima facie evidence of the unreasonableness of the payment. Given the pervasive use of this provision, this "damned if you do or don't" assertion is absurd and, if carried to its logical extension, would negate all tax planning which was based upon a written assertion of the tax results being sought.

Option 1 (Preferred as a Matter of Practical Experience)

The Secretary shall make part of the minute book a copy of the same.

Option 2 (Not Preferred for Smoothly Running Closely Held Corporations)

The following Officers are authorized to execute the same: President and Secretary.

Option 3 (Not Preferred Unless There Is to Be a Consent Meeting and All Those Voting Won't Actually Review the Transaction)

The President shall do all things reasonable and necessary to carry out the purposes of the Qualified Retirement Plan and to that end he shall:

(a) Distribute the necessary Notice and summary to participants.

(b) Execute and file the necessary form with the Department of Labor.

(c) Execute and file the Application for determination of tax status with the Internal Revenue Service.

(d) Deliver the initial contribution to the Trustees of said plan.

(e) Establish procedures for (and carrying out such procedures) the execution by all participants of beneficiary designations and the election or refusal of a joint and survivor benefit.

COMMENT TO (e)

Modify if a joint and survivor benefit is not offered.

(f) Deliver Internal Revenue Service Form 1099 to all participants to reflect insurance economic benefit.

Option 4 (Not Preferred for Smoothly Running Closely Held Corporations)

The following vote on the above resolution was counted:

(a) Yes: [*Number*];

(b) No: [*Number*];

(c) Abstentions: [*Number*];

(d) Persons demanding that their objections be noted and the reasons for their objections: __________.

§ 48.126 Ratifying Transaction

Resolved, that the action of the Officers and Directors of this Corporation in [*Describe*] is ratified and approved.

COMMENT

Resolutions of Stockholders ratifying or adopting specific transactions are often obtained to "shore up" transactions between interested directors and the Corporation. Such resolutions may render reasonable transactions immune from attack, but will not prevent minority Stockholders from attacking transactions that involve fraud, waste, or probably manifest unfairness to the Corporation.

§ 48.127 Ratification and Approval of Transaction in Which a Director Has a Personal Interest

RESOLUTION RATIFYING AND APPROVING

[*Here Insert Appropriate Title*]

1. ______ [*Name of director(s) financially interested in transaction*] is now a Director of ______ Corporation.

2. The Stockholders of this Corporation have considered the following transaction. [*Here state facts of the proposed transaction. E. g., the rental of real property by the Corporation as lessee.*]

3. ______ [*Name of director(s) financially interested in transaction*] is interested in the transaction in that ______ [*Here state facts showing interest of Director. E. g., the interested Director is the owner and proposed lessor of the real property to be leased by the Corporation.*]

4. ______ [*Name of Interested Director*] has disclosed his interest to the Stockholders.

or

[4. The interest of [*Name of Director*] in this transaction is known to the Stockholders.]

5. The undersigned, constituting holders of a majority of the outstanding voting shares of the Corporation, find the transaction in the best interests of the Corporation and have resolved to, and do hereby, ratify and approve the acts of the Directors and Officers of the Corporation in entering into this transaction.

[The approving Stockholders should personally sign the minutes wherein such a resolution is stated, and the number of shares owned by each approving Stockholder should be indicated.]

Option 1 (Not Preferred for Smoothly Running Closely Held Corporations)

The following vote on the above resolution was counted:

(a) Yes: [*Number*];

(b) No: [*Number*];

(c) Abstentions: [*Number*];

(d) Persons demanding that their objections be noted and the reasons for their objections: ______________.

§ 48.128 Redemption

Resolved that the [*Board of Directors/Stockholders ratify as executed/adopt as proposed*] a stock redemption which has the following features:

(a) Stock to be redeemed: __________.

(b) Assets to be distributed for stock: ______ per [*common/preferred*] share.

(c) Closing date: __________.

COMMENT

See Chapters 61 et seq., infra, for forms.

Option 1 (Preferred as a Matter of Practical Experience)

The Secretary shall make part of the minute book a copy of the same.

Option 2 (Not Preferred for Smoothly Running Closely Held Corporations)

The following Officers are authorized to execute the notice to Stockholders: President.

Option 3 (Not Preferred Unless There Is to Be a Consent Meeting and All Those Voting Won't Actually Review the Transaction)

The President shall do all things reasonable and necessary to carry out the purposes of the redemption and to that end he shall:

(a) Notify the Stockholders of the redemption.

(b) Transfer documents and warrants of title.

(c) Distribute Internal Revenue Service form 1099 to all Stockholders redeemed and filing the same with the Internal Revenue Service.

Option 4 (Not Preferred for Smoothly Running Closely Held Corporations)

The following vote on the above resolution was counted:

(a) Yes: [*Number*];

(b) No: [*Number*];

(c) Abstentions: [*Number*];

(d) Persons demanding that their objections be noted and the reasons for their objections: __________.

§ 48.129 Reducing Capital Stock and Declaring Partial Liquidating Dividend

Whereas, this Corporation presently is the owner of certain properties;

Whereas, the Board of Directors deem it good business and advisable to make a partial liquidation of the Corporation and to pay out certain properties of the Corporation as a dividend in kind, ratably to the Stockholders of record on the ______ day of ______, 19__; and

Whereas, the payment of a partial liquidating dividend will impair the capital stock of the Corporation,

Now, therefore, be it resolved, that a partial liquidating dividend be declared and paid as of ______, 19__, said dividend to be paid in properties in kind and consisting of the following described properties: [*Here Describe*].

Be it further resolved, that the Articles of Incorporation of this Corporation be amended, reducing the capital stock of the Corporation from ______ shares of the par value of $______ per share to ______ shares of the par value of $______ per share; and that of the net book value of the assets paid out as a liquidating dividend $______ of such amount be charged against the capital stock account and the remainder be charged against the paid-in surplus account.

Option 1 (Not Preferred for Smoothly Running Closely Held Corporations)

The following vote on the above resolution was counted:

(a) Yes: [*Number*];

(b) No: [*Number*];

(c) Abstentions: [*Number*];

(d) Persons demanding that their objections be noted and the reasons for their objections: ______________.

§ 48.130 Registered Officer and/or Resident Agent

Resolved that the [*Board of Directors/Stockholders ratify as executed/adopt as proposed*] a Certificate of Change of [*Registered Office and/or Resident Agent*] which has the following features:

(a) New agent: __________.

(b) New address: __________.

(c) Applicable State: __________.

Option 1 (Preferred as a Matter of Practical Experience)

The Secretary shall make part of the minute book a copy of the same.

Option 2 (Not Preferred for Smoothly Running Closely Held Corporations)

The following Officers are authorized to execute the same: President.

Option 3 (Not Preferred Unless There Is to Be a Consent Meeting and All Those Voting Won't Actually Review the Transactions)

The President shall do all things reasonable and necessary to carry out the purposes of the Certificate of Change of Registered Office and/or Resident Agent and to that end he shall file the same with the relevant State.

Option 4 (Not Preferred for Smoothly Running Closely Held Corporations)

The following vote on the above resolution was counted:

(a) Yes: [*Number*];

(b) No: [*Number*];

(c) Abstentions: [*Number*];

(d) Persons demanding that their objections be noted and the reasons for their objections: ______________.

§ 48.131 Regular Meeting of the Board

Resolved, that the regular meetings of the Board of Directors be held on the ________ in every month at the Company's office in ________, at ________ o'clock ___. m. and that no notice of such meetings need be given.

Option 1 (Not Preferred for Smoothly Running Closely Held Corporations)

The following vote on the above resolution was counted:

(a) Yes: [*Number*];

(b) No: [*Number*];

(c) Abstentions: [*Number*];

(d) Persons demanding that their objections be noted and the reasons for their objections: ______________.

§ 48.132 Reimbursement of Employment Expenses

Resolved, that the following expenses be reimbursed to the following employees:

(a) Expenses of Conferences and Seminars.

Employee	Conference & Location	Date	Amount

(b) Medical Expenses.

Employee	Amount

(c) Miscellaneous Expenses.

Employee	Expense	Amount

(b) Any salary payment or other payment made to or on behalf of an Officer of the Corporation which shall be disallowed in whole or in part as a deductible expense for Federal income tax purposes, shall be reimbursed by such Officer to the Corporation to the full extent of the disallowance. It shall be the duty of the Board of Directors to enforce payment of each such amount disallowed.

COMMENT TO (b)

One question that arises in the case of an employee benefit is the reasonableness of the benefit in light of the total compensation paid. If it is reasonable, the deduction will be available; if the total compensation is not reasonable, the deduction will not be available. The Internal Revenue Service will attempt to claim, in the case of a Corporation, that an unreasonably high payment was in the nature of a dividend to a Stockholder-employee, which was both not deductible to the Corporation and not subject to the maximum tax limitations on earned income. The popular solution to this problem is a "double dip" provision (the government is dipping twice into the transaction) in the corporate minutes which requires repayment of the disallowed benefit to the Corporation leaving the Corporation and the employee in the same position they would have been in if the payment had not been made. The government is presently trying to thwart the use of such a provision by asserting that its existence is prima facie evidence of the unreasonableness of the payment. Given the pervasive use of this provision, this "damned if you do or don't" assertion is absurd and, if carried to its logical extension, would negate all tax planning which was based upon a written assertion of the tax results being sought.

Option 1 (Not Preferred Unless There Is to Be a Consent Meeting and All Those Voting Won't Actually Review the Transaction)

The Secretary shall make part of the minute book a copy of the same.

Option 2 (Not Preferred for Smoothly Running Closely Held Corporations)

The following vote on the above resolution was counted:

(a) Yes: ______________

(b) No: ______________

(c) Abstentions: ______________

(d) Persons demanding that their objections be noted and the reasons for their objections: ______________.

§ 48.133 Reimbursing Promoter

Resolved, that all costs and expenses incurred by ________, in or about the promotion, formation, and incorporation of this Corporation, amounting to $________, be forthwith repaid to him by the Corporation.

Option 1 (Not Preferred for Smoothly Running Closely Held Corporations)

The following vote on the above resolution was counted:

(a) Yes: [*Number*];

(b) No: [*Number*];

(c) Abstentions: [*Number*];

(d) Persons demanding that their objections be noted and the reasons for their objections: ____________________.

§ 48.134 Removal of Director

Be it resolved that pursuant to section ________ of the By-laws of the Corporation, ________ be and he hereby is removed from office as a Director of this Corporation and that ________ be and he is hereby appointed a Director of the Corporation in his place to hold office during the unexpired term of ________.

Option 1 (Not Preferred for Smoothly Running Closely Held Corporations)

The following vote on the above resolution was counted:

(a) Yes: [*Number*];

(b) No: [*Number*];

(c) Abstentions: [*Number*];

(d) Persons demanding that their objections be noted and the reasons for their objections: ____________________.

COMMENTS

Removal of Directors without cause is commonly permitted under the state business corporation acts if appropriate provision is included in the Articles of Incorporation or By-laws.

Such a resolution may be adopted only at a meeting expressly called for that purpose (Model Business Corporation Act § 39).

§ 48.135 Removal of Officers by Resolution of Directors

Upon motion duly made, seconded, and carried, the following resolution was adopted by the affirmative vote of a majority of the Directors present, at the time of the vote, at a meeting of the Board, a quorum being present:

Resolved, that [*Name of Officer*] be and he hereby is removed from the office of [*Title of Office*].

Option 1 (Not Preferred for Smoothly Running Closely Held Corporations)

The following vote on the above resolution was counted:

(a) Yes: [*Number*];

(b) No: [*Number*];

(c) Abstentions: [*Number*];

(d) Persons demanding that their objections be noted and the reasons for their objections: ____________.

§ 48.136 Removal of Entire Board of Directors and Electing Their Successors

Resolved that [*Here insert names of Directors to be removed*] be and they are hereby removed from office as Directors of this Corporation effective upon the election and qualification of their respective successors; and

Further resolved, that [*Here insert names of the new Directors*] be and they are hereby elected as Directors of this Corporation to serve until the annual meeting of Stockholders in 19__, or until their successors shall have been elected and qualify.

Option 1 (Not Preferred for Smoothly Running Closely Held Corporations)

The following vote on the above resolution was counted:

(a) Yes: [*Number*];

(b) No: [*Number*];

(c) Abstentions: [*Number*];

(d) Persons demanding that their objections be noted and the reasons for their objections: ________.

§ 48.137 Renewal of Corporate Existence

Resolved that the [*Board of Directors/Stockholders ratify as executed/adopt as proposed*] a Certificate of Renewal of Corporate Existence which has the following features:

(a) New corporate term: ________.

Option 1 (Preferred as a Matter of Practical Experience)

The Secretary shall make part of the minute book a copy of the same.

Option 2 (Not Preferred for Smoothly Running Closely Held Corporations)

The following Officers are authorized to execute the same: President.

Option 3 (Not Preferred for Smoothly Running Closely Held Corporations

The following vote on the above resolution was counted:

(a) Yes: [*Number*];

(b) No: [*Number*];

(c) Abstentions: [*Number*];

(d) Persons demanding that their objections be noted and the reasons for their objections: ________.

Library References:

C.J.S. Corporations § 79.
West's Key No. Digests, Corporations 🔑37.

§ 48.138 Reorganization—Exchange of Assets for Stock

Resolved that the [*Board of Directors/Stockholders ratify as executed/adopt as proposed*] an Agreement to Corporate Assets Exchange Assets for Stock of Another Corporation which has the following features:

(a) Effective Date: ________.

(b) Amount and description of corporate stock to be received: __________.

(c) Assets to be transferred: __________.

(d) Closing Date: __________.

(e) Special Features: __________.

Option 1 (Preferred as a Matter of Practical Experience)

The Secretary shall make part of the minute book a copy of the same.

Option 2 (Not Preferred for Smoothly Running Closely Held Corporations)

The following Officers are authorized to execute the same: President and Secretary.

Option 3 (Not Preferred Unless There Is to Be a Consent Meeting and All Those Voting Won't Actually Review the Transaction)

The President shall do all things reasonable and necessary to carry out the purposes of the Agreement to Corporate Assets Exchange Assets for Stock of Another Corporation and to that end he shall:

(a) Execute all transfer documents, warranties of title and representations.

(b) Cause the Corporation to apply for an Internal Revenue Service ruling as to the tax effect of the same.

Option 4 (Not Preferred for Smoothly Running Closely Held Corporations)

The following vote on the above resolution was counted:

(a) Yes: [*Number*];

(b) No: [*Number*];

(c) Abstentions: [*Number*];

(d) Persons demanding that their objections be noted and the reasons for their objections: __________.

Library References:

C.J.S. Corporations §§ 1583, 1584.
West's Key No. Digests, Corporations 🔑574.

§ 48.139 Reorganization—Exchange of Corporate Stock for Assets/Stock

Resolved that the [*Board of Directors/Stockholders ratify as executed/adopt as proposed*] an agreement to exchange Corporate Stock for [*assets/stock*] which has the following features:

(a) Effective Date: __________.

(b) Amount and description of corporate stock to be distributed: __________ for each [*Describe Assets or Stock to Be Received*].

(c) Closing Date: __________.

(d) Special Features: __________.

COMMENT

See Chapter 59, infra.

Option 1 (Preferred as a Matter of Practical Experience)

The Secretary shall make part of the minute book a copy of the same.

Option 2 (Not Preferred for Smoothly Running Closely Held Corporations)

The following Officers are authorized to execute the same: President and Secretary.

Option 3 (Not Preferred Unless There Is to Be a Consent Meeting and All Those Voting Won't Actually Review the Transaction)

The President shall do all things reasonable and necessary to carry out the purposes of the Reorganization and to that end he shall:

(a) Execute the proper transfer documents and representations.

(b) Cause the Corporation to apply for an Internal Revenue Service ruling as to the tax effect of the same.

Option 4 (Not Preferred for Smoothly Running Closely Held Corporations)

The following vote on the above resolution was counted:

(a) Yes: [*Number*];

(b) No: [*Number*];

(c) Abstentions: [*Number*];

(d) Persons demanding that their objections be noted and the reasons for their objections: __________.

§ 48.140 Reservation of Corporate Name

Resolved that the [*Board of Directors/Stockholders ratify as executed/adopt as proposed*] an application to Reserve Corporate Name which has the following features:

Name being reserved: ________.

Option 1 (Preferred as a Matter of Practical Experience)

The Secretary shall make part of the minute book a copy of the same.

Option 2 (Not Prefrered for Smoothly Running Closely Held Corporations)

The following Officers are authorized to execute the same: President.

Option 3 (Not Preferred Unless There Is to Be a Consent Meeting and All Those Voting Won't Actually Review the Transaction)

The President shall do all things reasonable and necessary to carry out the purposes of the Application to Reserve Corporate Name and to that end he shall: file the same with the States which the Corporation is to do business in.

Option 4 (Not Preferred for Smoothly Running Closely Held Corporations)

The following vote on the above resolution was counted:

(a) Yes: [*Number*];

(b) No: [*Number*];

(c) Abstentions: [*Number*];

(d) Persons demanding that their objections be noted and the reasons for their objections: ________.

§ 48.141 Resident Agent Change

Resolved, that as of the ____ day of ____, 19__, [*Name*] be and is hereby appointed the new agent for this Corporation in charge of the resident office of the Corporation and that the new resident office be located at [*Address*].

Option 1 (Not Preferred for Smoothly Running Closely Held Corporations)

The following vote on the above resolution was counted:

(a) Yes: [*Number*];

(b) No: [*Number*];

(c) Abstentions: [*Number*];

(d) Persons demanding that their objections be noted and the reasons for their objections: ______________.

§ 48.142 Resignation of Director

Resolved, that the resignation of ______ as Director of this Corporation be accepted to take effect on ______, 19__, and that the secretary be and he hereby is directed to notify ______ of such acceptance.

Option 1 (Not Preferred for Smoothly Running Closely Held Corporations)

The following vote on the above resolution was counted:

(a) Yes: [*Number*];

(b) No: [*Number*];

(c) Abstentions: [*Number*];

(d) Persons demanding that their objections be noted and the reasons for their objections: ___________.

§ 48.143 Resignation of Director and Appointing Successor

Resolved, that the resignation of ______ as a Director of this Corporation be and it hereby is accepted as of ______, 19__; and

Further resolved that the Secretary be and he hereby is directed to inform ______ of the acceptance of his resignation; and

Further resolved that ______ is hereby appointed a Director of this Corporation to fill the vacancy in the Board of Directors caused by the resignation of ______.

Option 1 (Not Preferred for Smoothly Running Closely Held Corporations)

The following vote on the above resolution was counted:

(a) Yes: [*Number*];

(b) No: [*Number*];

(c) Abstentions: [*Number*];

(d) Persons demanding that their objections be noted and the reasons for their objections: ___________.

§ 48.144 Restated Articles of Incorporation

Resolved that the [*Board of Directors/Stockholders ratify as executed/adopt as proposed*] restated Articles of Incorporation which have the following features:

(a) Purpose: [*Describe*].

(b) Summary of Provisions: [*Describe*].

COMMENT

See Chapter 51, infra, for form.

Option 1 (Preferred as a Matter of Practical Experience)

The Secretary shall make part of the minute book a copy of the same.

Option 2 (Not Preferred for Smoothly Running Closely Held Corporations)

The following Officer is authorized to execute the same: President.

Option 3 (Not Preferred Unless There Is to Be a Consent Meeting and All Those Voting Won't Actually Review the Transaction)

The President shall do all things reasonable and necessary to carry out the purposes of the Restated Articles of Incorporation and to that end he shall: file the same with the State of Incorporation and any other States the Corporation is registered to do business in.

Option 4 (Not Preferred for Smoothly Running Closely Held Corporations)

The following vote on the above resolution was counted:

(a) Yes: [*Number*];

(b) No: [*Number*];

(c) Abstentions: [*Number*];

(d) Persons demanding that their objections be noted and the reasons for their objections: __________.

§ 48.145 Retired Lives Reserve Plan

Resolved that the [*Board of Directors/Stockholders ratify as executed/adopt as proposed*] a Retired Lives Reserve Plan which has the following features:

Covered Employees	Benefit

Any salary payment or other payment made to or on behalf of an Officer of the Corporation which shall be disallowed in whole or in part as a deductible expense for Federal income tax purposes, shall be reimbursed by such Officer to the Corporation to the full extent of the disallowance. It shall be the duty of the Board of Directors to enforce payment of each such amount disallowed.

COMMENTS

One question that arises in the case of an employee benefit is the reasonableness of the benefit in light of the total compensation paid. If it is reasonable, the deduction will be available; if the total compensation is not reasonable, the deduction will not be available. The Internal Revenue Service will attempt to claim, in the case of a Corporation, that an unreasonably high payment was in the nature of a dividend to a Stockholder-employee, which was both not deductible to the Corporation and not subject to the maximum tax limitations on earned income. The popular solution to this problem is a "double dip" provision (the government is dipping twice into the transaction) in the corporate minutes which requires repayment of the disallowed benefit to the Corporation leaving the Corporation and the employee in the same position they would have been in if the payment had not been made. The government is presently trying to thwart the use of such a provision by asserting that its existence is prima facie evidence of the unreasonableness of the payment. Given the pervasive use of this provision, this "damned if you do or don't" assertion is absurd and, if carried to its logical extension, would negate all tax planning which was based upon a written assertion of the tax results being sought.

See Employee Benefit Plans Volume for form.

Option 1 (Preferred as a Matter of Practical Experience)

The Secretary shall make part of the minute book a copy of the same.

Option 2 (Not Preferred for Smoothly Running Closely Held Corporations)

The following Officers are authorized to execute the same: President and Secretary.

Option 3 (Not Preferred Unless There Is to Be a Consent Meeting and All Those Voting Won't Actually Review the Transaction)

The President shall do all things reasonable and necessary to carry out the purposes of the Retired Lives Reserve Plan and to that end he shall:

(a) Distribute the necessary disclosure summary to participants.

(b) Execute and file the necessary form with the Department of Labor.

(c) Pay plan expenses as required or reasonably necessary.

(d) Deliver Internal Revenue Service Form 1099 to all participants to reflect insurance economic benefits.

Option 1 (Not Preferred for Smoothly Running Closely Held Corporations)

The following vote on the above resolution was counted:

(a) Yes: [*Number*];

(b) No: [*Number*];

(c) Abstentions: [*Number*];

(d) Persons demanding that their objections be noted and the reasons for their objections: ________.

§ 48.146 Salary Adjustments

Resolved, that the following salary adjustments for the present fiscal year be ratified:

Employee	Amount	Date Effective

Further, any salary payment or other payment made to or on behalf of an Officer of the Corporation which shall be disallowed in whole or in part as a deductible expense for Federal income tax purposes, shall be reimbursed by such Officer to the Corporation to the full extent of the disallowance. It shall be the duty of the Board of Directors to enforce payment of each such amount disallowed.

COMMENT

One question that arises in the case of an employee benefit is the reasonableness of the benefit in light of the total compensation paid. If it is reasonable, the deductible will be available; if the total compensation is not reasonable, the deduction will not be available. The Internal Revenue Service will attempt to claim, in the case of a Corporation, that an unreasonably high payment was in the nature of a dividend to a Stockholder-employee, which was both not deductible to the Corporation and not subject to the maximum tax limitations on earned income. The popular solution to this problem is a "double dip" provision (the government is dipping twice into the transaction) in the corporate minutes which requires repayment of the disallowed benefit to the Corporation leaving the Corporation and the employee in the same position they would have been in if the payment had not been made. The government is presently trying to thwart the use of such a provision by asserting that its existence is prima facie evidence of the unreasonableness of the payment. Given the pervasive use of this provision, this "damned if you do or don't" assertion is absurd and, if carried to its logical extension, would negate all tax planning which was based upon a written assertion of the tax results being sought.

Option 1 (Not Preferred Unless There Is to Be a Consent Meeting and All Those Voting Won't Actually Review the Transaction)

The Secretary shall make part of the minute book a copy of the same.

Option 2 (Not Preferred for Smoothly Running Closely Held Corporations)

The following vote on the above resolution was counted:

(a) Yes: __________

(b) No: __________

(c) Abstentions: __________

(d) Persons demanding that their objections be noted and the reasons for their objections: __________.

§ 48.147 Sale of Assets

Resolved that the [*Board of Directors/Stockholders ratify as executed/adopt as proposed*] an Agreement to Sell Assets which has the following features:

(a) Buyer: __________.

(b) Price: __________.

(c) Terms: __________.

(d) Special features: __________.

(e) Closing date: __________.

Option 1 (Preferred as a Matter of Practical Experience)

The Secretary shall make part of the minute book a copy of the same.

Option 2 (Not Preferred for Smoothly Running Closely Held Corporations)

The following Officers are authorized to execute the same: President and Secretary.

Option 3 (Not Preferred Unless There Is to Be a Consent Meeting and All Those Voting Won't Actually Review the Transaction)

The President shall do all things reasonable and necessary to carry out the purposes of the Sale of Assets and to that end he shall be responsible to:

(a) Execute all necessary transfer documents, warrants of title and representations.

(b) Execute all security liens and UCC–1 security statements and the proper recording of the same.

Option 4 (Not Preferred for Smoothly Running Closely Held Corporations)

The following vote on the above resolution was counted:

(a) Yes: [*Number*];

(b) No: [*Number*];

(c) Abstentions: [*Number*];

(d) Persons demanding that their objections be noted and the reasons for their objections: ____________.

Library References:

C.J.S. Corporations § 1095.
West's Key No. Digests, Corporations ⚷439.

§ 48.148 Sale of Stock

Resolved, that [*Name(s)*] having offered to transfer to this Corporation all of the net assets described in the Offer attached hereto, for issuance to [*him/them*], fully paid and nonassessable [*Number*] shares (this being all of the issued capital shares) of the Corporation and it being determined that such property is necessary for the use and lawful purposes of this Corporation, this Corporation is hereby authorized to accept the Offer of [*Names*], and upon receipt of the necessary documents transferring the following assets to [*Name*] in exchange for [*Number*] shares of this Corporation in full payment thereof: [*Describe Assets*].

Option 1 (Not Preferred for Smoothly Running Closely Held Corporations)

The following vote on the above resolution was counted:

(a) Yes: [*Number*];
(b) No: [*Number*];
(c) Abstentions: [*Number*];
(d) Persons demanding that their objections be noted and the reasons for their objections : ____________.

§ 48.149 Seal

Resolved, that the Seal, the impression of which is herewith affixed, be adopted as this Corporation's corporate seal:

[*Imprint Seal Here*]

COMMENT

In most states a seal is no longer needed to have a validly executed document.

§ 48.150 Seal and Regulating Its Use

Resolved, that the seal now produced by the Secretary, an impression whereof is now made in the minute book of the Company, be adopted as the seal of the Company, and that such seal shall not be affixed to any deed or instrument of any description, except in the presence of an Officer, or Director, and the Secretary of the Company, who shall respectively sign said deed or instrument.

Option 1 (Not Preferred for Smoothly Running Closely Held Corporations)

The following vote on the above resolution was counted:

(a) Yes: [*Number*];
(b) No: [*Number*];
(c) Abstentions: [*Number*];
(d) Persons demanding that their objections be noted and the reasons for their objections: __________.

§ 48.151 Security for Faithful Performance of Duties

Resolved, that ______, who has been duly appointed as ______, shall give to the Corporation security for the faithful performance of his duties as ______, and that the security shall be in the form of a bond in the penal sum of $______, with two good and sufficient securities to be approved by this board, or a surety company bond of like amount to be approved by this board, or he may deposit with the Treasurer of this Corporation as such security the sum of $______ with his personal bond.

Option 1 (Not Preferred for Smoothly Running Closely Held Corporations)

The following vote on the above resolution was counted:

(d) Yes: [*Number*];
(b) No: [*Number*];
(c) Abstentions: [*Number*];

(d) Persons demanding that their objections be noted and the reasons for their objections: ____________.

§ 48.152 Security from Officer—Requirement

Resolved, that [*Name of Officer*], who has been duly appointed as [*Title of Officer*] shall give to the Corporation security for the faithful performance of his duties as [*Title of Officer*], and that the security shall be in the form of a bond in the sum of _______ ($_______) Dollars, with two good and sufficient securities to be approved by this board, or a surety company bond of like amount to be approved by this Board, or he may deposit with the Treasurer of this Corporation as such security the sum of _______ ($_______) Dollars with his personal bond.

Option 1 (Not Preferred for Smoothly Running Closely Held Corporations)

The following vote on the above resolution was counted:

(a) Yes: [*Number*];

(b) No: [*Number*];

(c) Abstentions: [*Number*];

(d) Persons demanding that their objections be noted and the reasons for their objections: ____________.

§ 48.153 Settlement of Claim

Whereas, [*Name*] claims to have been severely injured by [*Describe*], and [*Name*] (the Corporation's attorney) recommends the Corporation's acceptance of an offer to settle for $[*Dollars*].

Resolved, that the Treasurer be authorized and directed to pay $[*Dollars*] to [*Name*] on his signing and delivering to the Treasurer a proper release of all claims against this Corporation, the form of the release to be approved by said attorney.

Option 1 (Not Preferred for Smoothly Running Closely Held Corporations)

The following Officer is authorized to execute the same: President.

Option 2 (Not Preferred for Smoothly Running Closely Held Corporations)

The following vote on the above resolution was counted:

(a) Yes: [*Number*];

(b) No: [*Number*];

(c) Abstentions: [*Number*];

(d) Persons demanding that their objections be noted and the reasons for their objections: __________.

§ 48.154 Sinking Fund

Whereas, there will be available in the Treasury of this Company on ______, 19__, the sum of ______ Dollars:

Resolved, that the Treasurer of this Company is authorized and directed to place such sum in a sinking fund hereby created for the purpose of retiring the preferred stock of this Corporation, that the Secretary is further directed to give to each Stockholder notice of the amount of the sinking fund, and that it will be used for the retirement of preferred stock at the lowest price the same is offered, and stating that on ______, 19__, the Treasurer will receive sealed tenders of said preferred stock.

Further resolved, that at said last mentioned time the Secretary and Treasurer open any sealed tenders received, and use said sinking fund for the purchase of preferred stock, accepting the lowest tenders received, and, in the event the sinking fund is not exhausted, they are to use the balance in redeeming at its call price the preferred stock of Stockholders whose names are successively drawn by lot.

Option 1 (Not Preferred for Smoothly Running Closely Held Corporations)

The following vote on the above resolution was counted:

(a) Yes: [*Number*];

(b) No: [*Number*];

(c) Abstentions: [*Number*];

(d) Persons demanding that their objections be noted and the reasons for their objections: ______________.

Library References:

C.J.S. Corporations § 1169.
West's Key No. Digests, Corporations ⚿486.

§ 48.155 Specific Indemnification of Officer, Director, Employee or Agent

Resolved that the [*Board of Directors/Stockholders ratify/authorize*] that (but only to the extent to which set forth below) [*Name*] shall be indemnified for:

(a) Transaction or claim: __________.

(b) Limits of liability indemnification: $__________.

(c) Limits of indemnification for legal fees incurred: $________.

The following Officer is authorized to carry out the above resolution: Treasurer.

Option 1 (Not Preferred for Smoothly Running Closely Held Corporations)

The following vote on the above resolution was counted:

(a) Yes: ________.

(b) No: ________.

(c) Abstentions: ________.

(d) Persons demanding that their objections be noted and the reasons for their objections: ________.

COMMENT

See § 8.1 and § 8.2 of the form at § 34.14, infra, for the relevant By-law provisions.

§ 48.156 Split Dollar Plan

Resolved that the [*Board of Directors/Stockholders ratify as executed/adopt as proposed*]:

(a) A Split Dollar Plan with following features:

(1) Name of Plan: ________

(2) Type of Plan:

Alternative A–1

Collateral Assignment

Alternative A–2

Endorsement Method

Alternative A–3

Fractional Assignment

Alternative A–4

Revise Split Dollar

(3) Type of policy:

Alternative B–1

Face value of $________.

Alternative B–2

Premium of $________.

(4) Corporation's contribution shall be:

Alternative C–1

the increase, if any, in the tabular cash surrender value of the policy which will result from the premium payment in question and the application of dividends toward the purchase of additional insurance.

Alternative C–2

the difference, if any, in the premium then due and the "PS–58" costs of the policy in question.

Alternative C–3

the total premium, net of dividends and premium waivers.

(5) The insured's obligation shall be:

Alternative D–1

the PS–58 cost.

Alternative D–2

none.

Alternative D–3

the difference between the premium due and the Corporation's obligation set forth above.

(6) The "total loan" shall be defined as

Option 1

the total amount actually paid by the Corporation,

Option 2

$______ plus interest at ______ percent per annum.

COMMENT TO (6)

There is a loan only with a collateral assignment split dollar program.

(7) Participant description: ____________.

(b) Any salary payment or other payment made to or on behalf of an Officer of the Corporation which shall be disallowed in whole or in part as a deductible expense for Federal income tax purposes, shall be reimbursed by such Officer to the Corporation to the full extent of the disallowance. It shall be the duty of the Board of Directors to enforce payment of each such amount disallowed.

COMMENT TO (b)

One question that arises in the case of an employee benefit is the reasonableness of the benefit in light of the total compensation paid. If it is reasonable, the deduction will be available; if the total compensation is not reasonable, the deduction will not be available. The Internal Revenue Service will attempt to claim, in the case of a Corporation, that an unreasonably high payment was in the nature of a dividend to a Stockholder-employee, which was both not deductible to the Corporation and not subject to the maximum tax limitations on earned income. The popular solution to this problem is a "double dip" provision (the government is dipping twice into the transaction) in the corporate minutes which requires repayment of the disallowed benefit to the Corporation leaving the Corporation and the employee in the same position they would have been in if the payment had not been made. The government is presently trying to thwart the use of such a provision by asserting that its existence is prima facie evidence of the unreasonableness of the payment. Given the pervasive use of this provision, this "damned if you do or don't" assertion is absurd and, if carried to its logical extension, would negate all tax planning which was based upon a written assertion of the tax results being sought.

Option 3 (Preferred as a Matter of Practical Experience)

(c) The Secretary shall make part of the minute book a copy of the same.

Option 4 (Not Preferred for Smoothly Running Closely Held Corporations)

(d) The following Officers are authorized to execute the same: President and Secretary.

Option 5 (Not Preferred Unless There Is to Be a Consent Meeting and All Those Voting Won't Actually Review the Transaction)

(e) The President shall do all things reasonable and necessary to carry out the purposes of the Split Dollar Plan and to that end he shall:

(1) Distribute the necessary disclosure summary to participants.

(2) Execute and file the necessary form with the Department of Labor.

(3) Pay plan expenses as required or reasonably necessary.

(4) Deliver Internal Revenue Service Form 1099 to all participants to reflect insurance economic benefit.

(5) Execute the necessary *assignment/endorsement* forms of the insurance company.

Option 6 (Not Preferred for Smoothly Running Closely Held Corporations)

(f) The following vote on the above resolution was counted:

(1) Yes: [*Number*];

(2) No: [*Number*];

(3) Abstentions: [*Number*];

(4) Persons demanding that their objections be noted and the reasons for their objections: ________.

§ 48.157 Stock Certificates

Resolved, that the Board of Directors having reviewed the proposed [*common/preferred*] stock certificate form, the same is hereby adopted and a copy shall be inserted in the minute book by the Secretary.

COMMENT

Insert Sample Stock Certificate. See Chapter 41, supra.

§ 48.158 Stock Dividend

Whereas, there has been accumulated from undistributed profits of the Corporation an earned surplus of $______, which in the opinion of the Board of Directors can be advantageously used for the benefit of stockholders for acquiring property and goods for extending the company's business operations.

Therefore, resolved that $______ of the earned surplus be transferred to capital and ______ shares of common stock, Class C, of the par value of $______ per share, be issued and held as treasury stock until disbursed as hereinafter provided.

Be it further resolved that a dividend be and the same hereby is declared payable to Stockholders of record as of ______, 19__, one share of Class C common stock of the par value of $______ per share shall be distributed as such dividend to the holder of each outstanding share of common stock of Class A and Class B of the par value of $______ each, and to the holder of each share of nonpar preferred stock, the stock dividend to be extra and additional to any cash dividend now or hereafter declared.

Option 1 (Not Preferred for Smoothly Running Closely Held Corporations)

The following vote on the above resolution was counted:

(a) Yes: [*Number*];

(b) No: [*Number*];

(c) Abstentions: [*Number*];

(d) Persons demanding that their objections be noted and the reasons for their objections: ____________.

COMMENTS

Unlike a cash or in kind dividend, a share dividend does not reduce the assets of a Corporation. The only restrictions on a share dividend is that there must be authorized but unissued shares (or treasury shares reacquired out of surplus) and unrestricted surplus sufficient to permit the transfer to stated capital of an amount equal to the aggregate par value of the shares to be issued as dividend.

A pure share dividend does not constitute taxable income. However, as a result of the Tax Reform Act of 1969, virtually any election on the part of any Stockholder to take the dividend in cash or property rather than shares will render the entire dividend taxable income. Internal Revenue Code of 1954, § 305. Where a share dividend is taxable, the amount is determined by the fair market value of the shares received. See Chapter 57, infra.

A stock split is in some respects similar to a share dividend. However, the latter increases the stated capital of the Corporation while the former usually reduces the par value of each share so that the stated capital remains unaffected. A stock split usually requires an amendment to the Articles of Incorporation. See Chapter 57, infra, with respect to stock splits.

Library References:

C.J.S. Corporations § 466 et seq.
West's Key No. Digests, Corporations ⚷157.

§ 48.159 Stock Dividend—Another Form

Resolved, that a stock dividend consisting of *one-fifth* of one share of the capital stock of the par value of *$1.00* per share of this Corporation, on each share of the capital stock of this Corporation be and the same hereby is declared, payable to the holders of record of shares of this Corporation as of the ______ day of ______, payable on the ______ day of ______.

Resolved further, that the sum of $______, equal to the aggregate par value of the shares being issued pursuant to the stock dividend previously declared, be and the same is hereby transferred from earned surplus to stated capital of the Corporation, and the Treasurer of the Corporation is instructed to debit the earned surplus account of the Corporation and to credit the stated capital account of the Corporation in such sum.

Option 1 (Not Preferred for Smoothly Running Closely Held Corporations)

The following vote on the above resolution was counted:

(a) Yes: [*Number*];

(b) No: [*Number*];

(c) Abstentions: [*Number*];

(d) Persons demanding that their objections be noted and the reasons for their objections: ________________.

§ 48.160 Stock Dividend—Another Form

Whereas, this Corporation desires to transfer a portion of its retained earnings to stated capital,

Resolved, that a stock dividend of ______ percent be paid to Stockholders of record on ______. Said dividend is to be issued and paid within ______ days of said record date.

Resolved, that the retained earnings account be charged with $______, and that stated capital be credited in a like amount.

Resolved, that no fractional shares are to be issued pursuant to this dividend, but cash payments shall be made to each Stockholder based on the value of one whole share on the issuance date.

Option 1 (Not Preferred for Smoothly Running Closely Held Corporations)

The following vote on the above resolution was counted:

(a) Yes: [*Number*];

(b) No: [*Number*];

(c) Abstentions: [*Number*];

(d) Persons demanding that their objections be noted and the reasons for their objections: ________________.

§ 48.161 Stock Dividend—Another Form

Whereas, the financial statements furnished by the Treasurer of this Corporation to the Board of Directors are believed by the Directors to be an accurate statement of the financial condition of the Corporation on the last day of the fiscal year ending the ______ day of ______, 19__, and

Whereas, the balance sheet shows that this Corporation has unreserved surplus, of $______, which in the opinion of the Board of Directors can advantageously be used for the benefit of Stockholders for acquiring property and goods for extending the Corporation's business,

Therefore, be it resolved, that $______ of said surplus be transferred to capital and ______ shares of common stock, Class C, of the par value of *$5* per share, be issued and held as treasury stock until disbursed as hereinafter provided, and

Be it further resolved, that a stock dividend be and the same hereby is declared payable to Stockholders of record as of the ______ day of ______, 19__, one share of Class C common stock of the par value of *$5* per share to be distributed as such stock dividend to the holder of each outstanding share of common stock of Class A and Class B of the par value of *$100* each, and a like amount to the holder of each share of non-par preferred *$6* per share stock, said stock dividend to be extra and additional to any cash dividend now or hereafter declared.

Option 1 (Not Preferred for Smoothly Running Closely Held Corporations)

The following vote on the above resolution was counted:

(a) Yes: [*Number*];

(b) No: [*Number*];

(c) Abstentions: [*Number*];

(d) Persons demanding that their objections be noted and the reasons for their objections: ______________.

§ 48.162 Stock Dividend—Another Form

Whereas, there has been accumulated from undistributed profits of the Corporation a surplus of $______, which in the opinion of the Board of Directors can be advantageously used for the benefit of Stockholders for acquiring property and goods for extending the Corporation's business operations:

Resolved, that $______ of said surplus be transferred to capital and ______ shares of common stock, Class C, of the par value of *$5* per share, be issued and held as treasury stock until disbursed as hereinafter provided.

Further resolved, that a stock dividend be and the same hereby is declared payable to Stockholders of record as of the ______ day of ______, 19__, one share of Class C common stock of the par value of *$5* per share to be distributed as such stock dividend to the holder of each outstanding share of common stock of Class A and Class B of the par value of *$100* each, and a like amount to the holder of each share of no par preferred stock of the par value of *$100* each, said stock dividend to be extra and additional to any cash dividend now or hereafter declared.

Option 1 (Not Preferred for Smoothly Running Closely Held Corporations)

The following vote on the above resolution was counted:

(a) Yes: [*Number*];

(b) No: [*Number*];

(c) Abstentions: [*Number*];

(d) Persons demanding that their objections be noted and the reasons for their objections: ______________.

§ 48.163 Stock Dividend—Another Form

Whereas, there has been accumulated from undistributed profits of the Corporation a surplus of ______ ($______) Dollars, which in the opinion of the Board of Directors cannot be advantageously used for the benefit of Stockholders for acquiring property and goods for extending the Corporation's business operations;

Therefore be it,

Resolved that ______ ($______) Dollars of said surplus be transferred to stated capital and ______ shares of common shares, class "______", of the par value of ______ ($______) Dollars per share, be issued and held as treasury shares until disbursed as hereinafter provided, and be it further,

Resolved that a share distribution be and the same is hereby declared payable to Stockholders of record as of the ______ day of ______, 19__, one share of common shares, class "______" of the par value of ______ ($______) Dollars per share to be distributed as such share distribution to the holder of each outstanding share of common shares, class "______" of the par value of ______ ($______) Dollars each, said share distribution to be extra and additional to any cash dividend now or hereafter declared.

Option 1 (Not Preferred for Smoothly Running Closely Held Corporations)

The following vote on the above resolution was counted:

(a) Yes: [*Number*];

(b) No: [*Number*];

(c) Abstentions: [*Number*];

(d) Persons demanding that their objections be noted and the reasons for their objections: ______________.

§ 48.164 Stock Dividend—Another Form

Resolved, that the Board of Directors be and hereby are authorized and requested to direct the President and Secretary of the Corporation to issue ______ shares of the Class [*Number*] [*common/preferred*] stock of the Corporation to be divided pro rata among the Stockholders of record on the ______ day of ______, 19__.

DIRECTORS' RESOLUTION

Whereas, there has been accumulated from undistributed profits of the Corporation a surplus of $______, which in the opinion of the Board of Directors can be advantageously used for the benefit of Stockholders for acquiring property and goods for extending the Corporation's business operations;

Option 1

Resolved, that $______ of said surplus be transferred to capital.

Option 2

And resolved that shares of [*common/preferred*] stock, Class [*Number*], be issued and held as treasury stock until disbursed as hereinafter provided.

Further resolved, that a stock dividend be and the same hereby is declared payable to Stockholders of record as of the ______ day of ______, 19__, one share of Class [*Number*] [*common/preferred*] stock to be distributed as such stock dividend to the holders of outstanding share of Class [*Number*] [*common/preferred*] of the Corporation.

Option 3 (Not Preferred for Smoothly Running Closely Held Corporations)

The following vote on the above resolution was counted:

(a) Yes: [*Number*];

(b) No: [*Number*];

(c) Abstentions: [*Number*];

(d) Persons demanding that their objections be noted and the reasons for their objections: __________.

§ 48.165 Stock Dividend—Stockholders' Resolution—Another Form

Whereas, at the annual meeting of the Stockholders of this Corporation held on the ______ day of ______, 19__, a resolution was adopted requesting the Board of Directors to issue additional capital stock of this Corporation to the amount of $______ to be divided pro rata among the present Stockholders, and based upon the fact that during the last ______ years more than $______ of the net earnings of the Corporation have been expended for permanent improvements and betterments, thereby adding to the amount of assets of the Corporation which belong to the Stockholders:

Resolved, that the President and Secretary of this Corporation are hereby directed to issue ______ shares of the capital stock of the Corporation to the Stockholders of record on the ______ day of ______, 19__, in proportion to the amount of stock then owned by them respectively.

Option 1 (Not Preferred for Smoothly Running Closely Held Corporations)

The following vote on the above resolution was counted:

(a) Yes: [*Number*];

(b) No: [*Number*];

(c) Abstentions: [*Number*];

(d) Persons demanding that their objections be noted and the reasons for their objections: ______________.

§ 48.166 Stock Dividend—Stockholders' Resolution—Another Form

Whereas at the annual meeting of the Stockholders of this Corporation held on the ______ day of ______, 19__, a resolution was adopted requesting the Board of Directors to issue additional shares of this Corporation to the amount of ______ ($______) Dollars to be divided pro rata among the present Stockholders, and based upon the fact that during the last ______ years more than ______ ($______) Dollars of the net earnings of the Corporation have been expended for permanent improvements and betterments, thereby adding to the amount of assets of the Corporation which belong to the Stockholders; therefore be it,

Resolved, that the President and Secretary of this Corporation are hereby directed to issue ______ shares of the authorized but unissued shares of the Corporation to the Stockholders of record on the ______ day of ______, 19__, in proportion to the amount of shares then owned by them respectively, and be it further,

Resolved, that there be transferred from surplus to stated capital ______ ($______) Dollars, being the aggregate par value of the shares distributed.

Option 1 (Not Preferred for Smoothly Running Closely Held Corporations)

The following vote on the above resolution was counted:

(a) Yes: [*Number*];

(b) No: [*Number*];

(c) Abstentions: [*Number*];

(d) Persons demanding that their objections be noted and the reasons for their objections: ________________.

§ 48.167 Stock Dividend—Stockholders' Resolution—Another Form

Whereas, there has been expended for improvements and betterments during the years ______ more than $______, all of which sum has been furnished from the net earnings of the Corporation and fairly belongs to the Stockholders:

Resolved, that the Board of Directors be and hereby are authorized and requested to direct the President and Secretary of the Corporation to issue ______ shares of the capital stock of the Corporation, to be divided pro rata among the Stockholders of record on the ______ day of ______, 19__.

Option 1 (Not Preferred for Smoothly Running Closely Held Corporations)

The following vote on the above resolution was counted:

(a) Yes: [*Number*];

(b) No: [*Number*];

(c) Abstentions: [*Number*];

(d) Persons demanding that their objections be noted and the reasons for their objections: ________________.

COMMENT

Such resolution acts as notice of the wishes of the Stockholders, but does not compel the directors to declare such dividend, which they may or may not do in their discretion.

§ 48.168 Stock Dividend—Stockholders' Resolution—Another Form

We, the undersigned, being a majority of the holders of the outstanding shares to be distributed of [*Class*] shares of ______, a domestic Corporation organized under the laws of the State of ______, do hereby consent, there being no outstanding preemptive rights, that the following action permitted to be taken by vote, be taken without a meeting on written consent, to wit:

The Board of Directors of [*Name of Corporation*] is hereby authorized to direct the President and the Secretary of the Corporation to issue [*Number*] shares of [*Class*] shares of the authorized but unissued shares of said Corporation to the amount of ______ ($______) Dollars, to be distributed among the present holders of record of [*Class*] shares as of the ______ day of ______, 19__, in proportion to the amount of shares then owned by them respectively.

Option 1 (Not Preferred for Smoothly Running Closely Held Corporations)

The following vote on the above resolution was counted:

(a) Yes: [*Number*];

(b) No: [*Number*];

(c) Abstentions: [*Number*];

(d) Persons demanding that their objections be noted and the reasons for their objections: ______________.

§ 48.169 Stock Offering Plan

Resolved that the [*Board of Directors/Stockholders ratify as executed/adopt as proposed*] a Plan of Stock offering which has the following features:

(a) Description of Stock to be offered: [*Describe*]:

(b) Number of shares to be offered: Minimum: __________; Maximum: __________.

(c) Persons who are to get a specific offer and number of shares to be offered and consideration to be paid by them: [*Describe*]

(d) Criterion for rest of offering: __________.

(e) Agent to handle offering: __________.

(f) Commission to be paid to agent: __________.

(g) Time limit of offering: __________.

COMMENT

See Chapter 29, supra, for form of promoters agreement.

Option 1 (Preferred as a Matter of Practical Experience)

The Secretary shall make part of the minute book a copy of the same.

Option 2 (Not Preferred for Smoothly Running Closely Held Corporations)

The following Officer is authorized to execute the same: President.

Option 3 (Not Preferred for Smoothly Running Closely Held Corporations)

The following vote on the above resolution was counted:

(a) Yes: [*Number*];

(b) No: [*Number*];

(c) Abstentions: [*Number*];

(d) Persons demanding that their objections be noted and the reasons for their objections: ____________.

§ 48.170 Stock Option

Resolved that the [*Board of Directors/Stockholders ratify as executed/adopt as proposed*] a Stock Option which has the following features:

(a) Person issued to: ____________.

(b) Consideration: ____________.

(c) Stock which can be bought: ____________.

(d) Option price: ____________.

(e) Expiration date: ____________.

(f) Transfer restrictions: ____________.

(g) Earliest date of option exercise: ____________.

COMMENT

See Employee Benefit Plan Volume for form.

Option 1 (Preferred as a Matter of Practical Experience)

The Secretary shall make part of the minute book a copy of the same.

Option 2 (Not Preferred for Smoothly Running Closely Held Corporations)

The following Officer is authorized to execute the same: President.

Option 3 (Not Preferred for Smoothly Running Closely Held Corporations)

The following vote on the above resolution was counted:

(a) Yes: [*Number*];

(b) No: [*Number*];

(c) Abstentions: [*Number*];

(d) Persons demanding that their objections be noted and the reasons for their objections: ____________.

§ 48.171 Stock Split

Resolved, that Article *Fourth* of the Certificate of Incorporation be and the same is hereby amended as follows:

"Fourth:" * * * [*Number*] shares shall be [*Describe*] common stock.

At the time this amendment becomes effective, and without any further action on the part of the Corporation or its Stockholders, each share of common stock without par value then issued and outstanding shall be changed and reclassified into [*Number*] fully paid and nonassessable shares of [*Describe*] common stock. The capital account of the Corporation shall not be increased or decreased by such change and reclassification. To reflect the said change and reclassification, each certificate representing shares of common stock without par value theretofore issued and outstanding shall represent a like number of shares of [*Describe*] stock without par value issued and outstanding after such change and reclassification; and the holder of record of each certificate shall be entitled to receive a new certificate representing a number of shares of [*Describe*] stock without par value of the kind authorized by this amendment, equal to the number of shares represented by said certificate for theretofore issued and outstanding shares, so that upon this amendment becoming effective each holder of record of a certificate representing theretofore issued and outstanding [*Describe*] stock of the Corporation will have or be entitled to certificates representing in the aggregate [*Number*] shares of [*Describe*] stock without par value of the kind authorized by this amendment for each share of [*Describe*] stock without par value of which he was the holder prior to the effectiveness of this amendment.

Option 1 (Not Preferred for Smoothly Running Closely Held Corporations)

The following vote on the above resolution was counted:

(a) Yes: [*Number*];

(b) No: [*Number*];

(c) Abstentions: [*Number*];

(d) Persons demanding that their objections be noted and the reasons for their objections: __________.

§ 48.172 Stock Split—Another Form

Whereas, the Articles of Incorporation now authorize the issuance of *1,000* shares of *$100* par value common stock, of which *500* shares are now issued and outstanding; and

Whereas, it is deemed to be in the best interest of this Corporation and its Stockholders to split the outstanding shares into 5,000 shares of the same class;

Therefore, be it resolved, that Article ______ of the Articles of Incorporation of this Corporation be amended to read:

The aggregate number of shares which the Corporation is authorized to issue is *10,000 shares* consisting of one class. The designation of each class, the number of shares of each class, and the par value, if any, of the shares of each class, or a statement that the shares of any class are without par value, are as follows:

Class	**Number of Shares**	**Par Value Per Share**
Common		

Be it further resolved, that on the effective date of said amendment each share of *$100* par value common stock outstanding before the amendment is subdivided and reclassified into *10* shares of *$10* par value common stock.

Be it further resolved, that the Officers of this Corporation are hereby authorized and directed to take any steps necessary to submit the foregoing amendment to the Stockholders for approval and to perform all acts and execute all instruments necessary and proper to carry out these resolutions.

Option 1 *(Not Preferred for Smoothly Running Closely Held Corporations)*

The following vote on the above resolution was counted:

(a) Yes: [*Number*];

(b) No: [*Number*];

(c) Abstentions: [*Number*];

(d) Persons demanding that their objections be noted and the reasons for their objections: ________________.

§ 48.173 Stock Split—Another Form

Whereas, it is desirable that the authorized shares of this Corporation be increased from *50,000* shares to *200,000* shares, and that each presently issued and outstanding share of stock, [*of the par value of $20.00*] be divided and split up into four shares [*of the par value of $5.00*];

Resolved, that Article ______ of the Articles of Incorporation is hereby amended to read as follows:

> "This corporation is authorized to issue *200,000* common shares [*of a par value of $5.00 each and an aggregate par value of $1,000,000.00*]. Upon the amendment of this article to read as hereinabove set forth, each outstanding share [*of a par value of $20.00*], is split up and converted into four shares [*of a par value of $5.00 each*]."

Option 1 (Not Preferred for Smoothly Running Closely Held Corporations)

The following vote on the above resolution was counted:

(a) Yes: [*Number*];

(b) No: [*Number*];

(c) Abstentions: [*Number*];

(d) Persons demanding that their objections be noted and the reasons for their objections: ________________.

§ 48.174 Stock Split—Another Form

Resolved, that article ______ of the certificate of incorporation shall be amended to provide as follows:

"______: The aggregate number of shares which this Corporation shall have authority to issue is ______ (______) common shares which shares are to be without par value."

At the time this amendment becomes effective, and without any further action on the part of the Corporation or its Stockholders, each share of common shares without par value then issued and outstanding shall be changed and reclassified into [*Two*] fully paid and nonassessable shares of common shares, without par value. The capital account of the Corporation shall not be increased or decreased by such change and reclassification. To reflect the said change and reclassification, each certificate representing shares of common shares without par value theretofore issued and outstanding shall represent [*Twice*] the number of shares of common shares without par value issued and outstanding after such change and reclassification; and the holder of record of each such certificate shall be entitled to receive a new certificate representing a number of shares of common shares without par value of the kind authorized by this amendment, equal to [*Twice*] the number of shares represented by said certificate for theretofore issued and outstanding shares, so that upon this amendment becoming effective each holder of record of a certificate representing theretofore issued and outstanding common shares of the Corporation will have or be entitled to certificates representing in the aggregate [*Two*] shares of common shares without par value of the kind authorized by this amendment for each share of common shares without par value of which he was the holder prior to the effectiveness of this amendment.

Option 1 (Not Preferred for Smoothly Running Closely Held Corporations)

The following vote on the above resolution was counted:

(a) Yes: [*Number*];

(b) No: [*Number*];

(c) Abstentions: [*Number*];

(d) Persons demanding that their objections be noted and the reasons for their objections: ___________.

§ 48.175 Stock Split—Another Form

Resolved, that Article ______ of the Articles of Incorporation be and the same is hereby amended as follows:

* * * *two million (2,000,000)* shares shall be common stock, without par value.

At the time this amendment becomes effective, and without any further action on the part of the Corporation or its Stockholders, each share of common stock without par value then issued and outstanding shall be changed and reclassified into two fully paid and nonassessable shares of common stock, without par value. The capital account of the Corporation shall not be increased or decreased by such change and reclassification. To reflect the said change and reclassification, each certificate representing shares of common stock without par value theretofore issued and outstanding shall represent a like number of shares of common stock without par value issued and outstanding after such change and reclassification; and the holder of record of each such certificate shall be entitled to receive a new certificate representing a number of shares of common stock without par value of the kind authorized by this amendment, equal to the number of shares represented by said certificate for theretofore issued and outstanding shares, so that upon this amendment becoming effective each holder of record of a certificate representing theretofore issued and outstanding common stock of the Corporation will have or be entitled to certificates representing in the aggregate two shares of common stock without par value of the kind authorized by this amendment for each share of common stock without par value of which he was the holder prior to the effectiveness of this amendment.

Option 1 (Not Preferred for Smoothly Running Closely Held Corporations)

The following vote on the above resolution was counted:

(a) Yes: [*Number*];

(b) No: [*Number*];

(c) Abstentions: [*Number*];

(d) Persons demanding that their objections be noted and the reasons for their objections: ___________.

§ 48.176 Termination of Assumed Name

Resolved that the [*Board of Directors/Stockholders ratify as executed/adopt as proposed*] a Certificate of Termination of Assumed Name which has the following features:

(a) Name withdrawn: __________.

(b) Effective date of withdrawal: __________.

Option 1 (Preferred as a Matter of Practical Experience)

The Secretary shall make part of the minute book a copy of the same.

Option 2 (Not Preferred for Smoothly Running Closely Held Corporations)

The following Officer is authorized to execute the same: President.

Option 3 (Not Preferred for Smoothly Running Closely Held Corporations)

The following vote on the above resolution was counted:

(a) Yes: [*Number*];

(b) No: [*Number*];

(c) Abstentions: [*Number*];

(d) Persons demanding that their objections be noted and the reasons for their objections: ________.

§ 48.177 Transact Business in Foreign State

Resolved that the [*Board of Directors/Stockholders ratify as executed/adopt as proposed*] an Application for Authority to Transact Business in Foreign State which has the following features:

(a) Effective date: __________.

(b) State business is to be done in: __________.

Option 1 (Preferred as a Matter of Practical Experience)

The Secretary shall make part of the minute book a copy of the same.

Option 2 (Not Preferred for Smoothly Running Closely Held Corporations)

The following Officers are authorized to execute the same: President and Secretary.

Option 3 (Preferred as a Matter of Practical Experience)

The President shall do all things reasonable and necessary to carry out the purposes of the Application for Certificate of Authority to Transact Business in Foreign State and to that end he shall:

(a) File all necessary registration and tax forms.

Option 4 (Not Preferred for Smoothly Running Closely Held Corporations)

The following vote on the above resolution was counted:

(a) Yes: [*Number*];
(b) No: [*Number*];
(c) Abstentions: [*Number*];
(d) Persons demanding that their objections be noted and the reasons for their objections: __________.

§ 48.178 Vacancy on Board for Mental Illness or Felony Conviction

Whereas, ______, a Director of this Corporation, was declared of unsound mind by order (convicted of a felony by judgment) of the ______ Court, dated ______, 19__.

Resolved, that the office of ______ as a Director of this Corporation be and it hereby is declared vacant; and further,

Resolved, that Mr. ______ be and he hereby is appointed a Director of the Corporation in the place of ______ to hold office for the remainder of the term of ______, and until his successor is elected and qualified.

Option 1 (Not Preferred for Smoothly Running Closely Held Corporations)

The following vote on the above resolution was counted:

(a) Yes: [*Number*];
(b) No: [*Number*];
(c) Abstentions: [*Number*];
(d) Persons demanding that their objections be noted and the reasons for their objections: __________.

§ 48.179 Vacancy on Board for Failure to Accept Office

Whereas, ______ was elected a Director of this Corporation on ______, 19__, and has not accepted the office of Director, either in writing or by attending a meeting of the Board of Directors [*or* state here any other requirements of the bylaws for qualification of directors which Mr. ______ has not fulfilled].

Resolved, that the office of Director held by ______ be and hereby is declared vacant; and

Further resolved, that ______ be and he hereby is appointed a Director of the Corporation in place of ______ to hold office for the remainder of the term to which ______ was elected, and until his successor is elected and qualified.

Option 1 (Not Preferred for Smoothly Running Closely Held Corporations)

The following vote on the above resolution was counted:

(a) Yes: [*Number*];

(b) No: [*Number*];

(c) Abstentions: [*Number*];

(d) Persons demanding that their objections be noted and the reasons for their objections: __________.

§ 48.180 Vacation and Sick Day Plan

Resolved that the [*Board of Directors/Stockholders ratify as executed/adopt as proposed*] a Vacation and Sick Day Plan which has the following features:

(a) Employee Categories	Vacation Days during Employer Year	Sick Days during Employee Year

(b) Vacation days must be taken before [*Describe*] of the following Employee Year. If not taken, they are:

Alternative A–1

lost

Alternative A–2

to be paid for at [*percent*] % of base pay:

Alternative A–3

[*percent*] % cumulated.

(c) Pay for each Vacation day taken is to be paid for at [*percent*] % of base pay.

(d) Sick days must be taken before [*Describe*] of the following Employee Year. If not taken, they are:

Alternative B–1

lost.

Alternative B–2

to be paid for at [*percent*] % of base pay.

Alternative B–3

cumulated.

(e) Pay for each sick day taken is to be paid for at [*percent*] % of base pay.

COMMENT

See Volume on Employee Benefit Plans for form.

Option 1 (Preferred as a Matter of Practical Experience)

The Secretary shall make part of the minute book a copy of the same.

Option 2 (Not Preferred for Smoothly Running Closely Held Corporations)

The following Officers are authorized to execute the same: President and Secretary.

Option 3 (Not Preferred Unless There Is to Be a Consent Meeting and All Those Voting Won't Actually Review the Transaction)

The President shall do all things reasonable and necessary to carry out the purposes of the Deferred Compensation Plan and to that end he shall:

(a) Distribute the necessary notice and summary to participants.

(b) Execute and filing of the necessary EBS–1 form with the Department of Labor.

(1) Execute and File the necessary EBS–1 form with the Department of Labor.

(c) Deliver the initial contribution of $[*Sum*] to the Trustees of said plan.

(d) Establish procedures for (and carrying out such procedures) the execution by all participants of beneficiary designations and the election or refusal of a joint and survivor benefit.

Option 4 (Not Preferred for Smoothly Running Closely Held Corporations)

The following vote on the above resolution was counted:

(a) Yes: [*Number*];

(b) No: [*Number*];

(c) Abstentions: [*Number*];

(d) Persons demanding that their objections be noted and the reasons for their objections: __________.

§ 48.181 Warrants/Options

Resolved that the [*Board of Directors/Stockholders ratify as executed/adopt as proposed*] a [*Warrants/Options*] which has the following features:

(a) Person issued to: __________.

(b) Consideration: __________.

(c) Stock which said warrant'(s) can be converted into: __________.

(d) Conversion price: __________.

(e) Expiration date: __________.

(f) Earliest exercise date: __________.

COMMENT

See Chapter 42, supra, for form.

Option 1 (Preferred As a Matter of Practical Experience)

The Secretary shall make part of the minute book a copy of the same.

Option 2 (Not Preferred For Smoothly Running Closely Held Corporations)

The following Officer is authorized to execute the same: President.

Option 3 (Not Preferred For Smoothly Running Closely Held Corporations)

The following vote on the above resolution was counted:

(a) Yes: [Number];

(b) No: [Number];

(c) Abstentions: [Number];

(d) Persons demanding that their objections be noted and the reasons for their objections: __________.

§ 48.182 Withdrawal of Foreign Corporation (Corporation Registered to Do Business in a Foreign State)

Resolved that the [*Board of Directors/Stockholders ratify as executed/adopt as proposed*] an Application for Certificate of Withdrawal of Foreign (Corporation Registered to do Business in a Foreign State) Corporation which has the following features:

(a) State withdrawn from: __________

(b) Effective date of withdrawal: __________.

Option 1 (Preferred as a Matter of Practical Experience)

The Secretary shall make part of the minute book a copy of the same.

Option 2 (Not Preferred for Smoothly Running Closely Held Corporations)

The following Officer is authorized to execute the same: President.

Option 3 (Not Preferred Unless There Is to Be a Consent Meeting and All Those Voting Won't Actually Review the Transaction)

The President shall do all things reasonable and necessary to carry out the purposes of the Application for Certificate of Withdrawal of Foreign Corporation (Corporation registered to do business in a Foreign State) and he shall also file all related tax and other forms.

Option 4 (Not Preferred for Smoothly Running Closely Held Corporations)

The following vote on the above resolution was counted:

(a) Yes: [*Number*];

(b) No: [*Number*];

(c) Abstentions: [*Number*];

(d) Persons demanding that their objections be noted and the reasons for their objections: __________.

Library References:

C.J.S. Corporations § 1843.
West's Key No. Digests, Corporations ⚷651.

§§ 48.183–49.0 are reserved for supplementary material.

CHAPTER 49

INSPECTION OF BOOKS AND RECORDS

Table of Sections

Library References:

C.J.S. Corporations §§ 501 et seq., 779, 780.

West's Key No. Digests, Corporations ⚿181, 311.

§ 49.1 Inspection by Directors and Stockholders Compared [1]

Both Stockholders and Directors have the right to inspect corporate books and records in certain circumstances. However, the right of a Director is considerably broader than the right of a Stockholder and rests on an entirely different theoretical base. A Director is a manager of the Corporation and owes certain duties to it and to all the Stockholders. Indeed, he may be liable for negligent mismanagement if he does not adequately acquaint himself with the business and affairs of the Corporation. Hence, the Directors' right to inspect books and records is virtually absolute and unqualified. However, as with many supposedly absolute principles, there are exceptions.

1. This Section, and Sections 49.2–49.7, have their source in Hamilton, Corporations in a Nutshell (1980), Ch. 15.

Courts have sometimes denied inspection rights to Directors where it was clear that the Director was acting with manifestly improper motives and adequate information prepared by unbiased persons was available to the Director. Such cases, however, are exceptional and unusual.

The right of a Stockholder to inspect books and records, on the other hand, is considerably narrower. A Stockholder of course has a financial interest in the Corporation, and the common law recognizes a right to inspect books and records to protect this interest. However, because the Stockholder is not charged with management responsibility and is not subject to a broad fiduciary duty, his right to inspect is available only for "proper purposes," and is otherwise hedged with restrictions. The balance of this chapter deals exclusively with the more limited inspection rights of Stockholders.

§ 49.2 Common Law and Statutory Rights of Inspection

From the standpoint of the Corporation, a Stockholder's demand to inspect books and records almost certainly will be viewed as a hostile and threatening act. The practice therefore developed of denying the request out-of-hand and compelling the Stockholder to litigate, relying on whatever pretext may be available for the denial. In an effort to combat this attitude, the statutes of most states supplement the common law right of inspection with a statutory right of inspection which includes a "penalty" on corporate Officers who arbitrarily refuse to permit proper examination of books and records.

The statutory right of inspection is typically available to persons (1) who have been Stockholders of record for at least six months prior to the demand or (2) who own at least five per cent of the outstanding shares of the Corporation.[2] Some states use different numbers but the principle is the same. The statutory right to inspect, like the common law right, also requires a showing of "proper purpose" for the inspection which must be stated in the Stockholder's written demand. However, in the event a Stockholder qualifies for the statutory right of inspection the Corporation has the burden of showing the plaintiff does not have a proper purpose; Stockholders who do not qualify under the statute continue to have the common law burden of establishing that their purpose is a proper one.

Under the Model Act, a corporate Officer or agent who refuses to grant a statutory right of inspection is liable for a "penalty" equal to ten per cent of the value of the shares owned by the Stockholder.[3] State statutes vary widely: several states have made the penalty one or two per cent of the value of the plaintiff's shares; others have im-

2. Model Bus.Corp.Act § 52; West's Ann.Calif.Corp.Code § 1600 et seq.; McKinney's N.Y.Bus.Corp.Law § 624.

3. Model Bus.Corp.Act § 52.

posed a maximum penalty of *$500*; still others have imposed a per diem penalty of *$25* or some other amount. Several states require five days written demand in advance. As a practical matter, these provisions are pretty much a dead letter because the basic test of eligibility—a proper purpose—is a vague and uncertain one. While the potential of a substantial penalty may have a healthful effect, there appears to be little support for the imposition of the penalty.

§ 49.3 What Records May Be Examined?

Business Corporation acts require each Corporation to keep minutes of meetings, books and records or accounts, and information about Stockholders.[4] The Model Act, and the statutes of many states,[5] permit these records to be kept on tape or machine-readable form capable of being converted into written form in a reasonable time.

The right to inspect extends not only to all such records but to corporate records in general. Case law, for example, has authorized the examination of "records, books of account, receipts, vouchers, bills and all other documents evidencing the financial condition of the Corporation." Another case authorized the examination of the books of a subsidiary controlled by the Corporation. Corporate contracts and even the correspondence of the chief executive officer have been held to be subject to inspection in appropriate cases. The right generally extends to all relevant records necessary to inform the Stockholder about corporate matters in which he has a legitimate interest. The Corporation cannot defeat this right by offering summaries, substitute papers, or financial statements prepared by the Corporation's auditors.

§ 49.4 What Is a "Proper Purpose"?

The basic test of inspection by Stockholders is a "proper purpose." A purpose is proper if it is directed toward obtaining information bearing upon or seeking to protect the Stockholder's interest and that of other Stockholders of the Corporation.[6] The inspection may be to determine the worth of the Stockholder's holdings. It may be to seek reasons for a decline in profits. It may be to communicate with other Stockholders. It may be to ascertain whether there has been mismanagement or alarming transactions. All of these are "proper purposes."

4. Model Bus.Corp.Act § 52; McKinney's N.Y.Bus.Corp.Law § 624; West's Ann.Calif.Corp.Code § 1500.

5. Id.

6. E. g. Minn.Bus.Corp.Act § 302A.461 (4) provides that: "A 'proper purpose' is one reasonably related to the person's interest as a shareholder, beneficial owner, or holder of a voting trust certificate."

A Corporation cannot deny the right to inspect by arguing that the Stockholder has an improper purpose simply because he is unfriendly to management. An improper purpose is one with ulterior or vindictive motives. Obvious examples are general harassment of management or a desire to obtain trade secrets for a competitor. Probably mere idle curiosity is not a proper purpose, though it is a rare Stockholder who cannot allege a more specific purpose. Some courts appear to be more willing than others to countenance "fishing expeditions."

Obviously, substantial and difficult factual issues arise as to the Stockholder's true purpose. The issue may come down to predominant motive and intent. The burden of proof, discussed earlier, may be significant. It is probably fair to conclude that careful coaching of testimony may lead to the conclusion that the purpose for inspection is proper, while the outspoken or unusually forthright witness may run into difficulty.

§ 49.5 Who Is Entitled to Inspect?

A person who is a beneficial owner of shares but is not the record owner has a common law right of inspection, and depending on the wording of the statute, may have a statutory right as well. In some states, pledgees or judgment creditors have a statutory right to inspect.[7] Holders of voting trust certificates also have a statutory right to inspect under the Model Act (§ 52) and the statutes of many states.

§ 49.6 Inspection of Stockholders' Lists

Every Corporation must maintain "a record of its Stockholders, giving the names and addresses of all Stockholders and the number and class of the shares held by each."[8] This record is subject to the statutory or common law right of inspection possessed by every Stockholder [unlike the voting list compiled immediately before the meeting which is automatically open to inspection].[9] There has been a substantial volume of litigation over Stockholders lists in publicly held Corporations since such lists are, to quote a colorful phrase, "the line of scrimmage for contests involving incumbent management, dissident Stockholders, acquisition-minded Corporations, and those who have been described in current fiction as 'corporate raiders'."

7. Del.Gen.Corp.Law § 221 provides for inspection rights for bondholders and debenture holders.

8. Model Bus.Corp.Act § 52, See also McKinney's N.Y.Bus.Corp.Law § 624; West's Ann.Calif.Corp.Code § 1500.

9. See e. g. Model Bus.Corp.Act § 52; Del.Gen.Corp.Law §§ 219, 220; West's Ann.Calif.Corp.Code § 1600; McKinney's N.Y.Bus.Corp.Law § 624.

Also, a list of names and addresses of numerous well-to-do persons (as Stockholders are likely to be) is itself valuable, and may be sought in order to sell it to mail-solicitation firms. Indeed, some state statutes specifically provide that a Stockholders list need not be produced if the applicant has offered to sell or assisted another person in the sale or offering for sale of a Stockholders list within the preceding five years.

Much of the litigation dealing with Stockholders lists also involves the "proper purpose" test. Generally it has been held that it is a proper purpose to desire to communicate with other Stockholders about matters of corporate concern: to solicit proxies, to initiate a proxy contest, to publicize mismanagement, to discuss a derivative suit, to discuss proposals of management, to form a protective committee and the like. It has also been held to be a proper purpose to offer to purchase the shares of the Corporation. Courts probably tend to be more lenient in granting access to Stockholders lists than to other books and records. However, it is not a proper purpose to seek to sell to the Stockholders securities of unrelated Corporations. Similarly it is not a proper purpose to seek the list in order to communicate one's own social or political views to Stockholders. The mere fact that the Stockholder making the request is a competitor of the Corporation does not necessarily make his purpose improper though such a demand may raise suspicions.

§ 49.7 Demand for Inspection of Minutes and Records by Stockholders

To: [*Name of Corporation*]

The undersigned, being a Stockholder of record of [*Name of Corporation*] and holding [*Number*] shares of [*Class*] shares therein for at least six months immediately preceding this demand, hereby demands, pursuant to ______ of the ______ Business Corporation Law, the right to examine, in person or by agent or attorney, during usual business hours, the minutes of the proceedings of the Stockholders and the record of Stockholders of [*Name of Corporation*] and to make extracts therefrom at least five (5) days from the date of this demand.

Dated: ______, 19__.

____

§ 49.8 Demand to Inspect Books and Records

To: ______ Corporation

[*Address*]

The undersigned Stockholders of record do hereby demand that they be permitted to examine the books and records of the Corporation at a reasonable time and place, to be designated by you in writing. Without limiting the generality of the foregoing, the undersigned Stockholders desire particularly to examine the books of account of the Corporation and the minutes of Directors' meetings.

This inspection is for proper purposes, namely: (1) to ascertain the value of the shares owned by the undersigned; (2) to examine all expenditures in order to determine their reasonableness and wisdom; (3) to determine whether excessive compensation is being paid to Officers, Directors and others closely associated with management; and (4) to determine the extent and causes for the recent [*Describe*].

The undersigned Stockholders own of record more than *5* per cent of the outstanding shares of the Corporation and have owned such shares for more than *6* months.

The undersigned Stockholders do hereby appoint ______ and ______ as their agents to conduct the examination on their behalf and to make extracts from the corporate records so examined.

A response within five days establishing the time and place for this inspection would be appreciated. The response may be addressed to ______.

Name of Stockholder	Number of Shares Owned of Record

Dated: ______, 19__.

____

____

____

COMMENT

Even though a proper purpose is alleged, the Corporation may claim that the stated purpose is not the Stockholder's "true" purpose. The Corporation may also decline to grant permission to inspect upon a claim that the Stockholder is not acting in "good faith" or that the requesting Stockholder improperly used information obtained from a previous inspection of any Corporation. See § 49.4, supra.

§ 49.9 Authorization for Inspection of Minutes and Records

AUTHORIZATION FOR INSPECTION

The undersigned, being the holders of at least *five* percent of the [*Class*] shares of the outstanding shares of [*Name of Corporation*], do hereby authorize [*Name of Person Authorized*], pursuant to § ______ of the ______ Business Corporation Law, to examine, in our names and in our place and stead, in person or by agent or attorney, during usual business hours, the minutes of the proceedings of the Stockholders and the record of Stockholders of said [*Name of Corporation*], and to make extracts therefrom.

Dated: ______, 19__.

[*Signature*]

____

Stockholder

[*Signature*]

____

Stockholder

§ 49.10 Request for Annual and Published Interim Financial Reports

To: ______ Corporation

Please mail to me at the address set forth below the annual statement of the Corporation for its last fiscal year showing in reasonable detail the Corporation's assets and liabilities and the results of its operations. Also, please send the most recent interim statements which have been filed in a public record or otherwise published.

This request is made pursuant to § ______ of the ______ Business Corporation Act.

The undersigned is the holder of record of ______ shares of the common stock of the Corporation.

Dated: ______, 19__.

____

Stockholder

____

____

Address

COMMENTS

It should be noted that the Model Business Corporation Act has been amended to add the following provision to § 52:

> Each Corporation shall furnish to its Stockholders annual financial statements, including at least a balance sheet as of the end of each fiscal year and a statement of income for such fiscal year, which shall be prepared on the basis of generally accepted accounting principles, if the Corporation prepares financial statements for such fiscal year on that basis for any purpose, and may be consolidated statements of the Corporation and one or more of its subsidiaries. The financial statements shall be mailed by the Corporation to each of its Stockholders within 120 days after the close of each fiscal year and, after such mailing and upon written request, shall be mailed by the Corporation to any Stockholder (or holder of a voting trust certificate for its shares) to whom a copy of the most recent annual financial statements has not previously been mailed. In the case of statements audited by a public accountant, each copy shall be accompanied by a report setting forth his opinion thereon; in other cases, each copy shall be accompanied by a statement of the president or the person in charge of the Corporation's financial accounting records (1) stating his reasonable belief as to whether or not the financial statements were prepared in accordance with generally accepted accounting principles and, if not, describing the basis of presentation, and (2) describing any respects in which the financial statements were not prepared on a basis consistent with those prepared for the previous year.

§ 49.11 Request by Stockholder for Financial Statement

To: The Treasurer of [*Name of Corporation*]

You will please take notice that I am a Stockholder of [*Name of Corporation*], and that I hereby request you to furnish me with the most recent financial statements showing in reasonable detail the assets and liabilities and the results of operation of said Corporation, pursuant to and in accordance with the provisions contained in § ______ of the ______ Business Corporation Law.

Yours, etc.

____

§ 49.12 Request by Stockholder for Financial Statement—Another Form

To: [*Name of Corporation*]

The undersigned, ______ residing at No. ______ ______ Street, City of ______, County of ______, State of ______, does hereby request, pursuant to § ______ of the Business Corporation Law, that the [*Name of Corporation*] either give or mail to him an annual balance sheet and profit and loss statement for the preceding fiscal year, to wit: ______, 19__ to ______, 19__, and, if any interim balance sheet or profit and loss statement has been distributed to the Stockholders of said Corporation or otherwise made available to the public, the most recent such interim balance sheet or profit and loss statement, and in connection therewith does hereby state that the undersigned, ______, is and has been a Stockholder of record of [*Name of Corporation*] for at least *six* months immediately preceding his request [*or is a person holding, or is authorized in writing by the holders of, at least five percent of* [*Class*] *shares of* [*Name of Corporation*]].

Dated: ______, 19__.

[*Signature*]

§ 49.13 Demand for List of Stockholders

To: ______ Company

The undersigned, ______, owner and holder of ______ shares of the capital stock of ______ Company, having received a notice of a meeting of Stockholders to be held at ______, on the ______ day of ______, 19__, at ______ o'clock, __.M. for the purpose of voting upon the proposition of selling all or substantially all of the property of said Corporation, not in the regular course of business; and being of the opinion that it is against the best interests of Stockholders that all or substantially all of said Corporation's assets be sold; and

Being informed and advised by numerous other Stockholders who are of like opinion as the undersigned, that said Stockholders should communicate with other Stockholders for the protection of their investment; and for the purpose of having a meeting of such Stockholders as may share the views of the undersigned and others of like opinion; and being of the opinion that the Directors of said Corporation, who favor the sale of all or substantially all of the assets of said Corporation, are planning and conspiring to sell said assets to another Corporation in which the Directors of this Corporation have a financial interest, so that they may reap a substantial benefit to themselves at the expense of minority Stockholders; and

The Stockholders of this Corporation, being numerous and widely scattered and their names and addresses being exclusively in the possession and control of the officers of said Corporation and the undersigned being unable to communicate with said Stockholders for the proper purpose of discussing and presenting to said Stockholders an alternative plan, which will constitute fair and equitable treatment to all Stockholders and which will discriminate against none;

Now, therefore, I hereby demand that, for the purpose of enabling me to communicate with and call a meeting of Stockholders for a discussion of the plan proposed by the directors and to submit to said Stockholders an alternative plan which will protect the rights and interests of all Stockholders and discriminate against none, that you make available to me, my agent or attorney, a correct and complete copy of the list of Stockholders to be used for the purposes aforesaid, and in sufficient time before the Stockholders' meeting called for the ______ day of ______, 19__.

Dated: ______, 19__.

[*Signature*]

§ 49.14 Demand for List of Stockholders—Another Form

To: ______ Corporation

[*Address*]

The undersigned Stockholders of record do hereby demand that they be provided with a reasonably current list of Stockholders of record, including their addresses and the number of shares held by each person. In the alternative, the undersigned Stockholders of record demand that they be provided with access to such a list at a convenient time so that the list may be reproduced by xerography or photographic process without cost to the Corporation.

This demand is made for proper purposes, namely: to communicate with other Stockholders about matters of corporate concern, including current mismanagement of the Corporation by its Directors and Officers, the need to form a Stockholders protective committee, and the possible advisability of soliciting proxies in opposition to the solicitation by management.

The undersigned Stockholders have owned of record for more than *six* months the number of shares referred to below.

The undersigned Stockholders do hereby appoint ______ and ______ as their agents to receive the Stockholder list or to be given access to the list for reproduction purposes.

A response within five days is requested. The response may be addressed to ______.

Name of Stockholder	Number of Shares Owned of Record

Dated: ______, 19__.

____

____

____

§ 49.15 Demand for List of Stockholders—Another Form

I [We], the undersigned, holding of record the number of shares of [*Name of Corporation*] set opposite my [*our*] respective signature(s), and [collectively] holding of record at least five per centum of all of the outstanding shares of said [*Name of Corporation*], do pursuant to the power vested in me [us] by § ______ of the ______ Business Corporation Law, hereby appoint ______, for and in my [our] name[(s) and in the name of each of us], my [our] agent to inspect the stock book or record of Stockholders of [*Name of Corporation*] and to make extracts therefrom.

Dated ______, 19__.

Signature(s)	No. of Shares
______________	______________
______________	______________
______________	______________

§ 49.16 Affidavit of Purpose of Inspection

To: [*Name of Corporation*]

STATE OF ____________ }
County of ____________ } ss

______, being duly sworn, deposes and says:

1. That the inspection of the minutes of the proceedings of the Stockholders and record of Stockholders of [*Name of Corporation*], pursuant to a written demand therefor submitted to said Corporation by the deponent on the ______ day of ______, 19__, is not desired for a purpose which is in the interest of a business or object other than the business of the Corporation.

2. That the deponent has not within five years sold or offered for sale any list of Stockholders of any domestic Corporation or foreign Corporation or aided or abetted any person in procuring any such record of Stockholders for any such purpose.

[*Signature*]

____

[*Type Name of Deponent*]

[*Jurat*]

§ 49.17 Refusal to Permit Inspection

To: __________

____

____

The Board of Directors of ______ Corporation has considered your request to examine certain records of the Corporation and has concluded that it should be denied on two grounds: (a) ______, one of the requesting Stockholders, within *five* years improperly used information secured through a prior inspection of the books and records of ______ Corporation in that he disclosed it to a competitor of the Corporation, doing serious injury to it; and (b) your request is not made in good faith or for a proper purpose.

Dated: ______, 19__.

______ Corporation

By ______________

§ 49.18 Authorization for Inspection of Minutes and Records

AUTHORIZATION FOR INSPECTION

The undersigned, being the holders of at least *five* percent of the [*Class*] shares of the outstanding shares of [*Name of Corporation*], do hereby authorize [*Name of Person Authorized*], pursuant to § ______ of the ______ Business Corporation Law, to examine, in our names and in our place and stead, in person or by agent or attorney, during usual business hours, the minutes of the proceedings of the Stockholders and the record of Stockholders of said [*Name of Corporation*], and to make extracts therefrom.

Dated: ______, 19__.

[*Signature*]

____

Stockholder

[*Signature*]

____

Stockholder

§§ 49.19–50.0 are reserved for supplementary material.

†

BV 1

WEST'S LEGAL FORMS

SECOND EDITION

VOLUME 2

BUSINESS ORGANIZATIONS

With Tax Analysis

JOINT VENTURES

CORPORATIONS

1983 Pocket Part

By

PAUL LIEBERMAN
of the Michigan Bar

Sections 26.1 to 49

Insert this Pocket Part in back of Volume

ST. PAUL, MINN.
WEST PUBLISHING CO.
1983

2 West's Legal Forms 2d Ed.
1983 P.P.

SUMMARY OF CONTENTS

(Table of New or Retitled Sections)

Volume 1

DIVISION I. CHOICE OF BUSINESS FORM

DIVISION II. TAX LAWS—SOURCES AND ADMINISTRATION

DIVISION III. INDIVIDUALS IN BUSINESS (PROPRIETORSHIPS)

DIVISION IV. PARTNERSHIPS

PART A. FORMATION AND OPERATION OF PARTNERSHIP

SUMMARY OF CONTENTS

PART C. CORPORATE FINANCE—GENERALLY

Volume 3

PART F. OPERATION OF CORPORATION

PART G. NON-OPERATING METHODS OF TAKING ASSETS OUT OF THE CORPORATION

SUMMARY OF CONTENTS

DIVISION VIII. SUBCHAPTER S CORPORATIONS

DIVISION IX. BUSINESS TRUSTS

SUMMARY OF CONTENTS

DIVISION X. COOPERATIVES

DIVISION XI. U.S. TAXATION OF INTERNATIONAL ACTIVITIES

Volume 6

EMPLOYEE BENEFIT PLANS

EMPLOYEE BENEFIT (WELFARE) PLANS

SUMMARY OF CONTENTS

*

WEST'S LEGAL FORMS

SECOND EDITION

VOLUME 2

BUSINESS ORGANIZATIONS

With Tax Analysis

JOINT VENTURES

CORPORATIONS

*

DIVISION V
JOINT VENTURES

CHAPTER 26
JOINT VENTURES

§ 26.3 Comprehensive Joint Venture Agreement

Page 32

(New § 3.6).

§ 3.6 Extent of Services

The Managing Venturer(s) shall devote *his/her/their* entire time, attention, and energies to the business of the Venture, and shall not during the term of this Agreement be engaged in any other business activity whether or not such business activity is pursued for gain, profit, or other pecuniary advantage; without the prior written consent of the Venturer(s) first obtained; but this shall not be construed as preventing the Managing Venturer(s) from investing, when such investment will not interfere with the Managing Venturer(s) full time employment by the Venture.

(New § 3.7).

§ 3.7 Tax Matter Partner

(a) Name. The Tax Matters Partner shall be [*Name*], who shall be succeeded upon death or unwillingness or inability to act (as shall be determined by the Managing Venturer(s), or in their absence, by [*Name*]), by [*Name*].

(b) Duties. The Tax Matters Partner shall have the following rights and duties:

(1) Provide to the Internal Revenue Service any or all information which is within the knowledge of the Tax Matters Partner as to the organizations, operations and/or liquidation of the Venture.

COMMENT

This authority may be too broad in many circumstances.

(2) To adjust, arbitrate, negotiate, compromise, sue or defend, abandon or otherwise deal with and settle any and all claims in favor of or against the Venturers and the Venture as the Tax Matters Partner shall deem proper which shall directly relate to the organization, operations and/or liquidation of the Venture.

(3) Do all other things which may be granted to the Tax Matters Partner by Internal Revenue Code §§ 6221 through 6232, as they may be now or hereafter amended or supplemented.

COMMENT

This authority may be too broad in many circumstances.

DIVISION VI
CORPORATIONS

PART A
PREINCORPORATION MATTERS
INTRODUCTION

Page 43

(New text, page 43, line 10 from the top, after "and real property"*).*

The cost of eligible * * * type of property. In general, eligible personal and real property (except safe harbour leased and finance leased property) is broken down into the following four categories:

Stock, Securities and Short Term Debt

Page 48

Alternative Minimum Tax

(New text, page 48, line 6 from the top, after the heading "Alternative Minimum Tax") and before ***Tax Rates—Preference Tax on Individuals (Generally)****.*

After 1982 [15.5] individual taxpayers will pay (unreduced by credits but reduced by any "minimum tax" net operating tax carryover—see (F) below) a tax which is the greater of the tax as calculated above or the alternative minimum tax. The alternative minimum tax is equal to 20% of the amount by which the following calculation exceeds $30,000 ($40,000 in the case of joint returns and surviving spouses):

(A) Adjusted gross income (before any net operating loss carryback or forward deduction),

(B) Plus, a long list of preference items which, in general, include:

(i) The bargain element of any incentive stock option (see Volume 6, Chapter 5).

(ii) IRC § 174 R & D expenditures and IRC §§ 616 and 617 mining and exploration expenditures in excess of 10 year straight line.

(iii) One-half capital gains.

(iv) Depreciation in excess of straight line on real property and leased personal property and of certified pollution control facilities.

(v) Percentage depletion in excess of adjusted basis.

(vi) Intangible drilling costs not capitalized.

(C) Less, the following:

(i) Medical expenses and casualty losses to the extent each are in excess of 10% of adjusted gross income.

(ii) Charitable contributions.

(iii) The IRC § 691 estate tax deduction.

(iv) Interest to buy, build or rehabilitate taxpayers' or their family's principal residence.

(v) Interest generally to the extent it relates to (and does not exceed) investment income included in the taxpayer's minimum taxable income.

(D) Further, net operating loss carryovers have special treatment.

(E) To the extent to which taxpayers do not use a credit to reduce their tax, the credit can be carried back or over.

(F) The minimum tax will be reduced by the following minimum tax net operating loss carry back or forward:

(i) The loss is calculated by adding back to adjusted gross income tax preference items (see (B) above) and subtracting tax preference deductions (see (C) above).

(ii) Pre-1983 regular net operating loss carry forwards may be carried forward against the minimum tax subject to the IRC § 56(b) add on minimum tax.

15.5 IRC §§ 55, 57 and 58(i).

Tax Rates—Preference Tax on Individuals (Generally)

(Revised text, page 48, after above heading).

Individuals may pay a tax only on pre-1983 net operating loss carry forward preferences (as used) in part based upon the *preference ("minimum") tax* [16] of 15%. This is charged * * *.

17. *(Disregard footnote 17 in main volume).*

Page 49

Ordinary Income Tax on Corporations (Generally)

(New text, page 49, line 7 from the bottom, after "$25,000–$50,000 * * * 18"*).*

In addition, there is [18.10] after 1982 a 15% reduction in certain tax benefits available to Corporations, with an offsetting adjustment to the corporate minimum tax (see below) to prevent the minimum tax from applying to the amount the benefit is reduced. These include:

(1) A 15% reduction in the IRC § 613(b) depletion for coal.

(2) A 15% increase in the amount deemed distributed (and thus taxed) from a DISC to its Stockholders.

(3) A 15% ordinary tax on the capital gains portion of depreciable residential realty.

(4) A 15% reduction in the amount that IRC § 169 pollution control facilities can be amortized over 60 months; the rest must now be depreciated.

(5) 15% reduction in the deductibility of certain intangible drilling costs; the net must now be deducted over 3 years (subject to later recapture).[18.15]

(6) 15% of the IRC §§ 616 and 617 mineral exploration and development expenditures must be depreciated over 5 years rather than deducted (subject to later recapture). *Note:* This 15% portion can not be used for the taxpayer's cost depletion deduction.

18.10 IRC §§ 291, 57(b) and 263(c).

18.15 IRC § 1254.

Accumulated Income Tax on Corporations (Generally)

(Revised text, page 49, line 2 from the bottom, after "of the first"*).*

Corporations may pay a tax [19] in part based upon any income which is not distributed but is *"unreasonably accumulated"* (see Chapter 53, infra, for a more complete explanation) equal to an additional 27½% of the first $250,000 ($150,000 in the case of a service Corporation) of unreasonable accumulation and 38½% of the rest.

19. IRC § 531 et seq. (see § 53.9).

20. *(Disregard footnote 20 in main volume).*

Page 50

Preference Tax on Corporations (Generally)

(New text, page 50, line 19 from the bottom, after "more complete explanation."*).*

Corporations may pay a tax in part based upon a preference ("minimum") tax [22] equal to 15% of the amount by which the following items exceed the greater of $10,000 or the full amount of the normal income tax which would otherwise be paid in the year in question:

(1) Accelerated depreciation on real property over straight lined depreciation.

(2) As to S Corporations and Personal Holding Companies only, accelerated depreciation on leased personal property over straight line depreciation.

(3) 71.6% of the accelerated amortization of certified pollution control facilities.

(4) As to S Corporations and Personal Holding Companies, certain mining exploration and development costs.

(5) As to S Corporations and Personal Holding Companies, certain circulation and research and experimental expenditures.

(6) 71.6% of the depletion of iron and coal and 100% of the depletion of other mineral property over the adjusted basis of the property.

(7) 71.6% of the capital gains "savings" achieved by the Corporation's use, if any, of the alternative capital gains tax.

(8) The amount by which the fair market value of a share of stock transferred pursuant to the exercise of an incentive stock option exceeds the option price.

(9) As to S Corporations and Personal Holding Companies, certain intangible drilling costs.

(10) As to S Corporations and Personal Holding Companies, certain amounts which relate to the accelerated cost recovery deduction and, as to all Corporations, certain amounts which relate to the fifteen year real property accelerated cost recovery deduction.

Page 52

Dividend Income Generally

(Revised text, page 52, line 13 from the bottom, after "in the Corporation"*).*

(3) Redemptions of stock * * * situations are present.[25] The factual situations are intended to allow the redeeming Stockholder to receive capital gains treatment for the gain on his stock in those situations where (A) it is thought that the Stockholder has significantly reduced his percentage of economic ownership in the Corporation or that the distribution was of one or more independent businesses, or their proceeds, or (B) special tax treatment was thought to be unreasonable because of the circumstances of the redemption.

(New text, page 52, line 8 from the bottom, after "above are applicable."*).*

It should be * * * above are applicable. (See Chapters 56 and 57, infra, for more complete description).

Page 53

Earnings and Profits

(Revised text, page 53, line 2 from the top, after "redemptions of stock"*).*

Non-deductible distributions include dividends paid and distributions for capital redemptions of stock (which include partial liquidations) and life insurance premiums paid which do not increase cash values. The amount * * *.

Page 54

Redemptions (Generally)

(Revised text).

A *redemption* will be considered as not essentially equivalent to a dividend if[27] and only if:

(1)(A) A limited set of circumstances exist concerning the nature of the redemption, and

(B) The persons or entities whose stock ownership the Internal Revenue Code deems [28] (that is, arbitrarily and artificially implies) as being *"constructively"* owned by the redeeming Stockholder after the redemption either (i) do not in fact own such stock or (ii) if they do own such stock, the amount of stock which they own both before and after the redemption is statutorily *deemed* to entitle the Stockholder to claim that he falls within the circumstances which are necessary for him to avoid dividend treatment.

Briefly, the circumstances which will avoid dividend treatment (described more extensively at Chapter 63 et seq., infra) are circumstances where Internal Revenue Code provides that the Stockholder's actual (and deemed) ownership percentage was, as a result of the redemption, materially reduced. Briefly, the circumstances where stock will be *deemed* to be owned by the redeeming Stockholder are those where the family or entity who actually own the stock are thought to have such a close economic relationship to the redeeming Stockholder that the redeeming Stockholder and the "constructively redeeming Stockholder(s)" are probably acting in tandem with one another.

And the Corporation is not a *"collapsible Corporation"*,

Or (2) the Corporation distributes one or more separate businesses, or their proceeds, which have been operated for at least five years.

Under IRC § 302(b)(4) what was previously thought of as a partial liquidation (and for these volumes continues to be dealt with under that topic) is now a redemption (since it carries redemption type tax treatment).

CHAPTER 29

PREINCORPORATION AGREEMENTS

A. AGREEMENTS—GENERALLY

§ 29.1 Types of Preincorporation Agreements

(New text, page 79, line 4 from the bottom, after "(b)" *and before* "(d)" , *add* "(c) Stockholder Agreements."*).*

CHAPTER 30

SPECIAL PROBLEMS OF CLOSE CORPORATIONS

A. INTRODUCTION

§ 30.2 One-Man Corporation—Incorporated Partnership

(Revised § 30.2).

(a) Basic Recognition of Corporation Status. One, two, or more individuals might desire to form a business Corporation.

Where one person is involved, except for possible nominal stockholdings in others when necessary to qualify them to serve as Directors, the incorporation results in a "one-man corporation".

Where two or more persons are involved, the resulting close Corporation is sometimes loosely called an "incorporated partnership" or "chartered partnership". The associates might be all members of the same family, giving rise to the term "family corporation"; or members of two or more families; individuals who are completely unrelated; or even a combination of Corporations or of Corporations and individuals (including so-called "joint venture" corporations).

An entity may be given corporate tax status for state law purposes even though it is not entitled to (and does not want) corporate status. In addition, a Partnership or Business Trust or other entity may be given tax status unwittingly and unwillingly. The foundation for this determination is the Kintner Regulations (see Chapter 31, infra, for a more complete description of the Kintner Regulations).

(1) Basically, these Regulations provide for the following tests:

(A) Does the entity in question have centralized management? If so, this is considered a corporate characteristic.

(B) Do the owners of the entity in question have limited liability? If so, this is considered a corporate characteristic.

(C) Do the owners of the entity in question have free transferability of their ownership interests? If so, this is considered a corporate characteristic.

(D) Does the entity in question continue in its theoretical status as an entity for state law purposes in all cases even if one or more owner dies, is disabled, withdraws or become bankrupt? If so, this is considered a corporate characteristic.

(E) Does the entity have associates (i.e., more than one owner)? If so, this is considered a corporate characteristic.

(F) Is the object of the equity's existence to carry on a business for profit? If so, this is considered a corporate characteristic.

The purpose of the Kintner Regulations is to use the above characteristics to classify the entity in question for tax purposes as a Corporation or not.

(2) Generally, the Kintner Regulations are applied as follows:

(A) The characteristics that are shared by both types of entities are ignored. Thus, items (E) and (F) above are ignored if the question is Partnership or Corporation and items (A), (B), (C) and (D) above are ignored if the question is Business Trust or Corporation.

(B) The entity label is presumed to control. Thus, if 50% or more of the relevant characteristics match the entity's format, the entity's format will control the tax results. If less than 50% of the relevant characteristics match the entity's format, the alternative entity's tax rules will be applied.

(3) Even if the Kintner Regulations substantiate the Corporation's claim to corporate tax treatment, this treatment may be denied if the facts of corporate operation (not status) do not have enough "indices" of corporate being.

Thus, indices of corporate being are important for two reasons:

(A) Their lack of existence may be used under state law to pierce the corporate veil and deny corporate benefits to Stockholders, and

(B) Their lack of existence may be used under the tax law to disallow corporate tax status and tax benefits.

(4) What are these corporate indices? Generally, corporate indices will be the same for both tax and state law. As one might expect, they are physical acts which Corporation generally do. Therefore, the indices are many of the incorporation actions and documents described in this text.

Since some of these documents and actions are more important than others, the important ones have been noted below:

These are:

(A) Articles of Incorporation properly filed and accepted by the state of incorporation.

(B) Issuance of stock certificates.

(C) Adoption of By-laws.

(D) Filing corporate tax returns.

(E) Using the corporate name and executing documents by corporate agents in the name of the Corporation.

(F) Use of a corporate bank account, and when other assets are titled, holding them in the corporate name.

(G) The existence of a reasonable ratio of debt to equity (3 to 1 is reasonable; 9 to 1 is often thought to be unreasonable).

CHAPTER 31

ENTITIES TREATED AS CORPORATIONS FOR STATE LAW AND TAX LAW PURPOSES

Table of New or Retitled Sections

---

§ 31.4 General Indices of Corporate Status

In any case, corporate status will not be denied because of the taxpayer's desire to incorporate to obtain tax benefits.[1]

1. Silvano Achiro, 77 T.C. 881 (1981).

§ 31.5 Form Corporations

A related problem is the problem of taxpayers trying to ignore the corporate tax attributes of a transaction. This problem often arises when the Corporation was created in order to meet a usury law requirement. The courts have held that the Corporation will not be ignored for tax purposes if either (1) the Corporation was created to serve a taxpayer's purpose or (2) the Corporation engages in any business activity.[2]

2. Lomas Santa Fe, Inc. v. Commissioner, 74 T.C. 662 (1980).

CHAPTER 37

TAXATION OF INCORPORATION TRANSACTIONS

Table of New or Retitled Sections

---

§ 37.1 Introduction

(New text, page 379, line 5 from the bottom, after Paragraph "(3)"*).*

(4) Internal Revenue Code § 304 rules governing the incorporation of a holding company. These rules are discussed infra at § 59.12.

Note: If stock of a Corporation is being acquired as part of the transaction, the loss carryover of that Corporation may be reduced or lost (see Chapter 60).

(New text, page 379, bottom line, after "planning is simply"*).*

(b) Utilizing § 351. Effective tax * * * Code provisions. The most important question in planning is simply: assuming a holding company is not to be the result, does compliance (as discussed herein) with the requirements of IRC § 351 yield the desired tax result and, if so, can we comply?

Page 381

(New text, page 381, end of page).

(d) Incorporating a Partnership. Rev.Rul. 70–239, 1 CB 74 provides that the incorporation of a Partnership will result in the Corporation's basis in the Partnership's assets being equal to the Partnership's basis no matter how the transfer is accomplished. If the Partner's basis in the Partnership is higher than the Partnership's basis in its assets, it may be worthwhile liquidating the Partnership (which should, under IRC § 732(b), give the assets a basis equal to the Partner's basis), and then having the Partners contribute the assets to the Corporation. If the two steps are not dependent upon each other, the taxpayer should succeed.

§ 37.2 Tax Free Incorporations

Page 384

(New text, page 384, line 13 from the top, after "classes of stock.[13]"*).*

(7) Incorporation of a Holding Company. The incorporation of a holding company where property (which is described in IRC § 317 as assets excluding stock in the Corporation making the distribution (i.e. the subsidiary) or a right to

acquire such stock) is distributed, it will generally be taxed as a distribution of a dividend (ordinary income to the extent of E & P, then no tax to the extent of the surrendered stock's basis, then exchange treatment—see § 56.10 for a further discussion of dividends). See infra for a more complete description of these holding company incorporations.

See § 38.3, infra for a definition of stock.

Page 385

(New text, page 385, line 8 from the top, after "property of cash."*).*

(2) "Stock and securities" * * * property or cash. The IRS will generally not rule that an exchange is tax free under IRC § 351 if the term of the debt is less than 10 years or if the debt must be classified as equity in order to meet the test.[19.5]

19.5 Rev.Proc. 81–10, 1981–13 IRB 44.

(New text, page 385, line 17 from the top, after "product of services.[22]"*).*

The following property may not be transferred tax free:[22.5] (i) any indebtedness of the transferee Corporation (i.e.: the stock or securities' issuer) which was not evidenced by a security; (ii) interest on indebtedness owed by the transferee Corporation which accrued on or after the date of the transferor's debt's holding period; (iii) to the extent the transferor indirectly receives stock and securities which are transferred directly to the transferor's creditors to satisfy the transferor's indebtedness while the debtor is under court jurisdiction.

22.5 IRC § 351(d) and (e).

Page 390

(New subsections (j)–(m)).

(j) Creation of Holding Companies. A tax planning technique which is becoming increasingly popular is the creating of a holding company. The creation is often referred to as a creation of a personal holding company, which will own the stock of the operating Corporation, since (in these instances) the resulting operations will result in the holding company being subject to taxation under the personal holding company rules (since its only income will be IRC § 543(a)(1) dividend income—see § 53.10, infra).

The goal here may be one or more of the following:

(1) To allow the issuance of stock to senior Stockholders who want to freeze the estate tax value of such stock as a result of the fact that they will own preferred stock (rather than common). This same objective can often be met by a recapitalization (see Chapter 59, infra). (2) In this regard the advantages of a holding company are:

(A) It may not be necessary to leave the senior Stockholders with preferred stock only, as seems to be the Internal Revenue Service's position in the case of a recapitalization.

(B) The Internal Revenue Service should be willing to rule on the tax attributes of the transaction, although they will generally no longer rule in the case of recapitalizations.

(3) The issuance of preferred stock or securities may also result in a gift or income to (generally) one or more of the resulting common Stockholders.

(k) Internal Revenue Code § 382. Under the Internal Revenue Code changes to be effective in 1984, there will be a reduction or elimination of the tax loss carryover of a Corporation upon the reduction of certain owner's share of such carryovers (see Chapter 60, infra). One such reduction may occur as a result of a tax free (or taxable) incorporation after 1983.

(*l*) § 481 Recapture. Under Internal Revenue Code § 481 there is a ten year proration of certain adjustments required under that Section when the taxpayer changes (before incorporation) from the cash to accrual basis of accounting. Upon incorporation, there will be a "recapture" of the postponed tax.

(m) Income in Respect to a Decedent. If income in respect to a decedent is transferred to the Corporation, this will be taxed.

§ 37.3 Partially Tax Free Incorporations

Page 391

(New text, page 391, line 15 from the top, after "classes of stock.[11]"*).*

(5) Incorporation of a Holding Company. The incorporation of a holding company where property (which is described in IRC § 317 as assets, excluding stock in the Corporation making the distribution (i.e. the subsidiary) or a right to acquire such stock) is distributed will generally be taxed as a distribution of a dividend (ordinary income to the extent of E & P, then no tax to the extent of the surrendered stock's basis, then exchange treatment—see § 56.10 for a further discussion of dividends). See § 59.12, infra for a more complete description of these holding company incorporations.

See § 38.3, infra for a definition of stock.

Page 393

(New text, page 393, line 18 from the bottom, after "is applicable).[54]"*).*

(E) The amount of [54.5] (i) any indebtedness of the transferee Corporation (ie: the stock or securities' issuer) which was not evidenced by a security; (ii) interest on indebtedness owed by the transferee Corporation which accrued on or after the date of the transferor's debt's holding period; (iii) to the extent the transferor indirectly receives stock and securities which are transferred directly to the transferor's creditors to satisfy the transferor's indebtedness while the debtor is under court jurisdiction.

54.5 IRC § 351(d) and (e).

Page 394

(New text, page 394, line 11 from the top, after "on the transfer.[60]"*)*.

(5) In determining the * * * on the transfer.[60] However, a case can be made for the proposition that, if the Corporation has Earnings and Profits for the year in question, dividend treatment will result. This rule is fraught * *.

Page 395

(New text, page 395, line 6 from the top, after "sports player contracts."*)*.

(B) Internal Revenue Code § 1250 and § 291 property recapture at ordinary rates (but not in excess of the gain) of a certain percentage of the post 1963 real estate depreciation previously taken which is in excess of what straight line depreciation would have provided (depreciation faster than straight line is called *accelerated* depreciation). This *excess depreciation* is recaptured as follows:

(i) With certain government financed apartments and low income housing there will be graded recapture if the holding period was at least 100 months; otherwise there will be 100% recapture of depreciation in excess of straight line.

(ii) As to other types of post 1969 real estate depreciation, there will be a total recapture of the depreciation taken in excess of straight line. Pre 1970 recapture has special rules.

As to post 1980 real property, depreciation will be recaptured under Internal Revenue Code § 1245(a)(5) except as to:

(I) New residential property depreciated over 15 years.

(II) In general, property used outside of the United States.

(III) Property when there is an election to straight-line depreciate it over 15, 35 or 45 years.

(IV) Certain government financed apartments and low income housing.

15% of any straight line depreciation is also recaptured.

Page 397

(New text, page 397, line 18 from the bottom, after "property or cash."*)*.

(2) "Stock and securities" * * * property or cash. The IRS will generally not rule that an exchange is tax free under IRC § 351 if the term of the debt is less than 10 years or if the debt must be classified as equity in order to meet the test.[63.5]

63.5 Rev.Proc. 81–10, 1981–13 IRB 44.

Page 401

(New text, page 401, line 12 from the bottom, after "property (see supra)."*)*.

(i) Creation of Holding Companies. A tax planning technique which is becoming increasingly popular is the creating of a holding company. The creation is often referred to as a creation of a personal holding company, which will own the stock of the operating Corporation, since (in these instances) the resulting operations will result in the holding company being subject to taxation under the personal holding company rules (since its only income will be IRC § 543(a)(1) dividend income—see § 53.10, infra).

The goal here may be one or more of the following:

(1) To allow the issuance of stock to senior Stockholders who want to freeze the estate tax value of such stock as a result of the fact that they will own preferred stock (rather than common). Although this same objective can often be met by a recapitalization (see Chapter 59, infra), the advantages of a holding company are:

(A) It may not be necessary to leave the senior Stockholders with preferred stock only, as seems to be the Internal Revenue Service's position in the case of a recapitalization.

(B) The Internal Revenue Service should be willing to rule on the tax attributes of the transaction, although they will generally no longer rule in the case of recapitalizations.

The issuance of preferred stock or securities may also result in a gift or income to (generally) one or more of the resulting common Stockholders.

(j) Internal Revenue Code § 382. Under Internal Revenue Code § 382 as it is in effect prior to 1984, to the extent to which a § 351 transaction is taxable (i.e.: a result of a deemed purchase), there will be a reduction or elimination of the tax loss carryover of a Corporation upon the reduction of certain owner's share of such carryovers (see Chapter 60, infra).

Under the Internal Revenue Code changes to be effective in 1984, there will be a reduction or elimination of the tax loss carryover of a Corporation upon the reduction of certain owner's share of such carryovers (see Chapter 60, infra). One such reduction may occur as a result of a tax free (or taxable) incorporation after June 30, 1984.

(k) § 481 Recapture. Under Internal Revenue Code § 481 there is a 10 year proration of certain adjustments required under that Section when the taxpayer changes (before incorporation) from the cash to accrual basis of accounting. Upon incorporation, there will be a "recapture" of the postponed tax.

(*l*) Income in Respect to a Decedent. If income in respect to a decedent is transferred to the Corporation, this will be taxed.

§ 37.4 Non Tax Free Incorporations

Page 401

(New text, page 401, line 7 from the bottom, after "exchange of assets."*)*.

(a) Generally. If a Corporation * * * exchange of assets.[78.5] Although a case can be made for the proposition that if the Corporation has earnings and profits for the year in question, dividend treatment will result. Although the * * *.

78.5 IRC § 1001.

Page 402

(New text, page 402, top line, after "(b) Taxes."*).*

(b) Taxes. Under IRC § 267, in many situations, no loss can be recognized—see § 54.8 for further discussion.

The following is * * *.

(New text, page 402, line 16 from the bottom, after "sports player contracts."*).*

(2) Internal Revenue Code § 1250 and § 291 property recapture at ordinary rates (but not in excess of the gain) of a certain percentage of the post 1963 real estate depreciation previously taken which is in excess of what straight line depreciation would have provided (depreciation faster than straight line is called *accelerated* depreciation). This *excess depreciation* is recaptured as follows:

(A) With certain government financed apartments and low income housing there will be graded recapture if the holding period was at least 100 months; otherwise there will be 100% recapture of depreciation in excess of straight line.

(B) As to other types of post 1969 real estate depreciation, there will be a total recapture of the depreciation taken in excess of straight line. Pre 1970 recapture has special rules.

As to post 1980 real property, depreciation will be recaptured under Internal Revenue Code § 1245(a)(5) except as to:

(I) New residential property depreciated over 15 years.

(II) In general, property used outside of the United States.

(III) Property when there is an election to straight-line depreciate it over 15, 35 or 45 years.

(IV) Certain government financed apartments and low income housing.

15% of any straight line depreciation is also recaptured.

(New text, page 404, line 14 from the bottom, after "(IRC § 341)."*).*

(13) A transfer of income in respect of a decedent (IRC § 691(a)(2)).

Page 405

(New subsections (e)–(g)).

(e) Creation of Holding Companies. A tax planning technique which is becoming increasingly popular is the creating of a holding company. The creation is often referred to as a creation of a personal holding company, which will own the stock of the operating Corporation, since (in these instances) the resulting operations will result in the holding company being subject to taxation under the personal holding company rules (since its only income will be IRC § 543(a)(1) dividend income—see § 53.10, infra).

The goal here may be one or more of the following:

(1) To allow the issuance of stock to senior Stockholders who want to freeze the estate tax value of such stock as a result of the fact that they will own preferred stock (rather than common). Although this same objective can

often be met by a recapitalization (see Chapter 59, infra), the advantages of a holding company are:

(A) It may not be necessary to leave the senior Stockholders with preferred stock only, as seems to be the Internal Revenue Service's position in the case of a recapitalization.

(B) The Internal Revenue Service should be willing to rule on the tax attributes of the transaction, although they will generally no longer rule in the case of recapitalizations.

The issuance of preferred stock may also result in a gift or income to (generally) one or more of the resulting common Stockholders.

(f) Internal Revenue Code § 382. Under Internal Revenue Code § 382 as it is in effect prior to 1984, to the extent to which a § 351 transaction is taxable (i.e.: a result of a deemed purchase), there will be a reduction or elimination of the tax loss carryover of a Corporation upon the reduction of certain owner's share of such carryovers (see Chapter 60, infra).

Under the Internal Revenue Code changes to be effective in 1984, there will be a reduction or elimination of the tax loss carryover of a Corporation upon the reduction of certain owner's share of such carryovers (see Chapter 60, infra). One such reduction may occur as a result of a tax free (or taxable) incorporation after 1983.

(g) § 481 Recapture. Under Internal Revenue Code § 481 there is a 10 year proration of certain adjustments required under that Section when the taxpayer changes (before incorporation) from the cash to accrual basis of accounting. Upon incorporation, there will be a "recapture" of the postponed tax.

§ 37.8 Cross References

Page 414

(New text, page 414, bottom line, after "Chapter 38, infra)."*)*.

(3) Discussion of the possibility that the stock issued upon the incorporation of a holding company will be § 306 stock (see § 59.12, infra).

§ 37.9 Section 482 Allocation

Internal Revenue Code § 482 is more fully discussed at § 54.2. In the context of an incorporation, the Internal Revenue Service has tried to use § 482 (which allows the Service to reallocate income, deductions and credits to properly reflect transactions) in cases where the timing of the incorporation improperly separates income from related expenses or where some assets or liabilities are retained by the Stockholder (with a sheltering effect) (Rev.Rul. 80–198, 1980–2 C.B. 113). Thus when the Stockholder transfers accounts receivables or other rights to future income to the Corporation, and retains the associated liabilities or other assets which will be used by (rented to?) the Corporation, the Stockholder will be taxed on the assigned income (this was an application of the "assignment of income" doctrine (Ltr.Rul. 8139073)).

However, where the expense assumed by the Corporation relates to the asset transferred, the assumption will be recognized (Rev.Rul. 80–240, 1980–2 C.B. 116).

§ 37.10 Delayed Taxation Resulting From Certain Stock Issues

It is possible for the Corporation to issue stock upon incorporation which (by its own terms) will result in later dividend taxation to the holders (without the payment of a dividend as such). The rule is that a dividend tax will be payable by Stockholders who own stock when:

(1) The conversion ratio of such stock increases by its own terms.

Example. Corporation M is organized with two classes of stock outstanding, class A and class B. Each class B share may be converted, at the option of the holder, into class A shares. During the first year, the conversion ratio is one share of class A stock for each share of class B stock. At the beginning of each subsequent year, the conversion ratio is increased by 0.05 share of class A stock for each share of class B stock. Thus, during the second year, the conversion ratio would be 1.05 shares of class A stock for each share of class B stock, during the third year, the ratio would be 1.10 shares, etc.

M pays an annual cash dividend on the class A stock. At the beginning of the second year, when the conversion ratio is increased to 1.05 shares of class A stock for each share of class B stock, a distribution of 0.05 shares of class A stock is deemed made with respect to each share of class B stock, since the proportionate interests of the class B Stockholders in the assets or earnings and profits of M are increased.[84]

(2) Preferred stock has a call[85] (that is the Corporation may force a redemption) or put[86] and the call or put price is in excess of the fair market value of the stock when issued plus a reasonable call premium (presumed to be 10% of the fair market value if redemption will not take place for at least 5 years).

Example. Corporation V is organized with two classes of stock, class A common and class B convertible preferred. The class B stock is issued for $100 per share and is convertible into class A at a fixed ratio that is not subject to full adjustment in the event stock dividends or rights are distributed to the class A Stockholders. The class B stock pays no dividends but is redeemable in 10 years for $200. There are no facts to indicate that a call premium in excess of 10 percent of the issue price is reasonable. $90 of the redemption price (i.e., the excess of the redemption price over the sum of the issue price and a reasonable call premium) is deemed to be a distribution of preferred stock which is taxable as a dividend. This amount is considered to be distributed ratably over the 10-year period.

84. Reg. § 1.305–3(e) (Example (6)).

85. Ibid. (Example (15)).

86. Reg. § 1.305–5(b).

§ 37.11 Substance Over Form

(a) Use of § 351 to Acquire a Corporation. When the substance of a transaction is an incorporation, but the form is otherwise, the transaction will be taxed according to its substance. Thus in Rev.Rul. 80–284, 1980–2 C.B. 117, when the dust settled, some Stockholders of T received cash and some received preferred stock. The transaction could not be cast as a joinder reorganization (see Chapter 72 et seq., infra) because a substantial portion of the consideration paid by the acquiring Corporation was not its stock. Thus the parties did the following (which was not recognized because of the application of the substance over form rule):

> T, a manufacturing Corporation, had outstanding 1,000x shares of capital stock. The fair market value of T was 100,000x dollars, and the fair market value of each share of its outstanding stock was 100x dollars. T's President and Chairman of the board, A, owned 140x shares of its capital stock (14 percent). The remaining 860x shares of T's capital stock (86 percent) were publicly held. P, a large publicly traded Corporation unrelated to T, wished to purchase the stock of T and thereafter to have T's business continued by a wholly owned subsidiary. While the other stockholders of T were willing to accept cash for their T stock, A, who was of an advanced age and who had a very low basis in his 140x shares, was unwilling to sell the T stock for cash because the sale would result in recognition of taxable gain.
>
> In order to accommodate A's wish to avoid recognition of gain, P and A agreed in January, 1980, to organize a new Corporation, S, for the purpose of acquiring and holding all of the stock of T. Several months later, pursuant to the agreement, P transferred 86,000x dollars in cash together with other property to S solely in exchange for all of S's common stock, and A transferred his 140x shares of T stock to S solely in exchange for all of S's preferred stock. It was intended that this transaction would be a tax-free exchange under section 351(a) of the Code. Thereafter, and as part of the overall plan, S organized a new Corporation, D, by transferring the 86,000x dollars in cash to D solely in exchange for all of D's stock. D was then merged into T under applicable state law, and pursuant thereto each share of T stock, except those shares transferred by A to S, was surrendered in exchange for 100x dollars in cash. The T stock acquired by D for cash was cancelled and, pursuant to state law, each share of D stock was converted into stock of T. Although S could theoretically have acquired the remaining 86 percent of the T stock directly from the T stockholders for cash, the acquisition was made pursuant to the state merger laws because this method was more expeditious and convenient. T remains in existence as an operating company, and S remains in existence as a holding company.

Similarly in Rev.Rul. 80–285, 1980–2 C.B. 119 what in substance was an asset for stock transaction was not recognized as a § 351 incorporation.

However, in the Ltr.Rul. 7839060 the Internal Revenue Service did follow the form of a plan whereby the acquiring Corporation (for cash) and some of the acquired Corporation's Stockholders (for acquired Corporation stock) formed a subsidiary. The acquiring Corporation received the new subsidiary's common and the acquired Corporation's Stockholders received the subsidiary's preferred. The subsidiary created its own subsidiary which merged into the acquired

Corporation and distributed cash to the other acquired Corporation Stockholders. It is not clear if this ruling would be followed any longer.

§ 37.12 No Rulings

The Internal Revenue Service will not rule upon the tax effect of the transfer when part of the consideration received by the transferors consists of bonds, debentures, or any other evidence of indebtedness of the transferee and the term of the "indebtedness" is either less than ten years or a determination as to whether the "indebtedness" is properly classified as debt or equity is required in order to establish that the requirements of IRC § 351 are met (Rev.Proc. 80–37, 1980–1 C.B. 51).

PART C

CORPORATE FINANCE—GENERALLY

CHAPTER 38

CORPORATE FINANCE

Table of New or Retitled Sections

D. TAX IMPLICATIONS OF THE ISSUANCE OF STOCK AND DEBT

A. METHODS OF FINANCING—GENERALLY

§ 38.3 Dividing Investment Between Shares and Debt

Page 423

(Page 423, line 18 from the top, after "of it being" *disregard the word* "stock" *and add the words* "a loan"*).*

22. Culberson's Inc., 79–2 USTC § 9694.

Page 424

(Deletion, page 424, line 17 from the top through line 23 from the top, after "area often contradictory."*).*

As the foregoing suggests, * * * area often contradictory.

29. *(Disregard footnote in main volume).*

Page 425

(Disregard page 425 in its entirety).

(Page 426, disregard from first line from the top through line 28 from the top).

Leveraging can be obtained * * *.

36. Rev.Proc. 82–22, 1982–13 IRB 16.

§ 38.4 Allocation of Stock Between Capital and Services

Page 430

(Revised text, page 430, line 2 from the bottom, after "for C's assets"*.)*

The question then * * * for C's assets, unless the Corporation being formed is a holding company (see § 59.12, infra). Debt (securities) * * *.

§ 38.5 Division Between Junior Executives and Retiring Management

Page 432

(The cross reference, at end of first paragraph, to Chapters "57" and "59" should be to Chapters "59" and "61").

B. EQUITY (STOCK)

§ 38.12 Classes of Equity Securities

Page 432

(New text, page 433, line 2 from the top, after "of equity securities"*.)*

(a) Common Shares. * * *

Only common shares may qualify for IRC § 1244 treatment (IRC § 1244(c)(1) —see § 39.4, infra).

Page 433

(New text, page 433, line 12 from the bottom, after "dividends and liquidation."*)*.

For Internal Revenue Code purposes, preferred stock (in addition to having preferences) does not significantly participate in corporate growth.[3.5]

3.5 Rev.Rul. 81–95, 1981–12 IRB 15.

Page 436

(New text, page 436, line 10 from the top, add footnote "4.5" *after* "Secretary of State"*.)*

4.5 Upon the filing of such statement, the resolution establishing and designating the series and fixing and determining the relative rights and preferences thereof shall become effective and shall constitute an amendment of the Articles of Incorporation.

Page 437

(New text, page 437, line 2 from the bottom, after "further discussion of"*)*.

For further discussion of broadly held stock options, rights and warrants, see Chapter 42, infra. For a further discussion of stock options as employee benefits see Volume 6, Chapter 5.

§ 38.13 Preferred Stock

Page 438

(New text, page 438, line 19 from the bottom, after "stock after incorporation"*).*

Caveat: The issuance of preferred stock after incorporation or in the context of the incorporation of a holding company is fraught with danger. See Chapter 58, infra.

§ 38.21 Oppressive Issuance of Shares

Page 452

(New text, page 452, line 11 from the bottom, after "to benefit management"*.).*

In some situations minority Stockholders will have the right to be bought out (see Chapter 50, infra).

C. DEBT FINANCING

§ 38.33 The Trust Indenture

Page 457

(New text, page 457, bottom line, after "are parties"*.).*

Debt securities * * * are parties. See § 43.24 et seq., infra. The issuer of * * *.

§ 38.34 Classification of Debt Securities

Page 462

(Revised text, page 462, line 11 from the bottom, after "made noninterest-bearing"*).*

In unusual situations, debt securities might be made noninterest-bearing. However, this may create problems (see § 54.2(b), infra).

23. *(The cross reference to Chapter* "61" *should be to Chapter* "62"*).*

D. TAX IMPLICATIONS OF THE ISSUANCE OF STOCK AND DEBT

§ 38.49 Registration Bonds

(a) In General. Under the Tax Equity and Fiscal Responsibility Act of 1982, the ownership of the principal and interest of certain bonds must be registered on the books of the issuing Corporation.

(b) Definition. The term "registration-required obligation" means [16] any obligation (including any obligation issued by a governmental entity) other than an obligation which—

(1) Is issued by a natural person; or

(2) Is not of a type offered to the public, except if such obligation is of a type which the Secretary has determined by Regulations to be used frequently in avoiding Federal taxes; or

(3) Has a maturity (at issue) of not more than 1 year, except if such obligation is of a type which the Internal Revenue Service has determined by Regulations to be used frequently in avoiding Federal taxes; or

(4)(A) There are arrangements reasonably designed to ensure that such obligation will be sold (or resold in connection with the original issue) only to a person who is not a United States person, and

(B) Interest on such obligation is payable only outside the United States and its possessions, and

(C) On the face of such obligation there is a statement that any United States person who holds such obligations will be subject to limitations under the United States income tax laws.

Except if such obligation is of a type which the Internal Revenue Service has determined by Regulations to be used frequently in avoiding Federal taxes.

(c) Taxation. If any registration-required obligation is not in registered form:

(1) Any gain on the sale or other disposition of such obligation will be treated as ordinary income (unless the issuance of such obligation was subject to tax under IRC § 4701).[17]

(2) No interest deduction is allowed to the issuer.[18]

(3) The obligation can not have tax exempt status. NOTE: there is no natural person exemption (see (b)(1) above in order to escape registration in this case).[19]

16. IRC § 163(g).

17. IRC § 1232(d).

18. IRC § 163(f).

19. IRC § 103(i).

CHAPTER 39

SUBSCRIPTIONS AND ISSUANCE OF SHARES

§ 39.6 Preincorporation Subscription Agreement—Another Form

Page 479

(New text, page 479, line 8 from the top, after "Features of Corporation to" *add the word* "Be"*).*

CHAPTER 43

DEBT FINANCING

C. BONDS

§ 43.23 Debt Security Trust

COMMENT

Under the Trust Indenture Act of 1939, if the bond issue is intended for public distribution, the "trustee" must be a financially responsible bank with capital and surplus of at least $150,000 which has no affiliation with the issuer.

†